Biographical Dictionary of American Sports

FOOTBALL

Biographical Dictionary of American Sports

FOOTBALL

Edited by David L. Porter

GP

GREENWOOD PRESS

New York • Westport, Connecticut • London

Library of Congress Cataloging-in-Publication Data

Biographical dictionary of American sports. Football.

Bibliography: p.
Includes index.
1. Football—United States—Biography—Dictionaries.
2. Football—United States—History. I. Porter,
David L., 1941– .
GV939.A1B56 1987 796.332'092'2 [B] 86–29386
ISBN 0–313–25771–X (lib. bdg. : alk. paper)

British Library Cataloguing in Publication Data is available.

Library of Congress Catalog Card Number: 86–29386
ISBN: 0–313–25771–X

First published in 1987

Greenwood Press, Inc.
88 Post Road West, Westport, Connecticut 06881

Printed in the United States of America

The paper used in this book complies with the Permanent Paper Standard issued by the National Information Standards Organization (Z39.48–1984).

10 9 8 7 6 5 4 3 2

Contents

Preface

This book, the second of four companion volumes, provides brief biographies covering around 520 of the nation's most notable football figures. The subjects excelled at the college and/or professional level as football players, coaches, club executives, league administrators, rules developers, or promoters (some football announcers and writers are covered in the forthcoming Outdoor Sports volume). The biographies, listed in alphabetical order, range from 300 to 900 words depending on the relative importance of the football subject. All football subjects performed after the 1870s, with most from the twentieth century. The football subjects typically are deceased or retired, but several are still-active players, coaches, executives, or administrators as of June 1987. Biographical entries detail both major statistical achievements and career background data.

Each football subject meets three general criteria for inclusion. First, they were either born or grew up in the United States. A few exceptions were made when foreign-born figures resided most of their adult lives in the United States and played an important role in the development of American football. Second, the subject must have had exceptional accomplishments in college and/or professional football. Principal measurement standards included memberships in national football halls of fame, notable statistical achievements and records, major honors earned, and championship teams performed for. Third, the figure must have made an important impact on college and/or professional football. The essays describe the major accomplishments, achievements, and impact of the biographical subjects in college and/or pro football.

Selection of football entries proved very challenging. Before making final choices, the editor thoroughly researched football encyclopedias, halls of fame, records, and history books.[1] The football figures ultimately chosen excelled as players, coaches, administrators, and/or promoters and met several of the following specific criteria:

1. They belong to the Pro Football Hall of Fame in Canton, OH, the National Football Foundation College Football Hall of Fame in King's Mills, OH, and/or the Helms Athletic Foundation Pro and College Football Hall of Fame in Los Angeles, CA. All Pro Football and many National Football Foundation College Football Hall of Fame members are included;
2. They won major college football honors, such as the Heisman Trophy, the Maxwell, Lombardi, or Outland Award, and/or All-American designation, and appeared in post-season bowl and/or All-Star games. All Heisman Trophy winners through Vincent Jackson are included;
3. They earned individual major professional football honors, such as All-Pro and Pro Bowl selections and Most Valuable Player awards, and/or appeared in post-season playoff games;
4. They were selected to All-Time and/or All-Decade college or pro teams;
5. They compiled outstanding offensive statistical achievements and ranked high in career NCAA college conference, and/or pro league rushing, passing, and receiving yardage, and touchdowns scored;
6. They excelled defensively in tackles, quarterback sacks, interceptions, fumble recoveries, and/or other categories;
7. They starred as kickoff, punt, and/or extra point specialists.

The Pro Football Researchers Association and College Football Researchers Association helped immeasurably in the selection process. Robert Carroll provided invaluable assistance in determining the pro football entries, while Bernie McCarty, James Whalen, and the late Tony Cusher supplied excellent background material on college football figures. In several instances, contributors suggested biographical entries worthy of inclusion. Of course, the editor assumes ultimate responsibility for any significant football figures inadvertently excluded from this book. Several promising football players still in the early stages of their active careers are not included. Publication deadlines did not permit the inclusion of any college players performing after the 1985 season.

Around 90 contributors, mostly participants in the Pro Football Researchers Association, College Football Researchers Association, or the North American Society for Sport History, submitted biographical entries. Numerous contributors are university or college professors; many are authorities on college and/or pro football and teach courses in American sport history. Other contributors include public and private school teachers and administrators, writers, publishers, editors, journalists, librarians, consultants, and government employees. Contributors are mentioned following each essay and are listed alphabetically with occupational affiliation, if known, in the appendix.

Entries usually indicate the subject's (1) full given name at birth; (2) date and place of birth and, where applicable, date and place of death; (3) parental background, if available; (4) formal education; (5) wife and children, where applicable; and (6) major personal characteristics. Authors typically searched diligently and persistently for this often elusive data. In many instances, however, contributors could not ascertain all the above information. Essays describe the subject's football career through the 1986 season and usually include his (1) entrance into college and/or pro football; (2) positions played; (3) teams performed for with respective conferences and leagues; (4) lifetime rushing, passing, and reception yardage, touchdowns scored, and defensive, kicking, and punting statistics, where applicable; (5) notable individual records set, awards won, college and Pro Bowl appearances, All-American and All-Pro selections; and (6) personal impact on football history. Major college conferences frequently represented include the Atlantic Coast, Big Eight (formerly Missouri Valley, Big Six, Big Seven), Big Ten (formerly Western, Big Nine), Border, East-West Athletic, Ivy League, Mid-American, Missouri Valley, Pacific Coast, Pacific Ten (formerly Pacific Eight), Rocky Mountain, Skyline (formerly Mountain States Athletic), Southeastern, Southern, Southwest Athletic, Southwestern Athletic, and Western Athletic. American pro leagues covered include the National Football League (1919–), American Football League (1926, 1936–1937, 1940–1941, 1960–1969), All America Football Conference (1946–1949), World Football League (1974–1975), and United States Football League (1983–1986). Less biographical and statistical data typically were available on late nineteenth- and early twentieth-century figures. In the case of coaches, entries describe their (1) teams guided with inclusive dates; (2) major statistical achievements; (3) career won/loss records and percentages; (4) premier players coached; and (5) coaching philosophy, strategy, and innovations. Sketches on club executives and league officials concentrate on their positions held, notable accomplishments, and impact on football development.

This volume contains several additional features. Brief bibliographies list the most pertinent sources about each biographical subject. Several authors benefited from oral interviews or correspondence with the biographical subject, relatives, or acquaintances. Other contributors utilized primary source material at the Pro and National Football Foundation and Helms Athletic Foundation college football halls of fame, pro club offices, college and university athletic and alumni offices, daily newspapers, and various libraries across the United States. Second, asterisks are used whenever an essay cites a biographical subject covered elsewhere in the book. If a biographical subject is treated in a companion volume, the particular book is noted in parentheses as follows: (BB) for Baseball, (OS) for Outdoor Sports, and (IS) for Indoor Sports. Third, the Appendix lists (1) all entries by main category (player, coach, executive) selected; (2) player by main position played; (3) entries by place of birth; (4) entries who played professional football; (5) National Football Foundation College Football Hall of Fame members; (6) Pro Football Hall of Fame members; and (7) Major College Conferences, Professional Leagues, and Associations.

Several groups and individuals contributed very generously to this project at various stages. The Pro Football Hall of Fame, National Football Foundation College Football Hall of Fame, Professional Football Researchers Association, College Football Researchers Association, college and university alumni and athletic offices, pro club offices, daily newspapers, and libraries supplied significant information to essay contributors. Many unnamed football subjects, relatives, and acquaintances kindly furnished invaluable personal data and reminiscences for essay contributors. The editor deeply appreciates the enormous amount of time, energy, and effort expended by contributors in searching for sometimes rather inaccessible information. I am particularly indebted to John L. Evers and James D. Whalen, who continually consented to do football essays. Dennis A. Booher, William A. Borst, Albert J. Figone, Leonard Frey, John Hanners, John David Healy, Charles R. Middleton, Luther W. Spoehr, and Robert B. Van Atta graciously assisted in the latter stages. Stan W. Carlson, Robert N. Carroll, John L. Evers, Leonard Frey, William A. Gudelunas, Jay Langhammer, Bernie McCarty, Charles R. Middleton, Jerome Mushkat, Robert B. Van Atta, and James D. Whalen contributed at least ten essays each. William Penn College, notably librarians Ed Goedeken, Marion Rains, and Jim Hollis, made the atmosphere more conducive for working on this project. Mary Sive, Cynthia Harris and Neil Kraner again furnished adept guidance and numerous valuable suggestions in the planning and writing of this volume. Above all, the editor deeply appreciates the understanding and support that his wife Marilyn and children Kevin and Andrea have shown throughout the project.

NOTES

1. Sources consulted include *Official NFL Record & Fact Book, 1985* (New York, 1985); Bill Barron et al., *The Official NFL Encyclopedia of Football* (New York, 1982); Roger Treat, ed., *The Encyclopedia of Football*, 16th rev. ed., rev. by Pete Palmer (New York, 1979); Ronald L. Mendell and Timothy B. Phares, *Who's Who in Football* (New Rochelle, NY, 1974); Harold Claassen and Steve Boda, eds., *Ronald Encyclopedia of Football* (New York, 1960); L. H. Baker, *Football: Facts and Figures* (New York, 1945); Edwin Pope, *Football's Greatest Coaches* (Atlanta, GA, 1956); *The College Game* (Indianapolis, IN, 1974); John T. Brady, *The Heisman: A Symbol of Excellence* (New York, 1984); Frank G. Menke, *The All-Sports Record Book* (New York, 1950); Min S. Yee and Donald K. Wright, eds., *The Sports Book* (New York, 1975); David S. Neft et al., eds., *All-Sports World Record Book* (New York, 1976) and *The Complete All-Time Pro Football Register* (New York, 1975); Bob Oates, Jr., ed., *The First 50 Years: NFL* (New York, 1969); Ted Brock and Larry Eldridge, Jr., *25 Years: The NFL Since 1960* (New York, 1985); George Allen with Ben Olan, *Pro Football's 100 Greatest Players* (Indianapolis, IN, 1982); and Michael Rathet and Don R. Smith, *Their Deeds and Dogged Faith* (New York, 1984).

For history of college football, see Allison Danzig, *The History of American Football: Its Great Teams, Players, and Coaches* (Englewood Cliffs, NJ, 1956); John D. McCallum and Charles H. Pearson, *College Football U.S.A., 1869–1973* (New York, 1973); Ivan Kaye, *Good Clean Violence: A History of College Football* (Philadelphia, 1973); Parke H. Davis, *Football: The American Intercollegiate Game* (New York, 1911); and Alexander M. Weyand, *American Football: Its History and Development* (New York, 1926). For history of pro football, see Harold Claassen, *The History of Professional Football* (Englewood Cliffs, NJ, 1963); Robert M. Smith, *Pro Football: The History of the Game and the Great Players* (Garden City, NY, 1963); David S. Neft, Richard M. Cohen, and Jordan A. Deutsch, *Pro Football: The Early Years, an Encyclopedic History, 1895–1959* (Ridgefield, CT, 1978), and *The Sports Encyclopedia, Pro Football: The Modern Era, 1960 to the Present* (New York, 1982); Joe King, *Inside Pro Football* (Englewood Cliffs, NJ, 1958); Myron Cope, *The Game That Was: The Early Days of Pro Football* (New York, 1974); George Sullivan, *Pro Football's All-Time Greats: The Immortals in Pro Football's Hall of Fame* (New York, 1968); and Arthur Daley, *Pro Football's Hall of Fame* (Chicago, 1963).

Abbreviations

LEAGUES AND ASSOCIATIONS

AA	American Association
AAC	Atlanta Athletic Club
AAFC	All America Football Conference
AAU	Amateur Athletic Union
AAWU	Athletic Association of Western Universities (Big Five)
ABL	American Basketball League
ACC	Atlantic Coast Conference
ACFL	Atlantic Coast Football League
AFC	American Football Conference
AFCA	American Football Coaches Association
AFL	American Football League
AIC	Arkansas Intercollegiate Conference
AL	American League
AOO	American Officials Organization
APFA	American Professional Football Association
AnL	Anthracite League
AtBA	Atlanta Baseball Association
BC	Border Conference
BEC	Big Eight Conference (also Missouri Valley Intercollegiate Athletic Conference—formerly BSC)
BNC	Big Nine Conference (also WC)

BSC	Big Six/Seven Conference (also Missouri Valley Intercollegiate Athletic Conference)
BTC	Big Ten Conference (also WC, formerly BNC)
CaCAA	California Collegiate Athletic Association
CBCA	College Baseball Coaches Association
CFL	Canadian Football League
CIAA	Central Intercollegiate Athletic Association
CIF	California Interscholastic Federation
CoL	Continental League
ConFL	Continental Football League
CrL	Carolina League
CSB	Citizens Savings Bank
CSL	Cotton States League
ECAC	Eastern College Athletic Conference
ECL	Eastern Carolina League
EIAA	Eastern Intercollegiate Athletic Association
EL	Eastern League
FC	Frontier Conference
FWAA	Football Writers Association of America
FWC	Far Western Conference
GAA	Greensburg Athletic Association
GSC	Gulf States Conference
HAF	Helms Athletic Foundation (Citizens Savings Bank)
IC4A	Intercollegiate Association of Amateur Athletics of America
ICAC	Independent College Athletic Conference
ICC	Illinois College Conference
IL	Ivy League
IntL	International League
ISL	Interstate League
LSC	Lone State Conference
LTC	Little Three Conference
MAA	Midwest Athletic Association
MAAAU	Middle Atlantic Amateur Athletic Union
MAC	Mid-American Conference
MAL	Middle Atlantic League

MEL	Mexican League
MIAA	Michigan Intercollegiate Athletic Association
MIAC	Missouri Intercollegiate Athletic Association
MnIAC	Minnesota Intercollegiate Athletic Conference
MOL	Michigan–Ontario League
MSAC	Mountain States Athletic Conference (also Skyline Conference)
MVC	Missouri Valley Conference
MWC	Midwestern Conference
NAAF	National Amateur Athletic Federation
NACAD	National Association of Collegiate Athletic Directors
NAIA	National Association of Intercollegiate Athletics
NBA	National Baseball Association
NBL	National Basketball League
NCAA	National Collegiate Athletic Association
NCC	North Central Conference
NCFCA	National Collegiate Football Coaches Association
NCSIC	North Carolina State Intercollegiate Conference
NeCC	Nebraska College Conference
NFC	National Football Conference
NFF	National Football Foundation
NFHSAA	National Foundation of High School Athletic Associations
NFL	National Football League (formerly APFA)
NIBA	National Interscholastic Basketball Association
NIL	Negro Interscholastic League
NL	National League
NSC	North State Conference
NTCAC	Northern Teachers College Athletic Conference
NYPL	New York–Pennsylvania League
NWC	Northwestern Conference
OC	Ohio Conference
OSL	Ohio State League
OVC	Ohio Valley Conference
PCAA	Pacific Coast Athletic Association
PCC	Pacific Coast Conference
PCL	Pacific Coast League

PCPFL	Pacific Coast Professional Football League
PEC	Pacific Eight Conference (formerly PCC)
PFWAA	Professional Football Writers Association of America
PiL	Piedmont League
PSC	Pacific Southwestern Conference
PTC	Pacific Ten Conference (formerly PEC)
RMC	Rocky Mountain Conference
SA	Southern Association
SAC	Southwestern Athletic Conference
SC	Southern Conference (formerly SIAA)
SCAC	Southern California Athletic Conference
SDC	South Dakota Conference
SE	Southeast Conference
SEC	Southeastern Conference (formerly part of SC)
SEL	Southeastern League
SIAA	Southern Intercollegiate Athletic Association
SIAC	Southern Intercollegiate Athletic Conference
SL	Southern League
SLC	Skyline Conference (also Mountain State Athletic Conference)
SoC	Southland Conference
SWC	Southwest Athletic Conference
TIAA	Texas Intercollegiate Athletic Association
TL	Texas League
TSC	Tri-State Conference
UFL	United Football League
USFL	United States Football League
WA	Western Association
WAC	Western Athletic Conference (formerly CaCAA)
WC	Western Conference (also BTC, formerly BNC)
WFL	World Football League

WL	Western League
WSJCC	Washington State Junior College Conference

CROSS REFERENCE TO OTHER VOLUMES OF BIOGRAPHICAL DICTIONARY

BB	Baseball Volume
IS	Indoor Sports Volume
OS	Outdoor Sports Volume

FREQUENTLY CITED REFERENCE SOURCES

AP	Associated Press
CB	*Current Biography*
DAB	*Dictionary of American Biography*
INS	International News Service
NCAB	*National Cyclopedia of American Biography*
NEA	Newspaper Enterprises Association
NYT	*New York Times*
SEP	*Saturday Evening Post*
SI	*Sports Illustrated*
TSN	*The Sporting News*
UPI	United Press International
WWA	*Who's Who in America*

FREQUENTLY CITED FOOTBALL TERMS AND UNIVERSITIES

AC	Athletic Club
JC	Junior College
LSU	Louisiana State University
MVP	Most Valuable Player
SMU	Southern Methodist University
TCU	Texas Christian University
UCLA	University of California at Los Angeles

Biographical Dictionary of American Sports

FOOTBALL

A

ADDERLEY, Herbert A. "Herb" (b. 8 June 1939, Philadelphia, PA), college and professional player, announcer, and coach, is the son of Charles and Rene (White) Adderley and gained All-City honors in football, basketball, and baseball at Northeast High School in Philadelphia. At Michigan State University (1957–1961), the 6 foot, 200 pound offensive back earned three football letters and in 1961 received a B.S. in Education there. Adderley co-captained the 1960 squad and led the Spartans in rushing (1959) and receiving (1959–1960). An All-BTC selection in 1960, Adderley played in the East-West Shrine game, Hula Bowl, and Coaches' All-America and College All-Star games.

Adderley was selected by Green Bay on the first round of the 1961 NFL draft. He played for the Packers (1961–1969) before being traded to the Dallas Cowboys (1970–1972). Converted to a defensive back, Adderley performed on five NFL title teams (1961–1962, 1965–1967) and two Super Bowl championship squads with Green Bay (1966–1967). He also played on two NFC title teams (1970–1971) and one Super Bowl championship squad (1971) with the Dallas Cowboys. In Super Bowl II against Oakland, Adderley's 60-yard touchdown return of an intercepted pass was the first such feat in Super Bowl history. Adderley played in four of the first six Super Bowls, performing on the winning team three times.

Besides pacing the NFL in touchdowns by interceptions (1962, 1965) and yards gained by interceptions (1965, 1969), Adderley led Green Bay in kickoff returns (1961–1964) and interceptions (1963–1965) and holds the Packers season record for most touchdowns on interceptions (three). At Dallas in 1971, Adderley tied the Cowboys mark for most interceptions in one game (three) and topped their defensive backs with six interceptions for 182 yards. An All-NFL defensive back (1962–1963, 1965–1968), Adderley played in five Pro Bowl (1963–1967) and seven College All-Star games. Adderley recorded 48 career interceptions, returning them 1,046 yards for an average of 21.8 yards per runback and seven touchdowns. He also returned 120 kickoffs for 3,080 yards. In 12 NFL seasons, Adderley's teams won 127 times, lost 46, and tied five for a .713 winning percentage.

Adderley, who is married and has one daughter, subsequently announced football games for Temple University and the Philadelphia Eagles (NFL) and served as an assistant coach for the Temple Owls and Philadelphia Bell of the defunct WFL. Later an assistant radio station manager and special consultant for Schlitz Breweries, in 1980 Adderly was elected to the Pro Football Hall of Fame and to its AFL-NFL 1960–1984 All-Star second team.

BIBLIOGRAPHY: George Allen with Ben Olan, *Pro Football's 100 Greatest Players* (Indianapolis, IN, 1982); Fred W. Stabley, *The Spartans: A Story of Michigan State Football* (Huntsville, AL, 1975); *TSN Football Register—1972.*

John L. Evers

ALBERT, Frank Culling (b. 27 January 1920, Chicago, IL), college and professional player and coach, is the son of insurance executive Nevin and Blanche (Marshman) Albert. Albert grew up in Glendale, CA, where he won All-Southern California honors as a prep football and track star. Although initially rejected as "too small" for high school football, the persistent Albert was named Southern California's 1937 Prep Athlete of the Year. He entered Stanford University in 1938 and played single-wing tailback his sophomore year. Clark Shaughnessy,* who became head coach in 1940, switched to the T formation and installed the left-handed throwing Albert at quarterback. Stanford's 1940 team, "The Vow Boys," finished undefeated, won the PCC crown, was ranked number two nationally, and defeated Nebraska 21–13 in the Rose Bowl.

A pinpoint passer, the 5 foot, 10 inch, 166 pound Albert excelled as a ball handler, faker, placekicker, defensive back, punter, and team leader. He still holds the Stanford record with a 79-yard punt against Oregon State in 1940. Besides leading Stanford in minutes played (525), Albert made consensus All-American and placed third in the 1940 Heisman Trophy balloting. During his senior year Albert guided "The Vow Boys" to another good season and repeated as a consensus All-American. Named HAF Southern California 1941 Athlete of the Year, he placed fourth in the Heisman Trophy race and played in the Shrine All Star East-West Game. After graduation he joined the U.S. Navy as a deck officer. He married Martha Jean Barringer on July 21, 1942, and has three daughters, Nancy, Jane, and Terryl.

Upon discharge from the Navy, Albert signed with the San Francisco 49ers of the new AAFC. During the AAFC's four-year existence, Albert led the 49ers to a record 108 touchdowns. In 1948 he passed for 29 touchdowns and was named AAFC Co-MVP with Otto Graham.* Named Pro Player of the Year by *Sport* magazine in 1948, he made All-AAFC in 1949 and tossed five touchdown passes against the Cleveland Browns in a 1949 game.

An excellent punter, he booted an 82-yarder against the Buffalo Bills in 1948 and paced the AAFC in 1949 with a 48.2-yard average.

When the AAFC disbanded after the 1949 season, San Francisco joined the NFL. Following the 1950 season, Albert played in the first Pro Bowl and then split 49er quarterback duties with Y. A. Tittle* the next two seasons. In 1953 he moved to the Calgary Stampeders of the CFL for his final pro season. During his entire pro career, Albert completed 935 passes in 1,789 attempts for 12,363 yards and 127 touchdowns. He made 347 punts for a 42.6-yard average and rushed for 29 touchdowns.

Albert returned to the 49ers in 1954 as a radio-TV broadcaster and director of promotion. After serving as a 49ers assistant coach in 1955, at age 36 he became the NFL's youngest head coach in 1956. That same year, he was elected to the NFF College Football Hall of Fame. His second season as 49ers head coach produced an 8–4 record, tying the Detroit Lions for the Western Conference crown. In the playoff, Detroit defeated San Francisco 31–27 on a last-minute comeback. Albert, who resigned after his 1958 team finished 6–6, compiled a three-year 19–16–1 record. He remained with the San Francisco organization as a limited partner through 1976.

BIBLIOGRAPHY: Don E. Liebendorfer, *The Color of Life Is Red* (Palo Alto, CA, 1972); John D. McCallum and Charles H. Pearson, *College Football U.S.A., 1869–1973* (New York, 1973); Fred Merrick, *Down on the Farm: A Story of Stanford Football* (Huntsville, AL, 1975); *San Francisco 49ers Press Guides, 1950, 1956, 1958.*

Jay Langhammer

ALDRICH, Charles Collins "Ki" (b. 1 June 1916, Temple, TX; d. 12 March 1983, Temple, TX), college and professional player, was the second son of Riley Lee and Monta Vera (Pressley) Aldrich. His father worked in real estate, operated an auto repair shop, and owned several restaurants and clubs. Aldrich cried frequently as a child and was called "Ki baby" by his older brother, who had trouble saying the word "cry."

An All-State football player at Temple High, Aldrich entered TCU in the fall, 1935, and made All-SWC center for three years. As a sophomore in 1936, he helped the Horned Frogs win the first Cotton Bowl game 16–6 against Marquette. A consensus All-American in 1938, he helped TCU capture the national championship with an 11–0 record and 15–6 victory over Carnegie Tech in the Sugar Bowl. He also played in the College All-Star Game and the Dallas Southwest All-Star Game. At 5 feet, 11 inches, and 215 pounds, Aldrich became a quick, hard-hitting linebacker. TCU coach Leo "Dutch" Meyer* said, "Ki was the best man I've ever seen at sizing up plays"; he considered Aldrich, Sammy Baugh,* and Davey O'Brien* his three finest pupils. Aldrich was elected to the NFF College Football Hall of Fame in 1960, HAF College Football Hall of Fame, and Texas Sports Hall of Fame.

The first SWC lineman ever picked in the pro football draft's first round, Aldrich joined the Chicago Cardinals (NFL) in 1939 and played regularly there for two seasons. He performed for the Washington Redskins (NFL) in the 1941–1942 seasons before going into the U.S. Navy during World War II. He returned to the Redskins in 1945 and retired following the 1947 campaign. During his pro career, he averaged 50 minutes per game. Aldrich married Dorothy Pope on June 6, 1939 and had one daughter, Lisa, and one son, John. After being divorced in 1951, he wed Helen Patricia Criss on January 4, 1962. Following his pro career, he worked as superintendent of the Lena Pope Home for Orphans in Fort Worth, TX, and director of the Coffeyville, KS, Boys Club. He also operated a gas station and restaurant and owned a car dealership.

BIBLIOGRAPHY: John D. McCallum and Charles H. Pearson, *College Football U.S.A., 1869–1973* (New York, 1973); *Texas Christian University Football Press Guide, 1983; Texas Sports Hall of Fame Yearbook, 1981.*

Jay Langhammer

ALEXANDER, Joseph (b. 1 April 1898, Silver Creek, NY; d. 12 September 1975, New York, NY), college and professional player and coach, combined medicine and sports in a distinguished career. From upstate New York, Alexander played varsity football five seasons (1916–1920) at Syracuse University and won All-American honors at both center and guard. A 6 foot, 210 pound lineman, he once made eleven consecutive tackles against Colgate and helped the Orangemen record eleven shutouts. In naming his 1919 All-American team, Walter Camp* lauded Alexander and Swede Youngstrom of Dartmouth as "the greatest pair of defensive guards that have ever been seen on the gridiron."

After receiving a medical degree from Syracuse in 1921, Alexander delayed full-time practice to play in the fledgling NFL. In the NFL's third season (1921), Alexander joined the Rochester Jeffersons, one of the founding and short-lived franchises. After spending the next season with the struggling Milwaukee Badgers, he left football to begin his medical practice in New York City. When Tim Mara* purchased a franchise for $500 in 1925 and established the New York Giants, Alexander came out of retirement and was the first player to join the club. With Jim Thorpe* on the team, the Giants won eight of twelve games in their first season. In 1926 Alexander played guard and center and coached the Giants to a similar record. In Alexander's last playing season (1927), the Giants compiled a 11–1–1 record and won the NFL championship. New York's line also included Cal Hubbard* and Steve Owen.*

Except for a few brief coaching stints at City College of New York, Alexander devoted the rest of his career to medicine. He helped found one of New York City's first tuberculosis clinics and perfected the pneumothorax procedure for treating the disease. He served as instructor of medicine at Fifth Avenue Hospital from 1925 to 1962 and as consulting physician for several other New York City hospitals. In 1962 the New York City Commissioner of Hospitals conferred the Distinguished and Exceptional Service Award on him. Alexander, whose medical career spanned 51 years, married Vera Carley and had two daughters and one son. George Trevor placed Alexander on his All-Time All-American 1919–1929 team, while the New York *World Telegram* named him its All-Time All-American guard in its second balloting (1954). He also was selected to the NFF College Football Hall of Fame.

BIBLIOGRAPHY: Allison Danzig, *The History of American Football: Its Great Teams, Players, and Coaches* (Englewood Cliffs, NJ, 1956); *NYT*, September 14, 1975; Philadelphia *Inquirer*, September 15, 1975; Ken Rappoport, *The Syracuse Football Story* (Huntsville, AL, 1975); Paul Soderberg and Helen Washington, eds., *The Big Book of Halls of Fame* (New York, 1977); Syracuse University, *Lettermen of Distinction* (Syracuse, NY, 1969); Roger Treat, ed., *The Encyclopedia of Football*, 16th rev. ed., rev. by Pete Palmer (South Brunswick, NJ, 1979).

Bruce Leslie

ALEXANDER, William Anderson "Bill" (b. 6 June 1889, Mud River, KY; d. 23 April 1950, Atlanta, GA), college player and coach, spent his entire football coaching career at Georgia Tech. When William was six, his father, a coal mine manager, died; the boy was then brought up by his mother, a teacher. Since his high school background proved deficient, he entered Georgia Tech (SIAA) in 1906 as an apprentice student and needed six years to graduate. In 1912 he earned a B.S. in Engineering. Of mediocre football talent, he captained "the scrubs" and played enough to earn a letter.

From 1912 to 1920 he served as assistant coach at Georgia Tech under John Heisman.* In 1920 he became head coach and remained in that position through 1944. Alexander's players feared him on the field and idolized him off the gridiron. Besides having considerable football knowledge, he understood others well and was considered a clearinghouse for personal matters of every Georgia Tech player, coach, and athletic department employee. From 1920 to 1928 he coached exceptional teams to a record 58–17–7. Between 1929 and 1938, however, his squads dropped to a 36–55–8 mark. During twenty-five years Alexander's Georgia Tech squads won 134, lost 95, and tied 15. Under Alexander, the Yellowjackets won or shared eight SC and SEC championships, finished undefeated and untied in 1928, and won the national championship.

Georgia Tech, during Alexander's tenure, became the first team to play in all four major Bowls (Rose, Sugar, Orange, and Cotton). Alexander's squads captured three of five Bowl contests, including a famous 8–7 Rose Bowl victory over the University of California. In this game, Roy Riegels of California recovered a Georgia Tech fumble, was spun around by several would-be tacklers, and headed for the wrong goal line, sixty-five yards away. Teammate Benny Lom caught up with Riegels at the one-yard line and tried to turn him around. Several Georgia Tech players hit Riegels and caused him to fumble the ball into the end zone, where the Yellowjackets recovered for an apparent touchdown. The officials, however, denied the touchdown and placed the ball on the one-yard line. Lom tried to punt on the next play, but Georgia Tech blocked the ball out of the end zone. The play was ruled a safety, ultimately leading to the Yellowjackets victory.

Georgia Tech won the 1940 Orange Bowl 21–7 over Missouri, led by Paul Christman. In 1943 they lost the Cotton Bowl 14–7 to Dana X. Bible's* Texas Longhorns. Georgia Tech defeated Tulsa University 20–18 in the 1944 Sugar Bowl but lost 20–12 to Tulsa in the 1945 Orange Bowl in Alexander's last game as coach. Besides being Coach of the Year in 1942, Alexander received the Georgia Tech alumni Distinguished Service Award. He also was given the Amos Alonzo Stagg Award in 1946 and the Touchdown Club of New York Award in 1948. A longtime member of the NFL Rules Committee, he served as president of the AFCA and was elected to the HAF and NFF College Football Halls of Fame.

Alexander spent 44 years at Georgia Tech, including six as a player, eight as assistant coach, twenty-five as head coach, and five as athletic director. With Frank Broyles* at quarterback, Alexander's final 1944 squad won eight of ten games. Alexander, who was replaced by Bobby Dodd,* became athletic director until his death.

BIBLIOGRAPHY: Tim Cohane, *Great College Football Coaches of the Twenties and Thirties* (New Rochelle, NY, 1973); *Georgia Tech Football Media Guide, 1979;* John D. McCallum and Charles H. Pearson, *College Football U.S.A., 1869–1973* (New York, 1973); Edwin Pope, *Football's Greatest Coaches* (Atlanta, GA, 1956).

John L. Evers

ALLEN, George Herbert (b. 29 April 1922, Detroit, MI), college athlete and professional football coach, is the son of auto plant worker Earl and Loretta Allen. Allen graduated from Lake Shore (MI) High School, where he lettered in football, basketball, and track and boasted a perfect attendance record. The versatile Allen made All-Conference center in basketball and set a school record in the long jump. Allen attended Alma College and Marquette University as an officer trainee in the U.S. Navy's wartime V–12 program and played end for both schools. He served as athletic adjutant at the Farragut (ID) Navy base until his discharge in 1946 and then graduated with an M.S. in Physical Education in 1947 from the University of Michigan, where he lettered in wrestling and assisted football coach Fritz Crisler.* Allen married Etty Lombroso on May 26, 1951, and has four children.

Allen's head coaching career began in 1948 at Morningside (IA) College

(NCC), where he built a 15–2–2 record in three years. From 1951 to 1956 he compiled a 32–22–5 mark at Whittier (CA) College (SCAC). In 1957 he coached receivers with the Los Angeles Rams (NFL) but lost his position in a staff shakeup. Allen operated a car wash before George Halas* hired him as an assistant coach for the Chicago Bears (NFL) in 1958. Allen directed the Bear defense when Chicago won the NFL championship in 1963 and was awarded the game ball. In a controversial move causing Halas to file a breach of contract suit, Allen became head coach of the Los Angeles Rams (NFL) in 1966. He compiled a 49–17–4 record over five seasons (the best NFL mark during that period), won his division twice, and gave the Rams their first winning seasons in eight years. During his Rams tenure, Allen made fifty-one trades. He was temporarily fired after producing a 21–4–3 record with the Rams but was rehired within two weeks because of irate community and player reaction. In 1971 Allen took the head coaching reins of the Washington Redskins (NFL) and guided them to a second place Eastern Division finish with a 9–4–1 mark and to the playoffs for the first time since 1945. Under Allen, Washington won three straight Eastern Division titles before dropping to third place in 1975 and lost to the Miami Dolphins after the 1972 season in Super Bowl VII. In post-season games, Allen's NFL teams won four and lost seven. As Redskins coach, Allen built a 67–30–1 record in seven years by utilizing veterans. The Redskins, which included many ex-Rams acquired in numerous trades, were tabbed the Over-the-Hill Gang. Allen, whose prolific trading caused him to be fined in 1973 for dealing the same draft choices twice, was named NFL Coach of the Year in 1967, 1969, 1971, and 1972.

After a five-year absence from football, Allen became head coach of the Chicago Blitz in the new USFL and finished 12–6–0 in the 1983 inaugural season. When the Blitz and the Arizona franchises were exchanged, Allen became head coach of the Arizona Wranglers and led them to the 1984 USFL WC championship. The Wranglers lost the title game to the Philadelphia Stars and finished 12–9–0, after which Allen resigned. In fourteen pro seasons including post-season games, Allen compiled a 144–69–5 record.

Allen, an inspirational coach known for thorough preparation and intense devotion to duty, often did not go home during the football season. The physically fit Allen, who loves ice cream and milk, utilized numerous slogans. His best remembered slogans include "pay the price," "there is no detail too small," and "every time you win, you're reborn; when you lose, you die a little." Allen founded and supports the Red Cloud Athletic Federation to furnish athletic equipment for Sioux children, a service for which he has been made an honorary Sioux chief. He has also authored ten books.

BIBLIOGRAPHY: George Allen with Joe Marshall, "A Hundred Percent Is Not Enough," *SI* 39 (July 9, 1973), pp. 74–75; George Allen with Ben Olan, *Pro Football's 100 Greatest Players* (Indianapolis, IN, 1982); "The Attitude of a Winner," *Nation's*

Business 63 (September, 1975), 44–46ff; George Frazier IV, "Portrait of the Super-Coach as a Sweetheart," *Esquire* 70 (September, 1968), pp. 116–17ff; William Gildea and Kenneth Turan, *The Future Is Now* (Boston, MA, 1972); John Underwood, "The Ice-Cream Man Cometh," *SI* 35 (October 25, 1971), pp. 71–72, 74, 77.

John E. DiMeglio

ALLEN, Marcus (b. 26 March 1960, San Diego, CA), college and professional player, starred in football at the University of Southern California and with the Los Angeles Raiders (NFL). His parents are Harold, a general contractor, and Gwen Allen, a registered nurse. Allen began his illustrious football career at Lincoln High School in San Diego as a quarterback and safety. In 1977 he led Lincoln to the San Diego City championship with a 12–0–1 record. Besides passing for 1,900 yards and 18 touchdowns, he ran for 1,198 yards and 12 touchdowns, intercepted 11 passes for four touchdowns, and led the team in tackles. A 34–6 victory in the championship game over Keamey featured Allen's 197 yards rushing and his scoring all five Lincoln touchdowns. The only player in Lincoln High School history to have his jersey retired, he made the *Parade* and several other All-American teams.

Allen was recruited highly on a national scale and chose the University of Southern California (USC), where he majored in public administration. John Robinson, then USC head coach, originally recruited Allen as a defensive player. After his fourth day of practice, however, Allen was shifted to tailback. Allen started his career slowly as the number two tailback his freshman year, rushing for 171 yards and one touchdown. During his sophomore year (1979) Allen shifted to fullback, gained 649 yards rushing, and made eight touchdowns. He primarily served as a blocker for teammate and eventual Heisman Trophy winner Charles White.* In 1980 Allen returned to the tailback position and began to achieve stardom. During that season he rushed for 1,563 yards, scored 14 touchdowns, and became the nation's number two rusher behind Heisman Trophy winner George Rogers.* The number one all-purpose runner, Allen averaged 179.4 yards per game.

Allen's senior year (1981) established him as the game's premier college player with 15 new NCAA records, including most yards gained rushing in a season (2,342), highest per game rushing average (212.9 yards), most 200-yard games in a season (8), most carries in a season (403), most all-purpose yards in a season (2,550), highest rushing average per carry in a season (5.81 yards), and most 200-yard games in a career (11). Allen's 1981 statistics included 22 rushing touchdowns and 34 receptions for 256 yards and one touchdown. Allen's collegiate career ended with a Fiesta Bowl appearance and his recognition as the premier player in collegiate football as he won the Maxwell Memorial Award and the Heisman Trophy. The UPI Player of the Year, he was named to seven All-American teams.

The Los Angeles Raiders selected the 6 foot, 2 inch, 210 pound Allen as the tenth player chosen in the 1982 NFL draft. Allen's pro career, unlike his collegiate record, was marked by star performances from the outset. In his rookie season (1982) he led the NFL in touchdowns (14), was named *TSN* Rookie of the Year, and played in the Pro Bowl. During the 1983 season Allen rushed for 1,014 yards, scored 12 touchdowns, and helped lead the Raiders to the Super Bowl. In Super Bowl XVIII against the Washington Redskins, Allen rushed for 191 yards and was named MVP. He appeared in the 1984 Pro Bowl, having rushed for 1,168 yards and scored 15 touchdowns. In 1985 he led the Raiders to a 12–4 record, setting an NFL mark for most combined yards running and receiving (2,314). Allen rushed 380 times for 1,759 yards (4.6-yard average) and scored 11 touchdowns to become the first Raider to lead the NFL in rushing, and caught 67 passes for 555 yards (8.3-yard average) and 3 touchdowns, fumbling just 3 times. Besides making both All-Pro and the Pro Bowl, he tied Walter Payton's* NFL record with his ninth consecutive 100-yard rushing game and won both NFL MVP and Player of the Year honors. Allen rushed over 100 yards in his first two 1986 NFL games to extend his consecutive streak to 11 games before the New York Giants held him to 40 yards. The 8–8 Raiders failed to make the playoffs, as Allen rushed 208 times for 759 yards, scored 5 touchdowns rushing, and again made the Pro Bowl. Through the 1986 season, he had rushed 1,289 times for 5,397 yards and 49 touchdowns and caught 279 passes for 2,757 yards and 15 touchdowns.

BIBLIOGRAPHY: Timothy Carlson et al., "Allen," *Inside Sports* 3 (November 1981); Des Moines *Register*, December 24–25, 1985, and January, 1986; John Hall, "Football Traditions," *Trojans Illustrated* 1 (June–July, 1983); Beau Riffenburgh, "Marcus Allen and the U.S.C.: Tailback Legacy," *Pro* 2 (December, 1982); *TSN Football Register—1984, 1985, 1986;* University of Southern California, Press Releases, Los Angeles, CA.

William A. Sutton

ALWORTH, Lance D. "Bambi" (b. 3 August 1940, Houston, TX), college and professional player, is the son of Richard R. Alworth, an oil field construction foreman and superintendent, and teacher Elizabeth Louise (Parrish) Alworth. An all-around athlete, he graduated from Brookhaven (MS) High School and made scholastic All-American in football there in 1957. Alworth was recruited by Al Davis* to play football at the University of Arkansas (SWC, 1960–1962), where he annually made the All-American squad. He led the NCAA with 61 punt returns his senior year and was selected an All-American running back.

The extraordinarily fast 6 foot, 180 pound Alworth was recruited highly in 1962 by the rival NFL and AFL. He also was offered pro baseball contracts by the New York Yankees (AL) and Pittsburgh Pirates (NL). He was drafted in the second round by the San Diego Chargers (AFL) and played there until 1970; he then was traded to Dallas (NFL) and played with the Cowboys until retiring in July 1973. Alworth earned his sobriquet in pro football camp because of his innocent, youthful features. Despite his appearance, he proved extremely tough. Alworth played with two broken hands for much of the 1966 season until a hamstring injury sidelined him but he still led the AFL in all pass-receiving categories. An artist on the field, he outraced defensive backs and made spectacular catches with a grace unsurpassed in his time and rivaled by few others thereafter. He gathered many personal records, some of which still stand. An "efficient receiver," he scored 87 touchdowns (85 via the pass) and made 542 receptions for 10,266 total yards to rank fourth on the all-time receiving list at his retirement. His other AFL records included consecutive games scoring a touchdown (9), seasons leading the league in touchdowns (3), consecutive games with one or more pass receptions (96), games making touchdown catches (9), game touchdown receptions (tied with 4), and game receptions (13). He became the only AFL player to gain over 1,000 yards receiving for seven consecutive seasons, leading the AFL three times. An All-Pro each year from 1963 to 1969, he played in two AFL championship games and one Super Bowl (1971, with one TD pass reception). Alworth, a member of the All-Time AFC team, saw his number 19 retired by the Chargers.

Alworth studied law one year and became a successful businessman with diversified interests. Alworth and his first wife Betty Jean, to whom he was married in 1958 while still in high school, had two children, Lance, Jr., and Kelly. Divorced in 1969, he married Marilyn Joyce Lewis Gallo in 1970. This marriage also ended in divorce in 1979. He had three children by this second marriage, Lacy Elizabeth and Meles Faith, both of whom died as infants in 1973, and one daughter, Rian Faith, born in 1975. Alworth was elected to the NFF College Football and Pro Football Halls of Fame and was selected to the latter's AFL-NFL 1960–1984 All-Star team. He owns Space Saver, an industrial real estate company in San Diego.

BIBLIOGRAPHY: Kelly A. Alworth to Charles R. Middleton, September 3, 1985; Gerald Astor, "Lance Alworth: Charger Goes Groovy," *Look* 33 (December 2, 1969), pp. 91–92ff.; Herman L. Masin, "Fawn-Loving Roving Boy," *Senior Scholastic* 89 (September 16, 1966), p. 24; Ronald L. Mendell and Timothy B. Phares, *Who's Who in Football* (New Rochelle, NY 1974); *NYT*, July 4, 1974; Roger Treat, ed., *The Encyclopedia of Football*, 16th ed., rev. by Pete Palmer (New York, 1979).

Charles R. Middleton

AMECHE, Alan Dante "The Horse" (b. 1 June 1933, Kenosha, WI), college and professional player, is the son of factory worker August and Elizabeth (Lentini) Ameche, both Italian immigrants. Ameche attended Kenosha public schools and graduated in 1951 from Kenosha Bradford High School, where he made All-State fullback in football and excelled at track and field. He attended the University of Wisconsin from 1951 to 1955 and received a physical education degree in 1955. Ameche played fullback under coach Ivy Williamson at Wisconsin, where he set a four-year NCAA rushing record of 3,212 yards, averaged 4.8 yards per carry, and scored 25 touchdowns. The strong, durable, 6 foot, 215 pound Ameche played linebacker and fullback his junior and senior years, averaging 55 minutes a game. Nicknamed "The Horse," he rushed for at least 100 yards a game 16 times and achieved a high of 200 yards against Minnesota in 1951. A two-time All-American and three-time All-BTC selection, Ameche won the Walter Camp Memorial Trophy in 1953 and 1954 and Heisman Trophy in 1954.

As a freshman Ameche broke the Wisconsin rushing record in 1951 with 824 yards and the BTC mark with 774 yards. In 1952 he ran for 946 yards and again led the BTC with 721 yards. In the 1953 Rose Bowl he gained 133 yards in Wisconsin's 7–0 loss to Southern California. Ameche married Yvonne Molinaro in November 1952 and had six children, Brian, Alan, Jr., Michael, Catherine, Elizabeth, and Paul (deceased). In 1953 Ameche rushed for 802 yards, made All-American, and was named to the All-Academic team. His senior year, he gained 641 yards and scored nine touchdowns. In 1954 Ameche was chosen BTC MVP and made unanimous All-American. The quiet, modest Ameche accepted the public acclaim in a sincere, unassuming manner.

From 1955 to 1960 Ameche played pro football for the Baltimore Colts (NFL). He rushed for 4,045 yards in 964 carries for a 4.2-yard average, scored 44 touchdowns, and caught 101 passes. In 1955 Ameche led the NFL with 961 rushing yards, made All-Pro, and won Rookie of the Year honors. An excellent blocker and power runner, Ameche played on the 1958 and 1959 Baltimore Colts championship teams under coach Weeb Ewbank.* He scored the winning touchdown in the famous 23–17 sudden-death NFL title game in 1958 against the New York Giants.

Ameche joined two Colt teammates in establishing a chain of successful restaurants, which he later sold. He lives in Malvern, PA, where he owns three indoor tennis facilities, and he has a restaurant and bar in WI. Ameche, whose hobbies include tennis, classical music, and bridge, was elected in 1975 to the NFF College Football Hall of Fame. Ameche ranks among the greatest fullbacks, with his football and business accomplishments attesting to his determination and competitive spirit.

BIBLIOGRAPHY: Alan Ameche to Edward J. Pavlick, January, 1974; Oliver E. Kuechle with Jim Mott, *On Wisconsin! Badger Football* (Huntsville, AL, 1977); Herman L. Masin, "They Yell Themselves 'Horse,' " *Senior Scholastic* 65 (November 10, 1954), p. 22; Milwaukee *Journal*, January 11, 1979; Murray Olderman, *The Running Backs* (Englewood Cliffs, NJ, 1969); University of Wisconsin, Athletic Information Office files, Madison, WI.

Edward J. Pavlick

ANDERSON, Edward Nicholas "Eddie" (b. 13 November 1900, Oskaloosa, IA; d. 26 April 1974, Clearwater, FL), college and professional athlete and college coach, was the son of Edward M. and Nellie (Dinon) Anderson and coached football thirty-nine years with a composite 201–128–15 (.606 percent) record at Columbia College (Loras), De Paul University, Holy Cross College, and the University of Iowa (WC). Chosen 1939 Coach of the Year by the AFCA, Anderson compiled the seventh highest football victory total in college history. Anderson, a member of the HAF College Hall of Fame, was elected in 1971 to the NFF College Football Hall of Fame. He coached the Chicago *Tribune* College All-Stars twice, losing in 1940 to the Green Bay Packers 45–28, and defeating in 1950 the Philadelphia Eagles 17–7.

Anderson grew up in Mason City, IA, where he starred on the Mason City High School football team and graduated in 1918. Anderson started at end his freshman year at the University of Notre Dame (1918) for rookie Irish head coach Knute Rockne.* During Anderson's playing career (1918–1921), Notre Dame achieved a composite 31–2–2 record, in his second and third years perfect 9–0–0 seasons as Champions of the West, and a 22-game undefeated streak. WC champion Iowa ended the string with a 10–7 upset in 1921. At Notre Dame Anderson played with halfback George Gipp,* guard Heartley "Hunk" Anderson,* and tackle Lawrence "Buck" Shaw.* He led the Fighting Irish in pass receptions (43) and touchdowns (5) in 1920 and 1921 and captained the 1921 Irish team. Rockne praised the 5 foot, 10 inch, 166 pound Anderson: "I never saw him knocked off his feet." Anderson made 1921 All-American first team (*Football World* magazine) and second team (INS) and also performed as a two-year regular basketball guard, baseball catcher, gymnast, and boxer.

After earning a B.S. in Pre-Medicine at Notre Dame in 1922, Anderson played pro football at end with the Rochester Jeffersons (1922), Rock Island Independents (1923), and Chicago Cardinals (1923–1925) of the NFL. The Cardinals won the NFL championship with an 11–2–1 record Anderson's final year. He coached Columbia College to an undefeated season his first year there (1922) and a 16–6–2 composite record (1922–1924). He piloted De Paul University to a combined 21–22–3 record (1925–1931) while attending Chicago's Rush Medical College, from which he graduated in 1929. Anderson practiced medicine throughout his coaching career and specialized in ear, nose, and throat medicine. He served as head coach at Holy Cross College (1933–1938), producing an outstanding 47–7–4 composite record, two undefeated seasons, and AP poll ninth and fourteenth rankings. Star backs Bill Osmanski and Ronnie Cahill played under Anderson. The only Crusader loss in Anderson's final year, a 7–6 setback to Carnegie Tech, denied Holy Cross a Sugar Bowl bid. Although in contention for the Notre Dame head coaching post in 1934, Anderson was involved with medical research in Boston hospitals and at Harvard University and removed himself from consideration.

The University of Iowa, meanwhile, had won only three of twenty-five WC games between 1934 and 1938, causing fans to speculate that the Hawkeyes might join University of Chicago in dropping WC affiliation. When Anderson was given a three-year contract in 1939 as head coach at a $10,000 annual salary, no one expected that Iowa would finish with a 6–1–1 mark, become WC runner-up, and rank ninth in the AP poll Anderson's first season. Iowa defeated Wisconsin, Minnesota, Purdue, Indiana, and Notre Dame, the latter a 7–6 triumph in the first encounter with the Irish since the sensational 1921 Hawkeyes victory. Heisman Trophy winner Nile Kinnick* incurred a shoulder injury in the Hawkeyes' final game with Northwestern, a 7–7 tie that denied the Hawkeyes a WC co-championship with Ohio State. Iowa won five games in the last quarter in 1939, as "Iron Men" regular end and captain Erwin Prasse and tackle Mike Enich played sixty minutes of several games.

Anderson enlisted in the U.S. Army during World War II (1943–1945) and served as a major in the Medical Corps. He returned to Iowa from 1946 to 1949 and kept the Hawkeyes in or near the BTC first division. In Anderson's eight seasons at Iowa, his teams achieved a combined 35–33–2 record. After Holy Cross finished 1–9–0 under Coach Osmanski in 1949, the Crusaders persuaded Anderson to return in 1950 as head coach. He stayed fifteen years and compiled a combined 82–60–4 record. His three best seasons came in 1951 (8–2–0 and nineteenth AP rank), 1952 (8–2–0), and 1961 (7–3–0). Anderson married Mary Broderick, a Manchester, NH, model, in 1929, and had three sons and one daughter. In 1955 the AP named him to an All-Time Medical All-American team. After retiring from coaching in 1965, he continued as senior physician at Mansfield (CT) State Training School. He and his wife moved in 1970 to Indian Rocks Beach, FL, where he lived in retirement.

BIBLIOGRAPHY: L. H. Baker, *Football: Facts and Figures* (New York, 1945); Chuck Bright, *University of Iowa Football: The Hawkeyes* (Huntsville, AL, 1982); Tim Cohane, *Great College Football Coaches of the Twenties and Thirties* (New Rochelle, NY, 1973); Ronald L. Mendell and Timothy B. Phares, *Who's Who in Football* (New Rochelle, NY, 1974); *Notre Dame All-Americans* (Des Plaines, IL, 1979); *Notre Dame University Football Guide, 1984*; Notre Dame University, Sports Information Office files (South Bend, IN, August 13, 1985).

James D. Whalen

ANDERSON, Heartley William "Hunk" (b. 22 September 1898, Tamarack, MI; d. 24 April 1978, West Palm Beach, FL), college and professional player and coach, was the son of a railroader and made the All-State football team as a senior at Calumet (MI) High School. Notre Dame stars George Gipp,* "Ojay" Larson, and "Dolly" Gray, all Calumet graduates, arranged a football scholarship with coach Knute Rockne* for the financially struggling

Anderson. Anderson starred in the Fighting Irish line from 1919 through 1921, performing on the undefeated 1919 and 1920 squads. At a 1921 pep rally he reportedly told the student body, "You do the best you can, and I'll do the best *we* can." Another legend has the 5 foot, 11 inch, 165 pound Anderson knocking out giant center and teammate George Trafton* in an amateur boxing match. Rockne recognized Anderson as a fine, courageous athlete and an unusually intelligent player.

In 1922 Anderson officially turned pro with the Chicago Bears (NFL), although he previously had played for money under an assumed name—a then common practice. With the Bears, he played guard and coached the line under George Halas* from 1922 through 1925. He may also have played some exhibition games in 1926–1927 because Bears records list him for those seasons, despite his not appearing in any NFL games. Anderson weighed only 192 pounds as a Bear, was rather small even then for a pro lineman, and consequently often relied more on guile than muscle. To counter larger opponents, he invented the cross-body block in 1922.

In 1926 Anderson became a full-time Notre Dame assistant under Rockne. For several years he had returned to South Bend, IN, through the week to help at practices. That year Rockne left Anderson in charge for the Carnegie Tech game and traveled to Chicago to scout the Army-Navy game. When Carnegie Tech upset the Irish, Rockne was criticized for being absent. Nonetheless, Rockne kept faith in Anderson's abilities. Anderson reciprocated by building the powerful forward walls forming the backbone of Rockne's 1929 and 1930 national championship teams.

When Rockne was killed in a March 1931 plane crash, Anderson was named Notre Dame's head football coach and compiled a three-year 16–9–2 record. From 1934 through 1936, he garnered an 11–17–1 mark as head football coach at North Carolina State University (SC). Anderson served as line coach at the University of Michigan (WC) in 1937 and the University of Cincinnati in 1938. In 1939 he returned to pro football as line coach for the Detroit Lions (NFL) and was hired the following year by Halas to coach the Chicago Bears line. Anderson remained with the Bears through 1950 and impressed others as perhaps the nation's most formidable coach of linemen. When Halas served in the U.S. Navy during World War II, Anderson was one of three Bears co-coaches.

Anderson, a member of the NFF College Football Hall of Fame, usually is credited with inventing the line blocking system that made the T formation so successful during the 1940s and initiated the practice of blitzing linebackers to disrupt an opponent's offense. His greatest legacy, however, remains the numerous All-American and All-Pro linemen, who owed much of their success to his coaching. After leaving football, Anderson worked in the steel industry. He was survived by his wife, Marie, one son, William, and two daughters, Mrs. Sebring Simpson and Mrs. Jo Ann Wilcox.

BIBLIOGRAPHY: "A Hunk of History," *The Coffin Corner* 3 (February, 1981) pp. 1–3; Heartley Anderson File, Pro Football Hall of Fame, Canton, OH; Heartley W. "Hunk" Anderson with Emil Klosinski, *Notre Dame, Chicago Bears, and "Hunk"* (Oviedo, FL, 1976); Emil Klosinski, Ronald L. Mendell and Timothy B. Phares, *Who's Who in Football* (New Rochelle, NY, 1974).

Robert N. Carroll

ANDERSON, Kenneth Allan "Ken" (b. 15 February 1949, Batavia, IL), college athlete and professional football player, is the son of Erik and Jean (Phillips) Anderson, of Swedish descent. His father, a second-generation American, worked as the custodian at the local high school. Anderson entered athletics on the Little League level and played all sports through high school in Batavia. He participated in high school basketball with Dan Issel* (IS), who starred at the University of Kentucky and in the NBA. Anderson was recruited to play basketball at small, non-scholarship Augustana College (ICC) and asked permission to play football. He enrolled in 1967 and starred in both sports, scoring over 1,000 points in basketball in three years and setting several NCAA college division passing records.

In 1971 he was drafted in the third round by the Cincinnati Bengals (NFL). He married Bonnie Ziegler on June 17, 1972 and has three children, Matt, Megan Elizabeth, and Molly. After earning a B.S. in Mathematics from Augustana in 1972, he received a law degree from the Chase Law School at Northern Kentucky University in 1981. Early in his second season (1972), he became the Bengals' starting quarterback and held that position for most of his career. His first five years were played under head coach Paul Brown,* and quarterback coach Bill Walsh.* The 6 foot, 3 inch, 212 pound Anderson led the NFL in passing in 1975–1976, 1981, and 1982. In 1982 he set an all-time single-season pass completion percentage (70.3) and completed 20 consecutive passes for another NFL mark, both of which still stand. The holder of every Bengals club passing record, he entered the 1986 season leading the NFL in pass interception percentage. Only 3.58 percent of his 4,475 passes were intercepted.

Anderson ranks seventh on the all-time NFL passing list, completing 2,654 passes for 32,838 yards and 197 touchdowns through the 1986 season, throwing to receivers Charlie Joiner,* Isaac Curtis, Cris Collinsworth, Bob Trumpy, and Dan Ross. One of the era's leading quarterback rushers, he has gained 2,220 yards for a 5.6-yard average and 20 touchdowns. The self-effacing Anderson truly represents the model of a team player and aw-shucks hero usually seen only in fiction. Anderson, who donates much time to charitable causes around his adopted Cincinnati home, in 1975 became the youngest ever named NFL Man of the Year. In his first fifteen years Anderson helped the Bengals reach the playoffs four times, including two Central Division championships. In 1981 he led Cincinnati to the AFC championship and Super Bowl XVI, which his team lost 26–21 to the San Francisco 49ers.

Anderson, a consensus All-Pro and NFL Player of the Year in 1981, performed in the Pro Bowl in 1974, 1976–1977, and 1981–1982. In the off-season Anderson operates a beer distributorship. He wrote of his experiences and passing techniques in a book entitled *The Art of Quarterbacking* (1984). One of the premier quarterbacks in NFL history, he ranked high in all passing categories and is among only six players to win at least three passing titles. Anderson retired following the 1986 season.

BIBLIOGRAPHY: Ken Anderson and Jack T. Clary, *The Art of Quarterbacking* (New York, 1984); "Another Ideal Quarterback," *Time* 119 (January 25, 1982), pp. 64–65; Vince Aversano, "Ken Anderson: Player of the Year," *Football Digest* 11 (April, 1982), pp. 18–25; Pete Axthelm, "Super Bowl: Duel of Wits," *Newsweek*, 99 (January 25, 1982), pp. 62–67; Tom Callahan, "Bengal, Bengal Burning Bright," *Time* 119 (January 4, 1982), p. 67; *Cincinnati Bengals Media Guides, 1972–1984;* Jack T. Clary, *Main Men of the Seventies: The Quarterbacks* (New York, 1975); Weeb Ewbank, Jack Buck, and Bob Broeg, *Football Greats* (St. Louis, 1977); Ronald L. Mendell and Timothy B. Phares, *Who's Who in Football* (New Rochelle, NY, 1974); Lou Sahadi, *Pro Football's Gamebreakers* (Chicago, 1977); Rick Telander, "Walsh's Boys Go Head to Head," *SI* 56 (January 25, 1982), pp. 28–31.

Bruce W. Wasem

ANDERSON, Ottis Jerome "OJ" (b. 19 January 1957, West Palm Beach, FL), college and professional player, is the son of a hardworking motel worker and suffered two traumatic events as a young boy. His father abandoned his wife and five children when Anderson was only eight, and some years later a brother drowned in a swimming accident. Anderson, whose first name is spelled with a double "t" because of the haste of the attending physician at his birth, led the "back of the projects gang" in West Palm Beach. His mother instilled a healthy parental fear in him after he went to a local mall with a friend to steal a pair of shorts. As a strapping athlete with uncanny football moves for West Palm Beach High School in nearby Forest Hills, Anderson was actively recruited by the universities of Notre Dame and Oklahoma. He chose Miami University, however, to remain close to his family and received a B.A. in Physical Education.

Anderson played his final two college seasons as a running back under the much-traveled Lou Saban, who stressed that Ottis needed more discipline to succeed as a pro. Even though Anderson only made *TSN* and the AFCA All-American teams as a senior, St. Louis Cardinals (NFL) head scout George Boone made him the eighth player chosen in the first round of the 1979 player draft. The highlight of his bruising career with St. Louis ironically occurred in his first regular-season game against the Dallas Cowboys at hometown Busch Stadium. Before a sellout crowd of nearly 50,000, Anderson, nicknamed "OJ" because of his stylistic likeness to Orenthal James Simpson,* rushed for 193 yards. The disbelieving Cowboy team had prided itself on checking most opposing backs. When the season ended, he had amassed an incredible 1,605 yards in 16 games.

Over the next six years, Anderson experienced criticism, complaint, and popular ovation. Most fans believe he has not lived up to the great things forecast for him in 1979, when *TSN* both voted him Rookie of the Year and NFC Player of the Year and selected him on its NFC All-Star Team, honors he has not enjoyed since. Nevertheless, he rushed for over 1,000 yards during four of the past seven seasons. Only in the strike-abbreviated 1982 season, his injury-plagued (toe, calf, and knee) 1985 campaign, and in 1986 has OJ failed to amass 1,000 yards. The criticism has stemmed not from the bottom line of his performance but from his refusal to endure extra hits to gain that extra yard. Knowledgeable fans claim that he has seemed more intent on garnering yards than winning. Anderson's philosophy of survival has largely resulted from his conversations with former Pittsburgh Steeler (NFL) running back Franco Harris,* who lasted thirteen seasons in a game with a life expectancy under four years. Harris often stepped out of bounds to avoid hits that might have sidelined him for the next game.

The 6 foot, 2 inch, 220 pound Anderson possesses lightning speed and power, instilling a healthy fear even in the toughest defender. In 1984 he showed a new dimension with 70 catches, mostly from quarterback Neil Lomax out of the backfield. The Cardinals improved that year to 8–7–1, nearly making the playoffs. However, drug scandals, owner threats of a possible move, and injuries plagued the Cardinals in 1985. After St. Louis won three of its first four games, Anderson spent most of his time wrapped in his warm-up jacket on the sidelines. The Cardinals, picked first in the Eastern Division, finished with a dismal 5–11 mark, sparking owner Bill Bidwill to consider moving the franchise. During the 1986 season the Cardinals traded Anderson to eventual Super Bowl winner Giants for whom he saw limited duty.

Anderson's impressive eight-year NFL totals include 8,087 yards rushing on 1,810 carries for a 4.31-yard average in 113 games. He has scored 47 touchdowns rushing and another 5 on passes to go with his 2,797 yards on 308 receptions and 9.1-yard average per catch. He was the most prolific Cardinals back ever. Although wearing number 32, he really wanted jersey number 40 in 1979 because Gale Sayers* was his favorite player. The stepbrother of former TCU quarterback Mike Taliferro, Ottis remains one of the best liked Cardinal players for his quiet, friendly demeanor. Rarely, if ever, does he swear. During his first few seasons he joined teammate Theotis Brown to form the clever "Ottis and Theotis Show" on KMOX radio. He played in the 1979 and 1980 Pro Bowls and appeared briefly in the 1986 playoffs as the Giants routed the San Francisco 49ers 49–3 and the Washington Redskins 17–0 on their way to a victory over the Denver Broncos in Super Bowl XXI.

BIBLIOGRAPHY: *Newsweek* 94 (December 24, 1979), p. 81; *NYT*, December 5, 1984,

p. 28; *TSN*, December 8, 1979, p. 3; *TSN*, October 17, 1981, p. 51; *TSN*, December 12, 1981, p. 20; *TSN*, December 5, 1983, p. 11; *TSN Football Register—1985*.

William A. Borst

ANDERSON, Richard Paul "Dick" "Andy" (b. 10 February 1946, Midland, MI), college and professional player, grew up in Boulder, CO. He attended Boulder High School and the University of Colorado, graduating with a B.S. in Business in 1968. Anderson, whose brother Bobby played for the Denver Broncos (NFL), is the son of chemist Herman C. and Mariette G. (Moser) Anderson. Anderson, an all-around athlete in high school, played football, basketball, golf, and skiing and performed at fullback in a backfield which included Hale Irwin* (OS), the only Colorado golfer who could defeat him. "Andy," as he was known then, established his reputation as a "Big Play" player. At the University of Colorado, coach Eddie Crowder converted him to strong safety, a position where he excelled thereafter. Upon finishing his college career, he held several Buffalos records including 14 career interceptions (7 his senior year) and 113 unassisted tackles in a single season (1967). He twice was named to the All-BEC Academic Team and, his senior year, was chosen by both the AP and UPI as All-BEC, second team All-American by the FWAA, first team All-American by the NEA and AP, and All-Bowl Team by UPI. He played in the Senior Bowl, being defensive captain of the North squad, and was selected Colorado College Athlete of the Year. After scoring two touchdowns on punt returns in the Blue-Gray game, he was chosen MVP for that contest and assured that he would be picked high in the AFL-NFL combined draft.

Selected by the Miami Dolphins (AFL), Anderson played his entire pro career there as a safety. The smart 6 foot, 2 inch, 200 pounder often successfully defensed more physically talented opponents. After earning AFL Defensive Rookie of the Year honors in 1968, he played on the no-name defensive teams which took Miami to Super Bowls VI, VII, and VIII and one undefeated season in the early 1970s. His career was interrupted briefly when he was forced to sit out most of the 1975 and all of the 1976 season because of knee injuries, but he returned for a final year of competition before retiring in 1977. Anderson's records with the Dolphins remain impressive. He ranks second behind his business partner and backfield mate Jake Scott* in team career interceptions (34) and tied NFL records by making four interceptions in a single game and returning two for touchdowns. His career yardage on interception returns (792 for a 23.3-yard average), 230 yards returned in 1968, single-game 121 yards returned (1973), and three career interceptions returned for touchdowns (including one of 96 yards) all set Dolphins records. He thrice was named All-Pro (1972–1974) and entered the Colorado Sports Hall of Fame in 1980. The Pro Football Hall of Fame selected him to its AFL-NFL 1960–1984 All-Star Second Team.

Always a leader on and off the field, Anderson became president of the NFL Players Association from 1975 to 1977 and effectively led that organization through those difficult years of strikes and negotiations of expanded player benefits. Perhaps this experience encouraged him to serve from 1978 to 1981 as a Florida state senator as a self-described conservative Democrat. In this capacity, he was selected as the Most Valuable Senator by the Florida Farm Bureau. Anderson, a self-made millionaire, lives in Miami and remains active in numerous business and civic organizations. He is a recognized and successful investment consultant and owns property in Colorado and elsewhere. He married Lois Bruce, whom he met in college, on August 25, 1967, and with whom he had two sons, Christopher and Blakley. He later wed Joy Chiles in 1977 and has one son, Ryan.

BIBLIOGRAPHY: Boulder (CO) *Daily Camera*, 1966–1985; Eddie Crowder, Interview with Charles R. Middleton, Boulder, CO; Ronald L. Mendell and Timothy B. Phares, *Who's Who in Football* (New Rochelle, NY, 1974); *NYT*, 1975–1976; Dave Plati, Director of Sports Information, University of Colorado, Boulder, CO to Charles R. Middleton, 1985; *WWA*, 40th ed. (1978–1979); *Who's Who in American Politics* (1985–1986); *Who's Who in the South and Southwest* (1984).

Charles R. Middleton

ANDREWS, William Luther (b. 25 December 1955, Thomasville, GA), college and professional player, is the son of pulpwood worker Azell and Ethel (Glenn) Andrews. He has three brothers, Roosevelt, Azell, Jr., and Thomas, and two sisters, Mattie and Rosetta. Andrews attended Thomasville High School, where he starred in football, basketball, and track. After enrolling at Auburn University (SEC) in 1975, he lettered in football three years and received the Outstanding Senior Player Award in 1978. The Auburn *Media Guide* called him "one of the classiest men ever to wear an Auburn jersey" and "one of the most complete backs in Auburn history." Although primarily used as a blocker for Joe Cribbs and James Brooks (who rank second and third among Auburn's all-time leading rushers), Andrews still gained 1,347 yards rushing on 267 carries (5.0-yard average) to rank fifteenth on the list.

Andrews joined the Atlanta Falcons (NFL) in 1979 and made the NFL's All-Rookie Team, second team All-NFL in 1981 and 1982, and first team in 1983. Andrews played in the Pro Bowl from 1980 through 1983 but spent the 1984 season on the injured reserve list after a pre-season knee injury and remained sidelined the entire 1985 season. Andrews saw limited action during the 1986 season. From 1979 through 1983, he ranked as the most productive NFL back with 8,381 yards gained (5,772 rushing and 2,610 receiving). His excellence in blocking, running, and receiving established him as the best all-around NFL back. Andrews, the second player in NFL history to gain over 2,000 yards two different seasons (O. J. Simpson* was the first), holds

Falcons records in yards rushing (5,986), rushing attempts (1,315), rushing/receiving yards (8,596), and most games over 100 yards rushing (22). During his career, Andrews has scored 30 touchdowns rushing and caught 11 touchdown passes. In 1981 he set the Falcons record for pass receptions (81), an extremely rare mark for a running back. He has been selected twice as the Falcons' MVP. Andrews married Lydia Elzy on January 1, 1980, and has two sons, Andy and Micah. Andrews lives in Atlanta, where he is actively involved with the Special Olympics, Boy Scouts, Alliance Theatre, and Childrens Hospital.

BIBLIOGRAPHY: William Andrews, Interview with Robert T. Bowen, December 17, 1984; Auburn University *Media Guide, 1977, 1978, 1984*; Auburn University Sports Information Office files, Auburn, AL; *Atlanta Falcons Media Guide, 1984;* Charles Dayton, Atlanta Falcons Director of Public Relations and Promotions, Interviews with Robert T. Bowen, December 5 and 10, 1984.

Robert T. Bowen

ATKINS, Douglas L. "Doug" (b. 8 May 1930, Humboldt, TN), college and professional player, performed as a defensive end. The 6 foot, 8 inch, 270 pound Atkins proved a fine all-around athlete at Humboldt High School, excelling as a basketball player and track high jumper. From 1949 to 1953 he attended the University of Tennessee (SEC) on a basketball scholarship. He also played football at Tennessee for the legendary Robert Neyland,* and in 1952 made All-American at tackle. After graduating from Tennessee in 1953, he became the first-round draft choice of the Cleveland Browns (NFL).

Atkins played for the Cleveland Browns in 1953 and 1954 and was traded to the Chicago Bears (NFL), where from 1955 to 1966 he enjoyed his greatest years. The Bears traded Atkins to the New Orleans Saints, and he played his final three seasons there. He retired at age 39 after 205 NFL games, trailing only Lou Groza* in longevity. Atkins and Bears coach George Halas* waged many widely publicized contract disputes, causing Atkins' eventual departure to New Orleans. Atkins was selected All-Pro for 1960, 1961, and 1963, and played in the Pro Bowl from 1958 through 1963 and in 1965. Besides being named Lineman of the Year in 1958, he made the All-Pro team for the 1960s decade and the AFL-NFL 1960–1984 All-Star second team.

Atkins participated in NFL title games with Cleveland in 1953 and 1954 and was on the 1954 championship squad. He also performed in NFL title games with Chicago in 1956 and 1963, the latter squad winning the NFL championship. According to veteran George Halas, Atkins was the best defensive player he ever saw. Atkins earned legendary acclaim as a devastating pass rusher and often leapfrogged blockers to rush the passer. His defensive coach George Allen* remarked that Atkins looked so big and awesome he frightened the opposition. Often intimidating opponents and dominating games, Atkins ranked among the most effective players Allen had ever seen. Atkins, who on February 9, 1954, married Joyce Gay Floyd, was elected in 1982 to the Pro Football Hall of Fame and in 1985 to the NFF College Football Hall of Fame.

BIBLIOGRAPHY: George Allen with Ben Olan, *Pro Football's 100 Greatest Players* (Indianapolis, IN, 1982); Howard Balzer, "Defensive Class of '82 at Canton," *TSN* (August 16, 1982); Ronald L. Mendell and Timothy B. Phares, *Who's Who in Football* (New Rochelle, NY, 1974); George Vass, *George Halas and the Chicago Bears* (Chicago, 1971); Richard Whittingham, *The Chicago Bears—An Illustrated History* (Chicago, 1979).

John L. Evers

B

BADGRO, Morris Hiram "Red" (b. 1 December 1902, Orillia, WA), college and professional athlete and coach, was the son of a Washington dairy farmer and married Dorothea Taylor of Kent, WA. At the University of Southern California he twice was selected All-PCC at football end, was named to Coach Howard Jones'* All-Time Trojans Football Team, and also starred in baseball and basketball. In 1927 the 6 foot, 190 pound redhead joined the New York Yankees (NFL) but soon switched to pro baseball. After playing for Tulsa, OK (WL), in 1928, he compiled .284 and .239 batting averages as a part-time outfielder in 1929 and 1930 with the St. Louis Browns (AL). Badgro left pro baseball following the next season with Wichita Falls, TX (TL).

In 1930 he returned to pro football with the New York Giants (NFL). In six seasons there, he achieved respect as a hard-tackling and sure defender, strong blocker, and clutch receiver. Although the Giants passed infrequently, he in 1934 tied the NFL leaders with sixteen receptions. Badgro's Giants contended for the NFL championship every year, winning Eastern Division titles in 1933, 1934, and 1935 and the NFL championship in 1934. In 1933 he caught a 40-yard pass from Harry Newman for the first touchdown scored in the initial NFL championship game. Badgro was selected to several unofficial All-Pro teams in 1930 and the next year made the first official NFL squad. After again making the All-NFL squad in 1933 and 1934, Badgro finished his pro career in 1936 with the Brooklyn Dodgers (NFL). From 1933 to 1936 he caught 28 passes for 441 yards (15.8-yard average) and scored three touchdowns.

After serving as end coach at Southern California in 1937, the next year he coached football, basketball, and baseball at Ventura Junior College (CA). He assisted Lou Little* at Columbia University from 1939 to 1942 and held a similar job at the University of Washington from 1946 to 1953. For the next fourteen years, he worked with the State of Washington Department of Agriculture. With his election to the Pro Football Hall of Fame in 1981, he became both the oldest nominee ever chosen (age 78) and the nominee who waited the longest following retirement to be enshrined (45 years).

BIBLIOGRAPHY: Red Badgro file, Pro Football Hall of Fame, Canton, OH; Bob Braunwart and Bob Carroll, "Red Badgro," *The Coffin Corner*, 2 (June, 1980), pp. 1–2; "Guest of Honor," *Pro!*, San Francisco–Seattle Football Game Program, August 5, 1981; "Hall of Fame Profile," *Pro!*, New York Giants–Pittsburgh Football Game Program, September 29, 1981.

Robert Carroll

BAKER, Terry Wayne (b. 5 May 1941, Pine River, MN), college and professional football and basketball player, the first West Coast Heisman Trophy winner was the youngest of three sons born to Max and Laura (White) Baker, who divorced when he was age seven. His mother brought up the children in a lower middle-class neighborhood of Portland, OR. Brother Gary encouraged Baker to participate in sports at the local park. Because he lacked gloves, left-handed Terry learned to throw a baseball with his right hand and became ambidextrous. Through Ockley Green Grade School and Jefferson High School, Baker followed the path taken by Stanford great Bobby Grayson.* His high school teams won state titles in football, basketball, and baseball. As a senior, Baker was selected a *Senior Scholastic* All-American in both basketball (20 points per game) and football and broke George Shaw's Portland city football records.

Despite his football credentials, he was recruited to Oregon State University on a basketball scholarship. As a football walk-on, the 6 foot, 3 inch, 198 pound Baker began the 1960 season as the second-string tailback. When the regular quarterback was injured, he moved there and compiled 1,473 yards rushing and passing to finish sixth nationally. He subsequently led Beaver gridiron squads to a 5–5 season in 1961 and a 9–2 log his senior year. Baker guided Oregon State to a 6–0 victory over Villanova in the 1962 Liberty Bowl and scored the winning touchdown. In 1962 Baker represented the epitome of Saturday's college football hero. He led the nation in total offense (2,276 yards) and won numerous awards, including the Heisman Trophy and Maxwell Award, several Player of the Year citations, every major All-American team, and the NFF's Scholar-Athlete Award. *SI*, in its Sportsman of the Year issue, especially noted Baker's scholastic accomplishments.

A varsity basketball player, Baker led the freshman team in scoring. He became a starter and playmaker on Oregon State's 1962 and 1963 NCAA tournament teams, averaging 10.7 and 10.4 points per game. He remains the only Heisman Trophy winner to play in the NCAA basketball tournament the same season. Although he was the first player chosen in the 1963 NFL draft, Baker experienced an undistinguished pro football career. He spent three seasons as reserve quarterback for the Los Angeles Rams. Not disillusioned by the experience, he used it as a means to further his education. In 1968 he earned a law degree from the University of Southern California and returned to Portland, where he is now a senior law partner. In 1964 he married Diane Davis and has two children, Brian and Wendy. Baker, who was divorced in 1983, has been elected to the NFF College Football and Oregon Halls of Fame.

BIBLIOGRAPHY: Bob Clark, "Living Legend," Eugene (OR) *Register-Guard* (October 10, 1982), pp. 1–5C; Herman L. Masin, "The Baker Who Cooks with Gas!," *Senior Scholastic* 79 (November 29, 1961), p. 34; Alfred Wright, "Sportsman of the Year: Terry Baker," *SI* 18 (January 7, 1963), pp. 16–21; Alfred Wright, "With Terry You Stop and Think," *SI* 15 (October 16, 1961), pp. 52–58.

Dennis Clark

BAKKEN, James Leroy "Jim" (b. 2 November 1940, Madison, WI), college and professional football and baseball player, starred at West High School in Madison, WI. At the University of Wisconsin (BTC) from 1958 to 1961, he participated in football and baseball and received a B.S. in Education. A seventh round NFL draft pick as a placekicker–defensive back in 1962, he was released by the Los Angeles Rams and signed as free agent with the St. Louis Cardinals. As the Cardinals' regular placekicker from 1963 through 1978, Bakken led St. Louis in scoring 16 consecutive seasons and holds nearly all club season scoring and field goal records. His team career records included 234 consecutive games played (ranking third behind Jim Marshall and Mick Tingelhoff), 534 of 553 extra points (ranking third behind George Blanda* and Lou Groza*), 282 of 448 field goals (tied for fourth with Fred Cox behind Blanda, Jim Turner, and Jan Stenerud), and 1,380 points (ranking fifth behind Blanda, Groza, Turner, and Stenerud).

The 6 foot, 199 pound Bakken led the NFL in scoring with a team record 117 points (1967) and in field goals with 25 (1964) and a team record 27 (1967). Besides kicking a career-high 54-yard field goal in a pre-season win over the New York Jets in 1973, he booted a 51-yarder in regular season against the Cleveland Browns in 1964. Bakken holds club records of 17 full seasons as a Cardinal and scoring in 79 consecutive games. In a 28–14 win over the Pittsburgh Steelers in 1967, he set NFL records for most field goals attempted (9) and most field goals made (7). In 1973 he made six of seven field goals against the Atlanta Falcons. Bakken won the Paul Christman Award in 1975 and the Cardinals' MVP honor in 1976. He made *TSN* NFL Eastern Conference All-Star team in 1967 and 1968 and the NFC All-Star team in 1975 and 1976 and participated in the 1965, 1967, 1975, and 1976 Pro Bowls.

Bakken, a strong character with self-confidence, possessed a winning attitude and was not bothered by pressure. Although not cocky, he expected to do well in nearly every situation. The past president of the NFL Players Association, he lives with his wife, Hope, and two children in St. Louis.

BIBLIOGRAPHY: *St. Louis Football Cardinals Guide and Record Book, 1977; TSN Football Register—1978*; Jack Zanger, *Pro Football 1970* (New York, 1970).

John L. Evers

BARWEGAN, Richard J. "Dick" (b. 25 December 1921, Chicago, IL; d. 3 September 1966, Baltimore, MD), college and professional player and coach, ranked among the greatest interior linemen of the late 1940s and early 1950s. The son of George Barwegan, he graduated from Fenger High School in Chicago and entered Purdue University (WC) in 1943. Barwegan played with the College All-Stars that year under wartime regulations allowing undergraduate participation in the annual game and helped them defeat the NFL Washington Redskins 27–7. Purdue posted a perfect 9–0 record during his freshman year, with Barwegan being named MVP. An offensive and defensive guard and sometime linebacker, Barwegan made the College All-Stars four times, captained the 1944 and 1947 squads, and starred in the 16–0 victory over the Chicago Bears in 1947.

After graduation from Purdue in 1947, Barwegan joined the New York Yankees (AAFC). A year later he moved to the Baltimore Colts in an egalitarian movement within the AAFC and became one of the squad's first stars. He gained All-AAFC honors as offensive guard with the Colts' 1948 7–7 and 1949 1–11 clubs. When the Colts disbanded in 1950, Barwegan played the next three years with the Chicago Bears (NFL). He earned All-NFL honors in 1950 and 1951, as the Bears posted 9–3 and 7–5 records. On the Bears, he played with George Connor,* Johnny Lujack,* and other luminaries.

In 1953 Barwegan was traded back to the reassembled Baltimore NFL franchise and finished his playing career there the next year. He returned in 1962 as assistant coach of the Chicago Bulls of the AFL and completed the season as head coach after Ed Sprinkle joined the New York Titans. Barwegan established a seafood business in Baltimore and worked as sales manager of a paint company. Named with Jim Parker* and Dick Stanfel* as a guard on the Pro Football Hall of Fame Selection Committee's All-Pro Squad of the 1950s, Barwegan exhibited outstanding mobility and competitive leadership. The 6 foot, 1 inch, 228 pound Barwegan excelled at opening up the middle line and as a wide-ranging linebacker. Barwegan, who died of a heart attack, was survived by his wife Elizabeth (Ferguson), four children (two sons and two daughters), one brother, one sister, and his father.

BIBLIOGRAPHY: Tom Bennett et al., eds., *The NFL's Official Encyclopedic History of Professional Football* (New York, 1977); Chicago *Tribune*, September 4, 1966; George Sullivan, *Pro Football A to Z* (New York, 1975); Roger Treat, ed., *The Encyclopedia of Football*, 16th rev. ed., rev. by Pete Palmer (New York, 1979).

Leonard Frey

BASTON, Albert "Bert" (b. 3 December 1894, St. Louis Park, MN; d. 16 November 1979, St. Cloud, MN), college and professional player and coach, came from a family that pioneered St. Louis Park, a Minneapolis suburb. He played football at St. Louis Park High School and starred at end from 1914 through 1916 for the University of Minnesota (WC) gridiron teams. In his junior and senior years, he made All-American on Walter Camp's* team and became the first Gopher so honored twice. Baston, cited for his outstanding offensive and defensive play, came to Minnesota when the forward pass first became effective. Quarterback "Pudge" Wyman combined with Baston to form one of the greatest all-time college football passing duos.

In Baston's sophomore year, Minnesota celebrated its first homecoming as it upset a favored University of Wisconsin eleven. The formidable 1914 Gophers lost only to WC titlist Illinois. In 1915 Minnesota finished undefeated, tied with Illinois, providing coach Henry Williams* his last WC championship team. Senior Baston captained the 1916 Gophers squad, considered Coach Williams' best aggregate and one of the greatest all-time Minnesota teams. After defeating South Dakota State, North Dakota, and South Dakota, the Gophers trounced Iowa 67–0 and then suffered a 14–9 loss from overconfidence to Illinois. In one of the finest school exhibitions ever, Minnesota routed Wisconsin 54–0. Baston electrified the crowd by returning the opening kickoff of the second half for an 85-yard touchdown.

Baston received his Bachelor's degree from Minnesota in 1917 and graduated from the law school. After serving in the U.S. Marines in World War I, he played in the NFL with the Hammond Pros in 1919, Buffalo All-Americans in 1920, and Cleveland Indians in 1920 and 1921 before a service injury forced his retirement. Baston assisted football coaches Williams and W. H. "Doc" Spaulding at Minnesota in the 1920s and became end coach there in 1930. Under Baston's leadership, Minnesota fielded very fine offensive and defensive ends. Baston figured prominently in Bernie Bierman's* five national championships and six WC titles and trained All-American ends Frank "Butch" Larson (1933–1934) and Ray King (1937). Baston, who bought a car dealership in St. Cloud, MN, in 1939 and moved there in 1950, was voted into the NFF College Football Hall of Fame. He and his wife Ruby (died 1974) had one son Frederick, likewise a college football player at Minnesota.

BIBLIOGRAPHY: George Barton, *My Lifetime in Sports* (Minneapolis, MN, 1957); Stan W. Carlson, *Dr. Henry L. Williams* (Minneapolis, MN, 1938); Stan W. Carlson, *Minnesota Huddle Annual 1936–1938* (Minneapolis, MN, 1936–1938); Richard Fisher, *Who's Who in Minnesota Athletics* (Minneapolis, MN, 1941); Minneapolis *Star & Tribune*, November 17, 1979; University of Minnesota, *One Hundred Years of Golden Gopher Football* (Minneapolis, MN, 1981).

Stan W. Carlson

BATTLES, Clifford Franklin "Cliff" (b. 1 May 1910, Akron, OH; d. 28 April 1981), college and professional player and coach, was the son of a saltworks laborer with Goodrich and Firestone and graduated in 1927 from Kenmore High School in Akron, OH. For the next four years Battles starred as a halfback at West Virginia Wesleyan, a small Methodist college. Battles, who captained the basketball, track, baseball, and football teams, majored in English, graduated Phi Beta Kappa, and was a Rhodes Scholarship candidate.

Upon graduation in 1932, the 6 foot, 1 inch, 195 pound Battles joined the Boston Braves (NFL) as a halfback. During his rookie season Battles started at quarterback and finished second in the NFL in rushing. Battles moved to halfback the following season and led the NFL in rushing with 737 yards and an outstanding 5.0-yard average. Named to the All-NFL team in 1933, Battles quickly gained respect as a fast, elusive, brainy runner. Battles led Boston to an Eastern Division championship in 1936 but was injured during the first quarter in the Redskins loss in the championship game to the Green Bay Packers.

Poor attendance caused the Redskins to move to Washington for the 1937 season. Once again Battles led the NFL in rushing with a career-high 874 yards and was named to the All-NFL team. Along with quarterback Sammy Baugh,* Battles helped Washington win its first championship with a 28–21 victory over the Chicago Bears. The following spring, premier football running back Battles attempted to negotiate a raise with Redskins owner George Marshall.* Since Marshall refused to budge, Battles retired from pro football at age 28.

Battles became assistant football coach under Lou Little* at Columbia University (IL) in 1938 but left his coaching job in 1942 to serve in the U.S. Marines during World War II. Battles coached the El Toro Marines in California in 1944 and finished his sports career in 1946 and 1947 as the head coach of the Brooklyn Dodgers (AAFC). Subsequently, Battles became a manufacturer's representative for heavy machinery and the manager of civic relations for General Electric. He died of heart complications, leaving his wife, Edith, and two daughters, Pat Carlson and Judith Dowd.

Battles' pro career statistics included 3,542 yards gained in 846 rushing attempts (4.2-yard average) and 27 touchdowns and 37 passes caught for 546 yards (14.8-yard average) and 4 touchdowns. He scored 31 touchdowns and 4 extra points for 190 career NFL points. In 1955 Battles was named to the NFF College Football Hall of Fame, the first small college player so honored. The three-time All-NFL halfback and first player to rush for over 200 yards in a game was selected to the Pro Football Hall of Fame in 1968.

BIBLIOGRAPHY: Cliff Battles file, Pro Football Hall of Fame, Canton, OH; Myron Cope, *The Game That Was: The Early Days of Pro Football* (New York, 1970); *NYT*, April 29, 1981; Murray Olderman, *The Running Backs* (Englewood Cliffs, NJ, 1969);

George Sullivan, *Pro Football's All-Time Greats: The Immortals in Pro Football's Hall of Fame* (New York, 1968).

Daniel Frio

BAUGH, Samuel Adrian "Slingin' Sammy" (b. 17 March 1914, Temple, TX), college and professional athlete and football coach, became the nation's most celebrated passing star. As an All-American tailback at TCU in 1935 and 1936 and quarterback star with the Washington Redskins (NFL), Baugh revolutionized the sport. The 6 foot, 2 inch, 180 pound Baugh remained cool under intense pressure, stood poised with his arm cocked, ready to strike like an ancient gladiator, and influenced a generation of young passers. Don Smith of the Pro Football Hall of Fame stated, "More than any other person, the transformation of pro football from an infantry-type game to a pass-punctuated offensive extravaganza can be traced to Baugh." Football expert Grantland Rice* (OS) named Baugh the finest quarterback of all time in both college and pro football. Baugh's slingshot throws forced receivers to adopt new pass-catching techniques. Rice once wrote, "There were times when you couldn't even follow the flight of the ball. On one occasion he apparently knocked his receiver down with as much speed as [baseball pitcher] Dizzy Dean* [BB] ever saw." When *SI* marked the anniversary of college football's first one hundred years in 1969, Baugh was chosen the All-Century quarterback.

Redskins owner George Preston Marshall* promoted his first draft choice as a cowboy to the Washington fans. Baugh really grew up in a farming town, where his father, J. V. Baugh, worked for the railroad. Only after marrying high school sweetheart Edmonia Smith in 1938 and building a 6,300-acre ranch near Rotan, TX, with his grid earnings did he learn to ride and rope cattle in true cowboy fashion. Nationwide adulation and his cowboy reputation led to a starring role in the 1941 Republic movie serial *King of the Texas Rangers*. Baugh resembled a classic movie cowboy, being ruggedly handsome, tall, and lean. The Baughs moved in 1931 to Sweetwater, TX, where Sam played baseball, basketball, and football. Since baseball was his favorite sport, he played two years in the St. Louis Cardinals (NL) chain between football seasons. A tailback initially for Sweetwater High, Baugh practiced long hours polishing his passing skills. During his senior year (1932) he was relegated to blocking back.

Leo "Dutch" Meyer,* the TCU (SWC) freshman coach when Baugh arrived on campus in 1933, immediately recognized his passing talent. Years later Meyer commented, "Why, I've never seen anybody in his class as a passer. He could drop the ball on a dime from 30 yards with no more than wrist action." When Meyer took over as head coach in 1934, sophomore Baugh became a starting tailback. In three varsity campaigns Baugh completed 274 of 594 aerials for 3,437 yards and 40 touchdowns. Baugh's figures were unmatched even in the "pass crazy" SWC. Fifteen years later his national completion record finally was broken by a passer playing four varsity seasons. With Baugh at the helm, the Horned Frogs compiled a 29–7–2 record and scored Sugar and Cotton Bowl triumphs over LSU and Marquette in 1936 and 1937.

Baugh's most famous collegiate passing performance came against SMU on November 30, 1935, with the national championship at stake. After unbeaten SMU scored a stunning 20–14 victory, Grantland Rice termed it "one of the greatest football games ever played." Baugh completed only 17 of 45 passes for 177 yards but displayed incredible accuracy. Bill Cunningham of the Boston *Post* calculated that Baugh found his receivers on all but two passes. Said Cunningham, "He merely lifted his arm, cracked his wrist like a whip and there through the sunlight went the shining, spinning spheroid." Football writer Wilton Hazzard accused Baugh of possessing "uncanny accuracy that smacked of witchcraft," while George White of the Dallas *News* commented, "Visitors sat back and marveled at his accurate throws, but his over anxious receivers could not hold his bullet throws."

Baugh, a complete football player, displayed his other amazing talents before a national audience in the 1936 Sugar Bowl, as the Frogs defeated LSU 3–2 in a driving rainstorm. UPI writer George Kirksey remarked, "The almost unbelievable exploits of Sammy Baugh caused coaches, critics and just plain football fans to hail him as one of the year's greatest gridiron players. Passing is only one of Baugh's many accomplishments. He booted the heavy, waterlogged ball 14 times for an average of 48 yards." Yale coach Raymond "Ducky" Pond termed Baugh the best kicker he had ever seen in "adverse weather conditions." Baugh played just as impressively on defense, twice intercepting passes deep in TCU territory and making eight tackles from his safety post. Baugh prevented one touchdown with a spectacular open-field tackle at the Horned Frogs' two-yard line. He stalled another threat after LSU had gained a first down at the four-yard line by tackling the fullback for a three-yard loss. Baugh made the day's longest run, 42 yards from scrimmage. Baugh climaxed his collegiate career by passing for the lone touchdown, as the 1937 college All-Stars upset the defending NFL champion Green Bay Packers 6–0 in Chicago.

Baugh once held literally every NFL game, season, and career passing record. During 16 seasons with the Washington Redskins (1937–1952), Baugh completed 1,693 of 2,995 passes for 21,886 yards and 187 touchdowns and paced NFL passers six times. His top single-game performances included 29 completions against Los Angeles in 1949, 446 yards against Boston in 1948, and hurling six-touchdown aerials twice. Although many of his passing records have been erased, Baugh remains the greatest punter in NFL history. His punting records include a 45.1-yard career average, a 51.4-yard season average (1940), and leading the NFL four consecutive years. In 1943 Baugh achieved a rare triple crown by leading the NFL in passing, punting, and interceptions (11 in just 10 games). His record of four pass thefts in one game against Detroit in 1943 has since been tied.

Named All-Pro six times, Baugh directed the Redskins to five Eastern Division crowns and NFL championships in 1937 and 1942. When the Redskins switched from the single wing to the T formation in 1944, he moved to the quarterback spot and gradually quit playing on defense. Baugh rated the 1937 championship game against the favored Chicago Bears at ice-covered Wrigley Field as his biggest football thrill. Both clubs wore sneakers. Baugh tried passing the ball with numb fingers and was hobbled by a leg injury, as Chicago led 14–7 at halftime. Baugh hurled three touchdown passes in the third period, completed 18 of 33 passes for 335 yards, and helped the Redskins emerge a 28–21 victor.

Washington fans gave Baugh his "day" and presented him with a new station wagon in 1947, as he reached the pinnacle of his magnificent career. The contest matched a weak Redskin team against the finest outfit in Chicago Cardinals history. Baugh devastated the Cardinals, connecting on 25 of 33 passes for 355 yards and 6 touchdowns. Despite the humiliating 45–21 defeat administered by Baugh's squad, the Cardinals still won the 1947 NFL championship.

Baugh later served as assistant coach at Hardin-Simmons University and became head coach there in 1955. After moving to the AFL, he coached the New York Titans in 1960–1961 and Houston Oilers in 1964. Baugh was elected to the NFF College Football Hall of Fame in 1951, the HAF College Football Hall of Fame, and Pro Football Hall of Fame as a charter inductee in 1963.

BIBLIOGRAPHY: Bob Addie and George W. White, "The Saga of Slingin' Sam," *Sport Life* 1 (December, 1948); Steve Boda, Jr., *College Football All-Time Record Book* (New York, 1969); Bob Cunningham, "Pony Band Should Have Played 'California Here I Come,' " Boston *Post*, December 1, 1935; Murray Goodman and Leonard Lewin, *My Greatest Day in Football* (New York, 1948); Wilton Hazzard, "The Football Stars of 1936," *Illustrated Football Annual* (1936); Bruce Jacobs, "Baugh—Perennial of the Pros," *Sport Life* 4 (December, 1951); George Kirksey (UPI), "Great Punting Played Prominent Part in Win," Dallas *News*, January 3, 1936; Grantland Rice, "The Eleven Greatest Football Players of All Time," *Sport* 7 (November, 1949), pp. 32–37, 93; Grantland Rice, "Rice Calls Game One of Greatest in Sports History," Dallas *News* (December 1, 1935); Robert H. Shoemaker, *Famous Football Players* (New York, 1953); Don Smith, *The Pro Football Hall of Fame Souvenir Yearbook 1980–1981;* George W. White, "Wilson, Baugh Battle Thrills 35,000," Dallas *News*, December 1, 1935.

Bernie McCarty

BEBAN, Gary Joseph "The Great One" (b. 5 August 1946, San Francisco, CA), college and professional player, quarterbacked UCLA and won the 1967 Heisman Trophy. The son of truck driver Frank and Italian-born factory worker Anna (Consani) Beban, he grew up in Redwood City, CA, attended Sequoia High School (1960–1964), and played baseball, basketball, and football there. Beban won honorable mention on the 1963 All-American High School football team for his play as tailback at Sequoia. Beban, a highly recruited high school player, accepted a football scholarship offer from UCLA (PEC). Beban became varsity quarterback his sophomore year and led the Bruins to a 9–1 record and Rose Bowl berth. The Bruins' only loss came in their first game against top-ranked Michigan State, despite a stellar performance by Beban. UCLA avenged its defeat in the Rose Bowl by upsetting previously unbeaten Michigan State 14–12. That season Beban set UCLA records in offensive yardage (2,073), passing yardage (1,483), and touchdowns passing (14).

Beban, nicknamed "The Great One," led the Bruins to a combined 16–3–1 record the next two seasons. One of the most anticipated confrontations in college athletics occurred in November 1967 when Beban's Bruins played archrival University of Southern California, captained by running back O. J. Simpson.* UCLA lost the game 21–20, but Beban's play before a national television audience secured his fame. Beban outpolled rival Simpson in the Heisman Trophy balloting, won the Maxwell Award, and ended his college career with 5,358 total yards and 58 touchdowns. Although some football scouts questioned his size, the 6 foot, 190 pound Beban was selected by the Los Angeles Rams in the first round of the 1968 NFL draft. After a contract impasse, Beban was traded to the Washington Redskins (NFL) in June 1968. With the Redskins, Beban played backup running back and wide receiver and retired after the 1970 season. Beban, who received his B.A. in History, married UCLA classmate Kathleen Hanson on June 14, 1968, and has two children, Paul and Mark.

BIBLIOGRAPHY: Gary Beban to Eric C. Schneider, 1984; *CB* (1970), pp. 29–30; Herman L. Masin, "UCLA's Mad Bomber," *Senior Scholastic* 91 (October 19, 1967), p. 19; Gary Ronberg, "Wobbly Way to the Great One's Great Day," *SI* 29 (July 8, 1968), pp. 50–51.

Eric C. Schneider

BEDNARIK, Charles Philip "Chuck" (b. 1 May 1925, Bethlehem, PA), college and professional player and coach and broadcaster, is the son of open-hearth steelworker Charles A. and factory worker Mary (Pivovarnicek) Bednarik, both Czechoslovakian immigrants. Bednarik graduated in 1943 from Liberty High School in Bethlehem, where he lettered in football, basketball, and baseball. In 1949 he graduated from the University of Pennsylvania (IL) with numerous football honors. He married Emma Margetich on June 5, 1948, and has five daughters. During World War II, Bednarik enlisted in the U.S. Army Air Force and flew thirty combat missions over Germany as a B–24 waist gunner. At the University of Pennsylvania he played center and linebacker, made All-East his three varsity years, and was selected an All-American in 1947 and 1948. In 1948 he won the Maxwell Award as the nation's top college player, finished runner-up to Doak Walker* in Heisman Trophy balloting, and was named by Christy Walsh and a board of coaches to a 25-year All-American team. He played in the Blue-Gray, North-South Shrine, and College All-Star games and was picked in the 1949 NFL draft in the first round by the Philadelphia Eagles.

Noted for his bear-hug tackles, the 6 foot, 3 inch, 233 pound Bednarik tackled players decisively and made 20 career interceptions. George Allen* ranked Bednarik as the best linebacker in NFL history, with Dick Butkus* as one of the "two hardest-hitting tacklers [he had] ever seen" and as the era's best center. Bednarik played fourteen seasons for the Philadelphia Eagles, spending his rookie season mainly as backup center and the remainder as an outside linebacker. He made All-Pro from 1950 through 1956 and in 1960, six seasons as a linebacker and two as a center. Bednarik played in seven Pro Bowl games, was selected its MVP in 1954, and helped the Eagles win NFL championships in 1949 and 1960.

Bednarik's eighth All-Pro season in 1960 brought him the greatest attention and achievement. Bednarik had volunteered to play offense *and* defense in 1955 but did not start both ways until the fifth game of the 1960 season. Injuries to Eagles linebackers forced coach Lawrence "Buck" Shaw* to start Bednarik at middle linebacker. At age 35 Bednarik became pro football's last iron man, captivating a nation. En route to the 1960 NFL title, Bednarik hit New York Giant receiver Frank Gifford* with a legal but ferocious blindside tackle. Gifford missed the rest of that season and the entire following year before returning for two more years. Gifford fumbled and the Eagles recovered, to ensure Philadelphia the win. Bednarik provoked controversy by celebrating, while an unconscious Gifford required hospitalization. In the NFL title game against Vince Lombardi's* Green Bay Packers, Bednarik played continuously except for kickoffs. On the game's last play Bednarik bear-hugged hard-hitting Packer great Jimmy Taylor* to the turf in the secondary at the Philadelphia nine-yard line to preserve a 17–13 Eagles victory. That season, Bednarik won the Wanamaker Award as Philadelphia's outstanding athlete.

The down-to-earth, open, honest, energetic, competitive Bednarik made *Sport* magazine's All-Time All-American team in 1960, the ECAC's All-Time team, and the All-Time 50-year NFL team in 1969. The recipient in 1962 of the Hickok Award as the greatest pro lineman of the decade, he was named to the NFF College Football Hall of Fame in 1967 and the Pro Football Hall of Fame in 1969.

BIBLIOGRAPHY: George Allen with Ben Olan, *Pro Football's 100 Greatest Players* (Indianapolis, IN, 1982); Chuck Bednarik as told to Dick Schaap, "Who Says Pros Can't Play 60 Minutes?," *SEP* 234 (November 25, 1961), pp. 54–56ff; John D. McCallum with Chuck Bednarik, *Bednarik: Last of the Sixty-Minute Men* (Englewood Cliffs, NJ, 1977).

John E. DiMeglio

BELL, De Benneville "Bert" (b. 25 February 1894, Philadelphia, PA; d. 11 October 1959, Philadelphia, PA), college player and professional coach, club owner and commissioner, was the son of John Cromwell and Fleurette de Benneville (Myers) Bell, a Philadelphia Main Line family. He married Frances Upton in 1934 and had two sons and one daughter. At Haverford, PA, Prep School, Bell played football, basketball, and baseball. He entered the University of Pennsylvania (IL) in 1915 and played quarterback on the football team. Under his guidance Pennsylvania upset a mighty Michigan eleven in 1915 and lost to Oregon in the Rose Bowl. After serving in the U.S. Army in World War I, Bell captained the 1919 Pennsylvania squad and left the university in 1920 without a degree. From 1920 through 1928 he served as a volunteer assistant football coach of Pennsylvania's team.

In 1933 Bell entered the then treacherous pro football world. Bell joined six friends in purchasing the Frankford Yellow Jackets (NFL) franchise for $2,500 and promptly moved the team to Philadelphia. They renamed it the Eagles in honor of the Blue Eagle, the symbol of the National Recovery Administration. Bell bought the team outright in 1936 for $4,500 and served as both Eagles general manager and coach. During his coaching tenure (1936–1940) the Eagles won only 10 games, lost 44, tied 2, and suffered financial setbacks. Following the 1940 season, Bell sold the Eagles and obtained half interest in the Pittsburgh Steelers (NFL). In 1946 he sold his share of the Steelers to become NFL commissioner.

Bell made major contributions to the NFL's success. In 1936 Bell helped institute an NFL draft system, a system also adopted after World War II by pro baseball, basketball, and hockey. From 1946 to 1949 he guided the NFL through a costly war with the AAFC. Above all, he formulated the basic television policy guiding the NFL to the present day. The NFL blacked out home games, telecast outside games in a team's home territory, and controlled television rights. In 1953 a Federal District Court struck down the commissioner's power to control the telecasts of member franchises but upheld game blackouts.

As commissioner, Bell used broad authority. From his Philadelphia home, the shirt-sleeved Bell united the faction-prone football owners into sport's strongest single economic cartel. Despite his upper-class origins, he possessed a common touch that charmed hostile owners, reporters, players, and congressmen. Under his guidance the NFL prospered and average game attendance nearly doubled between 1946 and 1959. By the late 1950s some 30 million fans regularly watched NFL games on television. While watching a game between his beloved Philadelphia Eagles and Pittsburgh Steelers in 1959, Bell suffered a fatal heart attack.

BIBLIOGRAPHY: Bert Bell files, NFL Office, New York, NY, and Pro Football Hall of Fame, Canton, OH; Tom Bennett et al., *The NFL's Official Encyclopedic History of Professional Football* (New York, 1977); W. C. Heinz, "Boss of the Behemoths," *SEP*

228 (December 3, 1955), pp. 47, 72–75; Al Hirshberg, "He Calls the Signals in Pro Football," *NYT Magazine* (December 23, 1958), pp. 28, 30, 32, 35.

Benjamin G. Rader

BELL, Madison A. "Matty" (b. 22 February 1899, Fort Worth, TX; d. 30 June 1983, Dallas, TX), college player and coach, became an outstanding SWC football mentor. An all-around athlete at Fort Worth's North Side High School, he played under Centre College alumnus Robert L. "Chief" Myers. In 1916 Myers brought Bell, "Bo" McMillin,* "Red" Weaver, and Bill James among others from Fort Worth to Danville, KY. Under coach Charlie Moran,* Centre College lost only three games in four years and upset heavily favored Harvard University 6–0 in 1921. Bell planned to become a lawyer but needed money to attend law school. He coached Haskell Institute in Lawrence, KS for two years to a 12–5–2 record and Carroll College (Wisconsin) for one year to a 4–3–1 mark. He became assistant coach at the University of Texas (SWC) in 1923, expecting to finish his law study. The same year, though, TCU became a member of the SWC and named Bell head coach. From 1923 to 1928 Bell compiled a 33–17–5 record at TCU. Bell coached defensive end Raymond Matthews, one of the all-time great SWC players.

As head coach at Texas A&M University (SWC) from 1929 to 1933, Bell had a mediocre 24–21–3 record and was fired. In 1934 he served as line coach under Ray Morrison* at SMU (SWC). When Morrison left for Vanderbilt University in 1935, Bell became head coach and inherited an outstanding team. In 1935 the Mustangs won all twelve games and were ranked number one, winning the national championship. The Mustangs suffered their first defeat in the 1936 Rose Bowl, losing 7–0 to Stanford University. No other Texas team played in a Rose Bowl game. From 1935 to 1941 Bell compiled a successful 47–23–3 record at SMU. During World War II, Bell served as a lieutenant commander in the U.S. Navy. Bell returned to SMU from 1945 to 1949, coaching consecutive SWC champions in 1947 and 1948. His 1947 team tied Penn State University 13–13 in the Cotton Bowl, while his 1948 squad defeated the University of Oregon 21–13 in the Cotton Bowl. His most outstanding players were Doak Walker* and Kyle Rote. As a coach for twenty-six years, Bell compiled a 152–86–19 career record. From 1949 to 1964 he served as full time athletic director of SMU.

Bell's capacity for leadership and friendship overshadowed his record as a football coach. Bell, whose nickname "Moanin' Matty" came from his predominant pessimism, dealt with his players calmly and methodically. He was elected to the NFF College Football Hall of Fame and HAF College Football Hall of Fame. He served as president of the AFCA longer than any other person and also served many years on the NFL Rules Committee.

BIBLIOGRAPHY: Tim Cohane, *Great College Football Coaches of the Twenties and Thirties* (New Rochelle, NY, 1973); Wilbur Evans and H. B. McElroy, *The Twelfth Man: A Story of Texas A&M Football* (Huntsville, AL, 1974); Will Grimsley, *Football: The Greatest Moments in the Southwest Conference* (Boston, 1968); John D. McCallum and Charles H. Pearson, *College Football U.S.A., 1869–1973* (New York, 1973).

John L. Evers

BELL, Robert Lee "Bobby" (b. 17 June 1940, Shelby, NC), college athlete and professional football player, was considered by many authorities the finest defensive player of his era as a linebacker for the Kansas City Chiefs (AFL, 1963–1969; AFC of NFL, 1970–1974). Bell excelled as an all-around athlete and All-State quarterback in both six-man and eleven-man football at Cleveland High School (Shelby, NC). He in 1959 accepted an athletic scholarship to the University of Minnesota (BTC), where he played quarterback, offensive and defensive lineman, and linebacker, started every game in three years of varsity football, and garnered several national honors. He twice played in the Rose Bowl, was named the 1963 UPI College Lineman of the Year, and received the 1963 Outland Award as the nation's outstanding lineman. In 1961 he became the first black varsity basketball player at Minnesota.

Although only a seventh-round draft pick of the AFL Dallas Texans (later Kansas City Chiefs) in 1963, the 6 foot, 4 inch, 225 pound Bell quickly became one of the most versatile performers of the modern era. With a running back's speed and lineman's strength, he became a cornerstone in Coach Hank Stram's* innovative defensive formations. During his first two seasons, Bell played on the line and dropped back into a linebacker's position in forward pass situations. This alignment, consisting of three linemen and four linebackers, was called the stack defense and pioneered the use of four linebackers in pro football. He also played center and snapped the ball on punts. Bell in his third season moved permanently to left linebacker, where he won All-League designation for the next nine years. He starred on two AFL championship teams (1966, 1969), played in Super Bowls I and IV (1967, 1970), and was named to the last six AFL All-Star games and the first three AFC-NFC Pro Bowl contests. In Super Bowl IV, Bell led the Chiefs' defensive unit to a hard-fought 23–7 win over the NFL Minnesota Vikings.

After 168 games spanning 12 seasons Bell retired in 1975 to manage a restaurant in the Kansas City, MO, area. During his career, he intercepted 26 passes and returned them 479 yards (18.4-yard average per return) and scored six touchdowns by interception, one by fumble, and one by kickoff return. Bell's official statistics did not reflect his leadership qualities, uncanny ability to disrupt well-planned offensive formations through anticipation, or skill at tackling ballcarriers. He in 1969 was named to the All-Time AFL Team and in 1983 became the first Kansas City Chief inducted into the Pro Football Hall of Fame. The Pro Football Hall of Fame chose Bell on the 1960–1984 AFL-NFL All-Star second team.

BIBLIOGRAPHY: Bobby Bell file, Pro Football Hall of Fame, Canton, OH; Kansas City (MO) *Star*, November 2, 1966; May 23, 1967; December 12, 1968; Ruth Ann Lewellen, "Getting to Know Bobby Bell," *Chiefs Insider* (August 10, 1973), pp. 29–30; Joe McGuff, "Bobby Bell: Blood, Sweat, and Tears," *Quarterback* (September, 1970), pp. 70–72; "Manhandler from Minnesota," *Sport* 33 (November, 1962), pp. 42–43; Don Smith, "Bobby Bell, 1983 Enshrinee," Pro Football Hall of Fame *News Release*, April, 1983, Canton, OH.

John Hanners

BELLINO, Joseph Michael "Joe" (b. 13 March 1938, Winchester, MA), college and professional player and coach, is the son of Sicilian immigrant–factory worker Michele and Sarah Bellino. A 1957 graduate of Winchester High School, Bellino played on the state championship basketball team. At the U.S. Naval Academy he scored five touchdowns as a sophomore and eight touchdowns with a 5.6-yard rushing average as a junior. Neither Middies team looked impressive, but Navy drubbed Army 43–12 in 1959. Bellino's 1960 season, however, ranks among the most spectacular ever by a college player. Navy compiled an 8–1 record; as halfback Bellino rushed for 834 yards, passed for two touchdowns, caught 17 passes for 280 yards and three touchdowns, returned punts and kickoffs, and punted. He set Navy records for most points in a season (110) and game (24, against the University of Virginia), most carries in a season (168), and most yards rushing (834). He won the Heisman Trophy as College Football Player of the Year, easily outpolling Mike Ditka* and Billy Kilmer. The 5 foot, 9 inch, 180 pound Bellino was ranked with Fred "Buzz" Borries as the greatest Navy running back. The strong-legged Bellino proved difficult to stop, but in Navy's 1961 Orange Bowl loss to Missouri, he gained only four yards rushing. Bellino made a spectacular diving catch for a touchdown, but otherwise Missouri contained him.

Bellino fulfilled his Navy obligation after the 1960 season, served briefly as assistant football coach there, and began playing professionally in 1965. Bellino was drafted by the Washington Redskins (NFL) and Boston Patriots (AFL). Bellino played for the Patriots from 1965 through 1967, but primarily returned kickoffs and punts and scored only one touchdown in his entire pro tenure. Bellino, Roger Staubach*, and Napoleon McCallun might be the last Naval Academy football superheroes. The service commitment prevents the armed forces academies from competing for the best athletes, while American attitudes toward military service and personnel have shifted. Bellino, who married high school girlfriend Ann Tansey on June 11, 1961, is in the NFF College Football Hall of Fame and lives in Bedford, MA.

BIBLIOGRAPHY: Cynthia Laraway Barone, *Navy's Joe Bellino* (Winchester, MA, 1961); Roy Terrell, "Army, Navy and Joe Bellino," *SI* 13 (November 28, 1960), pp. 37–40; Washington (DC) *Evening Star*, 1960–1961.

John David Healy

BENBROOK, Albert "Benny" (b. 24 August 1887, Dallas, TX; d. 16 August 1943, Dallas, TX), college athlete, captained the 1910 undefeated University of Michigan (WC) western football champions. The two-time Walter Camp* All-American became the sixth player selected from a non-eastern school. During his football career (1908–1910), Michigan lost only three games. The catlike, 6 foot, 3 inch, 240 pound Benbrook ranked with Pudge Heffelfinger* (Yale) and Truxton Hare* (Pennsylvania) as the greatest guards in early gridiron history. Benbrook led interference as a pulling guard, backed up the line on defense, and occasionally plunged in short yardage situations.

In 1909 Benbrook led the Wolverines to a 12–6 upset victory over Pennsylvania, non-loser in 23 consecutive games. He showed outstanding sportsmanship by using his body on one play to shield the prostrate Minnesota Gophers All-American quarterback John McGovern, who was playing with a broken collar bone. In one of the long rivalry's greatest games (1910), Benbrook piloted the Wolverines to a 6–0 victory over the Gophers in the season's finale. He helped stop a Minnesota drive at the eighteen-yard line by blocking a field goal attempt. After Michigan made two unsuccessful attempts from the three-yard line, he insisted that the ball be plunged over his position in the fourth quarter. The resulting touchdown marked the only points scored the entire season against the heretofore undefeated Gophers.

Benbrook, a member of the Michigan track team (weights) and Michigamua Society, graduated in 1911. After joining his father's furniture firm, Monroe Benbrook and Company, he was commissioned a first lieutenant in World War I and served overseas with a machine gun battalion. Benbrook joined the American Seating Company, where he remained until his untimely death of heart failure. He and his wife lived in Chicago, IL, and had one son, James. Benbrook was named to the NFF College Football Hall of Fame in 1971 and made George Trevor's 1949 All-Time Midwest Team. The FWAA selected him in 1970 to the Early (1869–1920) All-Time Midwest Team, while Bob Zuppke* named him in 1951 to his All-Time All-American Team. Clark Shaughnessy* and Walter Eckersall* rated Benbrook with the greatest guards of all time. Walter Camp boasted: "He is a born player showing great strength and dash, an ability to follow the ball. There is no match for him on the gridiron."

BIBLIOGRAPHY: Stan W. Carlson, *Dr. Henry L. Williams* (Minneapolis, MN, 1938); Will Perry, *The Wolverines: A Story of Michigan Football* (Huntsville, AL, 1980); Clark Shaughnessy, *Football in War and Peace* (Clinton, SC, 1943); *Spalding's Official Intercollegiate Football Guides, 1910–1911;* University of Michigan, Library Archives, Ann Arbor, MI.

James D. Whalen

BENTON, James "Big Jim" (b. 25 September 1916, Carthage, AR), college and professional player, performed for the University of Arkansas Razorbacks (SWC) football squad from 1935 to 1937 and led the nation with 47 pass receptions in 1937. Benton's 47 receptions as an end set the standard for measuring future performances. Benton's collegiate performance was overshadowed by tackle Ed Franco of Fordham, whose Rams gained more attention from the eastern press.

In 1938 the NCAA's pass-catching champion joined the Cleveland Rams (NFL). He combined with quarterback Bob Waterfield* to lead the Rams to their only NFL title in 1945 by a 15–14 margin over the Washington Redskins. Benton's pro football career was interrupted in 1941 by World War II service. After rejoining the Cleveland Rams in 1942, he performed for the Chicago Bears when the Rams temporarily disbanded in 1943 and helped quarterback Sid Luckman* amass an NFL-leading 2,310 passing yards. Benton caught a touchdown pass in the 1943 championship game against the Washington Redskins.

In 1944 the 6 foot, 3 inch, 200 pound end returned to the Cleveland Rams and two years later led the NFL in pass receptions with 63, ranking second then to Don Hutson's* all-time high of 74 set in 1942. Benton in 1945 established a single-game pass-receiving record with 303 yards on ten receptions against the Detroit Lions. The Rams led the NFL in rushing that year, contributing to the successful passing game and a 9 win, 1 loss mark. The title game against the Redskins saw Benton catch a 37-yard touchdown aerial from Waterfield. The Rams in 1946 moved to Los Angeles, where Benton played through the 1947 season. During nine pro seasons, Benton caught 288 passes for 4,801 yards (16.7-yard average) and scored 45 touchdowns.

BIBLIOGRAPHY: *Lincoln Library of Sports Champions*, 14 vols. (Columbus, OH, 1974); Frank G. Menke, ed., *The Encyclopedia of Sports*, 5th rev. ed., rev. by Suzanne Treat (New York, 1975); David S. Neft et al., *The Complete All-Time Pro Football Register* (New York, 1975); Roger Treat, ed., *The Encyclopedia of Football*, 16th rev. ed., rev. by Pete Palmer (South Brunswick, NJ, 1979).

John R. Giroski

BERRY, Charles Francis "Charlie" (b. 18 October 1902, Phillipsburg, NJ; d. 6 September 1972, Evanston, IL), college and professional baseball player, coach, manager, and official, attended Lafayette (PA) College and played end on Walter Camp's* 1924 All-American football team. Besides being elected to the NFF College Football Hall of Fame in 1980, he was named to the Pennsylvania Sports Hall of Fame in 1969 and became a charter member of the Lafayette Athletic Hall of Fame in 1976. The son of Charles and Addie (Bartch) Berry, he graduated from Phillipsburg High School in 1921 and earned a Bachelor of Science degree from Lafayette in 1925. A four-year football player (1921–1924) under coaches Jock Sutherland* and

Herb McCracken, Berry started every game at end as a freshman on Lafayette's undefeated (9–0–0) national co-championship 1921 team. During his football career, the Leopards attained a 29–5–2 composite record and defeated Pennsylvania, Pittsburgh, Fordham, Rutgers, and Washington and Jefferson. Berry caught for the Lafayette baseball team four years, captained the football team, and served as class president his senior year.

The 6 foot, 185 pound Berry was team captain, leading scorer (108 points), and All-Pro end in 1925 with the Pottsville (PA) Maroons, NFL runner-up with a 10–2–0 season. He coached Grove City (PA) College (1927–1931) to three TSC football championships and a composite 27–7–8 record. During the summer Berry caught for the Philadelphia Athletics (AL, 1925, 1934–1938), Portland, OR (PCL, 1926), Dallas, TX (TL, 1927), Boston Red Sox (AL, 1928–1932), and Chicago White Sox (AL, 1932–1933), and managed Wilmington, DE (ISL, 1939–1940). He compiled a .267 batting average in 709 major league games over 12 seasons and coached for the Philadelphia Athletics from 1936 to 1940. Berry became a respected football and baseball official, serving as an NFL head linesman 24 seasons and an AL umpire 21 years. He worked 13 NFL championship games, 9 Chicago College All-Star football games, and several baseball World Series. Once he officiated a baseball doubleheader and an All-Star football game the same day.

After Berry retired in 1962, the AL retained him as a consultant to the supervisor of baseball umpires. An AL associate once said, "He was one of the greatest fellows for helping others, the type who would take you in tow and try to teach you. They didn't come any better as a gentleman." Berry married Helen S. Smith of Phillipsburg, NJ, in 1926 and had three daughters. After Berry suffered a stroke in July 1972, he and his wife lived with a daughter in Evanston, IL.

BIBLIOGRAPHY: Ritter Collet, Dayton (OH) *Journal-Herald*, September 19, 1972; Arthur Daley, "Sports of the Times," *NYT*, February 6, 1965; Lafayette College, Library Archives, Easton, PA; Francis A. March, Jr., *Athletics at Lafayette College* (Easton, PA, 1926); Ronald L. Mendell and Timothy B. Phares, *Who's Who in Football* (New Rochelle, NY, 1974); *Spalding's Official Intercollegiate Football Guides, 1928–1932*.

James D. Whalen

BERRY, David J. (b. 1870, Greensburg, PA; d. November 1938, San Francisco, CA), professional player, coach, and executive, was "the true father of professional football," according to historian Robert W. Smith. The son of John D. Berry, Jr., and his first wife, David Berry followed his father into the newspaper business. During the early 1890s Berry founded and served as editor and publisher of the weekly Latrobe (PA) *Clipper* when pro football started from Pittsburgh area club rivalry. In 1895 he promoted organization of the first pro football team at Latrobe. When his quarterback could not play in the opening game because of a conflict, Berry recruited eighteen-year-old John Brallier* from Indiana, PA, for $10 plus expenses to fill that position. Brallier was recognized until recently as the first pro football player.

The successful 1895 Latrobe team inspired Berry to recruit other college football stars to play for pay there. Berry initially played but retired to coaching and management after breaking a jaw in practice. He led the Latrobe team to enormous success, winning 40 of 55 games from 1895 through 1900 against top teams from Pennsylvania and nearby states. The tall, dark, and "rail thin" Berry, "tried to cover his youthful features by affecting a scraggly U. S. Grant beard." When Latrobe could no longer support a pro team, he persuaded the major league baseball ownership at Pittsburgh and Philadelphia to help him organize the NFL in 1902. Connie Mack's* (BB) Philadelphia Athletics squad included several of his baseball players. Berry served as both NFL president and general manager of the Pittsburgh Stars. Berry's club practiced 35 miles away at Greensburg, PA, possibly because of his newspaper publishing business and church deacon's position there, but this strategy cost him fan support at Pittsburgh.

According to Berry, the Stars won the NFL title in late November with an 11–0 victory over Philadelphia. Some newspaper accounts verify this, but others do not support it. After one loosely organized year, the NFL collapsed because of inadequate financing and the disappearance of some natural rivalries. Mack and Ben Shibe* (BB) lost $4,000 with their Philadelphia team and dropped out of the NFL.

Berry married Carrie Saxman of Latrobe, PA, and had one son, Meredith. Berry served as editor and publisher of daily newspapers at Greensburg and Uniontown, PA, and the *National Labor Journal* at Pittsburgh. In the early 1900s he moved to San Francisco, CA, and was publishing the *Industrial Labor Review* at the time of his death.

BIBLIOGRAPHY: Robert B. Van Atta, Interviews, with Berry family members, 1984–1985; Paul B. Beers, *Profiles in Pennsylvania Sports* (Harrisburg, PA, 1975); Robert Carroll, "Dave Berry and the Philadelphia Story," *First Annual Historical and Statistical Review of the Professional Football Research Association* (Canton, OH, 1980); Greensburg (PA) Newspapers, 1890–1902; Latrobe (PA) Newspapers, 1890–1902; Personal Scrapbook, Dr. John K. Brallier; Pittsburgh newspapers, 1890–1902; Robert M. Smith, *Illustrated History of Pro Football* (New York, 1972); Robert M. Smith, *Pro Football; The History of the Game and the Great Players* (Garden City, NY, 1963).

Robert B. Van Atta

BERRY, Raymond Emmett "Ray" (b. 27 February 1933, Corpus Christi, TX), college and professional player and coach, is the son of M. Raymond and Beth (Huggins) Berry. His father, a high school football coach, later became athletic director for the Paris, TX, school system. Berry played for his father at Paris High and made All-District end. After attending Schreiner Institute in Kerrville, TX, for one year, he enrolled at SMU (SWC) in 1951.

After playing just 56 minutes as a sophomore, Berry caught 11 passes for 144 yards his junior year. His teammates liked his leadership ability and elected him co-captain for 1954, although he had never started a game. He was named to the All-SWC team, earned Academic All-American honors, and played in the Shrine All Star (East-West) game.

A twentieth-round draft choice of the Baltimore Colts (NFL) in 1955, Berry spent hours perfecting his receiving skills and made the team. According to Dallas Cowboys head coach Tom Landry,* "Raymond Berry was the guy who started moves in the NFL. He worked on and perfected those moves which started the demise of man-to-man coverage." Berry overcame several physical problems—one leg shorter than the other, back problems, and poor vision—and was one of the first professional football players to wear contact lenses.

In his second season with the Colts, Berry made 37 receptions for 601 yards. In 1957 he ranked among the NFL's best receivers, catching 47 passes for 800 yards. Against the Washington Redskins, he caught 12 passes for 224 yards. An All-NFL end the next three seasons, he led the league in receiving each year. In 1958 he made 56 catches for 794 yards and 9 touchdowns during the regular season and 12 receptions for 178 yards in the dramatic NFL title game overtime victory against the New York Giants. During the 1959 season he caught 66 passes for 959 yards and scored 14 touchdowns. Berry made 74 catches for 1,298 yards and 10 touchdowns in 1960. He married Sally Ann Crook on August 19, 1960, and has three children, daughters Suzanne and Ashley and son Mark.

Berry enjoyed his best single-season mark in 1961, catching 75 passes to rank second in the NFL. He remained a productive receiver for the Colts until retiring after the 1967 season. He ranks high among NFL career receivers with 631 receptions for 9,275 yards and 68 touchdowns. Berry, who played in three NFL championship games and five Pro Bowls, was inducted into the Pro Football Hall of Fame in 1973 and the Texas Sports Hall of Fame in 1974. The Pro Football Hall of Fame selected him to the AFL-NFL 1960–1984 All-Star Team.

After retiring as a player, Berry served as an assistant coach with the Dallas Cowboys (NFL) in 1968–1969, the University of Arkansas (SWC) for three seasons, and the Cleveland Browns (NFL) in 1976. From 1979 through 1981, he was an assistant coach with the New England Patriots (NFL). He also co-authored *Ray Berry's Complete Guide for Pass Receivers.* After being a training camp assistant coach for the Minnesota Vikings (NFL) in 1984, he replaced Ron Meyer as head coach of the New England Patriots that October and guided them to a 4–4 record and second place finish in the Eastern Division of the AFC. In 1985 he was named AFC Coach of the Year, as the Patriots finished with their best mark (11–5) in franchise history. The Patriots then upset the New York Jets and Los Angeles Raiders in the playoffs and defeated the Miami Dolphins to capture the AFC title before losing to the Chicago Bears in Super Bowl XX. The next year, New England finished first in the AFC Eastern Division with an 11–5–0 mark before the Denver Broncos defeated them in the playoffs. Through the 1986 season, Berry has compiled a 26–14–0 coaching mark.

BIBLIOGRAPHY: *Baltimore Colts Press Guides, 1955, 1967, 1983;* Raymond Berry and Butch Gilbert, Jr., *Ray Berry's Complete Guide for Pass Receivers* (Englewood Cliffs, NJ, 1982); Ronald L. Mendell and Timothy B. Phares, *Who's Who in Football* (New Rochelle, NY, 1974); John Steadman, *The Baltimore Colts* (Virginia Beach, VA, 1978).

Jay Langhammer

BERTELLI, Angelo Bortolo "The Arm" "The Springfield Rifle" "Mr. Accuracy" (b. 18 June 1921, West Springfield, MA), college and professional player, is the son of Italian immigrants and attended Cathedral High School in Springfield, winning All-Conference honors in football, baseball, and hockey. Bertelli received pro hockey honors but preferred to play football. He entered the University of Notre Dame in 1940 and became one of its all-time best football passers. In his varsity debut as a sophomore against the University of Arizona, he completed 11 of 14 passes for 145 yards and one touchdown. Bertelli led the Fighting Irish to 8 wins and 1 tie and a number three national ranking by completing 70 passes in 123 attempts for 1,027 yards and 8 touchdowns. Bertelli's sophomore passing performance was lauded nationwide, earning him runner-up status in the Heisman Trophy race. In Bertelli's junior year, Notre Dame switched to the T formation from the old Knute Rockne* box-type offense. Bertelli completed 74 of 165 passes for 1,044 yards and 11 touchdowns. His performance paced Notre Dame to a 7 win, 2 loss, 2 tie season, and earned him All-American honors.

Bertelli's unique senior year saw him play in only six games before being called into the U.S. Marine Corps in November 1943. Notre Dame remained undefeated in those six games, as Bertelli completed 25 passes in 36 attempts for 511 yards and 11 touchdowns. The Fighting Irish won the national championship, while Bertelli was named All-American and won the coveted Heisman Trophy despite his shortened season. The 6 foot, 1 inch, 190 pound Bertelli served in the Pacific Theater and returned to Notre Dame upon his discharge to complete his education. Bertelli played one year with the Los Angeles Dons (AAFC) and two years with the Chicago Rockets (AAFC). Knee injuries curtailed his pro career, which consisted of 76 completions in 166 attempts for 972 yards and 8 touchdowns. Nicknamed "The Arm," "The Springfield Rifle," and "Mr. Accuracy," Bertelli was inducted into the NFF College Football Hall of Fame in 1972 and presently lives in Clifton, NJ.

BIBLIOGRAPHY: Jim Beach, *Notre Dame Football* (New York, 1962); Bill Libby, *Cham-*

pions of College Football (New York, 1975); *Notre Dame University Media Guide, 1982;* Francis Wallace, *Notre Dame from Rockne to Parseghian* (New York, 1967).

James R. Fuller

BERWANGER, John Jacob "The Flying Dutchman" "The Man in the Iron Mask" (b. 19 March 1914, Dubuque, IA), college athlete, coach, and official, was an All-American football halfback at the University of Chicago and won the first Heisman Trophy in 1935. The son of John Berwanger, a blacksmith of German descent, Berwanger entered the University of Chicago (WC) in 1932. An outstanding high school athlete, Berwanger was recruited widely by Northwestern, Iowa, Purdue, and other midwestern schools. A Chicago alumnus from Dubuque influenced Berwanger to choose that institution, hoping that the latter would compete in track there. According to Berwanger, he chose Chicago because of its strong academic programs and his desire to begin his business career in the Chicago metropolitan area.

Berwanger competed on the varsity football and track teams at Chicago from 1933 to 1935. He played football under Clark Shaughnessy,* who had replaced Amos Alonzo Stagg* after the 1932 season. Shaughnessy later used the team's single-wing formations to exploit Berwanger's strengths as a running back. Berwanger attributed his success to effectively combining running with kicking, passing, and defense. "I was able to do everything," Berwanger recalled. "Against Minnesota in 1935, I made 15 or 16 unassisted tackles, and that was one reason Grantland Rice* [OS] put me on his All-America team."

Nicknamed "The Man in the Iron Mask" for his face protector, Berwanger won principal acclaim as a runner. The 6 foot, 1 inch, 190-plus pound Berwanger recalled, "I was considered a big half-back." He also ran the 100-yard dash in just over 10 seconds, considered fast in the 1930s. His longest, best-known run came his senior year against Ohio State. After the Chicago defense had stopped an Ohio State drive on its 15-yard line, Berwanger scored on an 85-yard touchdown over right tackle. "I got hit several times, but managed to get away from them and go 85 yards for the touchdown," he later commented. Berwanger attributed Chicago's defeat in that game partially to the limited substitution rule. Although physically exhausted, he was forced to stay in the contest until near the end of the quarter. In his final game against Illinois, Berwanger gained over 100 yards to help Chicago defeat Bob Zuppke's* squad 7–6 and set up the winning touchdown. After being tackled just short of the goal line, he scored on the next play.

During his three-year career as a halfback, Berwanger played in 24 varsity games and gained over a mile in total yardage. Normally a linebacker on defense, he dropped back on fourth down to field punts. Berwanger suffered only two injuries. During his freshman year he broke his nose and consequently wore a face mask. His ankle was injured against Purdue in 1934, causing him to play the next game with a leg brace. Ironically, Berwanger's Chicago teams never enjoyed a winning season. The 1934 Chicago squad started the season with four victories, including a 28–0 defeat of the defending WC champion, the University of Michigan, but lost its final four games. The Heisman Trophy initially excited Berwanger most because of the two free airplane tickets to New York City he received. Although the Chicago Bears (NFL) obtained the draft rights to Berwanger from the Philadelphia Eagles, Berwanger skipped a pro football career because businessmen were paid higher salaries then. Berwanger lacked interest in using pro football as a springboard for a coaching career.

Berwanger entered business after graduating in 1936 but associated with athletics on a part-time basis. From 1936 until Chicago dropped football in 1939, he coached the freshman team. He joined the U.S. Naval Air Corps as a flying instructor in World War II and subsequently served as a BTC official. In the 1948 Rose Bowl game, he made a controversial touchdown call in the contest between Northwestern University and the University of California, Berkeley. When the Northwestern player appeared to cross the goal line, Berwanger signaled a touchdown. The Northwestern back, however, fumbled the ball and California recovered it.

In 1940 he married Philemina Baker and has two sons and one daughter. After his first wife's death, he married Jane Fulton Temple in 1984. He established a sales agency and rubber manufacturing business in Chicago after World War II. He was inducted into the NFF College Football Hall of Fame in 1954 and the HAF College Football Hall of Fame and frequently attended the NFF Hall of Fame inductions and Heisman Trophy ceremonies. The Heisman Trophy assumed more significance in later decades than when he received the first such award.

BIBLIOGRAPHY: Jay Berwanger and Bob Graf, "I Was So Scared . . . ," *SEP* 209 (December 5, 1936), p. 33; Howard Roberts, *The Big Nine: The Story of Football in the Western Conference* (New York, 1948); John S. Watterson, Interview with Jay Berwanger, Oakbrook, IL, October 29, 1984.

John S. Watterson

BEZDEK, Hugo Frank (b. 1 April 1884, Prague, Bohemia; d. 19 September 1952, Atlantic City, NJ), college football player, athletic coach, and administrator (baseball manager), came to America with his Czechoslovakian parents at age 5, grew up in the rough Chicago South Side, and attended school there. As University of Chicago (WC) fullback from 1902 to 1905, he exhibited pile-driving running for coach Amos Alonzo Stagg* and was named on the 1905 third All-American team. In 1905 Chicago defeated the University of Michigan 2–0 for Fielding Yost's* first defeat in 56 games. During Bezdek's four years, Chicago compiled a 38–4–2 record.

In 1906, Bezdek coached the University of Oregon to an undefeated season. From 1908 through 1912 he garnered a 29–13–1 record at the University of Arkansas. His 1909 Razorbacks finished 7–0, while the 1910 squad won seven of eight games. Bezdek returned to Oregon from 1913 to 1917 with a 25–10–3 overall record. His unbeaten 1916 Ducks defeated the University of Pennsylvania 14–0 in the Rose Bowl. At the 1918 Rose Bowl, Bezdek coached the Mare Island Marines to a 19–7 triumph over the Camp Lewis soldiers.

Along with football, Bezdek also coached basketball, baseball, and track. At Penn State University from 1920 to 1930, he coached the baseball team to a 129–76 record and a 29-game winning streak. His leadership skills impelled the Pittsburgh Pirates (NL) to hire him as manager. Bezdek, who managed the Pirates to a 166–187 record from 1917 through 1919, took over a last place team and elevated it to fourth. After the 1919 season Bezdek left Pittsburgh to concentrate on Penn State football. As Penn State's football coach from 1918 to 1929, he compiled a 65–29–9 record. Under Bezdek's leadership, Penn State made a 40–10–7 record from 1919 through 1924 and went undefeated for 30 consecutive games. The controversial, innovative, exciting coach was respected and hated, pictured as both savior and dictator. His 1922 Nittany Lions lost the Rose Bowl 14–3 to the University of Southern California. During his 24-year college coaching career, Bezdek's squads finished 127–58–15 for a .672 percentage.

From 1930 to 1936 he served as athletic director at Penn State until the Board of Trustees dismissed him because they disliked some of his policies. In 1937 and 1938 he coached the Cleveland Rams (NFL) to a 5–17–0 record. In 1949 he became coach and athletic director at the National Agricultural College in Doyleston, PA.

Bezdek exploited the spread formation, screen pass, quick kick, and onside kick. He also helped initiate the half spinner and full spinner series, where the tailback received the ball, faked a hand-off, performed a half or full turn, kept the ball, and turned into the line. Bezdek was a member of the HAF and the NFF College Football Halls of Fame. He and his wife Victoria had two children, Hugo Jr., and Frances.

BIBLIOGRAPHY: Tim Cohane, *Great College Football Coaches of the Twenties and Thirties* (New Rochelle, NY, 1973); John D. McCallum and Charles H. Pearson, *College Football U.S.A., 1869–1973* (New York, 1973); Ken Rappoport, *The Nittany Lions: A Story of Penn State Football* (Huntsville, AL, 1973).

John L. Evers

BIBLE, Dana Xenophon (b. 8 October 1891, Jefferson City, TN; d. 19 January 1980, Austin, TX), college player, coach, and administrator, was the son of Jonathan and Cleopatra Bible. His father served as professor of Greek and Latin at Carson-Newman (TN) College, where Bible played quarterback and earned his Bachelor's degree in 1912. Bible also coached the local high school team and occasionally, surreptitiously entered the lineup. In his early career, Bible earned a reputation as a "snarling perfectionist." With success over time, his bullfrog voice became more "mellow" and "courtly." He turned this to advantage, quoting biblical scriptures and preaching the merits of basic football. He did not employ fancy plays except for the fake punt on third down, his only concession to razzle-dazzle. Due partly to his family's educational background, he approached the game thoughtfully. Initially self-taught, Bible gradually developed his skill as a coach by visiting and seeking advice from the era's great coaches, including Fielding Yost.* Later in his career Bible scouted potential players, insisted on lengthy written reports on their talents, and instituted the scouting of future opponents. He began coaching football successfully at Mississippi College (1913–1915), where he also served as Latin professor, and at LSU (SIAA, 1916). At Texas A&M (SWC, 1917–1928), he was football coach and professor of English. Bible's winning seasons there included two campaigns of shutting out opponents altogether. Bible joined Nebraska (1929–1936), where the Cornhuskers lost only three BSC games. He concluded his coaching career at the University of Texas (SWC, 1937–1946) and became the state's highest paid official. As a coach, he accumulated 14 conference championships, won two Cotton Bowl games and tied one, and amassed a 205–73–20 overall record. His book, *Championship Football* (1947), proved a classic.

Despite considerable success as a coach, Bible made his most lasting mark on the sport as an administrator. He spent 27 years on the NCAA Rules Committee and helped modernize the game after World War II. As athletic director at the University of Texas, he built the school's athletic programs to a level of excellence. He utilized alumni to recruit players from remote Texas towns by emphasizing the importance of their education, the so-called Bible Plan of securing student-athletes.

Bible retired from active service in 1957 but was consulting athletic director until 1961. An influential leader of his generation in American college sport, he received numerous honors and was elected to the HAF and NFF College Football Halls of Fame and six others. When Bible died of a stroke, he was mourned widely. His wife pre-deceased him in 1942 and left two children, Barbara and Bill.

BIBLIOGRAPHY: "Bible Plan," *Newsweek* 28 (October 14, 1946), pp. 98–99; Frank X. Tolbert, "Longhorn's Bible," *Colliers* 118 (November 30, 1946), pp. 16–17; Ronald L. Mendell and Timothy B. Phares, *Who's Who in Football* (New Rochelle, NY, 1974); *NYT*, January 23, 1942, January 22, 1961, January 20, 1980; Edwin Pope, *Football's Greatest Coaches* (Atlanta, 1956).

Charles R. Middleton

BIDWILL, Charles W., Sr. (b. 16 September 1895, Chicago, IL; d. 19 April 1947, Chicago, IL), college athlete and professional executive, owned the Chicago Cardinals (NFL). Bidwill participated in athletics at St. Ignatius High School and Loyola University in Chicago. Following graduation from Loyola in 1916, he entered law practice and served as assistant prosecutor for Chicago and corporation counsel. He continued his law practice until 1925, when he pursued the sports world. He purchased the Cardinals franchise in 1933 from David Jones and served as owner-president until his death. Bidwill once loaned close friend George Halas* money to buy the Chicago Bears outright. Bidwill, a nonstop, nighttime person, wore dark blue shirts everywhere. The spendthrift, busy Bidwill worked and sometimes drank too hard. Besides owning a racetrack and managing two other tracks, he operated a printing company, dog racing tracks, and a girls softball team. With Halas, he operated the Chicago Bruins (ABL) franchise.

During Cardinals games the composed Bidwill sat quietly in his box. He did not visit the dressing room, letting the coaches direct the team. Until 1946 the Cardinals experienced little NFL success. After James Conzelman* became head coach, he and Bidwill assembled a championship-caliber team. The Cardinals owner acquired the "Dream Backfield" of Paul Christman, Marlin "Pat" Harder,* Charley Trippi,* and Marshall Goldberg.* After Bidwill died, the Cardinals won the NFL championship in 1947 with a 9–3 record. In 1948 the Cardinals finished 11–1 but lost the title game to the Philadelphia Eagles. As an NFL owner, Bidwill exhibited progressive attitudes in helping the Cardinals and the NFL achieve many goals. In 1967 he was elected to the Pro Football Hall of Fame. After Bidwill's death, his wife Violet Fultz assumed club ownership and moved the Cardinals to St. Louis before the 1960 campaign. Upon Violet's death in 1962, adopted sons Charles and William controlled the team.

BIBLIOGRAPHY: "The Chicago Cardinals—A Thumbnail History," *St. Louis Football Cardinals Magazine* (September, 1968), p. 74; Bill Gleason, "Charlie's Team," *Pro!*, November 1979, pp. 10E–16E; "Pro Football's Immortal Roll," *The Pro Football Hall of Fame Souvenir Yearbook, 1983–1984.*

John L. Evers

BIERMAN, Bernard William "Bernie" (b. 11 March 1894, Springfield, MN; d. 8 March 1977, Laguna Hills, CA), college athlete and football coach, was born of sturdy German ancestry, the son of William August and Lydia (Ruessler) Bierman. Bierman graduated from Litchfield High School in 1912, but a leg bone infection kept him from participating in athletics until his senior year. Besides competing in basketball and track, he lettered in football and captained the gridiron team. At the University of Minnesota he earned three letters each in football and track and one letter in basketball. Under Coach Henry Williams,* Bierman captained the 1915 football squad. Minnesota won the WC championship with an undefeated season, and Bierman received the WC medal for all-around athletic and scholastic achievement.

Bierman began his football coaching career at Butte (MT) High School in 1916. Butte outscored opponents 300–6 and captured the state championship by trouncing Billings 54–0. When the United States entered World War I, he enlisted as a private in the Marine Corps. After basic training at Quantico, VA, he was commissioned a second lieutenant on July 1, 1917, and promoted the next day to captain. When discharged in 1919, he became head football coach at the University of Montana and installed Williams' Minnesota shift system there. In 1922 Bierman resigned from coaching and entered the bond business in Minneapolis, MN. In 1921 he married Clara McKenzie, a Minnesota graduate from Havre, MT, and had two sons, William and James. William later played football under his father at Minnesota.

In 1923 Bierman became assistant football coach at Tulane University (SEC) under Minnesota teammate Clark Shaughnessy.* He became head football coach at Mississippi A&M in 1925 and returned to Tulane in that capacity two years later. After two moderately successful seasons, the Green Wave from 1929 through 1931 lost only to Northwestern and the 1931 Rose Bowl game to Southern California. Upon returning to his Minnesota alma mater in 1932 as head football coach, Bierman proved his coaching genius. His first Gophers squad won 5 and lost 3, but Minnesota went 28 games without defeat from the close of the 1932 season until the 1936 Northwestern game and garnered 21 consecutive victories. The 1934 team captured the WC and national championships and ranks among the greatest all-time college squads. National championship accolades followed in 1935 and 1936, 1940, and 1941, with Minnesota earning six BTC titles in that span. From 1942 to 1945 Bierman served in the U.S. Marine Corps as a colonel during World War II. He retired from head coaching after the 1950 season with a 162–57–11 record overall and a 92–34–6 mark at Minnesota.

Bierman used a single-wing formation with variations, often featuring an unbalanced line. His teams stressed top condition, discipline, precision executions, crisp blocking, hard tackling, and excellence in fundamentals. He produced four All-Americans at Tulane and fifteen at Minnesota, including backs Pug Lund and Bruce Smith,* tackles Leo Nomellini,* Ed Widseth,* and Dick Wildung,* and end Frank Larson. A member of the NFF and HAF College Football Halls of Fame, he often co-coached the East team in the Shrine All-Star games and twice coached the College All-Stars. He won College Coach of the Year awards, served as president of the AFCA, and authored a popular text, *Winning Football.* He then spent twenty years in southern California before moving in 1969 into a retirement community south of Los Angeles. Bierman Field Athletic Building on the University of Minnesota campus is named for him and has plaques honoring his five national championships. A bronze bust and plaque with his records are displayed in the lobby, a gift of 276 former players.

BIBLIOGRAPHY: George Barton, *My Lifetime in Sports* (Minneapolis, MN, 1957); Bernard Bierman and Frank Mayer, *Winning Football* (New York, 1937); Stan W. Carlson, *Dr. Henry L. Williams* (Minneapolis, MN, 1938); Stan W. Carlson, *Minnesota Huddle Annual 1936–1938* (Minneapolis, MN, 1936–1938); Richard Fisher, *Who's Who in Minnesota Athletics* (Minneapolis, MN, 1941); James P. Quirk, *Minnesota Football, The Golden Years* (Minneapolis, MN, 1984); University of Minnesota *Gopher Gazette*, October, 1976; University of Minnesota, *One Hundred Years of Golden Gopher Football* (Minneapolis, MN, 1981).

Stan W. Carlson

BILETNIKOFF, Frederick (b. 23 February 1943, Erie, PA), college and professional player, is the son of Ephraim and Natalie (Karuba) Biletnikoff. His father, a former AAU boxing champion, worked as a welder 43 years. A football, basketball, baseball, and track star at Erie's Technical Memorial High, Biletnikoff enrolled at Florida State University in 1961 and saw limited football action as a sophomore. The following season, he led Florida State in receptions with 24 and tied a Seminole record with a 99-yard interception return against the University of Miami. Team co-captain his senior year, Biletnikoff won consensus All-American honors and ranked fourth nationally with 57 catches for 987 yards and 11 touchdowns. In his best college performance he caught 13 passes for 192 yards and scored 4 touchdowns to lead the Seminoles to a 36–19 victory over the University of Oklahoma in the 1965 Gator Bowl. The 6 foot, 1 inch, 190 pound Biletnikoff, whose college career included 87 catches for 1,463 yards and 16 touchdowns, played in the College All-Star Game.

The second-round draft pick of the Oakland Raiders (AFL) in 1965, Biletnikoff saw considerable action as a reserve receiver his first two pro years. He became one of pro football's top receivers in 1968, catching 61 passes for 1,037 yards and making a career-best 82-yarder. In a 1968 playoff game with the New York Jets, he caught 7 passes for a career-high 190 yards. Not blessed with great speed, he relied on good hands, deceptive moves, and precise pass routes to achieve success. Biletnikoff enjoyed ten straight seasons with 40 or more catches and led the NFL in 1971 with 61 receptions for 929 yards and 9 touchdowns. He led the AFC the next year with 58 catches and was named NEA Outstanding Offensive Player. An All-NFL pick in 1970–1972 and All-AFC four times, he played in two AFL All-Star games and made four Pro Bowl squads.

Biletnikoff, who retired from the Raiders after the 1978 season, remains their regular-season career leader with 589 receptions for 8,974 yards and 76 touchdowns. In post-season play he caught 70 passes for 1,167 yards and 10 touchdowns. The MVP in Super Bowl XI, he caught four passes for 79 yards and helped the Raiders defeat the Minnesota Vikings 32–14. Biletnikoff came out of retirement in 1980 to play for the Montreal Alouettes (CFL), being the club's second-leading receiver with 38 catches for 470 yards and

4 touchdowns. Subsequently, he performed public relations work, part-time coaching, and small parts in movies and television. He wed Jerryln O'Connor on January 7, 1965, and has one son, Fred, Jr., and one daughter, Tanya. Following a divorce, he married Jennifer Lysengen on August 22, 1974, and has two daughters, Tracy and Natasha.

BIBLIOGRAPHY: *Florida State Football Press Guide, 1983; Los Angeles Raiders Press Guide, 1983*; Ronald L. Mendell and Timothy B. Phares, *Who's Who in Football* (New Rochelle, NY, 1974); *Oakland Raiders Press Guides, 1967, 1979.*

Jay Langhammer

BLAIK, Earl Henry "Red" (b. 15 February 1897, Detroit, MI), all-around college athlete and football coach, excelled as a football coach for twenty-five years at Dartmouth College (IL) and the U.S. Military Academy (Army) and compiled a 166–48–14 career record (.759 percent) and seven undefeated seasons. He coached thirty-five All-Americans, three Heisman Trophy, and three Maxwell, two Rockne, and one Outland Award winners, two national championship squads, and seven Lambert Trophy eastern championship teams. Three Dartmouth and thirteen Army teams ranked among the top twenty in final AP polls. William Douglas Blaik, his father, migrated from Glasgow, Scotland, to Canada, where he married Margaret Purcell. The Blaiks moved to Detroit and, when Earl was four years old, to Dayton, OH, where his father established a real estate business. At Steele High School, Blaik lettered in football, basketball, and baseball and graduated in 1914.

At Miami University (OH) Blaik starred in three sports and played end on the Redskins' 1916–1917 undefeated OC championship football teams. In 1918 he graduated from Miami with a Bachelor of Arts degree. Blaik was appointed to the U.S. Military Academy, where he was awarded the Saber as the outstanding athlete in his class. A basketball center-forward and baseball left fielder, the 6 foot, 2 inch, 190 pound Blaik was chosen third team All-American in football at end in 1919 by Walter Camp.* He graduated in 1920 with a Bachelor of Science degree, ranking 108 in a class of 271.

Blaik served as first lieutenant with the First Cavalry Division, Fort Bliss, TX, that patrolled the Mexican border. By 1922 the U.S. Army was reduced and officers were encouraged to resign. Consequently, Blaik joined his father's home-building business and served part-time as a football assistant coach at Wisconsin (WC, 1926) and West Point (1927–1933). After debating between home-building and football careers, he became head football coach at Dartmouth (IL) in 1934. Blaik reversed a mediocre Dartmouth football program by compiling a 22-game undefeated streak, unofficial IL championships in 1936–1937, and a seven-year 45–15–4 record. He coached the Big Green's first victory over the Yale Elis in 1935 and stopped Cornell's undefeated string at 18 games in 1940 with the sensational fifth down decision reversal.

Blaik became the first civilian Army head football coach in 1941, inheriting a 1–7–1 squad and attaining a 6–3–0 record his first year. From 1944 to 1950 Blaik's teams compiled an astonishing 57–3–4 record and 32- and 28-game undefeated strings. Army won national championships in 1944 and 1945, amassing 504 and 412 points with all-time stars Felix "Doc" Blanchard* and Glenn Davis.* In 1946 the AFCA named Blaik Coach of the Year. In 1951 ninety cadets were expelled from West Point for technical violations of the Honor Code. Forty-four of them, including Blaik's son, regular quarterback Robert, played football. With his squad completely decimated, Blaik coached the Cadets in adversity in perhaps his finest hour. President Dwight D. Eisenhower in 1952 said, "He is a very great man. If he had been thinking only of himself, he would have resigned long ago." By 1953 Army finished 7–1–1 and ranked fourteenth nationally, earning Blaik the Washington (DC) Touchdown Club Coach of the Year Award. In his final coaching season (1958), Blaik enjoyed his last undefeated season, saw his team ranked third nationally, and received the Touchdown Club of New York's annual award. In 18 seasons at Army, Blaik compiled a 121–33–10 mark.

A member of the HAF College Football Hall of Fame, Blaik was named to the NFF College Football Hall of Fame in 1965 and received the NFF's Gold Medal Award in 1966 for "significant contributions and highest ideals." The retired colonel became vice president and chairman of the executive committee of Avco Corporation in 1959. He helped solve racial problems in Birmingham, AL, in 1963 and served on the Clark Board rewriting the draft laws in 1966. Blaik married Merle J. McDowell of Piqua, OH, in 1923 and has two sons, William and Robert. The author of *You Have to Pay the Price* (1960) and *The Red Blaik Story* (1974), he resides in Colorado Springs, CO. In May 1986 President Ronald Reagan presented the Presidential Medal of Freedom (the nation's highest civilian award) to Blaik.

BIBLIOGRAPHY: Army-Navy College Football Game Program, November 29, 1919; Earl H. Blaik and Tim Cohane, "Red Blaik Speaks Out," *Look*, 23 (October 27, 1959), pp. 48–50; Tim Cohane, *Great College Football Coaches of the Twenties and Thirties* (New Rochelle, NY, 1973); John D. McCallum and Charles H. Pearson, *College Football U.S.A., 1869-1973* (New York, 1973); Ronald L. Mendell and Timothy B. Phares, *Who's Who in Football* (New Rochelle, NY, 1974); Jim Murray column, *Los Angeles Times*, November 30, 1974; Edwin Pope, *Football's Greatest Coaches* (Atlanta, GA, 1956); Marshall Smith, "Blaik and Son," *Look* 29 (October, 1950), pp. 59–62; U.S. Military Academy, Alumni Records, Association of Graduates, West Point, NY; Stanley Woodward, "The Man Behind the Army Team," *Sport* 9 (November, 1950), pp. 24–29, 85–88.

James D. Whalen

BLANCHARD, Felix Anthony, Jr. "Doc" (b. 11 December 1924, McColl, SC), college athlete and a three-time Army All-American fullback (1944–1946), is the son of Felix A. and Mary Blanchard. He was nicknamed "Little Doc" after his father, a small-town physician and star fullback for Tulane and Wake Forest. His father's first gift to his son was a football. At St. Stanislaus Prep School in Bay St. Louis, MS, Blanchard impressed dozens of college football recruiters by earning All-GSC honors and playing in two New Orleans Toy Bowls. After starring for North Carolina's (SC) freshman team in 1942, Blanchard served in the U.S. Army Air Corps and was appointed to West Point in 1944. Blanchard combined with halfback Glenn Davis* to form the immortal "Mr. Inside and Mr. Outside" duo and carry Army to three straight unbeaten campaigns. Army was named AP national champion in 1944 and 1945. Many grid historians rate the 1945 team the best collegiate squad ever.

The 6 foot, 205 pound Blanchard, blessed with tremendous muscle development, an explosive start, astounding speed, and fine agility, made an ideal T-formation football player. A versatile superstar, "Doc" often lined up at a flanker post, delivered crushing blocks on Davis' sweeps, and made long pass receptions downfield. Despite playing under thirty minutes per game in 1944 and 1945, he gained 1,666 career yards rushing (5.9-yard average) and scored 38 touchdowns. Notre Dame scout Jack Lavelle, who witnessed Blanchard destroy opponents for three years, pictured the Army star as a devastating runner with atomic-type power. Lavelle termed Blanchard "a pulverizing blocker and tackler, a deft punter who gets the ball off as quick as anyone I've seen, a nimble pass-receiver and a smart defensive man. But most impressive is his wrecking power."

Blanchard first rocketed into national headlines in 1944, when Army routed Notre Dame 59–0. Blanchard did not score and rarely carried the ball, but he attracted the crowd's attention. One press account noted, "Blanchard, employed mainly as a decoy in the Army attack, played a spectacular game, bursting half the eardrums of the 74,437 spectators in the third period with a block that made possible [a] scoring return of a punt." Besides smothering 6 foot, 7 inch, 242 pound tackle John "Tree" Adams on a kick return, he knocked over head linesman Dave Reese. Reese sustained a broken arm and dislocated elbow and was carried off the field. The great long-range kicker booted one kickoff over 70 yards in the stands.

In the 1944 Navy game Blanchard showed he would rank with the most awesome power runners in the game's history. With Army leading 9–7 in the fourth quarter, Blanchard carried on nearly every play and helped the Cadets move from their own 48-yard line for the clinching touchdown. Although Navy knew Blanchard would carry the ball, "Doc" swept 22 yards and then penetrated the Middie wall for gains of three, five, three, four, and three yards. Blanchard ran the final nine yards, carrying three Navy defenders into the end zone with him. Blanchard peaked in 1945, scoring 19 touchdowns and rushing for 718 yards (7.1-yard average). He won every grid award, including the Heisman Trophy, Maxwell Award, and Walter Camp Trophy, emblematic of Player of the Year status. He became the first football player to receive the prestigious Sullivan Award, given the nation's top amateur athlete.

Following the 1945 season, Temple coach Ray Morrison* remarked, "Doc Blanchard was a colossus who, experts insist, is the greatest fullback of all time. Blanchard turned loose more raw power against Army opponents than has been seen since the days of Bronko Nagurski.* In addition, Blanchard ran with greater speed and finesse than even the great Nagurski." Blanchard missed two contests with a serious knee injury in 1946, but still gained unanimous All-American recognition again. Blanchard made a 92-yard kick-off return against Columbia University in 1946, the best single play of his career. He simply bolted down the middle of the field, brushing aside six or seven tacklers along the way.

Blanchard also ran the 100-yard dash in ten seconds and tossed the shot put in track. Although he had never participated in the shot put before, Blanchard increased his distance in one season by 20 feet and won the 1945 IC4A indoor championship. Blanchard, who entered military service upon graduation from West Point, married his wife, Jody, in 1948 and has three children, Felix A. III, Jo, and Mary Theresa. A jet fighter pilot, Blanchard served in Alaska and Vietnam and retired in 1971 as a colonel. Blanchard was elected to the NFF College Football Hall of Fame in 1959 and the HAF College Football Hall of Fame.

BIBLIOGRAPHY: "Army's Super-Dupers," *Time* 46 (November 17, 1945) pp. 57–58; Jim Beach and Daniel Moore, *Army vs. Notre Dame* (New York, 1948); Earl H. Blaik and Tim Cohane, *You Have to Pay the Price* (New York, 1960); Doc Blanchard to Bernie McCarty, January 7, 1984; Steve Boda, Jr., *College Football All-Time Record Book, 1869–1969* (New York, 1969); Murray Goodman and Leonard Lewin, *My Greatest Day in Football* (New York, 1948); "Irish Suffer Worst Defeat in History," Grand Rapids (MI) *Herald*, November 12, 1944; Jack Lavelle and Tim Cohane, "I Scout Blanchard and Davis for Notre Dame," *Look* 10 (October 1, 1946); Ed Linn, "Mr. Inside and Mr. Outside," *Sport* 20 (December, 1955), pp. 52–61; Pete Martin, "Portrait of a Fullback," *SEP* 218 (December 1, 1945), pp. 18–19; Ray Morrison, "All-American Team," *SEP* 218 (December 29, 1945), pp. 18–19.

Bernie McCarty

BLANDA, George Frederick (b. 17 September 1927, Youngwood, PA), college and professional player, the son of coal miner Michael Blanda, attended Youngwood High School and received a B.A. in Education from the University of Kentucky. Blanda married Betty Harris on December 17, 1949, and has eleven children. Blanda played tailback for the Youngwood High School Railroaders, running, passing, and kicking with equally fine skill. At Kentucky (SEC) he started at quarterback his freshman year on a poor 1–9 squad. After the legendary Paul "Bear" Bryant* became coach, the 6 foot, 1 inch, 210 pound Blanda played on the second-string unit for most of his sophomore year. During his senior year he again became the starting quarterback on an 8–3 Kentucky squad.

Blanda was selected by the Chicago Bears in the twelfth round of the 1949 NFL draft and played third string quarterback behind Sid Luckman* and Johnny Lujack.* He was traded to the Baltimore Colts (NFL) in 1950 but was soon released. After rejoining the Bears, he became Chicago's regular kicker and reserve quarterback. Frustrated at not being given a chance as starting quarterback, he persuaded Bears coach George Halas* to play him on defense at linebacker and cornerback. Early in the 1952 season Blanda started one game at quarterback and engineered a last-minute drive to defeat the powerful Detroit Lions 24–23. He returned to the bench, however, for the next game. After the 1952 season he almost signed with Hamilton (CFL). Halas and NFL commissioner Bert Bell* ultimately persuaded him to stay with the Bears. Blanda started at quarterback the 1953 season, but the Bears compiled a dismal 3–8–1 record. The Bears signed quarterbacks Zeke Bratkowski and Ed Brown, who started the next few years. Blanda never started again for the Bears at quarterback but consistently appeared late in games to engineer victories. In 1960 he joined the Houston Oilers in the first AFL season. He started at quarterback and kicked for the Oilers, guiding Houston to a 26–24 win over the Los Angeles Chargers in the first AFL championship game. With Blanda at the helm, the Oilers repeated as 1961 champions and were upset in the 1962 championship game by Dallas. After Houston experienced four poor seasons, Blanda in late 1966 was replaced at quarterback by Don Trull. Blanda was traded in 1967 to the Oakland Raiders (AFL), who used him as the kicker and reserve quarterback behind Daryle Lamonica. He surpassed Lou Groza* to become pro football's leading scorer with a field goal against the Kansas City Chiefs on October 31, 1971. He participated in the AFC championship games from 1973 through 1975 and in Super Bowl II, which the Raiders lost to the Green Bay Packers. He played reserve quarterback behind Ken Stabler* in 1975 and then retired at age 48.

Blanda, an honest man, endorsed only products he had already used. He came from a tough background and was thus capable of ignoring even the most serious injuries. The habitual Blanda liked his regular restaurants and regular trips to the racetrack to relax before a game. A solid kicker and aggressive, bold quarterback, Blanda excelled as a winner and entertainer. His many career records include most pro games played (340), most consecutive games (224), and scoring over 500 points for three separate teams. His record of most points scored in a pro career (2,002) was broken on August 5, 1983, by Dave Cutler of the Edmonton Eskimos (CFL). Blanda was named *TSN* AFL Player of the Year in 1961 and selected on *TSN* AFL All-Star teams in 1961 and 1967. During his career Blanda completed 1,911 of 4,007 passes (47.7 percent) for 26,920 yards and threw 236 touchdown aerials.

Blanda scored 9 touchdowns and kicked 943 extra points and 335 field goals. He was elected to the Pro Football Hall of Fame in 1981 and was named to its AFL-NFL 1960–1984 All-Star second team.

BIBLIOGRAPHY: *Los Angeles Times* (August 8, 1983), pt. III, p. 2; Harold Rosenthal, ed., *AFL Official History, 1960–1969* (St. Louis, MO, 1970); *TSN Football Register—1976;* Wells Twombly, *Blanda Alive and Kicking* (New York, 1972).

Keith Hobson

BLOUNT, Melvin "Mel" (b. 10 April 1948, Vidalia, GA), college and professional player and executive, is the son of farmer James and Alice (Sharpe) Blount. A 1966 graduate of Lyons (GA) Industrial High School, he majored in physical education at Southern University (SAC). The 6 foot, 3 inch, 205 pound defensive back was selected to the All-American football team in 1969 and named the Jaguars' MVP his final two seasons.

After being selected by the Pittsburgh Steelers in the third round of the 1970 NFL draft, Blount performed with Pittsburgh for 14 seasons (1970–1983). He played in 200 games, intercepted 57 passes for 736 yards and 2 touchdowns, and returned 36 kickoffs for 911 yards (25.3-yard average). Blount's 29.7-yard average for kickoff returns in 1970 ranked as second best in Steeler history. He paced the Steelers in interceptions (1975–1977, 1981), leading the NFL with 11 in 1975 and establishing an all-time team record for one season. Blount holds the Pittsburgh career record for interceptions (57) and ranks ninth on the all-time NFL list. He became the eleventh player in NFL history to intercept a pass in six straight games. Very aggressive in his man-to-man coverage in the Pittsburgh secondary, Blount led the Steelers to Super Bowl triumphs following the 1974, 1975, 1978, and 1979 seasons. He in 1975 was named the NFL's Most Valuable Defensive Player and Steelers' MVP. An AFC All-Star team selection from 1975 through 1977, Blount played in the Pro Bowl following the 1975–1976, 1978–1979, and 1981 seasons. He established a Pro Bowl record with two interceptions in 1977 and was named the game's MVP.

Blount and his wife, Leslie, have one daughter, Tanisia. He has a son, Norris, whose mother was Blount's high school girlfriend. Blount breeds quarter horses on a farm in Toombs County, GA, and has established a youth home there to assist troubled children. Blount in 1984 was named Director of Player Relations for the NFL to replace the late Claude "Buddy" Young* and acts as liaison between the NFL and players. The Pro Football Hall of Fame selected him to its AFL-NFL 1960–1984 All-Star second team.

BIBLIOGRAPHY: Roy Blount, Jr., "The Steeler Is Really a Cowboy," *SI* 59 (July 25, 1983), pp. 59–74; *Pittsburgh Steelers Media Guide, 1977; TSN Football Register—1984.*

John L. Evers

BOOTH, Albert James, Jr. "Albie" "Little Boy Blue," "The Mighty Atom" (b. 1 February 1908, New Haven, CT; d. 1 March 1959, New York, NY), college athlete and football coach and official, became one of the nation's most exciting halfbacks (1929–1931) at Yale University (IL) in helping his teams achieve a composite 15–5–5 record. A product of the Golden Age of Sports, Booth set a single-game standard of excellence against the U.S. Military Academy (Army) his sophomore season that even he found difficult to duplicate. He became the only Yale student to captain five teams (freshman and varsity football, freshman and varsity basketball, freshman baseball), won eight varsity letters, and was inducted in 1966 into the NFF College Football Hall of Fame. The son of Albert, Sr., a Winchester Repeating Arms Company foreman, and Mary Louise (Frank) Booth, he early starred on a New Haven Boys Club football squad. At Hillhouse High School he captained the varsity baseball nine and played basketball, but was too small for football. He captained all three sports at Milford Prep School before graduating in 1928 and entering Yale University (IL) the same year.

Booth's freshman football team lost a close 7–6 contest to the Harvard freshmen. Nicknamed "Little Boy Blue" and "The Mighty Atom," the 5 foot, 6 inch, 144 pounder played single-wing tailback and called the plays. Although not exceptionally fast, he could stop quickly, pivot, sidestep, and shift speeds; he frequently fooled tacklers. An adequate passer, he excelled at coffin corner punting, dropkicked accurately at 50 yards, kicked off over the goal line, and proved a sure defender. Booth displayed his exceptional ability by scoring every point in Yale's 14–6 triumph over Brown his sophomore year. Chris Cagle,* Army's three-time All-American halfback, sparked the Cadets to two easy touchdowns against Yale. The Cadets led 13–0 late in the first half before Yale coach Marvin "Mal" Stevens sent Booth into the fray. Booth inspired his teammates by his presence, driving the Elis to two touchdowns, scoring both himself, and dropkicking the extra points to put Yale in front 14–13. Late in the game he returned a punt 75 yards on a zigzag course that electrified 80,000 spectators in Yale Bowl and sealed the victory for the Elis. He gained 223 yards on 33 carries (6.8-yard average) and received a spirited ovation upon retiring to the sidelines. Admirers deluged him with mail, as his spectacular runs were highlighted in newsreels throughout the nation and newspaper headlines blared "Booth 21, Army 13." Booth followed his brilliant performance against Army with 32- and 47-yard runs that led to touchdowns against Dartmouth, scored a touchdown and sparked two scoring drives against Maryland, and passed 23 yards for a touchdown against Harvard. Crimson All-American center Ben Ticknor tackled Booth from behind after he had returned a second-half kickoff 55 yards, preserving a 10–6 triumph for Harvard.

Yale suffered two defeats in 1930, losing by four points to Georgia and 13–0 to Harvard. The Elis tied Dartmouth and Army, ranked eighth and ninth respectively by the Frank G. Dickinson System. Booth was bothered with injuries his junior season when special defenses were set up to stop him. He threw two touchdown passes and dashed for three touchdowns of 55, 40, and 45 yards against Maryland. His 18-yard dropkicked field goal provided the winning margin in a 10–7 triumph over Princeton. The Harvard jinx still dogged him, however, as he gained only 22 yards in 10 attempts.

Booth's rewarding final season saw Yale finish 5–1–2 with its best record and first Big Three title in four years and an eighth-place ranking by Dickinson. Yale won early games over Maine and Chicago and tied strong Army and Dartmouth teams for the second consecutive year. Yale extended its undefeated string to 15 games in a wild 33–33 encounter with Dartmouth. Booth gained over 500 yards and scored three touchdowns on a 94-yard kickoff return, 22-yard pass reception, and 54-yard run from scrimmage. Sixth-rated Georgia inflicted the only Yale defeat.

In the fiftieth game of the long Yale-Harvard series in 1931, Booth finally tasted victory (3–0) over the undefeated seventh-ranked Crimson at Cambridge. Besides dropkicking the game-winning 22-yard field goal with three minutes remaining, he made several fine runs against the Crimson and passed 28 yards to end Herty Barres to set up the field goal. Booth missed the final game with Princeton because he was hospitalized with pneumonia, but the Elis achieved a Big Three record 51–14 score against the hapless Tigers. In three years Booth rushed for 1,428 yards on 344 carries (4.1-yard average), returned 63 punts for 718 yards (11.4 average) and 13 kickoffs for 420 yards (32.3 average), made 8 interceptions, and scored 137 points (17 touchdowns, 23 extra points, 4 field goals). Although ranking among all-time Yale greats, Booth ironically never made first team All-American and made only a few second teams.

Booth, a member of Yale's Sheffield Scientific School, served on the Freshman Student Council and Senior Prom Committee. A baseball shortstop, he hit a grand-slam home run his last game in a Yale uniform to defeat Harvard 4–0. He majored in applied economic science and graduated from Yale in 1932. On July 4, 1932, he married high school sweetheart Marion Gertrude Noble and eventually had two daughters. He joined the Sealtest Corporation in New Haven, CT, and became general manager of the ice cream division of southern New England. Booth became part-time assistant football coach at Yale (1932–1933, 1945–1947) and New York University (1934–1935). Booth, a top football official, served as director of the Eastern Association of Officials, treasurer of the Yale Football Association, director of the New Haven Boys Club, and vice president of the First Offenders Club, founded to help prevent juvenile delinquency. While returning from a Broadway show with friends, he suffered a fatal heart attack. The Albie Booth Memorial Football Game, played between two professional teams in Yale Bowl to help the New Haven Boys Club, was named in his honor.

BIBLIOGRAPHY: L. H. Baker, *Football: Facts and Figures* (New York, 1945); Morris A. Bealle, *The History of Football at Harvard, 1874–1948* (Washington, DC, 1948); Thomas G. Bergin, *The Game* (New Haven, CT, 1984); Tim Cohane, *The Yale Football Story* (New York, 1951); John D. McCallum, *Ivy League Football Since 1872* (New York, 1977); Yale-Army Football Game Program, October 25, 1930; Yale-Harvard Football Game Program, November 21, 1931.

James D. Whalen

BRADSHAW, Terry Paxton (b. 2 September 1948, Shreveport, LA), college and professional player and broadcaster, starred as quarterback of the formidable Pittsburgh Steelers (NFL) and led them to four Super Bowl titles. During his 14 years with the Steelers, Bradshaw broke every club passing record and ranked among the game's all-time greats. Bradshaw, the second of shipyard welder William and Novis Bradshaw's three sons, attended Shreveport's Woodlawn High School. He played football there and in 1966 also set the national high school record for the javelin toss. At Louisiana Tech University (GSC), he broke every school football passing record. In 1969 he was named second team All-American by UPI and *TSN* and chosen MVP of the Senior Bowl. Bradshaw was the first player selected in the 1970 NFL draft.

Bradshaw joined a young, talented Pittsburgh Steeler team that gained maturity under Coach Chuck Noll.* In 1972 he experienced his first pro success by leading the Steelers to their first AFC Central Division championship: in an AFC playoff game Pittsburgh defeated the Oakland Raiders by Bradshaw's stunning "Immaculate Reception" pass to Franco Harris.* With quarterback Bradshaw, the Steelers captured eight divisional titles, earned ten playoff berths, and won Super Bowls in 1974, 1975, 1978, and 1979. During his career Bradshaw completed 2,205 of 3,901 pass attempts for 27,989 yards and 212 touchdowns. The muscular, rawboned, 6 foot, 3 inch, 215 pound Bradshaw also ran for 32 touchdowns.

Bradshaw excelled in post-season play, establishing the NFL's all-time post-season career records for passes attempted (417), completions (233), yards passing (3,508), and touchdown passes (28). In his four Super Bowl appearances he completed 49 of 84 passes for a record 9 touchdowns. A two-time Super Bowl MVP, he completed 17 of 30 attempts for 318 yards and 4 touchdowns against the Dallas Cowboys in 1978. In 1979 he completed 14 of 21 passes for 309 yards and 2 touchdowns against the Los Angeles Rams. In 1978 AP and *Sport* named Bradshaw NFL Player of the Year. A year later he shared *SI*'s Man of the Year award with the Pittsburgh Pirates' Willie Stargell* (BB). The three-time Pro Bowl squad member (1976, 1979, 1980) was selected quarterback of the Steelers' all-time team. The Pro Football Hall of Fame selected him on its AFL-NFL 1960–1984 All-Star second team.

Although initially viewed as a country bumpkin, the devout Christian eventually won over the critical Steelers fans. Upon retiring in July 1984, due to chronic elbow problems, Bradshaw became a football broadcaster-analyst for CBS. During the off-season he lives on his 400-acre cattle ranch and quarter horse breeding farm at Grand Cane, LA. The twice-divorced Bradshaw was married in 1972 to Melissa Babish, a former Miss Teen-Age America, and in 1976 to Jo Jo Starbuck, an ice skating star. In 1986 he married Charla Hopkins of Denton, TX.

BIBLIOGRAPHY: Tom Barnidge, "Bradshaw Was the Best," *TSN*, June 18, 1984; Terry Bradshaw with Charles Paul Conn, *No Easy Game* (Old Tappan, NJ, 1973); Terry Bradshaw with David Diles, *Terry Bradshaw: Man of Steel* (Grand Rapids, MI, 1979); Ronald L. Mendell and Timothy B. Phares, *Who's Who in Football* (New Rochelle, NY, 1974); Pittsburgh *Press*, July 15, 1984; Lou Sahadi, *Super Steelers* (New York, 1980); Roger Treat, ed., *The Encyclopedia of Football*, 16th rev. ed., rev. by Pete Palmer (New York, 1979).

Frank W. Thackeray

BRALLIER, John Kinport (b. 27 December 1876, Cherry Tree, PA; d. 17 September 1960, St. Petersburg, FL), college and professional player and coach, was the son of Emanuel and Lucy M. (Kinport) Brallier. His father, a physician and Civil War veteran, was born in Cambria County, PA, received his medical degree in 1868, and practiced medicine at Cherry Tree in adjoining Indiana County, where his wife's family was prominent. Brallier began his football career with the Indiana, PA, public school team in 1890, the year after his father died. By 1892 he captained and played halfback as a sophomore. In 1893 Brallier attended both the public high school and Indiana Normal so he "could play on the (normal school) team." Alex Stewart, the normal school's left guard, fathered movie star Jimmy. With Brallier at quarterback, Indiana Normal in 1893 compiled a 3–1 record. Although his team did not fare as well against more formidable opponents, Brallier impressed the Washington and Jefferson College coach.

After graduation from Indiana High School in 1895, Brallier accepted an offer for "all expenses for the entire year" to play football at Washington and Jefferson. Before school started that fall, however, Latrobe, PA, pro football promoter David Berry* contracted Brallier to fill a vacancy at quarterback for a September 3 game. Offered $10 plus expenses, the nearly 19-year-old Brallier accepted because his fatherless family possessed limited financial resources. Brallier played well, especially in kicking and tackling, for two games with Latrobe and reported to Washington and Jefferson College. As varsity quarterback, Brallier guided Washington and Jefferson to a 6–1–1 season and was cited frequently for his play in news accounts as "little Brallier." Before the 1896 season Brallier received football scholarship offers from Washington and Jefferson, West Virginia University, Grove City College, and several pro teams and clubs including Latrobe. He chose West Virginia because "the inducements were better than other schools" to play under coach Thomas "Doggie" Trenchard.* After a few games, however, he left West Virginia and finished the season as a player-coach at Latrobe.

During U.S. Army service in 1898, Brallier was stationed near home and played at Latrobe for $150 plus expenses. The University of Pennsylvania initially sought him but regarded his amateur status as too questionable. Penn hoped to schedule Harvard, which had questioned the amateur status of other Quakers players. Brallier attended Medico-Chirurgical Dental School (Philadelphia, PA), later part of Penn. He captained a quite successful Medico-Chi football team for three years and played basketball there. In 1900 he declined a football coaching offer from the University of Maryland. In 1902 Brallier declined pro offers from Franklin and Oil City, PA, to open a dental office at Latrobe, PA, and rejoined the team there as player-coach. He married Bess Garnette Moorhead of Indiana, PA, in 1904 and retired three years later as a player. He coached several Latrobe area teams in both football and basketball and served twenty years on the Latrobe School Board.

When both Latrobe and Canton, OH, were competing for the planned Pro Football Hall of Fame after World War II, Brallier was presented the first lifetime NFL pass in recognition of his early pro status. After his retirement from dentistry and his wife's death in an automobile accident, Brallier divided his time between Canada and Florida.

BIBLIOGRAPHY: Robert B. Van Atta, "Pioneers in Pro Football," *Indiana County Heritage* (Winter, 1979–1980); Brallier family members and family Bible; Latrobe (PA) *Bulletin*, 1895–1899; Scrapbooks of Dr. John K. Brallier.

Robert B. Van Atta

BRANCH, Clifford, Jr. "Cliff" (b. 1 August 1948, Houston, TX), college athlete and professional football player, is the son of Clifford Branch, Sr., who works for the Port of Houston, and Hattie M. (Jack) Branch, a schoolteacher. A speedster, the young Branch once ran a 9.2-second 100-yard dash for Houston Worthing High School. He consistently was clocked at 9.3 seconds, defeating 1972 Olympic Silver Medalist Robert Taylor in five out of six competitions. He won the State 4–A high school 100-yard dash championship in 1966 and 1967. Initially, Branch intended to matriculate at the University of California at Berkeley but returned home after a visit to the school. He studied at Wharton County (TX) Junior College in 1968 and 1969 and was recruited by coach Eddie Crowder of the University of Colorado (BEC).

After sitting out one year of ineligibility in 1969, Branch literally raced into the college record books during his final two years of competition at Colorado. As a flanker and kick returner, he became a genuine quadruple football threat with his running, passing, receiving, and kick returning. The

5 foot, 11 inch, 170 pound Branch averaged 17.9 yards each time he touched the football in the 1970 and 1971 seasons. His 26.1-yard average per rushing carry remains a Buffalo record, while his eight career kick returns for touchdowns (three others were called back because of penalties) remains an NCAA record.

Branch also proved very successful in track competition at Colorado, sharing the then world indoor record for the 60-yard dash (5.9 seconds) and outdoor 100-yard dash (9.2 seconds). He competed on relay teams, which set records for the indoor mile and the outdoor 440-yard dash. These accomplishments earned him in 1971 many honors, including Colorado College Athlete of the Year, All-BEC and BEC Outstanding Senior Player, and *Football News* All-American.

Although qualifying in the 1972 Olympic trials, winning the 100-yard dash in both the Texas and Kansas relays, and setting a world indoor record (9.3 seconds) in the same event that year, Branch decided to forgo the trip to the Munich Olympic games. Branch is divorced from his wife, Essie, who had studied French and psychology at Colorado. He was drafted and signed by the Oakland Raiders (NFL), where he was a premier wide receiver. His success was enhanced by the effectiveness of the Oakland throwing game, which combined the swift Branch with the steady, clever Fred Biletnikoff.* In 1974 he led the NFL in pass receiving yards (1,092) and touchdowns (13). In 1976 his 12 touchdowns were also an NFL best. He was selected All-Pro each year from 1974 through 1977 and played in the 1976, 1980, and 1983 Super Bowls and the 1973–1975 and 1977 playoffs with the Oakland–Los Angeles franchise, and he caught 501 passes for 8,685 yards (17.3-yard average) and 67 touchdowns. He missed most of the 1985 season with a hamstring injury and retired before the next season. Branch underwent drug rehabilitation in 1981 and lives in Santa Barbara, CA.

BIBLIOGRAPHY: Boulder (CO) *Daily Camera* (1970–1984); Denver (CO) *Post* (June 6, 1981); R. F. Jones, "Raiders Hold the Winning Edge," *SI* 45 (December 13, 1976), pp. 26–45; *NYT Biographical Service* (December 21, 1974), p. 1678; Dave Plati to Charles R. Middleton, 1985; *Who's Who Among Black Americans* (Northbrook, IL, 1985); *WWA* 41st ed. (1980–1981), p. 394.

Charles R. Middleton

BRAZILE, Robert Lorenzo, Jr. "Bob" (b. 7 February 1953, Mobile, AL), college and professional player, was an outstanding 6 foot, 4 inch, 238 pound football linebacker. Brazile excelled in football at Vigor High School in Mobile, AL, and from 1971 to 1974 at Jackson State University, (SAC) where he played with Walter Payton.* Although originally a tight end, he moved to linebacker his sophomore year. In 1974 Brazile set a school record with 129 tackles and 79 assists. Besides leading the SAC with nine interceptions, he in 1974 also made All-American and was a unanimous SAC selection. Following the 1974 season, he participated in the Senior Bowl and College All-Star games. The Houston Oilers selected Brazile in the first round of the 1975 NFL draft.

Brazile, a starter for the Oilers from the outset, made 7 sacks, 138 total hits, 2 forced fumbles, and 4 fumble recoveries his rookie (1975) season. On virtually every All-Rookie squad, he was named AFC Rookie of the Year, NFL Defensive Rookie of the Year, and NFL Rookie of the Year. His coach, O. A. "Bum" Phillips, commented, "He could start for this football team in about three or four different places. He's that kind of athlete, he's not only big and fast, he's a great athlete. He could play tight end, defensive line and any one of the linebackers."

Blessed with 4.6-second speed in the 40-yard dash, Brazile excelled on special teams, recovered 10 opponent fumbles, and intercepted 12 passes for 199 yards. He made *TSN* AFC All-Star team in 1976, 1978, 1979, and 1982 and the NFL All-Star team in 1980. Following the 1978 and 1979 seasons, the Oilers lost AFC championship games to the Pittsburgh Steelers 34–5 and 27–13. From 1976 through 1982 he played in the Pro Bowl. Brazile retired before the 1985 regular season. Brazile, who resides in Jackson, MS, is married to the former Alice Cook and has two children, Sherri and Robert III.

BIBLIOGRAPHY: *Houston Oilers Fact Book 1977: TSN Football Register—1982*.

John L. Evers

BREWER, Charles "Charlie" (b. 8 March 1873, Honolulu, HI; d. 13 June 1958, Waltham, MA), college athlete, was a three-time Walter Camp All-American football halfback (1892–1893, 1895) at Harvard University and was named in 1971 to the NFF College Football Hall of Fame. Brewer, chosen on Harvard's (IL) three-deep All-Time Football Teams of 1945 and 1948, played an instrumental role in one of football's most controversial plays, the flying wedge. He starred two years at fullback and then performed at halfback the last two seasons on Crimson teams that amassed a composite 41–6–1 record. The son of John Davis and Nannie Roberta (Harris) Brewer, he grew up in Boston, MA, and studied at nearby Hopkinson's School. The star halfback of the prep school eleven, Brewer graduated from Hopkinson's in 1892.

Brewer proved an immediate backfield sensation as a freshman on Harvard's 1892 varsity football team that won its first ten games. One of Brewer's finest performances was against Cornell at Harvard's Jarvis Field, where he scored all three touchdowns in a hard-fought 20–14 triumph. Harvard and Yale were tied 0–0 at halftime of the season's finale at neutral Hampden Park in Springfield, MA, before a then huge crowd of 20,000 spectators when Harvard captain Bernie Trafford stood in kickoff formation as usual at the 55-yard line (midfield of the 110-yard gridiron) to open the second half. To the amazement of the crowd, the other ten Crimson players were divided into two columns parallel to the sidelines. The closest players of each column were stationed fifteen yards behind Trafford. The 1892 rules regarding kick-offs did not require that the ball actually be kicked. As Trafford touched the ball with his toe and picked up the pigskin, the two columns converged just in front of him to form an inverted V. After Trafford handed the ball to Brewer inside the wedge, the moving V ripped apart the Elis until Brewer was downed at the Yale 25-yard line. The brainchild of Harvard alumnus and chess expert Lorin Deland, who never played football, the formation added momentum to mass and replaced the stationary V wedge at the center of the field. The play caused serious injuries, however, and was banned after the 1893 season. Undefeated national champion Yale scored a touchdown in the second half to defeat Harvard 6–0.

The 5 foot, 10 inch, 150 pound Brewer, a strong punter and ballcarrier, hit the opposition's defensive line like a battering ram. He teamed with NFF College Hall of Fame tackle Marshall Newell,* All-American center William Lewis, guard-tackle Bert Waters, end Norm Chabot, halfback Edgar Wrightington, and end Arthur Brewer, his younger brother who captained the 1895 varsity. Harvard and Yale remained undefeated again when they met in 1893, but captain Frank Hinkey's* Elis overcame the Crimson's continued inventiveness to duplicate the previous year's triumph. Instead of wearing the usual canvas or moleskin uniforms, Harvard donned leather outfits that shed water and made tackling difficult. Harvard also employed Deland's new oval-shaped "turtle-back" mass play, but Yale players countered by rubbing resin on their hands and prevailed 6–0.

Brewer in 1894 scored one touchdown (worth four points) and kicked three conversions (each worth two points) in the 22–0 triumph over Dartmouth in the first game played at Harvard's new Soldiers Field. He scored on an 85-yard gallop in the 18–4 triumph in the mud against Brown, a 70-yard touchdown run in the 32–0 shutout over Williams, and two touchdowns in the 40–0 rout of the Boston Athletic Association. In Harvard's final practice before the Yale game, Brewer severely sprained an ankle and could not play full-time in the Yale and Pennsylvania games. The Crimson missed Brewer's booming punts and suffered continually with poor field position, dropping the last two games 12–4 and 18–4. The ankle injury kept Brewer off the All-American team and prevented him from becoming one of only five four-time consensus All-Americans.

Harvard in 1895 won all of its early season games, as Brewer returned to full-time efficiency. The Crimson, however, lost two games (Princeton and Pennsylvania) and tied one (Boston Athletic Association) in its last four outings and finished the season with an 8–2–1 mark. Brewer ran relays on the Harvard track team and performed three years with his class crew before graduating from Harvard University with a Bachelor of Arts degree in 1896. Brewer, who married Laura Holdredge Morse of Falmouth, MA, in 1898 and had one son and four daughters, served in World War I as a corporal in the Motor Corps of the Massachusetts State Guard. He joined Charles Brewer and Company exporting and shipping, Warren and Company steamship agents, and worked in the real estate business for a time. Brewer served as assistant treasurer of Massachusetts General Hospital and from 1929 to 1955 as president of the Warren Institution for Savings in Boston. He resided in suburban Weston, MA, where he was an active member of the Weston Golf Club.

BIBLIOGRAPHY: Morris A. Bealle, *The History of Football at Harvard, 1874–1948* (Washington, DC, 1948); Thomas G. Bergin, *The Game* (New Haven, CT, 1984); John A. Blanchard, ed., *The H Book of Harvard Athletics* (Cambridge, MA, 1923); Harvard-Pennsylvania Football Game Program, November 23, 1895; Harvard University Archives, Harvard University Library, Cambridge, MA.

James D. Whalen and Daniel Frio

BRICKLEY, Charles Edward (b. 24 November 1891, Boston, MA; d. 28 December 1949, New York, NY), college athlete and professional football player, ranked among the nation's top field goal kickers and led the championship 1912–1914 Harvard University (IL) football teams to undefeated seasons. Brickley's versatile performances included frequent fine runs and excellent blocks enabling teammates Eddie Mahan* and Fred Bradlee to advance the ball into scoring position. His blocking helped Harvard as much as his ball carrying, field goals, and defensive play altogether. Brickley graduated in 1910 from Everett (MA) High School, where he excelled in football, baseball, and track and performed as a three-sport star the following year at Phillips Exeter Academy. At Harvard University in 1911 he captained the freshman team that tied Yale 0–0.

A unanimous All-American halfback in 1912 and 1913, the 5 foot, 10 inch, 186 pound Brickley was selected 1913 Player of the Year by HAF and made J. C. Kofoed's All-Time Team (1913) and the Harvard All-Time Team (1948). Brickley scored 10 touchdowns and 13 field goals as a sophomore in 1912, dropkicked a field goal to defeat Dartmouth 3–0, and scored the only touchdown in a 7–0 win over Maine. In Harvard's 16–6 triumph over Princeton, he gained 106 yards (twelve less than Princeton) and kicked three field goals. During the season finale 20 to 0 victory over Yale, Brickley ran 18 yards for a touchdown with a recovered fumble and kicked two field goals.

As a junior in 1913, Brickley scored six touchdowns and three field goals in early victories over Penn State, Cornell, and Brown. On a muddy field, Brickley's 19-yard dropkick field goal defeated host Princeton 3–0 and gave Harvard its first triumph there. In the season finale 15–5 victory over Yale, he tied an all-time one-game record by kicking five field goals (35, 38, 32, and 24-yard dropkicks and a 40-yard placekick). Besides scoring all Crimson points, he kicked the last three field goals with blurred vision from an accidentally scratched eye. *NYT* writer Arthur Daley* (OS) in 1950 called Brickley "the greatest field goal kicker of them all," while Grantland Rice* (OS) remarked "he could dropkick and hit targets [Sam] Baugh* or [Sid] Luckman* might miss throwing." Although team captain in 1914, Brickley participated in only three games because of an emergency appendectomy. In the 36–0 season-ending triumph over Yale, he faked a field goal, enabling Huntington Hardwick* to score the final touchdown, and kicked the extra point.

Besides winning three football letters, Brickley threw the shot put three years for the track team and played left field in baseball his final year. In 1915 he hit a double and scored the winning run against Yale. A member of the 1912 U.S. Olympics team, he did not place in the hop, step, and jump. In 1918 Walter Camp* selected Brickley as fullback on his All-Service football team. Brickley played pro football briefly in 1917 with the Massillon (Ohio) Tigers and led his All-Stars in an exhibition game in 1921 with the Cleveland Indians. Brickley married Katherine A. Taylor in 1917 and had two sons, Charles E., Jr., and John T. He operated his own Wall Street stock brokerage firm, managed the Roosevelt Health Club in New York City, and was working as an advertising salesman when he died of a heart attack.

BIBLIOGRAPHY: L. H. Baker, *Football: Facts and Figures* (New York, 1945); Morris A. Bealle, *The History of Football at Harvard 1874–1948* (Washington, DC, 1948); John A. Blanchard, ed., *The H Book of Harvard Athletics* (Cambridge, MA, 1923); Tim Cohane, *The Yale Football Story* (New York, 1951); Ralph Hickok, *Who Was Who in American Sports* (New York, 1971); Ronald L. Mendell and Timothy B. Phares, *Who's Who in Football* (New Rochelle, NY, 1974); Alexander M. Weyand, *American Football: Its History and Development* (New York, 1926); Alexander M. Weyand, *The Olympic Pageant* (New York, 1952); Yale-Harvard Football Game Program, November 23, 1912.

James D. Whalen

BRODIE, John Riley (b. 14 August 1935, San Francisco, CA), college and professional athlete and sports commentator, is the first of three children of a Bay Area stockbroker. Brodie attended Oakland (CA) Technical High School, where he was chosen for the All-City teams in football, basketball, and baseball and was an outstanding golf and tennis player. Brodie entered Stanford University (PCC) in 1953 and received a B.S. in Physical Education from there in 1957. A consensus football All-American in 1956, Brodie led the NCAA in passing with 139 completions in 240 attempts for 1,633 yards, a .579 percentage, and 12 touchdowns. He also paced the nation that year in total offensive plays with 295 for 1,642 yards. As a junior, the versatile 6 foot, 1 inch, 210 pound Brodie ranked ninth nationally in total offense, punted, and played safety on defense. He finished his collegiate career with 296 completions in 536 attempts for 3,594 yards and 19 touchdowns. Besides throwing 37 interceptions, he gained 3,560 yards in total offense on 652 plays and surpassed all the passing records held by Frankie Albert.* Brodie, a member of the NFF College Football Hall of Fame, was chosen MVP in the 1956 Shrine All-Star (East-West) Game and 1957 College All-Star Game.

Brodie was selected in the first round by the San Francisco 49ers in the 1957 NFL draft. He performed 17 years (1957–1973) with San Francisco, becoming the regular quarterback in 1961. The successor to Y. A. Tittle,* Brodie owned or shared 17 of the 49ers' 22 listed passing records. He was named All-Pro twice and in 1970 won the Jim Thorpe Trophy as the NFL's MVP. He led San Francisco to the NFC championship game in 1970 and 1971, losing both times to the Dallas Cowboys. Brodie paced the 49ers in passing (1960–1962, 1964–1971, 1973) and holds the club record of 30 touchdown passes in 1965. He also passed for five touchdowns in one game, equalling the 49er mark. Brodie led the NFL in passing percentage (59.9) in 1958 and in average yards per pass completion (9.14) in 1961. In 1965 he paced the NFL in passing attempts (391), completions (242), passing percentage (61.9), yards (3,112), and touchdown passes (30). Topping the NFL in 1968, Brodie completed 234 of 404 passes for 3,020 yards. Again, he paced NFL passers in 1970 with 223 completions for 2,941 yards and 24 touchdowns. He finished his NFL career with a 55 percent completion average, 2,469 completions on 4,491 attempts for 31,548 yards, 214 touchdowns, and 224 interceptions, all club records. Only six other NFL quarterbacks have passed for over 30,000 yards.

Brodie played in only three games in 1963 because of an automobile accident and nearly jumped to the AFL in 1965. He remained with the 49ers and became one of the richest pro players in 1966 upon signing for over $1 million. A two-time Pro Bowl performer (1966, 1971), Brodie retired in 1973 and since has worked as an NBC-TV sportscaster for pro football and pro golf tour events. Brodie and his wife, Susan, have five children; he now pursues a career as a pro golfer on the Senior Tour.

BIBLIOGRAPHY: Lud Duroska, ed., *Great Pro Quarterbacks* (New York, 1972); *TSN Football Register—1974;* Herbert Wilner, "Long Live the King," *SEP* 240 (November 18, 1967), pp. 85–89.

John L. Evers

BROWN, James Nathaniel "Jimmy" "Jim" (b. 17 February 1936, St. Simons Island, GA), college and professional football player and lacrosse player, is the son of Swinton and Theresa Brown. At age 7, Brown journeyed north with his mother to Manhasset, Long Island, New York. Athletics became a dominant factor in his life as a teenager. At Manhasset High School, Brown excelled in every sport he tried and won 13 varsity letters. He averaged 38 points a game in basketball and 14.9 yards per carry in football; 45 colleges offered him scholarships. Brown held the Long Island basketball scoring record until Art Heyman broke it.

Brown attended Syracuse University and in 1956 made All-American in both football and lacrosse. In his senior season Brown set a still-standing major college record by scoring 43 points (6 touchdowns and 7 extra points) against Colgate University. The Orangemen played in the 1957 Cotton Bowl, where Brown dominated. Brown rushed for 132 yards and scored 21 points in Syracuse's 28–27 loss to TCU. During his collegiate career (1954–1956), Brown compiled 2,091 total yards, 25 touchdowns, and 187 points. A high scorer on the basketball team, Brown tallied 563 points in 43 games. He also placed fifth in the national decathlon championship in track. The Cleveland Browns selected Brown in the first round of the 1957 NFL draft, after which he played in the College All-Star Game.

Brown performed for Cleveland from 1957 to 1965 as one of the greatest ballcarriers in NFL history. The 6 foot, 2 inch, 228 pound fullback, often compared to Jim Thorpe* and Bronko Nagurski,* demonstrated power, speed, and quickness. His running power was most evident to the outside as he moved around and over people on a sweep or pitchout. Although targeted by every opponent, Brown never missed a pro game in nine years because of injuries, and he was seldom stopped. His duals with linebacker Robert "Sam" Huff of the New York Giants and Washington Redskins were unrivaled. Besides being NFL Rookie of the Year in 1957, Brown led Cleveland in rushing (1957–1965), scoring (1958–1959, 1962–1963, 1965), and receiving (1963). In seven different seasons, he rushed for over 1,000 yards. Brown paced the NFL in scoring with 108 points (1958) and holds team season records for most attempts (305), yards (1,863), and touchdowns (17). He also holds club rushing records for most attempts (37), yards (237), and touchdowns (5) in one game. On November 1, 1959, Brown scored 5 touchdowns against the Baltimore Colts.

Brown established NFL records for most seasons, leading the NFL in rushing (8), consecutive seasons pacing the NFL in rushing (5), career rushing attempts (2,359), career rushing yards (12,312), games with 100 or more yards rushing (58), career yardage average per gain (5.2), rushing touchdowns in a season (17), lifetime rushing touchdowns (106), and rushing yards in one season (1,863). Although many of these records have since been broken, Brown's 5.2-yard average gain and 106 career rushing touchdowns remain NFL records, the latter shared with Walter Payton.* His 12,312 career rushing yards stood until Payton surpassed it during the 1984 season. Brown's lifetime statistics for 118 games also included 262 receptions, 15,459 combined yards, and 756 points scored.

The two-time NFL MVP (1958, 1965) played in three NFL championship games (1957, 1964–1965). Cleveland lost to the Detroit Lions (1957) and Green Bay Packers (1965) but captured the 1964 crown with a 27–0 triumph over the Baltimore Colts. An All-NFL selection eight years, Brown was named to the Pro Bowl every year and selected the game MVP twice (1962–1963). Brown won the Jim Thorpe Trophy in 1958 and 1965 and shared it with Y. A. Tittle* in 1963. With Green Bay's Jim Taylor,* he was selected at fullback on the All-Pro Squad of the 1960s by the Pro Football Hall of Fame committee. In 1971 Brown was elected to the Pro Football Hall of Fame. Brown, who is also a member of the National Lacrosse Hall of Fame, was named to the Pro Football Hall of Fame's AFL-NFL 1960–1984 All-Star Team. Brown married Sue Jones in 1958 and has three children, Kim and Kevin (twins), and Jim. Brown now concentrates on his motion picture career, having appeared in *The Dirty Dozon*, *The Mercenaries*, and *Ice Station Zebra*, and actively promotes black economic causes.

BIBLIOGRAPHY: *Cleveland Browns Media Guide, 1977;* George Sullivan, *The Great Running Backs* (New York, 1972); *TSN Pro Football Guide*, 1985); *WWA*, 41st ed. (1980–1981), p. 447.

John L. Evers

BROWN, Paul E. (b. 7 September 1908, Norwalk, OH), college and professional coach and executive, was a very successful, innovative football mentor. Brown won few popularity contests with his cool, strict demeanor but made truly outstanding accomplishments. After graduation from Massillon (OH) High School, Brown received his B.A. in Education in 1930 from Miami University (OH). Although an undersized, ordinary player, he compiled a sparkling 16–1–1 coaching record at Severn Prep School in 1930–1931. From 1932 to 1940 Brown coached Massillon High School to an outstanding 80–8–2 record and several state championships. In 1940 he received his M.A. in Education from Ohio State University. The next year he became head football coach at Ohio State (WC). Besides capturing the 1942 national championship, Brown's Buckeyes won 18 of 27 games and tied one over three seasons. His Great Lakes Naval teams recorded a 15–5–2 mark in the 1944–1945 seasons.

Although still in military service, Brown was asked to coach the new Cleveland franchise of the proposed AAFC. The new AAFC hoped to challenge the NFL. Since Brown's reputation in Ohio was so highly esteemed, fans named the new team after him. Upon joining pro football in 1946, Brown made the gridiron world aware of his many coaching innovations. These techniques included employing intelligence tests as guides to a player's learning potential, using notebooks and classroom methods, utilizing film clip statistical studies, grading his own players from films, and having "messenger guards" so that plays could be called from the sideline. He formulated very innovative, detailed pass patterns and, when other teams copied his patterns, devised defenses to stop them. Several fine running backs were moved to defense because, according to Brown, "they were so good I didn't want to waste them on offense." In a highly significant contribution to pro football, he in 1946 began hiring black players for his new team. The NFL had instituted a color ban after 1933, denying talented black stars the opportunity to play pro football.

His unprecedented success with the Browns doomed the AAFC. During the AAFC's four-year existence, Cleveland won every championship and compiled an amazing 52–4–3 record. Since the Browns dominated the AAFC, spectators in other cities lost interest in the championship race. With the demise of the AAFC, the Browns in 1950 joined the NFL. Although many experts fully expected Cleveland to falter when meeting the "real pros," the Browns started the season by upsetting the 1949 NFL-champion Eagles, 35–10, at Philadelphia and won the 1950 championship. The Browns repeated as title winners in 1954 and 1955 and won Eastern Conference crowns in 1951, 1952, 1953, and 1957. During his outstanding coaching career with Cleveland, Brown compiled a 114–48–5 record and experienced only one losing season. After having several non-title seasons, however, Cleveland owner Art Modell in late 1962 fired Brown.

Brown left coaching for five years and was named in 1967 to the Pro Football Hall of Fame. In 1968 he returned to pro football as coach and general manager of the expansion Cincinnati Bengals (NFL). Despite having a squad of castoffs and raw recruits, he still won a Central Division title by 1970 and repeated in 1973. Although recording only a 55–59–1 mark in eight seasons there, Brown coached well for an expansion team. Since 1976 he has concentrated on his general managing duties. His great players included Pro Football Hall of Famers Otto Graham,* Marion Motley,* Bill Willis,* Dante Lavelli,* Lou Groza,* Jim Brown,* and Len Ford.* Brown and his late wife Kathy had three sons. After her death, he remarried. His controversial 1979 autobiography (with Jack T. Clary) made the best-seller lists.

BIBLIOGRAPHY: Paul Brown file, Pro Football Hall of Fame, Canton, OH; "Quarterback/Interview," *Quarterback* (November, 1969), pp. 24–29; George Sullivan, *Pro Football's All-Time Greats: The Immortals in Pro Football's Hall of Fame* (New York, 1968); Marty Williams, "First Came George Halas, Then Paul Brown," *Football Digest* 5 (April, 1976), pp. 50–54; Bob Younkers, "The Man from Massillon," *Sport Life* 3 (Fall, 1950), pp. 12–13, 92; Paul Brown with Jack T. Clary, *PB: The Paul Brown Story* (New York, 1979); Ray Buck, "Has Paul Brown Ruined the Bengals?" *Football Digest* 8 (June, 1979), pp. 34–38; Robert Diendorfer, "Has Pro Football Passed by Paul Brown?" *Sport* 33 (June, 1962), pp. 33, 84–86; Doug Grow, "Paul Brown Has Mellowed at 66... A Little," *Sport* 59 (November, 1974), pp. 75–76, 78–79; Ed Hershey, "That Old Brown Magic," *Newsday* (November, 1968), pp. 19–25; Joe Marshall, "The Bengals' Bungles," *SI* 51 (November 5, 1979), pp. 80–83; Tex Maule, "A Man for This Season," *SI* 17 (September 10, 1962), pp. 33–41; Jack Newcombe, "Paul Brown: Football's Licensed Genius," *Sport* 17 (December 1954), pp. 51–59.

Robert N. Carroll

BROWN, Robert Stanford "Bob" (b. 8 December 1941, Cleveland, OH), college and professional player, made football All-American at the University of Nebraska (BEC) and was selected All-Pro seven times. From a ghetto, the 6 foot, 4 inch, 280 pound offensive tackle attended East Technical High School in Cleveland and was recruited by Bill Jennings in 1960 to play for a perennially losing Nebraska team. When Bob Devaney* became head coach in Brown's junior year (1962), Nebraska returned to its ancient winning ways. Brown had not shown much gridiron skill at Nebraska and had nearly convinced Devaney that he liked being in the trainer's room better than playing football. As Brown was being taped by the trainer one day, he told Devaney that he could not make practice. On the practice field Devaney noticed a stranger in a three-piece suit watching the drills intently and got an idea. When Brown hobbled out on the field, Devaney whispered confidentially to him, "You see that guy over there? He's a scout from the Philadelphia Eagles. He's been asking about you." When Devaney mentioned that the scouts were concerned about his being injury-prone, Brown replied, "Coach, maybe I can go today." Brown quickly exhibited a remarkable attitude change, hitting hard and tackling ferociously. Before long, real scouts showed up to watch Brown perform.

Brown played well for Nebraska and helped the Cornhuskers defeat Miami 36–34 in the 1962 Gotham Bowl and triumph over Auburn in the 1963 Orange Bowl. Brown made All-American at offensive guard in 1963 and was voted Lineman of the Year by the Washington Touchdown Club. In 1964 he earned a Bachelor of Science degree in Education from the University of Nebraska. A high draft choice of the Philadelphia Eagles, he played there through the 1968 season and made All-NFL offensive tackle in 1964, 1965, and 1968. He joined the Los Angeles Rams in 1968, making All-NFL again. In 1971 he moved to the Oakland Raiders and made All-AFC three consecutive seasons. Brown, who earned an M.A. in Educational Administration at the University of Pennsylvania, retired after the 1973 season and became a California businessman.

BIBLIOGRAPHY: Bob Devaney, *Devaney* (Lincoln, NE, 1981); Hollis Limprecht et al., *Go Big Red: The All Time Story of the Cornhuskers* (Omaha, NE, 1966); Lincoln (NE) *Journal-Star*, 1962–1963; Omaha (NE) *World-Herald*, 1962–1963; *University of Nebraska Football Guides, 1962–1963.*

Jerry D. Mathers

BROWN, Roosevelt, Jr. "Rosie" (b. 20 October 1932, Charlottesville, VA), college athlete and professional football player, coach, and scout, is the son of Southern Railroad employee Roosevelt Brown, Sr., and excelled as a lineman. Since an uncle had died in a football game, his father wanted him instead to play trombone in the high school band. When the elder Brown's railroad duties kept him away from home, however, the son played football one full season without injury, unbeknownst to his father. At Morgan State College (CIAA), he captained the wrestling team, lettered in baseball, and twice was named to the Black All-American Football Team at tackle.

Pro teams rarely scouted at black colleges then. The New York Giants (NFL) selected Brown in the twenty-seventh round of the 1953 player draft when a team executive saw his picture in a black newspaper. An imposing physical specimen, Brown stood 6 feet, 3 inches, weighed 255 pounds, and had a 29-inch waist. Brown's size and quickness made him an exceptional blocker on either passes or runs. Brown started at left offensive tackle for the Giants as a rookie and excelled there from 1953 to 1965, helping lead New York to six Eastern Conference titles and one NFL championship. Besides being honored as 1956 NFL Lineman of the Year, he was named from 1956 to 1963 to the AP All-NFL Team. With the exception of 1960, UPI honored him similarly. *The Sporting News* named him All-Eastern Conference from 1956 through 1961 and again in 1965. Brown, who played in nine Pro Bowls, in 1975 became only the second "pure" offensive lineman to be enshrined in the Pro Football Hall of Fame. After retiring as a player, he served as a Giants' assistant coach through 1970 and still scouts for them. He lives in Teaneck, NJ, with his wife, the former Thelma Curenton.

BIBLIOGRAPHY: Roosevelt Brown file, Pro Football Hall of Fame, Canton, OH; "Roosevelt Brown," *Pro!*, Cincinnati-Washington Football Game Program, August 2, 1975; Harold Rosenthal, "Rosie Brown, Offensive Tackle," *Sport*, 40 (December, 1965), pp. 52–55, 92–93.

Robert N. Carroll

BROWN, William Ferdie "Willie" (b. 2 December 1940, Yazoo City, MI), college athlete and professional football player and coach, was a 6 foot, 1 inch, 210 pound defensive back. After attending Yazoo City High School, he played for Grambling College (SAC) from 1959 to 1962. Besides winning four football letters at Grambling, he also earned two track letters. He served as senior class president and earned a B.A. in Health and Physical Education. A free agent, he was cut by the Houston Oilers (AFL) in 1963 and joined the Denver Broncos (AFC). In 1964 he became a star defensive back with nine interceptions and tied the AFL one-game record with four against the New York Jets. During four seasons with Denver, he made 15 interceptions for 195 yards. After being traded in 1967 to the Raiders (AFL), he became Oakland's all-time leading interceptor with 39 in 12 seasons. In 16 pro seasons, he intercepted 54 passes for 472 yards and two touchdowns and set a record by pilfering at least one pass each season. The Raiders' defensive captain, he won the 1969 Gorman Award as the Player Who Best Exemplifies the Pride and Spirit of the Raiders.

Brown participated extensively in post-season competition, including the AFL championship games (1967–1969) and AFC championship games (1970,

1973–1977). He played in Super Bowls II and XI, setting a record in the latter by scoring on a 75-yard interception return against the Minnesota Vikings. During other post-season games, he scored on interception returns against the Miami Dolphins in 1970 and Pittsburgh Steelers in 1973. Brown, who was named to *TSN* AFL All-Star teams (1964–1969) and the AFC All-Star teams (1970–1973), played in five AFL All-Star games (1964–1965, 1967–1969), and four Pro Bowls (1970–1973). The Pro Football Hall of Fame named him to its AFL–NFL 1960–1984 All-Star Team.

Subsequently, Brown served as assistant coach with the Raiders during their victories in Super Bowls XV and XVIII. Besides being honored with a Willie Brown Day in his hometown, he was recognized for his work in the 1972 NFL drug campaign. Brown was elected to the Pro Football Hall of Fame on the eve of Super Bowl XVIII, making him the third free agent so honored. He is married, has one son and two daughters, and lives in Los Angeles, CA.

BIBLIOGRAPHY: *NFL Media Information Book, 1983; Oakland Raiders Media Guide, 1977; TSN Football Register—1979;* Jack Zanger, *Pro Football 1970* (New York, 1970).

John L. Evers

BROYLES, John Franklin "Frank" (b. 26 December 1924, Decatur, GA), college athlete, football coach, and athletic administrator, is the son of grocery store owner O. T. and Louise Broyles. An all-around athlete at Decatur High School, Broyles starred in football, basketball, and baseball at Georgia Institute of Technology (1944–1947) and earned ten letter awards there. An All-SEC quarterback in 1944 and 1946, he in 1944 led Georgia Tech to the SEC championship. He married Barbara Day in May 1945 and has four sons, Jack, Hank, Dan, and Tommy, and twin daughters, Betsy and Linda. A staunch family man, Broyles has participated in the Fellowship of Christian Athletes for a long time. Broyles, who graduated from Georgia Tech in 1947 with an industrial management degree, rejected pro baseball and football offers for coaching. Broyles apprenticed as football assistant to Bob Woodruff at Baylor University (SWC, 1947–1949), defensive backfield coach at the University of Florida (SEC, 1950), and offensive backfield coach for Bobby Dodd* at Georgia Tech (SEC, 1951–1956).

He landed his first football head coaching position at the University of Missouri (BEC), posting a 5–4–1 record in 1957. In January 1958 University of Arkansas athletic director John Barnhill named Broyles head coach, a selection that revitalized that school's athletic program. Under Broyles' guidance from 1958 through 1976, Arkansas won seven SWC football championships and appeared in ten bowl games. In 1964 the Razorbacks captured their only national title with an 11–0 season. Broyles, whose Arkansas record was 144–58–5 for a .707 percentage, compiled a career 149–62–6 (.699) mark. The most prestigious honors afforded a college coach have been won by

Broyles. Besides sharing National College Coach of the Year in 1964 with Notre Dame's Ara Parseghian,* he was named in 1983 to the NFF College Football Hall of Fame. An outstanding athletic administrator, Broyles has developed one of the nation's prominent all-around programs. From 1979 through 1983 Arkansas won five straight SWC all-sports championships. During the 1982–1983 season, Arkansas finished in the top ten nationally in six of its nine competitive athletic programs. A noted ABC television commentator on college football telecasts, Broyles is a fine amateur golfer and has served on the prestigious Board of Directors of the Master's Tournament.

BIBLIOGRAPHY: *Arkansas Basketball: 1983–84;* Roger L. Mendell and Timothy B. Phares, *Who's Who in Football* (New Rochelle, NY, 1974); University of Arkansas, Sports Information Office, Fayetteville, AR; *WWA*, 41st ed., (1980–1981), p. 457.

Joe Lee Smith

BRYANT, Paul William "Bear," "The Man" (b. 11 September 1913, Moro Bottoms, AR; d. 26 January 1983, Tuscaloosa, AL), college player and coach, was the son of truck farmer Wilson and Ida (Kilgore) Bryant. Nicknamed "Bear" because he wrestled a bear at Fordyce, AR, for money, Bryant participated in football, basketball, baseball, and track at Fordyce High School. He played on the state championship football team in 1930 as an offensive end and defensive tackle. From 1932 to 1936 Bryant attended the University of Alabama (SEC). As a starting offensive football end (1933–1935), he played on Crimson Tide teams that won 23 games, lost 3, and tied 2. He played with All-Americans Don Hutson* and Dixie Howell and performed on the 1935 Rose Bowl team that defeated Stanford University 29–13.

In 1936 Bryant married the former Mary Harmon Black and had two children, Paul, Jr., and Mae Martin. Bryant the same year joined the Alabama staff as an assistant football coach and in 1940 moved to Vanderbilt University (SEC) to work under Henry R. "Red" Sanders.* After the 1941 season, Bryant enlisted in the U.S. Navy. In 1945 he was named the head football coach at the University of Maryland (SC). Following a 6–2–1 record in his only year there, Bryant coached eight seasons at the University of Kentucky (SEC). Bryant's teams compiled a 60–23–5 record, including wins in the 1947 Great Lakes Bowl, 1951 Sugar Bowl, and 1952 Cotton Bowl. At Kentucky, Bryant developed All-Americans George Blanda,* Bob Gain,* and Vito "Babe" Parilli and guided the 1950 Wildcats to his first SEC championship. Bryant moved to Texas A&M University (SWC) in 1954 and enjoyed four successful seasons (25–14–2) there, winning the SWC crown in 1956. All-American Heisman Trophy winner John David Crow* and Jack Pardee led the Aggies in a 3–0 loss to the University of Tennessee in the 1957 Gator Bowl.

Bryant's Alabama tenure began in 1958 and ended with the Crimson Tide's 21–15 victory over the University of Illinois in the 1982 Liberty Bowl. As head coach at Alabama, Bryant guided six national championship (1961, 1964–1965, 1973, 1978–1979) and eight unbeaten teams during regular-season play (1956, 1961, 1964, 1966, 1971, 1973–1974, and 1979). His teams either won or shared the SEC title thirteen times. When Bryant relinquished the head coaching duties to former player Ray Perkins after the 1982 season, he had achieved an overall 323–85–17 record and was intercollegiate football's then all-time winningest coach. He surpassed Amos Alonzo Stagg's* record of 314 victories on November 28, 1981, when his team defeated Auburn University 28–17. In Bryant's twenty-five years at Alabama, his teams compiled a remarkable 232–46–9 record. Between 1971 and 1981 Alabama won 116 games and lost only 15, finished undefeated in 1979, and lost only one game in each of six other seasons. From 1959 to 1982 Alabama appeared in post-season competition twenty-four consecutive years under Bryant's leadership. His composite 15–12–2 record in major bowl games leads all other coaches in appearances, victories, and losses. Bryant's outstanding performers at Alabama included John Hannah,* Lee Roy Jordan,* Joe Namath,* and Ken Stabler.*

Bryant thrice was named National Coach of the Year (1961, 1971, and 1973) and eight times SEC Coach of the Year (1961, 1964, 1971, 1973–1974, 1977, 1979, and 1981). Nicknamed "The Man" because he proved a tough disciplinarian with integrity and fairness, he excelled at getting the most out of people. One of his rival coaches used to say, "Bryant could take his'n and beat your'n, and take your'n and beat his'n." He could win with either group. Bryant authored *Bear Bryant on Winning Football* and co-authored *Bear*. In 1986 he was elected to the NFF College Football Hall of Fame in his first year of eligibility.

BIBLIOGRAPHY: Clyde Bolton, *The Crimson Tide: A Story of Alabama Football* (Huntsville, AL, 1973); Paul W. Bryant and John Underwood, *Bear* (Boston, 1974); Mickey Herskowitz, *The Legend of Bear Bryant* (New York, 1976); John A. Peterson and Bill Cromartie, *Bear Bryant: Count Down to Glory* (New York, 1983).

John L. Evers

BUCHANAN, Junious "Buck" (b. 10 September 1940, Gainesville, AL), college athlete, professional football player, and coach, starred in football at Grambling (LA) State University (SAC, 1960–1963) and as a defensive tackle with the Kansas City Chiefs (AFL, 1963–1969; AFC of NFL, 1970–1975). Buchanan, a basketball and football star at Birmingham (AL) Parker High School, enrolled in 1960 at Grambling and played three years there at defensive and offensive football tackle for coach Eddie Robinson.* One of the finest all-around performers in small college athletic history, Buchanan joined fellow lineman Ernie Ladd in making the all-black college a nationally prominent football power. He earned All-SAC honors in football from 1960 through 1962 and was named unanimously to the 1962 NAIA All-American team. He participated on the 1963 College All-Star team that defeated the world champion Green Bay Packers (NFL) in an exhibition game in Chicago. Buchanan lettered one year in basketball and ran sprints in track at Grambling. In 1962 the 6 foot, 7 inch, 274 pounder ran the 440-yard dash in 49.2 seconds. Six years later he was named to the NAIA Hall of Fame.

Buchanan married his wife, Elizabeth, a Grambling student, in 1963 and has three children. Drafted in 1963 as the number one pick of the AFL Dallas Texans (later Kansas City Chiefs), Buchanan played on a powerful defensive unit that achieved winning seasons and national acclaim. His consistent play and domination of opposing linemen established new standards for defensive linemen in the era of the passing game. Combining intelligence, speed, and size, Buchanan developed new techniques for rushing an opposing quarterback in passing situations. Buchanan started in six AFL All-Star games (1964–1969) and the first two AFC NFC Pro Bowl games. Coach Hank Stram* in 1968 named him team co-captain. Buchanan led Stram's team to a .857 (12–2) win-loss percentage, the highest in Kansas City Chiefs history. Buchanan also started at defensive tackle in the 1966 and 1969 AFL championship games and the 1967 Super Bowl I against the Green Bay Packers and 1970 Super Bowl IV against the Minnesota Vikings. He continued his college studies during his pro football career and in 1969 graduated with a Bachelor's degree from Grambling. After 181 pro games spanning 13 years, Buchanan retired following the 1975 season because of several minor injuries and kidney stone problems. He then directed the Kansas State Special Olympics for the mentally and physically handicapped, coached for the NFL New Orleans Saints (1975, 1977) and Cleveland Browns (1978), and operated his own promotion and marketing company in the Kansas City, MO, area.

BIBLIOGRAPHY: Buck Buchanan file, Pro Football Hall of Fame, Canton, OH; Gary Cartwright, "Buck Buchanan: Steady as a Courthouse," *Sport* 20 (December, 1967), pp. 83–84; Kansas City (MO) *Times*, July 31, 1973; September 12, 1973; November 6, 1975; New York *Herald Tribune*, December 3, 1963.

John Hanners

BUCHANON, Willie James (b. 4 November 1950, Oceanside, CA), college and professional player, ranked among pro football's premier cornerbacks. A graduate of Oceanside High School, he attended Mira Costa (CA) Junior College and San Diego State University (CaCAA) from 1970 to 1971. The 6 foot, 1 inch, 196 pound Buchanon, an All-CaCAA and All-American performer in 1971, captained the Aztec defense, led them in interceptions, and punted regularly in 1970 and 1971. After the 1971 season he participated in the College All-Star, Senior Bowl, and Coaches All-America games. In the Shrine All-Star (East-West) game, he intercepted three passes and was named MVP.

The Green Bay Packers selected Buchanon, one of the best cornerback prospects in a decade, in the first round of the 1972 NFL draft. With the Packers from 1972 through 1978, he started at left cornerback except for fracturing his left leg in the 1973 and 1975 campaigns. As a rookie, he shared the Packer lead in interceptions, returned a blocked field goal attempt 57 yards for a touchdown against the New Orleans Saints, and was named AP Rookie of the Year. A highly effective tackler with 4.5-second speed in the 40-yard dash, he made *TSN* NFC All-Star team in 1978 and played in the 1974 and 1978 Pro Bowls.

In 1979 Buchanon was traded to the San Diego Chargers (NFL) for first- and seventh-round draft choices. With the Chargers four seasons, he participated in the 1980 and 1981 AFC championship game losses to the Oakland Raiders and Cincinnati Bengals. In eleven pro seasons, Buchanon made 28 interceptions for 278 yards, 2 touchdowns, and 15 fumble recoveries. Buchanon, who is single, teaches high school in San Diego, CA, and does graduate work at San Diego State. One of pro football's more flamboyant dressers, he keeps over forty plants in his apartment.

BIBLIOGRAPHY: *Green Bay Packers Media Guide, 1977; San Diego State University Football Media Guide, 1976; TSN Football Register—1982.*

John L. Evers

BURRIS, Paul "Buddy" (b. 20 January 1923, Rogers City, OK), college and professional player, was selected three years (1946–1948) as All-BSC guard at the University of Oklahoma and the first Sooner three-time All-American. Burris was named to the *Pic* magazine Scouts All-American team as a sophomore and to the Chicago *Tribune* Football Players team the following year and was made a consensus choice as a senior. During Burris' varsity career, the Oklahoma Sooners amassed a composite 25–6–1 (.797 percent) record and captured Gator and Sugar Bowl victories. Burris played with the Green Bay Packers (NFL) from 1949 to 1951 on mediocre teams placing no better than fifth in the NFC.

His parents, farmer Paul "Pop" and Myrtle Burris, had six sons and five daughters. All his brothers played football at Oklahoma—namely, consensus All-American center Kurt (1954); All-BSC fullback Bob (1955); twins Lynn and Lyle, center and halfback (1956); and Don, one year of junior varsity. Burris attended the two-room Riverside Country School through the eighth grade and entered Muskogee (OK) Central High School in 1938. He was heartbroken at not being made a halfback because he had always fancied himself as a ballcarrier, but he became a star end and tackle on the powerful Muskogee eleven. After graduating from high school in 1942, Burris enrolled at Tulsa University (MVC) and immediately made the Hurricane varsity. Coach Henry Frnka's Tulsa squad compiled a perfect (10–0–0) season, outscoring opponents 434–46. Tulsa placed fourth in the AP poll but lost 14–7 to Tennessee in the Sugar Bowl. Burris logged 167 minutes playing time behind sensational one-armed All-American guard Ellis Jones and excelled in the Hurricanes routs of Oklahoma (23–0) and Oklahoma (State) A&M (34–6). Quarterback Clyde LeForce, fullback Bobby Dobbs, and All-American halfback Glenn Dobbs operated behind a forward wall that held seven opponents scoreless.

Burris served thirty-four months with the U.S. Army Engineers in the European and Pacific theaters during World War II. Oklahoma (BSC) coach Jim Tatum,* who was building a Sooners dynasty, persuaded the 5 foot, 11 inch, 215 pound Burris to enter there in 1946. The season opener came against two-time national champion Army, featuring the heralded "Inside-Outside" running of Doc Blanchard* and Glenn Davis.* Behind 14–7 in the fourth quarter, the Sooners drove to the Army 14-yard line. An errant lateral pass was intercepted and returned 86 yards for an Army touchdown, giving the Cadets the hard-earned 21–7 victory. Army rated Burris "the toughest guard we've ever met, and that goes for their center [John] Rapacz. Both were bad news." Oklahoma tied Kansas for the 1946 BSC championship, defeated North Carolina State 34–13 in the Gator Bowl (the Sooners' first post-season game in eight years), and finished 8–3–0 as fourteenth-ranked in the nation. Under first-year coach Charles "Bud" Wilkinson,* Oklahoma repeated in 1947 as BSC co-champions with the Jayhawks, posted a 7–2–1 record, and ranked sixteenth in the final AP poll. For Oklahoma, Burris kicked off, targeted linebackers with explosive blocks, and proved a stalwart on defense. Long-time NFL New York Giants' coach Steve Owen* observed, "Burris is one of the best defensive linemen I've ever seen in college football." The low-slung, durable, square-jawed Burris, who sported a burr haircut, was hardworking, good-natured, and easy to coach; he kept the Sooners relaxed with his sense of humor.

The 10–1–0 Sooners won the BSC championship outright in 1948 (the first of twelve consecutive) and ranked fifth nationally. After Santa Clara upset the Sooners 20–17 in the opener, Oklahoma embarked on a 31-game undefeated streak under Wilkinson. Burris led the rushes that sacked the Texas quarterback four times to help the Sooners defeat the Longhorns 20–14 for the first time in nine years. Inspired by halfbacks Jack Mitchell and George Thomas, tackle Wade Walker, and end Jim Owens, Oklahoma defeated third-ranked North Carolina 14–6 in the Sugar Bowl. After the game North Carolina star Charlie Justice* stated, "Oklahoma is by far the best team we faced." A good student with a B-plus grade average, Burris graduated in 1949 with a B.S. in Business Administration. After playing three seasons with the Green Bay Packers (NFL), he worked from 1951 to 1957 with Dowell, a light industrial concern. Since then he has been a civilian employee at Tinker (OK) Air Force Base. Burris married Betty Jane Short in August 1947, and has two children.

BIBLIOGRAPHY: Volney Meece and Bill Bryan, *Thirteen Years of Winning Oklahoma Football* (Oklahoma City, OK, 1960); Hal Middlesworth, "Buddy Burris of Oklahoma," *Sport* 5 (November, 1948), pp. 34–35, 103; Sugar Bowl Football Game Programs, (January 1, 1943; January 1, 1949); University of Oklahoma, Alumni Records Office, Norman, OK, January, 1986.

James D. Whalen

BUTKUS, Richard Marvin "Dick" (b. 9 December 1942, Chicago, IL), college and professional player and broadcaster, is the son of electrician John and Emma (Goodoff) Butkus. At Vocational High School in Chicago, Butkus excelled in football as a fullback, was named to the football All-American team, and in 1960 was selected by the AP as Prep Football Player of the Year. The 6 foot, 3 inch, 245 pound center and linebacker attended the University of Illinois (BTC), earning a B.S. in 1965. Butkus, who captained the 1964 Fighting Illini football squad, was chosen team MVP, All-BTC, and All-American (1963–1964). Besides receiving the BTC MVP Award (1964), Butkus was named *TSN* Player of the Year. Butkus ranked sixth (1963) and third (1964) in the Heisman Trophy voting and won the Knute Rockne Trophy (1963–1964) as the nation's top lineman. On January 1, 1964, Butkus starred defensively in Illinois' 17–7 triumph over the University of Washington in the Rose Bowl.

Butkus, defensive captain for the College All-Stars (1965), became the first-round draft choice of the Chicago Bears (NFL). After receiving a reported $200,000 as a rookie, Butkus played with the Bears from 1965 through 1973. He represented an era that saw his position glamorized. The premier middle linebacker of the 1960s and 1970s and perhaps the best of all time, Butkus excelled as a defensive quarterback and became the heart and soul of the Bears' defense both physically and spiritually. Butkus, considered the greatest defensive player in Illinois history and an all-time BTC great, was called by coach George Halas* "one of the greatest defensive players in the history of the Bears." In 1969 against the Pittsburgh Steelers, Butkus enjoyed one of his typical games by making 15 unassisted tackles, assisting on 10 more tackles, and downing the quarterback for a safety. Respected by his teammates and opponents for his bruising play, Butkus once held the NFL record for most opponents' fumbles recovered in a career (25) and made 22 lifetime interceptions. He played in nine Pro Bowls (1965–1973) and made All-Pro six times (1965, 1967–1970, 1972) and the All-Pro squad of the 1960s and the AFL-NFL 1960–1984 All-Star Team, the latter two chosen by the Pro Football Hall of Fame selection committee.

Knee injuries forced Butkus to retire following the 1973 season. Since 1973 he has conducted sports radio shows in Chicago and pursued a television acting career. Butkus married Helen Essenburg and has three children, Nicole, Richard, and Matthew. The co-author of *Stop-Action*, Butkus was elected to the Pro Football Hall of Fame in 1979 and the NFF College Football Hall of Fame in 1983 and is a radio color analyst for Chicago Bears games.

BIBLIOGRAPHY: Robert W. Billings and Richard Butkus, *Stop-Action* (New York, 1972); *TSN Football Register—1974;* George Vass, *George Halas and the Chicago Bears* (Chicago, 1971).

John L. Evers

BUTLER, John "Jack" (b. 12 November 1927, Pittsburgh, PA), college and professional player, coach, and scout, starred as a defensive back with the Pittsburgh Steelers (NFL) from 1951 through 1959. Butler, whose father played sandlot football with Steelers owner Art Rooney,* never played high school football. He began his gridiron career at St. Bonaventure University; he was not selected in the NFL college draft and signed with the Steelers as a free agent in 1951. Quickly gaining a starting position with Pittsburgh, the 6 foot, 1 inch, 195 pound Butler anchored the Steelers' defensive backfield during the 1950s and led the team in interceptions in 1952–1953 and 1956–1958. In 1957 Butler tied for the NFL lead in interceptions with 10. He made 52 career interceptions, trailing only Mel Blount* among Steelers defenders.

Butler's 10 interceptions in 1957 rank him second on the Steelers' all-time list. His 11 steals occurred in 1957, after the NFL had expanded its schedule from 12 to 14 games. Butler returned 52 interceptions 871 yards for a Steelers record. Three interceptions were returned for touchdowns, tying the team record. Butler's greatest game came on December 13, 1953, when he set a club record, intercepting four passes against the Washington Redskins. The sure, punishing tackler was named All-NFL defensive halfback by UPI and All-NFL safety by AP in 1957. In 1958 and 1959 both UPI and AP named Butler All-NFL defensive halfback. Butler made four consecutive Pro Bowl appearances from 1956 through 1959.

Butler, who spent his off-seasons coaching at Dayton University, made the Steelers' all-time team selected for the club's fiftieth anniversary season in 1982. Earlier the Pro Football Hall of Fame Selection Committee named him to the All-Pro squad of the 1950s. After retiring from the Steelers, Butler was associated with the BLESTO-V organization. Butler resides in Pittsburgh and remains active as a pro scout.

BIBLIOGRAPHY: Ray Didinger, *Pittsburgh Steelers* (New York, 1974); Pat Livingston, *The Pittsburgh Steelers: A Pictorial History* (Virginia Beach, VA, 1980); Roger Treat, ed., *The Encyclopedia of Football*, 16th rev. ed., rev. by Pete Palmer (New York, 1979).

Frank W. Thackeray

BUTTS, James Wallace, Jr. "Wally" (b. 7 February 1905, Milledgeville, GA; d. 17 December 1973, Athens, GA), college athlete, football coach, and administrator, was the son of draying service operator James Wallace, Sr., and Anna Lousetta (Hutchinson) Butts. The 5 foot, 6 inch, 155 pound Butts was a small football player even for his era. As a prep school player at Georgia Military College, he captained the football, basketball, and baseball teams. At Mercer University he competed in football, basketball, baseball, wrestling, and boxing under Bernie Moore. Moore, who later coached at LSU and became the first SEC commissioner, called Butts the "greatest blocking end I ever coached." Butts coached ten years in prep schools (Madison A&M, Georgia Military College, and Male High, Louisville, KY) and lost only ten games. He became an assistant football coach at the University of Georgia (SEC) in 1938 and head coach and athletic director in 1939. His 140–86–9 record over 21 seasons resulted in four SEC championships and eight bowl games, including the Rose, Sugar, and Orange Bowls.

Butts' Georgia teams set seven SEC club season records and ten individual season records. Close friend Frank Leahy* appraised Butts as "college football's finest drill master and passing coach . . . I've learned much from him." Butts produced twelve All-Americans and seven All-Pro players and once had College Hall of Famers Frank Sinkwich* and Charley Trippi* in the same backfield. He was named SEC Coach of the Year three times (1942, 1946, 1959) and finished runner-up for National Coach of the Year in 1946. Butts coached four College All-Star teams against the NFL champions, winning three times. In 1961 he was elected to the HAF College Football Hall of Fame. Butts served on the NCAA Football Rules Committee for six years and as president of the AFCA in 1959.

Butts, who married Winifred Taylor on February 19, 1929, and had three daughters, Faye, Jean, and Nancy, retired as head football coach after the 1960 season and resigned as athletic director in 1964. Butts entered the insurance business and owned a company at his death. His players perceived him as an iron man on the field and a soft touch off the field. Despite his severe discipline and practices, Butts deeply cared for his players throughout their lives. Paul "Bear" Bryant* said, "He pioneered the passing game in the South," while Fran Tarkenton* stated, "After 13 years in the pros, I still have not met anyone who knows as much football as Coach Butts."

BIBLIOGRAPHY: Atlanta *Constitution*, December 17–31, 1973; Jesse Outlar, *Between the Hedges: A Story of Georgia Football* (Huntsville, AL, 1973); Ed Thilenius and Jim Koger, *No Ifs, No Ands, A Lot of Butts* (Atlanta, GA, 1960); Jack Troy, *Leading a Bulldog's Life* (Atlanta, GA, 1948); University of Georgia, Sports Information Department files, Athens, GA.

Robert T. Bowen

C

CAGLE, Christian Keener "Red" "Chris" (b. 1 May 1905, DeRidder, LA; d. 23 December 1942, Queens, NY), college and professional player, coach, and executive, was a three-time All-American football star. Cagle was nicknamed "Red" because his hair was often exposed when his helmet dangled from the back as he streaked down the field. At Southwestern Louisiana Institute in 1925, he scored 108 points and ranked as the nation's fifth highest scorer. From 1926 through 1929 Cagle won national acclaim as the famed number 12 at the U.S. Army Academy under head coach Lawrence "Biff" Jones.* At 5 feet, 11 inches, and 178 pounds, the extremely quick back ran to his right and left equally well, blocked and tackled effectively, and led the Cadets to a 30–8–2 record. Once referred to as "Onward Christian" Cagle for his upfield running ability, he was selected consensus All-American in 1927 and 1929, unanimous All-American in 1928 by Grantland Rice* (OS), and HAF Player of the Year.

Cagle figured in the cancellation of the Army-Navy rivalry in 1928 and 1929, when the Midshipmen requested all contestants be limited to three years of college football experience. Several Army stars, including Cagle, already had reached this plateau and would have been ineligible to compete against Navy. Since Army rejected this proposal, the rivalry was suspended for two years. Cagle was forced to leave West Point in 1929, when it was discovered that he had secretly married Marian Haile on August 25, 1928, on a furlough at Gretna, LA. Following his resignation, he coached briefly at Mississippi A&M.

From 1930 through 1932 Cagle starred in pro football with the New York Giants (NFL). The Giants had signed him for $7,500, then a lucrative amount. Cagle completed his playing career with the rival NFL Brooklyn Dodgers (1933–1934), where he became team co-owner with John Sims "Shipwreck" Kelly. After one year he sold his interest and entered the insurance business. In 1938 he became manager of the brokerage department of the Fidelity-Phoenix Fire Insurance Company. Cagle helped organize the Touchdown Club of New York and was selected to the HAF and NFF College Football Halls of Fame. At age 37, Cagle fractured his skull in a fall down subway stairs and died in Physicians Hospital in Queens, NY, from a brain hemorrhage. Besides his wife, Marion, he left two sons, Christian Keener, Jr., and Galyn.

BIBLIOGRAPHY: Tim Cohane, *Gridiron Grenadiers: Story of West Point Football* (New York, 1948); Ronald L. Mendell and Timothy B. Phares, *Who's Who in Football* (New Rochelle, NY, 1974); Frank G. Menke, ed., *The Encyclopedia of Sports*, 5th rev. ed., rev. by Suzanne Treat (New York, 1975); *NYT*, December 24, 1942; Paul Soderberg and Helen Washington, eds., *The Big Book of Halls of Fame in the U.S. and Canada Sport* (New York, 1977).

Donald E. Kosakowski

CALDWELL, Charles William, Jr. "Charlie" (b. 2 August 1901, Bristol, VA-TN (border); d. 1 November 1957, Princeton, NJ), college athlete and football coach, served as Princeton University (IL) football player–coach. Caldwell became the Tigers' first coach to win six Big Three championships and accomplished the feat consecutively between 1947 and 1952. A member of the HAF College Football Hall of Fame, Caldwell was named to the NFF College Football Hall of Fame in 1961, selected AFCA Coach of the Year in 1950, and received the New York Touchdown Club Award in 1952. Princeton won 24 consecutive games over four years. His 1950–1951 undefeated teams featured Heisman Trophy winner Richard Kazmaier,* was ranked sixth in AP polls, and won Lambert Trophies as eastern champion. The son of public accountant Charles William, Sr., and Lena Hoge (Snapp) Caldwell, he lived in Yonkers, NY, and played football and baseball at Yonkers High School. He added basketball to his sports participation at Mercersburg Academy, where he graduated in 1921.

A three-year (1922–1924) regular fullback and center at Princeton (IL), Caldwell played on the Tigers' 1922 undefeated national co-champion "Team of Destiny" that upset Yale 3–0 and Chicago 21–18. The 5 foot, 10 inch, 176 pound Caldwell won three letters as a baseball pitcher and slugged against Harvard the longest home run ever (520 feet) at Princeton Field. Besides lettering as a basketball guard, he served as senior class president and graduated in 1925 with a Bachelor of Science degree. Caldwell, a relief pitcher in 1925 for the New York Yankees (AL) served as Bill Roper's football assistant at Princeton from 1925 to 1927. He was head football coach from 1928 to 1942 at Williams College (LTC), where his teams compiled a 76–37–6 composite record and lost 14 games to major schools. Williams won eight LTC championships and recorded eight one-loss seasons in fifteen years.

One of the last successful single-wing offense proponents, Caldwell compiled a 70–30–3 record as Princeton (IL) head football coach from 1945 to

1956. In 1946 his Tigers handed Rutgers one of its two defeats and upset thirteenth-ranked Pennsylvania 17–14. In 1949 Princeton lost by two points to twelfth-ranked Cornell and handed Brown its only loss. Although rejected from World War II duty because of defective eyesight, Caldwell performed civilian work with Navy V–5 and V–12 programs. He married Ruth Bishop (1926), Marion Taylor (1941), and Lucille McCarthy Wheeler (1952) and had one son, Charles W. II, and one daughter, Mary Jane. The author of *Modern Single Wing Football* (1951) and *Modern Football for the Spectator* (1952), he compiled an outstanding coaching 146–67–9 career record (.678 percent). He died of cancer in 1957.

BIBLIOGRAPHY: Allison Danzig, *The History of American Football: Its Great Teams, Players, and Coaches* (Englewood Cliffs, NJ, 1956); Jay Dunn, *The Tigers of Princeton: Old Nassau Football* (Huntsville, AL, 1977); Ralph Hickok, *Who Was Who in American Sports* (New York, 1971); "Leader of a Revival," *Life* 31 (November, 1951), pp. 130–34; John D. McCallum and Charles H. Pearson, *College Football U.S.A., 1869-1973* (New York, 1973); Red Smith, "They Weep No More at Princeton," *SEP* 220 (October 11, 1947), pp. 26–27; "A Victory Parade Ends," *Life* 33 (October 20, 1952), pp. 30–31; Yale-Princeton Football Game Program, November 15, 1924.

James D. Whalen

CAMP, Walter Chauncey (b. 7 April 1859, New Britain, CT; d. 14 March 1925, New York, NY), college athlete, football coach, and administrator, was the son of schoolmaster-publisher Leverett L. and Ellen (Cornwell) Camp. After attending Hopkins Grammar School in New Haven, CT, Camp graduated from Yale University with a B.A. in 1880 and studied medicine for two years there. In 1882 he joined the Manhattan Watch Company in New York. The following year he began a lifetime career with the New Haven Clock Company, becoming president in 1903. Camp on June 30, 1888, married Alice Graham Sumner, sister of the famed Yale social Darwinist William Graham Sumner, and had two children, Walter, Jr. (1891) and Janet Camp Troxell (1897). Camp, the "Father of American Football," also performed in baseball, track, class crew, and tennis at Yale. He played doubles in the first intercollegiate tennis tourney but attracted national recognition in football.

Camp participated in football at Yale (IL) for six years, the final two as a medical school student. In 1876 he played halfback in the first Harvard-Yale game played under Rugby Union rules. The team captain three years, he shaped the rules transforming rugby football into American football. Camp attended the intercollegiate football conventions from 1877 to 1925, dying of a heart attack during the 1925 convention. As a football innovator, Camp proposed changing the number of players from fifteen to eleven. More important, he made football more rational with his 1880 proposal creating the scrimmage, in which one team had undisputed possession of the ball. The scrimmage replaced the chance possession found in the rugby scrum. Possession unfortunately made it possible for one team to keep the ball an entire half, prompting Camp in 1882 to propose a downs system. A team was given three downs to make five yards or surrender possession, the lines creating a gridiron effect on the field. Camp's rules committee leadership led to the present point system for touchdowns, field goals, and safeties. He also proposed permitting tackling below the waist.

From the 1880s to around 1910, Camp achieved acclaim as Yale's advisory football coach. Although not paid, he held nightly sessions advising the Yale captain and key players with his strongly analytical mind. Regarded as the coach of coaches, he gave continuity to Yale's dominating intercollegiate football teams. Camp contributed to Yale's athletic stability as its graduate advisor of athletics and paid treasurer of the Yale Financial Union, founded in 1893 to consolidate all athletic teams under one organization. He held the complete confidence of Yale's president in influencing Yale athletic policy.

Camp may have been the strongest promoter of commercialized athletics on the college campus. He applied business methods to college athletics in producing both spectator interest and victories and used innovative playing strategy and novel methods of promoting the game to the public. Through his prolific writing Camp promoted football to a mass audience. He produced voluminous newspaper articles, wrote over 200 magazine articles, and edited *Spalding's Official Intercollegiate Football Guide*. From 1891 to 1921 Camp wrote nearly thirty books including seven fiction works. His most popular fiction effort was *Jack Hall at Yale*. His nonfiction book *Football* (1896), co-authored with former Harvard coach Lorin F. Deland, described football playing techniques. From 1889 to 1925 Camp selected All-American football teams and consequently generated vast interest in the sport's stars.

The football crisis of 1905–1906 reduced the power Camp had achieved over football rules. Camp was reluctant to change the rules drastically to remove the game's brutality. He opposed the forward pass rule created in 1906 but ironically helped develop its use during that season. Camp lost control as secretary of the football rules committee in 1906, when opponents of Camp's conservative administration formed the NCAA.

After 1910 Camp withdrew from most aspects of Yale's athletic program. When the United States entered World War I, Camp directed the U.S. Navy Training Camps Physical Development Program and conducted a very popular Daily Dozen exercise program. He remained active on the football rules committee until his death. On November 3, 1928, the $300,000 Walter Camp Memorial Gateway was dedicated at the Yale Bowl to the Father of American Football. He is a member of both the HAF and NFF College Football Halls of Fame.

BIBLIOGRAPHY: Robert O. Anthony, *Guide to Walter Camp Papers* (New Haven, CT: Yale University Archives, 1982); Richard Borkowski, "Life and Contributions of Walter Camp to American Football," Ph.D. diss., Temple University, 1979; Walter

Camp, *American Football* (New York, 1891); Walter Camp, *The Book of Foot Ball* (New York, 1910); Walter Camp, comp., *Football Facts and Figures* (New York, 1894); Walter Camp and Lorin F. Deland, *Football* (Boston, MA, 1896); Walter Camp papers, Yale University Archives, New Haven, CT; Parke H. Davis, *Football; The American Intercollegiate Game* (New York, 1911); John S. Martin, "Walter Camp and His Gridiron Game," *American Heritage* 12 (October, 1961), pp. 50–55, 77–81; *NCAB*, vol. 21, pp. 193–94; Harford Powell, Jr., *Walter Camp* (Boston, MA, 1926).

Ronald A. Smith

CAMPBELL, Earl Christian (b. 29 March 1955, Tyler, TX), college and professional player, is the sixth of eleven children born to Burk C. (B. C.) and Ann (Collins) Campbell. Named after the white doctor who delivered him (Earl Christian), he grew up in a small, weather-beaten farmhouse six miles north of Tyler. His father held odd jobs and his mother cleaned houses to supplement the family's meager income from cultivating two acres of roses. When B. C. died of a heart attack in 1966, the family plunged deeper into poverty and "Bad Earl" endured a troubled childhood marked by delinquency. The courage and character of his deeply religious mother and the influence of football coaches, however, produced attitudinal changes by his senior year in high school. In leading John Tyler High School to a 15–0 record and the state 4A championship in 1973, Campbell rushed for 2,036 yards (6.6-yard average), scored 28 touchdowns, and was named All-State and All-American.

He then attended the University of Texas and became the first player named All-SWC for four years. His achievements for three years as a fullback in the wishbone offense paled compared with his performance as a senior. Shifted to tailback in the new Veer and I formations, he was named All-American and awarded the Heisman Trophy after leading the nation in 1977 in both rushing (1,744 yards) and scoring (114 points on 19 touchdowns).

Selected by the Houston Oilers of the AFC as the first player chosen in the 1978 NFL draft, Campbell immediately excelled in the I formation designed for him by coach O. A. "Bum" Phillips. Besides setting eight team records, he accounted for over half of Houston's rushing yardage. Campbell's NFL-leading 1,450 yards in 302 attempts, the most yards ever gained by a rookie and the first time a rookie had led the NFL since Jim Brown* in 1957, earned him Rookie of the Year and MVP honors. In 1979 he again led the NFL in rushing, gained over 100 yards in a then record seven consecutive games, and repeated as MVP. In 1980 he earned his third straight MVP award and rushing title with the finest offensive performance of his career. Besides gaining over 200 yards in four games, he led the NFL in every rushing category—attempts (373), yards (1,934), average yardage per carry (5.2), and touchdowns (13).

By 1981 his productivity began to decline because of the physical toll of his powerful running style and personal frustrations due to disagreements with new head coaches, the lack of team success, and public criticism of his efforts and abilities. He was traded in October 1984, to the New Orleans Saints (NFL) and reunited there with his friend and ex-coach, "Bum" Phillips. He retired before the 1986 season, 593 yards short of 10,000 career rushing yards. In eight pro seasons, Campbell gained 9,407 yards on 2,187 carries (8th best) for a 4.3-yard average and 74 touchdowns. Campbell, who caught 121 passes for 806 yards (6.7-yard average), was named to the Pro Bowl as an AFC All-Star annually from 1978 to 1983.

The 5 foot, 11 inch, 225 pound Campbell was not a graceful, elusive, broken-field runner but a pure power back. He utilized the brute strength of massive forearms and thighs, along with deceptive quickness and speed, to overpower defenders with a smashing, punishing running style. In return, he absorbed an unusually heavy physical pounding from the multiple tackles who blunt his bull-like charges. As Phillips said, "He's got absolutely no regard for his body—or anybody else's body." Averaging over twenty carries per game, Campbell throughout his career was largely a one-dimensional back. A workhorse, he ran like a stallion and was not adept at blocking or pass receiving.

In contrast with his explosive, reckless style on the gridiron, Campbell is a quiet, soft-spoken, even shy man shunning publicity and devoting considerable time to charitable and civic activities. In 1980 he graduated from the University of Texas with a Bachelor's degree in Speech Communication and married Reuna Smith, his girlfriend since junior high. The Campbells have one son, Earl Christian II.

BIBLIOGRAPHY: Sam Blair, *Earl Campbell: The Driving Force* (Waco, TX, 1980); John T. Brady, *The Heisman: A Symbol of Excellence* (New York, 1984); Michele Burgen, "Very Proud Man," *Ebony* 33 (March, 1978), pp. 56–58; David Casstevens, "Breaking in Earl Campbell," *Sport* 67 (November, 1978), pp. 72–74; *CB* (1983), pp. 45–48; Melissa Ludtke Lincoln, "The Real Earl Campbell Stands Up," *Sport* 69 (September, 1979), pp. 20–27; John McClain, "Earl Campbell: Deep in His Heart a Texan," *Football Digest* 14 (November 1984), pp. 20–26; *NYT*, December 9, 1977, November 5, 1979, December 5, 1982, and August 15, 1984; Bruce Newman, "Roots of Greatness," *SI* 51 (September 3, 1979), pp. 94–98ff.; Ron Reid, "This Oiler's a Gusher of a Rusher," *SI* 49 (September 18, 1978), pp. 24–25, and "Oilers Hit a Gusher," *SI* 49 (December 4, 1978), pp. 20–23; *TSN*, January 1 and November 21, 1983, October 22, December 10 and 17, 1984; *TSN Football Register—1985*.

Larry R. Gerlach

CANADEO, Anthony Robert "Tony" "The Grey Ghost of Gonzaga" (b. 5 May 1919, Chicago, IL), college and professional player and executive, is of Italian-American descent and began his football career at Chicago's Steinmetz High School. After graduating, he received no college football scholarship offers and joined his brother Savior in Milwaukee, WI. Several friends traveled by car to enroll at Gonzaga University (WA). Gonzaga officials consented to give a football scholarship only if Canadeo made the team. He made the Gonzaga squad as a freshman and earned All-Pacific Coast and Little All-American (1939) honors. Nicknamed "The Grey Ghost of Gonzaga," he possessed speed as a ballcarrier and premature streaks of grey hair.

When Notre Dame coach Charles "Gus" Dorais* saw Canadeo play, he contacted Green Bay (NFL) coach Earl "Curly" Lambeau.* The 5 foot, 11 inch, 190 pound Canadeo was drafted in the sixth round by the Green Bay Packers (NFL) and joined them after graduating in 1941. Canadeo played his entire eleven-year pro career with Green Bay. An offensive and defensive stalwart, Canadeo epitomized the all-around player. At a time when positions limited a player's contribution to the game, Canadeo brought a distinct versatility to the offense. Always a ballcarrier, Canadeo played quarterback, halfback, and receiver. A reserve quarterback to Cecil Isbell,* he served in 1944 and 1945 with the U.S. Naval Air Force and the Tank Corps of the U.S. Army in Europe. After World War II he became the starting halfback for the Packers and in 1949 became the first Packer and third NFL back to gain 1,000 yards.

Canadeo, the prototype for the total offensive player of the 1960s and 1970s, averaged 78.9 of the Packers' 125 yards and performed as a quarterback, halfback, receiver, defensive back, punt and kick returner, and punter. In 1,487 attempts, he averaged 5.8 yards per carry for 8,662 yards and scored 28 touchdowns. Besides gaining 4,197 yards and scoring 24 touchdowns as a rusher, he made 69 receptions for 579 yards and 4 touchdowns. As a punt returner, he netted 508 yards in 45 attempts for an 11.3-yard average. He returned 71 kicks for a 22.9-yard average, punted for a 37-yard average, and intercepted 9 passes. Canadeo was selected to the All-NFL team in 1943 and 1949 and retired following the 1952 season. He has served on the Green Bay Packers Board of Directors since 1957, belonging to its executive committee and being its treasurer (1980–1982) and vice president (1983). Canadeo was named to the NAIA Hall of Fame in 1957, Wisconsin Athletic Hall of Fame in 1973, Green Bay Packers Hall of Fame in 1973, and Pro Football Hall of Fame in 1974.

BIBLIOGRAPHY: "Canadeo," *Green Bay Packers Yearbook, 1974*, pp. 34–35; Art Daley, "8,000 Yards," Green Bay (WI) *Press Gazette* (1952); *Green Bay Packers Media Guide, 1952;* Chuck Johnson, "Packers of the Past," Milwaukee *Journal* (1965), p. 20; Keith Schroeder, "Grey Ghost of Gonzaga," *Sports Focus* (1975), p. 14.

Brian C. Gunn

CANNON, John Joseph "Jack" (b. 19 April 1907, Columbus, OH; d. 12 November 1967, Columbus, OH), college player, made unanimous All-American guard at the University of Notre Dame in 1929. The 5 foot, 11 inch, 193 pound Cannon played bareheaded, roved far and wide on defense, often was the first man under punts, and frequently made tackles after kicking off. A three-letter winner (1927–1929), Cannon starred in 1928 in the 12–6 upset over Army noted for Knute Rockne's* "Gipper" speech. In 1929 he made the key block enabling Jack Elder to score a 95-yard touchdown on an intercepted pass against Army. The 7–0 victory assured Notre Dame the national championship. Cannon was selected first team All-American by sportswriter Grantland Rice* (OS), the All-American Board, AP, UPI, INS, and NEA. The 1930 *Illustrated Football Annual* observed that Cannon was rated "the best of all-time by many experts who saw him in action."

Cannon starred in the East's 19–7 victory over the West in the 1930 Shrine All-Star Game. Bill Leiser of the *San Francisco Examiner* wrote: "It was impossible to take the play away from him. His was the most amazing demonstration of how valuable a guard may make himself to a football team that this observer has ever seen." In 1950 Cannon made the Shrine All-Time East Team. Among the most honored Notre Dame football players, Cannon was named to the HAF College Football Hall of Fame and in 1965 to the NFF College Football Hall of Fame. He made the All-Time All-American teams of Bill Edwards (1930) in *Illustrated Football Annual;* Grantland Rice (1939) in *Collier's;* George Trevor (1949); Pop Warner* (1951) for AP; and Professor Lacy Lockert (1951) in the Nashville (TN) *Banner*. In 1969, *SI* selected him to the 1920s decade team on the First Century All-Star Squad.

Cannon had attended Columbus Aquinas High School, where he had starred three years on the gridiron and graduated in 1926. Following graduation from Notre Dame in 1930, he worked as a florist in his Columbus hometown. "The Jack Cannon Flower Cart" became one of the largest floral establishments there.

BIBLIOGRAPHY: Richard M. Cohen, Jordan A. Deutsch, and David S. Neft, *The Notre Dame Football Scrapbook* (Indianapolis, IN, 1977); Ralph Hickok, *Who Was Who in American Sports* (New York, 1971); *Illustrated Football Annual 1930;* Ronald L. Mendell and Timothy B. Phares, *Who's Who in Football* (New Rochelle, NY, 1974); *75 Years of Notre Dame All-Americans* (Fairborn, OH, 1982); Maxwell Stiles, *Football's Finest Hour* (Los Angeles, CA, 1950); Alexander W. Weyand, *Football Immortals* (New York, 1962).

James D. Whalen

CANNON, William Anthony "Billy" (b. 8 February 1937, Philadelphia, MS), college and professional player, grew up in a blue-collar section of Baton Rouge, LA. His father was a janitor, while his mother worked as a domestic. Cannon attended Istrouma High School, excelling in football, track and field, and basketball. A gifted and popular athlete, Cannon made consensus high school All-American football halfback as a senior and received some fifty college scholarship offers. He and a friend experienced minor trouble with the law, received suspended sentences, and were placed on probation. The judge, a fanatical LSU (SEC) football supporter, supposedly required Cannon to attend that school. In 1955 Cannon matriculated at LSU.

From 1957 to 1959 the 6 foot, 1 inch, 210 pound Cannon starred at halfback on offense and defense and returned kickoffs and punts for the LSU Tigers. In 1957 Cannon set an LSU record with a 90-yard kickoff return against Texas Tech. The next year, he won All-American honors and led the Tigers to an 11–0 season and the national championship with a 7–0 victory over Clemson in the Sugar Bowl. Cannon again received All-American honors as a senior in 1959, directing the Tigers to a 9–3 season and a second consecutive Sugar Bowl appearance. The most memorable game of the 1959 campaign came in a 7–3 win over Mississippi. Late in the game, Cannon defied coach Paul Dietzel's rule against fielding punts inside the 15-yard line by catching the ball at the 11-yard line and returning it 89 yards for the winning score. This effort, among others, won Cannon the 1959 Heisman Trophy. In a rematch, Mississippi shut out LSU 21–0 in the 1960 Sugar Bowl. During his college career, Cannon gained 1,867 yards, scored 154 points, caught 31 passes for 522 yards, intercepted seven passes, returned 31 punts for 349 yards, and punted 111 times for a 36.7-yard average.

In 1960 Cannon was drafted in the first round by the NFL's Los Angeles Rams and the AFL's Houston Oilers. Los Angeles Rams general manager Alvin "Pete" Rozelle* disguised him in Philadelphia as Billy Gunn and signed him in late November 1959, to a three-year $50,000 contract. Under the goalpost at the Sugar Bowl, however, Cannon on January 1, 1960, signed with the Houston Oilers for $100,000. The Oilers won a lawsuit to secure Cannon's services from 1960 to 1965. Cannon's best season came in 1961, when he led the AFL in rushing with 948 yards and combined net yardage with 2,043. Cannon, whose performance helped the Oilers win the AFL championship, was named to the All-AFL squad. After a back injury and general dissatisfaction with the Oilers, Cannon was traded to the Oakland Raiders (AFL) in 1964 and converted to tight end. Cannon was named All-AFL with the Raiders in 1967 and released in 1970. Cannon signed with the Kansas City Chiefs (NFL) but retired after the 1970 season. In an 11-year pro career, Cannon rushed over 3,000 yards, caught 236 passes for 3,656 yards, scored 47 touchdowns for 392 points, and played in six AFL championship games. During the off-season, Cannon studied dentistry at LSU. Dorothy, his wife of twenty-nine years and mother of five children, helped him form a successful orthodontist practice in Baton Rouge. In July 1983 Cannon pleaded guilty to participating in a counterfeiting scam.

BIBLIOGRAPHY: Harold Claassen and Steve Boda, eds., *Ronald Encyclopedia of Football*, (New York, 1960); Douglas S. Looney, "In a Rush to Make a Big Gain," *SI* 59 (July 25, 1983), pp. 24–26, 31; Ronald L. Mendell and Timothy B. Phares, *Who's Who in Football* (New Rochelle, NY, 1974).

Jerry Jaye Wright

CAPPELLETTI, Gino Raymond Michael (b. 26 March 1934, Keewatin, MN), college and professional player, attended high school in Keewatin. He earned a B.S. in Recreation in 1955 from the University of Minnesota (BTC) where he was an offensive back and placekicker for the Gophers. He married Sandra Sadowsky on July 29, 1962, and has three daughters, Gina, Cara, and Christina. The 6 foot, 190 pound Cappelletti began his pro football career in Canada playing quarterback for the Sarnia Imperials in the Ontario Rugby Football Union in 1958. Just two years earlier, he had tried out with the Detroit Lions (NFL) before being released. He then sat out one year before signing in 1960 as a free agent with the Boston Patriots of the new AFL. He made the initial field goal in the AFL against the Denver Broncos on September 9, 1960. Cappelletti, tutored by offensive backfield coach Mike Holovak, broadened from being strictly a placekicker to a wide receiver also.

For six consecutive seasons (1961–1966), he scored over 100 points, a mark unequalled in pro football. During this period he won the AFL scoring title five times (1961, 1963–1966). Only Don Hutson* of the Green Bay Packers (NFL) had won that many titles. In 1964 Cappelletti scored an AFL- and career-record 155 points on 7 touchdowns, 38 extra points, and 25 field goals. That same year, he set two other AFL marks by kicking six straight field goals against the Denver Broncos. In addition to winning scoring titles, Cappelletti led the AFL in field goals three times (1961, 1963–1964). On November 11, 1968, he became the first and only player to score more than 1,000 career AFL points with a touchdown reception against the San Diego Chargers.

When the NFL merger was completed in 1970, he remained one of only three players to appear in every game in the AFL's ten-year history. A year later, he retired at age 36. His 1,100 points, 330 extra points, and 170 field goals all set AFL career records. Overall, he collected 1,130 points from 42 touchdowns, 342 extra points, and 176 field goals. He was selected for the AFL All-Star game following the 1961 through 1966 seasons but participated in only one championship game (1963).

BIBLIOGRAPHY: *Boston Patriots Press Guides, 1970; 1971;* Rick Gonsalves, *Specialty Teams* (New York, 1977); *TSN Football Register, 1967.*

Richard Gonsalves

CAPPELLETTI, John Raymond (b. 9 August 1952, Upper Darby, PA), college and professional player, is the son of John Anthony and Ann (Bianco) Cappelletti and currently resides in Westminster, CA. As a baby, Cappelletti was so pigeon-toed that he kept tripping himself. He wore corrective shoes and leg braces because he was also bowlegged. As he grew, however, he gained strength and his legs mended. At Monsignor Bonner High School in Upper Darby, PA, Cappelletti excelled in track, basketball, and football. In track, he threw the javelin and won All-Catholic League honors in 1967,

1968, and 1969. As a forward on the varsity basketball team, Cappelletti earned All-League honors in 1969. His greatest athletic achievements came in football, as he won All-League honors in 1967 and 1968 at halfback and made All-State quarterback for coach Jack Gottshalk in 1969.

Cappelletti received numerous football scholarship offers but narrowed his choices to Penn State, Ohio State, Miami (FL), and Virginia Tech. He selected Penn State because "it was close to home" and he thought "Coach Joe Paterno* would treat him more like an individual and not just a number." At Penn State, Cappelletti played defense during his freshman and sophomore years and moved to offensive running back his junior year. "I did not mind playing defense as a sophomore," he said. "In fact, it might have helped me recognize defenses better. It also gave me a chance to play. Nobody was going to play much at tailback behind Lydell [Mitchell].*" As a junior in 1972, Cappelletti gained 1,117 yards rushing for the third best season mark in Penn State history. In his first game as a ball carrier, he averaged 3.4 yards per rush for 74 yards. By midseason his game average exceeded 100 yards. He finished the season with a team-high 13 touchdowns and rushed 233 times for 4.8 yards per carry.

Cappelletti continued to improve his senior year, rushing for 1,522 yards. His two-year total of 2,639 yards placed him fifth on the all-time Penn State rushing list behind Curt Warner,* D. J. Dozier, Lydell Mitchell, and Matt Suhey, all of whom played at least three collegiate seasons. In his two-year career at running back, he gained 100 yards in 13 of his 22 starts, scored 29 touchdowns, and averaged 120 yards per game and 5.1 yards per carry. Following his senior season Cappelletti was named to the Kodak All-American Team and virtually every other All-American squad. He won the thirty-ninth Heisman Trophy, the only Penn State player to receive that coveted award. In his December 1973 acceptance speech, Cappelletti dedicated the award to his younger brother Joey, a leukemia victim. "If I can dedicate this trophy to him tonight and give him a couple days of happiness, this is worth everything." On April 30, 1977, he married Betty Ann Berry. Drafted by the Los Angeles Rams (NFL) in 1974, Cappelletti played four seasons (1974–1978) there and performed in the NFL championship games from 1974 through 1976. He sat out the 1979 season with a knee injury and finished his pro career with the San Diego Chargers (1980–1982). He retired in the spring 1983 with 2,957 yards rushing and 22 touchdowns on 824 carries. Presently, Cappelletti owns and operates a restaurant in Laguna Hignel, CA.

BIBLIOGRAPHY: Ron Bracken, "Walking Away," Centre *Daily Times* (State College, PA), January 24, 1984; "Cappelletti: Mr. Consistency," Beaver Stadium Pictorial, October 13, 1973; *DAC Journal*, 41, (December, 1973); Bill Lyon, "For Joey," Philadelphia *Inquirer*, April 5, 1977; Bill Lyon, "State's Cappelletti: Able But Reluctant Hero," Philadelphia 19Inquirer, August 19, 1973; Richard E. Peck, *Something for Joey*

(New York, 1983); *Penn State Orange Bowl Press Guide, 1974; Penn State Football Media Guide, 1985.*

Dennis A. Booher

CARIDEO, Francis F. "Frank" (b. 4 August 1908, Mt. Vernon, NY), college player and coach, was selected a unanimous All-American football quarterback (1929–1930) at the University of Notre Dame. He led Notre Dame to two undefeated seasons, two national championships, and nineteen consecutive victories. Besides being chosen HAF 1930 Player of the Year, he was named in 1931 to Parke H. Davis' All-Time All-American team. He rated honorable mention on the AP All-Time team (1951), made the All-Time Notre Dame team, and was elected to the NFF College Football Hall of Fame and the HAF College Football Hall of Fame. The son of Italian immigrant laborer Fred J. Carideo, Sr., he attended Dean Academy in Mt. Vernon. He was taught angle punting to the coffin corner by noted football kicking authority Leroy Mills, a New York City attorney and Princeton graduate. Carideo graduated from Dean Academy in 1927 with outstanding kicking and quarterbacking credentials.

Carideo played behind quarterback Jim Brady at Notre Dame his sophomore year (1928) but experienced considerable playing time under head coach Knute Rockne.* Notre Dame finished 5–4–0 in 1928 against strong opposition in a rebuilding year (Rockne's poorest season). The Fighting Irish lost to Southern California, rated first by Frank G. Dickinson; number 3, Georgia Tech; number 4, Wisconsin; and number 6, Carnegie Tech; but upset number 9 Army 12–6 in the classic game won for the "Gipper." Notre Dame achieved a spotless 9–0–0 record in 1929, when Carideo's talents fully blossomed. He completed a 10-yard touchdown pass to Jack Elder against Navy and scored touchdowns on a 75-yard punt return against Georgia Tech and 85-yard runback of an intercepted pass against Northwestern. His point after touchdown provided the 13–12 victory over Southern California before 112,912 spectators at Chicago's Soldier Field. In the final game with Army, Elder picked off a Cadet pass in the second quarter and returned it 96 yards for the game's only touchdown. Thereafter, Carideo directed a possession game and punted eleven times, including six inside the three-yard line, to preserve a 7–0 victory and perfect record.

In his final season (1930) against SMU, Carideo returned a punt 70 yards and completed a 25-yard pass to end Ed Kosky to set up two touchdowns. He scored a touchdown against Pennsylvania and kicked the extra point touchdown against Army in another thrilling triumph 7–6 on icy Soldier Field before 110,000 spectators. With five minutes to play against undefeated WC co-champion Northwestern, Notre Dame was playing for the national championship and was locked in a scoreless struggle. In his "greatest game," Carideo punted four times on first down with each landing inside the one-yard line. This broke Northwestern's spirit, as Carideo's subsequent punt return to the Wildcat 28-yard line set up the winning touchdown. Minutes later, a short Northwestern punt to the 30-yard line set up an insurance touchdown and enabled the Fighting Irish to triumph 14–0. Carideo closed his football career against Southern California before 73,967 spectators in the Los Angeles Coliseum. A 26-yard touchdown pass from Marchy Schwartz* to Carideo started a 27–0 Notre Dame rout of perhaps the best team in Trojan history. "Except for calling signals, passing, kicking, running, tackling, and blocking," wrote sportswriter-humorist John Kieran* (OS) in 1930, "this Carideo isn't much help to a football team."

The 5 foot, 7 inch, 175 pound, stocky Carideo possessed a dominating personality, strong leadership qualities, and a resonant voice. He led Notre Dame for three years in punt returns, his 92 returns for 947 yards setting an Irish record, and he holds the Notre Dame one-season (1929) record of five interceptions (151 total yards). Chicago *American* sportswriter Warren Brown in 1969 stated, "In the matter of the greatest quarterbacks who ever lived, I still like to think of Carideo." The 1930 backfield of Carideo, Schwartz, Marty Brill, and "Moon" Mullins compared favorably with the Four Horsemen, averaging 20 points heavier per player and being just as fast.

After his final season Carideo was feted at New York's Hotel Astor by friends from White Plains, NY, and appeared in the 1931 Universal picture *The Spirit of Notre Dame*. He graduated from Notre Dame in 1931 with a Bachelor of Science degree in Physical Education and served as backfield coach at Purdue University (WC, 1931), head coach at Missouri (BSC, 1932–1934), and backfield coach at Mississippi State (SEC, 1935–1938) and Iowa (WC, 1939–1942, 1946–1949). Carideo's efforts to institute the Notre Dame system proved too difficult for his limited material at Missouri, resulting in a 2–23–2 composite record. Carideo, who married Vera Crowley and had one daughter, Randy (1947), served in World War II as a U.S. Navy lieutenant. In 1950 he became an executive with Bankers Life Insurance Company, Cedar Rapids, IA, and handled commentary for several years at Iowa football games. He retired in 1971 and moved to Ocean Springs, MS, where he lives adjacent to a golf course that challenges his ability daily.

BIBLIOGRAPHY: Cameron Applegate, *Notre Dame vs. USC* (Hollywood, CA, 1977); Jim Beach and Daniel Moore, *Army vs. Notre Dame* (New York, 1948); Bob Broeg, *Ol' Mizzou: A Story of Missouri Football* (Huntsville, AL, 1974); *Notre Dame Football Guide, 1984;* Notre Dame University, Sports Information Office files, August 13, 1985, Notre Dame, IN; Gene Schoor, *A Treasury of Notre Dame Football* (New York, 1962).

James D. Whalen

CARMICHAEL, Lee Harold (b. 22 September 1949, Jacksonville, FL), college athlete and professional football player, grew up in Jacksonville and attended William H. Raines High School (1963–1967) there. Carmichael played quarterback and wide receiver on the football team and also excelled in basketball. He received a scholarship to Southern (LA) University (SAC), playing center in basketball and tight end in football. The 6 foot, 8 inch, 225 pound Carmichael caught 86 passes and scored 16 touchdowns in college. Despite his 4.7-second speed, 36-inch vertical leap, and imposing size, he was not drafted until the seventh round by the Philadelphia Eagles (NFL) in 1971.

Carmichael spent the 1971 and 1972 seasons as a backup wide receiver and tight end. The arrival of Boyd Dowler* as receiver coach and Roman Gabriel* as quarterback in 1973 transformed Carmichael's career. Dowler placed Carmichael permanently in the wide receiver slot, as Gabriel's passing allowed him to exhibit his pass-catching talents. Carmichael made an Eagle record and NFL-leading 67 receptions for 1,116 yards and 9 touchdowns. Recognition came with a 1973 Pro Bowl selection. On October 8, 1972, Carmichael began an NFL record of making a pass reception in 127 consecutive games. His streak, broken by Steve Largent,* was snapped in the final game of the 1980 season.

Although Carmichael prospered, the Eagles languished. Philadelphia won one-half of its games in 1974 but posted losing records the next three seasons. Carmichael caught 56 passes for 649 yards and 8 touchdowns in 1974. In 1975 he caught 49 passes for 639 yards and 7 touchdowns. The following year, he managed 42 receptions for 503 yards and 5 scores. Fans jeered him during the disappointing 1975 and 1976 seasons. Carmichael's marriage in 1976 to Bea, his involvement with the Fellowship of Christian Athletes, and the birth of son Lee Harold II transformed him. In 1980 he won the NFL's Man of the Year Award for his charitable efforts.

Carmichael quickly regained his previous form. Between 1977 and 1981 he averaged 52 receptions, 890 yards, and 8 touchdowns per season. During two of those seasons he gained over 1,000 yards. In post-season play from 1978 to 1981, Carmichael caught 29 passes and scored 6 touchdowns. Carmichael held Eagles team records for touchdown receptions (79), career receptions (589), and most yards gained receiving (8,978). He also finished the 1983 season tied with Fred Biletnikoff* for fifth place on the NFL's all-time pass reception list (589).

During 1982 and 1983 Carmichael caught fewer passes. Carmichael's age and loss of speed and the return to the "bump and run" defense, which tests a receiver's speed and agility, led to his being waived by the Eagles before the 1984 season. He signed with the New York Jets on August 9, 1984, in hopes of catching Charley Taylor,* the then all-time NFL leader in pass receptions with 649. After the Jets released him, he signed with the Dallas

Cowboys (NFL) and then retired at season's end. During his 14-year pro career he caught 590 passes for 8,985 yards (a 15.2-yard average), and 79 touchdowns.

BIBLIOGRAPHY: Ray Kennedy, "And the Streak Goes On," *SI* 53 (December 15, 1980), pp. 42–44; *NYT*, August 9, 1984; Philadelphia *Inquirer*, May 12, 1984; *Philadelphia Eagles Media Guide, 1983;* Ron Reid, "Philly Story: A Tall Tale," *SI* 49 (December 11, 1978), p. 88.

Eric C. Schneider

CARR, Joseph F. "Joe" (b. 22 October 1880, Columbus, OH; d. 20 May 1939, Columbus, OH), sports executive, was one of the nation's foremost professional athletic organizers, promoters, and administrators. After attending high school, he worked as a machinist for the Panhandle Division of the Pennsylvania Railroad. From 1900 to 1906 he wrote articles for the *Ohio State Journal*. In 1901 he organized the Panhandle White Sox, a Columbus semi-pro baseball team. He became secretary of the OSL in 1906 and two years later was selected its president. After disbanding in 1916, the league reorganized in 1922 with Carr again as president. Carr also served as president of the Columbus minor league baseball club through the 1931 season. From 1933 until his death, he served as promotional director of baseball's minor leagues and fostered the growth of the minor leagues from 12 to 41. He also belonged to the executive committee of the American Baseball Federation. An early advocate of professional basketball, Carr helped organize the ABL in 1925 and served for three years as its first president.

Carr made his greatest athletic contributions in pro football. In 1904 he organized the Columbus Panhandle football team, featuring the six Nesser brothers. For many years, the Columbus squad ranked among the nation's top pro teams and competed against the strongest elevens throughout the midwest. When the NFL (originally the APFA) was formed in 1920, Carr's Panhandles joined as charter members. Although urged to take the presidency, Carr preferred naming Jim Thorpe* because the Indian's fame would help the new APFA prosper. Since the APFA struggled its initial season, Carr was elected president the next year and remained in that post until his death. To a great extent, the survival and eventual prosperity of the NFL resulted from his farsighted administrative policies. Carr believed the public had an inherent right to know the NFL was being operated honestly and capably and that both players and owners deserved fair treatment at all times. When the Pro Football Hall of Fame opened in 1963, Carr was selected as one of its first enshrinees.

During his administration, the NFL grew from small-town to major league caliber. With the exception of Green Bay, all franchises by 1934 were located in major metropolitan centers. Carr took strong measures improving the NFL's prestige among those treasuring amateur ideals. When the original

Green Bay franchise owners employed college players under assumed names, Carr forced them to resign NFL membership. The new owners of a second Green Bay franchise clearly understood Carr's message. When Harold "Red" Grange* turned pro after his last college game in 1925, Carr refined the rules by stating that a player could not enter the NFL until his college class had graduated. In 1925 Carr also ordered the Milwaukee team owner to dispose of his holdings within ninety days for using four high school players in a game.

Carr also handled the territorial rights problem. Despite repeated warnings, the Pottsville, PA, team, seemingly on its way to the 1925 championship, insisted on playing an exhibition contest in another squad's territory. Carr suspended the franchise immediately, denying it the title. When Grange sought to put a team in Yankee Stadium the following year, Carr supported the New York Giants' territorial claim. The one-year "war" with Grange's hastily arranged AFL hurt the NFL temporarily but eventually strengthened it. As NFL president in the early 1930s, Carr administered the splitting of the NFL into eastern and western divisions and created an annual championship game and the annual player draft. Additionally, he backed many important rule changes and served as a tireless goodwill ambassador for pro football. He married Josephine Marie Sullivan in 1910 and had two children.

BIBLIOGRAPHY: Joe Carr file, Pro Football Hall of Fame, Canton, OH; Arthur Daley, *Pro Football's Hall of Fame* (Chicago, 1963); Richard P. McCann, *Pro Football's Hall of Fame Dedication Yearbook* (Canton, OH, 1963); Harry A. March, *Pro Football, Its "Ups" and "Downs"* (New York, 1934); Irven Scheibeck, "Joe Carr, Noted Figure in Sports World, Is Taken by Death after Heart Attack," Columbus (OH) *Sunday Dispatch*, May 21, 1939; George Sullivan, *Pro Football's All-Time Greats: The Immortals in Pro Football's Hall of Fame* (New York, 1968); Roger Treat, ed., *The Official Encyclopedia of Football*, 16th ed., rev. by Pete Palmer (South Brunswick, NJ, 1979).

Robert N. Carroll

CARTER, Anthony (b. 17 September 1960, Riviera Beach, FL), college and professional player, attended Sun Coast High School in Riviera Beach, where he excelled in football and scored fifty-four touchdowns in four seasons. The sixth of eight children, he was brought up by his mother Manita. Carter attended the University of Michigan (BTC, 1979–1982), majoring in recreation. The second three-time All-American wide receiver at Michigan (Bennie Oosterbaan* was the other), Carter placed second nationally in kickoff returns in 1980 (29.4-yard average) and third nationally in kickoff returns in 1981 (27.1-yard average), and second nationally in punt returns in 1982 (15.6-yard average). Carter averaged 18.2 yards each time he touched the ball, bettering by nearly three yards the NCAA record set by the University of Arizona's Theo Bell (1972–1975). Carter's 33 career touchdown catches (excluding bowl games) fell just one short of Elmo Wright's* NCAA record set at the University of Houston (1968–1970). If his receptions in four bowl games are included, nearly one of every four passes to him meant six points for the Wolverines. A four-year letterman at Michigan and three-time All-BTC receiver, Carter holds Michigan career records for most catches (161), receiving yards (3,076), and touchdowns (40). In 1982 he broke the 42-year-old scoring record held by Tom Harmon* (244 points to 237 points). On the all-time BTC list, Carter ranks first in reception yardage, second in receptions, and fifth in scoring, and holds the BTC season record of 11 touchdown receptions. Besides achieving All-American acclaim (1980–1982), Carter was selected the BTC's MVP in 1982 by the Chicago *Tribune*, named Michigan's MVP (1980, 1982), and chosen UPI's Collegiate Player of the Year (1982).

A 1983 territorial selection of the Michigan Panthers (the franchise merged with the Oakland Invaders in 1985) in the USFL, Carter made 60 receptions for 1,181 yards (second highest in the USFL) and scored nine touchdowns as a rookie. He brought back 40 punts for 387 yards and became the first USFL player to return a punt for a touchdown. Carter made nine receptions for 179 yards (club records) to lead the Panthers to the USFL championship with a 24–22 victory over the Philadelphia Stars. Named All-USFL by *Pro Football Weekly*, Carter also was selected All-USFL as best punt returner by *TSN*. Despite suffering a fractured arm during the 1984 season, Carter recorded 30 receptions, 538 reception yards, a 17.9-yard average per catch, and 4 touchdowns in six games.

Before the 1985 season he joined the Minnesota Vikings (NFL) as a game-breaking receiver. In 1985 he caught 43 passes for 821 yards (19.1-yard average) and 8 touchdowns and returned 9 punts for 117 yards (13-yard average), including a 41-yard return. For the 9–7 Vikings in 1986, Carter made 38 receptions for 686 yards (18.1 yard average) and led the club with 7 touchdowns. Through the 1986 season, he has caught 171 passes for 3,226 yards (18.9-yard average) and 28 touchdowns. Carter, who enjoys music, fishing, and bowling, is married to Ortancis Thomas and has two daughters, Tara and Nikki.

BIBLIOGRAPHY: *Oakland Invaders Press Guide, 1985;* John Papanek, "All the Way on Every Play," *SI* 57 (November 22, 1982), pp. 44–46, 49; *TSN Official USFL Guide and Register—1984; TSN Football Register — 1986.*

John L. Evers

CASANOVA, Thomas H. III "Tommy" (b. 20 July 1950, New Orleans, LA), college athlete and professional football player is the third of five children born to medical doctor and Mrs. Thomas H. Casanova, Jr. His father established a medical practice in Crowley, LA, where Thomas, III, graduated from Crowley High School in 1967. Casanova enrolled at LSU (SEC), played cornerback on the Tigers football team, and participated on the track squad, running the 100-yard dash in 9.7 seconds. In 1971 *SI* featured Casanova on its cover and called him the "Best Player in the Nation." He did his best to prove the magazine correct, making consensus All-American in 1970 and 1971. Casanova earned further individual recognition in the post-season Shrine (East-West) and College All-Star games and the Hula Bowl.

In the 1972 NFL draft, Casanova was unclaimed until the Cincinnati Bengals chose him in the second round. Other teams assumed he intended to forgo pro football for medical school. The 6 foot, 2 inch, 196 pound Casanova made a spectacular debut by returning a punt 52 yards for a touchdown in his first game. Before the season ended, he assumed the calling of defensive signals. Consequently, Cincinnati fans and teammates voted Casanova, who was named to the NFL's All-Rookie Team, the Bengals' MVP.

Casanova, meanwhile, finished his premedical courses and entered the University of Cincinnati's medical school. During the following four years he successfully combined football with his schooling. As a free safety and punt returner, he played in three Pro Bowl games until injuries forced his retirement in 1977. At that point, he completed his medical training by specializing in ophthalmology.

During his six pro years Casanova impressed others as an intelligent, hard-hitting safety whose speed made him a tough defender and dangerous punt returner. In 71 NFL games he intercepted 71 passes and averaged 16.2 yards a return. He also returned punts 784 yards for an 8.6-yard average and scored four touchdowns. A premier defensive back when healthy, he became one of the few pro athletes to attend and finish medical school.

BIBLIOGRAPHY: Chicago *Tribune*, July 1, 1972; *Cincinnati Bengals Media Guide, 1972–1977;* Cincinnati *Inquirer*, February 3, 1972, and September 16, 1973; Cleveland *Plain Dealer*, February 24, 1981; *SI* 35 (September 13, 1971), pp. 18–21; *TSN Football Register—1977*.

Jerome Mushkat

CASSADY, Howard "Hopalong" (b. 2 March 1934, Columbus, OH), college athlete and professional football player, excelled as an All-American halfback at Ohio State University. Cassady graduated from Central High School, where he starred in football, basketball, and baseball and impressed Ohio State football coach Woody Hayes.* Hayes convinced the redheaded Cassady to attend Ohio State (BTC), where he played baseball three years and from 1952 to 1955 became a football legend. In his first game against Indiana in 1952, the freshman back scored three touchdowns. He repeated the same feat in his final game as a senior against Iowa at Ohio Stadium in 1955. His overall college performance convinced Hayes that "the greatest player I ever had playing for me was Hop Cassady."

Although his nickname came from the popular movie and television character, it could have come from his explosive running style. For the Buckeyes,

Cassady gained 5.65 yards per carry and twice led the squad in pass receptions. In his senior year he rushed for 958 yards and scored 15 touchdowns. Cassady ranks first among Ohio State's all-time scoring leaders, third in career rushing, and fifth in total offense. Cassady also played defensive back, twice leading the Buckeyes in interceptions. During the 1954 season Cassady sparked Ohio State to an undefeated 10–0 season and the BTC championship, Rose Bowl game, and national title. Cassady received numerous honors during his college career. In 1953 he won the Ohio State Quarterback Club Trophy, awarded to the outstanding sophomore football player. A unanimous All-American selection in 1954 and 1955, he the latter year won the Heisman Trophy, Maxwell Award, Walter Camp Trophy, Chicago *Tribune* Trophy, AP Player of the Year, and *Los Angeles Times* College Player of the Year.

Although playing pro football for the NFL Detroit Lions (1956–1961, 1963), Cleveland Browns (1962), and Philadelphia Eagles (1962), Cassady experienced only modest NFL success because of his size. The 5 foot, 10 inch, 172 pound Cassady was used mainly as a defensive back and kick returner. During his pro career, he rushed 316 times for 1,229 yards (3.9-yard average) and 6 touchdowns and caught 111 passes for 1,601 yards (14.4-yard average) and 18 touchdowns. Cassady returned 77 kicks for 1,594 yards (20.7-yard average) and 43 punts for 341 yards (7.9-yard average). Cassady earned a Bachelor's degree in Education from Ohio State in 1957; he and his wife, Betty, have three children. Cassady, a member of the NFF College Football Hall of Fame served as a physical fitness director for the New York Yankees (AL) baseball club and now works for American Shipbuilding in Tampa, FL.

BIBLIOGRAPHY: Jerry Brondfield, *Woody Hayes and the 100-Yard War* (New York, 1974); Woody Hayes file, College Football Hall of Fame, King's Mills, OH; Woody Hayes, *You Win with People* (Columbus, OH, 1975); Harry Jebsen, Jr. Interview with Woody Hayes, Columbus, OH, 1984; Ronald L. Mendell and Timothy B. Phares, *Who's Who in Football* (New Rochelle, NY, 1974); Ohio State University, Sports Department, Columbus, OH; Robert Vare, *Buckeye* (New York, 1974).

Harry Jebsen, Jr.

CAVANAUGH, Francis W. "Frank" "The Iron Major" (b. 28 April 1876, Worcester, MA; d. 29 August 1933, Marshfield, MA), college player and coach, was the son of Patrick and Ann Cavanaugh and excelled as a football mentor. He starred in football at Worcester High School and played end from 1895 to 1897 at Dartmouth College. He wed Florence Ayers and had nine children. In 1898 Cavanaugh coached the University of Cincinnati football squad to a 5–1–3 season and an upset of Dartmouth. From 1899 through 1902 he directed winning teams for the Denver, CO, Athletic Club. At Holy Cross College the next three seasons, Cavanaugh's football clubs finished 16–10–2. After receiving a law degree from Boston University, Cavanaugh practiced law the next four years in Massachusetts and then returned to coaching in 1909 and 1910 at Worcester Academy. From 1911 to 1916 he coached Dartmouth (IL) to a 42–9–3 record. The Indians outscored opponents 1,397 to 247 points, never lost over two games a season, and made 28 shutouts.

During World War I he entered the U.S. Army in 1917 as a private and rose to the rank of major. Nicknamed the "Iron Major," he gained national acclaim as a war hero and was wounded in France. In 1919 Cavanaugh began coaching football at Boston College. From 1919 to 1926 Cavanaugh's Eagles posted a 48–14–5 record. His 1920 team, which won all eight games, claimed the Eastern region championship. From 1927 to 1932 Cavanaugh developed Fordham University into a national football power as head coach. Under the "Iron Major," the 1929 squad finished undefeated. The legendary Seven Blocks of Granite lines originated with Cavanaugh's 1930 team. Between 1929 and 1932 Cavanaugh's clubs posted a 27–4–4 record. Under Cavanaugh's direction, Fordham's overall record comprised 34–14–4. During his final years, Cavanaugh suffered near blindness from his World War I wounds.

On the football field, Cavanaugh demanded total effort both in practice and games. He expected superb physical conditioning and devised strenuous calisthenics, including grass drills. Vince Lombardi,* Fordham graduate, popularized these calisthenics in his successful program with the Green Bay Packers. Although Clark Shaughnessy* is credited for introducing the T formation to the college game at Stanford University, Cavanaugh had used the T and winged T eleven years earlier at Fordham. Cavanaugh completed his coaching career with a 145–48–17 record and was elected to the HAF and NFF College Football Halls of Fame.

BIBLIOGRAPHY: Tim Cohane, *Great College Football Coaches of the Twenties and Thirties* (New Rochelle, NY, 1973); *Dartmouth Football Press Guide, 1978;* John D. McCallum and Charles H. Pearson, *College Football U.S.A., 1869–1973* (New York, 1973).

John L. Evers

CHAMBERLIN, Berlin Guy (b. 16 January 1894, Blue Springs, NE; d. 4 April 1967, Lincoln, NE), college and professional player and coach, was the son of farmer Elmer E. and Anna I. (Tobyne) Chamberlin. He attended Blue Springs High School, which did not field a football team, and scrimmaged against the nearby Beatrice varsity squad. Chamberlin made All-State in football as a freshman at Nebraska Wesleyan University in 1912 before transferring to the University of Nebraska. A defensive end and offensive halfback, he scored 9 touchdowns his junior year and 15 his senior year for the undefeated Cornhuskers and twice earned All-American honors. He served in World War I and shortly afterward married Bernie W. Watkins.

Upon his discharge in 1919, the 6 foot, 2 inch, 210 pound Chamberlin joined the pro Canton (OH) Bulldogs. In 1920 and 1921 Chamberlin played for the Decatur (IL) Staleys of the new NFL. Chamberlin excelled for George

Halas'* first pro championship team in 1921, returning an interception 70 yards for a touchdown in a 10–7 victory to determine the NFL title. Chamberlin in 1922 returned to Canton as a player-coach and led the Bulldogs to the 1922 and 1923 NFL titles. In 1924 the Bulldogs moved to Cleveland and repeated as NFL champions. During this unprecedented championship string, Chamberlin's teams compiled an amazing 28–1–4 record. Coach Chamberlin, lauded as "the winningest ever" by distinguished mentor Steve Owen,* in 1925 directed the Frankford Yellowjackets. Chamberlin's club finished sixth in a twenty-team NFL, the first time his team failed to win the pro football championship since the NFL had declared champions.

The Frankford Yellowjackets rebounded in 1926, giving coach Chamberlin his fourth title in five years with a 14–1–1 record. The Yellowjackets defeated the Chicago Bears 7–6 in the NFL championship game, as Chamberlin blocked the conversion attempt and John "Paddy" Driscoll's* field goal try and scored in the game's waning moments. The Chicago Cardinals (NFL) signed Chamberlin in 1927 as a player only, but finished only ninth in a twelve-team NFL in 1927 and ninth in a ten-team NFL in 1928. Chamberlin allegedly coached the 1928 team, but research indicates Fred Gillies served as mentor. After 1928 Chamberlin farmed for many years in his native Nebraska and later served as a state livestock superintendent and state reformatory foreman.

Chamberlin compiled one of the most outstanding coaching records in NFL history. Ralph Vince, one of his Cleveland players, summarized, "Before Guy came, we just met on Sunday, had some lunch, and went out and played the game. Guy made us work; he made us practice every day." Chamberlin played very effectively as a two-way, sixty-minute pro end. Halas observed, "He was almost impossible to cover on a pass play." According to Owen, "Chamberlin had an uncanny ability to 'smell out' an opponent's play, and then be there to make the tackle." Besides being named as one end on the 1920s All-Decade team, he was inducted into the NFF College Football Hall of Fame in 1962 and the Pro Football Hall of Fame in 1965. After his death, the State of Nebraska established the Guy Chamberlin Athletic Scholarship, awarded each year to its most outstanding high school football player.

BIBLIOGRAPHY: George Sullivan, *Pro Football's All-Time Greats: The Immortals in Pro Football's Hall of Fame* (New York, 1968); Alexander M. Weyand, *Football Immortals* (New York, 1962).

Jim J. Campbell

CHANDLER, Donald G. "Don" "Babe" (b. 5 September 1934, Tulsa, OK), college and professional player, ranked among football's leading all-around kickers of the 1950s and 1960s. The son of a semi-pro fullback, he punted so well at Bacone Indian College (OK) that he won a football scholarship to the University of Florida. At Florida he made All-SEC in 1952, 1953, and 1955 and captured the NCAA punting championship in 1955 with a 44.3-yard average on 22 kicks. Drafted by the New York Giants (NFL) in 1956, he added placekicking to his punting skills and became one of the few double-duty pro football kickers. He led the NFL in punting in 1957 with a 44.6-yard average on 60 attempts and scoring (106 points) and points after touchdown (52) in 1963. He was traded to the Green Bay Packers (NFL) in 1965 for Bob Timberlake and reunited with Vince Lombardi,* who had coached him in New York.

As a Packer, he contributed significantly to the club's great seasons in the mid-1960s. He led the Packers in scoring in 1965 and 1966 with 88 and 77 points, respectively, setting a club record with 17 field goals in 1965. During the 1965 regular season, he established an NFL record with a 90-yard punt against the San Francisco 49ers. In the 1965 Western Division playoff against the Baltimore Colts, he tied and won the game with field goals. He then tied an NFL record with three field goals in the championship game against the Cleveland Browns. At 6 feet, 2 inches, and 215 pounds, Chandler participated almost yearly in championship games (1956, 1958–1959, 1961–1963, 1965–1967) and the first two Super Bowls (1967, 1968). He held Super Bowl game records for points after touchdown (5, 1967), field goals (4, 1968), and points (15, 1968). Greatly esteemed by such Packer teammates as Paul Hornung,* Jerry Kramer,* and Lee Roy Caffey, Chandler resides in Tulsa, OK. During his pro career, he punted 660 times for a 43.5-yard average, kicked 94 of 161 field goal attempts for 282 points, and booted 248 of 258 extra point attempts. The Pro Football Hall of Fame selected him as a specialist on its AFL-NFL 1960–1984 All-Star Second Team.

BIBLIOGRAPHY: Joe Falls, "Don Chandler, Kicker," *Sport* 41 (January, 1966), pp. 18–19, 74–75; Green Bay Packers, Sports Information Bureau files, Green Bay, WI.

Leonard Frey

CHANDLER, Wesley Sandy "Wes" (b. 22 August 1956, New Smyrna, FL), college and professional player, has been among the more spectacular wide receivers with the New Orleans Saints and San Diego Chargers of the NFL. After lettering in football, basketball, baseball, and track at New Smyrna High School, he became a star receiver at the University of Florida. His honors there included the All-SEC team in 1976 and 1977 and All-American squad in 1977. Named Florida Amateur Athlete of the Year in 1978, Chandler caught 92 passes for 1,944 yards and 22 touchdowns during his college career and rushed 353 yards for 6 touchdowns his senior year. At Florida, Chandler received a Bachelor's degree in Speech Pathology.

The New Orleans Saints (NFL) selected Chandler third in the 1978 draft behind Earl Campbell* and Art Still. In three seasons with the Saints, he caught 165 passes for 2,516 yards and 14 touchdowns. In 1979 he gained an outstanding 1,069 yards via aerials. Traded to the San Diego Chargers (NFL) for receiver Aundra Thompson and two future draft choices, he established himself in the 1981 season as John Jefferson's* successor and Dan Fouts'* best long threat. In the strike-shortened 1982 campaign, he compiled one of the greatest sets of receiving statistics in NFL history. He recorded 49 receptions in eight regular season games for 1,032 yards (21.1-yard average) and 9 touchdowns and amassed 260 yards on December 20 against the Cincinnati Bengals. During 1982 post-season competition, he gained 138 yards against the Los Angeles Raiders and 124 yards against the Pittsburgh Steelers. Chandler scored 8 touchdowns in four of his last five games that year.

Despite being plagued with injuries, he in 1983 still started 14 games and gained 845 yards. In 1984 Chandler played in 15 games with 708 yards in pass receptions. In 1985 he caught 67 passes for 1,199 yards (17.9-yard average) and 10 touchdowns. The next year, he made 56 receptions for 874 yards (15.6 yard average) and 4 touchdowns. He remains one of the most feared NFL deep receivers with at least 11 career receptions exceeding 40 yards each. Chandler's career highs included receptions of 85 yards against San Francisco in 1979, 66 yards against Cincinnati in 1982, and 63 yards against Pittsburgh in 1984.

The 6 foot, 182 pound Chandler received the Seagram's Sports Award as best NFL player for 1982, the Florida Sports Hall of Fame Award as Pro Athlete of the Year for 1982, and four Pro Bowl selections (1979, 1982–1983, 1985). With his wife, Bridget, he resides in New Orleans, LA. His civic activities there include socioeconomic service for the New Orleans Board of Distinction and chairing the New Orleans Recreation Department. Through the 1986 NFL season, Chandler had caught 516 passes for 8,216 yards (15.9 yard average) and 54 touchdowns. During his NFL career, he also returned 58 punts for 387 yards (6.7-yard average) and 47 kickoffs for 1,021 yards (21.7-yard average).

BIBLIOGRAPHY: San Diego Chargers, Sports Publicity Department, San Diego, CA; *TSN Football Register,—1986*.

Leonard Frey

CHRISTIANSEN, John LeRoy "Jack" (b. 20 December 1928, Sublette, KS; d. 30 June 1986, Stanford, CA), college athlete and professional football player and coach, proved a great pass defender and kick return specialist. After his father died in a 1930 grain elevator accident, he grew up at the Odd Fellows Orphanage in Canon City, CO. His football career nearly ended when he was a high school senior after he severely damaged his left arm in a shooting accident. At Colorado A&M (RMC), he initially concentrated on track and barely made the 44-member football traveling squad as a sophomore. After replacing an injured player in the regular lineup, he subsequently won All-Conference honors twice. A sixth-round draft choice of the Detroit

Lions (NFL) in 1951, he excelled from the outset. As a rookie, he led the NFL in punt returns with a record 21.47-yard average and set a record by scoring four touchdowns on long runs. He paced the NFL in pass interceptions with 12 in 1953 and 10 in 1957. Opponents were instructed not to throw in his area or punt to him. Nevertheless, he made 46 career interceptions, averaged 12.8 yards and a record 8 touchdowns for 85 punts returned, and averaged 22.5 yards for 59 kickoffs returned.

From 1951 to 1958 the 6 foot, 1 inch, 185 pound speedster led the "Chris Crew," the famous defensive backs who helped the Lions win four Western Conference titles and three NFL championships. After being named All-NFL by the AP in 1952, he made the AP and UPI squads from 1953 through 1957. *TSN* named him All-NFL from 1953 to 1955 and on its All-Western Conference team in 1956. He played in five consecutive Pro Bowls (1954–1958), in the 1956 game taking the opening kickoff 103 yards for a touchdown. He served as defensive backfield coach for the San Francisco 49ers (NFL) from 1959 through 1963 and head coach from 1963 through 1967, compiling a 26–38–3 record. After assisting at Stanford University from 1968 through 1971, he coached the Indians the next five years. After 1976 he was an NFL assistant coach. He and his wife, Doris Erickson, have four daughters. He was the seventh member elected to the Colorado Sports Hall of Fame in 1966 and was enshrined in the Pro Football Hall of Fame in 1970 and Michigan Sports Hall of Fame in 1986.

BIBLIOGRAPHY: Jack Christiansen file, Pro Football Hall of Fame, Canton, OH; Don Fair, "Seattle's Hall of Famer," *Pro!*, Seattle–San Diego Football Game Program, August 5, 1978, p. 82; Stan Grosshandler, "Chris' Crew," *Football Digest* 3 (November, 1973), pp. 54–58; Jack Newcombe, "You've Got to Be Good and Mean," *Sport* 20 (December, 1955), pp. 21, 62–65; Murray Olderman, *The Defenders* (Englewood Cliffs, NJ, 1973).

Robert N. Carroll

CLARK, Earl Harry "Dutch" (b. 11 October 1906, Fowler, CO; d. 5 August 1978, Canon City, CO), college athlete and professional football player and coach, was the son of Harry and Mary Etta (Lackey) Clark. His father, of Welsh descent, engaged in farming and railroading. Clark grew up in Pueblo, CO, and attended public schools there until age 14, when he quit to work as a "callboy" rousting out engineers and crew as trains were made up for a railroad. Two years later, he returned to Pueblo Central High School and toiled for the railroad and as a YMCA night desk clerk. Clark, who earned 16 letters, starred as a 137-pound football center and later halfback and also excelled in basketball, baseball, and track.

As a 20-year-old freshman, Clark briefly attended Northwestern University and then enrolled at Colorado College. Clark gained All-RMC honors despite the school's size, scoring at least one touchdown in 21 consecutive games. The winner of 12 varsity letters, Clark became a legitimate triple-threat football tailback. During his junior year (1929) Clark was named an All-American halfback over more highly touted backs from larger schools. Clark married Dorothy Schrader on June 11, 1930, and had no children.

Clark, who had grown to 6 feet, 183 pounds, signed his first pro contract in 1931 for $140 a game with the Portsmouth (OH) Spartans of the NFL. Clark played pro football for six seasons until retiring in 1937. Although considered a quarterback because he called signals and was an outstanding field general, Clark actually played single-wing tailback throughout his NFL career. Aside from the Green Bay Packers, Portsmouth remained the last "town team" in the NFL and maintained a franchise until its 1934 move to Detroit.

In 1932 Clark led the NFL in scoring, with 55 points on 6 touchdowns, 3 field goals, and 10 points after touchdown. Clark also paced the NFL in 1935 with 6 touchdowns, 1 field goal, and 16 extra points for 55 points and in 1936 with 7 touchdowns, 4 field goals, and 19 extra points for 73 points. Clark did not play pro football in 1933, serving instead as athletic director and head coach in football, basketball, and baseball at Colorado School of Mines (RMC). He returned to pro football in 1934, the first year his club competed as the Detroit Lions. In 1935 Clark scored a touchdown on a 40-yard run, as the Lions defeated the New York Giants 26–7 to win their first NFL title. Clark became player-coach in 1937 and twice guided the Lions to 7–4 records and second-place finishes in the Western Division. From 1939 through 1941 Clark compiled a mediocre 11–20–2 record as coach of the Cleveland Rams (NFL).

He later became athletic director at the University of Detroit but worked as a manufacturer's representative for a Detroit tool company after his wife's death in 1952. Clark subsequently returned to his native Colorado. The very modest, quiet Clark led more by example than by words. A fierce competitor, Clark seemed at his best in clutch situations in big games. From 1932 through 1937 Clark gained 2,757 yards rushing on 580 attempts for a 4.8-yard average per carry and 23 touchdowns. He passed for 1,235 yards on 97 completions in 197 attempts, and scored 42 touchdowns, 15 field goals, and 72 extra points for 369 career points. Clark was elected to the NFF College Football Hall of Fame in 1951, the HAF College Football Hall of Fame and the Pro Football Hall of Fame in the charter class of 1963.

BIBLIOGRAPHY: George Allen with Ben Olan, *Pro Football's 100 Greatest Players* (Indianapolis, IN, 1982); Myron Cope, *The Game That Was: The Early Days of Pro Football* (New York, 1970); Bob Curran, *Pro Football's Rag Days* (Englewood Cliffs, NJ, 1969); Arthur Daley, *Pro Football's Hall of Fame* (Chicago, 1963); Jerry Green, *Detroit Lions* (New York, 1973); Murray Olderman, *The Running Backs* (Englewood Cliffs, NJ, 1969); David Shapiro, *The 135 Greatest Pro Running Backs* (Berkeley, CA, 1978); George

Sullivan, *Pro Football's All-Time Greats: The Immortals in Pro Football's Hall of Fame* (New York, 1968); Alexander M. Weyand, *Football Immortals* (New York, 1962).

Harold L. Ray

COCHEMS, Edward B. "Eddie" (b. 24 January 1877, Sturgeon Bay, WI; d. 9 April 1953, Madison, WI), college player and coach, is recognized by the leading football authorities as the father of the forward pass. One of twelve children born to Matthias and Maria (Wegener) Cochems, he graduated from Sturgeon Bay High School in 1898 and entered the University of Wisconsin that fall. Four years later, he graduated with a B.S. in Business Administration. He married Mary Louise Mullen on August 20, 1902. At the University of Wisconsin (WC), Cochems played football under Princeton University graduate Phil King. The 165-pound Cochems played end his freshman year, but the following season he was moved to halfback because of his speed and aggressive play. Football was a dangerous game around the turn of the century because of the lack of protective padding and solid helmets. Since the principal style of play was the flying wedge, it was not unusual for players to be crippled for life or killed.

After graduating from Wisconsin, Cochems enjoyed two outstanding years (1902–1903) as football coach with the North Dakota Aggies, losing only one game there. In 1904 he followed John Heisman* as coach at Clemson College (SIAA) and experienced outstanding success there. The public outcry about the brutality of football attracted the attention of President Theodore Roosevelt in 1905. Roosevelt ordered rules makers to do something to make it less violent or he would have the game banned. A committee, including Cochems, was appointed to study ways of making football safer for the players and made two principal changes that year. First, the distance to be gained during the possession of the ball was increased from five to ten yards, and the number of downs from three to four. The second important change permitted a back behind the line of scrimmage to pass the ball forward. This change was made to eliminate mass formations.

The following year (1906) Cochems became coach at St. Louis University. His first act was to obtain permission to take the football team to Lake Beulah, WI, to help his players develop the skills to make the forward pass a reality. Footballs then were designed to fit the instep when being kicked and bore little resemblance to today's ball. When thrown, footballs resembled balloons. Cochems said, "I got the idea that the trajectory of the ball could be controlled if one could cause it to spiral as a baseball does when it is thrown. I felt that this could be done by grasping the ball at the laces and twisting the wrist when it was released."

After experimenting for some time, St. Louis fullback Brad Robinson mastered the technique so that he could throw it with a great deal of accuracy. The introduction of the forward pass altered the offensive strategy of football thereafter. On September 5, 1906, St. Louis used the pass effectively against Carroll College and won the game 22–0. St. Louis baffled every team it met that fall and finished with a season record of 11–0, scoring 407 points to 11 for opposing teams. Part of the success that season came because Cochems also introduced the triple threat, whereby two backs could pass, punt, or run the ball.

BIBLIOGRAPHY: Tom Butler, "Side Lines," Wisconsin *State Journal*, 1965; Arthur Daley, "Sports of the Times," *NYT*, 1963; Philip Dynan, "The Father of the Forward Pass," St. Louis University, St. Louis, MO, 1954; Stanley McGlynn, The Sports Parade, Milwaukee (WI) *Sentinel* (January 25, 1940); *Spalding Official Intercollegiate Football Guide, 1907;* "Wray's Column," St. Louis *Post Dispatch*, October 1, 1937.

Kendall J. Wentz

CODY, Joshua Crittenden "Josh" (b. 10 June 1892, Franklin, TN; d. 18 June 1961, Mt. Laurel, NJ), college athlete, football and basketball coach, and athletic director, performed at tackle for Vanderbilt University (SC) football squad. He made most all-time SIAA All-Star teams, including the FWAA Early Day (1869–1919) squad and George Trevor's Southern sectional teams of 1949 and 1970. A member of Walter Camp's 1915 and 1919 All-American third teams, Cody became only the fifth Southerner accorded the honor and first to be named twice. He made the All-SIAA squad three years, All-American first team in 1919 (Newark [NJ] *Sunday Call*), and Vanderbilt's All-Time team (Nashville [TN] *Banner*, 1933). The HAF College Hall of Fame member was elected in 1970 to the NFF College Football Hall of Fame.

Cody, regular varsity tackle under coach Dan McGugin* four years (1914–1916, 1919), captained the Commodores his final season. Vanderbilt (SIAA) finished 2–6–0 in 1914, when Cody scored field goals against Michigan and North Carolina and passed for a touchdown from fake field goal formation against Virginia. The Commodores achieved a combined 21–3–3 record his last three seasons and won the SIAA championship in 1915, averaging 51 points per game and boasting eight shutouts. Cody displayed outstanding punt coverage, scored one touchdown, and recovered two fumbles against Auburn. He blocked a Sewanee punt that set up a Vanderbilt touchdown and kicked one field goal against Virginia and against Auburn.

In 1916 and 1919 Cody blocked Auburn punts and recovered them for touchdowns. In 1919 he converted field goals against Tennessee (to gain a 3–3 tie), Alabama, and Virginia and kicked numerous points after touchdown, one of which gave the Commodores a 7–6 triumph over Auburn. His savage tackle and subsequent 60-yard run with an Alabama fumble set up the winning touchdown over the Crimson Tide. "Vanderbilt's team was built around the giant Josh Cody, a tackle whose superior has not been seen in this section for many a year," reported Georgia coach and athletic director

Herman J. Stegeman. The 6 foot, 4 inch, 225 pound Cody was all elbows and knees and possessed strong hands. Gentle off the field, he exhibited a smiling, unruffled amiability and ate heartily.

The son of a farmer, Cody became a four-sport star at Battle Ground Academy, Franklin, TN, and attended Bethel College in McKenzie, TN. His 13 athletic letters at Vanderbilt included basketball forward (4), baseball catcher (4), track shot put and discus performer (1), and football tackle (4). In 1917, he enlisted in the U.S. Army and served two years as second lieutenant during World War I. After graduating from Vanderbilt in 1920, he became head football and basketball coach (1920–1921) at Mercer (GA) College and served two stints (1923–1926, 1931–1935) as assistant football coach at Vanderbilt (SC, SEC) under McGugin.

Cody became a successful head football and basketball coach at Clemson University (SC, 1927–1930), where his gridders reversed three losing seasons with a composite 29–11–1 record and defeated archrival South Carolina all four years. His last Clemson team finished 8–2–0 and was considered about the best Tiger squad in history. He served as head football and basketball coach at the University of Florida (SEC, 1936–1939), where his elevens amassed a mediocre 17–24–2 mark. The Gators' 7–0 1939 upset of coach Frank Leahy's* otherwise undefeated, Cotton Bowl–bound Boston College highlighted Cody's Florida years.

Cody spent the next twenty years at Temple University as head basketball and assistant football coach (1940–1951), athletic director (1952–1959), and head football coach (1955). When Cody retired in 1960, Red Smith* (OS) wrote in the New York *Herald Tribune*, "Josh is remembered in the hush puppy belt as one of the greatest linemen ever to lay a cotton-picking paw upon a ball carrier." Cody married Elsa Hutcheson in 1923 and had one son, Ernest. The owner of a 200-acre farm near Mt. Laurel, he spent his remaining years cultivating the land and tending to his livestock.

BIBLIOGRAPHY: Kenneth N. Carlson, *College Football Scorebook* (Lynnwood, WA, 1981); Mrs. Ernest Cody, Telephone interview with James D. Whalen, August 30, 1985; John D. McCallum and Charles H. Pearson, *College Football U.S.A., 1869–1973* (New York, 1973); Tom McEwen, *The Gators: A Story of Florida Football* (Huntsville, AL, 1974); Ronald L. Mendell and Timothy B. Phares, *Who's Who in Football* (New Rochelle, NY, 1974); Fred Russell and Maxwell E. Benson, *Fifty Years of Vanderbilt Football* (Nashville, TN, 1938); Lou Sahadi, *The Clemson Tigers: From 1896 to Glory* (New York, 1983).

James D. Whalen

COLLINS, Gary (b. 20 August 1940, Williamstown, PA), college and professional player, came from a coal mining family. A natural athlete, Collins earned four letters each in football, basketball, and baseball at Williamstown High School. In high school football he played both fullback and defensive end and made All-Conference.

Collins attended the University of Maryland (ACC) from 1958 to 1962 on an academic scholarship and studied in the School of Physical Education, Recreation, and Health. After rejecting a pro baseball contract with the Philadelphia Phillies (NL), he graduated from Maryland. At Maryland he began playing football as a freshman, set Terrapins records for pass catching, and was acclaimed the best end in the school's history. Collins established every ACC record for an end—most touchdown passes caught, most pass receptions, and most yards gained on completed passes. Maryland's number 82, he made every All-American squad, usually on the first team. The 6 foot, 4 inch, 215 pound Collins was selected Maryland's Lineman of the Year in 1960 and Consensus All-American in 1961.

Despite having an exemplary record in college football, he appeared slow and lackadaisical in practice. According to Terrapin coach Tom Nugent, however, Collins stood "in a class all by himself" and defied the presumed rule that you play the way you practice. Collins, termed a "clutch guy," played best under the most pressure. This pattern continued in professional ranks. Drafted by Cleveland in the first round as the fourth overall NFL pick in 1962, Collins played with the Browns through 1971. He caught only 11 passes for 153 yards and 2 touchdowns his rookie year, appearing relaxed and almost indifferent before a game. In 1963 Collins was voted the Browns' outstanding player by Cleveland's Touchdown Club partly because previous winner, Jim Brown,* was ineligible for the award. Collins made the All-NFL team twice (1965, 1969) and was selected for the Pro Bowl game twice (1965, 1966). Besides leading the Browns four times in pass receiving, he holds a club record for catching a touchdown pass in seven consecutive games. Collins helped Cleveland defeat the Baltimore Colts 27–0 in the 1964 title game, but the Browns lost other title contests in 1965, 1968, and 1969. In 1965 Collins led the NFL in punting with a 46.7-yard average. In nine seasons through 1970, Collins caught 316 passes for 5,068 yards and 67 touchdowns. The Browns' all-time leader in touchdown receptions, Collins married his wife, Judy, his freshman year at Maryland and has two sons, Gary, Jr., and Kris. This outstanding end conducts a daily sports show on a suburban Cleveland radio station.

BIBLIOGRAPHY: Howard Coan, *Great Pass Catchers in Pro Football* (New York, 1971); Ronald L. Mendell and Timothy B. Phares, *Who's Who in Football* (New Rochelle, NY, 1974); *University of Maryland Football Handbook, 1959–1964; University of Maryland Terrapins Yearbook, 1961.*

Frederick J. Augustyn, Jr.

CONNOR, George (b. 21 January 1925, Chicago, IL), college and professional player and coach, starred as a football tackle and linebacker. The 6 foot, 4 inch, 250 pound Connor attended high school in Chicago and in 1942 entered Holy Cross College, becoming one of the first freshman All-Americans. Following a U.S. Navy stint, Connor transferred to Notre Dame and made All-American in 1946 and 1947. In 1946 he won the first Outland Award as the nation's finest lineman. Connor became the only Notre Dame player named to the All-Century team. The New York Giants (NFL) drafted him in 1946, but Connor remained at Notre Dame. The Giants traded his rights to the Boston Yanks (NFL), who sent Connor to the Chicago Bears (NFL) when he refused to play for them.

From 1948 to 1955 Connor played with the Bears and became pro football's premier tackle both offensively and defensively. During the 1950s he played linebacker and achieved the fame of quarterbacks and running backs. Following his retirement, he served in 1956 and 1957 as assistant coach for the Bears. Connor made All-Pro four straight years as a tackle and three seasons as a linebacker. Offensively and defensively, he was named to eight All-Pro teams at three different positions and participated in four Pro Bowl games. The captain of the 1947 Fighting Irish, he played on two national championship teams at Notre Dame. The Bears did not win an NFL title during Connor's eight-year tenure, but in 1950 tied for the division title and lost a playoff game to the Los Angeles Rams. The speedy Connor, a tremendous blocker and excellent tackler, often was used as tackle-eligible on pass plays and sometimes at fullback.

According to coach George Halas,* Connor earned the highest salary among NFL linemen as a rookie. The last of a vanished breed, Connor played both ways at tackle. He studied certain movements of the opposition, enabling him to diagnose and stop a play before it could develop. Connor belongs to the HAF and NFF College Football Halls of Fame. In 1975 he was selected to the Pro Football Hall of Fame.

BIBLIOGRAPHY: George Allen with Ben Olan, *Pro Football's 100 Greatest Players* (Indianapolis, IN, 1982); William Gildea and Christopher Jennison, *The Fighting Irish—Notre Dame Football through the Years* (Englewood Cliffs, NJ, 1976); Paul Musick, "Golden Boys," *Pro* (August 16, 1975), p. 5b; George Vass, *George Halas and the Chicago Bears* (Chicago, 1971); Richard Whittingham, *The Chicago Bears—An Illustrated History* (Chicago, 1979).

John L. Evers

CONZELMAN, James G. "Jimmy" (b. 6 March 1898, St. Louis, MO; d. 31 July 1970, St. Louis, MO), college and professional player and coach, was the son of James Dunn and Margaret Ryan and later assumed his stepfather's name. A star athlete at McKinley High School and Washington University in St. Louis (1916–1917), he quarterbacked the Great Lakes Navy team to a 17–0 victory over the Mare Island Marines in the 1919 Rose Bowl. The 6 foot, 180 pound Conzelman played and coached for several NFL teams. In 1920 Conzelman began his NFL career with the Decatur Staleys, joining his old friend and teammate George Halas.* He also played for the

Rock Island Independents (1921–1922), Milwaukee Badgers (1923–1924), Detroit Panthers (1925–1926), and Providence Steamrollers (1927–1929). As a player-coach, he compiled a 4–2–1 record for Rock Island in 1922, 15–10–3 for Milwaukee in 1923–1924, 9–14–2 for Detroit in 1925–1926, and 20–12–5 for Providence in 1927–1929. After his 1928 team won the NFL title, Conzelman received the MVP Award. He bought the Detroit franchise for $400 in 1925 and sold it two years later for $1,200.

In 1930 he became publisher of a St. Louis newspaper and coached the St. Louis Gunners semi-pro team. From 1934 to 1939 he served as head coach at Washington University of St. Louis and guided two squads to MVC championships. Conzelman returned to pro football in 1940 as head coach of the Chicago Cardinals (NFL). In 1947 he persuaded Cardinals owner Charles Bidwill* to secure the "Dream Backfield" of Paul Christman, Pat Harder,* Charley Trippi,* and Marshall Goldberg,* and won the club's only NFL title. Although they won the Western Division title the next year, the Cardinals lost the NFL championship game. Conzelman, who compiled a 34–31–3 mark with the Cardinals, guided his pro teams to a 82–69–14 career record.

Conzelman retired from coaching following the 1948 season and became an advertising and public relations executive in St. Louis. The colorful, versatile, talented Conzelman worked variously as an author, actor, sportswriter, boxer, baseball executive, songwriter, piano player, newspaper publisher, radio commentator, and after-dinner speaker. A member of the Pro Football Hall of Fame since 1964, he married Ann Forrestal and had one son, James, Jr.

BIBLIOGRAPHY: Ralph Hickok, *Who Was Who in American Sports* (New York, 1971); "Obituaries," *TSN*, August 15, 1970; "Pro Football's Immortal Roll," *The Pro Football Hall of Fame Souvenir Yearbook 1983–1984*.

John L. Evers

CORBUS, William "Bill," "The Baby-Faced Assassin" (b. 5 October 1911, San Francisco, CA), college player, is the son of accountant and mining engineer Adam and Olive (Longabaugh) Corbus. After starring in several sports at Vallejo, CA, High School, he entered Stanford University (PCC) in 1930. As a sophomore under legendary football coach Glenn "Pop" Warner,* he played guard superbly against the University of California and impressed Eastern writers with a near-perfect game in the season finale against Dartmouth. During his junior year, Corbus made All-American after great games against California and Pittsburgh. The talented guard also handled Stanford's extra point, field goal, and kickoff duties. A top student, he served as Stanford's student body president his senior year. Prior to his final season, Corbus was ranked among the nation's top football players. The tough blocker on offense and strong defender was nicknamed "the baby-faced assassin." One sports writer noted, "He had the face of a cherub and the strength of the devil."

Claude "Tiny" Thornhill replaced coach "Pop" Warner before the 1933 season. He was greeted by an outstanding group of sophomores, "The Vow Boys," who pledged to never lose a game to Southern California. As a senior on that squad, Corbus provided steadying influence on the nine sophomore starters. The real iron player performed a modern school record 550 minutes in eleven games. The 1933 Stanford squad compiled a fine 8–1–1 record and played in the first of three consecutive Rose Bowls. Corbus helped defeat the Southern California Trojans with two second-half field goals and provided the winning margin in a 3–0 win over UCLA. Corbus' outstanding play again earned him consensus All-American honors.

The magna cum laude graduate skipped pro football. He married Mary Louise Leistner on his birthday in 1934 and has two sons, William and George. In 1957 he was elected to the NFF College Football Hall of Fame. He also belongs to the HAF College Hall of Fame. Corbus spent over forty years with the national A&P grocery chain, retiring as vice-chairman in November 1977.

BIBLIOGRAPHY: Don E. Liebendorfer, *The Color of Life Is Red* (Palo Alto, CA, 1972); John D. McCallum and Charles H. Pearson, *College Football U.S.A., 1869–1973* (New York, 1973); Fred Merrick, *Down on the Farm: A Story of Stanford Football* (Huntsville, AL, 1975).

Jay Langhammer

CORYELL, Donald David "Don" (b. 17 October 1924, Seattle, WA), college and professional player and coach, began his football career at Lincoln High School in Seattle, WA. Upon graduation in 1943, Coryell joined the U.S. Army as a private in the ski troops and achieved the rank of first lieutenant in the paratroopers. Following discharge from the Army, Coryell entered the University of Washington (PCC) and played football as a 5 foot, 7 inch, 160 pound defensive back. He graduated with a B.A. in Education in 1950 and received an M.A. there in 1951.

Coryell's first coaching position came as an assistant coach for one year at Punahoe Academy in Honolulu, HI. This stint was followed by a head coaching position at Honolulu Farmington for one year and a two-year term at the University of British Columbia in Vancouver. In 1955 Coryell moved to Wenatchee (WA) Junior College (WSJCC). Although winless the previous year, Wenatchee finished undefeated under Coryell's supervision. Coryell became head coach and athletic director at the Fort Ord (CA) Army base in 1956. During his one season there, Fort Ord finished undefeated. At Whittier College from 1957 through 1959, he compiled a 23–5–1 record and won the SCAC championship each year. Following the 1959 season, Coryell spent one year as assistant coach at the University of Southern California (AAWU) and the next twelve seasons as head coach at San Diego State (CaCAA, PCAA).

At San Diego State, Coryell began to make his mark on the passing offense in collegiate football and later carried this same philosophy to the pro ranks. Coryell believed the best way to defeat an opponent with more physical talent and ability was to control the game with a strong passing attack. Coryell's tenure at San Diego State featured great offensive teams and the development of outstanding pro football prospects, especially at the quarterback and wide receiver positions. His twelve-year record included 104 wins, 19 losses, and 2 ties and three undefeated seasons (1966, 1968–1969). As a college coach, he compiled a 134–24–4 career record.

After succeeding with his offensive philosophy at the collegiate ranks, Coryell assumed his first professional head coaching position with the St. Louis Cardinals (NFL). At St. Louis, Coryell's offensive philosophy helped the Cardinals win two divisional championships during his five-year tenure. Following the 1978 season, Coryell became head coach of the NFL's San Diego Chargers. Coryell's offensive philosophy and talented offensive players helped create "Air Coryell," an offense almost totally dependent upon the passing game. Coryell has succeeded during his seven-year career with the Chargers, leading San Diego to Western Division championships three times. Coryell, the only coach to win over 100 games on both the collegiate and professional levels, resigned as San Diego coach in October 1986 after the Chargers lost seven straight games. He had a thirteen-year career pro record of 111 wins, 83 losses, and 1 tie. He and his wife, Aliisa, have one son and one daughter and reside in El Cajon, CA.

BIBLIOGRAPHY: Des Moines *Register*, October 30, 1986; *San Diego Chargers Media Guide, 1984; St. Louis Cardinals Media Guide, 1978; TSN Pro Football Register—1986.*

William A. Sutton

COWAN, Hector William "Hec" (b. 12 July 1863, Hobart, NY; d. 19 October 1941, Stamford, NY), college athlete, made tackle on the first football All-American team (1889) on which Walter Camp* and Casper Whitney collaborated and was named Player of the Year by HAF. A five-year regular (1885–1889) for Princeton University (IL), he scored 79 touchdowns and captained the Tigers in 1888. Chosen All-Time All-American by New York *Evening World* (1904), HAF (1930), John Heisman* (1932), Parke Davis (1934), and Frank Graham (1941), Cowan became a charter inductee in 1951 to the NFF College Football Hall of Fame and also belongs to the HAF College Football Hall of Fame. The son of farmer Hector and Helena Jane (Rich) Cowan, he graduated in 1884 from Delaware Academy, Delhi, NY. Since the Academy fielded no football team, Cowan's first exposure to the sport came his freshman year at Princeton while observing the final squad scrimmage. He was drafted to play for an absent scrub-team member opposite the captain at guard, where he showed outstanding ability and was encouraged to report for the varsity the following season.

The 9–0–0 1885 Princeton squad, the first Tiger team to use prearranged plays, triumphed (6–5) over Yale for the first time in seven years. Cowan blocked an attempted Eli field goal in that game. Undefeated in eight games the following year, the Tigers capitalized on Cowan's runs of 10, 40, 10, and 20 yards to defeat Harvard 12–0. A scoreless tie in the rain with undefeated Yale caused a deadlock with the Elis for the national championship. Cowan possessed a sterling character and trained for the ministry. In a bloody battle with Harvard in 1887, Cowan was ejected for the only time from a game by referee Wyllys Terry for an unintentional, illegal tackle below the knees. Cowan's absence caused Princeton to lose 12–0 to the Crimson. Tiger captain E. O. Wagonhurst exclaimed, "I would rather have any three men disqualified than Cowan." Princeton also lost to Yale 12–0, finishing 7–2–0 for the season.

Cowan, who earned a Bachelor of Arts degree in 1888, ranked fourth in his class and entered Princeton Theological Seminary. He continued playing football that fall because no rules governed eligibility of graduate students. As captain, Cowan moved from guard to tackle and used ballcarrying as a surprise element. He scored a touchdown and recovered a fumble in the Tigers' 18–6 triumph over Harvard, but his team lost again to Yale 10–0 to finish 11–1–0. The 5 foot, 10 inch, 189 pound Cowan possessed strong arms, shoulders, and chest and ran the 100-yard dash in 11 seconds. "His stubby legs drove like pistons when he carried the ball," Yale star "Pudge" Heffelfinger* recalled. "He could carry a couple of tacklers on his back, yet he was plenty fast in the open." Anxious for one more opportunity to oppose Yale, Cowan played on the undefeated (10–0–0) 1889 championship team. Against Harvard, Cowan scored two touchdowns and triggered a Crimson safety in Princeton's 41–15 victory. The Tigers also ended Yale's 48-game undefeated string with a 10–0 triumph. Cowan ran back fumbles for 20 yards and a short-yardage touchdown, carrying several Elis on his back. He also helped break Yale's V-formation plays and advanced 30 yards with a lateral pass from Knowlton Ames. In Cowan's five seasons, Princeton amassed a 44–3–1 record, outscored opponents 2,480 to 121, and finished 2–2–1 against Yale, 3–1–0 against Harvard, and 3–0–0 with Pennsylvania.

The class vice president his junior year, Cowan belonged to the debating society, Class Day committee, and lacrosse squad, and threw the hammer on the track team. After graduating in 1891 from Seminary, Cowan became a Presbyterian minister of churches in St. Joseph, MO; Spring Hill and Gardner, KS; and Buffalo, NY. He served as chaplain and football coach (1894–1896) at the University of Kansas (15–7–1 composite record) and chaplain–athletic director (1899–1906) at Potsdam (NY) State Normal School. He then returned to the Cowan family farm in Hobart, where his favorite recreation was operating the milking machine. During his last ten years, he served farmers as an area feed and grain merchant. He married Annie Louise Smith of Jamestown, NY, in 1892 and enabled his seven children to attend college. After a foot infection necessitated leg amputation, he died suddenly at a Stamford Hospital.

BIBLIOGRAPHY: Parke H. Davis, *Football: The American Intercollegiate Game* (New York, 1911); Jay Dunn, *The Tigers of Princeton: Old Nassau Football* (Huntsville, AL, 1977); William H. Edwards, *Football Days* (New York, 1916); Donald G. Herring, *Forty Years of Football* (New York, 1940); Ralph Hickok, *Who Was Who in American Sports* (New York, 1971); John D. McCallum, *Ivy League Football Since 1872* (New York, 1977); Ronald L. Mendell and Timothy B. Phares, *Who's Who in Football* (New Rochelle, NY, 1974); Seeley G. Mudd Manuscript Library, Princeton University Archives, Princeton, NJ: Alexander M. Weyand, *American Football: Its History and Development* (New York, 1926).

James D. Whalen

COY, Edwin Harris "Ted" (b. 23 May 1888, Andover, MA; d. 8 September 1935, New York, NY), college player, coach, and sportswriter, was the son of Edward G. Coy, headmaster of Hotchkiss School, and Helen Eliza (Marsh) Coy. After attending Hotchkiss, Coy followed family tradition and graduated from Yale College (IL) in 1910. His alumni connections included his father (class of 1869), brother Sherman, and two uncles, including ex-president Timothy Dwight. Coy played on the freshman football (captain), baseball, and track teams and varsity football (captain in senior year) and baseball squads. The 6 foot, 195 pound fullback proved a charging runner and an accurate, long, high punter. During his three varsity seasons (1907–1909), Coy played in only one losing game. In 1908 Harvard defeated Yale 4–0. The removal of Coy's appendix forced him to miss the first four games, but his dropkick field goals helped Yale record an undefeated season and shut out all ten opponents in 1909. Twice a first team All-American, he was elected to the NFF and HAF College Football Halls of Fame. Coy belonged to a select company of great fullbacks, including Ernie Nevers* of Stanford and Doc Blanchard* of Army.

He served on the Yale University Athletic Committee, Senior Council, and Junior Prom Committee and sang in the glee club and the Whiffenpoofs. He belonged to Delta Kappa Epsilon fraternity and to Skull & Bones, one of Yale's elite senior societies. After graduation, Coy was appointed head football coach by the new team captain. When the 1910 team suffered several defeats, however, Thomas L. Shevlin* (1906) replaced Coy as emergency coach. During the next twenty-five years Coy held a variety of positions: assistant sales manager of the Durham Coal and Iron Company, Chattanooga, TN (1911–1913); manager of the bond department at Munsey Trust Company, Washington, DC; financial editor of the Washington *Times;* office manager and member of Davies, Thomas and Company, a New York City stock exchange firm (1915–1924); investment broker with two other New

York City firms; field manager of Fuller Brush Company (1929–1931); and solicitor at Smyth, Sanford and Gerard, insurance agents, New York City (1931–1935).

In numerous civic activities, Coy served as a local volunteer with the New York City mounted police and later with the Justice Department; Yale alumni fund agent; treasurer and executive committee member of Girl Scouts; athletic director at Lenox Hill Settlement House, New York City (1920–1923); and active campaigner and member of the Ivy Republican Club. He contributed sporting articles, chiefly on football, to *St. Nicholas Magazine* (1910–1911), New York *World*, Boston *Globe*, Chattanooga (TN) *Times*, and Chicago *Herald & Examiner*. In 1928 he became special sports critic for the San Francisco *News* and wrote "Eastern and Western Football" for *Game and Gossip*.

Coy, who never equalled his earlier successes as a Yale football player, married three times. From his marriage to Sophie d'Antignac Meldrim of Savannah, GA (1913–1925, divorced) came two sons. He married Jeanne Eagles in Stamford, CT, in 1925 (divorced) and Lottie Bruhn in El Paso, TX, in 1928.

BIBLIOGRAPHY: Tim Cohane, *The Yale Football Story* (New York, 1951); "Edward H. Coy," biographical sketches in *History of the Class of 1910, Yale College* (New Haven, CT), vol. 1, senior year album (1910), p. 106, vol. 2, *Seven-Year Book* (1917), pp. 101–102, vol. 3, *Quindecennial Record* (1916), p. 116, and vol. 4, *Twenty-Five Year Record* (1935), pp. 59–60; Albert Beecher Crawford, ed., *Football Y Men—Men of Yale Series*, 3 vols. (New Haven, CT), vol. 1, *1872–1919* (1962), p. 95; Arnold Guyot Dana, "Yale Old and New," a compilation of articles and clippings in 100 volumes numbered 1–73, on microfilm (see reel #16 on football) and William Charles Wurtenberg, comp., scrapbook of newspaper clippings about Yale football (ca. 1902–1915), Manuscripts and Archives, Yale University Library, New Haven, CT.

Marcia G. Synnott

CREEKMUR, Louis "Lou" (b. 22 January 1927, Hopelawn, NJ), college athlete, professional football player, and announcer, is the son of James and Rose (Kaminski) Creekmur. His father, a delivery service owner, moved the family to Woodbridge, NJ, where Creekmur played tackle in high school football. He won a letter at tackle as a freshman for the College of William and Mary (SC) in 1944 and then joined the U.S. Army for two years. After returning to William and Mary in 1947, he started for the SC championship team. William and Mary finished 9–1 before losing 21–19 to Arkansas in the Dixie Bowl. Creekmur played in the Delta Bowl as a junior and scored the only touchdown of his career, running 70 yards after intercepting a pass. The recipient of the Jacobs Blocking Trophy in 1949, he played in the Senior Bowl and College All-Star Game. A track letter winner, he set a school record in the shot put and threw the discus.

When Creekmur's original class graduated in 1948, the Philadelphia Eagles (NFL) and Los Angeles Dons (AAFC) drafted him. Creekmur, however, stayed in school. After completing his eligibility, he was placed in a frozen player pool because the AAFC had disbanded. The Detroit Lions (NFL) selected him from the pool and Creekmur became a regular offensive guard as a rookie in 1950. Following the season, Creekmur made the Pro Bowl squad, the first of eight consecutive selections. Creekmur was named All-NFL from 1951 through 1954 as an offensive guard and tackle. He also played defense in key situations and spent part of the 1955 season at middle guard. He married Dolores Bell on June 24, 1951, and has two sons, Rex Louis and Corey Knox, and one daughter, Amy Glynn. After a divorce in 1975, he married Caroline Moore on July 24, 1976.

During his pro career, Creekmur played on three NFL championship teams (1952–1953, 1957). He made All-NFL offensive tackle in 1956–1957 and temporarily retired after the 1958 season. The Lions, however, encountered injury problems in 1959 and after the season began asked Creekmur to return. He played the final eight games before retiring permanently. The 6 foot, 4 inch, 250 pound, durable Creekmur relied on speed, strength, and quickness against line opponents. Besides being named to the *Football Digest* All-Time All-Pro football team, he was selected to the Detroit Lions Hall of Fame and the William and Mary Hall of Fame.

Creekmur began working as a district manager for Saginaw Transfer in 1958. He joined Ryder Truck Lines in 1964 as director of labor relations and shifted to their Jacksonville, FL, office. He moved to Miami with Ryder Truck Rental in 1969 and is currently director of customer and community relations. Creekmur also served as a color commentator on the Miami Dolphins radio network in 1972.

BIBLIOGRAPHY: *Detroit Lions Press Guides, 1950, 1953, 1958;* Jerry Green, *Detroit Lions* (New York, 1973); *William and Mary Football Press Guides, 1949–1983.*

Jay Langhammer

CRISLER, Herbert Orrin "Fritz" (b. 12 January 1899, Earlsville, IL; d. 19 August 1982, Ann Arbor, MI), college athlete, coach, and athletic administrator, was the son of devout Methodist farmers Albert and Catherine (Thompson) Crisler. Crisler's country doctor uncle encouraged him to study medicine at the University of Chicago on a full-tuition scholarship. Although he did not play high school football, he excelled as a nine-letter winner at Chicago (WC) in football, basketball, and baseball. Besides being named a third-team All-American football end, he was selected as an All-WC basketball player in 1920 and 1921 and led his 11–2 Chicago team to the WC championship. After graduating with honors, Crisler stayed at Chicago under Amos Alonzo Stagg* from 1922 to 1929 and coached three sports. After serving as head football coach and athletic director at Minnesota (WC) in 1930 and 1931, he became Princeton's (IL) first non-alumnus football coach and quickly reversed the Tigers' declining fortunes. From 1932 to 1937 he compiled 35 wins, 9 losses, and 5 ties and produced two undefeated teams (1933, 1935). He quickly demonstrated his fine tactical mind and forceful leadership qualities.

In 1938 he succeeded Harry G. Kipke as head football coach at the University of Michigan (WC, BTC). Crisler's terms included a $15,000 annual contract, a free hand in selecting assistant coaches, complete control over the program, and a future appointment as athletic director. During his decade as coach, Crisler produced a 71 win, 16 loss, 3 tie record and claimed the 1947 national championship with an undefeated season and a convincing 49–0 Rose Bowl win. Michigan won all nine games the next season, outscoring opponents by 606 to 97 over the two-year span. He relied on the older single-wing offense with its deception and multiplicity of plays and regularly produced All-Americans like Tom Harmon,* Bob Westfall, Bill Daley, and Bob Chappuis. Crisler's offense relied on careful execution, precision timing, and effective faking, causing alumni to flock back to the campus. His famous coaching clinics attracted thousands of high school coaches and steered top prospects to Michigan. An innovative, influential coach, he helped initiate the two-point conversion, the widening of goalposts, and the two-platoon system after 1945.

At the height of his success in 1947, Crisler became the athletic director and chairman of the athletic board. The talented administrator made Michigan one of the nation's most successful athletic programs with outstanding facilities and strong alumni identification. Before retiring in 1968, he financed new sports facilities, two stadium expansions, and a new all-events building named the Crisler Arena. In 1954 he was elected as a coach to the NFF College Football Hall of Fame. Crisler also belonged to the HAF College Football Hall of Fame and attracted national fame by almost single-mindedly shaping and directing the post–World War II destiny of Michigan's sports programs. Crisler's talents as a businessman, ambassador, and publicist produced a model program recognized as a monument to his diverse administrative talents and forceful personality. Unwilling to stand in Fielding Yost's* shadow, he achieved a stature and reputation forged out of a 30-year dedication to success and excellence.

BIBLIOGRAPHY: Tim Cohane, *Great College Football Coaches of the Twenties and Thirties* (New Rochelle, NY, 1973); Allison Danzig, *The History of American Football: Its Great Teams, Players, and Coaches* (Englewood Cliffs, NJ, 1956); John D. McCallum, *Big Ten Football Since 1895* (Radnor, PA, 1976); *NYT*, August 21, 1982; Will Perry, *The Wolverines: A Story of Michigan Football* (Huntsville, AL, 1980); Edwin Pope, *Football's Greatest Coaches* (Atlanta, GA, 1956).

Douglas A. Noverr

CROW, John David (b. 8 July 1935, Marion, LA), college and professional player, coach, and administrator, excelled as a running back. Crow grew up in Springfield, LA, where he became one of the state's greatest prep athletes. Among the nation's most avidly sought college recruits, he starred both offensively and defensively. From 1955 to 1957 he attended Texas A&M University (SWC), where he majored in business and played running back under legendary coach Paul "Bear" Bryant.* A unanimous All-American choice and UPI Back of the Year in 1957, he the same year won the coveted Heisman* Trophy, Washington Touchdown Club Award, and Walter Camp* Trophy. During his intercollegiate career, the 6 foot, 2 inch, 218 pound Crow gained 1,455 yards in 296 rushing attempts (4.9-yard average). Besides completing 7 passes in 16 attempts for 80 yards, he caught 13 passes for 280 yards, intercepted 8 passes for 45 yards, returned 21 punts for 248 yards and 11 kickoffs for 236 yards, and scored 115 points on 19 touchdowns and 1 extra point.

Crow, a first-round NFL draft choice, played with the Chicago Cardinals (1958–1959), St. Louis Cardinals (1960–1964), and San Francisco 49ers (1965–1968). An outstanding pro player for eleven seasons, he participated in four Pro Bowls and was named to the NFL team of the 1960s. In his first pro game, Crow set a Cardinals record with an 83-yard run from scrimmage. He gained 1,071 yards with the Cardinals in 1960, leading the NFL with 5.9 yards per carry. Crow scored 17 touchdowns for a Cardinals record in 1962 and holds the team's single-game rushing record with 203 yards. During his pro career he rushed for 4,963 yards on 1,157 carries and 38 touchdowns, caught 258 passes for 3,699 yards and 35 touchdowns, and completed 33 of 70 passes for 759 yards.

Following the 1968 season he assisted "Bear" Bryant at the University of Alabama (SEC). He returned to the NFL as an assistant football coach with the Cleveland Browns (1972–1973) and San Diego Chargers (1974). From 1975 to 1980 he served as athletic director and head football coach at Northeast Louisiana University (GSC) and became the only Heisman Trophy winner selected as collegiate head coach. Crow, who compiled a 20–34–1 record at Northeast Louisiana, resigned after the 1980 campaign to enter private business. Crow possessed an intense desire for the team to win, proved a hard-nosed football player, and exhibited an extreme willingness to pay the necessary price for victory. As a coach, he believed in hard work, discipline, and enthusiasm, and expected these qualities from his players. He remains a tireless promoter of football and is very active on the banquet circuit. Crow is married to Carolyn Gilliam and has three children, John David, Jr., Anna Lisa, and Jeanne. John David, Jr., played defensive back at the University of Alabama. Crow is a member of the NFF College Football Hall of Fame and Louisiana Sports Hall of Fame.

BIBLIOGRAPHY: Wilbur Evans and H. B. McElroy, *The Twelfth Man: A Story of Texas A&M Football* (Huntsville, AL, 1974); *Northeast Louisiana University Football Guide, 1976; Official Pro Football Almanac, 1965.*

John L. Evers

CROWLEY, James H. "Sleepy Jim." See under FOUR HORSEMEN.

CSONKA, Lawrence Richard "Larry" (b. 25 December 1946, Stow, OH), college and professional player, is the son of Joseph and Mildred (Heath) Csonka and received several college scholarship offers after excelling for the Stow High School football team. He selected Syracuse University, where he broke the rushing records of Jim Brown,* Ernie Davis,* Jim Nance,* and Floyd Little.* Csonka's offensive achievements seemed particularly impressive because Syracuse coach Ben Schwartzwalder* briefly converted him to middle linebacker his sophomore year. After returning to fullback, Csonka made some All-American teams as a junior in 1966. In 1967 he was unanimously selected All-American and placed fourth in the Heisman Trophy voting. His amateur career concluded at the 1968 College All-Star game, in which he was named the outstanding player.

The Miami Dolphins, entering their third year of NFL play, selected Csonka in the first round of the 1968 draft. With a new coaching system devised by Don Shula* after the 1969 season and new players acquired through trades and the draft, the Dolphins became a dominant NFL team during the early 1970s. They attained consecutive Super Bowl berths between 1971 and 1973, defeating the Washington Redskins and Minnesota Vikings after losing in their initial Super Bowl appearance to the Dallas Cowboys. The 1972 squad, which defeated Washington 14 to 7, won all 14 regular-season and 3 playoff games to become the first NFL club to complete a perfect season.

Analysts praised the Dolphins squads of the early 1970s as well coached and balanced with considerable depth. One of several All-Pro and Pro Bowl Dolphin players, Csonka was regarded as the team's pillar. By providing a powerful inside running game, the 6 foot, 3 inch, 235 pound Csonka forced opponents to play more tentatively against the pass and outside run. This permitted greater latitude for Bob Griese,* Paul Warfield,* Eugene Morris, Jim Kiick, and a stalwart offensive line. Csonka exceeded 1,000 yards in rushing each season between 1971 and 1973 and combined with Morris in 1972 as the first backfield tandem each of whose members gained over 1,000 yards rushing. In the 1973 Super Bowl contest, Csonka carried 33 times for 145 yards to set Super Bowl records and win the MVP award.

Csonka's talents as a bruising fullback capable of over 25 carries per game interested the entrepreneurs establishing a rival pro league. Memphis (WFL) acquired Csonka, Warfield, and Kiick in March 1974. Although completing their obligations to the Dolphins that year, they performed for Memphis in 1975 in the second (and last) year of the WFL's existence. Miami transferred its rights to Csonka to the New York Giants (NFL), who signed him for the 1976 season. Csonka played a smaller role within the Giants' offense than at Miami. He returned to the Dolphins as a free agent for the 1979 campaign, his last pro football season. Csonka's career 8,081 yards rushing (4.3-yard average) placed him tenth in NFL history as the 1987 season began. During eleven pro seasons, Csonka rushed for 64 touchdowns and caught 106 passes for 820 yards (7.7-yard average) and 4 touchdowns. Csonka was selected to the Pro Football Hall of Fame in 1987.

BIBLIOGRAPHY: *TSN Football Register—1979.*

Steven Tischler

D

DALY, Charles Dudley (b. 31 October 1880, Roxbury, MA; d. 12 February 1959, Pacific Grove, CA), college player and coach, starred at Harvard and Army for five years before becoming an influential coach. In his first college year (1898) he quarterbacked Harvard (IL) to its first victory over Yale since 1890. Daly made end runs to spearhead the offense and a downfield tackle to preserve the shutout. Although Daly was the youngest player on the field, Walter Camp* made him a first-team All-American. In 1899 the Carlisle Indians alone scored on Harvard and led until Daly's touchdown sparked a 22–10 victory. Harvard continued undefeated but settled for a tie against Yale. Harvard dominated only to squander two scoring opportunities created by Daly. He directed a 50-yard drive to the Yale one-yard line and handed off to the fullback, who hit the goal post. Later Daly returned a punt to Yale's 25-yard line, but a field goal attempt missed. Despite the scoreless draw, Daly enjoyed his second consecutive undefeated season and All-American selection.

The veteran 1900 team faltered late in the season. After recording seven shutouts, Harvard surrendered 44 points in the last four games. Again the Carlisle Indians broke the scoreless streak and took an early lead. Daly kept Harvard in the game with two field goals and threw the final block on the deciding touchdown. Against Army, Daly kicked a field goal and returned a punt for a 60-yard touchdown. Daly missed his penultimate game due to injury and probably was subpar for the Yale game, in which Harvard's three-year undefeated streak ended. After an extraordinary 33-game career, Daly finally had experienced defeat. In 1901 Daly began a long association with the U.S. Military Academy as player and coach. Daly's missed tackle ironically led to Harvard's defeat of Army, the latter's only loss that season. In 1902 Daly completed his playing career. In 1927 W. B. Hanna of the New York *Herald Tribune* named Daly one of the five best all-time quarterbacks.

After assisting former teammate Percy Haughton* at Harvard, Daly became head coach at Army in 1913. His first team lost only once, in one of college football's most famous games. Notre Dame unleashed several Gus Dorais*–to–Knute Rockne* passes for a 35–13 victory, establishing the Fighting Irish as a power and the forward pass as a dangerous weapon. The versatile Daly developed a passing attack and used it to defeat Navy. Daly's 1914 team won all nine games, outscoring opponents 219–20. With his passing combination of Vernon Prichard to Louis Merillat, Daly gained revenge over Notre Dame. The 1916 team again swept all nine games, outpointing the opposition 235–36. The 30–10 victory over an otherwise undefeated Notre Dame further avenged the famous loss. Daly's single-wing formation effectively enabled Army to mix their passing with the excellent running of Ollie Oliphant.* End Robert Neyland* later utilized many of Daly's great ideas as Tennessee coach. Daly, who concluded his coaching career in 1922, was elected to the NFF College Football Hall of Fame in its first election (1951) and also belonged to the HAF College Football Hall of Fame. From 1924 to 1926 he commanded a horse-drawn field artillery unit in Monterey, CA. He returned to Harvard as a professor of military science and tactics and then served tours of duty in Hawaii and attended the Army War College in Washington, DC. Daly, who retired from military service in 1933, was survived by his wife Beatrice, three sons, Charles, John, and Robert, and two daughters, Mrs. Robert Totten and Mrs. Peter Peca.

BIBLIOGRAPHY: Morris A. Bealle, *The History of Football at Harvard, 1874–1948* (Washington, DC, 1948); Allison Danzig, *The History of American Football: Its Great Teams, Players, and Coaches* (Englewood Cliffs, NJ, 1956); Paul Soderberg and Helen Washington, eds., *The Big Book of Halls of Fame* (New York, 1977).

W. Bruce Leslie

DAUGHERTY, Hugh Duffy (b. 8 September 1915, Emeigh, PA), college player and coach, performed as a football lineman three seasons at Syracuse University. He captained the Orangemen his senior year in 1939 and played one year under line coach Biggie Munn.* During World War II he served four years in the U.S. Army and saw duty in Australia and New Guinea in his thirty months overseas. He advanced from private to major, participated in three major campaigns, and was awarded the Bronze Star Medal. Daugherty returned to Syracuse as line coach under Munn in 1946 and accompanied him to Michigan State University (BTC) the next year. During the Spartan golden era, Munn's teams won 54 games, lost 9, and tied 2. Daugherty produced the outstanding Spartan lines, nicknamed "Duffy's Toughies." He developed several premier players, including All-Americans Ed Bagdon, Don Coleman, Don Mason, Dick Tamburo, Frank Kush,* and Larry Fowler.

Daugherty became Michigan State head football coach in 1954 and guided the Spartans for nineteen years. No football coach has served a longer tenure there. During that span, his teams won 109 games, lost 69 contests, and tied 5. Daugherty's squads annexed two outright BTC titles, placed second in the BTC four times, and ranked in the nation's top ten in final wire service polls seven times. Daugherty's two greatest Spartan teams were the 1965 and 1966 units, which finished undefeated in ten regular-season games, won BTC championships, and gained top national recognition. The 1965 Spartans lost to UCLA 14–12 in the Rose Bowl but was designated national champion by UPI, the NFF, and the HAF. The 1966 eleven was named National Co-Champion with Notre Dame by the NFF and the nation's best team with the most demanding schedule by the Columbus (OH) Touchdown Club. The Spartans were ranked second in the final AP and UPI polls.

Daugherty served as head coach of four North teams in the North-South Shrine Bowl, four East teams in the Shrine All-Star (East-West) games, and the Northern College All-Stars in the 1959 and 1968 Hula Bowl games. In his long Michigan State tenure, he was twice named Coach of the Year. As Spartans head coach, Daugherty produced 27 All-American players, including stars Earl Morrall,* Clinton Jones, Gene Washington, and Charles "Bubba" Smith.* He became one of the most popular banquet speakers, whose Irish wit and humor were widely quoted and printed, and a popular lecturer at football clinics. After the 1972 season he resigned as head football coach and served in 1973 and 1974 as special assistant to Michigan State's vice president for development. He and his wife Frances, son Danny, and daughter Dree left East Lansing, MI, in 1975 and reside in Santa Barbara, CA. He has been elected to the NFF College Football Hall of Fame as a coach.

BIBLIOGRAPHY: Michigan State University, Department of Information Services, Press Releases, July 1975, East Lansing, MI; NFF to Stan W. Carlson, 1984.

Stan W. Carlson

DAVIS, Allen "Al" (b. 4 July 1929, Brockton, MA), college athlete and professional football coach and executive, is the son of Louis and Rose (Kirschenbaum) Davis. Davis grew up in Brooklyn, NY, where he graduated from Erasmus Hall High School. He attended Wittenberg College and Syracuse University, earning an English degree in 1950. At Syracuse he participated in football, basketball, and baseball. From 1950 to 1951 he was line football coach at Adelphi College. He served in the U.S. Army, being head football coach at Ft. Belvoir, VA. In 1954 he joined the Baltimore Colts (NFL) on the player personnel staff. Davis married Carol Segal in July 1954 and has one son, Mark. After being football line coach at the Citadel (SC) from 1955 to 1956, he assisted three years at the University of Southern California (PCC).

In 1960 Sid Gillman* hired Davis as an assistant coach for the Los Angeles Chargers in the newly formed AFL. In 1963 Davis became general manager and head football coach of the Oakland Raiders (AFL). Although the Raiders had won only three of their last twenty-eight games, Davis guided the 1963 squad to a 10–4 mark and was named both Coach of the Year and Oakland's Young Man of the Year. As head coach there through 1965, Davis compiled a 23–16–3 record. In 1966 Davis became AFL commissioner. Eight weeks later, the AFL and NFL agreed to merge with a common draft and a championship game. Davis won acclaim nationally as the driving force bringing the leagues to the conference table. Following the merger, Davis resigned his position to become the Raiders' principal owner and chief executive.

As an executive for the past nineteen years, Davis has guided the Raiders' organization toward total commitment to excellence. Through 1986 the Raiders have experienced only one losing season and compiled an overall 224–88–7 record for a .718 percentage. They won the 1967 AFL championship and the 1976, 1980, and 1983 NFL championships. For an entire year, Davis waged a one-man battle against the NFL establishment to move his Oakland franchise to Los Angeles. In 1982 the courts permitted the move.

Davis is often questioned by the media and disliked by many owners because of his methods. Making winning the bottom line, he uses secrecy and trickery to achieve his ends. Davis is feared but respected, hated but loved, hard but understanding. A smart street fighter looking for an edge, he remains a maverick executive not bound by established practices.

BIBLIOGRAPHY: *The Oakland Raiders Media Guide, 1977;* Murray Olderman, "Oakland's Brash Owner Tells Why," *Sport* 72 (January, 1981), pp. 15–18; Lou Sahadi, *The Raiders: Cinderella Champions of Pro Football* (New York, 1981); *WWA* 42nd ed. (1982–1983), p. 766.

John L. Evers

DAVIS, Ernest "Ernie" (b. 14 December 1939, New Salem, PA; d. 18 May 1963, Cleveland, OH), college athlete, became the first black to win the Heisman Trophy. Davis grew up with his grandmother in Uniontown, PA, after his parents separated. He later joined his mother, Mrs. Arthur Radford, in Elmira, NY, where he excelled as a high school athlete. After being recruited by many schools, Davis finally chose Syracuse University, competed in both basketball and football, and earned his degree in business administration. A dedicated student, the popular Davis was chosen senior marshall at his graduation in 1962. Davis, at 6 foot, 2 inches, and almost 210 pounds, set Syracuse records for total yards gained, touchdowns, and points scored. Running from the winged T with an unbalanced line, he was a threat off tackle or around end and possessed speed in the open field. The excellent blocker and pass receiver also kicked extra points and played defensive back. He broke open several close games, including the 1960 Cotton Bowl and 1961 Liberty Bowl.

Selected for All-American teams three years and the Heisman Trophy recipient in 1961, Davis was drafted by the Buffalo Bills of the AFL and recruited by the CFL. He also was the first player selected in the 1961 NFL draft. Although chosen by the Washington Redskins (NFL), Davis was traded to the Cleveland Browns (NFL) by prior agreement and signed a reported $80,000 contract. He never played pro football, becoming ill with leukemia while preparing for the 1962 College All-Star game. After failing to respond to treatment, Davis died.

The quiet, cheerful, friendly, and gracious Davis refused to be drawn into racial issues, including alleged slurs aimed at him and his black teammates at the 1960 Cotton Bowl. His selection for the Heisman Trophy over black athlete Bob Ferguson of Ohio State signaled more complete recognition of minorities in college football. Never married, Davis was buried in his Elmira, NY, hometown.

BIBLIOGRAPHY: "Ernie Davis, Everybody's All American," *Ebony* 17 (December, 1961), pp. 73–74; Ernie Davis and Bob August, "I'm Not Unlucky," *SEP* 236 (March 30, 1963), pp. 60–62; *NYT*, January 2, 12, 1960, November 29, December 3, 5, 6, 1961, October 6, 7, 1962, and May 19, 22, 1963; Syracuse University, Sports Information Office files, Syracuse, NY; Alfred Wright, "Ernie Davis, A Man of Courage," *SI* 18 (May 27, 1963), pp. 24–25.

Daniel R. Gilbert

DAVIS, Glenn Woodward "Junior" "Mr. Outside" (b. 26 December 1924, Burbank, CA), college athlete and professional football player, made All-American football halfback as one of the greatest all-around Southern California athletes. The son of Irma and Ralph Davis, he attended Bonita High School (LaVerne, CA) and was appointed to the U.S. Military Academy in 1943. Besides being a four-year football starter, he participated on Army's baseball, basketball, and track teams. After military service Davis played pro football on the 1950–1951 Los Angeles Rams championship teams. The 5 foot, 9 inch, 175 pound Davis ranked among football's fastest players. Prior to a Rams game, Southern California track coach Jess Hill clocked Davis carrying a football for 100 yards in full uniform in 10 seconds flat. Nicknamed "Junior" because he was born nine minutes after athletic twin brother Ralph, Davis collected 16 varsity letters at Bonita High School. The CIF Football Player of the Year, he led Bonita in 1942 to the Southern California prep scoring record of 236 points. Besides winning All-CIF recognition as a centerfielder in baseball, he won the Knute Rockne Trophy as Southern California's outstanding high school track star in 1943.

After excelling on the varsity football team as a freshman at Army in 1943, Davis teamed with fullback Felix Blanchard* for the next three seasons as the most spectacular one-two combination in college football history. Dubbed "Mr. Outside and Mr. Inside," Davis and Blanchard propelled Army to three straight unbeaten campaigns and two AP poll national titles (1944–1945).

Many football authorities consider the 1945 Army team the finest college club ever assembled. Blazing speed and a shake of the hips freed Davis on sweeps or cutbacks inside end, while a powerful leg drive and stiff arm enabled him to shed tacklers. Davis exhibited the shiftiness of a classic broken-field runner and a remarkable change of pace, leaving tacklers grasping empty air. An all-around gridder, he excelled at passing, receiving, blocking, and defending. Davis, who set many national records, gained 6,464 yards in 637 carries for a 10.1-yard average, scored 59 touchdowns, and passed for 12 touchdowns. Amazingly, he produced one touchdown every nine plays.

In 1944 Davis scored 20 touchdowns and averaged 11.5 yards per rush. Besides winning the Maxwell Award and Walter Camp Trophy as Player of the Year, he placed second in the Heisman Trophy balloting and made the HAF All-Time All-American team. In 1945 Davis finished second on the Heisman Trophy list again, broke his own national record by averaging 11.51 yards per carry, and scored 18 touchdowns. Davis won the Heisman Trophy in 1946, was named Player of the Year by *TSN*, and, above all, was chosen Male Athlete of the Year by the AP. Army coach Earl Blaik* called Davis "the best player I have ever seen, anywhere, any time," while Columbia coach Lou Little* rated him "the best running back in football history."

Davis starred in every Army football game. He almost single-handedly helped undermanned Army defeat a powerful Michigan team 20–13 in 1946, when Blanchard and quarterback Arnold Tucker were slowed by injuries. Davis played 60 minutes, rushed for 105 yards including a 58-yard scoring dash, completed all seven of his aerials for 159 yards, threw a 31-yard touchdown pass, intercepted two passes, and made a game-saving defensive play at the finish.

The Brooklyn Dodgers (NL) tried to lure Davis into pro baseball with a $75,000 contract. On the same day in 1947, Davis played a baseball game against Navy and ran in a track meet against the Middies. Davis won the 100-yard event in 9.7 seconds, tying the Army record, and set a new school standard of 20.9 seconds in the 220-yard dash. In the Army Master of the Sword test comprising ten physical fitness events, Davis earned 926.5 of 1,000 possible points to break the school record.

Davis enjoyed one outstanding pro football year. In 1950 he led the Rams in rushing, ranked among the top NFL receivers with 42 catches, tallied 7 touchdowns, and passed for 2 scores. He scored on an 83-yard pass play in the NFL championship game against the Cleveland Browns. An old knee injury hampered Davis in 1951 and forced his premature retirement. During two pro seasons, he rushed for 616 yards in 152 carries (4.1-yard average) and 4 touchdowns and caught 50 passes for 682 yards (13.6-yard average) and 5 touchdowns.

Davis married Harriet Lancaster in 1953 and has one son, Ralph, and one stepson, John Slack. Since 1959 he has directed special events for the Los

Angeles *Times* and administered the newspaper's many charitable fund-raising activities. Davis was elected to the NFF College Football Hall of Fame in 1961 and belongs to the HAF College Football Hall of Fame.

BIBLIOGRAPHY: "Army's Super-Dupers," *Time* 46, (November 17, 1945), pp. 57–58; Hugo G. Autz, "The Quarterback All-America 1946," *The Quarterback* (December 7, 1946); Jim Beach and Daniel Moore, *Army vs. Notre Dame* (New York, 1948); Earl H. Blaik and Tim Cohane, *You Have to Pay the Price* (New York, 1960); Steve Boda, Jr., *College Football All-Time Record Book* (New York, 1969); Glenn Davis and *Los Angeles Times* to Bernie McCarty, December 20, 1983; Murray Goodman and Leonard Lewin, *My Greatest Day in Football* (New York, 1948); Richard C. Harlow, "All-American Team," *SEP* 219 (December 21, 1946), pp. 18–19; Ed Linn, "Mr. Inside and Mr. Outside," *Sport* 20 (December, 1955), pp. 52–61; John D. McCallum and Charles H. Pearson, *College Football U.S.A., 1869–1973* (New York, 1973); Bob Richelson, "The Truth about Glenn Davis," *Sport Life* 4 (December, 1951); Lawrence Robinson, "Army's Hot 3 Years End in a Bad Chill," *The Quarterback* (December 7, 1946); Wilbur Wood, "Indispensable Glenn Davis," *The Quarterback* (November 2, 1946).

Bernie McCarty

DAVIS, William Delford "Willie" (b. 24 July 1934, Lisbon, LA), college and professional player, is the son of Nodie Davis and one of three children. His mother, Nodie, brought up the children in Texarkana, AR, where Davis excelled in football, basketball, and baseball at Booker T. Washington High School. He received a football scholarship to Grambling College (SAC), serving as team captain two years and becoming a NAIA All-American. An industrial arts major, Davis in 1956 graduated from Grambling with a Bachelor of Science degree. The 6 foot, 3 inch, 245 pound defensive end was selected by the Cleveland Browns in the fifteenth round of the 1956 NFL draft, but was drafted into the U.S. Army. Davis in 1957 played service football and made the All-Army and All-Service teams.

Davis reported to the Cleveland Browns (NFL) in 1958 and was traded in 1960 to the Green Bay Packers (NFL); this trade marked the turning point of Davis' playing career. In his ten seasons with the great Packer teams, Davis proved an outstanding defensive player and one of the best NFL players. He possessed speed, agility, and size and exhibited intelligence, dedication, and leadership qualities as captain of the Green Bay defensive unit. By his retirement in 1969, he had recovered 21 opponents' fumbles, just one short of the all-time record. An All-NFL selection five times in a six-year span (1962–1967), Davis was chosen to the Pro Bowl five consecutive years (1963–1967). In twelve seasons (1958–1969), he remarkably did not miss any of his team's 162 games. Davis, who played in six NFL championship games (1960–1962, 1965–1967) and the first two Super Bowls, helped lead the Packers to championships in all title games except when the Philadelphia Eagles triumphed in 1960.

Davis in 1968 earned a Master's degree in Business at the University of Chicago and operated the Los Angeles distributorship for the Schlitz Brewing Company. Now living in Rancho Palos Verdes, CA, with his wife, Ann, and children, William, Duane, and Lori, he has greatly expanded his business interests. Davis received the Byron White Award, was named NAACP Man of the Year, and made the All-Pro team for the decade of the 1960s and the AFL-NFL 1960–1984 All-Star Team. In 1981 he was elected to the Pro Football Hall of Fame.

BIBLIOGRAPHY: Dave Anderson, *Great Defensive Players of the NFL* (New York, 1967); Don Smith, "Willie Davis: Speed, Agility, and Size," *The Coffin Corner* 7 (January/February, 1985), pp. 15–16.

John L. Evers

DAWKINS, Peter M. "Pete" (b. 8 March 1938, Royal Oak, MI), college athlete and coach, is the son of dentist Henry Dawkins and was stricken with polio in the seventh grade. The courageous Dawkins took intensive therapy and played a year later as junior high school quarterback. At Cranbrook Prep School the 110-pound junior became varsity quarterback and captained the baseball team as a first baseman. He was given little chance of making the varsity football team at the U.S. Military Academy, but he grew rapidly and dispelled skeptics with his right halfback running feats. As a sophomore, he scored 3 touchdowns and gained 30 yards on 6 carries. The next year he gained 665 yards rushing (5.36-yard average) for 8 touchdowns and caught 11 passes for 225 yards and 3 touchdowns. In his senior year (1958) Dawkins rushed 428 yards (5.48-yard average) for 12 touchdowns and caught 16 passes for 491 yards and 6 touchdowns. The senior captain returned 10 punts for 162 yards and 7 kickoffs for 132 yards in leading Army to an undefeated 8–0–1 record and third place national ranking in the AP and UPI polls.

Dawkins was awarded the Heisman Trophy and Maxwell Awards as the nation's outstanding college football player. Besides making six All-American teams, he was designated *SI* and *Sport* Player of the Year. Other honors his senior year included the Graham McNamee Award, Sports Lodge B'nai B'rith Award for High Principle and Achievement in Collegiate Football, Grantland Rice Trophy as the outstanding player in the Notre Dame–Army game, best player on the North squad in the North-South game, and the Academic All-American team. At Army he also excelled as a hockey defenseman, scoring 40 goals and 55 assists for 95 points and winning three varsity letters. Although he had never played hockey before, he in 1959 led ECAC defensemen in scoring and the All-East team. As a cadet, Dawkins graduated seventh in a class of 501, was brigade commander and president of the 1959 class, and participated in the chapel choir and Special Programs Committee. He was selected as a Rhodes scholar at Oxford University and became one of two Americans to win the coveted Double Blues Award for rugby. At age 36 he became the youngest player ever selected to the NFF College Football Hall of Fame.

Dawkins' Army service included two years of teaching social studies at West Point, duty in Korea, and two tours in Vietnam. He advised Vietnam Airborne units and was awarded two Bronze Star Medals, an air medal, and the Joint Service Commendation Medal. During his Academy teaching assignment, he helped coach the football halfbacks. At age 30 he enrolled at Princeton University for a Master's degree. After becoming the Army's youngest general at age 45 and being ticketed as a potential Army Chief of Staff, he quit the service to join the investment firm of Shearson Lehman/ American Express and ranks second in the public finance unit. He and his wife, Judi, have two sons, Noel and Sean.

BIBLIOGRAPHY: Army Football Game Programs, 1957–1958; North-South Shrine Football Game Program, 1958; Philadelphia *Enquirer*, January 20, 1959; Philadelphia *Sunday News* (November 23, 1958), 32–33; Trenton (NJ) *Times*, November 12, 1968; U.S. Military Academy, Press Release, 1958, West Point, NY; *Wall Street Journal*, October 15, 1984; "Where Are They Now?" *Newsweek* 67 (January 31, 1966), p. 14.

Stan W. Carlson

DAWSON, Leonard Ray "Len" (b. 20 June 1935, Alliance, OH), college athlete and professional football player and announcer, is the ninth of eleven children born to James and Annie Dawson, first-generation English immigrants. Dawson, whose father worked as a machinist in a pottery factory, excelled in athletics like his six older brothers. After graduating from Alliance High in 1953 with All-State honors in football and basketball, the young quarterback attended Purdue University (BTC) instead of Ohio State University because he preferred the Boilermakers' passing attack to the Buckeyes' running game. At Purdue, Dawson, who also lettered in basketball, starred on the gridiron. He led the BTC in passing and total offense for three years and finished his college career with 3,325 yards passing. After his senior season (1956), he was voted All-American and played in the North-South, Blue-Gray, Senior Bowl, and College All-Star games.

Selected in the first round of the 1957 NFL draft, Dawson spent his early pro career as reserve quarterback with the Pittsburgh Steelers (1957–1959) and Cleveland Browns (1960–1961). In 1962 he was acquired by the Dallas Texans of the new AFL on the recommendation of coach Hank Stram,* his backfield coach at Purdue. He promptly led the Texans to the championship and was named AFL Player of the Year. When the franchise moved to Kansas City in 1963, he continued to be successful. From 1962 through 1972 Dawson-led teams compiled the highest winning percentage in pro football and won AFL championships in 1966 and 1969. Although losing the first Super Bowl in 1966 to the NFL Green Bay Packers (35–10), the Kansas City Chiefs defeated the Minnesota Vikings (23–7) in Super Bowl IV and Dawson was named MVP.

Despite directing a controlled, balanced Chiefs offense and being overshadowed by Joe Namath* of the New York Jets, Dawson was the top-rated AFL quarterback. When the AFL and NFL merged in 1970, Dawson held AFL career records for passing efficiency (56.8), total passing yardage (18,899), touchdown passes (182), yards gained per pass (8.04), and lowest interception percentage (4.97). He led the AFL six times in completion percentage, four times in touchdown passes, and three times in average gain per pass. The only player to pace the AFL in passing more than once (1962, 1964, 1966, 1968), he ranks first and third in individual season passing efficiency (61.0 and 59.0) and threw for six touchdowns against Denver in 1964. He was named to the AFL All-Star team five times (1962, 1964, 1966–1968).

Lacking a strong arm and the ability to throw long passes, the 6 foot, 190 pound Dawson flourished under Stram's innovative offense of "play-action" passes and a "movable" pass pocket. He was noted for his coolness under pressure, quick release in throwing the ball, and passing accuracy. Stram lauded Dawson as "the most accurate passer I ever saw. He may be the most accurate passer football has known." Upon retiring after the 1975 season, Dawson held impressive pro career statistics: third in seasons as an active player (19), fourth in passing efficiency (57.1) and touchdown passes (244), seventh in games played (211), and eighth in completions (2,136) and passing yardage (28,711). He also held the third- and fourth-best season passing efficiency marks with 66.4 in 1975 and 65.3 in 1973.

Dawson married his high school sweetheart, Jacqueline Puzder in 1953 and has two children, Lisa and Len, Jr. For his support of numerous charitable activities and civic organizations, he was honored as the NFL's Man of the Year for 1973. He had a brief, lackluster career from 1978 to 1982 as a color commentator on NBC telecasts of NFL games and now broadcasts pro football games on radio. Dawson was elected to the Pro Football Hall of Fame in 1987.

BIBLIOGRAPHY: Larry Bortstein, *Len Dawson: Superbowl Quarterback* (New York, 1970); Dick Connor, *Kansas City Chiefs* (New York, 1974); Len Dawson with Bob Billings, *Inside Quarterbacking* (Chicago, 1972); Len Dawson with Lou Sahadi, *Len Dawson: Pressure Quarterback* (New York, 1970); Lud Duroska, ed., *Great Pro Quarterbacks* (New York, 1972); Howard Liss, *AFL Dream Backfield* (New York, 1969); Tex Maule, "Dallas Is a Loud Success with Its Silent Quarterback," *SI* 17 (December 24, 1962), pp. 82–83; *NYT*, December 27, 1973; Harold Rosenthal, ed., *American Football League: Official History, 1960–1969* (St. Louis, 1970); *TSN*, January 2, 1982.

Larry R. Gerlach

DEMPSEY, Thomas John "Tom" (b. 12 January 1947, Milwaukee, WI), college and professional player, excelled as a football placekicking specialist and is the son of Huey and LaVerne Dempsey. Although born with a deformed hand and foot, Dempsey was encouraged by his father to participate in sports. As he matured into a 6 foot, 1 inch, 255 pound adult, Dempsey overcame his physical handicaps. A 1965 graduate of San Diequito (CA) High School, Dempsey played defensive end in football and performed as a shot putter for the track squad. At Palomar Junior College, he in 1966 gained All-PSC defensive honors in football. Later, he played golf and wrestled professionally.

Dempsey in 1967 joined the semi-pro Lowell (MA) Giants as a football placekicker and began his NFL career in 1968 on the San Diego Chargers' taxi squad. His career blossomed in 1969 when the New Orleans Saints (NFL) hired him as a free agent. Dempsey emerged as one of the NFL's premier kickers with his selection to the Pro Bowl after that campaign. On November 8, 1970, Dempsey kicked a record 63-yard field goal against the Detroit Lions.

After being released by the Saints in 1971, he joined the Philadelphia Eagles (NFL) and enjoyed his most productive years there. Despite having impressive scoring and accuracy statistics, however, Dempsey disagreed with the team's management. His other NFL teams included the Los Angeles Rams (1975–1977), Houston Oilers (1977), and Buffalo Bills (1978). Dempsey's handicaps often received more media attention than his kicking prowess. Altogether, Dempsey kicked 158 of 252 field goals attempted for a .622 average, missed only 28 of 272 extra points, and scored 718 career points. The popular Dempsey won numerous civic and professional awards, including the George Halas Award in 1970 as Most Courageous Athlete. Dempsey also participated in philanthropic fund-raising activities. His career proved that physical obstacles do not limit a person with talent, determination, and desire for excellence.

BIBLIOGRAPHY: *Buffalo Bills Media Guide, 1979;* Canton (OH) *Repository*, September 24, 1974; *Gridweek*, December 18, 1970, September 26, 1971; *New Orleans Saints Media Guide, 1970; New Orleans Saints News Release*, December 16, 1969; Philadelphia *Inquirer*, August 28, 1974; *TSN Football Register—1979.*

Jerome Mushkat

DEVANEY, Robert S. "Bob" (b. 13 April 1915, Saginaw, MI), college player, coach, and athletic director, elevated the University of Nebraska's overall athletic program from last in the BEC to national status in gymnastics, baseball, wrestling, swimming, and women's sports. His father, Benjamin, worked as a Great Lakes sailor, insurance agent, bill collector, and factory worker at General Motors in Saginaw, and his mother, Grace (Rumbles) Devaney, also worked. His younger brothers included Arthur, a gifted pianist with the famous Freddie Martin Orchestra, and Ralph, who was killed parachuting over Omaha Beach in the 1944 Normandy invasion of Europe. Devaney, a mischievous child, graduated from Hill High School in Saginaw, making All-Conference in football. For three years he worked in the giant General Motors foundry in Saginaw, MI. Devaney graduated in 1939 from Alma College (MIAA), where he played football and was named MVP his senior year. After marrying Phyllis Wiley in 1939, he coached fourteen years at Big Beaver, Keego Harbor, Saginaw, and Alpena high schools in Michigan and brought up son Michael and daughter Pat.

Devaney pursued college coaching after meeting Duffy Daugherty* at coaching clinics. Daugherty persuaded athletic director Biggie Munn* to hire Devaney as an assistant football coach at Michigan State University (BTC). After four years at Michigan State, Devaney became head football coach at the University of Wyoming (MSAC). The humorous Devaney compiled an excellent 35–10–5 record in five years there. In 1962 he became head football coach at the University of Nebraska (BEC), which had fielded only three winning teams the previous 21 seasons. Oklahoma had replaced Nebraska in dominating the BEC and consistently overpowered the Cornhuskers. Cornhusker fans loved "Sweet Old Bob," who took the Nebraska team from a 3–6–1 mark in 1961 to a 9–2 record in 1962. In the Gotham Bowl, the Cornhuskers outscored the University of Miami 36 to 34.

Devaney achieved the best 11-year record of any college coach: an outstanding 101–20–2 mark for an .829 percentage. Besides winning eight BEC titles, Nebraska captured the national title in 1970 and 1971. The 1971 team, featuring Heisman Trophy winner Johnny Rodgers* and Outland Award and Lombardi Trophy winner Rich Glover, is considered perhaps the best college football squad of all time. Devaney coached numerous All-Star teams and in 1970 and 1971 won many Coach of the Year awards. Devaney has served over two decades as Athletic Director at Nebraska.

BIBLIOGRAPHY: Bob Devaney, *Devaney* (Lincoln, NE, 1981); Hollis Limprecht et al., *Go Big Red: The All-Time Story of the Cornhuskers* (Omaha, NE, 1966); Lincoln (NE) *Journal-Star*, 1962–1972; Omaha (NE) *World-Herald*, 1962–1972; *University of Nebraska Football Guides, 1962–1972.*

Jerry D. Mathers

DEVINE, Daniel John "Dan" (b. 23 December 1924, Augusta, WI), college athlete, college and professional football coach, and administrator, is the son of Jerome and Erma (Andrel) Devine and amassed a composite 172–57–9 (.742 percent) record at Arizona State University (BC, 1955–1957), University of Missouri (BEC, 1958–1970), and University of Notre Dame (1975–1980). He compiled a mediocre 25–28–4 record in four seasons (1971–1974) as head coach and general manager of the Green Bay Packers (NFL) and guided them in 1972 to their first NFC Central Division championship in five years. Devine was named Pro Football Man of the Year by *Football News* and NFC Coach of the Year by UPI and the PFWAA. Devine, who experienced only one losing season (Missouri, 1970) in 22 years of college coaching, garnered one unanimous national championship (Notre Dame, 1977), achieved two BEC titles (1960, 1969), captured one BC championship (1957), and finished with an outstanding 7–3–0 record in post-season play. He produced 24 All-Americans and 14 top-twenty teams in the AP poll.

Devine is the third of nine children of a small Augusta businessman. When his father became ill, 6-year-old Devine joined his uncle Johnson in Proctor, MN. A 135-pound sophomore center on the Proctor High School football team, Devine worked two summers as a railroad section hand. He moved to the backfield his last two seasons, growing to his present 5 feet, 8 inches, 175 pounds and captaining the team. Devine graduated from high school in 1942 and served as a B–29 bombadier in the U.S. Army Air Corps during World War II (1943 to 1945). A first lieutenant, he was sent to the Pacific Theater as the war ended. He enrolled at the University of Minnesota–Duluth (NTCAC), where he captained the football and basketball teams and served as president of the senior class and the student body. The Duluth eleven managed a 6–5–2 combined record for the 1946–1947 seasons in the NTCAC. Devine in 1947 married Duluth State student Joanne "Jo" Brookhart, granddaughter of former U.S. senator Smith Brookhart of Iowa. Devine worked two jobs in anticipation of the birth of their first child and laughs when he recalls that "Jo was elected a pregnant homecoming queen that year." He graduated in 1948 with a B.A. in Social Studies.

Devine began coaching football at East Jordan High School (MN), which had not won a football game in 1947. Devine produced two undefeated teams (1948–1949) and also coached the school's basketball squad. Clarence "Biggie" Munn* brought Devine to Michigan State University (BTC) as freshman football coach from 1950 to 1954. Devine learned organization, tactics, and player relations in the Spartan program that boasted a 35–2–0 record and a national championship in his first four years there. At Michigan State, Devine earned an M.A. in Guidance and Counseling in 1952. Devine compiled a 27–3–1 record from 1955 to 1957 at Arizona State, twice finishing second in the BC. In 1957 the Sun Devils achieved their first undefeated (10–0–0) season, national ranking (twelfth in the AP poll), and BC championship. The Sun Devils placed first nationally in 1957 in total offense (444.9 yards per game) and scoring (39.7 points per game). Devine's excellent years helped bring Arizona State a new 32,000-seat stadium and university status in a voter referendum.

Devine became the only major college coach whose football teams during the 1960s never lost more than three games in any season. His Missouri Tigers from 1958 to 1970 amassed a composite 92–38–7 record, placed second five times and third three times in the rugged BEC, and never finished lower than fourth. The Tigers in 1960 captured their first BEC title in 15 years and finished at 10–1. Missouri triumphed 21–14 over fourth-rated Navy in the Orange Bowl. For their first post-season triumph in eight tries, the Tigers were rated fifth nationally. In 1965 the sixth-ranked Tigers were led by All-American back Johnny Roland and scored a 20–18 Sugar Bowl victory over Florida. When Don Faurot* retired in 1967, Devine became Missouri athletic director. "Dan Devine is a very fine faculty man in every sense of the word," observed Missouri president Elmer Ellis. "He doesn't ask you to cut corners. He works within the system you set up for him."

Under constant and growing criticism at Green Bay, Devine did not enjoy his 1971 to 1974 pro football coaching venture. Packers fans expected a performance comparable to that of the legendary Vince Lombardi,* but Devine was considered too rigid and clumsy at handling players. When his two dogs were shot and his daughter was spat upon in a school bus, he returned to college coaching at Notre Dame. The low-keyed, assured, sensitive, emotional, and sincere Devine exhibited a soft-spoken dignity, acted tough but fair, and lacked color. From 1975 to 1980 he produced a 53–16–1 record at Notre Dame and coached star defensive end Ross Browner, the Outland, Maxwell, and Lombardi Awards winner, and right end Ken McAfee, the Walter Camp Trophy designate. Devine reinstated green jerseys not seen at South Bend in 14 years for one game in 1977 as a psychological ploy to whip Southern California 49–19. The Fighting Irish upset undefeated Texas 38–10 in the Cotton Bowl and finished the 1977 season with an 11–1–0 record. Notre Dame returned to the Cotton Bowl the following year ranked seventh nationally and captured an exciting come-from-behind 35–34 decision over Houston. Al Onofrio, Devine's assisant at Missouri, once said, "I've never seen Dan lose a game for which he especially pointed." The 1980 Irish, however, succumbed 17–10 to the undefeated national champion Georgia Bulldogs in the Sugar Bowl in Devine's final coaching effort. Before the 1980 season Devine had announced his retirement because of his wife's failing health and the pressures of coaching Notre Dame football. The seniors presented him with a plaque after the last home game that read, "What we gave, we have. What we didn't give, we have lost forever. Thanks for teaching us how to give."

Devine served as head coach at the 1961 and 1962 Shrine All-Star (East-West) Games, 1969 and 1978 Hula Bowls, and 1978 Japan Bowl. The Devines have six daughters and one son and live in Phoenix, AZ, where he is executive director of the Sun Devil Foundation at Arizona State University. Devine has served as national vice president of the Muscular Dystrophy Association of America, honorary chairman of the Kidney Foundation of Indiana, and a member of the executive board of the National Arthritis Foundation. An avid tennis player, Devine also enjoys fishing, golf, history, and politics.

BIBLIOGRAPHY: Bob Broeg, "The 'Talk Softly' Coach," *SEP* 234 (November 18, 1961), pp. 63–68; Ronald L. Mendell and Timothy B. Phares, *Who's Who in Football* (New Rochelle, NY, 1974); *NCAA Official Football Guides, 1947, 1948; Notre Dame*

Football Guide, 1980; Notre Dame–Georgia Football Game Program, November 8, 1975.

James D. Whalen

DICKERSON, Eric Demetric (b. 2 September 1960, Sealy, TX), college and professional player, is the son of Helen and Robert Johnson. He grew up with and legally was adopted by his great-aunt and -uncle, Viola and Kary Dickerson. At Sealy High he participated in football, basketball, and track, winning the state 100-yard dash as a junior in 9.4 seconds. As a senior football running back, he rushed for 2,653 yards and led Sealy to the Texas AAA championship. In the title game he scored four touchdowns and gained 311 yards rushing. *Parade* magazine named him All-American and the top high school running back of 1978.

In the fall, 1979, Dickerson entered SMU (SWC) and rushed 123 yards and scored three touchdowns in his first game against Rice University. Since injuries bothered him during much of his freshman year, he finished with 477 yards on 115 carries. As a sophomore Dickerson made the All-SWC second team and enjoyed five 100-yard games. He rushed 928 yards on 188 carries during the regular season and gained 110 yards versus Brigham Young University in the Holiday Bowl.

Dickerson earned second-team All-American honors as a junior and was selected SWC Player of the Year. He rushed for the second-best yardage (1,428) in SWC history and set SMU scoring records with 19 touchdowns and 114 points. His best game included 186 yards on 26 carries versus Rice, while his four touchdowns against Grambling tied a school record. SMU won the SWC championship but was banned from post-season play.

As a senior, Dickerson made consensus All-American, ranked third nationally with 147 rushing yards per game, and gained 1,617 yards for a 7-yard carry average. He enjoyed the second-best single-game performance in SMU history with 241 rushing yards against Houston, and scampered 80 yards against both Texas–El Paso and Texas A&M. After finishing third in the Heisman Trophy balloting, he gained 124 yards to help the Mustangs beat Pittsburgh 7–3 in the Cotton Bowl and also played in the Hula Bowl and Japan Bowl.

Dickerson's career 4,450 rushing yards on 790 carries broke the SWC marks of Earl Campbell* and are amazing because he alternated at tailback with Craig James all four years. James gained 3,742 yards, making the Mustangs twosome perhaps the most prolific backfield combination in college football history. Dickerson's 48 career touchdowns set an SMU record, while his 288 career points tied Doak Walker* as school leader.

The second player selected in the 1983 NFL draft, Dickerson gained immediate stardom with the Los Angeles Rams. He led the NFL in rushing with 1,808 yards, set a then NFL record for most carries in a season (390), and was named All-NFL. Dickerson, whose 20 touchdowns established a Rams record, was chosen the club's MVP. His best games included 199 yards against the Detroit Lions and 192 yards against the New York Jets. Dickerson's 85-yard scamper against the Jets stood out as the NFL's longest run during 1983. Besides recording impressive rushing totals, Dickerson also caught 51 passes for 404 yards. Other 1983 honors included unanimous Pro Bowl selection, *SI* Pro Player of the Year, *TSN* Pro Player of the Year and UPI NFC Player of the Year.

Dickerson enjoyed even more success in 1984, setting an NFL single-season rushing mark with 2,105 yards and breaking the record 2,003 yards set by O. J. Simpson* in 1973. His 2,244 combined rushing and receiving yards also established an NFL record. He rushed 100 or more yards in 12 games, breaking the mark of 11 by Simpson and Campbell. Dickerson's two best games of 1984 were a career-high 215 yards against the Houston Oilers and 208 yards versus the St. Louis Cardinals. He made All-NFL and became a unanimous Pro Bowl selection once again. At 6 feet, 3 inches, and 218 pounds, Dickerson combined outstanding speed, size, durability, and ambition to make him among pro football's top runners. The bachelor plans to pursue opportunities in commercials and acting during his football career.

In 1985 Dickerson missed the Rams' first two games because of a contract dispute and still rushed 292 times for 1,234 yards and 12 touchdowns and caught 20 passes for 126 yards to help the Rams finish first in the Western Division of the NFC. The Rams defeated the Dallas Cowboys in the playoffs, as Dickerson ran 55 and 40 yards for touchdowns, but lost to the Chicago Bears in the NFC title game. His 1986 statistics included an NFL-leading 1,821 yards rushing in 404 attempts (a 4.5 yard average) for 11 touchdowns and 26 pass receptions for 205 yards (a 7.9 yard average). Dickerson surpassed 2,000 all-purpose yards (2,026) for the third time in his 4-year pro career to lead the NFL. He gained 158 yards rushing in the Rams' 19–7 loss to the Washington Redskins in the NFC playoffs. Dickerson, who gained at least 100 yards in a game 11 times in 1986, was selected NFC Offensive Player of the Year, All-NFL, and to the Pro Bowl. Through the 1986 season, Dickerson had rushed 1,455 times for 6,968 yards (4.8-yard average) and 55 touchdowns and caught 118 passes for 874 yards (7.4-yard average) and two touchdowns.

BIBLIOGRAPHY: Ted Green, "Star Wars—L.A. Style," *Inside Sports* 6 (December, 1984); *Los Angeles Rams Press Guides, 1983–1984; Southern Methodist University Football Press Guides, 1981–1984;* Gene Wojciechowski, "Pointing toward Fame," Dallas *Morning News*, September 2, 1984; *TSN Football register—1986*.

Jay Langhammer

DIERDORF, Daniel Lee "Dan" (b. 29 June 1949, Canton, OH), college and professional player, is the son of John, an employee of Hoover Vacuum Cleaning Company, and Evelyn Dierdorf. He graduated from Glenwood High School in Canton, OH, and left the University of Michigan (BTC) one semester short of graduation, after being drafted in the second round by the St. Louis Cardinals (NFL). His greatest football thrill came in the 1970 Rose Bowl, which Michigan lost to the University of Southern California, 10–3. Dierdorf made seven All-American teams and played in several post-season classics, including the Shrine All-Star (East-West) Game and Hula Bowl.

The 6 foot, 3 inch, nearly 290 pound tackle anchored one of the best pro offensive lines of the 1970s that provided formidable protection for Cardinal quarterback Jim Hart.* Dierdorf in his thirteen-year career suffered only two major injuries, but one nearly crippled him permanently. In 1977 he broke his jaw but refused to let it heal properly on the bench. He continued playing, with special pads inserted in his helmet, despite having to sip most of his nourishment through a straw. Although his jaw was wired shut, he did not receive any sympathy from NFL defensive linemen.

During the 1981 season against the rival New York Giants, Dierdorf suffered a terrible knee injury in a pileup. The injury required immediate surgery and sidelined him for the rest of that season. The injury ultimately forced him to leave football, while he could still walk under his own power. Used sparingly his last two seasons, Dierdorf moved to center in 1983 to allow coach Jim Hanifan to insert younger players in the offensive line. After spending most of the 1983 season on the bench, Dierdorf retired. An intelligent player with a provocative moustache, the affable Dierdorf participated extensively in player union activities during the ill-fated strike of 1974. Besides walking picket lines, he later testified before a National Labor Relations Board hearing in New York that the Cardinals used illegal surveillance of striking veterans.

His honors included playing in the Pro Bowl from 1974 through 1978 and in 1980 and being named to *TSN* All-Star team from 1976 through 1978. Dierdorf has capitalized on his football fame as a very popular toastmaster, co-host on a KMOX-radio talkshow, and part owner of a posh steakhouse with former teammate Hart. The twice-married Dierdorf lives with his wife, Debbie, one son, and three daughters and is an ABC-TV color analyst for Monday night pro football games.

BIBLIOGRAPHY: Tom Barnidge, "Early Retirement," *St. Louis Magazine* (September, 1984), p. 56; Tom Barnidge and Douglas Grow, *The Jim Hart Story* (St. Louis, 1977); Bob Burnes, *Big Red: Story of the Football Cardinals* (St. Louis, 1975); *NYT* Biographical Service (December 8, 1977), p. 1620.

William A. Borst

DILWEG, Lavern Ralph (b. 11 January 1903, Milwaukee, WI; d. 2 January 1968, St. Petersburg, FL), college and professional player, was the son of Bernard and Alida (Winkler) Dilweg and excelled as a two-way football end during the 1920s and 1930s. Dilweg played football at Washington High School in Milwaukee and at Marquette University, being twice named to the Walter Eckersall* All-American Team. In the Shrine All-Star (East-West) Game after the 1925 season, he and All-American end Harold "Brick" Muller* of California shared game star honors. In 1926 Dilweg joined the Milwaukee Badgers (NFL) and immediately exhibited steady play offensively and defensively. When the Badgers disbanded after that season, he signed with the Green Bay Packers (NFL) and enjoyed his greatest years there. From 1927 through 1931 Dilweg made every important first-team All-NFL squad and was named to the first Official Team in 1931. During his nine-year pro career, he failed only once to make the first or second squad of at least one important All-NFL team, and that was his final (1934) season.

Although generally acknowledged as the best defensive end of his day, he exhibited steady rather than spectacular play. Offensively, he provided strong blocking when an end chiefly performed that function. Since Green Bay passed more than most pro teams, Dilweg also became an excellent receiver and in 1929 caught a then unusually high 25 passes. With the 6 foot, 3 inch, 199 pound Dilweg, the Packers won NFL championships in 1929, 1930, and 1931. Following the 1934 season, Dilweg entered law practice in Green Bay, WI. In 1942 he was elected to the U.S. Congress as a Democratic representative and served one term. Dilweg then built a lucrative law practice in Washington, DC, as a legal consultant on congressional legislation. In 1963 President John F. Kennedy appointed him to the U.S. Foreign Claims Commission, a post he held until his death. Dilweg and his wife, M. Eleanor (Coleman) Dilweg had three sons, Jon, Robert, and Gary and one daughter, Dianne.

BIBLIOGRAPHY: LaVern Dilweg file, Pro Football Hall of Fame, Canton, OH.

Robert N. Carroll

DITKA, Michael Keller "Mike" (b. 18 October 1939, Carnegie, PA), college athlete and professional football player and coach, is the son of Mike and Charlotte (Keller) Ditka. His father worked for the Aliquippa, PA, Southern Railroad. Ditka participated in football, basketball, baseball, and wrestling at Aliquippa High and entered the University of Pittsburgh in the fall of 1957. He became a regular end on the football team as a sophomore and played basketball and baseball briefly. The tough, aggressive, defensive player also became a capable pass receiver and good punter for the Panthers. As a senior in 1960, Ditka captained the Pittsburgh football squad, earned consensus All-American honors, and won the school's Chuck Hartwig Award for doing the most to promote athletics. Following his senior season, he played in the Shrine All-Star (East-West) Game, Hula Bowl, and College All-Star Game. He married Marge Dougherty on January 18, 1961, and had three sons, Michael, Mark, and Matt, and one daughter, Megan. Following a divorce, he married Diana Trantham on July 8, 1976.

The Chicago Bears first-draft choice, Ditka won NFL Rookie of the Year honors in 1961 by catching 56 passes for 1,076 yards and scoring 12 touchdowns. Against the Green Bay Packers, he made nine catches for 187 yards and scored three touchdowns. Named All-NFL his first four seasons, he played in five consecutive Pro Bowls. The prototype of the modern tight end, he caught short passes in a crowd and ran deep patterns. After posting 58 catches for 904 yards and five touchdowns in 1962, he then made 59 receptions for 794 yards and 8 touchdowns to help the Bears win the 1963 NFL championship. Ditka's career best came in 1964, when he made 75 receptions for 897 yards and 5 touchdowns. His single-game high of 13 catches for 168 yards occurred the same year against the Washington Redskins.

A calcium deposit on his right instep hampered Ditka's play in 1965 and 1966, causing the Bears to trade him to the Philadelphia Eagles (NFL). Following two injury-plagued years in Philadelphia, he was traded to the Dallas Cowboys (NFL). Ditka enjoyed several productive seasons there, including 30 receptions in 1971, and played in two Super Bowls. His fine 12-year career, which ended in 1972, included 427 receptions for 5,913 yards and 43 touchdowns. During off-seasons, Ditka worked as a stockbroker until Tom Landry* in 1973 appointed him specialty teams coach for the Cowboys. He remained on the Dallas staff through 1981, when George Halas,* his first NFL coach, named him Chicago Bears head coach. His first team posted a 3–6 record in the strike-shortened 1982 season but improved to 8–8 in 1983 and 10–6 in 1984. The Bears won the Central Division title in 1984 and defeated the Washington Redskins in the playoffs before losing the NFC championship game to the San Francisco 49ers. In 1985 Ditka was named AP and UPI Coach of the Year, guiding the Bears to a 15–1 regular-season record. The Bears, relying on their vaunted "46 Defense," defeated the New York Giants and Los Angeles Rams to capture the NFC crown and trounced the New England Patriots 46–10 in Super Bowl XX. Chicago captured the Central Division title again in 1986 with a 14–2 record but was upset by the Washington Redskins in the playoffs. As an NFL head coach through 1986, Ditka has compiled a 50–23 mark.

BIBLIOGRAPHY: *Chicago Bears Press Guides, 1961, 1966, 1983; Dallas Cowboys Press Guides, 1972, 1981;* Mike Ditka with Don Pierson, *Ditka* (Chicago, 1986); Jim O'Brien, *Hail to Pitt: A Sports History of the University of Pittsburgh* (Pittsburgh, 1982); Richard Whittingham, *The Chicago Bears: An Illustrated History* (New York, 1979); Richard Whittingham, *The Dallas Cowboys: An Illustrated History* (New York, 1981).

Jay Langhammer

DOBIE, Gilmour "Gloomy Gil" (b. 21 January 1879, Hastings, MN; d. 23 December 1948, Hartford, CT), college player and coach, was the son of well driller Robert and Ellen (Black) Dobie. After graduating from Hastings High School, he played quarterback in football from 1899 to 1902 for the University of Minnesota (WC). The outstanding quarterback assisted coach Henry L. Williams* from 1903 to 1905 at Minnesota. Dobie became head football coach at North Dakota State University in 1906 and guided the Bisons to two consecutive undefeated teams. In 1908 he assumed the head football coaching position at the University of Washington. His teams did not lose a single game from 1908 through 1916, winning 58 (including 39 in succession) and tying 3. The Huskies 63-game undefeated streak from 1907 to 1917 remains the college football record. At the U.S. Naval Academy between 1917 and 1919, he coached the Middies to 17 wins and only 3 losses.

He served as head football coach at Cornell University (IL) from 1920 through 1935 and became the first college mentor to receive a ten-year contract. At Cornell he compiled an 82–36–7 record and guided the 1921–1923 squads to no defeats in 24 games. After coaching at Boston College from 1936 through 1938, he retired because of a serious automobile accident. In 33 years of coaching Dobie compiled a 180–45–15 record (.781 winning percentage) and ranks as the sixteenth winningest coach. A record fourteen squads, including two at North Dakota State, nine at Washington, and three at Cornell, made undefeated marks.

In 1927 his wife died in an automobile accident. He had married Eva M. Butler on January 2, 1918, and brought up two daughters, Jane and Louise, and one son Gilmour, Jr.

Although not an inventive coach, Dobie proved a great teacher and drillmaster. The perfectionist mentor insisted on the power and flawless execution of blocking and tackling fundamentals. His teams relied primarily on the running game, resorting to passes sparingly. Nicknamed "Gloomy Gil" because of his pessimistic attitude, he always warned his squads of impending danger in the following game. Dobie claimed that none of his players were All-Americans and seldom admitted that any were good. Despite his gloomy outlook, hostility to the press (practices were always closed), and intense methods, Dobie exhibited friendly, sociable behavior between seasons and proved an interesting conversationalist. A learned man with a law degree, he exhibited keen intelligence, read habitually, and invested shrewdly in the stock market. Dobie, a member of the HAF College Football Hall of Fame, was elected in 1951 to the NFF College Football Hall of Fame.

BIBLIOGRAPHY: L. H. Baker, *Football: Facts and Figures* (New York, 1945); Tim Cohane, *Great College Football Coaches of the Twenties and Thirties* (New Rochelle, NY, 1973); John D. McCallum and Charles H. Pearson, *College Football U.S.A., 1869–1973* (New York, 1973); Edwin Pope, *Football's Greatest Coaches* (Atlanta, 1956).

John L. Evers

DODD, Robert Lee "Bobby" (b. 11 November 1908, Galax, VA), college athlete, football coach, and athletic director, is the son of furniture factory manager Edwin and Susan (Nuckolls) Dodd. Dodd, who had two brothers, Edwin, Jr., and John, and one sister, Ruth, attended public schools in Kingsport, TN, and earned sixteen letters in football, baseball, basketball, track, and gymnastics there. At the University of Tennessee (SC), Dodd participated in football, basketball, and baseball and was awarded nine varsity letters. His football teams compiled a 27–1–2 record, with Dodd being selected All-SC quarterback in 1929 and 1930 and a Grantland Rice* (OS) *Collier's* All-American in 1930. From 1931 to 1944 Dodd assisted the legendary football coach William Alexander* at Georgia Tech (SEC). He married Alice Davis of Atlanta, GA, in 1933 and has two children, Linda and Bobby, Jr. As head coach at Georgia Tech from 1945 to 1967, Dodd compiled an impressive 165–64–8 mark. His teams won nine of thirteen post-season games and participated in six consecutive major bowls.

Dodd's undefeated 1952 squad included six All-Americans and was named Team of the Year by HAF. Besides having two SEC championship teams, Dodd coached twenty-two All-American and eight Academic All-American players. Dodd served as an assistant coach in two College All-Star games and remains the only mentor to be head coach for two consecutive years. Eight Dodd assistants have been head coaches at major colleges. From 1968 to 1976 he served as Georgia Tech's athletic director. His maverick coaching style included making practice fun and using praise as the principal form of motivation. Nevertheless, he proved a strict disciplinarian and expected a complete performance on the field and in the classroom. He developed the "Belly Series" and considered the kicking game essential to winning.

Dodd was elected to the NFF College Football Hall of Fame as a player, the HAF College Football Hall of Fame as a player and coach, and state Halls of Fame in Virginia, Tennessee, and Georgia. For over thirty years he has led retarded children and Shriner's Crippled Children's programs. Dodd's charity work earned him the first Big Heart Award in Georgia for most significant long-term public service contributions.

BIBLIOGRAPHY: Atlanta *Journal-Constitution*, 1950–1976; Edwin Camp, *Alexander of Georgia Tech* (Atlanta, 1950); Bobby Dodd to Robert T. Bowen, 1984; Al Thomy, *The Ramblin' Wreck: A Story of Georgia Tech Football* (Huntsville, AL, 1973); Robert B. Wallace, Jr., *Dress Her in White and Gold* (Atlanta, 1963).

Robert T. Bowen

DONOVAN, Arthur "Art" (b. 5 June 1925, the Bronx, NY), college and professional player, is the son of boxing referee Arthur Donovan, and played football at St. Michael's High School in the Bronx, lettering for three years. He briefly attended the University of Notre Dame but left to join the U.S. Marines. After World War II, Donovan lettered at guard and tackle for Boston College and teamed with Ernie Stautner.* In 1950 the Baltimore Colts (NFL) drafted 26-year-old Donovan in the third round. The 6 foot, 2 inch defensive tackle played at 245 pounds early in his career but was listed later at 270 pounds. After the 1950 Colts won only a single game, the franchise was returned to the NFL. Donovan was sent to the Cleveland Browns (NFL) but was traded to the New York Yankees (NFL) before the 1951 season. The Yankees franchise was sold in 1952 to Dallas, but that team also folded. In 1953 Donovan returned to Baltimore with a new Colts NFL franchise.

With the Colts, Donovan became one of the NFL's best defensive linemen. He played in five Pro Bowls from 1953 to 1957, captaining the 1955 and 1956 Western Conference squads. The AP named him All-Pro from 1954 through 1957, while UPI selected him All-Pro in 1954–1955 and 1957. The Colts defensive line, featuring Donovan, Gino Marchetti,* and Gene "Big Daddy" Lipscomb,* ranked among the best in pro football history and played a significant role in Baltimore's 1958 and 1959 NFL championships. One of the most popular players in Colts history, the indefatigable, humorous Donovan spoke at boys clubs, service organizations, and church groups. Donovan, whose ability to keep morale high enhanced his value to the Colts, retired after the 1961 season and in 1968 became the first Colts player elected to the Pro Football Hall of Fame.

BIBLIOGRAPHY: "Art Donovan: A Colt Winner from the Word Go," *Pro!*, Atlanta-Baltimore Football Game Program, September 22, 1968; Art Donovan file, Pro Football of Fame, Canton, OH; "Hall of Fame Profile," *Pro!*, New York Giants–Baltimore Football Game Program, November 3, 1968; Jim Miller, "Yesterday's Heroes," *Pro!*, AFC Championship Football Game Program, January 11, 1981; Murray Olderman, *The Defenders* (Englewood Cliffs, NJ, 1973); Harold Rosenthal, "Little Arthur," *Extension* (September, 1959); John Steadman, "It's Always Story Time with Art Donovan," *Football Digest* 2 (November 3, 1972); George Sullivan, *Pro Football's All-Time Greats: The Immortals in Pro Football's Hall of Fame* (New York, 1968); Steve Weller, "Art Donovan: Watch Out for Groundhogs," *Quarterback* (February, 1970).

Robert N. Carroll

DOOLEY, Vincent Joseph "Vince" (b. 4 September 1932, Mobile, AL), college athlete, football coach, and athletic director, the son of electrician William and Nellie Dooley, is the third of four athletic children. Two older sisters, Margaret and Rosezella, excelled in high school basketball, while his brother, Bill, starred in college football and is head football coach and athletic director at Virginia Tech.

At McGill High School in Mobile, Dooley excelled in football and basketball. He twice led McGill to the Alabama State Tournament basketball finals and was chosen each time to All-Tournament teams. After completing high school in 1950, Dooley accepted a football scholarship to Auburn University (SEC). He started his first varsity game at safety during the 1951 season and intercepted two Billy Wade passes to help Auburn upset highly ranked Vanderbilt 25–14. Dooley set a Tigers record with six interceptions in 1951 and was selected to the All-SEC second defensive unit. The versatile Dooley started on Auburn's varsity basketball team as a sophomore. As a junior, Dooley suffered a knee injury during a football game against Mississippi and missed the remaining football and entire basketball seasons. As a senior in 1953, Dooley captained the football team to Auburn's first winning season (7–2–1) in seventeen years and a Gator Bowl appearance. Dooley completed his playing career in August 1954, by intercepting Detroit Lions' (NFL) Bobby Layne's* pass in the College All-Star game.

After graduating from Auburn with a degree in business administration, Dooley served as a second lieutenant in the U.S. Marine Corps from 1954 to 1956. Upon discharge, he returned to his alma mater as an assistant football coach under his old mentor, Ralph Jordan, and directed the varsity Tigers quarterback corps. In 1957 Auburn finished undefeated and won the national championship. After being quarterback coach from 1956 to 1959, Dooley coached the freshmen Tigers from 1961 to 1963 and produced two undefeated teams. Dooley married Auburn coed Barbara Meshad of Birmingham, AL, in 1960 and has four children, Deanna, Daniel, Denise, and Derek. Before leaving Auburn, Dooley completed an M.A. in History in 1963.

In 1964 Dooley became head football coach at the University of Georgia (SEC). During his first season he directed the Bulldogs to a 7–3–1 record and post-season appearance in the Sun Bowl and was named SEC Coach of the Year. Since 1964 Dooley has guided Georgia football and sustained only one season below .500 (5–6 in 1977). Through 1986 Dooley has compiled a career record of 183–70–10, won a national championship in 1980 and six SEC titles, and made 18 bowl appearances, including eight majors (five Sugar, three Cotton). The national championship, three SEC titles, and four major bowls (three Sugar, one Cotton) came from 1980 through 1983, when Georgia teams compiled a 43–4–1 record and finished in the top five of final national polls. Dooley, named NCAA Coach of the Year in 1980, SEC coach seven times, and NCAA district coach six times, coached in the Japan Bowl in 1982 and Hula Bowl in 1984.

Dooley also became Georgia athletic director in 1979 and developed one of the nation's best men's and women's sports programs. For these efforts, Dooley was honored as Sports Administrator of the Year in 1984. Dooley, elected to the Georgia Sports Hall of Fame in 1979 and the Alabama Sports Hall of Fame in 1984, has chaired the AFCA Ethics Committee and served on the board of trustees and as first vice president of the AFCA.

BIBLIOGRAPHY: *Georgia Bulldog Football, 1984.*

Jerry Jaye Wright

DORAIS, Charles Emile "Gus" (b. 2 July 1891, Chippewa Falls, WI; d. 4 January 1954, Birmingham, MI), college and professional player, coach, and administrator, the son of David Dorais, revolutionized football with the first effective use of the forward pass in 1913. After graduating from Chippewa Falls High School, he entered the University of Notre Dame in 1910 and roomed with freshman Knute Rockne.* The 5 foot, 7 inch, 140 pound quarterback and end Rockne led Notre Dame to its first undefeated season in 1912. Notre Dame, considered a small midwestern school with a second-rate, undefeated football team, met mighty, unbeaten Army at West Point on November 1, 1913. Utilizing the forward pass, Dorais riddled Army's vaunted defense with 13 completions in 17 attempts for 213 yards. The Fighting Irish stunned the eastern football establishment by routing the Cadets 35–13. The upset marked the legitimization of the forward pass as an offensive weapon and Notre Dame's rise to national football respectability.

After graduation from Notre Dame in 1914 with a Bachelor of Law degree, Dorais became athletic director; football, basketball, and baseball coach; and instructor of English and History at Dubuque (IA) College. Dorais, whose football team won 17, lost 9, and tied 2 in four years, married Vila Fettgather of Dubuque on May 20, 1917, and had three sons and two daughters.

Dorais entered the U.S. Army in 1918 and was appointed director of sports at Camp MacArthur in Waco, TX, where his football team won every game. Rockne, who became head football coach at Notre Dame in 1918, hired Dorais as his assistant for 1919. After one year there Dorais became athletic director and head football, basketball, and baseball coach at Gonzaga University in Spokane, WA. During five years there, his football teams won 20, lost 13, and tied 3 and captured the NWC championship in 1922. Dorais served as athletic director and head football coach at the University of Detroit from 1925 through 1942, when football was dropped because of World War II. During his eighteen-year tenure there, he transformed the Titans into a respected midwestern football power. From 1927 to 1929, Detroit won 19 consecutive games. Detroit was the only undefeated midwestern team in 1928. Dorais' overall record at Detroit included 113 wins, 48 losses, and 7 ties. In 1937 he coached the first college All-Stars to a 6–0 victory over the NFL champion Green Bay Packers. Dorais in 1943 became head coach of the struggling Detroit Lions (NFL) but fell short of his college achievements. Although enjoying winning seasons in 1944 and 1945, Dorais compiled a five-year pro record of 20 wins, 31 losses, and 2 ties. After his contract was not renewed in 1948, he served on the Detroit Common Council and operated an automobile agency in Wabash, IN. Dorais was elected to the HAF and NFF College Football Halls of Fame.

BIBLIOGRAPHY: L. H. Baker, *Football: Facts and Figures* (New York, 1945); Allison Danzig, *Oh, How They Played the Game: The Early Days of Football and the Heroes Who Made It Great* (New York, 1971); Jim Koger, *Football's Greatest Games* (New York,

1966); *The Notre Dame Scholastic*, 1910–1914; University of Detroit, Archives, Detroit, MI; University of Notre Dame, Archives, South Bend, IN.

Eugene C. Murdock

DORSETT, Anthony Drew "Tony" (b. 7 April 1954, Rochester, PA), college and professional player, became the first collegiate football running back to rush for over 6,000 yards and won the 1976 Heisman Trophy. The son of West and Myrtle Dorsett, he played two scholastic football seasons at Hopewell Township, PA, near Aliquippa. He was named first team All-State and Scholastic All-American by *Parade*, *Scholastic* magazine, and *Coach & Athlete*, and in 1972 set a one-game school rushing record (lasting 12 years) of 213 yards. Although weighing only 160 pounds, the 5 foot, 11 inch Dorsett became the first legitimate freshman All-American since 1944 in his first season at the University of Pittsburgh in 1973. In his third game that year, he ran for 265 yards in a driving rainstorm at Northwestern and set the rushing record for a freshman. Dorsett's outstanding collegiate game may have been in 1975, when he gained 303 yards in 23 carries against Notre Dame. Irish coach Dan Devine* called Dorsett's performance the finest he had seen in 28 years of coaching.

Dorsett's performance at Pittsburgh proved so outstanding that as of 1986 he still holds Panther records for rushing attempts, yards gained, and touchdowns for a game, season, and career; all-purpose running yards, points scored, and most games over 100 and 200 yards for a season and career; and average per carry for a game and season. He still holds the top three, and eleven of the top seventeen, game rushing performances, best three single-season rushing totals, and highest career scoring total; he ranked second only to passer Dan Marino* in total offense. Dorsett averaged 141.1 yards rushing per game in four years at Pittsburgh. He rushed for 2,150 yards his senior year counting his Sugar Bowl performance.

Dorsett, the first collegiate running back with four 1,000-yard seasons, led all NCAA scoring with 134 points in 1976. At Pittsburgh, he rushed 1,133 times for 6,082 yards and 58 touchdowns. He finished high in the Heisman Trophy voting all four years, with his lowest standing being thirteenth in his sophomore year. Beides winning the Heisman Trophy in 1976, he received the Maxwell Award, several other trophies and Player of the Year citations. He made All-American first teams each of his four years in college and was a virtually unanimous choice his junior and senior years. Dorsett was named *TSN* Player of the Year in 1976, when he led Pitt to the national championship. He played in the 1973 Fiesta Bowl, 1975 Sun Bowl, 1977 Sugar Bowl and the Hula and Japan Bowls. Dorsett's jersey, number 23, was retired by Pittsburgh.

The Dallas Cowboys (NFL) selected him in the first round of the 1977 draft after trading to get first choice. As a Cowboys running back, he continued gaining at least 1,000 yards yearly except for the strike-shortened 1982 season and often caught passes out of the backfield. Slightly heavier as a pro at 5 feet, 11 inches, and 189 pounds, he was chosen by *TSN* as NFC Rookie of the Year in 1977 and to *TSN*'s 1981 All-Pro team. Dorsett, named to the Pro Bowl in 1978 and 1981–1983, played in two Super Bowl games and five NFC title games through 1986. He established an NFL record for the longest run from scrimmage (99 yards) in a playoff game against the Minnesota Vikings on January 3, 1983. On October 13, 1985, against the Pittsburgh Steelers, Dorsett became the sixth NFL player to gain 10,000 career rushing yards. During the 1986 season Dorsett moved past Franco Harris* into third place on the NFL's career combined yardage list (14,835 yards). Through 1986 with Dallas, he has rushed 2,625 times for 11,580 yards (a 4.4-yard average) and 71 touchdowns and has caught 363 passes for 3,255 yards (a 9.0-yard average) and 12 touchdowns. From 1971 through 1986, excluding post-season games, Dorsett gained 19,934 yards rushing and scored 184 touchdowns in his scholastic, collegiate, and pro careers.

BIBLIOGRAPHY: *NCAA Football Guides, 1974–1977;* Jim O'Brien, *Hail to Pitt, A Sports History of the University of Pittsburgh* (Pittsburgh, 1982); *TSN Football Register—1986; University of Pittsburgh Football Media Guides, 1973–1977.*

Robert B. Van Atta

DOUGHERTY, Nathan Washington "Big 'Un" (b. 23 March 1886, Hales Mill, VA; d. 18 May 1977, Knoxville, TN), college athlete, captained the football, basketball, and track teams his senior year (1909) at the University of Tennessee (SIAA). The 6 foot, 2 inch, 190 pound star guard, tackle, and fullback was the largest player on the Volunteers football squad (1906–1909). He plunged for a touchdown in a 1907 victory over Georgia, returned the season-opening kickoff for a touchdown against Maryville College in 1908, and scored the only touchdown to defeat Transylvania in 1909. The Volunteers, led by Dougherty, enjoyed their first seven-win seasons in 1907 and 1908. Grantland Rice* (OS) and John Heisman* named Dougherty to their 1907–1908 All-SIAA Teams. He was inducted into the NFF College Football Hall of Fame in 1967 and made the FWAA Early (1869–1920) Southeastern Regional All-Time Team. According to Vanderbilt coach Dan McGugin,* "Dougherty was a splendid specimen of manhood at 190 pounds and used his great strength to best advantage. He was almost invincible on defense."

Dougherty's father, Samuel, moved his family to Knox County, TN, in 1898. Following graduation from Tennessee in 1909 with a B.S. in Civil Engineering, Dougherty taught at Cornell University and received an M.S. in Engineering there in 1914. The next two years, he served as assistant professor at George Washington University. At the University of Tennessee, Dougherty served as head of the engineering department from 1916 to 1940 and as dean of the college of engineering until retirement in 1956. He chaired for thirty-nine years the Tennessee Athletic Council. A vice president and early developer of the NCAA, Dougherty served as president of the SC. In 1933 he helped found and was secretary of the SEC. His best move came in 1925, when he hired Bob Neyland* as end coach under M. B. Banks. When Banks departed the following year, Neyland began the greatest head coaching career in Volunteers history. Dougherty, listed in *Who's Who in America*, *Who's Who in Engineering*, and *American Men of Science*, was Engineer of the Year for 1958. The Tennessee Board of Trustees named the largest engineering building the Nathan W. Dougherty Engineering Hall. Dougherty married Agnes Anna Monteith in 1913 and had five children.

BIBLIOGRAPHY: Russ Bebb, *The Big Orange: A Story of Tennessee Football* (Huntsville, AL, 1973); Bud Fields and Bob Bertucci, *Big Orange* (New York, 1982); Ronald L. Mendell and Timothy B. Phares, *Who's Who In Football* (New Rochelle, NY, 1974); Tom Siler, *The Volunteers* (Knoxville, TN, 1950); *Spalding's Official Intercollegiate Football Guide, 1909*; University of Tennessee, Library Archives, Knoxville, TN.

James D. Whalen

DOWLER, Boyd Hamilton (b. 18 October 1937, Cheyenne, WY), college athlete and professional football player and coach, is the son of Wyoming star halfback and high school coach Walter Dowler. Boyd excelled as an all-around athlete, earning ten varsity letters in track, basketball, and football. A football quarterback and tailback, he established state track records in the broad jump and high hurdles and participated in the 100-yard dash. The heavily recruited Dowler chose the University of Colorado (BEC) over Wyoming because of the Buffalos' track program. At Colorado, Dowler competed in the dashes and hurdles for the track team and made notable gridiron accomplishments. He led the Buffalos in passing, receiving, and interceptions and played several positions. The quarterback made the All-BEC squad and led Colorado to a victory over Clemson in the 1957 Orange Bowl. He also played in the Shrine All-Star (East-West) and College All-Star games prior to his 1959 graduation.

He was drafted by the Green Bay Packers (NFL) in 1959 in the third round, becoming the leading receiver on the first Vince Lombardi*–coached team and being named Rookie of the Year. In his eleven-year career, he led the Packers in receptions eight times. He also punted two seasons and competed in six NFL championship games and the first two NFL Super Bowls. The 6 foot, 5 inch, 224 pound Dowler, named to the Pro Bowl in 1966 and 1968, caught two touchdown passes in the 1967 NFL championship victory (21–17) over the Dallas Cowboys and a 62-yard touchdown pass in Super Bowl II. During his pro career (1959–1969), he made 449 receptions for 6,894 yards, scored 39 touchdowns, and played in 150 consecutive games. In 10 championship games, he caught 30 passes for 430 yards and 5 touchdowns. Among Packers receivers, only Hall of Famer Don Hutson* caught more passes. Dowler was selected to the second squad at flanker on the NFL's First Fifty Year Team and to the Green Bay Packers Hall of Fame in 1978. Dowler served as an assistant football coach with the NFL Los Angeles Rams (1969–1970), Washington Redskins (1971–1972), Philadelphia Eagles (1973–1975), Cincinnati Bengals (1976–1979), and Tampa Bay Buccaneers (1980–1984).

BIBLIOGRAPHY: Ken Harrnett, "Artful Dowler," *Green Bay Packers Yearbook, 1968*, p. 37; Chuck Lane, *Green Bay Packers Media Guide, 1968, 1970;* Len Wagner, "Dowler Always Second to Hutson," *Green Bay Packers Yearbook, 1970*, p. 27.

Brian C. Gunn

DRISCOLL, John Leo "Paddy" (b. 11 January 1895, Evanston, IL; d. 29 June 1968, Chicago, IL), college and professional athlete and football coach, starred as an All-WC halfback at Northwestern University and in early pro football. A small figure, Driscoll did not play football until his junior year at Evanston High School. He entered Northwestern University in 1914 and played halfback there in 1915 and 1916. In 1916 he led Northwestern to a second-place WC finish. The collegian specialized in open-field running and kicking and was selected team captain for his leadership. In defeating the University of Chicago in 1916, Driscoll scored 9 of Northwestern's 10 points with a touchdown and field goal. Led by Driscoll, the 1916 Wildcats won every game until losing 23–3 to Ohio State for the WC championship. Driscoll kicked a field goal for the only score. In 1915 Driscoll returned a kickoff 90 yards for a touchdown against Iowa. The 145-pound Driscoll also kicked 40- and 43-yard field goals in college games. In the summer of 1917, however, Driscoll ended his college eligibility by playing baseball with the Chicago Cubs (NL) as a utility infielder. In thirteen games, he made three hits and batted .107.

Driscoll enlisted in the U.S. Navy in 1917 and participated in the 1919 Rose Bowl for the Great Lakes Blue Jackets. After World War I, he played briefly for George Halas'* Decatur Staleys, predecessor of the Chicago Bears (NFL). In 1919 he joined the Chicago Cardinals (NFL) and played there until 1925. His most heralded game occurred against the Chicago Bears in 1925, when Red Grange* made his pro debut. Several times Driscoll punted the ball away from Grange and out of bounds. Since the fledgling AFL sought Driscoll, Halas bought his contract from the Cardinals for $3,500. Driscoll played with the Bears from 1926 to 1931, coached football at St. Mel's High School from 1924 to 1937, and in 1937 moved to Marquette University as head football coach. After joining the Bears' coaching staff in 1940, he took over as head coach when Halas temporarily retired in 1956. Driscoll's team won the 1956 WC championship but lost to the New York Giants 47–7 for the NFL title. When Halas returned as head coach the following season, Driscoll became director of research and planning for the Bears. He married Mary McCarthy in 1928 and had one son.

BIBLIOGRAPHY: "Chicago Sports Figure for More Than 50 Years," Chicago *Tribune*, June 30, 1968; "Honoring a Football Immortal," *Northwestern Alumni News* (December 15, 1956); "Legend Built by New Coach," Chicago *American*, December 23, 1956; "Was NU, Bear Grid Great," Chicago *Tribune*, July 3, 1968.

John Watterson

DRURY, Morley Edward (b. 5 February 1903, Midland, Ontario, Canada), college athlete and sportswriter, starred in football at the University of Southern California (PCC) and quarterbacked the Trojans (1925–1927) to a composite 27–5–1 record. Drury, 1927 team captain, was selected consensus All-American and HAF Player of the Year and was named to the HAF College Football Hall of Fame. Besides being elected in 1954 to the NFF College Football Hall of Fame, he made All-Time PCC teams chosen by George Trevor (1949) and the FWAA (1969). The son of seaman Edward and Marie (McCall) Drury, he moved to Long Beach, CA, at an early age. Drury won over 12 letters at Long Beach Poly High School in basketball, baseball, swimming, water polo, and football and twice captained the latter. Since Drury worked in the shipyards to finance his education, he was older than most classmates at graduation in 1924.

When Drury played football at Southern California, the Trojans progressed in the PCC from third place (11–2–0) to second place (8–2–0), to co-champions (8–1–1) his final season and suffered the five losses by only 12 total points. The 6 foot, 185 pound Drury's first varsity year (1925) coincided with a strengthened schedule and the arrival of coach Howard Jones.* The Trojans lost in 1925 to Stanford 13–9, as Drury watched on crutches because of a knee injury. The following season, the Trojans averaged 31.7 points per game and defeated California-Berkeley 27–0 for the first time since 1915. Similar 13–12 losses to national co-champion Stanford and third-ranked Notre Dame marked the only other blemishes in an otherwise successful season. Drury missed a point after touchdown that would have tied Notre Dame, a disappointment repeated the following season against the Fighting Irish. The extremely versatile Drury ran with power, punted, passed, tackled, kicked off, kicked field goals, and blocked for All-American halfback Mort Kaer.

In 1927 Drury scored two touchdowns and gained 250 yards to help the Trojans defeat California-Berkeley 13–0. Although playing with a wired broken jaw and wearing a special mask in a 13–13 tie with PCC co-champion Stanford, Drury intercepted 5 passes, gained 163 yards, and scored 1 touchdown. He played 60 minutes in a 7–6 loss to Notre Dame before a record 120,000 spectators in Soldier Field in Chicago. After throwing a pass for the Trojans' only touchdown against the Fighting Irish, he missed the extra point because the holder failed to position the ball properly in the mud. In the season's finale 33–13 victory against the University of Washington, Drury scored three touchdowns and gained 180 yards before 70,000 in Los Angeles

Coliseum. Upon leaving the field for the last time, Drury received a four-minute standing ovation that brought tears to his eyes.

Los Angeles *Examiner* sports editor Mark Kelly called Drury "The Noblest Trojan of Them All." Coach Jones praised Drury for great football instincts and insisted that he always call the signals. Drury ranks among the all-time Southern California career rushing leaders with 1,686 yards and 5.31-yard average. With the help of a stout line, Drury in 1927 made 1,163 yards rushing and 1,242 yards total offense. Drury, a Sigma Chi Fraternity member, won letters in basketball and water polo, traveled to Japan with the baseball team, and organized a local college ice hockey league. After graduating in 1928 with a Bachelor of Arts degree, he joined E. F. Hutton for two years as a securities salesman. Drury became a sportswriter for the Los Angeles *Express* in 1931 and worked from 1932 to 1973 in the real estate business. He married UCLA graduate Louise Mitchell of Santa Monica, CA, in 1940, has one son and one daughter, and enjoys retirement near Santa Monica.

BIBLIOGRAPHY: Allison Danzig, *The History of American Football: Its Great Teams, Players, and Coaches* (Englewood Cliffs, NJ, 1956); John D. McCallum and Charles H. Pearson, *College Football U.S.A., 1869-1973* (New York, 1973); Ronald L. Mendell and Timothy B. Phares, *Who's Who in Football* (New Rochelle, NY, 1974); Ken Rappoport, *The Trojans: A Story of Southern California Football* (Huntsville, AL, 1974); University of Southern California, Archives, Los Angeles, CA; USC–Stanford Football Game Program, October 30, 1926; USC–Washington Football Game Program, December 3, 1927; James D. Whalen, Telephone Interview, February 6, 1985.

James D. Whalen

DUDLEY, William McGarvey "Bullet Bill" (b. 24 December 1921, Bluefield, VA), college and professional player, starred at halfback in football at the University of Virginia and won the 1941 Maxwell Award and Walter Camp* Memorial Trophy. With the Pittsburgh Steelers (NFL) he won the Joe F. Carr MVP Trophy in 1946. Dudley received a similar award in 1944 playing service football with Randolph Field (TX) and made consensus All-American (1941), first team All-Service (1944), and All-Pro (1942, 1946). Dudley, a member of the HAF College Football Hall of Fame and Pro Football Hall of Fame, was elected in 1956 to the NFF College Football Hall of Fame. The FWAA named him in 1969 to the All-Time Southern Regional team, while Allison Danzig* (OS) included him at halfback in 1970 on his squad of all-time college specialists.

The son of James S. and Jewell (Jarrett) Dudley, he starred at halfback for Bluefield Graham High School and graduated from there in 1938. Dudley never missed an extra point and kicked a 35-yard field goal to defeat Princeton High School, one of the top West Virginia teams. Virginia Tech and Washington and Lee considered the 152-pound Dudley too small for college football, but coach Frank Murray persuaded him to attend the University of Virginia. Dudley played regular halfback as a sophomore (1939) when Virginia defeated Maryland, William and Mary, Chicago, and Washington and Lee and ran 45 yards for a touchdown in a 14–12 loss to Navy. The following year, he ranked as the nation's second best ground gainer and helped the Cavaliers defeat Yale, Maryland, Washington and Lee, and Lehigh. The 5 foot, 10 inch, 170 pound Dudley in 1941 was elected the nation's youngest college team captain. The Cavaliers finished 8–1–0 with five shutouts, a two-point loss to Yale, and their first triumph over Virginia Military Institute in six years. Virginia also defeated perennial rivals North Carolina and Virginia Tech for only the second time in fourteen years.

Although not fast over long distances, Dudley proved quick, shifty, determined, and fearless. The enthusiastic 60-minute performer called signals, punted and passed, and inspired teammates. He led the nation in scoring (1941) with 134 points (18 touchdowns, 23 conversions, 1 field goal) and made almost one-half of Virginia's points. He also paced the nation with 1,674 yards of all-purpose running and scored on an 89-yard punt return against Lafayette and a 79-yard run from scrimmage against North Carolina. He rushed for 968 yards (6.3-yard average), completed 57 passes (53 percent) for 856 yards, and gained 1,824 total yards from scrimmage. Dudley excelled for the East All-Stars in the 6–6 Shrine All-Star (East-West) game in January 1942. After intercepting four West passes and completing a 23-yard touchdown pass for the only East score, he was named to the All-Time All-East team. "His were the most brilliant forward pass interceptions. . . . [They] held the West at bay," declared sportswriter Bill Keefe. "Dudley proved himself one of the best all-around football players ever seen here."

Dudley earned a B.S. in Education in 1942 from the University of Virginia. He was named to the Chicago *Tribune* Charities College All-Star team that lost 21–0 to the NFL champion Chicago Bears. He joined the Pittsburgh Steelers (NFL) in 1942 and became NFL rushing champion by gaining 696 yards (4.3-yard average). Dudley served as flying instructor in the U.S. Army Air Corps (1943–1945) and flew missions in the Pacific Theater during World War II. A first lieutenant stationed at Randolph Field (1944), he was the leading back on the undefeated (12–0–0) Fliers. Randolph ranked third in the AP poll and triumphed 13–6 over Second Air Force in the post-season Bond Bowl in New York City. Dudley returned to the Steelers in 1945 and was the 1946 NFL rushing leader. He gained 604 yards (4.1-yard average) and topped the NFL in interceptions with 10. Dudley captained the NFL Detroit Lions (1947–1949) and finished with the NFL Washington Redskins (1950-1951, 1953). Altogether, Dudley rushed 765 times for 3,057 yards (4.0-yard average) and 19 touchdowns and caught 123 passes for 1,383 yards (11.2-yard average) and 18 touchdowns. He also completed 81 of 222 passes for 985 yards and 6 touchdowns.

Dudley, who married Libba Leininger in 1947 and has three children, worked as a Ford tractor plant executive in Detroit, MI, and an insurance sales executive in Washington, DC. A member of the Million Dollar Round Table, Dudley in 1964 received the prestigious National Sales Executive Club Sammy Award. He served in the Virginia legislature and was honored by the Chamber of Commerce in 1966 with a testimonial dinner in Lynchburg, VA, where he and his wife reside.

BIBLIOGRAPHY: John D. McCallum and Charles H. Pearson, *College Football U.S.A., 1869-1973* (New York, 1973); Robert Ours, *College Football Almanac* (New York, 1984); Randolph Field–Rice University Football Game Program, September 30, 1944; Robert Smith, "Bullet Bill Dudley," *Sport 37* (January, 1964), pp. 33–34, 58–60; Maxwell Stiles, *Football's Finest Hour* (Los Angeles, 1950); Roger Treat, ed., *The Encyclopedia of Football*, 16th rev. ed., rev. by Pete Palmer (New York, 1979); Virginia-Lafayette Football Game Program, September 27, 1941.

James D. Whalen

E

EASLEY, Kenny (b. 15 January 1959, Chesapeake, VA), college and professional player, ranks among the outstanding defensive backs in modern football. At Oscar Smith High School in Chesapeake, VA, he lettered in basketball and track and as a football quarterback and defensive back. Although offered basketball scholarships in both the ACC and BTC, he elected to play football at UCLA and enjoyed a spectacular gridiron career there. The three-time (1978–1980) consensus All-American was the first player named to the All-PTC team four times as a defensive star and kick returner. As a junior, he set a Bruins record with 336 yards on 27 punt returns. He made 105 tackles and returned an interception 62 yards for a touchdown against Oregon State as a senior. After graduating with a B.A. in Political Science, Easley joined the Seattle Seahawks (NFL) in 1981 and has been the mainstay of the team's defensive backfield since then.

In his first Seattle season he averaged 51.7 yards on three interception returns and ran back one for 82 yards against the Cleveland Browns. In the December 20 game against Cleveland, Easley netted 125 yards via interceptions for an NFL single-game record. During the next two seasons, his 11 pickoffs amounted to 144 yards and included 44- and 38-yard returns. Easley in 1984 made 10 interceptions for 126 yards, scored touchdowns against the New England Patriots and Kansas City Chiefs, and recorded a long gain of 58 yards. That same year, he intercepted three San Diego Charger passes in a single game. Before missing the last three games of the 1985 season due to an ankle injury, Easley had started 49 consecutive games. His 79 tackles in the 1985 season added luster to a career record that includes 10 contests with 10 or more tackles. Easley's 491 yards in 28 interception returns place him among the elite in NFL history. Easley missed part of the 1986 season with another injury. He has returned 26 punts for 302 yards (11.6 yard average).

The 6 foot, 3 inch, 206 pound Easley has won numerous pro honors, including AFC Defensive Rookie of the Year (1981), the NFL All-Rookie Team, first-team All-NFL (1982–1984), AFC Defensive Player of the Year (1983), and NFL Defensive Player of the Year (1984). He and his wife, Gail, reside in Bellevue, WA, where he is active in United Way and United Cerebral Palsy volunteer work.

BIBLIOGRAPHY: Seattle Seahawks, Publicity Department, Seattle, WA; *TSN Football Register—1986*.

Leonard Frey

ECKERSALL, Walter Herbert "Eckie" (b. 17 June 1886, Chicago, IL; d. 24 March 1930, Chicago, IL), college athlete and professional football player and official, quarterbacked the University of Chicago (WC) four years (1903–1906). He made Walter Camp's* and Casper Whitney's All-American teams from 1904 through 1906, the first Western player so honored. The Maroons captain and HAF Player of the Year in 1906, Eckersall in 1951 was selected a charter member of the NFF College Football Hall of Fame. His numerous All-Time All-American team honors included those of Walter Camp (1910), Fielding Yost* (1920), John Heisman* (1932), Parke Davis (1934), HAF (1950), the AP (1951), and the FWAA (1969).

From a pioneer Chicago family, Eckersall in 1897 carried the water bucket at University of Chicago football games. At Hyde Park High School, the 118 pounder starred at end as a freshman in 1899, played quarterback the next three years, and captained the team as a junior and senior. Hyde Park, one of the nation's top scholastic football teams, defeated the University of Chicago and lost to the University of Wisconsin. Hyde Park triumphed 105–0 over Eastern scholastic champion Brooklyn Poly Prep in a post-season game, making Eckersall the day's most promising prep athlete. A sprinter on the track team, he shared the national interscholastic record for the 50-yard (5.4 seconds) and 100-yard (10 seconds) dashes and held the Illinois state interscholastic record for the 220-yard dash (22 seconds). He graduated from Hyde Park High School in 1903.

The 5 foot, 7 inch, 142 pound Eckersall guided the University of Chicago football teams to a combined four-year 31–4–2 record. Chicago outscored opponents 1,047 to 127 points (33–4–2 and 1,107–127 if two 1905 games not generally listed but shown in the *Spalding's Official Intercollegiate Football Guide* are included). The four defeats came to teams with a 31–3–2 composite record. Chicago lost twice to WC co-champion Michigan "point-a-minute" teams (1903–1904) and once each to the U.S. Military Academy (1903) and WC co-champion Minnesota (1906).

Eckersall, a brilliant strategist, great punter and dropkicker, excellent blocker, and deadly tackler as safety, possessed unassuming modesty. He set a national record by dropkicking five field goals in games against Illinois

(1905) and Nebraska (1906), scored touchdowns on kickoff returns of 107 and 106 yards against Texas and Wisconsin on an 110-yard field, and made touchdown runs of 52 yards against Illinois (1903) and 95 yards against Iowa (1904). Eckersall twice scored every Chicago point against Wisconsin by dropkicking three field goals (worth 5 points each) in a 15–6 (1903) triumph and with one field goal in a 4–0 (1905) victory (field goal value reduced to 4 points). Besides punting 75 yards against Michigan (1904), he returned a fumble for a touchdown in the 22–12 defeat.

Chicago claimed the national championship with Yale in 1905 with an undefeated 11–0–0 season and ended Michigan's 56-game undefeated string with a thrilling 2–0 triumph before a record 25,791 at Chicago's Marshall Field, as Eckersall's punts stymied the Wolverines. Late in the game on third (final) down against a stiff wind, Eckersall stood behind his goal ready to punt. Since the Wolverines ends were attempting a blocked kick, he faked the punt and ran around right end to the 25-yard line. After moving the ball downfield, Eckersall punted over the Wolverines' goal. The Michigan back was tackled for a safety when attempting to run the ball back, permissible according to the day's rules.

All-Americans Mark Catlin (end), Hugo Bezdek* (fullback), and Walter Steffen (halfback) played variously with Eckersall under coach Amos Alonzo Stagg.* In 1906 forward passing was legalized to open up the game and reduce serious injuries. Stagg inserted over 40 passing plays for Eckersall to use against Minnesota, but heavy rains prevented his efforts. The undefeated Gophers kicked a field goal and took an intentional safety to win 4–2. The following week, Eckersall completed several passes mainly to Steffen in a 63–0 rout of Illinois. Grantland Rice* (OS) wrote "Eckersall was a noted sprinter, a great field general, a fine blocker, and one of the best drop kickers of all time. He was a great defensive man to keep back, either to nail the runner or to return punts through a broken field. No quarterback has shown a greater number of outstanding qualities than Eckersall showed in his all-around play."

Eckersall ran several 9.8-second 100-yard dashes in track, played third base and left field in baseball, participated as a speed skater, and bowled consistently at the University of Chicago. A student in the school of commerce and administration, he quit before graduation and became a major football authority with the Chicago *Tribune* (1907–1930). He played one year with a Chicago pro football team and three seasons at third base with Adrian "Cap" Anson's* (BB) independent Chicago Colts pro baseball team. A noted football official for many years, he worked Army-Navy, Army–Notre Dame, and BTC games. The bachelor Eckersall lived at the Chicago Athletic Association and remained loyal to his widowed mother. Her death in 1929 profoundly affected him and caused his health to fail. Within a year, he died in his suite of a heart attack.

BIBLIOGRAPHY: L. H. Baker, *Football: Facts and Figures* (New York, 1945); Tim Cohane, *Gridiron Grenadiers: Story of West Point Football* (New York, 1948); Parke H. Davis, *Football: The American Intercollegiate Game* (New York, 1911); Joseph Regenstein Library, University of Chicago, Chicago, IL; *Minnesota Alumni Weekly* 14 (November 9, 1914); Howard Roberts, *The Big Nine: The Story of Football in the Western Conference* (New York, 1948); Alexander M. Weyand, *Football Immortals* (New York, 1962); Kenneth L. (Tug) Wilson and Jerry Brondfield, *The Big Ten* (Englewood Cliffs, NJ, 1967).

James D. Whalen

EDWARDS, Albert Glen "Turk" (b. 28 September 1907, Mold, WA; d. 12 January 1973, Kirkland, WA), college and professional player, coach, scout, and executive, was of Scotch, English, and Irish descent. He played left tackle for the Washington State University Cougars (PCC) from 1929 to 1931. Washington State coach Babe Hollinberry nicknamed him "Turk." When Edwards was late for practice one day, Hollinberry remarked, "I wonder where that big Turk is." Edwards ended his college career in 1931, when he captained the Cougars to the Rose Bowl against Alabama. In 1932 the 6-foot, 2 inch, 260 pound tackle joined the Boston Braves (NFL) and played there until the franchise moved in 1937 to Washington as the Redskins. During the 1930s Edwards proved the preeminent NFL lineman and made the All-NFL teams in 1932, 1933, 1936, and 1937. The Redskins won Eastern Division championships in 1936, 1937, and 1940. On both the offensive and defensive lines, he displayed overwhelming strength and power. Although lacking superior speed, Edwards wore down his opponents with superior brute force, agility, and durability.

A freak injury in 1940 ended Edwards' nine-year pro-playing career; when he returned to the bench after a pre-game coin toss, his knee gave way. Edwards served as an assistant coach and scout with the Redskins until 1946 and compiled a 16–18–1 record as head coach there from 1946 to 1948. After being a vice president with the Redskins, he managed a sporting goods company in Seattle, WA. Edwards' pro career spanned seventeen years, during which time he earned accolades such as "the greatest football lineman of them all." Edwards received several awards, including being selected in 1941 to an All-Time All-West eleven, named to several college All-American teams, and picked as a tackle on the All-Time Rose Bowl team. In 1969 the Pro Football Hall of Fame enshrined Edwards. Edwards, also a member of the NFF College Football Hall of Fame, was survived by his wife, Bonnie (Beaudry), one son, and one daughter.

BIBLIOGRAPHY: Albert Edwards File, Pro Football Hall of Fame, Canton, OH; Corrine Griffith, *My Life with the Redskins* (New York, 1947); *NYT*, January 13, 1973; Alexander M. Weyand, *Football Immortals* (New York, 1962).

Daniel Frio

ELLER, Carl Lee (b. 25 January 1942, Winston-Salem, NC), college and professional player, is the son of mason Clarence McGee and Ernestine Eller. He graduated in 1960 from Atkins High School in Winston-Salem, where he made All-State in football, lettered in track, served as class president, and acted the lead role in Sophocles' *Antigone*. When Eller was in high school, his father died; Eller then worked summer construction jobs. After accepting a University of Minnesota (BTC) athletic scholarship, he joined fellow North Carolinian Bobby Bell* to give the Gophers a feared tandem at tackle. Eller twice married (Adreinne Coleman and Jaclynne Fasnacht) and has two children. Eller in 1962 anchored with Bell a Minnesota defense that compiled the nation's best record against rushing with only 52.2 yards allowed per game. Minnesota also set an all-time BTC mark by holding opposing BTC foes to 58.2 yards per game. Eller's 6 foot, 6 inch, 245 pound frame and speed made him a bulwark on defense and a standout blocker on offense. During his senior year (1963), Eller was selected an All-American tackle and played for the East in the Shrine All-Star (East-West) game.

Drafted by the Minnesota Vikings (NFL) in the first round, Eller became one of the sport's most respected defensive ends (1964–1979). Besides being named All-Pro five times and appearing in six Pro Bowl games, he occasionally joined the offensive line on short yardage situations. The Vikings' front four anchored a powerful defense, which led the NFC team to four Super Bowls. When the Vikings trailed the Los Angeles Rams at halftime in the playoffs en route to one of those titles, the ordinarily quiet Eller shouted a short speech and smashed his fist into a large, portable blackboard, breaking the latter. Teammate Fran Tarkenton* later described how intimidated he felt and declared that Eller's action marked a turning point in the contest. Eller played fifteen years through 1978 with the Vikings and finished his career with the Seattle Seahawks (NFL).

After completing his football career and overcoming personal problems, Eller started the career and management counseling program for NFL drug rehabilitation and developed his own Triumph Life Systems Company. In working with athletes, Eller discovered a condition he termed "hero-lism" and developed some of the principles of sport psychology. During the seventy-fifth anniversary BTC football season, Eller was named one of the BTC's twenty-two all-time greats along with Bronko Nagurski* and Alex Karras* at tackle. Eller worked as a businessman, acted dramatic roles, and made television commercials before entering the drug and alcohol counseling profession.

BIBLIOGRAPHY: John E. DiMeglio, Interview with Carl Eller, 1984.

John E. DiMeglio

ELWAY, John Albert (b. 28 June 1960, Port Angeles, WA), college and professional player, is the son of Jack and Janet (Jordan) Elway. His father served as head football coach at California State–Northridge and San Jose State and became head coach at Stanford University (PTC) in 1984. As a junior at Granada Hills (CA) High School, Elway passed for 3,039 yards and 25 touchdowns. He made All-City in baseball as an outfielder, hitting .551 to lead his team to the Los Angeles City crown. He missed one-half of his senior football year with injuries but still passed for 1,837 yards and 19 touchdowns. He batted .491 in baseball and was named Southern California Athlete of the Year.

Elway entered Stanford University (PTC) in 1979 and served as second-team quarterback as a freshman. In limited appearances, he completed 50 passes for 544 yards and 6 touchdowns. The next season, Elway became the first sophomore quarterback in eighteen years to make an All-American first team by completing 248 passes for 2,889 yards and 27 touchdowns. He was also selected as West Coast and PTC Player of the Year. A regular for the Stanford baseball team in 1981, the lefthanded-hitting outfielder batted .361 with 9 home runs and 50 runs batted in. The New York Yankees (AL) selected him in the first round of the free agent draft.

Against Purdue University in the opening game of his junior year, Elway passed for a career-high 418 yards and completed 33 of 44 passes. His Heisman Trophy chances dissipated the following week, as he passed for just 72 yards in a loss to his father's San Jose State team. He finished the season with 214 completions for 2,674 yards and 20 touchdowns and made the All-PTC West Coast squad. Elway signed a six-figure bonus contract with the Yankees and batted .318 for their Oneonta, NY, minor league club in the summer, 1982.

Elway returned to Stanford for his final football season in 1982 and ranked among the nation's leading passers. Besides leading NCAA Division I with 24 touchdown passes, he finished second in completion percentage, third in passing efficiency, and fourth in total offense. Elway, whose 262 completions and 3,242 passing yards set Indians records, finished second for the Heisman Trophy and made consensus All-American. He also established NCAA Divsion I career records for completions (774), passing attempts (1,246), interception avoidance (3.13 percent), and most games with 200 or more passing yards (30).

The first player with three seasons of at least 2,500 total offense yards, Elway compiled career figures of 9,349 passing yards, 9,070 total offense yards, 77 touchdown passes, and 62.12 completion percentage to rank high in college football history. A fine student, the tall, blond Elway won the NCAA Today's Top Five Award for athletic success, leadership qualities, and academic prowess. He also participated in the Fiesta Bowl–NCAA drug education program and served as an officer in Delta Tau Delta fraternity.

After finishing his college career, Elway debated whether to play pro football or continue with baseball. Football scouts rated him an excellent pro quarterback prospect, while some baseball experts predicted he would be only an average major leaguer. The first player chosen in the 1983 NFL draft, he refused to sign with the Baltimore Colts. He was traded within a week to the Denver Broncos (NFL), who signed him to a multiyear contract.

He became Denver's first-string quarterback in training camp but experienced several problems the early part of the 1983 season. He enjoyed several good games late in the year to help the Broncos make the NFL playoffs. He finished 1983 with 123 completions in 259 attempts for 1,663 yards and 7 touchdowns. The next year, he completed 214 of 380 passes for 2,598 yards and 18 touchdowns and threw 15 interceptions. In 1985 he guided Denver to an 11–5 record with 327 completions in 605 attempts for 3,891 yards and 22 touchdowns and threw 23 interceptions. The Broncos won the 1986 AFC Western Division title with an 11–5–0 mark, as Elway completed 280 of 504 passes for 3,485 yards and 19 touchdowns and threw only 13 interceptions. Elway passed for 257 yards to help Denver defeat the New England Patriots 22–17 in the AFC playoffs and then in the AFC championship game he completed 22 of 38 passes for 243 yards to help Denver defeat the Cleveland Browns 23–20 in overtime. In that game Elway spearheaded a crucial 98-yard touchdown drive at the end of the fourth quarter to tie the game and then led the Broncos into field goal position in the overtime but the Broncos lost Super Bowl XXI to the New York Giants. Through the 1986 season he has completed 944 of 1,748 passes for 11,637 yards (a 12.3-yard average) and has thrown 66 touchdown passes and 65 interceptions. He married Janet Buchan on March 3, 1984, and has one daughter, Jessica Gwen.

BIBLIOGRAPHY: *Denver Broncos Press Guides, 1983–1985; Stanford University Football Press Guides, 1979–1983; TSN Football Register—1986.*

Jay Langhammer

ENGLE, Charles Albert "Rip" (b. 26 March 1906, Elk Lick [now Salisbury], PA; d. 7 March 1983, Bellefonte, PA), college athlete and football coach, was the son of commercial building contractor Irvin and Cora Engle. Engle became a mule driver in a coal mine at age 14 and mine supervisor by age 19. He spent a year at Blue Ridge (MD) College (now defunct) and played there in the first football game he ever saw. He enrolled in 1925 at Western Maryland College, where he participated on the football team and excelled in basketball, baseball, and tennis before graduating in 1930. He captained the baseball and basketball teams and won recognition as an All-Maryland football end in 1929, the year Western Maryland finished 11–0.

Engle began his football coaching career at Waynesboro (PA) High School in 1931 and remained there eleven years, posting a 86–17–5 record. Waynesboro compiled three undefeated seasons and eight conference championships and lost only ten games from 1933 until 1940. After pursuing graduate work at Western Maryland College in 1941, he moved to Brown University (IL) as an assistant football coach in 1942 and assumed the head coaching job in 1944. He developed the winged-T offense, which his teams utilized almost exclusively until 1959, when he expanded his attack into a multiple T. His Brown teams won 28, lost 20, and tied 4 over a six-year span. In Engle's last two years at Brown, his teams won 15, and lost 3 games behind spindle-legged quarterback Joe Paterno.*

In 1950 Engle was offered the head football coaching job at Penn State University, provided he would retain the present coaches. He agreed, but brought Paterno fresh out of college. "Rip gave his assistant coaches responsibility and worked to keep them together," recalls 1958 and 1959 Nittany Lions starting quarterback Rich Lucas. "Hardly any of the assistants ever left; and it was probably because of respect and responsibilities they were given by Rip." Penn State's football program did not rank among the nation's best when Engle joined it in 1950. As Nittany Lions coach, Engle did not have a losing season; he compiled a 104–48–4 record and engineered three upsets over highly regarded Ohio State (1956, 1963, and 1964). His teams won three bowl games in four appearances and captured the Lambert Trophy as the best eastern college football team in 1961, 1962, and 1964.

Coach of the Year in NCAA District 2 in 1962, he also was elected president of the AFCA. Five times he journeyed abroad (Europe twice, Japan twice, and Far East once) to conduct clinics for the armed forces. He served as head coach for the Blue-Gray game in 1951, 1953, and 1963, joined the East staff for the 1955 and 1956 Shrine All-Star (East-West) games, and coached the East squad in 1957. Engle, who retired in 1966 in State College, PA, won the Amos Alonzo Stagg Award in 1970 for his contributions to football and was inducted into the NFF College Football Hall of Fame in 1974. Longtime friend and former Ohio State University football coach Woody Hayes* said of Engle, "His teams were always well coached.... But, more than that, he was a fine person and his teams reflected that quality."

BIBLIOGRAPHY: Beaver Stadium Pictorial Football Game Programs, November 13, 1965, and November 17, 1966; *Centre* (PA) *Daily Times*, March 8, 1983; Mrs. Charles A. Engle, Interview with Dennis A. Booher, June 11, 1984; Mervin D. Hyman and Gordon S. White, Jr., *Joe Paterno: "Football My Way"* (New York, 1978); *Penn State Drummer* (Fall 1983); Ridge Riley, *Road to Number One* (New York, 1977).

Dennis A. Booher

EWBANK, Wilbur Charles "Weeb" (b. 6 May 1907, Richmond, IN), college and professional football and basketball coach, is the son of Charles and Stella (Dickerson) Ewbank, who owned and operated two grocery stores. Nicknamed "Weeb" from a younger brother's mispronunciation of his given name, he played high school football, basketball, and baseball and delivered groceries in a horse-drawn wagon for his father. Ewbank entered Miami University (OH) in 1924, receiving a B.S from the newly established school of coaching in 1928. He played quarterback in football in high school and college (second string) and outfield in baseball. Ewbank married Lucy Massey in 1926 and has three daughters, Nancy, Jan, and Luanne.

After graduation, Ewbank coached football at Van Wert (OH) High School

(1928–1929) and football, baseball, and basketball at Miami University (OH) High School (1930–1943). Ewbank, who earned an M.A. from Columbia University in 1932, joined the U.S. Navy in 1943 and became assistant football coach at the Great Lakes Naval Training Station. He then served as backfield football and head basketball coach at Brown University (IL, 1946–1947) and head football coach at Washington University, St. Louis (MVC, 1947–1949). Ewbank moved to pro football ranks as line coach for the AAFC-NFL Cleveland Browns (1949–1954) and then as head coach of the NFL Baltimore Colts (1954–1962).

Ewbank made the Colts a powerhouse franchise by recruiting and developing stars Johnny Unitas,* Alan Ameche,* Raymond Berry,* Lenny Moore,* Gino Marchetti,* Gene Lipscomb,* Jim Parker,* Bill Pellington, and Arthur Donovan*. The Colts won the NFL championship in 1958 and 1959 and then slumped from 1960 through 1962, causing Ewbank to be fired. In 1963 the floundering New York Titans (AFL) acquired a new owner and new name (Jets), and hired Ewbank as coach and manager. Ewbank built the coaching staff and recruited star quarterback Joe Namath* (who won Super Bowl IV for the Jets over the Colts in 1969) and fullback Matt Snell. The 1969 Super Bowl victory made Ewbank the first AFL coach to defeat the NFL champions. With this victory, Ewbank became the only coach besides Paul Brown* to capture both AFL and NFL titles. Coach Ewbank also helped establish the Jets franchise and improve the status of the young AFL.

Of unprepossessing physical appearance, the short, pudgy, 5 foot, 7 inch, 186 pound Ewbank has a crewcut, pug nose, and sad blue eyes. Besides being emotionally involved with football and fatherlike toward his players, Ewbank very meticulously kept records and files of plays. He required each Colt to keep a notebook of his plays and fined each one $200 if he lost it. With the Jets, Ewbank graded his players on every play, a practice later adopted by many other coaches. Ewbank once joked that "football comes first and family is a necessary evil." He combined the two in 1973, hiring his son-in-law Charles Winner as Jets defensive coach. Ewbank handed the head coach position to Winner following that season but remained as general manager. His combined college and pro coaching record stood at 144–133–7, with his pro mark being 130–129–7. He authored *Weeb Ewbank's Pro Football Way to Physical Fitness* (1967) and *Goal To Go: The Greatest Football Games I Have Coached* (New York, 1972).

BIBLIOGRAPHY: Earl Blackwell, ed., *Celebrity Register* (New York, 1973); *CB* (1969), pp. 137–38; Ronald L. Mendell and Timothy B. Phares, *Who's Who in Football* (New Rochelle, NY, 1974); *NYT*, December 6, 1959; and December 30, 1968; *Who's Who in the East* (1974–1975).

Frederick J. Augustyn, Jr.

F

FAUROT, Donald Burrows "Don" (b. 23 June 1920, Mountain Grove, MO), college athlete, football coach, and administrator, is the second child of Fred W. and Charlotte (Burrows) Faurot. His father, a horticulturist, became one of the first county agents and then director of a fruit experiment station. Faurot attended high school in Mountain Grove and the University of Missouri (MVC), earning degrees in agriculture in 1925 and 1927. A tall, slender lad, he performed ably at fullback in 1923 and 1924 in a football program gaining national prominence.

After a successful stint as a football coach at Northeast Missouri State Teachers College (MIAC) from 1926 to 1934, Faurot returned to his alma mater (BSC) in 1935. At the University of Missouri from 1935 to 1956, Faurot became one of his era's most successful, innovative coaches. In nine seasons at Northeast Missouri, he had won 63 games while tying 3 and losing only 13. The Missouri Tigers had suffered losing seasons each year from 1930 to 1934. Faurot, whose predecessor had won only 2 games and lost 23 in three years, improved the Missouri situation immediately. After winning 3, losing 3, and tying 3 contests in 1935, the Tigers the following year enjoyed their first winning season since 1929 and placed second in the BSC.

Following a losing season in 1937, Faurot directed winning campaigns with talented, self-confident star Paul Christman. Faurot's policy was to rely on Missouri athletes. Christman played quarterback and safety, filled the air with footballs as a passer and kicker, and ran the ball effectively. As a sophomore in 1938, Christman led the Tigers to a 6–3 season. In his junior year, the Tigers lost only to formidable Ohio State. The Buckeyes were scheduled frequently to strengthen the program financially. Missouri won eight contests in 1939 and captured its first BSC championship, as Christman was named an All-American. Missouri was chosen for its first bowl game (the Orange Bowl), which the Tigers lost to Georgia Tech. Christman played superbly his senior year and again made All-American. The Tigers were not as strong, however, finishing with six wins and three losses.

Deprived of Christman's great passing talents, Faurot made a major innovation in 1941 by introducing the explosive split-T offense. The split-T, coupled with good athletes including All-American center Darold Jenkins and halfback Bob Steuber, enabled Missouri to lead the nation in rushing. The Tigers finished 8–1 in the regular season and won the BSC championship, but lost 2–0 to Fordham in the Sugar Bowl rain. The next year, Faurot's squad won eight games and another BSC title. Faurot coached in the U.S. Navy from 1943 to 1945. The position enabled him to teach his new offense to other coaches, most notably Jim Tatum* and Charles "Bud" Wilkinson.*

In 1946 Faurot returned to Missouri and enjoyed success for several more years. His teams produced four consecutive winning seasons and lost two bowl games. After declining an invitation to move to Ohio State University, he suffered five losing seasons in the next seven years. Although college football had entered a new era of high-pressure recruiting, Faurot still relied on Missourians. He coached only one All-American his final eleven years, namely, Harold Burnine.

After the 1956 season Faurot resigned as coach and served as Missouri athletic director. He had turned a debt into a surplus, enlarged the stadium, compiled a 101–79–10 record at Missouri, and introduced an offensive formation used successfully by Tatum at Maryland and Wilkinson at Oklahoma. Faurot's gridiron accomplishments led to his election as president of the AFCA and membership in the HAF and NFF College Football Halls of Fame. These feats, plus his identification with the state, resulted in his selection as a Missouri Squire. He remained an athletic director until mandatory retirement forced him out in 1967, but he still served in the Missouri alumni office and as a broadcaster at football games. Appropriately, the institution named its football field Faurot Field in 1972. Faurot, who shunned alcohol and tobacco, has enjoyed remarkably good health. He and his wife, Mary, have three children and eight grandchildren; the grandfather weighs no more than the athlete had six decades earlier.

BIBLIOGRAPHY: Bob Broeg, "The Old Master of Old Mizzou," *SEP* 223 (October 21, 1950), pp. 28–29ff.; Bob Broeg, *Ol' Missou: A Story of Missouri Football* (Huntsville, AL, 1974); Allison Danzig, *The History of American Football: Its Great Teams, Players, and Coaches* (Englewood Cliffs, NJ, 1956); Don Faurot, "The Best Player I Ever Coached," *SEP* 225 (November 29, 1952), p. 118; Don Faurot, *Football: Secrets of the "Split T" Formation* (New York, 1950); Don Faurot, "Is College Football Worth Saving?" *SEP* 231 (October 18, 1958), pp. 36ff.; Richard S. Kirkendall, Interviews with Don Faurot, 1984; John D. McCallum, *Big Eight Football* (New York, 1979); Frank Reck, "He Split the T," *Farm Journal* 78 (October, 1954), pp. 72–75; Maury

White, "Mizzou Fans Pay Tribute to Faurot's Contributions," Des Moines *Register*, September 30, 1984; Karen Worley, "Living Legends," *Missouri Alumnus* (1982).

Richard S. Kirkendall

FEARS, Thomas Jesse "Tom" (b. 3 December 1923, Los Angeles, CA), college and professional player and coach, excelled as a receiver with the Los Angeles Rams (NFL) from 1948 through 1956. He attended Manual Arts High School and won All-Southern California honors at end. Upon graduation, he lettered in football two years at the University of Santa Clara and served three years as a U.S. Air Force lieutenant during World War II. He enrolled at UCLA and made the All-PCC squad in both 1946 and 1947. The latter year, he was selected for the New York *Sun* All-American team and received a B.S. in Business from UCLA.

The Los Angeles Rams (NFL) drafted him as a defensive specialist in the eleventh round, but Fears was shifted to offensive end after intercepting two passes in the opening game of the 1948 season. He became one of few rookies ever to lead the NFL in pass receiving with 51 catches and paced the NFL the next two seasons with 77 and 84 receptions, respectively. On December 3, 1950, he caught an NFL-record 18 passes in a single game. He was named All-NFL in 1949 and 1950 by the AP and in 1950 by UPI.

The rugged 6 foot, 2 inch, 216 pound Fears compensated for lack of blazing speed by running extremely precise pass patterns. The buttonhook, his special pattern, exposed Fears to many blind-side tackles and several injuries his final six seasons. Nevertheless, he made clutch catches in important games. His three touchdown passes helped the Rams win the Western Division playoff game in 1950, while his fourth-quarter 73-yard pass reception provided the winning touchdown in the Los Angeles 1951 championship game victory over the Cleveland Browns. In the 1951 Pro Bowl, he caught two touchdown passes. Fears finished his playing career with 400 pass receptions for 5,397 yards and 38 touchdowns and then served as an assistant coach with several NFL teams. As head coach of the expansion New Orleans Saints from 1967 to 1970, he compiled a 13–34–2 mark. Fears, who married Lu Ella Kathreen in 1950 and has six children, was named to the Pro Football Hall of Fame in 1970.

BIBLIOGRAPHY: George A. Frazier, "Two for the Show," *Pro!* (1978); "Hall of Fame Profile," *Pro!* (1972); Tom Fears file, Pro Football Hall of Fame, Canton, OH.

Robert N. Carroll

FEATHERS, William Beattie (b. 4 August 1908, Bristol, VA; d. 11 March 1979, Winston-Salem, NC), college and professional athlete and coach, became the first NFL back to rush for 1,000 yards. Feathers excelled in Virginia prep football, earning All-State recognition four years at Bristol High School and All-Southern honors as a running back his last two years. At the University of Tennessee (SC, SEC), he started four seasons (1930–1933) and made football All-American honors as a senior. In 1933 he starred in the first College All-Star game. Feathers in 1934 became the first NFL player to break the 1,000-yard rushing mark in his rookie year with the Chicago Bears. He attributed his achievement to "just taking the ball and following Bronko [Nagurski*] wide." Behind Nagurski's blocking, Feathers led the Bears into the 1934 championship game. He rushed 1,004 yards that season despite missing two regular-season games with injuries.

George Halas* in 1937 adopted the T formation, making the single-wing star from Tennessee expendable. Feathers played for the Brooklyn Dodgers (NFL) in 1938 and 1939 and spent 1940 with the Green Bay Packers (NFL) before retiring. His NFL career statistics included hurling one touchdown pass and 12 completions in 43 attempts. Besides scoring 16 career touchdowns, he rushed 1,979 yards in 360 carries (5.5-yard average) and caught 14 passes for 243 yards.

Feathers began his football coaching career in 1941 at Appalachian State Teachers College (NCSIC), but lost his position when the United States entered World War II. In 1943 he joined North Carolina State University (SC) as backfield coach and physical training instructor in the U.S. Army Air Corps program. The following year, North Carolina State hired him as head football and baseball coach. The Wolfpack struggled through 1951 under Feathers but completed an 8–3 record in 1946 and received its first ever bowl bid to the Gator Bowl. From 1952 through 1960 Feathers served as assistant football coach at Texas Tech University (SWC). In 1961 he became the freshman coach at Wake Forest University (ACC). He joined the varsity staff in 1964 and served as head baseball coach from 1972 until his retirement in 1976. Feathers was named an initial member of the NFF College Football Hall of Fame.

BIBLIOGRAPHY: Charlotte (NC) *Observer*, March 13, 1979; Beattie Feathers file, Pro Football Hall of Fame, Canton, OH; *News & Observer* (Raleigh, NC), March 12, 1979; Roger Treat, ed., *The Encyclopedia of Football*, 16th rev. ed., rev. by Pete Palmer (New York, 1979); North Carolina State University, Archives, Raleigh, NC; North Carolina State University; Sports Information Office files, Raleigh, NC.

William H. Beezley

FENIMORE, Robert Dale "Blond Bob," "The Blond Bomber" (b. 6 October 1925, Woodward, OK), college and professional athlete, football coach, and official, became the greatest football player in Oklahoma State University (MVC) history. He guided the Cowboys to a school-record 21 consecutive victories, including triumphs in the 1945 Cotton Bowl and 1946 Sugar Bowl. A four-year star at tailback (1943–1946), Fenimore was selected as the first Oklahoma State All-American in 1944 and 1945. The first draft choice of the Chicago Bears (NFL) in 1947, he was hampered by a knee injury and played only that pro season. In 1947 he rushed 53 times for 189 yards (3.8-yard average) and one touchdown and caught 15 passes for 219 yards (14.6-yard average) and 2 touchdowns.

Fenimore excelled in football, basketball, and track at Woodward High School. In his senior year (1942), he made the All-State team by scoring 199 points and gaining 2,002 yards. In 1943 Fenimore made 72- and 61-yard touchdown runs in the All-State football game and led the North squad to a 20–6 win over the South. As an Oklahoma State ballcarrier, Fenimore combined sprinter speed, size (6 feet, 1 inch, 188 pounds), and the broken-field moves of a bunny rabbit. The triple-threat player proved an extraordinary passer, fine punter, and among the best midlands defensive backs.

Fenimore set 16 Cowboy records. In four seasons he rushed 472 times for 2,563 yards (5.4-yard average), completed 163 of 321 passes (51 percent) for 2,536 yards and 22 touchdowns, scored 33 touchdowns, kicked 10 conversions, and returned 18 interceptions for 422 yards. Fenimore led the nation in total offense in 1944 and 1945, and set a two-year national mark of 212.4 yards per game. He also paced the nation in rushing in 1945 with 1,048 yards (7.4-yard average).

Nicknamed "Blond Bob" and "The Blond Bomber," Fenimore gained national attention in 1944 when the Cowboys upset heavily favored Tulsa 46–40. He scored two touchdowns, including a 72-yard gallop, and passed for two touchdowns, the last covering 50 yards for the winning tally late in the contest. Tulsa had not lost a regular-season game since 1941. Veteran observers lauded Fenimore as the best all-around Cotton Bowl performer ever when he rushed and passed for 241 yards in a 1945 34–0 rout of TCU.

In 1945 Fenimore reached his peak. He gained 241 yards in the year's top single-game rushing performance to help the Cowboys edge Arkansas 19–14. Fenimore ran for 105 yards and 2 touchdowns, and passed for 143 yards in the 26–12 win over SMU. When Oklahoma State defeated TCU 25–12, he rushed for 178 yards and 2 touchdowns and added 168 yards in passing, receiving, and returning kicks and interceptions. The Cowboys defended their MVC title by trimming Tulsa 12–6, with Fenimore firing a 64-yard touchdown strike. Fenimore accounted for three touchdowns when the Cowboys handed Oklahoma its worst defeat ever, 47–0. Before the largest crowd ever to witness a southern football game, Fenimore scored two touchdowns, passed for a third tally, and gained 205 total yards to help the Cowboys defeat St. Mary's 33–13 in the Sugar Bowl.

Fenimore also participated in track in the dashes and long jump. He set an Oklahoma State freshman record of 9.7 seconds in the 100-yard dash and placed in that event at the Penn and Drake relays. His father, O. D. Fenimore, also had performed as a prep trackman. An honor roll student, Fenimore entered the insurance business and ranks among the top Oklahoma insurance executives with his own agency in Stillwater. He remained active in football as a coach and official, scouted the BEC for the Dallas Cowboys (NFL) and participated in community and church groups in Stillwater, OK. Fenimore married Veta Jo Cullen in 1947 and has two daughters, Elizabeth Ann and Jo Ellen. He was elected to the NFF College Football Hall of Fame in 1972 and the HAF College Football Hall of Fame.

BIBLIOGRAPHY: Steven Boda, Jr., *College Football All-Time Record Book* (New York, 1969); Allison Danzig, *The History of American Football: Its Great Teams, Players, and Coaches* (Englewood Cliffs, NJ, 1956); Robert Fenimore to Bernie McCarty, March 8, 1984; *Illustrated Football Annual*, 1944–1946; John D. McCallum and Charles H. Pearson, *College Football U.S.A., 1869–1973* (New York, 1973); Ray Morrison, "All-America Team," *SEP* 218 (December 29, 1945) pp. 18–19; *NCAA Football Guide, 1945–1946; Oklahoma State University Media Guide, 1973;* Grantland Rice, "1944 All-America Team," *Collier's* 114 (December 16, 1944) pp. 12–13; Chip Royal, "A.P. All-America Team," Orlando (FL) *Sentinel* (December 11, 1945); *Street & Smith's Football Yearbook, 1946*.

Bernie McCarty

FESLER, Wesley Eugene "Wes" (b. 29 June 1908, Youngstown, OH), college athlete, coach, and announcer, was selected three-time All-American football end (1928–1930) at Ohio State University (WC) and at guard on the 1931 All-American basketball team. The greatest all-around athlete in Buckeyes history, Fesler won nine letters in three sports and received the Potter Runmaker Cup for baseball three times. Fesler captained the 1930 football team and was awarded the 1930 Chicago *Tribune* Silver Football Trophy as the MVP in the WC. A member of the HAF College Football Hall of Fame, Fesler was elected in 1954 to the NFF College Football Hall of Fame and in 1977 to the Ohio State University Hall of Fame. Other honors included his being chosen an All-Time All-American football player by Parke H. Davis (1931 *Illustrated Football Annual*), Grantland Rice* (OS) (1939 *Collier's*), and Harry Stuhldreher* (1940). He was chosen All-Time All-Midwest by the FWAA (Modern Era, 1920–1969) and by George Trevor (1971) and was named to the Seventy-Fifth Anniversary All-Time BTC Team (1970). As Ohio State's head football coach in 1949, Fesler guided the Buckeyes to a BTC co-championship and 17–14 triumph over California in the Rose Bowl.

The son of steelworker Charles Martin and Sarah (Thomas) Fesler, he starred on the basketball, baseball, track, and tennis teams at Youngstown South High School and excelled at center on the football squad. In 1927 Fesler graduated and entered the Ohio State University School of Engineering. He starred on three football teams, amassing a composite 14–7–3 record (5–2–1, 4–3–1, and 5–2–1), but the Buckeyes placed no higher than fourth in the WC. Sophomore Fesler scored against Michigan on a pass from quarterback Allen Holman to help the Buckeyes defeat the Wolverines (19–7) for only the fourth time in 25 games. Ohio State lost the WC title when sixth-ranked Illinois defeated them 8–0 in the final game.

The Buckeyes opened the 1929 football season with four wins including a 7–0 triumph over Michigan on Fesler's 19-yard touchdown pass reception. Fesler saved the victory at Ann Arbor when he caught Willie Heston, Jr., from behind in the open field. A 60-minute performer in all eight games, Fesler picked a fumble out of the air and sped 98 yards for the Buckeyes' only score in an 18–6 loss to Northwestern. Fesler, a fullback, quarterback, and end in 1930, threw a 16-yard touchdown pass to halfback Lew Hinchman in a 16–7 triumph over Pittsburgh, completed a touchdown pass to end Dick Larkins to help Ohio State defeat Navy 27–0, scored a touchdown on a three-yard plunge against Indiana, and set up both touchdowns against Illinois with outstanding passing and rushing in the 12–9 Buckeyes triumph. The Buckeyes' only losses in 1930 came to WC co-champions Northwestern and Michigan. "Fesler was the greatest athlete I've ever seen," teammate Larkins once said. "I've never seen a human animal so well coordinated."

The handsome, 6 foot, 183 pound, curly-haired Fesler was mild-mannered, sensitive, and personable. He made All-WC guard three years in basketball and performed at first and second base and center field in baseball. In 1931 he drove in all the Buckeyes' runs in an 11–6 triumph against Illinois by hitting three home runs (two grand slams) and two doubles. The Phi Beta Kappan transferred after one year to the College of Commerce, delaying his graduation until 1932. Fesler, the varsity football end coach and assistant basketball coach (1931–1932) at Ohio State, tried out in 1931 with the St. Louis Cardinals (NL) baseball farm system.

Besides being head basketball coach at Harvard University (IL) from 1933 to 1940, Fesler served as end coach on Dick Harlow's* Crimson football staff. He served at Wesleyan (CT) University (1941–1942) as head football and basketball coach, but his gridders finished with a combined 7–9–0 record for last place in the LTC. Fesler joined the U.S. Army's Office of Strategic Services in Washington, DC (1943–1944), establishing and operating the physical and recreational program. The following year at Princeton University (IL), he was head basketball and assistant football and baseball coach. Fesler joined the University of Pittsburgh in 1946 as head football coach, hoping to revive the Panthers program that had suffered through six consecutive losing seasons. Fesler's Panthers lost three games to top-rated teams and finished with a 3–5–1 record. Although Pittsburgh lost 20–13 to the Buckeyes, Ohio State (BTC) hired Fesler as head coach.

Fesler inherited a Buckeyes squad depleted by graduation and pro talent raids. His first squad finished 2–6–1, but his next three achieved a composite 19–7–2 record, first- and second-place BTC finishes, and one sixth-place national AP ranking. Halfback Jerry Krall and fullback Fred "Curly" Morrison led the Buckeyes to a 14–7 margin over the University of California in the 1950 Rose Bowl, but the Bears then tied the score. Ohio State end Jimmy Hague kicked a 17-yard field goal with two minutes remaining to provide the winning margin.

Fesler used both the T-formation and single-wing attacks with an unbalanced line spiced with flankers and men in motion. SMU upset the Buckeyes 32–27 in the 1950 season opener, but Heisman Trophy winner Vic Janowicz* led them to victories in the next six games. Ohio State averaged nearly 40 points per game during that span and was rated number 1 nationally. The Buckeyes lost the last two games to nationally ranked Illinois and Michigan, the latter in the infamous "Blizzard Bowl" game at Columbus. Janowicz kicked a 28-yard field goal but suffered two punts blocked, one for an automatic safety and the other recovered by Michigan in the end zone for the winning touchdown in the 9–3 Wolverines victory. Michigan failed to make a first down or complete a pass in nine attempts, as both teams set a BTC record with 45 punts.

The constant pressure to win and Fesler's inability to defeat Michigan ultimately influenced his departure. His sons were taunted, while he received midnight telephone calls and stood on the verge of a nervous breakdown when he abruptly resigned. Ohio State athletic board chairman Frank Strong stated, "We keenly regret your decision. . . . You have exemplified fully the type of coaching leadership under which we desire our young men to participate in competitive sport." Six weeks later, he surprisingly filled the head coach's position vacated by Bernie Bierman* at the University of Minnesota (BTC). Fesler's three-year composite record at Minnesota from 1951 to 1953 produced a mediocre 10–13–4 mark, but the Gophers earned their first triumph (22–0) over Michigan in eleven years. His offense featured All-American halfback Paul Giel, 1953 runner-up for the Heisman Trophy. Fesler surprised the Gophers administration by resigning following the 1953 season to join Minneapolis, MN, radio station WDGY as partner, vice president, and sports director. His career composite ten-year record as head football coach was 41–40–8 (.506 percent).

Fesler left WDGY to become director of sales relations for Investors Diversified Services, a giant Minneapolis-based financial planning firm. He traveled extensively, giving motivational speeches to adult and youth groups before retiring in 1972. Fesler had two sons and one daughter by his first wife, a former Ohio State coed who died of cancer. In 1974 he married Myra Hallet and moved to Laguna Hills, CA, where he still resides and suffers from Parkinson's disease.

BIBLIOGRAPHY: Tim Cohane, "Can Fesler Rouse the Football Giant of the North?" *Look* 15 (October 9, 1951), pp. 64–68; Tim Cohane, "Ohio State—Football's High Pressure Area," *Look* 14 (February 28, 1950), pp. 48–52; Wesley E. Fesler, Telephone Interview with James D. Whalen (October 31, 1985); Bill Levy, *Three Yards and a Cloud of Dust* (New York, 1966); Ronald L. Mendell and Timothy B. Phares, *Who's Who in Football* (New Rochelle, NY, 1974); Wilbur Snypp, *The Buckeyes: A Story of Ohio State Football* (Huntsville, AL, 1974); Alexander M. Weyand, *Football Immortals* (New York, 1962).

James D. Whalen

FINCHER, William Enoch "Bill" (b. 12 November 1896, Spring Place, GA; d. 17 July 1978, Atlanta, GA), college player and coach, was the son of postman Samuel and Laura (Humphrey) Fincher and graduated in 1920 from Georgia Tech University (SIAA), where he lettered in football and served as class vice president. He married Leila Goodman on April 16, 1918, and had one daughter, Sue. Special World War I rules enabled Fincher, who played all line positions except center, to letter in five football seasons. His fifth season, approved by the SIAA, caused the University of Pittsburgh to sever its relations with Georgia Tech. The supercompetitive Fincher, described as a "holy terror on the field," possessed sight in only one eye and removed a porcelain eye before playing. Carlisle's starting eleven, led by Indian Joe Guyon,* converged on the feared 6 foot, 190 pound lineman in the game's opening play and tried to sideline him. Fincher's vicious tackling and blocking, however, reputedly sent several Carlisle team members to the sidelines with injuries as the game unfolded.

Under coach John Heisman,* Fincher participated as a substitute tackle his freshman year when Georgia Tech humiliated Cumberland in an ever-famous 222–0 matchup. Fincher made the All-SIAA team in 1917 at guard, 1918 and 1919 at end, and 1920 at tackle, and helped Georgia Tech attain the nation's top ranking in 1917. In 1918 Fincher captained Georgia Tech to a 6–1–0 record, including victories of 118–0 over Furman, 119–0 over the 111th Cavalry, and 128–0 over North Carolina State. Pittsburgh inflicted Georgia Tech's only loss (32–0) and became the only foe to score against them. After making second-team All-American in 1918, Fincher was named first-team All-American in 1920. Fincher also kicked extra points and made all thirteen attempts in one game. Fincher taught at Boys High and Tech High schools in Atlanta, GA, and served as line football coach at William and Mary (SC) and Georgia Tech (SC), including the 1928 Rose Bowl team. From 1932 to 1961 he worked as a soft drink corporation executive. He was elected to the Pioneer Division of the NFF College Football Hall of Fame, HAF College Football Hall of Fame, and Georgia Football Athletic Hall of Fame.

BIBLIOGRAPHY: Sue F. Barron and George C. Griffin to John E. DiMeglio, October 1984; Al Thomy, *The Ramblin' Wreck: A Story of Georgia Tech Football* (Huntsville, AL, 1973); Robert B. Wallace, Jr., *Dress Her in White and Gold* (Atlanta, 1963); Alexander M. Weyand, *Football Immortals* (New York, 1962).

John E. DiMeglio

FISCHER, William "Bill" "Moose" (b. 10 March 1927, Chicago, IL), college and professional player, is one of eight children of German immigrants. Fischer excelled in football and wrestling at Lane Technical High School in Chicago and became an All-State selection and the captain his senior football season. At the University of Notre Dame, Fischer became a four-year letterman (1945–1948) as a tackle and guard and two-time All-American (1947–1948). Under coach Frank Leahy,* Fischer led the Fighting Irish through three undefeated seasons and a composite 33–2–3 record. The 1946 team won eight games, held the powerful U.S. Military Academy to a scoreless tie, outscored opponents 271–24, and was declared national champion. With a perfect 9–0–0 record in 1947, Notre Dame again was voted the nation's best team. A 14–14 tie with the University of Southern California in 1948 broke Notre Dame's 21-game winning streak and resulted in a second-place finish behind Michigan in the national polls. Fischer in 1948 captained Notre Dame and was awarded the Outland Award as the outstanding college interior lineman by the FWAA. Teammates included Terry Brennan, George Connor,* Leon Hart,* Johnny Lujack,* Jim Martin, and Emil Sitko.

Following the 1948 season, the 6 foot, 2 inch, 248 pound Fischer captained the East team to a 14–12 victory over the West in the Shvine All-Star East-West game. He started at offensive guard in the College All-Star game in Chicago and was selected MVP. A first-round draft choice by the Chicago Cardinals in the 1949 NFL draft, Fischer excelled as an offensive lineman for five seasons (1949–1953) and twice was selected on the All-Pro Team (1951–1952). Fischer returned to Notre Dame as varsity line coach under Brennan and remained there until 1958. A Chevrolet employee for many years, he presently owns a dealership in Ishpemming, MI. Fischer, who married Roma Kainer in June 1949, and has one son, William Michael, was named a guard on the All-Time Notre Dame team and in 1983 was elected to the NFF College Football Hall of Fame.

BIBLIOGRAPHY: Joe Doyle, "Bill "Moose" Fisher," *Pittsburgh–Notre Dame Football Game Program*, November 5, 1983, pp. 6–8; NFF Hall of Fame Release, 1985, New York, NY; *Notre Dame Football Guide, 1983*.

John L. Evers

FISCUS, Lawson "Samson of Princeton" (b. 28 June 1866, Indiana County, PA; d. 31 August 1949, Youngwood, PA), college and professional player, was the son of Samuel and Catherine Fiscus, who lived on a family farm between Indiana and Shelocta in Indiana County, PA. One of 16 children, Fiscus attended Indiana Normal School before that school fielded its first organized football team in 1890. In 1891 he began his football career with the Allegheny Club at Pittsburgh, PA. Fiscus was recruited in 1892 by Princeton University, where he played guard and was nicknamed the "Samson of Princeton." At 5 feet, 11 inches, and 185 pounds, he exhibited great strength for his size.

The following year, Fiscus taught school at South Fork, PA, and commuted 150 miles round trip to Pittsburgh to play football. Later that season, he played halfback for "liberal" expenses for the Greensburg (PA) Athletic Association team, about halfway between Pittsburgh and Johnstown. In 1894

Fiscus accepted Greensburg's offer of $20 a game plus expenses. He played halfback and fullback for Greensburg through 1896, being joined periodically by brothers Ross and Newill.

In 1895 he was rewarded more handsomely for his Greensburg services and rejected offers of up to $125 monthly from Pittsburgh teams. After turning 30 years old, he in 1896 played one of his more spectacular games in his final pro football season. The Greensburg eleven, lauded by Pittsburgh newspapers as "perhaps the best in western Pennsylvania," defeated the formidable Pittsburgh Athletic Club, 14–0. Fiscus ran 30 yards for the first 4-point touchdown, tallied a second near the end of the first half, and ran 80 yards around left end in the second half for the final score, "one of the longest ever on the field."

Fiscus continued teaching school and moved to the "coal patch" community of Madison, PA, where he also operated a company store. In 1900 he married Ada Shumaker of Madison, where his football reputation helped him as a stern and effective disciplinarian in a tough mining town. They had eight children, Merle, Martha, Louise, Lurene, Dwight, Ruth, Elizabeth, and Don. A few years later, Fiscus and his wife moved to the nearby developing railroad town of Youngwood, PA. He operated stores there, and served as a highly respected police chief from 1928 to 1945. The town's youngsters, including George Blanda,* admired the "chief." Fiscus, who never sought recognition for his pioneer status as a paid football player, was inducted into the Westmoreland County Sports Hall of Fame.

BIBLIOGRAPHY: William E. Delserone, *Our Town: 75th Anniversary History of Youngwood, PA* (Youngwood, PA, 1973); Elizabeth Fiscus Gates and Don Fiscus, Interviews with Robert B. Van Atta, 1983–1985; Robert B. Van Atta, *The History of Professional Football at Greensburg, PA, 1894–1900* (Greensburg, PA, 1982); Robert B. Van Atta, "Pioneers in Pro Football," *Indiana County Heritage* (Winter, 1979–1980).

Robert B. Van Atta

FISH, Hamilton (b. 7 December 1888, Garrison, NY), college athlete, is the son of Hamilton F. Fish, U.S. representative and speaker of the New York Assembly. After attending St. Marks School, he entered Harvard University (IL) in 1906 and played tackle on the 1907–1909 football teams. Fish was selected by Walter Camp* to the 1908 and 1909 All-American teams. The 6 foot, 4 inch, 190 pounder excelled on defense and often broke through the opposing line. During his sophomore year he did not always prove effective. "I would break through very fast," Fish remembered, "and half the time I would get him [the ballcarrier] and half the time I wouldn't." Fish then learned from a Yale coach that he should penetrate only for about one yard. "Instead of going straight through," he recalled, "I got behind the line and then could move either way—in or outside end and nobody got by me."

In the early years of the forward pass, Fish was used as a pass receiver on offense by Harvard coach Percy Haughton.* The tall, fast Fish excelled on plays in which the tackle became eligible to catch passes. Fish considered catching passes the most dangerous part of his football career because the receiver could be tackled before reaching the ball. In a 1909 game with the U.S. Military Academy, Army team captain Eugene Byrne was killed. Byrne had run at Fish's side of the line on several plays and was exhausted. When Byrne was fatally injured, Fish had shifted to the weak side of the line and was not involved in the tackle. The game was suspended, with team captain Fish representing Harvard at the funeral.

At Harvard, Fish also played basketball and soccer and graduated cum laude in 1910. Fish studied law while teaching at Harvard during the 1910–1911 academic year. During World War I he served as an officer of the 369th Infantry, a black unit, and participated in the Battle of Champagne. He served as a Progressive in the N.Y. State Assembly from 1914 to 1916 and as a Republican in the U.S. House of Representatives from 1919 to 1945. In the election of 1940 President Franklin D. Roosevelt criticized him in the "Martin, Barton and Fish" speech. In 1921 he married Grace Chapin, daughter of a former Brooklyn mayor and has two children. A resident of New York City, Fish subsequently authored works and was engaged in the development business. Walter Camp* named him to his All-Time All-American football team.

BIBLIOGRAPHY: Morris A. Bealle, *The History of Football at Harvard, 1874–1948* (Washington, DC, 1948); Hamilton Fish, Interview with John S. Watterson, June 14, 1979.

John S. Watterson

FLAHERTY, Raymond "Ray" (b. 1 September 1904, Spokane, WA), college and professional player and coach, lettered four years in football at Gonzaga University and entered pro football with Los Angeles (AFL) in 1926. When the AFL failed, he played end with Red Grange's* New York Yankees (NFL) in 1927 and 1928 and the New York Giants (NFL) in 1929. Flaherty in 1930 coached football at Gonzaga University, compiling a 2–7–0 mark. After returning to the New York Giants in 1931, the 6 foot, 195 pound redhead enjoyed his best playing years and made the 1932 Official All-NFL team. New York coach Steve Owen* in 1933 made Flaherty his assistant and also a team captain through 1935. All three seasons, the Giants won Eastern Division crowns. The 1934 team won the NFL championship game, after Flaherty suggested they switch to basketball shoes for the second half on an ice-covered field. The better traction allowed New York to stage a rally from a 10–3 deficit and win convincingly 30–13. From 1932 to 1934 he caught 40 passes for 617 yards (15.4-yard average) and 6 touchdowns.

Boston Redskins (NFL) owner George Preston Marshall* hired Flaherty as head coach in 1936. In his initial season Flaherty led Boston to the Eastern

Division title. The Redskins moved in 1937 to Washington, DC, where they won the NFL championship with rookie quarterback Sammy Baugh.* In the championship game victory, the innovative Flaherty first used the modern screen pass. By 1939 Flaherty reportedly made $10,000, making him about the highest paid pro football coach. His Redskins won another Eastern Division title in 1940 and a second NFL championship in 1942.

He entered the U.S. Navy after the 1942 season and served there until the end of World War II. Flaherty in 1946 became head coach of the New York Yankees, becoming the new AAFC's first name pro coach. The Yankees captured Eastern Division titles his first two years, but injuries decimated the 1948 squad and Flaherty left before the season ended. In 1949 he coached the AAFC Chicago Hornets, which had won only two games in two years. Flaherty's 4–8–0 record represented significant improvement, but the Hornets were the only pro team he coached at least a full season to show a losing mark. In over ten pro coaching seasons, Flaherty's single-wing clubs compiled an 80–37–5 record. Flaherty and his wife Jackie have one son. After leaving pro football, Flaherty entered business in Spokane, WA, and has been semi-retired since 1964. In 1976 he was named to the Pro Football Hall of Fame.

BIBLIOGRAPHY: Sue English, "Flaherty Joins Hall of Fame," *Pro!*, Boston-Seattle Football Game Program, August 7, 1976; Ray Flaherty file, Pro Football Hall of Fame, Canton, OH; "Hall of Fame," *Pro!*, Pittsburgh-Cincinnati Football Game Program, October 17, 1976; "Ray Flaherty," *Pro!*, Denver-Chicago Football Game Program, July 31, 1976.

Robert N. Carroll

FLORES, Thomas Raymond (b. 21 March 1937, Fresno, CA), college and professional player and coach, was the first quarterback for the Oakland–Los Angeles Raiders (AFL-NFL) franchise and has ranked among the most successful NFL coaches since Raiders owner Al Davis* named him to succeed John Madden* in 1979. The son of Thomas and Nellie Flores, Mexican-American farm workers, he picked fruit through elementary and junior high school. After graduation from Sanger High School, he attended Fresno City College and earned his B.A. in Education from the University of the Pacific in 1958. After being released by the Calgary Stampeders (CFL) in 1958, Flores joined the Washington Redskins (NFL) in 1959 and signed as a free agent in 1960 with the Oakland Raiders of the newly formed AFL. He quarterbacked the Raiders through six seasons, completing 48.9 percent of his 1,715 passes for 11,635 yards and 92 touchdowns. On December 22, 1963, he enjoyed his greatest single performance by throwing six touchdown passes. Flores was traded with offensive end Art Powell* to the Buffalo Bills (AFL) for quarterback Daryle Lamonica in 1967 and finished his ten-year pro playing career with the Kansas City Chiefs (AFL) in 1969.

Flores' coaching career began in 1959 with the University of the Pacific freshman squad and included a year (1971) as assistant coach at Buffalo before Davis named him Madden's assistant with the Raiders in 1972. After seven years and one Super Bowl victory over the Minnesota Vikings (1977), Madden resigned following the 1978 season. In his 1979 debut as head coach, Flores posted a 9–7 mark. When the Raiders started 1980 with three losses in five games, rumors of dissatisfaction abounded. After popular quarterback Kenny Stabler* had been traded to the Houston Oilers (AFL) for Dan Pastorini, the latter suffered an early injury. Flores turned to veteran quarterback Jim Plunkett,* former San Francisco 49er (NFL) who had ridden the bench two years with Oakland. With Plunkett taking charge, the Raiders rallied for an 11–5 record, defeated Houston 27–7 and the Cleveland Browns 14–12 in the playoffs, and then bested the San Diego Chargers 34–27 in the AFC championship game. As underdogs against the Philadelphia Eagles in Super Bowl XV, the Raiders prevailed 27–10 to give Flores a title in his second year as head coach. After experiencing his only losing season (7–9) in 1981, he guided the Raiders to an 8–1 mark in the strike-shortened 1982 season and a 27–10 victory over Cleveland before losing 17–14 to the New York Jets in the playoffs. After a 12–4 regular-season record in 1983, the Raiders swept through the Pittsburgh Steelers (38–10) and Seattle Seahawks (30–14) and scored the most decisive Super Bowl win ever (38–9) over the Washington Redskins. In 1985 Flores guided the Raiders to a 12–4 mark and first-place finish in the Western Division of the AFC. The Raiders finished in fourth place in the AFC Western Division with an 8–8–0 mark in 1986 and missed the playoffs for the first time since 1981. After Flores' eight full seasons of head coaching, his record with the Raiders stands at 78–43 in the regular season and 8–3 in playoff and Super Bowl competition. A calm, familiar sideline figure on television, he epitomizes the stability and intelligent management that have made the Raiders franchise among the most successful in postwar pro sport.

BIBLIOGRAPHY: Los Angeles Raiders, Department of Sports Publicity, Los Angeles, CA; Lou Sahadi, *The Raiders: Cinderella Champions of Pro Football* (New York, 1981).

Leonard Frey

FLUTIE, Douglas Richard "Doug" (b. 23 October 1962, Manchester, MD), college and professional player, is the second of four children of Richard and Joan Flutie. His father works as a computer engineer, while his mother is a deli employee. He married secretary Laurie Fortier in 1985. Flutie grew up in Melbourne Beach, FL, where he played safety for the South Beaches Clubs. When he was in the eighth grade, his family moved to Natick, MA. He graduated from Natick High School in 1981 and was a student athlete. Although Flutie lettered in three sports, he was not considered a good college football prospect. The 5 foot, 9 3/4 inch, 173 pounder was termed too short and small to play quarterback in college.

Largely due to Flutie's small frame, no major college showed any interest in recruiting him. He planned to attend the University of New Hampshire when Boston College offered him their last athletic scholarship in 1981. Since Boston College could not get the two quarterbacks they were trying to recruit, new head football coach Jack Bicknell recruited him. Some Eagles' critics, however, viewed Flutie as a candidate for the defensive backfield rather than quarterback. Since Boston College was the only Division 1–A college that wanted him, Flutie accepted the scholarship offer.

During his freshman year Flutie began as the number 5 quarterback and became a starter within six weeks. He made his first college appearance in the fourth quarter in a 38–7 loss against Penn State and completed 8 of 18 passes for 135 yards, one touchdown, and one interception. Flutie played in just over one-half of the Eagles' games his freshman year, completing 105 of 192 passes for 1,652 yards and a 54.9 percent completion rate. He threw for 9 touchdowns, ninth best in the nation, and 8 interceptions. During his sophomore year Flutie played in eleven regular-season games and led Boston College to an 8–2–1 record. He completed 162 of 348 passes for 2,749 yards and a 46.6 completion percentage. Flutie threw 13 touchdown passes but tossed 20 interceptions. In a game against Penn State, he threw for 520 yards (a Boston College record) and the nation's single-game best for 1982. Flutie led the Eagles to the Tangerine Bowl (their first bowl appearance in 40 years), a 33–26 loss to Auburn. He completed 22 of 38 aerials for 299 yards, 2 touchdowns, and 2 interceptions and was named the Bowl MVP.

Flutie matured during his junior year, leading Boston College to a 9–2 record in 1983. At the Liberty Bowl, the Eagles lost 19–18 to Notre Dame. Flutie completed 17 of 36 passes for 287 yards, 3 touchdowns, and 1 interception. During the regular season Flutie completed 177 of 345 for 2,724 yards, 18 touchdowns, and 15 interceptions. He finished third in the Heisman Trophy balloting for that year's outstanding college player.

Flutie's best campaign came his senior year in 1984, when Boston College finished the regular season with a 9–2 record. He completed 233 of 386 passes for 3,454 yards, 27 touchdowns, and 11 interceptions and led the Eagles to a 45–28 victory over Houston in the Cotton Bowl, completing 13 of 37 passes for 180 yards and 2 touchdowns. In 1984 he broke single-season Boston College records for the most passes attempted and completed, total passing yards, and most touchdown passes. He was named *TSN* College Football Player of the Year and to *TSN* 1984 All-American Team. He received a prestigious NFF and Hall of Fame Scholar-Athlete grant for postgraduate study. Flutie, the most prolific passer in major college football history, won the coveted Heisman Trophy signifying the nation's best college player. A runaway winner, he secured 678 first-place votes of the 1,050 panelists from all phases of the sports media. Not since 1971 had a quarterback won this award.

His collegiate career statistics, excluding the Bowl games, included 677 completions in 1,271 attempts for 10,579 yards, 67 touchdowns, and 54 interceptions. He holds Eagle career records for most passes attempted and completed, passing yardage, and touchdown passes. His 10,579 yards passing broke an NCAA record. The Flutie era at Boston College included many last-minute game heroics, the most memorable being the last-second pass of 48 yards to give Boston College a 47–45 come-from-behind-victory over defending national champion Miami on November 23, 1984. Flutie's scrambling ability gave opponents a hard time in defending against him. He often took chances and secured several victories in the fourth quarters.

Like former Heisman Trophy winners Herschel Walker* and Mike Rozier,* Flutie signed a pro contract in the USFL, with the New Jersey Generals. The 50-page contract, reportedly worth $7 million for a five-year period, made him the highest paid pro football player and rookie in any sport. It covered everything from injuries to a possible merger between the USFL and the NFL. During his rookie season, Flutie completed 134 of 281 passes (48 percent) for 3,109 yards and 13 touchdowns and placed eleventh in USFL quarterback rankings. The Generals utilized Flutie's quickness and ability on rollout and bootleg plays to open up opportunities for running back Herschel Walker, who set the pro single-season rushing record. The USFL suspended its operations for the fall 1986 season while seeking a new trial in its suit against the NFL for damages or injunctive relief from the courts. The Los Angeles Rams held NFL draft rights to Flutie, but traded him in mid-season of 1986 to the Chicago Bears for an undisclosed draft choice. Flutie completed 23 of 46 passes for 361 yards in 1986 for the Bears and quarterbacked for the injured Jim McMahon* in the 27–13 NFC playoff loss to the Washington Redskins. Flutie, considered by most observers a smart, quick, optimistic, and decent individual, is a modest young man, does not drink or smoke, and is friendly and polite.

BIBLIOGRAPHY: Paul Attner, "Little Big Man," *TSN* 198 (November 12, 1984), pp. 2–3; Tom Callahan, "The Little Trophy Comes to Life," *Time* 124 (December 3, 1984), p. 71; Douglas Looney, "A Little Man on Campus," *SI* 59 (September 26, 1983), pp. 38–45; Cable Neuhaus, "Don't Sell Doug Flutie Short," *People Weekly* 22 (October 15, 1984), pp. 46–47; Ralph Wiley, "A Pocketful of Dreams," *SI* 62 (February 25, 1985), pp. 24–41; Steve Wulf, "Mr. Touchdown Scores Again," *SI* 62 (February 4, 1985), pp. 20–27.

Kant Patel

FOLLIS, Charles W. "The Black Cyclone" (b. 1879, VA; d. 1919, Cleveland, OH), professional athlete, became football's first black pro when he signed to play for the Shelby (OH) Athletic Club under manager Frank Schiffer in 1904. Many historians have, however, indicated Charles "Doc"

Baker of the Akron (OH) Indians (1906–1908) or Henry McDonald of Rochester (NY) in 1911 as the first black pro. Follis spent most of his life in Wooster, Shelby, and Cleveland (OH) and worked with his father, a farm laborer. The 6 foot, 200 pound Follis was the biggest of three brothers (including Curt and Joseph), who sang as a musical group. Follis played baseball three years with the Cuban Giants and graduated from Wooster High School in 1901. His football career began at Wooster High School (1899–1900), where he captained the team at right halfback and continued with the Wooster Athletic Association in 1901.

Follis, employed by Schiffer in a hardware store, played in 1902 and 1903 for the Shelby AC. His teammate Branch Rickey* (BB) later coached against him and broke major league baseball's color line by signing Jackie Robinson* (BB). In 1903 Follis enjoyed one of his best performances by running 20, 25, 25, and 70 yards against Rickey's Ohio Wesleyan collegians. Follis signed a contract on September 15, 1904, with the Shelby AC and ran 83 yards for a touchdown in his first pro game eight days later in a 29–0 victory over Marion, OH. In ten games Shelby scored 317 points and surrendered only 28 points in their lone loss to Massillon, OH. In 1906 Schiffer converted Shelby from an "amateur" to a pro team called the Blues. Since Follis was a black star, he was targeted by the opposition. Opponents tried to make sure he did not play the entire game. Frequent injuries and personal abuse eventually sidelined Follis. On Thanksgiving Day, 1906, he was helped off the field with another injury in his last-known football appearance.

Although appreciated by his teammates and loyal fans, Follis did not enjoy unanimous acceptance. He frequently kept alone, sometimes by choice but more often because of societal pressures. Despite his trials, he did not withdraw nor lash out in the eight years he was playing football. Follis died suddenly in the Great Flu Epidemic of 1919 and was buried in Wooster, OH. Although not appearing among the great black pro performers, he became one of the day's best runners and the first black pro football player.

BIBLIOGRAPHY: Milton R. Roberts and John Seaburn, with Dean Charles, "The First Black Pro" (1975), pp. 3D–6D; John Seaburn, "The First . . . at last," *Beacon Magazine* (March 2, 1975); Wooster (OH) *Daily Record*, September 17, 1965.

John L. Evers and Milton R. Roberts

FORD, Leonard Guy, Jr. "Len" (b. 18 February 1926, Washington, DC; d. 14 March 1972, Detroit, MI), college athlete and professional football player, was the son of federal employee Leonard Guy Ford, Sr. He began playing football at Armstrong High School in the nation's capitol, making All-City in 1942 and 1943. He enrolled at Morgan State University (CIAA) in February 1944, and became a regular on the school's championship basketball team his first day there. After achieving All-CIAA honors in football and success in baseball his first year there, he entered the U.S. Navy. Upon his discharge in 1945, he transferred to the University of Michigan (BTC). He earned All-American football honors at end in 1946 and 1947 and starred on the Wolverines' victorious Rose Bowl team his final season.

Ford signed with the Los Angeles Dons (AAFC), playing both offense and defense in 1948 and 1949. His great size and strength at 6 foot, 4 inches, and 240 pounds made him very formidable on defense. He also possessed outstanding speed and excellent hands for a gigantic figure, catching 67 passes in two years with the Dons. When the AAFC merged into the NFL in 1950, the Dons disbanded and players were placed in a special draft pool. Ford was picked by the Cleveland Browns, who used him exclusively on defense. In a game midway through the 1950 season, he suffered serious facial injuries that jeopardized his career. By wearing a special helmet, however, he played in the Browns' victorious championship game at the end of the season.

Ford became a key member of a Browns' defensive unit, which allowed the fewest NFL points six times and finished second twice from 1950 to 1957. He was named All-Pro by the AP and UPI from 1951 through 1954 and again by UPI in 1955. Ford, whose forte was rushing the passer, played in the Pro Bowl from 1952 through 1955 and retired after playing his final pro season with the Green Bay Packers (NFL) in 1958. At that time, he held the NFL record for most opposition lifetime fumbles recovered with 20. For a time, Ford studied law "so I can talk to my wife," a Detroit attorney and judge. The Fords had two daughters but were divorced a few years before his death. In 1976 he was named to the Pro Football Hall of Fame.

BIBLIOGRAPHY: Len Ford file, Pro Football Hall of Fame, Canton, OH; "Hall of Fame Len Ford," *Pro!*, Cleveland Browns–Pittsburgh Steelers Football Game Program, September 19, 1976; "Len Ford," *Pro!*, Denver Broncos–Chicago Bears Football Game Program, July 31, 1976; Murray Olderman, *The Defenders* (Englewood Cliffs, NJ, 1973).

Robert N. Carroll

FOREMAN, Walter Eugene "Chuck" (b. 26 October 1950, Frederick, MD), college and pro player, is the son of laborer William and cleaning woman Janet Foreman. He graduated in 1969 from Frederick High School, where he lettered in football, basketball, and track and set Maryland State High School high and low hurdle records. Currently unmarried and with a daughter, Foreman attended the University of Miami (FL), lettered in football, and achieved a 3.2 grade point average while majoring in Business. Foreman, a defensive tackle and tight end at Frederick High, was converted to the defensive secondary at Miami. After being timed as the fastest squad member at 40 yards, however, he soon became a running back. Foreman set a Miami rushing record his junior year and was touted as a Heisman Trophy candidate his final season. As a senior, Foreman played primarily wide receiver and compiled 1,555 yards by receiving, rushing, and returning kicks.

During his Miami career, he caught 56 passes for 732 yards and rushed for 1,631 yards. Foreman enjoyed outstanding North-South Shrine and Senior Bowl games, being named MVP in both, and was selected by the Minnesota Vikings (NFL) as their top draft choice.

The shy, quiet, determined Foreman possessed an ideal temperament for the Vikings. Although rookies rarely played key roles on coach Harold "Bud" Grant's* teams, Foreman started against the Chicago Bears in the second game of the season. He gained 116 yards in 16 carries, caught four passes for 46 yards, and received the game ball. The unanimous choice as Minnesota's Rookie of the Year, he was named the AP Rookie of the Year, received the Bert Bell Memorial Trophy as the NFC Rookie of the Year, and played in the Pro Bowl. Teammate Fran Tarkenton* became Foreman's biggest booster, lauding him as the Vikings' MVP and pro football's best and most versatile offensive player. In 1974 the Miami (FL) Touchdown Club named Foreman its Pro Football Player of the Year. During a seven-year career with Minnesota, the 6 foot, 2 inch, 210 pound Foreman enjoyed 17 100-yard rushing games and set Vikings records for career pass receptions (336, since broken) and rushing yardage (5,879). In 1975 Foreman led the NFL with 73 catches and scored a record-tying 22 touchdowns. From 1975 through 1977 Foreman rushed for 1,070, 1,155, and 1,112 yards, respectively. After being injured in the fourth game of 1978, he never regained his prime form. Handicapped by injuries, Foreman in 1979 rushed for only 215 yards, caught only 19 passes, and scored but 2 touchdowns. After that season, he was traded to the New England Patriots (NFL) and finished his pro career there in 1980. In his eight NFL years, he scored 53 touchdowns rushing and 23 touchdowns as a pass receiver, ran for 5,950 yards in 1,556 carries, made 3,156 yards on 350 pass receptions, and appeared in 5 Pro Bowls. Foreman operated a chain of Nautilus centers and has an interstate trucking business.

BIBLIOGRAPHY: Minnesota Vikings, New England Patriots, NFL, and Pro Football Hall of Fame, Canton, OH, Joe Soucheray, *Sooch!* (Minneapolis, MN, 1981).

John E. DiMeglio

FORTMANN, Daniel John (b. 11 April 1916, Pearl River, NY), college and professional player, is the son of wholesale food dealer Bernhardt Gerhardt and Emma Margaret Fortmann. Fortmann married Mary Annette Van Halperen on March 19, 1938, and has two sons, Thomas Edward and Stephen Paul. An outstanding student in the Pearl River public school system, Fortmann played football at halfback, end, and guard and graduated from high school at age 16. At Colgate University from 1932 to 1936, he studied premedicine and earned Phi Beta Kappa academic honors. Although a three-year varsity performer for coach Andy Kerr's* great teams, Fortmann attained little football recognition until his senior season. At age 19, the 6 foot,

190 pound Fortmann made All-East in 1935 and played in the Shrine All-Star (East-West) game, one of the era's few post-season games.

Fortmann planned to bypass pro football for medical school but was drafted by the Chicago Bears (NFL). Coach George Halas* selected Fortmann in the ninth and final round of the first college player draft in 1936 because "Dan Fortmann sounds like a good football name." Halas persuaded Fortmann to play with the Bears while attending the University of Chicago Medical School, citing that Bears' guard Joe Kopcha had done likewise in the early 1930s. Fortmann did not become a legal adult until after playing his entire rookie pro season. He made second-team All-Pro his first two seasons (1936–1937) and first-team All-Pro the remaining six seasons of his career (1938–1943). The 60-minute lineman made devastating blocks on offense and brilliantly diagnosed plays and vigorous tackles on defense. Fortmann played on the NFL championship Bears' teams in 1940, 1941, and 1943 and the Western Division title clubs of 1937 and 1942.

Fortmann was elected to the Pro Football Hall of Fame in 1965 and NFF College Football Hall of Fame in 1978. Fortmann served many years as the Los Angeles Rams' (NFL) team physician and recently retired from active medical practice at St. Joseph's Hospital in Burbank, CA, where he was chief of staff and one of the nation's leading surgeons. He resides with his wife in Pasadena, CA.

BIBLIOGRAPHY: George Allen with Ben Olan, *Pro Football's 100 Greatest Players* (Indianapolis, IN, 1982); Howard Roberts, *The Chicago Bears* (New York, 1947); George Sullivan, *Pro Football's All-Time Greats: The Immortals in Pro Football's Hall of Fame* (New York, 1968); Alexander M. Weyand, *Football Immortals* (New York, 1962).

Jim Campbell

FORTUNATO, Joseph F. "Joe" (b. 28 March 1931, Mingo Junction, OH), college and professional player and coach, excelled in football at Mingo Junction High School. After performing one season at Virginia Military Institute (SC, 1948), Fortunato transferred to Mississippi State University (SEC) and played football three seasons (1950–1952) there. A running back on offense and a linebacker on defense, the 6 foot, 1 inch, 225 pound Fortunato in 1951 was named All-SEC and All-American. In 1952 he led the Bulldogs in rushing with 779 yards on 128 attempts for a 6.1-yard average per carry. The durable two-way performer in 1950 paced Mississippi State with three interceptions. Against North Texas State University in 1952, he rushed for a Bulldogs-record 169 yards. In three seasons Fortunato rushed 187 times for 1,000 yards and 6 touchdowns and intercepted 4 passes for 37 yards.

Selected as a future choice in the seventh round of the 1952 NFL draft by the Chicago Bears, Fortunato finished at Mississippi State in 1953 and then joined the U.S. Army for two years. He played service football at Fort

Benning, GA, averaging 6.0 yards per carry, and then reported to the Bears for the 1955 season. In his twelve-year pro career, Fortunato played 155 games, made 16 interceptions for 156 yards, scored one touchdown, and recovered 22 opponents' fumbles to tie an NFL record. His 38 takeaways remain third best in Bears history. Fortunato became a key member of the Bears' linebacking corps (1955–1966), being selected for five Pro Bowl games and a unanimous All-Pro three straight years (1963–1965). As defensive captain for the Bears in 1963, Fortunato teamed with Bill George* and Larry Morris to form a linebacking corps allowing a modern record of only 144 points in 14 games. Chicago, boasting the best NFL defense, won the WC title easily and defeated Y. A. Tittle's* New York Giants 14–10 in the championship game. After retiring as a player in 1966, Fortunato remained with the Bears as a defensive coach and then defensive coordinator.

BIBLIOGRAPHY: George Allen with Ben Olan, *Pro Football's 100 Greatest Players* (Indianapolis, IN, 1982); William W. Sorrells, *The Maroon Bulldogs: Mississippi State Football* (Huntsville, AL, 1975).

John L. Evers

FOUR HORSEMEN, college football players from 1922 through 1924, became the most publicized backs in football history because of Grantland Rice's* (OS) imaginative prose and the inventiveness of Notre Dame student publicist George Strickler. Covering the 1924 Notre Dame 13 to 7 win over Army, Rice wrote, "Outlined against a blue-gray October sky, the Four Horsemen rode again," and forever immortalized the Notre Dame backs Harry Stuhldreher, James Crowley, Don Miller, and Elmer Layden. The following day Strickler photographed them astride rented horses, creating national attention.

The Four Horsemen did not play as a unit until the ninth game of their sophomore year in 1922. Between 1922 and 1924 the backfield made first-team All-American on one or more recognized teams. Notre Dame lost only two games during that span, won the 1924 national championship, and beat Stanford 27–10 in the Rose Bowl. Each back made the NFF College Football Hall of Fame; Layden, 1951, charter member; Stuhldreher, 1958; Crowley, 1966; and Miller, 1970. Stuhldreher also made the HAF College Football Hall of Fame. Although they weighed only 151 to 162 pounds each, they demonstrated outstanding speed, timing, and versatility. Miller, Crowley, and Layden ranked fifth, sixth, and fifteenth respectively among all-time Notre Dame rushers.

CROWLEY, James H. "Sleepy Jim" (b. 10 September 1902, Chicago, IL; d. 15 January 1986, Scranton, PA), halfback, coach, and executive, grew up in Denver, CO, and Green Bay, WI. Coached by Curly Lambeau* and captained by halfback Crowley, Green Bay East High School won the 1920 state football championship. A baseball pitcher, Crowley graduated in 1921 from East High. For Notre Dame, the 5 foot, 11 inch, 162 pound Crowley averaged 6.3 yards per carry and rushed 1,841 yards in three seasons. He led Notre Dame in passing in 1922 and 1923 and scoring in 1924 with 71 points. After graduating from Notre Dame in 1925, Crowley played that year with the Green Bay Packers and Providence Steamrollers (NFL). He served as assistant football coach three years at the University of Georgia (SC) and as head football coach at Michigan State (WC) from 1929 to 1932, compiling a 22–8–3 record. From 1933 to 1941 Crowley coached Fordham University to national football status with 56 wins, 13 defeats, and 7 ties. Fordham finished undefeated and third-ranked in 1937, rated among the top twenty for six consecutive years, and played in two major bowls. Crowley coached the legendary Seven Blocks of Granite, including future Hall of Fame linemen Vincent Lombardi,* Alex Wojciechowicz,* and Edmund Franco. Crowley's .761 career coaching percentage ranks eighteenth among college football mentors nationally. In 1945 Crowley became commissioner of the new professional AAFC. Five years later he became state industrial commissioner of northeastern Pennsylvania and managed a television station in Scranton, PA. He and his wife, Helen, had one son, Patrick Joseph, and lived in Scranton.

LAYDEN, Elmer F. "Thin Man" (b. 4 May 1903, Davenport, IA; d. 30 June 1973, Chicago, IL), fullback, coach, and executive, was a 6 foot, 161 pound slashing-type runner under coach Knute Rockne.* The son of Thomas and Rosemary Layden, he had two brothers and two sisters. He attended Sacred Heart Grade School and Davenport High School, where he made All-State in both football (halfback) and basketball (guard) and ran the dashes in track. After graduating in 1921, he followed his ex-coach Walter Halas to Notre Dame. Layden scored important touchdowns on pass interceptions once each against Princeton and Northwestern and twice against Stanford. His 71-yard punt against Wabash in 1924 remains among the longest in Notre Dame history. After setting an all-time Rose Bowl scoring record with 18 points against Stanford, he was named Co-Player of the Game. Following graduation from Notre Dame in 1925, Layden played the next year with the Brooklyn Horsemen (AFL). He coached Columbia College (now Loras) in 1925–1926 to an 8–5–2 football record and Duquesne University to a seven-year 48–16–6 record, including a 33–7 post-season victory over University of Miami (FL) in the 1934 Palm Festival. In 1934 Layden became Notre Dame head football coach and athletic director. His 8–1–0 1938 team was chosen national champion by the Dickinson System, while his 7–1–1 1935 squad won a last-minute 18–13 victory over Ohio State in one of the sport's outstanding games. Layden, whose seven-year record at Notre Dame comprised 47–13–3, compiled a career 103–34–11 college mark for .733 percent. Layden served as NFL commissioner from 1941 to 1946 and as an executive with General American Transportation in Chicago until his retirement in 1968. Layden, who wrote *It Was a Different Game* (1969), married his wife, Edythe, in 1926 and had four children.

MILLER, Donald C. "Midnight" (b. 2 March 1902, Defiance, OH; d. 28 July 1979, Cleveland, OH), halfback and coach, became the only Horseman to start every game for three years at Notre Dame. The first Horseman to receive All-American acclaim, he made the 1923 INS first team. He led Notre Dame twice in rushing, three times in pass receiving, and once in scoring. Miller's 6.8-yard career average per carry ranks best in Notre Dame history, while his 74.3-yard rushing average per game ranks third. Coach Rockne once called Miller "the greatest open field runner I ever coached." The 5 foot, 11 inch, 160 pound Miller played halfback four years and basketball center three years at Defiance High School before graduating in 1921. The son of Martin Harold and Anne (Riley) Miller, he was the youngest of five brothers to play football at Notre Dame. Miller, who also played basketball center and served as senior class president at Notre Dame, joined Crowley in 1925 with the Providence Steamrollers (NFL). He held the backfield coach post at Georgia Tech (SC) from 1925 to 1928 and at Ohio State (WC) from 1929 to 1932. After moving to Cleveland, OH, to pursue law, Miller served as national president of the U.S. Attorney's Association, U.S. attorney for the Northern Ohio District from 1941 to 1953, and judge and referee in Cleveland District Bankruptcy Court from 1965 to retirement in 1977. A U.S. district judge once said to him, "With all your legendary fame and national prominence, you still conduct yourself and your court with genuine humility, dignity and grace." The Millers had one son and four daughters.

STUHLDREHER, Harry A. "Stuly" (b. 14 October 1901, Massillon, OH; d. 26 January 1965, Pittsburgh, PA), quarterback, coach, and executive, was the son of William and Flora (Witt) Stuhldreher and proved a superior blocker at 5 feet, 7 inches, and 150 pounds, passed frequently, and returned punts. Touchdowns were scored in 1923 on his 40-yard pass to Layden against Army and 65-yard punt return against Butler, and in 1924 on his 75- and 50-yard passes to Crowley and Miller against Nebraska and a 40-yard pass interception return against Northwestern. At Massillon (OH) High School, Stuhldreher lettered as a football halfback, basketball forward, and track hurdler and graduated in 1920. After being a three-sport star the following year at Kiski (PA) Prep School, he in 1921 followed his brother Walter to Notre Dame. After graduating from Notre Dame in 1925, Stuhldreher the next year played with the NFL Brooklyn Dodgers. He coached football at Villanova (PA), attaining a 65–25–9 overall record and an undefeated season in 1928. In 1936 he became head football coach and athletic director at the University of Wisconsin (WC). He coached through 1948 with a 45–62–6 composite record and remained athletic director until 1950. His 1942 Badgers finished 8–1–1, defeated highly rated Ohio State, tied Notre Dame, and was named national champion by HAF. Stuhldreher became assistant to the president of the U.S. Steel Corporation in 1951. He and his wife, Mary, had four sons, Harry, Jr., Michael, John, and Peter. In 1931 Harry authored *Knute Rockne, Man Builder;* his wife Mary wrote *Many a Saturday Afternoon* (1964) and became dean of women at Duquesne University in Pittsburgh, PA.

BIBLIOGRAPHY: L. H. Baker, *Football: Facts and Figures* (New York, 1945); Richard M. Cohen, Jordan A. Deutsch, and David S. Neft, *The Notre Dame Football Scrapbook* (Indianapolis, IN, 1977); Ralph Hickok, *Who Was Who in American Sports* (New York, 1971); Oliver E. Kuechle with Jim Mott, *On Wisconsin!: Badger Football* (Huntsville, AL, 1977); Ronald L. Mendell and Timothy B. Phares, *Who's Who in Football* (New Rochelle, NY, 1974); *Notre Dame Football Guide, 1983;* Notre Dame–Georgia Tech Football Game Program, October 27, 1923; Notre Dame–Stanford Rose Bowl Football Game Program, January 1, 1925; Michael J. O'Donnell, *Villanova Football: A Statistical History* (Villanova, PA, 1964); *75 Years of Notre Dame All-Americans* (Fairborn, OH, 1982); *Spalding's Official Intercollegiate Football Guides, 1923–1925.*

James D. Whalen

FOUTS, Daniel Francis "Dan" (b. 10 June 1951, San Francisco, CA), college and professional player, is the son of sports broadcaster Bob and Julie Fouts. He attended St. Ignatius Prep School and the University of Oregon, where he earned a in Political Science in 1973. After becoming starting quarterback for Oregon (PEC) in 1970, he passed for 2,333 yards and guided the Ducks to a 4–7 record. In his last two years, Oregon finished with 5–6 and 6–4–1 records in the formidable PEC. During his Oregon career, Fouts broke nineteen school records and finished seventh on the NCAA's then all-time passing list and eleventh in total offense. The San Diego Chargers selected Fouts in the third round of the 1973 NFL draft.

Late in his rookie season with the Chargers, he replaced the aging Johnny Unitas* as starting quarterback. Although Fouts completed 87 of 194 passes for 1,126 yards and 6 touchdowns, San Diego finished with a dismal 2–11–1 record and placed last in the AFC Western Division. In 1974 he started at quarterback for the Chargers until being injured later in the season. The Chargers again finished last but with an improved 5–9 record, as Fouts passed for 1,732 yards. He continued as starting quarterback, although others doubted his ability to guide a successful team because the Chargers won only 2 of 14 games in 1975 and 6 of 14 contests in 1976.

In 1977 he refused to play and lost his starting position to former Los Angeles Rams quarterback Jamie Harris. Fouts took the Chargers to court over his contract terms but lost his case. After Harris was injured, Fouts returned to the starting lineup and passed for 199 and 237 yards in late season wins over the Seattle Seahawks and Cleveland Browns. When Don Coryell* replaced Tommy Prothro as Charger head coach during the 1978 season,

Fouts responded well. The Chargers won seven of their last eight games, as Fouts ranked third in passing efficiency. During their last three games, the Chargers averaged 41 points in victories over Chicago, Seattle, and Houston.

By 1979 the Chargers receiver corps included Kellen Winslow,* John Jefferson,* and Charlie Joiner.* With these excellent receivers, Fouts broke Joe Namath's* then single-season record with 4,082 passing yards. He led AFC quarterbacks with 82.6 rating points and guided the Chargers to the division title with a 12–4 record. In the playoffs the Chargers lost to the Houston Oilers. The following season, he broke his season passing record with 4,715 yards and helped the Chargers reach the AFC title game. In 1981 he broke his record again (since broken) with 4,802 yards, guiding the Chargers to their third consecutive division title. In 1983 Fouts signed a long-term contract with the club and completed 215 of 384 passes (63.2 percent) for 2,975 yards and 20 touchdowns. In 1984 he completed 317 of 507 passes (62.5 percent) for 3,740 yards and 19 touchdowns. The next year, he completed 254 of 430 aerials for 3,638 yards and threw 27 touchdown passes and 20 interceptions. His 1986 campaign included 252 completions in 430 attempts for 3,031 yards, 16 touchdowns and 22 interceptions. During the 1986 season he became the third player to record 40,000 yards in career passing and moved into second place ahead of Johnny Unitas on the NFL's all-time passing yardage list.

The bearded Fouts is characterized by his stocky build and shuffling style. With his superb passing, the Chargers triumphed over opponents in high scoring contests. In one of the NFL's classic games, the Chargers defeated the Miami Dolphins 41–38 in the 1981 playoffs. Besides being NFL Player of the Year in 1979 and 1982, he played in the Pro Bowl from 1979 through 1983 and in 1985. In 14 NFL seasons through 1986, Fouts has completed 3,091 of 4,240 passes for 40,523 yards and thrown 243 touchdown aerials and 227 interceptions. Fouts and his wife, Julie, have two children, Dominick and Suzanne. During the off-season he enjoys the country life at his rural Oregon home.

BIBLIOGRAPHY: Bob Fouts, "My Son Dan," *Gameday Magazine* (December 2, 1982), pp. 7D–9D; Earl Gustkey, "Air Coryell's Pilot Is Strictly Down to Earth," *Pro!* 2 (September, 1982) pp. 63–73; *Street & Smith College Football Yearbooks 1971–1973; Street & Smith Pro Football Yearbooks 1974–1985; TSN Football Register—1985.*

Keith Hobson

FRANK, Clinton Edward "Clint" (b. 13 September 1915, St. Louis, MO), college player, was a Yale University All-American tailback whose heroics rivaled those of fictional athlete Frank Merriwell. Frank, the nation's best college football player in 1937, won the Heisman Trophy and the Maxwell Award. When college football celebrated its centennial in 1969, he was named to the All-Decade backfield of the 1930s. His parents, baseball player Arthura

A. and Daisy Marian Frank, moved from St. Louis to Evanston, IL, where Clinton starred in high school football, basketball, and baseball and was elected senior class president. He attended Lawrenceville School (NJ) in 1933 and then entered Yale in 1934. A 5 foot, 10 inch, 175 pound sophomore, Frank started in the backfield and helped Yale (IL) compile a 6–3 record in 1935. He gained All-American honors in 1936 and 1937 and played his greatest games against formidable Princeton. Frank received numerous plaudits; the following is typical: "One of the greatest backs who ever carried the ball. Runs with the speed and power of a wild buffalo in mad flight. He's a sure-shot passer, at either long or short range. His defensive play was brilliant, his blocking outstanding. As shrewd and resourceful a field general as you'll find from coast to coast. He lifts the team by sheer personality."

In the first game his junior year, he set up all three touchdowns and a field goal in Yale's 23–0 win over Cornell. He passed for the lone tally on fourth down and intercepted two passes to help the Bulldogs upset Pennsylvania 7–0. Despite a broken finger, he scored both touchdowns in Yale's 12–6 conquest of Navy. Heavily favored Princeton jumped off to a 16–0 lead, but Frank spearheaded a comeback by plunging for a one-yard touchdown at the end of the first half. Lewis Burton of the New York *American* wrote, "Frank became a crazy, unfathomable devil doll late in the second period and from then on Princeton's fate was sealed." The Bulldogs surged ahead 20–16 in the third quarter, as Frank tossed a 60-yard scoring pass. After Princeton regained the lead, Frank hurled a 50-yard aerial to launch Yale on an 81-yard winning touchdown drive. He completed two more passes en route and ran the final 13 yards to climax the most exciting triumph in Yale football history. Frank completed six of seven passes in the second half, returned kickoffs 43 and 40 yards, and made two sensational goal-line tackles. The Bulldogs completed a 7–1 campaign the following week by edging Harvard 14–13. Frank ran 44 yards to set up the first touchdown and fired a 41-yard pass for the second score to put Yale ahead 14–0 at halftime. Harvard rallied after intermission, but Frank made two saving interceptions and ran out the clock.

Frank, elected captain, enjoyed an even more spectacular season in 1937. In victories over Maine, Penn, Army, and Cornell, he directly accounted for seven touchdowns, with scampers of 68 and 61 yards, and made a 78-yard aerial. The Bulldogs avenged their only loss of the previous year by tying Dartmouth 9–9. Dartmouth outplayed Yale, but Frank hurled a 35-yard touchdown pass on fourth down with three seconds remaining to produce bedlam at the Yale Bowl. He scored all three touchdowns in the 19–0 defeat of Brown. In the rain and mud against Princeton, Frank scored four touchdowns on runs of 79, 51, 5, and 4 yards, and gained 191 yards in 19 carries. Yale did not pass in the 26–0 rout of the Tigers. Frank tallied the lone Bulldogs touchdown in his farewell performance against Harvard, but the Crimson ruined Yale's unbeaten season, 13–6. Alan Gould of the AP commented, "Only the defensive prowess of Yale's captain Frank kept Harvard from running up a bigger score. A hero in defeat as he ended his All-American career, Frank twice broke up potential scoring plays when Harvard was running wild through a sagging Eli line."

Frank bypassed professional football and joined a Chicago advertising firm after graduation. A lieutenant colonel in the U.S. Army Air Force during World War II, he saw active duty in Africa, Italy, and England and aided General Jimmy Doolittle. Frank, who founded a successful Chicago-based advertising agency in 1954, chairs Bridlewood Corporation and is honorary chairman of the agency bearing his name. Although retired from the advertising business, he engages in various investment, charitable, and civic activities. Frank married Frances Calhoun Price in 1941 and has five children, Clinton, Jr., Marcia, Laurie Anne, Cynthia, and Arthur III. In 1967 he married Margaret Rathje Mullins, who also had five children by a previous marriage. Frank was inducted into the NFF College Football Hall of Fame in 1955 and into the HAF College Football Hall of Fame.

BIBLIOGRAPHY: Lewis Burton, "Yale Rallies to Down Princeton," New York *American* (November 15, 1936); Clinton Frank to Bernie McCarty, July 24, 1984; Alan Gould (AP), "Harvard Stuns Yale," Buffalo (NY) *Courier and Express* (November 20, 1937); Wilton Hazzard and George Trevor, *Illustrated Football Annual, 1937;* Dan Jenkins, "The First 100 Years," *SI* 22 (September 15, 1969), pp. 46–53; Robert F. Kelley, "Yale Routs Princeton," *NYT* (November 14, 1937); John D. McCallum, *Ivy League Football Since 1872* (New York, 1977); John D. McCallum and Charles H. Pearson, *College Football U.S.A., 1869–1973* (New York, 1973).

Bernie McCarty

FRIEDMAN, Benjamin "Benny" (b. 18 March 1905, Cleveland, OH; d. 24 November 1982, New York, NY), college athlete, professional football player and coach, and administrator, excelled at quarterback for the University of Michigan (WC, 1924–1926) and teamed with end Bennie Oosterbaan* to form one of the finest passing combinations in college gridiron history. Friedman made 1925–1926 consensus All-American, being Wolverines captain and WC MVP the latter year. He led the Wolverines to consecutive WC championships (one shared) with 7–1–0 records and second- and third-place national ratings by the Frank G. Dickinson System. Friedman, a member of Michigan Sports and HAF College Football Halls of Fame, was elected in 1951 a charter member of the NFF College Football Hall of Fame. He was named to Bill Edwards' All-Time All-American Team (1930 *Illustrated Football Annual*), George Trevor's All-Time Midwest Team (1949), and the Mid-Century University of Michigan squad (1950). A seven-year NFL veteran and four-time (1927–1930) All-Pro selection, Friedman was named to the All-Time NFL Team (1947 *Pro Football Illustrated*) and the Twenties Decade All-Pro Team (1973 *Pro Football Digest*).

Friedman's father Louis worked as a furrier and tailor in Cleveland, OH. "Benny" graduated in 1923 from Glenville High School, where he starred in football, basketball, and baseball. Glenville in 1922 won the Cleveland City football championship and defeated Chicago (IL) Oak Park High School in a post-season game of national championship significance. The 5 foot, 8 inch, 172 pound Friedman entered Michigan (WC) in 1923 and starred on the Wolverines freshman team. As a sophomore he became discouraged when he failed to start the first three varsity games under interim coach George E. Little and almost transferred to Dartmouth. Athletic director Fielding H. Yost* persuaded Little to start Friedman to put more passing into the offense, a move that paid handsome dividends. Michigan won the next four games convincingly by outscoring the opposition 77–6. Friedman completed touchdown pass plays of 62 and 35 yards in triumphs over Wisconsin and Minnesota, but nationally sixth-ranked Iowa upset the Wolverines 9–2 in the season's finale.

"The best team I ever coached was the Michigan team of 1925," Yost later told H. G. Salsinger of the Detroit *News*. The Wolverines were rated by Yost ahead of his "point-a-minute" 1901–1905 squads and outscored their opponents 227–3. Friedman passed for 760 yards and 14 touchdowns (mostly to sophomore Oosterbaan) and scored 52 points with 4 touchdowns, 2 field goals, and 22 extra points. Other Michigan stars included center captain Bob Brown, tackle Tom Edwards, guard Ray Baer, halfback Lou Gilbert, and fullback John "Bo" Molenda. Michigan was upset 3–2 by star-studded Northwestern in a driving rain-sleet storm and 55-mph gale at Chicago's Soldier Field. A punting duel ensued, as both teams played for breaks, attempted only one forward pass, and made one first down between them.

Friedman, an intelligent quarterback, threw a soft pass and exploited defensive weaknesses. The confident, outspoken Friedman never was injured and hated to lose. His outstanding performances and the successful 1925–1926 teams generated tremendous interest to build the mammoth Michigan stadium. Yost once stated, "In Benny Friedman I have one of the greatest passers and smartest quarterbacks in history. He never makes a mistake, and as for football brains, it's like having a coach on the field." Michigan won all its WC games in 1926 but dropped a 10–0 decision to undefeated national co-champion Navy before 80,000 spectators in Baltimore. Friedman completed several key touchdown passes to Oosterbaan during the season, highlighted by his performance in a 17–16 come-from-behind thriller at eighth-rated Ohio State before 90,411 witnesses.

Friedman, who majored in Literature, Science, and Arts, lettered in baseball his junior year and graduated from the University of Michigan in 1927. He played that fall with the 8–4–1 Cleveland Bulldogs (NFL) and in 1928 organized the Detroit Wolverines (NFL), who finished 7–2–1 and lasted only one season due to financial difficulties. He led the New York Giants (NFL) to two second-place finishes the next three years and a composite 31–11–2 record, largely keeping the New York franchise afloat during financially lean years. Friedman played his last two seasons with the Brooklyn Dodgers (NFL), who compiled a combined 8–13–1 record. He led the NFL four consecutive years (1927–1930) in scoring and touchdown passes and twice in extra points. Friedman finished with 70 career touchdown passes and scored 179 points.

Friedman served as part-time backfield football coach at Yale University (IL, 1931–1933) and head football coach (1934–1941) at City College of New York, where his charges compiled a 27–31–1 overall record. He was athletic director at Brandeis University (Waltham, MA) from 1949 to 1963, initiating the college sports program there, and served as the Judges' head football coach from 1951 to 1959. The Brandeis gridders made a composite 34–32–4 mark before the school discontinued the sport in 1960. Friedman in 1964 opened for boys in Oxford, ME, a thriving summer camp, which included the Kamp Kohut Football School for aspiring quarterbacks. Friedman stayed in top physical condition by demonstrating football techniques, exercising, and water skiing. In 1980 a blood clot formed in his left leg, which had to be amputated. He developed a heart condition and became despondent over ill health. Friedman was found in his East Side (NYC) apartment dead of a self-inflicted wound; he was survived by his wife, Shirley, one brother, and one sister.

BIBLIOGRAPHY: "Camp for Quarterbacks," *Sport* 40 (October, 1965), pp. 50–53; Robert N. Carroll to James D. Whalen, 1986; Michigan-Illinois Football Game Program, October 24, 1925; Will Perry, *The Wolverines: A Story of Michigan Football* (Huntsville, AL, 1980); Roger Treat, ed., *The Encyclopedia of Football*, 16th rev. ed., rev. by Pete Palmer (New York, 1979); University of Michigan, Alumni Records Office, Ann Arbor, MI (February 20, 1986).

James D. Whalen

FRYAR, Irving Dale (b. 28 September 1962, Mount Holly, NJ), college and professional player, graduated from Rancocas Valley Regional High School in Mount Holly and then attended the University of Nebraska (BEC) from 1980 through 1984. A wide receiver and punt-returning specialist, Fryar in 1983 was selected an All-BEC member and wide receiver on *TSN* College All-American Team. After ranking fourth nationally in punt returns as a sophomore in 1981, he finished third the following year. In Fryar's three varsity seasons, Nebraska posted a 33–5–0 overall record with three Orange Bowl appearances. In the 1984 national championship game, the Cornhuskers lost 31–30 to the University of Miami in the Orange Bowl.

The 6 foot, 200 pound Fryar was chosen by the Chicago Blitz in the first round (third player selected) of the 1984 USFL draft and by New England in the first round (first player selected) of the 1984 NFL draft. He was signed by the Patriots on April 11, 1984. In his first pro season, Fryar caught 11 passes for 164 yards and 1 touchdown and returned 36 punts for 347 yards (9.6-yard average). Fryar in 1985 led the NFL in punt returns with a 14.1-yard average. He returned 37 punts for 520 yards and 2 touchdowns, including an 85 yarder. His 2 punt-return touchdowns set a club record. Fryar, New England's third highest receiver, caught 39 passes for 670 yards (17.2-yard average) and made a 56-yard reception. He finished as the Patriots' second highest scorer with 60 points, including catching 7 touchdown passes.

New England, a wild card representative in the 1985 NFL playoffs, defeated the New York Jets and Los Angeles Raiders to reach the AFC championship game. Prior to the game, Fryar cut his right hand in a reported domestic argument with his pregnant wife, Jacqueline. He could not play in the Patriots' 31–14 triumph over the Miami Dolphins but participated in Super Bowl XX against the Chicago Bears. Although Fryar caught a touchdown pass, New England could not penetrate the Bears' vaunted "46" defense and suffered a 46–10 loss in the championship game. Following the Super Bowl, the Boston (MA) *Globe* reported that Fryar and five other Patriots admitted to coach Raymond Berry* that they had used drugs. The Patriots finished in first place in the AFC Eastern Division in 1986, as Fryar made 43 pass receptions for 737 yards (17.1 yard average and 6 touchdowns) and returned 35 punts for 366 yards and 1 touchdown. Fryar performed in the 22–17 AFC playoff loss to the Denver Broncos. Through 1986 Fryar caught 93 passes for 1,571 yards and 14 touchdowns. Fryar also scored one touchdown rushing and returned three punts for touchdowns.

BIBLIOGRAPHY: Carmi (IL) *Times*, January 9, 1986; *TSN Football Register—1986*.

John L. Evers

G

GABRIEL, Roman Ildefonzo, Jr. "Radar Roman" (b. 5 August 1940, Wilmington, NC), college and professional player and coach, is the son of Roman Ildefonzo Gabriel, Sr., a Filipino immigrant and cook on the Atlantic Coast Line Railroad, and Edna (Wyatt) Gabriel. At New Hanover High School (1954–1958), Gabriel starred as an All-State, All-American quarterback, All-Conference baseball player, and conference MVP in basketball. Nicknamed "Radar Roman," Gabriel attended North Carolina State University (ACC, 1958–1962) and led the nation as a sophomore in pass completions (60.4 percent). Gabriel made consensus All-American in 1960 and 1961 at quarterback, passing for 2,951 career yards.

The Los Angeles Rams (NFL) picked Gabriel in the first round in 1962. Although starting only four games, Gabriel was selected as quarterback on the NFL's All-Rookie Team and established an NFL record for allowing the fewest interceptions (2) in over 100 (101) passing attempts. Despite this impressive start, Gabriel rode the bench for most of the next three seasons. Under new head coach George Allen,* Gabriel in 1966 began starting at quarterback, and the Rams began to win. After compiling an 8–6 record in 1966, the Rams won the Coastal Division in 1967 and lost to the Green Bay Packers in the title game. Gabriel's best year came in 1969, when the Rams finished with an 11–2–1 record and lost to the Minnesota Vikings in the WC championship game. That year Gabriel completed 217 aerials, threw 24 touchdown passes, and suffered only 7 interceptions. He won the NFL's MVP award (Jim Thorpe Trophy) and honors from the AP, Maxwell Club, and Touchdown Club. Gabriel played most of the next three seasons with physical disabilities. Two knee operations, a separated rib, a collapsed lung, and a chronically sore passing arm hampered his performance. Despite these ailments, Gabriel completed over 50 percent of his passes and averaged 2,272 passing yards and 15 touchdowns per year.

The Rams traded Gabriel to the Philadelphia Eagles (NFL) in 1973. Gabriel enjoyed a superb year, winning the Comeback Player of the Year award and transforming an anemic offense into the NFL's second best. Gabriel played well in 1974 and 1975, but his physical problems continued. In 1976 he underwent a fifth operation on his right knee and played in only the last four games of the season. He retired after the 1977 season, with 30 touchdowns rushing, 201 touchdown passes, 149 interceptions, and 2,366 completions in 4,498 attempts for 29,444 yards.

The 6 foot, 4 inch, 220 pound Gabriel lives in Gilbert, AZ, with his wife, Lisa, and daughter, Amber, and has three sons by his first marriage. Gabriel coaches quarterbacks for the Arizona Wranglers (USFL) after spending three seasons (1980–1982) as coach at California Polytechnic University, Pomona, (CaCAA) and 1983 as offensive coordinator for the Boston Breakers (USFL).

BIBLIOGRAPHY: *Arizona Wranglers Media Guide, 1984; CB* (1975), pp. 148–50; Herman L. Masin, "Throw, Gabriel, Throw," *Senior Scholastic* 79 (September 27, 1961), p. 26; *Philadelphia Eagles Media Guide, 1977;* "The Rise of Roman's Empire," *Time* 94 (November 7, 1969), p. 84.

Eric C. Schneider

GAIN, Robert "Bob" (b. 21 June 1929, Akron, OH), college and professional player, won the 1950 Outland Award as the nation's Outstanding College Interior Football Lineman of the Year. Gain starred at tackle four years (1947–1950) at the University of Kentucky (SEC) and twelve years (1952, 1954–1964) with the Cleveland Browns (NFL). At Kentucky he won All-American honors his last two years (consensus in 1950) and co-captained the only Wildcats team to capture the SEC championship. The three-year All-SEC selection was chosen the best SEC lineman by the Atlanta (GA) Touchdown and Birmingham (AL) Quarterback Clubs. A stalwart defensive tackle on six Browns Eastern Conference and three (1954–1955, 1964) NFL championship teams, Gain starred in five Pro Bowl games. He was honored by the Pittsburgh (PA) Dapper Dan Club and was named to the West Virginia and the Cleveland Sports Hall of Fame. In 1980 he became the first Kentucky player to be inducted into the NFF College Football Hall of Fame.

The son of restaurant owner Zeman and Mary (Maletich) Gain, he graduated from Weir High School in Weirton, WV, made the All-State football team at tackle, and played center in basketball. The 6 foot, 3 inch, 230 pound Gain was one of the few two-way players performing for the immortal Paul "Bear" Bryant.* The Kentucky Wildcats compiled a composite 33–10–2 record, won two of three post-season games, and ranked eleventh and seventh nationally in AP polls Gain's last two seasons. Kentucky defeated Villanova 24–14 in the 1947 Great Lakes Bowl, was upset 21–13 by fifteenth-ranked Santa Clara in the 1950 Orange Bowl, and achieved its greatest triumph by defeating AP regular-season national champion Oklahoma 13–7 in the 1951 Sugar Bowl. Gain played with Wildcats stars All-American quarterback Vito

"Babe" Parilli, co-captain halfback Wilbur Jamerson, fullback Bill Leskovar, tackle Walt Yowarsky, center Harry Ulinski, and end Charlie McClendon. Gain in 1950 blocked and recovered two punts to set up touchdowns against North Texas and Georgia Tech. He kicked ten extra points against North Dakota to tie a SEC record. Gain graduated with a B.A. in Economics and Sociology from Kentucky in 1952.

The Green Bay Packers (NFL) drafted him in 1951, but Gain, unable to come to contract terms, starred one year with the Ottawa Roughriders (CFL). In 1951 Ottawa won its first CFL championship in several years with the help of Gain's field goals, rouges, and line play. Gain joined Cleveland (NFL) in a 1952 trade and helped the Browns win the American Conference Championship. He served a year in Korea and Japan as first lieutenant in the U.S. Air Force and then rejoined the Browns in 1954. Cleveland won two consecutive NFL championships by defeating Detroit 56–10 and Los Angeles 38–14 in title games. "Bob Gain became an excellent defensive tackle for us," Cleveland coach Paul Brown* stated. "He had such tremendous strength and big hands, he simply tossed aside an opposing lineman. Added to that strength was great quickness and mobility. Bob had a tremendous sense of humor, and few got the last laugh on him." Gain retired in 1964 after the Browns, under second-year coach Blanton Collier, won another NFL title by upsetting the Baltimore Colts 27–0 in the title game.

Gain married Mary Katherin Bastin in 1952 and has three daughters. Since leaving pro football, he has worked for the Pettibone Corporation, manufacturer of material handling equipment. He resides with his family in Cleveland's suburban Timberlake Village and has served the Heart Fund, Lake County Grand Jury, and other civic organizations.

BIBLIOGRAPHY: Jack T. Clary and Paul Brown, *PB: The Paul Brown Story* (New York, 1979); Robert Gain, Telephone Interview with James D. Whalen, February 18, 1986; Ronald L. Mendell and Timothy B. Phares, *Who's Who in Football* (New Rochelle, NY, 1974); Sugar Bowl Football Game Program (January 1, 1951); Roger Treat, ed., *The Encyclopedia of Football*, 16th rev. ed., rev. by Pete Palmer (New York, 1979).

James D. Whalen

GARBISCH, Edgar William "Ed" (b. 7 April 1900, Washington, PA; d. 13 December 1979, Cambridge, MD), college athlete, made All-American football center at the U.S. Military Academy. The HAF College Football Hall of Fame member was inducted in 1954 into the NFF College Football Hall of Fame and named in 1969 to the All-Time Modern (1920–1969) All-East Team by the FWAA. Garbisch started four years at guard (1917–1920) for Washington and Jefferson College and at center (1921–1924) for Army and captained his last year at both institutions.

Garbisch starred in the line four years on the Washington (PA) High School football team and graduated in 1917. His Washington and Jefferson teams finished with a combined 21–10–1 record, six losses coming from among the finest Pittsburgh, West Virginia, and Notre Dame teams ever. The Presidents, a leading eastern independent team, claimed victories over Penn State, Syracuse, Carnegie Tech, West Virginia, and Lehigh. Garbisch played his first three years beside all-time great tackle Wilbur "Fats" Henry* and excelled at kicking field goals and points after touchdowns. He made the Pittsburgh *Press* All-State team (1919–1920) and was chosen All-American (1920) by the Bethlehem (PA) *Times*.

The 1921 Washington and Jefferson graduate received an appointment at West Point. Although slender, the 6 foot, 185 pound Garbisch employed a cunning style that enabled him to hold his own against heavier opponents. The rugged tackler, punishing blocker, and tenacious, durable player alternated with captain Frank Greene at offensive guard and defensive center his first year and then played center full-time the last three years. Garbisch's Army teams produced a four-year composite 25–7–5 record. The Cadets' best seasons came under coaches Charles Daly* in 1922 (8–0–2) and John McEwan in 1924 (5–1–2), when Army defeated Navy twice and tied Notre Dame once.

In the final game at West Point's Cullom Field in 1922 against Notre Dame before an overflow crowd, Garbisch attempted a 44-yard field goal that fell one foot short of breaking the final 0–0 tie. His 47-yard placement from a difficult angle one yard from the sideline against Navy provided the 17–14 margin of victory. Garbisch developed the dropkick his last two years, allowing him more time and protection by one additional blocker. He dropkicked a field goal against Yale in 1923 and scored an extra point to tie the Elis in 1924. Against Notre Dame, he ran from a fake field-goal formation and dropkicked an extra point in 1924. The Irish, however, proved superior in their 13–7 triumph that inspired Grantland Rice* (OS) to call the Notre Dame backfield the Four Horsemen.* Before 80,000 spectators in Baltimore's new Municipal Stadium, Garbisch scored all Army's points against Navy by dropkicking four field goals (32, 42, 20, and 30 yards) in the 12–0 triumph. Garbisch's father, a Johns Hopkins University professor, saw his son lifted to the shoulders of admirers after the game and changed his mind about wanting his son to become a concert pianist.

Walter Camp* named Garbisch to his All-American first team in 1922 and 1924 and to the third team in 1923, although Garbisch was otherwise a consensus first team pick in 1923. He unfortunately played after the great reputations of centers "Germany" Schulz* (Michigan) and Bob Peck* (Pittsburgh) had been established or would have received more all-time acclaim. "He had a career total of 300 minutes against my alma mater," said Four Horseman Don Miller* in 1963, "and no other man can claim this distinction. He is the greatest lineman Notre Dame ever played against." Garbisch had played five games without substitution at Washington and Jefferson (1917) and Army (1921–1924) against the Irish.

Garbisch captained the Army tennis team and served as cadet captain commanding the First Battalion. After graduating from Army in 1925, he served in the armed forces the next twenty years and retired at the close of World War II with the rank of colonel. He became president of Grocery Store Products Company and served as vice-chairman and member of the board of directors of the NFF College Football Hall of Fame. Garbisch in 1930 married Bernice Chrysler and had one son, Edgar W., Jr., and one daughter, Gwynne. They maintained near Cambridge, MD, an estate that resembled an eighteenth-century Georgian home with authentic furnishings. They collected valuable American primitive paintings, many of which they gave to the National Gallery of Art (Washington, DC) and the Metropolitan Museum of Art (New York City). After Garbisch died of a massive stroke, his wife succumbed twelve hours later. Their art collection was sold at auction and brought nearly $4 million.

BIBLIOGRAPHY: Army-Yale Football Game Programs, October 28, 1922, November 3, 1923, November 1, 1924; Jim Beach and Daniel Moore, *Army vs. Notre Dame* (New York, 1948); Jack T. Clary, *Army vs. Navy* (New York, 1965); Tim Cohane, *Gridiron Grenadiers: Story of West Point Football* (New York, 1948); Tim Cohane, *The Yale Football Story* (New York, 1951); *Spalding's Official Intercollegiate Football Guides*, 1918–1921; Christy Walsh, *College Football and All-American Review* (Hollywood, CA, 1951); Washington *Post*, December 16, 1979.

James D. Whalen

GARRETT, Michael Lockett "Mike" (b. 12 April 1944, Los Angeles, CA), college and professional athlete, coach, and announcer, is one of six children and lived in poverty in the Boyle Heights section of Los Angeles. A top athlete at Theodore Roosevelt High School in Los Angeles, Garrett excelled in football and baseball at the University of Southern California (AAWU, 1962–1965) and earned a B.S. in Sociology there in 1967. As a sophomore running back (1963), Garrett averaged 13 carries a game and gained 833 yards for Southern California. He averaged 22 carries per contest for 948 yards in 1964 and 27 carries for 1,440 yards his senior season. In 1965 Garrett rushed 144 yards per game and led the nation in rushing. During his college career Garrett gained 3,221 yards to establish an NCAA record. He averaged 5.3 yards per carry, rushed for 25 touchdowns, caught 36 passes for 4 scores, and returned 44 punts for an 11.3-yard average and 2 touchdowns. Garrett set 14 NCAA, AAWU, and team records in his three seasons.

After passing quarterbacks had won the Heisman Trophy three consecutive seasons, Garrett returned the award to running backs in 1965. The unanimous All-American was recognized as the outstanding performer in college football and became the second black and second West Coast player to win the coveted trophy. Although performing on great Trojan teams under coach John McKay,* Garrett did not play in the Rose Bowl. The Kansas

City Chiefs (AFL) signed Garrett in 1966 to a five-year contract for a reported $450,000. Professionally, Garrett played for Kansas City (1966–1970) and the San Diego Chargers (1970–1973). He temporarily retired in 1970 to become a pro baseball player in the Pittsburgh Pirates' organization but retracted when he was traded to San Diego.

Garrett led the Kansas City Chiefs to the AFL championship in 1966 and played in the 35–10 loss to the Green Bay Packers in Super Bowl I. Garrett sparked Kansas City to the 1969 AFL championship and a 23–7 victory over the Minnesota Vikings in Super Bowl IV. Besides leading the AFL with a 5.5-yard rushing average (1966), Garrett paced Kansas City in rushing (1966–1967, 1969), receiving (1968–1969), and punt returns (1966) and topped San Diego in rushing (1971–1972). Garrett in 1967 established Kansas City records with 1,087 yards rushing in one season and 192 yards rushing in a single game and still holds the club record for rushing attempts (236) in 1967. An All-AFL selection in 1967, Garrett played in AFL All-Star games (1966–1967). In 104 games over eight seasons, he rushed for 5,481 yards and 35 touchdowns, made 238 receptions for 2,010 yards and 13 touchdowns, returned kicks for 558 yards and 1 touchdown, threw 1 touchdown pass, and scored 294 points.

Since his retirement, Garrett and his wife, Sherry, have operated a facility for juvenile delinquents and owned a real estate business. He has served as an analyst on football telecasts and volunteered as a football coach at Southern California. Garrett attends Western State Law School in San Diego, CA, and twice has been defeated for political office. In 1985 he was elected to the NFF College Football Hall of Fame.

BIBLIOGRAPHY: John Hall, "Football Traditions," *Trojans Illustrated* 1 (June/July, 1983), pp. 12–14; Bill Libby, *Heroes of the Heisman Trophy* (New York, 1973); John McKay with Jim Perry, *McKay: A Coach's Story* (New York, 1974); *TSN Football Register—1974*.

John L. Evers

GATSKI, Frank "Gunner" (b. 18 March 1923, Farmington, WV), college and professional player and scout, is the son of coal miner Louis and Ida Gatski, grew up in Number Nine Coal Camp, and worked in the soft coal mines one year. Gatski, who played center in football four years at Farmington High School, insisted, "You gotta be tough to play football." When Marshall University (WV) held a "survival-of-the-fittest" pre-season tryout in 1940, Gatski took the "only chance I had" to play college football. Gatski started at center for the freshman team in 1940 and the varsity squad the next two seasons. He saw military action in Europe during World War II, but his nickname "Gunner" came from Marshall announcer Gene Kelly. After being discharged in 1945, Gatski played football part of that season at Auburn University (SEC).

Gatski joined the Cleveland Browns (AAFC) in 1946. The Browns dominated the AAFC from 1946 to 1949 by winning 47, losing 5, and tying 2 games and captured four consecutive AAFC championships. Gatski scored his only touchdown in 1946 against the Chicago Rockets. When Moe Scarry retired after the 1947 season, Gatski started at center and linebacker for Cleveland. After the AAFC folded in 1949, the NFL absorbed the Browns, San Francisco 49ers, and Baltimore Colts. The Browns continued to dominate pro football, as Gatski played a significant role in the game plans of coach Paul Brown.* Cleveland's Big-T formation relied on fancy plays, accurate passing, fast receivers, and powerful centers. The 6 foot, 3 inch, 240 pound Gatski proved a fine blocker and, with his long legs, allowed the quarterback to receive the snap standing up and read defenses quickly. According to one sportswriter, he ranked among the finest centers in Cleveland Browns history. From 1946 to 1955 legendary Browns quarterback Otto Graham* completed 1,464 passes for 23,584 yards. Center Gatski contributed much to Graham's success story. Opponents greatly respected the rugged, strong, taciturn West Virginian. A serious competitor, Gatski never missed a game or practice in his college or pro career. He made All-Pro four times, played in eleven championship games (helping the Browns win eight), and was named by the Cleveland Touchdown Club as the team's MVP for 1955.

When Cleveland slumped in 1956, the Browns traded Gatski to the Detroit Lions (NFL). He retired after the 1957 season with his highest salary being $10,000 plus playoff money! In 1958 he ran unsuccessfully for the West Virginia State Legislature in the Democratic party primary. He scouted for the Boston Patriots (AFL) until 1961, when he became football coach at the West Virginia Industrial School for Boys (Pruntytown) and instituted a tight regimen for his players there. When the reform school closed in 1982, Gatski concentrated on hunting (archery) and fishing. He and his wife, Mae, live near Grafton, WV, and have seven children. Gatski, who has not much changed his perspective on life, said, "Getting in the mainstream, that's the real ball game. Life is much tougher than playing football which has plays." Gatski remarked, "There are no plays when you get out on the street."

When Gatski was named to the Pro Football Hall of Fame in 1985, he commented, "It's the best feeling I've had since we hung it on the [Los Angeles] Rams [30–28] in our first [1950] N.F.L. title game." He also made the All-Time Cleveland Browns team and was selected to the West Virginia Hall of Fame.

BIBLIOGRAPHY: Bob Barnett and Bob Carroll, "Frank Gatski," *The Coffin Corner* 6 (November–December, 1984), pp. 10–11; Cleveland *Plain Dealer*, September 24, 1951; October 19, 1955; December 13, 1958; July 24, 1972; November 16, 1977; December 2, 1977; January 23, 1985; Bill Levy, *Return to Glory: The Story of the Cleveland Browns* (Cleveland, 1965); Douglas A. Noverr and Lawrence E. Ziewacz, *The Games They*

Played: Sports in American History, 1965–1980 (Chicago, 1983); Vito Stellino, "Staubach, O. J. Join List of Elite," *TSN* (February 4, 1985), p. 32.

Frank Mazzella

GELBERT, Charles Saladin, Jr. "Charlie" "Miracle Man" (b. 24 December 1871, Hawley, PA; d. 16 January 1936, Philadelphia, PA), college player, was named three years as a first-team football All-American end at the University of Pennsylvania (IL) by Walter Camp.* A four-year regular with the Quakers (1893–1896), Gelbert played halfback on offense and end on defense. He was selected to Jack C. Kofoed's All-Time All-American Team for the Philadelphia *Record* (1912) and to the NFF College Football Hall of Fame (1960). The son of Charles S. and Barbara (Ott) Gelbert, he grew up in Scranton (PA) and graduated in 1893 from Lackawanna High School. His football career at the University of Pennsylvania coincided with some of the great Quaker grid teams. Between 1893 and 1896 Penn finished 52–4–0 and outscored opponents 1,594 points to 130. Penn captured the national championship in 1894 (12–0–0) and 1895 (14–0–0) and won 34 consecutive games before losing 6–4 to undefeated Lafayette College in 1896.

The 5 foot, 8 inch, 165 pound Gelbert was nicknamed "Miracle Man" by teammates because of his outstanding play against larger opponents. Sporting a full head of hair and handlebar moustache, he proved a deadly tackler and superb leader of interference. The 1895 Penn-Harvard football program stated, "Gelbert is undoubtedly one of the best ground gainers in the country." In the 1896 Penn 32–10 victory over Cornell, the versatile star tackled the punter for a safety and scored a touchdown on a short plunge. In 1895 Casper Whitney boasted, "Gelbert is very fast in getting down the field, sure in tackling and quick at breaking up interference." Gelbert's coach George Woodruff developed the guards back formation, putting Pennsylvania football on a par with the Big Three. During Gelbert's career, the Quakers defeated Cornell four times; Harvard, Penn State, Lafayette, and Navy three times each; Brown twice; Princeton once, and held 39 of 56 opponents scoreless. In 1939 the *Harvard Athletic Association News* stated, "Gelbert and [George] Brooke were chiefly responsible for the Red and Blue victories over Harvard in 1894 and 1895."

Although his son Charlie became a star major league baseball shortstop and coach for many years, Gelbert only substituted one year (1894) on the Quaker nine. He performed for the gymnastics team (1895–1896), which gave exhibitions prior to the organization of intercollegiate schedules. He graduated from the University of Pennsylvania in 1899 with a degree in veterinary medicine and practiced veterinary medicine as a lifelong career. Gelbert married Nida Florence Kelley of Scranton, PA, in 1902 and had three children.

BIBLIOGRAPHY: Edward R. Bushnell, *The History of Athletics at Pennsylvania* (Philadelphia, 1909); Allison Danzig, *The History of American Football: Its Great Teams, Players, and Coaches* (Englewood Cliffs, NJ, 1956); Parke H. Davis, *Football: The American Intercollegiate Game* (New York, 1911); John D. McCallum and Charles H. Pearson, *College Football U.S.A., 1869–1973* (New York, 1973); Ronald L. Mendell and Timothy B. Phares, *Who's Who in Football* (New Rochelle, NY, 1974); George W. Orton, *A History of Athletics at Pennsylvania* (Philadelphia, 1896); *Spalding's Official Intercollegiate Football Guides, 1895–1897*; University of Pennsylvania, Archives, Philadelphia, PA.

James D. Whalen

GEORGE, William "Bill" (b. 27 October 1930, Waynesburg, PA; d. 30 September 1982, Rockford, IL), college and professional player and coach, was a 6 foot, 2 inch linebacker. He excelled at football and wrestling at Waynesburg High School but rejected numerous wrestling scholarships to play football from 1948 to 1951 at Wake Forest University (SC). The two-way guard made the 1949 All-American team and was drafted in the second round in 1951 by the Chicago Bears (NFL). Clark Shaughnessy* summed up George's exceptional qualities: "He is a rare physical specimen both from the standpoint of power and agility. He's absolutely fearless on the field. He has a brilliant mind, an ability to size up a situation quickly and react to it, and also the ability to retain the complicated details of his job."

From 1952 to 1965 George played linebacker for Chicago as captain and quarterback of the Bears defense. He played with the Los Angeles Rams (NFL) in 1966 and in 1972 served as assistant coach for the Chicago Bears. George played 159 games, including 124 consecutive, with the Bears, intercepted 18 passes, and recovered 14 fumbles. In 1954 he booted 4 field goals and 13 extra points. George made All-Pro at middle guard and linebacker eight times, participated in eight Pro Bowl games, and played in two NFL championship games, helping the Bears win the 1963 title. George also made the All-Pro team for the 1950s decade. George, initially a middle guard on defense, backed up as a middle linebacker to read the plays better. He created that position, pioneering most of the techniques now used by middle linebackers. George, who saw the Bears retire his number 61 jersey, was selected in 1974 to the Pro Football Hall of Fame. In 1982 he was killed in an automobile accident south of Rockford, IL.

BIBLIOGRAPHY: George Allen with Ben Olan, *Pro Football's 100 Greatest Players* (Indianapolis, IN, 1982); George Sullivan, *Pro Football A to Z* (New York, 1975); George Vass, *George Halas and the Chicago Bears* (Chicago, 1971); *Wake Forest University Football Media Guide, 1978;* Richard Whittingham, *The Chicago Bears—An Illustrated History* (Chicago, 1979).

John L. Evers

GIBBS, Joe Jackson (b. 25 November 1940, Mocksville, NC), college player and college and professional coach, is the son of a sheriff and moved to the West Coast as a child. After graduating from Spring High School in Santa Fe, CA, he attended Cerritos (CA) Junior College and then transferred to San Diego State University (CaCAA). Under coach Don Coryell,* he played tight end, linebacker, and guard on San Diego State football teams that compiled a 22–6–1 overall record. Gibbs earned a B.S. in Physical Education in 1964 and an M.S. in 1966 from San Diego State. From 1964 to 1966 he worked with the offensive line as a graduate assistant coach at San Diego State under Coryell. San Diego State won 27 of 31 games, including an 11–0 record in 1966. In 1967 head coach Bill Peterson of Florida State hired Gibbs as his offensive line coach. The Seminoles compiled a two-year 15–4–2 record with a pass-oriented offense. Ron Sellers established many receiving records, including some still unbroken. University of Southern California (PEC) head coach John McKay* selected Gibbs in 1969 to coach his offensive line. The Trojans finished 15–4–1 during Gibbs' two-year stint there. In 1971 Arkansas (SWC) head coach Frank Broyles* hired Gibbs as an assistant. The next two years, the Razorbacks compiled a 14–8–1 record with Joe Ferguson at quarterback.

Gibbs' entrance into the NFL came in 1973 when St. Louis Cardinals head coach Coryell appointed him the offensive backfield coach. From 1973 to 1977 the Cardinals finished 42–27–1 with two NFC Eastern Division titles. The NFL's top offense featured quarterback Jim Hart,* running backs Terry Metcalf and Jim Otis, and wide receiver Mel Gray.* In 1978 Coach McKay hired Gibbs as offensive coordinator of the Tampa Bay Buccaneers (NFL). After one season there, he moved to the San Diego Chargers as offensive coordinator under Coryell. In two seasons, the Chargers won both Western Division AFC titles and set offensive records with quarterback Dan Fouts' passing. Gibbs spent eighteen years as an assistant coach on the collegiate and pro levels.

The Washington Redskins (NFL) in 1981 gave Gibbs his first head coaching job. Gibbs continued the phenomenal success he had enjoyed as an assistant. In six years through 1986, his 69–28 win-loss mark (.711) remains the second best of all active coaches. His clubs have won three Eastern Division NFC titles (1982–1984), two NFC crowns (1982, 1983), and one Super Bowl (1982). The Redskins triumphed in Super Bowl XVII against the Miami Dolphins 27–17 in 1982 and lost Super Bowl XVIII to the Los Angeles Raiders 38–9 in 1983. The 1983 Redskins set regular-season records for most points scored (541) and victories. From 1983 to 1986 Gibbs became one of just two NFL coaches to steer teams to four consecutive 10-victory seasons. He became the first head coach since Allie Sherman of the 1961–1962 New York Giants to be named AP Coach of the Year in successive seasons (1982–1983). In 1982 he guided the Redskins to their best finish in forty-two years, molding the offense around the running of John Riggins.*

The Chicago Bears defeated the Redskins in the 1984 playoffs. Washington triumphed over Los Angeles and Chicago in the 1986 playoffs before losing 17–0 to the New York Giants in the NFC Championship Game.

A racquetball enthusiast, Gibbs participates actively in church and youth programs and enjoys hunting and water skiing. Gibbs and his wife, Patricia, have two sons, Jason Dean and Cory Randle, and reside in Vienna, VA.

BIBLIOGRAPHY: *TSN Football Register—1985;* Washington Redskins, Publicity Office, Washington, DC.

Albert J. Figone

GIFFORD, Frank Newton (b. 16 August 1930, Santa Monica, CA), college and professional player and television sportscaster, is the son of former oil worker Weldon and Lola (Hawkins) Gifford. Gifford's early years were spent in various oil field communities until age 14, when his family settled in Bakersfield, CA. At Bakersfield High School (1944–1948), Gifford played football at halfback, quarterback, and end. He performed at tailback in the single-wing offense and led Bakersfield to the conference championship in his senior year. During a brief tenure at Bakersfield Junior College (1948), Gifford played halfback and participated in the Junior Rose Bowl game. Gifford studied at the University of Southern California (PCC, 1949–1952) with a full athletic scholarship. With his versatile physical skills, Gifford played offensive tailback and defensive halfback and kicked field goals and points after touchdowns. Gifford, an All-American in 1952 and participant in the North-South Shrine All-Star (East-West) games, was inducted into the NFF College Football Hall of Fame in 1976.

The top draft choice of the New York Giants (NFL), Gifford experienced a mediocre rookie year (1952), failing to score a point. The following season, however, he scored 47 points and made the All-NFL Defensive Team. In 1954 new offensive coach Vince Lombardi* designated Gifford as offensive halfback to run his power sweep. Lombardi's strategy enabled Gifford to become one of the NFL's most outstanding performers. In 1956 he ranked among the NFL's top ten in rushing (819 yards), pass receptions (51 for 603 yards) and points scored (65), and became the first NFL player to finish among the top five in both pass receptions and rushing categories. Gifford led the Giants to the Eastern Conferance title and NFL championship that season and was selected NFL Player of the Year.

Gifford's excellent performances helped the Giants capture Eastern Conference titles in 1958 (with 60 points) and 1959 (with 42 points). During the 1960 game against the Philadelphia Eagles, Gifford was blindsided while attempting to receive a pass and hospitalized with an acute brain concussion. After a brief retirement, he returned to the Giants at the flanker position and was named NFL Comeback Player of the Year (1963). Gifford made Pro Bowl appearances and was named the game's MVP in 1959. Gifford, who retired from football after the 1964 season, was named 1964 Sportsman of the Year. For his superior performances (484 points scored, 78 touchdowns, and 5,434 yards gained in pass receptions), Gifford was inducted into the Pro Football Hall of Fame in 1977. Gifford rushed 840 times for 3,609 yards (4.3-yard average) and 34 touchdowns and caught 367 passes (14.8-yard average) for 43 touchdowns. As a pro, he exhibited versatility and an exceptional skill to capitalize on opponents' weaknesses by rushing gains and touchdowns.

Since 1971 Gifford has been an ABC television sportscaster. Besides being the play-by-play announcer of NFL "Monday Night Football," he has been a commentator for ABC's coverage of the Olympic Games and other sports events and began anchoring "Wide World of Sports" in 1987. Gifford married Maxine Ewart in 1951 and has three children, Jeffry, Kyle, and Victoria. In 1973 Gifford wed his second wife, Astrid. Following their divorce, he married Kathie Lee Johnson, co-host of WABC's "The Morning Show," in October 1986.

BIBLIOGRAPHY: "Always Leave Them Limp," *Time* 82 (December 27, 1963), p. 40; Barbara Bannon, "Frank Gifford," *Publishers Weekly* 210 (October 11, 1976), p. 6; *CB* (1964), pp. 147–149; Stanley Frank, "Pro Football's All-Around Man," *SEP* 330 (October 26, 1952), p. 30; Frank Gifford, *Frank Gifford's Football Guidebook: Basic Plays and Playing Techniques for Boys* (New York, 1965); Frank Gifford, *Frank Gifford's NFL-AFL Football Guide for 1969* (New York, 1969); Frank Gifford with Charles Mansel, *Gifford on Courage* (New York, 1977); Edwin Shrake, "What Are They Doing to the Sacred Game of Football?" *SI* 35 (October 25, 1971), pp. 98–106; William N. Wallace, *Frank Gifford: The Golden Year, 1956* (Englewood Cliffs, NJ, 1969).

Joseph English
Eleanor English

GILL, Turner Hillary, Jr. (b. 13 August 1962, Fort Worth, TX), college and professional athlete, is the son of Turner Gill, Sr. One of the most highly recruited prep prospects in 1979–1980, Gill made All-State, All-County, and All-District quarterback at Fort Worth Arlington Heights High School and performed well enough on the baseball diamond at shortstop to be selected in the second round of the 1980 free-agent draft by the Chicago White Sox (AL).

At the University of Nebraska (BEC, 1980–1983), Gill majored in public relations and set a Nebraska freshman football team record with 981 total yards. He rushed 302 yards on 51 attempts for 3 touchdowns, and passed 679 yards on 34 completions in 52 attempts for 8 touchdowns. The first black quarterback at Nebraska, Gill started five games into the 1981 season and guided the Cornhuskers to six straight victories until suffering nerve damage to his right leg. He missed the final game against the University of Oklahoma and the Orange Bowl loss to Clemson University. In 1982 Gill earned consensus All-BEC honors, completed 90 of 166 passes for 1,182 yards and 11 touchdowns, threw just 3 interceptions (1.8 percent), and rushed for 497 yards and 4 touchdowns in 101 attempts. Gill was named the BEC Offensive Player of the Week twice in 1982 in consecutive performances against Penn State University and Auburn University. Against Kansas State University, Gill broke Dave Humm's eight-year-old Nebraska BEC single-game pass completion percentage record by completing 11 of 12 passes (.917 percent). Selected the outstanding back in the Orange Bowl, Gill completed 13 of 22 passes for 184 yards and 1 touchdown and rushed for 37 yards and 1 touchdown to lead Nebraska to a 21–20 come-from-behind victory over LSU. That same year, Gill earned honorable mention All-BEC baseball honors by batting .284 and ranking second on the team in hits.

Gill in 1983 completed 94 of 170 passes for 1,516 yards and 14 touchdowns and rushed for 631 yards in 109 attempts and 11 touchdowns to lead the Cornhuskers to a perfect (12–0–0) season. An All-BEC selection (1981–1983), Gill quarterbacked Nebraska to within one game of the national championship. When his two-point conversion pass attempt failed in the closing seconds of Nebraska's 31–30 Orange Bowl loss to the University of Miami, the Hurricanes became the national champion. Gill, fourth in the Heisman Trophy voting behind teammate-winner Mike Rozier,* led Nebraska to a 33–5–0 overall record in three seasons. He completed 231 of 428 passes for 3,317 yards and 34 touchdowns and rushed for 1,417 yards and 18 touchdowns in 290 attempts.

Although selected by the New York Yankees (AL) in the 1983 baseball draft and the Houston Gamblers of the USFL, Gill selected the CFL and signed a four-year contract estimated at $2 million. While learning the CFL intricacies, Gill performed as an alternate quarterback for the Montreal Concordes in 1984, with 199 completions in 375 attempts for 2,673 yards. Although hurling 17 touchdown passes, he threw 17 interceptions. The following season, he completed 212 of 352 passes for 2,255 yards and 17 touchdowns and suffered 15 interceptions. Joe Barnes replaced Gill as starting quarterback after the latter experienced three concussions. Montreal terminated his contract before the 1986 season because several doctors found him physically unfit to continue playing. In May 1986, Gill signed a contract to play baseball for the Cleveland Indians (AL) Class A affiliate in Waterloo, IA. In 1986 Gill batted .218 and made 32 errors at shortstop for the Central Division title club. He and his wife, Gayle, reside in Lincoln, NE.

BIBLIOGRAPHY: Des Moines *Register*, August 31, 1986; *Pro Football Weekly Scout's Notebook, 1984; University of Nebraska Football Media Guide, 1983;* Paul Witteman, "America's Top Team Turns to Turner Gill for Gridiron Guidance," *People Weekly* 20 (November 28, 1983), pp. 177–78.

John L. Evers

GILLMAN, Sidney "Sid" (b. 26 October 1911, Minneapolis, MN), college and professional player, coach, and executive, is the son of movie theatre owner David and Sarah Gillman. His father's career influenced Gillman in developing the use of game films to prepare for opponents. Gillman's contribution is now widely followed at all football levels. Gillman attended Ohio State University (WC) from 1931 until his graduation in 1934 and played in the first college All-Star game in 1934. An offensive end, he realized the potential importance of the forward pass in making football a more exciting spectator sport. Gillman played one season (1936) with the Cleveland Rams (NFL) and served as assistant coach at Ohio State University in 1934 and 1938–1940 and at Denison University (OC) from 1935 to 1937 and in 1941. His greatest opportunity came in 1944, when he was named head football coach at Miami (OH) after serving two seasons (1942–1943) as an assistant there. During four years (1944–1947), he compiled a 31–6–1 record and Sun Bowl victory his last season.

After a year as an assistant coach at Army (1948), he became head football coach at the University of Cincinnati (1949–1954). Under Gillman's leadership, Cincinnati became a major national power largely because of its offensive prowess. Gillman compiled a 50–13–1 record, including the Glass Bowl championship of 1950, and battled Woody Hayes* in the recruiting wars for high school talent. Gillman's success, built partly on rules violations resulting in NCAA probation for the university in 1955, impressed NFL owners. Gillman became head coach of the Los Angeles Rams (NFL) that year and held that position until 1960, making him the longest-serving Rams coach to that time. The intense, enthusiastic, determined, and self-confident Gillman was totally admired or thoroughly despised.

He further developed the use of the forward pass as the principal offensive weapon with the formation of the AFL in 1961. As head coach of the San Diego Chargers from 1961 to 1969 and briefly in 1971, he guided all but five of that team's AFL games. Gillman's clubs produced five Western Division titles and one AFL championship (1963), earning him a reputation as "perhaps the best passing coach ever." Gillman retired prematurely in 1969 because of health problems. His reputation and excellence as a coach, reflected in his election to the Pro Football Hall of Fame in 1983, grew. The energetic Gillman became special assistant at Dallas (NFL) under Tom Landry* in 1972 and served as offensive coordinator there in 1973 until becoming general manager of the Houston Oilers (NFL). He replaced Bill Peterson as head Oilers coach in midseason and was named 1974 UPI Coach of the Year after leading a team, which had won only twice the two previous years, to a 7–7 record. Nevertheless, he resigned as coach in January, 1975, and from the front office the next month. After serving as athletic director of the U.S. International University in 1979, he coached during the 1979–1980 seasons with the Philadelphia Eagles (NFL). He subsequently served as general manager of the San Diego franchise in the USFL in 1983 and became special assistant to the Los Angeles Express (USFL) in 1984. During eighteen pro seasons, Gillman's clubs compiled a 123–104–7 mark.

Gillman, an effective teaching coach, trained scores of assistants. Ara Parseghian,* Paul Dietzel, Chuck Noll,* and many others have become highly successful head coaches. Al Davis* also assisted him at one time. Gillman married high school sweetheart Esther Berg on August 20, 1935, and has four children, Lyle, Barbara, Terry, and Tommy.

BIBLIOGRAPHY: Melvin Durslag, "Beleaguered Boss of the Rams," *SEP* 232 (October 24, 1959), pp. 31ff; Mrs. Sidney Gillman to Charles R. Middleton, October 31, 1984; Earl Lawson, "Football's Man Without Mercy," *SEP* 228 (October 8, 1955), pp. 27ff; Ronald L. Mendell and Timothy B. Phares, *Who's Who in Football* (New Rochelle, NY, 1974); *NYT*, March 3, 1973, December 20, 1974, January 26, 1975, January 4, 1981, February 2, 1983, June 14, 1983, July 31, 1983, January 12, 1984.

Charles R. Middleton

GIPP, George (b. 18 February 1895, Laurium, MI; d. 14 December 1920, South Bend, IN), college player, was a famed Notre Dame football running back and the school's first All-American chosen by Walter Camp.* The son of carpenter-laborer Matthew Gipp, he grew up in a Michigan Upper Peninsula mining town and excelled in basketball and baseball for his Calumet High School team. One season, he led Calumet to a 24–1 basketball record and batted .494 for his hometown baseball team. One of eight children, he never graduated from high school and worked odd jobs as a taxi driver and telephone lineman. The restless Gipp rebelled against his parents' rigid Baptist and Methodist strictures and frequently visited pool halls and bars. Upon the advice of Notre Dame baseball player Bill Gray, Gipp enrolled at the Roman Catholic school in 1917 to play baseball.

At Notre Dame, Gipp played freshman football and made a 62-yard dropkick field goal in his first game. He also participated on the freshman basketball and track squads and engaged in pool at the local billiard parlors to earn spending money. Gipp played professional baseball in the summer, 1917, but his professionalism never became an issue or problem. He often bet on games for his poolroom cronies and collected commissions for placing and handling bets.

Under coach Knute Rockne's* influence and protective care, Gipp returned to Notre Dame. Since Gipp broke his leg in the third varsity football game, he avoided Army induction during World War I. During 1918 the casual, indifferent Gipp practiced only three days a week and avoided Rockne's harsh conditioning regimen. The patient Rockne tolerated Gipp's erratic behavior because of the latter's football intelligence and rare athletic ability. Although becoming an idolized hero during Notre Dame's undefeated 1919 season, Gipp ignored his academic studies and spent much time pool sharking, playing cards, and courting local girls. After Notre Dame expelled him in 1920, he contemplated playing pro baseball and looked at the University of Michigan and the University of Detroit for a better football scholarship arrangement. The U.S. Military Academy tried to recruit Gipp, but his family did not know where to forward the telegram. During the summer, 1920, Gipp became interested in Roman Catholicism and began realizing the security that Notre Dame had provided him. When Gipp passed an oral reentry examination, Rockne promised him an assistant coaching job the next year. In a topsy-turvy 1920 season, Gipp returned to betting and drinking heavily. Although physically unfit, he enjoyed memorable games against Army (332 total yards), Purdue, and Indiana. He never finished the season, catching strep throat that developed into pneumonia. Gipp died following a deathbed conversion to Roman Catholicism. During his final illness, he received a $3,580 baseball contract offer with the Chicago Cubs and was named an All-American football fullback.

The instinctive, shrewd, and intelligent Gipp became one of collegiate football's greatest runners and kickers. A four-year letterman, Gipp played in thirty-two consecutive football games and became a campus and national legend. Although an enigmatic and awkward loner with self-destructive private dissipations, he received plaudits for his football skills, instincts, and brilliant performances. He represented the indefatigable toughness of the Fighting Irish as the unknown, relatively poor school attracted national football prominence and established a winning tradition based on school loyalty. Whether Gipp's deathbed request to Rockne that he should ask them to "win one for the Gipper" is legend or fact, this gifted athlete's inspired and determined play became legend. Gipp's short, tragic life, with its misspent youth, was overshadowed by the loyal, unqualified love that Notre Dame people demonstrated for him. Although rejecting or being rejected by his school at various times, Gipp epitomized the pride and strength representing Notre Dame. Gipp was elected to the HAF and NFF College Football Hall of Fame.

BIBLIOGRAPHY: Jim Beach, "Gipp of Notre Dame," in Gene Schoor, ed., *A Treasury of Notre Dame Football* (New York, 1962); Patrick Chelland, *One for the Gipper: George Gipp, Knute Rockne, and Notre Dame* (Chicago, 1973); Dave Condon, Chet Grant, and Bob Best, *Notre Dame Football: The Golden Tradition* (South Bend, IN, 1982); Allison Danzig, *The History of American Football: Its Great Teams, Players, and Coaches* (Englewood Cliffs, NJ, 1956); George Gipp as told to Walter Kennedy, "My Greatest Football Game," in Gene Schoor, ed., *A Treasury of Notre Dame Football* (New York, 1962); Herbert T. Juliano, Clippings File, Sports Information Department, Notre Dame University, South Bend, IN; Ronald L. Mendell and Timothy B. Phares, *Who's Who in Football* (New Rochelle, NY, 1974); *NYT*, December 15 and 18, 1920; James A. Peterson, *Gipp of Notre Dame* (Chicago, 1959); Coles Phinizy, " 'Win One for the Gipper,' " *SI* 51 (September 17, 1979), pp. 40–48; Knute K. Rockne, "Gipp the Great," *Collier's* 86 (November 22, 1930), pp. 14–15, 63–64; Red Smith, "On Winning One for the Gipper," *NYT*, January 21, 1981.

Douglas A. Noverr

GOLDBERG, Marshall "Biggie" (b. 24 October 1917, Elkins, WV), college and professional player, starred as a University of Pittsburgh All-American football halfback and fullback from 1936 through 1938 and was named to the All-Decade Team of the 1930s by *SI*. The son of Sol and Rebecca Goldberg, he ranks among the most popular, respected athletes of all time. Goldberg's father even closed his movie theatre in Elkins during the fall to follow the Panthers around the nation. This father-son relationship captured the hearts of Depression-era fans, who desperately needed heroes to help make them forget the harsh reality of the times. A three-sport star at Elkins High School, Goldberg was nicknamed "Biggie" because he weighed only 110 pounds as a sophomore football player. He captained the Elkins' track, football, and basketball teams and won All-West Virginia honors in the latter two sports.

Pittsburgh enjoyed its greatest football era during Goldberg's three varsity campaigns, compiling a 25–3–2 record and routing Washington 21–0 in the 1937 Rose Bowl. Several polls named Pittsburgh the national champion in 1936, while the undefeated Panthers unanimously were chosen the best 1937 club. Noted football writer Wilton Hazzard typified press reaction concerning Goldberg's gridiron prowess: "Endowed with abnormal drive, Goldberg leaves his mark like a sprinter, picks his hole unerringly, and has the split-second acceleration needed to capitalize a breakthrough. Show him a sliver of light and he will show you his heels." Goldberg ranked among the nation's top defenders and blockers, being named to the All-American blocking team in 1938. He passed for touchdowns on those rare occasions when the Panthers machine could not overpower foes with its running attack. Although sportswriters delighted in mentioning his Blue Ridge Mountains birthplace, Goldberg proved an articulate, sensitive student leader, graduating with high honors.

The 5 foot, 11 inch, 185 pound Goldberg instantly succeeded at Pittsburgh. In his first varsity game as a sophomore halfback in 1936, he penetrated Ohio Wesleyan for 208 yards in 15 carries. In his most important performance of 1936, Goldberg set up two touchdowns and made a 50-yard run to help Pitt upset Notre Dame 26–0. Goldberg returned a kickoff 87 yards and scored two more touchdowns in routing archrival Carnegie Tech. According to historian James Mark Purcell, Goldberg led the nation's major-college rushers in 1936 with 860 yards. Official NCAA statistical record-keeping began in 1937.

Goldberg rushed 701 yards in 1937 for a 6.1-yard average, earning unanimous All-American recognition. Pittsburgh avenged its only loss of the previous year, when Goldberg slashed off tackle, twice reversed his field, and raced 77 yards to score as the Panthers defeated Duquesne 6–0. Pittsburgh rallied to beat Notre Dame 21–6, when a 51-yard Goldberg pass triggered a three-touchdown explosion in the fourth period. He rushed six times for 53 yards in the first scoring march to help the Panthers hand Nebraska its only loss, 13–7. Goldberg's two touchdowns, including a 63-yard scamper, helped defeat Wisconsin 21–0. The lone blemish on Pittsburgh's 1937 record came in a third straight scoreless tie with Fordham and its famous Seven Blocks of Granite forward wall.

In 1938 Goldberg asked to be switched to fullback and sacrificed headlines to block for his "Dream Backfield" mates, quarterback John Chickerneo and halfbacks Dick Cassiano and Harold Stebbens. Goldberg gained All-American honors again, but the Panthers backfield performed well only when he remained healthy. When Goldberg was injured, Pittsburgh lost games against Carnegie Tech and Duke. The Panthers finally defeated Fordham, however, by rallying 24–13 on Goldberg's two fourth-period touchdowns.

The struggling Chicago Cardinals (NFL) immediately moved Goldberg into their starting backfield. From 1939 through 1942 he excelled as an all-around NFL player. After serving three years as a U.S. Navy lieutenant during World War II, he returned to the Cardinals in 1946. Goldberg developed into a defensive ace and rugged tackler with "a nose for the ball." The Cardinals experienced their greatest period in pro football, winning the 1947 NFL crown and placing second in 1948. He retired at the end of the 1948 season, having rushed 476 times for 1,644 yards (3.5-yard average) and 11 touchdowns and caught 60 passes for 775 yards (12.9-yard average) and 5 touchdowns. Goldberg married his wife, Rita, in 1939 and has two children, Marshall, Jr., and Ellen Jane. The president of Marshall Goldberg Machine Tools, he was elected to the NFF College Football Hall of Fame in 1958 and the HAF College Football Hall of Fame.

BIBLIOGRAPHY: Allison Danzig, *The History of American Football: Its Great Teams, Players, and Coaches* (Englewood Cliffs, NJ, 1956); Marshall Goldberg to Bernie McCarty, March 18, 1984; *Illustrated Football Annual, 1937–1938;* Dan Jenkins, "The First 100 Years," *SI* 31 (September 15, 1969), pp. 46–53; John D. McCallum and Charles H. Pearson, *College Football U.S.A., 1869-1973* (New York, 1973); *Pittsburgh Media Guide, 1973;* James Mark Purcell to Bernie McCarty, March 6, 1984; Grantland Rice, "The All-America Football Team," *Collier's* 102 (December 17, 1938), pp. 13–15; Wilfrid Smith, "Pitt Routs Notre Dame," Chicago *Tribune*, October 25, 1936; Jock Sutherland, "Goldberg Has It All," Pittsburgh *Press*, October 26, 1937.

Bernie McCarty

GRAHAM, Otto Everett, Jr. "Mechanical Otto" (b. 6 December 1921, Waukegan, IL), college and professional athlete, football coach, and administrator, is the son of music teacher Otto Everett and Cordonna Ruthe (Hayes) Graham, and brother of Richard, Victor, and Eugene Graham. Young Otto was expected to pursue a music career, but enthusiasm for sports consumed him. In high school he earned All-State basketball honors and helped his team win the state title. Following his graduation from Waukegan Township High School in 1939, he attended Northwestern University (BNC) on a basketball scholarship.

As a touch football player, he impressed Northwestern coach Lynn "Pappy" Waldorf.* After a year's leave with a leg injury, Graham by 1941 played tailback in the football varsity's single-wing offense. In 1943 Graham made the All-American team by helping Northwestern finish second in the BNC. He set BNC records by completing 20 of 29 passes for 294 yards in one game and compiling 2,162 yards passing. Before the 1943 season, he played for the College All-Stars against the Washington Redskins and intercepted a Sammy Baugh* pass for a dramatic 97-yard touchdown. Although leaving in mid-year to join the U.S. Naval Flight Training Program, he received his B.A. from Northwestern in 1944.

A three-letter athlete in college, the 6 foot, 1 inch, 196 pound Graham played baseball and became the only athlete to make All-American status in both football and basketball (1943). Graham's scoring and playmaking abilities impressed basketball scouts, who signed him to play with the talented Rochester Royals (NBL). Graham played in 1945–1946 for Rochester with Al Cervi* (IS), Bob Davies* (IS), Red Holzman* (IS), Fuzzy Levane, and George Glamack* (IS). Starting in the backcourt with Holzman, he helped the Royals capture the NBL title.

Graham's football talents interested Paul Brown,* the first Cleveland Browns coach. After being released from the U.S. Navy, Graham became a T-formation quarterback with Brown's new Cleveland (AAFC) franchise. Before joining the Browns, Graham again led the College All-Stars in 1946 in defeating the Los Angeles Rams 16–0 and hurled a touchdown pass to Elroy "Crazy Legs" Hirsch.* Coach Brown designed his Cleveland team around Graham, who possessed outstanding peripheral vision for passing and who galvanized team spirit. Using Marion Motley,* Mac Speedie,* and Dante Lavelli,* Graham provided adept passing and leadership in steering the Browns to four straight AAFC championships. His AAFC statistics from 1946 to 1949 included 592 completions in 1,051 attempts for 10,085 yards, a 55.8 completion percentage, and a 9.51-yard average gain per pass. His 86 touchdown passes fell only two short of those of San Francisco's Frankie Albert.* Graham won the AAFC passing honors all four years, sharing 1946 accolades with Glenn Dobbs of Brooklyn. He was voted the AAFC MVP in 1947, 1948, and 1949, sharing the 1948 honor with Albert. No other player so dominated the AAFC in the late 1940s.

The Browns joined the NFL in 1950 and quickly succeeded. Although losing twice to the New York Giants because Steve Owen* devised a special "umbrella" defense to stop Graham's passing, Cleveland won its other ten games to capture the NFL title in the first year. After defeating the Giants in a playoff game, Cleveland beat the Rams 30–28 in a memorable game featuring the passing of Graham and Bob Waterfield.* In 1952 and 1953 the Browns lost the NFL title games. During the 1953 championship game, Graham played poorly and was replaced by quarterback George Ratterman. Graham quarterbacked Cleveland to NFL titles in 1954 and 1955 and then retired. Graham's impressive later achievements included leading the NFL in passing in 1953 and 1955. From 1951 to 1955 he won the All-NFL selection at quarterback and shared that honor with Bobby Layne* of Detroit in 1952. In 1953 and 1955 he was selected NFL Player of the Year. The 6 foot, 1 inch, 195 pound Graham, who still holds the highest lifetime passing rating (86.7) among pro players, passed for 174 touchdowns and 23,584 yards in 10 seasons. Graham completed 1,464 of 2,626 passes and threw 135 interceptions.

In 1959 he became football coach at the U.S. Coast Guard Academy. After rejecting many offers to enter the pro coaching ranks, he in 1966 joined the Washington Redskins (NFL) as general manager and coach. In three years Graham's teams won 17, lost 22, and tied 3. Graham also coached the annual College All-Star Team from 1958 through 1965 and again in 1969 and 1970. In 1970 he returned to the U.S. Coast Guard Academy as athletic director. Graham was elected in 1955 to the NFF College Football Hall of Fame and in 1965 to the Pro Football Hall of Fame. Graham married former Northwestern coed Beverly Jean Collinge on October 7, 1945, and has three children, Duey, Sandra Lee, and David. In December 1984 Captain Graham retired from the Coast Guard Academy.

BIBLIOGRAPHY: William Heuman, *Famous Pro Football Stars* (New York, 1967); Bill Levy, *Return to Glory: The Story of the Cleveland Browns* (Cleveland, 1965); Harry Molter, *Famous American Athletes of Today* (Boston, 1953); David S. Neft, Richard M. Cohen, and Jordan A. Deutsch, *Pro Football: The Early Years, An Encyclopedic History 1895–1959* (Ridgefield, CT, 1978); George Sullivan, *Gamemakers* (New York, 1971); Roger Treat, ed., *The Encyclopedia of Football*, 16th rev. ed., rev. by Pete Palmer (New York, 1979); *WWA*, 42nd ed., 1982–1983, p. 1278.

John D. Windhausen

GRANGE, Harold Edward "Red" "Galloping Ghost" "Wheaton Ice Man" (b. 13 June 1903, Forksville, PA), college and professional player, coach, and announcer, was nicknamed "Red," "Galloping Ghost," "Wheaton Ice Man," and "No. 77." Grange's mother, Sadie (Sherman), died when he was five. His father, Lyle, a lumber camp foreman, moved his family to Wheaton, IL, where he had relatives. Lyle became the police chief, while his son starred at Wheaton High School and won sixteen letters in football, basketball, baseball, and track. On the gridiron, Grange scored 75 touchdowns and made 82 conversions for 532 points. Even better known as a track star, in his senior year Grange won all 19 events he entered.

Grange enrolled at the University of Illinois (WC) in 1922 and enjoyed a spectacular career there, being named to the All-American football teams in 1923, 1924, and 1925. In his varsity debut against the tough University of Nebraska, he scored three touchdowns and gained 208 yards despite sitting out the fourth quarter. In seven games during the 1923 season, Grange scored 12 touchdowns and led the nation with 1,260 yards gained. On October 18, 1924, Illinois dedicated its new Memorial Stadium against the University of Michigan. Sixty-seven thousand fans witnessed Grange's finest performance and the most spectacular single-handed achievement in college football history. During the first 12 minutes, Grange scored four touchdowns, by taking the opening kickoff 95 yards and running 67, 56, and 44 yards from scrimmage. He carried the ball only six times and left the game before the end of the first quarter. He ran 15 yards for a fifth touchdown in the third period and threw a touchdown pass in the fourth quarter to lead Illinois to a 39–14 victory. In 41 minutes, Grange carried the ball 21 times for 402 yards and completed six passes for 64 yards.

"Number 77" made its last appearance on an Illinois football jersey against Ohio State University in 1925. In twenty games at Illinois, Grange scored 31 touchdowns, gained 4,085 yards, and completed 42 passes for 643 yards. Following the Ohio State game, Grange joined the pro Chicago Bears (NFL). Signed by George Halas* in 1925, Grange packed stadiums on a national barnstorming tour and earned well over $100,000 that year. After a salary dispute with Halas in 1926, Grange and his manager Charles C. Pyle* (OS) started the rival AFL with the New York Yankees. The AFL proved a financial disaster, however, and folded after one year. After New York was awarded an NFL franchise, Grange played for the Yankees in 1927 and sat out the 1928 season because of a knee injury. He played with the Bears between 1929 and 1934, participating on NFL championship teams in 1932 and 1933. Following a knee injury in a 1934 exhibition game, Grange never played again. Besides making the first All-Pro team in 1931, he scored 56 touchdowns and four conversions for 340 points during his pro career. From high school through pro football, Grange played in 247 games, carried the ball 4,013 times for 33,820 yards, and scored 1,058 points on 162 touchdowns and 86 conversions.

Grange served as an assistant coach with the Chicago Bears through 1937 and then entered private business. In 1942 Grange became an insurance broker and also announced Chicago Bears and college football games over radio and television. Since Grange suffered a heart attack in 1951, he and his wife, Margaret Hazelberg (whom he had married in October, 1941), have lived in retirement at Indian Lake Estates, FL, and enjoy golfing, fishing, and boating.

Grange, more than any other single player, focused public attention on the pro game. Teammates and opponents respected his record, ability, sportsmanship, and complete lack of exhibitionism. He was the last to take credit and the first to give it. Grange made three movies, *One Minute to Play*, *Racing Romeo*, *The Galloping Ghost*, and authored the books *Zuppke of Illinois* and *The Red Grange Story*. Grange, a member of the HAF and NFF College Football, and Pro Football Halls of Fame, was selected unanimously for the Modern All-Time All-American Team and named to Parke Davis' All-Time All-American Team.

BIBLIOGRAPHY: Lon Eubanks, *The Fighting Illini—A Story of Illinois Football* (Huntsville, AL, 1976); Harold E. Grange and Ira Morton, *The Red Grange Story* (New York, 1953); Richard Whittingham, *The Chicago Bears—An Illustrated History* (Chicago, 1979); Kenneth L. (Tug) Wilson and Jerry Brondfield, *The Big Ten* (Englewood Cliffs, NJ, 1967).

John L. Evers

GRANT, Harold Peter "Bud" (b. 20 May 1927, Superior, WI), college and professional athlete and football coach, excelled as a pro football mentor. Grant, an all-around athlete at Central High School in Superior, served in the U.S. Navy for one year. He played football and basketball at the Great Lakes Naval Training Center under coaches Paul Brown* and Weeb Ewbank.* Following his discharge, he attended the University of Minnesota (BTC) from 1946 to 1949 and won nine varsity letters there. He played end four years in football, forward three years in basketball, and pitcher-outfielder two years in baseball. Besides being named All-BTC twice in football, he was selected the MVP for the Minnesota 1949 football squad and 1948 basketball team.

Following graduation from Minnesota, he played pro basketball with the Minneapolis Lakers from 1949 through 1951 and belonged to the 1949–1950 NBA championship squad. With the Lakers he played in 96 regular-season games and scored 249 points and 54 playoff points. In 1952 he signed with the Philadelphia Eagles (NFL). The 6 foot, 3 inch, 199 pound Grant, the Eagles' first draft choice in 1950, started as a defensive end. After moving to offense in 1953, Grant ranked second in the NFL with 56 catches for 997 yards and seven touchdowns. In his first pro pass reception, Grant scored an 86-yard touchdown against the Pittsburgh Steelers. Since Grant encountered contractual difficulties with the Eagles, he the following year joined Winnipeg (CFL). He played four seasons there as a cornerback and wide receiver, making 216 receptions. Besides leading the CFL in receptions three times, he made a record five interceptions in one game. During six pro seasons, he played in 88 games and caught 272 passes for 4,197 yards and 20 touchdowns.

At age 29, Grant replaced Allie Sherman as head football coach at Winnipeg. Over ten seasons, Grant's Winnipeg teams compiled a 102–56–2 regular season and 20–10–1 playoff record and won six WC titles and four Grey Cup championships. In 1967 he became head coach of the Minnesota

Vikings (NFL). He guided the Vikings to eleven Central Division titles (1968–1971, 1973–1978, 1980) and twelve post-season playoff appearances, including the NFL championship in 1969 and NFC titles in 1973, 1974, and 1976. The Vikings lost Super Bowl IV to the Kansas City Chiefs 23–7, Super Bowl VIII to the Miami Dolphins 24–7, Super Bowl IX to the Pittsburgh Steelers 16–6, and Super Bowl XI to the Oakland Raiders 32–14.

In his first seventeen years as Minnesota head coach, Grant's teams won 161, lost 99, and tied 5 for a .608 percentage. Grant ranks sixth on the all-time NFL victory list behind George Halas,* Earl "Curly" Lambeau,* Tom Landry,* Don Shula,* and Paul Brown.* During Grant's entire career (1957–1983, 1985), his clubs compiled a 290–118–6 mark. Only George Halas, with a record 325 wins, compiled more coaching victories. In 1985 Grant began a second stint as Viking coach and compiled a 7–9 mark before retiring again.

Grant, generally portrayed as cold and humorless because of his stolid expression and penetrating eyes, is friendly and given to practical humor and wit. To Grant, football is a game of controlled emotion. In his estimation, the head coach cannot enjoy the luxury of emotion. If he panics or loses his poise, his team follows. Grant, an avid hunter and fisherman, spends much free time at the family lake home in northern Wisconsin. He and his wife, Pat, have six children and live in Bloomington, MN. Grant was named 1965 CFL Coach of the Year and 1969 NFL Coach of the Year by *TSN*. He also was selected Minnesota athlete of the first half century.

BIBLIOGRAPHY: *Minnesota Vikings Media Guide, 1976; NFL Media Information Book, 1983; TSN Football Register—1986; TSN NBA Guide, 1982–1983; University of Minnesota Media Football Information Guide, 1978.*

John L. Evers

GRAY, Melvin Dean "Mel" (b. 28 September 1948, Fresno, CA), college athlete and professional football player, excelled in football and track at Montgomery High School in Santa Rosa, CA. Following graduation, Gray attended Fort Scott (KS) Community College and the University of Missouri (BEC). Gray, who played football for the Tigers (1968–1970), set Missouri season records for receiving yardage (705), touchdowns (9), and average yardage per reception (27.1) as a junior. He established career records for most reception yardage (1,491) and touchdowns (14) and set the mark for most pass reception yardage in one game (171). He performed in Missouri's 1968 Gator Bowl victory and 1969 Orange Bowl loss. An All-BEC selection in 1969, Gray played in the Shrine All-Star (East-West) game in 1971. Gray also starred in track at Missouri, winning seven of nine 100-yard dash crowns on the major relay circuit and capturing nearly all BEC sprint titles. The outstanding athlete in a 1970 meet, he finished first in the 100- and 200-yard dashes and long jump and third in the triple jump.

Selected by the St. Louis Cardinals in the sixth round of the NFL draft,

Gray played 12 seasons there as a wide receiver (1971–1982). He made the *TSN* NFC All-Star team in 1975 and 1976 and played in the Pro Bowl following the 1974 through 1977 seasons. In 145 career games with the Cardinals, Gray rushed 15 times for 154 yards and 1 touchdown and caught 351 passes for 6,644 yards and 45 touchdowns. Gray also returned 9 punts for 49 yards and 51 kickoffs for 1,191 yards and recovered 7 fumbles. His career receptions place him third on the all-time Cardinals list, while his career receiving yards and touchdowns rank him second behind Jackie Smith* and Sonny Randle, respectively. Gray's best one-season output came in 1975, when his 48 receptions for 926 yards and 11 touchdowns led the NFC. That same season featured Gray's seven-catch, 187-yard, two-touchdown performance against the New York Giants. Gray led St. Louis in receiving (1975, 1977) and kickoff returns (1971) and paced the NFL with a 19.7 yard-per-reception average in 1974. The Philadelphia Eagles on December 5, 1982, held Gray without a pass reception for the first time in 121 games, ending the third-longest pass reception streak (to Steve Largent's* 139 and Harold Carmichael's* 127) in NFL history. Gray, a bachelor, missed most of the 1982 season with a knee injury and was granted free agency in 1983. He ended his pro career with the Oklahoma Outlaws (USFL) in 1984 and is considering a coaching career.

BIBLIOGRAPHY: Bob Broeg, *Ol' Mizzou: A Story of Missouri Football* (Huntsville, AL, 1974); *St. Louis Football Cardinals Media Guide, 1977; TSN Official USFL Guide and Register—1984.*

John L. Evers

GRAYSON, Robert Harry "Bobby" (b. 8 December 1914, Portland, OR; d. 21 December 1981, Portland, OR), college player and coach, was the second son of George and Jennie (Geller) Grayson. His father worked as an officer at a Portland leather goods company. At Portland's Jefferson High, Grayson set state track records in the 100- and 200-yard dash and starred in football and baseball. He entered Stanford University (PCC) in 1932 and became one of the freshman class "Vow Boys." After seeing the University of Southern California (USC) defeat Stanford, the "Vow Boys" pledged never again to lose to the Trojans. In his first varsity appearance against USC, Grayson scored the tying touchdown in the most exciting game of his career. Besides excelling as a runner, he began calling signals midway through his sophomore year and threw many passes from his fullback post. In the first of three consecutive Rose Bowl appearances, Stanford lost to Columbia, 7–0. Grayson, however, gained 152 yards on 27 carries, a Rose Bowl rushing record lasting 20 years.

During 1934 Grayson led the PCC in scoring, rushed for 711 yards, and won consensus All-American honors. After scoring three touchdowns and rushing for 161 yards against San Jose State, he gained 119 yards and scored twice in a 16–0 win over USC. He set a still-standing school record by intercepting four passes against Washington and returned two for touchdowns. In 1935 Grayson repeated as a consensus All-American. Stanford posted an 8–1 record, including a 7–0 win over SMU in the Rose Bowl and a third straight victory over USC. He set a Stanford career rushing mark of 1,547 yards, which lasted twenty years. In 1955 Grayson became the second Stanford player and first of four "Vow Boys" named to the NFF College Football Hall of Fame. Grayson is also a member of the HAF College Football Hall of Fame.

The Pittsburgh Steelers (NFL) made Grayson their top draft choice and sold his rights to the New York Giants, who offered only a $5,000 salary. His uncle, NEA sports editor Harry Grayson, advised him to skip pro football because of the low pay. Grayson attended Stanford University Law School and served as assistant football coach there before returning to Portland, OR. He and Sue Kessler married on November 8, 1946, and had one son, Dan. He worked with Greyhound Food Services and Cudahy Meats and from 1972 to 1980 headed the U.S. Savings Bond Division of Oregon.

BIBLIOGRAPHY: Don E. Liebendorfer, *The Color of Life Is Red* (Palo Alto, CA, 1972); John McCallum, *Pac-10 Football: The Rose Bowl Conference* (Seattle, WA, 1982); John D. McCallum and Charles H. Pearson, *College Football U.S.A., 1869–1973* (New York, 1973); Ronald L. Mendell and Timothy B. Phares, *Who's Who in Football* (New Rochelle, NY, 1974); Fred Merrick, *Down on the Farm: A Story of Stanford Football* (Huntsville, AL, 1975).

Jay Langhammer

GREEN, Hugh Donell (b. 27 July 1959, Natchez, MS), college and professional player, was named Collegiate Player of the Year in 1980 by *TSN* and later became an All-Pro linebacker. The son of Eltee and Lucy Green, he made first-team Mississippi All-State his junior and senior years (1975–1976) at Natchez North High School, was voted the state's top scholastic lineman in 1976, and led his team with 115 solo tackles as a senior.

At the University of Pittsburgh, he started his first varsity game in 1977 as a freshman against Notre Dame and debuted with eleven tackles and two sacks. After making All-East defensive selection and some All-American second and third teams that year, he became a first-team All-American for three years. Green played in the 1977 Gator Bowl, 1978 Tangerine Bowl, 1979 Fiesta Bowl, 1980 Gator Bowl, and the Hula and Japan Bowl games in January 1981. The University of Pittsburgh retired his jersey number 99 in recognition of his achievements. During his four years there, he made 45 sacks, 287 tackles, and 177 assists, recovered numerous fumbles, and made several interceptions. He played defensive end, rushing or dropping back as was deemed appropriate. Green, the first sophomore ever chosen to the Walter Camp Foundation All-American team, won the Maxwell Award, ranked quite high in Heisman Trophy and Outland Award voting, and was named to the All-Time Pitt team, updated.

After being selected by the Tampa Bay Buccaneers in the first round of the NFL draft in 1981, Green quickly became an established pro star. He was named to the 1982 and 1983 Pro Bowl games and made All-Pro at linebacker in 1983. That year, he scored two touchdowns on interception runbacks of 54 total yards, leading NFL linebackers in that category. Automobile accident injuries sidelined the 6 foot, 2 inch, 225 pound Green for much of the 1984 season. Despite stardom, Green is considered light for his position. Before the 1985 season, he was traded to the Miami Dolphins. Green intercepted one pass for 28 yards in 1985 as the Dolphins compiled a 12–4 regular-season mark and lost to the New England Patriots in the AFC title game. Miami finished with an 8–8 mark in 1986 and missed the AFC playoffs. The injury-riddled Green recorded four sacks, second highest on the club.

BIBLIOGRAPHY: Hugh Green, Interview with Robert B. Van Atta, October 1984; Pittsburgh *Post Gazette*, 1977–1981; Pittsburgh *Press*, 1977–1981; *TSN Football Registers—1982–1986; University of Pittsburgh Football Media Guides, 1977–1980.*

Robert B. Van Atta

GREENE, Charles Edward "Joe" "Mean Joe" (b. 24 September 1946, Temple, TX), college and professional player and coach, grew up in a poor black family and was reared by his mother. At Dunbar High School in Temple, he usually played middle linebacker in football. He attended North Texas State University (MVC) as a Physical Education major and was nicknamed "Mean Joe" after the football team's nickname "Mean Green." A consensus All-American in 1968, he also was named MVC Athlete of the Year and the nation's top defensive lineman. The Pittsburgh Steelers (NFL) drafted him in the first round in 1969, although some pro scouts questioned his competitiveness. That same year, he was selected UPI's NFL Rookie of the Year and played in the Pro Bowl. In 1970 he was named to the All-NFL team for the first of five consecutive seasons. Two years later, he received the George Halas Award as the NFL's most valuable player defensively.

The 6 foot, 4 inch, 260 pound Greene dominated at defensive left tackle with strength and quickness. Writer Roy Blount, Jr., commented that Greene was "too strong to be overpowered, too elusive to be hobbled, and too smart to be fooled." Noted for his intensity, he once grabbed the football from the center when offended by persistent holding and threw it into the stands. When playing under control, he became even more intimidating. In a crucial 1972 game against the Houston Oilers, he single-handedly made five quarterback sacks and a fumble recovery to ensure victory. Two years later, against the Cleveland Browns, he recovered a fumble and lateraled the ball to J. T. Thomas for the winning score. The Steelers added many defensive standouts to the "Steel Curtain" to win four Super Bowls (1975–1976, 1979–1980), but none overshadowed Greene. Named defensive captain in 1976, he was selected unanimously to the NFL's 1970s Team of the Decade. After being hampered by neck and shoulder injuries, he retired following the 1981 season.

Even before retirement, Greene appeared in minor films and television commercials. He received a Clio Award for a 1980 Coca-Cola commercial, in which he gave his jersey to a small boy. Since retirement he has served as an assistant coach with the Steelers. He lives in Duncanville, TX, with his wife, Agnes, and three children. Throughout his career, Greene proved a fearsome factor in the Steelers' defensive line. He once told an interviewer, "Intensity is a Pittsburgh tradition." Greene raised that tradition to the highest level. He was elected to the Pro Football Hall of Fame in 1987 and named to its AFL-NFL 1960–1984 All-Star Second Team.

BIBLIOGRAPHY: Roy Blount, Jr., "He Does What He Wants Out There," *SI* 43 (September 22, 1975), pp. 96–104; Diane K. Shah, "The Greene Machine," *Newsweek* 95 (January 21, 1980), pp. 60–61.

Luther W. Spoehr

GREGG, Alvis Forrest (b. 18 October 1933, Birthright, TX), college and professional player and coach, attended Sulphur Springs (TX) High School. The 6 foot, 4 inch, 250 pound Gregg earned a football scholarship from 1952 to 1956 at SMU (SWC). A two-way tackle, he captained the Mustangs in 1955 and made the All-SWC team in 1954 and 1955. In 1956 the Green Bay Packers (NFL) drafted him in the second round. During the 1960s Gregg figured prominently in the Packers' outstanding success. Gregg played with Green Bay in 1956 and from 1958 to 1970, spending 1957 in the military. In 1969 and 1970 he served as a Packers player-coach. The power of the great Packers offensive lines, Gregg played in 188 consecutive games. During his fifteen-year career he made All-Pro eight times and played in the Pro Bowl nine times. He was selected on the NFL team for the 1960s decade and the AFL-NFL 1960–1984 All-Star Team.

He participated in six NFL championship games with the Packers, helped his club win NFL titles in 1961, 1962, 1965, and 1967 and led them to Super Bowl titles in 1966 and 1967. Packer coach Vince Lombardi* once boasted, "Forrest Gregg is the finest player I ever coached." After the Packers released him in 1971, Gregg signed with the Dallas Cowboys (NFL) as a free agent. He helped lead the Cowboys that year to the championship, earning a third Super Bowl ring.

Following his playing career, he served in 1972 and 1973 as an NFL assistant coach with the San Diego Chargers and in 1974 with the Cleveland Browns. He became the Browns head coach in 1975 and the following year was named NFL Coach of the Year. After an 18–23–0 record in three years at the helm, he was replaced in December 1977 by Dick Modzelewski.*

Before coaching the Toronto Argonauts (CFL) in 1979, he joined the San Diego Chargers (NFL) as an assistant coach. In 1980 he became the head coach of the Cincinnati Bengals (NFL) and the next year guided the Bengals to a 12–4 record and a berth in Super Bowl XVI. Although the Bengals lost to the San Francisco 49ers 26–21, Gregg was acclaimed AFC Coach of the Year. In 1982 he again led the Bengals into the NFL playoffs. In his four years with the Bengals, he achieved a 34–27–0 record. He was named head coach of the Green Bay Packers following the 1983 season and compiled 8–8 records in 1984 and 1985. The Packers slipped to a 4–12 mark in 1986. As a pro coach, Gregg has compiled a career NFL 68–76 record.

A member of the Texas Sports Hall of Fame, he was selected in 1977 to the Pro Football Hall of Fame. Gregg and his wife, Barbara, have two children, Forrest, Jr., and Karen, both students at SMU. Forrest, Jr., played center on the SMU Mustangs football team.

BIBLIOGRAPHY: George Allen with Ben Olan, *Pro Football's 100 Greatest Players* (Indianapolis, IN, 1982); *Cincinnati Bengals—At Wilmington College Summer Camp, 1983; Cleveland Browns Media Guide, 1977; Official Pro Football Almanac, 1965; TSN Football Register—1982.*

John L. Evers

GRIER, Roosevelt "Rosey" (b. 14 July 1932, Cuthbert, GA), college athlete and professional football player, starred at defensive football tackle for the New York Giants (1955–1956, 1958–1962) and Los Angeles Rams (1963–1966) of the NFL. Born on a Georgia farm, he is the seventh of eleven children of Joseph and Ruth Grier. He moved north at age 13 to Roselle, NJ, where his father had settled three years earlier in search of work. After graduation from Roselle High School in 1950, Grier attended Penn State University to study psychology, music, and education; he also participated in football and track. In 1955 Grier received All-American honors as a football tackle and established an IC4A league shot-put track record of 58 feet. In 1955 he signed with the New York Giants (NFL) for a $6,500 salary and a $500 bonus. From 1955 until his 1968 retirement, the 6 foot, 5 inch, 300 pound Grier proved a dominant NFL defensive tackle. Combining aggressiveness with speed, Grier performed on a line that led the Giants to a 1956 NFL championship and made All-Pro. After serving in the U.S. Army in 1957, he played a major defensive role in helping the Giants win Eastern Conference titles in 1958, 1959, 1961, and 1962.

In a controversial move, the Giants in 1964 traded Grier to the Los Angeles Rams (NFL) for John Lovotere. Despite bitterness over the trade, Grier continued excelling for the Rams. The Rams line, which also included David "Deacon" Jones,* Merlin Olsen,* and Lamar Lundy and was nicknamed the "Fearsome Foursome," established new football standards for quickness, intelligence, and strength combined with enormous physical size. The four players arguably formed the greatest defensive line in pro football history. After playing in 142 NFL games and missing the 1967 season because of an achilles tendon injury, Grier retired. Grier married the former Beatrice Lewis and had one child, Denise, before being divorced. Grier wed Marge Grier, whom he divorced in 1978 and remarried in 1980, and has one son, Roosevelt Kennedy.

After his football retirement, Grier gained fame as an actor, television personality, and political activist. A published songwriter, singer, guitarist, and pianist, he performed in 1963 at New York's Carnegie Hall. He served on Senator Robert F. Kennedy's 1968 presidential campaign staff and acted in numerous films and television shows. He also authored *Rosey Grier's Needlepoint for Men* (1974). By the late 1970s Grier had withdrawn from show business to concentrate on charitable and religious causes.

BIBLIOGRAPHY: *CB* (1975), pp. 176–79; Roosevelt Grier file, Pro Football Hall of Fame, Canton, OH; Jerry LeBlanc, "Roosevelt Grier," Boston *Sunday Globe Magazine*, August 2, 1970, pp. 26–29; "Look Who's Needling Now!" *SEP* 246 (November, 1974), pp. 48–49, 94; "Takin' Care of Business: Rosy [sic] Grier," *Black Sport* (May 6, 1972), pp. 82, 86–87.

John Hanners

GRIESE, Robert Allen "Bob" (b. 3 February 1945, Evansville, IN), college athlete, professional football player, and sportscaster, is one of three children of plumber Sylverious and secretary Ida (Ulrich) Griese and graduated from Rex Mundi (Evansville) High School in 1963. He lettered in baseball, basketball, track, and football there and was named Indiana's best high school quarterback during his final two years. As a baseball pitcher, he compiled a 17–0 record before losing in the 1963 American Legion World Series. At Purdue University (BTC), Griese lettered in basketball and football. In football he was converted from a side-arm to overhand passer and made All-American twice. As a junior, he completed 19 of 22 passes, including 13 in a row, in a 25–21 upset over then top-ranked Notre Dame. The 6 foot, 1 inch, 190 pound Griese ended his college career with a 14–13 Rose Bowl triumph over Southern California. With the Boilermakers, he completed 348 of 609 attempts for 4,402 yards and also placekicked 75 conversions. Griese, who finished runner-up to Steve Spurrier* in the Heisman Trophy voting in 1966, graduated from Purdue in 1967 with a B.S. in Industrial Management. Griese married Judi Lassus on June 10, 1967, and has three sons.

Drafted by the Miami Dolphins (AFL), Griese quarterbacked during his first pro game when the starter was injured. Although he completed 12 of 19 passes and led Miami to a 35–21 victory, the Dolphins managed only ten more wins in Griese's first three seasons. After Don Shula* assumed the coaching reigns in 1970, Griese led the Dolphins to a 91–39–1 record until retirement. With a strong, accurate arm and an increasing ability to read defenses, Griese started eleven of twelve playoff games (including three straight Super Bowls). He quarterbacked the only NFL team to ever win all seventeen games in a single season, ending with the 1973 Super Bowl. An All-Pro in 1971 and 1977, Griese played in the Pro Bowl six times (1970–1971, 1973–1974, 1977–1978). Griese threw for 192 touchdowns and 25,092 yards and completed 1,926 of 3,429 passes for 56.2 percent in fourteen NFL campaigns. He never recorded a completion percentage below the 50.2 percent of his rookie year, and he reached his peak of 63 percent in 1978. On the day Griese became the 14th NFL passer to reach the 25,000-yard milestone, he ironically suffered a shoulder injury from which he never fully recovered. Major injuries had sidelined him four times previously for five games in 1969, nine contests in 1972, four games in 1975, and five contests in 1978. Some double vision and dizziness in 1976 forced Griese to wear eyeglasses thereafter. Griese in 1977 enjoyed his best year for throwing touchdowns (22) to pace the NFL. Griese was named as *TSN* AFC Player of the Year in 1971 and received the Maxwell Club's Bert Bell Memorial Trophy as NFL Player of the Year in 1977. Other honors included his induction into the Florida Sports Hall of Fame in 1979 and the NFF College Football Hall of Fame in 1985. Dolphins owner Joe Robbie called Griese the "cornerstone of the franchise" and retired his number 12 jersey. Griese believed his competitiveness, intelligence, determination, and desire ensured his success and maintained that a quarterback received too much credit for winning and too much blame for losing.

Griese, who joined NBC in 1982 as an analyst, works in investments, manages real estate holdings, and serves as director of visual education for American Optical. He is national sports chairman for the Muscular Dystrophy Association and regularly volunteers for other children's charities.

BIBLIOGRAPHY: Bob Griese to John E. DiMeglio, 1984; Dan Jenkins, "Spectacles Make Him Spectacular," *SI* 47 (October 10, 1977), pp. 111–112ff; National Broadcasting Company to John E. DiMeglio, 1984.

John E. DiMeglio

GRIFFIN, Archie Mason "Arch" "Butterball" (b. 21 August 1954, Columbus, OH), college and professional player and administrator, remains the only two-time Heisman Trophy winner (1974–1975) emblematic of the nation's outstanding College Football Player of the Year. A four-year (1972–1975) star halfback at Ohio State University (BTC), Griffin garnered several other Player of the Year honors including the UPI, Walter Camp Football Foundation (1974–1975), *TSN* (1974), and Maxwell Award (1975). The Chicago *Tribune* awarded Griffin the Silver Football Trophy as the MVP in the BTC (1973, the first sophomore honored, and 1974). The three-year All-American (the last two unanimous) and two-time Buckeyes co-captain in 1975 became the first college athlete to be named *TSN* Man of the Year. He was the first college player to surpass 5,000 career yards from scrimmage, gaining 5,177 yards on 845 carries (6.1-yard average), and to set an NCAA record with 31 consecutive games of 100-plus yards. Besides setting the Ohio State career rushing mark, Griffin ranked third in total offense and twelfth in scoring. He starred on two undefeated regular-season and four BTC championship teams (the first three shared with Michigan) and started in four Rose Bowl games. During that span, the Buckeyes lost only two games to BTC rivals, finished 3–0–1 with archrival Michigan, and compiled a 40–5–1 composite record.

The son of James and Margaret (Monroe) Griffin, Sr., he was the fourth of eight children (seven boys and the youngest a girl). All seven Griffin boys played major college football, three later performing in the NFL. His father often worked three jobs simultaneously, driving a sanitation truck during the day, working in a steel foundry at night, and filling in as part-time school custodian. An overweight child, Archie was called "Butterball" by his family and "Tank" by fellow football Little Leaguers. He performed in the line but found his niche in the backfield when the regular fullback failed to appear for a game. Griffin's junior high school English teacher once observed, "Archie is the most motivated, single-minded youngster I've ever seen. He got the best grades . . . was the most spontaneous . . . a model student." Griffin, a three-year regular halfback at Columbus Eastmoor High School, was named All-District as a junior and All-State his final year after leading Eastmoor to the City championship. He wrestled at 167 pounds and performed in the relays and sprints on the track team before graduating from high school in 1972.

The 5 foot, 8 inch, 182 pound Griffin planned to play football at Northwestern University but was persuaded by coach Woody Hayes* to enroll at Ohio State (BTC). Griffin played under two minutes in the 1972 opening triumph over Iowa, but was inserted midway through the first quarter of the second game with North Carolina when the inept Buckeyes fell behind 7–0. He exploded for a Buckeyes-record 239 yards and one touchdown to hand the twelfth-rated Tarheels their only season loss 29–14. Ohio State was outclassed 42–17 in the 1973 Rose Bowl by national champion Southern California, but finished 9–2–0 and ranked ninth nationally. Griffin began his remarkable string of 100-yard performances in the 1973 opener with Minnesota, gaining 129 yards in the 56–7 Buckeye triumph. He set a new Ohio State record with 246 yards against Iowa in a late-season encounter. Sixth-ranked BTC co-champion Michigan tied the Buckeyes 10–10 in the finale but lost the Rose Bowl bid to Ohio State. The Buckeyes gained a measure of revenge against Southern California by defeating the eighth-ranked Trojans 42–21, becoming the first BTC team to triumph over a PTC opponent in the Rose Bowl in five years. Griffin gained 149 yards on 22 carries and scored one touchdown. Ohio State finished the season 10–0–1, was ranked second nationally, and averaged 37.5 points per game.

Griffin fit well in Hayes' system that emphasized a strong running game.

Hayes credited him with exceptional blocking ability, especially in short yardage situations when fullback Pete Johnson sought to score. This strategy accounted for Johnson's Ohio State scoring record and Griffin's relatively modest 26-touchdown career production. The short, stocky Griffin had gapped front teeth, wore linemen's thigh pads, often played hurt, and seldom practiced before Wednesdays due to the constant physical pounding he received. "He'll catch the big pass that bails you out," Hayes declared. "He'll block. He'll run. That's why he's so enormously effective and valuable to our team, why our morale is so high."

Griffin gained 1,620 and 1,357 yards his last two seasons in leading the Buckeyes to fourth-place national rankings both years. Ohio State lost an 18–17 heartbreaker to the Trojans in the 1975 Rose Bowl, when Southern California quarterback Pat Haden completed late passes for a touchdown and two-point conversion. Ohio State was rated number 1 nationally in 1975 and defeated Michigan 21–14 to cap a perfect 11–0–0 season. The Wolverines ended Griffin's 100-yard games streak, however, holding him to 46 yards on 19 carries. The Buckeyes trounced UCLA 41–20 in midseason but lost to the fifth-ranked Bruins 23–10 in the Rose Bowl.

From a religious family, Griffin participated in the Fellowship of Christian Athletes and Campus Crusade for Christ. He earned a B.S. in Industrial Relations and graduated in 1976 one quarter earlier than scheduled. The Cincinnati Bengals made him second pick in the first round of the NFL draft. Griffin performed eight seasons with the Bengals, gradually converting from a ballcarrier to pass receiver. After suffering pulled stomach and groin muscles in 1983, he retired as the Bengals' fourth leading all-time rusher (2,808 yards, 4.0-yard average) and fifth best receiver (192 receptions).

Griffin and his brothers, James, Jr., and Ray, established six retail outlets for athletic footwear but expanded too rapidly and filed for bankruptcy in 1981. At Hayes' suggestion, Griffin joined the Ohio State staff in 1984 as special assistant to athletic director Rick Bay and specializes in public relations and fund-raising. He played part of the 1985 season with the USFL's Jacksonville Bulls—rushing 11 yards on 10 carries and catching 4 passes for 25 yards—but returned to Ohio State in midseason. Griffin, who in 1976 married college classmate Loretta Laffitte of Cleveland, OH, has one son, Anthony, and one daughter, Andrea.

BIBLIOGRAPHY: Edward F. Dolan, Jr., and Richard B. Lyttle, *Archie Griffin* (Garden City, NY, 1977); Archie Griffin and Dave Diles, *Archie: The Archie Griffin Story* (Garden City, NY, 1977); Dave Newhouse, *Heisman, After the Glory* (St. Louis, 1985); *Ohio State Football Media Guide, 1985.*

James D. Whalen

GROZA, Louis Roy "Lou" "The Toe" (b. 25 January 1924, Martins Ferry, OH), college and professional player, attended high school in Martins Ferry and received his B.S. in Business Administration from Ohio State University in 1949. He played football for the Buckeyes (WC) as an offensive lineman. In 1950 he married Jackie Lou Robbins and has four children, Jeff, Jill, John, and Jud. Groza, a 6 foot, 3 inch, 250 pound offensive tackle and placekicker, began his pro football career with Paul Brown's* Cleveland Browns (AAFC) in 1946. When the AAFC folded after the 1949 season, Cleveland joined the NFL. The Browns won the NFL title their first year on Groza's 16-yard field goal with 20 seconds left in regulation time to defeat the Los Angeles Rams 30–28 in the 1950 championship game. During that same season Groza had kicked a record 13 field goals. For the next several years Cleveland and Groza dominated the NFL. The Browns finished first seven out of eight times, as Groza led the NFL in field goals five times (1950, 1952–1954, 1957), a feat yet unmatched. No other kicker ever accomplished it three years in a row.

In 1953 he broke his own mark for most field goals (23) in only 26 attempts for a record 88.5 percentage. During the season Groza kicked an unprecedented 12 straight field goals. Due to his highly accurate placekicking, Groza was nicknamed "The Toe" by the press. He won his only scoring title in 1957, tying Washington's Sam Baker with 77 points. A back injury forced Groza to miss the entire 1960 season, but he returned to action in 1961. Groza made pro football history in 1964 by becoming the first player to score 1,000 career points and in 1965 by kicking his 200th career field goal.

After playing seventeen years in the NFL, Groza retired following the 1967 season. He had accumulated 1,349 points from one touchdown, 641 extra points, and 244 field goals, an NFL career record. With his AAFC output of 259 points (169 point after touchdowns and 30 field goals), he collected 1,608 career points. Groza also kicked 3 field goals in each of 21 games, an unprecedented record. Groza played on four championship teams (1950, 1954–1955, 1964) during his NFL tenure and was voted to the Pro Bowl an unequalled nine times (1950–1955, 1957–1959). During six of those years (1951–1955, 1957), he earned All-Pro honors. He appeared in a record nine championship games (1950–1955, 1957, 1964–1965), setting several marks in these contests. Groza was selected to the Pro Football Hall of Fame in 1974.

BIBLIOGRAPHY: *Cleveland Browns Press Guide, 1969;* Rick Gonsalves, *Specialty Teams* (New York, 1977); *TSN Football Register—1967.*

Richard Gonsalves

GUY, William Ray (b. 22 December 1949, Swainsboro, GA), college and professional athlete, ranks among the greatest punters in history and has been one of the Oakland–Los Angeles Raiders' (NFL) most valuable assets for the past decade. The first punter ever selected in the first round of the NFL draft (1973), he excelled as a baseball pitcher and football defensive back and kicker in high school (Thomson, GA) and college (University of Southern Mississippi, 1970–1972). A College All-American selection in 1972, he made the longest punt in NCAA history (93 yards against Mississippi in 1971) and a 61-yard field goal (against Utah State in 1972). He led the NCAA in punting in 1972 with 58 kicks for a 46.2-yard average and ranked second in NCAA career punting with 200 boots for a 44.7-yard average. Guy also made 51 of 59 career points after touchdowns, 25 of 59 career field goals, and 8 interceptions (fourth best nationally) for the 1972 season. As a baseball pitcher, the 6 foot, 3 inch, 195 pound Guy averaged better than one strikeout an inning in college and was drafted by the NL Cincinnati Reds (1969, 1973), Houston Astros (1971), and Atlanta Braves (1972).

After joining the Raiders in 1973, Guy embarked on a remarkably consistent punting career. He compiled a 42.4-yard punting average from 1973 through 1986 (with a minimum of 39.1 yards in 1982 and maximum of 45.3 yards in 1973), based on 1,049 kicks in 207 games. Only three of his punts have been blocked in a 14-year period. Described by a teammate as the Raiders' best offensive weapon, Guy enjoyed an outstanding game against the San Diego Chargers for the 1980 AFC championship by making four punts for a 50-yard average with a title-game record 71-yard effort that helped the Raiders to a 34–27 win. Known for his high hanging kicks, Guy once was suspected by the Houston Oilers of using a helium-filled football. The perennial All-Pro selection must be rated one of the superstars of specialty-team football. Guy participated in Super Bowls following the 1976, 1980, and 1983 seasons and played in the Pro Bowl from 1973 through 1978 and in 1980. The Pro Football Hall of Fame named him to its AFL-NFL 1960–1984 All-Star Team.

BIBLIOGRAPHY: Los Angeles Raiders, Sports Publicity Department, Los Angeles, CA; Lou Sahadi, *The Raiders: Cinderella Champions of Pro Football* (New York, 1981).

Leonard Frey

GUYON, Joseph N. "Joe" (b. 26 August 1892, Mahnomen, MN; d. 27 November 1971, Louisville, KY), college and professional player, was named to the Pro Football Hall of Fame (1966) and NFF College Football Hall of Fame (1971). The versatile Guyon starred at tackle and halfback for the Carlisle Indians (1912–1913) and Georgia Tech (SIAA, 1917–1918) and claimed All-American honors at both positions. Besides being chosen at halfback in 1970 on the NFL's 1920s Decade Team, Guyon was named All-Time All-American halfback by John W. Heisman* (1920), All-Time Specialist at running back by Allison Danzig* (OS) (1971), All-Time Southeastern Regional Early Era (1869–1919) fullback by the FWAA, and All-Time Carlisle Indian halfback by Glenn "Pop" Warner* (1914). A member of Georgia Tech's 1917 squad rated national champions by HAF, Guyon played in the backfield with quarterback Albert Hill, All-American halfback Everett Strupper, and fullback J. W. "Judy" Harlan. This backfield was judged one of the nation's all-time best by Clark Shaughnessy* (1943) and historian L. H. Baker (1945).

The 5 foot, 11 inch, 190 pound Guyon in 1912 was rated one of the finest tackles in the Middle States by noted University of Pennsylvania authority George W. Orton* (OS). Carlisle, led by legendary halfback Jim Thorpe,* finished 12–1–1; defeated Syracuse, Pittsburgh, Georgetown, Army, and Brown; and paced the nation scoring 504 points (36 average per game). The Indians averaged under 170 pounds per man and usually were outweighed, but they benefited from team speed, desire, pride of heritage, and Warner's coaching. Guyon replaced the departed Thorpe at halfback in 1913 and was named All-American by Parke H. Davis, coach Thomas J. Thorpe, and *Outing* magazine. Walter Camp* placed Guyon on his second team. Carlisle finished 10–1–1 and handed Dartmouth its only defeat 35–10. Guyon scored two touchdowns against Dartmouth and made the only touchdown in a 7–0 triumph over Cornell.

Guyon left Carlisle during the summer of 1914 to enroll at Keewatin Academy, a college preparatory school in St. Augustine (FL) not fielding an eleven. After transferring to Georgia Tech in 1917, Guyon played two years under coach John W. Heisman on 9–0–0 and 6–1–0 teams. The 1917 national champions (the first southern school to capture the title) fielded All-American tackle captain Walker Carpenter and end guard Bill Fincher,* averaged 54.6 points per game, and outscored opponents 491–17. Heisman employed his famous "jump shift" on offense, coaching his backs and linemen to barely pause before the ball was snapped. The Yellow Jackets overwhelmed perennial southern powers Auburn 68–7 and Vanderbilt 83–0, as Guyon sprinted to 48- and 75-yard touchdowns and amassed 344 yards on 12 carries (29-yard average). Pennsylvania (9–2–0) provided the high point of Georgia Tech's schedule. Before 10,000 spectators at Georgia Tech's Grant Field, the Yellow Jackets demolished 41–0 the East's second best team.

Guyon, halfback on the 1917 Atlanta *Constitution*'s All-American team, proved a big, fast, and excellent runner, passer, blocker, tackler, and punter. *Constitution* sports editor Ralph McGill wrote, "There is no doubt in my mind but that Guyon is the greatest football player the South ever saw." Paradoxically, however, the moody Guyon often lacked the inspiration to do his best. Guyon, consensus All-American tackle in 1918, and captain Fincher were the only returning regulars from the 1917 championship team. Most other squad members were freshmen, but Georgia Tech still lost only one game on the abbreviated wartime schedule and averaged 66 points per outing. The Yellow Jackets' 33-game undefeated streak, extending back to 1914, was broken in a 32–0 loss to Pittsburgh's national champions.

Guyon performed at halfback with the pro Canton Bulldogs (1919–1920) and received second-team All-Pro mention. He played with the Cleveland

Indians (1921) during the initial NFL season and then starred with the NFL Marion (OH) Oorang Indians (1922–1923). A member of the fifth-place 6–2–2 Rock Island (IL) Independents (1924), Guyon was named to the *Ohio State Journal*'s All-Pro third team. He performed with the Kansas City Cowboys (1925) and ended his pro career in 1927 with the 11–1–1 NFL champion New York Giants. Guyon's 95-yard punt in 1920 remained a pro record for fifty years. His parents, the Charles M. Guyons, were members of the Chippewa Tribe. Guyon lived in Harrah, OK, and then Flint, MI, where he served as a bank guard for the Citizens National Bank. Guyon, whose son Joseph F. was a Michigan physician, died from injuries received in an automobile accident in Louisville.

BIBLIOGRAPHY: Georgia Institute of Technology, Archives Library, Atlanta, GA; Joe Guyon file, National Archives, Washington, DC; Jim Koger, *National Champions* (Columbus, GA, 1970); John D. McCallum and Charles H. Pearson, *College Football U.S.A., 1869-1973* (New York, 1973); Ronald L. Mendell and Timothy B. Phares, *Who's Who in Football* (New Rochelle, NY, 1974); John S. Steckbeck, *Fabulous Redmen: The Carlisle Indians and their Famous Football Teams* (Harrisburg, PA, 1951); Al Thomy, *The Ramblin' Wreck: A Story of Georgia Tech Football* (Huntsville, AL, 1973); Roger Treat, ed., *The Encyclopedia of Football*, 16th rev. ed., rev. by Pete Palmer (New York, 1979).

James D. Whalen

H

HALAS, George Stanley "Papa Bear" (b. 2 February 1895, Chicago, Il; d. 31 October 1983, Chicago, IL), college and professional athlete, coach, and owner, was a pioneer and pillar of the NFL for over fifty years. He grew up in an ethnic, working-class neighborhood on Chicago's West Side, the last of eight children (four died in infancy) born to Frank J. and Barbara (Poledna) Halas, first-generation Bohemian immigrants. From his father's initial earnings as a tailor, the Halas family opened a grocery store and saloon and acquired real estate. While enjoying the comforts of a middle-class family, George learned the thrift, hard work, and loyalty that dominated his adult life. He married Wilhelmina "Min" Bushing in 1922 and had two children, Virginia and George, Jr. His son, "Mugs," served as treasurer and president of the Chicago Bears (NFL) from 1963 until his death in 1979.

Halas attended Crane Technical High School, where he lettered in football, basketball, and baseball. After graduating in 1913, he worked for a year in the payroll department of the Western Electric Company in Cicero, IL. Halas attended the University of Illinois (WC), where he received a B.S. in Civil Engineering in 1918. A three-sport letterman, Halas played football for Bob Zuppke,* captained the basketball squad, and starred on the championship baseball team. Forgiven his last six college credits, in January 1918 Halas joined the U.S. Navy as an ensign assigned to the sports program at the Great Lakes Naval Training Center. He was named the MVP in the 1919 Rose Bowl game, as Great Lakes defeated the Mare Island Marines 17–0. (Halas again volunteered for service in the U.S. Navy during World War II and from 1942 to 1945 served as a lieutenant commander in charge of the recreational operations for the Seventh Fleet in the Pacific.)

Discharged from the U.S. Navy in March, 1919, Halas participated in spring training with the New York Yankees and made the AL baseball team as a fleet, switch-hitting right fielder. After batting only .091 in twelve games, he spent the rest of the 1919 season with St. Paul, MN (AA). He then worked in the bridge design department of the Chicago, Burlington, and Quincy Railroad Company while playing semi-pro football on Sundays with the Hammond (IN) Tigers. In March 1920 he moved to Decatur, IL, to work for the A. E. Staley Company. Besides learning the starch products business, he served as athletic director and player-coach of the company's semi-pro football team. A year later he became co-owner of the team with Edward "Dutch" Sternaman and moved it to Chicago. In 1922 he renamed the team the Bears because they shared Wrigley Field with baseball's Chicago Cubs.

For sixty-three years Halas served the Bears as player, coach, and owner—the longest continuous association with a single team in sports history. Despite his slight build, he earned a spot on the All-NFL team of the 1920s because of his quickness and ferocity as an end for the Bears from 1920 to 1929. For four separate ten-year periods (1920–1929, 1933–1942, 1946–1955, 1958–1967), Halas effectively combined owner-coach duties to become the winningest coach in pro football history with a 326–150–31 career mark and .673 winning percentage. Exhibiting a rough, physical brand of football, his "Monsters of the Midway" won eight NFL championships (1921, 1932–1933, 1940–1941, 1943, 1946, 1963) and 11 Western Division titles. The Bears finished second fifteen times and below .500 only six times. The admitted highlight of his illustrious career came in Chicago's 73–0 victory over the Washington Redskins in the 1940 NFL championship game in a near flawless performance by the underdog Bears. After retiring from coaching in 1968 at age 73, Halas continued as active owner of the Bears. He also served from 1970 to his death as the first president of the NFC following the merger of the NFL and the AFL. The shrewd businessman became the wealthiest coach in pro football history due to his extensive investments in oil, real estate, and sporting goods.

Although the popular legend of Halas as the "Father of the NFL" is overdrawn, his dominant influence on the game as sport and business for over fifty years makes him the principal catalyst and primary symbol of modern pro football. In 1920 he attended the initial organizational meeting of the APFA (renamed the NFL in 1922). A longtime senior owner and member of the rules committee, he championed such far-reaching rules changes as creating hash marks, moving the goalposts to the goal line, and allowing the forward pass to be thrown from any place behind the line of scrimmage. The Bears owner brought unprecedented publicity and popularity to the pro game by signing collegiate star Harold "Red" Grange* in 1925 and was the first to broadcast games. As coach, he pioneered in conducting daily practice sessions, using classroom instruction and game films, locating spotters in the stands to suggest plays, and hiring full-time assistant coaches. With Clark Shaughnessy,* he developed the man-in-motion T formation that remains the basic offensive style of pro football.

The self-made Halas, for whom football symbolized life, has been called "the first buccaneer and the last puritan" of pro football. The nickname "Papa

Bear" signified no term of endearment because the crusty, combative, and often conniving curmudgeon frequently angered Bears personnel, opponents, and fellow owners alike. A parsimonious, paternalistic autocrat, he held personal loyalty and self-sacrifice as cardinal virtues. He admitted, "I like to win, and I fought for everything in the book. Nothing else mattered." In later years he was criticized as owner and coach for losing touch with the modern game and blamed for the declining success of the Bears after World War II. He may have been responsible for the unofficial racial segregation of pro football in the 1930s and 1940s; the Bears suffered in the 1950s and 1960s from a paucity of black players.

Although infrequently praised, Halas was respected universally as an innovative coach and entrepreneur. His leadership and influence in the NFL proved critical in elevating pro football from a Sunday diversion to a national sports industry. Fittingly, he was elected in 1963 a charter member of the Pro Football Hall of Fame.

BIBLIOGRAPHY: Myron Cope, ed., *The Game That Was: The Early Days of Pro Football* (New York, 1970); Frank Deford, "I Don't Date Any Woman under 48," *SI* 47 (December 5, 1977), pp. 36–38ff.; Ray Didinger, "George Halas: He Invented Pro Football," *Football Digest* 13 (February, 1984), pp. 32–35; George S. Halas, "My Forty Years in Pro Football," *SEP* 230 (November 23, 1957), pp. 34–35ff., (November 30, 1957), pp. 30ff., and (December 7, 1957), pp. 36ff.; George Halas with Gwen Morgan and Arthur Veysey, *Halas by Halas: The Autobiography of George Halas* (New York, 1979); Jerry Kirshenbaum, "Papa Bear," *SI* 59 (November 14, 1983), p. 17; *NYT*, December 30, 1963, November 1–2, 1983; *TSN*, January 2, 1982, August 16, 1982, November 14, 1983; George Vass, *George Halas and the Chicago Bears* (Chicago, 1971).

Larry R. Gerlach

HAM, Jack Raphael (b. 23 December 1948, Johnstown, PA), college and professional player, is the son of mining mechanic John and Caroline Ham. He graduated in 1966 from Bishop McCort High School in Johnstown, PA, where he participated on the football and track teams. At Penn State University, he majored in real estate and insurance and started three years at linebacker on the football team. During his senior year he served as defensive captain and was named an All-American. His Nittany Lions finished undefeated in 1968 and 1969 and won the post-season Orange Bowls. The Pittsburgh Steelers selected Ham in the second round of the 1971 NFL draft and used him at outside linebacker. His speed, quickness, and ability to anticipate plays made him especially effective against the pass. In the 1974 AFC championship game, he helped defeat the Oakland Raiders with two interceptions. His 32 career interceptions rank him third on the all-time list among NFL linebackers.

Although not big physically for an outside linebacker, the 6 foot, 1 inch, 220 pound Ham used intelligence, toughness, and speed to compensate for lack of size. He was selected to his first Pro Bowl in 1973 and became the only NFL linebacker named to the game eight straight seasons. Besides being NFL Defensive Player of the Year in 1975, he was the only unanimous defensive choice for the NFL's Team of the Decade. With Jack Lambert* and Andy Russell, Ham made Pittsburgh's linebacking corps a mainstay of the "Steel Curtain" defense that contributed to Super Bowl wins in 1975, 1976, 1979, and 1980. Ham suffered a broken ankle against Houston on December 10, 1979, and never regained his former mobility. After returning as a starter in 1980, he then broke his arm in a pre-season game against Cleveland in 1981. He returned again but retired after the 1982 season. He lives with his wife, Joanne (Fell) Ham, in Pittsburgh, where he works for the Neville Coal Company and helps raise funds for the American Cancer Society and other medical charities.

Although quiet and retiring off the field, Ham always seemed to be in the center of the football action. His critical tackles, interceptions, and fumble recoveries helped the Steeler defense of the mid-1970s become pro football's version of the immovable object.

BIBLIOGRAPHY: Pittsburgh *Press*, 1971–1982; Lou Sahadi, *Super Steelers* (New York, 1980).

Luther W. Spoehr

HANNAH, John Allen (b. 4 April 1951, Canton, GA), college athlete and professional football player, is the son of farming supply businessman Herb and Geneva Hannah. His father Herbert played tackle for the New York Giants (NFL) and his brother Charley performs at tackle for the Los Angeles Raiders (NFL). Hannah attended Baylor School for Boys in Chattanooga, TN, and Albertsville (AL) High School, where he starred in football, wrestling, and track. Hannah won the National Prep Wrestling Championship while at Baylor.

At the University of Alabama (SEC, 1969–1972), Hannah lettered in three sports. He remained undefeated as a freshman heavyweight wrestler, won the SEC shot put (61 feet, 5 inches) and discus (177 feet, 1 inch) track championship, and holds the SEC indoor shot put record. The three-time All-SEC grid choice twice made All-American (1971–1972). In 1972 Hannah was selected the Lineman of the Year by Touchdown Clubs in Columbus, OH; Miami, FL; Birmingham, AL; Washington, DC; and Atlanta, GA. He was also one of the four finalists for the Lombardi Award and received the Jacobs Award as the outstanding SEC blocker. The 6 foot, 3 inch, 265 pound offensive guard performed for the Crimson Tide in the Astro-Bluebonnet (1970), Orange (1971), and Cotton Bowls (1972). Following his career at Alabama, Hannah enjoyed outstanding performances in the College All-Star and Hula Bowl games.

Since being selected by New England in the first round of the 1973 NFL draft, Hannah performed for the Patriots through the 1985 season. Named to the All-Rookie team in 1973, Hannah earned wide recognition in 1976 as one of the best NFL guards. In 1977 he received the Mack Truck Award (given by players to the top offensive lineman) and has received virtually every honor accorded linemen in pro football. *TSN* honored Hannah on the AFC All-Star teams (1974, 1976, 1978–1979) and NFL All-Star teams (1980–1981, 1984–1985). He was named to the Pro Bowl following the 1976 and the 1978 through 1985 seasons. New England, the AFC Eastern Division co-champion in 1976 and champion in 1978, lost in the playoffs until 1985. In 1985 Hannah helped lead the Patriots to Super Bowl XX, where they lost 46–10 to the Chicago Bears.

Hannah and his wife, Page, a former Alabama cheerleader, were married in 1972 and have one son, Seth, and one daughter, Mary Beth. Hannah is also a stockbroker for the international firm of L. F. Rothschild in Boston, MA. He has approached his second career with the same determination for perfection that has led him to almost universal acclaim as pro football's finest offensive lineman. After undergoing operations on both shoulders to remove calcium deposits and arthroscopic surgery on his left knee, Hannah retired from pro football in June 1986. The Pro Football Hall of Fame named him to its AFL-NFL 1960–1984 All-Star Team.

BIBLIOGRAPHY: Jon Saraceno, "John Hannah," *USA Today*, January 20, 1986, p. 4C; *New England Patriots Media Guide, 1977; TSN Football Register—1985;* Paul Zimmerman, "John Hannah Doesn't Fiddle Around," *SI* 55 (August 3, 1981), pp. 47–62.

John L. Evers

HARDER, Marlin M. "Pat" (b. 6 May 1922, Milwaukee, WI), college and professional player and referee, is the son of Martin and Martha Harder. A 1940 graduate of Washington (Milwaukee) High School, he established several rushing and scoring records there. After enrolling at the University of Wisconsin (WC) that fall, the 5 foot, 11 inch, 205 pound Harder in 1942 became a football All-American at running back, led the WC in scoring, and was chosen the WC's MVP. Military service from 1943 through 1945 interrupted his collegiate but not his football career. Besides playing with Georgia Preflight, he participated in the 1943 college All-Star game and scored 15 of his team's winning 27 points.

Upon discharge as a sergeant in 1945, Harder waived his remaining college eligibility to sign with the Chicago Cardinals (NFL) and joined its "Dream Blackfield." The Cardinals won Western Division titles in 1947 and 1948 and the NFL championship in 1947, with Harder keying that success. As a halfback and placekicker, he led or tied the NFL in scoring for three consecutive years with 102 points (1947), 110 points (1948), and 102 points (1949)—a feat only three others had then accomplished. Harder married Margaret Austin on May 24, 1947, and has two children.

Traded to Detroit in 1951, Harder contributed substantially to the Lions' winning two National Conference championships. His greatest game perhaps occurred in the 1952 National Conference contest against the Los Angeles Rams, when Harder scored two touchdowns and kicked one field goal and four extra points. Hobbled by injuries, he retired in 1953 to join the Wayerhaeuser Company and eventually became a district manager. From 1965 to 1982 he also served as an NFL field umpire.

During eight pro seasons, Harder rushed for 3,016 yards, tallied 38 touchdowns (33 running and 5 receiving), kicked 198 extra points and 35 field goals for 531 points, and caught 92 passes for 864 yards and 9.4-yard average. In 1948 he kicked 53 extra points without a miss and established an NFL record with 9 extra points in one game. An All-NFL team selection in 1947, 1948, and 1949, Harder played in four college All-Star games and one Pro Bowl. In many ways, his achievements surpass those of subsequent kicking specialists. A complete player, Harder proved a jarring runner, skillful pass receiver, and exceptional blocker.

BIBLIOGRAPHY: *Chicago Cardinals Press Guides, 1946–1950; Detroit Lions Press Guides, 1951–1953; Football Digest* 1 (October, 1971); Oliver E. Kuechle with Jim Mott, *On Wisconsin!: Badger Football* (Huntsville, AL, 1977); Milwaukee (WI) *Sentinel*, December 2, 1953; Seattle (WA) *Post-Intelligencer*, January 16, 1977.

Jerome Mushkat

HARDWICK, Huntington Reed "Tack" (b. 15 October 1892, Quincy, MA; d. 26 June 1949, Cuttyhank, MA), college player, excelled on three of coach Percy Haughton's* golden era teams at Harvard University (IL). Hardwick, a 6 foot, 172 pounder from aristocratic family, was known for running, blocking, and tackling and made first-team All-American in 1914. Hardwick began his college career in 1911 as a right halfback on the Harvard freshman team. He moved to left halfback his sophomore year and scored in his second varsity game, a 19–0 victory over Holy Cross. After his 60-yard touchdown in a 46–0 romp over Amherst, he scored again in Harvard's first victory over Princeton since 1887. His lesser known but more unique defensive abilities played a central role in the victory over Yale to conclude the undefeated season. After his jarring tackle of an Eli punt returner knocked the ball loose, a teammate carried it into the end zone for Harvard's first score on the ground against Yale in eleven years. When the great Edward Mahan* and Paul Bradlee arrived his junior year, Hardwick moved to end and gained his greatest honors there. Although others made the headlines, Hardwick contributed as a formidable tackler and as a great blocker for Haughton's famous running offense.

In 1914 Hardwick completed an undefeated career with Haughton's greatest team. Although a first-team All-American end, Hardwick made his most notable performance at halfback. After crushing opponents 44–0 in the first two games, Harvard suddenly suffered backfield injuries and illness. Hardwick returned to halfback and scored all Harvard's points in a narrow 10–9 victory over Washington and Jefferson. Harvard was trailing late in the game when Hardwick led a long scoring drive and kicked the conversion to preserve the three-year unbeaten streak. Hardwick's versatility produced another close victory against Michigan, whom the Crimson played for the first time since 1895. Harvard generated few scoring opportunities. After Harvard briefly stalled on the Michigan 30-yard line, Hardwick threw a rare pass for a 12-yard gain. A few plays later, Hardwick ran 5 yards for the game's only score. In Hardwick's final game, Harvard routed Yale 36–0 and inhospitably spoiled the Elis' dedication of the Yale Bowl.

On three consecutive undefeated teams, Hardwick made his mark as a runner, blocker, pass receiver, and exceptionally hard tackler. In his senior year Hardwick and five teammates were selected first-team All-Americans. Hardwick's versatility helped Haughton make the most of this remarkable talent. Grantland Rice* (OS) said, "Of all the college players I have known since 1900 I would say he was top man in the matter of flaming spirit. He loved football with an intensity beyond belief. Tack was a great halfback and a great end. But above all, as a real tribute, he was a great blocker and a great tackler." In recognition of these talents Hardwick was elected to the NFF College Football Hall of Fame in its second election (1954).

Hardwick joined the Hayden Stone investment company in 1915 and served overseas as an artillery lieutenant and captain in World War I. After rejoining Stone and Company, he worked for Doremus investment company in the 1920s. In 1929 he helped found Boston Garden, an indoor sports facility, and served on the arena's executive committee. An ardent outdoorsman, he once headed a shark fishing trip to Galapagos. Hardwick, who participated in several sports promotion enterprises, was survived by his second wife, Manuela, and one daughter, Mrs. Edward Simmons, by his first marriage.

BIBLIOGRAPHY: Morris A. Bealle, *The History of Football at Harvard, 1874–1948* (Washington, DC, 1948); Allison Danzig, *The History of American Football: Its Great Teams, Players, and Coaches* (Englewood Cliffs, NJ, 1956); Allison Danzig, *Oh, How They Played the Game: The Early Days of Football and the Heroes Who Made It Great* (New York, 1971).

Bruce Leslie

HARE, Thomas Truxton "Trux" (b. 12 October 1878, Philadelphia, PA; d. 2 February 1956, Radnor, PA), college athlete, was one of only four Walter Camp* four-year All-Americans (1897–1900) as a star on the University of Pennsylvania (IL) football team. Hare played guard on the 1897 Penn undefeated (15–0–0) national championship squad that set the Quaker scoring record and was chosen team captain his last two seasons. Named

HAF 1900 Player of the Year, he was selected a charter member of the NFF College Football Hall of Fame in 1951 and the HAF College Football Hall of Fame. He made seventeen All-Time All-American teams, including those of John Heisman,* Fielding Yost,* Pop Warner,* George Trevor, Parke Davis,* and the HAF.

The son of prominent Philadelphia attorney Horace Binney and Emily Power (Beale) Hare, he attended St. Mark's Preparatory School, Southboro, MA. He participated in football, baseball, and track there and graduated in 1897. During Hare's four-year varsity football career at Penn (IL), the Quakers compiled a 47–5–2 composite record and held 32 opponents scoreless. Coach George Woodruff originated the guards-back formation, enabling Hare to become Penn's most dependable ground gainer, punter, and dropkicker. Besides calling signals, he played linebacker, kicked off, and booted conversions. According to Walter Camp,* Hare was the only player who could have made All-American at any position. His rushing yardage helped Penn triumph over Harvard 15–6 in 1897, while his excellent punting averted defeat against Cornell in 1898. In 1899 his two touchdowns helped defeat Michigan, and his defensive work preserved a tie with WC champion Chicago. He scored 65- and 35-yard touchdowns against Cornell and Harvard respectively in 1900.

The 6 foot, 2 inch, 200 pound Hare performed the hammer throw and shot put on the Quakers track team, which won three consecutive college championships. He placed second in the 1900 Paris Olympics with a hammer throw of 151 feet, 9 inches and first in the Tug of War. The soft-spoken Hare participated in dramatics, music, and literature and was elected "spoon man" by his senior classmates, one of the highest class honors.

After graduating in 1901 with a B.S. degree Hare earned a Bachelor of Law degree from the University of Pennsylvania Law School in 1904. He specialized in corporate law and joined the legal division of United Gas Improvement Company, Radnor, PA, in 1914. After retiring in 1941, he served as managing director of Bryn Mawr (PA) Hospital until 1946 and president until 1950. Hare married Katharine Sargent Smith of Philadelphia in 1906 and had four children. Besides enjoying golf and tennis, he painted for numerous exhibitions and wrote eight books for boys. He died at home after a prolonged illness.

BIBLIOGRAPHY: Edward R. Bushnell, *History of Athletics at University of Pennsylvania* (Philadelphia, 1909); Ralph Hickok, *Who Was Who in American Sports* (New York, 1971); John D. McCallum and Charles H. Pearson, *College Football U.S.A., 1869-1973* (New York, 1973); Ronald L. Mendell and Timothy B. Phares, *Who's Who in Football* (New Rochelle, NY, 1974); University of Pennsylvania, Library Archives, Philadelphia, PA; Alexander M. Weyand, *Football Immortals* (New York, 1962); Alexander M. Weyand, *The Olympic Pageant* (New York, 1952).

James D. Whalen

HARLEY, Charles Wesley "Chic" (b. 15 September 1895, Chicago, IL; d. 21 April 1974, Danville, IL), college athlete and professional football player, made three-time All-American (1916–1917, 1919) in football at Ohio State University (WC). Harley's 201 career points, including 23 touchdowns, 39 points after touchdowns, and 8 field goals, remained an Ohio State scoring record until broken by Howard Cassady* thirty-six years later. Ohio State won its first two WC titles in 1916 and 1917 and came within ten seconds of a third undefeated season and WC championship in 1919. In 1922 the Buckeyes completed the huge concrete stadium nicknamed the "House That 'Chic' Built."

A charter NFF College Football Hall of Fame member in 1951, the 5 foot, 9 inch, 158 pound Harley was named to the HAF and Ohio State University Halls of Fame. In 1956 he made the Miami (FL) *Daily News* All-Time All-American Team. The triple-threat performer failed to score in only three games. As a sophomore, he ran 20 yards for a touchdown and dropkicked the conversion to defeat Illinois 7–6. In a 14–13 victory over Wisconsin, Harley scored touchdown runs of 27 and 80 yards and dropkicked the final extra point. He scored touchdowns on a 20-yard run and 67-yard punt return and made a 34-yard field goal in a 23–3 triumph over John "Paddy" Driscoll's* previously undefeated Northwestern Wildcats. During his junior season he scored four touchdowns (40, 8, 11, and 33 yards) against Indiana, made two touchdown passes (25 and 32 yards) and a field goal against Wisconsin, and hurled a 17-yard touchdown pass and kicked 2 field goals against Illinois. Harley's blocking and decoying enabled Pete Stinchcomb to score three touchdowns in a 40–0 rout over Northwestern. In 1918 Harley enlisted in the U.S. Army Air Corps as a pilot. As team captain in 1919, he scored a 40-yard touchdown in Ohio State's first win (13–3) over Michigan. With ten seconds remaining in Harley's final collegiate game, however, Bobby Fletcher kicked a field goal to give Illinois a 9–7 victory and the WC title.

Harley moved with his family from Chicago to Columbus, OH, where he graduated from East High School in 1915. In three years, Harley's football teams lost only the final game of his senior year. Harley also played basketball, baseball, and track, winning the 100-, 220-, and 440-yard dashes, low hurdles, and long jump in one meet. At Ohio State he played guard in basketball and outfield in baseball and ran the sprints in track. Besides holding the Buckeyes' 50-yard dash record, he received a baseball offer from the St. Louis Browns (AL). Harley, who never married, had one brother, William, and one sister, Irene. After playing pro football in 1921 with the Chicago Bears (NFL), he began a lifelong struggle with mental illness. He entered the Veterans Hospital in Danville, IL, in 1938, where he stayed until his death from bronchial pneumonia.

BIBLIOGRAPHY: Si Burick, Dayton (OH) *Daily News*, April 23, 1974; Richard M. Cohen, Jordan A. Deutsch, and David S. Neft, *The Ohio State Football Scrapbook* (Indianapolis, IN, 1977); Dayton (OH) *Journal-Herald*, April 22, 1974; Ronald L.

Mendell and Timothy B. Phares, *Who's Who in Football* (New Rochelle, NY, 1974); Kenneth L. (Tug) Wilson and Jerry Brondfield, *The Big Ten* (Englewood Cliffs, NJ, 1967).

James D. Whalen

HARLOW, Richard Cresson "Dick" (b. 19 October 1889, Philadelphia, PA; d. 19 February 1962, Bethesda, MD), college athlete and football coach, was the son of Louis Francis and Eugenia (Prichett) Harlow, attended Episcopal Academy in Philadelphia and earned B.S. and M.S. degrees at Penn State University. He played from 1908 to 1911 at tackle under coach Bill Hollenback* and in 1911 set a record by blocking seventeen punts in five games. The courageous 195-pounder used his hands very effectively on defense and played an entire game against the University of Pittsburgh with his leg in a cast. He also participated on the track, baseball, and boxing teams.

After assisting Hollenback from 1912 to 1914, he served as head football coach the next three seasons at Penn State and compiled a 20–8–0 record. Harlow served as a lieutenant in the infantry during World War I and returned to Penn State from 1919 to 1921 as an assistant to Hugo Bezdek.* From 1922 to 1925 he coached Colgate University to an impressive 24–9–3 football mark. At Western Maryland from 1926 to 1934, Harlow's squads won 61 games, lost 12, and tied 7. His 1929, 1930, and 1934 squads finished undefeated, shutting out every opponent but one. From 1935 to 1942 he served as the first nongraduate head football coach at Harvard University (IL). In 1936 the AFCA named Harlow Coach of the Year. Despite being age 53, Harlow volunteered for overseas duty as a U.S. Navy submarine commander during World War II and drove himself so hard that he was hospitalized with physical exhaustion. Although not fully recovered, Harlow coached football at Harvard from 1945 through 1947. During 11 seasons at Harvard, Harlow's squads finished 45–39–7. Harlow, who coached football 27 seasons at Penn State, Colgate, Western Maryland, and Harvard, achieved an overall 150–68–17 record for a .667 percentage. He retired in 1948, the year he won the Amos Alonzo Stagg Award, and returned to Western Maryland a year later in an athletic advisory capacity.

A brilliant football mind, Harlow pioneered using the spinner series hidden-ball offense and specialized in deceptive faking, cross blocking, and defensive stunting. The great halftime orator rallied the entire student body and staff behind his team. Besides developing football maneuvers, the innovative Harlow pioneered intercollegiate boxing at Penn State. The rugged Harlow served as a professor of ornithology and for twenty-five years searched for rare birds' eggs. His own collection numbered over 850, valued at $40,000. Harlow, who died of a heart attack, married Lila Gilpin and had one daughter. He was named to the HAF College Football Hall of Fame and in 1954 was selected to the NFF College Football Hall of Fame.

BIBLIOGRAPHY: Tim Cohane, *Great College Football Coaches of the Twenties and Thirties* (New Rochelle, NY, 1973); John D. McCallum and Charles H. Pearson, *College Football U.S.A., 1869–1973* (New York, 1973); Ken Rappoport, *The Nittany Lions: A Story of Penn State Football* (Huntsville, AL, 1973).

John L. Evers

HARMON, Thomas D. "Tom" "Tommy" "Gary Ghost" "Old 98" (b. 28 September 1919, Gary, IN), college and professional player and announcer, is the son of Gary policeman Louis A. Harmon, an Irish high school sprint standout. His older brothers Lou and Harold starred in basketball and track at Purdue, and Gene in basketball at Tulane. Under coach Dick Kerr at Horace Mann High, Harmon earned fourteen varsity letters in four sports. He won state championships in the 100-yard dash and 220-yard low hurdles and the national interscholastic football scoring championship with 150 points. A three-year starter on his high school eleven, he added fifty pounds and hard-earned muscles to his six-foot frame between his freshman and senior year. Harmon's high school coach, a former football player at the University of Michigan, interested him in the Ann Arbor campus by taking the high school backfield every year to a football clinic held there during spring practices.

As a starter at Michigan (WC) from 1938 to 1940, Harmon performed gridiron exploits that made him a national figure. Dubbed the "Gary Ghost" and "Old 98," he demonstrated his triple-threat versatility in running, passing, and kicking and broke BTC records set by Red Grange.* During his remarkable, highly publicized career, he gained 2,134 yards rushing in 398 attempts, completed 101 of 233 passes for 1,396 yards, scored 237 points with 33 touchdowns, and led the nation in scoring in 1939 and 1940. In the 1939 game against Iowa, he scored all 27 points for the Wolverines, including a 95-yard pass interception. As a two-way 60-minute player, he performed superbly on defense and often took command of a game. In the 1937 victory over Pennsylvania he gained 203 yards, scored twice, and passed for a third touchdown. Although Michigan never won a BTC or national championship in Harmon's three years, coach Fritz Crisler* returned the Wolverines to national prominence. Harmon's post-season awards included All-American selections in 1939 and 1940, the Heisman Trophy, AP Athlete of the Year, and the Maxwell Award in 1940. Harmon's success came primarily from the superb blocking of quarterback Forest Evashevski and explosive single-wing offensive attack.

In 1941 Harmon was drafted first by the Philadelphia Eagles (NFL) but played instead with the New York Americans of the rival five-team AFL and broadcast the 1941 Michigan games with Harry Wismer. During World War II, he served in the U.S. Air Force and was awarded the Silver Star and the Purple Heart. Harmon survived bailouts from two destroyed planes in enemy-held territory. In 1946 and 1947 he played football professionally with the Los Angeles Rams (NFL), but showed only flashes of his former greatness because his legs had been badly burned and injured in the war. Despite his limitations, Harmon averaged 5.1 yards per rush (matching his college career average) and caught 15 passes for a 19.2-yard average. After retirement as a player Harmon pursued the career he had trained for as a speech and radio communications major at Michigan. As a television and radio broadcaster, he worked as sports director for KTLA in Los Angeles doing UCLA games, became the West Coast sports director for ABC, and worked with Mel Allen* (OS) on the NBC telecast of one Rose Bowl game. After World War II he married Hollywood film actress Elyse Knox, whom he met on the Bing Crosby radio show. Their children include Mark, who played quarterback for UCLA and is an actor; Christie, who was married to singer Ricky Nelson; and Kelly, a commercial actress and model. In 1954 Harmon was elected to the NFF College Football Hall of Fame. He also belongs to the HAF College Football Hall of Fame. After his college graduation he made an autobiographical movie called *Harmon of Michigan*.

BIBLIOGRAPHY: Allison Danzig, *The History of American Football: Its Great Teams, Players, and Coaches* (Englewood Cliffs, NJ, 1956); Tom Harmon, "This I Remember," *Michigan Football Game Program*, October 22, 1966, pp. 12–13, 45, 50, 52–53; John D. McCallum, *Big Ten Football Since 1895* (Radnor, PA, 1976); Ronald L. Mendell and Timothy B. Phares, *Who's Who in Football* (New Rochelle, NY, 1974); Herb Michelson and Dave Newhouse, *Rose Bowl Football Since 1902* (New York, 1977); "Midwestern Front," *Time* 34 (November 6, 1939), pp. 34–38; Will Perry, *The Wolverines: A Story of Michigan Football* (Huntsville, AL, 1980); Kenneth L. (Tug) Wilson and Jerry Brondfield, *The Big Ten* (Englewood Cliffs, NJ, 1967).

Douglas A. Noverr

HARPER, Jesse C. (b. 10 December 1883, Pawpaw, IL; d. 31 July 1961, Sitka, KS), college athlete, coach, and athletic director, attended Morgan Park Academy and entered the University of Chicago (WC) in 1902. His father moved to Iowa to work in the cattle business, enabling Jesse to secure free rides on cattle trains to Chicago. He played football his freshman year at Chicago under legendary coach Amos Alonzo Stagg.* After being sidelined with injuries in 1903 and 1904, he helped Chicago to an undefeated season and WC championship in 1905. Harper played halfback and backup quarterback to Walter Eckersall,* although only 5 feet, 10 inches, and 155 pounds. He also played college baseball four seasons, captaining the squad his senior year. After graduating in 1906, Harper coached football at Alma (MI) College (MIAA) and compiled a 10–4–4 mark in three seasons there. At Wabash (IN) College the next four seasons, his football teams won 15 games, lost 9, and tied 2. His 1910 aggregate outscored opponents 118–0 and won all four games. In 1911 Wabash held Notre Dame to a 6–3 score, surrendering the points in the last five minutes.

Harper became head football coach and athletic director at Notre Dame in 1913. During his first year there, he brought the Fighting Irish from obscurity to wide recognition by utilizing the forward pass. The forward pass, although known, had not been used previously by football powers. In a history-making game against Army, Notre Dame employed several Gus Dorais*–Knute Rockne* passes to win 35–13. The Fighting Irish defeated Army again 7–0 in 1915 and introduced young halfback George Gipp* against them in 1917 in his final game as coach. Harper made Notre Dame big time by scheduling Yale and Penn State and by taking his team southwest in 1915 for two victories in three days. Notre Dame defeated Texas 36–7 on Thanksgiving Day and then trounced Rice 55–2 on Saturday. Harper resigned as football coach and athletic director in 1917, having compiled a 33–5–1 mark. Nebraska and Army had inflicted two losses each. At Notre Dame, Harper coached the basketball squads to a 57–17 (.770) overall mark and the baseball teams to a 68–39 (.739) record. At age 33, Harper retired to operate a 30,000-acre ranch in Kansas. After Rockne's death in a 1931 plane crash, Harper returned to Notre Dame for two years as athletic director and instigated the no-transfer rule, a 77 grade point average, and stricter board, room, tuition, and books scholarship programs. In 1933 he resigned again to concentrate on his cattle ranch, which included twenty-five producing oil wells.

BIBLIOGRAPHY: Chicago *Sun Times*, August 4, 1961; Chicago *Tribune*, August 1–2, 1961; John Durant and Les Etter, *Highlights of College Football* (New York, 1970); South Bend (IN) *Tribune*, August 2, 1961; *University of Notre Dame Press Guide, 1983;* University of Notre Dame, Press Releases, 1931, July 3–9, 1955, South Bend, IN.

Stan W. Carlson

HARRIS, Clifford Allen "Cliff" (b. 12 November 1948, Fayetteville, AR), college and professional player, excelled as a scholar-athlete at Fayetteville High School. A football star at little Ouachita Baptist College (AIC), Harris earned a B.A. in Mathematics and Physics in 1970. Harris was skipped in the 1970 NFL draft, but the Dallas Cowboys signed him as a free agent. Harris, along with defensive backs Charlie Waters* and Mark Washington, outperformed many competitors to make the Cowboys roster. During ten seasons with the Cowboys, Harris achieved acclaim as one of the NFL's best-tackling, hardest-hitting safeties. Harris started for the Cowboys except when a military service call interrupted half of his rookie season.

As regular free safety for the Dallas Cowboys (1970–1979), Harris played in 141 regular-season games, made 29 interceptions for 281 yards, returned 66 punts for 418 yards and 63 kickoffs for 1,622 yards, and recovered 18 fumbles for 91 yards. He led the Cowboys in punt returns (1971), kickoffs (1972), interceptions (1974–1977, 1979), and combined assisted and unassisted tackles (1976). From 1974 to 1979 Harris made *TSN* NFC All-Star Team and participated in the Pro Bowl. Harris played in NFC championship games following the 1970–1971, 1973, 1975, 1977, and 1978 seasons and in five Super Bowls. Dallas lost Super Bowl V to the Baltimore Colts and Super Bowls X and XIII to the Pittsburgh Steelers, while defeating the Miami Dolphins in Super Bowl VI and the Denver Broncos in Super Bowl XII. Harris, who makes numerous personal appearances and speaking engagements, has worked with the Arthritis Foundation and Diabetes Association and performed environmental work in Dallas. Harris and his wife, Linda, live in Dallas, where he operates a shoe store and a steak house and is engaged in the oil business.

BIBLIOGRAPHY: *The Official Dallas Cowboys Handbook, 1977; TSN Football Register—1980.*

John L. Evers

HARRIS, Franco (b. 7 March 1950, Fort Dix, NJ), college and professional player, is the son of Cad Harris, a black with 20 years U.S. Army service, and Italian native Gina (Parenti) Harris. He graduated in 1968 from Rancocas Valley Regional High School in Mt. Holly, NJ, where he was named a high school All-American in football and played baseball and basketball. He majored in Hotel and Restaurant Management at Penn State University and played football there with Lydell Mitchell,* then considered the more promising pro prospect. Harris gained 2,002 yards on 380 carries, scored 24 touchdowns in three years, and helped lead Penn State to victories in the 1970 Orange and 1972 Cotton bowls.

The Pittsburgh Steelers made Harris the first running back chosen in the first round of the NFL's 1972 draft. Although starting only two of his first seven games that fall, he became the fifth NFL rookie to rush for over 1,000 yards. He gained national celebrity in the playoffs that year with his "Immaculate Reception" of a caroming pass, defeating the Oakland Raiders in the last seconds of a first-round AFC game. His longest pro run, a 75-yarder, also came in his rookie year against the Cleveland Browns. During seven of his first eight seasons, Harris rushed over 1,000 yards to tie Jim Brown's* record for most 1,000-yard seasons. He gained over 100 yards in 35 of those games. The Steelers, who had never before participated in post-season play, made the playoffs each of those years and won the Super Bowl in 1975, 1976, 1979, and 1980. Harris played his best in the playoffs, being the leading rusher in 13 of 19 post-season games. His finest game was against Minnesota in Super Bowl IX, when he ran 158 yards in 34 carries and was selected MVP.

The dependable, durable Harris carried the ball up to 41 times in a game but was rarely injured and missed only nine games in his first 12 seasons. At his retirement, he held the records (since broken) for most carries by a running back (2,881) and most 1,000-yard seasons (eight). With 12,120 yards rushing (4.1-yard average), he scored 91 touchdowns rushing, trailed only Walter Payton* and Jim Brown* in all-time rushing yardage, and ranked second behind Payton in most carries by a running back (2,949). Harris remains fourth in NFL career combined yardage with 14,622.

The 6 foot, 2 inch, 225 pound Harris possessed the size of a fullback, but his remarkable balance, quickness, explosive acceleration, and ability to cut back against the grain made him, in his prime, as elusive as any halfback. He eschewed the crunching, straight-ahead style of Jim Taylor* and other predecessors. Harris plunged ahead when necessary but usually avoided destructive direct hits from tacklers. Although not particularly noted as a blocker, he complemented his running skills with pass receiving and became adept at catching swing passes while circling out of the backfield. During his career he caught 307 passes for 2,287 yards (7.4-yard average) and 9 touchdowns. Lifetime, Harris scored 100 touchdowns for 600 points. In 1984 Harris closed his pro career with the Seattle Seahawks (NFL). He played in the Pro Bowls from 1972 to 1975 and 1977 to 1980 and missed the 1976 contest due to injury.

Harris lives on the North Side of Pittsburgh with his wife, Dana (Dokmanovich) Harris, and their son, Dok. An important civic figure, he works actively for Children's Hospital and other charities, has received many honors, and won the 1982 Whizzer White Humanitarian Award. With Terry Bradshaw,* Charles "Joe" Greene,* and other stalwarts, Harris anchored Pittsburgh's football dynasty in the late 1970s. He was named Player of the Decade for the 1970s by *College and Pro Football Newsweekly* and won similar recognition from other publications. His personal background and public-spirited off-field activities also made him a cultural symbol at a time of continuing racial tension. His dignified, congenial personality made him the personification of reconciliation. With a team that emphasized the work ethic, Harris represented success achieved the old-fashioned way.

BIBLIOGRAPHY: Roy Blount, Jr., "The Ascent of an Enigma," *SI* 51 (August 23, 1982), pp. 72–86.

Luther W. Spoehr

HART, James Warren "Jim" (b. 29 April 1944, Evanston, IL), college and professional player and broadcaster, began his football career as quarterback for Niles Township West High School in Morton Grove, IL. Hart lettered twice in football and baseball and three times in basketball. During his high school career, Hart was selected an All-Conference performer in football, basketball, and baseball and All-Suburban Area in football. Following graduation, Hart attended Southern Illinois University. Hart became the starting quarterback for the Salukis in the third game of his sophomore year and never relinquished that role. During his three-year career, Hart rewrote virtually every Southern Illinois passing record, including most completions (283), yardage (3,779), and touchdowns (34). Since the Salukis compiled only 8 wins and 21 losses, he was not selected during the 1965 NFL draft.

The 6 foot, 1 inch, 210 pound Hart was signed by the St. Louis Cardinals (NFL) as a free agent in 1966, spent the majority of that season on the taxi squad, and played briefly in the season's final game. In 1967 regular Cardinals quarterback Charlie Johnson was called into the U.S. Army on active duty. Hart, who had thrown eleven passes as a pro, became the regular quarterback and played pro football through the 1984 season. During Hart's career, he led the Cardinals to the playoffs twice and a first-ever Eastern Division championship in 1974. In 1974 Hart achieved a career-high 20 touchdown passes, attempted an NFL-leading 388 passes, and completed 51.5 percent of his aerials. Following the 1974 season, Hart was named NFL Player of the Year. During the mid-1970s under coach Don Coryell,* Hart quarterbacked the "Cardiac Cards" to exciting finishes.

In February 1984 Hart was signed by the Washington Redskins (NFL) as a free agent. Hart, who announced his retirement shortly after the 1984 season, is ranked as the number four quarterback of all time in passes completed (2,593) and yards gained (34,665) behind Fran Tarkenton,* Johnny Unitas,* and Dan Fouts.* Hart threw 209 career touchdown passes, made 247 interceptions, and scored 16 touchdowns.

A member of the Southern Illinois University Hall of Fame, Hart graduated with a B.S. degree in Education in 1967. Hart, active in civic and community affairs, received the 1976 Whizzer White Humanitarian Award (presented by the NFL Players Association). In 1980 he won the YMCA Brian Piccolo Award as the most civic-minded athlete in pro sports. Hart resides in St. Louis, MO, with his wife, Mary, son, Bradley, and two daughters, Katie and Suzanne, and is a restaurant owner.

BIBLIOGRAPHY: Bob Broeg, "Big Red Gotta Have Hart," St. Louis *Post Dispatch*, August 3, 1967; Mark Mulroy, "Peach Fuzz with a Difference," *SI* 47 (November 28, 1977); *St. Louis Cardinals Media Guide, 1983; Washington Redskins Media Guide, 1984.*

William A. Sutton

HART, Leon Joseph (b. 2 November 1928, Turtle Creek, PA), college and professional player, was awarded the 1949 Heisman Trophy as the nation's outstanding college football player and remains one of only two linemen to receive the prestigious honor. A four-year star end for the University of Notre Dame (1946–1949), Hart also won the Maxwell Award and Rockne Trophy his final season. The 1949 UPI Lineman of the Year, Hart was named Player of the Year by *TSN-Quarterback* and HAF. He was chosen the 1949 AP Male Athlete of the Year, far outdistancing Jackie Robinson* (BB) and Sammy Snead* (OS). In 1947 the FWAA selected sophomore Hart as an All-American for *Look*. Hart also made consensus All-American in 1948 and unanimous All-American in 1949 when he co-captained the Fighting Irish. He was chosen to several All-Time All-American teams, including *Sport* (1969), FWAA second-team modern (1919–1969), AP third team (1951), and Nashville (TN) *Banner* (1951), Miami (FL) *Daily News* (1956), and Notre Dame's all-time eleven (1962). In 1973 Hart was elected to the NFF College Football Hall of Fame.

The son of Westinghouse crane repairman Charles J. and Josephine (Lubert) Hart, he attended Wilkins Junior High and Turtle Creek High School and became the most sought athlete in the Pittsburgh area. The honor student won nine letters in football (captain), basketball, and baseball (captain) before graduating from high school in 1946 and fulfilled a boyhood ambition by attending Notre Dame. The Fighting Irish did not lose a game during Hart's four years, compiling a composite 36–0–2 record, achieving a 21-game winning streak, and capturing three national championships (1946–1947, 1949). As a 17-year-old freshman the 6 foot, 4 inch, 245 pound Hart alternated at end with veteran Jack Zilly. He scored a touchdown against Southern California on a 22-yard pass from George Ratterman and set up a touchdown against Iowa with a one-handed grab of a long Johnny Lujack* pass. The following season (1947), he caught touchdown passes to help Notre Dame triumph over Pittsburgh, Navy, and Northwestern and recovered two Navy fumbles to produce two additional touchdowns. Hart frequently played fullback in short yardage situations and became a "fifth back" on end around carries. During his junior season (1948), he scored on pass receptions against Pittsburgh, Michigan State, Washington, and Southern California. The latter touchdown came on a 35-yard run after the catch despite Hart's being hit four times by potential tacklers. "Tackling Hart was like trying to bulldog a fullgrown Brahma bull," said author Cameron Applegate. Hart caught 19 passes for 257 yards and 5 touchdowns his final season, rushed 18 times for 73 yards (4.1-yard average) and 1 touchdown, and recovered 3 fumbles. Teamed with some of Notre Dame's greatest players ever (Lujack, George Connor,* Bill Fischer,* Jim Martin, Bob Williams, and Emil Sitko), Hart proved a devastating blocker and monstrous defender. He made 49 career pass receptions for 742 yards and 13 touchdowns, led the Fighting Irish in pass receiving in 1948 and 1949, and produced 2 touchdowns on runs from scrimmage.

Hart served as senior class president at Notre Dame before graduating in 1950 with a B.S. in Mechanical Engineering. He played on two victorious post-season All-Star teams, helping the East All-Stars triumph 28–6 over the West and the Chicago *Tribune* College All-Stars defeat 17–7 over the Philadelphia Eagles. He bowled over two West defenders in the former on a 66-yard touchdown pass play. The only player to be chosen All-American (1949) and All-Pro (1951) by the same news service on both offense and defense in the same seasons, Hart starred at end eight years (1950–1957) with the Detroit Lions (NFL). He made All-Pro again in 1952 and played on three NFL championship teams (1952, 1953, 1957) and one Western Conference titlist (1954). Besides being one of the founders of the NFL Players Association, he served as president of the NFL Alumni Association. During his NFL career, Hart caught 174 passes for 2,499 yards (14.4-yard average) and 26 touchdowns and rushed 143 times for 612 yards (4.3-yard average) and 5 touchdowns. He married high school classmate Lois Newyahr in 1950, has five sons and one daughter, and resides in Birmingham, MI. Hart owned a Volkswagen dealership in Detroit and then became a market analyst for American Brakeblok Company in Troy, MI. In 1965 he formed his own manufacturing concern, Tire Tru, makers of wheel balancing material, in Birmingham, MI.

BIBLIOGRAPHY: John T. Brady, *The Heisman: A Symbol of Excellence* (New York, 1984); Bill Libby, *Heroes of the Heisman Trophy* (New York, 1973); *Notre Dame Football Guide, 1984;* Notre Dame University, Sports Information Office, August 13, 1985, South Bend, IN; Gene Schoor, ed., *A Treasury of Notre Dame Football* (New York, 1962).

James D. Whalen

HAUGHTON, Percy Duncan (b. 11 July 1896, Staten Island, NY; d. 27 October 1924, New York, NY), college athlete, football coach, and baseball executive, was the son of Malcolm G. and Mary N. (Lawrence) Haughton and graduated from Groton School (MA) in 1895 and Harvard University (IL) in 1899. Haughton married Gwendolen Whistler Howell in 1911 and had one daughter, Mrs. Alison Lawrence Derby. At Groton School from 1892 to 1895, Haughton excelled as a football player and team captain and baseball pitcher and first baseman. At Harvard (IL) he played two football seasons at tackle and one at fullback and developed into a great punter. In 1898 Haughton made second-team All-American at tackle and substitute tackle on Caspar Whitney's All-American team. He played baseball from 1896 to 1899 and captained the Harvard Crimson his senior year.

Following graduation he coached the Cornell University (IL) football team for two years and compiled a 16–5 record. Haughton joined a Boston bond broking firm and served as an assistant Harvard football coach without pay. In 1908, at age 32, he was appointed Harvard head coach. Since Harvard did not hire him, he was paid by interested alumni. From 1908 to 1916 Harvard reached its greatest heights in football prominence. Haughton's teams won 71 games, lost 7, and tied 5, outpointing opponents 1,427 to 106. His record against Yale, Harvard's chief opponent, stood at 5 wins, 2 losses, and 2 ties, while Haughton's Crimson won 5 and lost 1 against Princeton.

Haughton's commanding personality dominated the Harvard football scene. He organized practice with unsurpassed efficiency and emphasized skill and brains rather than brute force. Although Haughton seemed hard-hearted with his insistence upon discipline and drill, his teams displayed almost flawless execution on offense. Haughton modernized football by employing the single wing, Statue of Liberty play, running pass, and "trap" play. Defensively, he helped initiate the roving middle linebacker position and five-man line buffered by linebackers. With other coaches, Haughton challenged Rules Committee head Walter Camp* to liberalize rules by using four downs, continuing legalization of the forward pass, and realizing limits on substitutions.

Haughton became president of the Boston Braves baseball club in 1916, but still continued through the season as Crimson football coach. During World War I he served in the U.S. Army, was sent to France as a major, and was assigned to the headquarters staff, 26th Army division, as assistant chemical warfare officer. His war engagements included the Troyon sector and the Meuse-Argonne offensive. He entered private financial business following the war but became football coach in 1923 at Columbia University (IL) and compiled an 8–5–1 record there. On October 27, 1924, he died suddenly of angina pectoris shortly after a practice.

Above all, Haughton perfected the science of football by developing tricky, well-executed offensive maneuvers, a revolutionary change from the traditional straight-ahead attack that emphasized brawn and power. Haughton helped make football into an intricate spectator sport by instigating a more open style of play. In addition, he contributed syndicated newspaper articles and authored the book *Football and How to Watch It*.

BIBLIOGRAPHY: Frank D. Ashburn, *Fifty Years On, Groton School* (New York, 1934); Morris A. Bealle, *The History of Harvard Football, 1874–1948* (Washington, DC, 1948); Walter Camp, "*Collier's* First All-America," in Jack Newcombe, ed., *The Fireside Book of Football* (New York, 1964); Allison Danzig, *The History of American Football: Its Great Teams, Players, and Coaches* (Englewood Cliffs, NJ, 1956); Harvard University, *Harvard Class of 1899*, 50th Anniversary Report (Cambridge, MA, 1949).

Axel Bundgaard

HAYES, Wayne Woodrow "Woody" (b. 14 February 1913, Clifton, OH; d. 12 March 1987, Upper Arlington, OH), college player and coach, is the son of Wayne and Effie Hayes. Hayes, whose father was superintendent of schools in Newcombertown, OH, played tackle on the Newcombertown High School football team and captained the football squad his senior year. He received a B.A. from Denison University (OC), playing tackle on the football team and majoring in English and history. In 1935 and 1936 Hayes taught and served as assistant football coach at Mingo Junction High School in Ohio. After being assistant coach in 1937 at New Philadelphia (OH) High School, he was head football coach there from 1938 to 1940. Before joining the U.S. Navy in 1941, Hayes had received an M.A. in Educational Administration from Ohio State University in 1939. During World War II he commanded a patrol chaser and a destroyer escort and was discharged in 1946 as a lieutenant commander. Hayes married Anne Gross in 1942 and has one son, Stephen.

He became head football coach at Denison University in 1946, but his team won only one game. After Denison compiled undefeated 1947 and 1948 seasons, Miami University (MAC, Ohio) hired Hayes as head football coach in 1949 and won four of its last five games. In 1950 Miami finished undefeated, won the MAC title, and defeated Arizona State in the Salad Bowl. During this period Hayes impressed others as a super-recruiter, strict taskmaster, and totally dedicated football coach. With no major college experience, Hayes in 1951 was named head football coach at Ohio State University (BTC). Ohio State was considered the grave-yard of coaches before "Woody" arrived. He coached the Buckeyes twenty-eight years, during which his team finished 205–68–10. When Hayes resigned after the 1978 season, his 241 college victories ranked third among all-time coaches.

Despite the efforts of Heisman Trophy winner Vic Janowicz,* Ohio State won only four games in 1951. The Buckeyes improved to 6–3 marks in 1952 and 1953 and won the BTC title with a 10–0 mark in 1954. After defeating Southern California in the Rose Bowl, Ohio State was proclaimed national champion in both the AP and UPI polls. Hayes' club also won the national title in 1968. Hayes was named Coach of the Year in 1957, when Ohio State won the BTC title and Rose Bowl and ranked first in the UPI poll. During Hayes' tenure, the Buckeyes won or shared twelve BTC championships and played in eight Rose Bowls and one Sugar, Orange, and Gator Bowl. His outstanding players included Heisman Trophy winners Howard Cassady* (1955) and Archie Griffin* (1974–1975); Outland Award winners Jim Parker* (1956) and John Hicks (1973); and numerous other All-Americans.

Hayes' teams demonstrated sound execution of fundamentals, strong defense, conservative offense, a punishing running game ("three yards and a cloud of dust"), and disdain for the forward pass. The outspoken Hayes, who exhibited extreme competitiveness especially with archrival Michigan ("that team up north"), deeply regarded his players' personal interests, and battled officials, opposing players, coaches, reporters, and even the Ohio State faculty. He was forced to resign as head coach after striking an opposing player during the 1978 Gator Bowl. Hayes, a member of the NFF College Football Hall of Fame, authored *Football at Ohio State* (1957); *Hot Line to Victory* (1969); and *You Win with People* (1974). Since retirement he has frequently spoken at athletic banquets. Hayes delivered Ohio State's winter 1986 commencement address and was awarded an honorary Doctor of Humanities degree.

BIBLIOGRAPHY: Richard Cohen, Jordan Deutsch, and David Neft, *The Ohio State Football Scrapbook* (Indianapolis, IN, 1977); W. Woodrow Hayes, *You Win with People* (Columbus, OH, 1973); Bill Levy, *Three Yards and a Cloud of Dust* (Cleveland, 1966); John Underwood, "A Breath of Fresh Air after a Heavy Hayes," *SI* 50 (April 9, 1979), pp. 26–27; Ed Whipple, "The Great War, Part 73," *Toledo* (OH) *Blade Magazine* (November 14, 1976), 21–31; *WWA*, 40th ed. (1978–1979), p. 1,429.

James K. Skipper, Jr.

HAYNES, Abner "Butch" (b. 19 September 1937, Denton, TX), college and professional player, attended high school in Dallas and played football for North Texas State University (MVC) between 1957 and 1959. The 6 foot, 1 inch, 198 pound running back, an All-American selection in 1959, ranked seventh nationally in rushing and fifth in scoring. Haynes led the "Mean Green" in rushing and receiving from 1957 to 1959. In his collegiate career Haynes rushed 345 times for 1,864 yards and 25 touchdowns (club records) and made 46 pass receptions for 579 yards and 6 touchdowns. He gained 72 yards on 13 carries in a losing effort against New Mexico State University in the 1960 Sun Bowl.

Haynes was selected by the Oakland Raiders in the first round of the 1960 AFL draft. His draft rights were traded to the Dallas Texans (AFL), where he performed between 1960 and 1962. In his first season Haynes led the AFL in rushing and punt returns and was named Rookie of the Year and Player of the Year. In his third season, Dallas won the Western Division championship and met the Houston Oilers for the AFL crown. Haynes that season established an AFL record by scoring 19 touchdowns. After scoring two touchdowns in the championship game, Haynes nearly blundered when the contest went into overtime. The Texans won the coin toss, but confused captain Haynes elected to kick off and thus surrendered the wind advantage. Nevertheless, the Texans won 20–17 in the second overtime of the 77 minute, 54 second game. The Dallas franchise moved to Kansas City, MO, in 1963. Following the 1964 season Haynes was traded to the Denver Broncos and then topped the AFL in kickoff returns. In his final season (1967), he played for the Miami Dolphins (AFL) and New York Jets (AFL).

Haynes led Dallas–Kansas City in receiving and kickoff returns (1960), punt returns (1960–1961), scoring (1961–1962), and rushing (1960–1962, 1964). His 19 touchdowns in 1962 (13 by rushing) both still remain club records. He paced Denver in kickoff returns (1965) and rushing, receiving, and punt returns (1966) and led the Dolphins in rushing and punt returns (1967). A three-time All-AFL selection (1960–1962), Haynes played in the AFL All-Star game (1961–1962, 1964).

In AFL history, Haynes ranked third in rushing, ninth in receiving, and seventh in scoring. He in 1961 scored 30 points on 5 touchdowns to establish a one-game AFL record. During his eight-year pro career, Haynes scored an AFL-record 46 touchdowns by rushing, gained over 100 yards rushing in 14 games, and returned 121 kickoffs for 3,025 yards. He gained 12,065 yards by rushing, receiving, returning punts, and kickoffs, approached in the AFL only by Don Maynard's* 10,386 composite yards.

BIBLIOGRAPHY: *North Texas State University Media Guide, 1978;* Murray Olderman, *The Running Backs* (Englewood Cliffs, NJ, 1969); *TSN AFL Official History, 1960–1969.*

John L. Evers

HEALEY, Edward Francis, Jr. "Ed" (b. 28 December 1894, Indian Orchard, MA; d. 9 December 1978, Niles, MI), college and professional player and coach, was the son of Edward Healey, Sr., and grew up on a farm near Springfield, MA. The only boy in a family of nine children, he had seven older sisters. After attending Classical High School in Springfield, MA, and Holy Cross College, he was recruited to play football at Dartmouth College (IL) by Frank Cavanaugh* and transferred there in the fall, 1915. He played end under Cavanaugh and Clarence W. Spears beginning with the 1916 season. In 1917 he enlisted in the U.S. Army and served in the cavalry in France during World War I. He returned to Dartmouth in 1918 to play his final season and graduated the next year.

Following graduation, Healey moved to Nebraska to work part-time jobs and coach part-time at Creighton University. When the NFL was formed, he played for the Rock Island (IL) Independents for $100 per game from 1920 through 1922. The 6 foot, 3 inch, 220 pound Healey converted to tackle and in 1922 played across from Chicago Bears coach George Halas.* The much impressed Halas took Healey as payment for a $100 debt the Independents owed his club. Healey, the first player Halas ever purchased, played with the Bears from 1922 through 1927. An All-Pro five consecutive years from 1923 through 1927, he starred on the Bears' barnstorming tour following the 1925 season. Walter Camp* called Healey "the best I ever saw," while Halas praised him as "the most versatile tackle ever."

He married Louise Falk of St. Louis on November 17, 1927, and retired from pro football upon completion of that season. The father of two sons, Thomas and James, he already had become a salesman, quarry manager, and recruiter for the France Stone Company. Healey, who lived just outside South Bend, IN, coached for three years for Knute Rockne* at Notre Dame and remained a loyal Fighting Irish supporter thereafter. In 1937 he became the first president of the Chicago Bears Alumni Association. He was inducted into the Pro Football Hall of Fame in 1964 and was named in 1974 to the NFF College Football Hall of Fame in the Pioneers Category.

BIBLIOGRAPHY: Myron Cope, *The Game That Was: The Early Days of Pro Football* (New York, 1970); Allison Danzig, *Oh, How They Played the Game: The Early Days of Football and the Heroes Who Made It Great* (New York, 1971); Ronald L. Mendell and Timothy B. Phares, *Who's Who in Football* (New Rochelle, NY, 1974); Howard Roberts, *The Chicago Bears* (New York, 1947); Seymour Rothman, "Far from the Playing Fields, But Not Too Far," Toledo (OH) *Blade Sunday Magazine* (July 20, 1975), pp. 4–7; South Bend (IN) *Tribune*, 1977–1978; George Sullivan, *Pro Football's All-Time Greats: The Immortals in Pro Football's Hall of Fame* (New York, 1968).

Bruce W. Wasem

HEFFELFINGER, William Walter "Pudge" (b. 20 December 1867, Minneapolis, MN; d. 2 April 1954, Blessing, TX), college player and coach, was the son of Christopher B. and Mary Ellen (Totton) Heffelfinger, both of Scotch-Irish descent. His father operated a shoe manufacturing concern and speculated in real estate. Heffelfinger attended Minneapolis public schools and played baseball and football at Central High School. From 1888 to 1891 he attended Yale University (IL) and earned a degree from the Sheffield Scientific School in 1891. At Yale he performed spectacular football feats at guard. Named to Walter Camp's* All-American team three times, he subsequently was elected to nearly every All-Time All-American squad. As both a defensive and offensive linemen, Heffelfinger helped lead Yale to undefeated seasons in 1888 and 1891 and only one loss in 1889 and 1890. Heffelfinger allegedly introduced the "pulling guard" play, where the guard left the offensive line and led interference for the ballcarrier. On defense he ferociously penetrated blocks and tackled opposing-team ballcarriers. The 188 to 205 pound Heffelfinger towered over most other contemporary players.

Heffelfinger maintained a lifelong association with football. After playing briefly on semi-pro teams in the early 1890s, he coached football at the University of California (1893), Lehigh University (1894), and University of Minnesota (WC, 1895). From 1896 to 1910 he served as volunteer football line coach at Minnesota. Until 1917 he frequently helped Yale prepare for its key contests with Harvard and Princeton. At Yale practices he sometimes joined the substitutes in scrimmage. In the 1930s he founded Heffelfinger Publications, which produced football and baseball booklets for large manufacturers and dealers in sales promotion. In *This Was Football* (1954), Heffelfinger sharply criticized modern offensive and defensive line play. To enable defensive linemen to see the progress of a play and respond accordingly, he believed they should assume an upright position. In Minneapolis Heffelfinger became a successful business and political leader. The Republican served from 1924 to 1948 as a Hennepin County commissioner and was an unsuccessful candidate for the U.S. Congress in 1930. He married Grace Harriet Pierce on December 4, 1901, and had one son and two daughters.

BIBLIOGRAPHY: Evelyn Burke, "The Heffelfinger and Peavey Families," *Northwest Life* 16 (1945), p. 26; Tim Cohane, *The Yale Football Story* (New York, 1951); W. W. "Pudge" Heffelfinger as told to John D. McCallum, *This Was Football* (New York, 1954); W. W. "Pudge" Heffelfinger, "Football's Golden Era," *SEP* 211 (October 29, 1938), pp. 16–17, 80–82; W. W. "Pudge" Heffelfinger, "Nobody Put Me on My Back," *SEP* 211 (October 15, 1938), pp. 14–15, 32–34.

Benjamin G. Rader

HEIN, Melvin J. "Mel" "Old Indestructible" (b. 22 August 1909, Redding, CA), college and professional player, coach, and administrator, is the son of electrician Herman H. and Charlotte (Wilson) Hein. He moved at an early age with his family to Washington and was tutored while his father worked on a dam project. Hein later attended Burlington High School, where he excelled as a student and versatile athlete. Besides playing guard, center, halfback, and tackle in football, he participated in track, basketball, and baseball squads. Hein enrolled at Washington State College (PCC) in the fall, 1927. After playing freshman football, he starred on the varsity team the next three seasons and earned both All-PCC and All-American honors before graduating in 1931. He in 1931 captained the only Washington State team to ever play in the Rose Bowl. Before reporting to the New York Giants (NFL) training camp for the 1931 season, Hein married college sweetheart Florence Porter in Spokane, WA. They have one son, Melvin J., Jr., and one daughter, Sharon Lynn Wood.

Hein earned second-team All-Pro honors in 1931 and 1932 and first-team All-Pro center the next eight years. In 1935 he received more votes than any other All-Pro player, an incredible accomplishment for an interior lineman. Hein in 1938 became the only lineman ever to receive the official NFL MVP award. Although most pros spent just a few seasons in the NFL before entering another profession, Hein played fifteen years (1931–1945) as the Giants center. Nicknamed "Old Indestructible," Hein suffered only one injury of consequence—a broken nose in 1941. The large, 6 foot, 3 inch, 230 pound Hein performed well in all phases of the game. Besides being a fine blocker and accurate snapper offensively, defensively he pioneered a linebacking style practiced today. Hein's coverage checked the immortal Don Hutson* when the Giants played the Green Bay Packers in the 1930s and 1940s. Hein, a member of the HAF and NFF College Football Halls of Fame and a charter member of the Pro Football Hall of Fame, is cited as the center on most all-time teams.

After his active career, he spent four years each as head football coach at Union College (ICAC) and as pro assistant coach. Hein served as line coach at the University of Southern California (PCC, AAWU) from 1951 to 1966, when he became supervisor of officials for the AFL. He held a similar position with the NFL from 1970 to 1974 and then retired to San Clemente, CA.

BIBLIOGRAPHY: Robert Curran, *Pro Football's Rag Days* (Englewood Cliffs, NJ, 1969); Arthur Daley, *Pro Football's Hall of Fame* (Chicago, 1963); Gerald Eskenazi, *There Were Giants in Those Days* (New York, 1976); Robert Leckie, *The Story of Football* (New York, 1965); George Sullivan, *Pro Football's All-Time Greats: The Immortals in Pro Football's Hall of Fame* (New York, 1968); Alexander M. Weyand, *Football Immortals* (New York, 1962).

Robert N. Carroll

HEISMAN, John William (b. 23 October 1869, Cleveland, OH; d. 3 October 1936, New York, NY), college athlete, coach, and administrator, was the son of barrel manufacturer John M. and Sarah (Lehr) Heisman. Heisman, an outstanding baseball player at Brown University (IL) from 1887 to 1889, starred as a football tackle and end there. He then played the same positions at the University of Pennsylvania (IL) in 1890 and 1891, graduating from the Law School in 1892. Declining a law career, he began coaching football in 1892 at Oberlin College (OC) and led them to a perfect 7–0–0 record in their first year of varsity football. Heisman joined Akron University the following year and then returned to Oberlin College in 1894, achieving a 4–3–1 football record. At Auburn University (SIAA) he produced a 13–3–1 football record from 1895 through 1899. The next year found him at Clemson University (SIAA), where he immediately produced an undefeated 6–0–0 mark and four-year 19–3–2 record.

Heisman next moved to Georgia Tech (SIAA) and enjoyed his longest coaching tenure (1904–1919) there, building Georgia Tech into a nationally recognized power. His accomplishments there included three straight unbeaten teams (6–0–1 in 1915, 8–0–1 in 1916, and 9–0–0 in 1917) and a 32-game unbeaten string over a five-year period. In 1916 Georgia Tech defeated Cumberland College 222–0, the highest score ever recorded in college football. Heisman's record as Georgia Tech coach comprised 101 wins, 28 losses, and 6 ties. Besides coaching football, Heisman also coached baseball and basketball at Georgia Tech. In addition, he served as director of athletics at the AAC and from 1910 to 1914 as president of the AtBA. He also acted professionally, specializing in Shakespearian productions, and operated his own summer stock theatre for many years.

In 1920 Heisman returned to his alma mater and coached football at the University of Pennsylvania (IL) through the 1922 season. At Washington and Jefferson College in 1923, he compiled a 6–1–1 football record. From 1924 to 1927 Heisman was head football coach and director of athletics at Rice Institute (SWC). After 36 years of coaching, Heisman retired and became athletic director at New York's Downtown Athletic Club. His composite college coaching record comprised 184 victories, 68 losses, and 16 ties. Heisman, one of college football's greatest innovators, invented the center snap instead of rolling the ball on the ground. His greatest claim to football fame is as the "father of the forward pass." In the late 1890s and early 1900s football became rougher with wedge plays and mass movements. Heisman believed that the forward pass would save a sport in danger of being discontinued. He wrote letters and lobbied members of the Rules Committee for several years before the forward pass finally was legalized in 1906 and made the game less dangerous. The renowned Heisman Trophy, awarded each year to college football's best player, is named for him. Heisman was named to the NFF and HAF College Football and the Georgia Tech Hall of Fame.

BIBLIOGRAPHY: L. H. Baker, *Football: Facts and Figures* (New York, 1945); Allison Danzig, *The History of American Football: Its Great Teams, Players, and Coaches* (Englewood Cliffs, NJ, 1956); Bill Libby, *Champions of College Football* (New York, 1975); Howard Liss, *They Changed the Game* (New York, 1975); University of Pennsylvania, Archives, Philadelphia, PA.

James Fuller

HENDRICKS, Theodore Paul "Ted" "Mad Stork" (b. 1 November 1947, Guatemala City, Guatemala), college and professional player, is the son of Maurice Hendricks, a Pan-American Airlines mechanic, and Guatemalan native Angela (Bonatti) Hendricks. At Hialeah High School in Miami, FL, Hendricks made All-American end in football, excelled as a basketball player, and won honors as a student. He attended the University of Miami (FL) from 1965 to 1968, making All-American defensive end three times. Hendricks, the first sophomore at Miami to make All-American, in 1968 was voted Lineman of the Year by UPI and won the Washington (DC) Touchdown Club Award as the Outstanding College Lineman. The Hurricanes' MVP and a tri-captain in 1968, Hendricks holds the Miami career record for most fumbles recovered (12) and most tackles (227). He helped his team defeat Virginia Polytechnic Institute in the 1966 Liberty Bowl and performed in the 1967 Bluebonnet Bowl loss to the University of Colorado.

The 6 foot, 7 inch, 220 pound Hendricks was selected by the Baltimore Colts in the second round of the 1969 NFL draft. He played for the Colts until announcing in 1974 that he had signed a contract for the 1975 season with Jacksonville (FL) in the WFL. One week later, Baltimore traded him to Green Bay (NFL). Hendricks enjoyed one of his best seasons with the Packers in 1974, leading the club in interceptions (five) and blocking an NFL-record seven kicks. As a free agent in 1975, Hendricks signed with the Oakland Raiders (NFL) and played with the Oakland–Los Angeles franchise through the 1983 season before retiring.

One of the top NFL linebackers, Hendricks never missed an NFL game and played in 215 straight contests. Hendricks, the defensive captain for the Raiders in 1980, played in AFC championship games following the 1970–1971, 1975–1977, 1980, and 1983 seasons. He participated on Super Bowl championship teams with Baltimore in Super Bowl V and the Raiders in Super Bowls XI, XV, and XVIII. In sixteen pro football seasons, Hendricks intercepted 26 passes for 332 yards and 1 touchdown, recovered 17 fumbles, shared the all-time NFL career record with 4 safeties, and holds the NFL mark with 25 blocked kicks. A six-time All-Pro selection (1971–1974, 1980, and 1982), Hendricks played in the Pro Bowl following 1971 through 1974 and 1980 through 1983 seasons. Hendricks was selected to the NFF College Football Hall of Fame in 1987 and the Pro Football Hall of Fame named him to its AFL-NFL 1960–1984 All-Star Second Team. Hendricks and his wife, Jane, have two sons, and he operates a football camp for boys in the off-season.

BIBLIOGRAPHY: *Oakland Raiders Media Guide, 1977; TSN Football Register—1984;* Paul Zimmerman, "Who Is the Mad Hatter?" *SI* 59 (October 17, 1983), pp. 92–96, 98, 102, 104, 106.

John L. Evers

HENRY, Wilbur Frank "Fats" "Pete" (b. 31 October 1897, Mansfield, OH; d. 7 February 1952, Washington, PA), college and professional athlete, football coach, and administrator, began his athletic career as a 215-pound football fullback and basketball guard at Mansfield High School. The versatile Henry captained the 7–1 football team his senior year and played as a state championship basketball finalist. In 1915 he enrolled at Washington and Jefferson College at Washington, PA, then a leading national football power. He was converted to tackle because of his 6 foot, 225–250 pound frame and played varsity football in 1915–1917, 1919, and an abbreviated military training season in 1918. Henry's college career featured his aptitude for blocking punts, causing football coach John Heisman* in 1923 to characterize him as "the greatest punt blocker the game has ever known." After receiving All-American mention as a sophomore, he made Walter Camp's* 1917 and 1919 first-team All-American squad at tackle. As a senior, he refused to listen to pro offers until completing the track season because the weight man did not want his team to lose any points. He won four letters in each of four college varsity sports: football, basketball, baseball, and track.

Henry was selected All-Pro tackle after his first season in 1920 with the Canton Bulldogs in the new NFL, formed that year. He made All-Pro each year at Canton until 1924, when he refused to accompany the team on its transfer to Cleveland, OH. Instead, he played with Pottsville, PA, winners of the AnL title that year. Henry met Marie Floding at a Canton, OH, hospital when she treated him for a football injury and married her September 23, 1923. Henry joined a newly formed Canton Bulldogs team (NFL) in 1925 as a star player and club president, but the club folded after the 1926 season because of lagging attendance. He split 1927 with the New York Giants and Pottsville club (NFL) and ended his playing career with Pottsville in 1928. An ankle injury suffered with the Giants shortened his career.

Noted for his exceptional punting and dropkicking skills and all-around offensive and defensive ability at tackle, Henry kicked a 55-yard field goal to give Pottsville a 3–0 exhibition win over Coaldale, PA, and booted a then NFL-record 52-yard field goal for Canton against Akron. He also made an NFL-record 94-yard punt against Akron in 1923, a mark unsurpassed until 1969. With Canton in 1923, he scored a then quite remarkable 59 points on one touchdown, 26 extra points, and 9 field goals to help the Bulldogs win the NFL championship.

After returning to Washington and Jefferson as line coach in 1929, he in 1942 replaced Stu Holcomb aş head football coach and served as athletic director until his death. Henry, named a charter member of the Pro Football Hall of Fame in 1963, was elected to the NFF College Football Hall of Fame in 1951, the HAF College Football Hall of Fame, and Pennsylvania Sports Hall of Fame in 1972. Called the greatest all-time tackle by coaching immortals Lou Little,* Knute Rockne,* John Sutherland,* Glenn "Pop" Warner,* and Alfred "Greasy" Neale,* he made virtually every all-time college football team and the "first 50 years" squad selected by the NFF. With William "Pudge" Heffelfinger,* Henry was rated by Walter Camp as "top" all-time lineman. A Pro Football Hall of Fame selection committee chose him All-Pro for the 1920s decade. Henry, who played with a smile on his cherubic face, is memorialized at Washington and Jefferson by the physical education building named for him.

BIBLIOGRAPHY: Paul B. Beers, *Profiles in Pennsylvania Sports* (Harrisburg, PA, 1975); Bob Carroll, "Fabulous Fatman," *The Coffin Corner* 5 (October 1983), p. 8; John McCallum and Charles H. Pearson, *College Football U.S.A., 1869–1973* (New York, 1973); Lee North, *She Produces All-Americans; A History of W&J Football* (Washington, PA, 1947); *Washington* (PA) *Observer-Reporter*, 1915–1919, 1929–1942.

Robert B. Van Atta

HERBER, Arnold "Flash" (b. 2 April 1910, Green Bay, WI; d. 14 October 1969, Green Bay, WI), college and professional player, excelled as a football passer with the Green Bay Packers (NFL) in the 1930s. He starred in basketball and football at Green Bay's West High School and sold programs on Sundays at Packers games. After spending one year at the University of Wisconsin (WC), he transferred to Regis College in Denver, CO. When the Depression forced him to leave Regis, he returned to Green Bay and became a handyman around the Packers clubhouse. Green Bay coach Curly Lambeau* added the 6 foot, 200-pound Herber to the Packers roster in 1930 partly to draw home fans. Nicknamed "Flash," Herber quickly passed for a touchdown in his first Packers game. Herber's passing, running, and punting made the Packers stronger and helped them win NFL titles in 1930 and 1931. Despite his short fingers and the period's watermelon-shaped football, Herber became the NFL's top passer and specialized in throwing long aerials. He won the NFL passing title in 1932, the first year official statistics were kept, and repeated in 1934 and 1936. During the mid-1930s he combined with end Don Hutson* to form the NFL's first great pass-catching duo. Herber's first NFL pass to Hutson covered 83 yards for a touchdown. The Herber–Hutson duo spearheaded the Packers to the 1936 and 1939 NFL titles.

Herber, whose effectiveness was reduced by a leg injury, retired after the 1940 season. When World War II created player shortages, he made a comeback with the New York Giants (NFL) in 1944 and 1945. He could no longer run but still threw with authority and helped pass the Giants to the Eastern Division championship. Ironically, the Packers defeated the Giants 14–7 in the title game. Herber's career passing marks (counting from 1932) included 481 completions in 1,174 attempts for 8,033 yards and 79 touchdowns and easily outpaced other 1930s quarterbacks. In 1932 Herber was named to the official All-NFL team. He was elected to the Pro Football Hall of Fame in

1966, three years before his death. After retiring from pro football, Herber operated a soft drink business in Green Bay, WI, and conducted a weekly radio show.

BIBLIOGRAPHY: "Hall of Fame Profile," *Pro!*, San Francisco–Pittsburgh Football Game Program, November 1, 1981; Arnold Herber file, Pro Football Hall of Fame, Canton, OH; George Sullivan, *Pro Football's All-Time Greats: The Immortals in Pro Football's Hall of Fame* (New York, 1968); Jack Yuenger, "He Came to Play," *Green Bay Packers Yearbook, 1962*.

Robert N. Carroll

HESTON, William Martin "Willie" (b. 9 September 1878, Galesburg, IL; d. 9 September 1963, Traverse City, MI), college and professional player and coach, performed as halfback four years (1901–1904) at the University of Michigan (WC). Heston starred in the first Rose Bowl game in 1902, when the Wolverines trounced Stanford University 49–0. Heston, the second non-eastern player chosen by Walter Camp* on his All-American teams, made the third unit in 1901–1902 and first team in 1903–1904. The Michigan captain his final year, Heston was named HAF 1904 Player of the Year. He made several All-Time All-American teams, including those of Camp (1910), Glenn "Pop" Warner* (1920), Grantland Rice* (OS) for *College Humor* (1928), George Trevor (1937), and the FWAA (1969). In 1954 he was inducted into the NFF College Football Hall of Fame. He also was elected to the HAF College Football Hall of Fame.

As the main force on coach Fielding Yost's* "point-a-minute" teams for four years, Heston scored 93 (5-point) touchdowns for an astonishing 465 points and averaged around 136 yards per game. He combined speed and power, using his 5 foot, 8 inch, 185 pound frame to hit the middle of the line or skirt the ends. During Heston's career the Wolverines amassed a combined 43–0–1 record, outscored opponents 2,326 to 40 points, and averaged 53 points per game. Michigan finished 4–0–0 against Chicago, 3–0–0 over Wisconsin, and 1–0–1 against Minnesota, clubs previously dominating the WC. Heston remarked in 1947, "The T formation was pretty standard, although we shifted from it and we didn't throw passes. But we swept the ends and hit off tackle for good gains. And when those big Minnesota, Ohio and Chicago teams spread for us, we ripped up the middle." Besides winning four outright or shared WC crowns, Michigan shared the national championship with Harvard (1901) and Yale (1902). They administered the worst defeats in history to Buffalo (128–0), Ohio State (86–0), Michigan State (119–0), Iowa (107–0), and West Virginia (130–0).

Heston's father, a low-income Illinois farmer, moved his large family westward and ultimately settled in Grant's Pass, OR. Heston worked his father's farm and attended Grant's Pass High School, which had a boys choir but no athletics. After graduating in 1898, he entered San Jose Normal College and captained the football team in 1900. When San Jose and Chico State tied for the conference championship, Heston persuaded Stanford University coach Yost to direct San Jose in a playoff. Heston, shifted from guard to halfback, led the team to a 46–0 victory over Chico State. After becoming coach at University of Michigan (WC) the following year, Yost convinced Heston to forsake teaching, enter Michigan's Law School, and join the football team. Prior to the Rose Bowl game, Los Angeles sportswriters claimed that the Wolverines could not be very strong if Heston started with Michigan. Heston gained 170 yards in 18 carries for a 9.4 yard-average per carry against Stanford, however, before an estimated 8,000 spectators. Despite the 85-degree temperature, eleven Wolverines played the entire game without substitution.

The only blemish on Michigan's four-year record occurred in 1903, when they were tied 6–6 by undefeated WC co-champion Minnesota. The Gophers' Northrop Field was filled with 25,000 spectators when Heston ran 57 yards to set up the lone Wolverines score. He was injured in the intense battle with the Gophers, who were coached by Henry Williams* and line coach William "Pudge" Heffelfinger.* The Little Brown Jug competition was initiated in 1903, when Michigan forgot their water jug and Minnesota challenged them to win it back. When Chicago quarterback Walter Eckersall* lunged for Heston's legs in Michigan's 28–0 triumph in 1903, Heston hurdled the Maroons great and sped 75 yards for a touchdown. The quick-starting Heston led Michigan's 1904 Olympic 60, 100 and 200 meter gold medalist Archie Hahn* (OS) in impromptu races for the first 40 yards. In 1944 sportswriter Grantland Rice* (OS) noted, "Heston was a ball of fire off the mark. There were two occasions when he broke so quickly that he took the ball away from the quarterback who was lateraling to his halfback. Each time Willie ran for a touchdown."

After graduating with a Bachelor of Laws degree in 1905 from the University of Michigan Law School, Heston served as head football coach in 1905 at Drake University (4–4–0) and 1906 at North Carolina State University (SIAA, 3–1–4). He received an unprecedented $600 in 1905 to play one pro football game with the Canton Bulldogs against the Massillon Tigers. He captained an All-Star team in 1906 but broke his leg against Massillon and quit football. A Detroit lawyer, he served as assistant prosecuting attorney of Wayne County, MI (1911–1915), and was elected to the recorder's bench (1916–1923). He then concentrated on his private law practice and real estate business until retirement. Following his first wife's death in 1953, Heston in 1956 married his longtime secretary, Sarah E. Williams, of Bay City, MI. His two sons, William, Jr., and John, graduated from Michigan in 1932 and 1934, respectively, and played on four WC and two national championship football teams but lacked their father's outstanding ability. Heston stopped running one-half mile daily at age 75 but continued walking for exercise.

BIBLIOGRAPHY: L. H. Baker, *Football: Facts and Figures* (New York, 1945); Richard M. Cohen, Jordan A. Deutsch, and David S. Neft, *The University of Michigan Football Scrapbook* (Indianapolis, IN, 1978); Allison Danzig, *The History of American Football: Its Great Teams, Players, and Coaches* (Englewood Cliffs, NJ, 1956); Will Perry, *The Wolverines: A Story of Michigan Football* (Huntsville, AL, 1980); Maxwell Stiles, *The Rose Bowl: A Complete Action and Pictorial Exposition of Rose Bowl Football* (Los Angeles, 1947).

James D. Whalen

HEWITT, William Ernest "Bill" (b. 8 October 1909, Bay City, MI; d. 14 January 1947, Philadelphia, PA), college and professional player, attended Central High School in Bay City, MI. Hewitt in 1926 won All-State honorable mention at end for helping his football team win eight and tie one his senior year and excelled as a forward on the conference champion basketball team.

As a junior college student in 1927–1928 he coached the Essexville St. John High basketball team to a winning season. He then played varsity football three seasons for the University of Michigan (WC) under coach Harry G. Kipke. During his junior and senior years there, Hewitt nearly made All-American honors, but his fractured ankle in the 1930 season and shift from end to fullback in 1931 kept him from attaining the honor. Besides being the Wolverines' MVP his senior year, he helped his team become WC co-champions in 1930 and 1931. The versatile blocker, ballcarrier, and receiver proved a dedicated team player who led by his quiet example and dogged determination.

Hewitt played in the NFL for the Chicago Bears (1932–1936), Philadelphia Eagles (1937 to 1939), and Philadelphia–Pittsburgh Steagles merger team (1943). In 1937 Bears coach George Halas* traded Hewitt to the Eagles for first-round draft pick, fullback Sam Francis of Nebraska. The first player named All-NFL with two teams, Hewitt was selected All-Pro four times and excelled at defense and offense. He conducted a superquick defensive charge and pass rush and invented many trick plays to confuse the opposition. During his pro career he caught 101 passes for 1,606 yards for a 15.9-yard average per catch and scored 23 touchdowns. At Philadelphia Hewitt captained the Eagles, worked off-season, and earned more money than with the Bears. Hewitt feared becoming a "tramp athlete," but Eagles owner Bert Bell* gave him the security to become a team leader. He played without a helmet until the rules change mandated its use and helped lead the 1933 Bears to the NFL title. He married Mary Ellen Mulholland of Philadelphia in 1946, but died less than a year later in an automobile accident on a business trip. In 1971 he was enshrined in the Pro Football Hall of Fame.

BIBLIOGRAPHY: Bay City (MI) *Times*, January 15, 1947; Ronald L. Mendell and Timothy B. Phares, *Who's Who in Football* (New Rochelle, NY, 1974); Will Perry, *The Wolverines: A Story of Michigan Football* (Huntsville, AL, 1980); *The Pro Football*

Hall of Fame Souvenir Yearbook, 1979–1980; Richard Whittingham, *The Chicago Bears: An Illustrated History* (Chicago, 1979).

Douglas A. Noverr

HILL, Calvin (b. 2 January 1947, Baltimore, MD), college athlete and professional football player, is the son of construction foreman Henry Hill and grew up in a tough steel mill section, "Turner's Station," in East Baltimore. At age 14, Hill received a Schenley Foundation scholarship at the Riverdale Country School in New York City. For Riverdale, Hill played baseball, basketball, and football. He pitched and batted over .400 for the baseball team, made the All-City basketball squad with a 26 point average, and was named a high school All-American quarterback. After graduating with honors, Hill entered Yale University (IL) in 1965 on a scholarship.

Hill excelled in football and track at Yale. As a football running back, he compiled over 2,600 yards total offense on varsity squads with 4–5, 8–1, and 8–0–1 records. In track he recorded a long jump of 25 feet, 1.5 inches and a triple jump of 51 feet, 5.25 inches. Hill led the Elis in football rushing in 1967 and 1968 and compiled 1,512 career rushing yards to rank seventh on Yale's all-time list. An All-IL selection in 1967 and 1968, Hill scored 84 points in 1968 (tied for second), and recorded 24 career touchdowns for 144 points (fifth). He graduated in 1969 with a B.A. in American History.

The Dallas Cowboys (NFL) chose Hill in the first round of the 1969 player draft. The 6 foot, 4 inch, 227 pound running back broke the club's single-game rushing record in his second start and rushed for 942 yards in his first season to earn Rookie of the Year honors. Injuries slowed him down the next two seasons, but Hill in 1972 became the first Cowboys back to gain 1,000 yards. He ran for 1,036 yards to rank third in the NFC that year and enjoyed his best season in 1974, rushing for 1,142 yards. Hill led Dallas in rushing (1969, 1972–1974) and receiving (1972–1973) and remains tied with three others for most touchdowns scored in one game. In 1971 he recorded four touchdowns against the Buffalo Bills. Following the 1970 and 1971 seasons, he played in Super Bowls V and VI. The Cowboys lost to the Baltimore Colts in 1971 and defeated the Miami Dolphins in 1972 for the NFL title.

Hill played out his option with Dallas and signed as a free agent with the Hawaiians for the 1975 WFL season. He played in only three games there in 1975 and signed the next year with the Washington Redskins (NFL) after the WFL folded. Hill joined the Cleveland Browns (NFL) in 1978 and completed his playing career there in 1981. In thirteen pro seasons, he played in 159 games, compiled 6,301 rushing yards on 1,501 attempts, and scored 42 touchdowns. Hill recorded 275 pass receptions for 2,889 yards and 24 touchdowns and completed 5 of 13 passes for 204 yards and 3 touchdowns. An All-Pro selection in 1969 and 1973, he played in the Pro Bowl following the 1972–1974 seasons. Hill, who married Janet McDonald and has one son,

Grant Henry, has worked toward a degree in theology from the Perkins School on the SMU campus and has served as chairman of the National Association of Retarded Children.

BIBLIOGRAPHY: *Dallas Cowboys Media Guide, 1974; Lincoln Library of Sports Champions* (Columbus, OH, 1974); *TSN Football Register—1982.*

John L. Evers

HINKEY, Frank Augustus "Hink" or "Gussie" (b. 23 December 1871, Tonawanda, NY; d. 30 December 1925, Southern Pines, NC), college player and coach, twice captained Yale University's football eleven (IL) and became one of four players named four years to Walter Camp's* All-American teams (1891–1894). Hinkey was chosen at end on numerous All-Time All-American teams, including those of Camp (1910), Pop Warner* (1920), Bill Edwards (1930), Parke Davis (1934), the HAF (1950), and the FWAA (1969). The HAF 1891 Player of the Year as a freshman, he was selected a charter member in 1951 of the NFF College Football Hall of Fame. He was also elected to the HAF College Football Hall of Fame. Hinkey's German-born father, Lewis, was a partner and manager of the hardware firm of Nice and Hinkey. His mother, Mary Ann (Nice) Hinkey, was born in Clarence, NY, and resided at Grand Island, NY, before her marriage. After attending Tonawanda High School, Hinkey studied two years at Andover Preparatory School and starred at end on the football team at 135 pounds before graduating in 1891.

During Hinkey's four varsity years at Yale, the Elis compiled a combined 52–1–0 record, outscored the opposition 1,738 to 25, and captured the IL championship for 1891, 1892, and 1894. Yale played 34 consecutive games (two and a half seasons) without surrendering a point and finished 3–0 against Pennsylvania, 4–0 over Harvard, and 3–1 against Princeton. The undefeated 1893 Princeton Tigers upset the Elis 6–0. Hinkey, whose fierce tackle in the 1891 Harvard game caused a fumble that led to a Yale touchdown, blocked a Crimson field goal attempt near the end of the game. He recovered a Princeton fumble that led to a touchdown in Yale's 19–0 defeat of the Tigers. Harvard unveiled the flying wedge to open the second half against Yale the following year, but the Elis effectively neutralized it and Hinkey stopped a final Harvard rush at the 7-yard line to preserve the 6–0 victory. He grabbed a loose ball after a blocked kick to help defeat Princeton 12–0 and carried the ball occasionally, running for a touchdown against Penn in 1893. His defensive penetration of the Quakers' flying interference keyed Yale's 14–6 win.

Although playing cleanly and according to the rules, Hinkey exhibited such ferocity that he encouraged brutality. His teammates worshipped and even feared him, obeying every order. Yale center George Foster Sanford exclaimed, "Hinkey in action was a raving maniac who frothed at the mouth." He proved the key Elis player, causing opponents to gang up on him. Rough play caused a break in football relations with Pennsylvania (1893) for forty-one years and Harvard (1894) for two years. An editorial in the *New York Post* after the 1894 Yale-Harvard game stated, "No father or mother worthy of the name would permit a son to associate with the set of Yale brutes on Hinkey's football team." Physicians warned Hinkey early in life against competitive sports because of a consumptive condition, but he ignored their advice. Despite having a slim, sickly appearance and being slow afoot, the 5 foot, 9 inch, 152 pound Hinkey demonstrated fine coordination, muscular development, and combative instincts. Walter Camp observed, "He drifted through the interference like a disembodied spirit." Besides literally exploding when tackling, he proved effective in covering punts and boxing the tackle.

Off the field, the introverted Hinkey seldom spoke, avoided people, and had few close, devoted friends. Hinkey, whose brother Louis was a teammate his final year at Yale, played right field on the freshman baseball team and graduated from Yale in 1895. Hinkey sold real estate in Tonawanda, NY (1895–1903), became superintendent of the Zinc Smelting Works of Langon Zinc Company, Iola, KS (1903–1910), and of United Zinc and Chemical Company, Springfield, IL (1910–1913), worked as a stockbroker with Harris, Latter and Company, New York City (1913–1920), and was employed with the brokerage firm of DeWeese-Talbott, Dayton, OH (1920–1922). Hinkey served as Yale assistant football coach under Howard Jones* (1913) and became head coach the following year, posting a 7–2–0 record. An excellent teacher of offense, he utilized a baffling lateral pass attack borrowed from Canadian rugby and initiated the use of film to study plays. However, he neglected teaching football fundamentals. When his 1915 squad lost four early warm-up games, he was replaced by Tom Shevlin* for the final encounters with Princeton and Harvard. His cigar smoking, swearing, and heavy drinking bothered Camp, contributing to his ouster.

Hinkey married Elizabeth Thomas of Springfield, IL, in 1912 and had no children. His tubercular condition caused him in 1922 to enter a sanatorium in Southern Pines, NC. Former teammates Frank Butterworth and George Adee, who visited him toward the end, received a message from him the day he died: "Charon is at the crossing." Pop Warner once said of Hinkey, "He was the greatest football player of all time. He was the personification of two of the greatest attributes of the great football player: determination and fighting spirit."

BIBLIOGRAPHY: Morris A. Bealle, *The History of Football at Harvard, 1874–1948* (Washington, DC, 1948); Tim Cohane, *The Yale Football Story* (New York, 1951); Parke H. Davis, *Football: The American Intercollegiate Game* (New York, 1911); William H. Edwards, *Football Days* (New York, 1916); Ronald L. Mendell and Timothy B. Phares, *Who's Who in Football* (New Rochelle, NY, 1974); Alexander M. Weyand, *Football Immortals* (New York, 1962); Yale-Harvard Football Game Program, November 24, 1894; Yale University, Alumni Archives, Sterling Memorial Library, New Haven, CT.

James D. Whalen

HINKLE, William Clarke (b. 10 April 1912, Toronto, OH), college athlete and professional football player and coach, is the son of a steelworker and laboratory technician for the State Department of Highways. He graduated in 1928 from Toronto High School, where he played football, basketball, and baseball. From 1928 to 1932 he attended Bucknell College, where he played varsity football and baseball for three years and basketball forward his senior year. Hinkle, who graduated from Bucknell in 1932, married Emilie Cobden of Larchmont, NY, in 1936 and had no children. In 1929 Hinkle gained national prominence as a sophomore football fullback. During that season he led the East with 128 points and incredibly scored 50 in one game against Dickinson College. The next two seasons, Bucknell's football team finished undefeated and was voted the top eastern team. Hinkle was elected to three consecutive All-American teams and was voted the outstanding player in the 1932 Shrine All-Star (East-West) game.

From 1932 to 1942 Hinkle played professionally with the Green Bay Packers (NFL). The 5 foot, 11 inch, 200 pound fullback was noted for his versatility as an excellent runner, blocker, team punter, and placekicker. At defensive linebacker, he made punishing tackles. His legendary confrontations with Chicago Bears fullback Bronko Nagurski* caused Hinkle to remark, "My greatest day in pro football was the day I heard that Nagurski had retired." During Hinkle's pro career, the Packers compiled an impressive 80–35–4 record, won three Western Division titles (1936, 1938, and 1939), and captured two NFL championships (1936, 1939). In the 1938 NFL championship game, Hinkle carried the ball 18 times for 63 yards and scored one touchdown in the 23–17 loss to the New York Giants. The Packers trounced the Giants 27–0 in the 1939 NFL championship game, as Hinkle rushed 13 times for 23 yards and caught two passes for 23 yards. Although Hinkle never led the NFL in rushing, he was named to the NFL All-Pro team four seasons (1936–1938, 1941). He paced the NFL in scoring in 1938 with 58 points and in field goals in 1940 with 9 and 1941 with 6. During his career he rushed 1,138 times for 3,850 yards (3.4-yard average) and 35 touchdowns and caught 48 passes for 552 yards (11.5-yard average) and 9 touchdowns.

After the 1941 season Hinkle retired from pro football to join the U.S. Coast Guard. He served as an assistant football coach at the U.S. Coast Guard Academy one season and coached an industrial league football team in 1948–1949 in Weirton, WV. He worked many years in quality control in a steel mill and in industrial sales until retiring in 1973. Hinkle has been selected to nine Halls of Fame, including those of Bucknell University, Green Bay Packers, NFF College Football, and Pro Football. In 1981 he received the Ohio Governor's Award as an outstanding citizen in the state.

BIBLIOGRAPHY: Bob Barnett, "Playing for the Pack in the 1930s, An Interview with Clarke Hinkle," *Packer Report;* Bob Barnett, "The Packers First Playoff Game," *Packer Report;* Bill Barron, ed., *The Official NFL Encyclopedia of Football* (New York, 1982); Fran Connors, *The NFL Record Manual, 1983; Green Bay Packers Media Guide, 1983;* George Halas with Gwen Morgan and Arthur Veysey, *Halas by Halas* (New York, 1979); W. Clarke Hinkle, Interview with C. Robert Barnett, November 11, 1983; David S. Neft, Richard M. Cohen, and Jordan A. Deutsch, *Pro Football: The Early Years, An Encyclopedic History, 1895–1959* (New York, 1978); Roger Treat, ed., *The Encyclopedia of Football*, 16th rev. ed., rev. by Pete Palmer (New York, 1979).

C. Robert Barnett

HIRSCH, Elroy Leon "Crazylegs" (b. 17 June 1923, Wausau, WI), college athlete, professional football player, and sports administrator, is the son of Otto Peter and Mayme Sabena (Magnuson) Hirsch of German and Norwegian ancestry. He married childhood sweetheart Ruth Katherine Stahmer in 1946 and has two children, Win Stephen and Patricia Caroline. In 1951 Hirsch received a B.A. from Baldwin Wallace University. Previously, he had attended the University of Wisconsin (1941–1942, 1947) and the University of Michigan (1943–1944, as a Marine Corps officer candidate) and had served in the U.S. Marine Corps Reserve (1943–1946). After lettering in baseball, basketball, and football at Wausau High School, Hirsch excelled on the football gridiron at Wisconsin (WC) and then became the first four-sport (baseball, basketball, football, and track) letterman at Michigan (WC). As a halfback for the third-ranked Wisconsin Badgers in 1942, he gained 226 yards passing and 766 yards rushing and acquired the nickname "Crazylegs" for his unorthodox running style. Although Hirsch played football just one season for Wisconsin, state sportswriters in 1969 selected him to the Badgers' all-time backfield and named him the third best football player in Badgers history.

The 6 foot, 2 inch, 190 pound Hirsch scored both touchdowns and won the Outstanding Player award, as the collegians upset the Los Angeles Rams, 16–0, in the 1946 College All-Star game. With the Chicago Rockets (AAFC), Hirsch in 1946 began a twelve-year pro career as an end-halfback. The Rockets and the NFL's Rams had already offered him some $7,000. Hirsch had chosen the Rockets because of his friendship with their mentor, Dick Hanley, who had coached Hirsch during his year of military service football with the El Toro (CA) Marines.

When the AAFC folded after the 1948 season, Hirsch joined Los Angeles (NFL) in 1949. In nine years with the Rams, he caught 343 passes for 6,299 yards, averaged 18.4 yards per reception and scored 53 touchdowns. His greatest season came in 1951, when he led the NFL with 102 points scored and 66 passes received, set one NFL record by gaining 1,495 yards, tied another by snagging 17 touchdown passes, and captured Pro Player of the Year honors. Hirsch, a swift and sure-handed receiver, proved adept at catching footballs thrown over his head. He caught touchdown passes in a record 11 consecutive games (1950–1951) and helped popularize the long pass in pro football. During his pro career he caught 387 passes for 7,029 yards (18.2-yard average) and 60 touchdowns and rushed 207 times for 687 yards (3.3-yard average) and 4 touchdowns.

Perhaps inevitably, the handsome, popular Ram found his way to Hollywood, CA. Hirsch portrayed himself in a commercially successful movie, *Crazylegs—All-American*. Other off-field endeavors during his playing days included his own television and radio programs. Following his 1957 retirement as a player, Hirsch worked as sports director of the Union Oil Company of California (1958–1960) and general manager and assistant to the president of the Rams (1960–1969). From 1969 to 1987 he served as the athletic director at the University of Wisconsin. Hirsch is enshrined in the Pro and the NFF College Football Hall of Fame, HAF Pro Hall of Fame, and Wisconsin Athletic Hall of Fame.

BIBLIOGRAPHY: Steve Bisheff, *Los Angeles Rams* (New York, 1973); "Elroy 'Crazylegs' Hirsch Starts Crash Program for Wisconsin Talent," *Sports Focus Green Bay Packers Yearbook, 1969*, pp. 50, 52; Oliver E. Kuechle with Jim Mott, *On Wisconsin! Badger Football* (Huntsville, AL, 1977); John D. McCallum, *Big Ten Football Since 1895* (Radnor, PA, 1976); Robert M. Smith, *Illustrated History of Pro Football* (New York, 1977); Al Stump, "They Say He's Crazy to Play," *Sport* 18 (November, 1954), pp. 19–21, 84–86; George Sullivan, *Pro Football's All-Time Greats: The Immortals in Pro Football's Hall of Fame* (New York, 1968); *WWA*, 42nd ed. (1982–1983), p. 1,525.

Thomas D. Jozwik

HOGAN, James Joseph "Jim" (b. 31 October 1874, Glenbane, County Tipperary, Ireland; d. 20 March 1910, New Haven, CT), college athlete, performed at Yale University (IL) and thrice made Walter Camp's* All-American football squad (1902–1904). A four-year regular tackle, Hogan was named HAF 1902 Player of the Year as a sophomore and captained the 1904 Elis. Besides being elected in 1954 to the NFF College Football Hall of Fame, he was chosen All-Time All-American by J. C. Kofoed, Philadelphia *Record* (1912), and Walter W. Liggett, *Sportlife* (1925). Yale (IL) won Big Three championships twice (1902 and 1904) during Hogan's career and fielded among its best teams. The U.S. Military Academy (Army) prevented perfect seasons by tying the Elis 6–6 in 1902 and defeating them 11–6 in 1904. Yale lost only two other games, 22–0 to Harvard (1901) and 11–6 to Princeton (1903), and compiled a 22-game undefeated streak and 43–3–2 four-year record.

The 5 foot, 10 inch, 210 pound Hogan, a rugged ballcarrier with furious leg drive in the tackle-back formation, played with sleeves rolled up and a grim battle smile. John R. DeWitt of Princeton boasted, "You could hardly stop Hogan when he had the ball. He was the strongest tackle I ever saw."

Against Harvard and Princeton, Hogan scored five touchdowns and recovered two fumbles and one blocked punt. Hogan played on the famous 1902 "Irish Line" of Celtic extraction which included five All-Americans. In the New York *Sun* (1931), George Trevor noted, "Jim Hogan, barrel-chested, ox-necked, gorilla-armed tackle, had a flair for showmanship. He swung his huge hands like flails and cried like a child from sheer Celtic emotion when things went wrong." Hogan proved so vital a part of the Elis spirit that classmates called him "Yale."

The son of stonemason John F. and Bridget (Meehan) Hogan, he had three brothers and three sisters and moved to Torrington, CT, as a child. After graduation from Torrington High School, he worked for Union Hardware Company. At Phillips Exeter Academy, he became one of its greatest football players, captained the 1900 team, and graduated in 1901. Hogan participated in the shot put on the Yale track team, belonged to the debating society, and managed the Yale Dramatic Association. An honor student most of his four years and a faculty favorite, he held the John Benneto Scholarship as a junior and senior. The Delta Kappa Epsilon Fraternity member was appointed class agent for the Alumni Fund at graduation in 1905.

At Columbia University Law School he served on the *Law Review* staff and as football critic for the New York *World*. He earned a Bachelor of Law degree in 1908 and joined the law firm of Hatch and Clute in New York City. He was appointed deputy street cleaning commissioner of New York City in 1909 and resigned the following year to resume law practice, but he took ill suddenly with Bright's disease and died. Delta Kappa Epsilon in 1911 established the James J. Hogan Scholarship at Yale as a memorial to him. Yale president Arthur T. Hadley fondly referred to the 1905 graduates as "Hogan's class."

BIBLIOGRAPHY: L. H. Baker, *Football: Facts and Figures* (New York, 1945); Tim Cohane, *Gridiron Grenadiers; Story of West Point Football* (New York, 1948); Tim Cohane, *The Yale Football Story* (New York, 1951); Allison Danzig, *The History of American Football: Its Great Teams, Players, and Coaches* (Englewood Cliffs, NJ, 1956); Parke H. Davis, *Football: The American Intercollegiate Game* (New York, 1911); William H. Edwards, *Football Days* (New York, 1916); John D. McCallum and Charles H. Pearson, *College Football U.S.A., 1869–1973* (New York, 1973); Ronald L. Mendell and Timothy B. Phares, *Who's Who in Football* (New York, 1974); Yale–Harvard Football Game Program, November 19, 1904; Yale University Archives, Sterling Memorial Library, New Haven, CT.

James D. Whalen

HORNUNG, Paul Vernon (b. 23 December 1935, Louisville, KY), college athlete, professional football player, and announcer, grew up with his mother, Loretta, who separated from his father (an insurance agent) when Paul was two years old. At Flaget High School in Louisville, KY, Hornung excelled in basketball, baseball, and football. One of the most famous athletes in the school's history, Hornung was named the MVP in Kentucky his senior year. Hornung received a football scholarship from the University of Notre Dame and graduated in 1957 from there. Besides quarterbacking for the Fighting Irish, he also played defensive back in football and earned a basketball letter his sophomore year. The two-time collegiate football All-American (1955–1956) captured the Heisman Trophy his senior year, even though Notre Dame suffered through an injury-riddled season with only two wins. At Notre Dame, Hornung completed 105 of 214 passes for 1,660 yards and 12 touchdowns.

Hornung, the first player selected by Green Bay in the 1957 NFL draft, performed for the Packers from 1957 through 1966 but missed the 1963 season when he and Alex Karras* were suspended for gambling on NFL games. After Hornung proved ineffective his first two pro seasons, coach Vince Lombardi* moved him from quarterback to halfback. The triple-threat back played on three NFL championship teams (1961–1962, 1965) and in two Pro Bowls (1959–1960). In 1961 Hornung served in the U.S. Army and performed for the Packers on weekend passes. In the NFL title game, he scored 19 points against the New York Giants to tie a playoff game record and was selected the game's MVP by *Sport*. Hornung, injured most of the 1962 season, turned in a sensational performance in 1965 when Green Bay captured the NFL title game from the Cleveland Browns.

The versatile Hornung led the Packers in scoring (1958–1961, 1964) and paced the NFL three consecutive years (1959–1961) in points scored. In 1960 he scored 15 touchdowns, 15 field goals, and 41 extra points to establish an NFL season-record 176 points that has not been equalled. On October 8, 1961, Hornung scored 3 touchdowns, 6 extra points, and 3 field goals for 33 points to establish a single-game Packers record. His five rushing touchdowns on December 12, 1965, remain a club record, while his four field goals (twice) tied a team mark. Hornung in 1960 and 1961 made All-Pro and was selected the NFL's MVP. In nine pro seasons Hornung rushed 893 times for 3,711 yards and 50 touchdowns, completed 24 of 55 passes for 383 yards and 5 touchdowns, and made 130 receptions for 1,480 yards and 12 touchdowns. Hornung kicked 190 of 194 extra points, booted 66 of 140 field goals, and scored 760 points. He retired in 1967 after being selected by the New Orleans Saints (NFL) in the expansion draft.

Known almost equally for his escapades off the field, Hornung has settled into the business world. Married in 1967 to Pat Roeder and later divorced, Hornung wed again in 1980 and engages in real estate developments and other projects. He has succeeded as a sports commentator for Notre Dame telecasts, CBS-TV coverage of NFL games, and for college football games with Lindsey Nelson* (OS) for the Turner Broadcasting System. Hornung was elected in 1975 to the Green Bay Packers Hall of Fame, in 1985 to the NFF College Football Hall of Fame, and in 1986 to the Pro Football Hall of Fame.

BIBLIOGRAPHY: *CB* (1963), pp. 195–97; Evansville *(IN) Sunday Courier and Press* (March 24, 1985), pp. 1C, 7C; George Sullivan, *Pro Football A to Z* (New York, 1975).

John L. Evers

HORVATH, Leslie "Les" (b. 12 September 1921, South Bend, IN), college and professional player, graduated in 1939 from Cleveland Rhodes High School, where he starred in football, basketball, and track. At Ohio State University (WC) he played football four seasons (1940–1942, 1944) under coaches Francis A. Schmidt,* Paul E. Brown,* and Carroll C. Widdoes. Brown's 1942 squad won the national championship, while Widdoes' 1944 undefeated Buckeyes finished second nationally. The 1944 Heisman Trophy winner, the 5 foot, 11 inch, 160 pound Horvath won the WC MVP award and was selected to the HAF and in 1969 to the NFF College Football Halls of Fame. After being chosen the most valuable sophomore in 1940, Horvath averaged eight yards per carry against Pittsburgh, scored two touchdowns and passed for another against Illinois, and made various All-WC teams as a senior in 1942. WC coaches claimed the 1942 Buckeyes "had the most intense team speed ever seen in the Conference." Horvath, who entered a specialized U.S. Army dentistry training program as a graduate student at Ohio State in 1943, was granted another year of eligibility in 1944. Termed the "best civilian team in the nation," the "Baby Ducks" made a perfect 9–0–0 record with 31 freshmen and 12 upperclassmen. Horvath provided the highlight of the 1944 season by scoring two touchdowns in a come-from-behind 18–14 victory over Michigan.

A unanimous All-American, Horvath ranked second nationally rushing, third in total offense, and eleventh in scoring. The first Buckeye to compile 2,000 career yards, Horvath rushed for 1,546 yards and passed for 509. Due to World War II conditions, Horvath played twice in the Shrine All-Star (East-West) game. A member of Delta Tau Delta fraternity, he graduated from dental school in June 1945 and spent the next two years at the Great Lakes Naval Training Base and in Hawaii. He played halfback with the Los Angeles Rams (NFL) in 1947–1948 and Cleveland Browns (AAFC) in 1949 but retired after a rib injury. Horvath rushed 58 times for 221 yards (3.8-yard average) and 1 touchdown and caught 9 passes for 142 yards (15.8-yard average) and 1 touchdown.

Horvath, the son of a pharmacist, married in 1949 and a year later opened a private dental practice in Glendale, CA. After his first wife died in 1973, he remarried in 1975 and has no children. Horvath still practices dentistry in Glendale, CA.

BIBLIOGRAPHY: Richard M. Cohen, Jordan A. Deutsch, and David S. Neft, *The Ohio State Football Scrapbook* (Indianapolis, IN, 1977); Bill Libby, *Heroes of the Heisman Trophy* (New York, 1973); Ronald L. Mendell and Timothy B. Phares, *Who's Who in*

Football (New Rochelle, NY, 1974); *The Official NCAA Football Guide, 1943; The Official NCAA Football Guide, 1945;* Ohio State–Michigan Football Game Program, November 21, 1942; Ohio State–Minnesota Football Game Program, October 28, 1944; Kenneth L. (Tug) Wilson and Jerry Brondfield, *The Big Ten* (Englewood Cliffs, NJ, 1967).

James D. Whalen

HOUSTON, Kenneth Ray "Ken" (b. 12 November 1944, Lufkin, TX), college and professional player and coach, is the son of a dry cleaner and began high school at Lufkin playing in the band. He was offered an athletic scholarship at Prairie View College (SAC), then the leading institution for black athletes in Texas, because the high school football team captain insisted that Houston be made part of a two-player deal. Originally slated to play center, the 6 foot, 3 inch, 180-pounder was moved by defensive coach "Hoo" Wright to linebacker. Houston nearly quit school his junior year when his father suffered a stroke, but the family urged him to continue. Prairie View won the national championship three times, with Houston being named to several All-American teams. The Houston Oilers selected him in the ninth round of the 1967 AFL draft and moved him to safety. Houston, who was first named to the All-Star squad in 1968, made All-Pro for twelve of his fourteen seasons.

In 1971 Houston intercepted nine passes for the Oilers and set a single-season record by returning four for touchdowns. After that season, he entertained the American forces in Vietnam. Houston suffered a few injuries in 1972 and was traded to the Washington Redskins (NFL) for five players, including two regulars. Houston disliked leaving his native Texas but tied a record in his very first game by intercepting two John Unitas* passes for touchdowns to defeat the San Diego Chargers in the 1973 opener. Later that year Houston stopped Walt Garrison of the Dallas Cowboys on the one-yard line with sixteen seconds left to preserve a Redskins victory over their archrivals. Houston lifted Garrison, who had received a pass from Dallas quarterback Craig Morton, off his feet. Lifetime, Houston intercepted 49 passes and returned a record 9 for touchdowns. He also played in 183 consecutive games, the most ever by a defensive back. Houston, declared a free agent in 1981, returned to the Oilers as an assistant coach. He married Gustie Marie Rice of Houston, who holds a doctorate in mathematics, and has no children. During his Washington tenure, Houston was considered the best Redskins player and ranked by some writers as the greatest strong safety ever. He was elected in 1986 to the Pro Football Hall of Fame.

BIBLIOGRAPHY: Washington (DC) *Star*, August 5 and November 26, 1979, April 4, 1981.

John David Healy

HOWLEY, Charles Louis "Chuck" (b. 28 June 1936, Wheeling, WV), college athlete and professional football player, is the son of James and Mary Howley. At Wheeling's Warwood High, Howley played basketball, baseball, and track before trying out for football as a junior. As a senior he made All-State tackle for a football team winning only three games. Howley entered West Virginia University (SC) in the fall, 1954, and participated in several college sports. He played guard, center, and linebacker in football, earned All-SC honors three years, and participated in the Shrine All-Star (East-West) game, Senior Bowl, and College All-Star game. As a junior Howley was named SC Athlete of the Year and lettered in five sports. Besides being the SC one-meter diving champ, he sprinted for the track team and excelled in gymnastics and wrestling. After graduating with a Physical Education degree, he married Nancy Welch on June 28, 1958, and has one son, Scott, and one daughter, Robin.

The NFL's Chicago Bears drafted the 6 foot, 2 inch, 225 pound Howley in the first round. He played in every game as a reserve linebacker in 1958 but a knee injury in the third game of the 1959 season sidelined him. He returned to Wheeling, WV, to operate a gas station and remained on the retired list in 1960 while rehabilitating his knee. In the spring, 1961, he tested the knee in a West Virginia alumni game and decided to play pro football again. The Bears traded him for two draft choices to the Dallas Cowboys (NFL), where he became a starter during the 1961 season. Blessed with outstanding speed and agility, Howley excelled in pass coverage and proved a sure open field tackler. He made the All-Eastern Conference team in 1963, participated in the first of six Pro Bowls in 1965, and earned All-NFL honors from 1966 through 1970. Against Atlanta in 1967 he returned a fumble 97 yards for a touchdown. Howley intercepted 6 passes for 115 yards in 1968 and was named MVP in the 1970 Super Bowl, despite the Cowboys' 16–13 loss to the Baltimore Colts. The following year he intercepted 5 passes for 122 yards and helped the Cowboys defeat the Miami Dolphins, 24–3, in the Super Bowl.

Howley played with the Cowboys through the 1972 season and spent 1973 on the taxi squad before retiring. He finished his career with 24 interceptions for 395 yards. Howley, the fourth player named to the Cowboys Ring of Honor at Texas Stadium (1977), was also selected to the Wheeling Hall of Fame. During his playing career, Howley worked as a sales representative for Scott Manufacturing and opened his own dry cleaning company in 1969. The following year he formed a uniform company and now is president of Chuck Howley Uniform Rental.

BIBLIOGRAPHY: *Chicago Bears Media Guide, 1959; Dallas Cowboys Media Guides, 1962–1973, 1985; West Virginia University Football Press Guides, 1957–1958;* Richard Whittingham, *The Dallas Cowboys: An Illustrated History* (New York, 1981).

Jay Langhammer

HOWTON, William "Billy" "Red" (b. 5 July 1930, Littlefield, TX), college athlete and professional football player, was chosen All-Pro end in 1956 and 1957 with the Green Bay Packers (NFL). Howton caught 503 passes (13th best) for 8,459 yards (11th best) during his twelve-year pro career (1952–1963), scored 61 career touchdowns, and averaged 16.8 yards per reception. A star two-way end at Rice University (SWC), Howton made the 1951 *Collier's* (coaches), Chicago *Tribune*, and sportscaster Ted Husing's All-American teams. The 6 foot, 2 inch, 191 pound Howton grew up in Plainview, TX, where he starred in high school football. He played football at Rice University from 1949 to 1951 under coach Jess C. Neely* and was elected tri-captain his last season. Howton performed behind All-American end Jim "Froggie" Williams his sophomore year on the Owls' 10–1–0 SWC championship team. Fifth-ranked Rice trounced North Carolina 27–13 in the Cotton Bowl.

Rice finished 6–4–0 and 5–5–0 the next two seasons, with Howton winning All-SWC honors as the best all-around league wingman. Besides possessing outstanding pass-catching ability, Howton proved a clawing, scrambling defender always managing to stay on top of the play. Nicknamed "Red" due to his auburn hair, Howton adeptly dropped off the line to defend the flat zone in passing situations. He caught a 65-yard touchdown pass in 1950 in Rice's 27–7 triumph over Santa Clara. In his senior year Howton scored on a 74-yard pass play in Rice's 21–14 victory over Navy and caught 3 touchdown passes to help the Owls overwhelm SMU 28–7. Howton set Rice records in 1951 with 33 receptions for 747 yards (22.6-yard average) and 7 touchdowns. His Rice career totals included 64 receptions for 1,289 yards (20.1-yard average) and 12 touchdowns. Bill Fay observed, "Howton was known among jittery Southwest defensive backs as a great head-and-shoulders faker. An Arkansas player said that Howton would jigger around until he got you going the wrong way, then he'd take off and leave you. He's tremendously fast on the getaway." One of only three two-time winners of the Martin Trophy awarded to Rice's MVP, Howton also competed in the hurdles and relays on the Owls track team and ranked among the best softball pitchers in Texas. He caught 27- and 35-yard passes to set up a West touchdown in a 15–14 loss to the East in the Shrine All-Star (East-West) game and started at end for the College All-Stars in their 10–7 loss to the NFL Los Angeles Rams at Chicago's Soldier Field.

Howton, an immediate star with Green Bay in 1952, led the NFL with 1,231 yards (second highest one-year yardage in NFL history) on 53 receptions and scored 13 touchdowns. He gained 257 yards against the Los Angeles Rams in 1956 for the third highest one-game reception yardage in NFL history and led the NFL that season with 1,188 yards in pass receptions. Howton performed with losing Green Bay squads consistently between 1952 and 1958 under three head coaches. He was termed the "new Don Hutson,"* ranking second only to the latter in Packers pass receptions. He was traded to the Cleveland Browns (NFL) in 1959 and served as a decoy on many pass patterns for the Eastern Conference co–runner-up, finishing with 39 receptions, 510 yards, and 1 touchdown. Howton joined Dallas (NFL) in the 1960 expansion draft and performed at wide receiver for the Cowboys the next four seasons. He retired after the 1963 season and became a building contractor in Houston.

BIBLIOGRAPHY: East-West All-Star Football Game Program, 1951; Ronald L. Mendell and Timothy B. Phares, *Who's Who in Football* (New Rochelle, NY, 1974); David S. Neft et al., *The Complete All-Time Pro Football Register* (New York, 1975); *Official NFL Record Book, 1983;* Don Schiffer, ed., *1960 Pro Football Handbook* (New York, 1960).

James D. Whalen

HUARTE, John Gregory "Jack" (b. 20 May 1943, Anaheim, CA), college and professional player, made consensus All-American at quarterback at the University of Notre Dame and was awarded the 1964 Heisman Trophy as the nation's most outstanding player. Besides being the 1964 UPI Player of the Year, Huarte received the most votes for a college football player in the AP Athlete of the Year poll of sportswriters. Huarte set two NCAA and nine Notre Dame records in 1964, when the Irish rebounded from a 2–7–0 record to finish 9–1–0. His single-season 10.1 completions per game and 18.1 yards passing per attempt led the nation. Huarte's 114 completions in 205 attempts (55.6 percent) for 2,062 yards and 16 touchdowns and 2,080 total yards gained highlight his Irish records.

His father, Joseph Dominic Huarte, was perhaps the best shortstop to play pro baseball with the Roanoke (VA) Tars (ECL) and maintained a .267 lifetime batting average until the ECL folded in 1933. Joseph moved his wife and six children to California, where he purchased a ranch and grew oranges. John starred at Santa Ana Mater Dei High School as a baseball pitcher and football quarterback. He was chosen CIF football player of the year (1960) and captained the South squad in the state's North-South high school contest. The 6 foot, 1 inch, 1980 pound Huarte followed an older brother to Notre Dame but found his football success there slow developing. Huarte was injured most of his sophomore season (1962) and played only five minutes. He logged an additional forty-five minutes as a junior, failing again to win a monogram. Ara Parseghian,* named Notre Dame head coach the following year, was impressed by Huarte's 1963 spring practice performances. Huarte won the 1964 Hering Award as the outstanding quarterback in spring practice but suffered a shoulder separation of his passing arm in his final scrimmage. Huarte's shoulder mended without surgery, enabling him to throw passes that summer to his favorite receiver, Jack Snow.

Huarte in 1964 led Notre Dame to nine consecutive wins and a number 1 national ranking in the AP and UPI polls. In the season's final game, the

Southern California Trojans came from a 17–0 halftime deficit to score a 20–17 upset and spoil a perfect Irish season. Notre Dame averaged 28.7 points per game in outscoring opponents by a three-touchdown margin and ranked third in the final AP and UPI polls. After the post-season bowls, the Irish were ranked second by the FWAA and received the NFF College Football Hall of Fame's (General Douglas) MacArthur Bowl, emblematic of the national championship. Huarte teamed with several All-Americans, including Snow, guard Tom Regner, halfback Nick Eddy, tackle Kevin Hardy, end Alan Page,* linebackers Jim Carroll and Jim Lynch, and safety Nick Rassas.

Huarte possessed a quick release and good footwork and faked exceptionally well with sleight-of-hand efficiency. His touchdown pass to Snow in the last minute of play at Miami, FL, won the North-South All-Star Shrine game 37–30 for the North squad. Huarte earned a B.A. in Business Administration at Notre Dame in 1965. He directed the College All-Stars on two 80-yard touchdown drives (completing six consecutive passes at one point) in a 24–16 losing effort against the Cleveland Browns and was named the Chicago *Tribune* charity game's MVP.

The New York Jets (AFL) signed Huarte to a pro contract with a $200,000 bonus. (He was also drafted in the sixth round by the NFL's Philadelphia Eagles). Huarte was waived and spent most of the next seven seasons on taxi squads with the AFL Boston Patriots (1966), NFL Philadelphia Eagles (1967–1968), NFL Minnesota Vikings and AFL-NEL Kansas City Chiefs (1969–1971), NFL Chicago Bears (1972), and Memphis of the WFL (1973). Huarte, his wife, Eileen, and their five children live in Tempe, AZ, where he owns and operates Arizona Tile Supply, a thriving imported–ceramic tile business.

BIBLIOGRAPHY: John T. Brady, *The Heisman: A Symbol of Excellence* (New York, 1984); Bill Libby, *Heroes of the Heisman Trophy* (New York, 1973); Ronald L. Mendell and Timothy B. Phares, *Who's Who in Football* (New Rochelle, NY, 1974); *Notre Dame All-Americans* (Des Plaines, IL, 1979); *Notre Dame Football Guide, 1984;* Francis Wallace, *Notre Dame from Rockne to Parseghian* (New York, 1967).

James D. Whalen

HUBBARD, Robert Cal (b. 31 October 1900, Keytesville, MO; d. 19 October 1977, Milan, MO), college and professional football player and coach and professional baseball umpire, was the son of farmer Robert P. Hubbard and Sally (Ford) Hubbard. Hubbard graduated from Keytesville High School in 1919 and then worked on farms and odd jobs. He enrolled at Centenary College (LA) in 1922 and was coached there by his athletic hero Alvin (Bo) McMillin.* When McMillin left for Geneva College (PA), the 6 foot, 5 inch, 240 pound Hubbard accompanied him. Although primarily a tackle in college, he also played at end. Hubbard performed his tackle position like today's linebacker, playing off the line of scrimmage in a roaming, roving fashion.

Hubbard joined the NFL in 1927 with the New York Giants and developed into one of the game's best linemen under coach Steve Owen.* Hubbard married Ruth Frishkorn after the season and had two sons, Robert Cal, Jr., and William Ford. Although Hubbard had grown to 265 pounds, the Giants installed a screen pass, making the mobile tackle an eligible receiver. During the 1928 season Hubbard's Giants visited Green Bay for a game with the Packers. Hubbard, who never really liked big cities, so liked the small-town atmosphere of Green Bay that he threatened retirement if the Giants did not trade him to the Wisconsin team. Giants owner Tim Mara* dealt Hubbard, who reported to the Packers in 1929 and helped them win three consecutive NFL championships. He played both offensive and defensive tackle in those pre-free-substitution days and made the NFL's All-Pro team from 1928 to 1933. He became line coach at Texas A&M (SWC) in 1934 but returned to the Packers in 1935 and split the 1936 season with the New York Giants and Pittsburgh Pirates (NFL).

He umpired baseball games in the minor leagues in the off-season and from 1936 to 1951 in the AL. After a hunting accident left him with impaired sight in his right eye, the AL made the highly respected Hubbard supervisor of umpires. Hubbard held that position until retiring in 1969. Hubbard, the only figure elected to the NFF College and Pro Football Halls of Fame and National Baseball Hall of Fame, in 1969 was voted the NFL's greatest tackle for the league's first fifty years.

BIBLIOGRAPHY: Martin Appel and Burt Goldblatt, *Baseball's Best: The Hall of Fame Gallery* (New York, 1977); Arthur Daley, *Pro Football's Hall of Fame* (Chicago, 1963); Chuck Johnson, *The Greatest Packers of Them All* (New York, 1968); NFL Properties, *The First Fifty Years* (New York, 1969); Robert M. Smith, *Pro Football* (Garden City, NY, 1963); George Sullivan, *Pro Football's All-Time Greats: The Immortals in Pro Football's Hall of Fame* (New York, 1969); Alexander M. Weyand, *Football's Immortals* (New York, 1962).

Jim Campbell

HUFF, Robert Lee "Sam" (b. 4 October 1934, Edna Gas, WV), college and professional player and coach, starred as a 6 foot, 1 inch, 230 pound football linebacker. He attended Farmington (WV) High School, where he excelled in football and married while a senior. He attended West Virginia University (SC) from 1952 to 1955, working his way through school by waiting on tables. Huff captained and made All-American for the 1955 Mountaineers and was drafted by the New York Giants (NFL) in the third round. Rookie Huff almost left the Giants camp, but assistant coach Vince Lombardi* persuaded him to stay. Huff became one of the greatest and most publicized linebackers in pro football history and the first defensive pro football player to make the *Time* magazine cover. CBS produced a half-hour pro football documentary entitled "The Violent World of Sam Huff." They placed a microphone on him during a game to show the danger inherent in playing his position. Huff proved an inspirational leader, possessed great speed and tackling ability, and delighted fans with his vicious play. He engaged in hard-hitting duels with the premier running backs, notably Jim Brown* of the Cleveland Browns. Tom Landry* boasted, "Sam Huff became the symbol of defensive football."

After playing for the Giants from 1956 to 1963, Huff was traded to the Washington Redskins (NFL). The move by coach Allie Sherman, who claimed Huff had slowed down, enraged the Giant fans. From 1964 to 1967 Huff played for the Redskins. Until 1967 he had not missed a game since becoming a regular for the Giants. He retired in 1968, but coach Vince Lombardi convinced him in 1969 to return to the active ranks. Huff, who served as a Redskins assistant coach from 1968 to 1971, completed his career with 30 interceptions. Huff played in six NFL title games, helping the Giants win the championship in 1956. He made All-Pro in 1958 and 1959 and played in Pro Bowl games from 1958 through 1961 and in 1964, being named Lineman of the Game in 1960. Huff was named to the NFF College Football Hall of Fame and to the All-Pro squad of the 1950s and was selected in 1982 to the Pro Football Hall of Fame.

BIBLIOGRAPHY: George Allen with Ben Olan, *Pro Football's 100 Greatest Players* (Indianapolis, IN, 1982); Howard Balzer, "Defensive Class of '82 at Canton," *TSN*, August 16, 1982; Gerald Eskenazi, *There Were Giants in Those Days* (New York, 1976); Ronald L. Mendell and Timothy B. Phares, *Who's Who in Football* (New Rochelle, NY, 1974); *Official Pro Football Almanac, 1965*.

John L. Evers

HUMPHREY, Claude B. (b. 29 June 1944, Memphis, TN), college and professional player, is the son of Dosie and Millie Ann (Hayes) Humphrey. He starred in football at Lester High School in Memphis and then from 1965 to 1967 at Tennessee State University (MWC), where the Tigers compiled a 35–3–1 record. Humphrey, a defensive tackle on *TSN* College All-American football team in 1967, performed in the Senior Bowl, and Blue-Gray, Coaches All-America, and College All-Star games. Although a lineman, he was selected by the Atlanta Falcons in the first round of the 1968 NFL draft. The 6 foot, 5 inch, 258 pound Humphrey performed at defensive end for the Falcons from 1968 through 1978, when he was traded to the Philadelphia Eagles (NFL). A feared pass rusher, Humphrey made NFL Defensive Rookie of the Year in 1968. His most rewarding moment came in 1976, when his teammates selected him the MVP after he had been sidelined the previous season with a knee injury. In his comeback year, he incredibly made a career-high 18 sacks of opposing quarterbacks. During eleven years with the Falcons, he made *TSN* NFC All-Star team (1971–1974) and played in the Pro Bowl (1970–1974, 1977).

Humphrey nearly retired from pro football following the 1978 season, but played the next three campaigns for the Eagles. He participated in the NFC championship game following the 1980 season and Super Bowl XV, which Philadelphia lost 27–10 to the Oakland Raiders. During his 13-year, 171-game career, he made 2 interceptions for 11 yards, 11 fumble recoveries for 68 yards, 1 touchdown, and 2 safeties. Humphrey collects antique cars, including his treasured 1956 Cadillac, raises Dobermans, and works with underprivileged children. He and his wife, Sandra, have two children.

BIBLIOGRAPHY: *Atlanta Falcons Fact Book, 1978; TSN Football Register—1982;* Jack Zanger, *Pro Football 1970* (New York, 1970).

John L. Evers

HUNT, Lamar (b. 2 August 1932, Eldorado, AR), professional sports executive, is the son of oil billionaire H. L. and Lyda (Baker) Hunt and attended SMU, (SWC) where he played end on the Mustang football team and graduated in 1956. The private, unassuming Hunt is an ambitious and very competitive sportsman. Frustrated by his inability to acquire an NFL franchise, Hunt in 1959 formed the rival AFL. As AFL president, he largely guided the AFL to its ultimate success. The sole owner and founder of the Dallas Texans (now Kansas City Chiefs), he has served both as club president and chairman. He has presided over the AFC since the two leagues merged in 1970. In 1969 Kansas City defeated the Minnesota Vikings 23–7 in Super Bowl IV.

Hunt's accomplishments as a prominent sports figure transcend pro football. Besides holding interest in the Dallas Tornado Soccer Club, he founded World Championship Tennis in 1967 and served as a minor stockholder in the Chicago Bulls (NBA) club. Hunt was selected Southwesterner of the Year in 1969 by the Texas Sportswriters Association. President Gerald Ford appointed him to the President's Commission on Olympic Sports in 1975. He was elected to the Pro Football Hall of Fame in 1972, the tenth owner and first AFL person in any category so chosen.

Hunt, atypical of figures with such wealth and influence, developed a sports empire reportedly worth about $25 million in 1975. Hunt then devoted about 70 percent of his time to these ventures, spending the rest of his time on his oil operations. Although one of America's thirteen billionaires in 1982, he "lives frugally, stays out of the limelight," and generally leaves daily management of his teams to his pro employees. Hunt married Rose Mary Carr in 1956 but they were divorced in 1962. His second wife is Norma Lynn Knobel, whom he married in 1964. The Hunts have four children, Lamar, Sharron, Clark, and Daniel.

BIBLIOGRAPHY: Art Detman, "The Quiet Success of Lamar Hunt," *Dun's Review* 105 (January, 1975), pp. 42–45; *Forbes Magazine* 130 (September 13, 1982); Lamar Hunt to Charles R. Middleton, November 19, 1984; Don Kowet, *The Rich Who Own Sports* (New York, 1977); Ronald L. Mendell and Timothy B. Phares, *Who's Who in*

Football (New Rochelle, NY, 1974); *NYT*, July 29, 1970, February 9, 1972, July 23, 1972, June 2, 1975; *WWA*, 41st ed. (1981–1982), p. 1,648; *Who's Who in the Midwest* (1984–1985).

Charles R. Middleton

HUTSON, Donald Montgomery "Don" (b. 31 January 1913, Pine Bluff, AR), college athlete and professional football and baseball player, graduated from Pine Bluff High School in 1931 and the University of Alabama (SEC) in 1935. Hutson married Julia Richards on December 14, 1935, and has three daughters. At Pine Bluff High School, he became an outstanding baseball player and track and field performer. Considered too frail for football, he did not make his high school team until his senior year. Hutson enrolled at the University of Alabama in 1932, planning to play baseball. He made the football team as a 160-pound freshman because he possessed 9.8-second speed in the 100-yard dash, but he played little as a freshman or sophomore. As a junior in 1933, he played extensively and made the starting lineup late that season.

Hutson blossomed during his senior football season at Alabama. The Crimson Tide, fielding outstanding performers Millard "Dixie" Howell, Riley Smith, guard Charlie Marr, end Paul "Bear" Bryant,* and Hutson, won all nine games and defeated Stanford University 29–13 in the Rose Bowl. An outstanding receiver, he also ran the football occasionally on end-around plays. Against Clemson University, he caught six passes and scored two touchdowns. Later in the season he scored the winning touchdown against the University of Tennessee on a nine-yard end around. The Rose Bowl game marked Hutson's best college performance. He scored on a 54-yard touchdown pass late in the second period, insured the 29-13 victory with a fourth-quarter touchdown reception, and caught six passes for 165 yards. He was named to the 1934 All-American team. At Alabama, Hutson also played centerfield on the baseball team and sprinted for track team. Occasionally, he participated in both a track meet and a baseball game on the same day. He later played three seasons (1940–1942) of minor league pro baseball with the Pine Bluff (AR) Judges of the Class C CSL.

Hutson signed NFL contracts with both the Green Bay Packers and Brooklyn Dodgers in 1935. Both contracts arrived the same day in the office of NFL commissioner Joe Carr,* who upheld the Packers contract because it was postmarked seventeen minutes earlier than the Dodgers contract. Since Hutson carried only 178 pounds on a 6 foot, 1 inch frame, skeptics questioned whether he could play in the physical pro football games. Hutson quickly established himself, however, by catching an 83-yard touchdown pass on his first play as a Packer to give Green Bay a 7–0 victory over the Chicago Bears. From there, Hutson became the premier receiver of his 11 NFL years and led the NFL in receptions eight seasons and receiving yardage seven seasons. During his pro career he caught 488 passes for 7,991 yards and 100 touchdowns. George Halas,* owner and coach of the Chicago Bears, said, "Hutson is so extraordinary that I concede him two touchdowns a game and just hope we can score more."

Due to his small size and formidable pass-catching ability, Hutson was used as a defensive safety in that period of two-way football. During his last four seasons (1942–1945), he intercepted 23 passes. Hutson also placekicked for the Packers from 1940 through 1945. Besides leading the NFL in scoring from 1940 through 1944, he recorded 105 career touchdowns and 823 career points and made the All-Pro team in 1936 and from 1938 to 1942. With Hutson's help, the Packers finished either in first or second place in the Western Division ten times. The Packers won the Western Division in 1936, 1938, 1939, and 1944 and defeated the then Boston Redskins 21–6 in the 1936 NFL championship game. Green Bay also won championships by defeating the New York Giants 27–0 in 1939 and 14–7 in 1944.

As of 1986, Hutson held eight NFL receiving and scoring records as the forerunner of the speedy, evasive wide receiver. His elusiveness in the open field moved former Philadelphia Eagles coach Alfred Earle "Greasy" Neale* to remark, "Hutson is the only man I ever saw who can run in three different directions at the same time." Following his retirement from the NFL in 1945, he purchased a Chevrolet and Cadillac automobile agency in Racine, WI. He was inducted into the HAF and NFF College Football, Arkansas, Alabama, Wisconsin Athletic, and Green Bay Packers Halls of Fame and became a charter member of the Pro Football Hall of Fame in 1963.

BIBLIOGRAPHY: Bill Barron et al., *The Official NFL Encyclopedia of Football* (New York, 1982); Harold Claassen and Steve Boda, eds., *The Ronald Encyclopedia of Football* (New York, 1960); Fran Connors, ed., *The NFL Record Manual, 1983;* "The Era of Hutson," Green Bay Packers–Chicago Bears Football Game Program, 1957; *Green Bay Packers Media Guide, 1984;* Don Hutson file, Pro Football Hall of Fame, Canton, OH; David S. Neft, Richard M. Cohen, and Jordan A. Deutsch, *Pro Football: The Early Years, An Encyclopedic History, 1895–1959* (Ridgefield, CT, 1978).

C. Robert Barnett

I

ISBELL, Cecil (b. 11 July 1915, Houston, TX; d. 23 June 1985, Hammond, IN), college and professional player and coach, entered Purdue University (WC) in 1934 and became one of the Boilermakers' greatest football forward passers. Throughout his college career, Isbell directed an explosive offensive attack, guiding Purdue to a 13–9–2 record. Isbell, an effective runner and punter and premier passer, figured in 15 of 23 Purdue touchdowns his junior year as either a passer or a runner. Besides being named to several All-WC or All-Midwest teams, Isbell led the College All-Star squad in 1938 to a 28–16 triumph over the NFL Washington Redskins. Isbell completed one 39-yard touchdown pass and was awarded the first All-Star Trophy as the game's outstanding collegian.

Following his graduation in 1938, Isbell signed a pro contract with the Green Bay Packers (NFL). He started at left halfback in the 1938 NFL championship game, which Green Bay lost 23–17 to the New York Giants, and in the 1939 NFL title contest, in which Green Bay defeated the Giants, 27–0. In 1940 Isbell passed for three touchdowns and ran for a fourth score to help Green Bay defeat the College All-Stars, 45–28. During a brilliant 1941 season, Isbell set an NFL record by throwing at least one touchdown pass in every game. He led the NFL with 15 touchdown passes and completed 117 of 206 attempts for 1,479 yards. In Isbell's final pro season (1942), he set NFL records with 146 completions, 2,021 yards gained, and 24 touchdown passes. He threw touchdown passes in 23 consecutive games in 1941 and 1942, still a Green Bay Packers record. Isbell, known as the "home run hitter" because of his long, accurate passes, retired after the 1942 season to become an assistant coach at his Purdue University alma mater. During his pro career, Isbell completed 411 of 818 passes (50.2 percent) for 5,945 yards and 61 touchdowns. Isbell became head football coach at Purdue in 1944 and compiled a 14–14–1 record in a three-year period. In 1947 Isbell moved to Baltimore as first head coach of the Colts (AAFC). After two and one-half years as head coach, he served as backfield football coach for the Chicago Cardinals (NFL) in 1950 and 1951 and at Louisiana State University (SEC) the next two years before entering the business world. The 6 foot, 1 inch, 190 pound Isbell was inducted into the NFF College Football Hall of Fame in 1967 and Green Bay Packers Hall of Fame in 1972.

BIBLIOGRAPHY: Joe King, *Inside Pro Football* (Englewood Cliffs, NJ, 1958); Steve Owen, *My Kind of Football* (New York, 1952); Howard Roberts, *Story of Pro Football* (New York, 1953); Roger Treat, *The Encyclopedia of Football*, 16th rev. ed., rev. by Pete Palmer (New York, 1979); Arch Ward, *The Green Bay Packers* (New York, 1946).

James Fuller

J

JACKSON, Harold (b. 6 January 1946, Hattiesburg, MS), college athlete and professional football player and coach, attended Rowan High School in Hattiesburg. At Jackson State (SAC) the 5 foot, 10 inch, 175 pound Jackson excelled in track and football. He ran the 100–yard dash in 9.5 seconds and set Tiger records with 57 pass receptions in 1966 and 132 career receptions from 1964 through 1967. The two-time All-SAC wide receiver in 1968 received a B.S. degree in Secondary Education from Jackson State. Jackson was selected by the Los Angeles Rams in the twelfth round (323rd player chosen) of the 1968 AFL-NFL draft. He performed for the Rams (NFL) in 1968 and from 1973 through 1977, Philadelphia Eagles (NFL) from 1969 through 1972, New England Patriots (NFL) between 1978 and 1981, Minnesota Vikings (NFL) in 1982, and Seattle Seahawks (NFL) in 1983.

Jackson spent most of 1968 on the ready reserve list for the Rams and was traded the following year to Philadelphia. Besides leading the Eagles in pass receptions (1969, 1971–1972), Jackson caught 215 passes in four seasons. He led the NFL in 1969 with 1,116 pass reception yards, in 1972 with 62 pass receptions for 1,048 yards, and in 1973 with a 21.3–yard average per reception and 13 touchdowns. Jackson returned to the Rams in a trade for quarterback Roman Gabriel* before the 1973 season. The leading Ram pass receiver (1973, 1975–1977), Jackson played in the NFC championship game losses to Minnesota following the 1974 and 1976 seasons. In 1973 the major polls named him All-NFL and All-NFC. That same season, he tied a club record (with Bob Shaw and Elroy Hirsch*) for single-game touchdown receptions by catching four from John Hadl for 63, 19, 67, and 36 yards in a 37–31 triumph over the Dallas Cowboys. Jackson scored 78 points on 13 touchdown receptions during the 1973 season to lead all receivers.

After being traded on August 16, 1978, to New England, he the following year led the Patriots in pass receiving. In 1982 he was granted free agency. The San Diego Chargers (NFL) signed and released him, after which he played one game for Minnesota (NFL). Seattle (NFL) inked him as a free agent in 1983. In his final pro season (1983), Jackson performed in fifteen games for the Seahawks and played in the AFC championship game loss to the Los Angeles Raiders. In sixteen pro seasons Jackson compiled 579 pass receptions (seventh best all-time NFL), 10,372 reception yards (fourth), 17.9–yard average per reception (third), 76 touchdown receptions (ninth), and scored 456 points. He was named to *TSN* NFC All-Star team in 1972, 1973, and 1977 and played in the Pro Bowl following the 1969, 1972, 1973, 1975, and 1977 seasons. The Foxboro, MA, resident serves as receiver coach for New England. As a member of the Patriots' staff, he helped New England reach Super Bowl XX in 1986. The Patriots ultimately lost 46–10 to the Chicago Bears.

BIBLIOGRAPHY: *The Los Angeles Rams Official Media Guide, 1977; TSN Football Register—1984.*

John L. Evers

JACKSON, Vincent E. "Bo" (b. 30 November 1962, Bessemer, AL), college athlete and professional baseball player, won the 1985 Heisman Trophy as the nation's outstanding college football player. The four-year (1982–1985) Auburn University (SEC) running back also captured the 1985 UPI, Walter Camp Foundation and *TSN* Player of the Year awards. Jackson, named consensus (1983) and unanimous (1985) All-American, three times won All-SEC first-team honors. A shoulder separation during the second contest of his junior season caused him to miss six games and prevented his clean sweep of All-SEC nominations. Jackson dominated for Auburn in the Tangerine, Sugar, Liberty, and Cotton bowls and was named MVP of the last three. He received a similar honor for his outstanding performance at the 1986 post-season Japan (All-Star) Bowl, after gaining 171 yards on 18 carries and scoring 3 touchdowns. Jackson, Auburn's all-time leading career rusher with 4,303 yards, broke the Tigers record by 780 yards. He made 650 career carries for a 6.6–yard average and scored 43 touchdowns in three and one-half seasons. His 1985 1,786 rushing yards marked the second highest single-season performance in SEC history.

Jackson, the first three-sport letterman at Auburn in thirty years, starred in track and baseball. He holds a career best time of 6.18 seconds for the indoor 60–yard dash in track and twice made the semi-finals of the NCAA meet in that event. He ran the outdoor 100–meter dash in 10.39 seconds, the seventh best time in Tigers history, and participated on the 4 × 100 meter relay team. One of the premier college baseball players in 1985, he batted .401 with 17 home runs and 43 runs batted in. The Auburn center fielder led the Tigers with 6 triples, 5 doubles, 55 runs scored, and 9 of 10 bases stolen. Jackson was named All-District and All-Region by the CBCA and received the highest rating of any player eligible for the June, 1985, player draft. He was picked by the California Angels (AL) but chose to complete his last year of eligibility at Auburn.

The son of steelworker A. D. Adams and domestic Florence Bond, Jackson has five brothers and four sisters. A three-sport star at McAdory High School in McCalla, AL, he gained 1,173 yards on 108 carries in football and scored 17 touchdowns his senior year. Jackson, an All-State selection, was named as the Birmingham Touchdown Club's Back of the Year for Jefferson County. The two-time state high school decathlon champion set state track and field records in the 60–yard run, 60–yard hurdles, 100–yard run, 120–yard hurdles, long jump, and high jump. He batted .450 and .447 on the baseball diamond his last two years, stole 90 bases in 91 attempts in his career, and set a national high school record with 20 home runs in one season. Although drafted by the New York Yankees (AL) in the second round of the 1982 baseball draft, Jackson rejected a multiyear contract in order to attend Auburn.

"When Bo came to Auburn, we didn't realize the impact he would have," Tigers football coach Pat Dye stated. "According to our scouting reports, he wasn't the top back to come to Auburn that year." Dye used a fine-tuned triple-option wishbone offense through the 1984 season but switched to the I-formation that enabled Jackson to utilize his running ability. Jackson led the Tigers to a composite 37–12–0 record, winning the SEC title in 1983 and twice finishing in third place. Auburn remained competitive with highly regarded traditional foes Georgia Tech 4–0–0, Tennessee 3–1–0, Georgia 3–1–0, Alabama 2–2–0, and Florida 1–3–0. Other premier Auburn performers included running back Lionel "Little Train" James, tackle Doug Smith, and quarterback Pat Washington. Jackson scored the winning touchdown in the 1982 Tigers 23–22 triumph against Alabama, the first over the Crimson Tide in ten years. Auburn defeated Boston College 33–26 in the 1982 Tangerine Bowl.

Auburn completed a perfect SEC slate in 1983, lost only to fifth-ranked Texas, defeated Michigan 9–7 in the Sugar Bowl, finished 11–1–0, and ranked third in the national polls. Jackson rushed 1,213 yards during 1983 on 158 carries and scored 12 touchdowns. Despite his early injury in 1984, Jackson finished the season with 475 yards on 87 carries and scored 5 touchdowns. He helped the Tigers defeat Arkansas 21–15 in the Liberty Bowl, rushing 88 yards and scoring two touchdowns. His two touchdowns and 129 yards rushing in the 1986 Cotton Bowl game fell short against Texas A&M, however, as the Aggies defeated the Tigers 31–17. "I don't pay any attention to how much yardage I have while I'm in the game," Jackson stated. "I'm not running for records or the Heisman Trophy, I'm out there running for Auburn." The 6 foot, 1 inch, 222 pound Jackson majored in family and child development at Auburn University. In 1986 he led the Auburn baseball team in home runs (7) in 20 games and batted only .246. His career baseball statistics at Auburn included a .335 batting average and 70 home runs.

Jackson was drafted first by the Tampa Bay Buccaneers (NFL) but lost his remaining amateur baseball eligibility when he flew to Tampa for a medical exam in the private plane of team owner Hugh Culverhouse. SEC rules require that a player forfeit his amateur status if he accepts a plane ride paid for by a professional team. Jackson was selected in the fourth round by the Kansas City (American League) baseball club and signed with the Royals in June 1986. Jackson began his pro baseball career with the Memphis (TN) Chicks of the Class AA Southern League and in September joined the Royals, where he batted .207 with 2 home runs and 9 runs batted in.

BIBLIOGRAPHY: *Auburn Football Media Guide, Cotton Bowl Edition, 1985;* Auburn University, Sports Information Department, Auburn, AL, 1985; Herschel Nissenson, AP Article, September 25, 1985.

James D. Whalen

JAMES, Donald Earl "Don" (b. 31 December 1932, Massillon, OH), college player and coach, is the son of stonemason Thomas and Florence James. At Washington High School in Massillon, James earned four letters in football and two each in basketball, baseball, and track and participated on Ohio state (BTC) champion football teams in 1948 and 1949. James played football four years at Miami University (FL) and set five school passing records as Hurricanes quarterback (1952–1953). He graduated with several academic and athletic honors, including the Optner Trophy for being Miami's top scholar-athlete. James played one year of football and baseball in the U.S. Army (1954–1956).

Following his Army discharge, James enrolled at the University of Kansas (BSC) and served as freshman football coach while earning his Master's degree (1956–1957). He moved to Southwest High School in Miami, FL, as head football and basketball coach. After two years on the prep scene, James spent seven years at Florida State University as assistant football coach and defensive coordinator. A defensive mastermind, James moved to the University of Michigan (BTC) as head defensive coach (1966–1967) and University of Colorado (BEC) as defensive coordinator (1968–1970). His first head coaching break materialized in 1971, when he moved to Kent State University (MAC). His 1972 club produced the school's first MAC championship and earned an invitation to the Tangerine Bowl, where the Golden Flashes lost to the University of Tampa 21–18. The 1973 squad compiled a 9–2 record for the best mark in Kent State history, breaking thirty-six individual, team, and season records. In four seasons James compiled an overall 25–19–1 record and was named MAC and Ohio Coach of the Year in 1973.

After the 1974 season James replaced Jim Owens as head football coach at the University of Washington (PEC). In twelve seasons (1975–1986), James' teams have compiled a 99–39–1 record to make his overall career record 124–58–2. The Huskies have won ten or more games four different seasons and captured the PEC championship (1977, 1980–1981). They have appeared in nine bowl games since 1977, winning the Rose (1978, 1982), Sun (1979), Aloha (1982), Orange (1985), and Freedom (1986) bowls, and losing the Rose (1981), Aloha (1983), and Sun (1986) Bowls. James in 1977 was named National Coach of the Year by the AFCA. After a 28–17 victory over the University of Oklahoma in the 1985 Orange Bowl, the Huskies were ranked the nation's second team behind Brigham Young University.

James' football philosophy includes a strong defense, aggressive kicking game, and diversified offense that relies primarily on running the football and uses passes at any time. Married to the former Carol Hoobler, James has one son, Jeff, and two daughters, Jill and Jennifer.

BIBLIOGRAPHY: Jack Hicks, "Leader of the Pack," *Sport* 72 (December, 1981), pp. 51–53; *University of Washington Football Media Guide, 1978.*

John L. Evers

JANOWICZ, Victor Felix "Vic" (b. 26 February 1930, Elyria, OH), college and professional athlete and broadcaster, is one of nine children of Polish-born Felix and Veronica Janowicz. Janowicz competed in track, baseball, and football in Elyria secondary schools. A star halfback, he led Elyria High School to an undefeated season in football in 1947 and made the All-Ohio high school team twice. Janowicz aspired to a pro baseball career and even worked out with the Detroit Tigers (American League) and Cincinnati Reds (National Leagul) as a teenager but decided to play football at Ohio State University (BTC). John Galbreath (BB), a wealthy patron of the Ohio State football program, influenced Janowicz's decision. Upon entering Ohio State in 1948, the 5 foot, 8 inch, 185 pound Janowicz possessed power, speed, and agility. As a sophomore in 1949, he started occasionally as a left halfback and fullback in the single-wing formation, but an injury at mid-season limited his play.

The next year proved Janowicz's great football season, as coach Wes Fesler* gave him diverse responsibilities. Janowicz ran, passed as a quarterback and left halfback, called offensive signals, punted, kicked extra points and field goals, and keyed the defense as a safety. His greatest game came against Iowa, as he ran for two touchdowns, passed for four touchdowns, kicked ten extra points, and recovered two fumbles. In the final "blizzard bowl" loss to Michigan, he punted 21 times with four blocked. He led the BTC in total offense for the season, with 561 yards passing and 314 yards running. Although Ohio State did not capture the BTC championship, Janowicz won the Heisman Trophy. His versatility and performance against Iowa undoubtedly earned him substantial support for the award. A *NYT* sportswriter described Janowicz as a "strong runner," "accurate passer," "deadly tackler," and "canny signal-caller." Years later, a veteran Ohio sportswriter remembered Janowicz as the best all-around football player ever to perform for Ohio State.

The glory of the Heisman season did not prelude greater success for Janowicz. In 1951 he played for new coach Woody Hayes,* who converted the offense to the split T. As Janowicz recalled, the split T was too complicated for the Buckeyes to master in a few months and did not utilize his abilities adequately. Consequently, he and the Buckeyes played to a mediocre record. After graduating from Ohio State in 1952, Janowicz entered military service for a year and then pursued a pro baseball career. He spent the winter of 1953 in the MEL and played for the Pittsburgh Pirates (National League) in 1953 and 1954. Used as a catcher and third baseman, he appeared in 83 games, batted .214, and made 42 hits. In 1955 Washington Redskins owner George Preston Marshall* offered him an NFL contract. That year he rushed and kicked the ball for 88 points to finish second in NFL scoring. Just before the 1956 season, he suffered serious injuries in an automobile accident and never played pro football again.

After his athletic career ended, Janowicz engaged in various ventures. From 1959 to 1961 he served as the "color" man for broadcasts of Ohio State football games. Later he worked as public relations director for a beverage company and as sales executive for a manufacturing firm in Columbus, OH. In 1976 he was elected to the NFF College Football Hall of Fame. The next year he was enshrined with a charter group of athletes in the Ohio State University Sports Hall of Fame. He and his wife, Marianne, are the parents of one son and one daughter. Janowicz resides in Columbus not far from the stadium where thousands of fans saw him play.

BIBLIOGRAPHY: Carl M. Becker, interview with Si Burick, Sports Editor, Dayton (OH) *Daily News*, October 17, 1985; Carl M. Becker, interview with Vic Janowicz, October 16 and October 28, 1985; "Janowicz Honored at Heisman Dinner," *NYT*, December 13, 1950; "Janowicz Named to Hall of Fame," Dayton (OH) *Daily News*, April 2, 1976; "Time Treats Janowicz Well," Dayton (OH) *Journal Herald*, March 1, 1977; "Vic Janowicz—A Chin-Up Guy," Dayton (OH) *Daily News*, December 6, 1964.

Carl M. Becker

JEFFERSON, John Larry (b. 3 February 1956, Dallas, TX), college and professional player, grew up in Dallas with his parents, James, a manager, and Patsy Jefferson. He attended Roosevelt High School, where he helped his teams win the district championship in 1972 and 1973 and also earned All-District and All-American honors those seasons. After enjoying a successful prep career, Jefferson was recruited by many colleges and chose to attend Arizona State University (WAC). As a Sun Devil, the 6 foot, 1 inch, 200 pound Jefferson continued in the tradition of talented Arizona State wide receivers Charley Taylor* and J. D. Hill. During his Arizona State career he set many Sun Devils records and received several national honors. Jefferson led the Sun Devils in pass receptions from 1975 through 1977 and holds the career record for most receptions with 175 for 2,824 yards. Jefferson also caught passes in 42 consecutive games. His collegiate football career culminated with Consensus All-American honors in 1977.

In 1975 Jefferson made perhaps the single greatest play in Arizona State football history. The Sun Devils entered the final regular-season game against traditional rival University of Arizona with a perfect 10–0 record. With only seconds remaining in the first half, the Sun Devils trailed 14–3. Quarterback Dennis Sproul unleashed a pass to Jefferson deep in the end zone. Launching himself parallel to the ground, Jefferson used his outstretched arms to catch the ball an inch above the turf. The play has become known to Sun Devils football fans as simply "the catch." Jefferson's play marked the turning point of the game, as Arizona State defeated Arizona 24–21. Jefferson also caught a touchdown pass in the Fiesta Bowl that year, helping Arizona State defeat Nebraska 17–14. The Frank Kush*–coached Sun Devils finished the 1975 season 12–0 and ranked second nationally.

The San Diego Chargers selected Jefferson in the first round of the 1978 NFL draft. He immediately led the NFL in touchdown receptions (13) his first season. He starred on the Chargers, which already boasted talented wide receiver Charlie Joiner* and excellent quarterback Dan Fouts.* Tight end Kellen Winslow* later joined the Chargers, giving San Diego the most explosive passing attack in the NFL. In 1980 Jefferson led the NFL in receptions (82) and touchdown receptions (13). He also became the first player in NFL history to compile at least 1,000 yards receiving in each of his first three seasons and made the AFC Pro Bowl team from 1978 through 1980.

In 1981 Jefferson held out of the San Diego training camp, hoping to renegotiate his contract. Unable to come to terms, the Chargers traded him to the Green Bay Packers (NFL). At Green Bay Jefferson was overshadowed by teammate James Lofton* but played well enough to be selected for his fourth Pro Bowl in 1983. The 1984 season saw Jefferson make only 26 receptions for 334 yards. Following the 1984 season, Jefferson became a free agent. Unable to settle a contract problem, Green Bay traded him to the Cleveland Browns (NFL) three games into the 1985 season. Jefferson caught 3 passes for 30 yards with the Browns and was released before the 1985 season ended. The Houston Oilers (NFL) waived Jefferson during the 1986 preseason. Through 1986 he had caught 351 passes for 5,714 yards (16.3-yard average) and 47 touchdowns.

BIBLIOGRAPHY: *Arizona State Sun Devils—Media Guide, 1984;* David S. Neft, Richard M. Cohen, and Jordan A. Deutsch, *The Sports Encyclopedia: Pro Football—The Modern Era, 1960 to the Present* (New York, 1982); Dean Smith, *The Sun Devils—Eight Decades of Arizona State Football* (Tempe, AZ, 1979); *TSN Football Register—1986.*

Curtis R. Mang

JEFFERSON, Roy Lee (b. 19 November 1943, Texarkana, AR), college and professional player, excelled as a wide receiver for the Pittsburgh Steelers, Baltimore Colts, and Washington Redskins (NFL). He played defensive tackle for Compton (CA) High School with wide receiver Marv Fleming, who later played for the Green Bay Packers. In 1961 he matriculated at the University of Utah, where he played end and halfback and performed the placekicking duties. Jefferson, who led Utah (WAC) in scoring for three seasons, in 1964 was named All-American and helped the Utes to the Liberty Bowl. After his senior year Jefferson quickly signed a contract with the Pittsburgh Steelers (NFL) for a $15,000 bonus. Jefferson later regretted the move because the San Diego Chargers (AFL) drafted him first and made him a more lucrative offer. In 1968 and 1969 he was named to the Pro Bowl and paced the NFL both years in yardage gained. His 67 receptions in 1969 led the NFL and established a then Steelers record.

In 1970 Jefferson was traded to the Baltimore Colts (NFL) and played well for the Super Bowl champions, catching passes from John Unitas.* Following differences with Colts' owner Carroll Rosenbloom, Jefferson was traded to the Washington Redskins (NFL). In a typical George Allen*–era move, the Redskins had acquired an accomplished veteran for an untested player and a draft choice. In Jefferson's first year with Washington, he was named All-Pro, led the Redskins in receptions as a primary target for Sonny Jurgensen* and Billy Kilmer, and played in his second straight Super Bowl. Jefferson played for Washington through the 1976 season and remained high on the list of NFC receivers, but he spent most of his Redskins career in the shadow of the sensational Charley Taylor.* A knee injury in 1975 caused Jefferson's career decline. Lifetime, Jefferson caught 451 passes for 52 touchdowns and an amazing 18.7–yard average. Jefferson received 208 Redskin passes for 3,119 yards to place high on Washington's all-time list. The father of two children, Jefferson married Camille Gordon and remains active in Washington civic affairs. Jefferson starred in a movie called *Brotherhood of Blood*, apparently never commercially released.

BIBLIOGRAPHY: *Washington Redskins Press Guide, 1977;* Washington (DC) *Star-News*, 1971–1980.

John David Healy

JENNINGS, William Morley "Jopsey" (b. 23 January 1890, Holland, MI; d. 13 May 1985, Lubbock, TX), college and professional athlete, football coach, and administrator, was selected to the HAF College Football Hall of Fame and in 1973 to the NFF College Football Hall of Fame. Jennings graduated from Albion (MI) High School in 1908, attended Albion College (MIAA) one year, and followed his football coach to Mississippi A&M College (SIAA, now Mississippi State University). The first Maroons athlete to win letters in four sports, Jennings starred as a football halfback, baseball shortstop, and track hurdler and discus thrower, and captained the basketball team. In 1910 he returned a kickoff 95 yards for a touchdown and converted 11 of 13 extra points in an 82–0 rout of Howard University. During Jennings' two football seasons (1910–1911), Mississippi A&M compiled a 14–4–1 composite record and defeated LSU, Tulane, Tennessee, Sewanee, and Mississippi. He made All-SIAA football halfback in 1911 and won both hurdle events in the 1912 SIAA track meet.

After graduating with a B.S. degree in Industrial Education from Mississippi A&M in 1912, he played pro baseball at shortstop with Minneapolis, MN (AA), for eight years. The head football coach at Ouachita (AR) College (1912–1925), he compiled a 72–17–12 composite record (.772 percent) and fielded two consecutive undefeated teams (1924–1925). Dana X. Bible,* Mississippi A&M mentor, recommended Jennings for the head coaching job at Baylor University (SWC). As Baylor head football coach for 15 years (1926–1940), Jennings amassed a respectable 83–60–6 (.577 percent) composite record, four SWC runners-up, and four third-place finishes. His 1930 Bears missed the title by one-half game, but included first consensus SWC All-American guard Burton Koch. An early proponent of the five-man line defense against passing attacks, Jennings coached one of the nation's leading passers, All-SWC quarterback Billy Patterson.

The son of Methodist minister William Jennings and Annie (Sophia) Jennings, he coached in a quiet, workmanlike, and gentlemanly manner. He served as athletic director at Texas Tech University (SWC, 1941–1950) and chaired the men's physical education department until retirement in 1965 at age 75. Jennings scheduled nearly all SWC schools to provide the foundation for Tech's acceptance as an SWC member in 1956. During his administration, Jones Stadium was dedicated and financial stability was brought to the entire athletic program. The well-known, well-liked Jennings was respected in the South and Southwest, married Elizabeth Autrey in 1914, and had one son. An active golfer, he resided in Lubbock, TX, until his death.

BIBLIOGRAPHY: John W. Bailey, *The M Book of Athletics* (State College, MS, 1930); Denne H. Freeman, *That Good Old Baylor Line: Baylor Football* (Huntsville, AL, 1975); Ronald L. Mendell and Timothy B. Phares, *Who's Who in Football* (New Rochelle, NY, 1974); Ralph L. Sellmeyer and James E. Davidson, *The Red Raiders; Texas Tech Football* (Huntsville, AL, 1978); William W. Sorrels, *The Maroon Bulldogs: Mississippi State Football* (Huntsville, AL, 1975); James D. Whalen, telephone interview with William Morley Jennings, June 28, 1984.

James D. Whalen

JOHNSON, John Henry (b. 24 November 1929, Waterproof, LA), college athlete and professional football player, performed with the Calgary Stampeders (1953) of the CFL, San Francisco 49ers (1954–1956), Detroit Lions (1957–1959), and Pittsburgh Steelers (1960–1965) of the NFL, and Houston

Oilers (1966) of the AFL. His father, a Pullman porter, moved his family to Pittsburg, CA, near Oakland, in the early 1930s. An exceptional athlete at Pittsburg High School, Johnson in 1949 set a California discus record in track and field and earned twelve letters in four sports. The Oakland (CA) *Tribune* in 1972 named him Eastbay Area High School Athlete of the Century. Johnson attended St. Mary's College (CA), where in 1951 his 84–yard kickoff return earned a 7–7 tie with the heavily favored University of Georgia. When St. Mary's dropped football, Johnson played briefly at Modesto Junior College (CA) and Arizona State University (BC). Johnson, who participated in the 1952 Olympic track decathlon trials, led the nation in punt returns his senior year and received a Bachelors degree in Education from Arizona State in 1955.

Although drafted in 1953 by the Pittsburgh Steelers (NFL), he signed instead for $11,000 with the Calgary Stampeders (CFL). The next season he joined the NFL San Francisco 49ers, beginning a 14–year pro career as a fullback. The 49ers backfield of Johnson, Joe Perry,* Hugh McElhenny,* and Y. A. Tittle* ranked among the finest offensive units in pro football history. Johnson, who married Barbara Flood in 1950 and had four children before being divorced, later married Leona Johnson and has one son.

Johnson played for the 1957 world champion Detroit Lions and rushed for 1,141 yards in 1962 for Pittsburgh, becoming the first Steelers and ninth pro back to surpass 1,000 yards in a season. He also participated in the 1963 through 1965 Pro Bowl games. After being released in 1965 by the Steelers, Johnson spent the 1966 season with the Houston Oilers. Upon retiring in 1967 at age 37, he ranked as the fourth leading rusher in NFL history. In 143 games over 14 seasons, he gained 6,803 yards rushing on 1,751 carries for a 4.3–yard rushing average and 48 touchdowns. He caught 136 passes, including 32 in 1964, for 1,478 yards and 7 touchdowns.

A punishing blocker and durable, explosive runner, the 6 foot, 2 inch, 225 pound Johnson defined modern standards for fullbacks (especially with Marion Motley* and Jim Brown*) by combining powerful inside running with exceptional outside speed and agility. Opponents feared and respected Johnson's aggressive play. After retiring, Johnson worked eleven years as a public relations and urban affairs expert with a Pittsburgh utility company. He also founded the John Henry Johnson Foundation, an organization aiding disadvantaged children. In 1987, he was named to the Pro Football Hall of fame.

BIBLIOGRAPHY: John Henry Johnson file, Pro Football Hall of Fame, Canton, OH; Evan Pattak, "In Recognition of John Henry Johnson," *Pittsburgh Steelers Weekly* (August 9, 1980), pp. 26–27; Jim Scott, "Yesterday's Hero: John Henry Johnson," *Pro Quarterback* (January, 1971), pp. 44–46, 48.

John Hanners

JOINER, Charles Jr. "Charlie" (b. 14 October 1947, Many, LA), college and professional player and coach, in 1984 became the leading pass receiver in NFL history, surpassing Charley Taylor's* 649 receptions. At age 38, Joiner was among the oldest active NFL players with seventeen seasons and played his last ten seasons with the San Diego Chargers. Joiner grew up in Lake Charles, LA, and attended Boston High School there. At Grambling State University (SAC) he won four varsity letters and teamed with future NFL quarterback James Harris. Drafted as a defensive back by the Houston Oilers (NFL) in 1969, Joiner suffered arm and collarbone injuries his first few seasons. He was traded from Houston to the Cincinnati Bengals (NFL) in 1972, after making 66 receptions for 1,174 yards in three seasons. Joiner established consistent patterns that he maintained throughout his career by making 98 receptions for 1,769 yards as a Bengal from 1972 to 1975.

He joined the Chargers in 1976 in a trade for defensive end McCoy Bacon. At San Diego, Joiner steadily improved his career statistics by participating in 180 consecutive regular-season games and appearing in the 1976, 1979, and 1980 Pro Bowls. From 1979 to 1985 he averaged over 62 catches per season. Joiner's 12,162 career receiving yards ranks him first ahead of Don Maynard's* 11,834 figure. Joiner surpassed the career reception yardage mark in the same game that Steve Largent* of Seattle broke Harold Carmichael's* mark for consecutive games with a catch. Joiner retired following the 1986 season and became receiver's coach for the Chargers. Besides scoring 65 touchdowns, he caught an NFL-record 750 passes in his career and averaged 16.2 yards per catch. He enjoyed around 30 100–yard reception games and regularly starred in playoff competition. In 1979 against Denver he helped clinch San Diego's first AFC West title with a 32–yard touchdown catch from Dan Fouts.* The next year against Buffalo and Oakland in the playoffs, he caught 10 passes for 213 yards and 3 touchdowns. He gained 106 yards on 6 receptions in a victory over Miami in 1981 and opened the scoring the next year with a 28–yard reception from Fouts in the Chargers' playoff loss to Miami.

At 5 feet, 11 inches, and 180 pounds, Joiner mastered all the basic wide receiver moves and patterns. According to San Francisco coach Bill Walsh,* Joiner was the most intelligent and perceptive receiver the game has seen. During the off-season he worked as a management trainee (accounting) for Gulf Oil in Houston, TX. He has been named NFL Man of the Year by his Chargers teammates and most valuable and inspirational player in 1983. He resides in Houston with his wife, Dianne, and daughters Jynaya and Kori.

BIBLIOGRAPHY: San Diego Chargers, Sports Information Department, San Diego, CA; *TSN Football Register—1986*.

Leonard Frey

JONES, Bertram Hayes "Bert" (b. 7 September 1951, Ruston, LA), college and professional player, is the son of William A. "Dub" and Schumpert Jones. His father played for the Cleveland Browns (NFL) in the early 1950s and tied an NFL record by scoring six touchdowns in a game, while his grandfather "Hap" Barnes made football All-American at fullback for Tulane University. Jones first became involved with pro football as a ball boy for the Browns, although his family resided mainly in Ruston. He attended Ruston High School and entered LSU (SEC) in 1969. As backup quarterback in 1971, Jones fumbled and threw an interception in LSU's Orange Bowl loss to Nebraska. He led the 1972 LSU squad to a Sun Bowl victory over Iowa State. By his 1973 graduation, Jones had set numerous Tigers career records, including most yards, total offense (3,202), touchdown passes (28), and highest pass completion percentage (.526). Named Player of the Year by *TSN* his senior year, he quarterbacked the College All-Stars in 1973 against the Miami Dolphins.

General manager Joe Thomas of the Baltimore Colts made Jones his first NFL draft choice in 1973. The selection enabled Thomas to trade the venerable John Unitas* to the San Diego Chargers and provided a backup for new starting quarterback Marty Domres. On December 15, 1974, Jones completed a then-record 17 consecutive passes against the New York Jets, but the mark received little recognition at the time because the Colts lost the game 45–38. In 1975, 1976, and 1977, the Colts led the Eastern Division of the AFC. The Colts fielded a strong team including receiver Roger Carr, Bill Olds, Lydell Mitchell,* Raymond Chester, Don McCauley, and Fred Cook, but failed to win an AFC championship. In 1976 Jones was named All-Pro quarterback and received the NFL Players Association MVP Award. The team dropped in the standings after 1977, causing Jones' considerable talents to go unnoticed. Jones was traded to the Los Angeles Rams (NFL) in 1982, but a back injury forced him to retire after one season. Jones, a bachelor, later made beer commercials.

In pro football Jones completed 1,430 of 2,551 passes for a 56.1 completion percentage. He passed for 18,190 yards (7.17–yard average) and 124 touchdowns but suffered 101 interceptions. As of 1986, Jones' 78.2 rating ranked thirteenth on the all-time NFL list. His talents became obscured because he followed the superb Unitas and his club never advanced to the Super Bowl. The steady, workmanlike player threw everything on a straight line and seldom made the big play.

BIBLIOGRAPHY: Larry Fox, *Bert Jones and the Battling Colts* (New York, 1977); George Sullivan, *Bert Jones: Born to Play Football* (New York, 1977).

John David Healy

JONES, Calvin Jack (b. 7 February 1933, Steubenville, OH; d. 9 December 1956, near Hope, British Columbia, Canada), college and professional player, captained the University of Iowa (BTC) football team in 1955. The 6 foot, 220 pound guard in 1954 and 1955 attained All-American honors and made the All-BTC squad. One of the finest athletes ever produced at Steubenville High School, he led the Big Red to a 10–1 gridiron record in 1951 and carried the Steubenville basketball squad to 23 consecutive victories before losing to Middletown in the Ohio Interscholastic championship game. He also played in the Ohio All-Star football game in 1952.

Jones originally planned to attend Ohio State University but instead joined two high school teammates in enrolling at Iowa under football coach Forest Evashevski. The BTC consequently investigated Iowa's recruiting procedures. Jones, a great leader, played offensively and defensively for the Hawkeyes. Evashevski called Jones the greatest lineman he ever coached, while teammate Alex Karras* considered him the greatest college player he ever saw. Jones was named to 22 All-American squads and in 1955 won the Outland Award, symbolic of the nation's outstanding college lineman. In 1955 he played in the Shrine All-Star (East-West) game in San Francisco, CA, and Hula Bowl in Honolulu, HI. Iowa's first black captain, Jones in 1970 was selected to the All-Time Hawkeyes football eleven.

Although drafted by the Detroit Lions (NFL), he signed professionally with the Winnipeg Blue Bombers (CFL). While returning from the East-West All-Star game in Vancouver, British Columbia, he was killed in an airplane crash. Jones was elected to the HAF College Football Hall of Fame in 1962, the NFF College Football Hall of Fame, and the Iowa Sports Hall of Fame in 1971. His uniform number (62) was retired by the University of Iowa.

BIBLIOGRAPHY: Akron (OH) *Beacon Journal*, December 11, 1956; HAF College Football Hall of Fame; *NYT*, December 10–12, 14, 1956; Steubenville (OH) *Herald-Star*, December 11–12, 1956; University of Iowa, Sports News, Iowa City, IA.

Allan Hall

JONES, David "Deacon" (b. 9 December 1938, Eatonville, FL), college and professional player, ranks with Gino Marchetti* as possibly the greatest defensive ends in pro football history. One of eight children of carpenter-handyman Ishmael and Mattie Jones, he grew up in straitened circumstances and turned to football, basketball, and track at Hungerford High School in Orlando, FL. He attended Mississippi Vocational College and South Carolina State College, where he gained his nickname for leading the football team in prayers. Generally overlooked by pro football scouts, he was drafted by the Los Angeles Rams (NFL) in the fourteenth round in 1961 and made the team as a defensive tackle and backup for ends Lamar Lundy and Gene Brito.

Upon Brito's serious illness, Jones was moved into the 1961 starting lineup at left end. After a comparatively slow start compounded with weight problems, he began to show his best skills by 1964. He then teamed with Lundy, Merlin Olsen,* and Roosevelt Grier* as the "Fearsome Foursome," one of the greatest defensive lines in pro football history. Through a study of Baltimore Colts' game films, Jones patterned his defensive attack after Gino Marchetti's. Jones became, if anything, even deadlier in his quickness and speed (he sprinted 9.7 seconds for the 100–yard dash in high school) combined with tremendous strength. His forte proved the pass rush. In his eleven seasons with the Rams, he became renowned for his hard, clean tackling, introducing the familiar term "sack" to the modern game. A unanimous All-NFL selection from 1965 to 1970, he was named NFL Defensive Player of the Year in 1967 and 1968. Teammate Olsen and opponent Gale Sayers* called him the greatest of defensive football players.

At 6 feet, 4 inches, and around 250 pounds, Jones compiled several impressive statistics by participating in 143 consecutive games until injured in 1971, recovering over one dozen fumbles in his Los Angeles career, scoring safeties in 1965 and 1967, and returning an intercepted pass 50 yards in 1966. He played for the San Diego Chargers (NFL) in 1972 and 1973 and finished his pro career with the Washington Redskins (NFL) in 1974. Jones, a golf, table tennis, and jazz enthusiast, married Iretha Oberton in 1962 and was elected to the Pro Football Hall of Fame in 1980. The Pro Football Hall of Fame named him to its AFL-NFL 1960–1984 All-Star Second Team.

BIBLIOGRAPHY: Arnold Hano, "The Awesome Power of Deacon Jones," *Sport* 47 (January, 1969), pp. 58–64; *TSN Football Register—1974.*

Leonard Frey

JONES, Howard Harding "Head Man" (b. 23 August 1885, Excello, OH; d. 27 July 1941, Toluca Lake, CA), college athlete, football coach, and administrator, coached six national championship or co-championship teams and 30 All-Americans over 29 seasons. Jones, who finished with a composite 194–64–21 (.733 percent) record at six universities, was selected to the HAF College Football Hall of Fame and became a charter member in 1951 of the NFF College Football Hall of Fame. He played halfback with his brother Thomas Albert Dwight (Tad) Jones* at nearby Middletown (OH) High School and graduated in 1903. In two years at Phillips Exeter Academy and three seasons at Yale University (IL), Howard and Tad played together on undefeated teams. Jones played end and teamed with Tom Shevlin* and Edwin "Ted" Coy* to help Yale win three national championships (1905–1907). A member of Sheffield College and Class Day Committee, he caught for the Elis baseball team and graduated in 1908 from the three-year Select Course.

Walter Camp* recommended Jones in 1908 for head football coach at Syracuse University. Syracuse tied Princeton and beat Michigan but lost to

Pop Warner's* Carlisle Indians 12–0 and finished 6–3–1. Yale captain Coy asked Jones to coach the Elis football squad in 1909. Yale finished undefeated (10–0–0), won the national championship, and placed six players on Camp's All-American first team. The following year Jones coached Ohio State (WC) to a 6–1–3 record and held powerful Michigan with All-Americans Albert Benbrook* and Stanfield Wells to a 3–3 tie. Jones returned to Excello, OH, and worked in the paper business four of the next five years (1911–1915). Yale's newly formed Graduate Committee in 1913 hired Jones as its first paid football coach at a $2,500 annual salary. The Elis finished 5–2–3 with substandard material, tied Princeton, and lost 15–5 to undefeated Harvard on Charlie Brickley's* five field goals. Crimson coach Percy Haughton* had taught Jones earlier that the first law of coaching is to obtain good material.

From 1916 to 1923 Jones served as head football coach and athletic director at University of Iowa (WC) and brought grid respectability to the Hawkeyes. His outstanding players included tackle Frederick Duke Slater* and backs Aubrey Devine and Gordon Locke. In eight seasons his Iowa teams compiled a 42–17–1 record (.708 percent), finished undefeated (7–0–0) to win the WC 1921–1922 championships, and shared the national championship both years. Jones' two favorite career victories came against Notre Dame, the first in 1921 when Iowa triumphed 10–7 to end a Fighting Irish 20–game winning streak. Ten years later his Southern California Trojans halted a Notre Dame 26–game undefeated string with a thrilling 16–14 come-from-behind victory. His 1922 Hawkeyes defeated brother Tad's Yale team 6–0, but Illinois with Red Grange* broke Iowa's 20–game winning streak 9–6 a year later. Jones introduced his two-runner (quarterback-fullback) and two-blocker (halfbacks) system at Iowa and became the first to succeed with 6–2–2–1 and 6–3–2 defenses. He taught clean, hard football and drove his players, but remained sensitive and considerate. He left Iowa because of his disagreement with a member of the Athletic Board and his wife disliked Iowa City life.

Jones coached football at Trinity College (SC, now Duke University) in 1924 with sparse material and played underclassmen exclusively, recording only a 4–5–0 season. The University of Southern California (PCC) hired Jones as coach in 1925 with a mandate to defeat University of California–Berkeley, which had not lost to the Trojans in eight games under coach Andy Smith.* Southern California also faced Stanford's legendary Pop Warner and Notre Dame's Knute Rockne.* Between 1925 and 1932 the Trojans finished 5–1–1 against California and 5–2–1 against Stanford. All five victories over Stanford came consecutively at the end and drove Warner to another coaching position in the East. Jones did not fare as well against Rockne, finishing 2–4–0 including the Iowa victory.

During 16 years at Southern California (1925–1940), Jones compiled a combined 121–36–13 (.750 percent) record. His players included All-American tackles Jesse Hibbs and Ernie Smith, guards Aaron Rosenberg* and Harry Smith, and backs Morley Drury,* Erny Pinckert,* and Cotton Warburton. The Trojans won three national championships (1928, 1931–1932) and seven PCC championships, and captured five Rose Bowl encounters with distinguished coaches Jock Sutherland* (Pittsburgh), Bernie Bierman* (Tulane), Wallace Wade* (Duke), and Bob Neyland* (Tennessee). A dramatic last-second touchdown pass gave the Trojans a 7–3 victory in the 1939 Rose Bowl, spoiling Duke's undefeated and unscored upon record.

The quiet, chain-smoking Jones, who did not drink and whose strongest expression was "gol-dang," maintained dignity and bearing, kept his feelings to himself, and found relaxation difficult. Football so preoccupied his mind that he frequently forgot appointments and the location of his parked automobile. After Iowa City spectators became hostile in 1923 over a referee's adverse decision, he dispatched his players to hotels and restaurants to advise occupants that he agreed with the call that lost the game for the Hawkeyes. He told Stanford's All-American Bobby Grayson* in 1935 to wear only one sock and to put it on his injured leg so that the Trojans would know which one to protect. After Southern California's Johnny Baker kicked a field goal to upset Notre Dame in 1931, Jones visited Rockne's grave in South Bend (IN) Highland Cemetery and led his entire squad in prayer.

The son of paper executive Thomas Albert and Adelaide (Harding) Jones, he married Leah Bissell Clark in Denver, CO, in 1911 and had one son, Clark Harding. After their divorce (1925), he married Jane Dean Ridley in Lankershim, CA (1926). He wrote *How to Coach and Play Football* (1923) and *Football for the Fan* (1929). Jones, who enjoyed fishing and bridge and golfed in the mid-1970s, died of a heart attack.

BIBLIOGRAPHY: Chuck Bright, *University of Iowa Football: The Hawkeyes* (Huntsville, AL, 1982); Tim Cohane, *Great College Football Coaches of the Twenties and Thirties* (New Rochelle, NY, 1973); Tim Cohane, *The Yale Football Story* (New York, 1951); Dick Lamb and Bert McGrane, *75 Years with the Fighting Hawkeyes* (Dubuque, IA, 1964); Edwin Pope, *Football's Greatest Coaches* (Atlanta, 1956); Ken Rappoport, *The Trojans: A Story of Southern California Football* (Huntsville, AL, 1974); *Yale Pot Pourri* (Yearbook), 1907; Yale University, Archives, Sterling Memorial Library, New Haven, CT.

James D. Whalen

JONES, Lawrence McCeney "Biff" (b. 8 October 1895, Washington, DC), college player and coach, was a successful football mentor and Army colonel. Jones graduated in 1917 from the U.S. Military Academy, where he played left tackle on the 1915 and 1916 teams. The undefeated 1916 squad claimed the national championship. Jones, elected captain of the 1917 unit, instead served as a field artillery lieutenant with the American Expeditionary Force in France. After World War I, he returned to West Point and assisted football coaches Charles Daly* and John McEwan. From 1925 to 1929 he served as Army head coach with an impressive 30–8–2 record. His 1926 and 1927 teams lost only one game, while his 1928 squad was beaten twice. Jones coached Christian "Red" Cagle,* who made the 1927–1929 All-American teams. Earl "Red" Blaik,* his assistant coach, directed the fabled Army teams from 1941 to 1958. In 1930 and 1931 Jones served as a field artillery officer and assistant graduate manager of athletics at the Academy.

From 1932 to 1934 he coached LSU (SEC) to a 20–5–6 mark. His 1933 football team finished undefeated but tied three times. LSU played post-season games in 1933 and 1934 with Tennessee, where coach Robert Neyland* had built a dynasty. In 1933 the LSU Tigers defeated the Volunteers 7–0, shutting out a Neyland-coached team for the first time in 77 games. In 1935 the University of Oklahoma (BSC) hired 39-year-old Jones to modernize its athletic facilities and teach military courses. During two years there, he coached the Sooners to a 9–6–3 record and started Oklahoma toward big-time football. Following the 1936 season, Jones was transferred to Fort Leavenworth, KS. From 1937 to 1941 he coached the University of Nebraska (BSC) to a 28–14–4 record. His 1937 and 1940 Cornhuskers won the BSC championship, the latter team becoming the first Nebraska Bowl squad. In the Rose Bowl, the Cornhuskers lost 21–13 to Clark Shaughnessy's* Stanford University squad.

In 135 games over 14 seasons from 1926 to 1941, Jones achieved 87 victories, 33 defeats, and 15 ties for a .700 winning percentage. The 6 foot, 3 inch, 215 pounder exhibited his West Point training in coaching techniques. A very intelligent, staunch coach and drillmaster, he employed the "organize, deputize, supervise" theory and always expected an all-out performance. Jones retired from the U.S. Army as a major in 1937 but returned as a colonel in 1942 and served as graduate manager of athletics at West Point until June 1948. He was elected to the HAF and NFF College Football Halls of Fame.

BIBLIOGRAPHY: Tim Cohane, *Great College Football Coaches of the Twenties and Thirties* (New Rochelle, NY, 1973); John D. McCallum and Charles H. Pearson, *College Football U.S.A., 1869–1973* (New York, 1973); Jim Weeks, *The Sooners: A Story of Oklahoma Football* (Huntsville, AL, 1974).

John L. Evers

JONES, Thomas Albert Dwight "Tad" (b. 21 February 1887, Excello, OH; d. 19 June 1957, Hamden, CT), college athlete and football coach, molded outstanding Yale University teams. His brother Howard* excelled as coach at the Universities of Iowa and Southern California. In 1902 the Jones brothers played halfback on the Middletown (OH) High School team, coached by a Yale graduate who encouraged them to attend his university. After attending prep school, they entered Yale (IL) in 1904. As a sophomore at Yale, "Tad" started at quarterback and caught for the baseball team. The New York Giants (Natonal League) offered him a $5,000 baseball contract, but he preferred football. From 1905 through 1907 the Jones brothers helped their undefeated Elis teams to 28 victories and 2 scoreless ties. In his final season Jones was named All-American at quarterback.

After graduating in 1908 Jones remained at Yale as backfield football coach. As head coach at Syracuse University in 1909 and 1910, he guided the Orangemen to a 9–9–2 mark. From 1911 to 1915 he coached football at prep schools in the East. In 1916 he was named head football coach at Yale and guided the Elis to their best record since 1909. Yale lost only one game and defeated Harvard 6–3 in the Yale Bowl. The Elis had not scored a touchdown against Harvard in nine years nor defeated a Percy Haughton*–coached team. Jones called the 1916 team the "most courageous Yale team of all time." Jones also engaged in the shipbuilding business. During the World War I era, the U.S. government requested him to build ships in Seattle, WA. He remained there until 1920, when he returned as Yale coach.

Jones' 1923 squad became the greatest in Yale history. Besides having strong freshman teams in 1920 and 1921, the Elis benefited from transfers Century Milstead, Mal Stevens, Lyle Richeson, and William Neale. Utilizing a fast, powerful offensive attack and an equally impressive defense, Yale won all eight games and blanked five opponents. At age 40, Jones expected another outstanding team in 1927 for his final season. Yale lost only one game, giving him a career 66–24–6 coaching record. Until his death, he operated an industrial coal and oil company.

Jones, who remained devoted to his players, Yale, and football, believed the game could develop strong men. Although often a center of coaching-policy disputes, he built one of the sport's lasting reputations, wrote widely syndicated football articles, and was elected to the HAF College Football Hall of Fame. In 1958 he was named to the NFF College Football Hall of Fame. Jones married Betty Shearn and had one son and one daughter.

BIBLIOGRAPHY: Tim Cohane, *Great College Football Coaches of the Twenties and Thirties* (New Rochelle, NY, 1973); John D. McCallum and Charles H. Pearson, *College Football U.S.A., 1869–1973* (New York, 1973); *NYT*, June 19, 1957.

John L. Evers

JORDAN, Lee Roy (b. 27 April 1941, Excel, AL), college and professional player, starred in football at Excel High School. At the University of Alabama (SEC, 1959–1963) under coach Paul "Bear" Bryant,* Jordan played both offensively and defensively as a center-linebacker. The Crimson Tide won 29 games, lost 2, and tied 2 in Jordan's three varsity seasons. With a perfect 11–0–0 record in 1961, Alabama captured the SEC title and national championship. Besides performing in the 1960 Bluebonnet Bowl tie against Texas and the 1962 Sugar Bowl victory against Arkansas, Jordan made 31 tackles against the University of Oklahoma in the 1963 Orange Bowl and was named the game's Outstanding Player. The fourth-place finisher in the 1962 Heisman Trophy balloting was named the nation's outstanding lineman that year and selected All-SEC and All-American in 1961 and 1962. Jordan in 1963 played in the Coaches All-American and Senior Bowl games.

Jordan was chosen in the first round of the 1963 player draft by the Dallas Cowboys (NFL). The 6 foot, 1 inch, 220 pound linebacker performed for the Cowboys from 1963 through 1976. He played in NFL championship game losses to the Green Bay Packers in 1966 and 1967 and losses in Super Bowl V to the Baltimore Colts in 1971 and Super Bowl X to the Pittsburgh Steelers in 1976. As Cowboys defensive team captain, Jordan led Dallas in interceptions in 1973 and 1975 and established individual records for most unassisted tackles (100) in 1975 and combined tackles (163) in 1973. On October 28, 1973, he made 14 unassisted and 21 combined tackles against the Philadelphia Eagles, both one-game records. One week later Jordan intercepted three passes against the Cincinnati Bengals to tie a Cowboys mark.

Jordan, who played fourteen pro seasons, ranks third in team history with 472 yards and 3 touchdowns on interceptions and recovered 16 opposition fumbles. A Pro Bowl participant following the 1968–1970 and 1974–1975 seasons, Jordan was selected an All-Pro in 1966, 1968–1969, 1973, and 1975. Jordan and his wife, Biddy, have three sons, David, Patrick Lee, and Christopher. He works with a Dallas real estate firm and belongs to the NFF College Football Hall of Fame.

BIBLIOGRAPHY: Clyde Bolton, *The Crimson Tide; A Story of Alabama Football* (Huntsville, AL, 1973); Paul W. Bryant and John Underwood, *Bear* (Boston, 1974); *Dallas Cowboys Media Guide,1976; TSN Football Register—1976.*

John L. Evers

JURGENSEN, Christian Adolph III "Sonny" (b. 23 August 1934, Wilmington, NC), college and professional player and broadcaster, is the son of Christian Adolph II and Lola (Johnson) Jurgensen. At New Hanover High School in Wilmington, Jurgensen excelled as a football quarterback and basketball player and was considered a major league baseball prospect as a catcher. Jurgensen's passing earned him a football scholarship at Duke University (ACC), where he graduated in 1957 with a Bachelor's degree in Education. Jurgensen threw only 6 touchdown passes in three seasons (1954–1956) and only 59 passes as a senior because the Blue Devils relied on a ground-attack. Married in 1957, Jurgensen divorced in 1964; he married Margo Hurt in June 1967 and has four children, Gregory, Scott, Eric, and Gunnar.

The Philadelphia Eagles selected Jurgensen in the fourth round of the 1957 NFL draft. Jurgensen spent three seasons (1958–1960) as quarterback Norm Van Brocklin's* understudy. When the Eagles won the NFL title in 1960, Jurgensen held for placekicks. As the Eagles' regular quarterback (1961–1963), Jurgensen in 1961 led the NFL in passing with 235 completions for

3,723 yards and 32 touchdowns and paced with 3,261 passing yards in 1962. His 1961 passing yards and touchdowns remain Eagles' records.

Following his trade to the Washington Redskins (NFL) in 1964, the gregarious Jurgensen became very popular and played there through the 1974 season. Jurgensen in 1966 led the NFL in pass attempts (436), completions (254), and yards (3,209). He set NFL passing records in 1967 with 508 attempts, 288 completions, and 3,747 yards and passed for 31 touchdowns. Jurgensen in 1968 tied the NFL mark for the longest pass completion with a 99–yard touchdown toss to Gerry Allen against the Chicago Bears. Jurgensen again led the NFL in passing in 1969 with 274 completions in 442 attempts for 3,102 yards and 22 touchdowns. Besides pacing the Redskins in passing (1964–1970, 1974), Jurgensen twice threw five touchdown passes in one game and exceeded 400 yards passing on five occasions and 300 yards 23 times. He holds Washington single-game records for most passing attempts (50) and most completions (32). His 508 passing attempts, 3,747 yards, and 31 touchdowns in 1967 set club records, the last of which remains, the Redskins standard.

Besides playing for mediocre teams most of his eighteen seasons, the frequently injured Jurgensen underwent nine operations. He was sidelined with injuries when Washington lost to the Miami Dolphins in Super Bowl VII and never threw a pass in a championship game. An All-Pro in 1961, Jurgensen played in the Pro Bowl (NFL All-Star Game) following the 1964 season. His 255 touchdown passes rank him third on the all-time NFL list behind Fran Tarkenton* and Johnny Unitas.* He remains seventh in total yards (32,224) and sixth in passing attempts (4,262) and completions (2,433). Since retiring as an active player (1974), Jurgensen has served as a sports commentator and television analyst for CBS Sports and broadcasts Washington Redskins games. He was named to the North Carolina Hall of Fame and elected in 1983 to the Pro Football Hall of Fame.

BIBLIOGRAPHY: Jack T. Clary, *Washington Redskins* (New York, 1974); *The Pro Football Hall of Fame Souvenir Yearbook, 1983–1984; TSN Football Register—1974.*

John L. Evers

JUSTICE, Charles "Choo Choo" (b. 18 May 1924, Asheville, NC), college and professional player and coach, is the son of Parley Whittington and Nell (Foster) Justice. Justice, whose father worked fifty-two years for the Southern Railroad, has four brothers, Jack, Joe, Bill, and Neil, and one sister, Frances. Justice attended Lee Edward High School in Asheville, NC, where he led the football team his senior year to an undefeated season outscoring opponents 400–6. Upon completing high school in 1943, he joined the U.S. Navy. He played football two years for the Bainbridge (MD) Naval Training Station squad, which finished undefeated against college and service teams. With the exception of Justice, all team members came from college or pro ranks.

The Service Rookie of the Year in 1943, he made the second AP All-Service Team in 1944 and played in 1945 for the Pearl Harbor Navy All-Stars.

In the fall, 1946, he enrolled at the University of North Carolina (SC). During the next four years, the 5 foot, 10 inch, 176 pound Justice played tailback and helped the Tarheels compile an impressive 32–9–1 record. A historic clash with Georgia and its great Charlie Trippi* in the 1947 Sugar Bowl was followed by appearances in the 1949 Sugar Bowl and 1950 Cotton Bowl. At North Carolina he set the then NCAA total offense record of 5,176 yards gained (3,774 rushing and 2,362 passing), averaged 42.5 yards punting, returned punts 1,200 yards and kickoffs 909 yards, and scored 39 touchdowns. In 1948 and 1949 Justice was named to the All-American team. In the 1950 College All-Star game, he led his team to a 17–7 victory over the Philadelphia Eagles and was selected MVP. Carl Snavely,* Justice's college coach, remarked, "I doubt if there has been a finer all-around player in football than Charlie." Justice played in a game of "giants" and succeeded with speed, deception, and a will to excel.

He joined the Washington Redskins (NFL) midway through the 1950 campaign and led them in rushing the remainder of the season. After being an assistant coach at North Carolina in 1951, he returned to the Redskins from 1952 to 1954 and in 1953 led Washington in rushing and ranked second in pass receiving. During his brief pro career, he gained 1,284 yards rushing (4.9–yard average), caught 63 passes for 962 yards (15.3–yard average), and punted for a 40.4–yard average. In addition, he also was used as a passer and punt and kickoff returner. Subsequently, he became a distributor for Amoco Oil and operated an insurance agency in North Carolina. He married his wife, Sarah, in 1943 and has two children, Charles R. "Ronnie" and Barbara Elizabeth.

BIBLIOGRAPHY: Robert T. Bowen, interviews with Charles Justice, 1984; *The Carolina Football Brochure, 1983;* Charles Justice to Robert T. Bowen, 1984; David S. Neft, Richard M. Cohen, and Jordan A. Deutsch, *Pro Football: The Early Years: An Encyclopedic History, 1895–1959* (New York, 1978); Bob Quincy and Julian Scheer, *Choo Choo: The Charlie Justice Story* (Chapel Hill, NC, 1958).

Robert T. Bowen

K

KARRAS, Alexander George "Alex" "Tippy Toes" "Mad Duck" (b. 15 July 1935, Gary, IN), college and professional athlete and announcer, is the son of George Karras, a first-generation Greek immigrant. His father studied medicine at the University of Chicago, married a Canadian-born nurse, and in 1926 set up a general practice in Gary, IN. Karras, the fourth of five children (his older brother Louis was an All-American football lineman at Purdue), excelled at Emerson High School in Gary. Karras, an All-State fullback recruited by over one hundred colleges, chose the University of Iowa over Indiana University. At Iowa, Karras became the toughest, smartest, and most agile tackle in the BTC. The quick-footed, tenacious Karras developed various incredibly quick moves and countermoves on defense. Besides being named a two-time All-American and winning the Outland Award in 1957, he helped lead the Hawkeyes to the top ten final season rankings in 1956 and 1957, a BTC championship, and Rose Bowl win.

As the Detroit Lions' first-round NFL draft pick in 1958, Karras quickly gained respect as a defensive tackle by mastering the outside pass rush. A relatively light 6 foot, 2 inch, 250 pounder with poor eyesight, Karras carefully studied films of opposing guards to learn their blocking techniques. Karras' remarkable agility earned him the nickname "Tippy Toes," while his tough, belligerent behavior won him the appellation "Mad Duck." After gaining All-Pro status from 1960 through 1962, Karras and Paul Hornung* were suspended indefinitely by commissioner Pete Rozelle* in April, 1963, for allegedly betting on NFL games. During his suspension Karras worked as a bartender at Detroit's Lindell AC, where he held a share of the ownership, and he wrestled professionally. Rozelle demanded that Karras sell his partnership in Lindell's AC as a condition for reinstatement. Karras and his first wife, Joanie, whom he had married in the spring of 1958, went to her family's house in Clinton, IA. In March 1964, Karras and Hornung finally were reinstated. Karras played with Detroit until the Lions placed him on waivers in September 1971. Karras, who brought a colorful, controversial personality to pro football, used intelligence, quickness, agility, and guile to compensate for lack of weight.

Since retirement, Karras has worked as a sportswriter, color analyst on ABC "Monday Night Football" broadcasts for three years, and actor. He achieved fame with his role in *Paper Lion* and has gained recognition as a film and television actor. Karras appeared in an ABC situation comedy series, "Webster," with his second wife, Canadian-born actress Susan Clark, whom he met on a cruise to Greece and married in 1979. They have one daughter, and Karras has five older children by his first marriage. Karras and Clark co-starred in *Babe*, with Clark as Babe Didrikson Zaharias* (OS) and Karras as George Zaharias. They have their own film production company called Georgian Bay.

BIBLIOGRAPHY: "Back in Bounds," *Newsweek* 63 (March 30, 1964), pp. 54–55; Alex Karras and Herbert Gluck, *Even Big Guys Cry* (New York, 1977); John McCallum, *Big Ten Football Since 1895* (Radnor, PA, 1976); Patrice Maloney, "Alex Karras and Susan Clark," *Cable Today* 3 (December, 1983), pp. 26–27; Tex Maule, "A Gigantic Midget among Men," *SI* 21 (November 30, 1964) pp. 46–52; Tex Maule, "Players Are Not Just People," *SI* 18 (April 29, 1963), pp. 22–26; Tex Maule, "The Shadow over Pro Football," *SI* 18 (January 26, 1963), pp. 10–11; Ronald M. Mendell and Timothy B. Phares, *Who's Who in Football* (New Rochelle, NY, 1974); George Plimpton, *Mad Ducks and Bears* (New York, 1973); George Plimpton, *Paper Lion* (New York, 1966).

Douglas A. Noverr

KAVANAUGH, Kenneth "Ken" (b. 23 November 1916, Little Rock, AR), college and professional athlete, football coach, and scout, excelled as a "big play" end with the Chicago Bears (NFL) during their most successful era and made numerous touchdown receptions. Kavanaugh graduated from Little Rock High School in 1936 and entered LSU (SEC) that fall. He played football three varsity seasons at LSU, making All-SEC each year and twice becoming a Sugar Bowl All-Star. In his final season, Kavanaugh finished seventh in the Heisman Trophy balloting and won the Rockne Trophy given by the Washington Touchdown Club. During that season, he caught 30 passes for 467 yards and eight touchdowns and was selected to play in the *Chicago Tribune* College All-Star game for 1940. At LSU he also starred in baseball and later played minor league baseball for the St. Louis Cardinals organization.

Kavanaugh was drafted by the Chicago Bears (NFL) in the second round and joined them for the 1940 season. Coach George Halas* already had assembled a deep, talented roster and employed Kavanaugh as an integral part on offense. In view of Sid Luckman's* powerful arm, the incredibly speedy Kavanaugh was used almost exclusively as a long-distance touchdown threat. In the 1940 and 1941 seasons the Bears won the NFL championship. Kavanaugh then entered the U.S. Air Force and served three and one-half years, reaching the rank of captain. While stationed in England, he flew thirty missions. In 1946 Kavanaugh returned to the Bears to help Chicago capture another NFL championship. The 6 foot, 3 inch, 205 pound speedster enjoyed perhaps his greatest season in 1947, catching 32 passes for 818 yards and an NFL-leading 13 touchdowns. He made most All-NFL teams in both 1946 and 1947 and enjoyed his finest game in his final season (1950), catching 8 passes for 177 yards against the New York Yanks on October 29. His career 162 receptions netted 3,626 yards (22.4–yard average) and 50 touchdowns. One Kavanaugh touchdown came on a fumble recovery.

Kavanaugh is married and has one son and one daughter. He served as an assistant football coach with the Chicago Bears in 1951, Boston College in 1952–1953, Villanova University in 1954, and the New York Giants (NFL) from 1955 through 1970. Besides becoming a scout for the Giants in 1971, he also pursued several successful business enterprises.

BIBLIOGRAPHY: Ken Kavanaugh file, Pro Football Hall of Fame, Canton, OH; Ronald L. Mendell and Timothy B. Phares, *Who's Who in Football* (New Rochelle, NY, 1974).

Robert N. Carroll

KAZMAIER, Richard William, Jr. "Dick" (b. 23 November 1930, Toledo, OH), college player, is the son of businessman Richard W. and Marion A. (Greenlese) Kazmaier, Sr., and attended Maumee (OH) High School (1944–1948), where he participated in five sports. He played at quarterback on the football team, shortstop on the baseball squad, second man on the golf team; ran the 100–yard dash for the track team; and led the basketball team in scoring with 23 points per game. Kazmaier, a relatively small 5 foot, 11 inch, 170 pound football back, attended Princeton University (IL, 1948–1952). He did not make the first-string football team until the final game of his freshman season. In the third game of his sophomore year (a 14–13 loss to the powerful University of Pennsylvania), Kazmaier showed coach Charles Caldwell* that he could handle varsity competition. He delighted Palmer Stadium fans by scoring both Tiger touchdowns, averaging 9 yards per run, and completing 8 of 12 passes for 79 yards.

A tailback in Princeton's single-wing offense, Kazmaier proved a dominant force in college football from 1949 through 1951. In 27 games he ran for 20 touchdowns and threw 35 scoring passes. Besides carrying the ball 368 times for 1,964 yards, he completed 179 of 289 passes for 2,393 yards. The versatile, all-purpose back also punted 102 times for a 36.2–yard average. Jesse Abramson of the Philadelphia *Inquirer* perhaps described Kazmaier's talents best when he called him, "the indestructible senior tailback executioner of Charles Caldwell's single wing." Over the three-year period, Kazmaier led Princeton to 22 consecutive victories. Kazmaier earned All-American honors in 1950 and 1951, was selected AP Male Athlete of the Year in 1951, received the 1951 Maxwell Award, and won the Heisman Trophy his senior year, leading balloting in every region. Kazmaier's legacy as a great college football player was assured with his election to the NFF College Football Hall of Fame in 1966.

Although the Heisman Trophy can mean instant cash, two modern winners (Kazmaier and Pete Dawkins*) have skipped pro football. Kazmaier made his decision well before he graduated cum laude from Princeton to serve as a U.S. Aviation Ground Officer. He then trained for a business career by earning an M.B.A. from Harvard University. An article in *TSN* on December 10, 1984, indicated that Kazmaier expressed "no regrets" about his decision.

After successful experiences heading divisions of large corporations, Kazmaier in 1975 established his own marketing and financial services business specializing in the sports, recreation, leisure, health, and fitness industries. Kazmaier, who contributed to football in particular and sports in general, married Patricia Hoffman on June 20, 1953, and has six daughters. Kazmaier's key athletic activities include being president of the NFF and Hall of Fame, a member of the board of advisors of the President's Council on Physical Fitness and Sports, past director of the Sporting Goods Manufacturers Association, U.S. delegate to World Federation of the Sporting Goods Industry, member of the International Sports Organization Committee, and past chairman of the Athletic Institute. The Concord, MA, resident received the first Massachusetts Amateur Patron of the Year Award in 1985.

BIBLIOGRAPHY: Furman Bisher, "Bottom Line for Kazmaier: No Regrets," *TSN*, December 10, 1984; John T. Brady, *The Heisman: A Symbol of Excellence* (New York, 1984); Jay Dunn, *The Tigers of Princeton: Old Nassau Football* (Huntsville, AL, 1977); Jerry Izenberg, "The Homecoming," New York *Post*, February 25, 1984; Jeff Krasner, "Football Great Scores in Business," Boston *Herald*, December 9, 1984; "Life After the Heisman: One Winner's Story," *Christian Science Monitor*, November 23, 1984; Philadelphia *Inquirer* (1949–1951).

John G. Muncie

KELLEY, Lawrence Morgan "Larry" (b. 30 May 1915, Conneaut, OH), college athlete and football coach, is the son of Lawrence Wemple and Gladys Morgan Kelley and has one sister. He attended Williamsport (PA) High School and Peddie School. An honor student and scholarship recipient (Yale Club of New York and Mory's Association), he graduated in 1937 from Yale College. At Yale (IL) the versatile Kelley earned letters in baseball (first base and captain), basketball, and football. The first end to captain Yale's football team in twenty-five years, he was selected an All-American in 1936 by UPI, AP, and sportswriter Grantland Rice* (OS). A 6 foot, 1½ inch, nearly 200 pound right end, he used his wide shoulders, long arms, and great speed as a two-way player. Kelley played "a capable defensive end" and became "one of the best forward pass receivers of all time." In 1934 he made five of Yale's sixteen touchdowns, helping the Elis to a 5–3 season. During the next two seasons the wisecracking Kelley finished either high or co-high scorer. He scored against archrivals Harvard and Princeton from 1934 through 1936, as Yale beat Harvard three consecutive years and Princeton twice. In 1936 he became Yale's first Heisman Trophy winner.

In numerous extracurricular activities, Kelley served on the Undergraduate Athletic Association and Board of Control and the Senior Prom Committee and chaired the Class Day Committee. Besides belonging to Delta Kappa Epsilon fraternity, he was elected to Skull & Bones, an elite senior society. After pursuing graduate studies one year at Princeton, Kelley became from 1937 to 1942 a master in history and football coach at Peddie School. From 1942 to 1958 he served as manager for an aeronautical company and executive officer for two glove manufacturing companies. In 1958 he returned to teaching as mathematics instructor and alumni director of Cheshire Academy in Connecticut. Kelley married three times: in 1939, to Katharine Maria Duncan, from which union came a daughter; in 1946, to Anne Goodwin; and in 1961, to Lovdie Augusta Welsh, who had attended Dickinson Seminary. Kelley, now retired, resides in Pensacola, FL. At his twenty-fifth college class reunion in 1962, Kelley expressed content, despite his "vicissitudes," and kept "a full and happy recollection of the privileges which were accorded [him] because of [his] fortunate athletic happenstance."

BIBLIOGRAPHY: Tim Cohane, *The Yale Football Story* (New York, 1951); Albert Beecher Crawford, ed., *Football Y Men—Men of Yale Series*, Vol. 2, *1920–1939* (New Haven, CT, 1963), p. 83; Arnold Guyot Dana, "Yale Old and New," a compilation of articles and clippings in 100 volumes numbered 1–73, on microfilm (see reel #16 on football) in Manuscripts and Archives, Yale University Library, New Haven, CT; "Lawrence M. Kelley," biographical sketches in *History of the Class of Nineteen Thirty-Seven, Yale College*, Vol. 1, senior year album (New Haven, CT, 1937), pp. 413–14, Vol. 2, *Seven-Year Book* (New Haven, CT, 1944), p. 94, and Vol. 3, *Twenty-Five Year Book* (New Haven, CT, 1962), pp. 244–45.

Marcia G. Synnott

KELLY, Leroy (b. 20 May 1942, Philadelphia, PA), college and professional player, is the son of S. Orvin and Argie (Watson) Kelly. He excelled as football running back for the Cleveland Browns (1964–1973), led the NFL in rushing twice, and finished runner-up once in rushing. Besides being a great runner, he proved a fine pass receiver and blocker. The 6 foot, 205 pound Kelly did not have large size for a running back, but by using explosive initial speed he often penetrated the opposing line before the defense could react. Kelly's speed and shiftiness then made him difficult to tackle. An All-City quarterback and baseball shortstop at Simon Gratz High School in

Philadelphia, Kelly entered Morgan State College (CIAA) in Baltimore in the fall, 1960. During his career there, he won four football letters and made the All-CIAA team in 1963. He was named MVP in the 1963 Orange Blossom Classic in Miami, although Morgan State lost 30–7 to Florida A&M. In 1965 he received his B.S. degree from Morgan State.

Kelly, the eighth-round draft pick of the Cleveland Browns in 1964, played behind Jim Brown* that fall and consequently enjoyed little opportunity to display his skills. During 1964 and 1965, however, he became an outstanding returner of punts and kickoffs. In 1965 he led the NFL in punt returns by averaging 15.6 yards for 17 returns, and ran 2 kicks in for touchdowns. With Brown's retirement after the 1965 season, Kelly blossomed into one of the NFL's top running backs and enjoyed three consecutive outstanding seasons. In 1966 he gained 1,141 yards in 209 carries, losing the NFL rushing title to Gale Sayers* of the Chicago Bears on the last day of the season. He led the NFL with 5.5 yards per carry and 15 touchdowns.

Kelly asked for a $40,000 contract before the 1967 season, but the Browns offered him only $35,000. After negotiations broke down in August, Kelly played out his option at a 10 percent reduction on his $23,000 1966 contract and became a free agent. In 1967 he led the NFL with 1,205 rushing, 5.1 average yards per rush, and 11 touchdowns. The Browns, who then recognized Kelly's worth, in March 1968 signed him to a four-year $320,000 contract, and paid him the $40,000 he had sought for the 1967 season. In 1968 he again led the NFL with 1,239 yards rushing and 16 touchdowns. Kelly injured a leg in the first game of the 1969 season, and although he gained respectable yardage in 1969, 1971, and 1972, he never again possessed the same quickness. He played infrequently in 1973 and was waived to the Oakland Raiders (NFL) on July 9, 1974, but never played another pro game.

During his ten-year career, Kelly amassed 7,274 yards rushing to place fourth on the then all-time list. Kelly averaged 4.2 yards per rush, scored 74 rushing touchdowns, and enjoyed 27 100–plus yard games. A gifted pass receiver, he caught 190 passes for 2,281 yards (12–yard average) and 12 touchdowns. He also averaged 10.5 yards on 94 punt returns and 23.5 yards on 76 kickoff returns, passed for several touchdowns, and served as the Browns' backup punter. Kelly's diverse talents were praised by standout Lance Alworth,* who said, "I've never seen a better all-around player than Kelly. He seems to do everything well—protecting the passer, blocking for the fullback, running up the middle or going wide on sweeps, and catching passes." Kelly, selected All-Pro in 1966, 1967, and 1968, was named to the Pro Bowl from 1966 through 1971. A bachelor, he resides in Philadelphia and operates a Burger King restaurant franchise there.

BIBLIOGRAPHY: Cleveland Browns, Information Office Archives, Cleveland, OH; *Cleveland Browns Press Book, 1965–1974; NCAA Official Collegiate Football Record Book, 1961–1964; NFL Record Manual, 1965–1974; TSN Football Register—1966–1974.*

Eugene C. Murdock

KERR, Andrew "Andy" (b. 7 October 1878, Cheyenne, WY; d. 16 February 1969, Tucson, AZ), college athlete and coach, was the son of a cattle stockman Andrew and Mary (Fagan) Kerr and attended Carlisle, PA, elementary schools. A graduate of Dickinson College in 1900, he competed in football, baseball, and track there. Kerr taught mathematics and coached football at the high school in Johnstown, PA. After marrying Mary Meister of Scotdale, PA, in 1913, he had two sons, Andrew and William. His college coaching career began in 1914 at the University of Pittsburgh, where he directed freshman football under Glenn "Pop" Warner* and also coached varsity basketball and track. In 1921 Warner accepted a position with Stanford University. Since Warner would not break his existing contract with Pittsburgh, he sent Kerr to serve as Stanford (PCC) head coach in 1922 and 1923. Kerr also became head basketball coach there. Kerr installed Warner's tricky double-wing offensive football formation and became an authority on it. When Warner arrived at Stanford University in 1924, Kerr assisted him until 1926. Kerr joined Washington and Jefferson (PA) as head football and basketball coach the next three seasons. When the Shriners developed their East-West All-Star football game, Kerr coached the first East All-Star team and continued in that capacity for twenty consecutive years.

He was appointed head football coach at Colgate University in 1929 and lost only four games his first five seasons there. His "unbeaten, untied, unscored on and uninvited" 1932 team, which shut out opponents 264 to 0, gained permanent fame because the Rose Bowl snubbed it. Kerr's bewildering double-wing established him among the foremost exponents of razzle-dazzle football. His running game proved clever and deceptive, while his forward-passing plays exhibited fine execution. An exact taskmaster, he believed in constant repetition to achieve the precision timing his plays required, effectively used the double spinner and reverses, and promoted the lateral pass as much as any coach. He considered the development of the screen pass as one of his finest contributions to football. During his eighteen years at Colgate University, he never missed a squad practice session or game. Kerr compiled a 95–50–7 record there and a 137–71–14 overall coaching mark. After leaving Colgate, he coached Lebanon Valley College (PA) for three seasons. He received the Amos Alonzo Stagg Award in 1963 and was elected to the HAF and NFF College Football Halls of Fame. In 1966 the football field at Colgate University was renamed Kerr Stadium.

BIBLIOGRAPHY: Tim Cohane, *Great College Football Coaches of the Twenties and Thirties* (New York, 1973); Allison Danzig, *The History of American Football: Its Great Teams, Players, and Coaches* (Englewood Cliffs, NJ, 1956); Howard Liss, *They Changed the Game* (New York, 1975); John McCallum, *Ivy League Football Since 1872* (New York, 1977).

James Fuller

KEYES, Marvin "Leroy" (b. 18 February 1947, Newport News, VA), college and professional player, is the son of Henry Paul and Mae (Huggins) Keyes and excelled in several sports at George Washington Carver High School in Newport News, VA. Although attending Purdue University (BTC) on a football scholarship, he also attracted the attention of college basketball recruiters and was scouted as a shortstop by both the Baltimore Orioles (AL) and Pittsburgh Pirates (NL) in baseball. In addition, he holds the Virginia State high school long jump record (24 feet, 7 inches).

Keyes made his mark in college football. He enrolled in 1965 at Purdue University, where he majored in physical education. Keyes proved a multitalented athlete on the football field as a defensive back and running back and flanker on offense. In 1966 the 6 foot, 3 inch, 210 pound Keyes was used almost exclusively at defensive back and carried the ball only twelve times. Nevertheless, he averaged 8.4 yards per carry and completed 3 passes (2 for touchdowns). During the 1967 season Keyes played mainly at offensive running back and flanker. He scored 114 points on 13 rushing touchdowns and 6 receiving touchdowns to lead the nation in scoring. In addition, he passed for 3 touchdowns, rushed for 986 yards, and made 758 yards in pass receptions to earn consensus All-American honors.

The next year, Keyes again made All-American by rushing for 1,003 yards, making pass receptions for 428 yards, and playing more on defense. In one of the most remarkable all-time sports performances (September 28, 1968) versus Notre Dame, Keyes participated in an incredible 82 plays—24 at running back, 47 at flanker, and 11 at defensive back. He accounted for three touchdowns by running for two tallies and passing for another. Keyes finished second in the Heisman Trophy balloting to O. J. Simpson* and holds numerous Purdue season and career records. In 1969 Keyes was selected as the number 1 draft pick by the Philadelphia Eagles in the combined NFL-AFL draft. He played professionally with the Eagles (1969–1972) and NFL Kansas City Chiefs (1973), but injuries shortened his career as a running back and prevented him from achieving previous levels of success. In his pro career, Keyes rushed 125 times for 369 yards (3.0–yard average) and 3 touchdowns, and caught 30 passes for 270 yards (9.0–yard average).

BIBLIOGRAPHY: John Bansch, "Boilermakers Boom When Leroy Turns Key," *TSN*, October 12, 1968; Richard Dozer, "Laughing Leroy—Purdue's Grid Prize," *TSN*, November 25, 1967; *Kansas City Chiefs Media Guide, 1974; Philadelphia Eagles Media Guide, 1972;* Purdue University, Department of Sports Information, West Lafayette, IN.

William A. Sutton

KIESLING, Walter A. "Walt" "Big Kies" (b. 27 May 1903, St. Paul, MN; d. 2 March 1962, Pittsburgh, PA), college and professional player and coach, ranked among early NFL stars from the upper midwest. Kiesling prepped at Cretin High School and then matriculated at St. Thomas College,

(MnIAC) both in St. Paul, MN. The huge Kiesling debuted professionally at guard for Ole Haugsrud's Duluth Eskimos (NFL) in 1926. Although weighing over 200 pounds, the deceptively fast Kiesling used his speed to become one of pro football's archetypal pulling guards. During thirteen pro seasons the 6 foot, 2 inch, 246 pound Kiesling appeared with Duluth, 1926–1927; the Pottsville Maroons, 1928; Boston Braves, 1929; Chicago Cardinals, 1929–1933; Chicago Bears, 1934; Green Bay Packers, 1935–1936; and Pittsburgh Pirates (Steelers), 1937–1938. Kiesling's best pro years came with the Chicago Cardinals, where he became a perennial All-NFL selection. In his greatest game, he blocked for Ernie Nevers* when the powerful fullback ran for a record six touchdowns against the Chicago Bears in 1929. He played an integral role on the legendary Monsters of the Midway fielded by George Halas* in 1934 and in 1937 joined Pittsburgh (NFL) as a player–assistant coach.

Kiesling, Pittsburgh head coach on three different occasions, first assumed the reins midway through the 1939 season because the flamboyant Johnny "Blood" McNally* suddenly resigned. Thereafter, Kiesling always remained available whenever Steelers' owner Art Rooney* needed help. Guiding the Pittsburgh squad through the 1940 season, Kiesling compiled a 3–13–3 record in his first stint as head coach. After being relegated to assistant coach in 1941, Kiesling again rescued Rooney in midseason as the third Steelers coach that year. Despite this chaotic situation, Kiesling's 1942 club finished with a 7–4–0 mark for the first winning record in Steelers history. When the Steelers merged in 1943 with the Philadelphia Eagles to form the Steagles, Kiesling and Eagles coach Greasy Neale* split coaching duties. In 1944 he shared the head coaching post with Phil Handler, when the Steelers combined with the Chicago Cardinals. This club produced the worst record in Steelers history, finishing 0–10–0. Although relieved of his post before the 1945 season, Kiesling once again served as Steelers head coach from 1954 through 1956. His teams finished 14–22–0, giving him a career 30–55–6 coaching record. Kiesling, selected for the Pro Football Hall of Fame in 1966, was survived by his wife, Irene.

BIBLIOGRAPHY: Ralph Hickok, *Who Was Who in American Sports* (New York, 1971); Pat Livingston, *The Pittsburgh Steelers: A Pictorial History* (Virginia Beach, VA, 1980); Ronald L. Mendell and Timothy B. Phares, *Who's Who in Football* (New Rochelle, NY, 1974); *NYT*, March 3, 1962; Pittsburgh *Post-Gazette*, March 3, 1962; Pittsburgh *Press*, March 2, 1962; George Sullivan, *Pro Football A to Z* (New York, 1975); George Sullivan, *Pro Football's All-Time Greats: The Immortals in Pro Football's Hall of Fame* (New York, 1968); Roger Treat, ed., *The Encyclopedia of Football*, 16th rev. ed., rev. by Pete Palmer (New York, 1979); Joe Tucker, *Steelers' Victory after Forty* (New York, 1973).

Frank W. Thackeray

KILROY, Francis Joseph "Bucko" (b. 30 May 1921, Philadelphia, PA), college and professional player, coach, scout, and administrator, is the eldest of five children born to Joseph Francis and Agnes Kilroy, both of Irish descent. A hometown football star and 1939 graduate of Northwest Catholic High School, Kilroy briefly entered the University of Notre Dame and then returned to Philadelphia because of his father's illness. Kilroy played football lineman at Temple University and graduated from the V–12 Program in 1942 from Columbia University (IL). The 6 foot, 1 inch, 250 pound Kilroy was overlooked in the NFL draft but joined the Philadelphia Eagles as a free agent in 1943. He played with the Eagles for his entire pro career (1943–1956), except for wartime service as a merchant marine officer.

Kilroy initially played offensive guard and tackle and made All-Pro from 1947 through 1949. At defensive middle guard, however, he emerged as a dominant force. Kilroy, considered by his peers as the era's toughest lineman, again earned All-Pro honors from 1952 through 1954. In his first 12 seasons encompassing 200 games, the extremely durable Kilroy missed only one contest and appeared in 146 consecutive games. During his final three campaigns, he combined as a player-coach, until an ankle injury forced his retirement in 1956. By now the father of seven children, Kilroy remained with the Eagles as a full-time defensive coach and talent scout until 1962 and then joined the Washington Redskins (NFL) as director of player personnel. From 1966 to 1970 he worked for the Dallas Cowboys (NFL) as a "super scout" and then joined the New England Patriots (NFL) as director of player personnel. Kilroy became general manager in 1979 and vice president four years later.

Although a knowledgeable talent judge and able administrator, Kilroy made his principal impact on the field. As a versatile offensive and defensive lineman, he set a demanding standard of excellence with stamina and competitiveness. Kilroy's selection to the All-Decade team for the 1940s and to Temple University's Hall of Fame (1976) reflected his remarkable abilities.

BIBLIOGRAPHY: *Inside Football, 1979; New England Patriots Media Guide, 1979; New England Patriots Yearbook, 1984; Philadelphia Eagles Press Guides, 1946–1955.*

Jerome Mushkat

KIMBROUGH, John Alec "Jarrin' John" (b. 1918, Haskell, TX), college and professional player, helped lead Texas A&M University to SWC football championships in 1939 and 1940, a two-year 20–1 record, and Sugar and Cotton Bowl victories. Every poll awarded the undefeated Aggies the 1939 national college championship. The gigantic 6 foot, 2 inch, 222 pound back rushed with destructive power into the line, head down with knees pumping high. He ran with intelligence and often moved along the line to the outside, when the hole was not there. Despite his size, Kimbrough scampered as quickly as most scatbacks. The Aggies often isolated Kimbrough with a lateral in the flat, where smaller secondary defenders could not match his brute strength and speed. Football writer Wilton Hazzard called Kimbrough "a great plunger . . . a devastating blocker, a facile pass-snatcher, and one of the most dependable defensive backs in A&M history."

The youngest of seven children of W. A., a doctor, and Elizabeth Kimbrough, John played with his brother Jack, an end, at Texas A&M. After attending Haskell High School for two years, he transferred to Abilene High School and did not become eligible for football there until midway through his senior year (1936). Kimbrough nevertheless led Abilene to a Texas district championship and missed being named to the All-District team by one vote. In high school Kimbrough also participated in basketball and track.

Kimbrough began attracting attention as a powerful runner in late 1938, his sophomore season at Texas A&M. Most football forecasts, however, relegated the Aggies to the SWC 's second division for 1939. A versatile attack spearheaded by Kimbrough, along with a rugged defense allowing only 18 points, produced 10 straight Aggies victories in 1939. The Aggies trounced 1938 national champion TCU 20–6, as the latter suffered many injuries. According to one press report, "Kimbrough's bull-like rushes did most of the injuring." He played 455 minutes in 1939 and performed 60 minutes in the season's key 6–2 victory over SMU. In the muddy contest, Kimbrough ran, blocked, and defended with determination. With the ball at SMU's 10–yard line, Kimbrough penetrated the massed Mustang defense twice for eight yards. While the entire Aggies team ran to the right, Kimbrough sped to the left, broke free of the only remaining defender, and raced into the end zone. He won the SWC scoring title in 1939 with 10 touchdowns.

Kimbrough enjoyed his greatest performance in a 14–13 win over unbeaten Tulane in the 1940 Sugar Bowl. Besides tallying both Aggie touchdowns, he rushed 26 times for 152 yards. AP writer Felix R. McKnight reported, "Bull-shouldered John Alec Kimbrough, sturdy son of the Texas cow country, gathered his fading Texas Aggies for a dramatic fourth-period surge. The Southland's largest football throng saw one of the most destructive fullbacks the game has ever known simply crush a Tulane team that had pulled ahead, 13–7. No one knew how much he actually did gain, for he added many yards on the tailend of cunning Aggie lateral passes. Only once was he stopped without a gain." When Kimbrough grabbed a lateral, "Tulane players fell like tenpins as Kimbrough lowered his head and waded 10 yards" for the winning touchdown.

Texas A&M stretched its undefeated string to 19 games in 1940. The Aggies edged UCLA 7–0, when Kimbrough intercepted a pass and scampered nine yards into the end zone. In a 17–0 win over Arkansas, he carried five straight times from the 17–yard line for the first touchdown and later broke the game open with spectacular 47– and 38–yard interception returns. SMU, the SWC's second-ranked club, succumbed again 19–7, as Kimbrough gained 103 yards in 20 carries. Kimbrough staged another one-man assault on the winning touchdown drive, carrying eight consecutive times from the Mustangs 30–yard line. The next week against Rice, he gained 108 yards in 18 attempts through the vaunted Owl line. With the score 0–0 in the second quarter, the Aggies faced a fourth down and one situation on their own 45–yard line. Kimbrough gained three yards, causing Rice's defense to collapse. The Aggies tallied three touchdowns before halftime en route to a 25–0 win.

Texas ended the Aggies string, 7–0, on Thanksgiving Day, but Kimbrough penetrated the Longhorn line for 59 yards in nine straight carries. In nine regular-season games Kimbrough gained 611 yards in 162 rushes and returned 6 pass interceptions for 142 yards. Kimbrough finished his college career with another superb New Year's Day effort, plunging for the winning touchdown in a 13–12 Cotton Bowl triumph over Fordham. The two-time All-American (1939–1940) was named among the college game's three greatest fullbacks on the 1950 AP All-Time team and was elected to the NFF College Football Hall of Fame in 1954 and the HAF College Football Hall of Fame.

Upon graduation, Kimbrough signed a then-enormous estimated $37,500 contract to play one year for the New York Yankees (AFL). His contract included personal appearances set up by promoter and club president Douglas G. Wertz. In 1941 Kimbrough starred in the Twentieth Century Fox movie *Lone Star Ranger*. Kimbrough entered the U.S. Army as an infantry second lieutenant in 1942, transferred to the U.S. Air Corps, and served as a pilot in the Pacific until discharged as a major in 1945. After World War II, he excelled as a fullback for the Los Angeles Dons (AAFC). He ranked among the AAFC's leading rushers and scorers from 1946 to 1948, running for 1,224 yards in 329 carries, catching 35 passes for 574 yards, and tallying 138 points.

Kimbrough and his wife, Barbara, have two children, John Dudley and Barbara Banner. After retiring from pro football, Kimbrough served one year in the Texas legislature and engaged in farming and ranching. His business interests in the Haskell area included the Sportsman Parade Award Company, of which he served as president.

BIBLIOGRAPHY: Harold Claassen and Steve Boda, Jr., eds., *Ronald Encyclopedia of Football* (New York, 1960); Wilbur Evans, *Texas Sports Hall of Fame Yearbook* (1981); Gail Fowler, "Review of Season's Football Statistics," San Antonio (TX) *Express* (December 22, 1940); Wilton Hazzard, *Illustrated Football Annual* (1940); John Kimbrough to Bernie McCarty, September 27, 1984; Felix R. McKnight, "The Aggies' Rally Trips Tulane," St. Louis *Globe-Democrat* (January 2, 1940); *Pro Football Illustrated* (1947–1949); Alexander M. Weyand, *Football Immortals* (New York, 1962).

Bernie McCarty

KINARD, Frank "Bruiser" (b. 23 October 1914, Pelahatchie, MS; d. 7 September 1985, Jackson, MS), college athlete, coach, and professional football player, was described by a former coach as "the best lineman ever to play football." The 6 foot, 1 inch, 212 pound all-around athlete utilized his quickness and agility as a guard on the basketball team in 1936 and quarter miler for the track squad at the University of Mississippi (SEC). The first of four brothers to play football for "Ole Miss," Kinard made the 1936–1937 All-American football teams to become the first athlete from his school to gain this honor. Mississippi lost 20–19 to Catholic University of America in the 1936 Orange Bowl. Kinard, a rather large lineman, was nicknamed "Bruiser" because of his size, toughness, aggressiveness, and penchant for contact. Kinard's size and speed (10.4 seconds while running the 100-yard dash in uniform) greatly contributed to his athletic success and selection to "Pop" Warner's All-Time team. Playing both offensively and defensively, the durable Kinard averaged 55 minutes playing time per game at Mississippi.

The Brooklyn Dodgers selected Kinard in the second round of the 1938 NFL draft. Kinard, an outstanding blocker and tackler, made the All-NFL team at tackle in 1940–1941 and 1943–1944 with Brooklyn and the first AAFC squad in 1946 with the New York Yankees. No other player had made all-league honors in both the NFL and AAFC. In 1945 Kinard served in the U.S. Navy and made the All-Service football squad. In 1948 Kinard returned to the University of Mississippi as a football line coach. Kinard, who never earned over $2,000 for a pro football game, was named to the Pro Football Hall of Fame in 1966 and also is a member of the HAF and NFF College Football Halls of Fame.

BIBLIOGRAPHY: Frank G. Menke, ed., *The Encyclopedia of Sports*, 5th rev. ed., rev. by Suzanne Treat (New York, 1975); David S. Neft et al., *The Complete All-Time Pro Football Register* (New York, 1975); Mike Rathet and Don R. Smith, *Their Deeds and Dogged Faith* (New York, 1984); Roger Treat, ed., *The Encyclopedia of Football*, 16th rev. ed., rev. by Pete Palmer (New York, 1979).

John R. Giroski

KINNICK, Nile Clarke, Jr. (b. 9 July 1918, Adel, IA; d. 2 June 1943, Gulf of Paria, Venezuela), college athlete, was the son of Nile C. and Frances A. (Clarke) Kinnick and grew up in a family with roots deep in Iowa history. Kinnick, who lived in Adel until the Great Depression forced the family to move to Omaha in 1934, combined extraordinary athletic achievement with outstanding scholarship at Benson High School in Omaha. An All-State in both basketball and football, he played catcher in baseball and graduated with academic distinction in 1936.

He also excelled academically and athletically at the University of Iowa (WC). As a sophomore quarterback, the 5 foot, 10 inch, 175 pound Kinnick made the All-WC team and earned All-American mention in a practically moribund football program. Kinnick proved equally proficient as a basketball forward. By his senior year in 1939, Kinnick became the nation's premier all-purpose football back. As a passer, runner, punter, and dropkicker, he missed only 18 minutes of play in eight games, proved instrumental in making

107 of the Hawkeyes' 130 points, and led the nation in kickoff returns and interceptions. During his 22–game career, Kinnick rushed 254 times for 724 yards, completed 88 of 229 passes for 1,445 yards, intercepted 18 passes for 91 yards, averaged 41.1 yards on 167 punts, and returned 66 punts for 621 yards and 22 kickoffs for 563 yards. In addition, he passed for 13 touchdowns, scored 7 touchdowns, and kicked 11 extra points. Besides making All-American, he won the Heisman and Walter Camp Trophies and Maxwell Award and was chosen America's Athlete of the Year. An excellent student, Kinnick graduated Phi Beta Kappa in 1940.

After starring in the College All-Star game that year, he bypassed a pro career as the Philadelphia Eagles' (NFL) first draft choice to attend Iowa Law School and serve as an assistant football coach. He remained active in Republican politics and perhaps hoped to emulate his grandfather, a former Iowa governor. World War II tragically changed those plans. A member of the U.S. Naval Reserve, the bachelor Kinnick entered active duty shortly after Pearl Harbor and was killed in a plane crash. Although his career epitomized that of a true scholar-athlete, his many virtues especially impressed contemporaries. He symbolized fair competition, moral behavior, excellence of character, and bright promise. Kinnick's memory was kept alive by his selection to the HAF and NFF College Football and Iowa Sports Halls of Fame and by the Iowa stadium's being named in his honor.

BIBLIOGRAPHY: Dick Lamb and Bert McGrane, *75 Years with the Fighting Hawkeyes* (Dubuque, IA, 1964); John D. McCallum, *Big Ten Football Since 1895* (Radnor, PA, 1976); *The NCAA Official Football Guide, 1939, 1943;* D. W. Stumpp, *Kinnick: The Man and the Legend* (Iowa City, IA, 1975); University of Iowa, Sports Information Release, Iowa City, IA, August, 1977.

Jerome Mushkat

KNOX, Charles R. "Chuck" (b. 27 April 1932, Sewickley, PA), college and professional player and coach, is the son of an Irish steelworker and starred as a tackle on the Sewickley High School football team. He received a B.A. degree in History at Juniata College (PA), where he played offensive lineman from 1950 to 1953 and served as co-captain. After graduating in 1954, Knox spent one season each as assistant football coach at Juniata and line coach at Tyrone (PA) High School and three years as head coach at Elwood City (PA) High School. Knox, who did not play pro football, assisted in football at Wake Forest University (ACC) the 1959 and 1960 seasons and held a similar job at the University of Kentucky (SEC) from 1961 to 1963. Under Weeb Ewbank,* Knox served as offensive line coach from 1964 through 1966 for the New York Jets (AFL). The next six seasons, Knox won acclaim as Detroit Lions (NFL) offensive line coach. At both New York and Detroit, Knox developed outstanding offensive lines.

He became head coach of the Los Angeles Rams (NFL) in 1973, guiding the club to a 12–2 record. Besides achieving the most single-season victories in the franchise's history, Knox won Coach of the Year honors. With the Rams through the 1977 season, Knox compiled a 57–20–1 record. For the first time in NFL history, Knox's clubs won five consecutive NFC Western Division championships. In 1978 he joined the Buffalo Bills as head coach and led them to the 1980 AFC Eastern Division title. From 1978 to 1982 Knox coached the Bills to a 38–38–0 record. In 1983 Knox became head coach of the Seattle Seahawks (NFL). After leading the Seahawks to the playoffs for the first time in the franchise's history, Knox won the 1983 AFC Coach of the Year award with a 9–7–0 regular-season record and 2–1 playoff mark. Seattle lost to the Los Angeles Raiders, 30–14, in the 1983 AFC championship game. The Seahawks compiled a 12–4–0 record in 1984, an 8–8–0 mark in 1985, and at 10–6–0 in 1986 to bring Knox's overall coaching record to 136–84–1. The 1984 squad defeated the Raiders in the wild card game in the playoffs before being defeated by the Miami Dolphins. Knox, who ranks high in all-time NFL-coaching victories, became the first coach to lead three different teams to the playoffs.

The winner of *TSN* NFL Coach of the Year awards in 1973 and 1980, Knox stressed hard work and enthusiasm in three decades of coaching football. Knox has participated in several community fund-raising projects and exhibits poise, warmth, and dignity. He and his wife Shirley live in Seattle, WA, and have four children, Chris, Kathy, Colleen, and Chuck.

BIBLIOGRAPHY: *Los Angeles Rams Official Media Guide, 1977; NFL Media Information Book, 1983; TSN Football Register—1986.*

John L. Evers

KRAMER, Gerald Louis "Jerry" (b. 23 January 1936, Jordan, MT), college and professional player, attended high school in Sandpoint, ID, and performed as offensive football tackle and placekicker there. After overcoming several childhood injuries, Kramer became an excellent football player at the University of Idaho (PCC). The business administration major was selected to play in the East-West and North-South games and captained the West team. He married Barbara Joseph in 1956 and has six children, Tony, Diane, Danny, Alicia, Matt, and Jordan.

At 6 feet, 3 inches, 250 pounds, Kramer was drafted by the Green Bay Packers as a guard in the fourth round of the 1958 NFL draft and teamed with Fred Thurston to give the Packers among the game's best set of guards. In 1961 he missed eight games because of a broken ankle. Besides playing guard full-time in 1962, he later became the Packers' placekicker when Paul Hornung* injured his knee. Kramer made 9 of 11 field goal attempts and 38 of 39 extra points for 65 total points. He capped the season by kicking three field goals and one extra point in Green Bay's 16–7 win over the New York Giants for the NFL championship. The following year, Kramer assumed the placekicking duty full-time because Hornung was suspended for betting on NFL games. Kramer placed fourth among the NFL scorers with 91 points on 16 field goals and a team-record 43 extra points. The 1963 season, though, marked his last as Green Bay's kicking specialist.

Medical problems returned after the opening game of the 1964 season. Kramer was sidelined with several intestinal infections, which took eight operations to cure. During one operation, wood splinters were discovered from an injury sustained as a teenager. Kramer finally returned to action midway through the 1965 season. Against Dallas in the 1967 NFL title game, Kramer threw the crucial block on the Cowboys' Jethro Pugh, allowing quarterback Bart Starr* to score the winning touchdown for the Packers' third straight championship. Kramer appeared with Green Bay in the first two Super Bowls, won by the Packers. Before retiring in 1968, he played on five championship teams (1961–1962, 1965–1967), was named All-Pro five times (1960, 1962–1963, 1966–1967), and participated in three Pro Bowls (1962–1963, 1968). He has written four books based on his football experiences, *Instant Replay* (1968), *Jerry Kramer's Farewell to Football* (1969), *Distant Replay* (1985), and *Lombardi* (1986).

BIBLIOGRAPHY: Rick Gonsalves, *Specialty Teams* (New York, 1977); *Green Bay Packers Press Guide, 1968;* Jerry Kramer, *Farewell to Football* (New York, 1969).

Richard Gonsalves

KRAMER, Ronald John "Ron" (b. June 24, 1935, Girard, KS), college athlete and professional football player and announcer, is the son of auto forge plant foreman John and Adeline (Tschiltch) Kramer and grew up in East Detroit, MI. He graduated from East Detroit High School and starred as an All-State performer in football, basketball, and track. Kramer attended the University of Michigan from 1953 to 1957 and received a B.S. degree in Psychology there. A great all-around athlete at Michigan (BTC), Kramer won three letters each in football, basketball, and track. He excelled in football under coach Benny Oosterbaan* and became a two-time All-American and three-time All-BTC selection. Kramer played center in basketball as Michigan's MVP three years and captained the Wolverines his senior year. In track he competed in the high jump, shot put, and discus.

Kramer's three-year football career at Michigan included 53 pass receptions for 880 yards, 31 punts for a 40.6 yard-average, and 9 touchdowns, 43 extra points, and 2 field goals for 103 points. A sure-handed receiver, he proved a standout blocker and hard tackler as defensive end. The 6 foot, 3 inch, 220 pound Kramer exhibited good speed, great coordination, and strength, and was an average student, a quiet, serious-minded, blunt, and popular person. As a sophomore in 1954, Kramer caught 23 passes for 303 yards, punted 19 times for a 41.2–yard average, and scored 32 points. In 1955 he received 12 passes for 224 yards, scored 36 points, and won All-American honors. His senior year he caught 18 passes for 353 yards, scored 35 points, was named All-BTC for the third straight year, and was selected unanimously as an All-American.

Kramer played pro football with the Green Bay Packers (NFL) from 1957 to 1964 (except for 1958 in the U.S. Air Force) and Detroit Lions (NFL) from 1965 to 1967. At 240 pounds, he excelled as a powerful blocker and was considered the prototype modern tight end. Kramer played on the 1961 and 1962 Green Bay NFL championship teams coached by Vince Lombardi.* His best season came in 1962, when he caught 37 passes for 555 yards and 7 touchdowns and was named All-Pro. During ten pro seasons, he received 229 passes for 3,272 yards and scored 16 touchdowns.

Now divorced, Kramer married Nancy Lee Cook of Jackson, MI, in 1957 and has two children, Kurtis and Cassandra. Formerly an executive with a Detroit steel company, he owns a manufacturers' representative firm. Kramer, who has served on the board of directors of several civic and charitable organizations, was honored by the March of Dimes and Boys Club of Detroit and received the NCAA's Silver Anniversary Award. Michigan's greatest all-around athlete, Kramer was elected to the NFF College Football Hall of Fame in 1978 and is a color analyst for BTC football games.

BIBLIOGRAPHY: Detroit *News*, May 21, 1984; *SEP* 229 (October 20, 1956), pp. 31ff; Al Silverman, ed., *The Specialist in Pro Football* (New York, 1965); *Sports Review: Football, 1955;* University of Michigan, Athletic Information Office, Ann Arbor, MI.

Edward J. Pavlick

KUECHENBERG, Robert John "Bob" (b. 14 October 1947, Gary, IN), college and professional player, is one of nine children of Rudolph Frederick and Marion (Nels) Kuechenberg. His father, a professional fighter and circus and rodeo performer, worked in a steel mill. His brother Rudy also played in the NFL with Chicago (1967–1969), Green Bay and Cleveland (1970), and Atlanta (1971). Kuechenberg excelled in football at Hobart (IN) High School and at the University of Notre Dame (1965–1968). In 1969 he received a B.A. degree in Economics there. A member of the 1966 national championship team, Kuechenberg in 1968 was named Notre Dame's outstanding defensive lineman and also played offensive tackle.

Kuechenberg, a fourth-round selection of Philadelphia in the 1969 NFL draft, was released by the Eagles. He was signed by the Atlanta Falcons (NFL) but released a week later. Kuechenberg in 1969 played seven games with the semi-pro Chicago Owls (CoL) and joined the Miami Dolphins (NFL) in 1979 as a free agent. The 6 foot, 2 inch, 255 pound offensive guard performed for the Dolphins from 1970 through 1984. Kuechenberg, whose tremendous strength, quickness, and aggressiveness intimidated opponents, became one of the NFL's best run-blockers. He played in more games than any other Dolphin and performed in four Super Bowl games. The Dolphins lost in Super Bowls VI and XVII but recorded consecutive triumphs in Super Bowls VII and VIII. In 1972 Miami completed its perfect season (17–0) with a Super Bowl victory over the Washington Redskins. The six-time All-Pro selection played in the Pro Bowl following the 1974–1975, 1977–1978, and 1982–1983 seasons and was named to the AFL-NFL 1960–1984 All-Star Second Team. After being married in 1969 and later divorced, Kuechenberg wed Marilyn Nix in 1975 and has two sons, Brian and Erik. He has formed Creative Interiors of Florida, where he sells original oil paintings and continues the restoration of his manor by the sea at Miami Beach's Star Island.

BIBLIOGRAPHY: *Miami Dolphins Media Guide, 1977; TSN Football Register—1984;* Paul Zimmerman, "The Star of Star Island," *SI* 57 (December 13, 1982), pp. 34–45.

John L. Evers

KUSH, Frank Joseph (b. 20 January 1929, Windber, PA), college and professional player and coach, grew up in the small mining Pennsylvania town about 35 miles from Johnstown. As one of fifteen children living in a company-owned house, he early learned to deal with adversity. Kush, whose father died when he was only 14 years old, excelled in football at Windber High School, attended Washington and Lee University, and earned a scholarship to Michigan State University (BTC). For the Spartans, the 5 foot, 7 inch, 175 pound Kush proved that determination could overcome lack of size when he was selected as a first-team All-American guard. Kush received a B.S. degree from Michigan State and an M.S. degree from Arizona State University. Kush served in the U.S. Army and acted as the player-coach at Fort Benning, GA, in 1953 and 1954. During this time Kush married Frances Theroux and has three children, Dave, Dan, and Damien. From 1955 to 1957 Kush served under Dan Devine* as line football coach at Arizona State (BC).

Following the 1957 season, Devine became head football coach at Missouri and Kush was selected as his replacement. During Kush's first year as head coach, the college was renamed Arizona State University. As Arizona State head coach, he became one of the toughest, most successful mentors in America. Notorious for driving his players to the limit, he demanded excellent physical conditioning. Kush remained at the Arizona State helm for 22 years, compiling an impressive 176–54–1 record. Kush built a strong winning tradition at Arizona State in the BC, WAC, and PTC Conferences. His teams consistently ranked at or near the top in many offensive categories, including averaging 46.6 points per game for a 10–2 record in 1972. During the 1970s Kush's Sun Devils became a national, almost unbeatable, powerhouse. In 1970 they concluded a perfect 11–0 season with a 48–26 victory over North Carolina in the Peach Bowl. Arizona State secured a 61–9 record from 1970 through 1975 and won all 12 games in 1975. That season culminated in perhaps Arizona State's greatest victory, a 17–14 win over powerful Nebraska in the Fiesta Bowl and a number 2 national ranking. Kush accumulated a 6–1 mark in bowl games.

At Arizona State Kush developed many talented offensive and defensive performers, including many All-Americans and subsequent NFL stars. The impressive list included Charley Taylor* (1961–1963), Ben Hawkins (1963–1965), Curly Culp (1965–1967), J. D. Hill (1967–1970), Woody Green (1971–1973), Danny White (1971–1973), Bob Breunig (1972–1974), Mike Haynes (1972–1975), and John Jefferson* (1974–1977). Kush's tenure at Arizona State abruptly ended in 1979, when he was fired in midseason after being accused of punching a player during a 1978 game and trying to cover it up. Kush finished in style, winning a dramatic 12–7 decision over nationally ranked University of Washington in his final game as head coach. Although a jury later cleared Kush of any wrongdoing, no NFL team initially wanted his services. With his love of coaching still strong, he pursued other avenues. In 1981 he became head football coach of the Hamilton Tiger-Cats (CFL) and led them to an 11–4–1 record playoff berth.

In 1982 Kush became head coach of the Baltimore Colts (NFL) and guided them to a 7–17–1 record his first two seasons. After the club shifted to Indianapolis and garnered a 4–12 mark in 1984, Kush became head coach of the Arizona Outlaws (USFL) and compiled an 8–10–0 mark for the 1985 season. The USFL suspended operations for the fall, 1986 season, while seeking a new trial in its suit against the NFL for damages or injunctive relief from the courts. As a college or pro coach, Kush utilized mental toughness and physical conditioning as his basic philosophy.

BIBLIOGRAPHY: Peter Bonventre and Janet Huck, "Did the Coach Play Too Rough?" *Newsweek* 94 (October 29, 1979), p. 91; "Hit 'em High," *Time* 114 (October 29, 1979), pp. 46, 51; Dean Smith, *The Sun Devils—Eight Decades of Arizona State Football* (Tempe, AZ, 1979); *TSN NFL Register—1983; Who's Who in the West*, 12th ed. (1970).

Curtice R. Mang

L

LACH, Stephen John "Steve" (b. 6 August 1920, Altoona, PA; d. 12 July 1961, Altoona, PA), college athlete and professional football player, was the son of Polish immigrants John and Catherine (Suja) Lach. His father, a railroad worker, died when Steve was seven; his mother then operated a grocery store. Lach graduated from Altoona High School, where he starred as fullback in football and shot putter and discus and hammer thrower in track. He attended Duke University from 1938 to 1942 and received a B.A. degree in History from St. Francis College (PA) in 1958.

Lach played football three years at Duke under coach Wallace Wade* and lettered in track, setting SC shot put records. A rugged, 6 foot, 2 inch, 200 pound triple-threat back, Lach excelled as a power runner, pass receiver, punter, blocker, and defensive standout. He rushed for 954 yards in 141 carries and a 6.8–yard average, caught 50 passes for 720 yards, punted 86 times for a 41.2–yard average, and scored 16 touchdowns. Besides being an All-American halfback in 1941 and All-SC in 1940 and 1941, Lach won the Teague Award in 1941 as the top Carolinas' athlete. The premier wingback finished second nationally in pass receiving in 1940 with 26 receptions and 335 yards. In 1941 he caught 22 passes for 366 yards, rushed for 537 yards and an 8.7–yard average, intercepted 3 passes, punted for a 45.8 average, and scored 10 touchdowns in leading Duke to a 9–1 season. In the Rose Bowl, Lach rushed for 129 yards and punted 8 times for a record 47.1–yard average. His quiet manner, determination, and consistent play won much admiration.

Lach played for the Chicago Cardinals (NFL) in 1942 before entering the U.S. Navy. As tailback for Great Lakes in 1943, Lach threw a 47–yard touchdown pass in the closing seconds to upset top-ranked Notre Dame. In 1946 and 1947, he played fullback for the Pittsburgh Steelers (NFL). During his pro career, he rushed 192 times for 580 yards (3.0–yard average) and 13 touchdowns and caught 31 passes for 349 yards (11.3–yard average) and 5 touchdowns.

An avid golfer, the popular Lach operated a tavern in Altoona, PA, until his death and coached football at Highland Hall Prep School in 1956. Lach, who married Faye Mountain of Altoona in 1957 and had one son, Stephen, was elected in 1980 to the NFF College Football Hall of Fame. Lach's versatility and quality play offensively and defensively made him one of football's finest all-purpose backs.

BIBLIOGRAPHY: Altoona (PA) *Mirror*, July 13, 1961, and April 15, 1980; Chicago *Sun*, December 31, 1941; Allison Danzig, *The History of American Football: Its Great Teams, Players, and Coaches* (Englewood Cliffs, NJ, 1956); Duke University, Athletic Information Office, Durham, NC; Duke–Wake Forest Football Game Program, November 8, 1980; Durham (NC) *Herald*, July 15, 1961, and April 10, 1980; Maxwell Stiles, *The Rose Bowl: A Complete Action and Pictorial Composition of Rose Bowl Football* (Los Angeles, 1946).

Edward J. Pavlick

LAMBEAU, Earl Louis "Curly" (b. 9 April 1898, Green Bay, WI; d. 1 June 1965, Sturgeon Bay, WI), college and professional player, coach, and executive, was the son of contractor Marcel and Mary Lambeau. He starred for and even coached Green Bay's East High School during his senior year after the regular coach entered the armed forces. In 1918 he matriculated at Notre Dame on a football scholarship but withdrew from school his freshman year after playing first-string fullback during coach Knute Rockne's* rookie season. Lambeau returned to Green Bay and never resumed his college career.

In 1919 Lambeau helped organize the semi-pro Green Bay Packers football club. The Indian Packing Company contributed money for uniforms and allowed the team to use its grounds for practice. The versatile Lambeau served as Packers' coach, general manager, personnel director, ticket manager, captain, runner, and passer. "We just wanted to play for the love of football," he recalled. "We agreed to split any money we got and each man was to pay for his own doctor bills." Green Bay won 10 of its 11 games that year as Lambeau earned $16.75. In 1921 the Packers entered the APFA, forerunner of the NFL. During the early 1920s, Lambeau also coached Green Bay East High School's football team.

From 1922 through 1928 the Packers won 48 games, lost 23, and tied 11. This success stemmed in large measure from Lambeau's imaginative, demanding coaching. Besides being the first pro coach to hold daily practices, he helped initiate the use of game films for preparation and pioneered the forward pass. Lambeau's Packers quickly became an exciting team to watch. From 1929 to 1931 the Packers won three consecutive NFL championships. This feat was not duplicated until Vince Lombardi's* Packers accomplished it in the mid-1960s. Lambeau's Packers also won NFL championships in

1936, 1939, and 1944. No other pro football coach won as many titles. His premier players included quarterbacks Cecil Isbell* and Arnie Herber,* running backs Johnny Blood McNally,* Clarke Hinkle, and Tony Canadeo,* linemen Buckets Goldenberg and Cal Hubbard,* and legendary end Don Hutson.*

The Packers' fortunes declined rapidly after World War II, with the 1949 team winning only two games. Club management was deeply disturbed by Lambeau's spendthrift ways, the team's record and decline in home attendance, and the excessive time that "the Earl of Hollywood" spent on his southern California ranch. Differences between Lambeau and the front office caused his brief resignation in 1949. In December 1949 he signed a new two-year contract and then resigned two months later to become coach of the Chicago Cardinals (NFL). Lambeau's switch ended the longest coaching tenure in pro football history.

Lambeau did not duplicate his early success. During his two seasons in Chicago, the Cardinals won only eight games and lost sixteen. Lambeau resigned in December, 1951, and was promptly hired to coach the Washington Redskins (NFL). Lambeau's 1952 Redskins squad triumphed in only 4 of twelve contests, but his 1953 team won 6 games, lost 5, and tied 1. Washington's success on the field, however, was marred by quarrels between Lambeau and several key players. At the end of the season, defensive end Gene Brito and quarterback Eddie LeBaron defected to the CFL. Redskins' owner George Preston Marshall* concluded that Lambeau had lost control of his players and fired him before the 1954 season. Lambeau, who never coached another pro team, compiled a composite career coaching record of 236 victories, 111 losses, and 23 ties. He joined sixteen other charter members elected in 1963 to the Pro Football Hall of Fame. Lambeau prudently invested his football earnings in real estate and spent his remaining years in comfort on his California ranch, following the fortunes of the Packers, playing golf, and fishing. After his death, Green Bay's City Stadium was renamed Lambeau Field.

BIBLIOGRAPHY: Morris A. Bealle, *The Redskins, 1937–1958* (Washington, DC, 1959); Chuck Johnson, *The Green Packers* (New York, 1961); Milwaukee (WI) *Sentinel*, June 3, 1965; *NYT*, February 12, 1950, December 28, 1951, June 2, 1965; Washington (DC) *Evening Star*, June 3, 1965; Herbert Warren Wind, "The Sporting Scene: Packerland," *New Yorker* 38 (December 8, 1962), pp. 213–20ff.

Edward S. Shapiro

LAMBERT, John Harold "Jack" (b. 8 July 1952, Mantua, OH), college and professional player, became an outstanding NFL linebacker despite being a relatively light 220 pounds and 6 feet, 4 inches. Lambert began his football career as a quarterback at Crestwood High School in Mantua, OH, and also played basketball and baseball there. In the fall of 1970 he played as a freshman defensive end at Kent State (OH) University (MAC). For the next three years, he started at middle linebacker and served as tri-captain his senior year. Lambert made All-MAC first team as a junior and senior. In 1972 as a junior, he was chosen as the MAC Player of the Year and his team's MVP in the Tangerine Bowl. As a senior, Lambert played in the North-South and All-American Bowl post-season games.

He was selected by the Pittsburgh Steelers in the second round of the NFL 1974 draft, the 46th player chosen overall. Lambert became an immediate standout at inside linebacker, making virtually every NFL All-Rookie team and being chosen the NFL's Defensive Rookie of the Year. He was the only rookie starter on the Steelers' first Super Bowl championship team that year. In 1975 Lambert unanimously made All-NFL for the first time. Lambert was named to the Pro Bowl for the first of nine consecutive years, a record for an individual linebacker. That season, he also set an AFC playoff record by recovering three fumbles in the AFC championship game.

Lambert in 1976 was selected the NFL's top defensive player, and in 1981 his teammates named him the Steelers MVP. He missed three games due to knee injuries in 1977 but repeated as top NFL defensive player in 1979. Lambert in 1979 and 1981 made six interceptions, an unusual number for a linebacker, en route to 28 career interceptions. By 1983, Lambert had made All-Pro linebacker for the fifth consecutive year and had achieved more recognition than any of his contemporaries at that position. On the second play of the 1984 regular season, he severely dislocated his left big toe and then aggravated his injury by returning too soon to action. Consequently, in July 1985 he retired as a player.

Lambert led the Steelers in tackles each year he played from 1974 through 1983. He served as defensive captain for eight years, played in AFC championship games six years, and participated on four Super Bowl championship teams. The stadium at his alma mater, Crestwood High, was named in his honor in 1980. Lambert visited military bases in the Far East and Europe with NFL player groups during the off-season in 1976 and 1977 and has participated in charity work, particularly the Ronald McDonald House in Pittsburgh, PA. The unmarried Lambert owns an 85–acre farm he works northeast of Pittsburgh in Armstrong County. Upon announcing his retirement, Lambert said that he wanted to be remembered "simply as someone who played the best he could." Steeler fans attest that he did. The Pro Football Hall of Fame named him to its AFL-NFL 1960–1984 All-Star Team.

BIBLIOGRAPHY: Pittsburgh *Post Gazette*, 1974–1983; Pittsburgh *Press*, 1974–1983; *Pittsburgh Steelers Media Guides, 1974–1983; TSN Football Register—1985.*

Robert B. Van Atta

LANDRY, Thomas Wade "Tom" (b. 11 September 1924, Mission, TX), college and professional player and coach, is the son of Ray and Ruth (Coffman) Landry and began his career as an All-Regional fullback at Mission High School. After one semester at the University of Texas (SWC), he joined the U.S. Air Force and flew in thirty B–17 missions in World War II. In November 1945 he was discharged as a first lieutenant and returned to Texas. Landry was switched from quarterback to fullback when Bobby Layne* arrived at Texas. He earned All-SWC honors as a junior in 1947, was elected co-captain in 1948, and helped the Longhorns defeat Alabama in the 1948 Sugar Bowl and Georgia in the 1949 Orange Bowl.

In 1949 the 6 foot, 1 inch, 195 pound Landry joined the New York Yankees (AAFC), where he played defensive back and made 51 punts for a 44.1–yard average. The New York Giants in 1950 selected Landry and four other Yankees as payment for allowing an NFL franchise to occupy nearby Yankee Stadium. From 1950 through 1955 he played for the Giants and spent the last two seasons as a player-coach. He made 31 interceptions, leading the club with 8 in 1952 and tying Emlen Tunnell* with 8 in 1954. Landry also tied two Giants records by scoring touchdowns on interceptions in two consecutive games (against the Cleveland Browns, October 28, 1951, and New York Yankees, November 4, 1951) and intercepted three passes against the Philadelphia Eagles on November 14, 1954. He made 389 career punts for a 40.9–yard average, was selected All-Pro in 1954, and appeared in one Pro Bowl. From 1956 to 1959 he became the Giants' defensive coach under head coach Jim Lee Howell and worked with the famed Vince Lombardi.* Landry became the NFL Dallas Cowboys' first and only head coach in 1960 and guided them from an 0–11–1 expansion team to a record five Super Bowl appearances (V, VI, X, XII, and XIII), including victories over the Miami Dolphins in VI and Denver Broncos in XII.

Through the 1986 season, the dean of NFL mentors had coached 26 campaigns. Landry ranks as the second winningest coach of all-time with an NFL career record of 260–157–6, which includes a playoff record of 20–16. He guided the Cowboys to 21 consecutive winning seasons, including 19 playoff campaigns and 14 division championships, from 1966 to 1985. In 1986 the Cowboys finished 7–9–0 for the Cowboys first losing season since 1964. One of football's greatest innovators, Landry has kept the Cowboys winning despite constant turnover in player personnel. In 1962 he introduced the shuttling quarterback offense by alternating Eddie LeBaron and Don Meredith* (OS) on every play. To supplement the losses of Calvin Hill* and Walt Garrison in 1975, he installed the shotgun formation. His coaching tenure helped produce Cowboys stalwarts Bob Lilly,* Meredith, Don Perkins,* Mel Renfro, Chuck Howley,* Hill, and Roger Staubach.* In 1966 and 1971 UPI named Landry NFC Coach of the Year.

Landry earned degrees in business at Texas and industrial engineering from the University of Houston and also holds honorary degrees from California Lutheran College, John Brown University, Southwest Baptist College, and Indiana Central University. In 1978 he was inducted into the Texas Sports Hall of Fame.

In 1981 he received an award for distinguished service from the NFL Alumni Association, the *Football News* Man of the Year Award, and the Washington Touchdown Club Board of Governors Award. Mission, TX, in 1984 named its high school football stadium after him, while the NFL Alumni Association named Landry national chairman of its Youth of America Week. Landry has resided in Dallas, TX, since 1957 with his wife, Alicia Wiggs, whom he married in January 1949, and their three children, Tom, Jr., Kitty, and Lisa.

BIBLIOGRAPHY: Ronald L. Mendell and Timothy B. Phares, *Who's Who in Football* (New Rochelle, NY, 1974); *New York Giants Media Guide, 1982; Pro!* Giants Edition, 14 (October 30, 1985), p. 75; *TSN Football Register—1986*.

Donald Kosakowski

LANE, Richard "Night Train" "Dick" (b. 16 April 1928, Austin, TX), college and professional player, grew up with a foster mother and starred in football and basketball at Anderson High School in Austin. In 1947 the 6 foot, 2 inch, 210 pound Lane made Little All-American offensive end at Scottsbluff (NE) Junior College. He served four years in the U.S. Army, catching eighteen touchdown passes in 1951 for Fort Ord, CA. Following his military discharge, he walked on with the Los Angeles Rams (NFL) on a conditional contract and was switched to defensive back. As a rookie in 1952, he set the present NFL record by making fourteen interceptions. The twice-traded Lane played for the Chicago Cardinals (NFL) from 1954 to 1959 and Detroit Lions (NFL) from 1960 through 1965. Lane ranked second to Emlen Tunnell* among all-time interception leaders with 68 thefts for 1,207 yards and 5 touchdowns.

He received his nickname as a Rams player by often seeking help from end Tom Fears.* Fears owned a record of "Night Train," which always seemed to be playing when Lane arrived. Teammates started saying, "Here's Night Train visiting us again." Lane made All-Pro in 1956 and from 1960 through 1963, played in six Pro Bowls, and was selected on the All-Pro team for the 1950s decade. Lane gambled on the field and usually prevailed because of his great speed and coordination. He excelled as a tackler and mastered the ring-neck tackle, grabbing the ballcarrier around the neck and riding him to the ground. Vince Lombardi* called Lane the best cornerback he had ever seen. Lane was married to famous blues singer Dinah Washington until her death in December 1963. A member of the Black Athletes Hall of Fame, he in 1970 was named by sportswriters as the top NFL cornerback of all time. In 1974 he was inducted into the Pro Football Hall of Fame, which named him to its AFL-NFL 1960–1984 All-Star Team.

BIBLIOGRAPHY: George Allen with Ben Olan, *Pro Football's 100 Greatest Players* (Indianapolis, IN, 1982); Chicago Cardinals–Philadelphia Eagles Football Game Program, October 25, 1959; *The Lincoln Library of Sports Champions*, Vol. 10 (Columbus, OH, 1974); George Sullivan, *Pro Football A to Z* (New York, 1975); Washington Redskins–Chicago Cardinals Football Game Program, October 14, 1956.

John L. Evers

LANGER, James John "Jim" (b. 16 May 1948, Little Falls, MN), college and professional player, graduated in 1966 from Royalton (MN) High School, where he headed the football squad and pitched for the baseball team. He received a B.S. degree in Economics from South Dakota State University in 1970. At South Dakota State, he played linebacker in football, pitched and played first base in baseball, and worked in an all-night service station. The South Dakota State (NCC) football team finished with 4–6 marks in 1967 and 1968 and a 3–7 record in 1969. Erv Huether, Langer's baseball coach, arranged a tryout for the left-hander with the Cleveland Browns (NFL). Cleveland signed the 6 foot, 2 inch, 250 pounder as a free agent in 1970 and converted him to a guard. After the Browns placed Langer on the taxi squad, the Miami Dolphins (NFL) picked him up on waivers.

Langer became starting offensive center in 1971 and played in each of Miami's regular season games until sidelined with a leg injury for seven games during the 1979 campaign. Besides calling blocking assignments for the interior offensive linemen, he blocked very effectively for quarterback Bob Griese* on passing plays and enabled backs Larry Csonka,* Mercury Morris, and Jim Kiick to run up the middle. His assets included enormous physical strength, quick reflexes and acceleration, and a professional, no frills approach. Langer neutralized linebackers with his quickness and overcame nose tackles with his strength. He helped Miami win the AFC Eastern Division titles from 1971 through 1974 and appeared in the 1971–1973 Super Bowls. The 10–3–1 1971 Dolphins squad won the AFC Championship before losing 24–3 to the Dallas Cowboys in Super Bowl VI. In 1972 Langer played every offensive down, as Miami became the only undefeated modern NFL team. After enjoying a 14–0 regular season, Miami defeated Cleveland 20–14 in the AFC playoffs, Pittsburgh 21–17 in the AFC championship game, and Washington 14–7 in Super Bowl VII. Langer helped the 1973 Dolphins to a 12–2 regular season mark, the AFC championship, and a 24–7 victory over Minnesota in Super Bowl VIII. Miami repeated as AFC Eastern Division champion in 1974, but lost to Oakland in the AFC playoffs. Langer's club almost won AFC Eastern Division titles in 1975, 1977, and 1978, barely missing the playoffs each time.

During the 1970s, Langer excelled as the NFL's dominant center. According to a 1979 *Sport* Magazine poll, NFL centers overwhelmingly listed Langer as the best performer at his position in the 1970s. In 1979 Miami coach Don Shula* remarked, "I think everybody in the NFL acknowledges

Jim Langer as the finest center ever to play the game." Langer's honors included being offensive center on the *TSN* AFC All-Star Team (1973–1977), consensus All Pro selection (1974–1978), and Pro Bowl AFC squad member (1973–1978). Miami experienced only one losing season (1976) during Langer's tenure as starting center. In September 1980 he was traded to the Minnesota Vikings (NFL) for two future draft picks. Langer, who played with the Vikings in 1980 and 1981 before retiring, was named to the Pro Football Hall of Fame in 1987 in his first year of eligibility. Jim Otto* of Oakland remains the only other pure offensive center so honored. Langer lives with his wife Lynne in Royalton, MN, and has worked as a bank loan officer, real estate salesman, and small airplane-leasing service operator.

BIBLIOGRAPHY: Norman Aaseng, *Football's Crushing Blockers* (Minneapolis, MN, 1982); Dave Anderson, "It All Starts With the Center," *Sport* 68 (January, 1979), pp. 74–78; Gerald Astor, "Center Must Hold," *Esquire*, 84 (October, 1975), pp. 184–187, 214–215; *NFL Official Record and Fact Book, 1985; TSN Football Register—1982.*

David L. Porter

LANIER, Willie Edward "Honeybear" (b. 21 August 1945, Clover, VA), college and professional player, is the son of shipping clerk Robert and beautician Florine Lanier. Lanier, one of four children including one younger sister and two older brothers, attended Maggie Walker High School (1959–1963) in Richmond, VA, where the family had moved when he was a toddler. Although raised in a very religious environment, he made his own decisions at an early age. Lanier attended Morgan State University (CIAA, 1963–1967) because of its strong football program and played under coach Earl Banks. After suffering a knee injury there, Lanier realized the tenuous nature of his football career. Consequently, he developed additional interests and received his B.S. degree in Business Administration in 1967.

A second-round draft choice of the Kansas City Chiefs (AFL), Lanier quickly became the first black middle linebacker star. Nicknamed "Honeybear," the 6 foot, 1 inch, 245 pound Lanier possessed enough quickness to drop back on passes and cover outside sweeps. He also had enough strength and size to stop the run, a definite Chiefs' weakness before his arrival. He teamed with Bobby Bell* and Jim Lynch to form one of the most successful linebacking trios in football history. One of his best games occurred in a 16–3 win over the Denver Broncos in 1971, when Lanier made eight unassisted tackles, assisted on two others, broke up one pass, and recovered one fumble. For his feats, he was named Defensive Player of the Week. He intercepted a pass in the Chiefs' victory over the Minnesota Vikings in Super Bowl IV in 1970. Lanier made three post-season All-AFC teams at middle linebacker and played in the Pro Bowl from 1970 through 1974. In 1972 Kansas City fans voted the affable, highly articulate Lanier the leading citizen for his work in the area's Drug Abuse Campaign. He retired after the 1977 season to Richmond, VA, where he has sold real estate and currently works as an account executive for the brokerage house Wheat First Security. Now divorced, Lanier has two sons and one daughter. In 1986 he was elected to the Pro Football Hall of Fame.

BIBLIOGRAPHY: *Christian Science Monitor*, August, 1973; *Ebony Magazine* 38 (December, 1982); Bill Gutman, *Gamebreakers in the N.F.L.* (New York, 1973).

William A. Borst

LARGENT, Steve M. (b. 28 September 1954, Tulsa, OK), college and professional player, has ranked among the premier recent wide receivers. At Putnam High School in Oklahoma City, he lettered in football and baseball. At Tulsa University he topped the nation in touchdown receptions for the 1974 and 1975 seasons (14 each year), made second team AP All-American in 1975, and was named All-MVC twice. The collegian caught 126 passes for 2,385 yards and 32 touchdowns.

After being drafted by the Houston Oilers (NFL), Largent was traded to the Seattle Seahawks (NFL) during the 1976 pre-season. A remarkably consistent performer, he caught 471 passes for 7,608 yards and 60 touchdowns over the next eight seasons. In 1984 he made 74 receptions for 1,164 yards and 12 touchdowns for the 12–4 Seahawks. The next year, he caught 79 passes for 1,287 yards and six touchdowns. The Seahawks finished at 10–6 in 1986 as Largent caught 70 passes for 1,070 yards and 9 touchdowns. In October 1986 Largent broke Harold Carmichael's* record by catching at least one pass in 128 consecutive games. By the close of 1986 he had continued the streak to 139 games. Largent's eighth 1,000–yard season surpassed Lance Alworth* for all-time best. Through the 1986 season Largent has caught 694 passes for 87 touchdowns (3rd) and ranks as the second leading receiver in NFL history. He holds the NFL record for most seasons with at least 50 catches (8).

A six-time All-Pro selection (1978, 1979, 1981, 1984–1986), the 5 foot, 11 inch, 184 pound Largent resembles Raymond Berry* and Fred Biletnikoff* with his sure hands and pattern moves compensating for a lack of blinding speed. He has averaged over 16 yards per reception in his career and has made numerous long-gain plays from 40 to 74 yards. One Largent reception in the 1983 playoffs helped Seattle advance to the AFC championship game against the Los Angeles Raiders. He has led the Seahawks in receptions and yards in each of the club's first eleven years. Largent is extremely active in community service, including the Fellowship of Christian Athletes, Pro Athletes Outreach, United Way, and the Tulsa Police Department forensics laboratory. He has studied toward a secondary teaching degree and assisted in the University of Washington (PCC) football program. Largent enjoys mountaineering and has climbed Mount Rainier with former teammate Jim Zorn.

BIBLIOGRAPHY: Tom Bennett et al., *The NFL's Official Encyclopedic History of Professional Football* (New York, 1977); Seattle Seahawks, Office of Public Relations, Seattle, WA.; *TSN Football Register—1986.*

Leonard H. Frey

LARY, Robert Yale, Sr. (b. 24 November 1930, Fort Worth, TX), college and professional player, is the son of Yale Buster and Kathryn Helen (Capps) Lary, of Scotch-Irish descent. He graduated in 1948 from North Side High School in Fort Worth, where his father had captained the 1928 football team. At Texas A&M Lary received a B.S. degree in Physical Education in 1952 and earned six varsity letters (including three in baseball). He married Mary Jane (Janie) Boothe on January 24, 1952, and has two children, Robert, Jr., and Nancy. The 5 foot, 11 inch, blond, 189 pound right-hander was considered the most coordinated athlete at Texas A&M and loved baseball passionately. A consistent power-hitting first baseman, Lary slugged a bases-loaded home run his first time at bat for the Aggies and was named All-SWC and All-District 6 NCAA baseball. Many assumed Lary would pursue a pro baseball career. After playing minor league baseball from 1953 to 1957, however, Lary concentrated on pro football.

At Texas A&M (SWC) Lary scored four touchdowns against Arkansas in 1950 and two touchdowns in 1951 to help deny the Texas Longhorns the Sugar Bowl. Voted MVP by his teammates in 1951, he twice was named All-SWC defensive back and twice received All-American honorable mention honors. Lary, who never had a punt blocked in 184 college attempts, ranked fifth nationally in punt returns. A third-round choice of the Detroit Lions (NFL) in 1952, Lary signed for $6,500. The Lions dominated the NFL in the mid-1950s, winning championships in 1952, 1953, and 1957. Lary missed the 1954 and 1955 seasons due to U.S. Army service and was discharged in May 1956 as a first lieutenant. A great punter and punt return threat, Lary became a mainstay of the Lions' defensive backfield. One of the sport's top three punters, Lary made a lifetime 44.28–yard average on 503 punts and ranked only eight-tenths of a yard behind all-time leader Sammy Baugh.* He led the NFL in punting in 1959, 1961, and 1963, with his 48.9–yard average in 1963 being the second highest ever. Since his punts combined distance and hang time, Lion opponents in 1960 averaged under one yard per punt return! Named to the All-NFL defensive team four times, he played in nine Pro Bowls in eleven seasons with the Lions. At Lary's 1965 retirement, only four players exceeded his 50 career interceptions. In 133 games he returned 126 punts for 753 yards, once punted 74 yards, and returned a punt the same distance.

Lary's on-the-field versatility was matched off the field. In 1958 he upset a veteran Democratic incumbent in Tarrant County for a seat in the Texas State Representatives. Lary also won a second two-year term as state representative but declined a third because politics took too much time from football. Upon retirement at age 34, Lary joined longtime friend Tommy Helms in opening a Ford agency in Hurst, TX. Since selling the car agency in the late 1970s, Lary has operated an investment business with interests in real estate, oil, and gas. Lary resides in the Fort Worth area and enjoys golf, swimming, and Shriners' work. Besides being honored by Texas A&M on May 14, 1964, with a Yale Lary Day, he was named in 1975 to the All-Time Texas Pro Team. In 1979 Lary was inducted into the Pro Football Hall of Fame, the fifth defensive back so elected. Two of these defensive backs, Jack Christiansen* and Dick Lane,* played with Lary. Possessed of speed and a special élan, this outstanding defender and kicker made the punt a key weapon in modern football. The Pro Football Hall of Fame named him to its AFL-NFL 1960–1984 All-Star Team.

BIBLIOGRAPHY: Detroit Lions, News Release, June 27, 1952; "Ex-Lions Are Promoting Shrine Game in Pontiac," Pontiac (MI) *Times*, November 18, 1976; "Five Lions on All-Time Texas Pro Team," *Pro!* (1975); Jerry Green, *Detroit Lions* (New York, 1973); "In the Lions' Lair Lary Is King," *Sports All Stars/Football* (1968), pp. 48–49; Eddie Jones, "Yale Lary: The Big Little Man from Texas," Toledo (OH) *Blade Sunday Magazine* (December 10, 1961), pp. 22–23; Doug Kelly, "Chris's Crew," *Pro!* (1975), pp. 11D–15D; Yale Lary, Personal Correspondence, Detroit Lions, Archives, Pontiac, MI; "Yale Lary Retires as Lions Star," *Detroit News*, July 23, 1965; Yale Lary, "The Ways of a Pro Punter," *SI* 17 (September 10, 1962), pp. 44–49; "Leading Candidates 1951 Aggie Team," *Texas Aggie* (1951), pp. 21–22; "NFL Personnel Survey," Detroit Lions' Yale Lary, 1952; Publicity Questionnaire, Detroit Lions' Yale Lary, 1951; "Remember: Yale Lary," *Detroit News* (July 22, 1975); Don Smith, "Canton Enshrinees," Pro Football Hall of Fame, News Release, January 29, 1979.

Harold L. Ray

LATTNER, John Joseph "Johnny" (b. 24 October 1932, Chicago, IL), college and professional athlete and coach, starred at halfback in football for the University of Notre Dame (1951–1953) and was selected a unanimous All-American his last two seasons. He was awarded the Heisman Trophy as the nation's outstanding player of 1953 and won the Walter Camp Memorial Trophy and *TSN* and Touchdown Clubs of Washington (DC), Cleveland, and Detroit awards for his outstanding performance. In 1952 and 1953 he became the only two-time winner of the Maxwell Award. A member of HAF College Fottball Hall of Fame and Notre Dame All-Time Team, he was elected in 1979 to the NFF College Football Hall of Fame. Lattner attended Chicago's St. Thomas Aquinas Elementary School and Fenwick High School, where he made All-City basketball at center and All-State football twice at end and halfback. He captained both Fenwick squads, scoring 20 touchdowns and rushing for 1,300 yards in football his senior year. The son of Oak Park (IL) printer's machinist William L., Sr., and Mary Catherine Lattner, he graduated from Fenwick in 1950.

The 6 foot, 2 inch, 195 pound Lattner starred on Notre Dame football teams with a composite 23–4–2 record under head coach Frank Leahy.* Lattner led the Fighting Irish his sophomore season (1951) in rushing, interceptions, fumble recoveries, and playing time. His fourth down pass from punt formation against Iowa proved the key play that kept alive a 65–yard scoring drive to tie the Hawkeyes 20–20. Notre Dame finished 7–2–1 in 1952, ranked third in the AP and UPI polls, and defeated four nationally ranked conference champions: Oklahoma, Southern California, Texas, and Purdue. The Fighting Irish tied IL titlist Pennsylvania but were outclassed 21–3 by national champion Michigan State. "Lattner is my bread and butter player," Leahy declared. "He's a wonderful competitor and clutch performer." Lattner scored the only touchdowns against Southern California and Pennsylvania, returned a punt 86 yards for a touchdown against Iowa, and achieved touchdowns against Purdue and Texas. In 57 minutes against Oklahoma, he rushed for 98 yards, caught two passes for 46 yards, punted 8 times (38–yard average), and made 6 open field tackles and 2 all-important interceptions.

Notre Dame was ranked second in the final 1953 AP and UPI polls taken before number 1 Maryland lost in the Orange Bowl. The undefeated (9–0–1) Fighting Irish were declared national champions by the HAF and by football experts Dick Dunkel, Paul Williamson, and Frank Litkenhous. In their second year as a unit, the Notre Dame backfield of Lattner, quarterback Ralph Guglielmi, halfback Joe Heap, and fullback Neil Worden resembled the celebrated 1924 Four Horsemen* and 1930 backfields. The last defender against an Oklahoma screen pass, Lattner sliced through three Sooners blockers in an open field to make the tackle in the "defensive play of the season." Later, he intercepted a Sooners pass at the Notre Dame 32–yard line to preserve the 28–21 triumph. When Georgia Tech came to South Bend, IN, with a 31–game undefeated streak, the Fighting Irish triumphed 27–14. Lattner celebrated his twenty-first birthday by setting up the first touchdown by returning the opening kickoff 80 yards, gaining 101 yards (5.0–yard average) from scrimmage, and scoring one touchdown. He returned kickoffs for touchdowns of 86 yards against Purdue and 92 yards against Pennsylvania and scored four touchdowns to help the Fighting Irish defeat Southern California 48–14 before 98,000 spectators at the Los Angeles Coliseum.

Tommy Devine of the Detroit (MI) *Press* (1953) observed, "The heat has been on Notre Dame all season long and Lattner has played his finest football when things were toughest." Although not unusually fast or shifty, nor a great passer, Lattner usually found a way to win and used consistency as his greatest asset. He threw passes on the run, made extremely high punts that prevented runbacks, and ran with intelligence in the open field. For a self-imposed penalty, he carried a football around the Notre Dame campus for a week in 1952 after fumbling five times against Michigan State. With free substitution that year, he made All-American on both offense and defense. In three college seasons he scored 120 points on 20 touchdowns, amassed 1,724 yards on 350 carries (4.9–yard average), and gained 3,116 yards of all-purpose running to rank second on the all-time Notre Dame list.

Lattner played basketball at Notre Dame as a sophomore and scored the winning basket (75–74) against New York University with nine seconds of overtime remaining. He received Air Force ROTC training and was commissioned a second lieutenant at graduation in 1954. Lattner majored in accounting and earned a B.S. degree in Business Administration. The Pittsburgh Steelers' (NFL) first draft choice in 1954, he played pro football one year and competed in the Pro Bowl. Lattner rushed 69 times for 237 yards (3.4–yard average) and 5 touchdowns and caught 25 passes for 305 yards (12.2–yard average) and 2 touchdowns. He served two years (1955–1956) in the U.S. Air Force but seriously damaged his knee in a service football game. Although returning to the Steelers in 1957, he quit football because his knee swelled and failed to respond to treatment.

Lattner served as head football coach at St. Joseph High School, Kenosha, WS (1958), and assistant coach at Denver University (RMC, 1959) before that school discontinued the sport. In Chicago he sold chemicals and opened Johnny Lattner's Steak House in 1962 in the downtown area. His Heisman Trophy melted in a restaurant fire but was replaced by the award sponsors. He operated restaurants for eleven years (one in Chicago's Marina Towers) before becoming vice president of Pal Business Forms. Lattner married Margaret (Peggy) McAllister of Chicago in 1958 and has four sons and four daughters. He still exhibits enthusiasm, a boyish face with pink cheeks, and a shock of white hair and resembles a mature Huckleberry Finn. Lattner lives with his family in Oak Park, IL, and serves on the State of Illinois Physical Fitness Committee.

BIBLIOGRAPHY: "All-American," *Time* 62 (November 9, 1953), pp. 58, 65–66, 68, 71; John T. Brady, *The Heisman: A Symbol of Excellence* (New York, 1984); William B. Furlong, "The Bashful Terror of Notre Dame, *SEP* 226 (November 14, 1953), pp. 27, 111–12; Bill Libby, *Heroes of the Heisman Trophy* (New York, 1973); Ronald L. Mendell and Timothy B. Phares, *Who's Who in Football* (New Rochelle, NY, 1974); *Notre Dame Football Guide, 1984;* Notre Dame University, Sports Information Office, August 13, 1985, South Bend, IN.

James D. Whalen

LAVELLI, Dante Bert Joseph "Gluefingers" (b. 13 February 1923, Hudson, OH), college and professional player, is the son of blacksmith Angelo and Emily Lavelli. As a teenager, Lavelli led Hudson High to three undefeated football seasons and played baseball well. He planned to attend the University of Notre Dame but enrolled at Ohio State University (WC) in 1941 after Paul Brown* was named head football coach. As a sophomore in 1942, he was injured after only a few varsity games. Lavelli joined the U.S. Army during World War II and served in France, Belgium, and Germany.

Following the war, he signed with the Cleveland Browns of the new AAFC and under coach Paul Brown. Lavelli, one of the AAFC's star players during its four-year existence, led receivers with 40 catches in 1946 and twice earned All-AAFC honors. In 1949 against the Los Angeles Dons, he caught seven passes for 209 yards and four touchdowns. He married Joy Wright on April 21, 1949, and has three children, Lucinda, Eddie, and Lisa.

Nicknamed "Gluefingers," Lavelli, according to Coach Brown, "had the strongest pair of hands I've ever seen. Nobody could take [the football] away from him once he had it in his hands." When the Browns joined the NFL in 1950, Lavelli remained among pro football's top ends. In championship games, he caught 24 passes for 340 yards and made 11 catches in the 1950 title contest. Lavelli, who was named All-NFL in 1951 and 1953 and played in three Pro Bowls, led Cleveland in receiving four times. Counting his AAFC years, he became the then Browns' career leader with 386 catches for 6,488 yards and 62 touchdowns. He was named to the NFL All-Pro squad of the 1940s and inducted in 1975 into the Pro Football Hall of Fame.

Since retiring from pro football after the 1956 season, Lavelli has owned a furniture and appliance store in Rocky Ridge, OH. He also served as assistant coach for the College All-Stars in five games and as director of NFL Alumni Association.

BIBLIOGRAPHY: Jack T. Clary, *Cleveland Browns* (New York, 1973); *Cleveland Browns Press Guides, 1950, and 1983;* Ronald L. Mendell and Timothy B. Phares, *Who's Who in Football* (New York, 1974).

Jay Langhammer

LAYDEN, Elmer F. "Thin Man." See under FOUR HORSEMEN.

LAYNE, Robert Lawrence "Bobby" "Gadabout Gladiator" (b. 19 December 1926, Santa Ana, TX; d. 1 December 1986, Lubbock, TX), college and professional player, coach, and scout, is the son of a used car salesman who died suddenly at age 37. Layne, then around seven years old, was adopted by his uncle Wade and aunt Livinia Hampton. The Hamptons eventually moved to Dallas, TX, where Layne played football with Doak Walker* at Highland Park High School. The versatile Layne played guard and single-wing tailback and held for kicker Walker. An all-around athlete, Layne played basketball and pitched an American Legion baseball team to the state championship. Layne entered the University of Texas (SWC) on a baseball scholarship in 1944 but soon joined the U.S. Merchant Marines with Walker. When World War II ended, Layne returned to Texas and Walker to SMU. Although Walker scored on a 50–yard touchdown in their first encounter in 1945, quarterback Layne made two touchdown passes to help Texas win 12–7 and capture the SWC championship. After new coach Blair Cherry introduced the T formation, Layne made several All-American football teams as a senior. Layne completed 11 of 12 passes as Texas defeated Missouri 40–27 in the 1946 Cotton Bowl. On August 17, 1947, he married coed Carol Ann Kreuger, daughter of a pioneer west Texas surgeon. They had two sons, Rob and Alan. Rob was a place-kicker for the University of Texas, while Alan played tight end at TCU.

The 6 foot, 1 inch, blue-eyed, blond, 195 pound Layne compiled a 28–0 baseball pitching record at Texas. During Layne's four years, Texas never lost an SWC baseball game. Although offered a pro baseball contract, he instead signed in 1948 with the Chicago Bears (NFL). After one season behind quarterback John Lujack,* Layne played one year with the New York Bulldogs (NFL) and was traded in 1950 to the Detroit Lions (NFL). Layne earned over $20,000 annually when the NFL mean salary was $7,500. Under the fiery leadership of the 24-year-old Layne, the Lions barely missed the National Conference title in 1951. The Lions won the NFL championship in 1952 for the first time since 1935 and repeated the next year with a 10–2 record and in 1957. With the Lions from 1950 until October 1958, Layne guided Detroit to four conference titles and three (1952, 1953, 1957) NFL crowns. From 1958 through 1962 Layne finished his career with the Pittsburgh Steelers (NFL) under Raymond "Buddy" Parker.*

During 15 NFL seasons Layne played 175 games, completed 1,814 of 3,700 passes for 26,769 yards and 196 touchdowns, and set an NFL record with 243 interceptions. Besides kicking 34 of 50 field goals and earning 120 of 124 extra points, Layne rushed for 4 yards per carry, scored 25 touchdowns, and compiled 372 career points. Layne, who played in the Pro Bowl three times (1953, 1954, 1957), and was named to three All-Pro teams (1954, 1956, and 1958), became the premier pressure-quarterback in football. In the 1953 NFL title game, Layne's late-game heroics rallied the Lions to a memorable 17–16 win over the Cleveland Browns. George Halas* stated, "If I wanted a quarterback to handle any team in the final two minutes, I'd have to send for Layne." Paul Brown* considered him "the best third down quarterback in football." Layne later coached quarterbacks for NFL Pittsburgh (1963–1965), the NFL St. Louis Cardinals (1965), and scouted for the (NFL) Dallas Cowboys (1966–1967).

Nicknamed the "Gadabout Gladiator," Layne became the original bad boy of pro football. Known for partying, he needed only five hours sleep; he once said, "I sleep fast and wake up movin'." Quarterbacks Joe Namath* and Ken Stabler* followed his controversial lead. His colorful lifestyle purportedly cost him the TCU head coaching job in the 1980s. The NFL's most spectacular quarterback of the 1950s, Layne in 1956 was elected to the Michigan Sports Hall of Fame, to the NFF College Football Hall of Fame, and in 1967 to the Pro Football Hall of Fame. He also was a member of the Pennsylvania Hall of Fame. Layne's plaque claims he "invented the beat the clock" by achieving more feats in the closing seconds than any other quarterback. On November 17, 1968, the Lions retired his uniform number, 22.

Following ventures in sporting goods and oil, the "Texas Tycoon" administered his late father-in-law's extensive estate from the Texas Commerce Bank in Lubbock. In 1962 the determined Layne co-authored *Always on Sunday*, recounting his three head-on automobile crashes. A cataract operation blinded Layne in one eye, while two throat cancer operations left his voice raspy. His flamboyant style and reputation as "Mr. Clutch" lend credibility to the belief that Layne set the standards for judging today's quarterbacks. In 1986 Layne died two days after surgery to stop hemorrhaging in his lower esophagus.

BIBLIOGRAPHY: "Bobby Layne," Detroit *News* (August 21, 1968), pp. 16, 18, 21–23; Detroit Lions, Press Release, July 13, 1950; Jerry Green, *Detroit Lions* (New York, 1973); Jim Klobuchar, "Memory Layne: Life was a Cabaret for Bobby," *Pro!* (1975), pp. 3c–6c; Bobby Layne and Bob Drum, *Always on Sunday* (Englewood Cliffs, NJ, 1962); Bobby Layne, Personal Correspondence, Detroit Lions' Archives, Pontiac, MI; "A Pride of Lions," *Time* 64 (November 29, 1954), pp. 56–62; *Quarterback* (April, 1970), pp. 58–62, 77–79; Jim Taylor, "Layne Gains Hall of Fame," Detroit *Free Press* (February 9, 1967); *TSN Football Register—1966;* Larry Upshaw, "The Heroes of Highland Park High," Dallas *Life*/Dallas *Morning News* (October 17, 1982), pp. 10–11.

Harold L. Ray

LEA, Langdon "Biffy" (b. 11 May 1874, Germantown, PA; d. 4 October 1937, Paoli, PA), college player and coach, starred as regular football tackle four years at Princeton University (IL, 1892–1895) and made the Walter Camp All-American team the last three. The Tigers captain as a senior, he played on teams compiling a combined 41–5–1 record, outscoring opponents 1,135 to 104, and holding 35 opponents scoreless. Noted coach Pop Warner* in *Leslie's Weekly* (1920) chose Lea on his All-Time All-American team. Lea, a member of the HAF College Football Hall of Fame, was named in 1964 to the NFF College Football Hall of Fame. Lea's father, Joseph Tatnall Lea, was president of Philadelphia First National Bank; his mother was Anna (Cabeen) Lea. Lea attended St. Paul's Preparatory School (Concord, NH), where he was a gridiron star at fullback and captained the team in 1891. He graduated in 1892.

Princeton won 12 games Lea's freshman year but lost to Pennsylvania and Yale. Pennsylvania's 6–4 triumph over Princeton marked the first over a Big Three power and served notice that the Quakers could compete on a regular basis. Princeton introduced wide laterals against Yale to spread the attack. Although Lea blocked an attempted field goal, Princeton succumbed to the undefeated Elis 12–0. In 1893 Princeton won the national championship with an 11–0–0 record and defeated Yale, Pennsylvania, Army, and Cornell. The Tigers' 6–0 triumph over Yale, the first in four years, ended the Elis' string of 37 consecutive victories. Lea, quarterback Phil King, and end "Doggie" Trenchard* employed the ends-back formation in handing Yale's great end

Frank Hinkey* his only career loss. "In the Yale game Lea was one of the cleverest linemen ever seen in New York," sportswriter Casper Whitney observed. "Biffy's all-around tackle play—his blocking and tackling—was unsurpassed."

Hard feelings among alumni and spectators following undefeated Pennsylvania's 12–0 victory over Princeton in 1894 caused a break in the series until 1935. The Tigers lost also to undefeated Yale, 24–0, but triumphed over eight other opponents. Captain Lea in 1895 rushed for substantial yardage against Harvard but suffered a broken collarbone and was forced to leave the game, won by Princeton 12–4. Wearing a protective brace, Lea played with sheer fortitude and nerve against Yale. Lea kicked off and played end until reinjured in the second half, as the Elis triumphed 20–10. The Tigers finished 10–1–1, being tied by Orange Athletic Club and defeating Cornell, Lafayette, and Rutgers. Lea served as Princeton freshman class president and sophomore vice president, belonged to the Ivy Club, and probably graduated in 1896. His classmates voted him the "best football player" and "handsomest and most popular man of '96."

Former stars then assisted the captain in preparing the football varsity each fall. Lea helped coach Princeton (1896–1899) to a share of three national championships and then coached (1900) the University of Michigan (WC) to a 7–2–1 record. His players formed the nucleus of Fielding Yost's* first "point-a-minute" Wolverines the following year. Lea returned to Princeton (1901) as head coach, leading the Tigers to a 9–1–1 record. He joined the Cannelton Coal Company, Cannelton, WV, in 1896 and served as manager, general superintendent, and member of the board of directors until retirement in 1934. He married Lavilla Belknap Lyons of Charlottesville, VA, in 1902 and had three sons and one daughter. His sons later played regular at end on outstanding Princeton football teams (Francis, 1927; Langdon, 1932; and Gilbert, 1936). Lea died of a heart attack.

BIBLIOGRAPHY: Richard M. Cohen, Jordan A. Deutsch, and David S. Neft, *The University of Michigan Football Scrapbook* (Indianapolis, IN, 1978); Parke H. Davis, *Football: The American Intercollegiate Game* (New York, 1911); Jay Dunn, *The Tigers of Princeton: Old Nassau Football* (Huntsville, AL, 1977); Ronald L. Mendell and Timothy B. Phares, *Who's Who in Football* (New Rochelle, NY, 1974); Princeton–Pennsylvania Football Game Program, November 2, 1892; Princeton–Yale Football Game Program, November 23, 1895; Seeley G. Mudd Manuscript Library, Princeton University Archives, Princeton, NJ; Alexander M. Weyand, *American Football: Its History and Development* (New York, 1926).

James D. Whalen

LEAHY, Francis William "Frank" (b. 27 August 1908, O'Neill, NE; d. 21 June 1973, Portland, OR), college player and coach, amassed a composite 107–13–9 record (.864 percent) to rank second to Knute Rockne* among college football coaches with a minimum of ten years service. As coach two seasons at Boston College (1939–1940) and eleven campaigns at Notre Dame (1941–1943, 1946–1953), Leahy fielded seven undefeated and five national championship teams. Twenty-two of his players made consensus All-American, while seventeen won national trophy awards, including the Heisman (4), Camp (5), Maxwell (3), Rockne (3), and Outland (2). The AFCA Coach of the Year (1941) and FWAA Man of the Year (1949), Leahy was named to the NFF College Football Hall of Fame (1970) and the HAF College Football Hall of Fame. He served as head coach of the 1947–1948 College All-Stars, which defeated the NFL Chicago Bears 16–0 and lost to the Chicago Cardinals 28–0.

The son of Frank and Mary Winifred (Kane) Leahy, he grew up in Winner, SD. His articulate, pioneer-rugged father owned a freight and produce business and wrestled all challengers. Leahy attended Winner grammar school and played halfback three years at Winner High School. Lacking some courses necessary to enter Notre Dame, Leahy spent his final year at Omaha (NE) Central High School. He was shifted to tackle on the football team and graduated in 1927. After being Notre Dame freshman class president and football center, Leahy played three games at tackle as a 6 foot, 190 pound sophomore and started at tackle as a junior on the Fighting Irish 1929 9–0–0 national championship team. A pre-season knee injury requiring surgery prevented his playing in 1930. Ailing coach Rockne invited Leahy to share a room at Mayo Clinic, where he learned football tactics from one of the game's immortals. Leahy graduated in 1931 from Notre Dame with a B.S. in Physical Education.

Leahy served as football line coach at Georgetown (DC) University (1931), Michigan State College (WC, 1932), and Fordham University (1933–1938) under coach Jimmy Crowley.* Leahy helped develop the famous Seven Blocks of Granite line, which lost two games in three years and boasted three future NFF College Football Hall of Fame members. After becoming head football coach in 1939 at Boston College, he directed the Eagles with quarterback Charlie O'Rourke and end Gene Goodreault to their first Bowl games (a 6–3 Cotton Bowl loss to Clemson and 19–13 Sugar Bowl upset win over Tennessee), an undefeated season (1940), and number 5 national ranking.

Leahy coached Notre Dame to an undefeated season and number 3 national ranking his first year (1941) there and startled many Fighting Irish alumni and friends in 1942 by switching from the Rockne system to the T formation. "If Rock were alive," Leahy declared, "he would be the first to try it." Leahy's first national championship squad came the following season, when quarterback Angelo Bertelli* and halfback Creighton Miller led the Fighting Irish to a 9–1–0 record and played seven of the top twelve AP poll teams. After serving in the Pacific as a U.S. Navy lieutenant during World War II (1944–1945), Leahy returned to Notre Dame. Over the next four seasons (1946–1949), his Irish teams achieved a 37–0–2 record and featured all-time great quarterback Johnny Lujack,* tackle George Connor,* guard Bill Fischer,* and end Leon Hart.*

The perfectionist introvert proved overly modest and was known well by very few. Rockne had won the admiration of defeated opponents, but Leahy unintentionally alienated foes with his predictions of doom and the aloofness and stilted manner of speech inherited from his father. When Heisman Trophy winner Johnny Lattner* fumbled five times against Michigan State, Leahy admonished, "Oooooh, Jonathan Lattner. Oooooh, you heretic, Jonathan Lattner. What am I to do with you?" When Leahy used the sucker shift (1952) against Southern California and feigned injuries (1953) against Iowa to gain a tie, he created a furor. Memorable games of Leahy's coaching career included Boston College's 19–18 triumph over undefeated Georgetown (1940), Notre Dame's 35–12 rout of undefeated Michigan (1943), Great Lakes' 19–14 last-minute victory (1943) that spoiled a perfect Fighting Irish season, Notre Dame's much-publicized 0–0 tie with Army (Doc Blanchard* and Glenn Davis*) that spoiled two perfect records (1946), its last-minute comeback 14–14 tie with Southern California preserving an undefeated season (1948), its hard-earned 27–20 victory over SMU to complete a perfect season (1949), and its 27–21 triumph over coach Charles "Bud" Wilkinson's* otherwise undefeated Oklahoma Sooners (1952).

Leahy married Florence "Floss" Reilly of Brooklyn, NY, in 1936 and had five sons and three daughters. Leahy left coaching at the end of his final undefeated season (1953), having collapsed with acute pancreatitis during halftime of the Georgia Tech game. He became an insurance executive, president of All-Star Sports Associates public relations firm, and vice president of the Merritt, Chapman and Scott construction firm. He enjoyed amateur boxing as a youth and was appointed by Pope Pius XII in 1949 to the Knights of Malta, an exclusive worldwide Catholic clergy–lay group. Leahy, who wrote the book *Notre Dame Football, The T-Formation* (1949), developed leukemia and died of heart failure.

BIBLIOGRAPHY: Si Burick, Dayton (OH) *Daily News*, March 19, 1954; Edward Fitzgerald, "Frank Leahy . . . The Enigma of Notre Dame," *Sport* 8 (November 1949), pp. 16–21, 72–78; Edwin Pope, *Football's Greatest Coaches* (Atlanta, 1956); Wells Twombly, *Shake Down the Thunder: The Official Biography of Notre Dame's Frank Leahy* (Radnor, PA, 1974).

James D. Whalen

LEEMANS, Alphonse E. "Tuffy" (b. 12 November 1912, Superior, WI; d. 19 January 1979, Hillsboro Beach, FL), college and professional player, was the son of a Belgian miner-immigrant. Leemans, who built up his body as a youngster by juggling iron ore, was nicknamed "Tuffy" because he once dumped two larger, older boys in football. At George Washington University (SC) from 1932 to 1936, he gained 2,382 yards on 490 attempts and earned

MVP honors his final year. In the 1936 College All-Star game, he helped the collegians to a 7–7 tie with the 1935 NFL champion Detroit Lions. Upon the recommendation of 19–year old Wellington Mara, the New York Football Giants drafted him second in 1936 (NFL's first draft) and signed him for $3,000.

From 1936 to 1943 the 6 foot, 185 pound Leemans played for the Giants under coach Steve Owen.* He became an integral part of the Giants by calling signals from his right halfback position, where he ran, passed, and received, and also played defense with the era's best. As a rookie he became the first Giant to lead the NFL in rushing with 830 yards. Careerwise, Leemans rushed for 3,117 yards, compiled five 100–yard rushing games, passed for 2,324 yards, and scored 19 touchdowns. He made the All-Pro team in 1936, the only rookie to do so, and repeated in 1939. During his tenure the Giants posted a 53–27–8 record, appeared in three championship games (1938–1939, 1941), and captured the 1938 NFL title by defeating the Green Bay Packers. For his accomplishments, the Giants retired his number 4 jersey.

In 1942 against the Chicago Bears, he suffered a severe blow to his head and lost the hearing in one ear. This injury kept him out of military service. Following his 1943 retirement, he resided in the Washington, DC, area, became a successful businessman, and owned a mini-bowling lane in suburban Maryland. He and his wife, Theodora, had one daughter, Diane, and one son, Joseph. The first Giant to rush for over 3,000 career yards, Leemans was inducted in 1978 into the Pro Football Hall of Fame. According to *NYT* sportswriter Arthur Daley* (OS), Leemans "was a marvel, always the clutch guy for the fourth-down slash and rarely failing."

BIBLIOGRAPHY: Dave Klein, *The New York Giants: Yesterday, Today, and Tomorrow* (Chicago, 1973); Ronald L. Mendell and Timothy B. Phares, *Who's Who in Football* (New Rochelle, NY, 1974); *New York Giants Media Guide, 1982; NYT*, January 20, 1979, p. 26; Paul Soderberg and Helen Washington, eds., *The Big Book of Halls of Fame in the U.S. and Canada Sport* (New York, 1977).

Donald E. Kosakowski

LILLY, Robert Lewis "Bob" (b. 26 July 1939, Olney, TX), college and professional player, is the son of John and Margaret Louise (Redwine) Lilly. His father worked as a garage owner–mechanic, bulldozer operator, and haybailer contractor. Lilly starred in football, basketball, and track at Throckmorton (TX) High School before his family moved to Pendleton, OR. In his senior year at Pendleton High School, he made All-American end in football, All-State in basketball averaging 27 points a game, and won the state javelin championship. Lilly entered TCU (SWC) on a football scholarship in the fall, 1957. As a sophomore, he started at tackle and played in the Cotton Bowl against the Air Force Academy. During his junior year

Lilly was elected All-SWC by averaging eight tackles a game and recovering seven fumbles. He was named the outstanding lineman in the first Bluebonnet Bowl, although TCU lost 23–7 to Clemson. Lilly, a consensus All-American as a senior, played in the post-season Shrine All-Star (East-West), Hula Bowl, College All-Star, and Coaches All-America games. TCU coach Abe Martin called Lilly the best tackle he ever coached.

The Dallas Cowboys' first-round draft pick in 1961, Lilly played defensive end and was named to the NFL All-Rookie team. He married Katharine Waltman in December 1961 and has three children, Robert, Jr., Katharine Michelle, and Christienne Marie. He later divorced and then wed Margaret Ann Threlkeld on June 22, 1972, and has one son, Mark. Following his second season, Lilly made the Pro Bowl squad, the first of eleven such selections. Midway through the 1963 season, Cowboys head coach Tom Landry* shifted Lilly to defensive tackle. Lilly developed into one of the premier linemen in NFL history. Relying on upper body strength and quickness, the very durable 6 foot, 5 inch, 260 pounder played in 196 consecutive regular season games. He earned All-Pro honors seven times and played in two Super Bowls before retiring after the 1974 season.

Lilly was elected to the Pro Football Hall of Fame in 1980 and the NFF College Football Hall of Fame the following year. A member of the Texas Sports Hall of Fame, he was the first player named to the Dallas Cowboys Ring of Honor. Since retiring, Lilly has appeared frequently on television as a spokesman for numerous products. He also was engaged in a beer distributorship in Waco, TX, for several years and in 1983 co-authored *Bob Lilly: Reflections*, a book of photos taken during his pro career. The Pro Football Hall of Fame named him to its AFL-NFL 1960–1984 All-Star Team.

BIBLIOGRAPHY: *Dallas Cowboys Press Guides, 1961, 1975;* Bob Lilly and Sam Blair, *Bob Lilly: Reflections* (Dallas, TX, 1983); *Texas Christian University Football Press Guides*, 1960, 1983; Richard Whittingham, *The Dallas Cowboys: An Illustrated History* (New York, 1981).

Jay Langhammer

LIPSCOMB, Gene Allen "Big Daddy" (b. 9 November 1931, Detroit, MI; d. 10 May 1963, Baltimore, MD), professional football player and wrestler, never knew his father, who reportedly died in a Civilian Conservation Corps camp when Gene was a youngster. When Gene was 11 years old, his mother was murdered by a male acquaintance who stabbed her 47 times while she waited for a bus. He grew up with his maternal grandfather, who yelled at him and whipped him throughout much of his adolescence. As a youth, Lipscomb loaded trucks at a construction site and worked as a junkyard helper and dishwasher. He toiled at a steel mill from midnight to eight before going to class at Miller High School. At age 16 he quit school to join the U.S. Marine Corps and continued participating in football. Lipscomb had played football only one season at "Miller Tech," as he later referred to it when his teammates kidded him about his lack of a college education. Miller awarded Lipscomb his diploma in 1960 when he was 28.

At Camp Pendleton, CA, Lipscomb first made his gridiron reputation. His teammates started calling him "Big Daddy" because he could not remember any of his teammates' names and always referred to them as "little daddy." The Los Angeles Rams (NFL) signed him as an unseasoned rookie in 1953, but Lipscomb never established himself. The Baltimore Colts (NFL) signed him for the $100 waiver price in 1956. He made All-Pro three times (1957–1959) as a Colt, leading them to two championships. Lipscomb was fast and agile for a 6 foot, 6 inch, 288 pounder whose play made him one of the first defensive linemen to develop a separate personality much like the flashy halfbacks he terrorized. His philosophy was "I just grab an armful of men, pick them over until I find the one with the ball, and then I throw him down." Lipscomb, a good sportsman, always helped up the back he had just tackled because he did not want people to regard him as a mean player. He participated in the great Baltimore front four, which included Gino Marchetti,* Art Donovan,* and Don Joyce. He made a key play in the highly publicized championship game against the New York Giants on December 28, 1958, recovering a Frank Gifford* fumble.

The Colts traded Lipscomb in 1961 to the Pittsburgh Steelers (NFL), to whom he belonged when he experienced an acute reaction to a $12 bag of heroin on May 10, 1963, near the "Block" in Baltimore. His friends had a very hard time believing he died that way. A non-intoxicating amount of liquor in his system contributed to his death. Lipscomb was known for his fast cars, three wives, and many girlfriends and was divorced three times. Lipscomb once said of his second wife, "I don't mind losing her so much, but I sure minded losing my 1956 Mercury to her." He earned a peak $15,000 playing football, supplemented by over $40,000 earned each year in pro wrestling. He made one interception and scored two points in his 10–year pro career.

BIBLIOGRAPHY: Weeb Ewbank, *Goal to Go: The Greatest Football Games I Have Coached* (New York, 1972); Mickey Herskowitz, *The Golden Age of Pro Football* (New York, 1974); Ed Linn, "The End of Big Daddy Lipscomb," *SEP* 236 (July 27, 1963), p. 734; "Milestones," *Time* 81 (May 17, 1963), p. 101; Daniel Schwartz, "A Requiem for Big Daddy," *Esquire Magazine* 60 (September, 1963), pp. 88–89.

William A. Borst

LITTLE, Floyd (b. 4 July 1942, New Haven, CT), college and professional player, is the son of Fred Little, a factory worker who died in 1948, and Lula Little, who supported her family by becoming a clothes presser. Little, an explosive running back with great speed and exceptional balance, remained shy and introspective from childhood. Little's early poor health and lack of interest in school delayed his graduation from Hill House High School in New Haven, where he was named a prep school football All-American in 1962. He subsequently attended Bordentown (NJ) Military Academy to prepare for college. The 5 foot, 10 inch, 196 pound Little was recruited highly by several major colleges when it became clear that he could succeed scholastically in university work. He narrowed his choice to Notre Dame and Syracuse University, choosing the latter because of a personal appeal by Ernie Davis* shortly before leukemia killed him. Like Davis and Jim Brown* earlier, Little wore number 44 at Syracuse. He combined with Larry Csonka* to form the mid-1960s most formidable backfield.

At Syracuse, Little earned a double major in History and Religion and became both an extremely popular player and team leader. The three-time football All-American (1964–1966) scored five touchdowns in his first college game and recorded 46 tallies for his college career. His nineteen touchdowns in 1965 led the nation. He starred in the 1967 Gator Bowl, setting the then single-game rushing record for that event. His 5,529 total yards over his career at Syracuse guaranteed him high recruitment by both the NFL and AFL. Little signed with the Denver Broncos (AFL) in 1967, making him the first number 1 draft choice ever signed by that club. He played with Denver until retiring in 1975, when his 6,323 total career yards placed him twentieth among all-time leading rushers in NFL history. He scored 54 career touchdowns and made the All-NFL squad (1969–1971), the only 1,000–yard season in his career. In 1971 he led the AFC in rushing and was named Outstanding Pro Back by the FWAA. An All-Pro selection in 1971–1972 and 1974, he tied for the AFC lead in passing receptions (12) in 1973 and won the coveted Brian Piccolo Award.

Little's popularity in Denver reflected his athletic prowess. His constant dedication to community service projects captured the hearts of Denver residents. He worked in drug abuse programs and with disadvantaged children, whose lives resembled his own. The exemplary family man married Joyce Green, whom he met at Syracuse and who teaches biology, and has two daughters, Christy and Kyra. The personally modest Little possesses a rare sense of perspective on the importance of athletics in society. On several occasions he publicly has criticized other players for their avarice. He earned a Master's degree from Denver University School of Law in 1975, entered management training with the Adolph Coors Company, worked for two years for NBC Sports, and subsequently worked for Ford Motor Company. Since 1979 Little has operated successful Lincoln/Mercury dealerships in California. He is a member of the NFF College Football Hall of Fame.

BIBLIOGRAPHY: Gerald Astor, "Floyd Little: Portrait of an All-American," *Look* 30 (November 1, 1966), pp. 90–92; Pete Axthelm, "The Year of the Runner," *Newsweek* 80 (December 4, 1972), pp. 76–84; *Black Sports* (May, 1976); Myron Cope," Half a Glass of Fresh Blood on Saturday Morning," *SEP* 239 (November 19, 1966), pp. 84–86; "Floyd Little on the Run," *Ebony* 21 (December, 1965); Floyd Little to Charles

R. Middleton, October 19, 1984; Ronald L. Mendell and Timothy B. Phares, *Who's Who in Football* (New Rochelle, NY, 1974); Roger Treat, ed., *The Encyclopedia of Football*, 16th ed., rev. by Pete Palmer (New York, 1979); *WWA*, 38th ed. (1974–1975), p. 1,895.

Charles R. Middleton

LITTLE, Louis Lawrence "Lou" (b. 6 December 1893, Boston, MA; d. 28 May 1979, Delray Beach, FL), college and professional player and coach, was a 6 foot, 2 inch, 220 pound University of Pennsylvania (IL) football player and coached Columbia University (IL) to one of the greatest upsets in football history in the 1934 Rose Bowl. The son of contractor Michael and Theresa Little, he grew up in Leominster, MA, played football, basketball, and baseball at Leominster High School before graduating in 1912, and studied one year at Worcester (MA) Academy. Seeking a pre-medical degree at the University of Vermont, southpaw Little studied dentistry and later switched to the liberal arts. Little enrolled at the University of Pennsylvania in 1915 and starred at tackle on the 1916 and 1919 teams, which compiled a composite 13–5–2 record and lost 14–0 to the University of Oregon in the 1919 Rose Bowl. He received first team All-American mention in 1916 from *The Pennsylvanian*, Nathan A. Tufts (football official), and the Philadelphia *Evening Telegraph* and played with Bert Bell,* Howard Berry, and Heinie Miller. Little left Pennsylvania before graduation in 1920 and joined the Buffalo All-Americans, who finished second in the 1921 NFL season with a 9–1–2 record. He served as football player-coach of the Frankford (PA) Yellow Jackets in 1922–1923 and worked as a bond salesman during the off-seasons.

From 1924 to 1929 Little coached the Georgetown Hoyas (Washington, DC) to a 41–12–3 composite football record (.759 percent). Georgetown defeated Fordham, Syracuse, West Virginia, Boston College, Duke, and New York University, tied Pittsburgh and Navy, and produced 275–pound consensus All-American guard, Harry Connaughton. In 1930 Little was lured to Columbia University as football coach and athletic director for a reported $18,000 salary, among the highest at the time. Little developed outstanding teams, losing only one game each year from 1931 through 1934. His 1933 squad, quarterbacked by Cliff Montgomery, defeated highly favored Stanford University 7–0 in the Rose Bowl on the storied reverse 17–yard touchdown run by Al Barabas. Although the Lions encountered less success in later years, Little coached excellent passers Sid Luckman,* Maxwell Award winner Paul Governali, and Gene Rossides. Between 1945 and 1947 the Lions finished 21–6–0 and ended Army's 32–game unbeaten streak with a thrilling 21–20 victory. Four Little teams attained high ranking, namely, 1933 (9th), 1934 (8th), 1945 (20th), and 1947 (20th).

Known for his gourmet appetite, prominent nose, pince-nez, and husky voice, Little wore natty attire and once owned 50 suits. Besides insisting that his players be polite and neatly dressed, he wrote newsletters to his former players every three months. He was beloved at Columbia, despite his combined 27–year record of 110–116–10 (.487 percent). In 1956 *NYT* sportswriter Arthur Daley* (OS) wrote, "If he had a winning season, it was nice, but it wasn't necessary. Even the alumni could understand." Little, a member of the HAF College Football Hall of Fame, was elected in 1960 to the NFF College Football Hall of Fame. He chaired the AFCA rules committee (1934–1958) and presided over the AFCA (1939). The New York Touchdown Club (1943) honored Little for contributions to the game. He in 1954 became the first coach to receive a silver plaque from the FWAA. The plaque read "with esteem and affection" on his twenty-fifth anniversary as coach at Columbia.

During World War I, Little participated as an infantry captain and served in the Meuse-Argonne sector. Little, who married Loretta Tuttle in 1929 and had no children, retired from Columbia in 1957 and consulted for Canada Dry Company. The author of *Lou Little's Football* (1934) and *How to Watch Football* (1935), he left most of his estate to Columbia University.

BIBLIOGRAPHY: Morris A. Bealle, *The Georgetown Hoyas* (Washington, DC, 1947); Tim Cohane, *Great College Football Coaches of the Twenties and Thirties* (New Rochelle, NY, 1973); Lou Little, "Who's to Blame For Football's Troubles?" *Look* 21 (December 10, 1957), pp. 71–74; John D. McCallum and Charles H. Pearson, *College Football U.S.A., 1869–1973* (New York, 1973); Ronald L. Mendell and Timothy B. Phares, *Who's Who in Football* (New Rochelle, NY, 1974); William Peters, "Columbia Gets a Lot with a Little," *SI* 1 (November 29, 1954); Edwin Pope, *Football's Greatest Coaches* (Atlanta, 1956).

James D. Whalen

LOFTON, James David (b. 5 July 1956, Fort Ord, CA), college and professional player, ranks among the most versatile NFL receivers. He began his football career as a quarterback at Washington High School in Los Angeles. A wide receiver at Stanford University (PEC) during the mid-1970s, Lofton earned All-American honors his senior year by leading the PEC with 68 receptions for 1,216 yards and pacing the nation with 16 touchdown receptions.

A first-round draft choice of the Green Bay Packers (NFL) in 1978, Lofton quickly impressed the pros with three touchdown receptions against the New Orleans Saints on September 10, 1978. Lofton's play earned him the NFC Rookie of the Year title and All-Pro honors. Since 1979 he has appeared in six Pro Bowls. Lofton ranks first on the Packers' all-time reception list with 530 catches for 9,656 yards and has scored 49 touchdowns. In 1981 and 1982 he set individual records with 71 receptions. He led the NFL with a 22.4–yard average per reception in 1983 and 22.0 yards per reception in 1984 and a career-high 69 receptions in 1985. The versatile Lofton has rushed for 245 yards and one touchdown on 31 carries and scampered 83 yards against the

New York Giants in 1983 for the third longest run from scrimmage in Packers history. Against the Baltimore Colts in 1982, he demonstrated his quarterback skill with a 43–yard completion to John Jefferson.*

The very athletic Lofton enjoyed considerable success in track and field at Stanford. A world-class sprinter and long jumper, he won the 1978 NCAA long jump at 27 feet and clocked 20.7 seconds for 200 meters and 46.6 seconds for 400 meters. Like other talented football and track performers, Lofton chose the security of a pro athletic career over possible Olympic fame. In light of the 1980 Olympic boycott, he certainly made the right decision.

Holding a B.S. in Industrial Engineering from Stanford, Lofton serves as team representative and an officer in the NFL Players Association. Lofton, whose wife, Beverly, is a professional entertainer, has one son, David James. A successful businessman off the field, Lofton is both the chief executive of his own advertising and public relations firm and a television producer. He also participates in various charitable and cultural activities. Loften was suspended for the final game of the 1986 season because of an alleged sexual assault charge. In May 1987 he was traded to the Los Angeles Raiders (NFL).

BIBLIOGRAPHY: Tom Jordon, "The Clock Runs Out," *Track and Field News* (May, 1978); "NCAA Championships: They Don't Come Any Better," *Track and Field News* (August, 1978); Public Relations Office, Green Bay Packers, Green Bay, WI, September, 1984; *TSN Football Register—1986*.

Adam R. Hornbuckle

LOMBARDI, Vincent Thomas "Vince" (b. 11 June 1913, Brooklyn, NY; d. 3 September 1970, Washington, DC), college player and professional coach and general manager, guided the Green Bay Packers (NFL) to six Western Conference championships, five NFL titles, and two Super Bowl championships in nine years (1959–1967). He served as head coach one year (1969) with the Washington Redskins (NFL). Lombardi amassed a career composite 96–34–6 (.728 percent) regular season NFL record and finished 10–2–0 in post-season play. He received the Distinguished American Award in 1970 from the NFF Hall of Fame and was elected in 1971 to the Pro Football Hall of Fame. The son of Italian immigrants, Lombardi lived in modest comfort as a child. His father, Harry, the neighborhood butcher, remained supportive during Lombardi's five years of study for the Catholic priesthood at Brooklyn's Cathedral Preparatory Seminary. Lombardi's zest for football, developed during occasional sandlot games, helped influence his decision in 1932 to transfer to Brooklyn's St. Francis Prep for his final school year. The fullback became an All-City performer and earned a scholarship to Fordham University in New York City.

Switched to guard with the Fordham Rams, the 5 foot, 11 inch, 188 pound Lombardi proved a short-fused scrapper with a violent charge off the line of scrimmage. He failed to letter in 1934 as a sophomore but started the next two seasons under coach Jimmy Crowley.* Fordham achieved 6–1–2 and 5–1–2 records in 1935 and 1936 and finished eleventh (Dickinson) and fifteenth (AP) in final national ratings. The Rams played two scoreless ties with highly ranked Pittsburgh and spoiled New York University's perfect slate in 1935 with a season-ending 21–0 triumph, but suffered a similar setback 7–6 the following year to the Violets. Lombardi played on Fordham's famed Seven Blocks of Granite forward wall that included NFF College Football Hall of Fame members Alex Wojciechowicz* (center) and Ed Franco (tackle). The line held eight of 17 opponents scoreless and allowed 4.4 points per game. In 1936 the Rams defeated Purdue, SMU, and St. Mary's (CA) before being tied 7–7 by Georgia and losing the final game to New York University. Quarterback Andy Palau called a successful play repeatedly against Pittsburgh in which Lombardi trapped All-American tackle Tony Matisi. Lombardi caught an elbow in the mouth early in the fray but played sixty minutes with his mouth full of blood from a cut requiring thirty stitches.

Lombardi made the Dean's List four years at Fordham University and graduated cum laude in 1937 with a B.S. degree. He attended Fordham Law School at night, worked as an insurance investigator during the day, and played minor league football with the Brooklyn Eagles on weekends. From 1939 to 1946 Lombardi taught chemistry, physics, and Latin and coached varsity football, basketball, and baseball at St. Cecilia High School in Englewood, NJ. His football teams won thirty-six consecutive games and six state championships, while his 1945 basketball team garnered the New Jersey parochial school title. After serving as Fordham freshman football coach (1947) and varsity assistant coach (1948) under Ed Danowski, he became Earl Blaik's* offensive line coach (1949–1953) at the U.S. Military Academy. Army dropped one game in two years before losing forty-four players involved in the 1951 Honor Code violations. The Army football program rebounded and finished 7–1–1 in Lombardi's last season there. Blaik influenced Lombardi more than Danowski did, lessening Lombardi's temper and teaching him poise, self-control, organization, and total commitment.

Former Fordham classmate and New York Giants' owner Wellington Mara hired Lombardi to direct the offense for Jim Lee Howell's coaching staff. Lombardi served there from 1954 to 1958, helping the Giants win two Eastern Conference titles and their first NFL championship (1956) in eighteen years. Despite Lombardi's obvious coaching ability, he was bypassed when several excellent head coaching positions opened. In the meantime, the Green Bay Packers had played eleven years without a winning season, averaged under four victories a year, and finished 1–10–1 in 1958. Lombardi's coaching opportunity finally came in 1959, when he was chosen to lead the Packers. As head coach and general manager, he demanded and received absolute authority to set salaries, hire and fire personnel, and design uniforms. Through bold and shrewd trades, he guided the Packers to a 7–5–0 finish his first season. He made third stringer Bart Starr* his regular quarterback, promoted reserve fullback Jim Taylor* to the first team, and switched part-time quarterback Paul Hornung* to full-time running back. Hornung scored an NFL record 176 points in 1960 and won three consecutive scoring titles, while Taylor achieved 1,000–plus yards rushing during five seasons.

Lombardi's playbooks were slim. "Football is two things," he emphasized, "blocking and tackling." The coach of many moods knew intuitively what would work to inspire the Packers. The players always addressed him as "Mister" or "Coach," never "Vince." He was as stern on a veteran as on a rookie and displayed occasional humor, but most often his player sessions were strictly business. Green Bay finished 8–4–0 in 1960 to win the Western Conference title but lost 17–13 to the Philadelphia Eagles in the NFL championship game. Lombardi was named 1961 Pro Coach of the Year by the Washington (DC) Touchdown Club after guiding the Packers to the first of two consecutive NFL championships. Green Bay defeated the Giants 37–0 and 16–7 in the 1961 and 1962 title games. Lombardi built pride and mutual esteem among his players, including offensive guard Jerry Kramer,* running back Elijah Pitts, defensive end William "Willie" Davis,* offensive tackle Forrest Gregg,* linebacker Ray Nitschke,* and defensive back Herb Adderley.* Green Bay won three more NFL titles (1965–1967) under Lombardi, defeating the Cleveland Browns once and Dallas Cowboys twice in championship games. The Packers captured the first two Super Bowls in 1966 and 1967 with 35–10 and 33–14 triumphs over AFL champion Kansas City and Oakland.

Lombardi retired from coaching in 1968 but continued as the Packers' general manager. Anxious to return to coaching, he in 1969 became coach and general manager of the Washington Redskins (NFL) with 5 percent ownership of the club. Lombardi guided the Redskins, with star quarterback Christian "Sonny" Jurgensen* and linebacker Robert Sam Huff,* to a 7–5–2 finish and their first winning season in fourteen years. "Winning isn't everything, it's the only thing" was his credo. He pitted strength against strength and taught zone blocking to facilitate more efficient "runs to daylight." Since Lombardi demanded promptness, his players set their watches ahead 10 minutes on what they called "Lombardi time." "If he coached through fear," *NYT* sportswriter Arthur Daley* (OS) once said, "it has to be a left-handed tribute to the overwhelming strength of the man that he could command such iron discipline in an era when men sneered contemptuously at authority."

After a five-year courtship, Lombardi in 1940 married Marie Planitz of Red Bank, NJ. The deeply religious Lombardi displayed warmth and sentiment around his family and close friends. He took the Redskins job on condition that his son, Vincent, Jr., and daughter, Susan, would move their families to Washington, DC, so he could be near them. The sports world was shaken in 1970 when Lombardi died of cancer in Georgetown University Hospital. A funeral mass was held in his honor at New York's St. Patrick's

Cathedral. "It's like losing a father," Starr lamented. "Fellows that played under him are better people for it." The street on which the Packers offices are located was renamed Lombardi Avenue, while the Super Bowl Trophy is now called the Lombardi Trophy. Perhaps Jerry Kramer summed up the Lombardi mystique best in his book *Instant Replay:* "Lombardi was a cruel, kind, tough, gentle, miserable, wonderful man whom I often hate and often love and always respect." The Pro Football Hall of Fame named him co-coach of the AFL-NFL 1960–1984 All-Star team.

BIBLIOGRAPHY: Tim Cohane, *Bypaths of Glory: A Sportswriter Looks Back* (New York, 1963); Arthur Daley, "Sports of the Times," *NYT* (September 3, 1970); Fordham–Purdue Football Game Program, November 7, 1936; Ralph Hickok, *Who Was Who in American Sports* (New York, 1971); Ronald L. Mendell and Timothy B. Phares, *Who's Who in Football* (New Rochelle, NY, 1974); Al Silverman, ed., *Lombardi* (New York, 1970); *Time* 80 (December 21, 1962), pp. 56–61.

James D. Whalen

LONG, Charles "Chuck" (b. 18 February 1963, Norman, OK), college and professional player, is the son of Charles and Joan Long and graduated from Wheaton (IL) North High School in 1981. The seven-time letterman in football, basketball, and baseball captained the football and baseball teams as a senior. Long, whose football squad won the State 4A football title his junior season, was selected first team football All-State in 1980. The 6 foot, 4 inch, 213 pound quarterback graduated from the University of Iowa (BTC) in December 1985 with a Bachelor's degree in Business. In 1981 Long only played a few downs against Northwestern University and Washington in the Rose Bowl. After starting the 1982 season opener and then losing his job, he became the number 1 signal caller for the third game. Long set then-Iowa records for season pass completions (65.2) and consecutive completions (11 against Tennessee in the Peach Bowl). He set Peach Bowl records for yards passing (304) and total offense (306) and tied the mark for touchdown passes (3), being named the game's MVP. For the season, he threw for 1,678 yards, ran for 121 yards, and accounted for 15 touchdowns.

Long completed his second season (1983) as a starter, winning All-BTC honors and Iowa's MVP accolades. In 1983 he completed 157 of 265 passes for 14 touchdowns and 2,601 yards and finished second nationally in passing efficiency with a 160.4 rating. Besides surpassing 200 yards passing in eight games, he recorded a season-high four touchdown passes against the University of Wisconsin, tied the Hawkeyes mark with 11 consecutive completions, and was the only quarterback nationally to average over 10 yards per pass attempt (10.31 yards). The Hawkeyes lost 14–6 to the University of Florida in the Gator Bowl. Long in 1984 finished seventh in the balloting for the Heisman Trophy, being named first team All-BTC and honorable mention All-American. He passed for 2,871 yards (a Hawkeyes record), completed 216 passes with a 67.1 completion percentage (both school marks), finished fifth nationally in passing efficiency, and broke the NCAA record by completing 22 consecutive passes against Indiana. Long paced the BTC in passing efficiency and enjoyed a record-breaking performance in the Freedom Bowl victory over the University of Texas by completing 29 of 39 passes for 461 yards and 6 touchdowns (Hawkeyes school records). He set an all-time bowl record with six scoring passes against the Longhorns, earning him game MVP honors.

A consensus first team All-American in 1985, Long won the Maxwell Award, finished second in the Heisman Trophy voting, was named the BTC's first team quarterback and MVP, and received the Davey O'Brien National Quarterback Award. The Hawkeyes captain completed 260 of 388 passes (67.0 percent) for 3,297 yards and 27 touchdowns, all Iowa records. He was ranked third nationally in passing and second in BTC total offense. His 89–yard touchdown pass to Robert Smith was the second longest in Iowa history. The Hawkeyes lost 45–28 to the University of California at Los Angeles in the Rose Bowl, after which Long played in the Japan Bowl. A bachelor, Long holds the Hawkeyes football marks for yards passing, completions, touchdown passes, and total offense in a game, season, and career and for pass attempts in a season and career. He threw for over 200 yards in 27 games and surpassed 100 yards in 42 of his last 47 contests. Long's career passing totals included 1,203 attempts (first in Iowa history), 782 completions (first), 74 touchdowns (first), and 10,461 yards (first). The BTC's all-time leader in passing and total offense and BTC 1986 Men's Athlete of the Year, Long also set BTC records for touchdown passes in a game, season, and career. In NCAA history, he ranks third in career passing efficiency and sixth in passing yards. In 1986 he was selected by the Detroit Lions in the first round of the NFL draft. After holding out at spring training camp, Long signed a four-year contract worth $1.75 million and threw for a touchdown on his first professional pass. In 1986 Long completed 21 of 40 passes for 247 yards and 2 touchdowns and threw two interceptions for the 5–11 Lions.

BIBLIOGRAPHY: Des Moines (IA) *Register*, 1982–1986; University of Iowa, Press Release, Iowa City, IA, 1986.

John L. Evers

LUCKMAN, Sidney "Sid" (b. 21 November 1916, Brooklyn, NY), college and professional player and coach, is the son of Meyer Luckman, ranked among the best NFL quarterbacks for a decade and was the most talented and famous Jewish football player in American sports history. Luckman attended Erasmus High School and Columbia University, where he played under shrewd IL coach Lou Little* from 1936 through 1938. Luckman gained All-American honors his senior year despite the Lions' losing record. He played tailback and became a true triple-threat as a good runner, booming kicker (with one 72–yard punt), and brilliant passer. His college passing record included 180 completions in 376 attempts for 2,413 yards.

One of the smartest college football players, Luckman was selected by Chicago Bears (NFL) coach George Halas* as the team's first T formation quarterback. The 6 foot, 197 pound Luckman was not built in the classic quarterback mold, being a stocky, slow, short passer. He exhibited tremendous dedication, studied and mastered the T formation, and, according to Halas, made a marvelous field leader who never called a wrong play. Luckman rivaled Sammy Baugh* of the Washington Redskins for top NFL quarterback in the early 1940s. The Bears won four NFL championships in seven years with Luckman as quarterback from 1940 to 1946. Luckman made All-Pro four of those years and served in the U.S. Merchant Marine in 1944, occasionally playing during shore leave. Perhaps Luckman's most famous game was the Bears' 73–0 rout of the Washington Redskins for the title in 1940. Luckman led the Bears, playing only in the first half. His greatest game occurred in 1943 at the Polo Grounds, where he passed for seven touchdowns against the New York Giants, breaking Baugh's record of six in one contest. That year he passed for 28 touchdowns in 10 games, a record that stood for sixteen years. Subsequently, Luckman coached football for two decades at the U.S. Merchant Marine Academy. He retired as a pro player in 1947, having attempted 1,744 passes and completed 904 aerials for 14,686 yards and 139 touchdowns in 12 seasons. Luckman was elected to the NFF College Football Hall of Fame.

BIBLIOGRAPHY: Robert Slater, *Great Jews in Sports* (Middle Village, NY, 1983).

Eric Solomon

LUJACK, John C. Jr. "Johnny" (b. 4 January 1925, Connellsville, PA), college athlete and professional football player, quarterbacked the University of Notre Dame to national championships in 1943, 1946, and 1947, and never lost to a college foe. He won unanimous All-American honors in 1946 and 1947 and was awarded the Heisman Trophy his senior season. In 1947 Lujack climaxed a brilliant college career by being voted the AP Male Athlete of the Year. The first draft choice of the Chicago Bears (NFL), Lujack played four pro football seasons from 1948 through 1951. He earned the rare distinction of being named All-Pro as both defensive back (1948) and quarterback (1950).

The son of John and Alice Lujack, he has three older brothers and two sisters and became an honor student and senior class president at Connellsville High School. He won All-State mention in football, basketball, and track. In his best prep football game, he returned two successive punts 70 yards for touchdowns. He led his school in scoring as a basketball guard and was considered a pro baseball prospect as a shortstop but refused an offer from the Pittsburgh Pirates (NL) because he wanted to attend Notre Dame. As a sophomore, Lujack lettered in football, baseball, basketball, and track and became the first Notre Dame four-letter winner since 1912. In the spring 1944 he participated in a track meet against DePauw and a baseball game against Western Michigan the same day. Lujack made three hits in Notre Dame's 3–1 baseball victory and won the javelin throw between innings. He might have captured the high jump, but his baggy pants knocked down the crossbar.

Lujack began his varsity football career as a halfback in 1943 when All-American Angelo Bertelli* started at quarterback. Lujack's brothers, all fine athletes, had trained him in forward passing at an early age. When Bertelli was called to active U.S. Marines duty after six games, Lujack started against undefeated Army. Lujack's name made bold headlines across most sports pages nationally, as he directed Notre Dame to a dramatic 26–0 upset victory. He completed 8 of 15 passes for 237 yards and 2 touchdowns and plunged one yard for another tally. After being commissioned an ensign in the U.S. Navy in 1944, Lujack served eleven months on a submarine chaser in the Atlantic Ocean and later played 10 games for the Fort Pierce football team. Upon receiving his honorable discharge in June 1946, he guided Notre Dame to a new pinnacle of football glory the next two seasons.

A 6 foot, 180 pounder, Lujack in three total seasons completed 144 passes in 280 attempts for 2,080 yards. Called a "coach on the field" by Frank Leahy,* he provided leadership, poise, and daring. These qualities impressed the All-American selectors even more than his passing exploits. Notre Dame grid history author Jim Beach commented, "Johnny was the kind of quarterback who called runs when passes were expected, and passed on fourth down. He kept the defense in a state of confusion and his teammates on their toes. He knew the job of every man on every play." Rated the finest T-formation quarterback of all time by many grid experts, he made the All-American Board of Football's 25–year Anniversary Team in 1949 and the 1940s decade team selected by *SI* in 1969.

Despite his splendid offensive talent, Lujack may have performed even better defensively. He ranks with football's most awesome open-field tacklers and supposedly missed only one tackle in three varsity campaigns at Notre Dame. In his very first game after returning to Notre Dame in 1946, Lujack dominated defensively in a 26–6 victory over WC champion Illinois. Every time sensational Illini sprinter Claude "Buddy" Young* carried the ball into the secondary, he was tackled by Lujack. Young did not regain his old form until the end of the season and cited Lujack's jarring tackles as a major reason he earned the dubious Football Flop of the Year award.

In the historic 1946 scoreless tie with the famous Doc Blanchard*–Glenn Davis* Army team, Lujack made one of the most crucial tackles in football history. Sportswriter Jack Sher recounted: "Big Doc broke around end and headed down the sideline, completely in the clear. Lujack, with his usual deadly instinct, had seen the play coming. He cut across the field, the only man who had any chance at all of waylaying a back who was almost never stopped in the open. Blanchard thundered down the sidelines, while 70,000 spectators held their breath, and Lujack closed in. Johnny hit him like something shot out of a rifle, right at the ankles. Doc went down on the Irish 37–yard line, and he went down hard."

In four years with the Chicago Bears (1948–1951), Lujack completed 404 of 808 aerials for 6,295 yards and 41 touchdowns and possessed few peers as an all-around performer. He staged his greatest pro passing performance against the Chicago Cardinals in 1949, throwing for six touchdowns and a then NFL-record 458 yards. Lujack married Patricia Ann Schierbrock on June 26, 1948, and has three children, Mary Jane, John Francis, and Carolyn Elizabeth. Since 1954 he has owned a successful auto dealership in Davenport, IA, and relaxes by playing golf. Lujack was elected to the NFF College Football Hall of Fame in 1960.

BIBLIOGRAPHY: Jim Beach and Daniel Moore, *Army vs. Notre Dame* (New York, 1948); Jim Beach, *Notre Dame Football* (New York, 1962); Frank Graham, "Lujack of Notre Dame," *Sport* 7 (October, 1949), p. 36; Arthur F. Hayes, *The Quarterback* (December 3, 1947); Dan Jenkins, "The First 100 Years," *SI* 31 (September 15, 1969), pp. 46–53ff.; John Lujack to Bernie McCarty, May 25, 1984; Edward Prell, "Lujack and Leahy—All-Star Dynamite," Chicago *Tribune*, August 15, 1948; Jack Sher, "Lujack, Leahy and Notre Dame," *Sport* 3 (October, 1947), pp. 58–68.

Bernie McCarty

LYMAN, William Roy "Link" (b. 30 November 1898, Table Rock, NE; d. 28 December 1972, Los Angeles, CA), college and professional player and coach, was the son of farmer-rancher-realtor Edwin and Anna (Cleaveland) Lyman. He graduated in 1917 from McDonald (KS) Rural High, a school too small to have a football squad. At the University of Nebraska (MVC) he played football tackle in 1918–1919 and 1921. In 1920 he left Nebraska because of illness and financial problems. He married Grace Godwin on June 2, 1920, and had two daughters. At Nebraska he made several football All-Star teams (especially in 1921) and yet mysteriously missed the Walter Camp All-American eleven. Lyman's highlights at Nebraska included a 1918 scoreless tie against Knute Rockne's* Notre Dame squad with famed George Gipp,* a 1919 3–0 win over eastern champion Syracuse University, and a 1921 10–3 victory against Pop Warner's* formidable Pittsburgh team.

Lyman started his thirteen-year pro career with the Canton Bulldogs (NFL), where he teamed with Wilbur "Fats" Henry* for two consecutive titles. Lyman helped the Bulldogs win a third straight championship in 1924, when the Bulldogs transferred to Cleveland. Since the franchise encountered problems in 1925, Lyman and four others bought it for $3,500 and moved it back to Canton. They lost their investment, as the NFL took over the team. From 1926 through 1934 Lyman played with the Chicago Bears (NFL). After serving as football line coach at Nebraska (BSC, 1935–1941) and Creighton University (1942), he became a very successful insurance agent and owned his own agency years later. In sixteen college and pro seasons, Lyman experienced only one losing campaign. Lyman stressed, "I never seemed to accept the teachings of many coaches who, if we lost, said we played a good game and always learned something. To me, it was win or else." A blocker for Jim Thorpe,* Red Grange,* and Bronko Nagurski,* the 6 foot, 2 inch, 250 pounder won respect with his size, excellent speed, and rough play. He revolutionized line play by using a shifting, sliding style. His Pro Football Hall of Fame (1964) citation includes this statement: "To this day, they don't do things much different, nor any better." Lyman was also elected to the HAF College Football Hall of Fame, Nebraska Sports Hall of Fame, and Nebraska Football Hall of Fame.

BIBLIOGRAPHY: Link Lyman clippings file, University of Nebraska Alumni Association, Lincoln, NE; Alexander Weyand, *Football Immortals* (New York, 1962).

John E. DiMeglio

M

McAFEE, George Anderson "One Play" (b. 13 March 1918, Corbin, KY), college and professional player and official, performed at halfback and safety for Duke University and the Chicago Bears (NFL) and is the son of Clarence and Mary Lydia McAfee. McAfee, whose father was employed by the Chesapeake and Ohio Railroad, moved at age three or four to Ironton, OH, and grew up there. At Ironton High School he won letters in football, track, and baseball. His secondary school coach Dick Gallagher later served as director of the Pro Football Hall of Fame. McAfee entered Duke University (SC) in 1936 but saw little service his sophomore and junior years. An All-American his senior year, he started on a Rose Bowl–bound team with Eric Tipton and Tommy Prothro. Duke won nine straight games before losing 7–3 to Southern California at the Rose Bowl. At Duke, he was nicknamed "One Play" because of his blinding speed.

George Halas* of the Chicago Bears (NFL) drafted McAfee in 1940 but initially thought he had made a big mistake selecting the 5 foot, 11 inch, 182 pound halfback. The rookie calmed the skeptics his first regular season by running 93 yards for a touchdown against the archrival Green Bay Packers. The next season, McAfee gained 474 yards in 65 carries for an NFL-leading 7.3–yard average and was chosen All-Pro for the only time in his career. During his first two seasons, he ran 96 yards against Cleveland, surprised the Brooklyn Dodgers by running 75 yards with only 17 seconds left, and made other sensational long gains. McAfee entered the U.S. Navy after the 1941 season and did not return to the Bears until 1945. In his first game back, McAfee played only 17 minutes and yet scored two touchdowns. Although injured in 1946, he played full seasons from 1947 through 1950 and performed extensively at safety late in his career until a bone injury to his heel forced his retirement. A sensational punt returner, he gained 1,431 career yards for a 12.8–yard average and ranked first in that category for many years. In 1948 he led the NFL in punt returns (30) and total yards

(417). The excellent defender intercepted 21 passes for 294 yards and one touchdown and also punted and passed (left-handed) on occasion. Besides having blinding speed, McAfee defeated the opposition with technique. He developed a unique hip shift to elude tacklers and wore the low-cut running shoe now standard football gear. Lifetime, McAfee gained 1,685 yards in 341 rushes for a 4.9–yard average and scored 39 touchdowns, including 14 via rushing. He helped the Bears win championship games in 1940 (against the Washington Redskins) and 1941 (against the New York Giants) by scoring one touchdown in each contest. His 1941 score proved the deciding one of that game. He watched from the bench in 1946, as the Bears again defeated the Giants to become champions.

McAfee, an NFL head linesman from 1961 through 1966, was named to the NFF College Football Hall of Fame and in 1966 to the Pro Football Hall of Fame. He established the McAfee Oil Company in Durham, NC, where he still resides. He married Jeane Mencke on June 15, 1945, and has three children. Many opponents claim that McAfee was the greatest running back ever at the height of his career. McAfee, however, may have lost the best years of his career to World War II, cutting his actual career painfully short.

BIBLIOGRAPHY: *Chicago Bears Press Book, 1946.*

John David Healy

McCORMACK, Mike (b. 21 June 1930, Chicago, IL), college and professional player, coach, and executive, is the son of heat/frost insulator Michael and Georgia McCormack and moved to Kansas City, KS, as a youngster. McCormack attended De La Salle High School, where he participated in football and basketball. McCormack excelled in football at the University of Kansas, captaining the Jayhawks and making the All-BSC squad in 1950. McCormack, who played in the College All-Star game and captained the West squad in the 1951 Shrine All-Star (East-West) game, was also selected a tackle on the all-time Kansas All-Star team. The New York Yankees chose him in the first round of the 1951 NFL draft. The 6 foot, 4 inch, 250 pound McCormack spent two years in the U.S. Army following his rookie season with the Yankees. In a 15–player trade, McCormack was acquired by the Cleveland Browns (NFL) and from 1954 to 1962 achieved All-Pro status as a guard there. A mainstay in the Browns' offensive line, he played in the 1954, 1955, and 1957 NFL championship games and on the 1954 and 1955 title squads. McCormack played for Cleveland in the 1955 and 1956 College All-Star games and from 1962 through 1965 served as assistant coach for the All-Stars. Five times (1956–1957, 1960–1962) he played in the Pro Bowl.

Following his retirement as a player, McCormack entered private business for three years. McCormack began his pro coaching career as offensive line coach for the Washington Redskins (NFL) from 1966 through 1972 under Otto Graham,* Vince Lombardi,* and George Allen.* The knowledgeable, likable McCormack was head coach of the Philadelphia Eagles (NFL) from 1973 through 1975, compiling a 16–25–1 record. From 1976 through 1979 McCormack worked with the Cincinnati Bengals (NFL) as offensive line coach. The seventh coach in Baltimore history, he guided the NFL Colts in 1980 and 1981 to a 9–23–0 record. In 1982 he joined the Seattle Seahawks (NFL) as director of football operations and became their interim head coach when Jack Patera was dismissed following two games of the strike-ridden season. The Seahawks completed the 1982 campaign with a 4–3–0 record. In 1983 McCormack was named president and general manager of the Seahawks and saw Seattle make the playoffs for the first time. In 1984 McCormack was elected to the Pro Football Hall of Fame. A resident of Seattle, he and his wife, Ann (Helsby) McCormack, have four children, Michael, Timothy, Molly, and Colleen.

BIBLIOGRAPHY: *Cincinnati Bengals Football Guide, 1977; Seattle Seahawks Prospectus, 1983; University of Kansas Football, Press, Radio, TV Guide, 1977.*

John L. Evers

McCUTCHEON, Lawrence "Larry" (b. 2 June 1950, Plainview, TX), college and professional player, attended Plainview High School and Colorado State University (WAC) on a football scholarship from 1969 to 1972. During his excellent college career, the fullback gained 2,917 yards on 649 attempts for a 4.5–yard average and scored 22 touchdowns. Twice he amassed over 1,000 yards in a season and holds school rushing and scoring records. As a sophomore, he was named the outstanding back of the WAC. The Los Angeles Rams selected the 6 foot, 1 inch, 205 pound McCutcheon in the third round of the 1972 NFL draft. On the reserve squad his first season, he was activated for three games and performed on the special teams. In 1973 McCutcheon gained 120 yards in the opening game against the Kansas City Chiefs and made UPI's All-Rookie team and several All-NFL and All-NFC teams.

Rams backs have rushed over 1,000 yards at least thirteen times in a season, with McCutcheon accomplishing the feat four times between 1973 and 1977. He gained over 100 yards in 22 regular-season and three post-season playoff games. His best performance came in the 1975 NFC playoffs, when he rushed 37 times for 202 yards against the St. Louis Cardinals. Besides scoring 23 touchdowns, McCutcheon holds the all-time Rams rushing record with 6,186 yards on 1,435 attempts to surpass notable rushers Dick Bass, Deacon Dan Towler, Les Josephson, and Tank Younger. From 1973 through 1977 McCutcheon made the Pro Bowl and received the club's Outstanding Offensive Back Award. In 1974 he won the Rams' MVP Award. McCutcheon played in the 1974–1976 and 1979 NFC championship games and in Super Bowl XIV, which his team lost 31–19 to the Pittsburgh Steelers.

In 1980 McCutcheon played seven games with the Denver Broncos (NFL) and eight contests with the Seattle Seahawks (NFL). The next year, he appeared in six games for the Buffalo Bills (NFL) before knee injuries forced him to retire. During his ten-year pro career, he rushed for 6,578 yards on 1,521 attempts, compiled a 4.3–yard average, and scored 26 touchdowns. Besides ranking nineteenth on the all-time NFL rushing yardage list, he caught 198 passes for 1,799 yards and 13 touchdowns. McCutcheon, a bachelor, spends his free time with golf, tennis, and hunting. A low-key, controlled person, he loves nature and prefers the outdoor life. The nomadic McCutcheon enjoys moving around after being in a certain place for a length of time.

BIBLIOGRAPHY: *Colorado State University Football, 1979;* Doug Kelly, "The 'Plain' Is Gone from the Kid from Plainview—1,000 Yard Lawrence McCutcheon," *Profile* (1974), pp. 53–59; *Los Angeles Rams Media Guide, 1977; TSN Football Register—1982.*

John L. Evers

McDONALD, Thomas Franklin "Tommy" (b. 26 July 1934, Roy, NM), college and professional player, is the son of the Clyde McDonalds. His father, a farmer, pitched in semi-pro baseball. McDonald excelled in football, basketball, track, and baseball at Highland High School in Albuquerque, NM, where he set scoring records in football and basketball and earned five gold medals in the state track meet. McDonald, a 5 foot, 9 inch, 168 pound football halfback-flanker attended the University of Oklahoma (BSC) and majored in Industrial Education there. He led the Sooners to a 30–0–0 record (1954–1956) and two national championships and scored the winning touchdown against the University of Maryland in the 1956 Orange Bowl. A consensus All-American (1956), McDonald finished third in the Heisman Trophy voting and won the Maxwell Award as the nation's outstanding college player. The two-way performer scored in 20 of 21 games (1955–1956) and became the only Oklahoma back ever to rush for at least one touchdown in every game his junior season. In his college career, McDonald rushed for 1,683 yards, completed 28 of 44 running halfback passes (63.6 percent), and accumulated 2,254 total yards. He scored 102 points (1955) as the nation's fourth leading scorer. An All-BSC choice (1955–1956), McDonald was an All-American scholastic choice as a junior. Following his graduation, he played in the College All-Star game (tying the scoring record with three touchdowns), North-South game, and Hula Bowl.

McDonald was selected by the Philadelphia Eagles in the third round of the 1957 NFL draft and became a great pass receiver for the Eagles (1957–1963), Dallas Cowboys (1964), Los Angeles Rams (1965–1966), Atlanta Falcons (1967), and Cleveland Browns (1968). A member of the Philadelphia NFL champions in 1960, McDonald made All-Pro three times and appeared in the Pro Bowl (1959–1963, 1966). McDonald scored four touchdowns in 1959 against the New York Giants to tie a club record and compiled 237 pass reception yards in 1961 against the Giants for a one-game club record. McDonald led the Eagles in scoring (1959), pass receiving (1959, 1961–1962), punt returns (1957, 1959), and kickoff returns (1958–1959) and made 13 touchdown receptions (1960–1961) to equal a club record. He also paced the Rams (1965) and Falcons (1967) in pass receiving. A top NFL pass receiver, McDonald placed second (1959, 1965), fourth (1961), and fifth (1962). He finished first (1961) and third in (1959, 1962, 1965) in pass reception yardage, and paced the NFL (1961), tied for the lead (1958), and finished in the top five each season (1958–1962) in touchdown catches. During a streak of 93 consecutive games, he caught at least one pass. In 12 pro seasons, McDonald played in 152 games and ranks high on the all-time NFL lists for receivers. He compiled 495 pass receptions (19th), 8,410 reception yards (14th), 17–yard average gain per reception, and 84 pass reception touchdowns (5th).

McDonald operates an oil portrait firm, which includes portraits of all Heisman Trophy and Maxwell Award recipients. He was married to Ann Campbell (Miss Oklahoma) in 1957 but divorced three years later. McDonald married Patricia Gallagher in 1962 and has four children. In February, 1985, he was named to NFF College Football Hall of Fame.

BIBLIOGRAPHY: *Atlanta Falcons Media Guide, 1968;* Herman L. Masin, "The Sooner Who Gets There Sooner!" *Senior Scholastic* 69 (November 8, 1956), pp. 32–33; *Philadelphia Eagles Media Guide, 1977; University of Oklahoma Press Guide, 1956;* Joan Weckesser, "Ex-Eagles Star Turns Businessman," *Today's Shopper* (March 15, 1972), p. 30.

John L. Evers

McELHENNY, Hugh Edward, Jr. "The King" "Hurrying Hugh" (b. 31 December 1928, Los Angeles, CA), college and professional player, is the son of Pearl and Hugh McElhenny, Sr. His father owned a prosperous vending machine company. McElhenny showed an early interest in athletics, but his sports career seemed endangered because he stepped on a broken milk bottle at age 9 and severed every tendon in his left foot. McElhenny spent two years in a wheelchair and on crutches before recovering. McElhenny, a mediocre student, still enjoyed a brilliant athletic career at George Washington High School in Los Angeles. He was timed in 9.7 seconds for the 100–yard dash and set a world interscholastic record of 14 seconds flat for the 120–yard hurdles.

McElhenny received over forty football offers from major universities. Since his academic grades were not strong, McElhenny enrolled at nearby Compton (CA) Junior College. He also wanted to be close to Peggy Ogston, the childhood sweetheart he later married. Due to McElhenny's gate appeal, Compton drew 208,000 football fans in 1948. McElhenny scored 23 touchdowns, 12 on runs of 30 yards or longer. After his freshman year, McElhenny enrolled at the University of Washington (PCC). He played three seasons (1949–1951) there and helped lead the Huskies to an 8–2 record in 1950.

McElhenny, whose college football career was outstanding, holds the Huskies' single-game rushing record of 296 yards. In three years he rushed for 2,499 yards and remains Washington's career scoring leader with 233 points. "Hurrying Hugh" in 1981 became the fifth Husky player to be inducted into the NFF College Football Hall of Fame.

McElhenny was drafted by the San Francisco 49ers (NFL) in 1952 and played so well that he was chosen Rookie of the Year. McElhenny in the NFL performed nine seasons with San Francisco (1952–1960), two campaigns with the Minnesota Vikings (1961–1962), and one year each with the New York Giants (1963) and Detroit Lions (1964). At New York, he helped the Giants win the Eastern Conference title. During his pro career, McElhenny rushed 1,124 times for 5,281 yards (4.7–yard average) and 38 touchdowns and caught 264 passes for 3,247 yards (12.3–yard average) and 20 touchdowns. After retirement from football, McElhenny returned to Seattle as an executive for the Washington Transit Advertising Company. McElhenny was inducted into the Pro Football Hall of Fame in 1970, University of Washington Sports Hall of Fame, and Washington State Hall of Fame.

Probably the most famous football player ever at the University of Washington, McElhenny held 16 Husky records at one time. He enjoyed an even more distinguished pro career as a preeminent running back of the 1950s and later often was compared to Gale Sayers.* McElhenny could pivot, sidestep, change pace, and turn on a sudden burst of speed when needed. The 6 foot, 1 inch, 198 pounder also possessed power. McElhenny's punishing straight-arm and fierce dedication made him one of his day's most celebrated players. His son Lance starred as a quarterback at SMU in the early 1980s.

BIBLIOGRAPHY: George Allen with Ben Olan, *Pro Football's 100 Greatest Players* (Indianapolis, IN, 1982); Jack T. Clary, *Thirty Years of Pro Football's Great Moments* (New York, 1976); "Huskies' Hugh McElhenny Joins College Hall of Fame," Seattle *Times*, February 1, 1981, p. B11; *Lincoln Library of Sports Champions*, vol. 8 (Columbus, OH, 1974); John D. McCallum, *Pac-10 Football: The Rose Bowl Conference* (Seattle, 1982); *Official NFL Record Manual, 1983* (New York, 1983); *Official NFL Record and Fact Book, 1984* (New York, 1984); Murray Olderman, *The Pro Quarterback* (Englewood Cliffs, NJ, 1966); Paul Soderberg and Helen Washington, eds., *The Big Book of Halls of Fame* (New York, 1977); Roger Treat, ed., *The Encyclopedia of Football*, 16th rev. ed., rev. by Pete Palmer (New York, 1979).

James E. Odenkirk

McFADIN, Lewis Pate "Bud" (b. 21 August 1928, Iraan, TX), college and professional player and coach, graduated from Iraan High School in 1947. Several colleges recruited the 6 foot, 4 inch, 240 pound high school lineman, who enrolled at the University of Texas in 1947. In 1951 he graduated from Texas with a B.A. degree in Business Administration. The offensive guard and defensive tackle lettered on the 1948–1950 Longhorn (SWC) football squads, making All-American in 1949 and consensus All-American in 1950 at guard. Under coach J. Blair Cherry, the 6–3–1 1948 Texas team finished second in the SWC and defeated Georgia 41–28 in the Orange Bowl. The Longhorns compiled a 6–4–0 mark in 1949 and 9–1–0 slate in 1950, placing second on the UPI poll and third on the AP balloting. Texas captured the 1950 SWC title with a 6–0 record, but lost 14–13 to national champion Oklahoma and then 20–14 to Tennessee in the Cotton Bowl. McFadin, the MVP of the 1951 College All-Star game against the Cleveland Browns, made several 1950s All-Decade football teams and also won the Longhorn boxing and wrestling championships.

The Los Angeles Rams (NFL) drafted McFadin in the first round in 1951. After serving eighteen months in the U.S. Air Force, McFadin joined Los Angeles for the final two games of the 1952 season. The Rams utilized the versatile McFadin at middle guard and linebacker on their 8–3–1 1953 and 6–5–1 1954 squads. In 1955 new coach Sid Gillman* converted McFadin to defensive tackle to team with Gene Lipscomb.* The 8–3–1 Rams won the 1955 Western Conference crown before losing 38–14 to the Cleveland Browns for the NFL title. Following the 1956 campaign, a friend was showing McFadin an old-fashioned pistol when it accidentally discharged and lodged a .44 caliber bullet in McFadin's stomach. McFadin hovered near death for several days and retired from pro football to his Humble, TX, ranch.

In 1960 the Denver Broncos of the newly formed AFL persuaded McFadin to come back. The then 280–pound McFadin captained the inexperienced Denver aggregate and became the best AFL defensive lineman of the early 1960s. He made the All-AFL team at defensive tackle from 1960 through 1962, was a unanimous selection the first two seasons, and participated in five Pro Bowls. Despite McFadin's ability, knowledge, and determination, the youthful Broncos struggled with records of 4–9–1 in 1960, 3–11–0 in 1961, 7–7–0 in 1962, and 2–11–1 in 1963. On Thanksgiving Day, 1962, McFadin scored his first pro touchdown on a 69–yard return of a fumble against the New York Titans. Kansas City coach Hank Stram* remarked, "He has great quickness and mobility for a big man. And he's got years of experience to go along with that natural ability." Kansas City linebacker E. J. Holub stated, "He's the toughest lineman in the league. He covers the field from sideline to sideline." McFadin finished his pro career with the 4–10–0 Houston Oilers (AFL) in 1964 and 1965 and served as their defensive line coach from 1966 through 1970. He was named to the NFF College Football Hall of Fame, in 1973 to the Longhorn Hall of Fame at the University of Texas and in 1975 to the State of Texas All-Time Team for the Texas Sports Hall of Fame. The Del Rio, TX, resident is married to Patsy Blackburn, has two children, and works as a rancher and real estate broker.

BIBLIOGRAPHY: *The College Game* (Indianapolis, IN, 1974); *Denver Broncos Media Guides, 1961, 1963; Los Angeles Rams Official Press, Radio, and Television Guide, 1955; NCAA Official Collegiate Football Record Books, 1950, 1951;* Sheila Richardson to David

L. Porter, August 1, 1986; Don Schiffer, *Pro Football, 1963* (New York, 1963); Roger Treat, ed., *The Encyclopedia of Football*, 16th rev. ed., rev. by Pete Palmer (New York, 1979); University of Texas, Sports News Releases, November 4, 1973; October, 1980, Austin, TX; Bill Wise, ed., *1963 Official Pro Football Almanac* (New York, 1963).

David L. Porter

McGUGIN, Daniel E. "Dan" (b. 29 July 1879, Tingley, IA; d. 19 January 1936, Memphis, TN), college player, coach, and administrator, was the son of a Union officer Benjamin Franklin and Melissa Almeda (Critchfield) McGugin. McGugin's introduction to athletics came at Drake University because Tingley High School did not have a competitive sports program. After spending one year at Drake, McGugin played left guard from 1901 to 1903 for the University of Michigan's (WC) point-a-minute squads. Under coach Fielding Yost,* he participated on two undefeated, untied teams. The 1901 squad outscored opponents 550 points to none and demolished Stanford University 49–0 in the first Rose Bowl game. When McGugin married Virginia L. Fite of Nashville, TN, Yost served as his best man. Yost met Virginia's sister Eunice then and later married her. McGugin and his wife had three children, Daniel Jr., Leonard, and Lucy Ann.

Although a corporation lawyer, McGugin became head football coach in 1904 at Vanderbilt University (SIAA). With the exception of U.S. Army duty in 1918, McGugin coached and served as athletic director at Vanderbilt from 1904 until his untimely death in 1936 and combined his law career and football coaching for three decades. Under McGugin, Vanderbilt captured ten championships (1904–1907, 1910–1912, 1921–1923). McGugin's 1904 Vanderbilt squad won all nine games, led the nation in scoring, and outscored opponents 474 points to four. The 1910, 1921, and 1922 teams finished undefeated but tied, while the 1905–1906, 1911, 1915, and 1926 squads each lost one game. In 1907, 1912, and 1916, Vanderbilt lost one and tied one. Vanderbilt finished with a 2–6–0 record in 1915, the only losing season in McGugin's career.

In 30 years as coach at Vanderbilt, McGugin guided his clubs to 197 victories, 55 defeats, and 19 ties for a .762 percentage. Only 22 major college football coaches have compiled a better winning percentage, with only two coaching longer than McGugin. His teams incredibly outscored their opponents 6,673 points to 1,668. In the pre-Bowl era, McGugin's Vanderbilt squads pioneered intersectional football by playing Michigan, Ohio State, Yale, and Harvard. Several fine performers, including All-American blocking back and linebacker Lynn Bomar, played under McGugin. Other outstanding Vanderbilt players, including Ray Morrison,* Josh Cody,* Jess Neely,* and Henry "Red" Sanders,* became successful football coaches.

McGugin, a master psychologist, motivated players to achieve maximum potential. He spoke softly and slowly, gradually preparing his team. Few surpassed him in delivering pep talks. His undefeated 1921 team handed the University of Texas its only defeat (20–0) in Dallas after such a motivational speech. He respected the attitudes of others, did not criticize players until after the game, expertly handled his players, and showed constructive leadership. McGugin pioneered in speed and the forward pass, taught the South the Michigan punting game, and probably originated the Statue of Liberty play. Although a great playmaker, he refused to take credit for many of his innovations. McGugin retired from coaching in 1934 but remained as athletic director. He was president of the AFCA and a member of HAF College Football Hall of Fame. In 1951 he was elected to the NFF College Football Hall of Fame.

BIBLIOGRAPHY: Tim Cohane, *Great College Football Coaches of the Twenties and Thirties* (New Rochelle, NY, 1973); John D. McCallum and Charles H. Pearson, *College Football U.S.A., 1869–1973* (New York, 1973); *Vanderbilt Commodore Football Press Guide, 1979.*

John L. Evers

McKAY, John Harvey (b. 5 July 1923, Everettsville, WV), college and professional player and coach, is the son of coal mine superintendent John and Gertrude McKay. An All-State football running back and basketball guard at Shinnston (WV) High School, McKay served after graduation in the U.S. Air Force between 1942 and 1945. In 1946 he started as a football defensive back at Purdue University (WC). After transferring to the University of Oregon (PCC), McKay played offensively and defensively in 1948 and 1949. With Norm Van Brocklin* at quarterback, the 1948 squad compiled a 9–1 record and lost to SMU in the Cotton Bowl. McKay holds Oregon records for most touchdowns rushing in a game (3) and highest career average per carry (6.4 yards). Although drafted by the New York Yankees (AAFC), he instead entered college coaching.

In June 1950 McKay married Nancy "Corky" Hunter and has four children, Michelle, Terri, Richard, and John, Jr. (John, Jr., played college and pro football for his father.) McKay served as assistant coach at the University of Oregon from 1950 to 1958 and the University of Southern California (AAWU) in 1959 before becoming head coach of the Trojans in 1960. During McKay's sixteen years at Southern California, his teams won 127 games, lost 40, tied 8, and captured nine (AAWU, PEC) championships. His squads compiled three undefeated campaigns (1962, 1969, 1972) and won four national championships (1962, 1967, 1972, 1974). Only two other coaches (Frank Leahy* and Paul "Bear" Bryant*) have won four national titles. McKay, whose Trojans won six of nine bowl games and appeared in eight Rose Bowls, became the only coach ever to take a team to Pasadena four successive times (1967–1970). McKay coached 40 All-Americans and two Heisman Trophy winners (Mike Garrett* and O. J. Simpson*) and was named Coach of the Year in 1962 and 1972. His All-Americans included Hal Bedsole, Ricky Bell, Sam Cunningham, Anthony Davis, Clarence Davis, Pat Haden, Lynn Swann,* Richard Wood, and Ron Yary.*

In 1975 McKay was selected vice president and head coach of the Tampa Bay Buccaneers (NFL). Four years later, McKay guided Tampa Bay to the NFC Central Division title. Under his direction, Tampa Bay became the second expansion team to qualify for the playoffs within its first four seasons and the first expansion franchise to win ten games in one of its initial four seasons. In 1981 he led the Buccaneers to another Central Division title. His 1982 squad qualified for the playoffs but lost in the first round. In his nine year (1976–1984) professional coaching career, Tampa Bay has won 44 games, lost 88, and tied 1.

BIBLIOGRAPHY: John McKay and Jim Perry, *McKay: A Coach's Story* (New York, 1974); *Tampa Bay Buccaneers Media Guide, 1978; TSN Football Register—1984.*

John L. Evers

MACKEY, John (b. 24 September 1941, Brooklyn, NY), college and professional player, is the son of clergyman Walter Raymond and Dora (Hill) Mackey and developed into an all-around athlete at Hempstead High School, Long Island, NY. He graduated from Hempstead High School in 1959 and earned a B.A. in History/Political Science from Syracuse University in 1963. At Syracuse Mackey played right halfback for the undefeated football freshmen in 1959 and substitute back for the 7–2 Orangemen varsity squad. Back Ernie Davis,* Mackey's roommate, taught the latter how to handle tacklers and utilize his running speed to make large gains. In 1961 Mackey excelled as a starting end for the 7–3 Orangemen, 15–14 victors over Miami (FL) in the Liberty Bowl. The quiet, serious-minded Mackey almost single-handedly helped 5–5 Syracuse defeat Navy in 1962 and scored twice in the East's 25–19 triumph over the West in the Shrine All-Star (East-West) game. He married Syracuse coed Sylvia Ann Cole on December 28, 1963, and has three children, Lisa, John, and Laura.

The Baltimore Colts (NFL) drafted Mackey in the second round in 1963. The 6 foot, 2 inch, 220 pounder combined with quarterback John Unitas* to form one of the best pass-catch duos in pro football. Although a light tight end, Mackey caught 35 passes for 736 yards and 7 touchdowns as a rookie in 1963. He also paced the Colts in kickoff returns with 9 for 271 yards and was the only rookie to make the Pro Bowl. A thigh injury diminished Mackey's performance in 1964 for the 12–2 Colts, 27–0 losers to the Cleveland Browns in the NFL title game. In 1965 he caught 40 passes for 814 yards and 7 touchdowns. All-Pro honors were bestowed upon Mackey from 1966 through 1968. After catching 50 passes for a career high 829 yards in 1966, he the next season made a career-high 55 receptions for 686 yards. In 1968 he led the 13–1 Colts with 45 catches for 644 yards and 5 touchdowns. Coach

Don Shula* utilized Mackey's fine running ability, as the latter gained 103 yards on 10 end-around plays. The New York Jets, however, upset the Colts 16–7 in Super Bowl III. Bone chips were removed from Mackey's knee before the 1970 season, reducing the tight end's mobility. In the 16–13 Super Bowl V victory over the Dallas Cowboys following the 1970 campaign, Mackey set a game record for the 11–2–1 Colts by scoring on a 75–yard tipped pass from Unitas. He started the first three games in 1971 before an elbow injury limited his playing time. Mackey was traded in 1972 to the San Diego Chargers (NFL) and finished his playing career there that season.

During ten NFL seasons, Mackey caught 331 passes for 5,238 yards and 39 touchdowns. The NFL in 1970 named Mackey, whose 15.8–yard average per reception ranked him highest among tight ends with longevity, as the best tight end in pro football history. The Pro Football Hall of Fame named him to its AFL-NFL 1960–1984 All-Star Second Team. Mackey was the prototype of the modern tight end with the speed of a sprinter, sure hands of a wide receiver, and superb strength of a blocker and earned five Pro Bowl game selections. In 1970 Mackey was chosen president of the fledgling NFL Players Association and organized that year's player strike. His suit against the NFL destroyed the (Pete) Rozelle* rule, a compensation clause restraining the right of a player to bargain with another club, and provided the foundation for subsequent management-labor relations. The president of John Mackey Enterprises, he served on the board of advisors of Advance Federal Savings and Loan Association of Baltimore and on the board of directors of the Syracuse University Alumni Association and Big Brothers of Baltimore.

BIBLIOGRAPHY: Nathan Aaseng, *Football's Toughest Tight Ends* (Minneapolis, MN, 1981); George Allen with Ben Olan, *Pro Football's 100 Greatest Players* (Indianapolis, IN, 1982); *The Lincoln Library of Sports Champions*, vol. 8 (Columbus, OH, 1974); *TSN Football Register—1972; WWA*, 37th ed. (1972–1973), p. 1,979.

David L. Porter

McMAHON, James Robert "Jim" (b. 21 August 1959, Jersey City, NJ), college and professional player, is the second of six children born to James Francis and Roberta (Williams) McMahon. The McMahons moved to San Jose, CA, when Jim was three years old and then, just prior to his junior year in high school, to Roy, UT, where he lettered in football, basketball, and baseball. After graduating in 1977 with All-State MVP credentials in football, McMahon, a Catholic like his father, wanted to attend Notre Dame. When the Fighting Irish failed to recruit him, he chose Brigham Young University (WAC) because of its pass-oriented offense.

Although his mother is Mormon, McMahon chafed at the restrictive social atmosphere while excelling in football at the church-owned school. He won All-WAC honors as a sophomore in 1978 despite splitting quarterbacking duties. Following a red-shirt year, McMahon in 1980 recorded the finest offensive performance in collegiate history. The first player to pass for over 4,000 yards in a season, he set 32 NCAA season passing and total offense records and tied two other marks. His records included most touchdown passes (47), consecutive games over 300 yards passing (11), total offense yardage (4,627), yards passing per game (380.9), total offense per game (385.6 yards), yards per pass attempt (10.7), and, remarkably, both the most yards passing (4,571) and the highest passing efficiency (176.9). Despite missing two games and playing most of his senior season with a hyperextended knee, McMahon in 1981 again led the nation in passing and total offense. He was chosen All-WAC for the second consecutive year, named consensus All-American, played in the Hula and Senior Bowls, and received the first annual Davey O'Brien National Quarterback Award as the nation's top signal-caller.

In his two years as full-time quarterback, McMahon made All-WAC twice, led the Cougars to two WAC titles and Holiday Bowl victories, and passed for 8,126 yards and 81 touchdowns while maintaining a completion rate above 64 percent and an interception rate below 3 percent. He completed his college career with 56 individual NCAA records, far exceeding the previous mark of 18 held by a single player. His then career records included most yards passing (9,536), total yards offense (9,723), and touchdown passes (84).

The most prolific and accurate passer in NCAA history, McMahon was selected by the Chicago Bears as the fifth player taken in the first round of the 1982 NFL draft. In his first five pro seasons, McMahon completed 635 of 1,111 passes for 8,318 yards and 49 touchdowns. He emerged as a top-flight performer in 1984 with a 97.8 quarterback rating but was side-lined after nine games with a lacerated kidney. In 1985 he led the Bears to a 15–1 regular-season mark by completing 178 of 313 passes (56.9 percent) for 2,392 yards and threw 15 touchdown passes and only 11 interceptions. The Bears defeated the New York Giants and Los Angeles Rams to win the NFC crown and trounced the New England Patriots 46–10 in Super Bowl XX as McMahon completed 12 of 20 passes for 256 yards and scored 2 touchdowns. In an injury-riddled 1986 season, McMahon completed 77 of 150 passes for 995 yards and 5 touchdowns and threw 8 interceptions for the 14–2 Central Division champion Bears. McMahon underwent rotator cuff surgery on his shoulder in December 1986 after being slammed to the ground in a game against the Green Bay Packers, missing the playoffs. Despite being injury-prone throughout his athletic career, McMahon remains an intense competitor and is regarded by the Bears as a "franchise" quarterback. He married Nancy Daines in 1982 and has two children, Ashley and Sean.

BIBLIOGRAPHY: Kevin Lamb, "Jim McMahon: The Hungriest Bear of All," *Football Digest* 13 (December, 1983), pp. 24–31; Jim McMahon file, Brigham Young University Athletic Department, Salt Lake City, UT; Jim McMahon with Bob Verdi, *McMahon!* (New York, 1986); *NCAA Football Record Book, 1982; NYT*, November 25, 1981; Pat Putnam, "McMahon with a Golden Arm," *SI* 55 (November 30, 1981), pp. 88, 93;

Salt Lake City *Tribune*, November 17, 1981; Gene Sapakoff, "Armed and Dangerous: Jim McMahon," *Sport* 72 (October, 1981), pp. 81ff.; *TSN*, September 26, 1981, November 26, 1981, October 28, 1985; *TSN Football Register—1985*.

Larry R. Gerlach

McMILLIN, Alvin Nugent "Bo" (b. 12 January 1895, Prairie Hill, TX; d. 31 March 1952, Bloomington, IN), college and professional player and coach, was the son of meat packer Reubin T. and Matilda (Riley) McMillin. The devout Roman Catholic played quarterback for Fort Worth (TX) High School and earned a football scholarship at Centre College, where he played from 1919 through 1921 and graduated in 1937 with a B. A. degree. During his playing days, McMillin became a nationally known quarterback. Centre defeated the University of Kentucky 3–0 in 1919 on the only field goal McMillin ever attempted. The next year, he completed 119 of 170 passes by utilizing his quickness and bullet throws. His most important victory came in perhaps the "upset of the century" in 1921, when Centre defeated Harvard 6–0 on McMillin's 32–yard touchdown run. Kentucky Governor Edwin P. Morrow claimed it was more desirable to be McMillin than governor at that moment, while Ralph Paines memorialized the event and McMillin's career in *First Down Kentucky* (1921).

After playing professionally with the Milwaukee Badgers and Cleveland Indians (NFL) for a year, the 5 foot, 9 inch, 165 pound McMillin entered a college coaching career. Here he turned his ruggedness to advantage, becoming a "stern, tough" coach. McMillin's leadership won games, while his homespun West Texas phrases made him an instant success on the banquet circuit. McMillin coached at Centenary College (1922–1924), Geneva College (1925–1927), and Kansas State University (BSC, 1928–1933), always with winning records. McMillin's first contract was not renewed because the school's accrediting agency objected that his salary exceeded that of faculty members and the president. At Indiana (WC), he gained his greatest reputation by winning consistently as head coach from 1934 through 1947. In 1945 he guided the Hoosiers to their first undefeated season and WC championship and was selected Coach of the Year. The very popular McMillin was given two consecutive 10–year contracts (1935–1944, 1945–1954) and promised tenure in the physical education department when they ended.

McMillin instead became head coach of the Detroit Lions (NFL) in 1948 and built the team before management and disgruntled players forced him out in 1950. The Lions won three championships in four years after his departure. He became head coach of the Philadelphia Eagles (NFL) in 1951 but resigned after two games because of cancer. His fatal heart attack came the next year. McMillin's personal life revolved around his family. At Centre, he allegedly bet on games that he quarterbacked and failed to pass a single course his senior year. Yet he settled down and married childhood sweetheart Marie Myers on January 2, 1922. After she died unexpectedly in 1926, he married Kathryn Gillihan on October 6, 1930. Besides having a daughter ("Bo Peep") from his first marriage, he had four children from his second, Jerry, Janie, Nuge, and Mike.

McMillin, a sound football figure with an exceptional ability to exercise psychological control over his players and opponents, compiled a remarkable 146–77–13 college record, especially given the universities where he coached. His honors included being named All-American and HAF Player of the Year in 1919, second team All-American in 1920 and 1921, president of the AFCA in 1940, and FWAA Man of the Year in 1945. He was elected to both the HAF and NFF College Football Halls of Fame.

BIBLIOGRAPHY: *DAB*, Supp. 5 (1951–1955), pp. 457–59; William F. Fox, Jr., and Robert A. Cook, "Missing Man of the Year," *SEP* 219 (September 28, 1946), pp. 14–15; Ronald L. Mendell and Timothy B. Phares, *Who's Who in Football* (New Rochelle, NY, 1974); *NYT*, April 1, 1952; "Obituary," *Time* 59 (April 7, 1952); Ashton Reid, "Indiana's Bo," *Colliers* 118 (August 31, 1946), pp. 42ff.; *WWA*, vol. 3 (1951–1960), p. 585.

Charles R. Middleton

McNALLY, John Victor "Johnny Blood" (b. 27 November 1904, New Richmond, WI; d. 28 November 1985, Palm Springs, CA), college and professional player and coach, was perhaps the most flamboyant NFL player ever. McNally, the son of a successful flour mill general manager and schoolteacher and the nephew of the publishers of the Minneapolis (MN) *Tribune*, rejected bourgeois life. After completing high school at age 14, the highly intelligent McNally drifted for several years until enrolling at St. John's (MN) University. At St. John's he earned varsity letters in football, basketball, track, and baseball. McNally left St. John's and entered the University of Notre Dame as a freshman, hoping to play under legendary football coach Knute Rockne.* He ran afoul of Notre Dame's discipline code and quickly returned to Minneapolis as a stereotyper on his uncle's newspaper.

In the fall, 1924, he tried out for the East 26th Street Liberties, a Minneapolis semi-pro team. Young athletes then customarily played under an assumed name to protect their amateur status. En route to the tryout, McNally passed a movie marquee advertising the Rudolf Valentino film *Blood and Sand.* Since the title stuck in McNally's mind, he rechristened himself Johnny Blood. After the 1924 season, McNally began a fifteen-year NFL career with the Milwaukee Badgers. He played with the Duluth Eskimos (NFL) in 1926 and 1927 and jumped to the Pottstown Maroons (NFL) in 1928. The following year, he joined the Green Bay Packers (NFL) and achieved stardom there. With the exception of playing the 1934 season for the Pittsburgh Pirates (NFL), Blood performed with the Packers from 1929 through 1936. He scored 37 touchdowns and 224 points with Green Bay, including an NFL-record 13 touchdowns in 1931. Blood led the Packers to

NFL championships from 1929 to 1931 and 1936 and was designated "All-League" from 1928 through 1930. He was named All-NFL left halfback in 1931, the first year such a team was officially selected. From 1932 on, Blood rushed 383 yards on 121 attempts and caught 65 passes for 1,106 yards.

Blood proved no favorite of Packers coach Curly Lambeau* because curfews were habitually broken, inexcusable absences became commonplace, and the aura of alcohol seemed always present. Blood viewed money as a commodity to be spent as rapidly as possible and did not believe any rule applied to him. Nevertheless, the 6 foot, 1 inch, 187 pound Blood became a devastating player with his slashing running style, great speed, and elusiveness. Bolstered by unlimited self-confidence, Blood proved an outstanding pass catcher with exceptional leaping ability. A fine defensive backfield player, he excelled as a strong tackler.

In 1937 Lambeau shipped Blood to Pittsburgh (NFL), where he served as Art Rooney's* player-coach until mid-1939. Blood's Pittsburgh stint began auspiciously when he returned the opening game kickoff against the Philadelphia Eagles for a touchdown. Blood's once magnificent playing skills deteriorated rapidly amidst subpar Pittsburgh teammates. Blood proved a coaching disaster, perhaps the most inappropriate choice ever made by a pro team to fill a head coaching position. Discipline, training, organization, and planning did not fit Blood's style. Blood's coaching record at Pittsburgh came to 6–19–0. After playing at Kenosha in 1940 and 1941, Blood joined the military and served as a cryptographer in China. He failed in a 1945 comeback attempt with the Packers and returned to St. John's (MnIAC), completing his education and later coaching the football team. The twice-married Blood later operated an employment agency. In 1958 he lost a campaign for sheriff of St. Croix County, WI, on a platform of "honest wrestling." Blood, inducted into Pro Football's Hall of Fame in 1963, later lived in Palm Springs, CA.

BIBLIOGRAPHY: Myron Cope, *The Game That Was: The Early Days of Pro Football* (New York, 1970); Arthur Daley, *Pro Football's Hall of Fame* (Chicago, 1963); Ray Didinger, *Pittsburgh Steelers* (New York, 1974); Pat Livingston, *The Pittsburgh Steelers: A Pictorial History* (Virginia Beach, VA, 1980); Ronald L. Mendell and Timothy B. Phares, *Who's Who in Football* (New Rochelle, NY, 1974); Howard Roberts, *Story of Pro Football* (New York, 1953); George Sullivan, *Pro Football A to Z* (New York, 1975); George Sullivan, *Pro Football's All-Time Greats: The Immortals in Pro Football's Hall of Fame* (New York, 1968); Roger Treat, ed., *The Encyclopedia of Football*, 16th rev. ed., rev. by Pete Palmer (New York, 1979); Joe Tucker, *Steelers' Victory after Forty* (New York, 1973).

Frank W. Thackeray

MADDEN, John Earl (b. 10 April 1936, Austin, MN), college athlete, professional football coach, and announcer, the son of auto mechanic Earl and Mary (O'Flaherty) Madden, moved at age 5 to Daly City, CA, near San Francisco, and played both football and baseball at Jefferson High

School. Madden started as a two-way tackle on the 1957 and 1958 California Polytechnic College (San Luis Obispo) team, which compiled an 18–2 composite record. An All-CaCAA football tackle and baseball catcher, he earned a Bachelor's degree in 1959 and a Master's degree in 1961 from Cal Poly. The Philadelphia Eagles selected Madden in the twenty-first round of the 1958 NFL draft, but a knee injury that fall ended his playing career.

In 1960 and 1961 Madden served as assistant coach at Hancock Junior College in Santa Maria, CA. As head coach at Hancock (1962–1963), he compiled a 12–6 record and saw his 8–1 1963 squad finish among the nation's top ten JC teams. From 1964 through 1966, Madden coordinated the defense for San Diego State College (CaCAA). The Aztecs, ranked number 1 among small colleges, won 26 of 30 games during his tenure there.

Madden served as linebacker coach for the Oakland Raiders in 1967 and 1968 and at age 33 became the youngest head coach in AFL history. He compiled a 12–1–1 record his first season, before losing the AFL championship game to the Kansas City Chiefs 17–7, and was named AFL Coach of the Year. During his ten-year pro coaching stint, Madden compiled an outstanding 112–39–7 record for a .731 percentage. He guided the Raiders to seven Western Division championships, as his squads won 10 or more games seven times. In 1976 Madden led the Raiders to a 13–1 regular-season mark, playoff and championship game victories over the New England Patriots and Pittsburgh Steelers, and a 32–14 triumph over the Minnesota Vikings in Super Bowl XI. Besides being the youngest coach to direct an NFL team to a Super Bowl victory, in 1976 he was named Washington (DC) Touchdown Club's Coach of the Year.

Following the 1978 season, Madden suddenly left pro football to spend more time with his family. He joined CBS Sports as a television commentator-analyst and teamed with George "Pat" Summerall* to become one of the nation's most popular sportscasters. The shirt-sleeved, 6 foot, 4 inch, 270 pound redhead vividly displayed his emotions on the sidelines. He was totally involved in every play, and he was often emotional with referees, flapping his arms and bellowing. Although a demanding coach, he is a gentle family man. He and his wife, Virginia Fields, have two sons, Mike and Joe. Mike played wide receiver at Harvard University (IL) and Joe is an offensive tackle at Brown University (IL). As a television commentator, Madden utilizes an informed, straightforward approach. Claustrophobia in planes forces him to travel to games by train. He seldom wears coats and never ties his shoe laces. Madden received Emmys for Outstanding Sports Personality-Analyst in 1981 and 1982 and was named Sports Personality of the Year by the American Sportscaster's Association in 1985.

BIBLIOGRAPHY: Gail Buchalter, "Jock," *People Weekly* (January 17, 1982), pp. 99–101; John Madden, *Hey, Wait a Minute, I Wrote a Book* (New York, 1984); John

Madden, *One Knee Equals Two Feet* (New York, 1986); *The Oakland Raiders Media Guide, 1977; TSN Football Register—1978; WWA*, 42nd ed. (1982–1983), pp. 2103–04.

John L. Evers

MADIGAN, Edward Patrick "Slip" (b. 18 November 1896, Ottawa, IL; d. 10 October 1966, Oakland, CA), college player, coach, and executive, compiled a combined 118–58–13 (.659 percent) football coaching record at St. Mary's (CA) College (FWC, 1921–1939) and the University of Iowa (WC, 1943–1944). A member of the HAF College Football Hall of Fame, Madigan was elected in 1974 to the NFF College Football Hall of Fame. Besides producing two undefeated seasons and one Cotton Bowl championship, he piloted two top ten nationally ranked teams and five All-Americans at St. Mary's. The Gaels under Madigan fielded only two losing squads in his nineteen seasons there.

Madigan enrolled in 1915 in pre-law at the University of Notre Dame and played varsity football in 1916 under Fighting Irish head coach Jesse Harper,* but did not letter as backup center behind All-American Frank Rydzewski. Madigan started at guard in 1917, when the Irish achieved a 6–1–1 record. He served in 1918 as a U.S. Army lieutenant in France during World War I and returned to Notre Dame in 1919. Knute Rockne,* in his second year as Notre Dame head coach, guided the Fighting Irish to the first of two consecutive 9–0–0 seasons. The 5 foot, 11 inch, 160 pound Madigan alternated at center with George Trafton* on a team featuring halfback George Gipp,* end Eddie Anderson,* and guard Heartley "Hunk" Anderson.* Madigan earned a law degree in 1920 from Notre Dame and that fall coached the Columbia Prep School eleven in Portland, OR.

Before Madigan became football coach and athletic director at St. Mary's College in 1921, the Gaels played mostly club, service, and freshman teams. Between 1918 and 1920, the 900–student Moraga, CA, independent college had finished with a 3–13–0 record and winless mark the last year. Madigan produced a 4–3–0 record his first season at St. Mary's, reducing California's and Stanford's point advantages to 21–0 and 10–7, respectively. By 1924 Madigan guided the Gaels to a 9–1–0 slate. That year St. Mary's defeated seventh-ranked Southern California 14–10 and lost 17–7 to second-rated, undefeated California.

St. Mary's finished undefeated (9–0–1) in 1926 and achieved its first triumph (26–7) over California in nine years. Center Larry Bettencourt in 1927 became the Gaels' first consensus All-American and led St. Mary's to a 16–0 upset victory over Stanford. St. Mary's frequently scheduled two or three West Coast teams rated in the nation's top ten. In 1928 the Gaels lost 19–6 to national champion Southern California and 7–0 to number 2 rated and Rose Bowl participant California. The following year, St. Mary's (8–0–1) achieved a scoreless tie with fourth-ranked California, defeated UCLA,

Oregon, Santa Clara, and San Francisco, and was rated ninth nationally by the William F. Boand System.

St. Mary's inaugurated a colorful intersectional rivalry with Fordham in 1930 at New York City's Polo Grounds and ended the Rams' 15–game undefeated streak. After St. Mary's fell behind 12–0 at halftime, fullback Angelo Brovelli spearheaded the Gaels' three-touchdown surge in the second half for a 20–12 triumph. A one point loss to California prevented an undefeated season, but the Gaels' 8–1–0 finish in 1930 earned them a thirteenth-place national ranking by Boand. Madigan's strongest team may have been the 1931 aggregation, ranked fifth nationally by Dickinson despite losing two of ten games. St. Mary's upset 13–7 national champion Southern California, regarded as one of the finest Trojan squads ever. The Gaels also defeated the PCC runner-up California and third-place Oregon and edged SWC champion SMU 7–2 on December 5 in San Francisco before 50,000 spectators. Otherwise, these four highly rated elevens finished with a composite 33–2–3 record. St. Mary's boasted its finest backfield in 1931 with All-American Brovelli, quarterback Jimmy Ahern, and halfbacks Bud Toscani and Bill Beasley and was captained by tackle Toby Hunt. The Gaels, however, were upset by mediocre Olympic Club and UCLA elevens.

Madigan epitomized the most flamboyant era of college football. St. Mary's famed annual junkets to New York City prompted journalist Westbrook Pegler* (OS) to dub the times "the era of wonderful nonsense." Eighteen Pullman cars transported the entourage from San Francisco, while all hotels, restaurants, and other accommodations were first class. The humorous Madigan, who always gave bright interviews to sportswriters, espoused gaudy uniforms and helped introduce silk pants and tearaway jerseys. Madigan sensed the coming popularity of Sunday football and scheduled games with Santa Clara on the Sabbath before capacity crowds of 60,000 in San Francisco's Kezar Stadium. He also sold tickets and suited up friends to sit on the bench to give the appearance of squad depth.

St. Mary's held its own between 1929 and 1939 with traditional rivals and frequently ranked among the nation's top 15 teams. Madigan's 1937 squad lost only to the nation's second-ranked (California), third-ranked (Fordham), and ninth-ranked (Santa Clara) teams in the AP poll. In Madigan's last eleven years at St. Mary's, the Gaels finished 7–3–1 with Santa Clara, 3–5–1 with Fordham, 4–5–2 with California, 1–1–0 with Southern California, 9–1–1 with San Francisco, 4–3–0 with UCLA, 6–1–0 with Oregon, and 2–0–0 with SMU. Halfback Ed Heffernan starred in the Gaels' 1939 Cotton Bowl 20–13 triumph over eleventh-rated Texas Tech. That summer Madigan served as assistant coach of the College All-Stars, who lost 9–0 to the New York Giants (NFL).

The smiling, gracious Madigan, who possessed an infectious laugh, was a great storyteller and gridiron gambler. He used the Rockne formation, preferring deception through speed and clever ball handling. His ample salary was tied to a percentage of gate receipts. Football historian L. H. Baker in 1945 said, "There is no doubt that from the publicity alone which this college received, Madigan was worth all he got." When St. Mary's Board of Control withheld his gate receipt supplemental salary for four years, Madigan deposited St. Mary's $100,000 share of the 1939 Fordham game receipts into his personal bank account. The subsequent financial dispute caused Madigan to leave St. Mary's after amassing a 116–45–12 (.705 percent) record in nineteen seasons. By 1939 more ex-Gaels were employed as CA public school teacher-coaches than from any other California institution.

Madigan in 1940 served as general manager of San Francisco's new Golden Gate Fields Race Track and then coached two wartime University of Iowa (WC) football squads, composed mostly of outmanned teenagers. Lacking service trainees and changing personnel frequently, his Hawkeyes produced a dismal 2–13–1 combined record. From 1944 to 1946 Madigan served as regional director of Small War Plants for three states. After helping launch the pro Los Angeles Dons (AAFC) in 1946, he in 1948 became a successful building contractor on the West Coast with his son Edward, Jr. A millionaire by 1958, Madigan built a 180–home development in Concord, CA, and named all of the streets for Notre Dame football heroes. Besides his son, he and his wife Charlotte had two daughters, Mary and Patricia. They lived in Oakland, CA, where Madigan died of heart failure.

BIBLIOGRAPHY: Patrick Chelland, *One for the Gipper: George Gipp, Knute Rockne, and Notre Dame* (Chicago, 1973); Ralph Hickok, *Who Was Who in American Sports* (New York, 1971); Dick Lamb and Bert McGrane, *75 Years with the Fighting Hawkeyes* (Dubuque, IA, 1964); *Notre Dame Football Guide, 1984;* Notre Dame University, Sports Information Office, South Bend, IN, October 1, 1985; Christy Walsh, *College Football and All-America Review* (Hollywood, CA, 1951).

James D. Whalen

MAHAN, Edward William "Eddie" (b. 19 January 1892, Natick, MA; d. 22 July 1975, Natick, MA), college player, athletic coach, and administrator, starred on the great Harvard University (IL) "golden era" football teams. After captaining the 1912 freshman squad to an 18–17 victory over Yale, Mahan started at varsity halfback the next year. He scored two touchdowns, including a 67–yard end run, in his first game. In the rout of Penn State, he even outshone famous teammate Charles Brickley* with brilliant open-field running on a muddy field. Coach Percy Haughton* deliberately kept the valuable Mahan out of the Cornell game to rest him for the Princeton contest. The strategy paid off, as Mahan ran fifty yards in Harvard's first victory at Princeton. A triumph over Yale gave Harvard an undefeated season and an astonishing 225–21 point advantage. Mahan, Brickley, and guard Stan Pennock* made the Walter Camp All-American team.

In 1914 Mahan's end runs again complemented Brickley's plunges to give

Harvard another undefeated, twice-tied season. When Brickley was sidelined by appendicitis, Mahan assumed the dropkicking and placekicking duties and converted two of each in the Princeton game. The final game for perhaps Harvard's greatest team came, ironically, at the dedication of the Yale Bowl. Mahan returned an early kick to Yale's 27–yard line and sparked Harvard to its greatest rout (36–0) to date over Yale. Mahan joined five teammates from the 7–0–2 squad, which outscored opponents 187 to 28, on Camp's All-American team.

From that extraordinary All-American list, Mahan alone remained in 1915. As team captain, Mahan scored the first touchdown of the season and led Harvard to four victories to extend the unbeaten streak to 33 games. In the last victory, Mahan's three field goals accounted for all of the Crimson's points in a 9–0 triumph over Virginia.

Mahan remained at Harvard as halfback coach and served in World War I with the U.S. Marine Corps in Europe. Following World War I, he performed relief work with Herbert Hoover in Europe. In 1924 he was named head baseball coach at Harvard. He joined the coaching staff of Choate School in Wallingford, CT, in 1926 and then was appointed director of athletics at Newman School in Lakewood, NJ. His subsequent investment banking career included stints with Hornblower and Weeks; Richardson, Hill, and Company; and Lee, Higginson, and Company. Mahan, who was survived by his wife and two daughters, worked with the Massachusetts Department of Natural Resources before retirement. He was elected to the HAF and NFF College Football Halls of Fame.

BIBLIOGRAPHY: Morris A. Bealle, *The History of Football at Harvard, 1874–1948* (Washington, DC, 1948); Allison Danzig, *The History of American Football: Its Great Teams, Players, and Coaches* (Englewood Cliffs, NJ, 1956); *NYT*, December 3, 1914; Paul Soderberg and Helen Washington, eds., *The Big Book of Halls of Fame* (New York, 1977).

Bruce Leslie

MARA, Timothy James "Tim" (b. 29 July 1887, New York, NY; d. 16 February 1959, New York, NY), professional owner, grew up on New York's lower East Side. Mara quit school at age 13 to support his widowed mother by selling newspapers and working as a theater usher. His newspaper route acquainted him with several bookmakers. Soon he became a runner for bookies, collecting debts for 5 percent and delivering winnings for tips. By age 18 he began taking bets. Mara's pleasant demeanor, quick mind, and unquestioned integrity made him a highly successful bookmaker, a legal pursuit then in New York. The NFL, meanwhile, had struggled through its first five years on a shaky financial foundation. NFL president Joe Carr* knew that the NFL needed a solid New York City franchise to prosper; thus, in 1925 Carr sought to interest New York City fight manager Billy Gibson in an NFL franchise for a bargain price of $500. Gibson rejected Carr's offer but suggested that Mara might consent. Mara joined the NFL, quipping, "A New York franchise to operate anything ought to be worth $500."

At the time, Mara knew nothing about football and admitted founding his New York Giants NFL franchise on "brute strength and ignorance." He hired capable personnel to handle field operations and saw his 1925 team produce a respectable 8–4–0 record. New York fans, still more enthralled by big-time college football, left the Giants with estimated losses of $40,000 to $45,000 with only one game left. In hopes of signing Red Grange* of the University of Illinois, college football's greatest star, Mara secretly traveled to Chicago. "The Galloping Ghost," though, already had joined the Chicago Bears. Mara arranged a game between the Bears and his Giants at the Polo Grounds. Nearly 70,000 fans saw the contest, giving Mara $143,000 net receipts and a respectable season profit.

The next year, however, Grange nearly destroyed the Giants financially. He and his manager Charles C. "Cash and Carry" Pyle* (OS) sought to put their own team into New York's Yankee Stadium, but Mara blocked this move at the NFL's winter meeting. They instead formed the rival AFL, centered on Grange and his New York team. Mara not only faced direct competition from football's greatest drawing card, but several of his stars defected to the new AFL. Although Mara lost $60,000, the AFL encountered more severe financial problems and disbanded after only one season. Mara's Giants emerged from the battle even stronger and won the NFL championship in 1927. Mara fought two more battles, winning easily a 1936–1937 skirmish with a second AFL. From 1946 to 1949, however, the rival AAFC hurt Mara's club and the entire NFL. Mara's Giants competed for fans with both an AAFC team in Yankee Stadium and a rival-league Brooklyn franchise. Despite heavy financial losses, Mara again emerged from the struggle strengthened.

Mara never forgot his early struggles. At the height of the Depression, he helped others less fortunate by arranging an exhibition game between the Giants and former Notre Dame stars, including the legendary Four Horsemen.* The contest, which the New Yorkers won easily, demonstrated the quality of pro football to a then skeptical public and raised $115,000 for the Unemployment Relief Fund. Mara, who resided with his wife, Lizette, and sons, Jack and Wellington, in New York, was named a charter member of the Pro Football Hall of Fame in 1963. His son Jack served as Giants president from 1953 until his death in 1965, while son Wellington has headed the club ever since.

BIBLIOGRAPHY: Arthur Daley, *Pro Football's Hall of Fame* (Chicago, 1963); Richard P. McCann, *Pro Football's Hall of Fame Dedication Yearbook* (Canton, OH, 1963); Timothy Mara file, Pro Football Hall of Fame, Canton, OH; Ronald L. Mendell and Timothy B. Phares, *Who's Who in Football* (New Rochelle, NY, 1974); Don Smith, "Mr. Mara," *The Coffin Corner* 6 (November/December 1984), pp. 7–8; George Sullivan, *Pro Football's All-Time Greats: The Immortals in Pro Football's Hall of Fame* (New York, 1968).

Robert N. Carroll

MARCHETTI, Gino John (b. 2 January 1927, Smithers, WV), college and professional player, was moved with his family to a California detention camp shortly before his fourteenth birthday during World War II because his father was an Italian immigrant. Marchetti never showed much football talent until his senior year at Antioch (CA) High School. Although named team MVP, he could not proceed directly to college and enlisted in the U.S. Army. Marchetti served in the infantry during the worst days of the Battle of the Bulge. After spending a year at Modesto (CA) Junior College, he was recruited by coach Joe Kuharich of the University of San Francisco. At San Francisco, Marchetti was a teammate of All-American Oliver Matson* and was named All-Pacific Coast and All-Catholic tackle in 1951.

Marchetti was drafted in the second round in 1952 by the Dallas Texans, a new NFL franchise. He attracted favorable notice as an offensive tackle, but the Texans seldom won and drew so poorly that they became a road team midway through the season. When the franchise was returned to the NFL for 1953, a new team named the Colts was formed in Baltimore. Here Marchetti switched to defensive end and became one of the premier players in pro history. He made 11 straight Pro Bowls (missing one because of an injury) and was named All-Pro seven times (1957–1962, 1964). At 6 feet, 4 inches and 245 pounds, Marchetti impressed others with his vicious pass-rushing. Coach Sid Gillman* called Marchetti "the most valuable man ever to play his position." In a 1969 poll, he was selected the top defensive end of the NFL's first fifty years. The Pro Football Hall of Fame named him to its AFL-NFL 1960–1984 All-Star Team.

Marchetti's father, a tavern owner, refused to watch him play for fear that his son would get hurt. He finally relented and watched the telecast of the famed 1958 NFL championship game, in which the Colts defeated the New York Giants in sudden-death overtime. Ironically, Marchetti broke his leg in two places while making a key tackle late in the fourth quarter. Marchetti retired after the 1964 season to concentrate on his flourishing restaurant business but returned for one more season when the Colts needed him in 1966. In 1972 he was selected to the Pro Football Hall of Fame.

BIBLIOGRAPHY: Bob Carroll, "Father Knew Best," *The Coffin Corner* 4 (February, 1982), p. 6; Gino Marchetti file, Pro Football Hall of Fame, Canton, OH; Ronald L. Mendell and Timothy B. Phares, *Who's Who in Football* (New Rochelle, NY, 1974).

Robert N. Carroll

MARINO, Daniel Constantine, Jr. "Dan" (b. 15 September 1961, Pittsburgh, PA), college and professional player, is the son of Pittsburgh *Post-Gazette* truck driver Daniel Constantine and Veronica Marino, of Polish descent, and has two younger sisters, Cindi and Debbie. After growing up in the Oakland working-class district, he graduated in 1979 from Pittsburgh Central Catholic High School and received a B.S. degree in Communications with a 3.0 cumulative grade point average four years later from the University of Pittsburgh. A Miami, FL, resident, Marino married longtime sweetheart Claire Veezey of Pittsburgh on January 30, 1985 in Oakland, PA, and has one son, Daniel Charles.

Marino started playing quarterback in the fourth grade for the St. Regis School football team, won the punt, pass, and kick competition at age 9, and guided his team in 1975 to a first place tie in the City Catholic Grade School League. At Central Catholic High School, Marino starred as a football quarterback and baseball pitcher. The Kansas City Royals (AL) selected Marino in the fourth round of the free agent baseball draft, but the heavily recruited 6 foot, 3 inch, 214 pounder instead accepted a football scholarship from the University of Pittsburgh coach Jackie Sherrill.

From 1979 through 1982 Marino guided Pittsburgh to 42 wins in 47 games and set Panthers career records for passing and total offense yardage (over 8,500). Despite not starting the first seven games as a freshman, the curly-haired Marino set a school season record for most yardage passing and ranked tenth nationally in aerials. The confident, candid quarterback completed 115 of 193 passes for 1,508 yards (59.6 percent) and threw 9 touchdown passes with only 7 interceptions. Sherrill's Panthers captured the Eastern title with an 11–1 record and finished sixth nationally. At the Fiesta Bowl, Marino guided Pittsburgh to a 16–10 triumph over Arizona State. In 1980 Marino made the All-East team by quarterbacking the Panthers to another 11–1 record. Marino completed 109 of 211 passes (51.7 percent) for 1,531 yards and 14 touchdowns. Pittsburgh overwhelmed South Carolina 37 to 9 in the Gator Bowl to finish second nationally. Marino enjoyed a sensational junior year and broke school career passing records, as the Panthers again finished 11–1 and ranked second nationally. The nation's second best passer and seventh best in total yardage, he completed 200 of 339 passes (59 percent) for 2,615 yards, tossed 34 touchdown aerials, and made several All-American teams. Pittsburgh was rated first nationally until Penn State handed the Panthers their first loss in 17 games. In the Sugar Bowl, Marino completed 26 of 41 passes for 261 yards and 3 touchdowns to defeat Georgia 24–20. Although initially a Heisman Trophy candidate, Marino disappointed fans, media, and pro scouts with a lackluster 9–3 1982 season. Pittsburgh, primed for a national championship, again lost to Penn State and 7–3 to Southern Methodist in the Cotton Bowl. Marino threw fewer touchdown passes, hurled 23 interceptions, finished only twenty-third nationally in total offense, and passed 341 times for 2,251 yards.

Miami Dolphins coach Don Shula,* impressed with Marino's strong arm, quick pass release, poise, and peripheral vision, picked him twenty-seventh in the first round of the NFL draft. Marino, the sixth quarterback chosen, signed an estimated $2 million four-year contract and replaced David Woodley as starter in the sixth game. In his debut, he passed for 322 yards and three touchdowns in a 38–35 overtime loss to the Buffalo Bills. Marino emerged as the most exciting NFL rookie, completing 173 of 296 passes for 2,210 yards and tossing 20 touchdown aerials. Wide receiver Mark Duper and running back Tony Nathan were Marino's leading receivers, with the former catching 51 passes for 1,003 yards and 10 touchdowns. Besides averaging 7.47 yards per throw, Marino suffered only 6 interceptions and was sacked only 6 times. The Dolphins won 9 of their last 10 regular-season games under Marino but lost to the Seattle Seahawks in the AFC playoffs. Marino, who possessed a better arm and more magnetic personality than former Dolphin star quarterback Bob Griese,* became the first rookie since the NFL merger to lead the AFC in passing (57.14 percent). The first rookie quarterback ever named to start in the Pro Bowl, he received the team's MVP award and was named *TSN* Rookie of the Year.

Marino shattered most NFL season passing records en route to winning the 1984 MVP award. The first NFL quarterback to exceed 5,000 passing yards in one season, he averaged 318 yards passing per game and completed 362 of 564 passes for 5,084 yards in leading the Dolphins to a 14–2 regular-season record and the AFC title. He threw 48 touchdown passes in 16 games, demolishing by 12 the mark shared by Pro Football Hall of Famers Y. A. Tittle* and George Blanda* in 14 games. An inspirational leader, Marino coolly handled blitzes, was sacked only 14 times, and hurled only 17 interceptions. He combined superb vision, quick releases, and exceptional control to throw over 400 yards a record 4 times and tossed at least 3 touchdown aerials in 9 different games. Marino used speedy wide receivers Mark Clayton and Mark Duper to burn secondary defenses, as the Dolphins scored an NFL season-record 70 touchdowns. Clayton caught 73 passes and a league season record 18 touchdown passes, while Duper made 71 pass receptions for 1,306 yards and 8 touchdowns. Besides recording 5 touchdown passes in the season opener against the Washington Redskins, he guided the Dolphins to victories in their first 10 games, passed for 470 yards in a 45–34 loss to the Los Angeles Raiders, and tossed 4 touchdown aerials in each of his last 4 games. In the AFC playoffs, he threw 3 touchdown passes in the semi-finals against Seattle and completed 21 of 32 passes for 421 yards and 4 touchdowns in the 45–28 championship game triumph over the Pittsburgh Steelers. His passing yardage and touchdowns set NFL championship game records and nearly matched in slightly over three quarters the 433 total yards that Dan Fouts* made in an overtime game. Although the San Francisco 49ers defeated the Dolphins 38–16 in the Super Bowl, Marino established game records for completions (29) and passing attempts (50). In 1985 he completed 336 of 567 passes for 4,137 yards, threw 30 touchdown passes and repeated as an All-Pro selection and Pro Bowl participant. Miami finished in first place in the Eastern Division of the AFC and defeated the Cleveland Browns in the playoffs before losing to the New England Patriots in the AFC title game. In 1986 Miami compiled an 8–8 record and failed to make the playoffs. Marino's 1986 statistics included 378 completions in 623 attempts for 4,746 yards, with 44 touchdown passes and 23 interceptions. Marino set NFL records for passes attempted and completions in a season and compiled the second best total for touchdown passes. His 4,746 passing yards marked the third highest total in NFL history, as Marino again made All-Pro. Marino became the NFL's leading career percentage passer while throwing for six touchdowns and 448 yards in a 51–45 overtime loss to the New York Jets and became the first NFL quarterback to throw for at least 30 touchdowns in three consecutive seasons. Through 1986 he has completed 1,249 of 2,050 passes (60.9 percent) for 16,177 yards (13.1–yard average) and has thrown 142 touchdown passes and 67 interceptions.

BIBLIOGRAPHY: Pete Axthelm, "The Year of the Rookie," *Newsweek* 102 (November 14, 1983), p. 79; Tom Callahan, "Twinkle in Two Men's Eyes," *Time* 124 (November 19, 1984), p. 109; Des Moines (IA) *Register*, 1983–1985; Jim O'Brien, *Hail to Pitt: A Sports History of the University of Pittsburgh* (Pittsburgh, 1982); *Street & Smith College Football Yearbooks, 1980–1983; Street & Smith Pro Football Yearbooks, 1983–1986*; Rick Telander, "Idol of the Marino Corps," *SI* 61 (December 24–31, 1984), pp. 86–91; John Underwood, "Miami's Set of Sparkling Studs," *SI* 61 (September 5, 1984), pp. 104–118; Paul Zimmerman, "The Class of Their Class," *SI* 59 (November 14, 1983), pp. 49–56.

Kevin R. Porter

MARSHALL, George Preston (b. 11 October 1896, Grafton, WV; d. 9 August 1969, Washington, DC), professional owner, was the son of West Virginia newspaper executive and later Washington, DC, laundry owner T. Hill Marshall. Young Marshall attended Friends Select School in Washington, DC, and Randolph-Macon College. After acting in stock company shows and serving in World War I, Marshall made a fortune in the laundry business in Washington, DC. His company expanded to fifty-seven branches before Marshall sold it in 1945.

He in 1932 became part-owner of the new Boston Braves (NFL) franchise. After suffering heavy financial losses the first year, Marshall's three partners quit. Marshall shifted the team from Boston's Braves Field to Fenway Park before the 1933 season and changed its name to the Redskins to capitalize on its association with baseball's Red Sox. Losses continued both on the field and at the turnstiles, despite the exploits of All-Pro runner Cliff Battles* and star tackle Albert "Turk" Edwards.* In 1936 Marshall hired Ray Flaherty* as coach and signed Notre Dame All-American end Wayne Millner.* The Redskins captured the NFL's Eastern Division title, but Marshall so disapproved of the club's poor attendance that he moved the championship game (which Boston lost) to a neutral site, New York's Polo Grounds.

For the 1937 season, he shifted his team to Washington, DC. The Redskins quickly became one of the NFL's most successful, popular operations. Marshall utilized fabulous halftime entertainments, including the Redskin Marching Band, pro football's first such unit. According to Marshall, "Football without a band is like a musical without an orchestra." He also pioneered in using pro publicity and public relations to "sell" the Redskins to the fans. In 1937 he signed TCU All-American passer "Slingin' Sammy" Baugh* amid a publicity blitz, making the quarterback pro football's most famous player before he ever played a game. Baugh fulfilled his notices by passing the Redskins to the NFL championship his rookie season. Baugh continued leading Washington's attack, helping the Redskins win another NFL championship in 1942 and Eastern Division titles in 1940, 1943, and 1945.

Marshall was married several times. His second wife, movie star Corinne Griffith, wrote a popular book, *My Life with the Redskins*. The flamboyant, fiery, competitive Marshall notoriously interfered with his coaches' decisions and sometimes lectured them on the field during the game. Flaherty largely ignored the owner's suggestions and left for the U.S. Navy following the 1942 season. Some Redskins coaching changes thereafter seemed more arbitrary than inspired. Owner Marshall paid players frugally. Star runner Battles retired after leading the NFL in rushing in 1937 because Marshall refused to give him a $500 raise. From 1946 through 1949 several Redskins players deserted Marshall for higher pay in the rival AAFC. Marshall also refused to sign black players until 1962, when All-Pro wide receiver Bobby Mitchell* joined the Redskins. Throughout the 1950s, the Redskins' lackluster record stemmed partly from their failure to sign black players.

Marshall nevertheless made numerous contributions to pro football. Besides his showmanship and successful Baugh-led teams, he directed the movement in 1933 to divide the NFL into Eastern and Western divisions and institute a championship game between division winners. He promoted rule changes that encouraged the passing game and field goals, returning the goalposts to the goal line from the end line. Failing health forced Marshall to retire in 1963, the same year he was named a charter member of the Pro Football Hall of Fame.

BIBLIOGRAPHY: Arthur Daley, *Pro Football's Hall of Fame* (Chicago, 1963); Richard P. McCann, *Pro Football's Hall of Fame Dedication Yearbook* (Canton, OH, 1963); George P. Marshall file, Pro Football Hall of Fame, Canton, OH; Ronald L. Mendell and Timothy B. Phares, *Who's Who in Football* (New Rochelle, NY, 1974); Don Smith, "George Preston Marshall," *The Coffin Corner* 6 (November/December, 1984), pp. 12–13; George Sullivan, *Pro Football's All-Time Greats: The Immortals in Pro Football's Hall of Fame* (New York, 1968).

Robert N. Carroll

MATSON, Oliver Genoa "Ollie" (b. 1 May 1930, Trinity, TX), college athlete and professional football player and scout, moved with his mother, Gertrude, a schoolteacher, from Texas to San Francisco, CA, as a teenager. Matson excelled in football and track at Washington High School in San Francisco and in 1948 scored 19 touchdowns as an All-American JC halfback at San Francisco City College. At the University of San Francisco (1949–1951), Matson in 1951 led the Dons through an undefeated nine-game schedule as a running back and was selected as a defensive All-American. Matson led the nation in rushing with 1,566 yards on 245 attempts and averaged 6.39 yards per attempt and 174 yards per game. The top all-purpose runner with 2,037 yards for 226.3 yards per game, Matson paced the nation in scoring with 126 points on 21 touchdowns. He tied an NCAA record with two kickoff return touchdowns in one game against Fordham University. Matson finished his career with a then all-time college rushing record of 3,166 yards on 547 plays in 30 games, averaging 105.5 yards per game and scoring 35 touchdowns.

Upon graduation in 1952, the 6 foot, 2 inch, 210 pound Matson was drafted in the first round by the Chicago Cardinals (NFL). At the 1952 Olympic Games in Helsinki, Finland, Matson finished third to win a bronze medal in the 400–meter run and captured a silver medal on the second place 1,600–meter relay team. Matson played for the Cardinals from 1952 to 1958, except for serving in 1953 in the U.S. Army. He led the Cardinals in scoring (1952, 1954, 1957–1958), rushing (1954–1958), punt returns (1955), and kickoff returns (1952, 1955–1956). With mediocre support most of his career, Matson enjoyed his greatest rushing season in 1956 with 924 yards. He tied the Cardinals record with two punt return and two kickoff return touchdowns in one season and in 1956 returned a kickoff 105 yards for a touchdown against the Washington Redskins. On March 23, 1959, Matson was traded to the Los Angeles Rams (NFL) for nine players. After leading the Rams in kickoff returns in 1959 and rushing in 1962, Matson became disillusioned with club methods and played out his option. Matson was traded to the Detroit Lions (NFL) after the 1962 season and in 1963 to the Philadelphia Eagles (NFL), where he performed for three seasons. At age 36, he returned 26 kickoffs for 544 yards. Matson retired following the 1966 season to operate a restaurant in Los Angeles and scout for the Eagles.

In his 14 NFL seasons, Matson only twice played on teams with winning records. The NFL Rookie of the Year in 1952 and All-NFL selection (1954–1957), Matson played in five Pro Bowl games and won the MVP award in 1956. As a pro, he recorded 12,844 combined net yards, 5,173 yards rushing, and 222 receptions; scored 438 points; and made 9 touchdowns on punt and kickoff returns. The quiet, calm, and friendly Matson married Mary L. Paige on August 22, 1954. He was enshrined in the Pro Football Hall of Fame in 1972 and is a member of the NFF College Football Hall of Fame.

BIBLIOGRAPHY: *Chicago Cardinals–Pittsburgh Steelers Football Game Program*, October 31, 1954; Murray Olderman, *The Running Backs* (Englewood Cliffs, NJ, 1969); *The Pro Football Hall of Fame Souvenir Yearbook, 1983–1984.*

John L. Evers

MAY, Mark (b. 2 November 1959, Oneonta, NY), college and professional player, is the son of bar owner Clarence and Ethel May and attended Oneonta public schools from 1965 through 1976 and the University of Pittsburgh from 1977 to 1981. At Oneonta High School, May participated in football, track, basketball, and wrestling. He played on Jackie Sherrill's first team as Pittsburgh head football coach and became the Panthers' starting left offensive tackle as a freshman. During May's successful career there, Pittsburgh lost only eight games in four seasons and made four bowl appearances. May impressed favorably the Pittsburgh area media. Besides being one of the most articulate Panthers and appearing at many public engagements, he became Pittsburgh's Lineman of the Week sixteen times and incredibly did not allow a quarterback sack his junior and senior seasons. In 1980 he won the Outland Award, awarded to the nation's best interior lineman, and made consensus first team All-American.

The Washington Redskins (NFL) in 1981 drafted the 6 foot, 6 inch, 288 pound May in the first round as an offensive left tackle, although the Pittsburgh lineman had played on the right side. May engaged in a contract dispute during his first training and reported late, causing him to fall behind schedule. Free agent Joe Jacoby won the starting job at left offensive tackle, but the persistent May eventually moved to his present right offensive guard position. May and the Redskins excelled in the strike-shortened 1982 season. The offensive line, nicknamed "The Hogs," helped the Redskins defeat the Miami Dolphins 27–17 in the Super Bowl XVII. May and the Redskins compiled an excellent 14–2 record during the 1983 campaign but lost to the Los Angeles Raiders 38–9 in Super Bowl XVIII. Washington repeated as Eastern Division champions with an 11–5–0 mark in 1984 before being upset by the Chicago Bears in the NFC playoffs. May's squad finished 12–4–0 in 1986 and defeated the Los Angeles Rams and the Bears in the playoffs before losing to the New York Giants 17–0 in the NFC championship game. May, a bachelor, has proven a major figure in the Redskins' success.

BIBLIOGRAPHY: *University of Pittsburgh Football Media Guide, 1980; Washington Redskins Press Guide, 1986.*

Michael J. Bodek

MAYNARD, Donald Rogers "Don" (b. 25 January 1935, Crosbyton, TX), college athlete and professional football player and coach, is the son of Ernest Thomas Maynard and Marian Arletta Sharpe. Since his father's cotton and construction businesses caused numerous moves, he attended public schools in Portales, NM; and Lamesa, Three-Way, and San Angelo, TX, before graduating from Colorado City (TX) High School in 1953. Maynard began participating in organized baseball and track in junior high school and playing both basketball and six-man football as a high school freshman. During his junior and senior years at Colorado City, he lettered in baseball, basketball, football, and track, won the state track championship in the high and low hurdles, and was twice named Best All Around Athlete in the high school.

Maynard accepted a track and football scholarship from Rice University (SWC) but transferred after one semester to Texas Western University, where he captured the BC track championship in the low and high hurdles. As a football left halfback and safety, he helped the Miners to a 1956 BC championship and appeared in the 1957 Sun Bowl. During his senior year Maynard led the Miners in scoring in 1957 with 52 points. Maynard married Marilyn Frances on December 13, 1956, and had two children, Terry Lynn and Tim Scott, before their 1978 divorce. Following college graduation, Maynard played in 1958 with the Eastern Conference–winning New York Giants (NFL). After the Giants released him, he played the 1959 season with the Hamilton Tiger-Cats, division winners (CFL).

Maynard in 1960 was the first player signed by the New York Titans, charter members of the newly established AFL. During his first AFL seasons, Maynard caught 72 passes for 1,265 yards and 6 touchdowns. When new owners renamed the Titans as the Jets and signed star quarterback Joe Namath,* Maynard became his most prolific receiver. In the 1968 AFL championship game that propelled the Jets to Super Bowl immortality, the 6 foot, 1 inch, 175 pound Maynard caught six Namath passes for 118 yards and the winning touchdown against the Baltimore Colts. During 13 seasons with the Titans/Jets, Maynard caught 627 passes for 11,732 yards and 88 touchdowns in 168 games and held all Jets receiving records upon retirement. He played for the St. Louis Cardinals (NFL) and Los Angeles Rams (NFL) in 1973 and served as player-coach for Shreveport (WFL) in 1974. Maynard returned to El Paso, TX, where he works in the life insurance business.

During his AFL–NFL career, Maynard played on five All-Pro Teams and held two league records: 11,834 career yards receiving and 50 games with at least 100 yards in receptions. He ranks second in career touchdown receptions (88) and fourth in career catches (633). Maynard was named to the All-Time AFL Team by the Pro Football Hall of Fame Selection Committee, and was inducted into the Texas Sports Hall of Fame in 1982 and to the Pro Football Hall of Fame in 1987.

BIBLIOGRAPHY: Tom Bennett et al., *The NFL's Official Encyclopedic History of Professional Football* (New York, 1977); Don Maynard file, Texas Sports Hall of Fame, Grand Prairie, TX; Don Maynard to Mary Lou LeCompte, 1984; Roger Treat, ed., *The Encyclopedia of Football*, 16th rev. ed., rev. by Pete Palmer (New York, 1979);

The University of Texas at El Paso, Sports Information Office, El Paso, TX.

Mary Lou LeCompte

MEADOR, Edward Doyle "Ed" (b. 10 August 1937, Dallas, TX), college athlete and professional football player, is the son of Euel Edgar and Esther (Cranford) Meador. His father, a mechanic who worked on heavy-haul equipment, moved the family from Dallas to Russellville, AR, midway through Meador's sophomore year in high school. At Russellville High, Meador was injured much of his junior year and then lettered in three sports as a senior. He was named All-District football halfback, earned all-district honors as a basketball guard, and ranked among the state's top track sprinters. Russellville High later enshrined him in its Hall of Fame.

Meador entered Arkansas Tech University (AIC) in the fall, 1955, and began an outstanding four-year career as a two-way halfback. During his sophomore year he returned a kickoff 102 yards against Southeast Missouri State to set a still-standing Arkansas Tech record. His 95–yard run from scrimmage against the College of the Ozarks and his 337 rushing yards against Hendrix College in 1958 remain school records. As a senior, he rushed 1,080 yards, scored 84 points, and earned NAIA All-American and Little All-American honors. A team co-captain as a junior and senior, Meador was named the state's Outstanding Amateur Athlete for 1958, won MVP honors in the 1958 Optimist Bowl, and earned the Neil Martin Award as top Arkansas athlete in 1959. The holder of several AIC records and many school marks, he made 3,448 career rushing yards, 45 touchdowns, and 272 points. He also passed for 949 yards, returned punts and kickoffs for a combined 1,619 yards, and intercepted 9 passes.

Besides his football exploits, Meador sprinted on the Arkansas Tech track team and participated in many campus activities. He served as president of the freshman class and the lettermen's club, was cadet commander of ROTC, belonged to Blue Key national honor society, and was named to Who's Who in American Colleges and Universities as a junior and senior. Meador, a member of both the NAIA and Arkansas Halls of Fame, married Paulette Mitchell on May 25, 1957, and has four children, Michael, Mark, William, and Victoria. After a 1976 divorce, he wed Annette Weiss in 1977.

Selected by the Los Angeles Rams in the seventh round of the 1959 NFL draft, Meador started at defensive back as a rookie. Blessed with outstanding speed, the blond, 5 foot, 11 inch, 195 pounder proved a vicious open-field tackler. Meador started 159 consecutive games for the Rams, played in five Pro Bowls, and earned five All-NFC selections. Although he had retired after the 1969 season, he was asked to return by the Rams during 1970 training camp and played his twelfth and final season with the club. Meador remains the Rams' career leader with 46 interceptions for 547 yards and 5 touchdowns. Following his retirement, he returned to Dallas, TX, and engaged in real estate development and investments. More recently, he and his wife have been involved in jewelry sales.

BIBLIOGRAPHY: *Arkansas Tech University Football Press Guide, 1984; Los Angeles Rams Press Guides, 1959, 1969, 1984;* Ronald L. Mendell and Timothy B. Phares, *Who's Who in Football* (New Rochelle, NY, 1974).

Jay Langhammer

MEYER, Leo Robert "Dutch" "The Saturday Fox" (b. 15 January 1898, Ellinger, TX; d. 3 December 1982, Fort Worth, TX), college athlete, coach, administrator, and professional baseball player, was the son of Robert Frederick and Julia (Lieck) Meyer and excelled as a mentor at TCU (SWC). Born of German parents in a German neighborhood, he spoke no English until grade school and participated in football, basketball, and baseball at a Waco, TX, high school. He graduated in 1922 with a degree in Geology from TCU, where he earned 11 varsity sport letters. As a pitcher, he won 30 of 34 decisions at TCU and signed a baseball contract with the Cleveland Indians (American League). After spending the 1922 season in the minor leagues and developing a sore arm, he began his coaching career at Polytechnic High School in Fort Worth, TX.

In 1923 Meyer became coach of all freshman sports at TCU (SWC). As TCU freshman football coach for 11 seasons, Meyer guided the Horned Frogs to 29 wins in 33 games. In 1934 Meyer succeeded Francis Schmidt* as TCU head football coach. As head coach for 19 years, Meyer became TCU's only football coach to win 100 games and developed 12 All-Americans, 39 All-SWC players, and Heisman Trophy winner Davey O'Brien.* Meyer's teams won three SWC championships, placed second four times, finished third four times, and upset so many teams that "Dutch" was nicknamed "The Saturday Fox." Seven times Meyer's Horned Frogs played in Bowl games. His 1938 team, which won all 10 games and defeated Carnegie Tech in the Sugar Bowl, remains TCU's only undefeated and untied team and won the national championship. From 1934 to 1952 Meyer's football teams compiled a 109–79–13 record.

Meyer served as TCU's athletic director from 1952 to 1963 and in 1956 coached the Horned Frogs baseball team to its first SWC title in 23 years. He also inspired the construction of a new stadium which bears his name and is nationally recognized as "Mr. Football, TCU." Meyer, a small, stocky coach, exhibited fiery, cocky, hell-raising characteristics. An excellent orator, he gave inspirational pep talks like those of Knute Rockne.* Besides showing his frustrations on the sidelines, he smoked cigarettes incessantly and was drained emotionally after games. Meyer was devoted to his players, who never forgot the spirit he instilled in them. An excellent teacher and strategist, he used imaginative, sound strategy. With All-American quarterbacks Sammy Baugh* and O'Brien from 1934 to 1938, he initiated "The Meyer Spread" that became the era's most advanced aerial development.

Meyer served as president of the NCAA and AFCA. He is a member of the HAF College Football Hall of Fame and in 1956 was elected to the NFF College Football Hall of Fame.

BIBLIOGRAPHY: Tim Cohane, *Great College Football Coaches of the Twenties and Thirties* (New Rochelle, NY, 1973); John D. McCallum and Charles H. Pearson, *College Football U.S.A., 1869–1973* (New York, 1973); *TCU Football Press Guide, 1979; TSN*, December 20, 1982; Kern Tips, *Football, Texas Style: An Illustrated History of the Southwest Conference* (Garden City, NY, 1964).

John L. Evers

MICHALSKE, August "Mike" (b. 24 April 1903, Cleveland, OH; d. 26 October 1983, Cleveland, OH), college and professional player and coach, made All-American fullback at Penn State University in 1925 and became an All-Time, All-Pro selection at guard. The New York Yankees (AFL) switched Michalske to guard in 1926 because of his speed and 6 foot, 2 inch, 209 pound size. The Yankees featured Red Grange* and were the top attraction of the short-lived AFL. When the AFL collapsed, the Yankees in 1927 joined the NFL.

Michalske, who made All-NFL guard in both 1927 and 1928, was owed $400 by Yankee owner Charles C. "Cash and Carry" Pyle* (OS) when the Yankees disbanded after two seasons. In lieu of money, the Yankees made Michalske a free agent to negotiate with another team. He signed with the NFL Green Bay Packers, which coach Curly Lambeau* had built into a juggernaut by adding stars Johnny Blood McNally* and Cal Hubbard.* The Packers won the NFL championships from 1929 through 1931, as Michalske made All-NFL each year to extend his personal string to five consecutive years. A 60–minute performer, Michalske remained a staunch blocker on offense and sure tackling linebacker on defense. He pioneered linebacker blitzes, joining tackle Hubbard among the first to use stunting extensively.

After being named All-NFL in 1935, Michalske became assistant football coach under Ernie Nevers* and head basketball coach at Lafayette College. In 1937 he returned to the Packers (NFL) for one final pro season. He coached football at St. Norbert College (WI) and from 1942 through 1946 at Iowa State University (BSC), where his Cyclones compiled an 18–18–3 record. He later served as line coach at Baylor University (SWC), Texas A&M (SWC), and the University of Texas (SWC) and as assistant coach for two seasons with the Baltimore Colts (NFL). In 1957 he left coaching because "I was always finding myself out of a job. I got tired of getting fired, so I quit." In 1964 he became the first guard ever elected to the Pro Football Hall of Fame.

BIBLIOGRAPHY: Chuck Johnson, *The Green Bay Packers* (New York, 1961); Richard P. McCann, *Football's Greatest Weekend* (Canton, OH, 1964); Ronald L. Mendell and Timothy B. Phares, *Who's Who in Football* (New Rochelle, NY, 1974); August Michalske file, Pro Football Hall of Fame, Canton, OH; George Sullivan, *Pro Football's All-Time Greats* (New York, 1968).

Robert N. Carroll

MILLER, Donald C. "Midnight." See under FOUR HORSEMEN.

MILLNER, Wayne Vernal (b. 31 January 1913, Roxbury, MA; d. 19 November 1976, Arlington, VA), college and professional player, coach and scout, was the son of the Charles E. Millners and entered the University of Notre Dame in 1932, becoming one of its all-time gridiron greats. After the first game of his sophomore year, he started at left end the rest of his three-year career. Millner made a historic, thrilling catch in the end zone of a William Shakespeare pass with five seconds left for an 18–13 victory over unbeaten Ohio State on November 2, 1935. Notre Dame scored three touchdowns in the fourth quarter, including two in the last three minutes, for the victory in perhaps the "Game of the Century." Besides earning nearly unanimous All-American honors in 1935 to conclude his college career, Millner played in the 1936 College All-Star game, as his squad tied the Detroit Lions 7–7.

In 1936 Millner joined the Boston Redskins (NFL) and played in the title game loss to the Green Bay Packers. The next year, the Redskins moved to Washington and performed in the championship game against the Chicago Bears. Millner caught 11 passes, including 55–yard and 77–yard aerials for touchdowns, to help Washington win 28–21. Millner became the top Redskins offensive end from 1936 through 1941, but he spent the next three and one-half years during World War II in the U.S. Navy as a gunnery officer. Upon his discharge in 1945, Millner rejoined Washington as a player-coach and ended his active career with 13 catches for 130 yards and 2 touchdowns in Washington's drive for an Eastern Division championship. Washington lost the title game 15–14 to the Cleveland Rams. During his pro career he caught 124 passes for 1,578 yards (12.7–yard average) and 12 touchdowns.

Subsequently, Millner held assistant coaching jobs with the Washington Redskins, Chicago Rockets (AAFC), Baltimore Colts (NFL), and Philadelphia Eagles (NFL). In 1956 he became head coach after the second game, when Alvin "Bo" McMillin* resigned because of illness. After Philadelphia finished the season with a 4–8 record, Millner retired as head coach because of illness. Millner spent many years as a part-time scout for the Washington Redskins and public relations director for an automobile dealer. A member of the HAF College Football Hall of Fame, the 6 foot, 189 pound Millner was inducted into the Pro Football Hall of Fame in 1968 and NFF College Football Hall of Fame in 1984.

BIBLIOGRAPHY: Jim Beach, *Notre Dame Football* (New York, 1962); Richard M. Cohen, Jordan A. Deutsch, and David S. Neft, *The Scrapbook History of Pro Football* (Indianapolis, IN, 1979); Bill Libby, *Champions of College Football* (New York, 1975); *A NYT Scrapbook History, The Complete Book of Football* (New York, 1980); *Notre Dame University Media Guide, 1982.*

James Fuller

MITCHELL, Lydell Douglas (b. 30 May 1949, Salem, NJ), college and professional player, excelled as a running back at Penn State University and professionally with the Baltimore Colts (1972–1977), San Diego Chargers (1978–1979), and Los Angeles Rams (1980) of the NFL. Mitchell attended Salem High School, where he performed well as a scholar-athlete. The president of his junior and senior classes, he scored 999 points in varsity basketball competition and in 1968 made All-State in football. At tailback under coach Joe Paterno,* the elusive, darting Mitchell broke all Penn State season and career football rushing records (Curt Warner* and D. J. Dozier have since surpassed Mitchell in career rushing yardage). In 1971 he established NCAA season records with 174 points, 26 touchdowns, by rushing, and 29 touchdowns combined rushing and pass receiving, and was named a consensus All-American. At the 1972 Cotton Bowl, he was voted outstanding offensive player for gaining 146 yards on 27 carries to lead the Nittany Lions to a 30–6 win over heavily favored Texas. Mitchell, who gained 2,934 yards rushing in his college career, earned a B.A. degree in Education in 1972.

Drafted in 1972 by the Baltimore Colts (NFL), the 5 foot, 11 inch, 198 pound Mitchell was considered too small for a running back and began his pro career slowly. By the mid-1970s, however, he ranked among the game's most consistent, versatile, and talented performers. In 1974 he established an NFL record for pass receptions by a running back with 72 catches. He in 1975 became the Colts' first 1,000–yard rusher in a season by gaining 1,193 yards on 289 carries. In 1977 he led the NFL in pass receptions with 71 catches. His Colts club records included most pass catches in a game (13, against New York Jets, 1974); most 1,000–yard seasons (3, 1975–1977); most carries in a game (40, against Jets, 1974); and most consecutive starts for a running back (63, 1973–1977). He also played in the 1975 through 1977 Pro Bowl games. In 1978 Mitchell was traded to the San Diego Chargers (NFL) and released after the 1979 season. He joined the Los Angeles Rams (NFL) in 1980 and retired in 1981 at age 31. During nine pro seasons and 111 NFL games, Mitchell gained 6,534 yards on 1,675 carries for a 3.9–yard rushing average. He caught 376 passes for 3,203 yards and scored 47 touchdowns for 282 points.

BIBLIOGRAPHY: Lydell Mitchell file, Pro Football Hall of Fame, Canton, OH; "Lydell . . . No Respect," *Cheerleader National Issue* (1978), pp. 118–20; "Preview Pro Football," *Newsday*, December 7, 1975; John F. Steadman, "Lydell Mitchell: The Colts' Record Slasher," *Football Digest* 5 (March, 1976), pp. 67–69.

John Hanners

MITCHELL, Robert Cornelius "Bobby" (b. 6 June 1935, Hot Springs, AR), college athlete and professional football player and executive, performed as a football halfback and wide receiver. From 1954 to 1958 the 6 foot, 195 pound Mitchell starred in football and track at the University of Illinois and in 1955 set a BTC record by averaging 8.6 yards per rush. In track, he established a BTC record in the indoor low hurdles and broke Harrison Dillard's* (OS) mark in the indoor 70–yard low hurdles. In 1958 he graduated from Illinois with a B.A. degree in Education.

The same year the Cleveland Browns (NFL) drafted him in the eighth round. Before reporting to the Browns, he shared the MVP Award for the 1958 College All-Star game with Jim Ninowski by scoring two touchdowns helping the All-Stars upset the NFL champion Detroit Lions, 35–19. At Cleveland from 1958 to 1961, he played 48 consecutive games at halfback alongside Jim Brown.* He was traded with Leroy Jackson to the Washington Redskins (NFL) for a number 1 draft choice, which the Browns used to select the late Ernie Davis.* Mitchell became the first black player for the Redskins, breaking Washington's color barrier. From 1962 through 1968 he played wide receiver for the Redskins. He joined the Redskins' personnel staff in 1968 and in 1981 was named their assistant general manager.

During his 11–year career, Mitchell made All-Pro from 1962 through 1964 and played in the Pro Bowl from 1961 through 1964. Mitchell gained 2,735 yards in 513 rushing attempts for 18 touchdowns and caught 521 passes for 7,953 yards and 65 touchdowns. He returned 102 kickoffs for 2,690 yards and 5 touchdowns and brought back 69 punts for 699 yards and 3 touchdowns. Mitchell scored 91 touchdowns for 546 points, ranking eighth behind Jim Brown,* Walter Payton,* Lenny Moore,* John Riggins,* Don Hutson,* Franco Harris,* and Jim Taylor.* He netted 14,078 combined yards, among the highest in NFL history. In 1962 Mitchell led NFL receivers with 72 catches for 1,384 yards and 11 touchdowns. For 10 seasons he ranked among the top 10 receivers. During his 7 years with the Redskins, Mitchell ranked first, second, fifth, fourth, sixth, and fourth and missed ranking only in 1968.

Mitchell, a multitalented offensive performer, possessed extremely shifty 9.5–second speed in the 100–yard dash and made spectacular long-distance scoring plays. In the opening game of the 1963 season, Mitchell caught a pass from quarterback George Izo and raced 99 yards for a touchdown against the Cleveland Browns to tie an NFL record. Mitchell and his lawyer wife, Gwendolyn Morrow, have two children: Terry Sue, a graduate student at Howard University, and Robert C., Jr., a student at Stanford University. Mitchell has been selected to Who's Who in Black America, the Arkansas

Hall of Fame, Washington, DC, All-Star Hall of Fame, and Washington, DC, Touchdown Hall of Fame. In 1983 he was inducted into the Pro Football Hall of Fame.

BIBLIOGRAPHY: Jack T. Clary, *Washington Redskins* (New York, 1974); Steve Guback, "Five for the Hall of Fame," *TSN*, July 25, 1983; *Official Pro Football Almanac, 1965* (New York, 1965); Don Smith, "Five Inductees Will Join Pro Football's Hall of Fame," *Football Digest* 12 (August 1983), pp. 54–55; *Washington Redskins Fan Guide, 1983*.

John L. Evers

MIX, Ronald Jack "Ron" "Intellectual Assassin" (b. 10 March 1938, Los Angeles, CA), college and professional player, is the second son of Sam and Daisy (Koskoff) Mix. His father, a Russian-Jewish immigrant, came to the United States at age 13 and became a tailor. At Hawthorne High, Mix excelled in football and track. He entered the University of Southern California (AAWU) in 1956 and played end as a freshman and sophomore. During his junior year he shifted to tackle and played 204 minutes there. He captained the Trojans squad as a senior, being named Most Valuable Lineman and All-American. He played in the Hula Bowl and was selected MVP in the Copper Bowl.

Although drafted in the first round by the Baltimore Colts (NFL), Mix spurned their offer and signed with the Los Angeles Chargers of the first-year AFL. As a rookie, he earned All-AFL honors and helped lead the Chargers into the AFL's first championship game. The club moved to San Diego for the 1961 season and played in another AFL title game, with Mix again making All-AFL. He shifted from tackle to offensive guard during 1962, making the All-AFL team and being the Chargers' MVP. The 6 foot, 4 inch, 255 pound Mix returned to tackle in 1963 and remained one of pro football's best offensive linemen until retiring after the 1969 season. Besides being named All-AFL each season from 1960 through 1968, he played in seven AFL All-Star Games and five AFL championship contests. He was selected to the All-Time AFL squad by the Pro Football Hall of Fame in 1970 and later to the AFL-NFL 1960–1984 All-Star Team.

Between seasons, Mix continued his education and received a Doctor of Jurisprudence degree in 1967 from the University of San Diego. Mix, whose article earned him the nickname "Intellectual Assassin," married Patricia Lanphier on February 14, 1965, and has three children, Carrie, Beth, and Darci. After completing law school in 1970, Mix returned to pro football. The Chargers traded him in July 1971 to the Oakland Raiders (NFL), where he performed capably in a reserve role. Following that season, he began his law practice and is a partner in the San Diego firm of Schall, Boudreau and Gore. He was inducted into the Pro Football Hall of Fame in 1979 and Jewish Sports Hall of Fame in 1980.

BIBLIOGRAPHY: Jack Horrigan and Mike Rathet, *The Other League* (Chicago, 1970); Ronald L. Mendell and Timothy B. Phares, *Who's Who in Football* (New Rochelle, NY, 1974); *Oakland Raiders Press Guide, 1972; San Diego Chargers Press Guides, 1960, 1969, 1983; University of Southern California Press Guide, 1959.*

Jay Langhammer

MODZELEWSKI, Richard "Dick" "Little Mo" (b. 16 February 1931, West Natrona, PA), college and professional player and coach, starred at football tackle. His older brother Edward played six pro seasons in the NFL and was nicknamed "Big Mo." From 1948 through 1952 "Dick" played for the University of Maryland (SC) and helped the Terrapins defeat Tennessee 28–13 in the 1951 Sugar Bowl. In 1952 he was selected to the All-American team and won both the Knute Rockne Trophy and Outland Award. A second-round NFL draft pick, he played with the Washington Redskins in 1953 and 1954. After Modzelewski signed with the Calgary Stampeders (CFL) in 1955, the Redskins and Stampeders signed a no raid agreement allowing "Little Mo" to remain with Washington. Modzelewski joined the Pittsburgh Steelers (NFL) in 1955 and then starred the next 8 seasons (1956–1963) for the New York Giants (NFL). From 1964 through 1966 he completed his playing career with the Cleveland Browns (NFL).

As a New York Giant, the outstanding 6 foot, 2 inch, 260 pound defensive tackle combined with Jim Katcavage, Roosevelt Grier,* and Andy Robustelli* to form the "Fearsome Foursome." During his fourteen-year pro career, he appeared in eight NFL championship games (six with the Giants and two with the Browns) and appeared on two NFL championship teams (1956 Giants and 1964 Browns). The ironman Modzelewski played in 180 consecutive games. Following retirement, he scouted for the Cleveland Browns in 1967 and served as their defensive line coach from 1968 through 1975 and defensive coordinator in 1976. Upon Forrest Gregg's* resignation late in 1977, Modzelewski became the Browns' interim coach. He returned to the New York Giants as defensive coordinator in 1978 and has served since 1979 as the defensive line coach of the Cincinnati Bengals (NFL). For his many accomplishments, he in 1985 was inducted into the Pro Football Hall of Fame and in 1986 into the National Polish-American Sports Hall of Fame. Modzelewski and his wife, Dorothy, have four children, Mark, Laurie, Terrie, and Amie.

BIBLIOGRAPHY: "Giants Edition," *Pro!* 9 (September 24, 1978), p. 41; Ronald L. Mendell and Timothy B. Phares, *Who's Who in Football* (New Rochelle, NY, 1974); Paul Soderberg and Helen Washington, eds., *The Big Book of Halls of Fame in the U.S. and Canada Sport* (New York, 1977).

Donald Kosakowski

MONTANA, Joseph C., Jr. "Joe" (b. 11 June 1956, Monongahela, PA), college and professional player, is the son of finance company executive Joseph, Sr., and Theresa Montana. At Ringgold High School in Monongahela, PA, Montana excelled in baseball and made All-American in football and All-State in basketball. The 6 foot, 2 inch, 195 pound quarterback entered the University of Notre Dame in 1974 and received a Bachelor of Business Administration degree in Marketing there in 1978. Due to a shoulder injury, Montana did not play football in 1976. He led the Fighting Irish to the national championship in 1977 and was one of Notre Dame's tri-captains in 1978. Montana led Notre Dame to a 38–10 victory over the University of Texas in the 1978 Cotton Bowl and rallied the Fighting Irish from a 23-point fourth-quarter deficit to a 35–34 miracle triumph over the University of Houston in the 1979 Cotton Bowl, being named the game's Most Valuable Offensive Player. Montana led Notre Dame in passing (1977–1978) and ranked second on Notre Dame's all-time list in passing yardage for one season with 2,010 yards (1978) and second in total offense (1978) with 2,114 yards on 332 plays. He remains second in career passing yards per game (1975, 1977–1978) with 4,121 yards and 25 touchdowns, fourth in pass completions with 268 of 515 passes, and fourth in total offense with 4,225 yards on 644 plays.

Selected by San Francisco in the third round of the 1979 NFL draft, Montana became the 49ers' regular quarterback in 1980. He led the NFL in completion percentage (1980–1981) and passes attempted and touchdown passes (1982). Montana established NFL career records for highest passer rating (92.7) and completion percentage (65.3), lowest interception percentage (2.60), and most consecutive 300–yard games in one season (5) in 1982. In seven pro seasons from 1979 through 1986, Montana has completed 1,818 of 2,878 passes for 22,408 yards and 141 touchdowns, thrown 76 interceptions, and compiled a 63.2 completion percentage. He has rushed 249 times for 905 yards and 12 touchdowns and at least twice has passed for over 400 yards in one game. His best performance came against the Atlanta Falcons on October 6, 1985, when he completed 37 of 57 passes for 429 yards and 5 touchdowns, all 49er records. Montana holds single-season club records with 3,910 passing yards in 1983 and a .646 pass completion percentage in 1984. Montana played in Super Bowls XVI and XIX following the 1981 and 1984 seasons. In 1981 he led the 49ers to a 26–21 triumph over the Cincinnati Bengals by running for one touchdown and passing for another. In 1984 he threw three touchdown passes and paced San Francisco to a 38–16 victory over the Miami Dolphins, setting a Super Bowl record with 331 passing yards. Montana was selected the MVP in both games. An All-NFC quarterback (1981, 1984–1985), Montana was named to the Pro Bowl team following the 1981 and 1983–1985 seasons. He underwent surgery for removal of a ruptured disc in September 1986 and missed several games. Upon returning to action in early November he led the 49ers to the NFC Western

Division title with a 10–5–1 mark. The New York Giants trounced San Francisco 49–3 in the playoffs as Montana was hospitalized with a concussion suffered in the second quarter.

Montana married Kim Moses in his second semester at Notre Dame but they divorced three years later. In 1981 he married stewardess Cass Castillo. After their divorce, in February 1985 he married actress/model Jennifer Wallace. He has no children.

BIBLIOGRAPHY: *CB* (1983), pp. 250–53; *Notre Dame Football Guide, 1984; TSN Football Register—1986*.

John L. Evers

MONTGOMERY, Wilbert (b. 16 September 1954, Greenville, MS), college athlete and professional football player, is the brother of Los Angeles Raiders (NFL) return specialist Cleo Montgomery. He graduated from Greenville High School in 1972, making All-State as a football defensive back. After briefly attending Jackson State University, Montgomery transferred to Abilene Christian University (LSC) and set a modern collegiate record by scoring 37 touchdowns as a freshman tailback in 1973. Lydell Mitchell* and Terry Metcalf had shared the previous mark with 29 touchdowns. The 11–1 Wildcats outscored opponents 466–206 and won the NAIA championship in their initial LSC season. At Abilene Christian, Montgomery rushed for 3,047 career yards, set a college record with 76 career touchdowns, scored at least one touchdown in 32 of 35 games, and gained over 100 yards 14 times. He also competed in track, achieving bests of 9.6 seconds for 100 yards, 20.8 seconds for 220 yards, and 25 feet, 6 inches for the long jump.

The Philadelphia Eagles (NFL) selected Montgomery as a running back in the sixth round of the 1977 draft. In 1977 the 5 foot, 10 inch, 195 pounder returned 23 kickoffs for 619 yards and an NFL-leading 26.9–yard average and recorded a 99–yard touchdown against the New York Giants. He the next season rushed for 1,220 yards (4.7–yard average) and 9 touchdowns, becoming the second Eagles player to surpass 1,000 yards rushing. The AP named Montgomery to the second team All-Pro. In 1979 Montgomery enjoyed his best pro season, rushing for a career-high 1,512 yards (4.5–yard average) and 9 touchdowns. The Eagles finished second to Dallas in the NFC Eastern Division with an 11–5 mark, as Montgomery became the fifth NFL player to rush at least 1,500 yards in a season and topped the 100–yard rushing mark seven times. Montgomery also caught 41 passes for 494 yards (12–yard average) and 5 touchdowns, making him the only NFL player with over 2,000 all-purpose yards that season. On November 4, 1979, he gained a career-high 197 yards against the Cleveland Browns. In 1978 and 1979 he tied club records by scoring 4 touchdowns in games against the Washington Redskins and was named to Pro Bowls.

In 1980 Montgomery helped the 12–4 Eagles win the NFC crown and a

Super Bowl berth by gaining 194 yards in the NFC title game against Dallas. No player had ever rushed 100 yards against the Cowboys in a playoff game. The next season, Montgomery rushed for 1,402 yards and 8 touchdowns and set an Eagles' record with eight 100–yard rushing performances. Knee injuries limited Montgomery's effectiveness in 1982 and 1983, but he in 1984 led the Eagles in rushing for the sixth time to tie Steve Van Buren's* club record. During 1984 Montgomery caught a career-high 60 passes for 501 yards (8.4–yard average) and passed Van Buren as the all-time Eagles rusher with 6,538 yards and 1,465 carries. The same season, he extended his club record of career 100–yard rushing games to 26. In August 1985 the Eagles traded Montgomery to the Detroit Lions (NFL). Montgomery, who retired after the 1985 season, rushed 1,540 times for 6,789 yards (4.4–yard average) and 45 touchdowns to rank fifteenth among all-time pro rushing leaders and had recorded three 1,000–yard rushing seasons. Montgomery also had caught 273 passes for 2,502 yards (9.2–yard average) and 12 touchdowns and returned 32 kicks for 814 yards (25.4–yard average) and 1 touchdown. Montgomery, who owns a meat market in Philadelphia, bested opponents with speed, dazzle, and desire, proving equally effective on long- and short-yardage situations. He and his wife, Cheryl, a former Dallas Cowboys cheerleader, have one daughter, Sherrita.

BIBLIOGRAPHY: Des Moines *Register*, January 13, 1981; *Detroit Lions Media Guide, 1986; Zander Hollander, ed., The Complete Handbook of Pro Football, 1984* (New York, 1984); *Philadelphia Eagles Media Guide, 1985; Street & Smith's College Football Yearbooks, 1973–1977; Street & Smith's Pro Football Yearbooks, 1978–1986; TSN Football Register—1986.*

David L. Porter

MOORE, Leonard Edward "Reading Comet" "Lenny" (b. 25 November 1933, Reading, PA), college and professional player and announcer, played in seven NFL Pro Bowls, made All-NFL running back or flanker five times, and scored 113 touchdowns for the Baltimore Colts. As an All-State running back at Reading High School, Moore led his football team to its best record in its first 75 years, played on a district championship basketball squad, and won a silver medal in the state track championships in the 1951–1952 season. From there, he matriculated at Penn State University and graduated in 1956. Moore set school football records or led the Nittany Lions from 1953 to 1955 in rushing, scoring, pass interceptions, and kick returning.

The "Reading Comet," as the speedy 6 foot, 1 inch, 190 pounder was known, compiled a career rushing average of 6.2 yards per carry at Penn State with 2,380 yards in 382 attempts over three years and paced the Nittany Lions in rushing all three seasons. In 1954 he set a then school record with 1,082 yards rushing, paced the team in kickoff returns, and also brought back punts. He led Penn State two years in pass interceptions and scoring.

Moore played in the Shrine All-Star (East-West) post-season game and received All-American mention his junior and senior years. His effectiveness was enhanced through his frequent use as a decoy by coach Charles "Rip" Engle.* He was the first black collegian to play at Fort Worth, TX, when the Nittany Lions visited TCU.

The first draft choice of the Baltimore Colts in 1956, Moore quickly became an NFL standout as a flanker and was named the NFL's Rookie of the Year with a 7.5–yard rushing average. After that successful pro debut, he married Frances Elizabeth Martin on December 25, 1956. His pro career with the Colts as a flanker through 1961 and then as a running back and occasional split end lasted through 1967. Called "Spats" by his teammates because of the appearance of tape wound tightly over his shoes, Moore experienced a subpar season in 1963 because of injury, health, and other problems. It was thought his career was over, but in 1964 he became the NFL Comeback Player of the Year, *TSN* NFL Player of the Year, and NFL MVP. Moore that year led the NFL with 20 touchdowns, including 16 via rushing, 3 on pass receptions, and 1 on a fumble recovery. He scored touchdowns in a record eighteen straight games from late 1963 into 1965. Moore's longest NFL touchdown run, however, came on a 108–yard kickoff return in 1957, his only return that season.

For his pro career, Moore set an NFL record for most years leading the league in rushing average (1956–1958, 1961). His 113 career touchdowns were surpassed at that point only by Jimmy Brown.* In 143 NFL games, Moore gained 11,213 yards—5,174 via rushing and 6,039 on pass receptions. He was selected to the Pro Football Hall of Fame in 1975. Colt quarterback John Unitas* called him "the best offensive back in the league," while split end Raymond Berry* said, "Lenny Moore has got to be the greatest athlete I've ever seen." Pennsylvania sports historian Paul Beers named Moore to a modern All-time, All-Pennsylvania offensive football team. At various times during and after his pro football career, Moore operated a tavern, served as a disc jockey and "jazz expert," and provided TV color commentary for Colt games.

BIBLIOGRAPHY: Paul B. Beers, *Profiles in Pennsylvania Sports* (Harrisburg, PA, 1975); David S. Neft et al., *The Sports Encyclopedia, Pro Football* (New York, 1977); Murray Olderman, *The Running Backs* (Englewood Cliffs, NJ, 1969); Tim Panaccio, *Beast of the East: A Game by Game History of the Penn State–Pitt Football Rivalry 1893 to 1891* (West Point, NY, 1982); *PIAA Guide Book of Pennsylvania High School Athletics, 1951–1952* (Vandergrift, PA, 1952); *Penn State University Football Media Guides, 1953–1956; Pro Football Hall of Fame Souvenir Yearbook, 1975;* Ridge Riley, *Road to Number One; A Personal Chronicle of Penn State* (Garden City, NY, 1977); *TSN Football Register*—1959–1967.

Robert B. Van Atta

MORAN, Charles Barthell "Uncle Charlie" (b. 22 February 1878, Nashville, TN; d. 13 June 1949, Horse Cave, KY), college and professional athlete and football coach, umpired NL baseball twenty-four seasons (1916–1939) and worked four World Series (1927, 1929, 1933, 1938). His eighteen-year college football coaching record (122–33–12) ranks twentieth nationally in winning percentage (.766) among all-time college coaches. The HAF College Football and Texas A&M Athletic Halls of Fame member guided tiny, 267–student Centre College (KY) in 1921 to a 6–0 upset of powerful Harvard University, undefeated in twenty-five games over two and one half seasons including a Rose Bowl triumph and national championship. In a poll of the nation's sportswriters in 1951, the AP voted this game the biggest football upset of the first half of the twentieth century.

Moran, a sensational Nashville, TN, high school football halfback and the son of an area farmer, was recruited by the University of Tennessee (SIAA) in 1897. He played football one year, producing several outstanding touchdowns during the Volunteers' 4–1–0 season before transferring to Bethel College (TN). He completed his higher education there over the next three years and served as player-coach of the Bethel football squad. He served as player-coach with the pro football Massillon (OH) Tigers and assistant grid coach at Carlisle Indian School under Pop Warner,* and pitched in baseball for Chattanooga, TN, and Little Rock, AR (Southern Association) and Dallas, TX (Texas League). The St. Louis Cardinals (National League) brought him to the majors in 1903 as a pitcher, but he developed a sore arm (0–1 record, 5.25 earned run average). In 1908 he rejoined the Cardinals as a catcher and batted .175 in twenty-one games. He also caught for Milwaukee, Brewers (American Association) and Montgomery, AL (Southern Association). From 1909 to 1914 Moran spent summers as a baseball umpire in the Texas League and autumns as head football coach at Texas A&M College (TIAA). The Aggies had defeated the University of Texas only once in seventeen games before Moran guided them to three consecutive triumphs. Texas A&M amassed a composite 38–8–4 (an all-time school-record .800 percent) under Moran, boasting one undefeated season, three TIAA championships, and a school-record 366 points in 1912.

The rough-talking and demanding Moran exploited liberal eligibility rules requiring transfer students to attend only one day of classes before joining the football squad. Although Moran was tremendously popular with his players and the students, his Aggies contract was not renewed. Texas had severed relations with the Aggies, accusing Moran of using ringers and coaching "dirty football." Some Texas A&M officials believed he "won too many games," but the Corps of Cadets honored him on his final day there with a full dress parade. A Charlie Moran Day was held at College Station, TX, in 1938 and the Class of 1913 at their thirty-fifth reunion in 1948 named his an honorary class member. Moran returned to pro football at Massillon the next three autumns (1915–1917) and in 1918 joined coach Robert L. "Chief"

Myers at Centre College as football assistant. Myers preferred promoting Centre athletics and insisted that Moran assume the football head coaching duties. During the next five seasons (1919–1923) under Moran, the Colonels amassed a combined 41–6–1 (.865 percent) record.

Centre achieved undefeated regular seasons in 1919 and 1921, when they were named Southern champions by football authority Parke H. Davis. During that span, Moran was the only Southern coach to place three players (quarterback Alvin "Bo" McMillin,* center Jim Weaver, and end Jim Roberts) on Walter Camp's* All-American first teams. Chief Myers in 1917 brought McMillin, Weaver, end Madison "Matty" Bell,* and tackle Bill James with him from Ft. Worth (TX) Northside High School to form the nucleus of the strong Centre teams of that period. Moran, a colorful, controversial figure, washed the uniforms, cut the grass, and lined the gridiron. His players were nicknamed the "Prayin' Colonels" after Moran suggested a prayer at halftime of a game with West Virginia. The 1921 squad was defeated 22–14 by SWC champion Texas A&M in the post-season Dixie Classic at Dallas, a forerunner of the Cotton Bowl. The Colonels took the contest too lightly, with McMillin being married the morning of the game. The comparative scores with common foe TCU had made Centre the overwhelming favorite.

Moran coached the Bucknell University football team (1924–1926) to a combined 20–9–2 record that included notable triumphs over Navy, Rutgers, and Georgetown (Washington, DC). After being co-coach in 1927 of the 6–9–3 seventh-place Frankford Yellow Jackets (NFL), Moran inherited a losing football program in 1930 at Catawba (NSC) College and produced an undefeated season his first year. In four seasons, his gridders finished 23–10–5 and captured two NSC championships.

Moran married Pearl McGee, whom he met at Bethel College; their one son, Tommy, played on the Centre College eleven. Moran took great pride in the baseball umpiring profession and stressed, "It ain't nothin' until I call it." His raspy voice resembled a buzz-saw when his decisions were disputed. He experienced early baptism of fire in 1918, when he called out a Philadelphia Phillies base runner in a close play at home plate in the Polo Grounds with the New York Giants holding a ninth inning 3–2 lead. Moran was jostled so roughly by several Phillies players that he used his fists in defense. Around 1,000 Giant fans rushed onto the playing field and massed around the beleaguered umpire to protect him as a near riot ensued. "If you umpire a game without calling attention to yourself, you have had a good day," he once said. "The public never notices you until it thinks you've called one wrong." Moran retired with a lifetime pension of $2,000 a year and spent most of his remaining years operating his farm outside of Horse Cave, KY. After being bedfast for three weeks, Moran died at home of a heart ailment.

BIBLIOGRAPHY: John Devaney, "The Praying Colonels," *Sport* 42 (November, 1966), pp. 44–45, 73–75; Wilbur Evans and H. B. McElroy, *The Twelfth Man: A Story of Texas A&M Football* (Huntsville, AL, 1974); Hart County (KY) Historical Society,

Horse Cave, KY, 1986; Ralph Hickok, *Who Was Who in American Sports* (New York, 1971); Charles Moran file, National Baseball Hall of Fame and Museum, Cooperstown, NY; Tom Siler, *The Volunteers* (Knoxville, TN, 1950); Kern Tips, *Football, Texas Style: An Illustrated History of the Southwest Conference* (Garden City, NY, 1964).

James D. Whalen

MORRALL, Earl Edwin "Mr. Eyebrows" (b. 17 May 1934, Muskegon, MI), college athlete and professional football player and coach, is the son of Arthur and Helen Morrall. Morrall established his athletic credentials at Muskegon Central High School, where he starred in football, basketball, and baseball. A fine student, Morrall received a football athletic scholarship in 1952 at Michigan State University. Under the tutelage of great Michigan State (BTC) coaches Clarence "Biggie" Munn* and Duffy Daugherty,* the 6 foot, 1 inch, 185 pound Morrall became one of the most notable quarterbacks in Spartans history. In 1969 he was named to the All-Time Michigan State team.

Although the starting quarterback in 1954, he enjoyed his greatest season his senior year in 1955. Nicknamed "Mr. Eyebrows," Morrall led the Spartans to the Rose Bowl. The Spartans recorded nine wins and one loss, including a fine 21–7 triumph over Paul Hornung's* Notre Dame and a dramatic 17–14 Rose Bowl victory over UCLA. In the Rose Bowl game, Morrall led the drive to set up Dave Kaiser's winning 41–yard field goal with seven seconds left. Morrall held the ball for Kaiser's kick. His 1955 statistics included 46 pass completions for 979 yards and 6 touchdowns. He compiled an exceptional 13.8–yard average per pass for the regular season. During the temporary return to one-platoon football, Morrall displayed his versatility as a safety on defense and a most effective punter. In 1955 he averaged 42.6 yards per kick, a Spartans record for over twenty years. He holds the Michigan State record for the longest fumble return, a 90–yard touchdown run against Purdue in 1955. As a quarterback, Morrall called most of his own plays for Michigan State's "multiple" offense and displayed intelligence, leadership, exceptional ball-handling abilities, and blocking skills. For his great season, Morrall was named to several All-American teams.

Morrall excelled as an infielder on the Michigan State baseball team, which participated in the College World Series in 1954. An honors student, he received a B.S. degree in Mechanical Engineering in 1957. He married Jane Whitehead in June 1956 and has five children: Matt, Mardi, Mindi, Mitchell, and Meghan.

The San Francisco 49ers (NFL) drafted Morrall as their first choice in 1956. For many seasons, Morrall's NFL career was a "checkered" affair. He was shuttled among teams and shared quarterback duties with heralded stars Y. A. Tittle* at San Francisco, Bobby Layne* at Pittsburgh, Fran Tarkenton* at New York, and Bob Griese* at Miami. Some have called Morrall the greatest relief quarterback in pro football history. Whenever called upon to start, Morrall proved a distinguished pro football quarterback. He was celebrated in George Plimpton's *The Paper Lion* as cerebral—generous to Plimpton with his special insights and to youngsters with his time. His 21-year NFL playing career, spanning 241 regular season NFL games, ranks among the longest in pro history. After one NFL season with the 49ers, he spent over one year with the Pittsburgh Steelers, almost seven with the Detroit Lions, three with the New York Giants, four with the Baltimore Colts, and five with the Miami Dolphins. Altogether, he completed an impressive 1,379 passes in 2,689 attempts for 20,809 career yards and threw for 61 touchdowns.

The high and low points of his career occurred during the 1968–1969 season. Under his favorite coach Don Shula,* he replaced injured Johnny Unitas* and led the Baltimore Colts to a 13–1 regular season record and 34–0 triumph over the Cleveland Browns for the NFL championship. During the season he completed 182 passes in 317 attempts for 2,909 total yards, led the NFL in passing, and was named MVP. As the Colts' starting quarterback in Super Bowl III, however, he was intercepted three times. The New York Jets established parity for the AFL with their 16–7 victory sparked by Joe Namath.* Morrall received redemption when he again replaced an injured Unitas and led the Colts to a 16–13 triumph over the Dallas Cowboys in Super Bowl V in 1971. Subbing for an injured Griese after Shula picked him up on waivers, Morrall directed Miami through 12 wins in an undefeated 17–0 season in 1972 and was chosen AFC Player of the Year and the Dolphins MVP.

Retiring after the 1976 season, Morrall became president of Arrowhead Country Club in Fort Lauderdale, FL, and part-time coach for the University of Miami Hurricanes. He also serves on the board of directors of Atlantic Service Group. In 1979 he was enshrined in the Michigan Sports Hall of Fame. Morrall's charisma and analytical intelligence are reflected in his autobiography, *In the Pocket: My Life as a Quarterback* (1969).

BIBLIOGRAPHY: Tom Bennett et al., *The NFL Official Encyclopedic History of Professional Football* (New York, 1977); Duffy Daugherty with Dave Diles, *Duffy: An Autobiography* (Garden City, NY, 1974); Ronald L. Mendell and Timothy B. Phares, *Who's Who in Football* (New Rochelle, NY, 1974); *Michigan State University Football Media Guides, 1953–1955;* Michigan State University, Sports Information Office, East Lansing, MI; Earl Morrall and George Sullivan, *In the Pocket: My Life as a Quarterback* (New York, 1969); George Plimpton, *Paper Lion* (New York, 1964); Fred W. Stabley, *The Spartans: A Story of Michigan State Football* (Huntsville, AL, 1975); *TSN Football Register—1976.*

Erik S. Lunde

MORRISON, Jesse Raymond "Ray" (b. 28 February 1885, Sugar Branch, IN; d. 19 November 1982, Miami Springs, FL), college athlete, coach, and administrator, coached football 34 years at SMU (SWC, 1915–1916, 1922–1934), Vanderbilt University (SC, 1918, SEC, 1935–1939), Temple University (1940–1948), and Austin (TX) College (1949–1952). His famed "Aerial Circus" at SMU broke with orthodox football and popularized passing as a major offensive weapon. Passes were thrown on any down regardless of field position. Morrison starred in football four years (1908–1911) at halfback and quarterback for Vanderbilt University, where he was team captain, three-time All-SIAA, and 1911 Grantland Rice* (OS) *New York Evening World* All-American. The FWAA chose Morrison Early (1869–1919) All-Time Southeastern Regional quarterback, while the Nashville (TN) *Banner* (1937) named him SEC Coach of the Year. Morrison was chosen quarterback on the Vanderbilt All-Time team (1933) and selected to the NFF College Football (1954), HAF College Football, NACAD, Texas Sports (1963), and Tennessee Sports Halls of Fame.

During Morrison's playing career, Vanderbilt achieved a composite 30–6–2 record, two SIAA titles, and one undefeated season. The Commodores tied Yale University 0–0, the first time the Elis were held scoreless at home. College Hall of Famers Edwin "Ted" Coy* and Walter Eckersall* were impressed by Morrison's play, while Commodore coach Dan McGugin* declared, "Ray is the best quarterback I have ever seen." The 5 foot, 11 inch, 157 pound Morrison served as president of the sophomore and senior classes, baseball captain, and track sprinter and won twelve letters before graduating with a B.A. degree from Vanderbilt in 1912.

The son of farmer James S. and Estella May (McHenry) Morrison, he grew up in McKenzie, TN, and attended McTyire Prep School there. Morrison quarterbacked teams that lost only two games in four years and graduated from McTyire in 1908. He taught mathematics and coached football (1912–1914) at Branham and Hughes Military Academy in Spring Hill, TN, where his gridders lost only two games in three seasons. Newly formed SMU (SWC) hired Morrison in 1915 to organize its athletic department, construct the football field, and become its first grid coach. The SMU president insisted upon an extremely difficult schedule, although the Mustangs fielded inexperienced material. Morrison consequently was fired after a two-season 2–13–2 record. Morrison served as U.S. Army YMCA secretary (1917) at Fort Oglethorpe, GA, and replaced McGugin (1918) as head coach, guiding Vanderbilt (SIAA) to a 4–2–0 mark. He insisted that McGugin return as head coach of the Commodores after the latter's business venture failed. After coaching and teaching mathematics at Gulfport (MS) Academy (1919), he returned to SMU as freshman football coach (1920–1921). He recruited at SMU the "Immortal Ten," seven of whom made All-SWC and lost only two SWC games in three years.

After being named Mustang head coach in 1922, Morrison guided the "Immortal Ten" with quarterback Logan Stollenwerck to a 9–0–0 season (1923) and SMU's first SWC championship. The Mustangs won two additional SWC titles under Morrison (1926, 1931), finished second three times, and placed no lower than fifth. They achieved five undefeated regular seasons with outstanding backs Gerald Mann, Redman Hume, and Weldon Mason, and tackle Marion Hammon. The Mustangs signaled the emergence of SWC members as football powers with close intersectional losses to ninth-ranked Army in 1928 and top-rated Notre Dame in 1930. SMU upset highly regarded Fordham 26–14 at the Polo Grounds in 1934. Morrison's composite record during his last 13-year stint at SMU comprised 82–31–20. His final Mustangs squad (1934) boasted future All-American halfback Bobby Wilson,* guard J. C. Wetsel, and tackle Truman Spain, who played in the Rose Bowl and shared the 1935 national championship under coach Matty Bell.*

Morrison replaced McGugin at Vanderbilt (SEC) in 1935, when the Commodores defeated Tennessee and Alabama for the first time in nearly a decade. Vanderbilt placed second in the SEC and missed a Sugar Bowl invitation by failing to gain twelve inches in three downs in a 7–2 loss to SEC champion Louisiana State University. Morrison's 1937 squad finished 7–2–0 with star tackle "Baby" Ray and All-American center Carl Hinkle, triumphed over LSU and Tennessee, but failed to receive a Rose Bowl bid after a 9–7 loss to Alabama. After scoring a field goal against the Commodores in the last two minutes, the Crimson Tide were chosen to represent the SEC at Pasadena. Morrison achieved a composite 25–20–2 record at Vanderbilt before becoming head coach and athletic director at Temple.

Morrison, scholarly in appearance and innovative, employed the trap play and five-man defensive line early in his career. His best seasons at Temple came in 1941 (7–2–0) and 1945 (7–1–0), but his material typically was substandard. The Owls lost several games to strong Penn State, West Virginia, Syracuse, Army, Michigan State, and Oklahoma and finished with a composite 31–38–9 record under Morrison. Sought by Yale as head coach, Morrison joined Austin College (TX) as coach because his wife wished to return to Texas. His four-year record there comprised an unspectacular 11–26–0, after which he retired from coaching in 1953. Morrison married Julia Goar and had two daughters and one son. He returned to SMU for the third time as vice president of public relations and development until retiring in 1964. He served on the NCAA rules committee for many years and was honored by the AFCA in 1980 as the oldest living past president. He lived his last four years with his son Jack in Miami Springs, FL, where he suffered a fatal stroke.

BIBLIOGRAPHY: Tim Cohane, *Great College Football Coaches of the Twenties and Thirties* (New Rochelle, NY, 1973); Zipp Newman, *The Impact of Southern Football* (Montgomery, AL, 1969); Temple Pouncey, *Southern Methodist Football: Mustang Mania* (Huntsville, AL, 1981); Harold V. Ratliff, *The Power and the Glory: The Story of Southwest Conference* (Lubbock, TX, 1957); Fred Russell and Maxwell E. Benson, *50 Years of Vanderbilt Football* (Nashville, TN, 1938); Kern Tips, *Football, Texas Style: An Illustrated History of the Southwest Conference* (Garden City, NY, 1964).

James D. Whalen

MOSES, Haven Christopher (b. 27 July 1946, Los Angeles, CA), college and professional player, ranked among Don Coryell's* greatest wide receivers at San Diego State University and among the most dangerous long yardage performers in the AFL-NFL during fourteen seasons with the Buffalo Bills and Denver Broncos. Moses, an outstanding high school athlete in San Pedro, CA, won four varsity letters each in football and baseball and two in basketball. After two years at Harbor Junior College in Los Angeles, he transferred to San Diego State (CaCAA) in 1966. The University of Southern California also had sought him, but as a defensive back. Under Coryell, he shone as an all-around player with outstanding blocking, punt returning, defensive, and receiving skills. He caught 62 Don Horn passes for 1,201 yards and 10 touchdowns in 1966 and made 54 receptions for 958 yards and 7 touchdowns in 1967.

After earning a degree in sociology, Moses was drafted by the Buffalo Bills (AFL) in 1968. In five seasons there, he exceeded 600 yards receiving three times and performed outstanding backfield blocking. After being traded to the Denver Broncos (NFL) in 1972 for wide receiver Dwight Harrison, Moses averaged over 30 receptions the next nine seasons and made a career-high 54 catches in 1979. His 302 receptions and 5,450 yards as a Bronco rank him with Lionel Taylor, Riley Odoms, and Steve Watson among the top four in Denver history. One of his greatest performances came against the Oakland Raiders on New Year's Day 1978, when his five receptions for 168 yards and two touchdowns advanced Denver to the Super Bowl against Dallas. In 14 AFL-NFL seasons, he caught 448 passes for 8,091 yards (18.1–yard average) and 56 touchdowns.

The 6 foot, 3 inch, 200 pound Moses epitomized the archetypal "athlete," who would have excelled in numerous football functions in a less specialized game. With his wife, Joyce, and sons, Christopher and Brian, he resides in North Carolina. Moses has worked for the Coors Brewing Company since his retirement from football in 1981 and participates in several community relations projects.

BIBLIOGRAPHY: Denver Broncos, Sports Information Department, Denver, CO.

Leonard Frey

MOTLEY, Marion (b. 5 June 1920, Leesburg, GA), college and professional football player, was elected in 1968 to the Pro Football Hall of Fame. Motley starred at fullback eight years with the Cleveland Browns (AAFC from 1946 through 1949 and NFL from 1950 through 1953), and completed his career with the Pittsburgh Steelers (NFL) in 1955. A three time (1946–1948) All-AAFC fullback, he made All-Pro in 1950. He led the AAFC in 1948 with 964 yards rushing on 157 carries (6.1–yard average) and the NFL in 1950 with 810 yards rushing on 140 attempts (5.8–yard average). Motley achieved a career 5.7–yard rushing average per carry with 4,720 total yards gained in

828 attempts and scored 31 touchdowns. Motley, the all-time AAFC leading rusher with 3,024 yards, helped Cleveland teams win four consecutive AAFC titles, one NFL championship, and four conference titles.

The son of foundry molder Shakeful and Blanche (Jones) Motley, he moved to Canton, OH, with his family as a three year old. Motley starred at fullback three years for Canton McKinley High School football teams that lost only three games, all to archrival Massillon (OH) High School coached by future Cleveland mentor Paul Brown.* Motley also participated in basketball at center before graduating from high school in 1939. From 1940 to 1942 he played football at the University of Nevada–Reno (FWC) under coach Jim Aiken. Motley produced long-distance touchdowns at Nevada with a 105–yard punt return in 1941 and 95-yard return of an intercepted pass against San Francisco in 1942. The latter year, *Illustrated Football Annual* placed him on the All-American Check List with one hundred other backs and stated that "Motley is a 22–karat back, but the ensuing cast is catch-as-catch-can." During Motley's three years, Nevada achieved a mediocre 12–12–3 composite record.

The 6 foot, 2 inch, 235 pound Motley joined the U.S. Navy in 1944 and was assigned to the Great Lakes Naval Training Station. He played football in 1945 with the Bluejackets under Coach Brown on a 6–3–1 team. Great Lakes achieved a resounding 39–7 triumph over Notre Dame in the season's finale, with Motley scoring on a 44–yard run up the middle. "Notre Dame simply could not handle Motley that day," Brown said, "and even had trouble knocking him down as he ran several trap plays that became his specialty over the years."

Motley signed with Cleveland (AAFC) in 1946, joining all-time Browns' players Mac Speedie* and Dante Lavelli* at the ends, tackle Lou Groza,* center Lou Saban, guard Bill Willis,* quarterback Otto Graham,* halfback "Dub" Jones, and defensive end Len Ford.* Motley possessed sprinter's speed but mostly ran plays inside the tackles. Besides being devastating on the "Motley trap," he excelled on draw plays and screen passes and was one of Cleveland's best defensive linebackers. The Browns completely dominated the AAFC, amassing a composite 47–4–3 record in four seasons. During Motley's four NFL years with Cleveland, the Browns finished 40–8–0 overall and defeated the Los Angeles Rams 30–28 for the 1950 championship. Cleveland lost title games the next three years to the Rams 24–17 and Detroit Lions 17–7 and 17–16. "Marion became our greatest fullback ever because not only was he a great runner, but also no one ever blocked better—and no one ever cared more about his team," Brown once stated. Motley, big enough to block defensive ends by himself, possessed the speed to run away from or trample linebackers and cornerbacks. A severe knee injury before the 1954 season sidelined him that year. He played his final campaign with the last place 4–8–0 Pittsburgh Steelers (NFL) mostly as a linebacker.

Motley married Eula Coleman in 1943 and has three sons. After retiring from pro football, he worked four years with the Cleveland Post Office, served eight years as safety director of an Akron, OH, construction company, and spent ten years with the State of Ohio Lottery. The widower lives in Cleveland but commutes to nearby Akron to work at the State of Ohio Department of Youth Services.

BIBLIOGRAPHY: Paul Brown with Jack T. Clary, *PB: The Paul Brown Story* (New York, 1979); Robert Carroll to James D. Whalen, March, 1986; Ronald L. Mendell and Timothy B. Phares, *Who's Who in Football* (New Rochelle, NY, 1974); James D. Whalen, telephone interview with Marion Motley, March 25, 1986.

James D. Whalen

MULLER, Harold Powers "Brick" (b. 12 June 1901, Dunsmuir, CA; d. 17 May 1962, Berkeley, CA), college athlete and professional football player and coach, made All-American three times at the University of California at Berkeley (PCC). He was the son of Edgar Eugene and Eulalie (Powers) Muller and attended public schools in San Diego and Oakland, CA, where his father served as superintendent of Almeda County Schools. At the University of California (PCC), Muller attained All-American status as an end on teams selected by Walter Camp.* After being a third team choice in 1920, he was named to the first team in 1921 and 1922. He starred for the Golden Bears Wonder Teams and never experienced defeat in his three-year career. California compiled a 27–0–1 record, tying Washington and Jefferson 0–0 in the 1922 Rose Bowl. From 1920 through 1922, California outscored opponents 1,220–81.

Muller's California coach Andy Smith* planned brilliant tactics based on series plays and interchanging players and positions. Muller's greatest notoriety ironically came from a pass he threw rather than any reception from his end position. In the 1921 Rose Bowl game, Muller threw a pass over 50 yards to Brodie Stephens for a touchdown to help California defeat Ohio State 28–0. Muller's passing, receiving, blocking, and tackling skills became legendary. At 6 feet, 2 inches, and 195 pounds, Muller ran swiftly and possessed large hands and a strong passing arm. Navy coach Bill Ingram called him "one of the two greatest ends ever seen in my time," while Smith considered him the greatest player he ever saw as a passer and receiver.

The all-around athlete placed second to win a silver medal in the high jump at the 1920 Antwerp, Belgium, Olympics. In the Columbus, OH, All-West All-Star game in December 1922 Muller scored the only touchdown by returning a fumble recovery. He also scored the only touchdown of the inaugural Shrine All-Star (East-West) game in December 1925 by catching a pass from teammate Tut Imlay. During 1926 Muller served as co-coach and played for the Los Angeles Buccaneers (NFL). The Bucs compiled a 6–3–1 record, as Muller scored one touchdown.

After graduating from California with a B.A. degree in 1923, Muller received his M.D. degree in Orthopedic Surgery from the University of California–San Francisco in 1928 and did postgraduate work at Temple University. He interned at the University of California–San Francisco Surgical Hospital in 1928–1929 and established a medical practice in Modesto, CA. In 1946 he moved his practice to Berkeley, CA. During World War II, Muller served five years in the U.S. Army as an orthopedic surgeon in France and England and was discharged as a lieutenant colonel. Muller married Zanita Campbell in 1928 and had one daughter, Marilyn, before their 1936 divorce. A marriage in 1946 to Mildred Carson produced one son, Scott Carson.

Muller, a charter member of the HAF and NFF College Football Halls of Fame (1953), served on the Sports Committee of the American Medical Association and as a diplomat of the American Board of Orthopedic Surgery. The "Brick" Muller Room is dedicated in his honor at the University of California Memorial Stadium.

BIBLIOGRAPHY: L. H. Baker, *Football: Facts and Figures* (New York, 1945); Allison Danzig, *The History of American Football: Its Great Teams, Players, and Coaches* (Englewood Cliffs, NJ, 1956); Deke Houlgate, *The Football Thesaurus* (Los Angeles, 1954); John McCallum and Charles H. Pearson, *College Football U.S.A., 1869–1973* (New York, 1973); *NCAB* (1951), p. 435; David S. Neft, Richard M. Cohen, and Jordan A. Deutsch, *Pro Football: The Early Years, An Encyclopedic History, 1895–1959* (Ridgefield CT, 1978); Maxwell Stiles, *Football's Finest Hour* (Los Angeles, 1950).

George P. Mang

MUNCIE, Harry Vance "Chuck" (b. Munsey 17 March 1953, Uniontown, PA), college and professional player, was named "Muncie" because of a misspelling on his birth certificate. He began his football career as a high school running back for the Uniontown Red Raiders. He played football three years but experienced problems with a new head football coach his senior year and by mutual agreement left the team. He played basketball his senior year and averaged 18 points per game as a guard. Muncie was not recruited heavily but was recommended to Stanford University (PEC) coach Mike White by Muncie's older brother, Bill, a running back for the British Columbia Lions (CFL). Muncie's other brother, George, played with the Minnesota Vikings (NFL), while Nelson performed with the Baltimore Colts (NFL). Due to a poor academic record, Chuck attended a junior college to strengthen his academic credentials. He briefly attended Arizona Western but transferred to Merritt Junior College in Oakland (CA) and improved his grades to become eligible.

During this time, Coach White had moved to the University of California–Berkeley (PEC). White kept his scholarship promise to Muncie, who enrolled there. During his three seasons, Muncie set California records in rushing (3,052 yards) and touchdowns (38). In 1975 Muncie finished second in the

Heisman Trophy voting behind Archie Griffin,* made All-American, was named offensive MVP in both the Shrine All-Star (East-West) game and Japan Bowl, and played in the Hula Bowl. He completed a B.S. degree in Criminology and was the third player chosen in the 1976 NFL draft, being selected by the New Orleans Saints. Muncie played for New Orleans for four and a half seasons, during which time he achieved periods of stardom and was suspended for suspected drug usage and other reasons. During his career with the Saints, Muncie reached a pinnacle in 1979 by becoming the first Saint to rush 1,000 yards and set a then-club record with 1,198 yards (since surpassed by George Rogers*). During that season, he also set then club records for touchdowns (11) and most yards rushing one game (161) and was named MVP of the Pro Bowl.

Following a disappointing start in 1980, continued erratic behavior, and drug allegations, Muncie was traded to the San Diego Chargers (NFL) for a second-round draft choice. Muncie's tenure with the Chargers was marked with highs and lows. Muncie was selected to play in the Pro Bowl following the 1981 and 1982 seasons. In 1981 he tied the NFL record for rushing touchdowns in a season (19). On the other hand, he has been suspended several times for missing team flights, practices, and even games. The rumors concerning his involvement with drugs finally were substantiated in 1982, when he was implicated in a cover story and entered drug rehabilitation centers twice. During his career, Muncie had carried 1,547 times for 6,651 yards (4.3–yard average) and scored 71 touchdowns in 109 games. Muncie caught 259 passes for 3,285 yards (8.8–yard average) and 3 touchdowns.

Early in the 1984 season, Muncie missed a team flight to Seattle and was traded on September 10 to the Miami Dolphins (NFL) for a second-round draft choice. On September 14 Muncie failed his physical examination when traces of drugs (cocaine, amphetamines, and marijuana) were found during blood and urine testing. The trade was invalidated, and Muncie was returned to the Chargers. Upon disclosure of the physical exam results to the NFL office, commissioner Pete Rozelle* suspended Muncie until he could complete a drug rehabilitation program. Muncie has undergone the rehabilitation program, but his future will be determined after a review by the commissioner's office.

BIBLIOGRAPHY: Bob Kravitz, "Chuck Muncie, The man with everything . . . but nothing," Pittsburgh *Press*, 1984; *New Orleans Saints, Media Guide, 1980; San Diego Chargers, Media Guide, 1984; TSN Football Register—1984.*

William A. Sutton

MUNN, Clarence L. "Biggie" (b. 11 September 1908, Grow Township, MN; d. 18 March 1975, Lansing, MI), college athlete, coach, and athletic administrator, was the son of H. B. and Jessie Munn and lived in Anoka, MN, near Minneapolis. At Minneapolis North High School, he made All-

City fullback three years (1925–1927) in football and captained the gridiron squad his senior year. He lettered in basketball three years and captained the track team as a senior, ranking among the greatest track performers in state prep history. In five track meets, he averaged four first places; set records in the javelin, shot put, and relays; and finished undefeated in the 100–yard dash.

At the University of Minnesota, Munn excelled in football and track. He set indoor and outdoor WC shot put records in 1931 and 1932 and broke the shot put mark at the Penn Relays, a record that stood twenty-seven years. Besides competing in the 1932 Olympic track finals, he was voted Minnesota's MVP in 1930 and 1931 as a football guard, won the Chicago *Tribune* trophy as the WC MVP in 1931, and earned unanimous All-American honors that year. Munn later was selected to the first *SI* Silver Anniversary All-American football team (1956) and the *Football News* 100–year All-American team (1969). Munn assisted Minnesota football coach Bernie Bierman* for three years (1932–1934) and also helped in track there. In 1935 and 1936 he served as athletic director and head football, basketball, and track coach at Albright College (PA). The next year, he became line football coach under Ossie Solem at Syracuse University. He was football line coach from 1938 to 1945 at the University of Michigan (WC) under Fritz Crisler* and served as head football coach in 1946 at Syracuse.

Munn became head football coach at Michigan State University (BTC) in 1947 and held that post until becoming athletic director in 1954. During that span he was selected Coach of the Year by the Detroit Quarterback Club and Washington, DC, Touchdown Club and named National Coach of the Year in 1952. He is enshrined in the NFF College Football Hall of Fame as a coach and Minnesota Sports Hall of Fame as a player and coach. Munn helped originate the Michigan Sports Hall of Fame, designing its plaque and being chosen to membership as a coach. At Michigan State (BTC), Munn guided the Spartans to a four-year 28–game winning streak from 1950 through 1953. In 1952 undefeated Michigan State captured the national championship. The next year, the Spartans shared the BTC title and won the Rose Bowl 28–20 over UCLA. Munn's teams collectively recorded an impressive 152–35 overall mark. His notable players included All-American ends Bob Carey and Don Dohoney, tackle Don Coleman, and guard Ed Bagdon.

Munn participated in the Boy Scouts, chaired many committees of the American Red Cross and the Fellowship of Christian Athletes, and belonged to Rotary, the Minnesota and Michigan Alumni associations, Masons, and Shriners. As athletic director, he developed one of the nation's best overall sports and intramural programs at Michigan State. His tenure was disrupted when he suffered a stroke on October 7, 1971. He suffered a second stroke on March 10, 1975, and died eight days later, being survived by his wife, Vera, and two children, Michael and Jane.

BIBLIOGRAPHY: George Barton, *My Lifetime in Sports* (Minneapolis, MN, 1957); Richard Fisher, *Who's Who in Minnesota Athletics* (Minneapolis, MN, 1941); Clarence Munn Career Biography Release, Michigan State University Athletic Department, East Lansing, MI, 1975.

Stan W. Carlson

MUSSO, George Francis "Moose" (b. 8 April 1910, Collinsville, IL), college athlete and professional football player, starred as a football tackle and guard. The son of a coal miner, the 6 foot, 2 inch, 270 pound Musso excelled in all sports at Collinsville High School and as an athlete at Millikin University (ICC). Besides being football captain in 1932, he earned twelve letters in four sports and was named to the NAIA Hall of Fame.

A fierce competitor, he played for the Chicago Bears (NFL) from 1933 to 1944. He played tackle for the Bears until 1937 and then moved to the guard position. Coach George Halas* publicly acclaimed Musso "the greatest guard in professional football ranks." During his rookie season, Musso made the All-Pro second team and became the talk of the NFL. Musso made the All-Pro team at tackle in 1935 and at guard in 1937, the first player chosen at two positions. In 1938 and 1939 he was selected on the second best eleven. As Bears captain nine years, Musso exhibited inspirational competitive leadership and was the only player Halas permitted to give pre-game pep talks. During Musso's twelve years, the Bears won the NFL crown four times (1933, 1940–1941, and 1943), and Western Division titles three times (1934, 1937, and 1942). In the 1940 championship game, Musso helped the Bears overpower the Washington Redskins, 73–0.

Musso remains the only person to play football against two future U.S. presidents. In a 1929 Millikin University game, he lined up against Eureka College guard Ronald Reagan. With the Bears a few years later, he played against University of Michigan center Gerald Ford in the College All-Star game. Subsequently, he engaged in the restaurant business and in 1958 was elected sheriff of Madison County, an office he held for several years. He was named to the HAF College Football Hall of Fame, and in 1982 to the Pro Football Hall of Fame.

BIBLIOGRAPHY: Myron Cope, *The Game That Was: The Early Days of Pro Football* (New York, 1970); *Pro Football Hall of Fame Souvenir Yearbook, 1983–1984*; George Vass, *George Halas and the Chicago Bears* (Chicago, 1971); Richard Whittingham, *The Chicago Bears—An Illustrated History* (Chicago, 1979); Alexander M. Weyand, *Football Immortals* (New York, 1962).

John L. Evers

N

NAGURSKI, Bronislaw "Bronko" (b. 3 November 1908, Rainy River, Ontario, Canada), college football player and professional athlete, was selected a charter member of the NFF College (1951) and Pro (1963) Football Halls of Fame and is enshrined at the HAF College Football Hall of Fame. A consensus All-American tackle (1929) with the University of Minnesota (WC), Nagurski was chosen All-Pro fullback (1932–1934) with the Chicago Bears (NFL). He starred on three Chicago championship teams, played in two other title games, and performed on one undefeated Minnesota eleven. Besides being fullback on Frank G. Menke's (1950) All-Time NFL team, Nagurski was named at tackle on most college All-Time All-American teams including George Trevor (1937), Clark Shaughnessy* (1943), AP (1951), *Sport* (1969), FWAA Modern Era (1920–1969), and *SI* (1969). Grantland Rice* (OS) in 1949 named Nagurski as All-Time fullback for *Sport*.

Few have engendered the myths, contradictions, and confusion surrounding Nagurski's playing career. The incredibly strong, durable Nagurski possessed massive legs, arms, and shoulders and a 19–inch neck. Stories abound regarding Nagurski's giving directions by pointing with a plow and cracking the wall behind the end zone at Chicago's Wrigley Field after exploding for a touchdown. Confusion surrounds his given name and performance at two positions with the Minnesota Gophers. In 1929 Rice and the three major news services named Nagurski All-American tackle, while Knute Rockne* placed him at fullback on his All-Midwestern team. The New York *Sun* set a precedent by choosing a ten-player All-American team with Nagurski at tackle and fullback. As a sophomore, he substituted at end for the injured Bob Tanner and then shifted to tackle at midseason. He played sporadically at fullback the following year but returned to tackle after suffering broken ribs in the 1928 Iowa game. He spent his final season at both positions, but Art Pharmer also played fullback and curiously made all Gopher short-yardage touchdowns listed in the 1930 *Spalding's Intercollegiate Football Guide*.

The 1930 *Illustrated Football Annual* stated, "Nagurski was a great all-around player of outstanding accomplishment. Not a success in his backfield attempt, but too good a tackle to miss top rating."

Nagurski's parents moved from Rainy River to International Falls, MN, when he was four years old. Originally from the Ukraine, they established a thriving mom-and-pop grocery store and brought up two sons and two daughters. Bronko played end, tackle, guard, and fullback two years on the winless International Falls High School team. He performed at guard and center on the basketball squad and participated in the shot put, discus, high jump, and relays on the track team. After the high school principal cancelled a trip to the district basketball tournament to punish two teammates, Nagurski transferred to Bemidji (MN) High School for his senior year. The state high school commission disallowed Nagurski's football participation because he lived outside the school district. He graduated from Bemidji High School in 1926 and enrolled the same year at the University of Minnesota.

The unheralded, unrecruited Nagurski in 1927 teamed with two year All-American fullback Herb Joesting and guard Harold Hanson to help Minnesota achieve a 6–0–2 record, second in the WC and third in Frank G. Dickinson's national rating. Nagurski blocked a Notre Dame punt before an overflow crowd of 25,000 at Cartier Field to set up Joesting's touchdown with one minute remaining to gain a 7–7 tie, the first time in 20 seasons the Fighting Irish had failed to defeat an intercollegiate foe at home. The Gophers produced 6–2–0 records and third place WC finishes the next two years, aided by Nagurski, halfback Fred Hovde, All-American end Ken Haycraft, and guard George Gibson. Following his midseason injury in 1928, Nagurski wore a girdle that enabled him to excel at tackle before returning to fullback for the final game with undefeated, fourth-rated Wisconsin. Nagurski caused a Badgers fumble, which he recovered at the Wisconsin 20–yard line. After five consecutive carries, he scored the game's only touchdown. He tackled "Bo" Cuisinier in the open field and intercepted a Wisconsin pass to preserve the 6–0 triumph. The 6 foot, 225 pound Nagurski in 1929 scored on a 41–yard gallop against Iowa by literally running over the Hawkeyes' All-American halfback Willis Glassgow in a 9–7 losing effort.

The Gophers amassed a combined 18–4–2 record during Nagurski's three years, losing four games by five total points. "Nagurski is the most versatile player of all time," Gopher head coach Clarence W. Spears declared. "He could be an All-American at any of the eleven positions." Nagurski ran his own interference and never tried to sidestep, preferring to lower his head and shoulders and plow into his opponent. He possessed a high-pitched voice, acted kind and gentle off the field, and rarely argued. In the 1930 Shrine All-Star game he gained 90 of the East's 175 yards in a 19–7 triumph over the West. Although listed in the game program at guard, he was named to the All-Time East team in 1940 at tackle by the FWAA and at fullback in

1950 by sportswriter Maxwell Stiles. He graduated from the University of Minnesota in 1930 and played pro football with the Chicago Bears (NFL) under owner-coach George Halas.*

Nagurski joined a star-studded Bears squad that included immortal halfback "Red" Grange,* All-Pro ends Bill Hewitt* and Luke Johnsos, and guards Joe Kopcha and George Musso.* The Bears had not won an NFL championship since 1921 and finished 4–8–2 in 1929. During Nagurski's nine seasons with Chicago, the Bears compiled a composite 79–20–12 (.766 percent) regular-season record and never lost more than five games each season. Nagurski's jump pass to Grange from a fake plunge in a 1932 playoff game with the Portsmouth Spartans for the NFL championship in Chicago Stadium accounted for the Bears' only touchdown in the 9–0 triumph. The NFL was divided in 1933 into Eastern and Western divisions, with the Bears in the latter. In the first division championship playoff game, Chicago defeated the New York Giants 23–21 on two Nagurski touchdown passes to end Bill Karr.

The Bears lost their next two NFL championship playoff games by 30–13 in 1934 to the Giants (although Nagurski scored on a one-yard plunge) and 28–21 in 1937 to the Washington Redskins. When Nagurski threatened retirement in 1937, Chicago increased his salary to $5,000. He quit before the 1938 season when Halas refused his demand for an additional $1,000 but came out of retirement in 1943 to bolster the tackle post on the Bears' World War II–depleted squad. He helped the Bears win another NFL championship by scoring a touchdown in the 41–21 triumph over the Redskins in the title game.

Nagurski's name symbolized the raw power and brute force of football. A large athlete for that era, he performed sixty minutes each game for the Bears primarily at fullback and linebacker. He amassed 3,947 career yards rushing with 856 carries for a 4.6–yard average. He completed 36 of 73 passes (mostly jump passes) for 9 touchdowns. After the first gridiron meeting of Nagurski and Don Hutson* in 1935, the Green Bay Packers' all-time great end declared, "On first down Nagurski ran straight over me. He ran me down and kept going without breaking stride. I'm not sure he even saw me!" New York Giants' All-Pro center Mel Hein* observed, "If you hit him low, he'd run over you. When you hit him high, he'd knock you down and run over you."

Nagurski in 1934 also became a pro wrestler. He provided the sport with a "name" and made the flying block maneuver his trademark. Recognized as the world's champion in some states, he found wrestling lucrative until his retirement in 1960. He in 1936 married Eileen Kane, the daughter of an International Falls, MN, mayor, and has four sons and two daughters. Nagurski purchased and managed a Pure Oil station in International Falls until 1968. The arthritic, shy, almost reclusive Nagurski wears thick-lensed glasses and requires two canes to move about. He used to enjoy hunting and fishing near the rugged Canadian border and still cooks, gardens, and watches sporting events on television.

BIBLIOGRAPHY: Frank Graham, "One for the Book," *Sport* 10 (October, 1950), pp. 37–38; Mervin D. Hyman and Gordon S. White, Jr., *Big Ten Football* (New York, 1977); Norman Katkov, "Bronko the Great," *Sport* 18 (November, 1954), pp. 51–59; Ronald L. Mendell and Timothy B. Phares, *Who's Who in Football* (New Rochelle, NY, 1974); Minnesota–Wisconsin Football Game Programs, October 29, 1927, and November 24, 1928; Bob Oates, Los Angeles *Times*, May 7, 1984; Maxwell Stiles, *Football's Finest Hour* (Los Angeles, 1950); Roger Treat, ed., *The Encyclopedia of Football*, 16th rev. ed., rev. by Pete Palmer (New York, 1979).

James D. Whalen

NAMATH, Joseph William "Joe" (b. 31 May 1943, Beaver Falls, PA), college and professional player and announcer, is the son of steelworker John and Rose (Juhasz) Namath. At Beaver Falls High School, Namath excelled in basketball, baseball, and football and was selected on the high school All-American football squad after quarterbacking his team to a perfect season and the Western Pennsylvania championship. Namath played outfield and pitcher and was offered a $20,000 bonus from the Baltimore Orioles (American League), but instead pursued a football career. At the University of Alabama, Paul "Bear" Bryant* called Namath "the greatest athlete I have ever coached." In three seasons (1962–1964), the 6 foot, 2 inch, 200 pound Namath completed 230 of 428 passes for 3,055 yards and 29 touchdowns and rushed for 597 yards and 15 touchdowns. Namath guided Alabama (SEC) to Orange Bowl appearances in 1963 and 1965, when he was named the game's MVP. He did not play in the 1964 Sugar Bowl because of his suspension for breaking training rules. An All-American in 1964, Namath led the Crimson Tide to a perfect season and the SEC title. Alabama won the national championship, although losing to the University of Texas in the Orange Bowl. After quarterbacking Alabama to a 28–3–0 record, Namath on January 2, 1965, signed with the New York Jets (AFL) for a reported $427,000. He was drafted in the first round by the Jets and St. Louis Cardinals (NFL).

With the Jets in the AFL and NFL (1965–1976), Namath was selected Rookie of the Year in 1965. He led the AFL (1966–1967) in passing attempts, completions, and yards gained and paced the NFL (1972) in yards gained and touchdown passes. Namath became the first player in pro football history to pass over 4,000 yards in a season by completing 258 of 491 passes for 4,007 yards and 26 touchdowns in 1967. Despite having four knee operations, Namath passed over 400 yards three times and more than 300 on 21 occasions. His best yardage day (496) came against the Baltimore Colts on September 24, 1972, when he threw for six touchdown passes. Namath once held an

NFL record of 15 consecutive completions and established 12 Jets' passing records, including most attempts in a game (62 in 1970), season (491 in 1967), and career (3,655); most completions in a game (34 in 1972), season (258 in 1967), and career (1,836); most passing yards in a game (496 in 1972), season (4,007 in 1967), and career (27,057); and most touchdown passes in a game (six in 1972), season (26 in 1967), and career (170). Following his victory prediction, he directed New York to the AFL championship in 1968 and led the Jets to a 16–7 upset victory over the Baltimore Colts in Super Bowl III. His 17 completions for 206 yards gave the AFL its first championship victory over the NFL.

Besides being named to the all-time AFL squad, Namath made All-Pro three times and was chosen for the Pro Bowl twice. Namath was selected three times to play in the AFL All-Star game, where he was chosen the MVP in 1965 and co-MVP in 1967. Following his Super Bowl triumph, Namath won the Hickok Belt, AFL and Super Bowl MVP awards, and George Halas* Award. Although offered $4 million to join the WFL in 1974, Namath remained with the Jets until being released in 1977. Namath, who finished his playing career in 1977 with the Los Angeles Rams (NFL), played in 143 games in 13 seasons, attempted 3,762 passes, completed 1,886 for 27,663 yards and 173 touchdowns, and rushed for 7 touchdowns. Namath was criticized by many for his flamboyant lifestyle. In 1969 he was ordered by NFL commissioner Pete Rozelle* to sell his interest in Bachelors III, a nightclub on Manhattan's East Side, because it was frequented by gamblers. Since his retirement, Namath has pursued an acting career, owns several restaurants and apartments, and is involved in numerous investments and endorsements. He co-authored *I Can't Wait Until Tomorrow 'Cause I Get Better Looking Every Day* (1979) and *A Matter of Style* (1973). In 1985 Namath was elected to the Pro Football Hall of Fame. Namath on November 7, 1984, married Deborah Lynn Mays, an aspiring actress, and has one daughter, Jessica. In 1985 ABC hired him to broadcast that year's Monday night pro football games. Two years later he joined NBC-Sports as an announcer.

BIBLIOGRAPHY: *Los Angeles Rams Official Media Guide, 1977;* Joe Willie Namath with Dick Schaap, *I Can't Wait Until Tomorrow 'Cause I Get Better Looking Every Day* (New York, 1979); Rose Namath Szolnoki with Bill Kushner, *Namath, My Son Joe* (Birmingham, AL, 1975); *TSN Football Register—1978*.

John L. Evers

NANCE, James Solomon "Jim" (b. 30 December 1942, Indiana, PA), college athlete and professional football player, attended Indiana (PA) High School. He starred at fullback in the Syracuse University backfield from 1962 through 1964 and gained his yardage by running over defensive players. The 6 foot, 1 inch, 235 pound Nance also wrestled for the Orangemen and won the NCAA heavyweight championship his senior year. Nance's weight caused an early problem in his pro football career. He reported to the Boston Patriots (AFL) in 1965 above 255 pounds and experienced a disappointing rookie season. Nance trimmed down the following year to 240 pounds, which allowed him to better use his cutting ability. For the next two years, he led the AFL in rushing yardage. In 1966 he set permanent AFL records in rushing attempts (299), yards gained (1,458), and yards per game (104) and paced the AFL in touchdowns with 11. In 1967 Nance again topped the AFL in rushing attempts (269) and rushing yardage (1,216). The workhorse fullback finished first in rushing attempts a third time in 1969.

Nance's running style evolved as he gained pro football experience and learned to read the defense better. Nance played for the Patriots from 1965 through 1971, leading Boston in rushing each of his first six years. Nance, later named the all-time Patriots fullback, played the 1973 season with the New York Jets (NFL) and finished his career the following season with Memphis of the short-lived WFL. Nance, an All-AFL fullback in 1966 and 1967, was honored as 1966 AFL Player of the Year for his record-setting performance. During 8 seasons, he ran 1,341 times for 5,461 yards and 45 touchdowns. After retiring from football, Nance engaged in several businesses. In 1983 he suffered a stroke while playing touch football. Although doctors doubted Nance would ever walk again, he regained the use of both legs.

BIBLIOGRAPHY: Larry Fox, *The New England Patriots, Triumph and Tragedy* (New York, 1979); Hal Higdon, *Pro Football USA* (New York, 1968); David S. Neft et al., *Sports Encyclopedia, Pro Football* (New York, 1977); Roger Treat, ed., *The Encyclopedia of Pro Football*, 16th rev. ed., rev. by Pete Palmer (New York, 1979).

Steve Ollove

NEALE, Alfred Earle "Greasy" (b. 5 November 1891, Parkersburg, WV; d. 1 November 1973, Lake Worth, FL), college and professional athlete and coach, was the son of a produce operator. A childhood friend, whom Neale called "Dirty," nicknamed him "Greasy." Neale, a mediocre student, graduated from Parkersburg High School, attended West Virginia Wesleyan College, and married college sweetheart Genevieve Horner. Although claiming to have limited baseball abilities, the hardworking Neale played baseball for West Virginia Wesleyan and spent eight seasons (1916–1923) as an outfielder in the major leagues. He played for the Cincinnati Reds (NL) from 1916 to 1920 and hit a career-high .294 in 1917. After starting the 1921 campaign with the Philadelphia Phillies (NL), he then returned to the Reds for parts of two more seasons. In the 1919 World Series, the 6 foot, 170 pound Neale made 10 hits and batted .357 for the victorious Reds against the Chicago "Black Sox." In 768 career games, he batted 2,661 times, slugged eight home runs, and compiled a .259 batting average. Neale also played basketball at West Virginia Wesleyan, scoring a then amazing 139 field goals in the 1912–1913 season.

Neale achieved notoriety as a college and pro football player but made his greatest achievements coaching. At the intercollegiate level, he served as head coach at West Virginia Wesleyan (1916–1917), Washington and Jefferson (1922), the University of Virginia (SC, 1923–1928), and the University of West Virginia (SC, 1931–1934) and as backfield coach at Yale (IL, 1934–1940). In 1922 his Washington and Jefferson team upset Jock Sutherland's* Lafayette squad by a 14–13 score before over 50,000 fans in New York's Polo Grounds. During that game, Neale introduced a "naked reverse" or "dance" play. The same year, his Washington and Jefferson squad tied a much heralded University of California team (0–0) in the Rose Bowl.

At the request of new Philadelphia Eagles owner Alexis "Lex" Thompson, Neale began an NFL head coaching career in 1941. Thompson, a wealthy sportsman and Yale alumnus, believed Neale could revitalize the traditionally weak franchise. Neale's successful career with the Eagles brought him national fame. From 1941 through 1950 Neale coached the Eagles to an impressive 63–43–5 record. (In 1943, World War II forced a one-year merger between the Eagles and Pittsburgh Steelers known as the "Steagles.") Under Neale, the Eagles won Eastern Division titles from 1947 through 1949 and captured the NFL crown in 1948 and 1949. The Eagles also finished second in the East three times and under .500 only twice during Neale's era. The Eagles lost the 1947 title game to the Chicago Cardinals but gained revenge by defeating them in the 1948 championship match by a 7–0 score under intolerable weather conditions. Neale's best season with Philadelphia came in 1949, when the Eagles won eleven of twelve regular-season games and defeated the Los Angeles Rams (14–0) in a driving rainstorm to capture the NFL title. In 1949 the Eagles outscored their opponents 362 to 134. Injuries ended the Eagles supremacy in 1950, when Philadelphia played only .500 football.

After the 1948 season Thompson sold the Eagles to a syndicate headed by Jim Clark. The new owners abruptly dismissed Neale following the 1950 season. Neale left the Eagles with "regrets," but made no apologies for his performance. Neale, one of football's great innovators, introduced or popularized the naked reverse, man-to-man shifting defenses, stutter series, triple reverse, false reverse, and a form of the 4–3 defense. He understood the psychology of football and its players, emphasizing confidence as imperative for success. Neale was inducted into the Pro Football Hall of Fame in 1967 and into the NFF College Football Hall of Fame.

BIBLIOGRAPHY: "Milestones," *Time* 102 (November 12, 1973), p. 118; Greasy Neale, "Football Is My Life," *Colliers* 128 (November 3, 1951, pp. 28–29ff.; November 10, 1951, pp. 30–31ff., November 17, 1951, pp. 24–25ff.); *Philadelphia Eagles Media*

Guides, 1942–1950; Joseph L. Reichler, ed., *The Baseball Encyclopedia,* 6th rev. ed. (New York, 1985).

William A. Gudelunas

NEELY, Jess Claiborne (b. 4 January 1898, Smyrna, TN; d. 9 April 1983, Weslaco, TX), college player, athletic coach, and administrator, was the son of farmer William and Mamie (Gooch) Neely. He starred in football at Smyrna High and the Branham and Hughes Prep Schools before entering Vanderbilt University (SIAA) in the fall, 1920. Under NFF College Hall of Fame coach Dan McGugin,* Neely played three years at halfback and end on a Vanderbilt squad that lost just one game. He captained the unbeaten 1922 Commodores squad, which held formidable Michigan to a tie. After earning his law degree in 1923, he engaged in the farm loan business and coached football part-time at Murfreesboro, TN. In 1924 he became athletic director and head coach of all sports at Southwestern College in Memphis, TN. After four years there, he joined the University of Alabama (SEC) as an assistant football coach and head baseball coach. Neely married Dorothy Doucher on January 2, 1930, and had two daughters, Joan and Mary.

Neely became head football coach at Clemson University (SC) in 1931, posting a 43–35–7 record through 1939 and a 6–3 victory over Boston College in the 1940 Cotton Bowl. He served as head football coach at Rice University (SWC) from 1940 through 1966 and compiled the most successful record in the Owls' history. With a 144–124–10 mark, Neely won six SWC titles and guided eight All-American players. Neely's Rice Owls participated in six bowl games, starting with an 8–0 win over Tennessee in the 1947 Orange Bowl. His 1949 squad, led by All-American Froggie Williams and Tobin Rote, finished 10–1 to break the Owls' record for most wins and defeated North Carolina, 27–13, in the Cotton Bowl. Neely's 1954 team, sparked by All-American Dicky Moegle, finished sixth nationally with an 8–2 record and defeated Alabama 28–6 in the Cotton Bowl. The 1957 Rice unit ranked eighth nationally but lost to Navy 20–7 in the Cotton Bowl. The Owls lost to Mississippi in the 1961 Sugar Bowl and to Kansas the following year in the Bluebonnet Bowl.

A quiet man of unquestionable character and integrity, Neely coached conservatively, stressed fundamentals, and shunned trick or deceptive plays. Although secretive and stubborn at times, he acted warm and gracious on other occasions. His fellow coaches respected him as an unyielding, hard-working competitor. He served a term as president of the AFCA and was given the Amos Alonzo Stagg Award for long and distinguished service. Neely, who retired at Rice after the 1966 season, compiled a 207–179–10 career football record. As athletic director at Rice, he oversaw the construction of a 70,000–seat football stadium and 6,000–seat fieldhouse. In 1967 he returned to his alma mater as athletic director. He retired on January 1,

1971, but remained with the athletic department as golf coach and athletic director emeritus. Neely was inducted into the NFF College Football Hall of Fame in 1971, HAF College Football Hall of Fame, Texas Sports Hall of Fame, and Clemson Hall of Fame.

BIBLIOGRAPHY: *Clemson Football Press Guide, 1983;* John D. McCallum and Charles H. Pearson, *College Football U.S.A., 1869–1973* (New York, 1973); Ronald L. Mendell and Timothy B. Phares, *Who's Who in Football* (New Rochelle, NY, 1974); *Rice University Football Press Guide, 1983; Texas Sports Hall of Fame Yearbook, 1981; Vanderbilt University Football Press Guide, 1983.*

Jay Langhammer

NEELY, Ralph Eugene (b. 12 September 1943, Little Rock, AR), college and professional player, is of Irish descent and the son of oil field employee Noah and Lottie (Lyon) Neely. At Farmington (NM) High School Neely won four letters as a two-way football tackle and earned All-State honors as a senior in 1960. He also received four basketball letters and captained the team as a senior. After playing baseball his first two years, he shifted to track and competed in the weight events as a junior and senior. Neely entered the University of Oklahoma in the fall of 1961 and earned BEC Sophomore Lineman of the Year honors as an offensive tackle in 1962. As a junior, he was selected All-BEC and second team All-American. In his senior year Neely made consensus All-American and played in the Hula Bowl and College All-Star game. The Sooners performed in the Gator Bowl his senior year, but Neely was ruled ineligible because he signed a pro contract prematurely.

Originally drafted by the Baltimore Colts (NFL) and Houston Oilers (AFL), Neely signed with the Oilers and then with the Dallas Cowboys (NFL). Dallas had acquired his rights from the Colts. He attended training camp with Dallas before a court ruled him Houston property, but Neely still remained with Dallas. The matter was resolved when the Cowboys gave the Oilers four draft choices in 1966. The 6 foot, 6 inch, 272 pound Neely possessed good speed, quickness, intelligence, and explosive blocking techniques. He started at offensive tackle in his first game with the Cowboys and was named to the NFL All-Rookie team in 1965. He earned All-NFL honors the next four seasons, played in two Pro Bowls, and was named to the NFL's All-Pro squad of the 1960s. Following the 1970 season, Neely appeared in Super Bowl V 16–13 loss to the Baltimore Colts on a last-second field goal.

At midseason in 1971, Neely broke his leg in a motorcycle accident and missed the Cowboys' Super Bowl win over the Miami Dolphins, 24–3. The next season, a broken hand caused him to miss one game. Neely, who participated in 13 NFL seasons, played in two more Super Bowls following the 1975 and 1977 seasons. After the Cowboys defeated the Denver Broncos 27–10 in Super Bowl XII, Neely retired.

Neely married Diane Forte on December 22, 1962, and has one son, Dale, and one daughter, Dedra. In the off-season as a player, he engaged in real estate and oil investments and owned a firm that manufactured custom boat trailers. He later worked for a computer company and marketing consultation firm. In June 1985 Neely entered the banking industry and moved to Quitman, TX, as an investor and officer of the First National Bank.

BIBLIOGRAPHY: *Dallas Cowboys Press Guides, 1965–1977; TSN Football Register—1977; University of Oklahoma Football Press Guides, 1962–1964.*

Jay Langhammer

NEVERS, Ernest Alonzo "Ernie" (b. 11 June 1903, Willow River, MN; d. 3 May 1976, San Rafael, CA), college and professional athlete and football coach, was the last of eight offspring of George and Mary Nevers. His Nova Scotian parents were innkeepers in several small northeastern Minnesota towns. He attended high school in nearby Superior, WI, where he became an outstanding basketball player. After his parents moved to Santa Rosa, CA, Nevers enrolled at Stanford University (PCC) and won letters there in baseball, basketball, and football. He first gained national football prominence in 1925, when Stanford played Notre Dame and their well-publicized Four Horsemen in the Rose Bowl game. Nevers, who had missed much of the 1924 football season with two broken ankles, played the full sixty minutes on specially bandaged legs and displayed a remarkable rushing performance in a 27–10 loss. As a senior, he played the full schedule as a fullback and defensive back under coach Glenn "Pop" Warner* and was named the nation's top college player.

Nevers turned pro in December 1925 when he was paid $25,000 to appear in an all-star football exhibition series against Red Grange* and the Chicago Bears. Later that winter, he played pro basketball in Chicago. He pitched baseball for the St. Louis Browns (American League) in 1926 and that fall led the Duluth Eskimos (NFL). He played in all thirteen regular-season games and sixteen non-league road games that helped popularize pro football nationally. He provided an outstanding one-man show with his passing, rushing, kicking, and relentless defensive play. His all-consuming desire for victory kept the 6 foot, 200 pounder in the lineup even when he was battered and hurt. In three sports in 1926, he netted about $60,000.

He again played both pro baseball and football in 1927, but his three-year stint with the Browns ended after the 1928 season. He skipped football that fall because of a back injury and instead returned to Stanford as assistant gridiron coach under Warner. In 1929 Nevers returned to the NFL as player-coach of the Chicago Cardinals. He led the NFL in scoring, making a record 6 touchdowns and 40 points in a decisive 40–7 victory over the Chicago Bears on November 28. Four days earlier, he had scored every point in a 19–0 win over Dayton. Nevers also starred for the Cardinals in 1930 and 1931, but his active career ended when he broke a wrist in an All-Star game after the 1931 season. In five NFL seasons, he made All-Pro at fullback each time and scored 301 points.

Nevers served as football backfield coach at Stanford from 1932 to 1935 and at Iowa (WC) in 1937 and 1938 and as head coach at Lafayette in 1936. He coached the Chicago Cardinals (NFL) in 1939, but his club won only one game. During World War II (1942–1945), he served as a captain in the U.S. Marine Corps with aviation ordnance duty in the South Pacific. After the war Nevers settled near San Francisco in Tiburon, CA, where he handled public relations for a wholesale liquor company. In 1926 he married Mary Elizabeth Heagerty, who died of pneumonia in 1943. He wed Margery Luxem in 1947 and had one daughter. The ideal American sports hero, Nevers was talented, versatile, courageous, handsome, modest, and non-controversial. His accolades and awards included being a charter member of the HAF and NFF College Football Halls of Fame, Pro Football Hall of Fame, and Stanford's Hall of Fame. Besides being named the best college player of all-time by *SI*, he made several all-time college football teams and the all-time NFL team.

BIBLIOGRAPHY: Chicago *Tribune*, November 29, 1929; Arthur Daley, *Pro Football's Hall of Fame* (Chicago, 1963); L. Robert Davids, interview with Ernie Nevers, December 9, 1965; Jack Hand, *Great Running Backs of the NFL* (New York, 1966); David S. Neft, et al., *The Sports Encyclopedia: Pro Football* (New York, 1977); Ernie Nevers, National Baseball Hall of Fame Questionnaire, Cooperstown, NY; Ernie Nevers file, Pro Football Hall of Fame, Canton, OH; Jim Scott, *Ernie Nevers, Football Hero* (Minneapolis, MN, 1969).

L. Robert Davids

NEWELL, Marshall "Ma" (b. 2 April 1871, Clifton, NJ; d. 24 December 1897, Springfield, MA), college athlete and football coach, remains one of only four four-year (1890–1893) first-team football All-American selections. The 5 foot, 7 inch, 168 pound Harvard University (IL) tackle possessed powerful legs and shoulders, used his hands well defensively, and handled larger players easily. The son of Samuel and Mary Lovejoy (Marshall) Newell, he grew up on his father's farm in Great Barrington, MA, and graduated in 1890 from Phillips Exeter Academy (NH). Newell played on a national championship football team his freshman year at Harvard (IL), when the 1890 Crimson amassed an 11–0–0 record and outscored opponents 555–12. Harvard defeated Yale 12–6 for the second time in the series, started in 1875. Newell spearheaded the Harvard line in dominating Yale's William "Pudge" Heffelfinger.* He made several gains on carries from scrimmage in Lorin F. Deland's flying interference and "turtle-back" formations. Although losing to Yale the other three times, Harvard compiled a combined four-year 46–3–0 record and defeated Pennsylvania, Dartmouth, Cornell, Brown, and all other scheduled teams. Newell, 1892 HAF Player of the Year, was elected to the NFF College Football Hall of Fame in 1957 and to the HAF College Football Hall of Fame. He made several All-Time All-American teams, including those of the *New York Evening World* (1904), Walter Camp* (1910), second team, Parke H. Davis in *Illustrated Football Annual* (1931), and Ray Byrne (1950). In 1948 he was selected to the Harvard All-Time Team.

Newell, a quiet, magnetic personality, belonged to the Harvard crew three years. Nicknamed "Ma," he helped lonely freshman players. An amateur naturalist, the bachelor walked through the woods Sunday mornings and kept a diary of poems and notes that have become part of the heritage of his 1894 graduating class. Newell became Cornell University's (IL) first paid football coach in 1894–1895, when Glenn S. "Pop" Warner (1894 captain),* Joseph W. Beachem, and Clinton R. Wyckoff used the ends-back formation. The strategy inspired Warner to develop the double-wingback a few years later. Newell joined the Boston and Albany Railroad, Springfield division, in 1896 as assistant superintendent, but tragically was killed in a snowstorm by a passing train on Christmas Eve, 1897.

Thirty years after Newell's tragic death, his name was still revered in Harvard Yard. Tributes to him include a memorial volume published by classmates in 1898 with excerpts from his diary, the Newell Gate entrance to Harvard Stadium dedicated in 1899, the Newell Boat Club in 1900, the Newell Prize in English established at Exeter in 1900, and the memorial picture and inscribed tablet placed in the Harvard Union by the Class of 1909. The inscription reads in part: "Although he died before he was twenty-seven years old, Newell had proved himself not only a great athlete and a loyal Harvard man, but also a lover of books, of nature, of mankind, and of the truth."

BIBLIOGRAPHY: Morris A. Bealle, *The History of Football at Harvard, 1874–1948* (Washington, DC, 1948); John A. Blanchard, ed., *The H Book of Harvard Athletics* (Cambridge, MA, 1923); Allison Danzig, *The History of American Football: Its Great Teams, Players, and Coaches* (Englewood Cliffs, NJ, 1956); William H. Edwards, *Football Days* (New York, 1916); Harvard University, Library Archives, Cambridge, MA; John D. McCallum and Charles H. Pearson, *College Football U.S.A., 1869–1973* (New York, 1973); Alexander M. Weyand, *Football Immortals* (New York, 1962); Yale–Harvard Football Game Program, November 25, 1893.

James D. Whalen

NEWSOME, Ozzie "Wizard of Oz" (b. 15 March 1956, Muscle Shoals, AL), college and professional player, is the cousin of pro football running backs Darrin and Kevin Nelson. A 1974 graduate of Colbert County High School in Leighton, AL, the nine-letter man won All-American honors in football and basketball and twice captained the football and basketball squads. As a football wide receiver, he scored touchdowns on one-third of his pass receptions and helped Colbert County win the state title his junior year.

Coach Paul "Bear" Bryant* recruited the wide receiver for the University of Alabama (SEC). As a freshman, Newsome in 1974 caught 20 passes for the 11–0 second-ranked Crimson Tide. Alabama won the SEC crown but lost 13–11 to Notre Dame in the Orange Bowl. Newsome converted one of every four receptions into touchdowns his sophomore year, as 10–1 Alabama captured another SEC title. The Crimson Tide ranked third nationally and defeated Penn State 13–6 in the Sugar Bowl. In 1976 Newsome gained 529 yards on 25 pass receptions and scored 6 touchdowns for the 8–3 Crimson Tide. The next year, 11–1 Alabama defeated Ohio State 35–6 in the Sugar Bowl. Newsome caught 36 passes for 804 yards, earning 1977 Alabama Amateur Athlete of the Year honors. At Alabama he made 102 career receptions for a school-record 2,070 yards (a SEC-record 20.3–yard average), scored 16 touchdowns, and led the Crimson Tide each year in passes caught. Newsome made the All-SEC team three times and earned All-American honors in 1976 and 1977. Coach Bryant's wishbone offense prevented Newsome from utilizing his full pass-receiving skills. Bryant lauded Newsome as "the best end I ever coached, because not only was he a great receiver, but he had exceptional concentration, fine speed, and great hands. Ozzie was a total player, meaning that he was a fine blocker and outstanding leader." In 1978 Newsome graduated with a B.S. degree in Recreation and Parks Management.

The Cleveland Browns (NFL) selected the 6 foot, 2 inch, 232 pounder in the first round of the 1978 draft and converted him to a tight end. In 1979 Newsome recorded a career-high 9 touchdowns on 55 receptions. The next year, he caught 51 passes for 594 yards and 3 touchdowns, helping the 11–5 Browns capture the AFC Central Division crown. Oakland defeated Cleveland 12–10 in the playoffs, but Newsome made 4 receptions for 51 yards. Newsome participated in the Pro Bowl following the 1981 season, during which he ranked third among NFL receivers with 59 catches and became the second Browns player to amass over 1,000 receiving yards. During the strike-shortened 1982 campaign, Newsome gathered in 49 passes for 633 yards and 3 touchdowns and made 4 catches for 51 yards in the 27–10 playoff loss to Oakland.

Although being double-teamed, Newsome recorded a career-high 89 pass receptions and 6 touchdowns for the second-place Browns in 1983. Newsome's 89 receptions ranked him second in the AFC that year and sixth best all-time. The Pro Bowl selected Newsome in 1984, when the tight end again snared 89 passes for 1,001 yards and 5 touchdowns. On October 14, 1984, against the New York Jets, he set club records by making 14 receptions for 191 yards. In 1985 Newsome became the tenth NFL player to catch at least 50 passes in six pro seasons and passed Jackie Smith* as the leading all-time

NFL receiver among tight ends. Newsome's pass catches dropped to 62 in 1985, but he scored once in the 24–21 playoff loss to the Miami Dolphins. The durable Newsome has captained the offensive team since 1984 and entered the 1986 campaign with receptions in 98 consecutive games, sixth longest in NFL history. Besides owning the top three single-season pass-catching performances for the Browns, he has ranked among the NFL's top ten receivers three times. In 1986 the injury-riddled Newsome made only 39 receptions for 417 yards and 3 touchdowns for the AFC Central Division winners. Newsome helped the Browns with 6 catches for 114 yards to beat the New York Jets in overtime in the playoffs, but the Browns lost, again in overtime, in the AFC championship game to the Denver Broncos, 23–20. Through the 1986 season, he has caught 541 career passes for 6,698 yards (12.4–yard average) and 42 touchdowns. Newsome, the Browns' all-time leading receiver, ranks eleventh among NFL all-time pass catchers and has rushed for two touchdowns on end-around plays. The Bratenhahl, OH, resident married Gloria Jenkins, an Alabama graduate, on March 4, 1983, and works off-seasons with the Employee Relations Department of Eastern Ohio Gas Company.

BIBLIOGRAPHY: Norman Aaseng, *Football's Toughest Tight Ends* (Minneapolis, MN, 1981); *Cleveland Browns Media Guide, 1986;* Zander Hollander, ed., *The Complete Handbook of Pro Football, 1984* (New York, 1984); "Pro Football's Leading Lifetime Receivers," *Football Digest* 15 (August, 1986), p. 87; *Street & Smith's College Football Yearbooks, 1975–1979; Street & Smith's Pro Football Yearbooks, 1979–1986; TSN Football Register—1986.*

David L. Porter

NEYLAND, Robert Reese, Jr. "Bob" "The General" (b. 17 February 1892, Greenville, TX; d. 28 March 1962, New Orleans, LA), college athlete, football coach, and athletic administrator, was the youngest of 12 children. The son of Greenville, TX, lawyer Robert Reese and Pauline (Lewis) Neyland, he hoped to become an engineer and attended Burleson College and Texas A&M before matriculating at the U.S. Military Academy at West Point, NY, in 1912. A good student, Neyland played varsity end in football in 1914 and 1915 and won the Academy heavyweight boxing championship three years. The outstanding baseball player helped Army defeat Navy four times and received pro bonus offers from the legendary major league baseball managers John McGraw* (BB) and Connie Mack* (BB). Upon graduation, he served with the Engineers in the Mexican campaign and fought overseas with the American Expeditionary Forces in 1917. After World War I he earned a B.S. degree in Civil Engineering at Massachusetts Institute of Technology in 1921 and returned to West Point as an assistant coach in various sports and as an aide to the superintendent general, Douglas MacArthur. In 1925 he moved to the University of Tennessee (SC) to head the ROTC program and coach football. From 1926 through 1935 his Volunteer football teams won 75 of 87 games. He also taught ROTC until 1931 and worked with the developing Tennessee Valley Authority.

Neyland returned to active duty in Panama in 1935 but resigned a year later to return to Tennessee. He then made the Volunteers (SEC) nationally prominent by winning 33 straight football games, holding opponents scoreless in 1939, and participating in several bowl games. During World War II he returned to military service, briefly coached an all-star game, and served in the China-Burma-India theatre as port officer in Calcutta, India. As a brigadier general and holder of numerous decorations, he in 1946 retired again to Knoxville, TN. His postwar Volunteers football teams initially did not enjoy success. After adopting the new, wide-open, two-platoon system ("rat race football"), he from 1949 through 1952 led Tennessee to a 36–6–2 record and coached the nation's best football team in 1951. Neyland retired from coaching in 1952, with a 173–32–12 record and five SEC titles, and spent his remaining years at Tennessee as athletic director. Elected to the HAF and NFF College Football Halls of Fame, he also was voted the Amos Alonzo Stagg Award by his fellow coaches.

Neyland discouraged media interviews and public appearances and did not lecture or write about football. A quiet force in the evolution of the sport, he belonged to the NCAA Rules Committee. He also served as an informal advisor to many others, including Tennessee alumni who pursued coaching. Neyland brought the organization and precision of military science to football and coaching. His approach included the careful analysis, planning, and execution of all phases of the game; development of superior equipment (including low-cut shoes, tearaway jerseys, lighter padding, and improved helmets); and recruitment and care of his athletes. He also innovated in the use of game films, covers for the playing field, and the utilization of a pressbox observer. A stern and commanding figure active in the development of the modern University of Tennessee, he was nicknamed "the General," held in awe, fear, respect, and affection by his players and associates. His close friends knew him as a convivial host, bridge player, and fisherman. Married to Ada (Peg) Fitch on July 26, 1923, he had two sons, Robert R. III and Lewis F. Long plagued with liver and kidney problems, Neyland died in Knoxville, TN.

BIBLIOGRAPHY: Ralph Hickok, *Who Was Who in American Sports* (New York, 1971); *NYT*, March 29, 1962; Tom Siler, *Tennessee: Football's Greatest Dynasty* (Knoxville, TN, 1961); Tom Siler, *Tennessee's Dazzling Decade, 1960–1970* (Knoxville, TN, 1970); University of Tennessee, Sports Information Office Files, Knoxville, TN.

Daniel R. Gilbert

NITSCHKE, Raymond Ernest "Ray" (b. 29 December 1936, Elmwood Park, IL), college and professional player and executive, is the son of surface lines employee Robert and Anna Nitschke. A brother brought him up after his parents died when he was a young boy. Nitschke attended Proviso High School in Maywood, IL, and excelled in baseball, basketball, and football there. He was offered a pro baseball contract by the St. Louis Browns (American League) and was an All-State quarterback in football. The 6 foot, 3 inch, 235 pound Nitschke received a football scholarship at the University of Illinois (BTC, 1954–1957) and was converted to fullback as a sophomore. Although primarily used as a blocking back, Nitschke gained 943 yards rushing in three years and averaged 6.5 yards per carry on 79 attempts as a senior.

After playing in the College All-Star game and Senior Bowl, Nitschke was selected in the third round in the 1958 NFL draft by the Green Bay Packers. He was switched to a linebacker position with the Packers from 1958 through 1972. Injuries plus military service prevented Nitschke initially from establishing himself in the NFL. In 1962 Nitschke became a star under coach Vince Lombardi.* He possessed good speed, and his rugged defensive play made him one of the game's most feared tacklers. Nitschke defended against the run and pass with a fierceness that intimidated opponents. As defensive captain, Nitschke steadily enhanced his reputation and teamed with Dave Robinson* and Lee Roy Caffey to form one of the top linebacking units in NFL history. An All-Pro (1964–1966), he played in the Pro Bowl (1965) and helped Green Bay capture five NFL titles (1961–1962, 1965–1967) and Super Bowl victories following the 1966 and 1967 seasons. The Packers in 1962 defeated the New York Giants in the NFL title game. Nitschke was named the MVP after deflecting a pass for an interception and recovering two fumbles. In fifteen seasons Nitschke played in 190 games and recorded 25 interceptions for 385 yards and 2 touchdowns.

Nitschke in 1961 married Jacqueline Forschette and resides in Oneida, WI, with their children John, Richard, and Amy. He publishes *Ray Nitschke's Pro Football Report* during the season and co-authored an autobiography, *Mean on Sunday*. Nitschke, currently a national accounts executive for a midwest trucking firm, also represents other companies at various conventions and gatherings. Named to the All-Pro Squad for the decade of the 1960s and the AFL-NFL 1960–1984 All-Star Team, he in 1967 was voted the outstanding player at his position and in 1969 was named the NFL's all-time top linebacker. In his first year of eligibility, Nitschke in 1978 was elected to the Pro Football Hall of Fame.

BIBLIOGRAPHY: George Allen with Ben Olan, *Pro Football's 100 Greatest Players* (Indianapolis, IN, 1982); Ray Nitschke with Robert W. Wells, *Mean on Sunday* (Garden City, NY, 1973); Mike Tully, *Where Have They Gone?: Football Stars* (New York, 1979).

John L. Evers

NOBIS, Thomas Henry, Jr. "Tommy" (b. 20 September 1943, San Antonio, TX), college and professional player and executive, is the son of Thomas Henry Nobis, Sr. A highly recruited prep football prospect, Nobis made All-State at Thomas Jefferson High School in San Antonio, the same school that produced Kyle Rote. The 6 foot, 2 inch, 240 pound Nobis attended the University of Texas (SWC, 1962–1966) and graduated with a Bachelor's degree in Speech. One of the best two-way linemen in Texas history, Nobis led the Longhorns to the 1963 national championship with an 11–0–0 record and a 10–1–0 mark in 1964. He harassed Roger Staubach* in the Longhorns' 28–6 triumph over the U.S. Naval Academy in the 1964 Cotton Bowl and flattened Joe Namath* in Texas' 21–7 upset over the number 1-ranked University of Alabama in the 1965 Orange Bowl. In Nobis' three varsity seasons, Texas recorded 28 victories and only 5 losses. Nobis, who averaged nearly 20 tackles per game as primary offensive blocker, was selected All-SWC (1963–1965), All-American (1964–1965), Most Valuable Longhorn Player (1964), team captain (1965), and seventh in the Heisman Trophy voting (1965). In 1965 he received the Outland and Maxwell awards, presented annually to the nation's best interior lineman and number 1 college player, respectively. *SI* selected him to the All-Century college football team (1869–1969). Nobis, runner-up to O. J. Simpson* as the greatest college player of the 1960s, performed in the College All-Star and Coaches All-America games (1966) following graduation.

Nobis received a reported $400,000 bonus contract as the number 1 choice of the Atlanta Falcons in the 1966 NFL draft. In 11 seasons with the Falcons, Nobis became one of the finest NFL middle linebackers and was respected for his tackling ability and bruising play. Nobis in 1966 won the Bert Bell Trophy as the most valuable rookie and was selected NFL Rookie of the Year. Besides being named Falcon Player of the Year (1966, 1968), Nobis in 1967 was chosen Texas Pro Athlete of the Year and made the All-Pro squad. He played in Pro Bowls (1966–1968, 1970, 1972) and made the Western Conference All-Star team (1966, 1968). During Nobis' pro career (1966–1976), the expansion Falcons won only 50 of 154 games. Due to surgery on both knees, Nobis retired following the 1976 season and joined the Falcons front office as an administrative assistant. He and his wife Lynn have two children. A member of the NFF College Football Hall of Fame, Nobis in 1976 was inducted into the Texas Longhorn Hall of Honor.

BIBLIOGRAPHY: Denne H. Freeman, *Hook 'Em Horns: A Story of Texas Football* (Huntsville, AL, 1974); Dan Jenkins, "There's No Show Biz Like Nobis," *SI* 23 (October 18, 1965), pp. 40–42, 47–48, 50, 55; Herman L. Masin, "The Nobis Roamer of Them All," *Senior Scholastic* 87 (October 14, 1965), p. 24; *TSN Football Register—1976.*

John L. Evers

NOLL, Charles Henry "Chuck" (b. 5 January 1932, Cleveland, OH), college and professional player and coach, played football at Benedictine High School in Cleveland and the University of Dayton. The football team captain, he received a Bachelor of Science degree in Education in 1953. Noll's pro football career began as a twenty-first round draft choice of the Cleveland Browns (NFL) in 1953. He played in 77 pro games spanning 7 seasons with the Browns as a linebacker and became one of coach Paul Brown's* famous messenger guards, relaying plays to the quarterback. Noll, unlike most coaches, permits his quarterback to select his own plays. During Noll's playing career with the Browns, Cleveland won five Eastern Conference championships and two of three NFL title games (1953–1955).

At age 27, the 6 foot, 1 inch, 218 pound Noll retired as a pro player and served as a defensive assistant coach under Sid Gillman* with the Los Angeles Chargers of the new AFL. Noll's coaching tenure with the Chargers in Los Angeles and later San Diego lasted six years, including four Western Division and two AFL titles. In 1966 he moved to the NFL, where he became the defensive backfield coach for the Baltimore Colts under Don Shula.* In Noll's three seasons there, the Colts lost just three regular season games, won an NFL title in 1968, and lost to Joe Namath's* New York Jets in Super Bowl III.

In 1969 Noll became head coach of the Pittsburgh Steelers (NFL), a perennially losing team. Prior to Noll, the Steelers had never played in the NFL championship game. During Noll's first season (1969), the Steelers won their first game and then lost 13 in a row to finish last. Noll used their first choice to draft quarterback Terry Bradshaw* and began making the draft his trademark. He rebuilt the Steelers through the draft rather than trading draft picks for players. During his first sixteen years as head coach, Noll made only ten trades with other teams. After Noll's team finished 5–9 and 6–8 in 1970 and 1971, the Steelers compiled an 11–3 mark in 1972 and won their first title of any kind by taking the AFC Central Division. The Steelers captured their first playoff game 13–7 over the Oakland Raiders on Franco Harris'* "Immaculate Reception," but then lost 21–17 to the undefeated (17–0) Miami Dolphins. In 1973 Noll once again led the Steelers to the Central Division title, with Oakland eliminating them in the first round of the playoffs.

The next year (1974) culminated Noll's efforts with the Steelers, as Pittsburgh won its first NFL championship by defeating the Minnesota Vikings 16–6 in Super Bowl IX. In 1975 Noll became the third coach to win consecutive Super Bowls when Pittsburgh defeated the Dallas Cowboys 21–17. After the Steelers made the playoffs in 1976 and 1977, Noll in 1978 became the first mentor to win three Super Bowls by guiding Pittsburgh to a 35–31 victory over Dallas. In 1979 he became the first coach to win four Super Bowls and record consecutive Super Bowl triumphs twice. Following the 31–19 victory over the Los Angeles Rams in 1979, Noll's Steelers were acclaimed the Team of the Decade. The Steelers enjoyed 13 consecutive winning seasons from 1972 to 1984, but suffered losing campaigns in 1985 and 1986.

Noll ranks seventh among all-time coaches and third among NFL active coaches with a 155–107–1 regular-season record and has led the Steelers to eleven playoff appearances in his 18 years and to a 15–7 post-season record. Noll and his wife, Marianne, have one son, Chris, and reside in Upper St. Clair, PA.

BIBLIOGRAPHY: *Pittsburgh Steelers Media Guide, 1984; TSN Football Register—1986.*

William A. Sutton

NOMELLINI, Leo "The Lion" (b. 19 June 1924, Lucca, Italy), college and professional athlete, was born near the Leaning Tower of Pisa and came to the United States with his parents at age four. The Nomellinis settled in Gilman, IL, where his father opened a candy store. Nomellini did not play high school sports because his parents feared that he would be injured and wanted him to work to support his family. He participated, however, in sandlot-type sports in the parks. After graduation from high school, he enlisted in the U.S. Marines and was stationed at Cherry Point, NC. He played left tackle on the base football team and was nicknamed "The Lion." After being discharged from the service, he enrolled at the University of Minnesota (WC) and, under postwar rules, was eligible to play four years. He started at guard on Bernie Bierman's* Golden Gophers as a freshman and later switched to tackle, being twice selected an All-American. At Minnesota, Nomellini also participated in track as a shot-putter and anchorman on the 440–yard relay team and won the WC heavyweight wrestling title. He later wrestled professionally during the off-season from pro football.

Nomellini's interest in football began when he saw the movie about renowned Notre Dame coach Knute Rockne.* Pat O'Brien starred as Rockne and Ronald Reagan depicted the fabled George Gipp.* Nomellini particularly was intrigued by the part where Gipp, not yet on the squad, walked by the bench in civilian clothes, picked up a football, and kicked it eighty yards. The Minnesota Golden Gophers disappointed both players and coach Bierman in 1949 because losses to Michigan and Purdue spoiled a possible national championship season. Nomellini played in the 1950 College All-Star game in Chicago.

In 1950 the 6 foot, 3 inch, 259 pound Nomellini became the first player ever drafted by the San Francisco 49ers (NFL) and received no bonus for signing. In filing for a divorce later, his wife Ruth stated that Nomellini loved football more than her and the children and with a passion that devoured him. He played for the 49ers from 1950 through 1963 without missing a game. Nomellini participated in 266 successive games, including pre-season, regular season, and post-season action, and appeared in 174 regular-season games. From 1951 through 1955 he played both offensive and defensive tackle without wearing protective pads. The loose, mobile Nomellini became one of few players ever selected All-NFL at both offensive and defensive positions. He was chosen for offensive team honors in 1951 and 1952 and defensive accolades in 1953–1954, 1957, and 1959. In perhaps his greatest season (1955), he was not selected to either the offensive or defensive squads despite playing the full sixty minutes of every game. Nomellini, who preferred to play on defense, was named an All-Time NFL defensive tackle, performed in ten Pro Bowl games, and was enshrined in the Pro Football Hall of Fame in 1969. He also is included in the NFF College Football Hall of Fame and now resides in San Francisco, CA.

BIBLIOGRAPHY: George Barton, *My Lifetime in Sports* (Minneapolis, MN, 1957); University of Minnesota, *100 Years of Golden Gopher Football* (Minneapolis, MN, 1981); Mike Rathet and Don R. Smith, *Their Deeds and Dogged Faith* (New York, 1984); San Francisco 49ers, Media Releases, San Francisco, CA, 1963.

Stan W. Carlson

NORTON, Homer Hill (b. 15 June 1891, Birmingham, AL; d. 26 May 1965, College Station, TX), college athlete and football coach, helped develop southwestern intercollegiate football. The son of Methodist minister John W. Norton, he graduated in 1916 from Birmingham Southern College. He starred there in football, basketball, track, and baseball and was named the best all-around athlete in the South. After playing minor league pro baseball as an outfielder from 1916 to 1919, he the next two seasons coached the Centenary College football team. The new Centenary College president, who wanted the school to build up its football and join the SWC, hired Alvin "Bo" McMillin* in 1922 to achieve these goals and made Norton assistant. McMillin, however, did not gain SWC membership and in 1926 moved to Geneva College. From 1926 to 1933 Norton served as head football coach at Centenary, compiled an outstanding 60–20–9 overall record, and had three undefeated teams. His squads won 20 consecutive victories and posted 14 successive shutouts.

Norton in 1934 accepted the head football coaching position at Texas A&M University, where he developed some of the finest SWC teams. His 1939 Aggies outscored opponents 198–18, defeated Tulane 14–13 in the Sugar Bowl, and won the national championship. Besides capturing three straight SWC titles and nineteen consecutive games, Norton's teams played in the 1941 and 1942 Cotton Bowls and 1944 Orange Bowl. From 1934 to 1947 Norton developed outstanding players John Kimbrough,* Marshall Robnett, Joe Routt,* Jim Thomason, and Joe Boyd. Altogether, his Texas A&M teams won 82 games, lost 53, and tied 9. During his 24–year college coaching career, Norton achieved a 142–73–18 composite mark. Following the 1947 season, Norton surrendered his coaching duties and pursued the motel and restaurant business. He operated a popular restaurant across from the main entrance of the Texas A&M campus.

Norton, an inspirational leader, worked hard and expected his players to do likewise. A devout football enthusiast, the strict disciplinarian firmly believed in the Golden Rule. Norton preached to his players, "It's how you show up at the showdown that counts." Norton, one of the first coaches to employ a "screwy" defense, used four- and five-man lines, the "blitz," and the "red-dog." Texas A&M squads established a season college record by holding opponents to only 1.71 yards per play. Norton is a member of the Texas Sports Hall of Fame, Texas A&M Athletic Hall of Fame, HAF and NFF College Football Halls of Fame.

BIBLIOGRAPHY: Tim Cohane, *Great College Football Coaches of the Twenties and Thirties* (New Rochelle, NY, 1973); Wilbur Evans and H. B. McElroy, *The Twelfth Man: A Story of Texas A&M Football* (Huntsville, AL, 1974); John D. McCallum and Charles H. Pearson, *College Football U.S.A., 1869–1973* (New York, 1973); Kern Tips, *Football—Texas Style: An Illustrated History of the Southwest Conference* (Garden City, NY, 1964).

John L. Evers

O

O'BRIEN, Robert David "Davey" (b. 22 June 1917, Dallas, TX; d. 18 November 1977, Fort Worth, TX), college and professional player, entered TCU (SWC) in 1935 and backed up great football quarterback Sammy Baugh* as a sophomore. The next year, his outstanding passing, running, punting, and defensive abilities earned him All-SWC honors at quarterback his junior year. In 1938 he directed TCU to the national championship with a 10–0 regular-season mark. O'Brien passed for 19 touchdowns, completed 110 passes in 194 attempts for 1,733 yards, and threw only 4 interceptions. He gained 466 yards rushing with 127 carries for a 3.4–yard average. His 1938 honors included a unanimous All-American selection, the Heisman Trophy, Walter Camp Memorial Trophy, Maxwell Memorial Trophy, and Washington, DC, Touchdown Club Award. *Liberty* Magazine presented him a Gold Football for being chosen on its All-Player, All-American team. O'Brien threw a touchdown pass and kicked a field goal to lead TCU to a 15–7 win over Carnegie Tech in the Sugar Bowl to highlight an 11–0 season.

Following graduation, O'Brien in 1939 joined the Philadelphia Eagles (NFL) for a $12,000 bonus. He was named quarterback on the 1939 NFL Coaches All-Star team as a rookie and on the All-Star second team in 1940, but then retired to join the Federal Bureau of Investigation (FBI). His final game against the Washington Redskins proved the highlight of his pro career, as O'Brien set longstanding NFL records by completing 33 of 60 passes. During his brief pro career, he completed 223 of 478 passes for 2,614 yards and 11 touchdowns and threw 34 interceptions. He spent 10 years with the FBI and then entered the Texas oil industry in 1950. The 5 foot, 7 inch, 150 pounder was elected to the NFF College Football Hall of Fame in 1955 and Texas Sports Hall of Fame in 1956 and joined twenty-four other recipients of *SI*'s Silver Anniversary All-American award in 1960.

BIBLIOGRAPHY: Allison Danzig, *The History of American Football: Its Great Teams, Players, and Coaches* (Englewood Cliffs, NJ, 1956); Bill Libby, *Champions of College*

Football (New York, 1975); Howard Roberts, *Story of Pro Football* (New York, 1953); *Texas Christian University Media Guide, 1981*.

James Fuller

O'DEA, Patrick John "Pat" "Kangaroo Kicker" (b. 16 March 1872, Kilmore, Australia; d. 4 April 1962, San Francisco, CA), college athlete and coach, grew up in Melbourne and starred in Australian Rules football for Xavier College and community football competition there. After coming to the United States in 1896, he attended the University of Wisconsin and earned a law degree in 1900. O'Dea played football four years at Wisconsin (WC) under coach Phil King and made legendary kicking feats as goal kicker and punter. He kicked 32 five-point field goals, including 31 by dropkick, and regularly punted at least 50 yards. Nicknamed the "Kangaroo Kicker," O'Dea kicked from any angle and on the dead run. The long, lithe 6 foot, 170 pounder possessed highly developed legs, proved a good kick returner, and starred as a high hurdler in track. His soft-spoken, gentle manner and winning personality made him a favorite on and off campus.

O'Dea became regular football fullback as a sophomore and captained the Badgers his junior and senior years. In 1897 he dropkicked a 57–yard field goal against the University of Chicago and punted the entire 110–yard field against Minnesota. The next year O'Dea dropkicked 10 field goals, including a record 62–yarder against Northwestern, and was chosen a second team All-American by Walter Camp.* As a senior in 1899, O'Dea dropkicked 13 field goals including 4 against Beloit College and 3 against Lawrence College. He dropkicked a 60–yarder against Minnesota, placekicked a 57–yard goal against Illinois, and was selected a third team Walter Camp All-American. In three years as a regular back, O'Dea led Wisconsin to a 27–4–0 record.

O'Dea coached football at Notre Dame in 1900 and 1901, compiling 8–1–1 and 6–2–1 marks, and guided Missouri in 1902 to a 5–3–0 record. He settled in San Francisco, CA, where he opened a law practice and coached the Stanford crew in 1913. From 1917 to 1934 O'Dea lived in Westwood, CA, under the assumed name of Charles J. Mitchell and worked as a statistician for a lumber company. Long believed dead, O'Dea revealed his true identity in 1934 and explained that he wanted to escape his football fame and failing business. The congenial O'Dea was honored at Wisconsin's homecoming celebration. O'Dea later returned to San Francisco, where he participated in Wisconsin alumni affairs and worked for a clothing firm until several years before his death. In 1962 he was elected to the HAF and NFF College Football Halls of Fame. Among football's most famous and spectacular stars, O'Dea established the importance of kicking in football strategy.

BIBLIOGRAPHY: Mervin D. Hyman and Gordon S. White, Jr., *Big Ten Football* (New York, 1977); Milwaukee (WI) *Journal*, April 5, 1962; Kenneth "Tug" Wilson and

Jerome Brondfield, *The Big Ten* (Englewood Cliffs, NJ, 1967); University of Wisconsin, *Wisconsin Athletic Review* (1954); *Wisconsin Alumnus* (May/June, 1979); *Wisconsin News*, September 19, 21, 1934.

Edward J. Pavlick

OLIPHANT, Elmer Quillen "Ollie" (b. 9 July 1892, Bloomfield, IN; d. 3 July 1975, New Canaan, CT), college athlete, professional football player, and administrator, starred seven years (1911–1917) at Purdue University (WC) and the U.S. Military Academy (Army). He made All-WC and All-Western halfback his last year at Purdue (1913), All-American second team halfback at Army (1915), and consensus All-American first team (1916–1917). A member of the State of Indiana Football Hall of Fame, Oliphant was chosen All-Time All-East by George Trevor (1949), and All-Time All-American by Fielding Yost* (1920), Knute Rockne* (of which he was most proud), and the FWAA (Early Day, 1869–1919) in 1969. The 1916 HAF Player of the Year, he was inducted into the HAF College Football Hall of Fame and in 1955 into the NFF College Football Hall of Fame. The son of Marion Ellsworth and Alice (Quillen) Oliphant, he moved at age nine to Washington, IN, and attended Washington High School three years. When his father's gristmill partner absconded with $62,000 of company funds, he transferred to Linton (IN) High School to work part-time in the coal mines to help with family finances. An All-State end in football at Linton, he placed first in the state track meet in the mile, quarter mile, low hurdles, and broad (long) jump, and graduated in 1910.

Oliphant concurrently waited on tables in the Kappa Sigma fraternity house, carried laundry, fired furnaces, and sold shoes to put himself through Purdue University. He won twelve varsity letters (three in each major sport), made All-WC baseball left fielder, HAF All-American basketball guard, and captained the football and baseball teams. In 1911 Oliphant helped the Boilermakers defeat Indiana (12–5) for the first time in seven years and with a broken ankle kicked a field goal against Illinois. Although winning only two WC games between 1906 and 1911, Purdue finished in fourth place the next two seasons. Oliphant scored 43 points against Rose Poly Institute (1912) with 5 touchdowns and 13 consecutive extra points and helped Purdue tie defending WC champion Wisconsin 7–7 (1913) with a brilliant 32–yard touchdown run. Sportswriter Harry Grayson joked, "Badger rooters woke up screaming, nightmared by a herd of pink Oliphants." Purdue, whose only loss in 1913 was 6–0 to national co-champion University of Chicago, finished the season 4–1–2 under coach Andy Smith* for the best Boilermaker record since 1905. Oliphant, named the greatest athlete in Purdue history, graduated in 1914 with a B.S. degree in Mechanical Engineering and won an appointment to West Point.

The blond, 5 foot, 8 inch, 178 pound Oliphant, who had a squat build, short legs, and devastating stiff-arm, hit with the impact of a medium-sized bull and proved a likable egotist who enjoyed playing before crowds. Oliphant appeared in five football games his first year at Army, scoring three touchdowns against Maine (70, 70, and 5 yards). Oliphant gained substantial yardage and completed a key pass in a 20–7 triumph over Notre Dame but did not letter because he did not play in the Navy game. Army coach Charles Daly* did not need Oliphant in the 20–0 triumph but undoubtedly intended to stifle some of the star plebe's enthusiasm. Army finished 9–0–0 and was rated 1914 national champions by HAF and Parke Davis.

The next three years, Oliphant dominated the Cadets offense with help from NFF College Football Hall of Fame greats Babe Weyand and Lawrence "Biff" Jones* at tackle, end Bob Neyland,* and center John McEwan. Army recorded 5–3–1, 9–0–0 (for another national championship), and 7–1–0 seasons and triumphed over Navy two years (the 1917 game was cancelled due to World War I). "Until Oliphant graduates, Annapolis will have to be twenty-five percent stronger than the Army in order to win," declared Walter Camp* in the 1917 *Spalding's Official Intercollegiate Football Guide*. Oliphant set still-existing school records: most touchdowns (6) and most points scored (45) in one game (against Villanova, 1916), and most points scored (125) in one season (1917) on 17 touchdowns, 20 conversions, and 1 field goal. He either scored or was responsible for all points scored against Georgetown (10 in 1915), Navy (14 in 1915, 15 in 1916), and Boston College (14 in 1917). Oliphant made 5 touchdown runs between 50 and 96 yards against Trinity (1916), contributed 21 of Army's points in a 30–10 triumph over Notre Dame (1916), and scored 112 points during the 1916 season.

Oliphant won 12 letters at Army in football, basketball, baseball, track, hockey, and boxing, and captained the football and baseball teams. An excellent all-around athlete, he batted .424 and .421 his last two seasons as a baseball outfielder, scored twice as many points as the next highest Cadet on the basketball hardcourt, broke Weyand's Army low hurdles record, and strongly challenged four-time heavyweight boxing champion Neyland. The only Cadet athlete to win letters in four major sports, he required a special act of the Athletic Council to design a suitable varsity letter containing a gold star and three stripes for him. Oliphant won the Edgerton Saber as football captain and the Athletic Association Saber as the outstanding athlete. The cadet captain of Company D, he served as acting major of the Second Battalion and his senior year as superintendent of Sunday School for children on the post. He married Barbara "Bobbie" Benedict on Graduation Day, June 12, 1918, and had no children.

Oliphant served in the U.S. Cavalry one year at Fort Sill (OK) and three years as physical education instructor at West Point. Appointed track coach (1921–1922) by superintendent Douglas MacArthur, Oliphant produced two undefeated seasons. While on duty at Army, he played with the NFL Buffalo All-Americans (1920–1921) and led them the second year to a second-place finish and 9–1–2 record. Due to governmental deemphasis, he left the military service and served as athletic director (1922) at Union College (NY).

In 1923 Oliphant joined the Metropolitan Life Insurance Company. Through tremendous drive and ambition, he became one of the highest salaried executives and headed the group insurance division for the New York area. He contributed to successful World War II bond drives and was honored by General Motors in 1969 with the establishment of the Elmer Q. Oliphant Scholarship. Oliphant retired in 1957 and died of cardiac arrest after a two-year illness.

BIBLIOGRAPHY: L. H. Baker, *Football: Facts and Figures* (New York, 1945); Jim Beach and Daniel Moore, *Army vs. Notre Dame* (New York, 1948); Harold Claassen and Steve Boda, Jr., *Ronald Encyclopedia of Football* (New York, 1961); Jack T. Clary, *Army vs. Navy* (New York, 1965); Tim Cohane, *Gridiron Grenadiers: The Story of West Point Football* (New York, 1948); Howard Roberts, *The Big Nine: The Story of Football in the Western Conference* (New York, 1948); U.S. Military Academy, Alumni Records, West Point, NY; Alexander M. Weyand, *Football Immortals* (New York, 1962).

James D. Whalen

OLSEN, Merlin Jay (b. 15 September 1940, Logan, UT), college and professional player and announcer, is the eldest of nine children of schoolteacher Merle Barrus and Lynn J. Olsen. At Logan High School, Olsen played football and ran the hurdles in track. Olsen, a Mormon, attended Utah State University on a scholarship. In 1961 the defensive tackle achieved consensus All-American status his senior year, won the Outland Award for defensive excellence, and made the Academic All-American team. A Phi Beta Kappa student, he graduated with a B.S. degree in Finance in 1962 and later earned an M.S. degree in Economics. On March 30, 1962, he married Susan Wakley. They have three children, Kelly Lynn, Jill Catherine, and Nathan Merlin.

A first-round NFL draft pick in 1962, Olsen played fifteen years with the Los Angeles Rams through the 1976 season. The 6 foot, 5 inch, 275 pound tackle was recognized as one of the best NFL linemen. In the 1960s he teamed with David "Deacon" Jones,* Lamar Lundy, and Roosevelt Grier* to form an outstanding defensive unit. He proved fast for such a large man, hardworking, and a natural leader. Selected for many All-Pro teams and MVP awards, he was chosen to the Pro-Bowl a record fourteen times. In his first year of eligibility (1982), Olsen was elected to the Pro Football Hall of Fame. He also is a member of the NFF College Hall of Fame and was named to the AFL-NFL 1960–1984 All-Star Team.

Unlike many retired athletes, Olsen has not faded from sight. A public relations executive, he owns a car dealership and heads numerous charities. He has appeared in numerous action films and television shows, especially playing regularly in the long-running "Little House on the Prairie" series as farmer-woodsman Jonathan Garvey. He is best known to the general public, however, as a top-rated sports analyst and football commentator on NBC-TV. Olsen, an extremely intelligent, energetic, literate, and versatile figure, enjoys hunting, fishing, and golf. The San Marino, CA, resident operates his business office in Los Angeles. His brother Phil played for the Rams and the Denver Broncos (NFL) from 1971 to 1976.

BIBLIOGRAPHY: Roger Kahn, "The Game without the Ball," *SEP* 240 (December 16, 1967), pp. 79–83; *Los Angeles Times*, 1962–1976; Ronald L. Mendell and Timothy B. Phares, *Who's Who in Football* (New Rochelle, NY, 1974); Bob Ottum, "Tackling a New Career," *SI* 54 (January 19, 1981), pp. 106–110ff; S. LaMar Wade, "The Country Gentleman," *SEP* 254 (November, 1982), pp. 63–65ff; *WWA* (1982–1983), p. 2523.

Frank P. Bowles

OOSTERBAAN, Benjamin Gaylord "Bennie" (b. 24 February 1906, Muskegon, MI), college athlete, coach, and administrator, is the son of Muskegon postmaster Benjamin Oosterbaan, of Dutch ancestry. Although his older brother Andrew died from a sports-related injury, he starred in four sports at Muskegon High School. In 1922–1923, he was selected forward on the Interscholastic All-American basketball team and played in an invitational tournament in Chicago. He made All-State in football and won the state discus championship. Oosterbaan entered the University of Michigan (WC) in 1924 without a scholarship, but became one of Michigan's greatest athletes. During his final three years, he earned nine letters in varsity football, basketball, and baseball. The 6 foot, 2 inch, 198 pound end combined with quarterback Benny Friedman* to produce one of the most productive passing duos ever in college football. Oosterbaan often drifted unnoticed through the defensive line into the open for a perfectly timed pass from Friedman. The 1925 Michigan team under Fielding Yost* outscored its opponents 227–3, lost only one game (3–2 to Northwestern), and claimed the WC championship. Oosterbaan, three-time All-American football end from 1925 to 1927, made All-American on a 10–2 WC champion basketball team in 1927, and won the WC batting championship in baseball.

After graduating in 1928, he rejected pro football and baseball contracts to serve as an assistant football coach under Yost and held that position until Fritz Crisler* became head coach in 1938. In 1933 he married Delmas Cochlin, a University of Michigan graduate and university hospital worker. They adopted a daughter, Anna, after a son, Bennie, Jr., died in 1946 of an incurable disease at age eight. Oosterbaan became head basketball coach in 1938, but in 1946 Crisler appointed him backfield football coach. With Oosterbaan's offensive innovations, Michigan recorded a perfect season in 1947, a Rose Bowl win, and its first national championship since 1933. When Crisler retired to become athletic director in 1948, Oosterbaan succeeded him as football coach and immediately produced another national championship team. Oosterbaan's squads compiled a 63–33–4 football record from 1948 to 1958, shared the BTC title in 1949, and won the BTC outright in 1950 with a Rose Bowl victory.

Coach Oosterbaan exhibited offensive wizardry with elaborate faking, spinner plays, tricky reverses, and formations requiring adept ball handling and intricate timing. The two-platoon system, pioneered by Crisler, was used effectively by Oosterbaan until the 1953 rule changes. After his coaching career, he became supervisor of public and alumni relations in the athletic department under Crisler. He served in this capacity until 1968, when Don Canham replaced him. Oosterbaan's major honors included being Coach of the Year in 1948, All-Time All-American end on a team selected in 1951 by national sportswriters and sportscasters, and inducted into the HAF and NFF College Football Halls of Fame. In contrast to Crisler, Oosterbaan seemed easygoing, quiet, relaxed, and intimate with his players.

BIBLIOGRAPHY: *CB* (1949), pp. 462–63; Allison Danzig, *The History of American Football: Its Great Teams, Players, and Coaches* (Englewood Cliffs, NJ, 1956); John D. McCallum, *Big Ten Football Since 1895* (Radnor, PA, 1976); Ronald L. Mendell and Timothy B. Phares, *Who's Who in Football* (New Rochelle, NY, 1974); Will Perry, *The Wolverines: A Story of Michigan Football* (Huntsville, AL, 1980); Walter W. Ruch, "Michigan's Unexpected Hero," *SEP* 22 (October 8, 1949), pp. 38ff; Kenneth L. (Tug) Wilson and Jerry Brondfield, *The Big Ten* (Englewood Cliffs, NJ, 1967).

Douglas A. Noverr

OSBORNE, Thomas William "Tom" (b. 23 February 1937, Hastings, NE), college and professional athlete and coach, is the son of businessman Charles and Erma Osborne. He married Nancy Tedermann in 1962 and has one son, Mike, and two daughters, Ann and Susie. The Nebraska Athlete of the Year at Hastings High School in 1954–1955, the 6 foot, 3 inch, 175 pound Osborne made All-State in football as a halfback and in basketball with a 19.2 per game scoring average and won the Class A discus title. He earned a B.A. degree in 1959 and played football and basketball at Hastings College (NeCC), where his father and grandfather had graduated. In 1959 he was named State College Athlete of the Year. After playing flanker two years for the Washington Redskins (NFL) and one season for the San Francisco 49ers (NFL), he joined coach Bob Devaney's* football staff at the University of Nebraska (BEC) in 1962 as a graduate assistant. Within three years, he earned his M.A. and Ph.D. degrees in Educational Psychology. In 1967 he coached receivers full-time and later became offensive coordinator.

When Devaney retired after a sensational eleven-year tenure as head coach, he chose Osborne as his successor. Several outstanding assistants from Devaney's staff had already become head coaches at other schools. Osborne compiled an outstanding 9–2–1 record his first season and coached Nebraska to a second-place finish in the BEC. Nebraska finished seventh in the final AP poll and defeated Texas 19–3 in the Cotton Bowl. Through the 1986 season, Osborne had made an exceptional record as Nebraska head coach:

Year	*Wins*	*Losses*	*Ties*	*BEC*	*AP Rank*
1973	9	2	1	2	7
1974	9	3	0	2	9
1975	10	2	0	1	9
1976	9	3	1	4	9
1977	9	3	0	2	12
1978	9	3	0	1	8
1979	10	2	0	2	9
1980	10	2	0	2	7
1981	9	3	0	1	11
1982	12	1	0	1	3
1983	12	1	0	1	2
1984	10	2	0	2	4
1985	9	3	0	2	11
1986	10	2	0	3	5
Career	137	32	2	.811	

Devaney and Osborne remain the only consecutive coaches from the same school to win over one hundred games. Osborne, a big redhead with conservative dress, speech, and beliefs, recruits athletes who work hard and graduate and has conducted a program known nationally as "squeaky clean." Nebraska is one of the few big-time college football schools never placed on NCAA probation. During Osborne's first 14 years, Nebraska has won or shared five BEC titles, finished second seven times, and barely missed national titles from 1981 through 1983. He has helped produce two Heisman Trophy winners (Johnny Rodgers,* Mike Rozier*) and four Outland Award winners (Rich Glover, Larry Jacobson, Dave Rimington* [twice], Dean Steinkuhler*). Osborne's squads consistently rank among national leaders in rushing and scoring offense and defense. Osborne coached the Cornhuskers to victories in the 1974 Cotton Bowl, 1975, 1985, and 1987 Sugar Bowls, 1976 Bluebonnet Bowl, 1980 Sun Bowl, and 1983 Orange Bowl. Nebraska suffered defeats in the 1979, 1982, and 1984 Orange Bowls, 1981 Sugar Bowl, and 1986 Fiesta Bowl. Osborne's Coach of the Year awards included BEC (1975, 1978, 1980); Bobby Dodd's National (1978); and Fellowship of Christian Athletes National (1983). In 1982 Osborne received the first Distinguished Nebraskalander Award.

BIBLIOGRAPHY: Bob Devaney, *Devaney* (Lincoln, NE, 1981); Hollis Limprecht et al., *Go Big Red: The All-Time Story of the Cornhuskers* (Omaha, NE, 1966); Lincoln (NE) *Journal-Star*, 1962–1984; Jerry Mathers, *Nebraska High School Sports* (Lyons, NE, 1980); Omaha (NE) *World-Herald*, 1962–1984; *University of Nebraska Football Guides, 1962–1984.*

Jerry D. Mathers

OTTO, James Edwin "Jim" (b. 5 January 1938, Wausau, WI), college and professional player, won All-State honors as a football center-linebacker for Wausau High School. At the University of Miami (FL), he set a Hurricanes record for most football tackles and received his Bachelor of Science degree in 1960. Since most scouts considered the 6 foot, 2 inch, 205 pounder too small for pro football, no NFL team drafted him or gave him a free-agent contract. The Minneapolis franchise of the new AFL drafted him in the twenty-fifth round, but the club became the Oakland (CA) Raiders by the time Otto reported to training camp.

Although unimpressed by Otto's size, scouts had underestimated his determination because he won the starting offensive center position and was named All-AFL his rookie season. By this time Otto had grown to 240 pounds, and most of his career he performed at 255 to 260 pounds. The 1960 season started two remarkable streaks for Otto. He won All-AFL center honors the entire ten years the AFL existed and All-AFC center accolades from 1970 through 1972 after the AFL merged with the NFL. Additionally, he started every regular-season game (210) for the Raiders until his retirement in 1975. When his 73 pre-season contests, 12 All-Star games, and 13 playoff games are included, he incredibly appeared in 308 consecutive contests. This amazing streak continued despite Otto's numerous injuries, including elbow bone chips, a ten-times broken nose, a broken jaw, numerous concussions, a dislocated knee, dislocated fingers, a severe pinched nerve in his neck, three left knee operations, and six right knee operations. He retired after an exhibition game in 1975 because his plastic right knee prevented him from playing up to his usual form.

After wearing uniform number 50 for the 1960 season, Otto requested the unusual number 00 for his remaining pro career. This move undoubtedly earned him recognition at an often obscure position. More important, he employed sure ball-snapping and superior blocking skills. In the Raiders' complicated offense, he also called all line-blocking assignments and was judged one season to have made only three errors in 650 plays called. Otto, who is married and has one daughter and one son, in 1980 became the third AFL player named to the Pro Football Hall of Fame. The Pro Football Hall of Fame named him to its AFL-NFL 1960–1984 All-Star Team.

BIBLIOGRAPHY: Ronald L. Mendell and Timothy B. Phares, *Who's Who in Football* (New Rochelle, NY, 1974); Jim Otto file, Pro Football Hall of Fame, Canton, OH; Don Smith, "Jim Otto," *The Coffin Corner* 6 (November/December, 1984), pp. 13–14.

Robert N. Carroll

OWEN, Benjamin G. "Bennie" (b. 24 July 1875, Chicago, IL; d. 26 February 1970, Houston, TX), college player, coach, and administrator, was considered the "father of football" at the University of Oklahoma. His family moved to St. Louis, MO, and then in 1892 to a Kansas farm. A pharmacy student at the University of Kansas, he quarterbacked Fielding Yost's* undefeated 1899 Jayhawks. Following graduation, he began his football coaching career at Washburn College and in 1901 assisted Yost at the University of Michigan (WC). The Wolverines won all eleven games and outscored opponents 550–0. From 1902 through 1904 he compiled a 22–2–2 record as coach at Bethany College (KS).

Owen became head football coach at Oklahoma in 1905, guiding the Sooners to an upset over the powerful Haskell Indians and to their first victory over the University of Texas. At Oklahoma from 1905 to 1926, Owen produced eighteen winning seasons and guided his 1911, 1915, 1918, and 1920 Sooners to unbeaten marks. The Sooners won SWC titles in 1915 and 1918 and MVC championship in 1920. Owen stressed offense, as his teams made record scores. His 1911 team outscored opponents 282–15 in eight games, while his undefeated 1918 squad averaged 46 points per game and held opponents to 7 points all season. During twenty-seven coaching seasons, Owen compiled a 155–60–19 mark for a .703 percentage.

Owen, a soft-spoken, clever tactician who lost his right arm in a hunting accident, became the first exponent of fast, wide-open offense in the Missouri Valley area. An imaginative innovator, he utilized the direct snap from center to a back behind the line and quickly mastered the forward pass. Owen adopted a wide-open, reckless attack, enabling his 1914 squad to lead the nation's major teams in points (435), complete one mile of forward passes, and score 25 touchdowns on aerials. In 1915 the Sooners averaged 35 passes per game and defeated ten straight opponents, convincing proof that passes could comprise a major part of the offense.

Owen's contagious spirit and enthusiasm inspired his players to hustle. The Sooners used the "hurry-up" offense, often starting the next play before the other team was ready. Since Owen advocated clean play, clean speech, and sportsmanship, Oklahoma opponents knew that he would treat them fairly. He recruited intelligent players and saw most of his athletes graduate. As director of athletics at Oklahoma from 1927 to 1934, he promoted construction of a new football stadium and many other athletic facilities. He retired in 1938 and lived in Houston, TX, from 1964 until his death. The "Mr. Football" of Oklahoma for whom Owen Field is named, he was elected to the NFF College Football Hall of Fame in 1951 and HAF College Football Hall of Fame in 1969.

BIBLIOGRAPHY: John D. McCallum, *Big Eight Football* (New York, 1979); John D. McCallum and Charles H. Pearson, *College Football U.S.A., 1869–1973* (New York, 1973); *TSN*, March 14, 1970; Jim Weeks, *The Sooners: A Story of Oklahoma Football* (Huntsville, AL, 1974).

John L. Evers

OWEN, Stephen Joseph "Steve" "Stout Steve" (b. 21 April 1898, Cleo Springs, OK; d. 17 May 1964, New York, NY), college and professional athlete, football coach, executive, and scout, was the son of James Rufus and Isabella (Doak) Owen and was born in the Indian Territory. His father had claimed rolling land when the Cherokee Strip was opened to settlers, while his mother had been the area's first schoolteacher. He graduated from Aline (OK) High School in 1916 and attended Phillips University (OK), serving in 1917 and 1918 as the football team's captain and star tackle. To earn college money, he wrestled professionally as Jack O'Brien to preserve his amateur standing. Following his discharge from the student army training corps, he coached football one year at Phillips University, worked briefly in the oil fields, and played pro football at tackle with the Kansas City Cowboys (NFL) in 1924 and 1925.

New York Giants (NFL) owner Tim Mara* purchased Owen's contract from Kansas City in 1926 for $500. Owen captained the 1927 Giants, which compiled an 11–1–1 record and limited opponents to an NFL record-low 20 points. The 5 foot, 10 inch, 260 pound Owen played tackle with the Giants from 1926 through 1931 and in 1933 and ranked among the NFL's finest defensive players. In 1931 Owen became New York's fifth head football coach. During the next twenty-three years (1931–1953), he guided the Giants to a 151–100–7 composite record, eight Eastern Division titles, and two NFL championships (1934, 1938). "Stout Steve," known for his wad of snuff, also worked as a foreman in Mara's coal yard in the Bronx during the off-season.

Owen emphasized fundamentals, blocking and tackling, and became an offensive and defensive innovator. In 1937 he devised the A Formation, his version of the single wing involving the splitting of his line. He placed four linemen to the right of center and two to the left, but inserted the majority of his backs on the weak side. To stop Cleveland Browns Otto Graham's* passing, Owen in 1950 introduced the umbrella defense, a forerunner of the standard 4–3–4 NFL defense. In 1950 the Giants recorded the first ever shutout (6–0) over the Cleveland Browns and then defeated them 17–13 to become the first team to defeat Cleveland twice in one season. A defensive expert, he became the first pro football coach to start a game by kicking rather than receiving. He drew criticism later in his career for trying field goals instead of gambling for a touchdown. Actually, Owen stood ahead of his time, as evidenced by the constant increase of field goal attempts.

Owen regarded the 1938 NFL championship team as his greatest squad. His backs included Alphonse "Tuffy" Leemans,* Ward Cuff, Hank Soar, Ed Danowski, Kink Richards, and Nello Felaschi, while linemen included Jim Lee Howell, Jim Poole, Tarzan White, Dale Burnett, John Del Isola, Ed Widseth,* and Mel Hein.* "Stout Steve" considered center-linebacker Hein as the greatest player he ever coached and credited him with much of the success of the A formation. With huge hands and considerable ability, Hein could easily snap the ball to any one of three backs. For this formation to succeed, a great center proved essential. No other team utilized this formation for any length of time. At the annual draft in 1951, Owen selected the special slip of paper entitling the Giants to the nation's number 1 pick. The Giants selected SMU's Kyle Rote. Owen considered the Rote selection his luckiest venture.

Following a disappointing 3–9 1953 season, the Maras relieved Owen of his coaching duties. He was given a five-year contract for a front office job, his first contract with the Giants after twenty-three years of handshakes. After one year, the contract was terminated by mutual agreement. Owen served as assistant football coach at Baylor University (SWC), as line coach for the Philadelphia Eagles (NFL) in 1956 and 1957, and coached the Toronto and Calgary entries in the CFL from 1958 through 1962 and the Syracuse Stormers (UFL) in 1963 before scouting for the Giants. Owen, who died at Oneida City Hospital in New York of a cerebral hemorrhage, married Miriam Virginia Sweeney on November 25, 1935 and had no children. His brother Bill played with the Giants from 1929 through 1936 and assisted Owen during the 1930s. In 1966 Owen was elected to the Pro Football Hall of Fame.

BIBLIOGRAPHY: Stan Grosshandler, "Conversations about the A," *The Coffin Corner* 5 (June, 1983), p. 8; *NYT*, November 22, 1950; December 11, 1953; May 18, 1964; *NFL Record Manual, 1983*.

Donald Kosakowski

OWENS, Loren Everett "Steve" (b. 9 December 1947, Gore, OK), college and professional player, is the fifth of nine children born to Cherry and Olen Owens and graduated in 1965 from Miami (OK) High School. The 6 foot, 2 inch, 215 pound Owens excelled as an all-around interscholastic athlete in track, baseball, and football and averaged 7.2 yards per carry as a football running back over three years. In 1965 he enrolled at the University of Oklahoma (BEC) and played unimpressively as a freshman. His collegiate football career blossomed, however, after he married his wife, Barbara, in 1966. By his senior year, Owens became the nation's finest power runner and gained more yards than any previous player. The durable Owens rushed 905 times for 3,867 yards, scored 56 touchdowns, ran for over 100 yards in 17 consecutive games, and set nine BEC and seven NCAA rushing records. In 1969 he was named a consensus All-American and won the prestigious Heisman Trophy.

The Detroit Lions (NFL) drafted him in 1970, but a pre-season separated shoulder limited his rookie action to 122 yards gained in 36 attempts in six games. In fourteen contests the next year, he gained a Lions-record 1,035 yards in 246 carries and ranked second in the NFC and fourth in the NFL in rushing. In addition, he in 1971 caught 32 passes, made a 74–yard touchdown reception, was named All-Pro, and played in the Pro Bowl. The following seasons proved both discouraging and anticlimactic. Several injuries, including bruised ribs and a pulled hamstring in 1972, leg muscle pulls in 1973, and ligament and cartilage damages requiring an operation in 1974, ironically disproved his collegiate durability. Consequently, Owens saw his playing time diminish from 1972 through 1974, missed the entire 1975 campaign, failed a comeback attempt, and then retired in 1977.

During six pro seasons, Owens carried 635 times for 2,451 yards and a 3.9–yard average and scored 20 touchdowns. He caught 99 passes for 861 yards (8.6–yard average) and made 2 touchdown receptions for 132 career points. Until plagued by injuries, Owens ranked among the NFL's most effective runners.

BIBLIOGRAPHY: Detroit (MI) *Free Press*, June 1, 1977; *Detroit Lions Media Guide, 1972–1976; Detroit Lions Press Release*, May 2, 1974, Detroit, MI; *Football Digest* 1 (January, 1972); Los Angeles *Times*, December 16, 1972; *Pro!*, November 10, 1974; *TSN*, November 30, 1968; George Sullivan, *The Great Running Backs* (New York, 1972).

Jerome Mushkat

P

PAGE, Alan C. (b. 7 August 1945, Canton, OH), college and professional player, is the son of Howard F. and Georgianna (Umbles) Page and graduated in 1963 from Canton Central Catholic High School, where he lettered in football and was named All-City, All-County, and All-State. Page graduated in 1967 from the University of Notre Dame, winning football All-American honors as a senior and majoring in Political Science. He received a law degree from the University of Minnesota in 1978. The twice-married Page wed Addie Johnson on December 17, 1966, and Diane Sims on June 5, 1973, and has four children.

Drafted by the Minnesota Vikings (NFL), Page captured Rookie of the Year honors in 1967. Page anchored one of the best front fours in pro football, with Jim Marshall, Carl Eller,* and Gary Larsen, collectively tabbed as the Purple People Eaters, the Purple Gang, and the Four Norsemen by the media. Perhaps the quickest defensive lineman off the ball in NFL history, Page helped the Vikings to four Super Bowl appearances, earned All-Pro status from 1970 to 1977, and appeared in the Pro Bowl from 1969 to 1977. He was named the NFL's Defensive Lineman of the Year and Defensive Player of the Year in 1970 and its MVP in 1971, the first time a defensive player ever won the prestigious award. After playing with the Vikings from 1967 into the 1978 season, Page was dealt to the Chicago Bears (NFL) and performed there from 1978 through 1981. Entry into long-distance running in mid-career led to Page's being the first NFL player to complete a marathon. His playing weight dropped from 245 to 210 pounds, partly influencing the Vikings to sell Page to the Bears. Page believed his union work influenced the sale. He served as player representative (1970–1974, 1976–1977) and as an NFL Players Association Executive Committee member from 1972 to 1975. During his fifteen-year career, Page set NFL records in safeties and blocked kicks. Page was selected among the Silver Anniversary Minnesota

Vikings in 1985. The Pro Football Hall of Fame named him to its AFL-NFL 1960–1984 All-Star second team.

In 1981, Page was honored by the U.S. Jaycees as one of America's Ten Outstanding Young Men. Page served as an associate in a law firm emphasizing a team approach (1979–1984) and was named special assistant attorney general for the State of Minnesota in 1985. He chaired the United Negro College Fund in 1972, participated on its advisory board, and acted as its Telethon co-host in 1984. The Minnesota Council on Physical Fitness chairman in 1972, he was a Chicago Multiple Sclerosis Read-A-Thon volunteer in 1979 and served on the Board of Directors of the Chicago Association of Retarded Citizens. Page also was an American Cancer Society state chairman, conducted a weekly commentary for "Morning Edition" on National Public Radio and color commentary for Turner Broadcasting System "Sports' College Football Game of the Week" in 1982, and is affiliated with many educational, law, civic, and charitable organizations.

BIBLIOGRAPHY: Alan Page to John E. Di Meglio, 1985; "Vikings Front Four," *Ebony* 25 (January 1970), pp. 83–86ff.

John E. DiMeglio

PARKER, Clarence McKay "Ace" (b. 17 May 1913, Portsmouth, VA), college and professional athlete and coach, was elected in 1955 to the NFF College Football Hall of Fame, to the HAF College Football Hall of Fame, and in 1972 to the Pro Football Hall of Fame. Parker in 1938 and 1940 made All-Pro halfback with the Brooklyn Dodgers (NFL) and was awarded the 1940 Joe F. Carr MVP Trophy. A three-year (1934–1936) single-wing star quarterback with Duke University (SC), Parker captained the 1936 Blue Devils team and was selected consensus All-American. He was chosen in 1971 to George Trevor's All-Time Intercollegiate South Sectional Team and to Allison Danzig's* (OS) list of All-Time Specialists as a punter and running back. The son of railroad general foreman Ernest R. and Mabel (McKay) Parker, he excelled in five sports at Portsmouth Woodrow Wilson High School and graduated in 1933. Besides being football halfback, basketball forward, baseball left fielder, and golfer, the versatile Parker competed in the high jump, long jump, and pole vault field events.

Parker played under coach Wallace Wade* on Duke teams that amassed a composite 24–5–0 record. Duke lost only one SC engagement in three years and won SC championships the last two seasons. Parker in 1935 produced nine runs of 40 yards or better and scored 60 points to lead all SC scorers. The Blue Devils, ranked eleventh in 1936 by the AP and ninth by Frank G. Dickinson, suffered their only defeat by 15–13 to Tennessee when the Volunteers' safety returned Parker's punt 75 yards for a last-minute touchdown. The 5 foot, 11 inch, 175 pound Parker teamed with All-American halfbacks Eric Tipton and Elmore Hackney and center Dan Hill. He produced the nation's longest run, a 105–yard kickoff return for a touchdown against North Carolina, returned a North Carolina State punt 75 yards for a touchdown, and in 1936 scored 52 points on 8 touchdowns and 4 extra points. The versatile performer showed exceptional ability running, blocking, passing, tackling, pass defending, punting, play selecting, and kicking points after touchdowns. A star of the East's 3–0 triumph over the West in the 1937 Shrine All-Star game at San Francisco, Parker made key gains from scrimmage to set up the winning field goal. He performed at forward one year on the basketball team and starred three years in left field for the varsity nine before graduating from Duke in 1937.

Parker played with the NFL Brooklyn Dodgers (1937–1941) and Boston Yanks (1945), and the AAFC New York Yankees (1946). Brooklyn finished as Eastern Division runner-up in 1940 and 1941 with 8–3–0 and 7–4–0 marks. The New York Yankees won the 1946 AAFC Eastern Division championship with a 10–3–1 record but lost 14–9 to the Cleveland Browns in the title game. "Parker is one of the greatest players I've ever coached," Wallace Wade declared. "And with his record in pro ball, he is one of the all-time greats."

A major league baseball player, Parker played shortstop and second base for the Philadelphia Athletics (1937–1938) of the American League and the Pittsburgh Pirates (1940) and Chicago Cubs (1947) of the National League. He hit a home run his first time at bat in the majors, one of the few to accomplish this feat, but compiled a meager .179 major league batting average. Parker served from 1942 to 1945 as a U.S. Navy lieutenant in the Physical Fitness Program at the Portsmouth (VA) Naval Base. He managed the Portsmouth (VA) baseball team (1947–1948) and the Durham (NC) Bulls (1949–1952), twice being named Manager of the Year.

Parker returned to Duke in 1948 to serve as offensive backfield coach under Wade and Bill Murray. In 1953 he became the Blue Devils baseball head coach, guiding Duke to several ACC titles and two trips to the NCAA World Series at Omaha, NE. Parker left Duke in 1966 to serve as a football talent scout for the San Francisco 49ers (NFL) and has served since 1977 in a similar position with the St. Louis Cardinals (NFL). Parker in 1942 married Thelma Sykes of Portsmouth, VA, where he resides; he has no children.

BIBLIOGRAPHY: Duke–Army Football Game Program, October 17, 1953; Duke University, Library Archives, Durham, NC, 1985; Ronald L. Mendell and Timothy B. Phares, *Who's Who in Football* (New Rochelle, NY, 1974); Roger Treat, ed., *The Encyclopedia of Football*, 16th rev. ed., rev. by Pete Palmer (New York, 1979); James D. Whalen, telephone interview with Clarence Parker, November 25, 1985.

James D. Whalen

PARKER, James Thomas "Jim" "Big Jim" (b. 3 April 1934, Macon, GA), college and professional player, is the son of Charles Parker, Sr., a track laborer for the Central of Georgia Railroad. Before his senior year in high school, Parker moved from Macon to Toledo, OH, to live with an uncle and aunt. Parker played football at Toledo Scott High School and impressed Ohio State University (BTC) football coach Woody Hayes,* who recruited him as an offensive guard and defensive linebacker. Nicknamed "Big Jim," the 6 foot, 3 inch, 248 pound Parker became the prototype of the modern offensive lineman because of his excellent size, mobility, and speed. Parker, a teammate of Heisman Trophy winner Howard "Hopalong" Cassady* in the mid-1950s, was credited by Hayes for "having much to do with Hop Cassady's success. . . . " Besides leading the Buckeyes to the BTC and national championship titles in 1954, Parker the next two seasons made consensus All-American teams. Parker, the first Ohio State lineman to win the Outland Award, received his B.A. degree in Physical Education in 1956. The gregarious, hardworking lineman found respect and friendship among teammates and opponents.

A first-round draft choice of the Baltimore Colts (NFL) in 1957, Parker made All-Pro left tackle from 1958 to 1961 and (now 275 pounds) at guard the next four seasons. Parker participated in Pro Bowl games from 1959 through 1966 and played pivotal roles on the Colts Western Conference championship teams in 1958–1959, 1964–1965, and 1967. Parker became a model for modern pro linemen by providing pass protection for Johnny Unitas,* thus enabling the quarterback to break modern passing records and become the era's most legendary player. Parker's pro career ended late in the 1967 season, when a knee injury failed to respond to treatment. Parker's team-motivated decision spurred his coach Don Shula* to comment that "It was one of the most unselfish moves ever made in sports." After the five-year mandatory waiting period, Parker was inducted into the Pro Football Hall of Fame in 1973. Parker, a member of the NFF College Football Hall of Fame, resides with his wife Mae in Columbia, MD, has four children, and owns the Parker Package Company in Baltimore. The Pro Football Hall of Fame named Parker to the AFL-NFL 1960–1984 All-Star Team.

BIBLIOGRAPHY: Jerry Brondfield, *Woody Hayes and the 100–Yard War* (New York, 1974); Woody Hayes, *You Win with People* (Columbus, OH, 1975); Harry Jebsen, Jr., interview with Woody Hayes, 1984; Ronald L. Mendell and Timothy B. Phares, eds., *Who's Who in Football* (New Rochelle, NY, 1974); Ohio State University, Sports Department files, Columbus, OH; Jim Parker file, NFF College Football Hall of Fame, Kings Mills, OH; Jim Parker file, Pro Football Hall of Fame, Canton, OH.

Harry Jebsen, Jr.
William Burke

PARKER, Raymond Klein "Buddy" (b. 16 December 1913, Kemp, TX; d. 22 March 1982, Kaufman, TX), college athlete and professional football player and coach, performed with the Detroit Lions (1935–1936) and Chicago Cardinals (1937–1943) and later coached the Cardinals, Lions, and Pittsburgh Steelers of the NFL. Born near Dallas, he was the son of a lumberyard owner and starred in three sports at Kemp High School. Parker won an athletic scholarship to North Texas JC, where he played baseball and football. In 1931 he joined his older brother Robert at Centenary College (LA) and achieved prominence there as a football running back. During his senior year (1934), he ranked among the nation's leading rushers and kicked a dramatic 18–yard field goal to upset the powerful University of Texas. In Parker's three varsity football seasons, Centenary lost only two games. In 1935 Parker signed with the Detroit Lions (NFL) for a $1,200 salary and played an instrumental role as a substitute running back in the Lions' 1935 NFL championship. Parker was traded after the 1936 season to the Chicago Cardinals (NFL), where he played as an offensive and defensive back until his retirement in 1943. Parker rushed 180 times for 489 yards (2.7–yard average) and 4 touchdowns and caught 40 passes for 378 yards (9.5–yard average). He married wife Jane in 1940 and had one son, Robert.

Chicago Cardinals coach Jimmy Conzelman* in 1943 named Parker player-coach. Parker's astute handling of the 1947 Cardinals backfield proved instrumental in the team's NFL championship that year. In an unusual move, Parker in 1949 was named Cardinals co–head coach with Phil Handler and assumed full duties as head coach midway through the season. He spent 1950 as assistant coach at Detroit (NFL) and was named Lions' head coach in 1951. At Detroit, Parker immediately built a powerful team for a franchise accustomed to losing money and games. The Lions easily won National Conference championships from 1952 through 1954 and NFL titles in 1952 and 1953, making Parker only the fourth NFL coach to win consecutive titles. After recording 48 wins, 24 losses, and 2 ties, Parker in 1957 resigned as Lions coach amidst disagreements between two factions of Detroit ownership. Named head coach of the Pittsburgh Steelers sixteen days later, he enjoyed moderate success there for eight seasons. Claiming he could no longer control his players, Parker resigned after compiling a 5–9 record in 1964 and five consecutive exhibition losses in 1965. His Steeler record (51–48–6) ranked then as the best eight-year record in the team's history. In fifteen seasons as an NFL head coach, Parker compiled a 102–72–9 mark for a .582 winning percentage.

Parker won respect as an intense competitor and innovative backfield coach, allowing his quarterbacks to call and develop their own plays during a game. He invented the "two minute offense," a strategy used before halftime and at the end of a game to confuse the defense by executing several offensive plays without a huddle. Never a strict disciplinarian, Parker allowed his players to form grievance committees, forbade rigid training rules and curfews, refused to conduct injury-causing drills during practice, and treated his players as pro businessmen. Parker, elected to the HAF College Football Hall of Fame in 1966, died in 1982 following complications from ulcer surgery.

BIBLIOGRAPHY: *CB* (1955), pp. 468–470; Tommy Devine and Bob Latshaw, "The Man Who Stirred Up the Lions," *Sport* 24 (October, 1954), pp. 80–83; Raymond Parker file, Pro Football Hall of Fame, Canton, OH.

John Hanners

PARRATT, George Watson "Peggy" (b. 1885, Cleveland, OH; d. 3 January 1959, Cleveland, OH), college athlete and professional football player, official, coach, and entrepreneur, made valuable contributions to pro football in Ohio between 1905 and 1916. After attending Cleveland schools, Parratt became a three-time All-Ohio college football star at Case School of Applied Science in Cleveland and simultaneously played pro football in 1905. Parratt violated his amateur status by playing for the pro Shelby (OH) Athletic Club and was barred from further college play, the first well-known star so disciplined by his school. Talented enough to play pro basketball and baseball at a later date, Parratt also was ruled ineligible in these sports at Case. He graduated from Case with an engineering degree in 1906 and later received a law degree from Baldwin-Wallace College.

After declining the head football coaching position at Marietta College, Parratt in 1906 joined the Massillon (OH) Tigers and immediately started at quarterback. Research indicates that Parratt threw pro football's first completed pass on October 25, 1906, to Massillon's Dan Policowski. Parratt played football for the Tigers and the Franklin AC in Cleveland and spent most of his time officiating games in 1907. Upon returning to Shelby in 1908, he helped organize and financially support the Blues team. The next season he played for and coached the Blues to a tie for state honors with the Akron (OH) Indians. In 1910 and 1911 Parratt recruited well-known Ohio college graduates and captured the state title. The following season he became player, coach, and owner-manager of the Akron Indians but lost the state title to Elyria. Through heavy recruitment, Parratt's teams won the state title in 1913 and 1914. His 1914 eleven consisted of several University of Notre Dame players, including Knute Rockne.* Parratt and Rockne combined for several successful forward pass plays on their way to the title. Parratt in 1916 returned to Cleveland, where he organized the Indians and directed a team for the last time as an active player.

After being inactive in Ohio football for several years, Parratt in 1925 represented the Cleveland Bulldogs at the NFL's annual meeting in Chicago. He served on a committee to re-draft the NFL constitution and met with the Intercollegiate Committee of Athletics. Parratt, who had publicized pro football, earned recognition from leaders of the game for his organizational skills and ability to conduct negotiations. An outstanding bridge player, Parratt earned a life master certificate from the American Contract Bridge League and won several major tournaments. Parratt, who married Harriet Bradley and had one daughter, Maryann, worked on the engineering staff with Ohio Crankshaft Company until his retirement.

BIBLIOGRAPHY: Cleveland *Plain Dealer*, January 6, 1959; Milt Roberts, "Peggy Parratt, MVP," *The Coffin Corner* 1 (August, 1979), pp. 3–7.

John L. Evers
Milton R. Roberts

PARSEGHIAN, Ara Raoul (b. 21 May 1923, Akron, OH), college athlete and professional football player and coach, coached football at Miami (OH) University (MAC, 1951–1955), Northwestern University (BTC, 1956–1963), and the University of Notre Dame (1964–1974) with a 170–58–6 (.739) win-loss record. His first Notre Dame squad finished 9–1–0 after the Fighting Irish had won only two games the year before. Parseghian was chosen 1964 Coach of the Year by the AFCA, FWAA, *Football News*, New York *Daily News*, and the Touchdown Clubs of Washington, DC, and Columbus, OH. He guided three national championship teams and 21 consensus All-Americans at Notre Dame and three All-Americans at Northwestern, and was named in 1980 to the NFF College Football Hall of Fame.

The son of Akron banker Michael and Amelia Parseghian, he starred in three sports at Akron South High School and graduated from there in 1941. After one year at Akron University (OC), Parseghian enlisted in the U.S. Navy V–12 program during World War II, commanded a company at Great Lakes Naval Training Station, and was discharged in December 1945. The 5 foot, 9 inch, 190 pound Parseghian entered Miami University (OH) and starred at halfback for the Redskins (MAC, 1946–1947). The latter year, he played on the undefeated MAC championship team, which triumphed 13–12 over Texas Tech in the Sun Bowl. Parseghian was named Redskins MVP and earned All-American honorable mention. Parseghian, the last athlete to win letters in three sports at Miami, excelled as a southpaw basketball and baseball player. The football captain-elect for 1948, he needed only six hours to graduate and postponed graduation six months to play pro football that fall with the Cleveland Browns. He played well with the 1948 AAFC champions, rushing 44 times for 166 yards (3.8–yard average) and one touchdown and receiving 3 passes for 33 yards (11–yard average) and one touchdown. Parseghian, however, suffered a serious pre-season hip injury in 1949 that forced him to quit playing.

Parseghian returned to Miami as freshman basketball and football coach, the latter under head coach Woody Hayes.* Parseghian's gridders finished undefeated. When Hayes became coach at Ohio State, Parseghian succeeded him as Redskins head football coach. His 5–year composite 39–6–1 record included two MAC championships; three runners-up; victories over Cincinnati, Marquette, Northwestern, and Indiana; a perfect 9–0–0 season in 1955; and fifteenth national ranking in the AP poll. Employing occasional psychology, he dressed the Redskins in tattered practice uniforms for final drills at Bloomington in front of sympathetic Indiana onlookers unprepared for the following day's 6–0 upset.

Northwestern University had experienced four consecutive losing seasons (the last one winless) and had lost 22 of its last 26 BTC games when Parseghian agreed to coach the Wildcats. Performance reversal and renewed respect came almost immediately, as the next eight years the Wildcats finished 4–3–1 over Minnesota, 3–3–0 with Hayes' Ohio State Buckeyes, 4–4–0 against Illinois, 2–4–0 with Michigan, and a complete 4–0–0 domination of Notre Dame. Northwestern stars included All-American halfback Ron Burton, guard Jack Cvercko, quarterback Tommy Myers, and wingback Paul Flatley. Northwestern won its first six games two seasons and ranked fourth in the AP poll at midseason (1958 and 1963), second for six weeks (1959), and first for two weeks (1962), but thin material and injuries caused late-season losses.

Notre Dame hired Parseghian, a French-Armenian Presbyterian, because the Fighting Irish had not enjoyed a winning season for six years. His teams lost no more than three games during any one season, amassed a composite 95–17–4 record, and ranked in the final AP top ten all but two seasons, finishing thirteenth and fourteenth those years. Parseghian strongly believed in placing the right man in the right job. Senior Heisman Trophy winning quarterback John Huarte* previously had not played enough to win a monogram and wide receiver Jack Snow had only performed at defensive end and halfback, but the two formed in 1964 the nation's finest passing combination. Team captain Jim Carroll in 1964 said, "Ara and his staff are the kind of people you hate to let down. They're young and enthusiastic and get close to the guys." Parseghian frequently shunned the coaches' practice field tower, led calisthentics, ran pass patterns, and demonstrated blocking. Memorable games included the last minute 20–17 loss to Southern California (1964) that spoiled a perfect season, the controversial 10–10 tie with Michigan State (1966), the Cotton Bowl 21–17 loss to Texas' 1969 national champions, the Cotton Bowl 24–11 triumph over Texas the following year that prevented a Longhorn repeat championship, and the thrilling 24–23 Sugar Bowl triumph (1973) over coach Paul "Bear" Bryant's* Alabama eleven. Irish stars under Parseghian included halfback Nick Eddy, end Alan Page,* quarterback Terry Hanratty, and linemen Mike McCoy, Larry DiNardo, Walt Patulski, and Greg Marx.

The physically and emotionally drained Parseghian left coaching after the 1974 season to become president of Ara Parseghian Enterprises, a specialty insurance firm in South Bend, IN. A frequent ABC-TV and CBS-TV sports commentator, he serves as a Miami University trustee and for several years was national chairman of the Multiple Sclerosis Society. He married a former Miami University student, Kathleen "Kate" Davis, and has two daughters and one son. He co-authored with Tom Pagna the book *Parseghian and Notre Dame Football* (1971), resides in South Bend, IN, and enjoys golfing winters in Marco Island, FL.

BIBLIOGRAPHY: Terry C. Bender and Lawrence W. Stiles, *Major College Football* (Bryn Mawr, PA, 1983); William B. Furlong, "Ara's New Era," *SEP* 237 (November 28, 1964), pp. 72–75; Robert Kurz, *Miami of Ohio—The Cradle of Coaches* (Troy, OH, 1983); Miami-Dayton Football Game Program, November 8, 1947; Tom Pagna, *Notre Dame's Era of Ara* (Huntsville, AL, 1976).

James D. Whalen

PATERNO, Joseph Vincent "Joe" (b. 21 December 1926, Brooklyn, NY), college player and coach, is the oldest of three children born to Angelo Lafayette and Florence (de LaSalle) Paterno. His Italian-American parents of modest means also were born and bred in Brooklyn. His father, Angelo, worked his way through law school during the early years of the Depression and was employed in the New York City courts, while his mother, Florence, was a housewife. Paterno attended Brooklyn Prep School and Brown University, where he earned a B.A. degree in English Literature. At Brown University (IL) he quarterbacked coach Charles A. "Rip" Engle's teams to 7–2 and 8–1 marks in 1948 and 1949.

Paterno planned to enter law school and perhaps pursue politics following graduation. Before earning his undergraduate degree in June 1950, however, he helped Coach Engle with the quarterbacks in spring practice. Engle, who already had accepted the head football position at Penn State University, asked him to be offensive back coach. Paterno, who needed the money for law school, decided "he had nothing to lose but a little time" and agreed to go to Penn State. The city-bred and city-wise Paterno initially was less than enthusiastic about State College, PA. After three months Paterno told Engle, "You'd better start looking around for another coach because I'm getting out of here. I'll go nuts in this town." Paterno never left State College.

After 16 years as assistant coach under Engle, Paterno became head coach in 1966. Since that time, Paterno has marched to a different drummer and has been considered a maverick by many colleagues. He believed that the intellectual and athlete could coexist and complement each other. He explained his attitude in the context of his "grand experiment": "We're trying to win football games . . . but I don't want it to ruin our lives if we lose. . . . I tell the kids who come here to play, enjoy yourselves. There's so much besides football. I want them to learn art and literature and music and all the other things college has to offer."

A demanding individual in practice and academic achievement, Paterno has molded the Penn State football program into a nationally recognized entity on both academic and athletic fronts. Over 90 percent of his players earn college degrees. "I think our people are flattered when we recruit them because they know we are going to ask them to do difficult things." His graduates include ten national postgraduate scholarship winners and six NFF College Football Hall of Fame scholar-athletes.

Besides achieving the second highest winning percentage (.819) of any active coach with a decade's service, Paterno has compiled a 199–44–2 career record and directed four undefeated teams (1968, 1969, 1973, and 1986), national championship squads in 1982 and 1986, and consecutive winning streaks of 31, 23, and 19 games. Penn State won national championships with a 27–23 victory over Georgia in the 1983 Sugar Bowl and a 14–10 triumph over Miami in the 1987 Fiesta Bowl. Paterno's Nittany Lion teams have been ranked among the nation's top ten in 15 of his 21 years, selected for bowl appearances 18 times, and compiled a 12–5–1 record in post-season play. In addition, his teams have won the Lambert Trophy as the top Eastern team 18 times.

Awards and honors have accumulated quickly. Paterno, AFCA National Coach of the Year in 1968, 1978, and 1982, FWAA National Coach of the Year in 1978, 1982 and 1986, and Eastern Coach of the Year seven times, received the prestigious Dapper Dan Man of the Year Award and the Art Rooney Award in 1983. In 1982 he received the Bobby Dodd Coach of the Year Award. *SI* selected him the 1986 Sportsman of the Year, the second coach so honored. Paterno's coaching philosophy emphasizes honesty, hard work, fun, and academic awareness. Although a football coach, he considers coaching very similar to teaching and believes himself a teacher first. With tenure and job security as professor of physical education at Penn State, Paterno has the freedom to stress his philosophy of "recruitment to graduation."

His concern for academic excellence is best typified by his 1983 campaign for the restoration of sanity to mainstream college football. Too often some schools resort to questionable recruiting and curriculum-rigging practices. His initial move was made at the NCAA Convention on January 17, 1983. Among the most controversial measures enacted at the convention was Proposition 48, which raised the academic eligibility standards for incoming freshman athletes. Paterno spoke in favor of the measure, with many citing his speech as the pivotal point for its passage. Paterno also spoke out for Proposition 49B, permitting college freshman athletes to receive a grant-in-aid but not compete.

Winning is important to Paterno, who ranks eighth on the all-time major college winning percentage chart, but the quest for excellence pervades the Paterno philosophy. This perhaps is best reflected in the advice he received as a youngster, the spirit of which he tries to inculcate within each of his players: "Whatever you do, don't sell yourself short. Your potential is as much as you want it to be." Under Paterno's leadership, Penn State has produced several especially fine linebackers and running backs. Some notable players have included running backs Lydell Mitchell,* Franco Harris,* John Cappelletti,* Curt Warner,* and D. J. Dozier, linebackers Dennis Onkotz, Jack Ham,* and Shane Conlan, and Outland Award winner Mike Reid.*

Paterno married Suzanne Pohland, a Penn State graduate, on May 12, 1962, has two daughters and three sons, and resides in State College, PA.

BIBLIOGRAPHY: Dennis A. Booher, interview with Joe Paterno, May 3, 1983; Thomas Granger, "Joe Paterno: The Lion in Autumn," *SEP* 255 (October, 1983), pp. 61–63, 98, 100; Mervin D. Hyman and Gordon White, Jr., *Joe Paterno: "Football My Way"* (New York, 1978); Eric Kaplan, "The Impossible Dreams of Football's Don Quixote," *Family Weekly* (September 4, 1983); Hank Nuwer, "Joe Paterno: Team Builder," *Success Magazine* (October, 1983); *Penn State Media Guide, 1983;* James A. Peterson and Dennis Booher, *Joe Paterno: In Search of Excellence* (New York, 1983); Jimmy Smith, "Joe Paterno: Football Coach, Teacher, Lawyer," New Orleans *Times-Picayune*, December 26, 1982; Ian Thomsen, "Now What Does Paterno Do?" *Boston Globe*, August 25, 1983.

Dennis A. Booher
Rocco Carzo

PAYTON, Walter Jerry "Sweetness" (b. 25 July 1954, Columbia, MS), college and professional player, is the son of Alyne Payton, who still lives in Columbia, and the late Peter Payton. At Columbia High School, Payton did not start playing football until his junior year. His great college and pro performances earned him the nickname "Sweetness." At Jackson State University (SAC) in 1973 he led all NCAA Division II in football scoring with 160 points. *The Football Roundup* College Player of the Year (1974) became the leading scorer in NCAA history with 464 points. In his college career Payton scored a then record 66 touchdowns, rushed for 3,563 yards (6.1–yard average), kicked 5 field goals and 54 points after touchdowns, caught 27 passes for 474 yards, punted for a 39–yard average, and averaged an incredible 43 yards per kickoff return. He completed 14 of 19 passes for 4 touchdowns, played in the College All-Star game 21–14 loss to Pittsburgh, and performed in the Shrine All-Star (East-West) and Senior Bowl contests. Payton received a Bachelor of Arts degree in Special Education, completing the academic work at Jackson State in three and one-half years.

He was selected in the first round by the Chicago Bears in the NFL draft. In 12 seasons with the Bears, he has started 172 of 178 games (156 consecutive starts) and established many records. Payton holds the single-game rushing record with 275 yards against the Minnesota Vikings in November 1977, and set the all-time NFL rushing record in 1984. Through 1986 Payton has rushed 16,193 yards on 3,692 carries (4.4–yard average) for 105 touchdowns. He exceeded Jim Brown's* record by 3,681 yards through 1986 and has netted 21,053 combined yards, bettering Brown's record by 5,594 yards. Payton owns most Bears' rushing records and at least five NFL records, including most yards rushing, most combined yards, most 100–yard games, and single-game rushing yardage and rushing attempts. In 1980 he earned an unprecedented fifth consecutive rushing title with 1,460 yards. At age 23, he in 1977 became the youngest player in pro history voted the NFL's MVP.

In 1976 Payton was selected *TSN* NFC Player of the Year and UPI's MVP runner-up. The next year, he was chosen UPI's Athlete of the Year, won the Thorpe Trophy as the NFL's MVP, and received several other MVP and Player of the Year awards. For several years he led All-Pro selections in votes. Payton appeared in the Pro Bowl for the ninth time in 1986 and was selected as 1984 Black Athlete of the Year. In 1985 he became the first player to accumulate 2,000 yards from scrimmage in three consecutive seasons and the only player to do it four times in a career. Payton finished third in rushing with 1,551 yards and 9 touchdowns (4.8–yard average) and caught 49 passes for 483 yards (9.9–yard average) to help the Bears post a 15–1 regular-season mark in 1985. The Bears defeated the New York Giants and Los Angeles Rams to capture the NFC title and trounced the New England Patriots 46–10 in Super Bowl XX. During the Bears' 13–10 overtime win over the Philadelphia Eagles in September 1986 Payton became the first NFL player to surpass 15,000 career rushing yards, scored his 100th rushing touchdown, and recorded his 75th 100–yard rushing game. Payton rushed 1,333 yards and finished third in total yardage (1,715) to help the 14–2 Bears capture the NFL Central Division title in 1986.

Payton and his wife, Connie, have one son, Jarrett, and one daughter, Brittany, and reside in suburban Barrington, IL. Payton, who is part-owner of a diner and bar in Schamburg, IL, has served as honorary chairman of the Illinois Mental Health Association and for Heart Association activities. He also has aided the Boy Scouts, March of Dimes, Piccolo Research Fund, United Way, and Peace Corps. He has tremendous strength, bench-pressing 390 pounds and leg-pressing 600 pounds plus. In 1978 he published his autobiography, "*Sweetness*," and in 1979 formed Walter Payton Enterprises, an investment firm. Payton won the Maxwell Club's Bert Bell Award as NFL Player of the Year in 1985 and set an NFL record (since broken) by gaining over 100 yards in nine consecutive games. The Pro Football Hall of Fame named him to its AFL-NFL 1960–1984 All-Star Second Team.

BIBLIOGRAPHY: AP, News Release, November 21, 1983; Chicago Bears, Press Releases, Summer 1985; Minneapolis (MN) *Star and Tribune*, September 23, 1985; *NYT*, October 8, 1984; Walter Payton, "*Sweetness*" (Chicago, 1978); *TSN Football Register—1986*.

Stan W. Carlson

PEARSON, Drew (b. 12 January 1951, South River, NJ), college and professional player and coach, is the son of Samuel and Minnie (Washington) Pearson and was possibly the greatest wide receiver in Dallas Cowboys' (NFL) history. He succeeded Joe Theismann* as quarterback for South River

(NJ) High School before being converted to flanker back at Tulsa University (MVC), where he caught 33 passes for a run-oriented offense in 1972. Signed as a free agent in 1973 by the NFL Dallas Cowboys, Pearson established Dallas records during his eleven-year career there for receptions (489) and total yardage (7,822) and averaged 16 yards per reception with 48 touchdowns. The clutch performer made some of the most memorable scoring plays in Cowboys history, including an 83–yard fourth-quarter catch to triumph over the Los Angeles Rams in the 1973 NFC playoffs, 50–yard last-second catches to defeat the Washington Redskins in 1974 and Minnesota Vikings in the 1975 playoffs, and two receptions in the last four minutes to oust the Atlanta Falcons from the 1980 playoffs.

Pearson's quarterbacking beginnings helped Dallas, as he completed a 46–yard touchdown pass in 1974, a 39–yard scoring strike in 1976, and two passes for 81 yards and 1 touchdown in 1981. Additionally, he tied an odd NFL career record of most touchdowns via recoveries of own fumbles (2). At 6 feet and 190 pounds, Pearson participated in three NFL championship games (1975, 1977, 1978) and seven NFC championships (1973, 1975, 1977–1978, 1980–1982). Pearson's three Pro Bowl appearances (1974, 1976–1977) contributed to his being named to the Pro Football Hall of Fame's All-Star team of the 1970s. After retiring from the Cowboys in 1983, Pearson worked as a radio and television sports broadcaster. In 1985 he joined head coach Tom Landry's* Dallas (NFL) staff as a wide receivers coach. He is the son-in-law of Marques Haynes* (IS), the famous Harlem Globetrotters basketball star, and has two children, Tori and Britni.

BIBLIOGRAPHY: Dallas Cowboys, Sports Information Bureau, Dallas, TX; *TSN Football Register—1983*.

PECK, Robert D., Jr. (b. 30 May 1891, Lock Haven, PA; d. 14 June 1932, Culver, IN), college and professional player and coach, received wide acclaim as college football's greatest center of its first 50 years. After playing football at Lock Haven (PA) High School, he matriculated at the University of Pittsburgh in 1913 and became the Panthers' first football All-American. He played regularly at center on the 1914 through 1916 Pittsburgh football teams, which lost only one game in three years. Peck captained the 1916 national championship unit, considered by coach Glenn "Pop" Warner* as his greatest squad. Peck, chosen by Walter Camp* as the first team center on his 1915 and 1916 All-American teams, played roving center on defense, a forerunner of the linebacker position of later years. The small, extremely aggressive Peck attracted attention by taping his wrists, ankles, and helmet so others could recognize him in a pileup. His yelling was heard throughout the stands, while his chatter and ferocity in making tackles inspired a Pittsburgh cheer, "When Peck fights, the team fights."

After completing his career at Pittsburgh, Peck played pro football for the Canton Bulldogs and 1919 Massillon Tigers of the APFA. Besides being named to the NFF College Football Hall of Fame in 1974 and to the HAF College Football Hall of Fame, he was chosen at center on the NFF's "first 50 years of collegiate football" eleven-man team and on Knute Rockne's 1906–1926 "collegiate best." Peck remains the center on Pittsburgh's all-time team, updated periodically by city sportswriters and broadcasters. The 1916 Panthers squad, which Peck led, was considered by Walter Camp* as the greatest to that time. Peck later served as head football coach and athletic director at Culver (IN) Military Academy, where he died suddenly.

BIBLIOGRAPHY: Paul B. Beers, *Profiles in Pennsylvania Sports* (Harrisburg, PA, 1975); Allison Danzig, *The History of American Football: Its Great Teams, Players, and Coaches* (Englewood Cliffs, NJ, 1956); John D. McCallum and Charles H. Pearson, *College Football U.S.A., 1869–1973* (New York, 1973); Jim O'Brien, *Hail to Pitt, A Sports History of the University of Pittsburgh* (Pittsburgh, 1982); *Owl*, University of Pittsburgh Student Yearbook, 1918, Pittsburgh, PA; *Pittsburgh Football Media Guides*, various years.

Robert B. Van Atta

PELLEGRINI, Robert "Bob" (b. 13 November 1934, Yatesboro, PA), college and professional player and coach, is the son of Henry M. and Gabrielle Pellegrini. A 1952 graduate of Shannock Valley High School, Pellegrini played all eleven football positions and performed most notably at quarterback. At the University of Maryland (ACC, 1952–1956), he played guard and center on offense and linebacker on defense. As a junior, the versatile 6 foot, 3 inch, 240 pound Pellegrini won All-ACC honors at guard and made equally strong contributions on defense. He co-captained the Terrapins the following year (1955), switching to center and winning All-American recognition. After the regular season he participated in the Senior Bowl and was selected as the MVP in the College All-Star game.

Pellegrini, first-round draft choice of the Philadelphia Eagles (NFL), started at offensive guard and entered military service shortly afterwards. As a player-coach at Fort Knox (KY) in 1957, he was named Service Player of the Year. He was discharged in 1958 and solidified his position as a middle and outside linebacker with the Eagles. His defensive play helped the Eagles unexpectedly win the Eastern Conference title in 1960, but a leg injury kept him out of the championship game. Pellegrini married Antoinette Taddeo on January 18, 1958, and has three children. The Eagles in 1962 traded him to the Los Angeles Rams (NFL) because of a coaching change. Since Pellegrini desired to play on the East Coast, however, the Rams traded him that year to the Washington Redskins (NFL). He remained with Washington until retiring in 1965.

During his 9–year pro career, Pellegrini impressed others with stiff defense and strong leadership. The new Miami Dolphins (AFL) hired Pellegrini as an assistant coach in 1966 but fired him two years later in a purported economy move. The disillusioned Pellegrini rejected a subsequent coaching offer from the Boston Patriots (AFL) and entered private business in New Jersey. He is now senior executive host at Resorts Hotel Casino in Atlantic City.

BIBLIOGRAPHY: *Miami Dolphins Media Guide, 1967; Philadelphia Eagles Media Guide, 1968; Pro!* (September 22, 1967); Washington *Post*, February 27, 1962; September 3, 1962; October 23, 1963; March 3, 1968; *Washington Redskins Media Guide, 1965;* Washington (DC) *Star*, September 4, 1962.

Jerome Mushkat

PENNOCK, Stanley Bagg "Stan" "Stan the Man" (b. 15 June 1892, Syracuse, NY; d. 27 November 1916, Newark, NJ), college player and coach, was the son of John R. Pennock. His father, a wealthy businessman, served as partner in the Aromatic Chemical Plant and general manager of the Solvay Process Company in Syracuse and had four other children. Stanley entered Harvard University (IL) in 1911 after graduating from Hackley School and played right guard on its freshman (1911) and varsity (1912–1914) teams. During the golden years of IL football, Pennock helped Harvard win 27 straight games and national co-championships his three varsity years. The exceptionally durable 195 pound guard, who played with fierce aggressiveness, was cited for his consistency and well-rounded 60–minute game by Walter Camp.* Pennock, nicknamed "Stan the Man," trained well and displayed a superior grasp of football fundamentals. At Harvard he roomed with running back Charles Brickley,* for whom he opened many holes in the Crimson line. Pennock also excelled as a student and participated actively in college life.

Pennock finished his varsity football career in 1914 and later served as assistant football coach there. After graduating from Harvard in 1915, he attended courses that fall at the chemical laboratories of Harvard. In 1916 he formed a partnership and opened a chemical plant in New York City. A subsequent plant was opened in Newark, NJ, where Pennock was killed in an explosion. Pennock, among Harvard's greatest guards, remains one of the Crimson's five three-time All-Americans. He was selected by Camp as the nation's best guard in 1913 and was named to the All-Time, All-American team by Knute Rockne* for the 1906–1926 period. Pennock is a member of the HAF and NFF College Football Halls of Fame.

BIBLIOGRAPHY: John Blanchard, ed., *The H Book of Harvard Athletics* (Cambridge, MA, 1923); Boston *Globe*, November 28, 1916; Boston *Herald*, November 28, 1916; John D. McCallum and Charles H. Pearson, *College Football U.S.A., 1869–1973* (New York, 1973).

Daniel Frio

PERKINS, Donald Anthony "Don" "Perk" "Mr. Consistent" (b. 4 March 1938, Waterloo, IA), college and professional player and announcer, is the son of Claude, a Rath Packing Company butcher, and Lilly Perkins. Nicknamed "Perk," he attended Waterloo West High School and earned four varsity letters each in football and track as a halfback and sprinter. In 1955 Perkins received All-State honors at halfback as a senior. One year later, Perkins entered the University of New Mexico (MSAC). He performed so impressively on the freshman team that head coach Marv Levy eagerly anticipated Perkins' becoming eligible for varsity play. The 5 foot, 10 inch, 190 pound Perkins received All-MSAC selection three seasons at halfback. Perkins set twelve career Lobos records, including rushing for an MSAC-record 2,001 yards and scoring 138 points. During his senior year (1959), Perkins led the nation in kickoff returns with 15 for 520 yards and became the first Lobos player to have his number (43) retired. Perkins in 1959 married Virginia Green of Waterloo, IA, and has three children, Tony, Karen, and Randall.

In 1960 the Baltimore Colts (NFL) traded their ninth-round draft rights to Perkins to the Dallas Cowboys (NFL). Perkins, however, missed the entire 1960 season with a chronic foot injury sustained in College All-Star camp. A halfback in his delayed rookie season, Perkins in 1961 led the Cowboys with 815 rushing yards, 32 pass receptions, and 5 touchdowns and also returned 22 kickoffs for 443 yards. The explosive, sure-handed Perkins rarely fumbled the football. During a two-season stretch (1965 and 1966), he fumbled only once. Most Cowboys partisans argued that Perkins had already crossed the goal line when the fumble occurred.

Perkins, who increased his playing weight to 204 pounds, became one of the best NFL pass blockers and virtually never missed a blocking assignment. His dedication and conscientious field performance earned him the title "Mr. Consistent." During his eight seasons with the Cowboys, Perkins finished among the NFL's top ten in rushing each time. He rushed 1,500 times for 6,217 career yards (4.1–yard average) and 42 touchdowns and caught 146 passes for 1,310 yards (9–yard average) and 3 touchdowns. Perkins, an All-Pro five times, competed in the 1962–1963 and 1966–1967 Pro Bowl Games. He also played in two NFL championship games (1966–1967) before retiring from football in 1968. Upon retirement, Perkins ranked fifth in NFL history with 6,217 yards rushing and saw the Cowboys retire his number. Since 1968 Perkins has worked as director of courtesy and information for the State of New Mexico and provided color commentary on football broadcasts.

BIBLIOGRAPHY: *Dallas Cowboys Press Guides, 1961, 1968;* Ronald L. Mendell and Timothy B. Phares, *Who's Who in Football* (New Rochelle, NY, 1974).

Jerry Jaye Wright

PERRY, Fletcher Joseph "Joe" "The Jet" (b. 27 January 1927, Stevens, AR), college and professional player, coach, and scout, is the son of Fletcher and Laura (Wheeler) Perry and grew up in Los Angeles, CA. Perry graduated in 1944 from Jordan High School, where he starred in track, football, basketball, and baseball. He attended Compton JC (CA) in 1944 and 1945. Perry, one of pro football's great running backs, played for the San Francisco 49ers (AAFC, NFL) from 1948 to 1960 and 1963 and Baltimore Colts (NFL) in 1961 and 1962. He gained a then career 9,723 yards rushing, averaged 5.0 yards per carry, caught 260 passes for 2,021 yards, and scored 84 touchdowns and 513 points. A 6 foot, 200 pound speedster, Perry led the AAFC once and NFL twice in rushing and was selected a three-time All-Pro fullback. Nicknamed "The Jet," for his extra fast starting speed, the soft-spoken Perry proved a keen student of the game. Although suffering numerous injuries throughout his career, he seemed extremely durable. Perry, one of the first blacks in modern pro football, received much verbal and physical abuse early in his career, then earned the respect of opponents and was well liked by teammates.

Before joining the U.S. Navy, Perry played football for two seasons at Compton JC and scored 14 touchdowns in 1944 and 11 touchdowns in 1945. He starred for the Alameda (CA) Naval Air Station team in 1947 and signed as a free agent with the San Francisco 49ers (AAFC). As a rookie in 1948, he gained 562 yards in 77 carries, led the AAFC with a 7.3 yard rushing average, and scored 10 touchdowns. In 1949 he paced the AAFC in rushing with 783 yards, averaged 6.8 yards rushing, and was named All-AAFC fullback. When the 49ers joined the NFL in 1950, Perry continued ranking among the top rushers. After finishing third in 1952 with 725 yards, he in 1953 gained 1,018 yards to top the NFL, scored 10 touchdowns, and was named All-Pro. In 1954 he rushed for an NFL-leading 1,049 yards to become the first runner to gain 1,000 yards in consecutive seasons, averaged 6.1 yards per carry, and scored eight touchdowns. He repeated as an All-Pro selection and was named UPI Player of the Year.

Perry, who sold cars and worked as a radio disc jockey in the off-season, played for the 49ers until traded in 1960 to Baltimore. After two seasons with the Colts, he returned to the 49ers in 1963 for one more year and then retired. Perry finished his sixteen-year career, longest of any running back, as pro football's all-time rushing yardage leader. Perry served as a scout and assistant coach for the 49ers from 1968 to 1976. The twice-divorced Perry is a salesman for Gallo Wines and lives in Daly City, CA. One of pro football's most durable players and greatest runners, Perry was elected to the Pro Football Hall of Fame in 1969.

BIBLIOGRAPHY: Melun Durslag, "Takes Two to Touchdown," *Collier's* 134 (September 3, 1954), pp. 34–36ff; Murray Olderman, *The Running Backs* (Englewood Cliffs,

NJ, 1969); San Francisco *Examiner*, January 12, 1984; *Sport* 10 (January, 1955), pp. 42–43, 86–87, George Sullivan, *Great Running Backs* (New York, 1972).

Edward J. Pavlick

PFANN, George Roberts (b. 6 October 1902, Marion, OH), college athlete and coach, starred in football at Cornell University (IL). He was named HAF 1923 Player of the Year and was elected in 1957 to the NFF College Football Hall of Fame. As football quarterback for three years (1921–1923), Pfann never experienced defeat. Cornell recorded three consecutive 8–0–0 seasons under coach Gilmour Dobie* and outscored opponents 1,051–81. The Big Red, named national co-champion by Parke H. Davis and HAF in 1921–1922, defeated Dartmouth, Columbia, and Colgate and broke the Franklin Field jinx in 1921 with a 41–0 triumph over Pennsylvania. In 1923 Pfann served as captain, made unanimous All-American, and scored 98 points and 15 touchdowns, the most by an eastern player. He proved an excellent field general, passer, receiver, and blocker, with his heavy, powerful legs and low center of gravity making him difficult to bring down. W. B. Hanna commented in the New York *Herald Tribune* (1927): "To my mind, one of the best of all quarterbacks was Pfann of Cornell." Allison Danzig* (OS, 1959) wrote: "Let anyone start a discussion as to the all-time quarterbacks and inevitably the names of [Walter] Eckersall* and Pfann come up." The 5 foot, 10 inch, 180 pound Pfann was chosen on Knute Rockne's* 1906–1926 Period Team and George Trevor's (1938) and FWAA's (1968) All-Time East teams.

The son of tailor John Martin Pfann, who died when George was three years old, and Ada M. (Roberts) Pfann, George starred in three sports at Marion (OH) High School (1916–1918) and Columbia (TN) Military Academy (1918–1920). In 1919 Columbia performed in the finals of the Southern Scholastic football championship. Pfann, who also played varsity lacrosse defenseman and basketball guard three years at Cornell, joined Sigma Alpha Epsilon Fraternity, served on the student council, and earned a Bachelor of Arts degree at graduation in 1924. Pfann studied law at Cornell Law School and was Big Red assistant football and freshman basketball coach. Selected as a Rhodes Scholar in 1926, he completed his study of law at Oxford (England) University. He played rugby and performed on the Oxford lacrosse team that won the Southern England championship.

Besides practicing law with the New York firm of Edwards and Smith, Pfann also became part-time head football coach of Swarthmore (PA) College (1931–1935). He served as a lieutenant colonel in World War II with the Third and Seventh armies under General George Patton, earning seven battle stars. After being counsel (1946–1964) for the Cooperative Grange League in Ithaca, NY, he was a professor of law (1964–1976) at Cornell until retirement. Pfann, a Cornell trustee for several years, married Betty Talmadge Wyckoff in 1929 and has two sons, George, Jr., and Bruce. He wed Louise McDermott in 1964 and still resides in Ithaca, NY.

BIBLIOGRAPHY: Cornell–Pennsylvania Football Game Program, November 29, 1923; Cornell University, Library Archives, Ithaca, NY; Allison Danzig, *Oh, How They Played the Game* (New York, 1971); John D. McCallum and Charles H. Pearson, *College Football U.S.A., 1869–1973* (New York, 1973); Ronald L. Mendell and Timothy B. Phares, *Who's Who in Football* (New Rochelle, NY, 1974); Alexander M. Weyand, *Football Immortals* (New York, 1962); James D. Whalen, telephone interview with George R. Pfann, June 29, 1984.

James D. Whalen

PIERCE, Bemus (b. 28 February 1873, Gowanda, NY; d. 15 February 1957, Riverside, CA), college and professional player and coach, became Carlisle Indian School's (PA) greatest football lineman (1894–1898) and only three-time team captain. The 6 foot, 1½ inch, 225 pound Pierce was the oldest of farmer Jacob and Jane Pierce's six children and belonged to the Seneca tribe. At Carlisle he played guard under coaches Vance McCormick, William Hickok, and Billy Bull, frequently carried the ball, and performed most field goal and extra point kicking. The 1898 All-American teams of Casper Whitney and Walter Camp* for *Harper's Weekly* and *Collier's*, respectively, rated Pierce just below those named.

Carlisle's composite five-year 22–22–2 record during Pierce's playing career proved deceptive. The Indians' first college football season came in 1894, when Carlisle finished 1–6–2. They played a very ambitious schedule the next four years, meeting Yale, Harvard, Princeton, and Pennsylvania in twelve games and losing by only 16.5 points per game. The Big Four's composite 137–10–5 record (.918 percent) included six undefeated seasons and four national championships. Whitney ranked the 1898 Indians fifth in the nation behind the Big Four. Carlisle defeated Illinois twice and Brown and Wisconsin once each, the latter in the first night game ever played before 15,000 at Chicago's Coliseum in 1896.

In 1899 Pierce married Carlisle student Anna Gesis of the Chippewa tribe. Pierce played pro football for three years with Pittsburgh, teaming with stalwart guard Glenn "Pop" Warner.* When Warner became head football coach at Carlisle in 1899, Pierce assisted him for two seasons. Lafayette High School in Buffalo, NY, named him head coach for the 1901 season. The next two years saw Pierce head the football program at the University of Buffalo. In 1904 Kenyon College (OC) lost its head coach four days before the season's first game. Pierce accepted the head coaching position and led Kenyon to a first-place tie with Western Reserve. After being assistant football coach at Carlisle in 1905, Pierce guided the Indians to a 9–2–0 mark as head coach in 1906. Carlisle defeated Pennsylvania, Syracuse, Minnesota, and Pittsburgh for a fifth-place national ranking but lost to Harvard (5–0) and Penn State. Pierce's next football head coaching assignment came at Haskell Institute of Lawrence, KS, where his club proved dominant for several years. From 1917 to 1921 Pierce retired to farming in Irving, NY.

accepted the head football coaching and assistant disciplinarian positions at Sherman Institute in Riverside, CA. He coached there until 1931, producing outstanding quarterback Wallace Newman. From 1931 to 1938 he taught farming at Sherman Institute. Pierce, whose wife died in 1938, resumed farming and resided with his daughter Lillian (Mrs. Pat McGill of La Sierra, CA) until his death. Pierce was survived by one son, Heston, and two daughters, Lillian McGill and Dorothy Wall.

BIBLIOGRAPHY: Jeanne Benson to David L. Porter, June 25, 1986; Allison Danzig, *The History of American Football: Its Great Teams, Players, and Coaches* (Englewood Cliffs, NJ, 1956); Bemus Pierce file, National Archives, Washington, DC; Riverside (CA) *Daily Enterprise*, February 19, 1957; John S. Steckbeck, *Fabulous Redmen: The Carlisle Indians and Their Famous Football Teams* (Harrisburg, PA, 1951); Arvel E. Wall to David L. Porter, June 13, 1986.

James D. Whalen
David L. Porter

PIHOS, Peter "Pete" (b. 22 October 1923, Orlando, FL), college and professional player and coach, grew up in Orlando and moved to Chicago, IL, his junior year in high school. At Chicago's Austin High School, Pihos developed into a fine football end and made the All-State team his senior season. Pihos then played football at Indiana University (WC) because he wanted to perform under coach Alvin "Bo" McMillin.* His career at Indiana encompassed 1941 through 1946 because of a military service stint in World War II, during which he received a battlefield commission and saw action in the Battle of the Bulge. For Indiana, Pihos made All-American at end in 1943 and fullback in 1945 and became the only Hoosier to earn such honors at two different positions. The 6 foot, 1 inch, 211 pound Pihos also displayed fine linebacking abilities at Indiana. In 1970 Indiana fans selected Pihos on the school's "all time" team and as the "all time greatest player" to perform for the Hoosiers. Pihos graduated from Indiana and joined the Philadelphia Eagles (NFL), who had drafted him in 1945.

Pihos enjoyed a fabulous career with the Eagles, making All-Pro six times (1948–1949, 1952–1955) until his retirement after the 1955 season. Pihos played mainly offensive end at Philadelphia but made All-Pro as a defensive back in 1952. Early in his career, he played both offensively and defensively. His receiving statistics looked as impressive as any end had achieved until that time. Pihos made 373 career NFL receptions for 5,619 yards and 61 touchdowns. He caught at least 60 passes in twelve game schedules in 1953 (63), 1954 (60), 1955 (62) and played in five consecutive Pro Bowls. He led NFL receivers in catches from 1953 through 1955 and retired at age 32 after one of his finest seasons.

Pihos subsequently held several football head coaching positions, including three seasons at Tulane University (SEC, 1958–1960). He also coached at

Delaware Valley College (PA) and worked with the Richmond Rebels (ConFL). The versatile Pihos pursued a career in the insurance business. Pihos has received many post-career honors, including being elected to the HAF College Football Hall of Fame (1966), NFF College Football Hall of Fame (1968), and Pro Football Hall of Fame (1970). George Allen,* author of *Pro Football's 100 Greatest Players, Past and Present*, selected Pihos as the "all-time greatest tight end." Pihos played on the 1948 and 1949 NFL–title winning Eagles teams.

BIBLIOGRAPHY: Ray Didinger, "The Greatest Team of the Greatest Years," *Pro!* 3 (January, 1983), pp. 69–75; Roger Treat, ed., *The Encyclopedia of Football*, 16th rev. ed., rev. by Pete Palmer (New York, 1979); *Philadelphia Eagles Media Guides, 1947–1955.*

William A. Gudelunas

PINCKERT, Erny (b. 1 May 1908, Medford, WI; d. 30 August 1977, Los Angeles, CA), college and professional player, was the son of Gerhart and Emma (von Graffel) Pinckert. He made two-time football All-American at the University of Southern California (PCC, 1930–1931) and ranked among the all-time premier blocking backs. When single- and double-wing formations prevailed, the triple-threat tailbacks received the most publicity. Pinckert, a wingback who mainly afforded interference, proved an exception to the rule and was voted the best 1931 player in a nationwide poll of college gridders. Pinckert came from a large, well-known San Bernardino, CA, family with five brothers and five sisters. Two of his sisters achieved fame, Jeanne Dixon as a noted astrologer and aviatrix "Pinky" Brier as a ferry pilot during World War II. Pinckert married Mildred Cadillac and had three children, Erny, Jr., Rickey, and Julie. After starring at football end and quarterback for San Bernardino High School, Pinckert enrolled at Southern California in 1928. He was famed on naked reverses and as a pass receiver, and tackler; supposedly no rival completed an aerial in his defensive territory in 1931. He averaged 11.7 yards per rush in 1930 (still a Trojans record) and carried the ball more often in 1931 (50 times), averaging 6.2 yards.

Pinckert's best individual running performance came in the 1932 Rose Bowl match against undefeated Tulane. Southern teams never had lost a Rose Bowl game before. Pinckert tallied the winning touchdown on a 28–yard reverse in the third period. A few plays later, Pinckert set up the clinching touchdown by recovering a fumble at Tulane's 28–yard line. He scampered 23 yards to paydirt as the Trojans recorded a 21–12 triumph. One press account noted, "You can put this down in your hatband, that but for Pinckert, the Trojans wouldn't have had a shadow of a chance. He was half the club." Pinckert was named the game's MVP. The victory earned Southern California recognition as the 1931 national champion. The Trojans compiled a 28–5 record during Pinckert's three varsity campaigns and routed

Pittsburgh 47–14 in the 1930 Rose Bowl. Notre Dame, the national champion in 1929 and 1930, inflicted two of those losses. According to Pinckert, his finest blocking performance came in the 16–14 Trojans win over Notre Dame in 1931.

Pinckert, a 5 foot, 11 inch, 194 pounder, starred with the Boston/Washington Redskins (NFL) from 1932 through 1940. He typified the rugged star player of pro football's early days and paid little attention to personal safety. Pinckert once remarked, "Hit a guy hard three times and the fourth time he will get out of your way." A 1933 game against the Bronko Nagurski*–powered Chicago Bears earned Pinckert the title "Mr. Tough Guy." Pinckert's coach "Lone Star" Dietz designed a special play for the contest, in which Boston scored a 10–0 upset. Guard Jack Riley let himself be blocked out of the play the first time Nagurski ran through his position, leaving a gaping hole. Pinckert, running full speed, hit Nagurski and forced the Chicago fullback to sit out the rest of the first half. Shortly after intermission, Nagurski charged at Riley's spot and was hit again by Pinckert. This time Nagurski was helped off the field. As a pro, Pinckert rushed 28 times for 114 yards (4.1–yard average) and one touchdown and caught 21 passes for 289 yards (12.8–yard average) and one touchdown.

Gentle and creative off the gridiron, Pinckert served as cartoonist for the Los Angeles *Examiner* as a collegian. Besides being known for a keen sense of humor, he was voted the best-dressed NFL player in 1937. After retiring from pro football, he owned a successful clothing business, Erny Pinckert California Designs. In 1959 Pinckert was elected to the NFF College Football Hall of Fame. He also belonged to the HAF College Football Hall of Fame.

BIBLIOGRAPHY: Bernie McCarty, "The Day They Clobbered the Bronk," *Reporter*, April 7, 1977; Erny Pinckert to Bernie McCarty, May 16, 1977; Ken Rappoport, *The Trojans: A Story of Southern California Football* (Huntsville, AL, 1974); "Southern California Gallops over Tulane," Dallas *Morning News*, January 2, 1932; *Spalding's Intercollegiate Football Guide, 1932;* "Tulane Lauded on Coast," Dallas *Morning News*, January 3, 1932.

Bernie McCarty

PLUNKETT, James William "Jim" (b. 5 December 1947, Santa Clara, CA), college and professional player, is the third child born to William and Carmen (Blea) Plunkett. His parents met at a school for the blind in Albuquerque, NM, before moving to California during World War II. His father operated a newsstand in San Jose, where Jim excelled in football, wrestling, and baseball at James Lick High.

He enrolled at Stanford University (PEC) in 1967 and, following a redshirt year, became starting quarterback as a sophomore. During his junior year, he threw for 2,673 yards and 20 touchdowns. Besides being named to the AP All-American second team, he won the Voit Memorial Trophy as the PEC's outstanding player and finished eighth in the Heisman Trophy balloting. As a senior in 1970, Plunkett earned many prestigious awards, including the Heisman Trophy, Maxwell Award, Walter Camp Player of the Year, and *TSN* Player of the Year. With 7,887 total offense yards, he became the first major college football player to surpass the 7,000 yard mark. Plunkett completed 530 passes in 962 attempts for 7,544 yards and 52 touchdowns. He led Stanford to a 27–17 Rose Bowl win over Ohio State and was named Player of the Game in both the Rose and Hula Bowls.

The New England Patriots (NFL) made Plunkett their first pick in the 1971 draft. He passed for 2,158 yards and 19 touchdowns, earning NFL Rookie of the Year honors. After suffering injuries the next four seasons, Plunkett was traded to the San Francisco 49ers for four draft choices and a player. Following two mediocre seasons, he was released by the 49ers. Plunkett's career appeared over until the Oakland Raiders signed him during the 1978 season. He saw no action that year and threw only 15 passes in 1979. In 1980, however, he replaced injured Dan Pastorini and led the Raiders into the Super Bowl. In a 27–10 win over the Philadelphia Eagles, Plunkett passed for 261 yards and three scores and was named Super Bowl MVP. The NFL also named him 1980 Comeback Player of the Year.

In 1981 a thumb injury limited Plunkett's action. He married Gerry Lavelle the following spring and has one son, James. After the Raiders moved to Los Angeles for the 1982 season, Plunkett led the team to an 8–1 record. In the playoff game against the Cleveland Browns, he threw for a career high 386 yards. Plunkett started well in 1983 but was benched in favor of Marc Wilson. When Wilson was injured, Plunkett directed the Raiders to an AFC title and 38–10 Super Bowl win over the Washington Redskins. He compiled his best single-season statistics, including 230 completions for 2,935 yards and 20 touchdowns. In 1986 he replaced Wilson as starting quarterback after the Raiders struggled at the start of the season. Through the 1986 season, Plunkett completed 1,943 passes in 3,601 attempts for 25,882 yards and 164 touchdowns and threw 198 interceptions. Throughout his personal life and athletic career, Plunkett has proved to be a courageous man who continually overcomes obstacles.

BIBLIOGRAPHY: *CB* (1982), pp. 322–25; Bill Gutman, *Jim Plunkett* (New York, 1973); Don E. Liebendorfer, *The Color of Life Is Red* (Palo Alto, CA, 1972); Jim Plunkett and Dave Newhouse, *The Jim Plunkett Story* (New York, 1981); Rick Telander, "A New Light on an Old Poll," *SI* 60 (January 23, 1984), pp. 44–45, 47–49; *TSN Football Register—1986*.

Jay Langhammer

POE BROTHERS, college players, were six sons of John Prentiss and Anne Johnson (Hough) Poe, Sr., who played football for Princeton University (IL) between 1880 and 1901. They participated in four national championships, three undefeated seasons, and four victories over Yale; three of the brothers were named to Walter Camp's* All-American teams. All attended George G. Carey Preparatory School in Baltimore and early learned football fundamentals at the Maryland AC.

John P. Poe, Sr., Princeton graduate in 1854 and father of nine children including three daughters, was a distinguished Baltimore lawyer and Maryland state attorney general. The nephew of the poet Edgar Allan Poe, he was a descendant of the De La Poer family of Ireland that emigrated from Waterford in the 1600s.

POE, Samuel Johnson (b. 27 March 1864, Baltimore, MD; d. 10 April 1933, Washington, DC), the eldest brother, played varsity football at Princeton (1880–1882) and made fierce tackles and runs of 40, 20, and 20 yards in the 1882 loss against Yale. The 5 foot, 6 inch, 150 pounder excelled in lacrosse at Princeton (1881–1883, captain 1884) and helped lacrosse become a recognized sport there. He played on the All-American lacrosse squad, which toured Europe in 1884 and won 24 of 25 games. Poe graduated from Carey School in 1880; Princeton (B.A.), 1884; Johns Hopkins University (M.A.), 1885; and University of Maryland Law School (LL.B.), 1887. He practiced law in Baltimore throughout his professional career.

Poe married Laura Lee Cromwell in 1900 and had two children, John P. III and Mary. A captain in the Maryland National Guard during the Spanish-American War, he served as infantry battalion commander at Spartanburg, SC, in World War I. He died in Walter Reed Hospital after a long illness.

POE, Edgar Allan "Pete" (b. 15 September 1871, Baltimore, MD; d. 29 November 1961, Chestnut Hills, PA) quarterbacked Princeton's football team (1888–1890) and made Walter Camp's first All-American team in 1889. That year the undefeated (10–0–0) Tigers won the national championship by defeating Yale 10–0, Harvard 41–15, and Penn 72–4. Princeton ended Yale's 37–game victory streak and amassed a 32–2–1 record during Poe's football career. The football and lacrosse captain his junior and senior years, the 5 foot, 4 inch, 138 pound Poe served as senior class president and represented Princeton at the Graduate Football Rules Advisory Committee meeting in New York in 1890.

Poe graduated in 1887 from Carey School, as Phi Beta Kappa in 1891 from Princeton, and earned a law degree from the University of Maryland in 1893. A corporate law specialist with his father's firm, he became attorney general of Maryland in 1911 and Princeton alumni trustee in 1922. His first wife, Annye Thornton McCay, whom he married in 1895, died in 1928. They had one son, Edgar Allan, Jr. Poe married Mrs. Marie L. McIlhenny, a Philadelphia widow, in 1932 and moved to Chestnut Hills, PA, after his retirement in 1951.

POE, John Prentiss, Jr. (b. 26 February 1874, Baltimore, MD; d. 25 September 1915, Loos, France) made the 1891–1892 All-American football second teams at halfback and helped Princeton attain a 24–3–0 record. After graduating in 1891 from Carey School, Poe enrolled at Princeton that fall and was elected freshman class president. Poe left school after two years and coached football at the University of Virginia (SIAA), the U.S. Naval Academy, and Princeton between 1893 and 1897. At halftime of the 1896 Harvard game, he told the undefeated Tigers varsity, "If you won't be beat, you can't be beat." Poe's famous remark was used in 1922 by coach Bill Roper to inspire another undefeated Tigers team.

The adventurous, 5 foot, 5 inch, 143 pound bachelor participated in the Spanish-American War (1898) and Philippine insurrection (1899), engaged in ranching in New Mexico (1900), gold mining in Nevada (1905), and surveying in Alaska (1910) before enlisting in the British Army (1914). Assigned to the famous Scottish infantry regiment "Black Watch," Poe was killed in action at the Battle of Loos in World War I. Poe, whose name is inscribed in the Black Watch roll of honor in Edinburgh Castle, Scotland, was honored by his Princeton classmates with an athletic field bearing his name.

POE, Neilson "Net" (b. 1 October 1876, Baltimore, MD; d. 22 September 1963, Baltimore, MD), a 5 foot, 4 inch, 142 pound left halfback, helped Princeton from 1894 to 1896 compile a composite 28–3–2 record. The undefeated 1896 squad, considered national champions, defeated Yale 24–6 and Harvard 12–0. Poe, given his grandfather's nickname "Net," graduated from Carey School (1893), Princeton (1897), and the University of Maryland Law School (1900). He coached football at Wesleyan University (1897), the University of Illinois (WC, 1899), and the U.S. Naval Academy (1900) and served as Princeton's first freshman coach (1904).

An officer in the American First Division in World War I, Poe was twice wounded, twice cited for gallantry under fire, and awarded the Distinguished Service Cross. Poe settled permanently on the Princeton campus in 1919 in Nassau Club bachelor quarters and continued as assistant football coach until retirement in 1943. Never far from his beloved Tigers, he daily observed practices until a fatal illness required his removal to the Baltimore Veterans Hospital.

POE, Arthur (b. 22 March 1879, Baltimore, MD; d. 15 April 1951, Cedar Rapids, IA), probably the greatest football player among the brothers, made Walter Camp's 1898 (second) and 1899 (first) All-American teams. After suffering knee injuries his freshman and sophomore years (1896–1897), he moved from quarterback to end. The 5 foot, 7 inch, 146 pound Poe stole the ball from a Yale back in 1898 and scored a 95–yard touchdown to defeat the Elis 6–0. He scored 80– and 40–yard touchdown runs against Navy and Brown, respectively, helping Princeton win the 1898 championship with an 11–0–1 record. With only thirty seconds remaining, Poe in 1899 dropkicked his first field goal (35 yards) to defeat Yale 11–10. The Tigers gained their first consecutive victories over the Elis and claimed the 1899 national championship with a 12–1–0 record. Named HAF 1899 Player of the Year, Poe was elected to the NFF College Football Hall of Fame in 1969. Poe graduated from Carey School in 1896 and Princeton in 1900 with a B.A. degree and served as an executive with the Quaker Oats Company in Cedar Rapids, IA, until his retirement in 1947.

POE, Gresham Hough (b. 30 July 1880, Loudon County, VA; d. 25 April 1956, Garrison, MD) was substitute quarterback (1899–1901) for Princeton and played a minor role in the 12–0 loss to Yale in 1901 when the Tigers compiled a 9–1–1 record. After graduating from Carey School in 1898, Poe was elected president of the Princeton freshman class, wrestled at middleweight, and excelled at wing three years on the Tigers hockey team. The 5 foot, 5 inch, 140 pound Poe graduated from Princeton with a B.A. degree in 1902. Poe, who coached the University of Virginia (SIAA) football team in 1903 to a 7–2–1 record, formed the Baltimore investment banking firm of Jenkins, Whedbee, and Poe in 1906 and continued there until retirement in 1953. He served overseas in World War I as captain in the Field Artillery and headed the Princeton Alumni Association of Maryland in 1925. Poe married Elizabeth Pattison Webb of Baltimore in 1924 and had no children.

BIBLIOGRAPHY: James R. Church, *University Football* (New York, 1893); Allison Danzig, *Oh, How They Played the Game: The Early Days of Football and the Heroes Who Made It Great* (New York, 1971); Allison Danzig, *The History of American Football: Its Great Teams, Players, and Coaches* (Englewood Cliffs, NJ, 1956); Parke H. Davis, *Football: The American Intercollegiate Game* (New York, 1911); Jay Dunn, *The Tigers of Princeton: Old Nassau Football* (Huntsville, AL, 1977); William H. Edwards, *Football Days* (New York, 1916); Donald G. Herring, Sr., *Forty Years of Football* (New York, 1940); Ralph Hickok, *Who Was Who in American Sports* (New York, 1971); John D. McCallum and Charles H. Pearson, *College Football U.S.A., 1869–1973* (New York, 1973); Ronald L. Mendell and Timothy B. Phares, *Who's Who in Football* (New Rochelle, NY, 1974); Princeton University, Archives, Seeley G. Mudd Manuscript Library, Princeton, NJ.

James D. Whalen

POLLARD, Frederick Douglas "Fritz" (b. 27 January 1894, Chicago, IL; d. 11 May 1986, Silver Spring, MD), college athlete and professional football player and coach, was elected in 1954 to the NFF College Football Hall of Fame and belonged to the HAF College Football Hall of Fame. Named All-New England halfback at Brown University (IL) in 1915, Pollard the next year was the second black player chosen consensus football All-American (center William Lewis of Harvard was the first black selected in 1892, 1893). Pollard, named first team All-Pro halfback in 1920 by the Rock Island (IL) *Argus* as a member of the Akron (OH) Indians, served as player-coach of the Akron Indians and Hammond (IN) Pros to become the first black mentor of a pro football team. A three-sport star at Chicago's Lane Technical High School, he was the son of barber John W. and Amanda Pollard. He starred on the football, baseball, and track teams, winning the Cook County (IL) hurdles and quarter mile championships three years (1910–1912), and graduated from high school in 1912.

The 5 foot, 8 inch, 150 pound Pollard played football two years (1915–1916) at Brown under coach Edward N. Robinson on 5–4–1 and 8–1–0 teams. The Bruins defeated Yale 3–0 in 1915 for only the second time and posted a 39–3 triumph over the Carlisle Indians, but lost decisions to 9–1–2 Syracuse (6–0) and 8–1–0 Harvard (16–7). Pollard's 20–yard punt return to the Crimson 12–yard line led to the Bruins' only touchdown against Harvard. When Michigan, Syracuse, and Nebraska declined invitations to play in the 1916 Rose Bowl game, Brown accepted with a mediocre record. The Bruins' triumph over Yale and Pollard's reputation as a crowd-pleaser influenced the Tournament Committee's decision to match Brown against undefeated Washington State. Only 7,000 spectators attended the game at 20,000–seat Tournament Park in a chilling rain and muddy field. The heavier Cougars outgained the Bruins nearly four to one and triumphed 14–0. Unable to effect his customary cuts and changes of pace, Pollard was held to 47 yards on 13 carries.

Seven regulars and three substitutes from the Rose Bowl squad returned in 1916 to produce Brown's best record to date. Besides Pollard, other stars included guard Wallace Wade,* quarterback C. J. Purdy, tackle captain Mark Farnum, and center Ken Sprague. Brown won its first eight games, including a 21–6 victory against Yale and its first triumph ever over Harvard, 21–0. Pollard scored two touchdowns against Yale on a 55–yard run from scrimmage and a 60–yard punt return giving the Elis their only 1916 defeat. He produced two touchdowns against Harvard the following week on runs of 47 and 3 yards and boasted additional gains of 42 and 22 yards. His open-field running displays prompted Walter Camp* in the 1917 *Spalding's Official Intercollegiate Football Guide* to write, "Pollard was the most elusive back of the year, or of any year. . . . So often his offensive work, on account of its very brilliancy, obscured his really sterling defense. He could always be relied upon to anticipate the spot where the runner would come, and his tackling was deadly." Colgate (8–1–0), whose only loss was by four points to Yale, defeated Brown 28–0 on a muddy field in the season's finale.

Pollard won the intercollegiate hurdles championship in 1916 and 1917 as a member of the Brown track team. He served with the U.S. Army as physical director at Fort Meade (MD) during World War I and then entered the University of Pennsylvania Dental School. Pollard soon left school to play pro football with the independent Akron Indians (1919–1920) prior to formation of the NFL and led them in 1920 to fifteen consecutive victories. In 1921 the Akron Pros boasted a 7–2–1 record under Pollard's guidance and finished third in the new NFL. Pollard played with the NFL Milwaukee Badgers (1922), Hammond Pros (1923–1925), and Providence Steamrollers

(1925) and finished his playing career with Akron (1926). All except Providence compiled losing records.

Pollard organized and coached the independent Chicago Brown Bombers pro football team (1927–1933) and then served as assistant film producer at Suntan Studio next to the Apollo Theater in New York City. Later, he became owner-president of the Pollard Investment Company and the Pollard Coal Company. Pollard married Ada Parker Laing of Chicago in 1914 and has one son, Frederick, Jr., and three daughters, Gwen, Leslie, and Elyner. His son won a bronze medal in the 110–meter hurdles event at the 1936 Berlin Olympics and was named Little All-American football halfback in 1937 at the University of North Dakota. When Pollard's wife died in 1982, he moved from their New Rochelle, NY, home to Silver Spring, MD, and lived with son Frederick and his family.

BIBLIOGRAPHY: John D. McCallum and Charles H. Pearson, *College Football U.S.A., 1869–1973* (New York, 1973); Ronald L. Mendell and Timothy B. Phares, *Who's Who in Football* (New Rochelle, NY, 1974); Maxwell Stiles, *The Rose Bowl: A Pictorial Exposition of Rose Bowl Football* (Los Angeles, 1947); Roger Treat, ed., *The Encyclopedia of Football*, 16th rev. ed., rev. by Pete Palmer (New York, 1979); James D. Whalen, telephone interview with Frederick D. Pollard, Jr., December 11, 1985.

James D. Whalen

POWELL, Arthur L. "Art" "King Pin" (b. 25 February 1937, Dallas, TX), college and professional player, caught 479 career passes to rank among pro football's all-time top ten receivers. He established an AFL career record with 81 touchdowns spanning eight seasons (1960–1967) and holds the AFL mark with four touchdowns in a single game. From 1963 through 1966 Powell made first team All-AFL and played in the AFL post-season All-Star games. He gained over 1,000 yards on pass receptions in five seasons and twice led the AFL in reception yardage and touchdowns. Including his two NFL seasons (1959, 1968), Powell caught 479 passes for 8,046 career yards and averaged 16.8 yards per reception.

Powell grew up in San Diego, CA, where he starred in high school football, basketball, and track. After one year at San Diego JC, Powell in 1956 entered San Jose State College. He played halfback in football and led the nation with 40 receptions, the first back in sixteen years to accomplish that feat. The first Spartan since 1939 to win a national statistical title of any kind, he gained 583 yards and scored 5 touchdowns for 2–7–1 San Jose State. The Spartans defeated only Drake and California Poly under coach Robert Bronzan. The 6 foot, 2 inch, 212 pound Powell left San Jose State after his sophomore year and played with Toronto and Montreal (CFL). In 1957 he rushed 7 times for 71 yards, returned 4 kickoffs for 73 yards, and intercepted 2 passes. He was selected by Philadelphia in the eleventh round of the 1959 NFL draft and appeared primarily on the kickoff and punt return teams for the 7–5–0 Eagles. In 1959 he returned 15 punts for 124 yards and 1 touchdown, returned 14 kickoffs for 379 yards, and intercepted 3 passes for 17 yards.

Philadelphia released Powell following that season, after which Powell signed with New York (AFL) as a wide receiver. Nicknamed "King Pin," Powell enjoyed an outstanding year in 1960 with 14 touchdowns and 1,167 yards gained under Titan coach Sammy Baugh.* Double-teamed much of the next season because of injuries to other receivers, Powell saw his offensive production suffer. Powell played out his option with New York in 1962 while gaining an AFL-leading 1,130 yards and signed with Oakland (AFL). Raiders' coach and general manager Al Davis* led Oakland from a dismal 1–13–0 record in 1962 to a 10–4–0 and second-place Western Division finish in 1963. Powell spearheaded the dramatic turnaround by leading the AFL in yards gained (1,304) and touchdowns (16). He averaged better than 11 touchdowns and produced two additional 1,000–plus yardage seasons the next three years.

Powell was traded to Buffalo (AFL) in 1967. Bills coach Joe Collier considered Powell "one of the most dangerous receivers in football," but Powell missed the last eight games of the season with injuries. After winning three consecutive Eastern Division titles, Buffalo won only four games in 1967 and finished in last place. Powell often experienced problems with management regarding his value as a player and was labeled a troublemaker. After Buffalo released him, Powell joined Minnesota (NFL) in August 1968. He caught only one pass for 31 yards for the Vikings and retired at the end of the season. Powell, an avid golfer, has one brother, Charlie, who played pro football at end with the NFL San Francisco 49ers and Oakland Raiders.

BIBLIOGRAPHY: Harold Claassen and Steve Boda, Jr., eds., *Ronald Encyclopedia of Football* (New York, 1960); Ronald L. Mendell and Timothy B. Phares, *Who's Who in Football* (New Rochelle, NY, 1974); *Official NCAA Football Record Book, 1957; Official NFL Record Book, 1983; TSN Football Register—1969*.

James D. Whalen

PRESNELL, Glenn (b. 28 July 1905, Gilead, NE), college and professional athlete and football coach, is the son of section railroad foreman James and Grace Presnell. Presnell graduated in 1924 from DeWitt (NE) High School, where he participated on the football, basketball, and track teams. From 1924 through 1927 he attended the University of Nebraska (MVC) and played basketball two seasons and football four seasons. A three-year football starter at tailback, the 5 foot, 10 inch, 193 pound Presnell made both the 1927 New York *Sun* All-American team and Walter Camp All-American Second Team squad and participated in the 1927 Shrine All-Star (East-West) game. In 1928 Presnell became player-coach with the semi-pro Ironton (OH) Tanks for $150 per game. The position included a $1,600 per year teaching post with the Ironton school system. Under Presnell, the Tanks over two years compiled 13 wins, 7 losses, and 2 ties. In 1930 Presnell continued as a player, but Alfred Earle "Greasy" Neale* was named coach. The Tanks finished with seven wins and three losses and defeated three NFL teams: the New York Giants 13–12, Chicago Bears 26–13, and Portsmouth Spartans 16–15.

After the Ironton Tanks disbanded in 1930, Presnell joined the Portsmouth Spartans (NFL) and initially was overshadowed by All-Pro tailback Earl "Dutch" Clark.* The Spartans placed second (11–3) in the NFL in 1931 and third (6–2–4) in 1932 after losing 9–0 to the Chicago Bears in the indoor Championship game. In 1933 he led the NFL in scoring with 63 points, tied for the NFL lead in field goals with five, and made the All-Pro team. Since the Portsmouth club became the Detroit Lions in 1934, Presnell moved to Detroit. During that season, he kicked a then NFL record 54–yard field goal to defeat the Green Bay Packers 3–0 and finished third in scoring with 63 points. Presnell performed in 1935 with the Lions, who defeated the New York Giants 26–7 to win the NFL championship. He retired from pro football following the 1936 season. During his six NFL seasons, he threw 16 touchdown passes, scored 20 touchdowns, and kicked 41 extra points and 15 field goals for 206 points.

Presnell began his college football coaching career in 1937 as an assistant at the University of Kansas (BSC). He subsequently served as an assistant coach at the University of Nebraska (BSC, 1938–1941, 1946), North Carolina Pre-Flight Training Center and Atlanta Naval Air Station (1943–1945), and Eastern Kentucky State University (OVC, 1947–1952). An acting head coach at Nebraska (BSC) in 1942, he later became head football coach (1953–1963) and director of athletics (1953–1974) at Eastern Kentucky (OVC). Presnell, who retired in 1974, was inducted into the University of Nebraska Football Hall of Fame. In 1929 Presnell married Lizbeth Gehrling of Ironton, OH, and had one son Daniel. After the death of his first wife, Presnell married Mary Ford in 1974 and now lives in Ironton.

BIBLIOGRAPHY: Bob Barnett, "The Game That Saved the NFL," *River Cities Monthly;* Bob Barnett, "The Portsmouth Spartans," *River Cities Monthly;* Bob Barnett, "The Tanks and Spartans," *Football Digest;* C. Robert Barnett, interviews with Glenn Presnell, 1979–1984; David S. Neft, Richard M. Cohen and Jordan A. Deutsch, *Pro Football: The Early Years, An Encyclopedic History, 1895–1959* (Ridgefield, CT, 1978).

C. Robert Barnett

PRUITT, Gregory Donald "Greg" (b. 18 August 1951, Houston, TX), college athlete and professional football player, is related to former NFL players Brig Owens, Marv Owens, and Beasley Reece and former NBA star Bob Love. Pruitt, whose parents, Herman and Maggie (Lee) Pruitt, were divorced when he was age 9, spent a considerable amount of time with his older brothers, who encouraged him to play football. Pruitt's organized football career began when he was a 4 foot, 4 inch freshman at Houston's B. C. Elmore High School. During his high school career, Pruitt caught 87 passes and scored 27 touchdowns as a quarterback, tight end, and wide receiver. Although heavily recruited by small black colleges, he attracted major scholarship offers from only Colorado, Houston, Arizona State, and Oklahoma. Pruitt accepted a football scholarship from Oklahoma (BEC), where he began as a wide receiver.

Coach Chuck Fairbanks switched to the wishbone offense and shifted Pruitt to running back. Pruitt played on the second team until an injury to a starter gave him his opportunity. For the remainder of his sophomore year, the 5 foot, 10 inch, 190 pound Pruitt gained 241 yards on 45 carries and was named the outstanding offensive player of the 1970 Astro-Bluebonnet Bowl versus Alabama. Pruitt, who made All-American at running back his junior and senior seasons at Oklahoma, finished third in the Heisman Trophy balloting as a junior and second as a senior. As a junior, Pruitt set a then-Oklahoma record for yards rushing with 1,665 (Billy Sims* broke that record with 1,762) and established an NCAA record for yards per carry with 9.35. His personal best performance comprised a Sooners-record 294 yards rushing on 19 carries versus Kansas State in 1971. In that game he averaged 15.4 yards per carry and scored three touchdowns. During his senior year he was the leading candidate for the Heisman Trophy until suffering an ankle injury with three games left in the season. He captained the Sooners his senior year and was selected MVP of the 1973 Hula Bowl. At Oklahoma, Greg performed on the freshman basketball team and ran the low hurdles on the track squad.

Upon completion of his eligibility, Pruitt was chosen by the the Cleveland Browns (NFL) in the second round of the 1973 draft. Pruitt played for the Browns nine seasons and was selected to the Pro Bowl four times. Pruitt ranks third on the all-time Browns' list in most yards rushing one game (214), career rushing average (4.74 yards), and career pass receptions (323). During his tenure with the Browns, Pruitt enjoyed seventeen 100–yard rushing games and three 1,000–yard rushing seasons. Following the 1981 season, Pruitt was traded to the Los Angeles Raiders (NFL). After joining the Raiders, Pruitt became very successful as a return specialist on kicks and punts. In 1983 he set an NFL record for punt return yardage by bringing back 58 punts for 668 yards and set a Raiders record with a 97–yard return versus the Washington Redskins. He was named to the Pro Bowl for the fifth time following the 1983 season and participated in the Super Bowl victory over Washington.

His career statistics included 5,672 yards gained rushing, 3,069 yards in receptions, and 4,523 return yards. Pruitt retired prior to the 1985 season after twelve NFL campaigns and ranks seventh in all-time combined rushing, receiving, and return yardage. During his career, he scored 47 touchdowns. He received a Bachelor's degree in Journalism from the University of Oklahoma following his third season with the Browns. He resides in Shaker Heights, OH, where he operates Pruitt Energy Sources, an electrical wire and cable distributing company.

BIBLIOGRAPHY: *Cleveland Browns Media Guide, 1982;* Al Eschbach, "Hello . . . Goodbye," Oklahoma *Journal*, November 10, 1971; *Los Angeles Raiders Media Guide, 1984;* Volney Meece, "Pruitt's No. 1 . . . on Foe's Stop List," *Oklahoma City* (OK) *Times*, September 21, 1972; *TSN Pro Football Register—1984; University of Oklahoma Press Guide, 1972;* Jim Weeks, "Pruitt and the Heisman Trophy—It Could Be Close," *Norman* (OK) *Transcript*, November 3, 1971; Jim Weeks, "Pruitt's Still Making Moves As NFL Career Winds Down," *Sooners Illustrated* (October, 1984).

William A. Sutton

PRUITT, Michael "Mike" (b. 2 April 1954, Chicago, IL), college athlete and professional football player, is the son of security guard John and Alberta Pruitt and has three brothers, Joe, Larry, and Robert, and one sister, Betty Jean. Pruitt graduated in 1972 from Wendell Phillips High School in Chicago, where he won three letters each in football and track and two letters in wrestling. After rushing over 1,000 yards in 1971, he made the All-State football team at running back. Pruitt also captained the track squad his junior and senior years, running the 100–yard dash in 9.5 seconds, and won the city wrestling championship at 185 pounds. The 6 foot, 1 inch Pruitt entered Purdue University (BTC) in 1972 and started at fullback in football the next year for coach Alex Agase's 5–6 Boilermakers. As a junior, Pruitt gained 613 yards rushing (6–yard average) for the 4–6–1 team. His 94–yard run against Iowa in 1974 remains the longest scoring play in Boilermakers history. In 1975 he was selected a tri-captain for the 4–7 Purdue squad. Pruitt rushed 217 times for 899 yards and three touchdowns and surpassed 100 yards rushing on five occasions to earn All-BTC honorable mention. Purdue's MVP, he gained 162 yards rushing and scored two touchdowns against Wisconsin. His career record at Purdue included 1,588 yards gained on 351 carries (4.5–yard average) and six touchdowns. Pruitt, who participated in the post-season College All-Star and Shrine All-Star (East-West) games and Senior and Japan bowls, also competed for Purdue in track and ran the 60–yard dash in 6.2 seconds. He in 1973 earned a Bachelor of Arts degree in Business Administration and minored in Theatre, having appeared in three college plays.

The Cleveland Browns (NFL) selected the 225 pound Pruitt in the first round of the 1976 draft. Pruitt spent the first two seasons as reserve fullback behind Cleo Miller and returned 12 kickoffs for 237 yards. In 1978 Pruitt started nine games at fullback, gaining 560 yards and scoring 5 touchdowns. For the next five seasons, he paced the Browns in rushing and ranked among the top four AFC rushers four times. In 1979 the UPI named Pruitt to its All-AFC first team, as he gained a career-high 1,294 yards for 9 touchdowns and caught 41 passes for 372 yards and 2 touchdowns. Besides finishing second to Earl Campbell* in AFC rushing, Pruitt accounted for over one-half of the 9–7 Browns' rushing yardage. Cleveland finished first in the AFC Central Division in 1980 with an 11–5 mark, as Pruitt placed third in the AFC with 1,034 yards rushing, scored 6 touchdowns, and caught a career-high 63 passes for 471 yards. Following the 1979 and 1980 seasons, Pruitt participated in the Pro Bowl.

In 1981 Pruitt again was the Browns' busiest offensive player with 247 carries for 1,103 yards and 63 pass receptions for 442 yards. His 1,545 combined yards comprised the tenth highest in NFL history. A groin pull hampered Pruitt's effectiveness in 1982 after he gained 136 yards and scored two touchdowns in the season opener against the Seattle Seahawks. Pruitt returned to full form in 1983, gaining 1,184 yards for third best in the AFC and his fourth 1,000–yard effort in five seasons. The same year, he also caught 30 passes for 157 yards and 2 touchdowns and recorded a career-high 12 touchdowns altogether. The UPI named Pruitt, who within eight seasons had become the twenty-second NFL player to rush for 6,000 career yards, to its All-AFC second team. Pruitt, whose offensive production declined the next two seasons, underwent arthroscopic knee surgery in November 1984 and split the 1985 NFL campaign between the Buffalo Bills and Kansas City Chiefs. Pruitt led Kansas City in rushing (448 yards) in 1986 as the Chiefs made the AFC playoffs for the first time since 1971. The New York Jets eliminated the 10–6 Chiefs in the AFC wild-card game.

Through the 1986 season, Pruitt ranks 12th in NFL career rushing with 7,378 yards in 1,846 carries (4.0–yard average) and 51 touchdowns. In 11 pro games he rushed for at least two touchdowns. Pruitt, the third best rusher and eighth highest scorer in Browns' history, was Cleveland's second leading receiver in the 1979–1984 period and has caught 262 career passes for 1,804 yards and 5 touchdowns. In 1980 he was selected Miller Man of the Year for his contributions to the Cleveland community. Pruitt, the president of a highway construction firm, married his wife, Karen, in 1976 and has two sons, Aaron and Kevin.

BIBLIOGRAPHY: Mark Adams to David L. Porter, July 16, 1986; *Cleveland Browns Media Guide, 1985;* Zander Hollander, ed., *The Complete Handbook of Pro Football, 1984* (New York, 1984); "Pro Football's Leading Lifetime Rushers," *Football Digest* 15 (August, 1986), p. 85; Purdue *Boilermaker Bulletin*, November 24, 1975; Purdue University, Sports Information Office, West Lafayette, IN; *Street & Smith's College Football Yearbooks, 1974–1977; Street & Smith's Pro Football Yearbooks, 1978–1986; TSN Football Register—1986.*

David L. Porter

R

RASHAD, Ahmad (b. Bobby Moore, 19 November 1949, Portland, OR), college and professional player and announcer, retained his given name until starting his pro career. He graduated from Mt. Takoma High School in Tacoma, WA, and enrolled at the University of Oregon. At Oregon he set 14 school records as a halfback, made the All-PEC team three successive years, and earned All-American recognition as a senior. He graduated with a Bachelor's degree in Education and has earned credits toward a Master's degree. Drafted in the first round by the St. Louis Cardinals (NFL) in 1972, the 6 foot, 2 inch, 200 pounder was converted to a wide receiver. After the 1973 season, the Buffalo Bills (NFL) acquired him for quarterback Dennis Shaw. He missed the entire 1975 season due to a knee injury and signed with the Seattle Seahawks (NFL). The Minnesota Vikings (NFL) acquired him just before the 1976 season in a trade with Seattle.

During his first six seasons with the Vikings (1976–1981), Rashad led NFL players in total pass receptions. In 1981 he broke Walter "Chuck" Foreman's* Vikings career record for pass receptions (336) and extended the figure to 400. Rashad's 495 career pass receptions tied him for 19th place with Tommy McDonald* on the NFL's all-time list. Rashad led the NFL in pass receptions in 1977 (51) and 1979 (80) and ranked 13th in 1981. From 1976 to 1980 he paced the Vikings in receiving yardage and/or receptions. His career 5,489 receiving yards as a Viking rank second to Sammy White's 5,513 yards. Rashad established the two best season Vikings pass reception yardage marks with 1,156 yards (1979) and 1,095 yards (1980). Rashad's four touchdowns against the San Francisco 49ers in 1979 established the club one-game record for touchdowns. In 1981 an injury prevented him from starting against the Kansas City Chiefs in the final game and broke his string of 88 consecutive starts. Rashad set a Vikings record by catching passes for over 100 yards in 13 games and caught at least one pass in 77 consecutive games. Rashad was selected to four consecutive Pro Bowls (1978–1981), being named MVP in his first appearance. During eleven pro seasons, he gained 6,831 yards and averaged 13.8 yards per catch. His 44 career touchdowns included four very long gains. After substituting in his first four pro games, he started all contests from 1976 through 1982 except the final 1981 season game.

During his playing career, Rashad worked off-seasons as a reporter for WCCO-TV and vice-president for special events for Jeno's in Minneapolis. He has participated in charity activities, including the Mental Health Association, Boys Club, Muscular Dystrophy Association, Special Olympics, and Challenge for Children. In 1980 fan balloting, he was named Miller National Football Man of the Year for Minnesota. Now employed by NBC Sports, the Lakeville, MN, resident remains an above average tennis player. In December 1985 he married Phylicia Ayers-Allen of "The Cosby Show." They have one daughter, Condola. Rashad has four other children from a previous marriage.

BIBLIOGRAPHY: Minneapolis (MN) *Star and Tribune*, 1976–1982; Minnesota Vikings Professional Football Game Programs, 1976–1981; Minnesota Vikings, Press Releases and Fact Sheets; St. Paul (MN) *Pioneer Press*, 1976–1982; *TSN Football Register—1983; USA Weekend*, November 21–23, 1986.

Stan W. Carlson

RAY, Hugh L. "Shorty" (b. 21 September 1884, Highland Park, IL; d. 16 September 1956), administrator, was the NFL Supervisor of Officials from 1938 through 1952. Although never playing or coaching in the NFL, he deserved much credit for the success the pro game achieved by the 1950s. Ray attended the University of Illinois, but the 5 foot, 6 inch, 138 pounder was too small even by early standards to play varsity football. Intensely interested in sports, he turned to officiating and officiated in the WC for over 30 years. Probably no other WC official officiated in three major sports—namely football, basketball, and baseball. In 1925 he organized the AOO to improve the quality of sports officiating. His useful innovations included conducting rules-interpretation seminars and requiring officials to submit written reports on each game they handled.

In football, Ray made his greatest contributions. The NFHSAA asked him to write its football rule book in 1929. Ray's successful code became the standard for all football rulebooks. In 1938 he became Technical Advisor on Rules and Supervisor of Officials for the NFL. Until then pro football simply used the college rules with few exceptions. A master of detail, Ray instituted the practice of touring the training camps to explain and clarify the rules. He traveled to countless games and practices, armed with a stopwatch, clipboard, binoculars, pencils, and charts, studying how the game was played and always seeking ways to improve it.

Many of his discoveries have become common football knowledge. The faster a game is played, for example, the more time it consumes. More plays are run in the second quarter than in the first and more in the fourth quarter than any other. A team can actually lose because it plays "too fast," the subject of a famous bet between Ray and Green Bay Packers coach Earl "Curly" Lambeau.* No doubt his most important achievement was improving the caliber of NFL officiating. Ray's proudest boast was that, when he began, only a few NFL officials could score 95 percent on a written rules test with the book open beside them. When Ray retired in 1952, all NFL officials could score better than 95 percent without using the book. In 1966 Ray was elected to the Pro Football Hall of Fame.

BIBLIOGRAPHY: Mike Rathet and Don Smith, *Their Deeds and Dogged Faith* (New York, 1984); Beau Riffenbaugh, *The Official NFL Encyclopedia* (New York, 1986); Howard Roberts, *The Story of Pro Football* (Chicago, 1953).

Robert N. Carroll

REEVES, Daniel Edward "Dan" (b. 19 January 1944, Rome, GA), college and professional player and coach, is the son of farmer–general contractor Charles and Ann (Horton) Reeves. He excelled as a football, basketball, and baseball player at Americus (GA) High School before enrolling at the University of South Carolina (ACC) in 1961. He became the Gamecocks' starting quarterback as a sophomore and earned All-ACC second team selection. Although injuries limited his playing time as a junior, he starred as a senior and again made All-ACC second team. His best single-game passing effort came against the University of Nebraska in 1964, when he completed 18 of 28 passes for 248 yards. Reeves, who finished his college career with 2,561 passing and 815 rushing yards, married Pam White on June 27, 1964, and has two daughters, Dana and Laura, and one son, Lee.

Reeves signed as a free agent with the Dallas Cowboys (NFL) in 1965 and made the club as a reserve running back. After becoming a starter in 1966, he rushed for 757 yards and caught 44 passes. He scored an NFL-leading 16 touchdowns, including four against the Atlanta Falcons. *TSN* named him to the Eastern Conference All-Star team. Reeves enjoyed another fine season in 1967, rushing for 603 yards and catching 39 passes. Although not particularly fast, he showed a knack for finding holes, stretching for extra yardage, and utilizing the halfback option pass.

In the fourth game of the 1968 season, Reeves suffered a knee injury that sidelined him for the year and hampered his running and cutting ability in later years. He remained a valuable spot player for the Cowboys until 1972 and played in four NFL title games and two Super Bowls. His pro career statistics included 532 rushing attempts for 1,976 yards, 129 receptions for 1,693 yards, and 253 points scored.

The Cowboys named him offensive backfield coach in 1970, although he still played until retiring early in the 1972 season. He pursued private business in 1973 but returned to the Cowboys prior to the 1974 campaign. Reeves, inducted into the University of South Carolina Athletic Hall of Fame in 1977, continued with Dallas (NFL) as an assistant coach through the 1980 season. In 1981 the Denver Broncos (NFL) named him as their head coach. His first team produced a 10–6 record to barely miss the playoffs, but fell to a 2–7 mark during the strike-shortened 1982 season. Denver made the AFC playoffs with a 9–7 record in 1983 and finished in first place in the Western Division with a 13–3 record in 1984. Denver was eliminated in the first round of the playoffs both years. After finishing second with an 11–5 mark in 1985, the Broncos won the AFC Western Division with an 11–5 record in 1986. The Broncos beat the New England Patriots in the playoffs and then came from behind to defeat the Cleveland Browns 23–20 in overtime in the AFC championship game. Reeves' team lost to the New York Giants, 39–20, in Super Bowl XXI. Through 1986, Reeves has compiled a 56–33 career mark.

BIBLIOGRAPHY: *Dallas Cowboys Press Guides, 1966–1967, 1980; Denver Broncos Press Guide, 1986;* Jim Hunter, *The Gamecocks: S.C. Football* (Huntsville, AL, 1975); Ronald L. Mendell and Timothy B. Phares, *Who's Who in Football* (New Rochelle, NY, 1974).

Jay Langhammer

REEVES, Daniel Farrell "Dan" (b. 30 June 1912, New York, NY; d. 15 April 1971, New York, NY), professional owner and administrator, was the son of Irish immigrant James, builder of a multimillion-dollar neighborhood grocery store chain, and Rose Reeves. Reeves captained his football team at Newman Preparatory School (Lakeland, NJ), where he graduated in 1929. He maintained his interest in football after graduating from Georgetown University (1933) and becoming a New York Stock Exchange member. After two futile bids to buy pro football teams, he in 1941 purchased the Cleveland Rams (NFL).

Military service during World War II interrupted his involvement with the Rams. After being discharged in 1945, he saw Cleveland win the NFL title and falter financially. At a subsequent acrimonious owners' meeting, he won grudging approval for an unprecedented franchise move to an entirely new market in Los Angeles, CA. Many people thought Reeves had erred by moving a championship team so abruptly, and other factors multiplied his mistakes. No other major league franchise yet existed on the West Coast, air travel seemed prohibitive, and Southern California appeared a collegiate preserve. The rival AAFC then placed the Dons in Los Angeles, seemingly verifying critics' claims. During the next three years, the Rams drew poorly, steadily lost money, and forced Reeves to enlist new partners.

Compelled to innovate, Reeves glamorized the Rams with bright uniforms, encouraged a crowd-pleasing passing attack, and created the NFL's first efficient scouting system. In the front office, he recruited Alvin Rozelle* and other bright public relations people. Although other owners hesitated, Reeves pioneered television broadcasting and broke the NFL's racial barriers by hiring Kenny Washington.* These moves popularized the Rams, particularly when the AAFC collapsed and made Los Angeles the first NFL franchise to draw over one million fans in a season.

During the mid-1950s the Rams' financial success created bitterness among the partners resenting Reeves' unilateral control. Commissioner Bert Bell* formed a custodianship to run the Rams until matters settled. In 1962 Reeves regained his position by buying out his old partners and refinancing. At times, turmoil on the field proved equally divisive. During Reeves' 25 years of ownership, the Rams hired 10 coaches with a combined record of 125 victories, 127 losses, and 7 ties, 6 Western Division or conference titles, and 1 NFL championship. Coach George Allen* especially experienced a trying relationship with Reeves. Throughout these problems, Reeves conducted his stock business. He married Mary Corroon on October 24, 1935, and brought up six children.

Reeves, a keen judge of talent, proved a pivotal figure in molding pro football and all sports. His innovations became standards, while his players and workers became influential figures on both the collegiate and pro levels. He provided new directions with his franchise move to the West Coast, early appreciation of television's commercial possibilities, and shattering of racial shibboleths. In 1967 these contributions collectively led to his induction into the Pro Football Hall of Fame.

BIBLIOGRAPHY: Baltimore *American*, December 15, 1963; Canton (OH) *Repository*, November 20, 1969; Los Angeles *Herald-Examiner*, February 8, 1967; August 10, 1968; Los Angeles *Times*, December 30, 1962; February 7, 1970; *Los Angeles Rams Media Guide, 1970; NYT*, April 16, 1971; *Pro* (September 19, 1971); St. Louis *Globe-Democrat*, January 31, 1969; *TSN*, June 27, 1970; April 17, 1971.

Jerome Mushkat

REID, Michael Barry "Mike" (b. 24 May 1947, Altoona, PA), college athlete and professional football player, is the second of three sons born to railroad man William and Charlotte Reid. He began his sports career at Altoona High School, where he excelled in wrestling and track (shot put) and made All-State offensive fullback and defensive tackle in football. After gaining nearly 1,000 yards and scoring 107 points as a senior, he was recruited by numerous universities. He chose nearby Penn State University, where he matriculated as a business major in 1966. By his sophomore year he was noted for his prowess in track, wrestling, and football. A knee injury, however, forced him to sit out the entire 1967 football season. Upon his return the 6 foot, 3 inch, 235 pound co-captain was converted from middleguard–linebacker to tackle and anchored the Penn State defensive line to undefeated seasons in 1968 and 1969 and two Orange Bowl victories. Mentioned for national honors in 1968, he was named a consensus All-American in 1969, won the Outland Award as the nation's outstanding lineman of the year, and received the Maxwell Award. Reid also finished fifth, ahead of all other linemen, in the balloting for the Heisman Trophy.

After graduation from Penn State in 1969, Reid was drafted in the first round by the Cincinnati Bengals (NFL). With his size and quickness, he excelled as a defensive tackle and pass rusher, was awarded All-Rookie (1970) and All-Pro (1973, 1974) honors, and played in the Pro Bowl games in 1973 and 1974. During these years, the Bengals twice (1970 and 1973) won the Central Division title and bowed in the playoffs each time to the eventual winner of the Super Bowl. Team tensions during the 1974 players' strike may have influenced Reid's early retirement from the pro ranks in 1975, but he had found football less personally rewarding than his developing music career. Reid had rediscovered this interest at Penn State, where he became a popular performer and graduated as a music major. By 1975 he had become a well-known entertainer and piano soloist with a classical and popular repertoire that included some personal compositions. From 1975 to 1979 he toured with small groups and then settled in Nashville, TN. Soon his songs were being performed by top recording artists, with his "Stranger in My House" receiving a 1984 Grammy award. Reid, who is married and has one son, defied the stereotype of the athlete. The thoughtful, imaginative, articulate Reid remained conscious of the seeming contradiction between his competitive athletics and musical talents. He was recognized as a twentieth-century Renaissance figure with outstanding accomplishments in his two major vocations. In 1987 he was named to the NFF College Football Hall of Fame.

BIBLIOGRAPHY: Elizabeth A. Bechtel, "Grammy & Pappy," *The Penn Stater* (May/June, 1984), p. 12; Frank Bilovsky, *Lion Country: Inside Penn State Football* (West Point, NY, 1984); Neil Offen, "Paying for It," *Esquire* 82 (October, 1974), pp. 82–84; Ron Reid, "Handy Pair of Brainy Bengals," *SI* 37 (October 16, 1972), pp. 46–48.

Daniel R. Gilbert

RETZLAFF, Palmer Edward "Pete" (b. 21 August 1932, Ellendale, ND), college athlete and professional football player, coach, executive, and announcer, is the son of German-born Fred W. and Ella Retzlaff. Retzlaff, nicknamed "Pete," graduated from Ellendale High School and attended Ellendale State College in 1949 and 1950. He transferred to South Dakota State College (SDC), where he earned B.S. (1953) and M.S. degrees. He captained the track and football squads, won MVP awards in both sports, and served as class president. As a running back, he gained Little All-American honors. Although drafted by the Detroit Lions (NFL) in the twenty-second round in 1953, he was released before the season. Retzlaff, who served in the infantry in 1954–1955, married Patty Kennard and has four children, Krisann, Carol, James, and Dani.

After signing again with Detroit in 1956, he was sold to the Philadelphia Eagles (NFL) for $100 as a reserve running back. In 1958 coach "Buck" Shaw* moved him to receiver. Teaming with quarterback Norm Van Brocklin,* he shared the NFL receiving title that same year with 56 catches and helped the Eagles win the 1960 NFL championship. He played in the Pro Bowl in 1958 and 1960 and was named to the All-Eastern Conference squad in 1958. The 6 foot, 1 inch, 211 pound Retzlaff won more recognition after he moved from split end to tight end in 1963, serving as player-coach and making the Pro Bowl and Eastern Conference All-Stars the next three years. Besides being the Eagles' MVP in 1963, he was named Pro Football Player of the Year in 1965 by the Washington Touchdown Club and several other groups.

He retired after the 1966 season as the then fifth leading receiver in NFL history, with 452 catches for 7,412 yards and 47 touchdowns. Retzlaff, whose jersey was retired by the Eagles, was selected to the Eagles All-Time team. Twice president of the NFL Players Association, he served as the Eagles' general manager from 1969 to December 1972. He later worked as a CBS football commentator and broadcaster on a Philadelphia radio and television station and pursued business interests, which have since occupied him full-time.

BIBLIOGRAPHY: Weeb Ewbank, Jack Buck, and Bob Broeg, *Football Greats* (St. Louis, 1977); Ronald L. Mendell and Timothy B. Phares, *Who's Who in Football* (New Rochelle, NY, 1974); "Pete Retzlaff Interview," *Quarterback* (December, 1969); Philadelphia *Eagles Magazine* (December 19, 1965), pp. 3–4; Philadelphia *Evening and Sunday Bulletin*, 1956–1972; Philadelphia *Inquirer*, 1956–1972.

Bruce W. Wasem

REYNOLDS, Robert O'Dell "Bob" "Horse" (b. 30 March 1914, Morris, OK), college and professional football player and sports executive, is the son of Clarence and Cynthia Evelyn (O'Dell) Reynolds. His father, an oil well drilling contractor, moved the family to Okmulgee, OK. Reynolds made All-State as a tackle in football and participated in wrestling and track. He entered Stanford University (PCC) in the fall of 1932 and became one of "The Vow Boys," pledged not to lose in football to the University of Southern California. Nicknamed "Horse," the 6 foot, 4 inch, 225 pounder earned All-American honors in 1934 and 1935 as a tough two-way tackle and kickoff specialist. His most remarkable feat, comprised playing the entire sixty minutes in three consecutive Rose Bowls against Columbia, Alabama, and SMU. He also participated in the College All-Star game and was elected to the NFF College Football Hall of Fame in 1961. He also belonged to the HAF College Football Hall of Fame.

Although drafted by the Chicago Cardinals (NFL) Reynolds refused to sign with them and skipped pro football in 1936. His rights were acquired by the Detroit Lions (NFL), whose owner Dick Richards promised to help Reynolds start a business career. After two seasons with the Lions, he took a sales position with Richards-owned radio station KMPC in Beverly Hills, CA, and later moved into management. He married Emma Lee McDaniel on June 14, 1941, and has three sons, Christopher, Daniel, and Kirkwood. In 1952 Reynolds joined film star Gene Autry in forming Golden West Broadcasters and remained the largest minority stockholder until the Signal Companies bought 49.9 percent of the stock in the fall, 1968. Shortly afterward, Reynolds opened his own office as a private investor in the oil industry. During this period he served as president of the California Angels (AL) baseball club (1961–1975) and as a vice president and director of the Los Angeles Rams football club (1963–1972). He also was a member of the Board of Regents for the University of California system for 15 years.

BIBLIOGRAPHY: Don E. Liebendorfer, *The Color of Life Is Red* (Palo Alto, CA, 1972); John D. McCallum, *Pac-10 Football: The Rose Bowl Conference* (Seattle, 1982); John D. McCallum and Charles H. Pearson, *College Football U.S.A., 1869–1973* (New York, 1973); Fred Merrick, *Down on the Farm: A Story of Stanford Football* (Huntsville, AL, 1975).

Jay Langhammer

RICHTER, Leslie Alan "Les" (b. 26 October 1930, Fresno, CA), college athlete, professional football player, and thoroughbred racing executive, was a fine three-sport athlete and honor student at Fresno High. A fullback, quarterback, and linebacker in football, he also played guard on the basketball squad and catcher on the baseball team. After entering the University of California at Berkeley (PCC) in the fall, 1948, he played fullback and linebacker on the freshman football squad. During his sophomore season, he played mainly on defense and helped the Golden Bears to a 10–0 season before losing to Ohio State in the Rose Bowl. Richter was shifted to guard as a junior and became a consensus All-American. He also played linebacker and kicked 24 of 31 extra point attempts, as the Golden Bears again won the PCC title with a 9–0–1 record. California returned to the Rose Bowl but lost to Michigan, 14–6.

As a senior, Richter served as team co-captain, again won consensus All-American honors, and also was named AP Outstanding Lineman of the Year and California's MVP. The Golden Bears' leader in minutes played, he kicked 40 of 44 extra points and later played in the Shrine All-Star (East-West) and College All-Star games. The NFF College Football Hall of Fame inducted him in 1982. He also was chosen to the PCC all-time first team. During his final two years at California, Richter became an outstanding rugby player and scored 150 of the team's 242 points. He served as team captain and earned All-American honors in the sport. A 1952 graduate with a Bachelor's degree in Business, Richter became the first athlete in California history to serve as valedictorian of his class.

The second player chosen in the 1952 NFL draft, Richter was traded by the Dallas Texans to the Los Angeles Rams for a record 11 players. He joined the U.S. Army as an officer for two years and did not report to the Rams until 1954. He was selected the team's outstanding rookie, playing at offensive guard and linebacker and handling the placekicking duties. Following the season, he appeared in his first of eight Pro Bowls. Richter led the Rams in scoring the next two seasons and played in the NFL championship game against the Cleveland Browns following the 1955 season. During the balance of his pro career, he performed primarily on defense as a linebacker and middle guard. The aggressive, vicious 6 foot, 3 inch, 238 pound tackler also called defensive signals and won several team awards, including most inspirational player in 1956 and MVP in 1960. During his final pro season (1962), he played center most of the year after an injury sidelined the starter. In his nine-year career, he kicked 104 of 107 extra point attempts and 29 of 55 field goal attempts and intercepted 16 passes.

Richter and stewardess Marilyn Shaw, who met on a team flight, were married in 1955 and have two children, Ann and John. During his playing career, Richter became interested in the business affairs of team minority owner Edwin Pauley, who later invested in Riverside Raceway. Richter took an off-season position with the track and became general manager after retiring from pro football. He later was named president of Riverside, one of the nation's most successful race tracks.

BIBLIOGRAPHY: Steve Bisheff, *Los Angeles Rams* (New York, 1973); *Los Angeles Rams Press Guides, 1954–1958, 1962;* Ronald L. Mendell and Timothy B. Phares, *Who's Who in Football* (New Rochelle, NY, 1974); *University of California Football Press Guides, 1948–1950, 1982.*

Jay Langhammer

RIGGINS, John "Diesel" (b. 4 August 1949, Centralia, KS), college and professional player, is the son of Franklin "Gene" and Mildred Riggins and brother of minor league baseball player Frank Riggins. Riggins, whose father worked for the Missouri Pacific Railroad, attended Centralia High School and twice achieved the state 100–yard dash championship. After entering the University of Kansas (BEC) in 1967, he broke Jayhawks records for career yardage (2,706) and season yardage (1,131) set by Gale Sayers.* The sixth overall pick in the 1971 NFL draft, Riggins signed with the New York Jets. Riggins promptly became New York's best offensive back, leading the Jets in rushing and receiving. During five seasons there, he rushed for a 4.2–yard average in 928 carries and alternated as a receiver for Joe Namath.* Namath's Jets, however, had declined from their 1968 Super Bowl peak.

In 1976 Riggins signed as a free agent with the Washington Redskins

(NFL), who already possessed Larry Brown and other backfield stars. After being a reserve in 1976 and injured in 1977, he excelled in 1978 with 248 carries for a 4.1–yard average and was named Comeback Player of the Year. In 1980 Riggins sat out the season in a contract dispute with Redskins management. He experienced a mediocre season in 1981, disappointing both Washington fans and his teammates. A midseason strike in 1982 threatened to eradicate a brilliant Redskins start. After the strike, Riggins gained 553 yards in eight games and scored three touchdowns. In the NFL playoffs, Riggins gained 185 yards against the Minnesota Vikings to set a Redskins post-season record. In Super Bowl XVII against the Miami Dolphins, Riggins set records for attempts (38), yards rushing (166, since broken), and attempts rushing and receiving (39). His record 43–yard run from scrimmage in the fourth quarter put the Redskins permanently ahead in that game. Riggins set the NFL record for touchdowns scored by rushing in a single season (24) in 1984, but his performance in the Super Bowl that year proved disappointing. The Los Angeles Raiders routed the Redskins 38–9, as Marcus Allen* broke Riggins' record of the previous year.

During his career, Riggins had carried 2,916 times (third all-time) for 11,352 yards (3.9–yard average, fifth all-time) and scored 104 touchdowns rushing. Riggins, who ranks third in total touchdowns behind Jimmy Brown* and Walter Payton,* also caught 250 career passes for 2,090 yards (8.4–yard average) and 12 touchdowns. Despite his Super Bowl record rush, the 6 foot, 2 inch, 230 pound Riggins seldom made long gains and recorded 66 yards as his career high. But he justifiably earned the title "Diesel" for his consistent ability to gain at least two or three yards in a given carry. A devastating player on a third down and one-yard situation, Riggins simply barreled into the left of the line for the first down. The shy Riggins averted publicity with a sense of humor. Before the 1986 season, the Redskins placed Riggins on waivers. Riggins is married to Mary Louise Kraft and has three children.

BIBLIOGRAPHY: *TSN*, December 26, 1983; Washington *Post*, 1977–1986; *Washington Redskins Press Guide, 1985*.

John David Healy

RIMINGTON, Dave Brian (b. 22 May 1960, Omaha, NE), college and professional player, is the son of packing plant employee Emile and Barbara Rimington. At South High School in Omaha, Rimington excelled in football, wrestling, track, and weight lifting; was named Athlete of the Year and Football Lineman of the Year; and earned All-State and All-Metro honors.

The heavily recruited Rimington attended the University of Nebraska (BEC, 1978–1982), where he majored in management. After missing the 1978 season because of knee surgery, Rimington lettered as a freshman in 1979 and started at center as a sophomore in 1980. In Rimington's four seasons, the Cornhuskers compiled a 41–8–0 overall record and played in four bowl games. He was selected as the Most Valuable Lineman in the 1983 Orange Bowl and then saw his jersey number 50 retired. Rimington became the first two-time winner of the prestigious Outland Award (1981–1982), awarded annually to the nation's best interior lineman by the FWAA. In his senior year, he also received the Vince Lombardi Rotary Award as the outstanding College Lineman of the Year. Rimington became only the second center (the other was North Carolina State University's Jim Ritcher* in 1979) and third junior to win the Outland Award. The other two juniors to win the award were Zeke Smith of Auburn in 1958 and Ross Browner of Notre Dame in 1976. Rimington became the Cornhuskers' fourth Outland winner, including Larry Jacobson (1971), Rich Glover (1972), and Dean Steinkuhler* (1983).

A dedicated weight lifter and among the strongest men ever to play football at Nebraska, Rimington was named Nebraska's Lifter-of-the-Year for 1980–1981. Besides receiving All-American honors (1981–1982), Rimington excelled as a student and was named to the Academic All-American Team (1981–1982) with a 3.25 grade point average. The three-time All-BEC lineman also was selected an Academic All-BEC three times. In 1982 he received the Fred Ware Award from the *Omaha World-Herald* as the outstanding collegiate athlete in Nebraska.

Since being chosen in the first round of the 1983 NFL draft, Rimington has played for the Cincinnati Bengals. Heralded as the greatest collegiate lineman of the decade, Rimington missed several games in 1983 with a foot injury and still made several All-Rookie teams. Rimington started in all 16 games in 1984 and 1985, recovering three fumbles the latter season. Married to Lisa Shaw in July 1981, Rimington is working on a Master's degree in Business Administration and hopes to own a fitness center.

BIBLIOGRAPHY: *Cincinnati Bengals Football Media Guide, 1984; TSN Football Register—1986;* Terry Todd, "A Man of Heft Who's Also Deft," *SI* 57 (November 8, 1982), pp. 40–42, 44–45; *University of Nebraska Football Media Guide, 1982.*

John L. Evers

RINGO, James Stephen "Jim" (b. 2 November 1932, Orange, NJ), college and professional player and coach, spent his formative years in Phillipsburg, NJ, and participated in varsity basketball, track, and football at Phillipsburg High School. Ringo excelled in football and was selected Scholastic All-State Center. At Syracuse University, Ringo was awarded an athletic scholarship for playing on the Orangemen's football team and accrued All-East honors at center.

After graduation in 1953 Ringo played fifteen years in the NFL. A seventh-round draft choice of the Green Bay Packers (NFL), Ringo played for legendary coach Vince Lombardi.* Under his aegis, the 6 foot, 1 inch, 232 pound Ringo starred at center on the NFL's championship teams of 1961 and 1962 and captained the Packers for eight years. After an 11 tenure with

Green Bay, he was traded to the Philadelphia Eagles (NFL) and played center there four years (1964–1967) until retiring as an active player. During his career Ringo made All-Pro eight times and appeared in ten Pro Bowl games. He established a then NFL endurance record by participating in 182 consecutive pro games. For his outstanding skills and particularly his strength at blocking on the offensive line, Ringo was elected to the Pro Football Hall of Fame in 1981 and to its AFL-NFL 1960–1984 All-Star Second Team.

Ringo has remained with the NFL in a coaching capacity. This new occupation began in 1969 with the Chicago Bears as offensive line coach and continued in 1972 with the Buffalo Bills. Ringo, a superb instructor of line play, at Buffalo initiated the design for the highly successful "Electric Company" that blocked for O. J. Simpson's* then record 2,003–yard season. The National 1,000 Yard Foundation named Ringo's 1973 offensive line NFL Blockers of the Year and cited him as the NFL Assistant Coach of the Year. Midway through the 1976 season, Ringo assumed head coaching duties with the Buffalo Bills and held this position through the 1977 season with a 3–18 composite mark. After NFL offensive line coaching stints with the New England Patriots, Los Angeles Rams, and New York Jets, Ringo returned to the Buffalo Bills as offensive line coordinator in January 1985. Ringo married Betty Martin in 1951 and has four children, Michelle, James, Anthony, and Kurt.

BIBLIOGRAPHY: "Can the Bills Survive Under Ringo?" *Olean* (NY) *Times Herald*, October 16, 1976; "Football Is All Consuming Passion of Coach Ringo," *Buffalo* (NY) *Evening News*, October 16, 1976; Jerry Kramer, *Instant Replay* (New York, 1965); "Saban, Bill's Coach Quits; Ringo, Aide, Named to Post," *NYT*, October 18, 1976.

Joseph English
Eleanor English

RITCHER, James Alexander "Jim" (b. 21 May 1958, Berea, OH), college and professional player, is the son of machine repairman Robert A. and public schoolteacher Joan (Noir) Ritcher. The 6 foot, 3 inch, 245 pound Ritcher graduated from Highland High School in Hinckley, OH, where he competed in football, wrestling, and track. He is completing his undergraduate degree in sociology with a criminal justice option at North Carolina State University (ACC). He and his wife Harriett live in Raleigh, NC, and have one son, John.

As a junior at North Carolina State in 1978, Ritcher was selected by the AP and the AFCA as a first-team All American and received the Jacobs Blocking Trophy as the ACC's top blocker. Despite injuries in 1978, he was graded high by his coaches in every game and credited for the Wolfpack's successful rushing attack. Ritcher, who exhibited mental and physical toughness and quickness off the ball, ranks among the best offensive centers ever to play college football.

Ritcher's play in 1979 earned him the Outland Award, given to the nation's top interior lineman by the FWAA. He became the first center and only the third ACC player so honored. Ritcher had wanted to play defensive end, his high school position. In 1979 he consistently surpassed 80 percent in the films at the center position, where 60 percent is considered a good performance. In 1979 Ritcher received first-team All-American recognition by the AP, UPI, FWAA, AFCA, Walter Camp Foundation, NEA, and *TSN*. His other honors and awards included being named AP National Lineman of the Week for his play against Syracuse on September 16, 1978, and All-ACC in 1978 and 1979. He also earned the H. C. Kennett Award as North Carolina State's outstanding student-athlete of the 1979–1980 year.

In 1980 Ritcher was drafted in the first round by the Buffalo Bills (NFL). After his rookie season, Ritcher was moved to offensive left guard partly because of his excellent speed (4.6 seconds for 40 yards). He became a starting offensive left guard in 1983 and was rated the team's most consistent lineman in 1984, and has appeared in nearly all the Bills games since 1983. Richter made honorable mention on the 1986 AP All-Pro team at offensive guard.

BIBLIOGRAPHY: Buffalo Bills Public Relations Office, Buffalo, NY, 1985; North Carolina State University Sports Information Office, Raleigh, NC, 1984; Jim Richter to Angela Lumpkin, March 7, 1985.

Angela Lumpkin

ROBESON, Paul Bustill (b. 9 April 1898, Princeton, NJ; d. 23 January 1976, Philadelphia, PA), college athlete and professional football player, was the son of Rev. William Drew Robeson, North Carolina runaway slave, and Anna (Bustill) Robeson, a teacher who died when Paul was nine. Robeson married Eslanda Cardozo Goode on August 17, 1921, and had one child, Paul, Jr. Robeson discovered early his superior mental and physical qualities. At a high school in Somerville, NJ, Robeson scholastically headed his class of 250 students. He proved a skilled high school debator, sang solos for the glee club, acted in the drama club, and excelled in several sports. During his senior year, he achieved the highest score on a statewide examination for a Rutgers College scholarship. From then on, as he later recalled, "Equality might be denied, but I *knew* I was not inferior."

His remarkable physical and mental abilities continued to blossom at Rutgers College (1915–1919). He was elected to Phi Beta Kappa his junior year, led his class academically, won every oratorical competition for which he was eligible, and delivered the graduation class oration. Robeson earned twelve varsity letters in football, basketball, baseball, and track and field, played catcher in baseball, and performed at center in basketball. In track and field he threw the discus and javelin, shot putted, and competed in the pentathlon. He became nationally known in football when Walter Camp* made him a two-time All-American at end. Robeson was only the third black to attend Rutgers and the sole Negro enrolled during his four years. His initial appearance on the Rutgers team resulted in a racial incident. In his first football scrimmage, one player smashed and broke Robeson's nose. Another player jumped on him when he was down, dislocating his shoulder. He eventually was accepted by his teammates. Washington and Lee, however, refused to play against a Negro, forcing Robeson to remain out of that game. Robeson eventually dominated his position, especially defensively. Walter Camp named him an All-American his junior and senior years, calling him the greatest defensive end of all time.

The 6 foot, 3 inch, 215 pound scholar-athlete financed his education at Columbia University Law School by playing pro football. On weekends he performed for the Akron (OH) Pros (APFA) with black ex-collegian "Fritz" Pollard.* On Thanksgiving Day, 1920, Robeson's Akron squad defeated Jim Thorpe's* Canton Bulldogs to remain undefeated and win the pro championship. He later played with the Milwaukee Badgers of the fledgling NFL while completing his law degree. Upon graduation from Columbia, Robeson briefly practiced law before attaining greatness in the performing arts. He was denied membership in the American Bar Association because of race and suffered other discriminatory practices in his New York City firm. He soon withdrew from law practice and began a famed singing and acting career. He starred in several Eugene O'Neill plays and gave concerts that featured his rich voice singing Negro spirituals and folk songs. By the 1930s Robeson became politically involved in opposing fascist policies, imperialism, and racism. After spending most of the 1930s in Europe, he returned to the United States at the outset of World War II.

During the war, Robeson attempted to desegregate pro baseball. At the major league annual meeting in 1943, Robeson and the Negro Publishers Association addressed commissioner Kenesaw Mountain Landis* (BB) and the owners. Robeson told them that if he could be the first black lead in an otherwise all-white cast of Shakespeare's *Othello* on Broadway, the allowing of blacks into baseball was not incredible. Action, however, awaited the conclusion of the war. Robeson's efforts to remove racial injustice in baseball and American life were partially met when Jackie Robinson* (BB) was signed by Branch Rickey* (BB) of the Brooklyn Dodgers (NL) in 1945 and joined the Dodgers in 1947. Ironically, two years later Robinson was asked to testify against Robeson before the House Un-American Activities Committee (HUAC). Robeson, the political activist, had spoken out against American racial injustice to a leftist congress in Paris, France. It was unthinkable, Robeson stated, that American Negroes would fight against the Soviet Union, which had shown human dignity to blacks. Robinson was asked by HUAC to "give the lie" to Robeson's statement. Robinson's testimony helped remove black support for Robeson. Later the U.S. State Department took away Robeson's passport and helped place Robeson's career into oblivion. Robeson's active career in America nearly was ended following his character assassination during the Cold War era. A victim of political ideology, he died in near obscurity and never was voted into either the NFF College or Pro Football Halls of Fame.

BIBLIOGRAPHY: *Afro-American Encyclopedia*, vol. 8, pp. 2244–45; Philip S. Foner, ed., *Paul Robeson Speaks, Writings—Speeches—Interviews, 1918–1974* (New York, 1978); Freedomways Associates, editors, *Paul Robeson: The Great Forerunner* (New York, 1978); Dorothy Butler Gilliam, *Paul Robeson: All-American* (New York, 1976); W. Augustus Low and Virgil A. Clift, *Encyclopedia of Black America* (New York, 1981), pp. 135, 576–578, 732; Paul Robeson, *Here I Stand* (London, 1958); Paul Robeson Papers, Rutgers University Archives, New Brunswick, NJ; Marie Seton, *Paul Robeson* (London, 1958); U.S. Congress, House, "Hearings Regarding Communist Infiltration of Minority Groups." *Hearings Before the Committee on Un-American Activities*, 81st Cong., 1st sess. July 13, 18, 1949.

Ronald A. Smith

ROBINSON, Edward Gay "Eddie" (b. 13 February 1919, Jackson, LA), college football player, athletic coach, and administrator, became the winningest coach in college football history on October 5, 1985, with his 324th triumph in the Grambling State University (SAC) "Tigers" 27–7 win over Prairie View A&M. Witnessed by 36,652 spectators at the Dallas, TX, Cotton Bowl, Robinson's victory broke legendary coach Paul "Bear" Bryant's* record. Robinson topped Chicago Bears' (NFL) coach George Halas'* 326 career victories the same season, giving Robinson more triumphs than any other coach above the high school level. The still active Robinson has coached 44 years (1941–1942, 1945–1986) at Grambling, produced 41 teams with winning records, and enjoyed 27 consecutive winning seasons to set an all-time NCAA record for Division I-AA schools. His squads won or shared 13 SAC championships, posted three undefeated and six single-loss seasons, and compiled a composite 336–113–15 (.748 percent) record through 1986. Robinson through 1985 sent a record 211 Grambling players to the NFL, including 25 All-Pro or Pro Bowl players and 13 NFL or conference statistical leaders. In 1969, 13 Tigers were drafted by NFL teams.

Robinson, former president of the AFCA and NAIA, is a member of the NAIA Hall of Fame and was cited by the FWAA in 1966 as "the man who made the greatest contribution to College Division football during the last 25 years." He was presented the Walter Camp Foundation's Distinguished American Award in 1982 and received the NCAA's Special Recognition Award in 1986 as college football's all-time winningest coach. Robinson was named in 1976 an assistant coach for the annual Shrine All Star (East-West) football game.

Robinson's father, Frank, worked at a Standard Oil Company plant in Baton Rouge, LA. "Eddie" quarterbacked three undefeated Baton Rouge McKinley High School football teams and starred as a baseball pitcher before graduating from high school in 1937. He attended Leland College, a small (now defunct) Baptist school in Louisiana. An accurate passer, Robinson excelled at quarterback four years and led Leland in 1939–1940 to a combined 18–1–0 record. He worked on a coal truck, hauled ice, toiled at a feed mill, and spent his last two years as a playing assistant coach under new head coach Rubin Turner. Robinson graduated from Leland College in 1941 and earned a Master's degree at the University of Iowa in 1954.

Grambling was known in 1941 as Louisiana Negro Normal and Industrial Institute and later adopted the name of the northern Louisiana city in which it is located. In 1941 Ralph Waldo Emerson Jones, longtime president of Grambling State University, hired Robinson as head football and basketball coach and physical education instructor for a monthly $63.75 salary. Robinson resembled one-man athletic departments of the times, mowing the grass, marking the lines, taping ankles, and writing game accounts for the local newspaper. After finishing 3–5–0 in Robinson's first season, the Tigers achieved a perfect 8–0–0 record in 1942. When football was discontinued the next two years due to World War II conditions, Robinson coached Grambling High School to the state tournament and recruited the entire team for his 1945 Tiger varsity. The squad included fullback Paul "Tank" Younger, who starred four years at Grambling and played nine years for the Los Angeles Rams (NFL).

Robinson continued to recruit successfully, although major colleges enjoyed the advantages of television exposure, major bowls, and training tables. Employing the winged-T attack, he guided future NFL star tackles Junious "Buck" Buchanan* and Ernie Ladd, defensive end Willie Davis,* wide receivers Charlie Joiner* and Trumaine Johnson, defensive backs William "Willie" Brown* and Rosey Taylor, and quarterbacks James Harris and Doug Williams. "When I left Grambling," Williams once said, "I felt like I had a degree in philosophy. It is amazing what that man knows, in addition to all the football he teaches."

Grambling and Morgan State University in 1968 became the first primarily black institutions to engage in a football game at New York's Yankee Stadium. The encounter, won 9–7 by Morgan State, attracted 64,204 fans. Grambling performed before other crowds in excess of 60,000 at the Los Angeles Coliseum, Houston Astrodome and Chicago's Soldiers Field. ABC-TV sportscaster Howard Cosell* (OS) in 1968 narrated the Grambling documentary "One Hundred Yards to Glory." After the 100–station Grambling Football Network was inaugurated in 1970, the Tigers appeared the next year in a nationally televised game for the first time, defeating Morgan State 31–13. Robinson displays tireless energy while maintaining an ambitious off-season speaking schedule. The extremely modest coach, an incurable sentimentalist, tears easily, speaks of the beauty of the American way of life and quotes Abraham Lincoln and Alfred Lord Tennyson. Robinson married his childhood sweetheart Doris Mott in 1941, has three children, and lives in a comfortable four-bedroom brick home at the edge of the Tiger practice field.

Grambling won its 300th victory under Coach Robinson in 1982 by defeating Florida A&M 43–21 at Bragg Memorial Stadium in Tallahassee, FL. The triumph tying Bryant's all-time victory record was achieved in a 23–6 victory over Oregon State at Independence Stadium in Shreveport, LA, in 1985. Unable to obtain a flight to Tuscaloosa, AL, in 1983 after Bryant died, Robinson drove the 400–mile distance all night to attend Bryant's funeral. "I don't want to be remembered as the guy who broke Bryant's record any more than Bryant wanted to be remembered as the man who broke [Amos Alonzo] Stagg's* record. I would like to be remembered as a guy who made the same contributions Bryant did, who influenced people's lives and made an impact on the game."

BIBLIOGRAPHY: O. K. Davis, *Grambling's Gridiron Glory* (Ruston, LA, 1983); Rick Reilly, "Here's To You, Mr. Robinson," *SI* 63 (October 14, 1985), pp. 32–39; *The NCAA News* (September 23, 1985), pp. 1–2; (January 8, 1986), pp. 1–2.

James D. Whalen

ROBINSON, Jerry (b. 18 December 1956, San Francisco, CA), college and professional player, was the first three-time consensus All-American football player in nearly 30 years. Indeed, this unique accomplishment came as a middle linebacker at UCLA (PEC), whereas previous triple choices attracted more attention as running backs and quarterbacks. Robinson attended Cardinal Newman High School in Santa Rosa, CA. His prep career demonstrated his outstanding versatility, as he captained the football, basketball, and track teams. As a football performer, he played split-end and was named to the All Redwood City and All Northern California All-Star teams. Robinson's track record exemplified his all-around abilities, with his 9.5–second time in the 100–yard dash and 6 foot, 5 inch, high jump marks. In basketball he also made the Northern California All-Star team.

The heavily recruited Robinson chose to attend college in his native California at UCLA (PEC). Prior to Robinson's sophomore year at UCLA, coach Terry Donahue and his staff moved Robinson from his customary offensive end position to defensive linebacker, a fortuitous move for both Robinson and the Bruins. At 6 feet, 3 inches, and 208 pounds, he was rather light for the linebacker position and made up for any size disadvantage with his superior athletic talents. Coach Donahue attributed the success of his defensive teams to Robinson's excellence at linebacker. Robinson was selected as NCAA consensus All-American from 1976 through 1978 and unanimous choice the last two years. As a sophomore, he played in the 36–3 loss to Alabama in the 1976 Liberty Bowl. As a senior, he anchored the UCLA defense in the Bruins 10–10 tie with Arkansas in the 1978 Fiesta Bowl. During his junior and senior years, Robinson was honored by the New York Downtown AC as its Linebacker of the Year. Robinson's senior-year excellence also brought him the Voit Award as the Best Player on the West Coast. The sociology major's athletic accomplishments were acknowledged when UCLA retired his uniform number 84.

The Philadelphia Eagles (NFL) made Robinson their first pick in the 1979 draft and twenty-first overall selection. His high selection proved justified when he was chosen linebacker on the All-Rookie team for 1979. He started for the Eagles in the 1980 NFL championship game and 1980 Super Bowl against the Oakland Raiders. In 1981 he recovered four fumbles for 59 yards and one touchdown, and was selected to the Pro Bowl. Robinson has totalled six career interceptions and 11 fumble recoveries. In September 1985 he was traded to the Los Angeles Raiders where he recorded two quarterback sacks. The measure of a star athlete also must include his non-athletic accomplishments. Robinson and his wife Cynthia have one daughter Jacqueline. An intense participant in civic activities, Robinson was named the Philadelphia Eagles' Man of the Year for 1984 for his community service.

BIBLIOGRAPHY: *The Football News*, September 13, 1977; *The NCAA Official Collegiate Football Record Book, 1979*, p. 109E; *The Philadelphia Eagles Media Guide, 1985; TSN Football Register—1986.*

George P. Mang

ROBINSON, Richard David "Dave" (b. 3 May 1941, Mt. Holly, NJ), college and professional player, excelled as an NFL linebacker for the Green Bay Packers (1963–1972) and Washington Redskins (1973–1974). He grew up in Mt. Laurel, NJ, and joined his three brothers in playing football at Moorestown (NJ) High School. His father, William Robinson, a road scraper operator, died when "Dave" was a high school freshman. Robinson won an athletic scholarship to Penn State University and earned a B.S. degree in Engineering there in 1963. The versatile Penn Stater played offensive and defensive tackle, guard, and end. In 1963 he was voted All-American and selected as the first draft choice of the Green Bay Packers (NFL). He in 1963 married Elaine Robinson and has three sons, twins Richard Edward and David Michael, and Robert.

Under Packers' coach Vincent Lombardi,* the 6 foot, 3 inch, 245 pound Robinson played a key role on the defensive unit leading Green Bay to 1965 and 1966 NFL titles and victories in the first two Super Bowls in 1967 and 1968. Robinson, a sure tackler, excellent pass defender, and aggressive rusher against the quarterback, particularly excelled in important contests. His timely defensive play insured Green Bay victories in numerous playoff and championship games. The outspoken, articulate Robinson was selected by his teammates as union player representative. An All-Pro in 1967, 1968, and 1970, he won the MVP award in the 1968 Pro Bowl game and played in the 1966–1967 and 1969 Pro Bowls. In a surprise move, Green Bay in 1973 traded Robinson to the Washington Redskins (NFL). Robinson refused to report to Washington, but Redskins coach George Allen* convinced him to play one more year. After the 1974 season, Robinson retired and became a brewing company executive in Akron, OH.

BIBLIOGRAPHY: John Devaney, "Dave Robinson and the Thief at His Door," *Sport* 46 (November, 1968), pp. 40–43; Bud Lea, "Anatomy of a Retiring Linebacker," *Milwaukee* (WI) *Sentinel*, February 23, 1973; Dave Robinson file, Pro Football Hall of Fame, Canton, OH; Barry Stainback, *How the Pros Play Football* (New York, 1970).

John Hanners

ROBUSTELLI, Andrew "Andy" (b. 6 December 1926, Stamford, CT), college athlete and professional football player, coach, and executive, excelled as a football defensive end. The 6 foot, 1 inch, 230 pound Robustelli graduated from Stamford High School, where he starred in football, and then attended LaSalle Military Academy in Oakdale, Long Island. After serving in the U.S. Navy from 1944 to 1945, he matriculated at Arnold College (now a part of the University of Bridgeport). Besides making Little All-American three consecutive years, he also lettered in baseball and was named to the NAIA Hall of Fame.

Robustelli unexpectedly achieved stardom in pro football. A nineteenth-round draft choice in 1951, he excelled at defensive end for the Los Angeles Rams (NFL) through 1955. He won All-Pro honors in 1953 and 1955 and played in the 1951 and 1955 NFL championship games, helping the Rams win the 1951 title. After being traded in 1956 to the New York Giants (NFL), he made All-Pro honors five more times through 1960. He appeared in six more championship games, helping the Giants capture the 1956 NFL title. Overall, he made seven Pro Bowl appearances. He captained the Giants' defensive team six years and in 1962 was named the NFL's MVP. Robustelli joined Dick Modzelewski,* Rosey Grier,* and alternating ends Walt Yowarsky and Jim Katcavage in comprising the Giants' "Fearsome Foursome." An exceptionally smart, quick, and strong defensive end, he became a superb pass rusher and recovered 22 opponents' fumbles. In 14 NFL seasons, he missed only one game.

Robustelli, who retired in 1964, spent his final seasons as a player-defensive coach. Since 1974 he has served as director of operations for the Giants and oversees coaching, scouting, signing of players, trades, and the pre-season training camp. Robustelli married Jean Dora and has nine children. He belongs to the HAF College Football Hall of Fame and in 1971 was enshrined into the Pro Football Hall of Fame.

BIBLIOGRAPHY: George Allen with Ben Olan, *Pro Football's 100 Greatest Players* (Indianapolis, IN, 1982); Gerald Eskenazi, *There Were Giants in Those Days* (New York, 1976); *New York Giants Media Guide, 1977;* Don Smith, *New York Giants* (New York, 1960); George Sullivan, *Pro Football A to Z* (New York, 1975).

John L. Evers

ROCKNE, Knute Kenneth "Rock" (b. 4 March 1888, Voss, Norway; d. 31 March 1931, near Bazaar, KS), college athlete and professional football player, coach, and administrator, amassed a career composite 105–12–5 football head coaching record at the University of Notre Dame from 1918 to 1930. His .881 winning percentage ranks highest all-time nationally among coaches. A member of HAF College Football Hall of Fame, Rockne was chosen a charter member of the NFF College Football Hall of Fame (1951) and was named the top all-time coach by the AP (1951), *Sport* (1969), and *Collier's* (1925–1950 era). Rockne captained the 1913 Fighting Irish football team and made Walter Camp's All-American third team squad at end. As coach, Rockne guided six Notre Dame national championship squads (three nearly unanimous), five perfect record teams, 20 All-Americans, and one Rose Bowl winner. Rockne's outstanding coaching ability, leadership, charisma, and wit placed him in the forefront of college football's rapid growth in popularity at the end of World War I. Rockne served in 1924 with Yale's Tad Jones,* Georgia Tech's Bill Alexander,* Stanford's Glenn "Pop" Warner,* and Christy Walsh on the first All-American Board of Football to select the nation's top players.

Rockne's father, machinist and renowned carriage-maker Lars Knutson Rokne (Norwegian spelling), won first prize after entering his carriage in competition at the Chicago 1893 Columbian World's Exposition. He sent for his wife Martha (Gjermo) Rockne and children to join him in Chicago, where they settled in the Logan Square section. Knute had four sisters, two born in the United States, and attended Chicago's North West Division High School. The small, wiry youth played varsity football one year but enjoyed greater success on the track team as a half-miler and pole vaulter. Rockne devoted too much time to athletics and failed to finish high school. Between 1905 and 1910 he worked nights as a clerk at the Chicago post office to earn money for college. He read books voraciously and kept in physical condition by entering club track meets.

Two track companions persuaded Rockne in 1910 to enroll at Notre Dame, where they believed their budgets would stretch the farthest. After passing a stringent entrance examination, Rockne failed to win a varsity letter as a lightweight freshman football fullback under coach Shorty Longman. The regular end in 1911 and 1912 under coach Jack Marks and 1913 under coach Jesse Harper,* the 5 foot, 8 inch, 165 pound Rockne played on three undefeated teams compiling a composite 20–0–2 record. Although Notre Dame badly outclassed several minor opponents on its schedule, the Fighting Irish also defeated Pittsburgh, Marquette, and Penn State. In 1913 Notre Dame spoiled two perfect records with notable triumphs over Texas and Army. Army boasted four Camp All-Americans but succumbed 35–13 to Notre Dame's surprise passing attack. Fighting Irish quarterback Charles "Gus" Dorais,* who had practiced throwing to Rockne the previous summer on the beach at Lake Erie's Cedar Point, used the forward pass under Harper's direction as an integral part of the Notre Dame offense. The forward pass had been used merely as a threat or desperation play since its legalization in 1906. Dorais completed 14 of 17 passes to both ends and halfbacks for 243 yards against the Cadets. When the Army defense spread to stop his passes, Dorais sent second team All-American fullback Ray Eichenlaub up the middle for huge gains. Rockne in 1930 wrote, "Notre Dame received credit as the originator of a style of play that we had simply systematized."

Besides participating in the half mile, long jump, and shot put on the Notre Dame track team, Rockne set the Fighting Irish pole vault record at 12 feet, 4 inches. He edited the school yearbook as a senior, played the flute occasionally with the band and orchestra, and served as a comedian with the Notre Dame Players Association. Besides waiting on tables and performing janitorial duties, he earned pocket money boxing in South Bend, IN, clubs. Rockne and Dorais roomed together in the basement of Corby Hall, where they charged naive, unsuspecting freshmen "radiator rent." After hinging a permanent screen to the window in their room, they exacted a toll for the use of the window after curfew. Rockne majored in chemistry, graduated magna cum laude with a four-year 92.5 cumulative average and a B.S. degree in Pharmacy in 1914.

During the next four years, Rockne served as a chemistry instructor at Notre Dame under brilliant scientist Father Julius Nieuwland and as head track coach and Harper's football assistant. On Sundays he played end for the pro Massillon Tigers and was outplayed in a storied clash with Canton's immortal halfback Jim Thorpe.* When Harper retired after the 1917 grid season, Rockne succeeded him as Notre Dame head football coach and athletic director. Author Francis Wallace divided the 13–year Rockne Era into six periods: 1918, the Informal Wartime Year, produced a 3–1–2 record; 1919–1921, the World War I returnees finished undefeated the first two seasons and 28–1–0 overall; 1922–1924, the Four Horsemen* and Seven Mules achieved a 27–2–1 record and concluded an undefeated national championship year in 1924 with a 27–10 Rose Bowl triumph over Stanford; 1925–1927, the Forgotten Men merely finished 23–4–2; 1928, the Bad Year, saw his gallant cripples win five of nine games and furnished his most dramatic victory; 1929–1930, the national championship squads won 19 games in two perfect seasons against the absolute best from every section.

As a child, Rockne had had his nose flattened by a baseball bat. In later years he frequently covered his bald head with a battered felt hat and wore baggy trousers. Using stabbing psychology and pulse-stirring halftime oratory to inspire his troops, Rockne believed that the right word to a player sometimes made a greater impact than hours on the practice field. In an era of raw beef and power, Rockne advocated mobile, swift-striking teams, brush blocking, and quick-opening plays. In testimony to Rockne's coaching, Princeton coach Charlie Caldwell* was amazed at how fresh he felt as a player in 1924 after the Fighting Irish swept through the Tigers 12–0. Rockne ran the Four Horsemen behind the third-string line to deflate egos, but he intended nothing personal in his criticism. A great believer in football as a means to an end, he proved the game's most influential defender when it came under public criticism.

Rockne strengthened the Notre Dame schedule with intersectional games throughout the nation. Notre Dame added Nebraska (1915), Georgia Tech (1922), Wisconsin (1924), Minnesota (1925), Southern California (1926), Navy (1927), SMU and Pennsylvania (1930). Notable games included the 33–7 Fighting Irish triumph over Northwestern in 1920 in legendary All-American halfback George Gipp's* final appearance before his premature death; the 10–7 loss to undefeated Iowa in 1921 ending Notre Dame's 22-game undefeated streak; Grantland Rice's* naming of the Four Horsemen in 1924 following Notre Dame's 13–7 conquest of Army; the 19–0 loss to underrated Carnegie Tech in 1926 while Rockne was scouting the Army-Navy game in Chicago; the 12–6 win for "the Gipper" over Army in 1928; Notre Dame's 27–0 routing of a fine Southern California aggregation in 1930 (Rockne's last game with the Irish), despite being without its top two fullbacks and using a second team halfback masquerading as the third-string fullback; and blocking back Marty Brill's scoring three touchdowns in 1930 in a 60–20 triumph over Pennsylvania, the school not considering him good enough to play there.

Rockne encouraged football participation and insisted that uniforms be issued to all 150–200 men that turned out for the first practice. Usually he carried only three assistant coaches to whom he could delegate authority and used his seniors to help coach the younger players. Rockne found coaching positions for many former Fighting Irish gridders after graduation. Nicknaming him the "Father of Coaches," the *NCAA News* in 1984 stated that Rockne's coaching influence peaked in 1934 when 18 of his former players coached football at major schools and many more directed minor programs. Rockne wrote three books, *Coaching—The Way of the Winner* (1925), *The Four Winners* (a 1925 novel), and *The Autobiography of Knute K. Rockne* (1931). Rockne also served as public relations spokesman for the Studebaker Corporation and partner in a brokerage firm, wrote magazine and syndicated newspaper articles, provided endorsements, and proved an articulate, dynamic banquet speaker.

Rockne and Bonnie Gwendoline Skiles met at Cedar Point and were married in 1914 at Sandusky, OH. They had three sons, William, Knute, Jr., and John, and one daughter, Mary Jean. Rockne in March 1931 boarded a Transcontinental and Western Air Line tri-motor at Kansas City, bound for Los Angeles to discuss production of the movie *The Spirit of Notre Dame*. The airliner exploded over a Kansas farm, hurtled to the ground and burned, killing all eight passengers and shocking the entire nation. Newspaper "extras" blared the tragic news, while the Chicago *Tribune* telephone lines were so jammed that the operator simply answered, "Yes, it's true about Rockne."

Notre Dame president the Reverend Charles L. O'Donnell's eulogy was broadcast nationwide. Former Notre Dame president the Reverend John L. Cavanaugh declared, "I think you will find, after all, that the man is really greater than the legend." Humorist Will Rogers observed, "It takes a mighty big calamity to shock this country all at once, but Knute, you did it!" The Rockne Memorial Building stands on the Notre Dame campus in lasting tribute. A memorial was erected in his native Voss, and at least eleven biographies have been written on his life. AP sportswriter Jerry Liska in 1951 wrote, "Rockne was 10 years ahead of the game in his era. And if he were living today, his scheming still would be 10 years in advance of coaching rivals."

BIBLIOGRAPHY: Jim Beach and Daniel Moore, *Army vs. Notre Dame* (New York, 1948); Arthur Daley, "Sports of the Times," *NYT*, August 2, 1952; Jack Newcombe, "Knute Rockne, The Man and the Legend," *Sport* 15 (November, 1953), pp. 18–21, 72–79; Coles Phinizy, "We Know of Knute, Yet Know Him Not," *SI* 51 (September 10, 1979), pp. 98–112; Knute K. Rockne, *The Autobiography of Knute K. Rockne* (Indianapolis, IN, 1931); Francis Wallace, *Knute Rockne* (Garden City, NY, 1960).

James D. Whalen

RODGERS, John "Johnny" (b. 5 July 1951, Omaha, NE), college and professional player, the son of Eddie Jones of Omaha, became perhaps college football's greatest punt returner at the University of Nebraska (BEC). When Rodgers won the 1972 Heisman Trophy by a landslide vote, some writers objected because of his off-the-field conduct. As a University of Nebraska freshman, Rodgers had participated in a gas station robbery. Coaches Bob Devaney* and Tom Osborne* became his unofficial godfathers during his two years probation. Later he committed several automobile violations. Rodgers' biological father left the premises early, and his mother was only age 16 at his birth. He grew up in the near northside Omaha ghetto area that spawned baseball star Bob Gibson* (BB), football star Gale Sayers,* Olympic sprinter Roger Sayers, pro basketball star Bob Boozer, and other outstanding athletes. Rodgers starred three years at Omaha Technical High School in football, basketball, and baseball and was named Nebraska High School Athlete of the Year in 1969.

Rodgers, who joined the greatest class of athletes in University of Nebraska history, proved the most dangerous weapon in a highly talented crew boasting a 31–game unbeaten streak. Nebraska won national titles in 1970 and 1971 and barely missed in 1972. Rodgers comprised the main long-range offensive threat on the 1971 team, rated as college football's all-time best squad. The holder of many Nebraska records that may stand for decades, he starred in the 1973 Orange Bowl.

Nicknamed "Johnny," Rodgers performed best in "must" games for Nebraska. In what sportswriters called "The Game of the Century" and "the best college football game of all time," Rodgers played an exceptional game against the University of Oklahoma Sooners in November 1971 at Norman, OK. With the BEC and national titles at stake, Rodgers broke a 72–yard punt return for a touchdown to give the Cornhuskers an early 14–3 lead. Oklahoma was ahead 31–28 late in the game when Rodgers made a sensational diving catch of a third-down, long-yardage pass to keep the drive alive. Nebraska eventually won that game 35–31 to retain the nation's number 1 ranking in the AP and UPI polls. In the 1972 Orange Bowl, Rodgers duplicated his Oklahoma punt return against the University of Alabama by dodging eight Crimson Tide tacklers in five yards and scoring a 77–yard touchdown. Nebraska defeated Alabama 38–6 and was ranked first in the final AP and UPI polls. BEC members Oklahoma and Colorado finished second and third, respectively. In the 1973 Orange Bowl, Rodgers performed even better against national title-seeking Notre Dame. Rodgers scored on runs of 8, 5, and 4 yards, threw a 52–yard touchdown pass, and caught a 50–yard touchdown pass to help Nebraska overwhelm the Fighting Irish 40–6. The Cornhusker regulars left the game with Nebraska ahead 40–0 and six minutes remaining in the third period.

Rodgers set or tied 19 Nebraska, 7 BEC, and 4 NCAA records. His key career Nebraska records included most points (300); touchdowns (50); all-purpose yards (6,210); all kick return yards (2,543); all kick return touchdowns (9); punt return yardage (1,651); passes caught (154 for 2,779 yards); and rushing (152 carries for 836 yards). His season marks comprised 58 passes caught for 1,013 yards (1972); 11 touchdown passes caught (1971); 684 yards and 4 touchdowns on punt returns (1971); 988 yards and 5 touchdowns on all kick returns (1971); and 2,213 all-purpose yardage (1971). His game marks included 290 all-purpose yardage against Colorado (1972), 170 yards in punt returns against Oklahoma State (1971), and a 92–yard punt return in the same game.

The Montreal Alouettes (CFL) outbid the San Diego Chargers (NFL) for Rodgers' services. The 5 foot, 9 inch, 165 pound Rodgers was considered too small for the NFL by the Chargers. Defying skeptics, Rodgers captured CFL Rookie of the Year honors and starred from 1973 through 1976 there. Rodgers played for the Chargers in the 1977 and 1978 seasons, but injuries prevented him from duplicating his collegiate running. The Bonita, CA resident owned an entertainment magazine similar to *TV Guide*, but filed for bankruptcy in 1986. His son Terry was California High School Player of the Year as a football running back for National City (CA) Sweetwater High School in 1985 and played football at the University of Nebraska in 1986. Rodgers, who lives with Sharon Collins, has six other children, including Kevin, Darrell, Latonia, John Stewart, Jerome, and Johnni.

BIBLIOGRAPHY: Des Moines (IA) *Register*, April 23, 1986; Bob Devaney, *Devaney* (Lincoln, NE, 1981); Kansas City *Star*, August 24, 1986; Lincoln (NE) *Journal-Star*,

1970–1972; Jerry Mathers, *Nebraska High School Sports* (Lyons, NE, 1980); Omaha (NE) *World-Herald*, 1970–1972; *University of Nebraska Football Guides, 1970–1972.*

Jerry Mathers

ROGERS, George Washington, Jr. (b. 8 December 1958, Duluth, GA), college and professional player, overcame tremendous adversity. The son of convicted murderer George Washington Rogers and welfare mother Grady A. Rogers, he observed that "for a kid brought up like me, football makes you or breaks you." Rogers left the Atlanta housing project, where his mother, two brothers, and two sisters lived, and returned to the Duluth home of an aunt, Otella Rogers. He graduated from Duluth High School, helping them win a Class AA football championship. Rogers then attended the University of South Carolina, from which he received an A.S. degree in 1981.

The 6 foot, 1¾ inch, 224 pound tailback, who ran the 40–yard dash in 4.5 seconds, rushed for 5,204 yards from 1977 to 1980 and set numerous Gamecocks records. In his best individual performance (1978), he gained 237 yards and scored two touchdowns against Wake Forest. During his best season (1980), he gained 1,894 yards rushing. Rogers often carried the ball 25 to 30 times a game and gained over 100 yards in 22 games his last two collegiate seasons. He played instrumental roles in eight Gamecocks victories in 1979 and 1980 to produce the school's best records and made All-American teams both years. Although South Carolina lost to the University of Pittsburgh in the 1980 Gator Bowl, Rogers was named the game's outstanding offensive player.

After placing seventh (and second among non-seniors) in the 1979 Heisman Trophy voting, Rogers (according to coach Jim Carlen) "beat the system" by winning the trophy in 1980. The first southern black to receive the Heisman, Rogers accomplished the feat at a university having almost no television coverage. In Rogers' first nationally televised game, South Carolina lost 13–10 to the eventual national champion, the University of Georgia. Nevertheless, ABC-TV named him the game's MVP. In 1980 he was selected Chevrolet/ABC's MVP and NCAA Back of the Year at the Pigskin Annual Awards banquet. Rogers joined five other college seniors on the NCAA/ABC-TV national tour promotion for college football.

In the first round of the 1981 NFL draft, the last place New Orleans Saints selected Rogers. After signing a five-year contract for one million dollars, he was touted as another Earl Campbell.* During his first pro season, he led the NFL in rushing with 1,674 yards in 378 carries and scored 13 touchdowns. Besides being named NFL Rookie of the Year, he also played in the NFL Pro Bowl. Rogers, along with other team members, admitted to federal investigators that in 1981 he had used over $10,000 worth of cocaine. After voluntarily undergoing drug rehabilitation treatment, he suffered an injury sidelining him much of the 1982 season. Before the 1985 season he was traded to the Washington Redskins and placed seventh in the NFC that year with 1,093 yards rushing. In 1986 he led the NFL in touchdowns (18) and placed seventh again in rushing (1,203 yards). The 12–4 Redskins defeated the Los Angeles Rams and then upset the Chicago Bears, 27–13, in the NFC playoffs, as Rogers gained 72 yards and scored one touchdown. The New York Giants limited Rogers' effectiveness in the NFC championship game, defeating the Redskins 17–0. Through the 1986 season Rogers has rushed 1,529 times for 6,563 yards (4.3–yard average), scored 48 touchdowns, and caught 48 passes for 321 yards (6.7–yard average). Although popular among teammates for his sense of humor and warmth, Rogers shies away from public speaking and contacts with sportswriters and crowds. The unmarried Rogers lives in Columbia, SC, and has one son and one daughter.

BIBLIOGRAPHY: Tom Callahan, "Coke and No Smile," *Time* 120 (August 9, 1982), p. 49; Mike Del Nagro, "Oh, No, Here He Comes Again," *SI* 53 (September 22, 1980), pp. 66–67; Mike Del Nagro, "Those Heisman High-Flyers," *SI* 53 (December 1, 1980), pp. 24–26; "George Rogers—1980 Heisman Winner," *University of South Carolina Sports Brochure*, pp. 148–149; John Papanek, "Another Campbell May Be Coming," *SI* 55 (August 3, 1981), pp. 20–22; Diane K. Shah with Vincent Coppola, "Two Southern Steamrollers," *Newsweek* 96 (November 17, 1980), p. 113; *TSN Football Register—1986*.

Marcia G. Synnott

ROONEY, Arthur Joseph, Sr. "Art" (b. 27 January 1901, Coultersville, PA), professional athlete and sports executive, owned and founded the Pittsburgh Steelers (NFL) and is the oldest of nine children (six boys and three girls) of Daniel and Kathleen Rooney. His father, of Welsh descent, operated a hotel and saloon on Pittsburgh's north side; his mother was of Irish descent. The Rooneys moved to the north side of Pittsburgh when Arthur was only one year old. He grew up and played near the present site of Three Rivers Stadium, the current home of the Pittsburgh Steelers. He attended St. Peter's Parochial School, Duquesne University Prep School (circa 1917), Indiana State (PA) Normal School, Georgetown University (one year), and Duquesne University. Rooney married Kathleen McNulty on June 11, 1931, and has five children, Daniel, Arthur, Jr., Tim, John, and Pat.

During the 1920s Rooney participated in semi-pro football, minor league baseball, and boxing. He reportedly held both the middleweight and welterweight AAU boxing championships. He played halfback for several Pittsburgh semi-pro football teams, including the Hope-Harvey's, Majestic Radio, and James P. Rooney's (named for his brother, a local politician). Around 1926 he played one memorable game against the Canton Bulldogs (NFL) with the legendary 38–year-old Jim Thorpe.* Rooney excelled at amateur baseball and played minor league baseball with Flint, MI (MOL) in 1921 and Wheeling, WV (MAL) in 1925. Art combined with younger brother Dan on the Wheeling Stogies to dominate the MAL. Outfielder Art finished second in hitting with a .369 average and led the MAL in runs (109), hits (143), stolen bases (58), and games played (106). Catcher Dan, who placed third in the MAL in hitting with a .359 average, later became a Catholic priest and served as a missionary in China. "I didn't continue in the minors because I made more money playing semi-pro," Rooney said.

In the late 1920s Rooney began betting seriously on horse racing. He later reportedly said "For a period of years after 1927 I was one of the country's biggest and most successful horse players." Rooney's interest in horse racing eventually changed direction. In the 1940s he purchased and operated Shamrock Farms, a horse breeding and training farm in Maryland. When parimutuel betting was legalized in Pennsylvania in the early 1950s, he purchased Liberty Bell (harness) and Keystone (flat) racetracks in Philadelphia. The Rooneys later added a harness racing track in New York and a dog racing track in Florida.

Rooney, best known as the founder and owner of the Pittsburgh Steelers, started the franchise as the Pirates and entered it in the NFL in 1933. In a 1981 interview, Rooney described the founding of the Steelers. "I had a semi pro team, the J. P. Rooneys, which compared favorably with the NFL teams," he said. "But we had the 'blue laws' in Pennsylvania, and you couldn't belong to an organized league and play on Sunday. I knew they were going to repeal the 'blue laws' in 1933 so I took my team and joined the NFL." In the first thirty-nine years, the Pittsburgh franchise failed to win a division or conference championship. Rooney attempted several solutions, but most ended in disaster. Byron (Whizzer) White* was signed for an exorbitant $10,000 salary in 1938 and led the NFL in yards gained rushing, but he accepted a Rhodes Scholarship in England the following year.

Rooney in 1940 sold the franchise to Alexis Thompson. The next year, however, he bought into the Philadelphia Eagles, traded his club share to Thompson for the Pittsburgh franchise, and then changed the team's name to the Steelers. During World War II, the Steelers merged unsuccessfully with the Eagles (1943) and Chicago Cardinals (1944) because of diminished manpower. Ill luck still plagued the Steelers after World War II. Tailback Bill Dudley,* who led the NFL in rushing in 1942 and 1946, was traded because of conflicts with head coach Jock Sutherland.* A former outstanding college coach, Sutherland led the Steelers to an 8–4 record in 1947 and then died suddenly in April 1948 from a brain tumor.

Through the 1950s and 1960s, the Steelers generally suffered losing seasons. By the late 1960s Rooney's sons Daniel and Arthur, Jr., assumed control of the team. In 1969 they hired as head coach Chuck Noll,* former assistant coach with the Baltimore Colts. After building the Steelers into a Central Division champion (11–3 record) by 1972, Noll coached Pittsburgh to Super Bowl victories in 1974, 1975, 1978, and 1979. Rooney, one of the most popular sports franchise owners, supported several pro football innovations, including the annual player draft and successful television package. He was inducted into the Pro Football Hall of Fame in 1964 for his many contributions to the game.

BIBLIOGRAPHY: C. Robert Barnett, personal interviews with Art S. Rooney, December 13, 1981, and October 7, 1984; Bill Barron et al., *The Official NFL Encyclopedia of Football* (New York, 1982); Bob Broeg, "Sports Comment," *St. Louis Post-Dispatch*, November 11, 1962; Arthur Daley, "Sports of the Times," *NYT*, December 13, 1963; Vince Johnson, "Rooney Unique in Pro Football Hall of Fame," *Pittsburgh Post-Gazette*, September 7, 1964; David S. Neft, Richard M. Cohan, and Jordan A. Deutsch, *Pro Football: The Early Years: An Encyclopedic History, 1895–1959* (Ridgefield, CT, 1978); Robert J. Oates, *Pittsburgh Steelers: The First Half Century* (Los Angeles, 1982); Vito Stellino, "Steelers 50 Seasons," *Pro!* (January 1982).

C. Robert Barnett

ROSENBERG, Aaron David "Rosy" (b. 26 August 1912, Brooklyn, NY; d. 1 September 1979, Los Angeles, CA), college player, starred three years (1931–1933) in football with the University of Southern California (PCC) and made All-American guard the last two seasons. His Trojans teams finished undefeated in 27 consecutive games, wielded a combined 30–2–1 record, won two Rose Bowl games, and captured two national championships. Rosenberg made the West Coast sports editors' All-Time PCC first team and the FWAA All-Time Far West second team. In 1966 he was elected to the NFF College Football Hall of Fame.

After moving to Los Angeles as a young boy, Rosenberg graduated from Fairfax High School in 1930. He entered Southern California and starred on the 1930 freshman football team. Although they dropped the 1931 season opener in Rosenberg's sophomore year 13–7 to fifth-rated St. Mary's College (CA), the Trojans won the remaining nine games and defeated California-Berkeley (6–0), Stanford (19–0), Washington (44–0), and Georgia (60–0). The Trojans ended Notre Dame's 26–game undefeated streak with a thrilling 16–14 come-from-behind victory. Southern California won the 1931 national championship, led by Rosenberg, senior backs Erny Pinckert* and Gus Shaver, and guard Johnny Baker. The Trojans represented the PCC in the 1932 Rose Bowl and triumphed 21–12 over undefeated, second-ranked Tulane.

The Trojans shared the national championship with Michigan in 1932 by completing a perfect 9–0–0 season. Rosenberg, tackles Ernie Smith and Tay Brown, and end Ray Sparling formed one of Southern California's finest defensive units and never allowed a point to be scored via rushing. Although two touchdowns were scored on the Trojans through the air, Southern California extended consecutive victories over Stanford and Washington (5), California-Berkeley (3), and Notre Dame (2). The PCC champion Trojans overwhelmed undefeated, third-ranked Pittsburgh 35–0 in the 1933 Rose Bowl. The 6 foot, 2 inch, 225 pound Rosenberg moved quickly for his size and played pulling guard on offense, leading the Trojans interference. He performed at linebacker on defense in coach Howard Jones'* 6–2–2–1 alignment. Rosenberg, assigned to cover the Stanford fullback, stopped coach Glenn "Pop" Warner's* fullback fake reverses that had devastated other opponents. "I give credit to Rosenberg," Jones stressed, "for playing a big part in the success of the team's defense against Notre Dame and Stanford in 1931 and 1932."

Rosenberg and Irvine "Cotton" Warburton, the only returning stars in 1933, led the Trojans to an outstanding 10–1–1 season and sixth-place national ranking in the Frank G. Dickinson System. Southern California defeated Notre Dame, Georgia, Washington, and California, but played a scoreless tie against a strong Oregon State team and lost to the PCC co-champion Stanford Indians 13–7. Stanford started seven sophomores, who kept a "vow never to lose to USC" during their playing careers. Rosenberg suffered a broken cheekbone, which Jones discovered at halftime of the Oregon State game. When he was asked why he did not leave the game, Rosenberg reminded Jones that one more time-out would have resulted in a five yard penalty. Rosenberg talked constantly on the playing field and enjoyed needling opponents. Bobby Grayson,* one of Stanford's "Vow Boys," maintained, "He was an exciting athlete and a true motivating influence in that USC line." Rosenberg, one of the Trojans' mightiest guards, for three years bulwarked lines that held 22 of 33 opponents scoreless.

After graduating from the University of Southern California School of Journalism in 1934, Rosenberg joined Twentieth Century Fox Studios as a second assistant film director at $40 a week. He served as a U.S. Navy officer during World War II (1942–1946) and then became a leading Hollywood movie producer with Universal Studios, creating the stars' salary-deferral system. He produced a remake of *Mutiny on the Bounty*, *To Hell and Back*, *The Detective*, *Winchester 73*, and *The Glenn Miller Story*, and for television, the "Daniel Boone" series. Rosenberg, who married Victoria Ann Astlett of Los Angeles, CA, had one son, Peter Anthony, and three stepchildren. He died of a stroke.

BIBLIOGRAPHY: Tim Cohane, *Great College Football Coaches of the Twenties and Thirties* (New Rochelle, NY, 1973); Allison Danzig, *The History of American Football: Its Great Teams, Players, and Coaches* (Englewood Cliffs, NJ, 1956); John D. McCallum and Charles H. Pearson, *College Football U.S.A., 1869–1973* (New York, 1973); Ronald L. Mendell and Timothy B. Phares, *Who's Who in Football* (New Rochelle, NY, 1974); Ken Rappoport, *The Trojans: A Story of Southern California Football* (Huntsville, AL, 1974); Rose Bowl (Southern California–Tulane) Football Game Program, January 1, 1932; Southern California–Notre Dame Football Game Program, December 10, 1932; Southern California–Stanford Football Game Program, November 11, 1933; University of Southern California Archives, Los Angeles, CA.

James D. Whalen

ROUTT, Joseph Eugene "Joe" (b. 18 October 1914, Chapel Hill, TX; d. 10 December 1944, Belgium), college football player and professional boxer, was the son of farmer Eugene Otis Routt and Anna Belle (Clay) Routt, attended public schools in Chapel Hill, and graduated in 1933 from nearby Brenham High School. He matriculated at Blinn JC in Brenham TX, and transferred in 1935 to Texas A&M University (SWC). Routt played football in high school, junior college, and at Texas A&M in 1935, 1936, and 1937. Although never on a championship squad, Routt made consensus All-American guard in 1936 and 1937 and captained the 1937 Aggies. He played in the 1937 College All-Star Game and Shrine All-Star (East-West) game, captaining the West squad and being selected the game's top lineman. In 1936 and 1937 Routt won the intramural light heavyweight boxing championship.

An outstanding student, Routt graduated from Texas A&M with a Bachelor's degree in Marketing and Finance and moved to Houston. He became a sales representative for Longhorn Portland Cement Company and launched a pro boxing career. After suffering a humiliating defeat in his first bout, the 6 foot, 210 pound Routt quit boxing. He joined the U.S. Army as a captain in 1940 and barnstormed the nation with an Army All-Star eleven against pro football teams. Routt married Marilyn Maddox in 1942 and had two daughters. Sent to Europe in 1944, he was killed leading his troops into the Battle of the Bulge and was posthumously awarded the Bronze Star. Routt in 1952 became one of three initial honorees and the first football player elected to the Texas Sports Hall of Fame. Membership in the NFF College Football Hall of Fame followed in 1962. His citation read in part: "In war as in football, Joe Routt was a true leader of men, ever prepared to make the ultimate sacrifice."

BIBLIOGRAPHY: Thad Johnson, "Joseph 'Joe' Routt," *Texas Sports Hall of Fame, Its Members and Their Deeds* (n.p., n.d.); "Obituary," Houston (TX) *Post*, December 21, 1944; Joe Routt file, NFF College Football Hall of Fame, Kings Mills, OH; Texas A&M University, Sports News Office, College Station, TX.

Mary Lou LeCompte

ROYAL, Darrell K. (b. 6 July 1924, Hollis, OK), college and professional player, coach, and administrator, guided the University of Texas (SWC) to three national football championships and four undefeated regular seasons. Besides being chosen Coach of the Year by the AFCA (1963, 1970) and FWAA (1961, 1963), he was named Coach of the 1960s Decade by an ABC-TV poll of sportswriters and was elected to the Texas Sports Hall of Fame (1976) and NFF College Football Hall of Fame (1983). Royal achieved a 23–year composite 184–60–5 (.749 percent) coaching record, ranking fifteenth in victories among coaches. He served as head coach at Mississippi State University (SEC, 1954–1955) and the universities of Washington (PCC, 1956) and Texas (1957–1976), amassing a Longhorns SWC record of 109–27–2 for the highest winning percentage (.792) in SWC history. He guided Texas to 11 SWC titles (three shared), including six in succession (also an SWC record).

Royal grew up in the Oklahoma dust bowl during the Depression and at night often slept with a wet dishrag on his face. His father, Burley Ray Royal, worked as a truck driver and night watchman; his mother, Katy Elizabeth (Harmon) Royal, died when he was four months old. Royal quarterbacked the 1942 undefeated Hollis High School eleven and graduated from there in 1943. He served as a staff sergeant with the U.S. Air Force during World War II (1943–1946) and played on the Third Air Force football team at Tampa, FL, while taking aerial gunner training. Royal won four football letters at the University of Oklahoma (BSC, 1946–1949) under coach Bud Wilkinson,* excelling at halfback and quarterback on Sooner teams that boasted a 36–6–1 composite record, 21–game winning streak, four BSC championships, and a 3–0–0 bowl record. The undefeated (11–0–0) and second-ranked 1949 Oklahoma Sooners fielded five All-Americans: Royal (INS and Paramount News), end Jim Owens, tackle Wade Walker, guard Stan West, and halfback George Thomas. The 5 foot, 10 inch, 170 pound Royal set Sooners records for career pass interceptions (17), single-season punt return average (32.8 yards), and longest game punt return (95 yards against Kansas State in 1948). He punted 81 yards against Oklahoma (State) A&M and achieved a 38.1–yard career punting average. "Royal probably is the best punter I've ever seen," observed Wilkinson. Royal completed 53.9 percent of his forward passes in 1949 and threw 76 consecutive passes without an interception.

After graduating from the University of Oklahoma in 1950, Royal held assistant football coaching posts at North Carolina State (SC, 1950), Tulsa (MVC, 1951), and Mississippi State (SEC, 1952). He guided the Edmonton Eskimos (1953) to a 17–5–0 season in the pro CFL and returned to Mississippi State as head coach, posting a two-year 12–8–0 record. He led Washington (1956) to a 5–5–0 record and fourth place in the PCC, the Huskies' highest finish in four years. Royal replaced Ed Price as Texas head coach after the Longhorns had completed a disastrous 1–9–0 season and promptly led them to their first winning season (1957) in four years and a Sugar Bowl invitation. Royal, whose colorful expressions delighted reporters, remarked, "We're gonna dance with the one who brung us" and "One does not take over a one and nine squad and inherit a warm bed." Although he had a low-key manner, he proved an outstanding administrator and meticulous planner. "When he explains something," observed Longhorns quarterback James Street, "it's like getting a lecture from a professor."

Royal emphasized in-state recruiting and produced thirty Longhorns All-Americans, two Outland Award winners (tackle Scott Appleton and guard Tommy Nobis*), and one Maxwell Award and Rockne Award winner (Nobis). His squads played in 16 post-season bowl games with an 8–7–1 mark and held a 6–1–0 edge over former mentor Wilkinson's Oklahoma and

14–5–0 dominance of Frank Broyles'* Arkansas. The 1963 Longhorns defeated 28–6 number 2 nationally ranked Navy in the Cotton Bowl to achieve their first national championship. Consecutive national titles followed in 1969–1970 (the latter shared) under the leadership of All-American fullback Steve Worster, end Cotton Speyrer, and tackle Bobby Wuensch. Texas came from behind in the final game of 1969 to post a sensational victory over undefeated Arkansas 15–14. In 1969–1970 they split with Notre Dame in consecutive Cotton Bowl engagements, registering a thrilling 21–17 triumph and a 24–11 loss. Royal initiated in 1961 the "flip-flop" offense, in which linemen and backs exchanged positions to gain maximum strength. He in 1968 adopted the wishbone-T offense, helping the Longhorns garner another SWC championship after a four-year drought.

Royal, who in 1963 wrote the book *Darrell Royal Talks Football*, in 1975 presided over the AFCA and retired from coaching in 1977. He resigned as University of Texas athletic director in December 1979 to become special assistant to the university president. Royal married Edith Marie Thomason of Hollis in 1944 and had two sons, Mack and David, and one daughter, Marian. Tragedy struck twice when Marian died in 1973 in an automobile accident and David was killed in 1982 in a motorcycle mishap.

BIBLIOGRAPHY: Denne H. Freeman, *Hook 'Em Horns: A Story of Texas Football* (Huntsville, AL, 1974); Lou Maysel, *Here Come the Texas Longhorns*, Vols. 1–2 (Austin, TX, 1970, 1978); Ronald L. Mendell and Timothy B. Phares, *Who's Who in Football* (New Rochelle, NY, 1974); Sugar Bowl Football Game Program, January 2, 1950; Jim Weeks, *The Sooners: A Story of Oklahoma Football* (Huntsville, AL, 1974).

James D. Whalen

ROZELLE, Alvin Ray "Pete" (b. 1 March 1926, South Gate, CA), college athlete, professional football executive, and commissioner, is the son of Raymond and Hazel (Healey) Rozelle. A 1944 graduate of Compton (CA) High School, Rozelle served in the U.S. Navy from 1944 to 1946. At Compton JC he played basketball and tennis and handled sports publicity. Rozelle entered the University of San Francisco in 1948 and served as athletic news director prior to his 1950 graduation. Between 1950 and 1952 he worked as assistant athletic director at San Francisco before joining the Los Angeles Rams (NFL) as public relations director. Rozelle entered private business from 1955 to 1957 and then was named general manager of the Rams. He held that position until January 26, 1960, when he was selected as NFL commissioner.

When the 33–year-old Rozelle became commissioner, pro football still perhaps lagged behind college football in popularity. Rozelle became a surprise compromise choice to succeed Bert Bell* when NFL officials Marshall Leahy and Austin Gunsel neither could gain the needed votes. The hard-working organizer and diplomat apparently proved just what the NFL needed. Rozelle's first action involved expanding the NFL from 12 to 14 teams. His greatest achievement in the first two years came in 1962, when he negotiated the NFL's first single-network television agreement. Rozelle convinced the team owners to pool television receipts so he could bargain for each one at the same time. Under his direction, NFL attendance rose from 3.1 million in 1960 to 10.7 million in 1973.

Rozelle controlled pro football in an ironclad fashion. He made several tough, sometimes unpopular decisions and acted independently of the owners who hired him. In 1963 he successfully handled the gambling scandal that included Paul Hornung* and Alex Karras.* Rozelle suspended players for gambling, associating with people of undesirable backgrounds, and being involved with drugs. He fined coaches for such offenses as criticizing officials. In December 1963 *SI* named Rozelle Sportsman of the Year for his role in preserving the NFL's integrity.

Besides maintaining the NFL's stability throughout the conflict with the AFL, Rozelle played key roles in the merger and restructuring of the NFL, conception and growth of the Super Bowl, and emergence of the NFL as the nation's most popular sports attraction. Once the merger was approved, Rozelle secured congressional action to make it exempt from antitrust prosecution. Rozelle presided over the organization of NFL Properties, which controls merchandise licensing for the clubs, and backed the movement to gain a more effective benefit plan for the players. Highly involved in getting federal legislation enacted to support the NFL, Rozelle lost a celebrated court case in 1982, when Al Davis* and the Oakland Raiders (NFL) were permitted to move to Los Angeles, CA. The "Rozelle Rule," invoked by the commissioner, involved athletes playing out their options with one team so they could be free to negotiate with another. If the two teams involved could not agree, Rozelle fixed the amount of compensation, usually in the form of draft choices or players. Although given a ten-year contract in 1977, Rozelle has been criticized severely in recent years due to the many problems facing pro football. Married to Jane Marilyn Coupe on June 11, 1949, Rozelle has one daughter, Ann Marie. In 1985 he was elected to the Pro Football Hall of Fame. The following year Rozelle instituted an NFL drug program that required mandatory random testing for players during the season, and he handed down his most severe penalty against an NFL player. Green Bay Packers defensive lineman Charles Martin was suspended for two games for roughing up Chicago Bears quarterback Jim McMahon. Rozelle also welcomed the outcome of an anti-trust suit brought by the rival USFL. The USFL, which had no contract with a major television network, protested that the NFL held a monopoly and consequently sought $1.6 billion in damages. A federal jury found the NFL guilty of anti-trust violations but ruled that the NFL had not used its muscle to keep rivals off the television screen and awarded the financially strapped USFL only $3. The jury decision left the USFL with only an $8 million cable-television contract, causing the league to suspend operations for the fall 1986 season. Herschel Walker,* Jim Kelly, Kelvin Bryant, and other USFL stars switched to the NFL for the fall 1986 season.

BIBLIOGRAPHY: *CB* (1964), pp. 381–83; Charles Leehrsen, "The USFL's Dark 'Victory,' " *Newsweek* 108 (August 11, 1986), p. 45; Beau Riffenburgh, "The Class of 1985," *Game Day*, Seattle Seahawks–Indianapolis Colts Football Program, August 10, 1985, pp. 3B, 5B; George Sullivan, *Pro Football A to Z* (New York, 1975).

John L. Evers

ROZIER, Mike (b. 1 March 1961, Camden, NJ), college athlete and professional football player, is the son of Garrison and Beatrice Rozier. At Woodrow Wilson High School in Camden, Rozier was selected an All-State and All-American football performer. After spending one year at Coffeyville (KS) JC, Rozier in 1981 entered the University of Nebraska (BEC). During his Nebraska career, Rozier excelled as a football running back and sprinter on the Cornhuskers' indoor track team. The 5 foot, 10 inch, 210 pound Rozier was selected on the All-BEC football team, BEC Offensive Player of the Year, and All-American (1982–1983). Rozier in 1983 won the coveted Heisman Trophy as the nation's outstanding college football player, joining O. J. Simpson* as the only other Heisman winner to have transferred from a junior college.

In 1981 Rozier helped lead Nebraska to a 9–3–0 record, including a 22–15 loss to Clemson University in the Orange Bowl. He rushed for 949 yards on 151 attempts and scored five touchdowns. Nebraska in 1982 defeated LSU 21–20 in the Orange Bowl to complete a 12–1–0 season. Rozier ranked fourth in the nation in rushing, recording 1,689 yards on 242 attempts, scoring 15 touchdowns, averaging 140.7 yards per game, and placing eighth nationally in all-purpose running. When Nebraska played for the national championship in the 1983 Orange Bowl, Rozier was injured during the game. The Cornhuskers lost 31–30 to the University of Miami. Rozier, that season, led the nation in rushing, compiling 2,148 yards on 275 attempts, scoring 29 touchdowns, averaging 179 yards per game, and placing second in all-purpose running. He paced the nation in scoring with 174 points, as his 29 rushing touchdowns set an NCAA record, and also established a then national mark for most yards gained in four consecutive games (929). As a player on the highest scoring college football team in history, Rozier averaged 7.81 yards per carry (an NCAA record) and tied Lydell Mitchell's* national season record of 29 touchdowns and 174 points scored. Rozier shares the NCAA season record for 100–yard games (11) with six others, including five Heisman Trophy winners. In three varsity seasons at Nebraska, Rozier ran for 4,780 yards, scored 50 touchdowns, and averaged 136.6 rushing yards per game and an NCAA-record 7.16 yards per carry.

Rozier, the first player chosen in the 1984 USFL draft, received a three-year contract valued at a reported $3.1 million with the Pittsburgh Maulers and rushed for 792 yards and three touchdowns in 14 games. When the Pittsburgh franchise disbanded, Rozier in 1985 signed for a reported $200,000 with the Jacksonville Bulls (USFL). He finished second in the USFL to Herschel Walker* in rushing with 1,361 yards on 320 attempts and scored 12 touchdowns. Rozier's best game came when he rushed for 199 yards and scored 4 touchdowns against the Orlando Renegades. He ranked fourth among the USFL all-time rushing leaders for one season. On July 1, 1985, Rozier signed a four-year contract with the Houston Oilers (NFL) for a reported $2.25 million. He led the 5–11 Oilers in rushing with 462 yards on 133 attempts and 8 touchdowns in 1985 and with 662 yards on 199 attempts and 4 touchdowns in 1986. In his three-year pro career, Rozier has rushed 875 times for 3,287 yards and scored 27 touchdowns.

BIBLIOGRAPHY: John T. Brady, *The Heisman: A Symbol of Excellence* (New York, 1984); Dan Levin, "This Debut Was a Real Debacle," *SI* 60 (March 5, 1984), p. 14; *TSN*, December 19, 1983, pp. 2, 35; *TSN Official USFL Guide and Register—1985; TSN Football Register—1986.*

John L. Evers

RYAN, Frank Beall (b. 12 July 1936, Fort Worth, TX), college and professional player and administrator, graduated from Paschal High School in Fort Worth and attended Rice Institute on a football scholarship. At Rice he received a B.A. degree in Physics in 1958, an M.A. degree in Mathematics in 1962, and Ph.D. degree in Mathematics in 1965. Under quarterback Ryan, Rice (SWC) lost to Navy 20–7 in the 1958 Cotton Bowl. The scholar-athlete, who researched the "boundary behavior of analytic functions" and published articles in numerous professional journals, was drafted as a quarterback in the fifth round by the Los Angeles Rams (NFL) in 1958. From 1958 to 1970 the 6 foot, 3 inch, 199 pound Ryan quarterbacked in the NFL. After playing four years with the Los Angeles Rams, he was traded in 1962 to the Cleveland Browns (NFL). He enjoyed his greatest pro football success there and made the 1964–1966 Pro Bowls. In 1969 and 1970 he played with the Washington Redskins (NFL). During 12 pro seasons, he completed 1,090 of 2,133 passes (51.1 percent) for 16,042 yards (7.5–yard average), 149 touchdowns, and 111 interceptions. Upon his retirement, Ryan ranked seventh among NFL passers.

Ryan's finest hour came in the 1964 NFL title game at Cleveland's Municipal Stadium. The Browns, Eastern Conference champions, played the heavily favored Baltimore Colts of the Western Conference. Although the Colts possessed all-around balance and team excellence, Ryan guided Cleveland to an incredible 27–0 upset victory. Following the game, Ryan commented, "They rushed but I never heard them." The Colts fearsome defensive line of Gino Marchetti,* Gene Lipscomb,* Art Donovan,* Ordell

Brasse, and Don Joyce could not stop the Browns' attack. Ryan characteristically credited Cleveland's offensive and defensive lines with the major role in the victory.

Ryan saw no contradiction between athletic and scholarly pursuits, enjoying his greatest success in pro football while performing most effectively in academics. Ryan researched highly complex areas of math and computer science and taught these subjects at Rice in 1966 and Case Western Reserve University from 1967 through 1970. His interest in computers was stimulated in 1960 while he was employed with Texas Instruments. In July 1969, he created a computer called *PROBE*. Two years later, his organization was providing computer support for the U.S. House of Representatives. In June 1977 Ryan joined Yale University as the director of athletics and lecturer in mathematics. He married Joan Busby, nationally syndicated columnist for the *Washington Post* and director of publications for the Yale School of Organization and Management. The Ryans live in New Haven, CT, and have four sons.

BIBLIOGRAPHY: Bill Levy, *Return to Glory: The Story of the Cleveland Browns* (Cleveland, OH, 1965); David S. Neft et al., *The Complete All-Time Pro Football Register* (New York, 1975); Roger Treat, ed., *The Encyclopedia of Football*, 16th rev. ed., rev. by Pete Palmer (New York, 1979); *TSN Football Register—1969*.

John R. Giroski

S

ST. CLAIR, Robert Bruce "Bob" "The Geek" (b. 18 February 1931, San Francisco, CA), college and professional player, became one of few pro athletes to play nearly their entire career in their hometown. St. Clair, who attended junior and senior high school in San Francisco, was judged too small at 5 feet, 9 inches, and 150 pounds to play varsity football as a high school sophomore. St. Clair's raw meat and health food diet, however, enabled him to blossom to 6 feet, 4 inches, and 210 pounds as a high school junior. He also possessed surprising speed, running the relays in track in high school. He enrolled at the University of San Francisco and in 1951 was named All-Pacific Coast end on an undefeated team that sent Gino Marchetti,* Ollie Matson,* Dick Stanfel,* and six other players into pro football. When San Francisco dropped football after that season, he transferred to the University of Tulsa (MVC) for the 1952 campaign and then joined the San Francisco 49ers (NFL) in 1953.

Nicknamed "The Geek" because of his 6 foot, 9 inch, 265 pound frame, St. Clair played offensive tackle with the 49ers through the 1964 season. He co-captained the 1957–1958 49ers with All-Pro defensive tackle Leo Nomellini* and helped San Francisco to a first-place tie in the Western Conference in 1957. San Francisco lost to Detroit 31–27 for the title in 1957 and usually finished from third to fifth place during St. Clair's seasons there. St. Clair was among the best remembered of a faceless band of offensive linemen because he was the era's tallest pro player. St. Clair's run and pass-blocking abilities, combined with his innate toughness and speed, earned him distinction as one of pro football's most durable offensive tackles. His unusual quickness was demonstrated in an exhibition game against the New York Giants at Seattle, WA, in 1955. St. Clair was not expected to play because three of his teeth had been extracted the day before, but he performed the whole game on offense. Defensive back Emlen Tunnell* intercepted a pass with a clear field ahead, but St. Clair tackled him from behind. After earning

All-Pro honors in 1955, he the next year set an NFL record by blocking ten field goal attempts. A foot injury forced him to retire from pro football following the 1964 season.

St. Clair worked as a sales manager for a San Francisco air freight concern and lived with his wife, Ann, and four children in Daly City, a San Francisco suburb. An effective speaker on the banquet circle, he was elected a city councilman and mayor of Daly City. St. Clair also maintained an active interest in juvenile problems because several of his junior high friends from the Mission District gang had ended up in prison. He frequently has visited detention homes and reform schools, where his message has made a far-reaching impact on juveniles. St. Clair now resides in Santa Rosa, CA, and supervises a liquor store chain.

BIBLIOGRAPHY: Mickey Herskowitz, *The Golden Age of Pro Football* (New York, 1974); Dan McGuire, *San Francisco 49ers* (New York, 1960); Don Schiffer, *Pro Football, 1963* (New York, 1963).

Albert J. Figone

SANDERS, Henry Russell "Red" "The Wizard of Westwood" (b. 7 March 1905, Asheville, NC; d. 14 August 1958, Los Angeles, CA), college athlete and football coach, professional baseball player, and athletic administrator, was the lone son of three children born to salesman Henry Edgar and Ida Virginia (Barr) Sanders and moved at age two with his family to Nashville, TN. The black-haired youngster acquired a lifelong nickname because of the red sweater he always wore in sandlot football games and because his aggressive behavior reminded adults of "a young red bull." He briefly attended Davidson County Central High and Duncan Preparatory School in Nashville before spending three years at the Riverside Military Academy in Gainesville, GA. Upon graduating from Riverside in 1923, he returned home to attend Vanderbilt University (SC). A good student and student body officer, Sanders earned four letters each in football, basketball, and baseball. Sanders captained the baseball team and spent his gridiron days as a backup quarterback, but he impressed coach Dan McGugin,* who thought Sanders had "one of the best football brains I have ever known."

After graduating from Vanderbilt in 1927, he spent the next three years as an assistant football coach at Clemson University (SC) and played pro baseball as a second baseman for Pensacola, FL (SEL), Muskogee, OK (WA), and Mobile, AL (SA). As head football coach at Columbia (TN) Military Academy (1931–1933) and his alma mater, Riverside (1934–1937), he compiled one of the best records (55–4–2) in southern prep history. He then coached freshman football at the University of Florida (SEC) in 1938 and the backfield at Louisiana State University (SEC) in 1939 before becoming head coach at Vanderbilt in 1940.

After suffering in 1940 his only losing season ever as a head coach, Sanders quickly built traditionally weak Vanderbilt into a regional power. An 8–2 record in 1941 earned him SEC Coach of the Year honors. After serving as a lieutenant commander in the U.S. Navy's preflight training program at Pensacola, FL, from 1943 to 1945, Sanders returned to Vanderbilt in 1946 as coach and athletic director. He again rebuilt the program with the Commodores, claiming a twelfth-place national ranking in 1948. Sanders, whose reputation far exceeded his modest 36–22–2 record in six years at Vanderbilt, then directed a faltering program at UCLA (PCC).

In nine seasons with the Bruins (1949–1957), Sanders brought national prominence to UCLA and West Coast football by posting a 66–19–1 record for a .773 winning percentage. His Bruins won three consecutive PCC titles (1953–1955) and finished second four times, and third twice. From 1952 through 1955 UCLA lost only three regular-season games by nine total points. After an undefeated (9–0) season in 1954, the Bruins were named national champions and Sanders national Coach of the Year. Dubbed "The Wizard of Westwood" by the press, Sanders changed Bruins uniforms from dark blue to the famous sky blue. He guided UCLA to the Rose Bowl in 1954 and 1956, losing both times to Michigan State.

Although soft-spoken, congenial, and witty off the field, Sanders proved a stern, caustic, discipline-minded coach who excelled at making strategic decisions during a game. He was greatly influenced by General Robert Neyland* of Tennessee. Sanders, whose favorite term for a good player was "animal," throughout his career advocated an aggressive defense and a balanced-line, single-wing offense. He retained the single-wing after virtually every other major college and even most high schools adopted the T formation. His attack, which he called "a horse-and-buggy offense with a TV set in the dashboard," boasted unusual versatility and scoring punch because of a complex set of fullback spinners and reverses.

An innovative coach, Sanders originated the 4–4 defense, developed the "squib kick," and popularized the spread formation. The universally respected Sanders served as an assistant coach in the 1946 Blue-Gray game, 1951 Shrine All-Star (East-West) game, 1952 College All-Star game, and 1952 North-South Shrine game and as head coach of the West in the 1956 Shrine All-Star (East-West) game. He also was elected president of the PCC Coaches Association and served on the Board of Trustees of the AFCA (1954–1957) and as vice president of the AFCA (1957). For Sanders, whose coaching career was ended abruptly at age 53 by a heart attack just prior to the 1958 season, football was his life and the players his family. He had no children by either marriage, to Kathleen McKinney in 1928 or Ann Daniel in 1945.

BIBLIOGRAPHY: Tim Cohane, "Single-wing Sanders," *Look* 17 (November 17, 1953), 104–8; *Los Angeles Times*, August 15–16, 1958; Edwin Pope, *Football's Greatest Coaches* (Atlanta, 1956); Red Sanders file, Vanderbilt University, Athletic Department, Nashville, TN; "Red's Way," *Newsweek* 44 (November 15, 1954), pp. 100–10; Fred Russell,

"They're All Rooting for Red," *SEP* 223 (November 11, 1950), pp. 34, 168–74; *UCLA Football Guide*, 1958; Hendrik Van Leuven, *UCLA Football: Touchdown UCLA* (Huntsville, AL, 1982).

Larry R. Gerlach

SAYERS, Gale Eugene (b. 30 May 1943, Wichita, KS), college athlete, professional football player, and administrator, is the son of auto mechanic Roger and Bernice (Ross) Sayers. The Sayerses moved to Omaha, NE, where Gale starred in football and track at Central High School. He attended the University of Kansas (BEC) and made All-American football halfback in 1963 and 1964 for the Jayhawks. As a sophomore, Sayers gained 1,125 yards on 158 carries to lead the nation with a 7.1–yard average. During his career, the 6 foot, 199 pound Sayers rushed for 2,675 yards and compiled a 6.5–yard average. He still holds two Kansas records, including longest run from scrimmage (99 yards against the University of Nebraska in 1963) and most yards rushing in a single game (283 against Oklahoma State University in 1962).

In 1965 the Chicago Bears (NFL) made Sayers their top draft choice. Sayers enjoyed a fabulous rookie season, firmly establishing himself as one of the game's greats. Sayers set an NFL record by scoring 22 season touchdowns and tied Dub Jones and Ernie Nevers* by making six touchdowns in a game against the San Francisco 49ers. The landslide choice for Rookie of the Year, Sayers tied or broke eight NFL records. A unanimous All-NFL selection from 1965 to 1969, he made Player of the Game in three Pro Bowls until knee injuries ended his career after the 1971 season. In a poll, sportswriters named Sayers the greatest running back in pro football's first 50 years. He led the NFL in rushing in 1966 and 1968 and kickoff returns in 1966. During his career he rushed for 4,956 yards on 991 carries (5–yard average) and scored 39 touchdowns. Sayers also caught 112 passes for 1,307 yards (11.7–yard average) and 9 touchdowns. As a kickoff returner, he compiled an NFL-record 30.6–yard average. Overall, he held 8 NFL and 15 Chicago Bears records. In 1968 he suffered the first of several unfortunate knee injuries. The following year, he led the NFL in rushing with 1,032 yards and won the George Halas Award as pro football's most courageous player. He dedicated the award to his teammate and friend Brian Piccolo, who was in the hospital dying of cancer.

Following his premature retirement, he joined the University of Kansas (BEC) athletic department as assistant athletic director. From 1976 to 1981 he served as athletic director at Southern Illinois University–Carbondale and then entered private business. Sayers authored the book *I Am Third*, taking the title from a sign over the office door of former University of Kansas track coach Bill Easton. The title means "God is first, my friends second, and I am third." He also co-authored with Bob Griese* another book, *Offensive*

Football. Sayers married Ardie Bullard of Omaha, NE, and has six children, Gary, Guy, Gaylon, Gayle Lynne, Scott, and Timmy.

He was inducted into the NFF College Football Hall of Fame for his outstanding career with the Jayhawks and into the Kansas Sports Hall of Fame and the Black Athletes Hall of Fame. In 1969 he was named one of the Ten Most Outstanding Men by the Jaycees for his work with poverty-stricken children.

In 1977 34–year-old Sayers became the youngest person ever inducted into the Pro Football Hall of Fame, which later named him a specialist on its AFL-NFL 1960–1984 All-Star Team.

BIBLIOGRAPHY: George Allen with Ben Olan, *Pro Football's 100 Greatest Players* (Indianapolis, IN, 1982); Gale Sayers, *I Am Third* (New York, 1970); *TSN Football Register—1972;* George Vass, *George Halas and the Chicago Bears* (Chicago, 1971), Richard Whittingham, *The Chicago Bears—An Illustrated History* (Chicago, 1979).

John L. Evers

SCHEMBECHLER, Glenn Edward, Jr. "Bo" (b. 1 April 1929, Barberton, OH), college athlete and football coach, ranks among the top 20 all-time gridiron coaches with a career .778 winning percentage on 207 wins, 57 losses, and 7 ties. His 24–year victory total tops active coaches and ties him for fifth place on the all-time list with Jess Neely* and Warren Woodson.* An offensive football tackle (1948–1950) at Miami University (MAC, OH), Schembechler served as head football coach at Miami (1963–1968) and at the University of Michigan (BTC) since 1969 without suffering a losing season. He was named Coach of the Year by the AFCA and FWAA (1969) and *TSN* (1985). The three-time BTC Coach of the Year (1972, 1980, 1982) served in 1983 as president of the AFCA. Besides being elected to the Miami University Athletic Hall of Fame (1972), Schembechler was named MAC (1965) and Ohio (1966) Coach of the Year. He guided two MAC co-champions and three runners-up at Miami and 11 BTC titlists (eight shared) and four runners-up at Michigan. Schembechler guided the Wolverines to 14 post-season games (11 consecutive), 2 undefeated regular seasons, and at least 10 victories ten times and coached at least 31 All-Americans (19 consensus).

The son of fireman Glenn E., Sr., and Elizabeth Schembechler, he along with his two older sisters attended Oakdale Grade School in Barberton. When one of his sisters as a child mispronounced "brother," "Bo" became his nickname. Schembechler started four years on the Barberton High School football team, as a wingback, guard, and tackle and made All-Ohio at the latter position his senior year. The left-hander pitched Barberton to the Ohio baseball semi-finals, when they lost 3–0 to Columbus Upper Arlington. Schembechler graduated from high school in 1947 and was recruited for Miami (OH) by coach Sid Gillman,* who left the following year. Schembechler substituted his first two varsity seasons on teams compiling a 12–5–1 record and one MAC championship. The 5 foot, 11 inch, 195 pound Schembechler was a mainstay with the 1950 MAC champions, coached by Woody Hayes* and led by quarterback Carmen Cozza and halfback John Pont. The 9–1–0 Redskins overwhelmed Gillman's Cincinnati Bearcats 28–0 and defeated Arizona State 34–21 in the Salad Bowl. The Miami baseball pitcher majored in natural science and physical education and graduated in 1951.

While earning a Master's degree in Physical Education in 1952 at Ohio State University, Schembechler served as graduate assistant on Hayes' Buckeye football staff and then entered U.S. military service at Camp Rucker, AL. After being player-coach of Rucker's undefeated regimental football champions, he was discharged during the summer, 1954. He served as line football coach at Presbyterian (SC) College (1954), Bowling Green University (MAC) under Doyt Perry (1955), Northwestern University (BTC) with Ara Parseghian* (1956–1957), and Ohio State (BTC) under Hayes (1958–1962). Schembechler stated that he learned more football from Parseghian than from any other source. As head football coach at Miami, he achieved a composite 40–17–3 (.691 percent) record and registered triumphs over Northwestern, Indiana, and Tulane. Outstanding quarterbacks Ernie Kellerman and Bruce Matte enabled Schembechler to hold 4–2–0 advantages over archrivals Cincinnati and Bowling Green.

Michigan athletic director Don Canham, who hired Schembechler as head football coach in 1969, commented, "I never met a man who had a more single-purpose mind than Bo." Schembechler, consumed by coaching, attacks things enthusiastically and remains impulsive, quick-tempered, and tough. Before Schembechler's arrival at Ann Arbor, MI, few crowds filled the 101,701–seat Michigan stadium. His 166–40–4 (.806 percent) composite record there made capacity crowds a regular occurrence. His greatest coaching triumph occurred in 1969, when the 8–3–0 Wolverines ended veteran defending national champion Ohio State's 22–game winning streak with a resounding 24–12 upset victory. Despite their often heated 6–4–1 rivalry, Schembechler once stated, "As adversaries on the football field, I would say Woody and I get along about as well as any two coaches could coaching at Michigan and Ohio State." Schembechler worked long hours recruiting while living on hamburgers and chili and gained twenty-five pounds his first year at Michigan. He suffered a heart attack on the eve of the 1970 Rose Bowl game and was hospitalized during the Wolverines' 10–3 loss to Southern California. After a 45–pound weight reduction, he submitted in 1976 to successful open-heart surgery.

The Wolverines have won many "big games" under Schembechler but have enjoyed little success in post-season play. Michigan stands 3–11–0 in all bowls and 1–7–0 in the Rose Bowl. The Wolverines have been ranked in the AP poll's top 20 all but two seasons and in the top ten 14 times. His highest ratings occurred in 1974 (third, 10–1–0), 1976 (third, 10–2–0), and

1985 (second, 10–1–1), the last following a mediocre 6–6–0 1984 season. In 1986 Michigan triumphed over Nebraska 27–23 in the Fiesta Bowl. Outstanding Wolverines players have included end Jim Mandich, tackles Dan Dierdorf,* Paul Seymour, and Dave Gallagher, guard Reggie McKenzie, running back Rob Lytle, and wide receiver Anthony Carter.*

Bo and Millie Schembechler, a widow from St. Louis with three sons (Chip, Geoff, and Matt), were married in 1969 and have one son, Glenn E. III, called "Shemmy." Schembechler has learned to pace himself, relax, and exercise self-discipline. His annual high school coaches clinic ranks among the nation's best. He is featured in a weekly television show in Detroit and a state television network called "Michigan Replay."

BIBLIOGRAPHY: Joe Falls, *Bo Schembechler, Man in Motion* (Ann Arbor, MI, 1973); Bob Kurz, *Miami of Ohio, The Cradle of Coaches* (Piqua, OH, 1983); Will Perry, *The Wolverines: A Story of Michigan Football* (Huntsville, AL, 1980).

James D. Whalen

SCHMIDT, Francis A. (b. 3 December 1885, Downs, KS; d. 19 September 1944, Seattle, WA), college athlete and coach, was the son of Francis Walter and Emma Katherine (Mohrbacher) Schmidt, attended high school at Fairbury, NE, and then enrolled at the University of Nebraska (MVC). He played football, basketball, and baseball for the Cornhuskers and earned a law degree from Nebraska in 1914. He began his coaching career at the University of Tulsa (formerly Kendall College) in 1915 and spent the 1915–1916 and 1919–1921 seasons there. This stint was interrupted for two years during World War I, when he enlisted in the U.S. Army. After being Division Bayonet Instructor of the 87th Division, he later commanded Headquarters Company of the 347th Infantry of the American Expeditionary Forces and captained and commanded Company B of the 50th Infantry of the Regular Army. Schmidt's Tulsa teams won three football championships in five seasons, lost only one of four games to the University of Oklahoma, and fielded one of the nation's best forward passing teams. His teams scored 576, 593, and 622 points in 1916, 1919, and 1920 for 1,791 points all together and held opponents to 88 tallies. His composite Tulsa record included 24 wins, only 3 losses, and 2 ties.

From 1922 to 1928 Schmidt coached football and basketball and at times baseball and track at the University of Arkansas (SWC). His football record there included 42 victories, 20 losses, and 3 ties. At TCU he coached the Horned Frogs football squad from 1929 through 1933 and garnered SWC championships in 1929 and 1932 and a co-title in 1933. His TCU football teams lost only five SWC games and one non-SWC contest and boasted an impressive overall record of 46 wins, 6 losses, and 5 ties. From 1922 to 1934 Schmidt-coached teams lost only once to SMU. He also proved an outstanding basketball coach, guiding TCU to two SWC titles.

Schmidt was hired as Ohio State University (WC) head football coach in 1934 at a $7,500 annual salary for three years and saw his contract renewed for another three years. In 56 games there, Schmidt's Buckeyes held opponents scoreless 25 times and were shut out only six times. His Ohio State composite record included 39 wins, 16 losses, and 1 tie. The Buckeyes shared the 1935 WC title and won the 1939 WC championship outright. Schmidt resigned under pressure in December 1940 and coached the University of Idaho (PCC) football squad to a 7–12 record the next two seasons. Schmidt sang in the Presbyterian church choir, kept active in youth organizations, belonged to Sigma Alpha Epsilon fraternity, Rotary, Elks, and the Chamber of Commerce, and was a 32–degree Mason. Schmidt, whose widow resides in Tulsa, OK, was elected to the HAF and NFF College Football Halls of Fame as a coach.

BIBLIOGRAPHY: George Barton, *My Lifetime in Sports* (Minneapolis, MN, 1957); NFF College Football Hall of Fame, News Release, September 16, 1951; Ohio State University, News Release, Columbus, OH, August 3, 1984; *Texas Christian University Football Media Guide, 1981.*

Stan W. Carlson

SCHMIDT, Joseph Paul "Joe" (b. 18 January 1932, Mt. Oliver, PA), college and professional player and coach, is the son of bricklayer Peter and Stella Schmidt, of German descent. His brother Robert died at age 11 in 1930 in a fall from a tree, and his brother William was killed by a sniper in 1944 in France. Brother John starred in football for Carnegie Tech (1937–1939) and the 1940 Pittsburgh Steelers (NFL). The elder Schmidt died in 1945, when Joe was age 13. Schmidt at age 14 played sandlot football with teams including World War II veterans. He performed as fullback in football at Brentwood (PA) High School, graduating in 1949. The heavily recruited Schmidt entered the nearby University of Pittsburgh that fall. A 6 foot, 218 pound linebacker, Schmidt survived numerous injuries and four different Panther head coaches to become the first elected football captain there since 1929. During his senior year, Schmidt led the Panthers to a 22–19 win over Frank Leahy's* Notre Dame team at South Bend by returning an interception 60 yards. Schmidt, an All-East (AP and UPI) and first team All-American (INS) selection, played in the 1952 North-South game.

In the 1953 Senior Bowl, Schmidt was scouted by Buster Ramsey and consequently drafted by the Detroit Lions (NFL) in the seventh round. After an inauspicious debut at the 1953 training camp, Schmidt later impressed coach Raymond "Buddy" Parker.* When injuries sidelined veteran linebacker Lavern Torgeson in midseason, Jack Saylor recalled, "Schmidt moved in and Torgy's job was deader than your front lawn in August." The Lions changed to a 4–3 defense, making Schmidt the key as middle linebacker. Parker commented, "Schmidt's mobility took some of the load off the defensive backs on pass defense. . . . , [his] style of play brought about the zone defense, revolving defenses, and the modern look of pro football." Vince Lombardi* labeled Schmidt a "cat" and "one of the top linebackers. A great diagnostician, a great tackler, and a strong defensive leader." Schmidt, who wore number 56, captained Detroit the last nine of his thirteen years, led the Lion defense to two NFL championships, intercepted 24 passes, and scored three touchdowns. He played in an NFL All-Star game eight times and the Pro Bowl nine straight years (1955–1963) and was selected team MVP four seasons. Schmidt, called "the best linebacker in the league" by Paul Hornung* of the Packers, retired after the 1965 season as the highest paid Lion with a $27,000 salary. The price paid, however, included shoulders laced with surgical scars.

After his thirteen-year playing career, Schmidt served as an assistant football coach with Detroit in 1966. When Harry Gilmer was fired January 6, 1967, owner William Clay Ford hired Schmidt on a five-year, $50,000 contract as head coach. Schmidt vowed to be fair and honest with his players and led the Lions to a 43–34–7 record. His 10–4 1970 squad lost a bitter 5–0 playoff game to the Dallas Cowboys. Jack Saylor opined that Schmidt was "snakebit as a coach." Amid a wave of acerbic media criticism and with his family receiving abuse in school and at games, Schmidt in 1973 quit at age 41. "I am not willing," Schmidt stated, "to make my family no. 2—to get to the Super Bowl." Schmidt married Marilynn Rotz in 1960 and lives in Grosse Point Woods, MI, with daughters Amy and Kerry and sons William, Mark, and Joseph, Jr. Quiet off the field, Schmidt is a highly successful businessman in the Detroit area directing a manufacturing agency. Schmidt, who was inducted into the Pro Football Hall of Fame in 1973, served the Lions for 20 years as player and coach. Schmidt's distinctive, red-dogging style of play led writer Jerry Green to term him "the greatest middle linebacker of his age, an epochal athlete, who helped change the Pro's philosophy of defense." The Pro Football Hall of Fame named him to its AFL-NFL 1960–1984 All-Star Second Team.

BIBLIOGRAPHY: Ben Dunn, "Sports Profile: Lions of Joe Schmidt," Detroit *News*, January 3, 1963; Joe Falls, "Schmidt Made the Right Decision," Detroit *Free Press*, January, 1973; Jerry Green, *Detroit Lions* (New York, 1973); Jerry Green, "Just a Guy Named Joe," Detroit *News* (February 6, 1973), p. 1d; Jerry Green, "Lions Coach Ready to Swing Ax," Detroit *News*, (January 12, 1967), pp. 1c–2c; Bill Halls, "Schmidt Reveals Why He Got Out," Detroit *News* (January 13, 1973), pp. 1b, 8b; Bill Halls, "Schmidt Quits the Lions," Detroit *News* (January 13, 1973), p. 1a; Jim O'Brien, *Hail to Pitt: A Sports History of the University of Pittsburgh* (Pittsburgh, PA, 1982); Joe Schmidt, personal correspondence, Detroit Lions Archives, Pontiac, MI; Joe Schmidt, Questionnaire, 1953; Jack Saylor, "How No Confidence Schmidt Became No. 1," Detroit *Free Press* (July 26, 1973), pp. 1d, 3d; Jack Saylor, "Schmidt Was a Snakebit Coach," Detroit *Free Press* (January 1973); Lyall Smith, "A Good Joe Makes the Hall of Fame," *Michigan State Hall of Fame* Program (1970), p. 11ff, Pete

Waldmeir, "Schmidt Makes Sure Ford, Thomas Know Russ' Place in Lion Picture," Detroit *News* (1953), p. 1c.

Harold L. Ray

SCHULZ, Adolph George "Germany" (b. 19 April 1883, Fort Wayne, IN; d. 14 April 1951, Detroit, MI), college player, coach, and administrator, made All-Time All-American football center at the University of Michigan (WC, 1904–1905, 1907–1908), was chosen HAF Player of the Year in 1907, and captained the 1908 Wolverines. Schulz, a charter member in 1951 of the NFF College Football Hall of Fame and member of the HAF College Football Hall of Fame, joined Yale guard William "Pudge" Heffelfinger* as the most honored interior linemen. He made at least eighteen All-Time All-American teams, including those of Walter Camp* (1910), John Heisman* (1920, 1932), HAF (1930, 1950), Grantland Rice* (OS) (1928, 1939, 1949), AP (1951), and the FWAA (1969).

Schulz developed unusual strength as a part-time worker in Fort Wayne, IN, steel mills while attending high school and played guard on the football team, gaining a wide reputation for outstanding play. Schulz joined coach Fielding Yost's* last two Michigan "point-a-minute" teams (1904–1905) as a regular guard and was shifted to center after seven games. His huge hands enabled him to snap the larger football with one hand and become one of the first centers to perfect the direct spiral pass (as opposed to end-over-end). Without consulting Yost, Schulz left the defensive line in 1904 to become one of the first linebackers. He performed so well that Yost never objected to the new defensive alignment. Michigan won all ten games, and Yost gave the 6 foot, 4 inch, 245 pound Schulz considerable credit for the Wolverines' staunch defense in easy wins over Wisconsin and Chicago. Grantland Rice (OS) in 1928 observed, "Schulz stands as the fastest giant that ever played football, a human bulwark fast enough to tackle at either end as he brought down his man after the manner of a hawk snaring a quail."

The Wolverines demolished their first twelve opponents in 1905, scoring 495 points and blanking the opposition. In the final game against Chicago, however, Michigan surrendered a safety and suffered its first loss (2–0) in five years. Short of funds for tuition in 1906, Schulz returned to work in the steel mill but reentered Michigan in 1907. By 1907 the forward pass had been legalized, the Wolverines had left the WC, and schedules had been shortened considerably. Michigan lost only to Eastern power University of Pennsylvania (6–0) but defeated Ohio State University and SIAA champion Vanderbilt University. Since the rules prevented movement of a dead ball from near the sideline to a hash mark further inbounds, Schulz occasionally snapped the ball from an end position and caught center-eligible passes.

Schulz missed the first three games his final year (1908) because of scholastic difficulties. Michigan finished 5–2–1, administered Notre Dame's only loss, tied undefeated Michigan (State) Agricultural College, and defeated Ohio State and repeat-Southern champion Vanderbilt the fourth consecutive year. Most Wolverines veterans had graduated a year earlier so that Schulz made a majority of the tackles in losing efforts against Syracuse and Pennsylvania. With All-American halfback Bill Hollenback, the Pennsylvania Quakers (11–0–1), rated national champions by Parke Davis, overwhelmed the young Wolverines 29–0. Despite suffering a physical bearing and torn hip muscle, Schulz still exhibited perhaps the greatest one-man defensive performance ever seen. Schulz begged to continue, but the referee stopped the game in the second half and advised Yost to remove him. Pennsylvania had scored only one touchdown until then, but added four more after Schulz departed. According to Hollenback, two to four players were assigned to him every play. Camp* named Schulz to his 1907 All-American team but bypassed him the following year. *Spalding's Official Intercollegiate Football Guide* listed fourteen metropolitan newspaper and other major 1908 sources that named Schulz All-American, while Camp significantly placed him on his All-Time team two years later. The cat-quick Schulz, who had an easy smile and friendly blue eyes, enjoyed boxing for recreation and relaxed before games by napping.

Leaving Michigan before graduation, Schulz in 1909 joined the staff of General Electric in Madison, WI. He served as line football coach at the University of Wisconsin (WC, 1911–1912) and the University of Michigan (WC, 1913–1915) and athletic director and line football coach at Kansas State University (MVC 1916–1919) and Tulane University (SC, 1920–1921). An insurance adjuster in the Detroit office of the Medical Protective Society of Fort Wayne in 1922, he was head football coach the following year of the 5–3–1 University of Detroit squad and thereafter devoted full time to the insurance business. Schulz, who with his wife, Emilie, had no children, remained active in American Legion baseball and the Tribe of Michigamua, a Michigan alumni society that helped secure positions for recent graduates. He succumbed to a malignant stomach ulcer at Henry Ford Hospital after a lengthy illness.

BIBLIOGRAPHY: University of Michigan, Alumni Records Office, Ann Arbor, MI; Richard M. Cohen, Jordan A. Deutsch, and David S. Neft, *The University of Michigan Football Scrapbook* (Indianapolis, IN, 1978); Allison Danzig, *The History of American Football: Its Great Teams, Players, and Coaches* (New York, 1956); Parke H. Davis, *Football: The American Intercollegiate Game* (New York, 1911); John D. McCallum and Charles H. Pearson, *College Football U.S.A., 1869–1973* (New York, 1973); Will Perry, *The Wolverines: A Story of Michigan Football* (Huntsville, AL, 1980); Alexander M. Weyand, *Football Immortals* (New York, 1962).

James D. Whalen

SCHWARTZ, Marchmont Howard "Marchy" (b. 20 March 1909, New Orleans, LA), college player and coach, excelled as a two-time (1930–1931) consensus All-American halfback at the University of Notre Dame. Schwartz starred on two national championship (1929–1930) squads and teams with a three-year composite 25–2–1 record. A member of the Notre Dame All-Time eleven (1962), Schwartz was elected in 1974 to the NFF College Football Hall of Fame. He led the Fighting Irish two years in scoring, rushing, and passing and rushed 7.5 yards per attempt in 1930 to rank second on Notre Dame's single-season all-time list. In three seasons (1929–1931), Schwartz produced 17 touchdowns, gained 1,945 yards rushing on 335 carries (5.8–yard average), and amassed 2,501 yards total offense. The son of New Orleans Equitable Equipment Company general manager Edward and Loretta (Klock) Schwartz, he attended St. Stanislaus High School in Bay St. Louis, MS. Schwartz played football there only two years because his parents frowned on gridiron competition. After graduating from high school in 1927, he played one year of freshman football at Loyola University (New Orleans) under coach Clark Shaughnessy.* Schwartz transferred to Notre Dame in 1928 and sat out that season.

In 1929 Notre Dame head coach Knute Rockne* alternated Schwartz with starting halfback Jack Elder. Schwartz on several occasions helped preserve Notre Dame's undefeated (9–0–0) season with key runs, passes, and defensive plays. His most spectacular performances, however, occurred in 1930 on "perfect play" off-tackle slants for touchdowns to win three close games. He scored twice from scrimmage against SMU, once against undefeated, fourth-ranked Northwestern on a 28–yard run with five minutes remaining, and once on a 54–yard carry against undefeated, ninth-ranked Army with six minutes left to play. Other outstanding plays included his touchdown runs of 60 yards (against Pittsburgh), 40 yards (against Pennsylvania), and 25 yards (against Indiana) and his touchdown passes to Frank Carideo* and Bucky O'Connor (against Southern California) and to Tom Conley and Ed Kosky (against Carnegie Tech). Notre Dame finished with its second consecutive perfect season (10–0–0) and extended its winning streak to 19 games.

In "Hunk" Anderson's* first year as head coach in 1931 following Rockne's untimely death, Notre Dame slipped to a 6–2–1 finish and was rated eleventh nationally by Frank G. Dickinson. Despite playing a scoreless tie with fourth-rated Northwestern in the second game of the season, the Fighting Irish extended their undefeated string to 26 until top-rated Southern California defeated them 16–14 on a fourth-quarter field goal. Schwartz was hurt in the Pittsburgh game, but later completed a touchdown pass that helped defeat the ninth-ranked Panthers 25–12. He achieved touchdown runs of 58 and 60 yards and averaged eight yards per carry against Carnegie Tech, gaining 188 yards on 23 carries. Against the Trojans, he passed to Chuck Jaskwich to set up the first touchdown and scored the other one. Army and Yankee Stadium mud alone limited Schwartz to short yardage in 1931, as the Cadets triumphed 12–0 in the final game of the season before 78,559 people. Schwartz set a Notre Dame single-game record of 15 punts against Army for 509 yards.

The 5 foot, 11 inch, 178 pound Schwartz, named for a racehorse, excelled as a punter and passer and proved the team's most consistent ground gainer. Chicago *Tribune* sportswriter Harvey T. Woodruff wrote (1931), "Marchy Schwartz was one of the greatest running backs in Notre Dame history." Schwartz earned a B.A. degree in Professional Studies in 1932 and a law degree from Notre Dame the following year. He served as Notre Dame backfield coach (1932–1933) and Shaughnessy's assistant coach (1934) at the University of Chicago (WC). As head coach the next five years at Creighton University, he produced a first and second place finish in the MVC and a mediocre 19–22–2 overall record. Shaughnessy brought Schwartz to Stanford (PCC, 1940–1941) as his assistant to help mold the undefeated Rose Bowl champions and re-introduce the T formation to college football.

Schwartz was appointed Stanford head coach in 1942 and guided the Indians to a 6–4–0 finish with All-American guard Chuck Taylor. Stanford triumphed over California, Washington, Southern California, and previously undefeated St. Mary's Pre-Flight, but a 20–7 loss to UCLA prevented a Rose Bowl appearance. Since Stanford did not field a football team the next three years due to World War II conditions, Schwartz worked in public relations with a Wichita, KS, oil firm. Stanford offered him a five-year contract in 1946 and persuaded him to return to Palo Alto as head football coach. Schwartz achieved mixed results from 1946 to 1950 and nearly won a Rose Bowl invitation in 1949 with a 7–3–1 record, led by sophomore backs Gary Kerkorian and Harry Hugasian and All-American end Bill McColl. A 0–9–0 finish in 1947, however, helped reduce his composite record to an even 28–28–4. Longtime Stanford sports information director Don Liebendorfer summed it up best; "Schwartz was head football coach at Stanford during two of the most difficult periods . . . immediate pre– and post–World War II. The polished, fluent, and handsome Schwartz did a very good job under trying circumstances."

Schwartz, assistant coach of the Chicago *Tribune* Charities All-Stars (1947, 1950) and head coach of the victorious West in the Shrine All-Star (East-West) game (1950), became immensely popular with sportswriters. Against the wishes of the Stanford president and athletic director, Schwartz spurned a new five-year contract in 1950 and retired from coaching. He wished to spend more time with his family and found the demands of high school recruiting distasteful. Schwartz married Rosemarie O'Donnell of Omaha, NE, in 1937 and has three children, Marchmont, Jr., and twins John and Mary Jane. Schwartz worked as senior account executive with Trans-America Title Insurance Company of San Francisco until 1980 and lives in Danville, CA.

BIBLIOGRAPHY: Cameron Applegate, *Notre Dame vs. USC* (Hollywood, CA, 1977); Jim Beach and Daniel Moore, *Army vs. Notre Dame* (New York, 1948); Don E. Liebendorfer, *The Color of Life Is Red* (Palo Alto, CA, 1972); *Notre Dame Football Guide, 1984;* Notre Dame University Sports, Information Office, South Bend, IN, August 13, 1985; Gene Schoor, *A Treasury of Notre Dame Football* (New York, 1962).

James D. Whalen

SCHWARTZWALDER, Floyd Burdette "Ben" (b. 2 June 1909, Point Pleasant, WV), college player and coach, is the son of nurseryman Michael and Hattie (Stewart) Schwartzwalder and played high school football in Huntington, WV. At the University of West Virginia (SC) he performed at center and linebacker on the Mountaineers' football team. After earning a B.S. degree in Physical Education in 1933 and an M.A. degree in 1934 from West Virginia, he taught and coached football at Sisterville, Weston, and Parkerville high schools in West Virginia and McKinley High School in Canton, OH, from 1941 through 1942. As a company commander in the 57th Parachute Infantry during World War II, Major Schwartzwalder was awarded the Bronze Star and Silver Star.

Schwartzwalder began his collegiate coaching career in 1946 at Muhlenberg College, where he won all but five games (1946–1948). He directed the Mules to his first bowl victory over St. Bonaventure University in 1946 at the Tobacco Bowl. He accepted the head coaching responsibilities of the Syracuse University football team, which had experienced a postwar decline. Schwartzwalder's first season (1949) at the helm continued this trend with a four win, five loss record. After persuading the administration to increase the number of athletic scholarships to acquire more high caliber players, he molded squads garnering national attention among the major college teams.

The 7–2 record in 1952 earned the Orangemen's first bowl bid and a 61–6 loss to the University of Alabama in the Orange Bowl. Syracuse's appearances against TCU in the 1956 Cotton Bowl and the University of Oklahoma in the 1958 Orange Bowl also ended in losses. The outstanding 1959 team produced an undefeated, untied season plus a post-season contest against the University of Texas in the Cotton Bowl. With future Heisman Trophy winner Ernie Davis* leading the way, Syracuse defeated Texas for its first bowl victory and number 1 national ranking. Schwartzwalder also was selected Coach of the Year by the nation's college football coaches.

At Syracuse (1949–1973), Schwartzwalder compiled 153 wins, 91 losses, and 3 ties and guided the Orangemen to three more bowl appearances (1962 against University of Miami in the Liberty Bowl; 1965 against LSU in the Sugar Bowl; 1967 against the University of Tennessee in the Gator Bowl). Syracuse also was awarded the Lambert Trophy as the best eastern team in 1952, 1956, 1959, and 1966. An outstanding tactician rooted in thorough football fundamentals, Schwartzwalder refined the skilled performances of several outstanding college and pro players, most notably, Jim Brown,* Larry

Csonka,* and Floyd Little.* Schwartzwalder, elected to the NFF College Football Hall of Fame in 1982, married Ruth Simpson in 1934 and has two daughters, Susan and Mary.

BIBLIOGRAPHY: "Coach Ben," *Time* 76 (October 31, 1960), p. 70; Mal Mallette, "Football's Absent Minded Professor," *SEP* 233 (October 29, 1960), pp. 30–33; *WWA*, 34th ed. (1966–1967), p. 1,894.

Joseph English
Eleanor English

SCOTT, Jacob E. III "Jake" (b. 20 July 1945, Greenwood, SC), college and professional player, is the son of pulpwood contractor Jacob E., Jr., and college professor Mary Bell (Hughie) Scott. Scott attended high school in Athens, GA, and Arlington, VA, where he played football, basketball, and baseball. He matriculated at Bullis Prep School in Silver Spring, MD, playing football there and being most outstanding prep player for the Washington, DC, area in 1964. Scott entered the University of Georgia (SEC) in 1965. At 6 feet, 1 inch and 185 pounds, he possessed potential for greatness on both offense and defense. Vince Dooley,* his college coach, described Scott as "the best safety man I've ever seen in college football." As a sophomore in 1967, he was named to the All-SEC team at safety and All-SEC Academic team. In 1968 Scott led the SEC with 10 interceptions (a Bulldog record) for 175 yards and two touchdowns. He also paced the SEC with 35 punt returns for 440 yards and one touchdown. He was selected consensus All-American and SEC Player of the Year.

In 1969 Scott performed for the Vancouver Tigercats (CFL). Vancouver qualified for the championship playoffs, but was defeated in the preliminary round. In 1970 he joined the Miami Dolphins (NFL). He played six years at Miami and three seasons for the Washington Redskins (NFL) before ending his career in 1978. Scott was named to the All-Pro Defensive Team five times (1971–1976) and chosen MVP of the 1972 Super Bowl, where Miami completed the only undefeated season (17–0) in modern pro football history. His career records included 49 interceptions returned for 551 yards. He returned punts for 1,390 yards and a 10.4–yard average and in 1971 led the NFL with 33 for 318 yards. Used sparingly on kickoff returns, he averaged 23 yards per return. In 1983 Scott was chosen on the Coaches All-Time Team as a defensive back. Upon retirement, he moved to a Colorado ranch and mostly hunts, skis, plays golf, and enjoys life. He is engaged also in real estate investment and development.

BIBLIOGRAPHY: George Allen with Ben Olan, *Pro Football's 100 Greatest Players* (Indianapolis, IN, 1982); Tom Bennett et al., *The NFL's Official Encyclopedic History of Professional Football* (New York, 1977); Robert T. Bowen, interviews with Dr. Mary Scott and Jake Scott, 1985; David S. Neft, Richard M. Cohen, and Jordan A. Deutsch, *Sports Encyclopedia: Pro Football* (New York, 1977); Jesse Outlar, *Between the*

Hedges: A Story of Georgia Football (Huntsville, AL, 1973); University of Georgia, Sports Information files, Athens, GA.

Robert T. Bowen

SEARS, Victor "Vic" (b. 3 March, 1919, Ashwood, OR), college and professional player and coach, is the son of Samuel and Petranela Sears, who farmed near Eugene, OR. The lanky, 6 foot, 3 inch, 190 pound Sears played tackle at Oregon State University, where he was selected All-PCC and All-American as a senior in 1940. In January 1941 Sears played in the Shrine All-Star (East-West) game in San Francisco. Sears was drafted fourth in 1941 by the Pittsburgh Steelers (NFL), whose franchise was sold and became the Philadelphia Eagles. During the early building phases, Sears played an instrumental role at offensive and defensive tackle under coach Alfred Earle "Greasy" Neale.* Neale, a "defensive specialist," developed his teams with strong defenses.

From 1941 to 1949 Sears averaged playing fifty minutes a game. His honors included being named to the first All-NFL team in 1943 and 1949 and to either the second team or honorable mention during 1941–1942, 1944–1948, and 1951–1952. Under Neale, the Eagles lost 28–21 to the Chicago Cardinals in the 1947 NFL championship game. The now 230 pound Sears anchored a strong defensive line as a left tackle and helped the Eagles defeat the Chicago Cardinals 7–0 for the 1948 NFL title. In 1949 the Eagles defeated the Los Angeles Rams 14–0 for the NFL championship in a driving rain. The Eagles in the late 1940s featured defensive prowess, and Sears performed as an outstanding two-way tackle. Neale described Sears as the greatest defensive tackle he had ever seen.

Sears, who married Grace Walder of Philadelphia in 1949, played through the 1952 season and then planned to quit. His retirement ended quickly, as he returned for the 1953 season. After his second retirement in 1953, Sears purchased a farm in Bucks County, PA. He and his wife brought up Brenda and sons Richard and Victor. Sears returned for brief coaching stints with the Eagles and worked as a representative for several manufacturing companies until moving to Eugene, OR, to farm berries. Sears was named in the 1960s to the All-Time Eagles Team as a two-way tackle, in 1977 to the All-Northwest Football Team, and in 1980 to the Oregon Hall of Fame.

BIBLIOGRAPHY: John D. McCallum, *Pac–10 Football: The Rose Bowl Conference* (Seattle, WA, 1982); Alexander M. Weyand, *The Saga of American Football* (New York, 1955).

Albert J. Figone

SELMON, Lee Roy (b. 20 October 1954, Eufaula, OK), college and professional player, is the son of sharecropper Jesse Selmon and brother of pro football players Dewey and Lucious Selmon. Selmon, who graduated from the University of Oklahoma with a Bachelor's degree in Special Education and was Academic All-BEC, is married to Claybra and has two children, Brandy and Lee Roy, Jr. A defensive football end, the 6 foot, 3 inch, 250 pound Selmon played on Oklahoma teams that never finished lower than third in the final polls and compiled a 43–2–1 record. The Sooners finished first twice (1974, 1975), both years in which Selmon made All-BEC. In the Orange Bowl game of 1976, his team defeated a strong Michigan club 14–6 for the national title. The exceptional player won the Outland and Lombardi awards as the outstanding college lineman in 1975, made *TSN* College All-American Team that year, and was the first player selected in the NFL draft in 1976.

He joined the Tampa Bay Buccaneers (NFL) in 1976 and made All-Pro from 1979 through 1984. He was named NFL Defensive Player of the Year by the AP in 1979, while *TSN* selected him as NFL Defensive MVP. He was chosen NFL Players Association NFC Defensive Lineman of the Year in 1980 and 1981 and NFL Defensive Lineman of the Year in 1980. He displayed outstanding quickness and ability to defend against both the pass and run and consistently led his team in sacks. Selmon recovered eight fumbles, scored one touchdown, and played in the 1980 NFL championship game. Selmon retired from pro football following the 1985 season.

Since 1978 Selmon has prepared for a business career by serving as a marketing, promotion, and commercial credit executive with the First National Bank of Miami. He chairs the United Negro College Fund Sports Committee and supports numerous community service projects, including the Ronald McDonald House and Special Olympics.

BIBLIOGRAPHY: Ronald L. Mendell and Timothy B. Phares, *Who's Who in Football* (New Rochelle, NY, 1974); *Tampa Bay Buccaneers Press Guide, 1984; TSN Football Register—1986; WWA*, 42nd ed. (1982–1983); *Who's Who Among Black Americans* (1980).

Charles R. Middleton

SHAUGHNESSY, Clark Daniel (b. 6 March 1892, St. Cloud, MN; d. 15 May 1970, Santa Monica, CA), college athlete and professional football player and coach, was the son of Edward and Lucy Ann (Foster) Shaughnessy and participated in football and track at the University of Minnesota. From 1911 through 1913 he played end, fullback, and two-way tackle at Minnesota (WC) under famed football coach Henry Williams.* He earned All-WC honors and made third team All-American at tackle in 1912. After graduation, Shaughnessy assisted Williams until becoming Tulane University (SIAA) head football coach at age 23. His Tulane career spanned 1915–1920 and 1922–1925, resulting in 57 wins, 28 losses, and 7 ties overall and an unbeaten

6–0–1 1919 season. Shaughnessy's 1925 team finished 9–0–1 and received a Rose Bowl invitation, but Tulane's president declined without consulting Shaughnessy. Loyola of the South became his football base from 1926 through 1932. Shaughnessy moved to the University of Chicago (WC) from 1933 to 1939, but the school deemphasized the athletic program with a resultant record of 18 wins, 33 losses, and 4 ties. At the University of Chicago, he befriended George Halas.* The owner-coach of the Chicago Bears (NFL), Halas had employed the T-formation offense for several years. Shaughnessy studied the T formation, expanded it, and devised terminology that greatly enhanced its value and effectiveness.

Stanford University (PCC) hired Shaughnessy for the 1940 football season, enabling him to install his improved version of the T formation. He led the Indians to an undefeated season, number 2 national ranking, and 9–0–0 record, and defeated Nebraska 21–13 in the Rose Bowl. Stanford's record and resultant publicity spurred both college and pro teams to adopt the T formation. Shaughnessy remained at Stanford through 1941, compiling 16 wins and 3 losses over two seasons. During this span Stanford outscored its opponents 356 to 180 points. Shaughnessy moved to the University of Maryland (SC) as head football coach and athletic director in 1942, switched to the University of Pittsburgh (1943–1945), and then returned to Maryland in 1946. During 31 college seasons, Shaughnessy's clubs compiled 149 victories, 106 defeats, and 14 ties. Shaughnessy entered pro ranks in 1947 as assistant coach of the Washington Redskins (NFL) and became head coach of the Los Angeles Rams (NFL) in 1948. The Rams won the 1949 Western Division title, lost the NFL championship 14–0 to the Philadelphia Eagles, and compiled a 14–7–3 overall record under Shaughnessy. Shaughnessy assisted Halas of the Chicago Bears (NFL) in the 1950s and 1960s and played a major role in developing the modern sophisticated pro football defenses, giving each player a specific assignment on every play. Widely known as the father of the modern T formation, Shaughnessy was elected to the HAF and NFF College Football Halls of Fame. He was survived by his wife, Louvania Mae Hamilton, whom he had married on December 5, 1917, and by three children, Clark, Jr., Jamie, and Maria Mae.

BIBLIOGRAPHY: Steve Bisheff, *Los Angeles Rams* (New York, 1973); Allison Danzig, *The History of American Football: Its Great Teams, Players, and Coaches* (Englewood Cliffs, NJ, 1956); George Halas, *Halas by Halas* (New York, 1979); Joe King, *Inside Pro Football* (Englewood Cliffs, NJ, 1958); Bill Libby, *Champions of College Football* (New York, 1975); Howard Roberts, *Story of Pro Football* (New York, 1953).

James Fuller

SHAW, Lawrence Timothy "Buck" "The Silver Fox" (b. 28 March 1899, Mitchellville, IA; d. 19 March 1977, Menlo Park, CA), college and professional player, coach, and administrator, was nicknamed "The Silver Fox" because of his silver hair. At 178 pounds, he played tackle under Knute

Rockne* at Notre Dame between 1919 and 1921 and teamed with George Gipp.* His football coaching career began as an assistant at North Carolina State (SC) in 1924, Nevada (FWC) from 1925 to 1928, and Santa Clara from 1929 to 1935. As head football coach at Santa Clara from 1936 to 1942, he became a master of his craft. Shaw's teams finished 47–10–2, highlighted by his 1936 and 1937 Sugar Bowl wins over LSU. His 1937 team set an NCAA record by holding opponents to 69.9 offensive yards per game.

After coaching at the University of California–Berkeley (PCC) in 1945, Shaw became the first head coach of the San Francisco 49ers (AAFC) in 1946. Shaw was fired in 1954, although his 49ers had compiled a 71–39–4 record. During this period he atypically coached for six months and spent the rest of the year as vice president of sales and promotion in a San Francisco corrugated box company. This dual career commitment as coach and corporation executive became a distinctive characteristic of his pro life. The genteel, dapper Shaw and his wife Marge moved to Colorado Springs, CO, in 1955. As director of athletics, he established athletic programs for the newly formed U.S. Air Force Academy. He also served as the Falcons' first head football coach in 1956 and 1957, producing a 9–8–2 record. Yet his principal interest remained in the NFL. He served as head coach of the Philadelphia Eagles from 1958 to 1960 and retired after winning the 1960 NFL championship. Shaw, whose career 90–55–5 NFL record made him one of the more successful earlier coaches, died of cancer after an extended illness. He was elected to the NFF College Football Hall of Fame.

BIBLIOGRAPHY: *Denver Post*, March 20, 1977; *Los Angeles Times*, March 20, 1977; Ronald L. Mendell and Timothy B. Phares, *Who's Who in Football* (New Rochelle, NY, 1974); *NYT*, December 27, 1960; March 20, 1977.

Charles R. Middleton

SHELL, Arthur "Art" (b. 26 November 1946, Charleston, SC), college and professional player, graduated from Bonds-Wilson High School in North Charleston, SC, and then attended Maryland State–Eastern Shore College (CIAA) from 1964 to 1968. A two-way football tackle, Shell was chosen All-American in 1966 and 1967 by the Pittsburgh *Courier* and *Ebony* magazine. Besides earning All-CIAA honors three times (1965–1967), Shell was named to the Little All-American football team as a senior. He also won two letters in basketball before receiving a B.S. degree in Industrial Arts Education from Maryland State in 1968.

The 6 foot, 5 inch, 285 pound Shell was chosen by the Oakland Raiders (AFL) in the third round (80th player selected) of the 1968 AFL-NFL draft. In 16 pro seasons with Oakland (AFL-NFL) from 1968 through 1982, Shell participated in 207 games. Shell was named to TSN AFC All-Star team in 1974, 1975, and 1977 and played in the Pro Bowl (NFL All-Star game) following the 1972 through 1978 and 1980 seasons. One of the outstanding pro football offensive linemen, Shell played in the 1969 17–7 AFL championship game loss to the Kansas City Chiefs. He also participated in AFC championship games following the 1970, 1973–1977, and 1980 seasons. In Oakland's 32–14 triumph over Minnesota in Super Bowl XI, Shell proved a key member of the offensive line that enabled the Raider backs to gain considerable yardage. The strong pass protector also played on the Raiders' Super Bowl XV championship team. With a 27–10 victory over the Philadelphia Eagles, Oakland became the first wild-card team to win the NFL title. Shell retired following the 1982 season.

Shell, who is married and has one son, was honored in 1976 as Oakland's Lineman of the Year and held the second longest consecutive game streak on the Raiders squad. Shell taught during the off-season and was named as offensive tackle on the second AFL-NFL 1960–1984 All-Star team.

BIBLIOGRAPHY: *The Oakland Raiders Media Guide, 1977; TSN Football Register—1982.*

John L. Evers

SHEVLIN, Thomas Leonard "Tom" (b. 1 March 1883, Muskegon, MI; d. 29 December 1915, Minneapolis, MN), college athlete and football coach, was the son of wealthy lumberman Thomas Henry and Alice (Hall) Shevlin and had two sisters. An above average student, Shevlin attended the Hill School (1897–1902) and graduated from Yale College (IL) in 1906. He married Elizabeth Brannin Sherley of Louisville, KY, in 1909 and had one daughter and one son. An all-around athlete in school and college, Shevlin played varsity football and baseball and placed among the top four in hammer throw in track meets. A 5 foot, 9 inch, and nearly 190 pounder, he proved extremely muscular and unusually fast and joined Yale's "Irish Line" as a freshman. After being moved from right tackle to right end, he often returned opponents' kickoffs to his 30–yard line. From 1902 through 1904 strong Yale teams won 32 games (including 26 shutouts), lost twice (to Princeton in 1903 and Army in 1904), and tied once (with Army in 1902). Yale finished undefeated under Captain Shevlin in 1905, as Princeton alone scored (23–4) against the Elis. Yale crushed Columbia 53 to 0. The three-time, first team All-American, who later was elected to the HAF and NFF College Football Halls of Fame, justifiably boasted: "In the four years I played football no one ever made a run around my end!"

Coach Walter Camp* described Shevlin as "one of the most magnetic characters that ever came to Yale," while president Arthur Twining Hadley noted that he spent "wisely" his princely allowance (enjoying fast cars and 40–cent cigars) and helped fellow students. Shevlin belonged to Alpha Delta Phi fraternity and was elected to his Class Cup Committee but was shunned by Yale's senior societies. After a year in the Northwest learning the lumber business, he entered his father's firm and became president of seven companies in 1912. One of the eight most heavily insured American men, Shevlin carried $1,500,000 in business and $75,000 in personal life insurance. An emergency football coach at Yale in 1910 and 1915, he converted losing teams to winning squads by teaching them the "Minnesota shift" and an aggressive game. Shevlin, who wore a big fur coat and derby and carried a diamond-studded cane, inspired players with his energy, enthusiasm, resourcefulness, and courage. The 1910 Yale team, tied by Vanderbilt and defeated by Army and Brown, became Big Three champion by defeating Princeton 5–3 and holding Harvard to a scoreless tie. In 1915 Shevlin coached Yale to victory over Princeton, but lost to Harvard. His cold, contracted in New Haven, CT, developed into pneumonia and caused his premature death.

BIBLIOGRAPHY: Tim Cohane, *The Yale Football Story* (New York, 1951); Albert Beecher Crawford, ed., *Football Y Men—Men of Yale Series*, 3 vols. (New Haven, CT, 1962), Vol. 1, *1872–1919*, p. 86; Arnold Guyot Dana, "Yale Old and New," a compilation of articles and clippings in 100 volumes number 1–73, on microfilm (see reel #16 on football) in Manuscripts and Archives, Yale University Library, New Haven, CT; New York *Morning Sun*, December 30, 1915; "Shevlin of Yale, A Model of the Modern College Athlete," Boston *Sunday Herald*, October 16, 1904; "Thomas Leonard Shevlin," biographical sketch in *History of the Class of 1906 Yale College*, Vol. 1, senior year album (New Haven, CT, 1906), p. 292; *Thomas Leonard Shevlin In Memoriam, 1883–1915* (New Haven, CT, 1916); "Thomas L. Shevlin Dies; Ill of Pneumonia Four Days," Minneapolis (MN) *Journal*, December 29, 1915; "Tom Shevlin," New York *Evening Mail*, December 30, 1915; "Tom Shevlin Dies in Minneapolis," New York *Evening Post*, December 29, 1915.

Marcia G. Synnott

SHOFNER, Delbert M. "Del" "T-Bone" (b. 11 December 1934, Center, TX), college athlete and professional football player, is one of seven children (two boys and five girls) and of German-English descent. At Center High School, Shofner excelled as an all-around athlete student. Shofner entered Baylor University (SWC) in 1953 on a basketball scholarship. His mother did not want him to play college football because of a knee injury to an older brother. Nevertheless, he earned freshman letters in football, basketball, baseball, and track. A versatile athlete with natural ability, he earned his track letter by running the 100– and 220–yard dashes in under 32 seconds combined. During the spring, 1954, the track coach invited him to the year's final meet against SMU and TCU at Fort Worth. With no baseball game that day, Shofner competed without a single workout and won both the 100–yard dash in 10 seconds flat and the 220–yard dash in 21.5 seconds.

The 6 foot, 3 inch, 185 pound Shofner was nicknamed "T-Bone" during his sophomore year. Baylor football coach George Sauer placed him on a diet of milk, vitamins, and two steaks a day to improve his underweight condition. Shofner averaged 6.2 yards per carry (545 yards on 88 carries) to set an all-time Baylor record and was unanimously chosen SWC Sophomore of the Year. Shofner, Baylor's first three-sport letterman in 14 years, won seven varsity letters (1953–1957): three in football, two in baseball, and two in track. In 1956 he led the Baylor football squad in rushing, scoring, receiving, punting, pass interceptions, and punt and kickoff returns. His 60 points and 40.7-yard punting average paced the SWC. As a running back in three varsity seasons, he averaged 6.1 yards per carry. In the 1957 Sugar Bowl against Tennessee, Shofner was selected the MVP. He also played in the Senior Bowl and College All-Star game. A 9.8–second track sprinter in the 100–yard dash, he ran the anchor leg on Baylor's half-mile relay team and on the 440–yard relay team that tied the world record at 40.2 seconds. Remarkably, Shofner accomplished these feats while suffering from anemia and ulcers.

In the 1956 draft, the Los Angeles Rams (NFL) secured the New York Giants' first selection by trading defensive end Andy Robustelli* and chose Shofner. As a Rams rookie in 1957, Shofner played defensive back. In view of his 9.8–second speed, the Rams switched him to offense in 1958. He caught 51 passes for an NFL-high 1,097 yards. After four years with the Rams (1957–1960), Shofner was traded to the Giants (NFL) in 1961 and combined with fellow Texan Y. A. Tittle* to help lead New York to three Eastern Conference titles (1961–1963). Unstoppable on the fly pattern, he paced the Giants in receiving three straight years (1961–1963) and established a club record in 1961 with 68 catches. Shofner retired in 1967 after 11 NFL years (1957–1967) with 349 receptions for 6,470 yards and 51 touchdowns and punted 153 times for a 42.0–yard average. The ex-Baylor star was named All-Pro five times (1958–1959, 1961–1963) and appeared in five Pro Bowls.

BIBLIOGRAPHY: Ronald L. Mendell and Timothy B. Phares, *Who's Who in Football* (New Rochelle, NY, 1974); *NYT*, August 29, 1961; David S. Neft et al., *The Sports Encyclopedia: Pro Football* (New York, 1977).

Donald Kosakowski

SHULA, Donald Francis "Don" (b. 4 January 1930, Grand River, OH), college and professional player and coach, is the third of six children born to Dan and Mary (Miller) Shula. His father, who immigrated to America as a child and changed the family name from Süle, worked as a nurseryman and Lake Erie fisherman. He and his wife, also a devout Catholic of Hungarian descent, emphasized discipline, hard work, and religion. Don grew up in nearby Painesville and attended St. Mary's Elementary School and Harvey High School, where he lettered in football, basketball, baseball, and track. After graduating in 1947, he accepted a football scholarship to John Carroll University, a Jesuit school in Cleveland, and starred as a defensive and running back.

Selected by Cleveland in the ninth round of the 1951 NFL draft, Shula proved an intelligent, aggressive defensive back during seven NFL seasons with the Browns (1951–1952), Baltimore Colts (1953–1956), and Washington

Redskins (1957). Shula, who had decided upon a football coaching career while in high school, then served as an assistant coach with the University of Virginia (ACC, 1958), University of Kentucky (SEC, 1959), and NFL Detroit Lions (1960–1962). In 1963 he was named head coach of the Baltimore Colts.

Although the youngest head coach in pro football, the 33-year-old Shula quickly became a success. After a third-place finish in 1963, the Colts in the next six years won two Western Conference titles and never finished below second place. The 1968 Colts posted a 13–1 record and won the NFL championship but were upset 16–7 by the New York Jets in Super Bowl III. After recording 71 wins, 23 losses, and 4 ties in seven years with Baltimore, Shula in 1970 joined the floundering Miami Dolphins of the AFC and promptly established himself as one of the finest coaches in pro football history. In 17 seasons with the Dolphins, he has won 12 Eastern Division titles (1971–1975, 1977–1979, 1981, 1983–1985), five AFC championships (1971–1973, 1982, 1984), and two Super Bowls (1972–1973). Shula has compiled a regular-season record of 177 wins, 73 losses, and 2 ties. His 1972 team, featuring a slashing running game and "No Names Defense," completed an unprecedented perfect 17–0 season by defeating Washington 14–7 in Super Bowl VII.

The first NFL coach to win 100 games in his first 10 years, Shula ranks first among active coaches in regular-season wins (247–94–6) and winning percentage (.724) through the 1986 campaign and stands second to George Halas* in career wins (264–106–6) and first in career winning percentage (.714). His teams have remained remarkably consistent winners, experiencing only one losing season (1976), never finishing lower than third place, and posting five unbeaten streaks of 10 or more games (no other team has recorded more than two such streaks).

Voted Coach of the Decade for the 1970s and co-coach on the AFL-NFL 1960–1984 All-Star Team, Shula attributes much of his coaching success to the influence of Paul Brown.* He believes that strict discipline, detailed preparation, and efficient organization ensure gridiron success. The pragmatic coach makes fundamental changes in offensive and defensive strategy according to the skills of available players and has consistently produced better results with less talent than any other coach in history. Although he has gained greater control over his fiery temper, he remains a workaholic, hates to lose, and imparts his drive and intensity to the players. Shula regards teaching as the most important aspect of coaching because "it's not what you know but what your ballplayers know that counts."

Shula, who received a B.S. degree in Sociology from John Carroll in 1951 and an M.A. degree in Physical Education from Western Reserve in 1953, married Dorothy Bartish in 1958. They have five children: David, Donna, Sharon, Annie, and Michael. The sons are following in their father's footsteps. David, a former receiver at Dartmouth and with the NFL Baltimore Colts, serves as an assistant coach with the Dolphins, and Mike quarterbacks at the University of Alabama.

BIBLIOGRAPHY: Jody Brown, *Don Shula: Countdown to Supremacy* (New York, 1983); *CB* (1974), pp. 366–69; Pete Dexter, "Don Shula, In Perspective," *Esquire* 100 (September, 1983), pp. 80–85; Larry Felser, "Don Shula," *Sport* 75 (November, 1984), pp. 17ff.; Tom Jackson, "The Ultimate Football Coach," *Sport* 74 (January, 1983), pp. 48–51; Morris T. McLemore, *The Miami Dolphins* (New York, 1972); Mark Ribowsky, "Shula Pride," *Sport* 67 (December, 1978), pp. 26–32; Don Shula with Lou Sahadi, *The Winning Edge* (New York, 1973); *TSN*, July 25, 1981, January 17, 1983, and December 10, 1984; *TSN Football Register—1986*; John Underwood, "Sitting on Top of the World," *SI* 39 (September 17, 1973), pp. 120–126ff.; John Underwood, "His Eyes Have Seen the Glory," *SI* 53 (September 29, 1980), pp. 48ff.; and John Underwood, "New Names But Still No Names," *SI* 55 (October 12, 1981), pp. 35–41.

Larry R. Gerlach

SIMPSON, Orenthal James "O. J." (b. 7 July 1947, San Francisco, CA), college athlete, professional football player, and announcer, is the third of four children of James and Eunice Simpson. His father, a bank custodian, separated from the family when "O. J." was five. Since "O.J." suffered a calcium deficiency as a baby, he wore braces and experienced difficulty learning to walk. A self-declared rebellious youngster, Simpson disliked school and was suspended five times. Nevertheless, he remained there to play sports. He graduated in 1965 from Galileo High School in San Francisco, where he had participated in track, baseball, and football. As a football player, Simpson displayed considerable speed and led the city in scoring his senior year. Yet his football teams compiled mediocre records, and the 5–4 mark his senior year was the only winning season during his high school career. He met his first wife, Marguerite, in high school and married her in 1967.

Few colleges recruited him, given his team's mediocre record and his academic grades. He attended City College in San Francisco, where he enjoyed a brilliant first season and received scholarship offers from 50 different colleges. Although the offers were enticing, he still did not meet the admission standards to the University of Southern California, his primary choice. He deferred transferring until his grades reached an acceptable level after the fall term. During that fall season at City College, he scored 54 touchdowns and gained 310 yards in a single game, both national junior college records then.

In the spring of 1967 he enrolled at Southern California (PEC) and participated on the NCAA championship track team. He sprinted on the 440–yard relay team, which established a new world mark. Simpson led the Trojans football team to a PEC championship and 14–3 victory over Indiana in the Rose Bowl. The 6 foot, 1 inch, 205 pound Simpson became an outstanding open-field runner with tremendous speed and exceptional peripheral vision, but he fumbled the ball frequently. Simpson's last year at Southern California under coach John McKay* proved better than his first, as he nearly carried the Trojans to another national championship. His Trojans career statistics included 649 rushes for 3,295 yards and 34 touchdowns in 22 games. The Trojans' impressive overall record in Simpson's two Southern California seasons was 19–2–1. He received the Heisman Trophy and the Maxwell Award as the nation's most outstanding college football player. Other recognition included his being named AP and UPI Player of the Year, *Sport* Man of the Year, and All-American for the second consecutive year.

In 1969 he was drafted in the first round by the Buffalo Bills (AFL). He wanted the Bills to trade him to one of the California teams, but he eventually signed with the Bills for an estimated $300,000. Simpson's first three pro years proved lackluster, and many analysts considered him a failure. In his second year, he was hampered by a knee injury. Under new head coach Lou Saban, Simpson rushed for over 1,000 yards in 1972. In 1973 Simpson reached the summit of pro football as the premier running back by setting three NFL records. Aside from being the first to surpass the 2,000–yard rushing mark (2,003 yards), he compiled (since broken) NFL records for the most games with 100 or more yards in one season (11) and most yards in one game (250).

Simpson's improved performance greatly enhnaced the Bills' record. Although they did not make the Super Bowl, the Bills challenged for playoff berths during the latter part of Simpson's career. After nine years at Buffalo, he played two seasons with the San Francisco 49ers (NFL) before retiring in 1979. During 11 NFL seasons, Simpson rushed for 11,236 yards (fifth best), caught 203 career passes for 2,142 yards, and scored 61 touchdowns rushing and 14 receiving. Since completing his playing career, Simpson has appeared in movies and served as an ABC television sports commentator and announcer on "Monday Night Football." In 1985 Simpson was inducted into the Pro Football Hall of Fame. He is also a member of the NFF College Football Hall of Fame. He married Nicole Brown, an interior decorator, on February 2, 1985, and has one daughter, Sydney. The Pro Football Hall of Fame named him to its AFL-NFL 1960–1984 All-Star Team.

BIBLIOGRAPHY: Pete Axthelm, "O. J., the Juice Really Flows," *Newsweek* 82 (November 26, 1973), pp. 67–70; Hal Bock and Ben Olan, *Football Stars of 1974* (New York, 1974); Chicago *Tribune*, August 4, 1985; Larry Felser, *O. J. Simpson* (New York, 1974); Larry Fox, *Born to Run: the O. J. Simpson Story* (New York, 1974); I. R. McVay, "O. J. Simpson: USC's Jet-Speed Powerhouse," *Look* 32 (October 14, 1968), p. 114; *NYT*, August 10, 1969; *NYT*, December 17, 1973; O. J. Simpson, *The Education of a Rich Rookie* (New York, 1974); "Year of the Okay-Doke," *Time* 102 (December 24, 1973), p. 57.

Tony Ladd

SIMS, Billy Ray (b. 18 September 1955, St. Louis, MO), college and professional player, grew up with his grandmother Sadie Sims after his parents divorced; he attended high school at Hooks, TX. Sims excelled in high school football, scoring 516 points and gaining 7,738 yards in three years. Sims' career rushing yards made him the second greatest runner in American high school history behind Ken Hall of Sugar Land, TX, who had rushed for 11,232 yards from 1950 to 1953. Sims always gained at least 123 yards in a game and twice exceeded 300 yards.

Sims studied at the University of Oklahoma (BEC, 1975–1980) and graduated with a B.A. degree in Recreational Therapy. Although injured in 1976 and 1977, Sims in 1978 broke the Sooners one-season rushing record of 1,665 yards set by Greg Pruitt* in 1971. Sims led the nation with 1,762 yards rushing (7.6 yard average) and 20 touchdowns, establishing a BEC single-season record in rushing yards. Sims tied an NCAA record by rushing at least 200 yards in three consecutive games and established an NCAA season record with 7.63 yards per rushing attempt and a career record with 7.09 yards per rush. Guard Greg Roberts, Sims' roommate and Outland Award winner, cleared his path. Selected as the Heisman Trophy winner, Sims became only the sixth junior and third Oklahoma player (after Billy Vessels* and Steve Owens*) to capture the award. Sims in 1979 again led the nation in scoring with 22 touchdowns and finished fourth in rushing with 1,506 yards. In 1979 and 1980 he helped Oklahoma to Orange Bowl victories and was named the Offensive MVP in the first game. He was selected *TSN* College Player of the Year in 1978 and made the All-BEC and consensus All-American teams in 1978 and 1979.

After being chosen by the Detroit Lions in the first round of the 1980 NFL draft, Sims was selected Rookie of the Year after rushing for 1,303 yards and played in three Pro Bowls (1980–1982). In five seasons with the Lions (1980–1985), Sims rushed 1,131 times for 5,106 yards (4.5–yard average) and 42 touchdowns and caught 186 passes for 2,072 yards (11.1–yard average) and 5 touchdowns. Sims broke Dexter Bussey's club career rushing mark by one yard and Terry Barr's club touchdown mark by nine. His 16 touchdowns in 1980 led the NFL, while his 1,437 yards rushing in 1981 surpassed the Detroit club record of 1,035 yards set by Steve Owens* in 1971. Sims also holds single-season team marks with 16 touchdowns (1980), 313 rushing attempts (1980), and 13 touchdowns by rushing (1980, 1981). He led the Lions in rushing (1980–1983) and receiving (1982). Sims injured his knee on October 21, 1984 against Minnesota and missed the last half of the 1984 season and the entire 1985 season before retiring in July 1986. He and his wife, Brenda, of New Boston, TX, were married in 1977 as students at Oklahoma and live in Bloomfield Hills, MI, just ten minutes from the Silverdome.

BIBLIOGRAPHY: Charles N. Barnard, "Simbo Leads the Charge of the Rookie Runners," *Sport* 72 (January, 1981), pp. 21–24; Des Moines *Register*, July 23, 1986; John

D. McCallum, *Big Eight Football* (New York, 1979); John Papanek, "Running For the Vote," *SI* 51 (September 10, 1979), pp. 34–39; *TSN Football Register—1986*.

John L. Evers

SIMS, Kenneth Wayne "Ken" (b. 31 October 1959, Kosse, TX), college and professional player, grew up in tiny Kosse, TX, where he participated in games and sports with his brothers. Sims, who attended public schools in Groesbeck, TX, from 1966 through high school graduation in 1978, cites his mother, Doris, as the major influence on his life. Sims played on the fifth, sixth, and seventh grade baseball teams and began participating in football in the seventh grade. Through junior and senior high school, he played at linebacker, tight end, kicker, and running back on the football team and performed on the basketball and track squads. Following his senior season, Sims made the All-District football team, Centex Player of the Year for Class AA, *Parade* All-American, and the Texas High School Coaches All-Star team.

Inspired by the success of Earl Campbell,* Sims played college football at the University of Texas (SWC) as a full-time student from 1978 through 1982. A three-year letterman at defensive end, he was named MVP on the Texas football team in 1980 and 1981 and made All-SWC and All-American in 1981. A co-captain of the 1981 team, he was named Lineman of the Year by both the Washington and Columbus Touchdown Clubs and MVP by the Entertainment and Sports Network. Sims also earned the Vitalis Award for Sport Excellence and won the prestigious Vince Lombardi Trophy. A leader on the field and in the classroom and community, Sims received numerous invitations as a speaker. He participated in the 1981 Fiesta Bowl Drug Education Program and was named by the NCAA as one of the top five Student Athletes of 1982.

The New England Patriots selected Sims first in the entire 1982 NFL draft, an unusual honor for a defensive lineman. Sims, who is single, attended the University of Texas in the off-season and has played defensive end for the Patriots since 1982. He made the All-Rookie team in 1982, tying for the Patriot lead in quarterback sacks. In recognition of his achievements, Kosse and Groesbeck held Kenneth Sims Day on June 3, 1982. In 1985 he recovered two fumbles and helped lead the Patriots to an 11–5 regular-season record but he missed the playoffs and Super Bowl XX with a broken leg. Following the Super Bowl, the *Boston Globe* reported that Sims and five other Patriots had admitted to coach Raymond Berry* that they had used drugs. The Patriots captured the AFC Eastern Division title with an 11–5 record in 1986 but were eliminated by the Denver Broncos 22–17 in the AFC playoffs.

BIBLIOGRAPHY: Mary Lou Le Compte, interview with Kenneth Sims, 1984, Austin, TX; Kenneth Sims file, Sports Information Office, Men's Athletics, The University of Texas, Austin, TX; *TSN Football Register—1986*.

Mary Lou Le Compte

SINGLETARY, Michael "Mike" (b. 9 October 1958, Houston, TX), college and professional player, attended Houston Worthing High School and graduated from Baylor University (SWC) with a B.A. degree in Management in 1981. An outstanding linebacker at Baylor, he averaged fifteen tackles per game. He was named consensus SWC Player of the Year in 1979 and 1980 and was the only SWC junior to achieve this recognition in that decade. As a senior, he was a finalist in the Lombardi Award balloting. The 5 foot, 11 inch, 230 pounder played in the Japan and Hula Bowls at Baylor and made several All-American teams in 1980.

Singletary has played middle linebacker with the Chicago Bears (NFL) since 1981, when he was named to several All-Rookie teams. Following in the footsteps of Dick Butkus,* he made consensus All-Pro in 1983, 1984, 1985 and 1986, and played in the Pro Bowl following each of those seasons. He was named UPI's NFC Defensive Player of the Year in 1984 and 1985 and usually led the Bears in tackles. From 1981 to 1985 he made four fumble recoveries and intercepted nine passes. Singletary helped the Bears capture the NFC Central Division title in 1984 with a 10–6 mark and played in the NFC championship loss to the San Francisco 49ers. In 1985 he spearheaded an incredible "46" defense as signal caller, helping the Bears compile a 15–1 regular-season record. The Bears defeated the New York Giants and Los Angeles Rams to capture the NFC title and trounced the New England Patriots 46–10 in Super Bowl XX, as Singletary recovered two fumbles. Singletary again led the Bears' defense in 1986, helping the team capture the NFC Central Division title with a 14–2 mark, but the Washington Redskins eliminated Chicago 27–13 in the playoffs. According to former Bears defensive coach Buddy Ryan, "not only is Mike Singletary the best defensive linebacker ever. But to me, he's the MVP of the NFL. Hands down." Perhaps equally important, he actively participates in the Fellowship of Christian Athletes and has been highly successful in organizing community projects, most notably Sports Teams for the Prevention of Drug Abuse. In 1985 he received the Mayor Daley Award for Community Service and the Brian Piccolo Award. He and his wife, Kim, live in Chicago.

BIBLIOGRAPHY: *Chicago Bears Media Guide, 1985; Who's Who Among Black Americans, 1985; TSN Football Register—1986.*

Charles R. Middleton

SINKWICH, Francis "Frank" (b. 20 October 1920, McKees Rocks, PA), college and professional player and coach, is the son of restaurant owner Ignatius and Veronica (Swetko) Sinkwich and has two sisters, Violet and Eleanor. He played high school football at Youngstown, OH, and enrolled at the University of Georgia (SEC) in 1939 as a 5 foot, 10 inch, 185 pound football halfback. He lacked great speed, but coach Wally Butts* said he possessed "the greatest acceleration of any back I have ever seen." As a sophomore in 1940, he was named to the UPI All-Southern team. In 1941 he was unanimously selected All-SEC, leading Georgia to a 40–26 victory over TCU in the Orange Bowl. Sinkwich set a total offense record of 382 yards, scored three touchdowns, and was selected the game's MVP. He led the NCAA in rushing with 1,103 yards and was named All-American.

Sinkwich dominated college football in 1942. He led the NCAA in total offense with 2,187 yards (1,392 via passing, 795 via rushing) and established SEC records for total offense, most touchdowns (16), most points (96), and average gain per game rushing and passing (198.8 yards). Despite two sprained ankles, he scored the only touchdown in Georgia's 9–0 defeat of UCLA in the Rose Bowl. Besides being elected unanimously to the All-SEC and All-American teams, he was selected UPI Player of the Year and awarded the Heisman Trophy. Sinkwich's career record at Georgia comprised 2,279 yards rushing (30 touchdowns) and 2,331 yards passing (30 touchdowns). His total offense yardage (4,610) and 60 touchdowns set SEC records.

In 1943 he entered the U.S. Marines but was given a disability discharge. He then joined the Detroit Lions (NFL) that season. In 1944 he led the NFL in punting, made the All-Pro team, and won the Joe F. Carr Trophy as MVP. Sinkwich, drafted in 1945, was assigned to the U.S. Army Air Force and was injured playing football. After his discharge, he played for the New York Yankees in 1946–1947 and Baltimore Colts in 1947 in the AAFC. Since injuries prevented him from regaining his quickness, he retired following the 1947 season. Sinkwich coached the University of Tampa football team in 1950–1951 to an 11–7–1 record and was elected in 1964 to the HAF College Football Hall of Fame. He also belongs to the NFF College Football Hall of Fame. In 1968 he was named to the All-Time All-SEC team as fullback and was joined by his college teammate Charlie Trippi* in the backfield. He married Adeline Weatherly in 1942 and has two children, Francine and Frank, Jr. He lives in Athens, GA, where he is owner of a beverage distributorship.

BIBLIOGRAPHY: Jesse Outlar, *Between the Hedges: A Story of Georgia Football* (Huntsville, AL, 1973); Ed Thilenius and Jim Koger, *No Ifs, No Ands, A Lot of Butts* (Athens, GA, 1960); Jack Troy, *Leading a Bulldog's Life* (Atlanta, 1948); University of Georgia, Sports Information Office, Athens, GA.

Robert T. Bowen

SISEMORE, Jerald Grant "Jerry" (b. 16 July 1951, Olton, TX), college and professional player, is the second of four sons of James and Anita (Allen) Sisemore. His father worked as a farmer, irrigational driller (for thirteen years), and security guard. At Plainview (TX) High School, Sisemore participated in football, basketball, and track. A second team All-State defensive tackle, he made the All-District second team in basketball and threw the shot put for the track team.

After entering the University of Texas (SWC) in 1969, Sisemore started as a sophomore at offensive tackle for the Longhorns' 1970 national championship football team. He earned All-SWC first team honors and played in the first of three consecutive Cotton Bowl games. The next two seasons, Sisemore made consensus All-American under coach Darrell Royal* and helped Texas win two more SWC crowns and high national rankings. A team tri-captain as a senior, he appeared in the Senior Bowl and College All-Star game. Sisemore, among the top linemen in school history, was elected to the Longhorn Hall of Honor in 1980.

The 6 foot, 4 inch, 260 pounder, blessed with size, strength, and quickness, was drafted in the first round by the Philadelphia Eagles (NFL) in 1973. He started at offensive tackle his first three pro years, spent the 1976–1977 seasons at offensive guard, and then returned to his natural position. On June 19, 1977, he married Ann Peebles and has one son, Grant, and one daughter, Ashley. A durable player, Sisemore appeared in 127 consecutive contests until a knee injury kept him out of two games in 1982. He played in Super Bowl XV against the Oakland Raiders following the 1980 season, made the All-NFC second team in 1981, and participated in two Pro Bowls. In May 1985 the Eagles released Sisemore.

BIBLIOGRAPHY: *Philadelphia Eagles Press Guides, 1973, 1983; University of Texas Football Press Guides, 1972, 1973.*

Jay Langhammer

SLATER, Frederick Wayman "Duke" (b. 19 December 1898, Normal, IL; d. 14 August 1966, Chicago, IL), college and professional player, made All-American tackle on the undefeated (7–0–0) University of Iowa 1921 football team and helped the Hawkeyes win their first undisputed WC championship. Slater was named to the HAF College Football Hall of Fame and made a charter member of both the NFF College Football Hall of Fame and Iowa Sports Hall of Fame (1951). Six hundred sportswriters named him in 1946 to an All-Time All-American team. He made All-Time teams chosen by Glenn "Pop" Warner* (1925), Chicago Sportswriters (1940), George Trevor (1949), David Reese (1951), the BTC (1970), and the University of Iowa (1970).

Slater, one of six children of the Reverend and Mrs. George W. Slater, Jr., lived in the Hyde Park district of Chicago before his family moved to

Clinton, IA. Slater initially quit Clinton High School at age 15 to cut ice for a commercial ice company on the Mississippi River in sub-zero weather, but he returned to graduate in 1916. Slater entered the University of Iowa (WC) in 1918 as a member of the wartime Student Army Training Corps. He starred that year on the first Hawkeyes team ever to triumph over Minnesota and the first to defeat Nebraska in 19 years. From 1918 to 1921 Slater helped Iowa to a composite 23–6–1 record and wins over Northwestern, Indiana, Illinois, Purdue, and Notre Dame. In Slater's senior year, the Hawkeyes ended a 20-game Fighting Irish victory streak by defeating Notre Dame 10–7 and claimed the 1921 national co-championship with Cornell and Lafayette. Iowa was invited to play in the 1922 Rose Bowl, but declined because of a WC ruling against post-season competition.

The large, rangy, 6 foot, 2 inch, 210 pound Slater possessed exceptional leg drive and a quick charge. He played without headgear and often was double- and triple-teamed. Although good-natured, courteous, and kindly, he did not exhibit a mild manner on the gridiron. Teammate Aubrey Devine in 1953 described the 1921 team, "The power of [Gordon] Locke driving behind Slater was the main strong point. Slater had a powerful offensive charge which, I doubt, has been equalled in the history of the game." His coach Howard Jones* never saw a greater tackle, while Fritz Crisler* claimed playing against none better at the University of Chicago. Slater made All-WC three years and was named to most 1921 All-American teams (Walter Eckersall*—Chicago *Tribune*, New York *Herald*, INS, NEA, Billy Evans). Walter Camp* chose Slater to his 1921 second and 1919 third teams. Camp allegedly wanted to allocate only one position on his first team to a Hawkeye in 1921 and designated the outstanding Devine.

Slater graduated from the University of Iowa Law School in 1928 with a Bachelor of Laws degree and simultaneously played pro football ten seasons in the NFL. Slater's teams produced a modest 39–45–13 composite record and never finished higher than fourth in the NFL. Slater starred with the Milwaukee Badgers (1922, 1926), Rock Island Independents (1922–1925), and Chicago Cardinals (1927–1931) and was named to All-Pro teams (1923–1926) by a panel of sportswriters. A Chicago lawyer from 1929 to 1948, Slater coached football in the early 1930s at Oklahoma City's Douglass High School. Slater, who served as judge of Cook County (IL) Superior Court from 1949 until his death in 1966, married Etta Searcy and had no children.

BIBLIOGRAPHY: Chuck Bright, *University of Iowa Football: The Hawkeyes* (Huntsville, AL, 1982); Allison Danzig, *The History of American Football: Its Great Teams, Players, and Coaches* (Englewood Cliffs, NJ, 1956); Ralph Hickok, *Who Was Who in American Sports* (New York, 1971); Dick Lamb and Bert McGrane, *75 Years with the Fighting Hawkeyes* (Dubuque, IA, 1964); John D. McCallum and Charles H. Pearson, *College Football U.S.A., 1869–1973* (New York, 1973); Howard Roberts, *The Big Nine: The Story of Football in the Western Conference* (New York, 1948); Howard Roberts, *Story of Pro Football* (Chicago, 1953); Roger Treat, ed., *The Encyclopedia of Football*, 16th rev. ed., rev. by Pete Palmer (New York, 1979); University of Iowa, Library Archives, Iowa City, IA.

James D. Whalen

SMITH, Andrew Latham "Andy" (b. 10 September 1882, DuBois, PA; d. 8 January 1926, Philadelphia, PA), college player and coach, excelled as football mentor at the University of California, Berkeley (PCC). After attending DuBois High School in Philadelphia, he played football at fullback in 1901 and 1902 for Penn State University and transferred to the University of Pennsylvania (IL) for the 1903 and 1904 seasons. In 1904 he made All-American at fullback for the 12–0 Quakers, who outscored opponents 222–4 and won the national championship. Smith studied chemistry in college but entered the real estate business upon graduation. At the University of Pennsylvania, he served as freshman coach in 1905 and 1906 and varsity backfield coach the next two seasons. As head coach at Pennsylvania from 1909 to 1912, Smith compiled a 29–11–3 record and developed outstanding players Ernest Cozens and Roy Mercer. His 1910 squad won 9 of 11 games and tied 1 contest. From 1913 through 1915 Smith coached Purdue University (WC) to a 12–6–3 record and developed star halfback Elmer "Ollie" Oliphant.*

From 1916 to 1925 he coached football at the University of California–Berkeley. His "Wonder Teams" (1920–1924) finished undefeated, winning 44 and tying 4 contests. California's undefeated string reached 50 games and ended in 1925 with a 15–0 loss to the Olympic Club of San Francisco. Smith compiled a 74–16–5 record at California and a 115–33–11 career mark. At California, he coached All-Americans Harold "Brick" Muller* and Edwin "Babe" Horrell. The 1920 "Wonder Team" outscored its opponents 482 to 14. Although they were underdogs in the 1921 Rose Bowl, the Golden Bears defeated the Ohio State Buckeyes 28–0 to claim the national championship. During this game Muller threw a 53-yard touchdown pass to "Brodie" Stephens. The West Coast had never witnessed a pass of this distance. Although favored to beat Washington and Jefferson in the 1922 Rose Bowl, the Golden Bears were held to a scoreless tie.

Smith knew football strategy and his rival coaches so completely that he accurately told his players what plays to expect before a game. Smith's philosophy led to the development of both football players and men. His criteria for success—aggressiveness, obedience, concentration, determination, and harmonious cooperation—made a real team. Gracious and modest in victory or defeat, he stressed truth and considered unfair victory worse than defeat. After the 1925 season Smith returned to Philadelphia for the Army-Navy game. He contracted pneumonia and died shortly thereafter in the University Hospital. His brother returned his body to Berkeley, where, memorial services were held outside the stadium. Smith belongs to the HAF College Football Hall of Fame and in 1951 was selected to the NFF College Football Hall of Fame.

BIBLIOGRAPHY: Tim Cohane, *Great College Football Coaches of the Twenties and Thirties* (New Rochelle, NY, 1973); John D. McCallum and Charles H. Pearson, *College Football U.S.A., 1869–1973* (New York, 1973); Brick Morse, *California Football History* (Berkeley, CA, 1937); *University of California Football Media Guide, 1979.*

John L. Evers

SMITH, Billy Ray, Jr. (b. 10 August 1961, Fayetteville, AR), college and professional player, is the son of investment bank manager Billy Ray Smith, Sr., and school purchasing secretary Carroll Smith and has one brother, Kevin, and two sisters, Shelly and Shannon. His father, an All-SWC football defensive tackle at the University of Arkansas, played professionally with the Los Angeles Rams, Pittsburgh Steelers, and Baltimore Colts (NFL). Smith grew up in Westminster, MD, and moved with his family in 1971 to Plano, TX, near Dallas. He graduated in 1979 from Plano High School, excelling in football, baseball, swimming, and soccer. Smith, who twice played in the Texas State 4A championship football game, demonstrated fundamental skills, agility, intellect, dedication, and an excellent attitude. The good-natured, confident, poised Smith also played the piano, bass guitar, and trombone.

Smith attended the University of Arkansas (SWC) from 1979 to 1983 and started every varsity football game for four seasons as a defensive lineman. The 6 foot, 3 inch, 231 pounder set Arkansas records by making 63 tackles behind the line of scrimmage for 343 yards in losses and became the first Razorbacks junior selected consensus All-American. Arkansas finished 10–2 in 1979, 7–5 in 1980, 8–4 in 1981, and 9–2–1 in 1982, making the top ten nationally in 1979 and 1982. The Razorbacks defeated Tulane 34–15 in the 1980 Hall of Fame Bowl and Florida 28–24 in the 1982 Bluebonnet Bowl, but lost to Alabama 24–9 in the 1980 Sugar Bowl and to North Carolina 31–27 in the 1981 Gator Bowl. Smith started off the snap of the ball so quickly and moved so unerringly that opponents routinely assigned two linemen to block him. He was named consensus All-American at defensive end in 1981 and 1982 and Washington Touchdown Club Defensive Player of the Year in 1982. Arkansas coach Lou Holtz lauded Smith as "the best football player I've ever been around," "a joy to coach," "a complete person," "a universal donor," and "an 11 on a scale of 10." A B-minus student academically, Smith left Arkansas following the Senior Bowl in January 1983, only one semester short of a Bachelor's degree in Finance and Banking.

In 1983 the Oakland Invaders (USFL) and San Diego Chargers (NFL) selected him in the first round of the respective pro drafts. After signing with the Chargers in May 1983 he was switched to right inside linebacker to utilize his speed. Smith in 1983 returned one kickoff ten yards and recovered one fumble for the defensively porous 6–10 Chargers. The Chargers finished 7–9 the next year, as Smith intercepted three passes for 41 yards (13.7–yard average) and recovered three fumbles. In 1985 he intercepted one pass for no yardage for the improving 8–8 San Diego club. During 1986 Smith recorded 11 quarterback sacks for the 4–12 Chargers and made the UPI AFC All-Star second team at inside linebacker. He married fellow Arkansas student Nina Dickinson of Houston, TX, in October 1983.

BIBLIOGRAPHY: *TSN Football Register—1986; Street & Smith's College Football Yearbooks*, 1980–1983; Rick Telander, "Like Father, Like Son," *SI*, 58 (April 25, 1983), pp. 46, 50, 62.

David L. Porter

SMITH, Bruce P. "Boo" (b. 8 February 1920, Faribault, MN; d. 28 August 1967, Minneapolis, MN), college and professional player, was awarded the 1941 Heisman Trophy as the nation's outstanding college football performer. A star halfback (1939–1941) at the University of Minnesota (WC), Smith performed on two national championship teams, made unanimous All-American, and captained the Golden Gophers his final season. The 1941 HAF Player of the Year received the Captain's Cup as the nation's top college player. Smith won the Chicago *Tribune* Trophy as the Most Valuable College All-Stars when the Chicago Bears defeated the Stars 21–0 before 101,103 at Chicago's Soldier Field. In 1972 Smith was elected to the NFF College Football Hall of Fame.

The 6 foot, 200 pound Smith was one of five children of Faribault attorney Lucius A. and Healy Smith. His father started at guard and substituted at fullback (1909–1911) on three Minnesota WC championship football teams. Bruce outgrew a bowlegged condition as a child and played on the Faribault High School varsity football team as an eighth grader. He ran the 100–yard dash in 10.0 seconds on the track squad and starred on the basketball and golf teams. An All-State basketball forward, Smith led the netters to the state high school tournament. He captained the football, basketball, and golf squads, winning a record fourteen letters. Before graduating in 1938, he also sang in the high school chorus and won a history contest.

During Smith's three varsity seasons at Minnesota, the Golden Gophers finished 3–4–1, 8–0–0, and 8–0–0 under noted coach Bernie Bierman.* Smith alternated with senior Harold Van Every at halfback his sophomore year, scoring six touchdowns and gaining 303 yards from scrimmage on 69 carries. Minnesota played four teams rated top 20 by the AP and lost four games by 20 total points. One of Smith's touchdowns in 1939 came against powerful Michigan in a 20–7 Golden Gopher upset victory. Minnesota in 1940 defeated four opponents rated in the AP top ten, including number 3 Michigan (7–6), number 7 Nebraska (13–7), number 8 Northwestern (13–12), and number

10 Washington (19–14). The Golden Gophers boasted a formidable backfield with All-Americans Smith, George Franck, and Bill Daley and rallied from behind in six of eight games. Although he completed a 41–yard touchdown pass against Nebraska and gained over 100 yards against Purdue, Michigan, and Ohio State, Smith made one carry against the Wolverines that left an indelible mark on college football history. Minnesota was behind 6–0 in the second quarter against undefeated Michigan in a contest to determine the national championship when Smith sloshed 80 yards in the mud on a weak side reverse for the tying touchdown. Joe Mernik's conversion sealed the one-point triumph before a capacity crowd of 64,000 spectators at Minneapolis. According to Coach Bierman, Smith made the big plays when they were most needed. Smith, a smooth, deceptive runner with great balance and change of pace, possessed powerful legs and used his interference well. Besides being one of the last dropkickers on conversions, he proved a true triple-threat performer as passer, runner, blocker, tackler, and punter.

A knee injury in 1941 did not deter Smith from amassing 936 all-purpose yards, averaging 4.9 yards per carry from scrimmage, and scoring six touchdowns. Minnesota was held to minus yardage without a first down in the first quarter against Iowa until Bierman inserted the lame Smith. Smith's running and passing then sparked the Golden Gophers to an overwhelming 34–14 triumph. Smith rushed for 93 and 97 yards respectively in victories over Illinois and Washington. His 68–yard punt against fifth-rated Michigan provided good field position. On the next possession, Smith completed a 44–yard pass to Herman Frickey at the Wolverine two-yard line. Frickey scored the only touchdown on the next play as the Golden Gophers triumphed 7–0. "The Smith to Frickey pass was the best executed play of the season, as close to a perfect play from every standpoint," Bierman observed. The modest, religious Smith practiced clean living and shunned personal glory. Minnesota All-American tackle Dick Wildung* once said, "Bruce was the true All-American boy. . . . Even when he got hurt and came back to play with a bad leg, he would really inspire the team. He was just a great leader."

Smith's three-year composite totals at Minnesota included 1,214 yards gained from scrimmage (4.86–yard average), 496 yards passing, 287 return yards (13–yard average), 2,074 all-purpose yards, 39.2-yard punting average, and 122 points scored. Enlisted in the Naval Reserve, Smith graduated from Minnesota in 1942 and served in the U.S. Navy during World War II. He starred on the 1942 Great Lakes Naval Training Station football team, averaging 5.9 yards per carry and being named Armed Services Player of the Year. He repeated on the All-Service team the following year with the St. Mary's (CA) Pre-Flight School while taking flight training. After being discharged in 1945, he joined the Green Bay Packers (NFL). Smith had been drafted in the eleventh round because his bad knee made his speed suspect. He played mostly on defense with the Packers (1945–1948) and Los Angeles

Rams (1949). His composite pro statistics included 660 yards gained on 108 carries (6.1–yard average), 8 pass receptions for 79 yards, and 2 touchdowns.

Smith starred in 1942 in Columbia Pictures' *Smith of Minnesota*, a movie about his life. He and his wife, Gloria, who were married in 1946, had two sons and two daughters. Smith worked in the clothing and sporting goods business in Philadelphia, Chicago, and Minneapolis. He preferred life in a small town and took a beer distributorship in Alexandria, MN, before dying of cancer at age 47. The Reverend William J. Cantwell of Minneapolis said, "This man was an inspiration to everyone at the hospital who had the good fortune to come into contact with him." In 1986 he was inducted into the Minnesota Sports Hall of Fame.

BIBLIOGRAPHY: John T. Brady, *The Heisman: A Symbol of Excellence* (New York, 1984); *Football at Minnesota* (Minneapolis, MN, 1914); Ralph Hickok, *Who Was Who in American Sports* (New York, 1971); Bill Libby, *Heroes of the Heisman Trophy* (New York, 1973); Ronald L. Mendell and Timothy B. Phares, *Who's Who in Football* (New Rochelle, NY, 1974); James P. Quirk, *Minnesota Football, The Golden Years, 1932–1941* (Minneapolis, MN, 1984); Richard Rainbolt, *Gold Glory* (Wayzata, MN, 1972).

James D. Whalen

SMITH, Charles Aaron "Bubba" "Interballistic Bubba" (b. 28 February 1945, Beaumont, TX), college and professional player, starred as a defensive football lineman at Michigan State University (BTC) and with the Baltimore Colts, Oakland Raiders, and Houston Oilers (NFL). The son of Georgia and Willie Ray Smith, he played football for his father at Charlton Pollard High School in Beaumont, TX. Under his father's tutelage, "Bubba" and his two brothers, Willie Ray, Jr., and Tody, won All-State football honors. During his senior year, Charlton Pollard compiled an 11–0 record.

At Michigan State University, Smith excelled on the outstanding 1965 and 1966 Spartans teams. The 6 foot, 8 inch, 280 pounder rushed opposing quarterbacks with such relentless ferocity that Michigan State students chanted "Kill, Bubba, Kill" whenever he took the field. The surprisingly agile, speedy Smith amazed fans and sportswriters in the Penn State game his junior year by tackling broken-field runner Mike Irwin on a kickoff return. The Pittsburgh *Press* commented that "what other eyewitnesses remember about Smith was the way he converted the Penn State offense into rubble by the end of the third quarter. At the start, [Rip] Engle's* blockers were holding him out. Each time is was just a little harder. Near the finish, Bubba was wading right through and clamping his huge paws around the neck of the Penn State quarterback." Nicknamed "Interballistic Bubba," Smith recorded 15 solo tackles, 45 assisted tackles, and dropped opposing runners ten times for 59 yards net losses his senior year. An All-American in 1965 and 1966, he was named MVP in both the College All-Star and the Senior Bowl games.

The number 1 draft choice of the Baltimore Colts (NFL), he made All-NFC in 1970–1972 and the 1971–1972 Pro Bowls. Smith recorded nine quarterback sacks and blocked four field goals in his best season (1971) and performed in the 1969 and 1971 Super Bowls with the Colts. Smith suffered a severe knee injury in 1972 when he ran into a dropped yard marker; he missed the entire season. He played from 1973 to 1975 with the Oakland Raiders (NFL) and from 1975 to 1977 with the Houston Oilers (NFL). Smith authored (with Hal De Windt) an autobiography, *Kill Bubba Kill*, (1983) and acts in television, movies, and commercials.

BIBLIOGRAPHY: Douglas F. Eilerston, *Major College Football Results 1957–81* (Kinston, NC, 1981); John D. McCallum, *Big Ten Football Since 1895* (Radnor, PA, 1976); John D. McCallum and Charles H. Pearson, *College Football U.S.A., 1869–1973* (New York, 1973); Ronald L. Mendell and Timothy B. Phares, *Who's Who in Football* (New Rochelle, NY, 1974); Bubba Smith and Hal De Windt, *Kill Bubba Kill* (New York, 1983); University of Michigan, Department of Information Services Releases, 1963–1983.

Lawrence Ziewacz

SMITH, Jackie Larue (b. 23 February 1940, Columbia, MS), college athlete and professional player, is the son of Jack Dempsey and Hazel (Gates) Smith and became a first-rate pro football tight end. At high school in Kentwood, LA, he earned four football letters as a tailback and three letters in track. He excelled in football and track at Northwestern Louisiana State College (GSC) and received a B.S. degree in Education in 1962. An excellent blocker and all-out competitor, the 6 foot, 4 inch, 230 pound Smith was selected by the St. Louis Cardinals in the tenth round of the 1963 NFL draft. Smith, one of the NFL's premier tight ends for over a decade, played with the Cardinals from 1963 through 1977. Smith's ability to combine speed along with blocking ability separated him from many talented tight ends. Smith became the all-time NFL tight end and Cardinals record-holder when he established the NFL record for pass receptions (475, since broken) and yards gained via pass receptions (7,869). He gained 7,918 yards on 480 receptions for a 16.5–yard average, ranking nineteenth among all-time NFL pass receivers. His 8,350 career combined net yards, including 327 rushing and 105 on kickoff returns, ranked second to Ollie Matson's* team record 8,509 yards.

As Cardinals offensive co-captain, Smith caught passes in 45 straight games and made 40 career touchdown receptions. In 1967 he made a career-high 56 catches for a Cardinals-record 1,205 yards and 9 touchdowns. He played in 198 games over 15 seasons, ranking second only to Jim Bakken.* A knee injury in 1971 halted his consecutive game streak at 121. From 1964 to 1966 he also handled Cardinals punting duties with a 39.1–yard average. He was named to *TSN* Eastern Conference All-Star team in 1966 and 1968 and made five successive Pro Bowls from 1967 to 1971. After being released in 1978 by the Cardinals, he played one season with the Dallas Cowboys (NFL). He appeared in the NFC championship game and Super Bowl XIII, with his team losing 35–31 to the Pittsburgh Steelers.

Smith played with tremendous enthusiasm and ideal mental approach and tried hard to be the best. A fierce competitor, he easily angered on the field if an opponent tried to intimidate him. Off the field, Smith is a soft-spoken, pleasant, drawling Southerner, a devoted family man, and a businessman. Smith, who strives for racial harmony, resides in St. Louis with his wife, Geraldine, and has four children.

BIBLIOGRAPHY: Jeff Meyers, "Like Fine Wine, Jackie Smith Gets Better With Age . . . and He Was Good to Begin With," *Profile* (1974), pp. 99–105; *St. Louis Football Cardinals Guide and Record Book, 1979; TSN Football Register—1979.*

John L. Evers

SNAVELY, Carl Grey "The Grey Fox" (b. 30 July 1894, Omaha, NE; d. 12 July 1975, St. Louis, MO), college athlete and football coach, was the oldest son of Methodist minister Charles Cameron and Jessie (Boggs) Snavely. He grew up in various Pennsylvania towns and attended high school in Danville, PA. At Lebanon Valley College (PA) he lettered in football, baseball, and basketball, belonged to the debate team and literary society, and served as senior class president. In 1915 Snavely received his B.A. degree and married Bernyce Clara Richardson. They had one child, Carl Grey, who was killed during World War II; they later adopted a son, also named Carl Grey. Snavely began his football coaching career at Kiski Prep School in 1915. From 1916 to 1923 he headed football programs at Vandergrift (PA) High, Franklin School (Cincinnati, OH), the University of Cincinnati, Marietta (OC) College, and Kiski Prep. Snavely spent the next three seasons at Bellefonte (PA) Academy, where his teams won national championships each year.

As head football coach at Bucknell University from 1927 to 1933, Snavely compiled a 42–16–8 record. His 1931 squad won the EIAA championship and included Clarke Hinkle,* one of Snavely's best-known players. At Bucknell he exhibited sound fundamentals and good organization and recruited talented players. These traits earned him the nickname "The Grey Fox." After completing his M.A. degree at Bucknell in 1933, Snavely coached the University of North Carolina (SC) to a 15–2–1 record over two seasons before moving to Cornell. Following a rare losing season in 1936, Snavely coached Cornell to three IL titles and the 1939 Lambert Trophy. Snavely, who guided Cornell to a 46–26–3 record over nine seasons, coached in the North-South game from 1938 to 1940 and headed the College All-Stars in 1941.

In 1945 Snavely returned to North Carolina, where he compiled a 44–33–4 record the next eight seasons. The Tarheels lost the 1946 and 1948 Sugar Bowls and 1949 Cotton Bowl and were paced by Charlie "Choo Choo"

Justice.* During his last three seasons at North Carolina, Snavely failed to achieve a winning record. In 1953 he moved to Washington University (St. Louis) and ended his coaching career there five years later. His overall college coaching record was 180–96–16.

Snavely, who served as president of the AFCA in 1952, was inducted into the NFF College Football Hall of Fame in 1965 and into the HAF College Football Hall of Fame. The serious-minded and hardworking Snavely keenly understood the game and excelled at adapting other systems of play for his own purposes. Snavely, a pioneer user of movies as a coaching tool, utilized lectures and quizzes to teach his players. Besides being reluctant to abandon the single wing for the T-formation, Snavely criticized the pressure exerted by alumni and administrators to win at any cost.

BIBLIOGRAPHY: Bucknell University, Athletic Public Relations, Lewisburg, PA; "Celebrating 100 Southern Conference Championships, 1888–1950," University of North Carolina at Chapel Hill, Chapel Hill, NC; Cornell University, Athletic Department, Ithaca, NY; *NYT*, July 14, 1975; "Sports News," Bucknell University February 2, 1976; Sunbury (PA) *Daily Item*, February 2, 1965, July 14, 1975; University of North Carolina at Chapel Hill, Sports Information Office, Chapel Hill, NC.

Mary I. Avery

SPEEDIE, Mac Curtis (b. 12 January 1920, Odell, IL), college athlete and professional football player and coach, suffered from a bone deficiency in his left leg at age 8. Doctors feared that Speedie would have to wear a brace for life, but after four years of painful rehabilitation with an orthopedist, he learned to walk and then run without a support. He starred in track, basketball, and football at South High School in Salt Lake City, UT. At the University of Utah, Speedie played football three years at end and was named twice to the All-RMC team. Nevertheless, he won most acclaim for his excellent track accomplishments in the dashes and hurdles, setting the RMC record for the 220–yard low hurdles.

He entered the U.S. Army in March 1942 and served until June 1946 with the rank of first lieutenant. While playing service football, he was "discovered" by coach Paul Brown* when Speedie's soldiers met Brown's Great Lakes team in 1945. Although Great Lakes won easily, Brown was extremely impressed by the young player with the apt name. After World War II, Coach Brown made his great Cleveland Browns the dominant team of the NFL-rival AAFC. The Browns won the AFFC championship each year from 1946 through 1949. When the NFL and AAFC made peace in 1950, the Browns joined the NFL and continued to win titles there.

Speedie, one of the Browns' most potent weapons, teamed with Dante Lavelli,* another unknown discovered by Brown. Speedie and Lavelli gave quarterback Otto Graham* the best tandem of receivers in pro football.

Speedie and/or Lavelli made every important All-League team from 1946 through 1952. Speedie, who set the AAFC record with 211 receptions, was named to the All-AAFC Team (1947–1949), the UPI squads (1946, 1948–1950, 1952), and the AP teams (1947–1949). He especially proved formidable after catching the ball because his speed and agility made him a real breakaway threat. After leading the NFL with 62 receiptions in 1952, Speedie played in the CFL with Regina in 1953 and 1954 and Vancouver in 1955. During his NFL career, he caught 349 passes for 5,602 yards (16.3-yard average) and 33 touchdowns.

In the early 1960s the 6 foot, 3 inch, 215 pound Speedie served as an assistant coach with both the Houston Oilers and Denver Broncos of the AFL. He became Bronco head coach after the fourth game of the 1964 season and held that post through the second game of 1966 with a 6–19–1 composite record. Speedie and his wife, Lynne, have one son and one daughter. After leaving the Broncos, he worked with Wilson Sporting Goods Company.

BIBLIOGRAPHY: Bob Braunwart and Bob Carroll, "Big Mac of the Browns' Attack," *The Coffin Corner* 4 (January, 1982), pp. 1–3; Ronald L. Mendell and Timothy B. Phares, *Who's Who in Football* (New Rochelle, NY, 1974); Mac Speedie file, Pro Football Hall of Fame, Canton, OH.

Robert N. Carroll

SPURRIER, Stephen Orr "Steve" (b. 20 April 1945, Miami Beach, FL), college and professional player and coach, is the son of Presbyterian minister and Erskine College football player Graham Spurrier. The 6 foot, 2 inch, 203 pound Spurrier attended Science Hill High School in Johnson City, TN, where he starred in football, basketball, and baseball. In 1963 Spurrier accepted a football scholarship at the University of Florida (SEC) and eventually broke every Gators game, season, and career passing and total offense record. Besides taking the Gators to consecutive 1966 Sugar and 1967 Orange Bowl appearances, he in 1966 set SEC season records for most pass attempts, completions, and passing yardage. His honors included being All-SEC Sophomore of the Year, SEC MVP in 1966, and All-SEC quarterback his junior and senior years. He in 1966 won the Heisman Trophy as college football's most outstanding player and made the 1965 and 1966 All-American squads. As a three-year starter, Spurrier completed 392 of 692 passing attempts for 4,848 yards and 36 touchdowns and compiled 5,290 yards total offense.

A first-round draft choice of the San Francisco 49ers (NFL), he played there from 1967 through 1975. After five seasons as John Brodie's* backup quarterback, he started the 1972 campaign, passed for 1,983 yards, and completed 54 percent of his attempts. Spurrier in 1976 and 1977 quarterbacked for the expansion Tampa Bay Buccaneers (NFL). Spurrier, a natural all-around athlete, possessed an even disposition and active brain, and functioned best in crucial situations. With all the fame he achieved, he remained largely unchanged in personality and outlook, a team player, humble, and unaffected.

After the 1977 campaign, Spurrier retired as an active player. He served as assistant football coach at the University of Florida (SEC) in 1978 and Georgia Tech in 1979 and spent 1980 through 1982 as Duke University's (ACC) offensive coordinator. In 1983 the Tampa Bay Bandits of the USFL named Spurrier its head coach. The youngest head coach in pro football at age 37, he completed the 1983 season with an 11–7–0 record to finish third in the Central Division. In 1984 Tampa Bay tied for first place in the Southern Division with a 14–4 record but lost to Birmingham 36–17 in the Eastern Division playoffs. The next year, Tampa Bay compiled a 10–8 mark and was defeated by Oakland 48–27 in the quarter-finals. The USFL suspended its operations for the fall 1986 season while seeking a new trial in its suit against the NFL for damages or injunctive relief from the courts. Spurrier married Jerri Starr, has three children, Lisa, Amy, and Steve, and resides in Tampa, FL.

BIBLIOGRAPHY: *Georgia Tech Football Media Guide, 1979;* Tom McEwen, *The Gators: A Story of Florida Football* (Huntsville, AL, 1974); *TSN Football Register—1976; USFL Media Guide, 1983; USA Today*, December 23, 1986.

John L. Evers

STABLER, Ken Michael "The Snake" (b. 25 December 1945, Foley, AL), college and professional player, is the son of shop foreman, Leroy Stabler, and a nurse and attended Foley High School, where he played quarterback. His team won two state championships and lost only once in his three varsity seasons. At the University of Alabama (SEC), he played under coach Paul "Bear" Bryant* as reserve quarterback behind Steve Sloan before assuming the starting position in 1966. In Stabler's first season as regular quarterback, Alabama won all eleven games and defeated Nebraska in the Sugar Bowl. In 1967 he was disciplined and later reinstated by Coach Bryant. Alabama compiled an 8–1–1 record and lost the Cotton Bowl to Texas A&M University. The 6 foot, 3 inch, 210 pounder graduated in 1968 with a Bachelor's degree in Physical Education.

In 1968 he was selected by the Oakland Raiders in the second round of the AFL-NFL draft. During his first season, he played on the taxi squad and with the Spokane, WA, Shockers (ConFL). Because of domestic problems, he did not perform in 1969. In 1973 Stabler became starting Oakland quarterback after the Raiders lost two of their first three games. Stabler guided the Raiders to the AFC playoffs, where they lost 27–10 to the Miami Dolphins. He directed the Raiders to the 1974 and 1975 AFC championship games and 1976 Super Bowl with a 13–1 regular season record. In the Super Bowl, Stabler led the Raiders to a 32–14 victory over the Minnesota Vikings by completing 12 of 19 passes for 180 yards and one touchdown. In 1977 the Raiders finished 11–3 in the regular season but lost 20–17 to the Denver Broncos in the AFC championship. For the next two seasons, the Raiders compiled 9–7 marks and failed to make the playoffs. Stabler experienced a subpar season in 1978 due to injuries and argued publicly with Raiders' owner Allen "Al" Davis.* Free of injury in 1979, he directed Oakland to season records in yards gained (3,615) and passes completed (498).

Before the 1980 campaign, Stabler surprisingly was traded to the Houston Oilers (NFL) for quarterback Dan Pastorini. Although completing 64 percent of his passes, he threw for only 13 touchdowns and 28 interceptions. He almost retired in 1981, but when reserve quarterback Gifford Nielson was injured in training camp, he returned and led the Oilers to a 7–9 mark. Before the 1982 season he was traded to the New Orleans Saints (NFL). He led the Saints to a 4–5 record in the strike-shortened season, passing for 1,343 yards and 6 touchdowns. He retained the starting quarterback position in 1983 despite competition from reserve Dave Wilson. Stabler, who retired after the 1984 campaign, completed 2,270 of 3,793 passes (60 percent) for 27,938 yards and 194 touchdowns and scored 4 touchdowns.

Nicknamed "The Snake" for his quick pass releases and swift movement afoot, Stabler was noted for his long hair, bearded appearance, and fast lifestyle before he married. He displayed rare touch and great passing accuracy in short to medium ranges, but he also seemed injury-prone and reluctant to run with the ball. Stabler threw left-handed, quite unusual for an NFL quarterback, and proved a natural field leader. His personal records included compiling an NFL passing rating of 103.7 in 1976 and being career passing leader for the Raiders (19,078 yards). Stabler led the NFL in passing percentage with 62.7 percent (1973) and 66.7 percent (1976) and touchdown passes with 26 (1974). He played in the 1973, 1974, and 1977 Pro Bowls and was named AFC Player of the Year by *TSN* in 1974 and 1976.

BIBLIOGRAPHY: Paul W. Bryant and John Underwood, *Bear* (New York, 1974); Zander Hollander, ed., *Complete Handbook of Pro Football, 1981* (New York, 1981); Murray Olderman, ed., *Super* (Oakland, CA, 1981); Jack Park, ed., *Football Action, 1983* (New York, 1983); Ken Rappoport, *Cowboys, Raiders* (New York, 1982); Lou Sahadi, *Ken Stabler and the Oakland Raiders* (New York, 1977); Ken Stabler and Dick O'Connor, *Super Bowl Diary: The Autobiography of Ken 'The Snake' Stabler* (Los Angeles, 1977); Ken Stabler with Barry Stainback, *Snake* (New York, 1986); *TSN Football Register—1982*.

Keith Hobson

STAGG, Amos Alonzo "The Grand Old Man of the Midway" "Mr. Integrity" (b. 16 August 1862, West Orange, NJ; d. 17 March 1965, Stockton, CA), college athlete and coach, was the son of shoemaker Amos L. and Eunice P. Stagg, both of English descent. The fifth of eight children, Stagg worked odd jobs during high school to augment the family's meager income.

After graduating from Orange High School, he received a scholarship to Phillips Exeter Academy and excelled there as a baseball player. He declined a baseball scholarship to Dartmouth College and entered Yale University (IL) to study for the ministry. He pitched Yale to five consecutive Big Three baseball championships and was named to Camp's first All-American football team in 1889. After graduation from Yale in 1888, he spurned a baseball offer from the New York Giants (NL) and entered Yale Divinity School. Upon learning that he was not a good speaker, Stagg became a physical educator. He enrolled at the YMCA Training School at Springfield, MA, where he studied and lectured from 1890 to 1892. He coached the football team and played in the first historic basketball game at Springfield. Stagg helped James Naismith* (IS) in the early development of basketball and in 1891 coached his Springfield team in the first indoor football game at Madison Square Garden in New York.

At age 30 in 1892, Stagg was appointed associate professor and director of physical culture and athletics at the University of Chicago (WC). Stagg, the first coach to have academic status, was promoted to professor in 1900 and remained at Chicago until 1932, when he reached the mandatory retirement age of 70. During his forty years there, Stagg made virtually unmatched contributions to athletics in general and football in particular. Chicago's faculty representative to the WC for fifteen years, he proved most influential in the formation and early growth of the WC. He served on the NCAA's first Rules Committee, making notable contributions. Besides being on Olympic committees from 1902 to 1932, he helped coach U.S. track athletes for the 1924 Olympic games. In 1910 and 1911 he presided over the Society of Directors of Physical Education, the national men's college physical education group, and belonged to the first Board of Governors as NCAA representative of the NAAF. Nicknamed "Mr. Integrity," he was renowned for his honesty. One BTC book dedicated to Stagg states that he "provided an example, without parallel, of what is right and fitting in college sports."

Some authorities consider Stagg the greatest name in football history. "The Grand Old Man of the Midway" became the game's most prolific inventor and master strategist. His innovations included the center snap, huddle, lateral pass, man in motion, unbalanced line, cross blocking, onside kick, T formation, hidden ball trick, placekick, spread punt formation, fake punt, Statue of Liberty play, backfield shifts, and over a thousand other football plays. Moreover, he became the first coach to write a football book with diagrams, have players do wind sprints, use a tackling dummy (which he invented), put numbers on players' jerseys, have players wear hip pads and knit pants, put lights on the practice field, and award letters to deserving players. He also designed the indoor batting cage in baseball and the troughs for overflow in swimming pools.

During Stagg's football career at Chicago, he coached four undefeated football squads, won seven WC titles, compiled 255 victories, and developed eleven All-Americans (subsequently five others). His 1894 team played the first post-season intercollegiate game, defeating Stanford 24–4 on Christmas Day in San Francisco. In 1914 the University of Chicago renamed the football field Stagg Field, the first time a football coach was so honored. He also introduced basketball at Chicago, coached seven WC basketball champions, and conducted the NIBA tournament in Chicago for thirteen years.

From 1933 to 1946 he coached football at the College of the Pacific (FWC). At age 81, Stagg in 1943 coached his team to seven victories against major opponents and was selected Coach of the Year. After resigning as head coach in 1946, he served the next six years as assistant coach to one of his sons at Susquehanna College (PA). Since his ailing wife, Stella, needed a warmer climate, Stagg returned to the West Coast and served six years as punting and kicking coach at Stockton JC. Following a remarkable 71 years of coaching, he retired at age 98. No active football coach served longer in the game's history. His phenomenal 314–181–35 record remained unchallenged until surpassed in 1982 by Paul "Bear" Bryant.*

Stagg received numerous other prestigious honors. Besides earning the Honor Award in 1931 from the present American Alliance for Health, Physical Education, Recreation, and Dance, he was granted honorary degrees from Springfield College and the College of Wooster. In 1939 the AFCA began presenting the Stagg Award to any person, group, or institution advancing football and perpetuating the example and influence of Stagg. In 1940 at age 78, Stagg was presented an award by the Touchdown Club of New York for meritorious service. He was inducted into the NFF College Football Hall of Fame in 1958 at age 96 as a coach and player, the only person honored in both categories. His picture appeared on the cover of *Time* that same year. Additional honors included induction into the HAF College Football Hall of Fame and being named at age 93 the greatest living American by the U.S. Chamber of Commerce. In 1959 he was elected to the Naismith Memorial Basketball Hall of Fame as a contributor. The first Heisman Trophy was awarded to one of his premier football players, John "Jay" Berwanger,* while the Stagg Bowl is played annually for the NCAA Division III national title.

Married for sixty-nine years to Stella Robertson of New York, he had two sons and one daughter. Stagg spent his last few years at a Stockton, CA, nursing home, suffering from Parkinson's disease and cataracts. The Dean of Coaches died at 102, having contributed perhaps more than any other football coach. As one source stated, "A. A. Stagg did not invent football, it only seems that way." No one contributed more to the game's evolution, as "The Grand Old Man" epitomized all that was fine and decent in intercollegiate athletics.

BIBLIOGRAPHY: "Coach," *Time* 59 (June 16, 1952), p. 58; Alfred Eisenstadt, "Adding to Years of Life," *Time* 72 (October 20, 1958), pp. 62–68, 73–76; "Grand Old Man," *Time* 32 (November 21, 1938), p. 47; Dean Hill, *Football Thru the Years* (New York,

1928); Arleen Keylin and Jonathan Cohen, eds., *New York Times Sports Hall of Fame* (New York, 1981); Robert Leckie, *The Story of Football* (New York, 1972); *NCAB* 18 (1922), p. 199; Ron Newsome, "Amos Alonzo Stagg—Football's Grand Old Man," *Journal of Health, Physical Education, and Recreation* 44 (January, 1973), pp. 77–78; "Stagg Saga," *Newsweek* 28 (December 16, 1946), pp. 90–91; "Stagg's Century," *Newsweek* 60 (August 13, 1962), p. 48; "Stagg Formulas," *Newsweek* 38 (August 27, 1951), pp. 76, 78; Kenneth L. "Tug" Wilson and Jerry Brondfield, *The Big Ten* (Englewood Cliffs, NJ, 1967).

Joanna Davenport

STALLWORTH, Johnny Lee "John" (b. 15 July 1952, Tuscaloosa, AL), college and professional player, has excelled at wide receiver for the Pittsburgh Steelers (NFL) since 1974. With Lynn Swann,* Jack Lambert,* and Mike Webster,* he was included in a draft that helped the Steelers capture four Super Bowl championships (1975–1976, 1979–1980) in a six-year period. Stallworth graduated from Tuscaloosa High School, where he played football. At Alabama A&M (SIAC) he made 103 career receptions, caught 48 passes for 925 yards and 7 touchdowns as a senior, twice earned All-SIAC recognition, and participated in the Senior Bowl. In 1974 he earned a B.S. degree in business administration and finance.

As a Steeler, Stallworth has twice been named MVP (1979 and 1984) and played in Pro Bowls following the 1979, 1982, and 1984 seasons. He holds club records for career receptions (492), receiving yardage (8,163) and touchdowns (61), passing Swann in these categories in 1984. Because of injury, he played only four regular-season games in 1983, but he dramatically rebounded with his best season. In 1984 he made 78 receptions for 1,356 yards, one of the 15 best single-season yardage totals in NFL history. His previous best effort came in the last Steelers championship season of 1979, when he caught a then-team record 70 passes for 1,183 yards. In 1985 he caught 75 passes for 937 yards and 5 touchdowns. In 1986 he caught only 34 passes and missed several games because of injuries. Stallworth's greatest games have included post-season play. In 1976 the AFC final against the Oakland Raiders was decided by his 20–yard touchdown reception. In the 1978 first round against the Denver Broncos, he caught a then-record 10 passes. In the 1979 Super Bowl against the Dallas Cowboys, he gained 115 yards on 3 receptions and scored 28–yard and 75–yard touchdowns. The following January against the Los Angeles Rams, he made one of his patented leaping catches of a Terry Bradshaw* aerial for 73 yards and gained 121 yards in the Super Bowl win. Stallworth also played in the AFC Championship game following the 1984 season.

At 6 feet, 2 inches, and 190 pounds, Stallworth combines great speed with various moves and ranks among football's most feared receivers. During the off-season he and his wife, Flo, and children, Natasha and John, Jr., reside in

Huntsville, AL. He engages in real estate development and civic service, including Multiple Sclerosis, the American Lung Association, and Sheriff's Boys' Ranch. In 1979 he was named Alabama's Professional Athlete of the Year.

BIBLIOGRAPHY: Tom Bennett et al., *The NFL's Official Encyclopedic History of Professional Football* (New York, 1977); Pittsburgh Steelers, Office of Public Relations, Pittsburgh, PA.

Leonard Frey

STANFEL, Richard "Dick" (b. 20 July 1927, San Francisco, CA), college and professional player and coach, is the son of a tavern owner and attended Commerce High School in his native city. After serving in the U.S. Army Signal Corps, Stanfel performed for Coach Joe Kuharich's outstanding University of San Francisco Dons (1948–1950) and was selected All-Pacific Coast and All-American guard in 1950. Following his collegiate career, he played in the College All-Star and Shrine All-Star (East-West) games (1951) and served as an assistant coach (1959–1963) to Otto Graham* for the College All-Stars.

A second-round selection of the Detroit Lions in the 1951 NFL draft, the 6 foot, 3 inch, 240 pound offensive guard excelled for the Lions (1952–1955) and Washington Redskins (1956–1958). The Lions won the Western Conference championship in 1953 and defeated the Cleveland Browns (17–16) for the NFL title. Detroit repeated as Western Conference champion in 1954 but lost the title to Cleveland 56–10 in 1955. Stanfel's excellent performance earned him the NFL's MVP Award (1954), the only offensive lineman ever to win that honor. The outstanding offensive guard made All-Pro five times (1953–1954, 1956–1958), played in five Pro Bowl games, and captained the Redskins three seasons. He was chosen to the All-Pro squad of the 1950s by the Hall of Fame selection committee.

Following the 1958 season, Stanfel became assistant football coach at the University of Notre Dame under Joe Kuharich (1959–1962) and the University of California–Berkeley (AAWU, 1963) under Marv Levy. Stanfel served as offensive line coach under Kuharich (1964–1968) and Jerry Williams (1969–1970) for the Philadelphia Eagles (NFL). Between 1971 and 1975 he was offensive line coach and coordinator for Dick Nolan with the San Francisco 49ers (NFL). Stanfel joined Hank Stram* (1976–1977) and Dick Nolan (1978–1980) as offensive line coach for the New Orleans Saints (NFL) and replaced Nolan as interim coach after 12 games, finishing the 1980 season with a 1–3–0 record. His only victory came in a 21–20 triumph over the New York Jets. Stanfel, who has served as the Chicago Bears' offensive line coach under Neil Armstrong and Mike Ditka* since 1981, married Marge Weber in December 1962, and has three sons, Richard, Scott, and Jon.

BIBLIOGRAPHY: *New Orleans Saints Media Guide, 1977; Official NFL Record and Fact Book* (New York, 1984); *Philadelphia Eagles Media Guide, 1964.*

John L. Evers

STARR, Bryan Bartlett "Bart" (b. 9 January 1934, Montgomery, AL), college and professional player, coach, and announcer, is the son of retired U.S. Air Force master sergeant Benjamin and Lula (Tucker) Starr. At Sidney Lanier High School in Montgomery, Starr in 1951 was named to the high school All-American team. Starr attended the University of Alabama (1952–1956), earning a B.S. degree. He led the Crimson Tide (SEC) to a 61–6 1953 Orange Bowl triumph over Syracuse University and 28–6 loss to Rice Institute in the 1954 Cotton Bowl.

The seventeenth-round choice of the Green Bay Packers in the 1956 NFL draft, Starr struggled to remain in the NFL. For four seasons he shared the quarterbacking duties before he gained regular status late in the 1959 season under first-year coach Vince Lombardi.* Starr played his entire career at Green Bay (1956–1971) and guided the Packers in six playoff appearances. The Packers in 1960 lost the NFL title to the Philadelphia Eagles but captured the 1961 and 1962 NFL crowns with victories over the New York Giants. Starr quarterbacked Green Bay to consecutive NFL titles in 1965, 1966, and 1967 and led the Packers to successive triumphs in the first two Super Bowls (1967–1968), being voted the game's MVP both times.

Starr paced the Packers in passing (1958–1970) and led the NFL three times (1962, 1964, 1966) in aerials. Named All-Pro once (1966) and to the Pro Bowl on four occasions (1961–1963, 1966), Starr established NFL marks for lifetime passing efficiency (57.4 percent) and lowest percentage of passes intercepted for a season (1.20) and shared the record for fewest passes intercepted in a season (3). He still holds the NFL record for most consecutive passes attempted without an interception (294). In 16 seasons Starr completed 1,808 of 3,149 passes (57.4 percent) for 24,718 yards and 152 touchdowns, ranked eighth on the all-time NFL pass rating list, and excelled in post-season play. During six NFL title games, he completed 84 of 145 passes (57.9 percent) for 1,090 yards, 11 touchdowns, and only 1 interception. At two Super Bowls, Starr completed 29 of 47 attempts (61.7 percent) for 452 yards, 3 touchdowns, and 1 interception.

Following his retirement as a player, Starr became the quarterback coach for the Packers until resigning in 1973. A successful automobile dealer, Starr also proved a popular analyst on CBS-TV's NFL football telecasts during the 1973 and 1974 seasons. He was named head coach of Green Bay in 1975 and held that position until being dismissed following the 1983 season. In nine NFL seasons Starr's teams won 52 games, lost 76, and tied 3. Green Bay's highest finish came in 1978, when the Packers tied for first place in their division and still did not make the playoffs. In 1982 the Packers gained a playoff berth but lost in the second round. Starr married Cherry Morton on May 8, 1954, and has two sons, Bart, Jr., and Bret. During his playing career, Starr won the NFL's MVP (1966), Byron White Award (1967), and NFL Gladiator Award (1969) and was named Pro Football Player of the Decade by the Columbus Touchdown Club (1970). Starr in 1977 was elected to the Green Bay and Pro Football Halls of Fame.

BIBLIOGRAPHY: *Green Bay Packers Media Guide, 1977; TSN Football Register—1983.*

John L. Evers

STAUBACH, Roger Thomas "The Dodger" (b. 5 February 1942, Silverton, OH), college athlete and professional football player, is the son of manufacturing representative Robert and Elizabeth (Smyth) Staubach. At Purcell High School in Cincinnati, OH, Staubach made All-Ohio in football, basketball, and baseball. After failing the U.S. Naval Academy entrance exam, Staubach attended New Mexico Military Institute in 1961, made the JC All-American football team, and was named All-Conference in basketball and baseball there. At the U.S. Naval Academy (1962–1965), Staubach his junior season quarterbacked the Midshipmen to a 9–1–0 record. Staubach appeared in the Cotton Bowl against the University of Texas, which defeated Navy 28–6. Staubach in 1963 was selected All-American, won the Heisman Trophy and Maxwell Award as the nation's outstanding college football player, and received the Walter Camp Trophy as the Player of the Year. Besides lettering in basketball and baseball, Staubach for three consecutive years received the Thompson Trophy as the best overall Academy athlete. As the outstanding senior athlete, Staubach was presented the Academy Sword and saw his jersey (number 12) retired. Staubach completed 292 of 463 passes for 3,571 yards during his college career, threw or ran for 35 touchdowns, and compiled 4,253 total yards on offense. His .631 pass completion percentage remains a Naval Academy record. After graduation in 1965, Staubach captained the College All-Stars against the Cleveland Browns.

Following his selection (as future choice) by the Dallas Cowboys in the tenth round of the 1964 NFL draft, Staubach spent four years in the U.S. Navy. After serving one year as backfield coach for the Plebes and one year in Vietnam, Staubach quarterbacked the Pensacola, FL Naval Air Station Goshawks in 1967 and 1968 before receiving his discharge in July 1969. After joining the Dallas Cowboys in 1969 as a 27–year-old rookie, the 6 foot, 2 inch, 197 pound Staubach served two seasons as a reserve quarterback and then replaced Craig Morton during the 1971 season. Staubach led the Cowboys to a 24–3 victory over the Miami Dolphins in Super Bowl VI and was named the game's MVP. After injuries sidelined him during the 1972 season, Staubach quarterbacked the Cowboys from 1973 through 1979 and guided them to Super Bowl appearances following the 1975, 1977, and 1978 seasons.

Dallas lost to the Pittsburgh Steelers in Super Bowls X and XIII (21–17 and 35–31) and captured Super Bowl XII with a 27–10 victory over the Denver Broncos. In four Super Bowls, Staubach completed 61 of 98 passes (a record) for 734 yards, 8 touchdowns and a .622 pass completion percentage. He led the Cowboys (1971, 1973–1979) and the NFL (1971, 1973, 1977–1979) in passing and in 1977 paced the NFL in nearly every passing department. In his 11 pro seasons, Staubach completed 1,685 of 2,958 passes for 22,700 yards and 153 touchdowns (all Cowboys records). Staubach, a scrambling quarterback, compiled a .570 pass completion percentage and rushed 410 times for 2,264 yards and 20 touchdowns. Besides being selected to *TSN* NFC All-Star Teams (1971, 1976–1977, 1979), Staubach was named NFC Player of the Year in 1971 and played in the Pro Bowl following the 1971, 1976, 1978, and 1979 seasons. In 1985 he was elected to the Pro Football Hall of Fame.

Staubach married Marianne Hoobler on September 4, 1965, and has five children, Jennifer, Michelle, Stephanie, Jeffrey, and Amy. Since his retirement, Staubach has served as a television sports commentator, been associated with a plastics company and the real estate business, and participates in numerous Dallas civic projects, including the Fellowship of Christian Athletes.

BIBLIOGRAPHY: Bill Libby, *Heroes of the Heisman Trophy* (New York, 1973); *Official Dallas Cowboys Handbook, 1977;* Roger Staubach with Sam Blair and Bob St. John, *Staubach First Down, Lifetime To Go* (New York, 1974); *TSN Football Register—1980.*

John L. Evers

STAUTNER, Ernest "Ernie" (b. 20 April 1925, Cham, Germany), college and professional player and coach, starred as a defensive tackle for the Pittsburgh Steelers (NFL) from 1950 through 1963. Although the Steelers never won a championship during Stautner's career, he led an NFL defensive unit regarded as the most rugged. The son of Bavarian immigrants who settled on an upstate New York farm, Stautner played high school football without his father's knowledge and against his expressed wishes. After graduating from high school, he served in the U.S. Marine Corps from 1943 to 1946. He attended Boston College and achieved All-American status there as a two-way lineman under coach Dennis Myers.

In 1950 the Pittsburgh Steelers (NFL) made him their second draft choice. Stautner spent his entire fourteen-year career with Pittsburgh, playing in 173 games and recovering 21 lifetime fumbles. His three career safeties tied him for second on the all-time NFL list. The 6 foot, 1 inch, 235 pound defensive tackle compensated for his smallish size with strength, aggressiveness, and durability. Stautner used huge, punishing hands to claw his way into the opponent's backfield and was named to nine Pro Bowls from 1953 through 1962. The UPI picked Stautner as All-NFL defensive tackle in 1956, while both the UPI and the AP selected him in 1958 for that honor.

Stautner, who owned and operated an open-air theatre in Lake Placid, NY, during off-seasons, was named to the Steelers' all-time team selected in 1982. He made the All-Pro squad of the 1950s, chosen by the Pro Football Hall of Fame Selection Committee. After retiring from the Steelers, Stautner joined the Dallas Cowboys (NFL) as an assistant football coach in 1966. As defensive coordinator at Dallas, Stautner developed the Cowboys' doomsday and flex defenses that proved key ingredients in the club's legendary long-term success. Stautner, the father of three children, was inducted into the Pro Football Hall of Fame in his first year of eligibility (1969).

BIBLIOGRAPHY: Ray Didinger, *Pittsburgh Steelers* (New York, 1974); Pat Livingston, *The Pittsburgh Steelers: A Pictorial History* (Virginia Beach, VA, 1980); Ronald L. Mendell and Timothy B. Phares, *Who's Who in Football* (New Rochelle, NY, 1974); George Sullivan, *Pro Football A to Z* (New York, 1975); Roger Treat, ed., *The Encyclopedia of Football*, 16th rev. ed., rev. by Pete Palmer (New York, 1979).

Frank Thackeray

STEINKUHLER, Dean Elmer (b. 27 January 1961, Syracuse, NE), college and professional player, is the son of Elmer and Maxine Steinkuhler. A five-position performer in eight-man football at Sterling (NE) High School, Steinkuhler earned All-Conference and Class D All-State honors. He was named State Defensive Player of the Year by the *Lincoln* (NE) *Journal-Star* and also lettered in basketball and track. Steinkuhler attended the University of Nebraska, where he majored in criminal justice. He started at offensive guard for the 1979 Cornhuskers (BEC) freshmen, was redshirted in 1980, lettered as a substitute in 1981, and started in 1982. The co-captain of the 1983 squad, Steinkuhler became the fastest lineman in Nebraska history with a 4.67 second time for 40 yards. Steinkuhler, an avid strength enthusiast, increased his bench press to 350 pounds and body weight to 275 pounds. In 1983 he spearheaded Nebraska's offensive line that helped the Cornhuskers capture a second straight national rushing and scoring title championship in Division I NCAA play.

In three varsity football seasons (1981–1983), Steinkuhler played on Cornhuskers teams with an overall 33–5–0 record and three Orange Bowl appearances. Nebraska was undefeated in 12 games prior to the 1984 Orange Bowl and ranked as the nation's number 1 team. A 31–30 loss to the University of Miami cost Nebraska the national championship. Steinkuhler's most memorable play came in this game when he picked up a purposely fumbled ball and ran 19 yards for Nebraska's first score. A devastating blocker, Steinkuhler helped pave the way for teammate Mike Rozier* to win the Heisman Trophy in 1983. The same year Steinkuhler won the Outland Award, given annually to the nation's best interior lineman by the FWAA.

It marked only the second time that linemen from the same school have won the award consecutive seasons. He also received the Vince Lombardi Rotary Award as the year's outstanding college lineman. For the first time, players from the same school also won this award in consecutive seasons. The All-American selection was voted UPI's Lineman of the Year, became a consensus All-BEC choice (1982–1983), and participated in the Hula and Japan bowls.

The finest offensive lineman in Nebraska football history, Steinkuhler was selected second in the entire 1984 NFL draft. For the third consecutive year, the Houston Oilers drafted the nation's top-rated lineman. Steinkuhler became a member of their offensive line at guard in 1984, until sidelined in early November with a knee injury. He spent much of the 1985 season on the injured reserve list with a knee injury, but returned to the active list for the 5–11 Oilers in 1986.

BIBLIOGRAPHY: *Houston Oilers Football Media Guide, 1984; University of Nebraska Football Media Guide, 1983; TSN Football Register—1986.*

John L. Evers

STOREY, Edward J. "Doc" (b. 10 May 1901, Somerville, MA), kicking authority, attended Brewster Academy and received a B.S. degree in Engineering from the University of New Hampshire in 1922. After earning his Doctorate of Education degree in Health Administration from New York University in 1941, he became known as "Doc." Storey was appointed director of health and physical education for the Mamaroneck (NY) public schools in 1926 and held the position thirty-five years. As football coach at Mamaroneck High School, he began studying the kicking game because his team was defeated badly by it. In 1928 he befriended former Princeton punter Leroy Mills, who later wrote *Kicking the American Football* (1932), the first full-length book on the subject.

He married Helen F. Farley in 1932 and had two children, Edward J., Jr., and Helen W. The same year at the World's Fair in New York, he conducted the famous Academy of Sport and held his first kicking camp. Storey taught punting, placekicking, and dropkicking with the help of Charles Brickley,* former Harvard kicking great. By applying his engineering and physics work to kicking, he made that skill a scientific study. As his reputation grew, so did the number of students attending his kicking camps. He has conducted camps since 1932 throughout the nation and has held his own camps in Fort Lauderdale, FL, and now in South Deerfield, MA. He has trained such pro kickers as Danny Miller and Al Del Greco.

Storey invented the baseball batting tee used by little leaguers and designed the small football used by elementary and junior high school players. He has written two books, *Secrets of Kicking the Football* (1971) and *How to Kick the Football* (1981). The *NYT* called the 5 foot, 3 inch author "the greatest living authority on kicking." During the past fifty years he has written many articles on kicking for the *Athletic Journal*. In 1979 he appeared in an *SI* article entitled "When in Doubt, Punt."

BIBLIOGRAPHY: Richard Gonsalves, interview with Edward J. Storey, January 15, 1986; Edward J. Storey, *How to Kick the Football* (West Point, NY, 1981); Rick Telander, "When in Doubt, Punt," *SI* 51 (November, 1979), pp. 100–102.

Richard Gonsalves

STRAM, Henry Louis "Hank" (b. 3 January 1924, Chicago, IL), college athlete, professional coach, and announcer, is the son of Henry L. and Nellie Stram and starred in baseball and as an All-State football halfback at Lew Wallace High School in Gary, IN. Stram entered Purdue University (WC) on a football scholarship in 1941 and served in the U.S. Army between 1942 and 1945. In 1946 he returned to Purdue and graduated two years later with a Bachelor's degree in Physical Education. At Purdue, Stram won four letters in baseball and three in football. In November 1953, Stram married the former Phyllis Pesha and has six children, Hank, Jr., Dale, Stu, Julie, Gary, and Mary Nell. Upon graduation, Stram served as backfield football coach at Purdue (BTC) for the next eight years. In 1956 Stram joined SMU (SWC) as assistant coach and spent two seasons at the University of Notre Dame in the same capacity. After a one-year stint as assistant coach at the University of Miami (FL), Stram became head coach of the Dallas Texans in the new AFL. As a college assistant coach, Stram helped develop All-American quarterbacks Dale Samuels and Len Dawson* of Purdue, George Izo of Notre Dame, and Fran Curci of Miami.

Under Stram, the Dallas Texans won the 1962 AFL championship with a 20–17 overtime victory over the Houston Oilers in the then longest football game over played (77 minutes and 54 seconds). In 1963 the Dallas franchise was moved to Kansas City. Three years later, the Chiefs captured the AFL flag and lost to the Green Bay Packers 35–10 in Super Bowl I. Stram again guided the Chiefs to the AFL crown in 1969 and experienced the highlight of his career in January 1970, when the Chiefs upset the Minnesota Vikings 23–7 in Super Bowl IV. As coach 15 years with the Dallas–Kansas City franchise and two seasons with the New Orleans Saints (1976–1977), Stram compiled one Super Bowl victory, three AFL championships, and five Western Division championships. He recorded 136 wins, 100 losses, and 10 ties, ranking him ninth on the all-time list of pro coaching victories. Stram, the only head coach to start and finish with the AFL (1960–1969), was named AFL and Pro Football Coach of the Year on three occasions. The inventive Stram proved an imaginative offensive and defensive tactician: he developed the moving quarterback pocket, had the tight end shift out of the backfield to create indecision, employed the famous "stack" defense to cause a change in blocking assignments, and devised several misdirection plays to counter the Minnesota Vikings' quick reaction and pursuit in Super Bowl IV.

Since retirement from coaching, Stram has earned acclaim with CBS Television Sports as an analyst commentator and played a major role in that network's award winning coverage of Super Bowl X. He works with veteran announcer Jack Buck* (OS) covering NFL games for CBS Radio Sports. Stram, who speaks frequently and travels countless miles, enjoys golf and paddle ball, both of which he plays exceptionally well.

BIBLIOGRAPHY: Joe McGuff, *Winning It All—The Chiefs of the AFL* (Garden City, NY, 1970); *New Orleans Saints Media Guide, 1977; TSN Football Register—1976.*

John L. Evers

STRONG, Elmer Kenneth, Jr. "Ken" (b. 6 August 1906, West Haven, CT; d. 5 October 1979, New York, NY), college and professional athlete and football coach, was the son of Elmer Kenneth Strong, Sr., and attended West Haven High School and New York University. In his senior year at NYU the 6 foot, 205 pound offensive back and placekicker led the East in scoring with 162 points. No points came from field goals. He was selected to the All-American football team and also excelled as a collegiate baseball hitter and outfielder. As a collegian, he married Amelia Hunneman in 1929. After that marriage dissolved, he wed Mabel Anderson in 1931 and had one son, Elmer Kenneth Strong III. His first pro contract, however, came with the New York Yankees baseball club (AL) upon his graduation from NYU in 1929. An outfielder with their New Haven, CT, farm team (EL), he batted .285 and belted 21 home runs. Strong played in 1930 with Hazelton (NYPL), where he compiled a .373 batting average with a league-record 41 home runs. On June 8, 1930, against Wilkes-Barre, he hit four successive home runs. A year later in Class AAA baseball, he suffered a severe, career-ending wrist injury on his throwing arm.

Strong, a versatile athlete, played two sports professionally. The New York Giants (NFL) offered him a contract in 1929, but he played instead for the Staten Island Stapletons (NFL). During his four-year period with Staten Island, he scored 45 percent of Stapletons' total points. After the Stapletons folded in 1933, Strong joined the Giants and shared the NFL lead in scoring that year (64 points) with Portsmouth's Glenn Presnell.* In the famous "sneakers game" against the Chicago Bears in 1934, he scored 18 points to set a championship game record. Following a salary dispute in 1936, Strong jumped to the New York Yankees (AFL). Upon trying to rejoin the Giants, he was banned from the NFL for three years. The Giants signed him in 1939, but Strong then retired in 1940 with more points scored (322) than anyone in NFL history. In 1943 the Giants enlisted Strong to help them through World War II. He agreed to play only as a placekicker and led the NFL with 6 field goals in 1944. Strong retired permanently in 1947, having gained 1,321 career yards on 363 rushing attempts for 24 touchdowns. His 479 career points came from 33 touchdowns, 167 extra points, and 38 field goals. With Emil Brodbeck, Strong wrote *Football Kicking Techniques* (1950), the first book to use motion picture studies of this skill. Strong returned to the Giants as a kicking coach from 1962 through 1965. Besides being elected to the HAF and NFF College Football Halls of Fame, he was inducted into the Pro Football Hall of Fame in 1967.

BIBLIOGRAPHY: Bob Carroll, "Ken Strong," *Coffin Corner* 1 (November 1979), pp. 2–4; *NYT*, October 6, 1979.

Richard Gonsalves

STUHLDREHER, Harry A. "Stuly." See under FOUR HORSEMEN.

STYDAHAR, Joseph Lee "Joe" (b. 17 March 1912, Kaylor, Armstrong County, PA; d. 23 March 1977, Beckley, WV), college athlete and professional football player and coach, excelled as an all-around athlete in scholastic and collegiate competition. He participated in all sports at Shinnston (WV) High School and briefly attended the University of Pittsburgh before transferring to University of West Virginia (SC). A three-year letterman in both football and basketball for the Mountaineers from fall 1933, until his 1936 graduation, Stydahar captained the 16–6 West Virginia basketball team his junior year and the football squad his senior year. The third-team All-American tackle played in the Shrine All-Star (East-West) game in 1936 and for the College All-Stars, who tied NFL champion Detroit Lions in the Chicago *Tribune* classic the following August. For his football and basketball accomplishments at West Virginia, Stydahar was chosen as the state's 1935 Amateur Athlete of the Year by the State Association of Sportswriters.

Chicago Bears (NFL) head coach George Halas* later recalled the 1936 draft: "In 1936, the Bears surprised everyone by making Joe Stydahar, a little known tackle from West Virginia, their first choice. . . . Stydahar was a giant of a man, standing 6–4 and weighing a solid 245. He was a perennial all-star at tackle." He played for the Bears through 1946 but missed two NFL seasons because he was called to active naval duty in late 1942. During 1943 and 1944 he was an officer on the USS *Monterey* in the Pacific. Early in his career Stydahar often played without a helmet, one of the last performers with that idiosyncrasy. A sixty-minute performer with the "Monsters of the Midway," as the Bears were then known, he excelled on both offense and defense. He played on five Western Division and three NFL championship teams and was named to the official All-NFL team from 1937 through 1940, when only eleven players were chosen. An occasional placekicker, he made 28 points on conversions in his NFL career. One came in the famous 73–0 Bear title win over the Redskins.

Following Stydahar's playing career, he became line coach of the Los

Angeles Rams (NFL) in 1948 and was promoted to head coach for the 1950 season. His 8–4 Rams won the 1950 National Conference championship but lost the title game 30–28 to the Cleveland Browns. The next year, the Rams boasted a 9–3 record and a 24–17 conquest of the Browns for the 1951 NFL championship. Stydahar left the Rams after the first game of the 1952 season to devote full time to the corrugated box and container business in Chicago. He returned to the game as an assistant coach with the Green Bay Packers (NFL) late in 1952. He served as head coach of the Chicago Cardinals (NFL) in 1953 and 1954, but a two-year record of 3–20–1 with mediocre talent prompted his return to business. In 1959 he became president of the Big Bear Container Corporation at Chicago. The Stydahars, who had three sons and one daughter, lived in suburban Glencoe and later Highland Park, IL.

Stydahar was named to the NFF College Football Hall of Fame (1972), Pro Football Hall of Fame (1969), Grantland Rice's All-Time team for the first fifty years of football, *SI*'s 1960 Silver Anniversary All-American team, the 1930–1950 University of West Virginia best, and the West Virginia Sports Hall of Fame (1954). He was survived by his four children, four sisters, and three brothers.

BIBLIOGRAPHY: Allison Danzig, *Oh, How They Played the Game: The Early Days of Football and the Heroes Who Made It Great* (New York, 1971); Doug Huff, *Sports in West Virginia* (Virginia Beach, VA, 1979); David S. Neft, Richard M. Cohen, and Jordan A. Deutsch, *The Sports Encyclopedia: Pro Football, 1977* (New York, 1977); *NYT*, March 25, 1977; *Pro Football Hall of Fame Souvenir Yearbook, 1969;* Roger Treat, ed., *The Encyclopedia of Football*, 16th rev. ed., rev. by Pete Palmer (New York, 1979); University of West Virginia, *Football and Basketball News Media Guides, 1933–1936.*

Robert B. Van Atta

SUFFRIDGE, Robert Lee "Suff" "Bob" (b. 17 March 1916, Fountain City, TN; d. 4 February 1973, Knoxville, TN), college and professional player and coach, remains one of the most honored post-1930 college football stars. A three-year (1938–1940) All-American guard at the University of Tennessee (SEC), Suffridge was named All-Time All-American first team by the AP (1951), *SI* (1969), coaches, writers, and players for *Sport* magazine (1969), *Collier's* Mid-Century (1900–1949), FWAA Modern Era (1919–1969), and Glenn "Pop" Warner's All-Era (1926–1950). In 1940 Suffridge was awarded the Knute Rockne Memorial Trophy as the nation's outstanding lineman and the SEC MVP Trophy, presented by the Atlanta Touchdown Club. A member of HAF College Football and the Rose, Sugar, and Orange Bowl Halls of Fame, he was elected in 1961 to the NFF College Football Hall of Fame.

The son of John B. Suffridge and the product of a broken home, he grew up with relatives and friends. Suffridge, a four-year regular guard for Knoxville Central High School, was acclaimed the school's greatest lineman. He played on Tennessee Volunteers teams that boasted three consecutive 10–0–0 regular seasons and were ranked second twice and fourth once by the AP. The outstanding Volunteers lines boasted four All-Americans, including end Bowden Wyatt, tackle Abe Shires, and guards Ed Molinski and Suffridge. Tennessee held 25 of 30 regular season opponents scoreless, 10 of them in succession in an unscored-upon 1939 season. Tennessee posted three consecutive victories over Alabama (the first since 1932), LSU, Vanderbilt, and Kentucky and two wins over Auburn, but proved less formidable in post-season bowls. Although defeating fourth-rated Oklahoma 17–0 in the 1939 Orange Bowl, the Volunteers lost 14–0 to third-ranked Southern California in the 1940 Rose Bowl and fifth-rated Boston College 19–13 in the 1941 Sugar Bowl. Between 1938 and 1940 Tennessee scheduled ten games with Mercer, Southwestern, Chattanooga, Sewanee, and the Citadel. The Volunteers may have fared better in post-season games if they had played a more demanding regular season schedule.

The 6 foot, 190 pound Suffridge proved an exceptional pulling guard and open-field blocker, leading Tennessee interference on coach Bob Neyland's* end sweeps. His defensive charge was so crisp, deadly, and quick that opposing coaches made erroneous claims of his being off-sides. He also blocked several punts and harassed opposing passers. Neyland, who was stingy with praise, once said, "Suffridge's defensive charge was the quickest and most powerful of any football player I ever saw." Suffridge, a fun-loving prankster with self-confidence, enjoyed needling Neyland and occasionally was in the General's doghouse. In his junior year (1939), Suffridge missed three games with a knee injury and wore a brace that cramped his style the rest of the season. During his final game for Tennessee the following year, he hit the Boston College safety with such force that the latter fumbled a punt. This move led to the Volunteers' first touchdown in the Sugar Bowl. Suffridge graduated from Tennessee in 1941 and played on the Chicago *Tribune* College All-Stars, which lost 37–13 to the Chicago Bears. He played pro football with the Philadelphia Eagles (NFL) in 1941 and 1945 under coach Alfred Earle "Greasy" Neale.* The latter year, the Eagles finished 7–3–0 and Eastern Division runner-up.

Suffridge served in the U.S. Navy (1942–1945) during World War II. He played football with the Georgia Navy Pre-Flight "Skyscrapers," the nation's third best service team with a 7–1–1 record, and made the 1942 UPI All-Service team. In 1944 he was given the rank of lieutenant and transferred to a naval armed guard detachment. He also served from 1946 to 1951 as football line coach at North Carolina State University (SC) under head coach Beattie Feathers.* From 1952 to his premature death from the effects of alcoholism, Suffridge sold insurance in Knoxville, TN. Divorced and in financial straits, he was survived by one son Robert Lee, Jr., and three daughters, Jean, Sarah and Martha.

BIBLIOGRAPHY: Russ Bebb, *The Big Orange: A Story of Tennessee Football* (Huntsville, AL, 1973); John D. McCallum and Charles H. Pearson, *College Football U.S.A., 1869–1973* (New York, 1973); Loran Smith, *Fifty Years on the Fifty: The Orange Bowl Story* (Charlotte, NC, 1983); University of Tennessee Sports Information Office, Knoxville, TN (September 5, 1985); Alexander M. Weyand, *Football Immortals* (New York, 1962).

James D. Whalen

SULLIVAN, Patrick Joseph "Pat" (b. 18 January 1950, Birmingham, AL), college and professional player, coach, and broadcaster, is the son of Jerry Sullivan and made All-State in football, basketball, and baseball at John Carroll High School in Birmingham, AL. He attended Auburn University (SEC, 1968–1972) and graduated in 1972 with a B.S. degree. A legend at Auburn, Sullivan quarterbacked the Tigers under Ralph "Shug" Jordan to a 25–5–0 record (1969–1971) and three bowl appearances. He was selected Auburn's Outstanding Player in the Tigers' 35–28 victory over the University of Mississippi in the 1971 Gator Bowl.

Sullivan combined with Terry Beasley to form one of the greatest pass-catch combinations in SEC football history. At Auburn, Sullivan established single-season passing marks with 281 attempts, 167 completions, 2,586 yards, 20 touchdowns, and a .590 completion percentage. He figured in 26 touchdowns and amassed 2,856 yards of total offense in 1970, both Tigers records. Sullivan established Auburn records by completing 454 of 817 passing attempts for 6,284 yards and compiled 6,843 yards of total offense, then third on the all-time list behind Chuck Hixson (6,884) and Jim Plunkett* (7,887). Besides being responsible for 71 career touchdowns, Sullivan tied an NCAA mark with Steve Ramsey and Glenn Davis,* and ranked third then in NCAA history with 53 touchdown passes. Sullivan led the nation in total offense (1970) and set a national mark by averaging 8.58 yards per play, breaking the old record set by John Huarte* of Notre Dame in 1964. Only twice in his college career did Sullivan throw for under 100 yards. He passed over 200 yards in 18 games and exceeded 300 yards in 4 games.

A consensus All-American (1971), Sullivan won the coveted Heisman Trophy as the nation's outstanding college football performer. Sullivan ranked sixth in the voting (1970) and became only the fourth SEC player to win the award. An All-SEC quarterback (1970–1971), Sullivan in 1971 was named National and SEC Player of the Year and Academic All-American; he also won the MVP Award in the Senior Bowl and College All-Star game. A second-round choice of the Atlanta Falcons in the 1972 NFL draft, Sullivan performed in a reserve quarterback role for four seasons. Sullivan played out his option in 1975 and had short stints with the NFL Washington Redskins and San Francisco 49ers before being released. In 30 pro games, Sullivan completed 93 of 220 passes for 1,155 yards and 5 touchdowns. Since leaving pro football, Sullivan has operated a State Farm Insurance agency. He and his wife, Jean, have three children and reside in Birmingham, AL. Sullivan broadcast Auburn football games and in 1986 was named quarterback coach for the Tigers.

BIBLIOGRAPHY: *Atlanta Falcons Fact Book, 1977;* Clyde Bolton, *War Eagle: A Story of Auburn Football* (Huntsville, AL, 1973); John T. Brady, *The Heisman: A Symbol of Excellence* (New York, 1984); *TSN Football Register—1976.*

John L. Evers

SUMMERALL, George "Pat" (b. 10 May 1930, Lake City, FL), college athlete, professional football player, and announcer, excelled as an NFL kicking specialist. The son of banker Allen and Cristelle (Wells) Summerall, he excelled in athletics at Columbia High School in Lake City, FL. In 1948 the 6 foot, 4 inch, 220 pound Summerall set a state football record with 73 pass receptions. Originally the University of Arkansas (SWC) recruited him for basketball and as an offensive-defensive football end. Besides being Razorbacks gridiron co-captain in 1951, he from 1949 to 1951 caught 43 passes for 670 yards and 7 touchdowns. Summerall was selected at end on the Arkansas all-decade team of the 1950s. Summerall unexpectedly became an athlete, being born with his right foot backward and the toes pointing to the rear. In an operation that made the medical journals, his right leg was broken and the foot reversed. Besides being a physical oddity, he showed intellectual ability by earning a Master's degree in Russian History from the University of Arkansas.

In 1952 the Detroit Lions (NFL) drafted Summerall in the fourth round as an offensive/defensive end on their championship team. After being traded to the Chicago Cardinals (NFL) in 1953, he served as their kicking specialist and played defensive end. With the Cardinals through the 1957 season, Summerall kicked 121 of 127 extra point attempts, booted 41 of 100 field goal attempts, and scored one touchdown on an interception return. In 1958 Summerall and Lindon Crow were traded to the New York Giants (NFL) for Dick Nolan and a first-round draft choice. From 1958 to 1961 Summerall kicked 136 of 138 extra points and 59 of 112 field goals for the Giants. He led the NFL with 20 of 29 field goals in 1959 and 46 of 46 extra points in 1961, made 126 consecutive extra points, and kicked field goals in 14 straight games. He booted one field goal and two extra points in the 1958 sudden-death NFL championship game, which the Giants lost 23–17 to the Baltimore Colts at Yankee Stadium. Summerall also played in the 1952, 1959, and 1961 NFL title games.

Three members of the Giants' 1958 team, Summerall, Kyle Rote, and Frank Gifford,* became successful sports announcers. Summerall started on CBS radio but later moved to the television side. Now CBS-TV's top NFL analyst, he covers basketball, golf, tennis, and other assignments and was named Sportscaster of the Year in 1977. Summerall has worked 20 of the 21 Super Bowls, either on radio or television, missing only Super Bowl VII. He and his wife, Katharine, have three children, Susan, Jay, and Kyle.

BIBLIOGRAPHY: *Arkansas Football Guide, 1977;* Gerald Eskenazi, *There Were Giants in Those Days* (New York, 1976); Ronald L. Mendell and Timothy B. Phares, *Who's Who In Football* (New Rochelle, NY, 1974); *New York Giants Media Guide, 1977.*

John L. Evers

SUTHERLAND, John Bain "Jock" (b. 21 March 1889, Coupar-Angus, Scotland; d. 11 April 1948, Pittsburgh, PA), college athlete, professional football player and coach, was the son of foundry worker Archibald and Mary (Burns) Sutherland. Sutherland, one of seven children, grew up with his widowed mother, knew poverty as a child, and emigrated at age 18 to Pittsburgh, PA. An authentic Horatio Alger, he attended high school during days and worked as a special policeman at a steel plant at night. The 6 foot, 1 inch, 200 pounder entered the University of Pittsburgh in 1914. Although he had never seen football played until he tried out for the Panthers team, he became an outstanding gridder. He originally played tackle but was moved by new coach Glenn "Pop" Warner* to guard in 1915 and gained All-American honors there. A scholar-athlete, Sutherland won the MAAAU heavyweight boxing championship and in 1918 the IC4A hammer throw. The Scot, who received American citizenship in 1917, studied dentistry at Pittsburgh and later became a fellow of the American Dental Society.

Sutherland's first football coaching assignment came in 1918 with a U.S. Army team. As Lafayette College coach from 1919 through 1923, he compiled a 33–8–2 record with shutout wins over Pittsburgh in 1921 and 1922. When Warner left Pittsburgh in 1923, Sutherland proved a popular replacement. Sutherland coached the Panthers fifteen years until resigning after the 1938 season because Pittsburgh deemphasized football. Sutherland produced a 111–20–12 record with four unbeaten squads, two national championship teams, and seven Lambert Trophies. Under Sutherland, the Panthers paid four visits to the Rose Bowl and declined a fifth opportunity. Sutherland recruited mostly from the mines and mills of western Pennsylvania and tutored 24 All-Americans. Sutherland, whose overall collegiate record comprised 144–28–14, experienced his only disappointments in the Rose Bowl. His Panthers lost three consecutive Rose Bowls before defeating Washington 21–0 in 1937. The quiet, unshakable, taciturn Sutherland, nicknamed "The Dour Scot," proved an exacting disciplinarian and drove his players relentlessly. The lifelong bachelor emphasized a stout defense and precision running game featuring devastating blocking.

In 1940 Sutherland coached the Brooklyn Dodgers to a second-place finish in the NFL's Eastern Division. After coaching the Dodgers through the 1941 season, Sutherland joined the World War II effort. In 1946 Sutherland returned to the pro coaching ranks with the Pittsburgh Steelers (NFL) and performed box office magic for the bedraggled club. Sutherland fielded successful teams that helped fill Forbes Field for Steelers owner Art Rooney.* The 1947 Steelers lost a playoff game to the Philadelphia Eagles for the Eastern Division crown. Sutherland's outstanding career came to a sudden and tragic end in April, 1948, when he unexpectedly died of a brain tumor. His pro 28–16–1 coaching record included a 13–9–1 mark with the Steelers. Sutherland was selected to the HAF and NFF College Football Halls of Fame.

BIBLIOGRAPHY: Tim Cohane, *Great College Football Coaches of the Twenties and Thirties* (New Rochelle, NY, 1973); Ralph Hickok, *Who Was Who in American Sports* (New York, 1971); Pat Livingston, *The Pittsburgh Steelers: A Pictorial History* (Virginia Beach, VA, 1980); Ronald L. Mendell and Timothy B. Phares, *Who's Who in Football* (New Rochelle, NY, 1974); *NYT*, April 12, 1948; Pittsburgh *Post-Gazette*, April 12, 1948; Pittsburgh *Press*, April 12–13, 1948; Pittsburgh *Sun-Telegraph*, April 12, 1948; Edwin Pope, *Football's Greatest Coaches* (Atlanta, 1956); Harry G. Scott, *Jock Sutherland: Architect of Men* (New York, 1954); Joe Tucker, *Steelers' Victory After Forty* (New York, 1973).

Frank Thackeray

SWANN, Lynn Curtis (b. 7 March 1952, Alcoa, TN), college athlete, professional football player, and announcer, is the son of Willie and Mildred (McGarity) Swann and excelled as a wide receiver with the Pittsburgh Steelers (NFL). Swann attended Serra High School in Foster City, CA, where he was named an All-American football player and won the state long jump championship. At the University of Southern California (PEC, 1970–1973), Swann received a Bachelor's degree in Public Relations. A three-year starter (1971–1973) and All-American wide receiver in 1973, Swann holds the all-time Trojans record with 95 receptions and ranks second in yardage with 1,562. He led the PEC in receiving in 1973 and caught six passes in the 1973 Rose Bowl and five in the 1974 Rose Bowl. Besides being Southern California's third leading all-time punt returner, he lettered for the Trojans in track as a long jumper and recorded a 24 foot, 10 inch jump his sophomore year.

Swann was selected by Pittsburgh in the first round of the 1974 NFL draft. As a wide receiver for nine seasons (1974–1982), Swann led Pittsburgh in pass catches six years. In his rookie season, he compiled a 14.1–yard punt return average, the fourth highest in Steeler history. His 41 returns and 577 yards remain team records, the latter ranking high in pro football history. After becoming a regular wide receiver by the end of the first season, Swann scored the winning touchdown against the Oakland Raiders in the AFC title game. Swann participated in AFC championship games following the 1974–1976 and 1978–1979 seasons and played for the victorious Steelers in Super Bowls IX, X, XIII, and XIV, making 16 receptions for 364 yards, 3 touchdowns, and a 22.8–yard average. A great competitor and clutch performer who performed best in crucial games, Swann enjoyed a sensational game in Super Bowl X against the Dallas Cowboys. He made 4 receptions for a game record 161 yards, including a 64–yard catch for the winning score. His performance won him the game's MVP Award and a new automobile.

During his nine-year NFL career, Swann played in 116 games and made 336 receptions for 5,462 yards, 51 touchdowns, and a 16.3–yard average per catch. His reception marks were Steelers career records until John Stallworth* broke them. He returned 61 punts for 739 yards and one touchdown and scored 318 points, including one touchdown by rushing. Swann was named to the AFC All-Star team (1975, 1977–1978) and played in the Pro Bowl following the 1977 and 1978 seasons but missed the 1979 contest because of an injury. Due to several brain concussions, Swann retired as an active player following the 1982 season. The Marina del Rey, CA, bachelor is pursuing a television career and is an ABC Television Sports football analyst with veteran announcer Keith Jackson. The Pro Football Hall of Fame named him to its AFL-NFL 1960–1984 All-Star Second Team.

BIBLIOGRAPHY: Ronald L. Mendell and Timothy B. Phares, *Who's Who In Football* (New Rochelle, NY, 1974); *Pittsburgh Steelers Media Guide, 1977; TSN Football Register—1983*.

John L. Evers

SWITZER, Barry (b. 5 October 1937, Crossett, AR), college player and coach, attended the University of Arkansas (SWC) from 1957 through 1960 and graduated with a B.A. degree in Business Administration. He played center linebacker in football there under coaches Jack Mitchell and Frank Broyles* and captained the 1959 Razorbacks team that won the SWC championship and Gator Bowl. A private man, he enjoys hunting, fishing, and golf and avoids publicity about his personal life. After serving one year in the U.S. Army, Switzer became an assistant football coach at Arkansas from 1960 to 1965. He was named assistant football coach (1966), offensive coordinator (1966–1972), and then assistant head coach at the University of Oklahoma (BEC) in 1970. His 1971 offensive unit set NCAA records for rushing and total yardage, guaranteeing his selection in 1973 as head football coach after the departure of Chuck Fairbanks.

Switzer, first named College Coach of the Year in 1973, received that honor in 1980 from *Football News* and was selected BEC Coach of the Year four times. His consecutive national championships after the 1974 and 1975 seasons marked the first time in history a team had taken consecutive titles twice. The Sooners also captured the national championship in 1985 by defeating top-ranked Penn State in the Orange Bowl and narrowly missed taking two other national titles. Under Switzer through 1986, Oklahoma has won or shared 11 BEC titles, and finished in the top six 11 times. Switzer also coached Heisman Trophy winner Billy Sims* Outland Award winners Greg Roberts and Tony Cassilas and Butkus Award winner Brian Bosworth. Other star players have included Leroy Selmon,* Rod Shoate, Joe Washington, Jamelle Holieway, and Keith Jackson.

Switzer developed the wishbone T, an offensive strategy enabling a powerful running game to dominate a contest by speed, fancy ball handling, and agility. It deemphasizes the forward pass as an offensive weapon, highlighting the quickness and power of the four-man offensive backfield. Since using it at Oklahoma, Switzer has never experienced a losing season. Through 1986 Switzer's Oklahoma squads have defeated Tom Osborne's Nebraska teams 11 of 15 times. Switzer's contract has been extended after every year except one (1983) since he became head coach. His Sooners teams have led the nation in rushing offense five times (1974, 1977–1978, 1981, 1986) and consistently ranked at or near the top in total defense Switzer coached the Sooners to victories in the 1976, 1979–1981, 1986, and 1987 Orange Bowls, 1976 Fiesta Bowl, and 1981 Sun Bowl. Oklahoma suffered defeats in the 1983 Fiesta Bowl and 1985 Orange Bowl. Switzer's 136–25–4 mark through 1986 gives him the best winning percentage (.831) among veteran active coaches. He in 1963 married Kay McCollum, whom he divorced in 1982, and has three children. Greg, Kathy, and Dove. He belongs to the Baptist Church and served from 1981 through 1983 on the Oklahoma Judicial Nominating Committee.

BIBLIOGRAPHY: Ronald L. Mendell and Timothy B. Phares, *Who's Who in Football* (New Rochelle, NY, 1974); *University of Oklahoma Press Guide, 1984; WWA* (1980–1981), p. 3,237.

Charles R. Middleton

T

TARKENTON, Francis Asbury "Fran" (b. 3 February 1940, Richmond, VA), college and professional player and announcer, is the son of Dallas and Frances Tarkenton. His father, a Pentecostal clergyman, served pastorates in Richmond, VA, Washington, DC, and Athens, GA. Tarkenton attended Athens High School, where he led his team to a state football championship. He graduated in 1961 from the University of Georgia with a Bachelor's degree in Business Administration. At Georgia (SEC) he played in the 1960 Orange Bowl and annual Blue-Gray game and made the All-American team. Tarkenton was chosen by the Minnesota Vikings in the third round of the 1961 NFL draft. He quarterbacked the newly organized Vikings from 1961 to 1966 and was traded in 1967 to the New York Giants (NFL). Tarkenton played in the 1964 and 1965 Pro Bowls with the Vikings and made four consecutive Pro Bowl appearances with the Giants from 1967 to 1970. After being traded back to the Vikings in 1972, he played his final seven seasons with Minnesota.

The diminutive, 6 foot, 185 pound Tarkenton enjoyed his greatest productivity and success during his second stint at Minnesota. He led the Vikings to three unsuccessful Super Bowl appearances in 1974, 1975, and 1977 and amassed many honors. *TSN* selected him the 1975 NFC Player of the Year and to the NFC All-Star team in 1972 and 1975. During his greatest season (1975), he won the Bert Bell Player of the Year, AP MVP, PFWAA MVP, and Washington Touchdown Club Awards. One of the first "scrambling" quarterbacks, he rushed 675 times for 3,674 yards, 32 touchdowns, and a 5.4–yard average per attempt to place among the top rushing quarterbacks in pro football history. The amazingly durable Tarkenton did not miss a game start because of an injury until his sixteenth season and played in 246 of 254 games.

The holder of prodigious passing records, he attempted more aerials (6,467), completed more passes (3,686), threw more touchdown aerials (342), and gained more yards passing (47,003) than any other pro football quarterback. In 1975, 1976, and 1978 Tarkenton led the NFL in completions. For a record 16 consecutive seasons he passed for 2,000 or more yards. In 18 seasons he set a record by passing for 1,000 or more yards each year. In 1978 he set new marks for season pass attempts (572) and most completions (345, since broken). During his career he completed nearly 57 percent of his aerials to rank highly among quarterbacks. For a long time he held the highest completion percentage (56.07) for a rookie. He held the Super Bowl records for most pass completions (18) in 1974 and most pass attempts (35) in 1977.

Tarkenton and his wife, Elaine, have three children, Angela, Matthew, and Melissa. Tarkenton retired to Atlanta, where he chairs the board of Behavioral Systems, a consulting firm. He served as TV color man on the ABC "Monday Night Football" sportscasting team and has appeared regularly on the "That's Incredible" television program. In 1986 he was elected to the Pro Football Hall of Fame. A year later he was named to the NFF College Football Hall of FAme.

BIBLIOGRAPHY: Jim Klobuchar and Fran Tarkenton, *Tarkenton* (New York, 1976); *Minnesota Vikings Media Guide, 1978; NFL Manual, 1983; TSN Football Register—1979.*

Axel Bundgaard

TATUM, James Moore "Big Jim" (b. 22 August 1913, McColl, SC; d. 23 July 1959, Chapel Hill, NC), college athlete and football coach, ranked among the leading ACC football mentors and attained a 14–year composite 100–35–7 (.729 percent) coaching record. He was named to the HAF College Football Hall of Fame and in 1984 to the NFF College Football Hall of Fame. Tatum's father, retail merchant Walter Robert Tatum, died when Jim was age 12. His mother was Jessie (Carmichael) Tatum, whose brother financed Jim's college education during the Depression. Tatum captained and played fullback for McColl High School's football team and maintained a 93 percent academic average before graduating in 1930. The 6 foot, 3 inch, 220 pound Tatum starred three years at the University of North Carolina as a baseball catcher and football tackle. Tatum, an All-SC selection and honorable mention All-American tackle in 1934 under coach Carl Snavely,* graduated in 1935 with a B.S. degree in Commerce.

Tatum assisted Snavely at North Carolina (1935) and Cornell (IL, 1936) and returned to the Tarheels (SC, 1937–1941) as assistant football coach under Raymond Wolf. After being Tarheels head coach in 1942, he served in the U.S. Navy as lieutenant junior grade and line coach under Don Faurot* at Iowa Pre-Flight (1943) and Jacksonville Naval Training Station (1944). As head coach at the latter base in 1945, he compiled a 9–2–1 record. Tatum became University of Oklahoma head football coach in 1946, installing Faurot's split-T formation, winning the BSC championship and Gator Bowl. Tatum started the machinery leading to the Sooners' phenomenal football reign. From 1947 to 1955 he served as head football coach at the University of Maryland (SC, ACC) and built the Terrapins into a football power with a composite 73–15–4 record. Under Tatum, Maryland fielded three undefeated teams, a national championship in 1953, four SC/ACC championships, five bowl teams, and consistent national ranking.

Tatum, named 1953 Coach of the Year by the AFCA, guided one Outland and one Camp Award winners, and four Rock Trophy winners and eight All-Americans. A hefty 260 pounds, Tatum became a forceful figure with superior teaching ability and displayed fine communication with his players and staff. Harry Byrd said, "He's an organizational genius. As an organizer, I have never seen his equal." Tatum, who married Edna Reed Sumrell of Ayden, NC, in 1936 and had three children, co-authored the book *Coaching Football and the Split-T Formation* in 1953. He returned in 1956 to coach at North Carolina, where he was stricken with a mysterious virus three years later and died at University Memorial Hospital.

BIBLIOGRAPHY: Paul Attner, *The Terrapins: Maryland Football* (Huntsville, AL, 1975); Morris A. Bealle, *Kings of American Football: The Complete Story of Football at the University of Maryland, 1890–1952* (Washington, DC, 1952); Booton Herndon, "Big Jim Tatum Is Home," *Sport* 21 (June, 1956), pp. 26–29, 74–79; Ralph Hickok, *Who Was Who in American Sports* (New York, 1971); Mal Mallette, "Jim Tatum of the Tarheels," *SEP* 230 (November 2, 1957), pp. 30ff.; Ronald L. Mendell and Timothy B. Phares, *Who's Who in Football* (New Rochelle, NY, 1974); Edwin Pope, *Football's Greatest Coaches* (Atlanta, 1956); Ken Rappoport, *Tar Heel: North Carolina Football* (Huntsville, AL, 1976).

James D. Whalen

TATUM, John David "Jack" (b. 18 November 1948, Cherryville, NC), college and professional player, grew up in Passaic, NJ, and saw football as his only escape from the ghetto. Tatum excelled as a football fullback at Passaic High School and won All-New Jersey and All-Metropolitan honors as a senior. The 5 foot, 11 inch, 205 pound freshman was switched to defense during spring drills at Ohio State University (BTC) and played on coach Woody Hayes'* 1968 national championship team. Tatum earned All-American designation at defensive back for the Buckeyes in 1969 and 1970 and All-BTC honors from 1968 through 1970. The Buckeyes finished 9–0–0 in 1968 and defeated Southern California 27–16 in the Rose Bowl. The 1970 Ohio State team also compiled a 9–0–0 record but lost 27–17 to Stanford in the Rose Bowl.

The Oakland Raiders (NFL) selected Tatum as their number 1 pick in the 1971 draft. Besides making the All-Rookie NFL team in 1971, Tatum was chosen for the Pro Bowl in 1973, 1974, and 1977 and *TSN* AFC All-Star squad from 1975 through 1977. He holds the NFL record for a fumble return, scampering 104 yards for a touchdown against the Green Bay Packers in 1972. Tatum played in the AFC championship games following the 1973 through 1977 seasons and in the 32–14 Super Bowl XI victory over the Minnesota Vikings in 1977. In April 1980 he was traded to the Houston Oilers (NFL) for running back Kenny King. Tatum led the Oilers with seven interceptions in 1980 but was released prior to the 1981 training camp.

During his pro career he intercepted 37 passes for 736 yards (19.9–yard average) and no touchdowns. His principal defensive accomplishments include intercepting at least four passes in a season six different times and making eight career fumble recoveries as a defensive back. In the 1978 exhibition season, Tatum tackled New England Patriots receiver Darryl Stingley so ferociously that the latter was paralyzed from the neck down. Tatum in 1980 published an autobiography, *They Call Me Assassin*, detailing his turbulent career as one of football's most feared tacklers.

BIBLIOGRAPHY: "The Assassin," *Time* 115 (January 28, 1980), p. 69; Larry Fox, "Yes, You Can Call Him Assassin," *Sport* 71 (August, 1980), pp. 20–23; *Oakland Raiders Media Guide, 1979; Ohio State University Football Media Guides, 1968–1970; TSN Football Register—1980;* Jack Tatum with Bill Kushner, *They Call Me Assassin* (Whittier, CA, 1980).

Allan Hall

TAYLOR, Charles Robert "Charley" (b. 28 September 1942, Grand Prairie, TX), college and professional player and coach, is one of seven children born to Tyree and Myrtle Taylor. His father held various jobs, including mechanic, porter, and bank employee. At Grand Prairie's Dalworth High, Taylor made All-State in football, led his team to the semi-finals of the NIL playoffs, and earned All-State recognition in basketball and track. After entering Arizona State University (WAC) in 1960, Taylor broke his neck as a freshman and nearly died. He wore a body cast for six months and brace for two more months. Remarkably, he still played halfback as a sophomore in 1961. Taylor, who made the All-WAC second team as a junior and All-WAC first squad as a senior, rushed 1,162 career yards on 194 carries. Besides being Arizona's Athlete of the Year in 1963, he played in the Shrine All-Star (East-West) game, Hula Bowl, and Coaches All-American game. In the College All-Star game he was named MVP.

The Washington Redskins' first draft choice in 1964, Taylor became NFL Rookie of the Year. Besides rushing for 755 yards, he caught 53 passes for 805 yards to set an NFL record for receptions by a running back. Midway through the 1966 season, Taylor shifted to end, led the NFL with 72 catches for 1,119 yards, and scored 12 touchdowns. Against the Dallas Cowboys that season, he enjoyed his best pro game with 11 receptions for 199 yards and 2 touchdowns. Taylor again paced the NFL in 1967 with 71 catches for 883 yards. After injuries (including a broken ankle) hampered him the next two seasons, he in 1972 caught 49 passes for 673 yards and made 50 or more catches the next three campaigns. A shoulder injury sidelined him during

1976, after which he played his final pro season in 1977 as a reserve wide receiver.

Taylor retired as the NFL's second leading career receiver, making 649 receptions for 9,130 yards and 79 touchdowns. Besides rushing for 1,488 yards, he scored 90 touchdowns to rank high on the NFL career list. He earned All-NFL first team honors six times (1964–1968, 1974) and second team honors twice (1969, 1975) and played in eight Pro Bowls and one Super Bowl. He caught 50 or more passes during seven seasons, held 10 Redskins records, and was inducted in 1984 into the Pro Football Hall of Fame and Texas Sports Hall of Fame. He also belongs to the Arizona State University Sports Hall of Fame. Following his retirement, Taylor remained with the Washington Redskins organization as a personnel scout for three seasons and became receivers coach in 1981. He married Patricia Grant in 1963 and has three children, Charley, Elizabeth Erin, and Erica.

BIBLIOGRAPHY: *Arizona State University Football Press Guide, 1983;* Jack T. Clary, *Washington Redskins* (New York, 1974); Ken Denlinger and Paul Attner, *Redskins Country: An Inside Look at Washington Redskins Football* (New York, 1983); David Slattery, *The Washington Redskins: A Pictorial History* (Virginia Beach, VA, 1977); *Washington Redskins Press Guides, 1966, 1977.*

Jay Langhammer

TAYLOR, James Charles "Jim" "Jimmy" (b. 20 September 1935, Baton Rouge, LA), college and professional player, attended Baton Rouge High School and earned All-State honors in basketball and football. Taylor in 1954 became the first athlete ever chosen to play in North-South High School All-American games in both sports and was selected MVP in the football contest. Taylor's father, an invalid, died when Jim was age 9, while his mother worked in a laundry. From age 10, Jim supported himself. Taylor entered LSU (SEC) in 1954 but recorded deficient grades. He transferred to Hinds Junior College (MS), where he led the football team in scoring. Upon returning to LSU as a junior, he became a two-way football player. The 5 foot, 11 inch, 215 pound fullback linebacker ranked third in the nation in scoring and eighth in rushing his senior year. He led LSU in rushing and scoring (1956–1957) and twice paced the SEC in scoring. In 1957 he was selected the Tigers' MVP, SEC Player of the Year, and first team All-American. In two seasons, Taylor recorded 20 touchdowns and kicked 22 extra points for 142 total points. He rushed 279 times for 1,314 yards and a 4.7–yard average.

Following his graduation in 1958 from LSU, Taylor played in the College All-Star game and was selected MVP in the Senior Bowl. Green Bay chose him in the second round of the 1958 NFL draft. Taylor played for the Packers from 1958 through 1966, when he played out his option. He signed with the New Orleans Saints (NFL) and retired after the 1967 season. Taylor teamed with running back Paul Hornung* to help Green Bay win four NFL championships (1961–1962, 1965–1966) and Super Bowl I following the 1966 season. Taylor's best season came in 1962, when he led the NFL in rushing attempts (272), rushing yardage (1,474), touchdowns (19), and scoring (114 points) and received the Jim Thorpe Trophy as the NFL's MVP. A disciple of the "run to daylight" theory, the weightlifting addict proved a punishing runner and fierce blocker. The prominent running back was named All-NFL once (1962) and played in the Pro Bowl five times (1962–1966). In 132 games he rushed 1,941 times (eighth on the all-time list), gained 8,579 yards (eighth), scored 83 rushing touchdowns (fifth), and enjoyed five consecutive seasons of 1,000 or more yards (tied for third). He caught 225 passes for 1,756 yards and 10 touchdowns. Besides compiling 10,538 combined yards, Taylor scored 93 total touchdowns and 558 points. He established records for NFL championship game carries (106) and yardage (392). Taylor holds the Green Bay single-game record for most rushing yards (186) and led the Packers in rushing seven consecutive seasons (1960–1966). His 1,474 rushing yards and 19 touchdowns in 1962 remain club season marks.

Taylor married Dixie Grant and has one daughter, Jobeth. After retiring from football, he started a construction company in Baton Rouge and a diving-and-salvage firm in Morgan City, LA. Taylor, a member of the LSU Athletic Hall of Fame and Louisiana Sports Hall of Fame, was elected in 1976 to the Pro Football Hall of Fame.

BIBLIOGRAPHY: George Allen with Ben Olan, *Pro Football's 100 Greatest Players* (Indianapolis, IN, 1982); *The Lincoln Library of Sports Champions*, Vol. 17 (Columbus, OH, 1974); Murray Olderman, *The Running Backs* (Englewood Cliffs, NJ, 1969); Dick Schaap, "Genius at Green Bay," *SEP* 235 (November 3, 1962), pp. 32, 34, 36, 38.

John L. Evers

TAYLOR, Lawrence "Kamikazee" "LT" (b. 4 February 1959, Williamsburg, VA), college and professional player, is the son of Iris and Clarence Taylor. His father, a Newport News, VA, shipyard supervisor, encouraged his three sons to participate in sports. A three-sport standout at Lafayette High School, the versatile Taylor became an All-State defensive end on Virginia's championship team his senior year and also caught ten touchdown passes as a tight end. From 1977 to 1981 Taylor attended the University of North Carolina (ACC). During his freshman year he earned the nickname "Kamikazee" for his ability to dive over the up-back to block punts. Originally a nose guard defensively, he switched permanently to outside linebacker his last two seasons and started every game there. During his college career he made 192 tackles, 21 quarterback sacks, 10 forced fumbles, 3 interceptions, and 3 fumble recoveries. In 1980 Taylor made consensus All-American and was named ACC Player of the Year. In addition, he played in the Shrine All-Star (East-West) game and the Japan Bowl.

Taylor in 1981 became the New York Giants (NFL) number 1 draft pick and second player chosen overall, and he made an immediate impact on the defense. During his rookie season, the 6 foot, 3 inch, 240 pound linebacker recorded 133 tackles, 10 ½ quarterback sacks, 1 fumble recovery, and 1 interception, adding 14 tackles and 2 sacks in the playoffs. His many post-season honors included being AP Defensive Player of the Year, NFL Rookie of the Year, and NFL Player's Association NFC Linebacker of the Year.

Nicknamed "LT," Taylor was voted the 1982 AP Defensive Player of the Year for an unprecedented second consecutive season. On Thanksgiving Day against the Detroit Lions, his 97–yard touchdown return on an interception became the longest in history by a Giants linebacker and gave New York a come-from-behind victory. Following the 1983 season, Taylor was selected UPI's NFC Defensive Player of the Year and unanimous All-Pro, playing in his third straight Pro Bowl. In 1984 Taylor helped lead the Giants to a surprising 9–7 record by pacing the squad in tackles (114), sacks (11½), and forced fumbles (6) and made his fourth consecutive Pro Bowl. Taylor recorded 13 sacks in 1985 and again made All-Pro and participated in the Pro Bowl as the Giants finished 10–6. In 1986 Taylor bounced back from rehabilitation for substance abuse to lead the NFL with 20 ½ quarterback sacks and fell only 1½ sacks short of breaking Mark Gastineau's season record. Taylor spearheaded a Giants defense that recorded 59 sacks and helped the club win the NFC Eastern Division with a 14–2 record. Taylor, the NFC Defensive Player of the Year, was again selected All-Pro and to the Pro Bowl. Taylor became the first defensive player named PFWAA MVP and the second defensive player named AP MVP. He led the Giants defense in the 49–3 NFC playoff rout of the San Francisco 49ers and helped the Giants to a commanding lead before missing the latter part of the 17–0 victory over the Washington Redskins in the NFC championship game. The Giants beat the Denver Broncos 39–20 in Super Bowl XXI.

Prior to the 1983 season, Taylor attempted to renegotiate his five-year contract and held out for three weeks. When the season ended, he signed a contract with the USFL's New Jersey Generals but bought it back, as the Giants extended his contract through the 1989 season. Taylor is married and has one son, T.J.

BIBLIOGRAPHY: *New York Giants Media Guides, 1982, 1983;* "The Loss of Innocence," *Inside Sports* 5 (November, 1983), pp. 26–34; *TSN Football Register—1986.*

Donald E. Kosakowski

TAYLOR, Lionel T. (b. 15 August 1936, Kansas City, MO), college athlete, professional football player, and coach, grew up in Lorado, WV. At New Mexico Highlands College (1955–1958), he excelled in football, basketball, and track. An All-FC flanker, the 6 foot, 2 inch, 215 pound Taylor joined the Chicago Bears (NFL) taxi squad in 1959. After being released in 1960, he signed with the Denver Broncos (AFL). Taylor performed for the Broncos through 1966 and the Houston Oilers (AFL) from 1967 to 1968, ranking among the finest receivers in AFL history. He led the AFL in pass catches a record five times (1960–1963, 1965) and in 1961 became the first pro player to receive 100 passes in a season. On November 29, 1964, he caught 13 passes against the Oakland Raiders to set an AFL mark.

During four different seasons Taylor made over 1,000 reception yards. He holds the AFL record with 567 lifetime receptions, ranking him ninth on the all-time pro football list. Taylor led Denver in scoring (1964) and most receptions and reception yardage (1960–1965). In 24 different games Taylor gained over 100 yards via passes. Taylor's best day came against the Buffalo Bills on November 27, 1960, when he set club records by amassing 199 yards and three touchdowns. With the Broncos, Taylor established career pass-receiving records by making 543 receptions, 6,875 reception yards, and 44 touchdowns. Taylor's lifetime statistics for 9 seasons included 567 receptions, 7,195 reception yards (fourth in AFL), a 12.7–yard average per catch, and 45 touchdowns. The three-time All-AFL selection (1960–1961, 1965) played with Houston in the 1967 AFL championship game 40–7 loss to the Oakland Raiders.

Taylor in 1970 became an assistant football coach for the Pittsburgh Steelers (NFL) and developed young pass receivers Lynn Swann* and John Stallworth.* Taylor coached for the Steelers seven seasons and became the senior member of Chuck Noll's* staff, assembling consecutive Super Bowl championship teams in 1974 and 1975 with triumphs over the Minnesota Vikings and Dallas Cowboys. In 1972 and 1976 the Steelers lost to the Miami Dolphins and Oakland Raiders in the AFC championship game. Taylor joined the Los Angeles Rams (NFL) in 1977 as receiving coach under Chuck Knox* and became Ray Malavasi's offensive coordinator in 1978. The Rams lost the AFC championship game to Dallas in 1978, but the next year played in the Super Bowl XIV 31–19 setback to the Steelers. In 1984 Taylor was named head football coach at Texas Southern University (SAC). After finishing 5–6 in 1984, Texas Southern compiled a 1–10 mark in 1985 and 2–8–1 in 1986. Taylor and his wife, Lorencita, have two daughters, Loretta and LaVern.

BIBLIOGRAPHY: *Los Angeles Rams Official Media Guide, 1977;* Lou Sahadi, *Broncos! The Team That Makes Miracles Happen* (New York, 1978); *TSN AFL Official History, 1960–1969.*

John L. Evers

TAYLOR, Otis, Jr. "Slug" (b. 11 August 1942, Houston, TX), college athlete, professional football player, and scout, is the son of school custodian Otis Taylor, Sr., and grew up with his mother, a domestic, and his aunt, a nurse. After graduating from Evan E. Worthing High School in 1961, Taylor attended Prairie View A&M College (SAC) on a basketball scholarship from 1961 through 1965. He enjoyed basketball the best and idolized Elgin Baylor* (IS) of the Minneapolis Lakers (NBA). Most experts agreed that Taylor's basketball talents enabled him to become a great leaping flanker in pro football. Taylor once drew with basketball star Willis Reed* (IS) in a one-on-one game.

Taylor quarterbacked in football until being switched to flanker to accommodate Jim Kearney, later his teammate with the Kansas City Chiefs (AFL). The Chiefs made Taylor, who belonged to the Philadelphia Eagles (NFL), their fourth draft pick in 1965. Before scout Lloyd Wells signed the 6 foot, 3 inch, 215 pound receiver, the Chiefs experienced difficulty finding him. He had been placed under the watchful eye of NFL "baby-sitters," who switched Taylor and other team prospects from Dallas motel to motel to keep them away from the upstart AFL. Despite being nicknamed "Slug" for sluggish, Taylor possessed 4.5–second speed for the 40–yard dash. Taylor, a flanker, electrified crowds with his acrobatic catches and snatched balls one-handed and even behind his back. A great open-field runner, he leaped, danced, and skipped to gain that extra yard.

During the first part of the 1965 season, starting receiver Chris Buford suffered a knee injury. Taylor replaced him and remained there until his retirement in 1975. He combined with quarterback Len Dawson* to form one of the most prolific passing tandems in pro football history and led Kansas City to two early Super Bowl appearances. Taylor set up a touchdown with a brilliant 31–yard reception in the Chiefs' 31–10 loss to Vince Lombardi's* Green Bay Packers in the first Super Bowl. In the AFL playoff on December 20, 1969 against the New York Jets, Taylor set up the winning score with a 61–yard catch. Two weeks later in the AFL championship match with the Oakland Raiders, his leaping catch enabled the Chiefs to drive for the winning score. Two weeks later, the Chiefs upset the Minnesota Vikings in Super Bowl IV. Taylor caught 410 career passes for 7,306 yards (17.8–yard average) and 57 touchdowns and rushed 30 times for 161 yards (5.4–yard average) and 3 touchdowns. He led the AFL in touchdown receptions (11) in 1967 and the NFL in reception yardage (1,110) in 1971, when he made *TSN* AFC All-Star team. The divorced Taylor, the father of one child and a dapper dresser, lives in Kansas City and scouts for the Chiefs.

BIBLIOGRAPHY: Robert H. Boyle, "Can it Catch-as-Catch-Can," *SI* 35 (November 15, 1971), p. 84; John Devaney, *Star Receivers in the NFL* (New York, 1972); *TSN* (December 11, 1971), p. 3.

William A. Borst

THEISMANN, Joseph Robert "Joe" (b. 9 September 1949, New Brunswick, NJ), college and professional player and announcer, is the son of liquor store clerk Joseph James and Olga (Tobias) Theismann and excelled as an all-around athlete at South River, NJ, High School. Quarterback Theismann teamed with receiver Drew Pearson* on an undefeated and top-ranked football team his senior year. An outstanding baseball pitcher, he received a pro offer from the Minnesota Twins (AL). Upon entering the University of Notre Dame, the 6 foot, 160 pound Theismann was given only a remote chance of becoming starting quarterback because of his size and weak throwing arm. During his sophomore year he returned punts and backed up All-American quarterback Terry Hanratty. Fighting Irish coach Ara Parseghian* liked Theismann's quick feet and moved him ahead of Coley O'Brien, the backup quarterback the previous season. In Theismann's best 1968 performance, he replaced the injured Hanratty against Pittsburgh, threw three touchdown passes, and scored on 9– and 10–yard runs. During that season he scored 5 touchdowns, rushed for 259 yards (4.4–yard average), and completed 55 percent of his 49 passes attempted.

Although 1969 initially looked like a rebuilding year, Theismann led Notre Dame to an 8–1–1 record and threw for more yardage than Hanratty had recorded in any of his three seasons as quarterback. His 13 touchdown passes surpassed by three Hanratty's best season effort. Notre Dame performed in the Cotton Bowl, ending a 45–year absence from post-season play. Despite being eight-point underdogs against the undefeated, number 1–ranked Texas Longhorns and hampered by the absence of three starters, Notre Dame led 17–14 until the final minute of play. The 21–17 loss provided football fans with one of the most exciting bowl games ever, as Theismann threw two touchdown passes.

In 1970 Theismann obliterated the Notre Dame single-season record for passes attempted (268), passes completed (155), and yards gained by passing (2,429) and tied the single-season mark for touchdown passes (16). Notre Dame finished the season 9–1, suffering a final game upset by archrival Southern California. In that game Theismann completed 33 of 58 passes for 526 yards and 2 touchdowns and scored 2 touchdowns. At the Cotton Bowl, the Fighting Irish upset undefeated Texas and ended the Longhorns' 30–game winning streak. Notre Dame's performance featured an innovative defense and inspired Theismann, who passed for one touchdown and scored two others. The final AP poll ranked Notre Dame second nationally, behind Nebraska and just ahead of Texas.

Theismann completed his Notre Dame career as the leader in passing percentage (57 percent), yardage (4,411), touchdown passes (31), and total offense (5,432). He finished second in completions (290), averaged 6.7 yards in total offense per play, and scored 15 touchdowns. Notre Dame sports information director Roger Valdiserri engineered a Heisman Trophy campaign, issuing "Theismann as in Heisman" bumper stickers. Nevertheless, Theismann finished second to Stanford quarterback Jim Plunkett* in the vote for the top collegiate football player. He made several All-American squads, including first team AP. An Academic All-American, he received a Bachelor of Arts degree in Sociology from Notre Dame in 1971. Theismann married Cheryl Lynn Brown on December 5, 1970 and has three children, Joseph, Amy, and Patrick. Since divorced, he now is engaged to Cathy Lee Crosby.

Pro football scouts projected Theismann as a possible defensive back or kick returner rather than quarterback because of his size. The Miami Dolphins (NFL) selected him in the fourth round. The persistent Theismann instead signed with the Toronto Argonauts (CFL), determined to play quarterback. His career statistics from 1971 to 1973 in Canada showed a 56.3 percent completion average, 40 touchdown passes, over 6 yards per carry rushing, and a championship game appearance his first year. He completed 382 of 679 passes for 6,093 yards and rushed 172 times for 1,051 yards and 3 touchdowns.

The Washington Redskins (NFL) obtained Theismann's rights from the Dolphins and indicated that he would be used as a quarterback. Theismann signed with them in 1974 and spent the first two seasons as backup to veterans Billy Kilmer and Sonny Jurgensen,* completing 19 of 33 passes for 2 touchdowns. He had developed a strong throwing arm to augment his already quick release and scrambling ability, but Redskins coach George Allen* preferred the veteran Kilmer. Theismann's first NFL start came during the fifth week of the 1976 season against the Kansas City Chiefs. He passed for 270 yards and two touchdowns and scored one touchdown in a losing effort. Jack Pardee replaced Allen as coach in 1978 and installed Theismann as starter. Theismann started the next seven and one-half seasons until a serious injury sidelined him.

From 1978 through 1984 Theismann passed over 2,000 yards each season. He far outdistanced contemporary quarterbacks with 1,815 yards rushing, as his 5.1 yards per carry rank highest for any ballcarrier in Redskins history. He finished in the top five of NFC quarterback rankings every year from 1979 to 1984. In 1982 Theismann led the Redskins to a 27–17 Super Bowl triumph over the Miami Dolphins and tied a Super Bowl record with eight consecutive completions. His 1982 honors included being the Pro Bowl starter, Bert Bell Award (MVP) winner, and NFL Miller Man of the Year for his off-the-field activities. He enjoyed an even better year in 1983, leading the Redskins to a 14–2 record and an NFL-record 541 points and repeating as NFL MVP. In the Super Bowl, however, the Redskins were annihilated 38–9 by the Los Angeles Raiders. Theismann rebounded in the Pro Bowl, leading the NFC to a 45–3 rout of the AFC. Besides completing a record 21 of 27 passes for 242 yards, he set another record with 3 touchdown passes.

After a slow start, Theismann led the Redskins to their third consecutive NFC title in 1984 and was named the AP NFL MVP. In the season's final four games, he completed 82 of 123 passes for over 900 yards and 7 touchdowns. Theismann started off poorly in 1985 and then an injury ended his career. In a nationally televised game on November 18 against the New York Giants, Theismann suffered a compound fracture of his right leg. During his NFL career, he completed 2,044 of 3,602 passes for 25,106 yards (12.3-yard average), 160 touchdowns, and 138 interceptions and rushed 355 times for 1,815 yards and 17 touchdowns. Theismann was waived by the Redskins in July 1986 and joined CBS-Television as a pro football analyst. The McLean, VA resident also won the Virginia State Class Racquetball championship and made the world finals in the television "Superstars" competition. Theismann also remains active in numerous charitable activities, operates three successful restaurants in northern Virginia, co-hosts a weekly television show, appears in television commercials, and has published a book, *Quarterbacking*.

BIBLIOGRAPHY: Baltimore *Evening Sun*, December 26, 1983; *Los Angeles Times*, December 14, 1983, January 9, 1984, November 20, 1985; Joe Theismann, *Quarterbacking* (New York, 1983); *TSN Football Register—1986;* Washington *Post*, July 26, 1986; *Washington Redskins Press Guide, 1985*.

Cappy Gagnon

THOMAS, Frank William "Tommy" (b. 15 November 1898, Muncie, IN; d. 10 May 1954, Tuscaloosa, AL), college athlete, football coach, and administrator, amassed a composite 141–33–9 (.795 percent) head coaching football record at the University of Chattanooga (SIAA, 1925–1928) and University of Alabama (SEC, 1931–1942, 1944–1946). A member of the HAF College Football Hall of Fame, Thomas was elected in 1951 as a charter member to the NFF College Football Hall of Fame. He led the Crimson Tide to three Rose Bowls and one Sugar, Cotton and Orange Bowl each and finished with a 4–2–0 post-season record. Thomas produced 4 SEC champions (one shared), 16 All-Americans, 26 All-SEC honorees, 4 undefeated regular seasons, 1 national co-championship, and 6 top twenty AP teams.

Thomas was the youngest of six children of ironworker James and Elizabeth (Williams) Thomas, who immigrated from Cardiff, Wales, in 1882. The smallest and finest player on the Hammond, IN, grade school basketball team, Thomas became the first four-sport star at East Chicago Washington High School. Besides being the top running back as a junior on the Indiana state championship football team, he excelled as a basketball guard, baseball shortstop, and track sprinter. Since Kalamazoo State Normal College (MIAA, now Western Michigan University) offered high school courses and a student jobs program, Thomas enrolled there in 1917 as a high school senior to alleviate family expenses because his father was temporarily unemployed. Thomas played on the Kalamazoo varsity football team, making an 85–yard run from scrimmage against the University of Michigan in a surprisingly close 17–13 loss and scoring a touchdown in a 14–0 triumph over Michigan State. He returned to Kalamazoo as a college freshman, captaining the football squad and starring on the basketball and baseball teams.

Fighting Irish varsity guard Maurice Smith persuaded Thomas in 1919 to enroll at the University of Notre Dame. Thomas roomed with the immortal George Gipp* and was saddened by his untimely death in 1920. Thomas played third-string quarterback (non-lettered) that year, alternated in 1921 with Chet Grant, and became regular quarterback his senior year. Coach Knute Rockne* was impressed with Thomas' keen memory and ability to call correct plays. Thomas led Notre Dame in 1922 with 21 punt returns for 196 yards and played on teams boasting a composite 27–2–1 three-year record. In 1923 he earned a law degree from Notre Dame. Before planning to embark on a law career, Thomas tried football coaching for one year. He became backfield coach at the University of Georgia (SC, 1923–1924) and successfully installed the Fighting Irish system at the request of head coach George Woodruff. Chattanooga (SIAA), which had achieved only one winning season in the previous seven years, hired Thomas as head football coach. The Moccasins finished 4–4–0 his first season and amassed a composite 22–5–2 record his last three seasons, winning outright or sharing the SIAA championship each year. Former Notre Dame teammate Harry Mehre, who was experiencing problems as the new head coach at Georgia, persuaded Thomas to return there in 1929 and 1930 as his backfield assistant. The Bulldogs finished 7–2–1 his second year at Georgia, enhancing Thomas' reputation as a talented, skillful coach.

Thomas was recommended for the head football coaching post at Alabama by successful departing coach Wallace Wade.* Although only three regulars returned in 1931 from Wade's undefeated Rose Bowl championship team, Thomas guided his first Crimson Tide squad to a 9–1–0 finish and third place in the 23–team SC. Alabama won the first two championships of the newly formed SEC with 7–1–1 (1933) and 10–0–0 (1934) seasons. Led by Crimson Tide star tackle Bill Lee, halfback Dixie Howell, and end Don Hutson,* Alabama outscored its opponents 31.6 to 4.5 points per game and defeated Stanford 29–13 in the 1935 Rose Bowl. The Dunkel and Williamson systems and the *Football Thesaurus* named Alabama national champions.

Thomas guided Alabama to two more Rose Bowls with undefeated seasons in 1937 and 1945. Alabama, ranked fourth in the 1937 AP poll, featured All-American guard Leroy Monsky, halfback Joe Kilgrow, and tackle Jim Ryba and lost 13–0 in the Rose Bowl to second-rated California. Thomas' World War II squads consisted mostly of 17–year-olds, too young to be drafted into military service. In 1944 Alabama lost to Duke in the Sugar Bowl in a surprisingly close 29–26 thriller. All-American halfback Harry Gilmer and center Vaughn Mancha led the sophomore-studded squad in 1945 to a perfect 10–0–0 finish and third-place ranking nationally. The Crimson Tide averaged 43 points per game and humiliated PCC champion Southern California 34–14 in the Rose Bowl. Thomas, who always let his squad members decide on bowl participation, built character and great teams and was loved and respected by his players. The short, chubby coach with a round face proved a great storyteller. "That 1934 team was my greatest," he once stated. "The

1937 outfit was my best-coached team—the team that went further on less material than any I ever coached. But my favorite of them all was that green 1944 eleven. Oh, how I loved those War Babies!"

Thomas in 1928 married Frances Rowe, the daughter of an Athens, GA, newspaper publisher, and had two sons Frank, Jr., and Hugh Rowe, and one daughter, Rita. In 1935 he served as head coach of the Chicago *Tribune* College All-Stars, which lost 5–0 to the NFL Chicago Bears. Thomas, a member of the Episcopalian Church, headed war bond drives, the March of Dimes, and a fund-raiser for the Crippled Children's Hospital in Birmingham, AL. He served as a director of the City National Bank of Tuscaloosa and a Lincoln-Mercury automobile agency and participated in the Exchange Club. Extremely high blood pressure forced Thomas to coach his last team in 1946 with a loud speaker from an elevated trailer (he had to stay off his feet and had developed a weak voice). Although his health continued to fail, he continued to serve as athletic director until January 1952. The practice field at Alabama bears his name as a lasting memorial.

BIBLIOGRAPHY: Clyde Bolton, *The Crimson Tide: A Story of Alabama Football* (Huntsville, AL, 1972); Ben Cook and Lawrence Wells, *Legend in Crimson: A Photo History of Alabama Football* (Oxford, MS, 1982); Ralph Hickok, *Who Was Who in American Sports* (New York, 1971); *Notre Dame Football Guide, 1984; Spalding's Official Intercollegiate Football Guides, 1918–1919, 1926–1929*; Naylor Stone, *Coach Tommy of the Crimson Tide* (Birmingham, AL, 1954).

James D. Whalen

THORPE, James Francis "Jim" (b. 28 May 1888, Indian Territory [c. Prague, OK]; d. 28 March 1953, Lomita, CA), America's finest all-around athlete, was the son of Hiram Thorpe, a farmer and trader of mixed Irish and Sac and Fox Indian descent. His mother, Charlotte (Vieux) Thorpe, was one-quarter French and claimed descent from Black Hawk, chief of the Chippewas. Given the Sac and Fox tribal name Bright Path, Thorpe had a twin brother who died at age 8 and 17 other siblings or half-siblings. An indifferent student, Thorpe attended the Sac and Fox Reservation School and Haskell Institute for Indians at Lawrence, KS. He loved to be outdoors, riding horses, swimming, hunting, and playing baseball. To stop Thorpe's periodic flights from school, his father enrolled the 16–year-old at faraway Carlisle Institute in Pennsylvania, the foremost American school for Indian youth.

A glorified trade school, Carlisle gave Thorpe minimal training in tailoring, subjected him to military-like discipline, and required him to live and work on farms in the surrounding area. Thorpe also discovered athletics at Carlisle, where he came under the tutelage of renowned track and football coach Glenn "Pop" Warner.* He first started on Warner's talented eleven in 1908, when he made two long touchdown runs in Carlisle's tie with powerful

University of Pennsylvania (IL). Despite increasing acclaim as a track star and football player, the bored, restless Thorpe left Carlisle in the spring, 1909. Until 1911 he pitched and played outfield at Rocky Mount, NC (Eastern Carolina League), and worked as a manual laborer in the southwestern states. In that period college athletes frequently played professional baseball in the summer months under aliases. That precaution the ingenuous Thorpe failed to take.

At Warner's urging, Thorpe returned to Carlisle for the 1911 football season. The 5 foot, 11 inch, 185 pound Thorpe combined power, speed, shiftiness, and kicking ability in leading Carlisle to 11 victories in 12 games. In an 18–15 triumph over Harvard (IL), Thorpe ran 70 yards for a touchdown and kicked four field goals. Walter Camp* named Thorpe to his authoritative All-American team. At the fifth modern Olympic Games in Stockholm, Sweden in the summer of 1912, Thorpe astonishingly won both the pentathlon of and decathlon, compiling 8,412 of 10,000 possible points. In presenting his two gold medals, King Gustav of Sweden pronounced Thorpe "the greatest athlete in the world." That fall Thorpe set a new college football scoring record of 198 points, as the Indians lost only to the University of Pennsylvania, and he was again selected All-American by Camp.

Soon thereafter reports surfaced that Thorpe had played pro baseball in 1909 and 1910. The AAU declared him pro when he competed in the Olympics, while the international Olympic authorities quickly removed his name from Olympic records and demanded the return of his medals. The disheartened Thorpe left Carlisle and joined the New York Giants baseball team (National League). Thorpe's major league career was undistinguished. As a part-time outfielder for six seasons with the Giants (1913–1915, 1917–1919), Cincinnati Reds (NL, 1917), and Boston Braves (NL, 1919), he batted .252. Thorpe also played with various minor league baseball teams and enjoyed his best season in 1920, when he hit .358 and drove in 112 runs for Akron, OH (International League). Thorpe not only encountered trouble with curveballs but drank and caroused excessively. He starred in the loosely organized pro football of the time, performing mostly with the Canton (OH) Bulldogs. In 1920 he helped found and was named honorary president of the APFA, which the next year became the NFL. Thorpe retired from pro football after the 1929 season as an occasional placekicker with the New York Giants.

Thorpe's last twenty-five years spelled difficulty. Married three times and divorced twice, he fathered seven children surviving into adulthood. Despite his considerable earnings as a pro athlete, he usually needed money and had to play bit roles in grade-B Hollywood movies. He also dabbled in Sac and Fox tribal politics, lectured on Indian life and his athletic career, and served during World War II in the U.S. Merchant Marine. Outside athletics, Thorpe experienced failure—a semiliterate alcoholic often dependent on his friends' charity. In 1950 an AP poll of American sportswriters named Thorpe the outstanding male athlete and best football player of the first half of the twentieth century. Three years later, Thorpe died of a heart attack at his trailer home in Lomita, CA. In 1982 the International Olympic Committee, after decades of petitions and pleas, returned Thorpe's medals to his family. Thorpe was elected to the HAF and NFF College and Pro Football Halls of Fame.

BIBLIOGRAPHY: *DAB*, supp. 5 (1951–1955), pp. 683–684; "Jim Thorpe at School," *Literary Digest* 45 (October 5, 1912), pp. 593–96; Jack Newcombe, *The Best of the Athletic Boys: The White Man's Impact on Jim Thorpe* (New York, 1976); Charles Paddock, "Chief Bright Path," *Collier's* 84 (October 5, 1929), pp. 16–17ff., (October 12, 1929), pp. 40ff., (October 19, 1929), pp. 30ff., (October 26, 1929), pp. 30ff.; Frank Scully and Norman Sper, "Jim Thorpe: The Greatest Athlete Alive," *American Mercury* 57 (August, 1943), pp. 210–15; *TSN*, April 8, 1953.

Charles C. Alexander

TINSLEY, Gaynell C. "Gus" (b. 1 February 1915, Ruple, LA), college athlete, coach, and professional football player, starred at football end for LSU (SEC). He was selected consensus football All-American (1935) and unanimous All-American (1936) at LSU and was named All-Pro (1937, 1938) with the Chicago Cardinals (NFL). Tinsley made several college all-time football teams, including the FWAA Southeastern Regional Modern Era (1919–1969), George Trevor's South Sectional (1949), *SI* Thirties Decade (1969), Glenn "Pop" Warner's* All-Era (1926–1950), Allison Danzig's* (OS) Specialists (1970), and the All-Time Sugar Bowl team. A member of the HAF College Football Hall of Fame, he was elected in 1956 to the NFF College Football Hall of Fame and in 1975 was the only player named to both the offensive and defensive LSU All-Time teams.

The son of farmer Thomas Clayton and Blanche (Worley) Tinsley, he starred in football and baseball at Haynesville (LA) Homer High School and graduated from there in 1933. The 6 foot, 1 inch, 195 pound Tinsley immediately started for the LSU eleven his sophomore year and played on Tigers teams amassing a composite 25–5–3 record from 1934 to 1936. LSU achieved SEC championships and played in post-season games in Tinsley's last two campaigns after posting a 19–game regular-season undefeated streak. The 9–2–0 Tigers were rated number 1 by Paul Williamson and number 4 by Frank G. Dickinson. The following year the AP and Dickinson rated 9–1–1 LSU number 2, while Williamson and Deke Houlgate named them national champions.

Tinsley blocked a punt against Mississippi his sophomore year and scored an LSU touchdown on the play. He blocked another punt in 1934 that led to a touchdown against SEC co-champion Tulane in a 13–12 loss at Tiger Stadium before a then SEC record 31,620 spectators. In the 1936 Sugar Bowl 3–2 loss to TCU, Tinsley rushed Horned Frog quarterback Sammy Baugh* into throwing an incomplete pass in the TCU end zone for an automatic safety. In his final season, Tinsley caught three touchdown passes against Tulane and one each against Auburn (15 yards), Mississippi State (20 yards), Georgia (20 yards), and Mississippi (33 yards) and one against Santa Clara (50 yards) in a losing 21–14 effort in the 1937 Sugar Bowl. The nation's highest scoring end, he led all LSU scorers with 48 points in 1936. "He's the greatest lineman I ever saw, someone who could have made All-American at any position," said LSU coach Bernie Moore. "He was so tough, he made blockers quit."

Regarded by admirers as a "big country boy," Tinsley exhibited a quick smile and flat, off-center nose. The powerful blocker scrambled opposing backfields on defense before plays could develop and cleared the path with three separate blocks on one play against Auburn, enabling the LSU halfback to run 90 yards for a touchdown. His teammates included star halfbacks Abe Mickal, Jess Fatheree, and "Pinky" Rohm and center Moose Stewart. Tinsley was chosen LSU MVP and was regarded as the Tigers' greatest lineman. Tinsley, who captained the Tigers baseball team and lettered three years in that sport, graduated with a B.A. degree in Mathematics in 1937. A member of the Chicago *Tribune* College All-Star team in 1937, Tinsley scored the game's only touchdown on a 47-yard pass from Baugh to upset the NFL Green Bay Packers 6–0. Tinsley played pro football three seasons (1937–1939) with the lackluster Chicago Cardinals and led the NFL in 1938 with 41 pass receptions for 516 yards and one touchdown, but a severe knee injury ended his playing career. He returned to LSU as end coach (1940–1941, 1945–1947) and served in the U.S. Navy (1942) before receiving a medical discharge. In 1943 and 1944, he served as head football coach at Haynesville (LA) High School.

In 1948 Tinsley succeeded Moore as LSU head coach but inherited a squad depleted of stars by graduation. His remarkable rebuilding job the following year earned him 1949 SEC Coach of the Year honors. In 1949 LSU finished 8–3–0, ranked ninth in the AP poll, and represented the SEC in the Sugar Bowl. The Tigers defeated conference champions Rice, North Carolina, and Tulane but were outclassed 35–0 by undefeated, second-ranked Oklahoma in the Sugar Bowl. Tinsley remained seven years (1948–1954) at LSU, coached three All-Americans (fullback Kenny Konz, tackle Sid Fournet, and center George Tarasovic), and achieved only two more winning seasons (7–3–1 in 1951 and 5–3–3 in 1953). Tinsley's 5–1–1 record against traditional rival Tulane could not save his job at LSU because his composite record was a mediocre 35–34–6. Tinsley, who left coaching in 1955 to teach Mathematics at Baton Rouge (LA) Tara High School, married Ann Tarver of Natchitoches, LA, in 1936 and has one son and one daughter. He maintains a stable of horses and bird dogs and never misses an LSU home football game. The Baton Rouge resident retired from teaching in January 1985.

BIBLIOGRAPHY: Peter Finney, *The Fighting Tigers: 75 Years of LSU Football* (Baton Rouge, LA, 1968); Dan Hardesty, *The Louisiana Tigers: LSU Football* (Huntsville, AL, 1975); John D. McCallum and Charles H. Pearson, *College Football U.S.A., 1869–1973* (New York, 1973); *Spalding's Official Intercollegiate Football Guides, 1935–1937;* Sugar Bowl Football Game Program, January 2, 1950; James D. Whalen, telephone interview with Gaynell C. Tinsley, September 4, 1985.

James D. Whalen

TITTLE, Yelberton Abraham, Jr. "Y. A." (b. 24 October 1926, Marshall, TX), college and professional player, is the son of Alma and Yelberton Abraham Tittle, Sr. His father, a rural postman, taught three sons and one daughter always to work hard in every task. With this upbringing and the inspirational guidance of his older brother Jack, Tittle became a 6 foot, 185 pound star tailback for Marshall High School. In 1944 the 17–year-old Tittle received a football scholarship from LSU (SEC). During his final game that year, Tittle completed 15 of 17 passes for 300 yards and three touchdowns to help defeat archrival Tulane University 25–6. In Tittle's sophomore season, coach Carl Brumbaugh helped change Tittle's football career by introducing the T formation at LSU.

Tittle utilized his most important asset, his passing ability, to rival Bobby Layne* of Texas, Charley Conerly of Mississippi, and Harry Gilmer of Alabama. He passed for 2,576 yards in four varsity seasons and led LSU to a 23–11–2 record. Besides receiving All-SEC honors in 1946 and 1947, he played in the Blue-Gray game in 1944 and 1945 and directed the Tigers to the Cotton Bowl in 1946. Against the University of Mississippi in 1947, Tittle showed his fine defensive ability by intercepting a Conerly pass late in the third period. He lost his pants before 40,000 fans, including his fiancée, when the intended receiver snatched his belt buckle. Tittle married his childhood sweetheart, Minnette DeLoach, on June 20, 1948, in Marshall, TX.

In 1947 Tittle signed with the Cleveland Browns (AAFC) for $10,000 and a $2,000 bonus. In a move to strengthen the weak Baltimore Colts franchise, rookie Tittle and several other AAFC veterans were dealt to the Colts for the 1948 season. Tittle played for Baltimore in 1948 and 1949 and was named AAFC Rookie of the Year. When the AAFC terminated, Tittle and Baltimore joined the NFL for the 1950 season. After the Baltimore franchise dissolved, the players were placed in a pool for the 1951 draft. The San Francisco 49ers selected Tittle in the first round, making him a top draft pick two different years.

From 1951 to 1960 Tittle quarterbacked the 49ers and combined with Pro Football Hall of Famers Joe Perry* and Hugh McElhenny* to produce one of the most potent NFL offenses. Tittle and receiver R. C. Owens in 1957 conceived the Alley-Oop pass, enabling the former to make the All-NFL team for the first time. In August 1961 the New York Giants obtained Tittle from the 49ers for lineman Lou Cordile, one of the most memorable trades.

Tittle, with the Giants from 1961 to 1964, led New York to three Eastern Conference titles (1961–1963) and captured the Jim Thorpe Trophy as the NFL's MVP in 1961 and 1963. In 1963 he set an NFL record by tossing 36 touchdown passes and tied another by throwing seven in one game against the Washington Redskins.

During his 17-year football career (1948–1964), he completed 2,427 passes for 22,070 yards and 242 touchdowns, passed for over 300 yards in 13 games, and scored 39 touchdowns. Tittle was selected to the All-NFL team three times (1957, 1962–1963) and appeared in six Pro Bowls. For his outstanding achievements, Tittle was enshrined in the Pro Football Hall of Fame in 1971 and in the Texas Sports Hall of Fame in 1986. Tittle's philosophy of working hard enabled him to be successful off the field too. He owns an insurance company and has made real estate investments in Atherton, CA. He and his wife, Minnette, have three children, Diane, Mike, and Pat.

BIBLIOGRAPHY: "Giants Edition," *Pro!* 9 (September 24, 1978), p. 125; Ronald L. Mendell and Timothy B. Phares, *Who's Who in Football* (New Rochelle, NY, 1974); David S. Neft, Richard N. Cohen, and Jordan A. Deutsch, *The Sports Encyclopedia: Pro Football* (New York, 1977); *NYT*, August 15, 1961; Don Smith, *Y. A. Tittle: I Pass!* (New York, 1964).

Donald Kosakowski

TRAFTON, George (b. 6 December 1896, Chicago, IL; d. 5 September 1971), college and professional athlete, football coach, and boxing promoter, attended Oak Park High School in suburban Chicago. He enlisted in the U.S. Army in 1896 and captained the Camp Grant team. In 1919 he enrolled at the University of Notre Dame and played for the undefeated football team of coach Knute Rockne.* Trafton called teammate George Gipp* "the greatest back I ever saw." Trafton allegedly was expelled from Notre Dame when Rockne caught him playing semi-pro football, a then common practice. In 1920 Trafton began his pro football career at center for the Decatur Staleys (NFL) under coach George Halas.* The 1920 season marked the first of thirteen consecutive campaigns that Trafton played for Halas' team, which subsequently became the Chicago Staleys and Chicago Bears (NFL). Trafton, the "iron man" of pro football, played every minute of each game for thirteen years. Throughout his career, Trafton defiantly wore the unlucky uniform number 13 and captained the Bears from 1923 to 1925.

During his first pro season Trafton gained his enduring reputation as a tough, dirty player. Teammate Red Grange* called Trafton "the toughest, meanest, most ornery critter alive." In 1920 the Rock Island Independents supposedly assigned one of their players to knock Trafton out of a game. After four Rock Island players in twelve minutes had been forced from the game due to injuries, the hostile crowd booed Trafton. Later Trafton explained, "I tackled a Rock Island halfback. He spun against a fence that was very close to the field and broke a leg. After that, the fans did get on me." The Rock Island fans were so infuriated that Trafton raced from the field when the game ended. He was handed a sweatshirt by the trainer as a makeshift disguise and grabbed two milk bottles as potential weapons. A cab waited outside the playing field and sped Trafton away from the rock-throwing mob. A few minutes later, he was offered a ride by a passing motorist. Halas allegedly gave Trafton the game receipts on the Bears' next visit to Rock Island. "I knew," said Halas, "that he'd be running for his life, whereas I have nothing to run for except the seven thousand dollars."

Trafton became one of the first centers to use the one-handed pass from center, possibly because he was missing the index finger on his left hand. He excelled with his invariably accurate snaps from center, proved an exceptional, unpredictable player on defense, and pioneered roving on defense to confuse his opponents. In a game against the Green Bay Packers, he once blocked a punt and then told them that another player was responsible. When the Packers keyed on the other player, Trafton blocked a second punt. While playing for the Bears, Trafton capitalized on his size and reputation to begin boxing. He defeated Arthur "Art the Great" Shires, baseball first-baseman for the Chicago White Sox (AL) in a five-round match in 1929 in Chicago. After seven consecutive victories, Trafton was knocked out by Primo Carnera in 54 seconds on March 26, 1930. Trafton later wrestled until he learned that the matches were fixed. He successfully promoted and managed fighters, handling the first professional fight of Joe Louis* (IS). Trafton, who played only one pro football game in 1933, coached football briefly for Northwestern University (WC) in 1922, served as line coach for the Green Bay Packers (NFL, 1944) and Los Angeles Rams (NFL), and was public relations director for the Rams. Trafton was elected to the Pro Football Hall of Fame in 1964.

BIBLIOGRAPHY: Howard Roberts, *The Chicago Bears* (New York, 1947); Harry Sheer, "Trafton in Camp of Ex-Enemies—Packers," *Chicago Daily News*, June 10, 1944; Morris Siegel, "This Trafton Was Tough as They Come," *Washington Post*, August 18, 1950; Don Smith, "The Toughest, Meanest and Most Ornery," *Coffin Corner* 7 (January/February 1985), pp. 7–8.

John S. Watterson

TRENCHARD, Thomas Gawthrop "Doggie" (b. 3 May 1874, Church Hill, MD; d. 16 October 1943, Lynbrook, NY), college athlete, professional football player, and coach, starred at football end three years (1892–1894) at Princeton (IL), captained the Tigers his last two years, and made Walter Camp's* 1892 second and 1893 first All-American teams. The son of George Ogden and Laura Newman Trenchard, he graduated in 1891 from Lawrenceville (NJ) Preparatory School and starred in football (captain) and baseball there. Nicknamed "Doggie" because of his long, shaggy hair, he was tight-lipped, grim, and daring. In the 1893 triumph over Yale that clinched the national championship for undefeated Princeton, Captain Trenchard told quarterback Phil King to call the earliest sleeper play on record. Trenchard threw a lateral pass from the Tigers' new ends-back formation to Frank Morse, who was "tying a shoe" near the sideline. Morse ran 50 yards around Frank Hinkey's* end, the only gain made on the Yale flanker in four years, to set up the game's lone touchdown. In *Harper's Weekly* (1893) Richard Harding Davis described the 6–0 Princeton win as the "greatest sports spectacle New York or America has ever witnessed, ending Yale's string of 37 victories." During Trenchard's varsity career, the Tigers compiled a combined 31–4–0 record. Trenchard represented Princeton in 1893 at three football rules conventions in New York City, played baseball at Princeton, and served as sophomore class president and master of ceremonies on Class Day at graduation in 1895.

The 5 foot, 7 inch, 146 pound Trenchard played pro football with Latrobe, PA (1897) and coached football at the Universities of North Carolina (SIAA, 1895, 1913–1915), West Virginia (1896), Pittsburgh (1897), and Washington and Lee (SIAA, 1902). Fielding H. Yost,* West Virginia player, lauded Trenchard as an excellent coach admired by his squad. Trenchard entered the lumber business at Gumberry, NC, where he became a partner in 1905 in the firm of W. E. and T. G. Trenchard and served as vice president of the Northampton and Hartford Railroad. During World War I, 43–year-old Trenchard became physical instructor with the American YMCA in France. From 1921 through 1940 he served as director of recreation for the Socony Vacuum Oil Company in New York. Trenchard married Rose Eleanor Lamdin of Baltimore in 1903, had two sons and two daughters, and resided many years in Long Island City, NY. He died suddenly from a heart attack en route to visit his daughter Sara in Lynbrook, NY.

BIBLIOGRAPHY: Allison Danzig, *The History of American Football: Its Great Teams, Players, and Coaches* (Englewood Cliffs, NJ, 1956); Parke H. Davis, *Football: The American Intercollegiate Game* (New York, 1911); Jay Dunn, *The Tigers of Princeton: Old Nassau Football* (Huntsville, AL, 1977); William H. Edwards, *Football Days* (New York, 1916); Princeton University, Archives, Seeley G. Mudd Manuscript Library, Princeton, NJ; Princeton–Pennsylvania Football Game Program, November 5, 1892.

James D. Whalen

TRIPPI, Charles Louis "Charley" (b. 14 December 1922, Pittston, PA), college and professional athlete and coach, is the son of coal miner Joseph and Jennie (Attardo) Trippi and has one brother, Sam, and three sisters, Angelina, Mary, and Jennie. He played football center and halfback at Pittston High School and attended LaSalle Academy on Long Island, NY for one year prior to enrolling at the University of Georgia (SEC) in 1941. The

5 foot, 11 inch, 185 pounder gained fame as one of football's most elusive runners. As a sophomore, Trippi was selected MVP in the Rose Bowl in helping Georgia defeat UCLA 9–0. He served in the U.S. Army Air Force from 1943 to 1945 and made the All-Service team in 1944 as a member of the Third Air Force team. In 1945 he returned to Georgia to complete his college career. Due to special rules during World War II, Trippi played in four College All-Star games for the collegians and with the pro champion Chicago Cardinals (NFL) in 1948. In 1946 against Georgia Tech, he gained 544 yards rushing, passing, and returning kicks. Georgia completed an undefeated, untied season with a 20–10 victory over North Carolina in the Sugar Bowl. A unanimous All-American, he received the Maxwell Award as the nation's outstanding college football player. His career record at Georgia included rushing 260 times for 1,669 yards and 32 touchdowns and completing 80 of 178 passes for 1,556 yards and 11 touchdowns. Trippi made All-American in baseball as a shortstop in 1946 with a .464 batting average, 11 home runs, and 27 stolen bases in 28 games.

He played one year of pro baseball in 1947 with Atlanta, GA (Southern Association), hitting .334 before joining the Chicago Cardinals (NFL) that fall. His four-year, $100,000 pro contract comprised the largest signed up to that time. The Cardinals won the NFL championship in Trippi's rookie 1947 season. He played with the Cardinals until 1955 and held nine team records. His career statistics with the Cardinals included 687 carries for 3,506 yards and 37 touchdowns; 205 completions in 434 passes for 2,547 yards and 16 touchdowns; 130 receptions for 1,321 yards; and 129 kick returns for 2,321 yards. After retiring as a player, he coached football for the Cardinals (1956–1957, 1963–1965) and the University of Georgia (1958–1962). Trippi, a member of the All-Time Rose and Sugar Bowl teams, was elected to the NFF College Football Hall of Fame in 1968 and named to the All-Time SEC team in 1968. In 1968 he was enshrined in the Pro Football Hall of Fame. Trippi married Virginia Davis in 1944 and had two daughters, Joanne and Brenda, and one son, Charles, Jr. After Virginia died in 1971, he married Peggy McNiven in 1977. They reside in Athens, GA, where Trippi is involved in real estate.

BIBLIOGRAPHY: Robert T. Bowen, interview with Charles Trippi, 1984, Athens, GA; Jesse Outlar, *Between the Hedges: A Story of Georgia Football* (Huntsville, AL, 1973); Ed Thilenius and Jim Koger, *No Ifs, No Ands, A Lot of Butts* (Athens, GA, 1960); Jack Troy, *Leading a Bulldog's Life* (Atlanta, 1948); University of Georgia, Sports Information Files, Athens, GA.

Robert T. Bowen

TUBBS, Gerald "Jerry" (b. 23 January 1935, Breckenridge, TX), college and professional player and coach, is the son of Vernon and Erma T. (Harbison) Tubbs. He graduated from Breckenridge High School in 1953 after leading his football team to the 1951 and 1952 state championships. At the

University of Oklahoma (BSC), the 6 foot, 2 inch, 220 pound Tubbs played linebacker on defense and center on offense. During his college career from 1954 through 1956, Oklahoma finished undefeated each season and twice won national championships. As a senior (1956), the speedy, competitive Tubbs made All-American, won the Walter Camp Trophy, and placed fourth in the Heisman Trophy balloting.

After being drafted in 1957 by the Chicago Cardinals (NFL) in the first round, Tubbs played there until traded in mid-1958 to the San Francisco 49ers (NFL). By 1960 he considered retirement because of a promising business opportunity. The 49ers consequently placed him on the expansion list for the Dallas Cowboys (NFL) franchise. When his commercial deal collapsed, Tubbs signed with the Cowboys. Dallas played Tubbs initially at outside linebacker to exploit his speed, but switched him to middle linebacker in 1960. Tubbs became a defensive stalwart, leading the Cowboys in assisted and unassisted tackles. The key player in the Dallas defense, Tubbs was named All-Pro in 1962 and starred in the 1963 Pro Bowl. Following the 1964 season, Cowboys management convinced him to become a player-coach rather than retire. Two years later a back injury forced him to end his playing career. Since 1967 Tubbs has served as Dallas linebacker coach and remains the only original Cowboys player still with the organization. During this period, he tutored numerous prominent linebackers and helped make the Cowboys one of the NFL's most dominant franchises.

BIBLIOGRAPHY: *Dallas Cowboys Bluebook, 1983;* Dallas *News,* August 16, 1961; Dallas *Times Herald,* October 12, 1962, July 17, 1963, June 15, 1965, September 5, 1967; *NYT,* November 4, 1969; St. Louis *Globe-Democrat,* February 20, 1971; Carlton Stowers, *Journey to Triumph* (Dallas, 1982); Richard Whittingham, *The Dallas Cowboys* (New York, 1981).

Jerome Mushkat

TUCKER, Young Arnold (b. 5 January 1924, Calhoun Falls, SC), college athlete and administrator, starred at quarterback for the incredible Army football teams (1944–1946) recording three straight unbeaten seasons and two national championships. Army's famous "Touchdown Twins," Glenn Davis* and Doc Blanchard,* usually captured the headlines. When Army lacked depth and Blanchard suffered a hobbling injury in 1946, Tucker often became the most valuable Cadets gridder. Besides making the All-American teams selected by Grantland Rice* (OS) and the New York *Sun* in 1946, he won the prestigious Sullivan Award as the nation's outstanding amateur athlete. Blanchard remains the only other football player to receive the Sullivan Award. The son of Floyd Allen and Sarah Victoria Tucker, he was born on a South Carolina farm where five or six generations of his family had lived. His father, an infantry captain during World War I, played baseball and boxed in the Army. After a military career, Floyd later worked for the U.S. Border Patrol and as a Treasury Department civil service employee.

Tucker performed brilliantly in football at Miami (FL) Senior High School. "The Florida towhead could match cross-steps, hip-shifts and straight-arms with the best of 'em in an open field," according to John D. McCallum and Charles M. Pearson, *College Football U.S.A., 1869–1973*. In guiding Miami High to the state title, Tucker ranked as "the most elusive climax runner ever developed in the Palmetto Glades" and outplayed football star Charley Justice* in an interstate game. An all-around athlete, he won All-State and All-South honors in football, twice earned All-State recognition in basketball, and participated as a sprinter, long jumper, and javelin tosser in track. An honor roll student on the dean's list, Tucker graduated in February 1943. As an apprentice seaman in the Navy V–12 program, Tucker attended the Universities of Notre Dame, Florida, Miami and North Carolina prior to entering Army in the summer of 1944. He played basketball at Florida (SEC) and football and basketball at Miami.

Tucker became starting Army quarterback in 1945 and led what many football experts consider the finest college club ever assembled. Army coach Earl Blaik* pictured Tucker as the Cadets' "forgotten man." Blaik added, "That kid from Florida made the T click, but sportswriters didn't play him up. He completed 60 percent of his passes. On a team which didn't boast a Blanchard and a Davis, this boy would have been a sensation as a broken-field runner." The 5 foot, 9 inch, 175 pound Tucker played his greatest game in 1946 in directing Army to a 21–7 victory over powerful BSC co-champion Oklahoma. Blanchard was sidelined, while Davis played receiver. Tucker passed for one tally and tossed another aerial to the one-yard line to set up the go-ahead touchdown. Oklahoma drove 73 yards to the Cadets four-yard line in the third period, before Tucker intercepted a pass. In the fourth quarter the Sooners marched to Army's nine-yard line, where safety Tucker anticipated the next play. Dashing between the Oklahoma quarterback and runner, he intercepted a lateral and ran 86 yards for the final score.

Tucker finally gained recognition as one of the nation's premier quarterbacks in Army's historic 1946 scoreless tie with perhaps the best Notre Dame team in history. The rival squads included four Heisman Trophy winners, three Outland Award winners, and 16 first-team All-American players. Game participants were named to 7 of the 11 positions on the team of the decade selected by *SI* in 1969 to mark college football's first 100 years. Tucker, the game's star, galloped 30 and 32 yards, tackled a Notre Dame runner from behind at Army's 12–yard line, and intercepted three Johnny Lujack* passes. Asked after the game why Tucker intercepted so many of his passes, Lujack replied, "He was the only man I could find open." Dan Daniel* (OS), *The Quarterback* writer, remarked, "Tucker was terrific. Army got all it could have out of its forces, which lacked Notre Dame's depth. Notre Dame did not get the most out of its personnel, chiefly because Lujack ran second to

Tucker." In 1946 Tucker also returned kicks for 78 and 76 yards against Cornell, passed for all 3 Army touchdowns in a 19–0 win over Duke, and completed 8 of 10 passes for 2 touchdowns in the first half against mighty Pennsylvania. Tucker tied for the national lead in interceptions (8), not including his score on a fumble recovery against Oklahoma. Coach Blaik summarized, "Tucker must rank near the top of all Army quarterbacks. As a competitor, he was simply superb—a fighter who carried on at times with enough injuries to sideline three quarters of a backfield." Tucker also played basketball three years at West Point, captaining the 1947 team, and participated in track three years.

Tucker married Patricia Small of Miami in 1947 and has two children, Arnold Thomas and Patricia Louise. Tucker, whose tour of military duty included assignments in Japan and Thailand, retired as an Air Force lieutenant colonel in 1974. From 1974 to 1976 Tucker served as assistant director of athletics at the University of Miami and still resides in Miami.

BIBLIOGRAPHY: Jim Beach and Daniel Moore, *Army vs. Notre Dame* (New York, 1948); Earl H. Blaik and Tim Cohane, *You Have to Pay the Price* (New York, 1960); Dan Daniel, "Tucker's Terrific Play for Army Rates Salute," *The Quarterback* (November 16, 1946); Allison Danzig, *The History of American Football: Its Great Teams, Players, and Coaches* (Englewood Cliffs, NJ, 1956); Dan Jenkins, "The First 100 Years," *SI* 31 (September 15, 1969), pp. 46–53; John D. McCallum and Charles H. Pearson, *College Football U.S.A., 1869–1973* (New York, 1973); Grantland Rice, "The 57th All-America Football Team," *Collier's* 118 (December 14, 1946), pp. 13–16; Arnold Tucker to Bernie McCarty, May 25, 1984.

Bernie McCarty

TUNNELL, Emlen "Em" (b. 29 March 1925, Bryn Mawr, PA; d. 22 July 1975, Pleasantville, NY), college athlete and professional football player, coach, scout, and executive, was elected in 1967 to the Pro Football Hall of Fame. A graduate of Radnor (PA) High School, Tunnell suffered a broken neck in his one football season at the University of Toledo (OC). He played basketball there and helped the Rockets advance to the championship game of the 1943 National Invitational Tournament before losing 48–27 to St. John's (NY) University. Following U.S. Coast Guard service, Tunnell resumed schooling at the University of Iowa (BTC). Tunnell played football his junior year but underwent eye surgery that sidelined him as a senior. After his 1948 graduation, Tunnell walked unannounced into the New York Giants (NFL) office and asked for a job.

A defensive back with unknown credentials, Tunnell was signed as a free agent and became the first black Giants player. The 6 foot, 3 inch, 190 pound Tunnell performed 11 years for the Giants and three seasons for the Green Bay Packers (NFL) before retiring in 1961. He in the 1950s keyed the Giants' famed "umbrella defense," a tactic that helped revolutionize pro football. This alignment shifted from the traditional six-man defensive line and dropped off two linemen for pass coverage to counter the era's great quarterbacks. Tunnell, along with Tom Landry,* Otto Schnellbacher, and Harmon Rowe, became known as the Giants' "offense on defense." In 1952 Tunnell gained 924 yards on defense, 30 yards more than Dan Towler of the Los Angeles Rams, the NFL's leading offensive ballcarrier. The next year, Tunnell gained 819 yards to surpass all but two offensive backs. Tunnell played in 167 NFL games altogether and 158 consecutive contests, both records at one time. He performed in four NFL championship games (1956, 1958, 1960–1961). New York defeated the Chicago Bears 47–7 in 1956 for the NFL title, and Green Bay won the crown in 1961 with a 37–0 victory over the Giants. The four-time All-NFL selection played in nine Pro Bowl games and set 16 Giants club records. Tunnell established pro marks for interceptions (79, second on the all-time NFL list), interception yardage (1,282, first), punt returns (258, first), and punt return yardage (2,209, fourth).

Married to Patricia Dawkins in 1962, Tunnell served as a scout and defensive coach for the New York Giants from 1962 to 1973 and became the club's assistant director of pro personnel in 1974. In 1969 Tunnell was named the NFL's best all-time safety. He became the first black assistant coach in the NFL, the initial black selected to the Pro Football Hall of Fame, and the first player named purely for defensive talents.

BIBLIOGRAPHY: Gerald Eskenazi, *There Were Giants in Those Days* (New York, 1976); *NYT* (July 24, 1975), 32; Paul Soderberg and Helen Washington, eds., *The Big Book of Halls of Fame in the United States and Canada* (New York, 1977); *TSN* (August 9, 1975), p. 40.

John L. Evers

TURNER, Clyde "Bulldog" (b. 10 November 1919, Stillwater, TX), college and professional player, graduated from Sweetwater High School in 1936, made the Little All-American football squad at Hardin-Simmons College (BC) and helped them earn two Sun Bowl berths. At the Sun Bowl, Hardin-Simmons tied New Mexico State in 1936 and defeated Texas Mines 34–6 in 1937. The Chicago Bears (NFL) drafted Turner in the first round in 1940. The Bears had selected George McAfee* earlier and sought a top-flight lineman to open up holes for the speedy back. This strategy yielded quick returns, as the 20–year-old Turner started at center and linebacker. The Bears finished the 1940 season with an 8 win, 3 loss record and shellacked Sammy Baugh's* Washington Redskins 73–0 in the NFL championship game. Mel Hein* of the New York Giants was named all-NFL center that year, but Turner earned the honor six times. By 1942 the 6 foot, 2 inch, 240 pound center had more than earned his nickname "Bulldog."

Turner, perhaps the fastest center in NFL history, often won races against backs. Chicago Bears coach George Halas* testified to Turner's defensive linebacking skills by lauding him as "the greatest pass rusher I'd ever seen." Turner led the NFL with 8 pass interceptions in 1942 and made 18 career interceptions for 3 touchdowns. Turner's entrance to the pros was marked by one of the first player tampering cases in NFL history. The Detroit Lions tried to lure Turner from the Bears, although the Chicago team had draft rights. After Turner spurned the Detroit offer, the incident was reported to NFL officials and the Lions were fined $5,000. Turner keyed an offensive line including Ed Sprinkle and Ray Bray, enabling quarterback Sid Luckman* to direct the Bears to NFL championships in 1940–1941, 1943, and 1946. In five NFL title games, Turner intercepted four passes. The Bears offense led the NFL in total yards gained five times during this period. Turner, who proved a terrific blocker, superb pass defender, and flawless ball snapper, was elected to the Pro Football Hall of Fame in 1966.

BIBLIOGRAPHY: Frank Menke, ed., *The Encyclopedia of Sports*, 5th rev. ed., rev. by Suzanne Treat (New York, 1975); David S. Neft et al., *The Complete All-Time Pro Football Register* (New York, 1975); Mike Rathet and Don R. Smith, *Their Deeds and Dogged Faith* (New York, 1984); Howard Roberts, *The Chicago Bears* (New York, 1947); Roger Treat, ed., *The Encyclopedia of Football*, 16th rev. ed., rev. by Pete Palmer (New York, 1979).

John R. Giroski

TWILLEY, Howard James, Jr. (b. 25 December 1943, Houston, TX), college and professional player, is the son of Howard and Bessie Twilley. He attended Tulsa University (MVC) from 1962 to 1968, earning a Bachelor of Science degree in Electrical Engineering. He received a Master's of Business Administration degree in 1971 from the University of Miami. He married Julie Laudon on December 28, 1968, and has three sons, Michael, Blaine, and Mark. The 5 foot, 10 inch, 180 pound Twilley never enjoyed exceptional speed and looked small for a receiver, but he used his intelligence to run great routes and possessed sure hands. At Tulsa he set ten NCAA pass reception records, including career catches (261), receiving yardage (3,343), and touchdown catches (32). Besides leading the NCAA University Division in pass receptions in 1964 and 1965, he in 1965 finished consensus All-American and Heisman Trophy runner-up, was selected UPI Lineman of the Year, and topped the nation in scoring. He also made Academic All-American in 1964 and 1965.

The Methodist family man always has supported education. He used part of his bonus money in 1966, when he signed as a twelfth-round draft choice of the Miami Dolphins (AFL), to establish a scholarship at Tulsa University. His initial pro contract, a no-cut, three-year arrangement, induced him to sign with Miami rather than the Minnesota Vikings (NFL). Twilley's survival as a pro in these early years was assured largely because of his contract. Twilley convinced Don Shula* that he was a clutch receiver, who ran superbly accurate routes splitting zone defenses apart. Twilley played his entire pro career with Miami before retiring in 1976 and was one of the original Dophins team members dominating pro football in the early 1970s. He played in three Super Bowls and made 150 career catches for 2,228 yards. He resides in Tulsa, OK, where he owns a sporting goods chain and operates shopping malls.

BIBLIOGRAPHY: Ronald L. Mendell and Timothy B. Phares, *Who's Who in Football* (New Rochelle, NY, 1974); *NYT*, November 8, 1972; Howard Twilley to Charles R. Middleton, November 7, 1984.

Charles R. Middleton

TYRER, James Efflo "Jim" (b. 25 February 1939, Newark, OH; d. 15 September 1980, Kansas City, MO), college and professional player, was the son of Efflo and Dorothy (Johnson) Tyrer. His father, a banker, served one term as Newark treasurer. At Newark High School, Tyrer excelled in football, basketball, and track. The two-way tackle and placekicker in football was named All-Central Ohio League twice and made the All-State squad as a senior. An All-League basketball second team center twice, Tyrer led the Newark squad in scoring as a senior with 327 points for a 17.2 per game average. He participated on the track squad as a junior and senior, consistently placing in the discus and shot put. Tyrer entered Ohio State University (BTC) in the fall, 1957, and started at football tackle as a sophomore. He made All-BTC as a junior and All-American in 1960, when he co-captained the Buckeyes' 7–2 squad and played in the Shrine All-Star (East-West) and College All-Star games. Tyrer married Martha Cline on August 17, 1960 and had four children, Tina, James Bradley, Jason, and Stephanie.

Drafted by both the Cleveland Browns (NFL) and the Dallas Texans (AFL), he signed with the Texans. Tyrer started at offensive tackle as a rookie in 1961 and moved with the club to Kansas City for the 1963 season. Tyrer made the All-AFL first team from 1962 through 1969 and played in eight consecutive AFL All-Star games, two Super Bowls, two Pro Bowls, and three AFL title games. At 6 feet, 6 inches, the 270 pound Tyrer possessed great speed and endurance for his size and played 12 straight years without missing a game. The Pro Football Hall of Fame named him to the All-Time AFL first team in 1970, the same year he became the first Newark High athlete selected to the school's Hall of Fame. In 1976 he was inducted into the Kansas City Chiefs Hall of Fame. Tyrer left the Chiefs after the 1973 season and played his final pro year with the Washington Redskins (NFL) in 1974. Subsequently, he owned an insurance agency and presided over Pro Forma, a merchandising firm representing athletes in commercial activities.

BIBLIOGRAPHY: Dick Conner, *Kansas City Chiefs* (New York, 1974); *Kansas City Chiefs Press Guides, 1963, 1973–1974; Ohio State University Football Press Guide, 1983;* Wilbur Snypp, *The Buckeyes: A Story of Ohio State Football* (Huntsville, AL, 1974).

Jay Langhammer

U

UNITAS, John Constantine "Johnny" (b. 7 May 1933, Pittsburgh, PA), college and professional player and announcer, is the third of four children from a family of Lithuanian descent. Judged in his era as the greatest pro quarterback of all time, Unitas truly fulfilled the legendary American dream of a poor boy rising from rags to riches. His father, Leon, who died in 1938, owned a small coal delivery business. His mother, Helen, supported her children by continuing that business, working at menial jobs, and serving as a bookkeeper after taking night accounting courses.

Vowing at age 12 to become a pro football player, Unitas worked unceasingly toward that goal. At St. Justin's High School in Pittsburgh, he made quarterback his senior year on Pittsburgh's All-Catholic High School team. Unitas received a football scholarship at the University of Louisville (1951–1955), after being rejected as too small by Notre Dame, Indiana, and other schools. He had failed the entrance exam at the University of Pittsburgh, whose football staff exhibited interest in him. At college, the 5 foot, 11 inch, 140 pound Unitas grew to 6 feet, 1 inch, and 196 pounds. During his senior year at Louisville, Unitas married high school sweetheart Dorothy Jean Hoelle. They had five children, Janice, John Constantine, Jr., Robert, Christopher, and Kenneth. After being divorced in 1971, Unitas married his second wife, Sandra, and has one son, Francis Joseph.

In 1955 the Pittsburgh Steelers (NFL) drafted Unitas as a quarterback in the ninth round but released him before the season began. Unitas played for the semi-pro Bloomfield (NJ) Rams for $6 a game on litter-strewn fields and supplemented his income by working at construction jobs. From 1956 to 1972 the legendary "Number 19" made his mark with the Baltimore Colts (NFL). Selected initially as understudy to star quarterback George Shaw, he rose to greatness. The NFL's MVP in 1957, 1964, and 1967, he won the Jim Thorpe Trophy in 1957 and 1967 and made All-Pro in 1957–1958, 1964–1965, and 1967. He directed the Colts to their sudden-death 23–17 overtime victory over the New York Giants for the 1958 NFL title, in what many sportswriters call the greatest pro football game ever played. Unitas also led the Colts to triumph over the Dallas Cowboys in the wild 1970 Super Bowl. Unitas quarterbacked the Colts to 47 consecutive wins from December 9, 1956, through December 4, 1960, and threw at least one touchdown pass each game, a record comparable to Joe DiMaggio's* (BB) 56 consecutive hits in baseball. The Colts won NFL championships in 1958–1959, 1968, and 1970–1971.

The records set by the cool, consistent Unitas remain virtually endless. In 1966 Unitas broke the mark for most touchdown passes and most yards gained in passing in a season. Boasting a lifetime pass completion average above 55 percent, he holds the NFL record with 27 300–yard passing games. Unitas was named AP Player of the Decade (1960s) and NFL Man of the Year (1970). In commemoration of the NFL's fiftieth anniversary in 1969, he was selected as "the Greatest Quarterback of All Time." Despite ripped arm tendons, punctured lungs, broken vertebrae, broken ribs and fingers, and torn knee cartilage, Unitas often played in pain and endured as long as he could. In 1968 he made a successful comeback after sustaining injuries. He underwent surgery in April 1971 after tearing an Achilles tendon while playing paddleball with running back Tom Matte. Although the injury did not permanently disable Unitas, the Colts benched him in midseason in 1972 and traded him to the San Diego Chargers (NFL). Unitas played with the the Chargers in 1973 and 1974 before becoming a CBS sports analyst.

By his retirement, Unitas had attempted more passes (5,186), completed more aerials (2,830) for more yardage (40,239), and thrown more touchdown passes (290) than any other quarterback in the NFL's history. Named to the Pro Football Hall of Fame in 1979, the eighteen-year pro veteran made the game more popular and affluent and achieved fame when quarterbacks were taking over pro football. Ironically, the serious, old-fashioned, crew-cut Unitas helped establish a football era characterized by Hollywood-like superstars, beneficiaries of a highly commercialized game. Always constructively critical of himself and teammates and forever self-driven on the gridiron, Unitas ceased active participation in football at age 41 when the game was changing. Unitas helped author two books, *Pro Quarterback: My Own Story*, with Ed Fitzgerald (1965) and *The Athlete's Handbook: How to be a Champion in Any Sport* (1979). The Pro Football Hall of Fame named him to its AFL-NFL 1960–1984 All-Star Team.

BIBLIOGRAPHY: Baltimore *News American*, July 25, 1974; Earl Blackwell, ed., *Celebrity Register* (New York, 1973); Hal Butler, *Sports Heroes Who Wouldn't Quit* (New York, 1973); *CB* (1962), pp. 430–32; Lud Duroska, ed., *Great Pro Quarterbacks* (New York, 1972); George Gipe, *The Great American Sports Book* (Garden City, NY, 1978); Ronald L. Mendell and Timothy B. Phares, *Who's Who in Football* (New Rochelle, NY, 1974); Miami *Herald*, July 26, 1974; *NYT*, January 17, 1971; Paul Soderberg, and Helen Washington, eds., *The Big Book of Halls of Fame in the United States and*

Canada (New York, 1977); *Webster's American Biographies* (Springfield, MA, 1974); WWA, 41st ed. (1980–1981), pp. 2, 3,352.

Frederick J. Augustyn, Jr.

UPSHAW, Eugene "Gene" (b. 15 August 1945, Robstown, TX), college and professional player and executive, is the son of Eugene and Cora (Riley) Upshaw and excelled in football, baseball, and track at Robstown High School and as an offensive lineman at Texas A&I College (LSC), where he was named to the NAIA and Coaches All-American teams. His strength, speed, and intelligence impressed pro scouts, as the Oakland Raiders selected him in the first round of the 1967 AFL-NFL draft. Upshaw's arrival in Oakland coincided with the Raiders' rise to prominence in pro football. Oakland had not appeared in post-season play prior to signing Upshaw, but captured the AFL title his rookie season before losing to the Green Bay Packers in the 1968 Super Bowl. The Raiders missed the playoffs only four times, as left guard Upshaw anchored their line. The Raiders twice captured the Super Bowl during Upshaw's tenure, defeating the Minnesota Vikings in 1976 and Philadelphia Eagles in 1980.

The 6 foot, 5 inch, 255 pound Upshaw retained his quickness throughout his career and proved a formidable opponent against the pass and run. Since football became a more cerebral game, he mastered the intricacies of line play strategy and adeptly called audibly to colleagues along the line in response to shifts in defensive formations. After the NFL and AFL merged, he was named to four All-Pro teams and five All-AFC squads. He was selected AFC Lineman of the Year in 1973 and 1974 and the top NFL lineman in 1977 and finished runner-up for the latter award in 1980. An extremely durable player, Upshaw participated in 209 consecutive games in his 16–season, 217–game career through the 1982 season.

Upshaw's leadership capabilities were recognized on the field, where he captained the Raiders for ten seasons, and off the field. A member of the Executive Committee of the NFL Players Association from 1976 to 1980, he was elected its president in 1980. When a breakdown in contract negotiations engendered an eight-week strike during the 1982 season, Upshaw helped to maintain membership morale in the face of intense media criticism of the players. Upshaw's colleagues selected him to head the NFL Players Association in June 1983, when he was named its executive director. The Pro Football Hall of Fame named him to its AFL-NFL 1960–1984 All-Star second team and inducted him into membership in 1987.

Upshaw's activities on behalf of several political, community, civic, and charitable organizations have earned him wider recognition. In 1980 he received the Byron "Whizzer" White Humanitarian Award for outstanding contributions to team, community, and nation. In 1982 he received the A. Philip Randolph Award as one of the outstanding Black leaders in America.

BIBLIOGRAPHY: *TSN Football Register—1983*.

Steven Tischler

V

VAN BROCKLIN, Norman " Stormin' Norman" "The Dutchman" (b. 15 March 1926, Eagle Butte, SD; d. 2 May 1983, Social Circle, GA), college and professional player, coach, and broadcaster, was the eighth of nine children born to middle-class farmers Mac and Ethel Van Brocklin and became one of football's supercompetitors. This hard-driving attitude won "The Dutchman" many honors as a player, but helped cause problems in two NFL head coaching stints. One of the sport's greatest passer-punters, Van Brocklin graduated in 1943 from Acalanes High School in Walnut Creek, CA, and began his football career there.

After a tour of U.S. Navy duty, Van Brocklin entered the University of Oregon (PCC) in 1946 and completed a B.S. degree in Physical Education in three years. He later married his biology instructor, Gloria Schiewe, and had six children. Athletically, "The Dutchman" experienced a frustrating freshman year at Oregon. Lacking running speed, he struggled with the single-wing system. After Jim Aiken became coach the next year and introduced the T formation, the 6 foot, 1 inch, 199 pound Van Brocklin began to excel on the gridiron. Van Brocklin made the All-PCC squad in 1947 and 1948 and guided the Ducks in a 21–13 loss to SMU in the 1949 Cotton Bowl. During three seasons at Oregon, Van Brocklin completed 144 of 316 passes for 1,949 yards and 16 touchdowns.

In 1949 the Los Angeles Rams (NFL) made the nationally recognized passer their fourth draft choice. "The Dutchman" spent a spectacular, controversial nine-year career with the Rams. Van Brocklin, who disliked sharing quarterbacking duties with Bob Waterfield* and later Billy Wade, led the Rams to their only NFL title in 1951. In the 1951 championship game, he threw a 73–yard touchdown pass to Tom Fears* to give the Rams a 24–17 triumph over the Cleveland Browns.

Dissatisfied with the Rams situation, Van Brocklin was traded to the Philadelphia Eagles (NFL) prior to the 1958 season. The Eagles made the biggest trade in their history, surrendering a first-round draft pick and veteran players Jimmy Harris and Buck Lansford for the volatile passer. The trade paid dividends, as Van Brocklin in 1960 led the Eagles to the NFL title. The 1960 Eagles relied on Van Brocklin's passing. "The Dutchman's" aerials to receivers Tommy McDonald* and Pete Retzlaff* propelled the Eagles to a 10–2 record and an Eastern Conference title. Van Brocklin starred in the NFL championship win over the Green Bay Packers and was voted 1960 NFL Player of the Year. At the peak of his career, the 34–year-old Van Brocklin abruptly retired.

Van Brocklin perhaps expected to replace retiring Eagles coach Buck Shaw* but was passed over and instead became head coach of the expansion Minnesota Vikings (NFL). "The Dutchman's" coaching career proved more controversial than his playing career. He coached the Vikings from 1961 through 1967 and the Atlanta Falcons (NFL) from 1968 through half of the 1974 campaign, compiling a lackluster 66–100–7 mark. As a head mentor, Van Brocklin dueled with Minnesota quarterback Fran Tarkenton,* other players, and newspapermen. After coaching Atlanta, Van Brocklin lived quietly in Social Circle, GA, broadcast for the Turner network, and assisted football coach Pepper Rodgers at Georgia Tech. Two serious surgeries in 1979 ended his active involvement in football.

Van Brocklin was elected to the NFF College Football Hall of Fame and in 1979 to the Pro Football Hall of Fame. During his illustrious career he passed for 23,611 yards and 173 touchdowns and averaged 42.9 yards per punt. Besides playing in 10 Pro Bowl games and five NFL championship contests, he led the NFL in passing three times (1950, 1952, 1954) and punting twice. In a single 1951 game he passed a record 554 yards against the New York Yankees. Although the NFL played only 12 games per season, Van Brocklin passed over 2,000 yards six times. Van Brocklin, who guided the 1951 Rams and 1960 Eagles to NFL championships, ranked among modern football's greatest quarterbacks.

BIBLIOGRAPHY: Bill Barron et al, *The Official NFL Encyclopedia of Football* (New York, 1982); *NYT* (May 5, 1983), p. D27; *Philadelphia Eagles Media Guides, 1958–1960;* Philadelphia *Inquirer* (May 3, 1983), pp. 1C, 5C.

William A. Gudelunas

VAN BUREN, Steve (b. 28 December 1920, La Ceiba, Honduras), college and professional player, saw his career flourish after adding 35 pounds by working in a steel mill as a high school student. When he entered LSU (SEC) in 1940, he had become a 6 foot, 1 inch, 200 pound runner capable of bruising opponent's tacklers. At LSU Van Buren played blocking back until his senior year and enabled tailback Alvin Dark* (BB) to make long runs. Coach Bernie Moore converted Van Buren to an offensive star his senior year. Van Buren broke the SEC rushing record that year and starred in the Tigers' 1944

Orange Bowl victory over Texas A&M. Van Buren, who ran 9.8 seconds in the 100–yard dash, scored two touchdowns and passed for a third in the game. In 1944 Van Buren received a Bachelor's degree in Mechanical Engineering from LSU.

Van Buren, first draft choice of the Philadelphia Eagles, played there from 1944 through 1951 and became one of the most devastating runners in NFL history. Termed a "1980s runner turned loose in the 1940s," the "boy from the bayous" held six NFL records and every Eagle rushing record by the end of the 1949 season. He won four NFL rushing titles and played on the 1948 and 1949 NFL championship Eagles. In the 1949 title game against the Los Angeles Rams, the powerful Van Buren gained 196 yards on 31 carries in a driving rainstorm to establish a then-NFL title game record.

Van Buren's pro coach Alfred Earle "Greasy" Neale* called him the greatest runner in football history. Van Buren's statistics justified that statement. By the end of the 1949 season, Van Buren held several all-time NFL marks: most yards gained rushing one season (1,146 in 1949); most career yards rushing (5,553); most rushes one year (263 in 1949); most career rushes (1,208); most touchdowns in one year (18 in 1945); and most touchdowns rushing in one year (16 in 1945). He also rewrote the Eagles' record book. As of 1985, Van Buren still held the all-time Eagles records for punt return average (13.9 yards), kickoff return average (26.7 yards), and career touchdowns (77).

Van Buren, a perennial All-Pro selection beginning in his rookie season, made the Pro Football Hall of Fame in 1965. Van Buren, who gained 5,860 yards rushing in his NFL career, became only the second runner in NFL history to gain 1,000 yards in a season and the first to rush over 1,000 yards in two seasons. Wilbert Montgomery* remains the only other Eagles back to gain over 1,000 yards in a season. Van Buren enjoyed his best rushing year in 1949 when he gained 1,146 yards on 236 carries in a 12-game season. He first surpassed the 1,000 yard mark in 1947 by garnering 1,008 yards on 217 rushes.

A crippling knee injury haunted Van Buren after his meteoric 1949 season, as he gained 629 yards on 188 carries in 1950 and only 327 yards on 112 rushes in 1951. He still attempted to play at training camp in 1953, but the knee problem worsened and forced perhaps the greatest Eagles runner of all time into retirement. Van Buren represented a modern-day big back, playing when runners of his size were uncommon. Van Buren's fabulous career demonstrated that men of his size and speed would be required on future teams, while his abilities helped modernize NFL offensive strategies. Van Buren, who married and had three children, still resides in the Philadelphia area.

BIBLIOGRAPHY: Bill Barron et al, *The Official NFL Encyclopedia of Football* (New York,

1982); Myron Cope, *The Game That Was: The Early Days of Pro Football* (New York, 1970); Ray Didinger, "The Greatest Team of the Greatest Years," *Pro* (January, 1983), 69–75; *Philadelphia Eagles Media Guides, 1944–1951.*

William A. Gudelunas

VAN EEGHEN, Mark (b. 19 April 1952, Cambridge, MA), college and professional player, is the son of a construction field superintendent and grew up in Cranston, RI. He attended Cranston West High School, where he made football All-American at running back and captained his high school basketball team to the state title. He and his wife, Nancy, his high school sweetheart, have three daughters, Brooke, Kady, and Amber. Van Eeghen graduated from Colgate University in 1974 with a B.A. degree in Economics. Freshmen could not play varsity football then, but van Eeghen started his sophomore year. The Red Raiders coach introduced the wishbone offense to eastern college football in 1971 to make best use of van Eeghen's talent. During his three years, van Eeghen established records for most yards gained rushing in a single season (1,089 in 1973) and career (2,591 from 1971–1973), most rushing attempts in a season (238 in 1973) and career (528 from 1971–1973), most rushing touchdowns in a season (14 in 1973), and most touchdowns in a season (15 in 1973).

The Oakland Raiders (NFL) made van Eeghen their third pick in the 1974 football draft. Van Eeghen spent eight seasons with the Raiders, averaging over 1,000 yards per season for his five full seasons as a starter (1976–1980). The first Raider to have gained over 1,000 yards three successive seasons, he in 1977 set a then-club record for single-season rushing (1,273 yards) and led the AFC in yardage gained. Van Eeghen played in 13 post-season games with the Raiders, including five AFC championship games and two Super Bowl victories (XI against the Minnesota Vikings and XV against the Philadelphia Eagles). Van Eeghen became the all-time Raiders rushing leader (5,907 yards) before being waived at the beginning of the 1982 season. Van Eeghen ended his pro playing career with two seasons for the New England Patriots (NFL). He rushed for 386 yards in 82 attempts in 1982 and carried 95 times for 358 yards and 2 touchdowns in 1983. He ended his career tied with Harry "Chuck" Muncie* for thirteenth place (6,651 yards) among all-time rushing leaders and with 37 rushing and four receiving touchdowns.

BIBLIOGRAPHY: Boston *Herald*, April 24, 1984; *Oakland Raiders Press Guide, 1981; New England Patriots, 1983 Fact Book;* Lee Woltman, "Mark van Eeghen: Raider with a Super Bowl Ring and a Colgate Smile," *The Colgate Scene* (February, 1977), pp. 10–11.

Eric C. Schneider

VAUGHT, John Howard "Johnny" "Harpo" (b. 6 May 1909, Ingleside, TX), college athlete and football coach, coached football over twenty-four seasons (1947–1970, part of 1973) at the University of Mississippi (SEC) and guided the Rebels to six SEC championships, four undefeated regular seasons, and ten wins in eighteen bowl games. The AP ranked his Rebels in the top ten nine times and top twenty seventeen times. Mississippi in 1960 won the FWAA Grantland Rice Trophy as national champions. Vaught's composite football coaching record included 190–61–12 (.745 percent), ranking him fourteenth in victories among all mentors.

One of eleven children of farmer Rufus and Sally (Harris) Vaught, he attended Ft. Worth Polytechnic High School. He played four-year regular gridiron end, tackle, and fullback and captained the football team his senior year. A star basketball player, he also served as senior class president and valedictorian and graduated in 1929. The 6 foot, 190 pound Vaught became an honor student at TCU and captained the 1932 SWC football champion Horned Frogs. Twice All-SWC guard, he became TCU's first All-American when chosen first team in 1932 by AP. Nicknamed "Harpo" by classmates because of his thick, curly hair, Vaught played three years as a basketball regular and graduated in 1933.

After coaching football two years at Ft. Worth (TX) Northside High School, Vaught in 1935 worked as an appliance salesman. He served as line coach (1936–1941) at the University of North Carolina (SC) under Raymond Wolf, as a lieutenant commander (1942–1945) in the World War II U.S. Naval Pre-Flight program, and as line coach at North Carolina Pre-Flight (1942) and Corpus Christi Naval Air Station (1945). After being line coach in 1946 for a 2–7–0 Mississippi squad under Harold Drew, Vaught became head football coach the following year and led the Rebels to a 9–2–0 record and their first SEC championship. In its first bowl game "Ole Miss" achieved its first victory (43–13) over Tennessee in 20 games (coach Bob Neyland's* worst loss) and a 13–9 Delta Bowl triumph over TCU. Chosen SEC 1947 Coach of the Year, Vaught guided the first two of his twenty All-Americans, quarterback Charlie Conerly and end Barney Poole, making an outstanding straight-T passing combination.

Mississippi had the smallest SEC enrollment and had never won more than three SEC games in a season before Vaught took charge. Most recruiting came within a 200–mile radius by the close-knit staff of former Rebels, including Frank "Bruiser" Kinard,* Buster and Ray Poole, and Junie Hovious. After Conerly graduated in 1948, Vaught adopted the split-T with a higher percentage of passes off the option. SEC championships followed in 1954 and 1955 under the leadership of quarterback Eagle Day and fullback Paige Cothren. The SEC "Game of the Year" in 1959 occurred when top-ranked LSU triumphed 7–3 over previously undefeated, third-rated "Ole Miss." In a Sugar Bowl rematch, the Rebels gained revenge 21–0 to finish 10–1–0 and with a second-place national ranking. Additional SEC titles came in 1960, 1962, and 1963 under quarterbacks Jake Gibbs and Glynn Griffing. Archie Manning became Vaught's last outstanding quarterback before the coach was forced to retire in 1970 because of a heart condition. Vaught was drafted to coach the last eight games of 1973 after mentor Billy Kinard was released.

A bluff, leather-faced perfectionist, Vaught imposed strict player regulations: "no marriage, no car, and 10:30 curfew six nights a week." He possessed no flair for laughter, making his points with earnestness and logic. In 1939 Vaught married Johnsie Stinson of Chattanooga, TN, an accomplished painter of birds. They have one son, John H., Jr., and live in University, MS, where Vaught is deacon of the First Baptist Church and enjoys golf, fishing, and dancing. He was elected to the NFF College Football Hall of Fame in 1979.

BIBLIOGRAPHY: Robert Ours, *College Football Almanac* (New York, 1984); Tom Siler, "He Made Ole Miss a Menace," *SEP* 229 (October 13, 1956), pp. 33, 129–131; William W. Sorrels and Charles Cavagnaro, *Ole Miss Rebels: Mississippi Football* (Huntsville, AL, 1976); John H. Vaught, *Rebel Coach* (Memphis, TN, 1974).

James D. Whalen

VESSELS, Billy Dale "Curly" (b. 22 March 1931, Cleveland, OK), college and professional player, suffered a youth of family hardships relieved only through athletics. He played basketball and baseball and won the state low-hurdle championship three consecutive years at Cleveland High School, where he graduated in 1949. The elusive, swift, 6 foot, 190 pound Vessels gained most prominence as a football player and won All-State honors both as a junior and senior. After enrolling at the University of Oklahoma (BSC) in 1949, he experienced academic difficulties and lost his eligibility. Once his grades improved, Vessels proved a hard-tackling football defensive back and a brilliant runner. Vessels led the Sooners to 27 victories in 31 games from 1951 to 1953, including Sugar and Orange Bowl triumphs and three BSC titles. During his senior year (1953), he finished second nationally in rushing (1,072 yards), total offense, and scoring (18 touchdowns) and made 111 yards passing. The consensus All-American won the Heisman Trophy and Maxwell Award and was selected Player of the Year by the AP and UPI.

Although he was drafted by the Baltimore Colts (NFL), Vessels disagreed with the team's management over his contract. Vessels, who married Susanne Wilson in 1953, joined the Edmonton Eskimos (CFL). Vessels enjoyed a sensational season, winning the Schenley Award as the CFL's best player. Military service at Fort Still, OK, in 1954 interrupted his pro football career. Although winning All-Army Service honors, he suffered a severe knee injury that shortened his career. He signed with the Baltimore Colts for the 1956 season upon his military discharge, but he never regained his former brilliance. Vessels rushed 44 times for 215 yards (4.9–yard average) and 2 touchdowns and caught 11 passes for 177 yards (16.1–yard average) and 1 touchdown. Subsequent difficulties with the Baltimore coaching staff caused Vessels to retire after that season and join the Mackle Corporation. Vessels, who resides in Coral Gables, FL, with his wife and three children, used his football aggressiveness, determination, and competitiveness to become a successful real estate developer. His selection to the NFF College Football Hall of Fame in 1974 proved a fitting tribute to his impressive career.

BIBLIOGRAPHY: *Baltimore Colts Media Guide, 1956; Congressional Record,* January 15, 1975; *Sport* 11 (September, 1951).

Jerome Mushkat

W

WADE, William Wallace (b. 15 June 1892, Trenton, TN), college athlete, coach, and administrator, is the son of farmer Robert Bruce and Sarah Ann (Mitchell) Wade. He attended Trenton's Peabody High School and Morgan Park Academy in Chicago, where he played football. Wade, who attended Brown University (IL) from 1913 to 1917 and received a B.A. degree in 1917, married Frances Bell in 1917 and has two children, William Wallace, Jr., and Frances Margaret. A lean, 6 foot, 180 pound guard, Wade played football three years at Brown under coach E. N. Robinson and participated in the 1916 Rose Bowl. After serving in the U.S. Army and attaining the rank of captain, Wade in 1919 and 1920 served as athletic director and head football, baseball and basketball coach at Fitzgerald and Clark Prep School in Tullahoma, TN. At Vanderbilt University (SC) in 1921 and 1922, he was assistant athletic director, assistant football coach, and head baseball and basketball coach.

Wade served as athletic director and head football coach at the University of Alabama (SC) from 1923 to 1930 and as head baseball coach from 1924 to 1927. His football squads compiled 61 wins, 13 losses, and three ties, fielded three undefeated teams, won four SC titles, and participated in the Rose Bowl three times. His outstanding Crimson Tide players included Pooley Hubert, Johnny Mack Brown, Fred Sington, and Johnny Cain. Wade's 1924 squad finished 8–1 and won the SC championship, while his 1925 team, led by backs Hubert and Brown, won the national championship with a 10–0 record and defeated Washington 20–19 in the Rose Bowl. Paced by end Wu Winslett, the 1926 squad repeated as national champions, compiled a 9–0–1 record, and tied Stanford 7–7 in the Rose Bowl. The 1930 team, featuring tackle Sington and back Cain, finished undefeated in ten games, triumphed over Washington State 24–0 in the Rose Bowl, and gave Wade his fourth SC and third national championship.

Wade served as athletic director and head football coach at Duke University

(SC) from 1931 to 1941 and then entered the U.S. Army. He returned as athletic director in 1945 and head coach from 1946 to 1950. During 16 years Wade's clubs won 110 games, lost 36, and tied 7, captured six SC championships, and twice appeared in the Rose Bowl. At Duke he developed Clarence "Ace" Parker,* Fred Crawford, Dan Hill, Eric Tipton, George McAfee,* and Steve Lach.* In 1933 Duke, led by tackle Crawford, finished 9–1 and won the SC championship. Halfback Parker paced the 1935 and 1936 Blue Devils to 8–2 and 9–1 records and SC titles. Wade's 9–1 1938 "Iron Dukes," starring back Tipton and center Hill, were undefeated and unscored on until losing 7–3 to Southern California in the Rose Bowl. Led by halfback McAfee, the 9–1 1939 team repeated as SC champions. Wade's 9–1 1941 squad, sparked by halfback Lach, led the nation in offense and lost only to underdog Oregon State 20–16 in the transplanted Rose Bowl at Durham, NC.

During World War II, Wade served with distinction as a battlefield commander and rose to lieutenant colonel. From participating in the Normandy Invasion, Battle of the Bulge, and Crossing of the Rhine, he earned the Bronze Star and French Croix de Guerre with Palm. Wade finished his football coaching career in 1950 with a 7–3 record. In 24 seasons at Alabama and Duke, he won 171 games, lost 49, and tied 10. An astute football analyst and defensive specialist, the taciturn Wade proved a tough drillmaster and stickler for detail and execution. The gruff, demanding, and patient teacher was highly respected by his players.

From 1947 to 1950 Wade served on the NCAA Football Rules Committee. After his first wife, Frances, died in 1947, he married Virginia Jones in 1950. He was SC commissioner from December 1950, to January 1960, before retiring to his Durham County, NC, farm. Wade was elected to the NFF College Football Hall of Fame in 1955 and to the HAF College Football Hall of Fame. Duke Stadium was renamed in 1967 in his honor. One of football's greatest coaches, Wade brought Alabama, Duke, and southern football into national prominence and helped popularize the Rose Bowl classic.

BIBLIOGRAPHY: "Bowl Man," *Time* 30 (October 25, 1937), pp. 32, 34–36; Tim Cohane, *Great College Football Coaches of the Twenties and Thirties* (New Rochelle, NY, 1973); Allison Danzig, *The History of American Football: Its Great Teams, Players, and Coaches* (Englewood Cliffs, NJ, 1956); *Duke University Football Press Guide, 1950;* George Langford, *The Crimson Tide* (Chicago, 1974); Zipp Newman, *The Impact of Southern Football* (Montgomery, AL, 1969); *WWA*, 31st ed. (1960–1961), p. 2,997.

Edward J. Pavlick

WALDORF, Lynn Osbert "Pappy" (b. 3 October 1902, Clifton Springs, NY; d. 15 August 1981, Berkeley, CA), college player and coach and professional administrator, became the first AFCA Coach of the Year in 1935 and finished runner-up in 1948 and 1949. He served as AFCA president in 1950 and was elected to the NFF College Football Hall of Fame in 1966 and to the HAF College Football Hall of Fame. The 5 foot, 11 inch, 210 pound Waldorf made Walter Camp's* All-American second team tackle as a sophomore (1922) and senior (1924) at Syracuse University. Under coach John Meehan, the Orangemen attained a three-year 24–4–3 composite record and defeated Wallace Wade's* Alabama, Jock Sutherland's* Pittsburgh, and Dick Harlow's* Colgate, Penn State, and Nebraska (the two years the Cornhuskers defeated Notre Dame's Four Horsemen*). The 1925 graduate served on the crew, as president of the Senior Council and Interfraternity Council, and participated in Phi Kappa Alpha fraternity.

Waldorf coached football at Academy High School in Erie, PA (1925), and Oklahoma City University (1926–1927), attaining the latter's best record (8–1–2) in 1927 despite fielding six regulars with no high school football experience. The 1927 squad shared the Oklahoma Collegiate Championship with Oklahoma Baptist. He never lost to Oklahoma, recording three victories and two ties. After being University of Kansas line coach (BSC, 1928), he coached Oklahoma A&M to a 34–10–7 record (1929–1933) and four MVC championships. As a mentor at Kansas State University in 1934, he guided the Wildcats to their only BSC championship with a 7–2–1 record. At Northwestern University (WC, 1935–1946), Waldorf fielded three top ten teams and another two in the top twenty and attained a combined 49–45–7 record. Northwestern won its first undisputed WC championship (1936), placed fourth or better eight seasons, and boasted eight All-Americans including quarterback Otto Graham.* Waldorf's clubs enjoyed eight victories over Illinois, five over Minnesota, four over Ohio State, two each over Michigan and Notre Dame, and one over Great Lakes Naval Training Station. The Wildcats spoiled undefeated seasons for Notre Dame, Ohio State, and Minnesota, ending the Golden Gophers' 28–game undefeated streak.

Waldorf coached football at the University of California–Berkeley (1947–1956), attaining a composite 67–32–4 record, three PCC championships and Rose Bowl appearances, and an outstanding 46–3–1 regular season mark his first five years. California had experienced three consecutive losing seasons before Waldorf's arrival. A portly 240 pounds, he displayed a calm demeanor, held high moral values, and remained one of the most liked by his peers. The son of Methodist bishop Ernest Lynn Waldorf and Flora Janet (Irish) Waldorf, he graduated from Cleveland (OH) East High School in 1921, married Louise Jane McKay in 1925, and had two daughters. The author of *This Game of Football* (1952), he left California after two losing seasons in the mid-1950s. He served as personnel director of the San Francisco 49ers (NFL) from 1957 until his retirement in 1972 and succcumbed to heart failure. Waldorf, who had survived several traditional coaching graveyards, compiled a 174–100–21 overall college coaching mark.

BIBLIOGRAPHY: Tim Cohane, "Those Golden Bears Are on the Go," *Look* 15 (October 23, 1951); Allison Danzig, *The History of American Football: Its Great Teams, Players, and Coaches* (Englewood Cliffs, NJ, 1956); Des Moines *Sunday Register*, September 7, 1986; Arthur L. Evans, *Fifty Years of Football At Syracuse University* (Syracuse, NY, 1939); John D. McCallum and Charles H. Pearson, *College Football U.S.A., 1869–1973* (New York, 1973); Ronald L. Mendell and Timothy B. Phares, *Who's Who in Football* (New Rochelle, NY, 1974); Walter Paulison, *The Tale of the Wildcats* (Evanston, IL, 1951); Ken Rappoport, *The Syracuse Football Story* (Huntsville, AL, 1975); Rube Samuelson, "Coast Compares Cal to Wonder Teams," *The Quarterback* (November 22, 1950); Collie Small, "Coaches Graveyard," *SEP* 220 (October 18, 1947), 24–25ff.

James D. Whalen

WALKER, Ewell Doak, Jr. "Dauntless Doak" "Dynamic Doak" (b. 1 January 1927, Dallas, TX), college and professional player, excelled in football for SMU (SWC, 1945, 1947–1949) and the Detroit Lions (NFL, 1950–1955). Nicknamed "Dauntless Doak" and "Dynamic Doak," the versatile Walker frequently made the "big" play. Walker grew up in a gridiron family, for his father, Ewell Doak, Sr., served as assistant football coach at North Dallas High School. Walker began his football career as a guard on the Highland Park Junior High team, but the coach wisely moved him to the backfield after several games. Walker led Highland Park High School of Dallas, TX, to the state playoffs before losing to Port Arthur in the 1944 finals.

Walker served briefly in the U.S. Merchant Marine in 1944 and entered SMU (SWC) five games into the season. After registering on a Monday, Walker played football on the following Saturday and scored the Mustangs' only touchdown on a 37–yard jaunt in their 12–7 loss to Texas. Walker served in the U.S. Army the 1945 season and played for the Brooke Army Medical Center team (San Antonio, TX) in 1946. He returned to SMU in 1947 and played there three more seasons. The 1947 SMU team is regarded among the SWC's greatest squads, finishing undefeated and being tied only by TCU. Walker's season highlight occurred when he caught a 54–yard pass to set up the winning touchdown against Texas. SMU won SWC championships in both 1947 and 1948.

During his SMU career, the versatile 5 foot, 11 inch, 173 pound Walker rushed for slightly over 1,950 yards for a 4.2–yard average per carry, threw 221 times for 1,638 yards, and returned 50 punts for 750 yards (15–yard average) and 2 touchdowns. He also returned 53 kickoffs for 1,080 yards and a 20.4–yard average, caught 26 passes for 449 yards, and punted 80 times for an average 39.5 yards per kick. Walker, who still holds the SMU career scoring record with Eric Dickerson,* made 288 points on 38 touchdowns, 57 of 63 extra points, and one field goal. His best game probably came in the 19–19 tie with TCU, as Walker amassed 471 yards total offense and galloped 80, 61, and 56 yards to give SMU a last-minute tie.

One mentor described Walker as a "coach on the field," who could "pass, run, block, punt, kick field goals and extra points, as well as call signals and play masterful defense." Walker's greatest asset was his ability to produce when the "chips were down." *SI* (September 15, 1969) stated: "Walker did more things well in football, including win—win with a mediocre team—than just about anyone who ever played. . . . They called him 'the miracle man; and he was precisely that in an age of perhaps the strongest football (the late 1940s) we have seen." Walker, an All-SWC four years and All-American from 1947 to 1949, won the Maxwell Award in 1947, Heisman Trophy in 1948, and Swede Nelson Award for Sportsmanship in 1949. Walker probably would have received the Heisman Trophy again as a senior in 1949, but was injured and played only 251 minutes.

After playing in the College All-Star game in 1950, Walker joined the Detroit Lions and starred in a brief, five-year NFL career. He led the NFL in scoring in 1950 and made All-Pro four of his five NFL seasons. Walker and former high school teammate and college rival Bobby Layne* led the Lions to NFL titles in 1952 and 1953. He gained 1,520 yards rushing (4.9–yard average) and 12 touchdowns and 2,539 yards in pass receptions (16.7–yard average) for 21 touchdowns. Walker also returned 18 punts for 284 yards (15.8–yard average) and one touchdown and 38 kickoffs for 968 yards (25.5–yard average). Walker retired at age 28, stating that he "wanted to get out while [he] had all [his] teeth and both [his] knees." The much honored Walker belongs to the Michigan Sports, Texas Sports, HAF, and NFF College Football and Pro Football Halls of Fame.

BIBLIOGRAPHY: Louis Cox and Bill Rives, *Text of Texas Hall of Fame Bibliography* (Grand Prairie, TX, 1959); Allison Danzig, *The History of American Football: Its Great Teams, Players, and Coaches* (Englewood Cliffs, NJ, 1956); John D. McCallum and Charles H. Pearson, *College Football U.S.A., 1869–1973* (New York, 1973); Ronald L. Mendell and Timothy B. Phares, *Who's Who in Football* (New Rochelle, NY, 1974); David S. Neft et al., *The Complete All-Time Pro Football Register* (New York, 1975); SMU College Football Game Program, 1983.

Lawrence Ziewacz

WALKER, Herschel Junior (b. 3 March 1962, Wrightsville, GA), college and professional athlete, is the son of Willis and Christine (Taylor) Walker. His father worked as a foreman in a kaolin clay plant, while his mother supervised in a clothing factory. He has three brothers, Willis, Jr., Kenneth, and Lorenzo, and three sisters, Sharon, Veronica, and Carol.

Walker attended Johnson County High School (Wrightsville), where he made consensus All-American in football and *Parade* magazine National Back of the Year. In high school he rushed 6,137 yards and helped his team win the 1979 state championship. He scored 45 touchdowns his senior year and 86 in his high school career, both national records. In track and field, he won the state championship in the 100–yard dash (9.9 seconds), the 220–yard dash (21.8 seconds) and in the shot put (53 feet, 3.25 inches) and participated on the state championship team. He played basketball and served as president of the Beta Club, national scholastic honor society.

At 6 feet, 2 inches, and 222 pounds, Walker combined size and speed never before seen in college football. After entering the University of Georgia (SEC) in 1980, he set an NCAA record as a freshman by rushing 1,616 yards, replacing Tony Dorsett* in the record book. Walker was named SEC Player of the Year, made All-American by consensus, and finished third in the Heisman Trophy balloting, the highest ranking ever achieved by a freshman. Walker became the first freshman ever selected to the FWAA and Kodak All-American teams. In the Sugar Bowl he led Georgia to the national championship. Georgia defeated Notre Dame 16–10, as Walker gained 150 yards, scored two touchdowns, and was named MVP. Later his freshman year, Walker qualified for the NCAA Indoor and Outdoor Track and Field Championships. He made All-American on Georgia's 400–meter relay team, which finished second in the championships. During the summer, 1981, he performed track in Europe and ran the 100 meters in 10.19 seconds.

As a sophomore in 1981, Walker made consensus All-American, was named SEC Player of the Year for the second time, and finished second in the Heisman Trophy voting. He achieved All-American recognition in Indoor Track for his performance in the 60–meter dash. Outdoors he nearly equalled the world record by running the 100 meters in 10.10 seconds. In his junior year Walker was named SEC Player of the Year and consensus All-American for the third consecutive season. He won the Heisman Trophy as the nation's outstanding collegiate football player, having set 4 NCAA, 7 SEC, and 14 Bulldog records in 1982 and established 10 NCAA, 15 SEC, and 30 Bulldog career records. He gained 5,259 yards rushing, ranking third on the NCAA all-time rushing list.

Walker passed up his senior year in college to enter pro football in the new USFL. With the New Jersey Generals in 1983, he led the USFL in rushing yardage (1,812), total yardage (2,370), and touchdowns by rushing (17). He also paced New Jersey's pass receivers with 53 catches for 558 yards and one touchdown. During a ten-month period, Walker gained 3,564 yards rushing for Georgia and New Jersey. In 1985 Walker shattered pro football single-season records by rushing 438 times for 2,411 yards in 18 games and was unanimously named USFL MVP. Walker also broke pro records with 11 consecutive and 14 total 100–yard rushing performances. His 22 touchdowns, including 21 rushing, 132 season points, and 233 yards rushing in a game against the Houston Gamblers also established USFL records. He led the Generals in receiving with 37 catches for 467 yards and one touchdown. During his USFL career (1983–1985), he rushed 1,143 times for 5,562 yards

(4.9–yard average) and 54 touchdowns and caught 130 passes for 1,484 yards (11.4–yard average) and 7 touchdowns. Walker was selected All-USFL in 1983 and 1985 and Player of the Year in 1985.

In August 1986 the Dallas Cowboys (NFL) signed Walker to a $5 million, five-year contract. Walker became the highest paid running back in NFL history. He rushed 184 times for 739 yards (4.9–yard average) in 1986, scored 12 touchdowns, and led the 7–9 Cowboys with 76 pass receptions for 837 yards (11.0–yard average) and 2 touchdowns. His twin 84–yard touchdowns against Philadelphia on December 14 demonstrated his enormous versatility. Changing direction on an end run, he split the Eagles defense with his blazing speed. The 84–yard reception came on a quick slant pass that he converted into a sprint to the end zone. Walker married Cindy de Angelis on March 31, 1983, and resides in Athens, GA, in the off-season.

BIBLIOGRAPHY: Athens (GA) *Banner Herald*, 1980–1983; Athens (GA) *Daily News*, 1980–1983; Atlanta *Constitution*, 1980–1983; Atlanta *Journal*, 1980–1983; *New Jersey Generals Public Relations Brochures, 1983;* University of Georgia, Sports Information files, Atlanta, GA; *USA Today*, August 14, 1986.

Robert T. Bowen

WALSH, William Ernest "Bill" (b. 30 November 1931, Los Angeles, CA), college and professional athlete and coach, is the son of a drifting laborer. Walsh attended George Washington High School in Los Angeles and Hayward (CA) High School, graduating in 1949. Although possessing only average athletic ability, Walsh participated in football and track. A quarterback at San Mateo (CA) JC for two seasons, Walsh then enrolled at San Jose State University and played end for the Spartans. He graduated from San Jose State in 1954 with a Bachelor of Arts degree in Education. Walsh in 1955 began his football coaching career as an assistant at Monterey Peninsula (CA) JC. After serving in the U.S. Army, Walsh became an assistant coach at San Jose State, where he also earned a Master's degree in Education in 1959. His first head coaching position came at Washington Union High School in Fremont, CA, from 1957 to 1959. In Walsh's first season his team won the conference championship with a 9–1–0 record.

Walsh began college football coaching at the University of California–Berkeley (AAWU) serving under Marv Levy from 1960 to 1962. In 1963 he joined John Ralston's Stanford University (AAWU) staff and worked with the defensive backfield for three seasons. Walsh started his pro football coaching career in 1966 as offensive backfield coach for the Oakland Raiders (AFL). In 1967 he was named head coach for the San Jose (CA) entry (ConFL), which finished in second place with a 7–5–0 record. Walsh returned to the AFL (later NFL), where he spent eight seasons (1968–1975) with the Cincinnati Bengals as quarterbacks and receivers coach. Walsh tutored Ken Anderson,* who became the NFL's leading passer for two consecutive seasons (1974–1975). With the San Diego Chargers (NFL) as an assistant coach in 1976, Walsh helped develop quarterback Dan Fouts.* Walsh returned to Stanford as head football coach in 1977 and directed the Cardinals to a two-year 17–7–0 record. Stanford registered a 24–14 victory over LSU in the Sun Bowl and a 25–22 triumph over the University of Georgia in the Bluebonnet Bowl.

Walsh has served as head coach of the San Francisco 49ers (NFL) since 1979. With Joe Montana* as a leading NFL quarterback, Walsh directed the 49ers to the NFC championship in 1981 and 1984 and to victories in Super Bowl XVI (26–21 over Cincinnati) and Super Bowl XIX (38–16 over the Miami Dolphins). The 49ers completed the 1984 season with an 18–1 record (second best in pro football history) and set Super Bowl records for most first downs (31), passing yardage (326), and total yards (537), and equalled the record for most touchdowns (5). The 49ers also finished first in the NFC Western Division in 1983 and 1986. Walsh, through 1986, has compiled a pro coaching record of 76 victories, 54 losses, and one tie, including 7 triumphs and 3 defeats in playoff games. Married in 1955, Walsh and his wife, Geri, and interior decorator, live in Menlo Park, CA, and have three children, Steve, Craig, and Elizabeth.

BIBLIOGRAPHY: Ben Kinley, "San Francisco's Gridiron Guru," *SEP* 257 (October, 1985), pp. 44–45, 80; Kenny Moore, "To Baffle and Amaze," *SI* 57 (July 26, 1982), pp. 60–72; *NFL Official Record and Fact Book, 1985; TSN Football Register—1986.*

John L. Evers

WALSTON, Robert Harold "Bobby" (b. 17 October 1928, Columbus, OH), college and professional player and executive, excelled as a football placekicker and end. He played football at the University of Georgia (SEC) from 1947 to 1950 at offensive end, defensive safety, and kicker. Walston appeared in the 20–20 Gator Bowl tie with Maryland following the 1947 season and the 41–28 Orange Bowl loss to Texas after the 1948 campaign. In 1950 he earned a B.S. degree in Physical Education and Psychology. From 1951 to 1962 he starred with the Philadelphia Eagles (NFL). His 94 points, made on 3 touchdowns, 28 extra points, and 6 field goals, paced the 1951 Eagles in total scoring for the first of 10 times there and earned him Rookie of the Year honors. By 1953 the 6 foot, 195 pound Walston became Philadelphia's leading kicker and short-yardage end. In 1954 Walston led the NFL with 114 points and the Eagles with 11 touchdowns. After a subpar 1955 season, Walston paced the Eagles in reception yardage in 1956. In 1960 Walston scored 105 points for the NFL's championship Eagles, catching 31 passes for 801 yards, scoring 13 touchdowns, and making 39 extra points and 14 field goals. He tallied 97 points in 1961 but broke his arm the next season while playing for the last place Eagles and retired from football. Lifetime, Walston scored 46 touchdowns, 365 extra points, and 80 field goals for 881 NFL points. He held the scoring record upon retirement, but contemporaries Lou Groza* and George Blanda* soon surpassed him. As a combined receiver and kicking threat, Walston perhaps compiled unparalleled statistics. The slow, unspectacular receiver possessed good hands and caught 311 career passes for 3,363 yards (10.8–yard average). Walston, like many placekickers, was underrated given his points scored. Walston's accomplishments would have received more publicity had he played for more championship teams. In 1960 and 1961 he appeared in the Pro Bowl. Walston was personnel scout (1963) and director of player personnel (1964–1967) for the Philadelphia Eagles, assistant coach (1967–1968) for the Miami Dophins (NFL), director of player personnel and assistant to the president (1968–1975) for the Chicago Bears (NFL), personnel scout (1978–1980) for the Edmonton Eskimos (CFL) and personnel scout (1983–1986) for the New Jersey Generals (USFL). Walston, who resides in Rosselle, IL, is married to Wikke Johannesson, and had three children, Bobbi, Mike, and Mark (deceased).

BIBLIOGRAPHY: David S. Neft and Richard Cohen, *Pro Football: The Early Years, 1895–1960* (New York, 1978); David S. Neft, Richard M. Cohen, and Jordan A. Deutsch, *The Sports Encyclopedia, Pro Football: The Modern Era, 1960 to the Present* (New York, 1982).

John David Healy

WARFIELD, Paul D. (b. 28 November 1942, Warren, OH), college athlete, professional football player, and executive, is the son of Lena Dryden and Amelia Bell (Fort) Warfield and was a premier NFL wide receiver. He became an All-American football back and excelled in baseball and track at Warren Harding High School. At Ohio State University (BTC) he starred at halfback on both offense and defense and made most All-American teams in 1963. In addition, he starred as a sprinter, broad jumper, and hurdler on the Buckeyes track squad. Besides making All-BTC in 1962 and 1963, he played in the Shrine All-Star (East-West), Coaches All-America, Hula Bowl, and College All-Star football games. The Cleveland Browns selected Warfield in the first round of the 1964 NFL draft. As a rookie, he made 52 receptions for 920 yards and scored 9 touchdowns. After being sidelined with a broken collarbone in 1965, he returned to previous form in 1966. He starred four more seasons with Cleveland, achieving season highs with 1,067 yards in pass receptions and 12 touchdowns in 1968. Warfield played in four NFL championship games with Cleveland. The Browns defeated the Baltimore Colts 27–0 for the 1964 NFL championship but lost the 1965, 1968, and 1969 title games.

The Browns traded the 6 foot, 188 pound Warfield to the Miami Dolphins (NFL) after the 1969 season to secure draft rights to quarterback Mike Phipps. Warfield enjoyed five years with the Dolphins, making 156 catches for 3,355 yards and 33 touchdowns. A fluid mover with 9.6–second speed in the 100–

yard dash, Warfield helped lead the Miami squad into the playoffs five straight years. The Dolphins lost Super Bowl VI but won Super Bowls VII and VIII. The outstanding receiver and blocker was named All-Pro with the Browns in 1968–1969 and the Dolphins from 1971 through 1973. He also played in seven Pro Bowls, including three with Cleveland (1964, 1968–1969) and four with Miami (1970–1972, 1974).

Following the 1974 season, Warfield played out his option and signed with the Memphis Southmen (WFL). He made 25 catches for 422 yards and scored 3 touchdowns, despite a hamstring pull, before the WFL folded during 1975. Upon returning to Cleveland in 1976, he made 38 catches for 613 yards (16.1-yard average) and scored 6 touchdowns. He retired following the 1977 season. His 20.1-yard average per catch on 427 career receptions remains an NFL record. He gained 8,565 yards and made 85 touchdowns with his regular-season receptions and caught 58 passes for 1,121 yards in post-season play.

Warfield married Beverly Ann Keys on September 6, 1964 and has two children, Sonja and Malcolm. With degrees from Ohio State and Kent State universities, Warfield prepared for a career in radio and television. He was named assistant to the president of the Cleveland Browns in 1981 and became their director of player relations in 1983. In his very first year of eligibility (1983), Warfield was elected to the Pro Football Hall of Fame. The Pro Football Hall of Fame named him to its AFL-NFL 1960–1984 All-Star Second Team.

BIBLIOGRAPHY: Dwight Chapin, "Class of 1983," *The Pro Football Hall of Fame Souvenir Book 1983–84* (July, 1983), pp. 3B–12B; *Cleveland Browns Media Guide, 1977;* Don Smith, "Five Inductees Will Join Pro Football's Hall of Fame," *Football Digest* 12 (August, 1983), pp. 52–55; *TSN Football Register—1978.*

John L. Evers

WARNER, Curtis Edward "Curt" (b. 18 March 1961, Wyoming, WV), college and professional player, grew up with his grandparents in the small southern West Virginia town of Wyoming and attended Pineville High School. An exceptional high school football, basketball, and baseball player, Warner scored 89 touchdowns and gained 2,532 career yards rushing before graduating in 1979.

From 1979 to 1982 Warner played running back for Penn State University. In his four seasons there, the 5 foot, 11 inch, 205 pound Warner became the best all-around Nittany Lions running back ever and set 41 school records. He rushed for 391 yards as a freshman, 922 yards as a sophomore, 1,044 yards as a junior, and 1,041 yards as a senior and set a career rushing mark with 3,398 yards. During his sophomore and junior campaigns, he was named the Most Outstanding Offensive Player in the Fiesta Bowl. Warner was named to the Walter Camp and UPI All-American first teams his junior season. As a senior, he received second-team All-American honors from UPI and *College and Pro Football News* weekly, made the Senior All-American team, and won *Football Roundup* magazine's Exemplary Player of the Year Award. Warner subsequently gained 91 yards in only 8 carries and scored 2 touchdowns in the Hula Bowl. He graduated with a major in Speech Communications and actively participated in youth groups and local churches near the Penn State campus.

The Seattle Seahawks (NFL) selected Warner third in the first round of the 1983 draft, the earliest a Penn State player had ever been chosen. Warner's high selection paid dividends because he enjoyed an outstanding rookie season. In his first pro football campaign, Warner rushed 1,449 yards to set a Seattle record, led the AFC in rushing, and scored 14 touchdowns to tie for the AFC lead. In leading the Seahawks to their first AFC playoff berth, Warner was named the AFC Player of the Year and the NFL Players Association Player of the Year. The same year, Warner also caught 42 passes for 325 yards and 1 touchdown. Several organizations honored him as their Offensive Player of the Year, while his teammates voted him their MVP. Warner became the first Seahawk selected for the Pro Bowl as a starter. The bachelor, who resides in Redmond, WA, sustained a season-ending injury in the first game of the 1984 season, but he rushed 291 times for 1,094 yards and 8 touchdowns in 1985. The UPI Offensive Player of the Year in 1986, he made the All-AFC team and participated in the Pro Bowl. Besides finishing second in the AFC with 13 touchdowns, he led the AFC in rushing yardage with 1,481 in 319 attempts (4.6–yard average). Warner also caught 41 passes for 342 yards (8.3–yard average) for the 10–6 Seahawks, who barely missed making the AFC playoffs. Through the 1986 season he had rushed 955 times for 4,064 yards (4.3–yard average) and 41 touchdowns and caught 131 passes for 993 yards (7.6–yard average) and 2 touchdowns.

BIBLIOGRAPHY: *Penn State University Football Media Guide, 1983; Seattle Seahawks Football Facts Book, 1984.*

Jon D. Sunderland

WARNER, Glenn Scobey "Pop" (b. 5 April 1871, Springville, NY; d. 7 September 1954, Palo Alto, CA), college athlete and coach, was the son of William Henry and Adeline (Scobey) Warner and entered Cornell University in 1892. Although he had never played football, he soon became a fine guard. At Cornell (IL) he also competed in baseball and won the college heavyweight boxing championship two years. After graduating from Cornell in 1895 with a law degree, he practiced law for a few months and then compiled a 7–4–0 record as head football coach at the University of Georgia (SIAA). In 1897 he returned to Cornell (IL) for two years (15–5–1 mark) before moving to Carlisle Indian School (34–18–3 record). He returned to Cornell five years later (21–8–2 mark) and then to Carlisle in 1907. The famed Jim Thorpe* played for Carlisle during this Warner regime. His Carlisle squad finished with a 74–23–5 record and outscored opponents 2,182 to 666 points.

Warner became head football coach at the University of Pittsburgh in 1915 and saw his 1916 Panthers ranked among the great college all-time teams. Jock Sutherland,* later renowned coach, started at guard for the 1916 Panthers. Warner produced three undefeated teams at Pittsburgh, including two generally considered national champions. Under Warner, Pittsburgh won 33 consecutive games, compiled a 59–11–4 overall mark, and outscored opponents 1,537 to 315 points. Warner stayed at Pittsburgh until 1923, although signing a contract with Stanford University (PCC) in 1921. Since Warner would not break his existing contract with Pittsburgh, he sent assistant Andy Kerr* to serve as Stanford head coach for two years. Warner arrived at Stanford in 1923, again selecting Kerr as his assistant. Warner guided Stanford (PCC) to the Rose Bowl three times, winning one, losing one, and tying one, and remained there through 1932. At Stanford, Warner's clubs won 71, lost 17, tied 8 and outscored opponents 1,974 to 594 points. He finished his head coaching career with a 31–18–9 mark at Temple University from 1933 through 1938, taking the Owls to the first Sugar Bowl in 1935. Warner's last coaching position came in an advisory capacity at San Jose State University for two years. His 44–year coaching career consisted of 312 wins, 104 losses, and 32 ties, as his squads outpointed opponents 8,795 to 2,810.

The creative Warner became one of the most fertile minds in college football history. Warner's innovations and contributions to the game remain legendary. He gave more technically to football than anyone else, using his contemplative, deliberative mind to devise plays and improve equipment. Above all, Warner developed the offensive wing-back system with single-wing and double-wing formations. These formations featured many fakes and spins and were used for years by many coaches. Warner blended power and deception in the wing-back series. Warner designed the reverse and three-point stance and saw the advantage of a player leaving his feet and using full body extension to execute the body block. He initiated the spiral punt and first used the famous hidden ball trick at Carlisle in 1903 against Harvard. Warner introduced play numbering, the dummy scrimmage, the first huddle, and football's first headgear, greatly improved protective padding, and produced the mousetrap play and unbalanced line. Away from football, Warner became a dedicated tinkerer, artist, and songwriter. Warner, elected to the HAF and NFF College Football Halls of Fame, in 1951 was voted Coach of All the Years. He married Tibb Lorraine Smith in 1899 and had no children.

BIBLIOGRAPHY: Tim Cohane, *Great College Football Coaches of the Twenties and Thirties* (New York, 1973); Allison Danzig, *The History of American Football: Its Great Teams, Players, and Coaches* (Englewood Cliffs, NJ, 1956); Bill Libby, *Champions of College Football* (New York, 1975); Howard Liss, *They Changed the Game* (New York, 1975);

John D. McCallum, *Ivy League Football Since 1872* (New York, 1977); Earl Schenck Miers, *Football* (New York, 1971).

James Fuller

WASHINGTON, Kenneth S. "Kenny" (b. 31 August 1918, Los Angeles, CA; d. 24 June 1971, Los Angeles, CA), college athlete and professional football player, in 1956 became the first UCLA (PCC) player named to the NFF College Football Hall of Fame. A member of the HAF College Football Hall of Fame, Washington starred at halfback three years (1937–1939) for UCLA. He gained All-American honors his last year and amassed 1,915 yards to break the all-time Bruins career rushing record. He was named 1939 Back of the Year by *Liberty* magazine and Southern California Athlete of the Year by HAF, and chosen to the All-Time PCC team. He brought national prominence to UCLA football, leading the Bruins in 1939 to their first undefeated season and topping the nation in total offense with 1,394 yards (812 rushing, 582 passing). Washington and UCLA teammate Woody Strode became the first post–World War II blacks to play in the NFL, the former performing at halfback three years (1946–1948) for the Los Angeles Rams. He led the NFL in 1947 in rushing average with 7.4 yards per attempt, gaining 444 yards in 60 carries.

Washington starred at halfback at Los Angeles Lincoln High School, where he graduated in 1936. In 1935 he was credited with a 60–yard touchdown pass against Garfield High School. He received mediocre support from UCLA teammates his first two varsity seasons, as the Bruins finished 2–6–1 and 7–4–1 under coach William H. Spaulding. UCLA won only five of fifteen PCC games, placing ninth and third respectively. UCLA was behind 19–0 in 1937 against Southern California with nine minutes remaining, when Washington completed 44– and 62–yard touchdown passes to halfback Hal Hirshon. The 62–yard pass set a Bruins record in the 19–13 loss to the Trojans. "Washington is by far the most accurate passer west of the Rockies," the *Illustrated Football Annual* stated in reviewing the 1937 season. Washington dashed 50 yards to a touchdown on an end sweep in a 27–14 loss against California. SMU players unanimously voted him the greatest individual they faced all season following the Mustangs' 26–13 triumph.

Washington in 1938 led the PCC by scoring 42 points in league play, but UCLA was trounced 42–7 by PCC champion Southern California. UCLA was invited to Hawaii for two post-season games, defeating the Honolulu Town Team 46–0 in a warm-up engagement and the University of Hawaii 32–7 in the Pineapple Bowl. Baseball's legendary Jackie Robinson* (BB) joined UCLA in 1939 at wingback in the single-wing offense employed by first year Bruins coach Edwin "Babe" Horrell. UCLA triumphed 6–2 over defending national champion TCU in the season's opener. Washington broke a 7–7 tie against California–Berkeley with a long touchdown dash to help

UCLA defeat the Golden Bears 20–7, only the second Bruins victory over California in seven engagements. Scoreless ties resulted from games with nationally ranked Santa Clara and third-ranked Southern California, the latter attracting the largest crowd (103,303) west of the Mississippi to the Los Angeles Coliseum. In one of the West Coast's most thrilling engagements ever, Southern California held the Bruins for four downs inside the Trojans three-yard line late in the season's final game to preserve the stalemate and earn the Rose Bowl invitation. After three UCLA plunges failed, the Bruins quarterback spurned a field goal attempt and threw an incomplete pass in the end zone. UCLA finished 6–0–4 and ranked seventh nationally in the final AP poll. Although some sources credit UCLA with the PCC co-championship, the Bruins played one more tie in the PCC than USC (5–0–3 to 5–0–2 for the Trojans) and thereby lost the PCC title by three yards and .045 percentage points.

The 6 foot, 1 inch, 195 pound Washington, large physically for a fleet halfback of that era, scored 19 career touchdowns and set five Bruins records, including career total offense (3,206 yards) and pass interceptions (6). He outshone wingback Robinson in gridiron versatility with his passing, punting, blocking, tackling, pass defending, and inside/outside ballcarrying. In a September 1962 *SI* article, "The Best College Player of All Time," Alfred Wright ranked Washington with all-time greats Ernie Nevers,* Jim Thorpe,* and Bronko Nagurski* for all-around performance.

Washington, an excellent baseball infielder at UCLA, batted .454 in 1937 and .350 in 1938, and tried out in 1950 with the New York Giants (National League) baseball club. After graduating from UCLA in 1940 with a B.A. degree in Letters and Science, Washington served as a Los Angeles police officer. He performed in 1940, 1941, and 1945 with the Hollywood Bears of the PCPFL, setting rushing, passing, and scoring marks and leading the Bears to two league championships. In 1944 he played with the San Francisco Clippers of the AFL. During Washington's three seasons with Los Angeles (NFL), the Rams placed second, fourth, and third in the Western Division under head coaches Adam Walsh, Bob Snyder, and Clark Shaughnessy* and finished with a composite 18–15–2 record. After retiring from pro football, Washington worked in Los Angeles as a business executive and civic leader. He died in UCLA Medical Center after a lengthy battle with a disease that crippled his heart and lungs.

BIBLIOGRAPHY: Jody Brown, *The Best Little Rivalry in Town* (West Point, NY, 1982); Robert N. Carroll to James D. Whalen, March, 1986; Ronald L. Mendell and Timothy B. Phares, *Who's Who in Football* (New Rochelle, NY, 1974); UCLA Sports Information Office, Los Angeles, CA, March, 1986; Hendrik Van Leuven, *UCLA Football: Touchdown UCLA* (Huntsville, AL, 1982).

James D. Whalen

WATERFIELD, Robert "Bob" "Rifle" (b. 26 July 1920, Elmira, NY; d. 25 March 1983, Burbank, CA), college athlete and professional football player, coach, and scout, was the son of Jack and Frances Waterfield, both of English descent. Waterfield's family moved to California where his father Jack operated the Van Nuys Transfer and Storage Company. When Waterfield was only 9, his father died, and his mother, Frances, a nurse, then supported the family. Waterfield attended Van Nuys High School, where he competed in football and gymnastics. Waterfield majored in Physical Education at UCLA but did not play freshman football. As a sophomore, Waterfield in 1941 became first string quarterback. In the spring of 1942 he competed for the Bruins undefeated gymnastics team in the long horse, rings, and hand balancing.

In 1942 Waterfield led UCLA (PCC) to its first victory over Southern California and a Rose Bowl berth. He set UCLA then single-game records for most passing yards, completions, and total offense and season marks for passing yards and touchdown passes, and total career passing. Waterfield was commissioned as second lieutenant in the infantry in 1943 and played football and basketball for the 176th Infantry at Ft. Benning, GA. After his discharge from the U.S. Army in 1944, the 6 foot, 1 inch, 190 pound Waterfield reentered UCLA and co-captained the 1944 football squad. During three years at UCLA, he completed 161 passes in 406 attempts for 24 touchdowns and 2,824 yards. He also punted 183 times for a 39.36–yard average.

Waterfield was drafted by the Cleveland Rams in 1945 and became the first quarterback in NFL history to lead his team to the championship his rookie season. Waterfield directed the Rams to the NFL title over the Washington Redskins, throwing two touchdown passes despite three broken ribs. In 1946 the Rams moved to Los Angeles, becoming the first major pro sports franchise to play on the West Coast. Waterfield signed a three-year contract for $20,000 a season, making him the highest paid NFL football player. In his eight seasons through 1952, Waterfield earned All-Pro honors three times and was named the NFL's MVP in 1945 and 1950. He led the Rams to another NFL championship in 1951.

Often called "Rifle" by his teammates, Waterfield played both offense and defense and combined excellent passing with outstanding punting skills. His NFL career statistics included 11,849 yards gained passing, 813 completions in 1,617 attempts, 98 touchdown passes, 573 points on 13 touchdowns, 315 extra points, and 60 field goals, and a 42.4–yard punting average. One highlight of Waterfield's illustrious playing career occurred on October 13, 1952, in Milwaukee. The Los Angeles Rams were behind the Green Bay Packers 28–6 with 12 minutes to play. Waterfield then passed for three touchdowns and kicked three extra points and one field goal, enabling Los Angeles to record a 30–28 victory. In 1965 Waterfield was unanimously selected to the Pro Football Hall of Fame.

After a brief stint as producer of his wife's film company, Waterfield later became head football coach of the Los Angeles Rams (NFL) in 1960. Waterfield's playing abilities did not transfer to the coaching sidelines, as Los Angeles finished 4–7–1 in 1960, 4–10 in 1961, and 1–7 in 1962, when he resigned in midseason. Waterfield married Jane Russell, his high school classmate and later movie actress, in 1943. They adopted three children, Thomas, Tracy, and Robert, before their marriage ended in divorce in 1968. Waterfield later wed Ann Mangus.

After his coaching career ended, Waterfield remained with the Rams as a scout and was responsible for drafting Roman Gabriel,* Merlin Olsen,* and David "Deacon" Jones.* Off the football field, Waterfield cherished privacy and shunned publicity. On the football field, the great competitor could run, kick, and pass and proved an outstanding defensive back. Former Ram teammate Don Paul once said, "I have always felt that the greatest all-around football player I have ever known is Bob Waterfield. He could do everything."

BIBLIOGRAPHY: Jack T. Clary, *30 Years of Pro Football's Great Moments* (New York, 1976); *Lincoln Library of Sports Champions*, Vol. 8 (Columbus, OH, 1974); John D. McCallum, *Pac-10 Football, The Rose Bowl Conference* (Seattle, WA, 1982); Jim Murray, "A Fable with a Sad End," *Los Angeles Times*, March 27, 1983, sect. CC, pp. 1, 10; *NYT Encyclopedia of Sport, Football*, vol. 1 (New York, 1979); *Official NFL Record Manual, 1983;* Murray Olderman, *The Pro Quarterback* (Englewood Cliffs, NJ, 1966); Paul Soderberg and Helen Washington, eds., *The Big Book of Halls of Fame* (New York, 1977); Larry Stewart, "Waterfield Remembered as an Outstanding Athlete and Loyal Friend," *Los Angeles Times*, March 26, 1983, pp. 1, 12; "Bob Waterfield, Quarterback and All-Pro Star of the Rams," *NYT*, March 26, 1983, sect. L, p. 28.

James E. Odenkirk

WATERS, Charles Tutan "Charlie" (b. 10 September 1948, Miami, FL), college and professional player and announcer, is the son of crane operator Marshall and Agnes (Fountain) Waters. At North Augusta (SC) High School, the good all-around athlete won three letters in baseball and basketball and two letters in football. Waters entered Clemson University (ACC) in the fall of 1966 and started at quarterback on the freshman football team. As a sophomore, he completed 11 passes in 23 attempts for 138 yards. In 1968 he played three games at quarterback and completed 16 of 38 passes for 162 yards. Waters then shifted to wide receiver, where he shared the Tigers leadership in receptions with 22 for 411 yards. Waters set a Clemson record as a senior by catching 44 passes for 783 yards and was named to the All-ACC team. He also won Clemson's Frank Howard Award in 1970 and was later elected to the Clemson Hall of Fame.

Drafted third by the Dallas Cowboys (NFL) in 1970, Waters started at defensive free safety and led Dallas with five interceptions as a rookie. He then played in the first of five Super Bowls, a record he shares with six others. Moved to cornerback in 1972, he intercepted six passes before breaking his arm in the NFC title game. The following year, he made five interceptions despite playing all season with a steel pin in his arm. In 1975 Waters returned to free safety and developed into an All-Pro performer. A smart player, the 6 foot, 2 inch, 200 pounder possessed great anticipation, outstanding mental toughness, and the ability to play with pain. He participated in the first of three Pro Bowls following the 1976 season and then achieved All-Pro status in 1977. Waters intercepted three passes in the 1977 NFC playoff game against the Chicago Bears to set an NFL record and shares the NFL mark for most interceptions (9) in post-season games. His 25 appearances in post-season contests ranks third-best in NFL history. South Carolina named him Pro Athlete of the Year for 1977, while an *SI* poll selected him the most underrated, unsung NFL player.

Waters repeated as an All-Pro safety in 1978 after leading Dallas in solo tackles and was chosen by Dallas fans as the Oak Farms Favorite Cowboy. After Waters played in 128 consecutive games, a torn knee ligament in a preseason game caused him to miss the entire 1979 campaign. He in 1980 tied for the Dallas interception lead with five, despite playing on a bad knee, and again was chosen by the fans as Oak Farms Favorite Cowboy. Waters, who retired after the 1981 season, played 12 seasons with Dallas and ranks second on the club with 41 career interceptions for 584 yards and 2 touchdowns in regular-season play. He was elected to the South Carolina Athletic Hall of Fame in 1980. Waters married Rosie Holotik in January 1977 and has three sons, Cody, Ben, and Cliff. He opened a sports talent agency, Pro-Motion, in 1978 and retains an interest in the company, now a Kim Dawson Agency division. Waters spent one season as a sportscaster for CBS-TV but now works as a real estate broker in Dallas.

BIBLIOGRAPHY: *Clemson University Football Press Guides, 1968, 1970, 1984; Dallas Cowboys Press Guides, 1970–1985.*

Jay Langhammer

WEATHERALL, James Preston "Jim" (b. 26 October 1929, Cushing, OK), college athlete and professional football player, graduated from White Deer (TX) High School and captained the football squad there. A two-way football tackle at the University of Oklahoma, the 6 foot, 4 inch, 245 pounder performed for the BSC champions from 1949 through 1951 and the 1950 national championship aggregate. He was selected an All-American in 1950 and 1951 by the AP, UPI, *Look*, and *Collier's* and captained coach Bud Wilkinson's* eleven his senior year. In 1951 he won the Outland Award, emblematic of being the outstanding lineman in college football. Oklahoma compiled 10–0–0 records in 1949 and 1950 and an 8–2–0 mark in 1951, losing only to Texas A&M and Texas. Weatherall appeared in the 35–0 victory over LSU and 13–7 loss to Kentucky in the 1950 and 1951 Sugar Bowls. Weatherall also lettered in wrestling for the Sooners as a heavyweight.

Although a first-round draft pick of the Philadelphia Eagles (NFL) Weatherall served two years in the U.S. Marines and played in 1954 with the Edmonton Eskimos (CFL). He joined the Philadelphia Eagles (NFL) for the 1955 season and played defensive tackle and end there through 1957. Weatherall was traded to the Washington Redskins (NFL) and temporarily retired following the 1958 season. He joined the Detroit Lions (NFL) four games into the 1959 campaign and performed there through 1960. With the exception of 1960, Weatherall's NFL clubs perennially finished with losing records.

BIBLIOGRAPHY: *Detroit Lions Media Guide, 1960; Philadelphia Eagles Press Guide, 1958;* Roger Treat, ed., *The Encyclopedia of Football*, 16th rev. ed., rev. by Pete Palmer (New York, 1979); University of Oklahoma, Sports Information Office, Norman, OK; *Washington Redskins Press Guide, 1958.*

Allan Hall

WEBSTER, George D. (b. 25 November 1945, Anderson, SC), college and professional player, starred defensively on Michigan State University's (BTC) national title 1965 and runner-up 1966 football teams. He in 1967 became the second Spartans player to have his uniform number retired and in 1975 was elected to the HAF College Football Hall of Fame. Webster played pro football with the Houston Oilers (AFL-NFL), Pittsburgh Steelers (NFL), and New England Patriots (NFL), but injuries hampered his career. Webster's father, George, worked in a textile mill, while his mother, Madge, was a domestic worker. A multisport star at Westside High School, he made All-State in football twice and once as a basketball forward. Westside captured the 1960 and 1962 state football championships and 1963 state basketball title. Webster won the state shot put championship in track his senior year and served as class president.

Webster lettered in football three years at Michigan State. During his final two seasons he played roverback on a defense featuring stalwarts Charles "Bubba" Smith,* Harold Lucas, Charlie Thornhill, and Bob Viney. This formidable defense held three opponents, including powerful Ohio State, to minus yardage. A consensus All-American in 1965 and 1966, Webster usually played his opponent's strong side. Webster's assignment allowed him to be involved in most plays and make jarring tackles of opposing runners seeking to challenge him. Although opponents directed their attack away from him, Webster still finished second in team tackles with 45, assisted on 48 others, and forced three fumbles his senior year. He in 1966 was selected Spartans MVP and finished second to Bob Griese* in the BTC's MVP balloting. During his last two years, the Spartans compiled 19 victories, 1 loss, and 1 tie. He played in the Shrine All-Star (East-West) and Hula Bowl games, being named MVP each time.

After signing in 1967 with the Houston Oilers (AFL), he promptly made AFC Rookie of the Year and earned All-AFL honors in 1967, 1968, and 1969.

He was traded to the Pittsburgh Steelers (NFL) in 1972 and played with the New England Patriots (NFL) from 1974 to 1976. Knee operations forced him to miss seven games in 1970 and four contests in 1971. He participated in the 1976 AFL championship game and was named to the All-Time AFL team. A bruising defender and hitter, Webster has stated, "I've been called a head hunter, that's unfair. Isn't running over people what the game's all about?" Since retiring, the bachelor has worked as athletic director for Gulf Coast Community Services and serves on the board of the Houston Council on Human Relations. He is a member of the South Carolina Athletic Hall of Fame.

BIBLIOGRAPHY: Michigan State University, Department of Information Services Releases, 1963–1975 (East Lansing, MI); Douglas F. Eilerston, *Major College Football Results, 1957–1981* (Kinston, NC, 1981); John D. McCallum, *Big Ten Football Since 1895* (Radnor, PA, 1976); John D. McCallum and Charles H. Pearson, *College Football U.S.A., 1869–1973* (New York, 1973), Ronald L. Mendell and Timothy B. Phares, *Who's Who In Football* (New Rochelle, NY, 1974), Fred W. Stabley, *The Spartans: A Story of Michigan State Football* (Huntsville, AL, 1975).

Lawrence Ziewacz

WEBSTER, Michael Lewis "Mike" (b. 18 March 1952, Tomahawk, WI), college and professional player, ranked among the NFL's top centers during the 1970s and the first half of the 1980s. A strong adherent of body and strength development, the 6 foot, 1 inch, 255 pound Webster became one of the strongest pro players. Webster participated in prep football at Rhinelander (WI) High School, where he was presented the prestigious University of Wisconsin Club award for scholarship and sportsmanship. He then attended the University of Wisconsin (BTC) and was an honor student in Physical Education. A three-year starter at center for Wisconsin from 1971 through 1973, he tri-captained the Badgers and received All-BTC honors and All-American mention his senior year. Following his senior season, Webster played in the Shrine All-Star (East-West), Hula Bowl, Senior Bowl, Coaches All-America, and College All-Star post-season games.

Selected by the Pittsburgh Steelers (NFL) in the fifth round of the 1974 NFL draft, Webster earned All-Rookie honors that fall. He became one of the top NFL centers by 1978 and was chosen for the Pro Bowl every year from 1978 through 1985. During that period, Webster made the All-AFC and All-NFL teams as first or second team center virtually every year because of his powerful blocking and pass protection ability. Webster played in the AFC championship games in 1974, 1975, 1976, 1978, 1979, and 1984 and on the Super Bowl championship teams of 1974, 1975, 1978, and 1979. A durable performer, he missed games in only two of 12 seasons through 1986. Injuries sidelined him for seven 1982 games and for several games at the start of the 1986 season. In 1980 he won the NFL "Strongman" competition.

Webster married Pamela Carlson on May 4, 1974, and has three children, Brooke, Colin, and Garrett. They live in McMurray, PA, a suburb of Pittsburgh.

BIBLIOGRAPHY: Pittsburgh *Post-Gazette,* 1974–1985; Pittsburgh *Press,* 1974–1985; *Pittsburgh Steelers Media Guides, 1974–1986; TSN Football Register—1985;* Robert B. Van Atta, interview with Michael Webster, August, 1985.

Robert B. Van Atta

WEEKES, Harold Hathaway (b. 2 April 1880, Oyster Bay, NY; d. 26 July 1950, New York, NY) college player, was the son of an aristocratic Long Island family. He enrolled at Columbia University (IL) in 1899, when the Lions revived football after an eight-year hiatus. Coach George Sanford, former Yale center who rebuilt the program, invented the "flying hurdle" play for back Weekes. Mounted on the shoulders of teammates "Wild Bill" Morley and Captain Berrien, Weekes was catapulted across scrimmage hopefully to land on his feet and scamper off. He other times launched himself feet first over the line. Although a great end runner, Weekes was famed for his patented airborne exploits.

Weekes' best-known game came in 1899 against Yale, which Columbia had not defeated since 1873. The Elis were unbeaten, untied, and unscored upon, making the streak look secure. After Columbia surprisingly held Yale scoreless through the first half, Weekes in the second half scampered for a 55–yard touchdown and gave the Lions a 5–0 upset victory. In another game, he ran 80 yards in Columbia's 22–0 triumph over Dartmouth. The Carlisle Indians, however, introduced the crouched stance to football in the Columbia game. The new strategy confused Columbia's line, as the Lions lost 45–0. Carlisle linemen also used the heels of their hands against Weekes' face to discourage his vaunted dives.

In his sophomore year, Weekes gained revenge over Carlisle with 60– and 80–yard touchdown runs to spark Columbia to a 17–6 victory. The Lions' greatest 1900 game may have been a defeat. Yale, which finished 12–0 and outscored opponents 336 to 10, faced their only real contest in the Columbia game. Weekes' early 50–yard touchdown gave Columbia a lead that remained until the second half, when greater depth gave the Elis a 12–5 victory. Walter Camp* placed him on the 1900, 1901, and 1902 All-American teams. Despite being hurt in almost every game his senior year, he scored six touchdowns against Fordham and returned a kick 107 yards against Hamilton.

In 1910 Camp placed Weekes on his All-Time, All-American team. Camp noted that "Weekes of Columbia was the best end runner for a man of his weight [210 pounds] that the game has ever seen." Weekes was elected in 1954 to the NFF College Football Hall of Fame in its second balloting. After graduating in 1903, Weekes became a very successful New York City stockbroker and belonged to various exclusive sporting and social clubs in the metropolitan area.

BIBLIOGRAPHY: Columbia University, Division of Intercollegiate Athletics, "Harold Hathaway Weekes," New York, NY; Allison Danzig, *The History of American Football: Its Great Teams, Players, and Coaches* (Englewood Cliffs, NJ, 1956); Paul Soderberg and Helen Washington, eds, *The Big Book of Halls of Fame* (New York, 1977).

Bruce Leslie

WEINMEISTER, Arnold "Arnie" (b. 23 March 1923, Rhein, Saskatchewan, Canada), college and professional player, is the son of German immigrants and moved to Portland, OR, before he was one year old. Weinmeister twice was named All-City tackle at Portland's Jefferson High School and received a football scholarship to the University of Washington (PCC), where he played end two years before joining the U.S. Army Artillery in 1943. Upon returning to Washington (PCC) in 1946, he was switched by coach Ralph Welch to fullback. Coach Ray Flaherty* of the New York Yankees (AAFC) drafted Weinmeister two years later as a fullback, but the Huskies' star injured a knee and was returned to tackle.

Joining the Yankees after the 1948 College All-Star game, he soon was considered the best tackle in football and made the All-AAFC team in 1949. When the AAFC merged with the NFL in 1950, he was awarded to the New York Giants. Although playing only four NFL seasons, he made All-Pro honors each year. The 6 foot, 4 inch, 250 pound Weinmeister awed observers by being the fastest NFL lineman and outrunning most backs. At training camp he often participated in match races. The Giants used him almost exclusively on defense, where his power and speed made him a devastating pass rusher. His versatility in rushing both inside and outside enabled Giant coach Steve Owen* to install his famous "umbrella defense," a formation only effective with an exceptionally fast, agile tackle.

Weinmeister left the Giants before the 1954 season to sign with the British Columbia Lions (CFL) for a substantial pay raise and retired after the 1955 campaign. Keenly interested in worker rights and wages, he since has worked as a teamster official. In 1984 he was elected to the Pro Football Hall of Fame.

BIBLIOGRAPHY: Bob Braunwart and Bob Carroll, "Arnie Weinmeister," *The Coffin Corner*, 4 (March, 1982), pp. 1–2; "Hall of Fame," *Gameday*, 15 (August 18, 1984); Ronald L. Mendell and Timothy B. Phares, *Who's Who in Football* (New Rochelle, NY, 1974); Arnold Weinmeister file, Pro Football Hall of Fame, Canton, OH.

Robert N. Carroll

WEIR, Edward "Ed" (b. 14 March 1903, Superior, NE), college athlete and professional football player and coach, played tackle for the University of Nebraska (MVC) from 1923 through 1925 and was the best football tackle coach Knute Rockne* ever saw. During Weir's varsity football seasons, Nebraska defeated Notre Dame two of three games. Although Notre Dame featured the fabled Four Horsemen,* the Fighting Irish lost 14 to 7 to the

Cornhuskers in 1923. In 1924 the Four Horsemen rode to a 34 to 6 win over Nebraska, but Weir's play impressed Rockne. After the game Rockne entered the quiet Nebraska dressing room, grabbed the downcast Weir, and commented, "You're the greatest tackle and cleanest player I have ever watched." In 1925 Weir once again wrecked the Notre Dame offense, leading the mediocre Cornhuskers to a 17–0 victory. In 1925 Weir's Nebraska shut out Illinois 14 to 0, limiting Red Grange* to 40 yards rushing.

These great games made the Nebraska farm boy an All-American in 1924 and 1925. The 6 foot, 1 inch, 191 pound Weir lacked the physical size for a lineman but compensated with exceptional speed, agility, and outstanding all-around athletic skills. During his senior year at Superior High School, he won the state pentathlon with a record score and captured five events in the state track meet. At Nebraska he excelled in the hurdles. In football he used his great power at tackle and occasionally ran tackle-around plays. He also excelled as a punter and placekicker, scoring five points in the final Notre Dame game. As an assistant coach at Nebraska later, he still could knock every lineman down. "He had a million tricks to take you off your feet," guard Bob Mehring declared. Weir did not contemplate playing pro football, but accepted an offer of $350 a game in 1926 from former Nebraska stalwart Guy Chamberlin* to join the Frankford Yellowjackets (NFL). He played with Frankford from 1926 through 1928, helping the 1926 squad win the NFL championship. Weir disliked big city life, however, and soon accepted an assistant football coaching position at Nebraska (BSC). Later he became head track coach there, producing ten BSC indoor and outdoor championships. The Lincoln, NE, resident is a member of the Nebraska Sports and HAF and NFF College Football halls of fame.

BIBLIOGRAPHY: Hollis Limprecht et al., *Go Big Red: The All-Time Story of the Cornhuskers* (Lincoln, NE, 1966); Lincoln (NE) *Journal-Star*, 1923–1925; Jerry Mathers, *Nebraska High School Sports* (Lyons, NE, 1980); John D. McCallum and Charles H. Pearson, *College Football U.S.A., 1869–1973* (New York, 1973); Omaha (NE) *World-Herald*, 1923–1925; Bob Snow, "I Want Ed Weir," *Nebraskaland* (March, 1970); *University of Nebraska Football Guides.*

Jerry Mathers

WEST, David Belford "Belf" (b. 7 May 1896, Hamilton, NY), college and professional player, is the grandson of a Civil War general and founder of National Hamilton Bank. His father, William Mott West, served as president of the bank and treasurer of Colgate University (1896–1910). After graduating from Peddie Institute in Hightstown, NJ, in 1914, he returned to Hamilton to play for Colgate. A halfback on the 1914 freshman team, West was switched to tackle the next season by coach Larry Bankart and supplemented great line play with extraordinary placekicking and punting. As a junior, he dropkicked a record 52–yard field goal against Syracuse for the Red Raiders great 1916 team that lost only to Yale. Although outgaining the Elis by a large margin, Colgate scored only on a West field goal in the 6–3 loss. In the season finale Colgate upset previously undefeated Brown. Colgate scored 28 points against the Brown defense, which had surrendered only 9 points in its first eight games. Colgate shut out the Brown offense, which had not scored under 18 points previously. West and Colgate tackle Steamer Horning confined Fritz Pollard* on a muddy field. West was named All-American, but two years of military service in World War I interrupted his football career.

In 1919 West returned to Colgate and captained another great Red Raiders team that remained undefeated until a final game loss to Syracuse. Despite playing with a knee brace, West again made All-American. During West's career, Colgate held 14 opponents scoreless, thanks largely to his extraordinary defensive abilities. He was elected to the HAF and NFF College Football Halls of Fame in 1954. After graduating in 1920, West played one pro football season for the Canton Bulldogs (NFL) and pursued a business career in Buffalo, NY. He married Maurita Lee in 1920 and had one daughter.

BIBLIOGRAPHY: Colgate University, Department of Athletics, "D. Belford West," Hamilton, NY; Allison Danzig, *The History of American Football: Its Great Teams, Players, and Coaches* (Englewood Cliffs, NJ, 1956); Paul Soderberg, and Helen Washington, eds., *The Big Book of Halls of Fame* (New York, 1977).

Bruce Leslie

WHITE, Byron Raymond "Whizzer" (b. 8 June 1917, Fort Collins, CO), college athlete and professional football player, is the son of Alpha Albert White, a lumberyard owner and mayor of Wellington, CO, and Maude (Burger) White. At Wellington High School, White succeeded in all areas of student life. President John F. Kennedy later claimed White "excelled in everything he has attempted." At the University of Colorado (MSAC), White headed the class of 1938 as valedictorian. The Phi Beta Kappan's scholastic achievements were matched by his gridiron skills. White comprised a true triple-threat whose exploits as a runner, passer, and punter excited football fans across the nation. In his senior year (1937) he led Colorado through an undefeated season and into the Cotton Bowl against Rice. The College champion in scoring, rushing, and total offense, he was chosen to the All-American team. Although best known for his football heroics, White enjoyed almost equal success on the Buffaloes' basketball and baseball teams.

After graduating with a Bachelor of Arts degree, he played the 1938 season for the Pittsburgh Pirates (now the Steelers) and was paid the NFL's highest salary ($15,800). After spending one year abroad at Oxford University on a Rhodes scholarship, he played two NFL seasons with the Detroit Lions (1940–1941). The 6 foot, 1 inch, 190 pound White led the NFL in rushing in 1938 (567 yards) and 1940 (514 yards) and earned All-NFL honors the latter year. During his pro career, White gained 1,319 yards in 387 attempts (3.4–yard average) and scored 11 touchdowns. He caught 16 passes for 301 yards (18.8–yard average) and one touchdown. He was named to the NFF College Football Hall of Fame in 1954 and the HAF College Football Hall of Fame.

Between 1942 and 1946 White served as a U.S. Navy intelligence officer in the Pacific and won two Bronze Stars and a Presidential unit citation. During World War II he renewed an acquaintance he had previously made in England with John F. Kennedy. After graduating from Yale magna cum laude with the Bachelor of Laws degree in 1946, White served briefly as law clerk to Chief Justice Fred M. Vinson. He then returned to Denver, CO, practicing primarily in corporate law. White supported Kennedy for Democratic presidential nomination in 1960 and early the next year was appointed Deputy Attorney General in Kennedy's administration. A year later, Kennedy selected White to fill the U.S. Supreme Court vacancy when Justice Charles Evans Whittaker resigned. White was sworn in on April 16, 1962. White, who married Marion Lloyd Stearns in 1946 and has two children, Charles and Nancy, resides in Washington, DC.

BIBLIOGRAPHY: "Balance Sheets of Supreme Court Justices," *U.S. News and World Report* 92 (May 31, 1982), 34; Kyle Crichton, "I'll Take Both," *Collier's* 102 (October 15, 1938), pp. 16ff.; Lance Liebman, "Swing Man on the Supreme Court," *NYT Magazine* (October 8, 1972), pp. 16–17ff; Ronald L. Mendell and Timothy B. Phares, *Who's Who in Football* (New Rochelle, NY, 1974); *WWA*, 42nd ed (1982–1983), II, p. 3543; Bob Woodward and Scott Armstrong, *The Brethren*, (New York, 1979).

Frank P. Bowles

WHITE, Charles Raymond (b. 22 January, 1958, Los Angeles, CA), college and professional player, graduated from San Fernando High School in 1976 and starred in interscholastic sports there. Although he was a record-setting low hurdler in track, he won more prominence in football. During his senior year, he became a *Scholastic Coach* All-American by running 1,155 yards on 121 carries. White was chosen Southern California High School Athlete of the Year in both track and football, one of only three athletes ever so honored.

After enrolling at the University of Southern California (PEC) in 1976, White became a football regular at midseason and led the Trojans to four straight bowl appearances (including three Rose Bowls). He reached his peak as a senior tailback in the Trojans' I formation by carrying 44 times and gaining 261 yards in a 42–33 triumph over Notre Dame and proving even more devastating in the 1980 Rose Bowl. Rushing 39 times for 247 yards, White scored the winning touchdown in a dramatic 17–16 comeback victory over Ohio State. Statistically, White enjoyed an outstanding season by rushing for 1,803 yards and averaging 180.3 yards per game. In his final six games, White averaged 214 yards. During his entire collegiate career, he ran for 5,598 yards on 1,023 carries (5.5–yard average) and scored 49 touchdowns. White ran over 100 yards on 30 occasions and surpassed 150 yards 20 other times. Consequently, White was named a consensus All-American in 1979, won the Heisman Trophy, and received the Walter Camp Trophy as Player of the Year. A communications major and aspiring actor, he appeared in several films and television series and used his athletic ability to win the 1980 Superstars' Competition on ABC-TV.

His pro career proved anticlimactic. The 5 foot, 10 inch, 183 pound White, although considered too slow and too small by scouts, was drafted by the Cleveland Browns (NFL) as the twenty-seventh player in the first round. After protracted salary negotiations, he signed a five-year contract. White started slowly, however, and never matched his collegiate exploits. During his first three seasons, White appeared in only 25 to 40 regular season games. When he was seemingly on the verge of stardom, injuries interfered. White lost the entire 1983 season with a broken ankle and saw his comeback the following campaign hurt by a knee sprain and back spasms. The Cleveland Browns released White on June 4, 1985, after which he joined the Los Angeles Rams (NFL). In 1985 he rushed 70 times for 310 yards (4.4–yard average) and 3 touchdowns and returned 17 kickoffs for 300 yards. The next season, he rushed 22 times for 126 yards and returned 12 kickoffs for 216 yards. During his pro career through 1986, he has rushed 368 times for 1,378 yards (3.7–yard average) and 12 touchdowns, caught 84 passes for 696 yards (8.3–yard average) and 1 touchdown, and returned 48 kickoffs for 859 yards (18.0–yard average). He played in the 1985 NFC Championship game and in the 1986 NFC playoffs.

Off the field, White made headlines in a different manner. Before the 1982 training camp he entered a drug rehabilitation program in Orange County, CA. Eventually, he became the only publicly known member of the Browns' "Inner Circle," a support group of Cleveland players with chemical dependency or alcohol abuse problems. White, who has a wife and three children, spends off-season speaking to youth groups about the dangers of such addictions.

BIBLIOGRAPHY: Akron (OH) *Beacon Journal*, April 30, 1980, December 1, 1984; Cleveland *Browns Media Guide, 1980–1984*; Cleveland *Plain Dealer*, September 18, 1980, July 30, 1982, October 25, 1982, September 16, 1984, October 15, 1984; Los Angeles *Herald Examiner*, August 8, 1979, December 4, 1979, December 13, 1979; Los Angeles *Times*, November 22, 1979; *Oakland* (CA) *Tribune*, February 7, 1980; San Francisco *Chronicle*, February 18, 1980; Seattle *Times*, August 8, 1979; *TSN Football Register—1986*.

Jerome Mushkat

WHITE, Randy Lee "The Monster" (b. 15 January 1953, Pittsburgh, PA), college and professional player, is the son of butcher Guy and Laverne (Lehman) White. At Thomas McKean High in Wilmington, DE, he made All-American fullback-linebacker in football, All-State center-forward in basketball, and All-Conference pitcher–first baseman in baseball. Although having college scholarship offers in all three sports, he elected to play football at the University of Maryland (ACC) and entered there in the fall, 1972. After being shifted to the defensive line, he made several All-American teams and the All-ACC squad as a junior. A consensus All-American defensive end as a senior, he won the Outland Award, Vince Lombardi Award, and ACC Player of the Year honors. He played in the Liberty and Peach bowls and College All-Star game.

White, the second player selected in the 1975 NFL draft, spent his first two pro seasons as a reserve middle linebacker with the Dallas Cowboys. After being shifted to defensive tackle prior to the 1977 season, he became one of the NFL's premier defensive performers. He was named the 1978 UPI NFC Defensive Player of the Year after making 123 tackles, including 16 sacks. Nicknamed "The Monster" by former Cowboys teammate Charlie Waters,* White consistently made the All-NFL or All-NFC team and was selected to every Pro Bowl from 1977 through 1985. He was voted Co-MVP with teammate Harvey Martin in Super Bowl XII following the 1977 season by helping Dallas defeat the Denver Broncos, 27–10. He appeared in other Super Bowl contests following the 1975 and 1978 seasons and appeared in the NFC Championship games following the 1980 through 1982 seasons. He was chosen the NFL Alumni Association Defensive Lineman of the Year in 1982. From 1984 through 1986, he recorded 29½ quarterback sacks. White's key abilities include great strength, speed, quickness, and constant high-intensity level. Coach Tom Landry* commented, "When Randy White lines up on you, he doesn't care whether you're All-Pro or whether you're a rookie. You're going to get the same treatment. That makes him unique in this game." White married model Vicki Haney on October 18, 1978, and has one daughter, Jordan Leigh.

BIBLIOGRAPHY: *Dallas Cowboys Press Guides, 1975, 1981, 1983; University of Maryland Football Press Guide, 1983;* Richard Whittingham, *The Dallas Cowboys: An Illustrated History* (New York, 1981). *TSN Football Register—1986.*

Jay Langhammer

WIDSETH, Edwin C. "Ed" (b. 5 January 1910, Gonvick, MN), college athlete and professional football player, is the son of farmer Erik and Caroline Widseth and milked cows as a youngster on his father's Clearwater County homestead. As a prepster, he won four letters in football at Northwest School of Agriculture, captained the 1932 team, and was voted MVP. He graduated from the Crookston, MN, school in 1933 and earned a Bachelor of Science degree in 1938 from the University of Minnesota. At Minnesota (WC), he won three letters in football and two letters in baseball. From 1934 through 1936 he played on three consecutive national championship Golden Gopher squads. The 6 foot, 1 inch, 223 pound tackle co-captained the 1936 team and was selected Minnesota MVP. Widseth earned a tackle berth on the 1935 and 1936 All-WC teams, was selected on some All-American teams as a junior, and was chosen unanimously as an All-American his senior year.

Widseth started as East tackle in the Shrine All-Star (East-West) game in January 1937, and also in the College All-Star game against the Green Bay Packers in August 1937. He rated the Minnesota game against Pittsburgh in 1934, one of the greatest all-time gridiron contests, as his most satisfactory contest. Widseth's Minnesota teams scored 667 points in three seasons and allowed opponents only 116 points. Starting tackles Widseth and Dick Smith are rated by some as the best pair of tackles in college football history. Writers described Widseth as "Minnesota's Seven Blocks of Granite" and the "Fifth Man in the Opponents' Backfield." In his three seasons, the Golden Gophers won 23 of 24 contests and lost only to Northwestern 6–0 on a muddy field in 1936.

Widseth played four NFL seasons (1937–1940) with the New York Giants. A powerful pro lineman, he was chosen the NFL MVP in 1938 and made either the first or second All-Pro team each year. He considered the 1938 game against the Chicago Bears at the Polo Grounds in New York as his best pro game. After a broken leg ended his pro career in 1941, he became an insurance agent with Equitable Life Assurance Company in St. Paul, MN, and later an owner-manager of Hart's Grocery in Minneapolis, MN. He has participated in the University of Minnesota "M" Club, Alumni Association, YMCA, Boy Scouts, Kiwanis, Minneapolis Athletic Club, and Central Avenue Commercial Association. He lives in the Minneapolis area with his wife Janet, whom he married in 1938, and has one daughter, Jane, and one son, E. George. His recreational activities in retirement include golf and bowling. He was elected to the NFF College Football Hall of Fame.

BIBLIOGRAPHY: George Barton, *My Lifetime in Sports* (Minneapolis, MN, 1957); Stan W. Carlson, *Minnesota Huddle Annual, 1936–1938;* Richard Fisher, *Who's Who in Minnesota Athletics* (Minneapolis, MN, 1941); *New York Giants Pro Media Guide, 1938;* University of Minnesota, *"One Hundred Years of Golden Gopher Football* (Minneapolis, MN, 1981); Ed Widseth to Stan W. Carlson, July, 1985.

Stan W. Carlson

WILDUNG, Richard "Dick" (b. 16 August 1921, St. Paul, MN), college and professional player, is the son of grocery store owner Harold F. and Adahlia M. Wildung. At Luverne (MN) High School, Wildung won four letters in football and three each in basketball and track. In 1938 he was selected on the All-State Prep Football team as a tackle and All-District basketball squad. At the University of Minnesota (WC) he played on the 1940 and 1941 national championship football teams and was chosen consensus All-American tackle in 1941 and 1942. One of his most satisfying games came in 1942 against Iowa Pre-Flight School. The Pre-Flights were coached by Bernie Bierman,* who had entered military service after Pearl Harbor. Bierman's Minnesota teams of 1940 and 1941 had finished undefeated, but the outmanned 1942 Golden Gophers eleven lost 7–6 to the service team. The Golden Gophers missed an opportunity to win the game in the last minute, bringing the first career loss for the entire Minnesota team. Wildung played in the Shrine All-Star (East-West) game in 1943, co-captaining the winning East team.

Wildung played seven pro seasons with the Green Bay Packers (NFL) from 1946 through 1951 and 1953. After the 1951 season, he worked in an Our Own Hardware store in Redwood Falls, MN, with his wife's oldest brother. Since his partner died in July 1952 Wildung could not leave the business unattended that fall. He returned to the Packers for the 1953 season just two weeks prior to the first NFL game and played defensive left tackle. A Green Bay captain for four seasons, he was considered an outstanding offensive and defensive player and one of the smartest NFL linemen. He won some All-Pro awards and performed in the Pro Bowl game following the 1951 season. During his first four pro seasons, Green Bay remained one of two NFL teams not using the T formation. The Packers still remained competitive. Late in the 1947 season against the formidable Chicago Cardinals, he played offensive left guard and defensive left tackle. Green Bay lost on the last play on a missed field goal, but coach Earl "Curly" Lambeau* claimed that Wildung performed the best game by a lineman in Packer history. Of German-Irish descent, Wildung and his wife, Margaret, have four children, Richard, Merrilee, David, and Kristine. After working in the hardware business from 1952 to 1959, he started selling road building equipment for a Minnesota heavy equipment distributor and has served as its vice president since 1968. Wildung, whose hobbies include handball and golf, was elected to the HAF and NFF College Football Halls of Fame.

BIBLIOGRAPHY: George Barton, *My Lifetime in Sports* (Minneapolis, MN, 1957); Richard Fisher, *Who's Who in Minnesota Athletics* (Minneapolis, MN, 1941); *Green Bay Packers Media Guide, 1951;* Dick Wildung to Stan W. Carlson, July, 1985.

Stan W. Carlson

WILKINSON, Charles "Bud" (b. 23 April 1915, Minneapolis, MN), college and professional athlete, coach, administrator, and announcer, is the son of real estate developer and mortgage dealer Charles P. and Edith (Lindbloom) Wilkinson. Wilkinson's mother died when he was only age eight. His father later married Ethel Grace, who enjoyed a warm relationship with stepsons "Bud" and William. At age 13 Wilkinson enrolled at Shattuck Military Academy in Faribault, MN. He captained the 1932 football team as a signal-calling tackle, won four letters in baseball as a center fielder, lettered three years as a goalie on the hockey squad, and played center his senior year on the basketball team. Besides being a first lieutenant in the cadet corps, the cum laude graduate was vice president of his class and business manager of the yearbook.

At the University of Minnesota (WC), he received a B.A. degree in English in 1937. Wilkinson won three letters in football on three consecutive national championship teams, lettered three years in hockey, and competed in golf his senior year. Wilkinson played guard on the Golden Gophers football squads as a sophomore and junior (1934–1935) but switched to quarterback his senior year (1936) as a single-wing signal caller and blocking back. As a guard, he made the All-WC squad and some All-American teams. At quarterback his senior year (1936), he made the All-WC team. He played on two WC championship hockey teams, co-captaining the 1935 aggregate. Wilkinson played in the 1937 College All-Star football game against the Green Bay Packers (NFL) and quarterbacked the collegians to their first victory over the pros. He also performed in the Texas All-Star game that year before starting his football coaching career as a line coach that fall at Syracuse under Ossie Solem.

In August 1938 Wilkinson married Mary Shiflett, whom he met after she transferred from Carleton College, and has two sons, Pat and Jay. At Syracuse, Wilkinson earned an M.A. degree in English in 1940 and his wife a B.A. degree in Philosophy. After leaving Syracuse in 1941 to enter the U.S. Navy pre-flight program, he became a hangar-deck officer on the aircraft carrier *Enterprise.* He saw action at Iwo Jima, Tokyo, Kyushu, and Okinawa and was commended in 1945 for high performance of duty when his ship was under attack. Before his sea duty, he had tutored the centers and quarterbacks on the famed Iowa Pre-Flight Seahawks.

Wilkinson became assistant football coach to Jim Tatum* at the University of Oklahoma (BSC) after his Naval discharge in 1946. He served as head coach from 1947 to 1964 and compiled impressive winning records. When the regents dismissed the athletic director, Wilkinson assumed that post too. Wilkinson's teams won 12 consecutive BSC titles and three national championships (1950, 1955, 1956). His system combined precision blocking, learned under Bernie Bierman* at Minnesota, with split-T tactics. He was among the first coaches to stress the T quarterback as a ballcarrier in a strong ground attack that included a spinner play. One of his greatest coaching performances came in 1950, after eighteen of his top twenty-five players had graduated. Although his fullback was the only returning starter, Wilkinson produced a national championship squad.

Wilkinson's record of 47 straight college victories (from 1953 to 1957) may never be broken. One of his most satisfying wins came in the 1954 7–0 Orange Bowl victory over Maryland. Wilkinson, who is enshrined in the NFF College Football Hall of Fame, was selected College Coach of the Year in 1949 and compiled a 145–29–4 mark in 17 seasons at Oklahoma. His best players included backs Tommy McDonald,* Clendon Thomas, and Billy Vessels,* center Jerry Tubbs,* guards Buddy Burris* and J. D. Roberts, tackle Jim Weatherall,* and end Max Boydston. After retiring from college coaching in 1964, he entered politics, served as an ABC network sports analyst, and headed the President's Physical Fitness program. Wilkinson, who married a second time at age 60 to his present wife, Donna, served as head coach of the St. Louis Cardinals (NFL) in 1978 and 1979 and compiled an unimpressive 11–21–0 overall mark. The St. Louis resident is engaged in business there.

BIBLIOGRAPHY: Stan W. Carlson, *Minnesota Huddle Annual 1936–1938;* Harold Keith, *Forty-Seven Straight* (Norman, OK, 1984); Minneapolis *Star,* August 10, 1978; James P. Quirk, *Minnesota Football: The Golden Years, 1932–1941* (Minneapolis, MN, 1984); University of Minnesota, *One Hundred Years of Golden Gopher Football* (Minneapolis, MN, 1981).

Stan W. Carlson

WILLIAMS, Henry Lane (b. 26 June 1869, Hartford, CT; d. 14 June 1931, Minneapolis, MN), college athlete, coach, and administrator, traced his paternal and maternal roots to the Salem, MA, colony. His father's forebears arrived from England in 1648, while his mother's ancestors came in the early 1630s and moved to Hartford, CT, in 1636. He graduated in 1887 from Hartford High School, where he played football and excelled in track. He enrolled in the fall, 1887, at Yale University (IL) and became a football teammate of William "Pudge" Heffelfinger* and Amos Alonzo Stagg* and lettered four years as a halfback. He performed college track four years, captaining the Elis as a senior and setting intercollegiate and world records in the high hurdles in 1891. As a junior and senior, he also edited the Yale University newspaper.

After graduating from Yale in 1891, Williams taught school and attended the University of Pennsylvania Medical School. In 1891 he became the first Army football coach to register a victory over Navy. Williams coached at Penn Charter School from 1892 to 1899, winning consecutive track championships and five league football titles. He married Nina Meadows Boyd during the 1890s and had one son, Henry Lane, Jr., who played center for the Minnesota football squad in 1917. Henry, Jr., followed his father's footsteps as a high hurler at Yale and medical graduate from Pennsylvania.

Minnesota (WC) football fortunes were at a low ebb in 1900 when Williams was hired with a three-year $7,500 contract as the first full-time Golden Gophers coach. Williams, recommended for the job by Stagg, coached there twenty-one seasons, becoming the "Father of Minnesota Football." He also became director of athletics, instructor in the University's Medical School with full faculty standing, and private medical doctor. Williams' first decade there produced better results than his last 10 years. In 1900 the undefeated Gophers triumphed in 10 games and tied 2 contests. The next year, Minnesota won 9 games and lost only to Wisconsin 18–0 in the opener. The

1902 Golden Gophers captured 9 victories and suffered setbacks to Michigan 23–6 and Nebraska 6–0. The outstanding 1903 squad won 13 contests, tied a great Michigan team 6–6, and outscored opponents 725–12. The Michigan game inaugurated the Little Brown Jug, the oldest college football trophy. In those days, teams brought their own water for sanitary purposes. The Michigan manager bought the jug at a store near the campus, but the Wolverines left it behind after the game. Michigan requested its return but was told it would have to win it back. The Wolverines recaptured it the next season and kept it until Minnesota trounced Michigan 34 to 7 in 1919 for the first Golden Gophers victory in the series since 1893.

The undefeated 1904 Golden Gophers won 13 games, shutting out all opponents except Nebraska and outscoring opponents 618–12. In 1905 Minnesota lost the home opener to Wisconsin and then triumphed in 10 consecutive contests. The next five seasons saw shorter schedules, as Minnesota finished 4–1 in 1906, 2–2–1 in 1907, 3–2–1 in 1908, and 6–1 in 1909 and 1910 (losing only to Michigan the last two seasons). Williams' squads compiled marks of 6–0–1 in 1911, 4–3–0 in 1912, 5–2 in 1913, 6–1 in 1914, and 6–0–1 (tied Illinois) in 1915. Although World War I cut into college football, Minnesota still fielded good teams. The Golden Gophers finished 6–1–0 (losing to Illinois) in 1916, 4–1–0 (losing to Wisconsin) in 1917, 5–2–0 in 1918, and 4–2–1 in 1919. Williams' last two teams produced mediocre 1–6 and 4–4 marks in 1920 and 1921.

During his long tenure at Minnesota, Williams frequently was criticized. His players loved him, but the aloof Williams did not mix well with people. At Minnesota from 1900 to 1921 he compiled an impressive 136–33–8 mark for a .905 winning percentage. All-American players there included John McGovern in 1909, James Walker in 1910, Bert Baston* in 1915 and 1916, and George Hauser in 1917. His clubs won WC championships in 1909 and 1911 and shared titles in 1900, 1903–1904, 1906, 1910, and 1915. Williams, an innovative coach, used ingenious and deceptive plays based on power and speed. He originated the Minnesota shift, crisscross plays, revolving wedge, and onside kick by the quarterback and was one of the early coaches to appreciate the forward pass. After retiring under pressure, he worked as a medical doctor in family practice and was elected to the HAF and NFF College Football Halls of Fame as a coach.

BIBLIOGRAPHY: George Barton, *My Lifetime in Sports* (Minneapolis, MN, 1957); Stan W. Carlson, *Dr. Henry L. Williams* (Minneapolis, MN, 1938); Stan W. Carlson, *Minnesota Huddle Annual*, 1936–1938; Richard Fisher, *Who's Who in Minnesota Athletics* (Minneapolis, MN, 1941); University of Minnesota, *100 Years of Golden Gopher Football* (Minneapolis, MN, 1981).

Stan W. Carlson

WILLIS, William K. "Bill" (b. 5 October 1921, Columbus, OH), college athlete, professional football player, and coach, is the son of Clement and Willana Willis. Since his father died when he was four years old, Willis grew up with his grandfather Clement, a laborer, and his mother. He graduated from Columbus East High School in 1940 and with a Bachelor's degree from Ohio State University in 1945. Willis married Odessa Porter in 1947 and has three sons, William, Jr., Clement, and Dan. A three-year regular and honorable mention All-State football player at Columbus East High School, Willis also played varsity basketball and performed field events in track. He worked for a year before entering Ohio State (WC) in 1941. Willis started at tackle on the 1942 Buckeyes team, which won the WC championship with a 9–1 record under coach Paul Brown.* The following season proved disastrous, however, as Ohio State won only three of nine games. Willis again started, but most experienced Buckeye players had been drafted into the armed services. Willis opened his senior season by playing in the College All-Star game at Chicago. That season the Buckeyes finished undefeated in nine games and won the WC championship. Although 6 feet, 2 inches, and 220 pounds, he ran fast enough to be a sprinter on the Ohio State track team.

Following his graduation Willis served as head football coach at Kentucky State University (MAA) for the 1945 season and then decided to play pro football the following year. No NFL teams had contacted Willis, despite his outstanding college record, because no black had played in the NFL from 1934 to 1945. Although Woodrow Strode and Kenny Washington* had signed with the Los Angeles Rams (following the franchise shift from Cleveland) in March 1946, the NFL appeared closed to Willis. He was offered a tryout in 1946 with the Montreal Alouettes (CFL). While traveling from Columbus to the Montreal training camp, he stopped in early August at the Bowling Green, OH, training camp of the Cleveland Browns of the newly organized AAFC to visit new Browns coach Paul Brown, who persuaded Willis to practice with the Browns that day. Willis played so impressively as a defensive middle guard in practice that he was signed to a pro contract. Nine days later, the Browns signed black fullback Marion Motley.* The Browns dominated the AAFC in 1946 with a 12–2 record and defeated the New York Yankees 14–9 for the championship, with Willis and Motley being named to the All-AAFC team. During the four-year AAFC existence, the Browns amassed 47 wins, 4 losses, and 3 ties and won all four AAFC championships. The Browns' success with Willis (four times All-AAFC) and Motley (three times All-AAFC) encouraged other AAFC teams to sign black players.

The AAFC disbanded following the 1949 season, but Cleveland, San Francisco, and Baltimore joined the NFL. The Browns quickly proved their strength when they crushed the defending NFL champion Philadelphia Eagles 35–10 in the opening game of the 1950 season. The Browns won 10 of 12 games that season and defeated the Los Angeles Rams 30–28 in the NFL championship game, as guard Willis was named All-Pro. During the next three seasons (1951–1953), the Browns recorded 30 victories and only 6 losses. Cleveland captured the American Conference championship each season but lost NFL championship games twice to the Rams and once to the Detroit Lions. Willis, who played primarily defensive middle guard during that period, made the All-Pro team each season and retired following the 1953 season.

During Willis' eight-year pro career, the Browns won eight division and five league championships. Willis was named All-Pro each season he played. Browns coach Paul Brown credits Willis with being the prototype of the big, mobile middle linebacker, who changed football defenses from five- to four-man lines in the middle 1950s. Willis was inducted into the NFF College Football Hall of Fame in 1971 and Pro Football Hall of Fame in 1977. Willis was employed as assistant director of recreation in Cleveland from 1954 until 1963 and then as deputy director and later director of the Ohio Youth Commission until his retirement in 1983.

BIBLIOGRAPHY: C. Robert Barnett, interviews with William Willis, June 7 and July 23, 1985; Bill Barron et al., *The Official NFL Encyclopedia of Football* (New York, 1982); Paul Brown with Jack T. Clary, *PB: The Paul Brown Story* (New York, 1979); Harold Claassen and Steve Boda, eds., *The Ronald Encyclopedia of Football*, (New York, 1960); David S. Neft, Richard M. Cohen, and Jordan A. Deutsch, *Pro Football: The Early Years, An Encyclopedic History, 1895–1959* (Ridgefield, CT, 1978).

C. Robert Barnett

WILSON, Lawrence Frank "Larry" (b. 24 March 1938, Rigby, ID), college and professional player and executive, grew up in rural Idaho and attended school in Rigby. Wilson excelled in high school athletics, winning four letters each in football, basketball, track, and baseball and becoming the greatest athlete in Rigby history. The high school football field has been named Larry Wilson Field. Wilson in 1956 entered the University of Utah (MSAC), where he starred in football and earned a B.S. degree in 1960. The two-way player was selected a third team All-American in 1959. As a fullback, Wilson holds Utah one-game records for most touchdowns (5) and points (32). His 13 touchdowns and 84 points in 1959 remain Utah season records, while his 20 touchdowns over three seasons established a career record.

A star in the 1959 Shrine All-Star (East-West) game, Wilson the next year was selected by the St. Louis Cardinals in the seventh round of the NFL draft. Wilson was converted to a defensive back and performed there from 1960 through 1972. Wilson became famous for the safety blitz, designed especially for him by Cardinals defensive coach Chuck Drulis. The deadly tackler and pass defender demonstrated great courage by playing against the Pittsburgh Steelers in 1965 with both hands in casts and made a key interception that led to a Cardinals victory. In 169 games Wilson intercepted 52 passes for 800 yards and 5 touchdowns. He pilfered 3 passes in one game twice, led the NFL with 10 interceptions in 1966, and tied an NFL mark by making thefts in 7 straight games. A five-time All-NFL selection (1963, 1966–1969), Wilson played in eight Pro Bowl games (1962–1963, 1965–1970). The premier NFL safety owns about all Cardinals interceptions records, including total thefts, career return yardage, scores, and longest single-return yardage. The Cardinals defensive captain twice was named their MVP (1966, 1968) and in 1966 finished second for the NFL MVP Award.

Wilson served as director of scouting for the Cardinals from 1973 to 1976 before being promoted to assistant director of operations. Since 1980 he has been the club's director of pro personnel. Besides being selected on the All-Pro squad of the 1960s and to the AFL-NFL 1960–1984 All-Star Team, Wilson in 1978 was elected to the Pro Football Hall of Fame. He and his first wife, Dee Ann, had two sons and one daughter. In 1980 Wilson married Nancy Drew.

BIBLIOGRAPHY: *St. Louis Football Cardinals Guide and Record Book 1977; TSN Football Register—1972; Utah Football Guide, 1973.*

John L. Evers

WILSON, Robert Edward, Jr. "Bobby" (b. 16 August 1913, Nacogdoches, TX), college athlete and professional football player, is the son of Robert and Luna (Wheeler) Wilson. His father owned cafeterias in several Texas towns. At Corsicana (TX) High School, Wilson made All-District halfback in football as a 128–pound sophomore. He led Corsicana to the state semifinals the next two seasons, earning All-State honors both years. He scored over 500 points in his high school football career and won All-Southern honors in 1931. A fine all-around athlete, Wilson captured the state long jump crown as a senior and started at guard on Corsicana's state-tournament-bound 1931 basketball squad.

After entering SMU in 1932, Wilson made All-SWC halfback in football the next year as a sophomore. He won the SWC long jump title in 1934 and placed eighth at the NCAA track meet. Despite missing four football games with a broken shoulder as a junior, Wilson led the SWC in scoring with 48 points and made several All-American teams. A 5 foot, 9 inch, 145 pounder as a senior halfback, the speedy Wilson became SMU's first consensus All-American and led the Mustangs to 12 straight wins and a Rose Bowl berth against Stanford. He again paced the SWC in scoring (72 points), passed frequently, returned punts, and excelled on defense. Besides being the SWC MVP, he also played in the College All-Star game.

Wilson played professionally one season (1936) with the Brooklyn Dodgers as the NFL's smallest two-way player and led the team in rushing with 505 yards on 104 carries (4.9–yard average). He married Betty Bailey on April 14, 1937, and has three sons, Robert, David, and Layton. Wilson joined

Sun Oil Company in 1937 and spent 37 years there before taking early retirement in 1973. For the next 10 years, he worked in real estate with his eldest son in the Houston area and then retired to Kerrville, TX, in 1983. Besides being elected to the NFF College Football Hall of Fame in 1973, Wilson is a member of the Texas Sports Hall of Fame, the Texas High School Football Hall of Fame, and the SMU/Dr. Pepper Hall of Fame.

BIBLIOGRAPHY: John D. McCallum and Charles H. Pearson, *College Football U.S.A., 1869–1973* (New York, 1973); Temple Pouncey, *Southern Methodist Football: Mustang Mania* (Huntsville, AL, 1981); *Texas Sports Hall of Fame Yearbook, 1981.*

Jay Langhammer

WINSLOW, Kellen Boswell (b. 5 November 1957, East St. Louis, IL), college and professional player, is the son of bus driver–dispatcher Homer and Odell Winslow. Winslow competed only in chess for East St. Louis High School because his parents feared that he might be injured and would not let him play football until his senior year. At the University of Missouri (BEC), Winslow played tight end in football and made the All-American squad in 1978. Winslow, who caught 29 passes that year, was drafted by the San Diego Chargers in the first round of the 1979 NFL draft. General Manager Joe Klein traded two picks to the Cleveland Browns (NFL) to secure draft rights to Winslow. The 6 foot, 5 inch, 245 pound speedster joined the Chargers as the prototype tight end and enjoyed many opportunities to show his skills because coach Don Coryell* favored throwing the football.

A great leaper with delicately soft hands, Winslow caught 25 passes in seven games in 1979 for the Chargers. He broke his leg and was placed on the injured reserve list for the remainder of the season. In 1980 he caught 89 passes for 1,290 yards and 9 touchdowns. During the next three seasons, including the strike-shortened 1982 campaign, Winslow averaged nearly 6 receptions a game and 1 touchdown pass reception in every other game and amassed nearly 3,000 receiving yards. His greatest regular-season performance came when he caught 5 touchdown passes against the Oakland Raiders on November 11, 1981. His best playoff game occurred in January 1982, against the formidable Miami Dolphins secondary for the AFC title. Although his team lost 41–38, Winslow caught 13 passes for 166 yards and 1 touchdown. Winslow was helped off the field a few times but blocked a field goal attempt to send the game into overtime. He led the NFL in receptions from 1980 through 1982, catching a career-high 89 in 1980. In 1980 and 1981 he made All-Pro and played in the AFL championship game and Pro Bowl. He also participated in the Pro Bowl following the 1982 and 1983 seasons. Winslow missed the first half of the 1985 campaign with a career-threatening knee injury, but returned at midseason to catch 25 passes for 318 yards (12.7–yard average). In 1986 he made 64 receptions for 728 yards (11.4–yard average) and 5 touchdowns. Through the 1986 season he has caught 488 passes for 6,222 yards (12.8–yard average) and 42 touchdowns. Winslow, a spectacular synthesis of size, speed, power, and courage, became the first tight end ever to lead the NFL in receptions for consecutive seasons.

With some Chargers teammates, he made a record album entitled "The Other Side of Us." Winslow also joined Billy Sims* of the Detroit Lions in forming an alliance to help needy youngsters in the Special Olympics. The one-time confirmed bachelor married Katrina McNight on December 20, 1981, but was divorced two years later. The Pro Football Hall of Fame named him as a receiver on the AFL-NFL 1960–1984 All-Star Team.

BIBLIOGRAPHY: St. Louis *Globe-Democrat*, January 1982; *TSN*, September 12, 1981; *TSN Football Register—1986*.

William A. Borst

WISTERT, Albert Alexander "Al" (b. 28 December 1920, Chicago, IL), college and professional player and announcer, is the son of Casimir and Josephine (Sukis) Wistert, both Lithuanian immigrants. Casimir, whose family name was originally Vistartius, worked as a sergeant on the Chicago police force and was killed on duty when Albert was a youth. Young Wistert came from a large family, having three sisters and two brothers, Alvin and Francis. The three Wistert brothers eventually played tackle at the University of Michigan (WC), achieved All-American status, and made both the Michigan Hall of Honor and the NFF College Football Hall of Fame.

In 1938 Albert graduated from Foreman High School in Chicago. Foreman did not have a football program, but Wistert excelled in basketball and baseball there. Although he played organized football for the first time after entering Michigan, he became one of the all-time great Wolverines linemen and made All-WC three times and various All-American teams (1940–1942). In 1940 Wistert's blocks helped Tom Harmon* win the Heisman Trophy and paced the Wolverines to wins in every game except a 7–6 thriller loss to Minnesota. Wistert graduated from Michigan in 1943 with a Bachelor's degree in Education.

Wistert, drafted by the Philadelphia Eagles (NFL) in 1943, played pro football from 1943 through 1951 and ranked among the greatest interior linemen of that era. The 6 foot, 2 inch, 212 pound Wistert made All-Pro six consecutive years between 1944 and 1949 and captained the winners of the 1947 Eastern Division title and the 1948 and 1949 NFL crowns. Many Wistert blocks enabled the legendary Steve Van Buren* to make long runs. Eagles' coach Alfred Earle "Greasy" Neale* always called Wistert the team's morale builder. One of the best NFL players at punt coverage, the durable Wistert played both offense and defense his first five years with the Eagles. Wistert co-captained the 1950 East squad in the first Pro Bowl and captained the 1943 College All-Star eleven, which defeated the world champion Washington Redskins.

Wistert, a model athlete and family man, enjoyed great success after his final NFL season (1951). He broadcast sports for WPTZ in Philadelphia and then entered the insurance field, becoming a successful agent-executive for Bankers Life of Nebraska. Wistert, who resides in Thousand Oaks, CA, married Marguerite Eleanor and has three daughters. He is deeply involved in the Tennis Association for the Mentally Retarded (TAMR), which is striving to become a national group. His daughter, Katharine Josephine Wistert, has been helped greatly by TAMR.

BIBLIOGRAPHY: Ray Didinger, "The Best Team of the Best Years," *Pro!* 3 (January, 1983), pp. 69–75; *Philadelphia Eagles Media Guides, 1944–1951;* Roger Treat, ed., *Official NFL Football Encyclopedia,* 16th rev. ed., rev. by Pete Palmer (New York, 1979).

William A. Gudelunas

WOJCIECHOWICZ, Alexander Francis "Wojie" (b. 12 August 1915, South River, NJ), college and professional player and coach, is the son of tailor Andrew and Anna (Chartowicz) Wojciechowicz, both Polish immigrants. He graduated in 1934 from South River High School, where he made All-State in both football and baseball. In September 1934, he entered Fordham University and began an outstanding football career. He twice made All-American at center (1936, 1937) and anchored the Rams' legendary Seven Blocks of Granite star-studded line, which included guard Vince Lombardi.* "Wojie" led Fordham to national prominence, losing only two games in his three varsity seasons. During his career, Fordham played powerful Pittsburgh to three consecutive scoreless ties.

His collegiate prowess led the Detroit Lions (NFL) to make him their number 1 draft pick in 1938. Wojciechowicz played both offensively and defensively for the Lions from 1938 through the first three games of the 1946 season. The 6 foot, 230 pounder was noted for his wide stance at center and devastating "chucking" ability as a linebacker. Early in the 1946 season he requested to play in the East because of business obligations and was acquired by the Philadelphia Eagles (NFL). Philadelphia coach Alfred Earle "Greasy" Neale* immediately made him a linebacker in an innovative defensive alignment. Neale's famed 5–2–4 defensive system featured Wojciechowicz and Joe Muha at linebacker. The defense keyed the Eagles to three consecutive Eastern Division titles (1947–1949) and two NFL crowns (1948–1949). "Wojie" defended solidly against the run, while his chucking made him strong against the pass. He became one of the era's most feared linebackers, earning All-Pro honors four NFL seasons.

Wojciechowicz, who retired after the 1950 season, entered the real estate business with the New Jersey Real Estate Department and coached briefly in the ACFL. Wojciechowicz in 1968 helped establish the NFL Alumni Association, which currently boasts over 7,000 members. Wojciechowicz married Katherine Mallen and has three sons and one daughter. Now retired in Forked River, NJ, he ranks among football's great two-way linemen both at the college and pro levels. He made seven Halls of Fame, including his 1968 induction into the Pro Football Hall of Fame and membership in the NFF College Football Hall of Fame. His greatness can best be summed up by saying Vince Lombardi* played "with" Wojciechowicz.

BIBLIOGRAPHY: Bill Barron et al.; The *Official NFL Encyclopedia of Football* (New York, 1982); Ray Didinger, "The Best Team of the Best Years," *Pro!* 3 (January, 1983), pp. 69–75; *Philadelphia Eagles Media Guides, 1946–1950;* George Sullivan, *Pro Football's All-Time Greats: The Immortals in the Pro Football Hall of Fame* (New York, 1968).

William A. Gudelunas

WOOD, William V. "Willie" (b. 23 December 1936, Washington, DC), college and professional player and coach, is the son of John and Amanda (Jones) Wood and attended Armstrong High School in Washington, DC; Coalinga (CA) Junior College; and the University of Southern California (PCC). He played football offensively at quarterback and defensively at halfback, but the small 5 foot, 10 inch, 189 pound Wood was not drafted in 1960 by either the NFL or the new AFL. Although he wrote to many pro teams, he received travel expenses for a tryout only from the rebuilding Green Bay Packers (NFL) under coach Vince Lombardi.* Wood made the 1960 Packers roster as a reserve defensive back and gained recognition with his reckless abandon as a punt returner. An injury to a Packers starter late in the 1960 season gave him a starting position he did not relinquish in his year career (1960–1971). He played in 166 consecutive games for Green Bay, making 48 interceptions and 2 touchdowns and leading the NFL in 1962 with 9 interceptions. Wood returned 187 punts for 1,391 yards and 2 touchdowns and led the NFL in 1961 with 16.1 yards per return. He was named All-Pro six consecutive years (1964–1969) and All-NFC (1970) and was selected to the 1964 through 1971 Pro Bowls. Besides playing in six NFL championship games (1960–1962, 1965–1967), he appeared in the first two Super Bowls (1966–1967) and holds three Super Bowl punt return records.

After retiring as a player in 1972, he served as an assistant coach with the San Diego Chargers (NFL) in 1973 and 1974 and became the first black pro head football coach in 1975 with the WFL's Philadelphia Bell. After the WFL collapsed financially in its initial season, Wood pursued private business and then joined former Packers teammate Forrest Gregg* with the CFL's Montreal Alouettes. When Gregg became Cincinnati Bengals' (NFL) head coach, Wood was named Montreal head coach and compiled a 6–20 record over the 1980–1981 seasons. Wood, dismissed as head coach in mid-1981, was selected to the Green Bay Packer Hall of Fame in 1977 and was named to the Pro Football Hall of Fame's AFL-NFL 1960–1984 All-Star Second Team.

BIBLIOGRAPHY: Gene Hintz, "Wood and Hart," *Green Bay Packers Yearbook, 1971*, p. 12; Chuck Johnson, "Wood," *Green Bay Packers Yearbook, 1970*, p. 23; Chuck Lane, *Green Bay Packers Media Guides, 1969–1971.*

Brian Gunn

WOODSON, Warren Brooks (b. 24 February 1903, Ft. Worth, TX), college athlete and coach, coached football 40 years at seven institutions and is a member of HAF College Football Hall of Fame. He was named 1960 Coach of the Year (college division) by the AFCA after guiding New Mexico State University to an 11–0–0 finish, BC title, and 28–8 Sun Bowl triumph over Utah State. Woodson's 32–season combined coaching record at four-year colleges (not counting eight years at the JC level) was 207–99–14 (.669 percent) for the sixth highest career victories. He served as head football coach at Arkansas (Conway) State Teachers College (AIC), Hardin-Simmons College (BC), the University of Arizona (WAC), New Mexico State University (BC), Trinity College (SoC), and New Mexico Highlands College. Woodson's clubs suffered only five losing seasons, compiled four undefeated regular campaigns, and fared 6–1–1 in bowl appearances.

The son of Baptist minister William Warren and Jeannette (Brooks) Woodson, he starred in football, basketball, baseball, and tennis at Temple (TX) High School and graduated from there in 1920. Woodson attended Baylor University (SWC) and started on the basketball and tennis teams four years. He qualified for the 1923 NCAA tennis tournament at Haverford, PA, and in 1924 captained the tennis squad. The 1924 All-SWC basketball forward earned a B.A. degree at Baylor the same year. Woodson learned the fundamentals of coaching and athletic administration at Springfield (MA) College, where he received a graduate degree in Physical Education in 1926. He coached Texarkana JC to a 40–13–6 football record from 1927 through 1934 and the basketball squad his last year to the JC state championship. Woodson created physical education programs at Texarkana and Arkansas State (AIC), where he served (1935–1940) as football and basketball coach. His gridiron elevens garnered a composite 40–8–3 record, while his netters won AIC championships every year.

As football coach at Hardin-Simmons (BC, 1941–1942, 1946–1951), Woodson guided the Cowboys in 1942 to their first victories over SWC foes in 28 games by defeating Baylor 13–6 and SMU 7–6. Woodson's 1942 and 1946 squads finished undefeated and featured national rushing champions Rudy Mobley and Wilton Davis. Under Woodson, the Cowboys amassed a composite 58–24–6 record and dominated contests with Arizona, Arizona State, and Kansas State. Woodson coached Arizona (WAC) to a combined 26–22–2 record (1952–1956) and guided halfback Art Luppino to two national rushing titles. Woodson, who emphasized offense, developed three more statistical champions at New Mexico State (BC) from 1958 to 1962. Backs Pervis Atkins, Bob Gaiters, and Jim Pilot led the nation in rushing and scoring. The Aggies ranked first nationally in total offense (1960) and rushing offense (1961) and finished with a composite 63–36–3 record under Woodson.

After a four-year hiatus, Woodson coached Trinity (SOC, 1972–1973) to a combined 16–5–0 record. A former New Mexico State player coaching at New Mexico Highlands persuaded Woodson in 1974 to assume the head coaching role at the latter school for one year so that he could study Woodson's methods. After a 4–4–0 season, Woodson retired from coaching. Woodson, who married Muriel Young and has one daughter, Dawn, lives in Dallas with his wife and follows sports via newspapers and television.

BIBLIOGRAPHY: Ronald L. Mendell and Timothy B. Phares, *Who's Who in Football* (New Rochelle, NY, 1974); *NCAA Official Football Guide, 1984;* James D. Whalen, telephone interview with Warren B. Woodson, June 30, 1985.

James D. Whalen

WRIGHT, Elmo "Elmo the Dancer" (b. 3 July 1949, Brazoria, TX), college and professional player, is the son of Lawrence and Lillie Bell (Woodard) Wright. His father works as a contractor, while his mother is employed as a dietitian. As a youngster, Wright participated more in music than in sports and became a talented saxophone player. At Brazoria's Sweeney High School, he performed as a two-time All-State split end in football, sprinter on the track team, and shortstop and pitcher in baseball. Wright entered the University of Houston in 1967. Blessed with outstanding speed, elusive moves, and good hands, the 6 foot, 195 pounder started at split end on the Cougars football team as a sophomore. In his first varsity game he caught three passes for 162 yards and 2 touchdowns against Tulane. Later that fall, he made seven catches for 249 yards and scored 4 touchdowns against Idaho and made 8 receptions for 244 yards versus Cincinnati. For the 1968 season he caught 43 passes for 1,198 yards and 11 touchdowns. His 27.9 yards per catch average set an NCAA Division I record for an end with 40 or more receptions.

As a junior, Wright was named to the All-American second team and ranked seventh in receiving with 63 catches for 1,275 yards and 14 touchdowns. All three marks established Cougars records. He also set Houston marks with 12 receptions for 200 yards versus Oklahoma State and gained 262 yards on 7 catches for 4 touchdowns against Wyoming. An Academic All-American, he helped Houston defeat Auburn 36–7 in the Astro-Bluebonnet Bowl. By his senior year Wright developed into college football's leading deep pass threat and big play specialist and was nicknamed "Elmo the Dancer" for his dancing routines in the end zone after scoring a touchdown. Despite facing double coverage as a senior, he caught 47 passes for 874 yards and 9 touchdowns and earned consensus All-American honors. Named Houston's MVP, he played in the Shrine All-Star (East-West) game, Hula Bowl, and College All-Star game. Wright holds most Houston receiving records, including 153 career catches for 3,347 yards. His 34 touchdown receptions and 21.9–yard career average per catch remain NCAA Division I records. Houston elected him to the Cougar Hall of Honor in 1976. Following graduation with a Bachelor's degree in Civil Engineering, Wright married Bobbie Wallace in 1971. He has one daughter, Eliza Monique, but was divorced in 1978.

The first Houston player ever drafted in the NFL's first round, he signed with the Kansas City Chiefs and won the Mack Lee Hill Award as the team's top rookie for 1971. He started every game, catching 26 passes for 528 yards and 3 touchdowns. Bothered by injuries in 1972, he played just seven games. Although he missed several games the next year, he caught 16 passes for 252 yards and 2 touchdowns. Wright played out his option after the 1974 season and signed with the Houston Oilers (NFL). Released after two games, he later played four contests for the New England Patriots (NFL). Following tryouts with the New York Giants (NFL) and New Orleans Saints (NFL) prior to the 1976 season, he retired from football with 70 career receptions for 1,116 yards and 6 touchdowns. After working in real estate development in Houston, he served as administrative aide to the Harris County commissioner and is completing an M.B.A. degree.

BIBLIOGRAPHY: *Kansas City Chiefs Press Guides, 1971–1974; TSN Football Register—1976; University of Houston Football Press Guide, 1983.*

Jay Langhammer

WYANT, Adam Martin (b. 15 September 1869, Montgomeryville, PA; d. 5 January 1935, Greensburg, PA), college and professional player, excelled in football at Bucknell University and the University of Chicago (WC) and performed from 1895 until 1897 on the first all-pro football team at Greensburg, PA. He may have been the first pro football player elected to the U.S. Congress. The son of Christian Y. and Elizabeth (John) Wyant, he was born on the family farm in rural Montgomeryville, PA. After completing studies at Reid Institute at Reidsburg, PA, he graduated in 1890 from Mt. Pleasant (PA) Classical and Scientific Institute. He attended Bucknell University for three years, playing on pioneer football teams there. The then imposing 6 foot, 196 pound Wyant transferred to the University of Chicago (WC) and played guard for new coach Amos Alonzo Stagg.*

In 1894–1895 he returned to teach at Mt. Pleasant Institute, where his top academic record as an undergraduate was remembered. Wyant signed with the GAA for a salary in 1895 and played quarterback for three seasons on the first completely pro football team. Wyant, who continued teaching while playing football, was elected the first principal of Greensburg High School in 1896 and then became the city's first superintendent of schools. After two terms as superintendent and summer law study at the University of Pittsburgh, he was admitted to the bar and opened a law practice at Greensburg in 1902. Eventually he became a director and/or officer of several industrial and financial corporations. He married Katherine N. Doty, daughter of a veteran Westmoreland County judge, at Greensburg on December 1, 1910, and had two children, Anna M. and Adam M., Jr.

In 1920 the popular Wyant became a candidate for U.S. Congress from Pennsylvania's 22nd District and was elected by the largest majority given a Republican candidate in the district's history. He served six terms from 1921 to 1933 and then continued his law practice at Greensburg until his death from cancer. His brother Andrew (1867–1963) graduated in 1892 from Bucknell University and in 1895 from the University of Chicago Divinity School with numerous academic honors. The second football captain at Chicago following Stagg,* Andrew served as a Baptist minister, graduated from the Chicago College of Medicine and Surgery in 1908, and practiced medicine.

BIBLIOGRAPHY: Addison B. Bowser, *The Bowser Family History* (Ford City, PA, 1922); *Sesquicentennial History of Greensburg, PA*. (Greensburg, PA, 1949); Robert B. Van Atta, *History of Professional Football at Greensburg, Pa., 1895–1900* (Greensburg, PA, 1982); Robert B. Van Atta, interviews with Wyant and related family members, 1983–1984.

Robert B. Van Atta

Y

YARY, Anthony Ronald "Ron" (b. 16 August 1946, Chicago, IL), college and professional player, is the son of Anthony and Clearcie Ethel (Golden) Yary and attended Bellflower High School and Cerritos (CA) JC. In 1967 he graduated from the University of Southern California (PEC) with a B.S. degree in Finance. He pursued postgraduate work at the University of California–Long Beach in 1970 and at UCLA in 1971. Yary, a consensus All-American football player for Southern California (PEC) in 1966 and 1967, led the blocking for O. J. Simpson* and in 1967 won both the Outland Award as the nation's top collegiate lineman and the Knute Rockne Memorial Trophy. At 6 feet, 6 inches, and 255 pounds, Yary proved the prototype of the ideal offensive tackle possessing strength, quickness, and durability. Yary participated in two Rose Bowls, the 14–13 loss to Purdue in 1967 and the 14–3 victory over Indiana in 1968.

The Minnesota Vikings (NFL) drafted him as the first player chosen in 1968. Yary's impressive collegiate credentials enabled him to become the first offensive lineman ever selected as the NFL's first pick. From 1969 to 1980 Yary anchored the Vikings' offensive line and never missed a regular-season game. The Vikings' offense featured Fran Tarkenton,* a quarterback reacquired by the Vikings from the New York Giants in 1972 and whose effective scrambling style made blocking more difficult. Critics alleged that Yary became an expert at illegally holding opponents. During his pro career Yary played offensive tackle with textbook precision. With the Vikings from 1968 through 1981, he played in 202 games and started 183 contests. Yary participated in four Super Bowls (following the 1969, 1973, 1974, and 1977 seasons) and seven Pro Bowl games (1971–1977). Besides being selected NFC Offensive Lineman of the Year from 1973 through 1975, he was named All-Pro seven times (1971–1977) and made *TSN* NFC All-Star team (1970–1978). In 1982 he was traded to the Los Angeles Rams (NFL) and retired after that season. The Cerritos, CA, resident works with his brother in the photography fund-raising business and is active in Big Brothers. The Pro Football Hall of Fame named him to its AFL-NFL 1960–1984 All-Star Second Team.

BIBLIOGRAPHY: George Allen with Ben Olan, *Pro Football's 100 Greatest Players* (Indianapolis, IN, 1982); *TSN Football Register—1980, 1985; WWA*, 41st ed. (1980–1981), pp. 3,608.

Albert J. Figone

YOST, Fielding Harris "Hurry Up" (b. 30 April 1871, Fairview, WV; d. 20 August 1946, Ann Arbor, MI), college athlete, football coach, and administrator, served as University of Michigan (WC) football coach and/or athletic director for forty-one years. The HAF College Football Hall of Fame member was elected in 1951 to the NFF College Football Hall of Fame as a charter designee. Yost coached the Michigan Wolverines (WC) to a 49–0 triumph over Stanford University in the first Rose Bowl game in 1902. From 1901 to 1905 his famous point-a-minute football teams finished undefeated in 56 games and outscored opponents 2,821 to 40 points. Chicago's undefeated eleven, with Walter Eckersall* at quarterback, defeated Michigan 2–0 in the final game of 1905. Although most early championship football was played in the East, Yost produced a national championship team his first year at Michigan (1901) and coached 18 All-Americans. His three All-Time All-Americans included Willie Heston* (1901–1904), Germany Schulz* (1904–1908), and Bennie Oosterbaan* (1925–1927).

The son of farmer and general store owner Permenus Wesley and Elzena Jane (Ammons) Yost, he graduated from Fairview High School in 1889 and attended Fairmont (WV) Normal School for two years. Yost left Fairmont to work in local oil fields and teach in the Mineral County (WV) School. After serving as school principal and police chief, he enrolled at Ohio (Northern) Normal College in 1893. The 6 foot, 195 pound Yost engaged in athletics for the first time as first baseman on the baseball team. Yost entered University of West Virginia Law School in 1895 and excelled at football tackle in 1895 and 1896 for the Mountaineers. Since eligibility rules were negligible, Yost was invited by Lafayette College coach Parke H. Davis to play for the Leopards against the University of Pennsylvania, which had been undefeated for three years. Yost's strong tackle play helped Lafayette upset Pennsylvania 6-4 and claim the 1896 national championship. A member of Sigma Chi fraternity, Yost earned a Bachelor of Laws degree in 1897 from the University of West Virginia. Between 1897 and 1900, he coached football conference champions at Ohio Wesleyan (7–1–1), Nebraska (7–4–0), Kansas (10–0–0), and Stanford (7–2–1). Ohio Wesleyan defeated Ohio State 6–0 and tied Michigan 0–0 in 1897. In 1900 he simultaneously coached the Stanford varsity and freshmen, San Jose Teachers College, and Lowell and Ukiah (CA) high schools to league championships.

Michigan athletic director Charles Baird in 1901 hired Yost, whose Wolverines (WC) compiled a combined 165–29–10 football record (.833 percent) over 25 seasons. Since the WC instituted a retroactive three-year eligibility rule in 1906, Michigan left the WC for the next 11 years and scheduled eastern schools. Michigan encountered limited success against Pennsylvania, Syracuse, Cornell, and Harvard with a combined 12–15–3 record. After recommending Dan McGugin* for the Vanderbilt head coaching position in 1904, Yost compiled a combined 8–0–1 record against the perennial SIAA champion Commodores. McGugin and Yost married the Fite sisters, Virginia and Eunice of Nashville, TN, in 1905 and 1906, respectively, and formed a law partnership there during the off-season.

Michigan triumphed over WC titlist Minnesota in 1909 and 1910 to determine the "championship of the West." Yost's use of quick kicks and long passes for good field position gave rise to the term "punt, pass, and prayer." Yost, whose nickname was a natural outgrowth of his accent on speed, aggressiveness, and frequent commands to "hurry up," displayed an amazing memory and uncanny inventiveness. Yost was appointed Michigan athletic director in 1921 and developed five more WC champions in the post–World War I years. The 1925 Wolverines, often rated by Yost as his best, defeated Red Grange's* Illinois 3–0 one year after his incredible five-touchdown performance against Michigan.

After being ordered by his physician to rest in 1924, he coached football two more years and then retired. His Michigan football teams had dominated the WC, winning ten of fourteen possible championships or co-championships. As athletic director, he built one of the nation's finest athletic plants substantially from football proceeds. The Yost Fieldhouse, the first ever built (1923), 85,000–seat Memorial Stadium, Women's Athletic and Intramural Sports buildings (1928), and golf course, gymnasium, and tennis courts (1930) stand as monuments to his leadership.

Yost retired in 1941 and held the title Professor Emeritus of the Theory and Practice of Athletics until his death. Coach Bob Zuppke* commented, "His greatest career at mighty Michigan extended from [Willie] Heston* to [Tom] Harmon* and back again. Try and erase that!" In 1948 George Little stated, "Yost had the ability to cope with sound football in the early century and made an adjustment successfully to stay at the top as a modern coach." The multitalented Yost worked as an architect (building designers conferred with him), developed a hydroelectric plant in Tennessee, was director of Dixie Cement Company and Cumberland Valley National Bank, served as Boy Scout commissioner, and received the highest Boy Scout award, Silver Beaver. He never smoked, drank, or cursed, but chewed on a stogie for hours. He was also an avid student of military history, and author of the book *Football for Player and Spectator* (1905). He and his wife, Eunice, had one son, Fielding, Jr.

BIBLIOGRAPHY: John Behee, *Fielding Yost's Legacy* (Ann Arbor, MI, 1971); Bill Cromartie, *The Big One* (Atlanta, 1979); Kent Kessler, *Hail West Virginia!* (Weston, WV, 1959); J. Fred Lawton, *"Hurry Up" Yost in Story and Song* (Ann Arbor, MI, 1947); Michigan–Minnesota Football Game Program, October 31, 1903; Will Perry, *The Wolverines: A Story of Michigan Football* (Huntsville, AL, 19); Edwin Pope, *Football's Greatest Coaches* (Atlanta, 1955).

James D. Whalen

YOUNG, Claude Henry "Buddy" (b. 5 January 1926, Chicago, IL; d. 4 September 1983, Terrell, TX), college athlete and professional football player and executive, was the son of pullman porter Claude and Lillian Young. At Englewood and Wendell Phillips High Schools in Chicago, Young excelled in football and track. The 5 foot, 4 inch, 175 pound Young attended the University of Illinois. (WC) Besides tying the world's indoor 60–yard dash record (6.1 seconds), he covered the 100–yard dash in 9.5 seconds. Young in 1944 won two sprints when Illinois captured the national track championship. A breakaway football runner, Young scored 13 touchdowns his freshman year to tie Red Grange's* twenty-year-old mark. Five Young touchdowns came on sprints exceeding 60 yards. Young ranked sixth among the nation's college scorers and second in rushing average (8.94 yards). He was named the MVP for the Fighting Illini and selected an All-American. Young served in the U.S. Merchant Marine in 1945 and scored 15 touchdowns for the Fleet City Training Base in Shoemaker, CA. Upon returning to Illinois in 1946, he led the Fighting Illini to a WC title. In the 45–14 Rose Bowl victory over UCLA, he was named MVP. Young paced Illinois in rushing and total offense in 1947 and holds the Fighting Illini mark for the longest run from scrimmage (93 yards). In his two college seasons, he scored 18 touchdowns, gained 1,308 yards, and averaged 6.6 yards per carry.

After opting to play pro football, Young was named the MVP in the 1947 College All-Star game. He performed for the New York Yankees (AAFC) from 1947 to 1949, New York Yanks (NFL) from 1950 to 1951, Dallas Texans (NFL) in 1952, and Baltimore Colts (NFL) from 1953 to 1955. In nine seasons Young compiled 9,601 total yards and scored 44 touchdowns for 264 points. He retired with a record 27.7–yard average on kickoff returns and led the AAFC in punt return average (1949). Young also paced the NFL in punt return yardage (1951) and kickoff returns and return yardage (1952). In 1953 Young returned an NFL kickoff 104 yards against Philadelphia still the Baltimore record. The Colts have retired his number 22 jersey. After scouting for Baltimore (1956–1963), Young joined the NFL front office in 1964 as director of player relations and remained there until his death. A member of the NFF College Football Hall of Fame and Chicago's Sports Hall of Fame, Young was killed in an automobile accident after attending a memorial service for Joe Delaney of the Kansas City Chiefs. He married Geraldine Young in 1945 and had four children, Claude, Jr., Paula, Jeffrey, and Zollie.

BIBLIOGRAPHY: *Chicago Tribune* (September 6, 1983), Sect. 2, p. 4; John D. McCallum, *Big Ten Football Since 1895* (Radnor, PA, 1976); David S. Neft et al., *The Sports Encyclopedia: Pro Football* (New York, 1977); Kenneth L. (tug) Wilson and Jerry Brondfield, *The Big Ten* (Englewood Cliffs, NJ, 1967).

John L. Evers

YOUNG, John Steven "Steve" (b. 11 October 1961, Salt Lake City, UT), college and professional player, is the oldest son of corporate lawyer LeGrande and Sherry Young and great-great-great grandson of Brigham Young University founder Brigham Young. His father, a running back, led Brigham Young University (BYU) in rushing in 1955. Steve grew up in Greenwich, CT, and excelled as a student and athlete at Greenwich High School. He captained the football, basketball, and baseball teams and earned honorable mention All-American as a wishbone football quarterback. After enrolling at BYU (WAC) in 1980, Young played behind All-American quarterback Jim McMahon* for two years and then started as a junior in 1982. Young quickly came into his own as a college quarterback, rushing or passing for 3,507 yards and 28 touchdowns. In 1982 he led BYU to a Holiday Bowl appearance, was named the WAC Offensive Player of the year, and made honorable mention AP All-American. He also ranked second nationally in total offense and sixth in passing efficiency.

A strong pre-season All-American candidate as a senior, Young in 1983 set or tied thirteen NCAA records. He led the nation in total offense with an average of 395.1 yards per game and in passing efficiency. Besides completing a phenomenal 71.3 percent of his passes, Young set records for most consecutive pass completions (18), most passes completed in a game (39) and season (306), and most yards rushing and passing in a game (497). He also completed touchdown passes in 22 consecutive games and compiled impressive senior year statistics, including for 4,346 yards rushing and passing and 41 touchdowns. Named WAC Offensive Player of the Year for the second time, Young also was honored as the first-team All-American quarterback by the AFCA, FWAA, AP, UPI, Walter Camp, *Football News*, Entertainment Sports Network Programming, and Gannett News Service.

Following his college career, Young played pro football with the Los Angeles Express of the newly formed USFL. His contract, considered the highest ever paid a pro athlete, approximated $44 million over 45 years and made Young instantly rich. Young completed 179 of 310 passes for 2,361 yards and 10 touchdowns in guiding the Express to the 1984 USFL playoffs. He then participated in the longest pro game, a 93–minute, 33–second contest against the Michigan Panthers. The Express won that game via Young's 295 passing yards but lost their next playoff game to the Arizona Wranglers. Following the 1984 season, the Express folded for financial reasons. Young awaited the outcome of his contractual agreement with Los Angeles before the left-hander joined the Tampa Bay Buccaneers (NFL). In 1985 Young took over starting quarterback duties for veteran Steve De Berg in the week 12 19–16 victory over Detroit. He completed 72 of 138 passes for 935 yards but threw 8 interceptions and only 3 touchdown passes. For the 2–14 Bucaneers in 1986, he completed 195 of 363 passes for 2,282 yards (6.29–yard average) and 8 touchdowns and threw 13 interceptions. The unmarried Greenwich, CT, resident spends the off-season studying for his degree in accounting at BYU.

BIBLIOGRAPHY: *Brigham Young University Football Media Guides, 1981–1983;* Teri Thompson, "Great, Great, Great Grandson . . . Great, Great, Great Quarterback," *Rocky Mountain News* (October 17, 1983), pp. 10–11; Ralph Wiley, "This One Was a Game and a Half," *SI* 61 (July 9, 1984), pp. 22–24, 29.

Jon Sunderland

Z

ZUPPKE, Robert Carl "Bob" "The Little Dutchman" (b. 2 July 1879, Berlin, Germany; d. 22 December 1957, Champaign, IL), college athlete, football coach, and administrator, was the son of jeweler Franz Simon and Hermine (Brocksbaum) Zuppke, both native Germans. In 1881 the Zuppkes immigrated to Milwaukee, WI, where Robert attended public school and Milwaukee Normal School for two years. He joined the art staff of the Normal School yearbook, beginning a lifetime devotion to and skill at drawing and painting. From 1901 to 1905 he attended the University of Wisconsin (WC) and received a Bachelor of Philosophy degree. Athletics likewise interested him. Although the short, light Zuppke was relegated to the reserves in football, he excelled at basketball. The quick, elusive runner, dribbler, and shooter won a letter on a championship hoop team. After a year as a commercial artist in New York City, he in 1906 became a high school history teacher, athletic director, and football coach in Muskegon, MI. A summer course in 1904 at the Chicago Art Institute enhanced his interest in art. Zuppke coached well at Muskegon from 1906 to 1909 and at Oak Park, IL, from 1910 to 1912. After Zuppke's third year at Oak Park High School, athletic directors at three WC universities, Illinois, Northwestern, and Purdue, sought him. Illinois athletic director George Huff persuaded Zuppke to become head football coach at $2,700 annually.

When the Fighting Illini held formidable Purdue to a scoreless tie in 1913, eyes quickly focused on "The Little Dutchman." During Zuppke's second and third years, Illinois won the WC championships. Other WC titles followed in 1918–1919, 1923, and 1927–1928. In 1918 Minnesota, which blanked Chicago 49–0, Wisconsin 54–0, and Iowa 67–0, lost 14–9 to Illinois in one of college football's biggest upsets. Zuppke coached football at Illinois until 1944. During Zuppke's first decade there, Illinois won four WC championships in seven seasons and otherwise finished near the top. In later gridiron seasons, Zuppke experienced problems and did not win WC titles.

Efforts to oust Zuppke began by 1938, while Illinois athletic director Wendell S. Wilson was released. After Illinois lost every game in 1941, Zuppke announced his retirement. During 29 years, Zuppke's teams won 131 games, lost 81, and tied 12 and captured national championships in 1914, 1918, 1923, and 1927. The innovative Zuppke originated or helped develop the pre-play huddle, and the screen, spiral, and flea flicker passes. Consequently, many coaches eyed Illinois each season and quickly applied the new strategies. Illinois attracted many outstanding players eager to participate on Zuppke teams. Harold "Red" Grange,* "Galloping Ghost" of the mid-1920s, became one of college football's best all-time backs.

Zuppke, the recipient of numerous awards, was elected to the NFF College Football Hall of Fame in 1951 and the HAF College Football Hall of Fame. Earlier he presided over the AFCA (1924–1925), coached the College All-Star football team (1942), and served as commissioner of sports programs at the Century of Progress Exposition at Chicago, IL (1933–1934) and New York World's Fair (1939–1940). In 1922–1923 Zuppke chaired the $2 million campaign for Illinois' War Memorial Stadium. "The Little Dutchman" was married twice. His first wife, Fanny Tillotson Erwin, whom he wed June 27, 1908, died in 1936. He married Leona Ray on September 10, 1956. Interest in art continued throughout his life, as Zuppke often painted Arizona canyons, deserts, and mountains. His landscapes and other works were exhibited in New York City, Chicago, Milwaukee, Toledo, Davenport, IA, and elsewhere. Few other figures have combined athletics and the arts so closely.

BIBLIOGRAPHY: *DAB*, Supp. 6 (1956–1960), pp. 727–28; Milwaukee *Journal*, October 31, 1940; *NYT*, December 23, 1957; Robert C. Zuppke, *Coaching Football* (Champaign, IL, 1930); Robert C. Zuppke, *Football Technique and Tactics* (Champaign, IL 1924); Robert C. Zuppke Papers, University of Illinois, Urbana, IL.

Irving Dilliard

APPENDIX 1

Football Entries by Main Category Selected

The following lists the football entries included in the book by the main category selected. The three categories listed are player, coach, and executive. A dagger following a name indicates a player who has also been a coach. A double-dagger indicates a player or coach who has also been an executive.

PLAYERS (421)

Herbert Adderley
Frank Albert†
Charles Aldrich
Joseph Alexander
Marcus Allen
Lance Alworth
Alan Ameche
Heartley Anderson†
Kenneth Anderson
Ottis Anderson
Richard Anderson
William Andrews
Douglas Atkins
Morris Badgro
Terry Baker
James Bakken
Richard Barwegan†
Albert Baston†
Clifford Battles†
Samuel Baugh†
Gary Beban
Charles Bednarik†
Robert Bell
Joseph Bellino
Albert Benbrook
James Benton
Charles Berry†
David Berry†
Raymond Berry†
Angelo Bertelli
John Berwanger
Frederick Biletnikoff
Felix Blanchard, Jr.
George Blanda
Melvin Blount‡
Albert Booth, Jr.
Terry Bradshaw
John Brallier†
Clifford Branch, Jr.
Robert Brazile, Jr.
Charles Brewer
Charles Brickley
John Brodie
James Brown
Robert Brown
Roosevelt Brown, Jr.†

William Brown†
Junious Buchanan†
Willie Buchanon
Paul Burris
Richard Butkus
John Butler
Christian Cagle†
Earl Campbell
Anthony Canadeo‡
John Cannon
William Cannon
Gino Cappelletti
John Cappelletti
Francis Carideo†
Lee Harold Carmichael
Anthony Carter
Thomas Casanova III
Howard Cassady
Berlin Guy Chamberlin†
Donald Chandler
Wesley Chandler
John Christiansen†
Earl Clark†
Edward Cochems†
Gary Collins
George Connor†
William Corbus
Hector Cowan
Edwin Coy†
Louis Creekmur
John David Crow†‡
James Crowley†‡
Lawrence Csonka‡
Charles Daly†
Ernest Davis
Glenn Davis
William Davis
Peter Dawkins
Leonard Dawson
Thomas Dempsey
Eric Dickerson
Daniel Dierdorf
Lavern Dilweg
Michael Ditka†
Arthur Donovan
Vincent Dooley†‡
Charles Dorais†
Anthony Dorsett
Nathan Dougherty
Boyd Dowler†
John Driscoll†
Morley Drury
William Dudley
Kenny Easley
Walter Eckersall
Albert Edwards†‡
Carl Eller
John Elway
Thomas Fears†
William Beattie Feathers†
Robert Fenimore†
Wesley Fesler†
William Fincher†
William Fischer
Lawson Fiscus
Hamilton Fish
Raymond Flaherty†
Douglas Flutie
Charles Follis
Leonard Ford, Jr.
Walter Foreman
Daniel Fortmann
Joseph Fortunato
Daniel Fouts
Clinton Frank
Benjamin Friedman†‡
Irving Fryar
Roman Gabriel, Jr.
Robert Gain
Edgar Garbisch
Michael Garrett
Frank Gatski
Charles Gelbert, Jr.
William George†
Frank Gifford
Turner Gill, Jr.
George Gipp
Marshall Goldberg

Otto Graham, Jr.†
Harold Grange†
Harold Grant†
Melvin Gray
Robert Grayson†
Hugh Green
Charles Greene, Jr.
Alvis Forrest Gregg†
Roosevelt Grier
Robert Griese
Archie Griffin‡
Louis Groza
William Ray Guy
Joseph Guyon
Jack Ham
John Hannah
Marlin Harder
Huntington Hardwick
Thomas Truxton Hare
Charles Harley
Thomas Harmon
Clifford Harris
Franco Harris
James Hart
Leon Hart
Abner Haynes
Edward Healey, Jr.†
William Heffelfinger†
Melvin Hein†
Theodore Hendricks
Wilbur Henry†‡
Arnold Herber
William Heston†
William Hewitt
Calvin Hill
Frank Hinkey†
William Clarke Hinkle
Elroy Hirsch‡
James Hogan
Paul Hornung
Leslie Horvath
Kenneth Houston†
Charles Howley
William Howton
John Huarte
Robert Cal Hubbard†
Robert Huff†
Claude Humphrey
Donald Hutson
Cecil Isbell†
Harold Jackson†
Vincent Jackson
Victor Janowicz
John Jefferson
Roy Jefferson
John Henry Johnson
Charles Joiner, Jr.
Bertram Jones
Calvin Jones
David Jones
Lee Roy Jordan
Christian Jurgensen
Charles Justice†
Alexander Karras
Kenneth Kavanaugh†
Richard Kazmaier, Jr.
Lawrence Kelley
Leroy Kelly
Marvin Keyes
Walter Kiesling†
Francis Kilroy†‡
John Kimbrough
Frank Kinard†
Nile Kinnick, Jr.
Gerald Kramer
Ronald Kramer
Robert Kuechenberg
Stephen Lach
John Lambert
Richard Lane
James Langer
Willie Lanier
Steve Largent
Robert Yale Lary
John Lattner†
Dante Lavelli
Elmer Layden†‡
Robert Layne†

Langdon Lea†
Alphonse Leemans
Robert Lilly
Gene Lipscomb
Floyd Little
James Lofton
Charles Long
Sidney Luckman†
John Lujack, Jr.
William Lyman†
George McAfee
Mike McCormack†‡
Lawrence McCutcheon
Thomas McDonald
Hugh McElhenny, Jr.
Lewis McFadin†
John Mackey
James McMahon
Alvin McMillin†
John (Blood) McNally†
Edward Mahan†‡
Gino Marchetti
Daniel Marino, Jr.
Oliver Matson
Mark May
Donald Maynard†
Edward Meador
August Michalske†
Donald Miller
Wayne Millner†
Lydell Mitchell
Robert Mitchell‡
Ronald Mix
Richard Modzelewski†
Joseph Montana, Jr.
Wilbert Montgomery
Leonard Moore
Earl Morrall†
Haven Moses
Marion Motley
Harold Muller†
Harry Muncie
George Musso
Bronislaw Nagurski
Joseph Namath
James Nance
Ralph Neely
Ernest Nevers†
Marshall Newell†
Ozzie Newsome
Raymond Nitschke‡
Thomas Nobis, Jr.‡
Leo Nomellini
Robert David O'Brien
Patrick O'Dea
Elmer Oliphant‡
Merlin Olsen
Benjamin Oosterbaan†‡
James Otto
Loren Owens
Alan Page
Clarence Parker†
James Parker
George Parratt†‡
Walter Payton
Drew Pearson
Robert Peck, Jr.†
Robert Pellegrini†
Stanley Pennock†
Donald Perkins
Fletcher Joe Perry†
George Pfann†
Bemus Pierce†
Peter Pihos†
Erny Pinckert
James Plunkett
Poe Brothers†
Frederick Pollard†
Arthur Powell
Glenn Presnell
Gregory Pruitt
Michael Pruitt
Ahmad Rashad
Daniel E. Reeves†
Michael Reid
Palmer Retzlaff‡
Robert Reynolds‡
Leslie Richter

John Riggins
Dave Rimington
James Ringo†
James Ritcher
Paul Robeson
Jerry Robinson
Richard David Robinson
Andrew Robustelli
John Rodgers
George Rogers, Jr.
Aaron Rosenberg
Joseph Routt
Mike Rozier
Frank Ryan‡
Bob St. Clair
Gale Sayers†
Joseph Schmidt†
Adolph Schulz†‡
Marchmont Schwartz†
Jacob Scott III
Victor Sears†
Lee Roy Selmon
Arthur Shell
Thomas Shevlin†
Delbert Shofner
Orenthal James Simpson
Billy Sims
Kenneth Sims
Michael Singletary
Francis Sinkwich†
Jerald Sisemore
Frederick Slater
Billy Ray Smith, Jr.
Bruce Smith
Charles Smith
Jackie Smith
Mac Speedie†
Stephen Spurrier†
Ken Stabler
Johnny Stallworth
Richard Stanfel†
Bryan Bartlett Starr†
Roger Staubach
Ernest Stautner†
Dean Steinkuhler
Elmer Kenneth Strong, Jr.
Harry Stuhldreher†
Joseph Stydahar†
Robert Suffridge†
Patrick Sullivan†
George Summerall
Lynn Swann
Francis Tarkenton
John Tatum
Charles Taylor†
James Taylor
Lawrence Taylor
Lionel Taylor†
Otis Taylor, Jr.
Joseph Theismann
James Thorpe‡
Gaynell Tinsley†
Yelberton Abraham Tittle, Jr.
George Trafton†
Walter Trenchard
Charles Trippi
Gerald Tubbs†
Young Arnold Tucker
Emlen Tunnell†
Clyde Turner
Howard Twilley, Jr.
James Tyrer
John Unitas
Eugene Upshaw‡
Norman Van Brocklin†
Steve Van Buren
Mark van Eeghen
Billy Vessels
Ewell Doak Walker, Jr.
Herschel Walker
Robert Walston
Paul Warfield
Curtis Warner
Kenneth Washington
Robert Waterfield†
Charles Waters
James Weatherall
George Webster

Michael Webster
Harold Weekes
Arnold Weinmeister
Edward Weir†
David Belford West
Byron White
Charles White
Randy White
Edwin Widseth
Richard Wildung
William Willis†
Lawrence Wilson‡
Robert Wilson, Jr.
Kellen Winslow
Albert Wistert
Alex Wojciechowicz
William Wood†
Elmo Wright
Adam Wyant
Anthony Ronald Yary
Claude Young‡
John Steven Young

COACHES (97)

William Alexander
George Allen‡
Edward Anderson
Madison Bell
Hugo Bezdek
Dana Bible‡
Bernard Bierman
Earl Blaik
Paul Brown‡
John Franklin Broyles‡
Paul Bryant
James Wallace Butts, Jr.‡
Charles Caldwell, Jr.
Walter Camp‡
Francis Cavanaugh
Joshua Cody‡
James Conzelman
Donald Coryell
Herbert Crisler‡
Hugh Duffy Daugherty
Robert Devaney‡
Daniel Devine‡
Gilmour Dobie
Robert Dodd
Charles Engle
Wilbur Ewbank
Donald Faurot‡
Thomas Flores
Joe Gibbs
Sidney Gillman‡
George Halas‡
Richard Harlow
Jesse Harper‡
Percy Haughton‡
Wayne Woodrow Hayes
John Heisman‡
Donald James
William Morley Jennings‡
Howard Jones‡
Lawrence Jones
Thomas Jones
Andrew Kerr
Charles Knox
Frank Kush
Earl Lambeau‡
Thomas Landry
Frank Leahy
Louis Little
Vincent Lombardi‡
Daniel McGugin‡
John McKay
John Madden
Edward Madigan
Leo Meyer‡
Charles Moran
Jesse Raymond Morrison‡
Clarence Munn‡
Alfred Earle Neale
Jess Neely‡
Robert Neyland, Jr.
Charles Noll
Homer Norton
Thomas Osborne

Benjamin Owen
Stephen Owen‡
Raymond Parker
Ara Parseghian
Joseph Paterno
Edward Robinson‡
Knute Rockne
Darrell Royal
Henry Sanders‡
Glenn Schembechler, Jr.
Francis Schmidt
Floyd Schwartzwalder
Clark Shaughnessy
Lawrence Shaw
Donald Shula
Andrew Smith
Carl Snavely
Amos Alonzo Stagg
Edward Storey‡
Henry Stram
John Sutherland
Barry Switzer
James Tatum
Frank Thomas‡
John Vaught
William Wallace Wade‡
Lynn Waldorf‡
William Walsh
Glenn Warner
Charles Wilkinson
Henry Williams‡
Warren Woodson
Fielding Yost‡
Robert Zuppke‡

EXECUTIVES (11)

De Benneville Bell†
Charles Bidwill, Sr.
Joseph Carr
Allen Davis†
Lamar Hunt
Timothy Mara
George Marshall
Hugh L. Ray
Daniel F. Reeves
Arthur Rooney, Sr.
Alvin Rozelle

APPENDIX 2

Football Entries by Main Position Played

The following lists the football entries included in the book by the main position played. The categories listed are Quarterback, Back, Linebacker, End, Tackle, Guard, Center, and Miscellaneous. A dagger following a name indicates the player played primarily on defense.

QUARTERBACKS (80)

Frank Albert
Kenneth Anderson
Terry Baker
Samuel Baugh
Gary Beban
De Benneville Bell
Angelo Bertelli
George Blanda
Terry Bradshaw
John Brallier
John Brodie
John Franklin Broyles
Francis Carideo
Earl Clark
Charles Daly
Leonard Dawson
Gilmour Dobie
Robert Dodd
Charles Dorais
Morley Drury
Walter Eckersall
John Elway
Wilbur Ewbank
Thomas Flores
Douglas Flutie
Daniel Fouts
Benjamin Friedman
Roman Gabriel, Jr.
Turner Gill, Jr.
Otto Graham, Jr.
Robert Griese
James Hart
Arnold Herber
John Huarte
Cecil Isbell
Donald James
Bertram Jones
Thomas Jones
Christian Jurgensen
Andrew Kerr
Nile Kinnick, Jr.
Robert Layne
Charles Long
Sidney Luckman
John Lujack, Jr.
James McMahon

Alvin McMillin
Daniel Marino, Jr.
Joseph Montana, Jr.
Earl Morrall
Jesse Raymond Morrison
Joseph Namath
Robert David O'Brien
Benjamin Owen
George Parratt
Joseph Paterno
George Pfann
James Plunkett
Edgar Allan Poe
Gresham Poe
Glenn Presnell
Edward Robinson
Darrell Royal
Frank Ryan
Henry Sanders
Stephen Spurrier
Ken Stabler
Bryan Bartlett Starr
Roger Staubach
Harry Stuhldreher
Patrick Sullivan
Francis Tarkenton
Joseph Theismann
Frank Thomas
Yelberton Abraham Tittle, Jr.
Young Arnold Tucker
John Unitas
Norman Van Brocklin
Robert Waterfield
John Steven Young

BACKS (164)

Herbert Adderley†
Marcus Allen
Alan Ameche
Ottis Anderson
Richard Anderson†
William Andrews
Clifford Battles
Joseph Bellino
John Berwanger
Hugo Bezdek
Bernard Bierman
Felix Blanchard, Jr.
Melvin Blount†
Albert Booth, Jr.
Charles Brewer
Charles Brickley
James Brown
William Brown†
Willie Buchanon†
John Butler†
Christian Cagle
Charles Caldwell, Jr.
Walter Camp
Earl Campbell
Anthony Canadeo
William Cannon
John Cappelletti
Anthony Carter
Thomas Casanova III†
Howard Cassady
John Christiansen†
Edward Cochems
James Conzelman
Donald Coryell†
Edwin Coy
John David Crow
James Crowley
Lawrence Csonka
Ernest Davis
Glenn Davis
Peter Dawkins
Eric Dickerson
Vincent Dooley†
Anthony Dorsett
John Driscoll
William Dudley
Kenny Easley†
Donald Faurot
William Beattie Feathers
Robert Fenimore
Charles Follis

Walter Foreman
Clinton Frank
Michael Garrett
Frank Gifford
George Gipp
Marshall Goldberg
Harold Grange
Robert Grayson
Archie Griffin
Joseph Guyon
Marlin Harder
Charles Harley
Thomas Harmon
Jesse Harper
Clifford Harris†
Franco Harris
Abner Haynes
William Heston
Calvin Hill
William Clarke Hinkle
Paul Hornung
Leslie Horvath
Kenneth Houston†
Vincent Jackson
Victor Janowicz
William Morley Jennings
John Henry Johnson
Charles Justice
Richard Kazmaier, Jr.
Leroy Kelly
Marvin Keyes
John Kimbrough
Stephen Lach
Earl Lambeau
Thomas Landry†
Richard Lane†
Robert Yale Lary†
John Lattner
Elmer Layden
Alphonse Leemans
Floyd Little
George McAfee
Lawrence McCutcheon
Thomas McDonald
Hugh McElhenny, Jr.
John McKay
John (Blood) McNally
Edward Mahan
Oliver Matson
Edward Meador†
Donald Miller
Lydell Mitchell
Robert Mitchell
Wilbert Montgomery
Leonard Moore
Charles Moran
Marion Motley
Harry Muncie
James Nance
Jess Neely
Ernest Nevers
Patrick O'Dea
Elmer Oliphant
Loren Owens
Clarence Parker
Raymond Parker
Ara Parseghian
Walter Payton
Donald Perkins
Fletcher Joe Perry
Erny Pinckert
John Prentiss Poe, Jr.
Neilson Poe
Frederick Pollard
Gregory Pruitt
Michael Pruitt
Daniel E. Reeves
John Riggins
John Rodgers
George Rogers, Jr.
Arthur Rooney, Sr.
Mike Rozier
Gale Sayers
Marchmont Schwartz
Jacob Scott III†
Donald Shula
Orenthal James Simpson
Billy Sims

Andrew Smith
Bruce Smith
Henry Stram
Elmer Kenneth Strong, Jr.
John Tatum†
James Taylor
James Thorpe
Charles Trippi
Emlen Tunnell†
Steve Van Buren
Mark van Eeghen
Billy Vessels
Ewell Doak Walker, Jr.
Herschel Walker
Curtis Warner
Kenneth Washington
Charles Waters†
Harold Weekes
Byron White
Charles White
Henry Williams
Lawrence Wilson†
Robert Wilson, Jr.
William Wood†
Claude Young

LINEBACKERS (22)

Robert Bell
Robert Brazile, Jr.
Richard Butkus
Joseph Fortunato
William George
Jack Ham
Theodore Hendricks
Charles Howley
Robert Huff
Lee Roy Jordan
John Lambert
Willie Lanier
Raymond Nitschke
Thomas Nobis, Jr.
Leslie Richter
Jerry Robinson
Richard David Robinson
Joseph Schmidt
Michael Singletary
Lawrence Taylor
Gerald Tubbs
George Webster

ENDS (100)

Lance Alworth
Edward Anderson
Douglas Atkins
Morris Badgro
Albert Baston
James Benton
Charles Berry
Raymond Berry
Frederick Biletnikoff
Earl Blaik
Clifford Branch, Jr.
Paul Bryant
James Wallace Butts, Jr.
Gino Cappelletti
Lee Harold Carmichael
Francis Cavanaugh
Berlin Guy Chamberlin
Wesley Chandler
Gary Collins
Herbert Crisler
William Davis
Lavern Dilweg
Michael Ditka
Boyd Dowler
Albert Edwards
Carl Eller
Thomas Fears
Wesley Fesler
William Fincher
Raymond Flaherty
Leonard Ford, Jr.
Irving Fryar
Charles Gelbert, Jr.
Sidney Gillman
Harold Grant

Melvin Gray
Hugh Green
George Halas
Huntington Hardwick
Leon Hart
William Hewitt
Frank Hinkey
Elroy Hirsch
William Howton
Claude Humphrey
Donald Hutson
Harold Jackson
John Jefferson
Roy Jefferson
Charles Joiner, Jr.
David Jones
Howard Jones
Kenneth Kavanaugh
Lawrence Kelley
Ronald Kramer
Steve Largent
Dante Lavelli
James Lofton
John Mackey
Gino Marchetti
Donald Maynard
Wayne Millner
Haven Moses
Harold Muller
Alfred Neale
Robert Neyland, Jr.
Ozzie Newsome
Benjamin Oosterbaan
Thomas Osborne
Drew Pearson
Peter Pihos
Arthur Poe
Arthur Powell
Ahmad Rashad
Palmer Retzlaff
Paul Robeson
Andrew Robustelli
Knute Rockne
Lee Roy Selmon
Thomas Shevlin
Delbert Shofner
Kenneth Sims
Billy Ray Smith, Jr.
Jackie Smith
Mac Speedie
Amos Alonzo Stagg
Johnny Stallworth
George Summerall
Lynn Swann
Charles Taylor
Lionel Taylor
Otis Taylor
Gaynell Tinsley
Walter Trenchard
Howard Twilley, Jr.
William Walsh
Robert Walston
Paul Warfield
Kellen Winslow
Elmo Wright

TACKLES (71)

Robert Brown
Roosevelt Brown, Jr.
Junious Buchanan
Joshua Cody
George Connor
Hector Cowan
Daniel Dierdorf
Arthur Donovan
William Fischer
Hamilton Fish
Robert Gain
Charles Greene, Jr.
Alvis Forrest Gregg
Roosevelt Grier
Louis Groza
Richard Harlow
Percy Haughton
Wayne Woodrow Hayes
Edward Healey, Jr.
John Heisman

Wilbur Henry
James Hogan
Robert Cal Hubbard
Lawrence Jones
Alexander Karras
Francis Kilroy
Frank Kinard
Langdon Lea
Frank Leahy
Robert Lilly
Gene Lipscomb
Louis Little
William Lyman
Michael McCormack
Lewis McFadin
John Madden
Mark May
Ronald Mix
Richard Modzelewski
Bronislaw Nagurski
Ralph Neely
Marshall Newell
Merlin Olsen
Stephen Owen
Alan Page
Mcihael Reid
Robert Reynolds
Bob St. Clair
Glenn Schembechler
Victor Sears
Clark Shaughnessy
Lawrence Shaw
Arthur Shell
Gerald Sisemore
Frederick Slater
Charles Smith
Ernest Stautner
Joseph Stydahar
James Tatum
James Tyrer
Lynn Waldorf
James Weatherall
Edward Weir
Arnold Weinmeister
David Belford West
Randy White
Edwin Widseth
Richard Wildung
Albert Wistert
Anthony Ronald Yary
Fielding Yost

GUARDS (41)

Joseph Alexander
Heartley Anderson
Richard Barwegan
Albert Benbrook
Paul Burris
John Cannon
William Corbus
Louis Creekmur
Nathan Dougherty
Lawson Fiscus
Daniel Fortmann
John Hannah
Thomas Truxton Hare
Walter Heffelfinger
Calvin Jones
Walter Kiesling
Gerald Kramer
Robert Kuechenberg
Frank Kush
Vincent Lombardi
Daniel McGugin
Edward Madigan
August Michalske
Clarence Munn
George Musso
Charles Noll
James Parker
Stanley Pennock
Bemus Pierce
Aaron Rosenberg
Joseph Routt
Richard Stanfel
Dean Steinkuhler
Robert Suffridge

John Sutherland
Eugene Upshaw
John Vaught
William Wallace Wade
Glenn Warner
Charles Wilkinson
William Willis

CENTERS (20)

Charles Aldrich
Charles Bednarik
Edgar Garbisch
Frank Gatski
Melvin Hein
James Langer
James Otto
Robert Peck, Jr.
Robert Pellegrini
Dave Rimington
James Ringo
James Ritcher
Adolph Schulz
Floyd Schwartzwalder
Barry Switzer
George Trafton
Clyde Turner
Michael Webster
Alex Wojciechowicz
Adam Wyant

MISCELLANEOUS (16)

James Bakken
Madison Bell
David Berry
Donald Chandler
Hugh Duffy Daugherty
Thomas Dempsey
Robert Devaney
Daniel Devine
Charles Engle
William Ray Guy
Charles Knox
Leo Meyer
Homer Norton
Samuel Poe
Francis Schmidt
Carl Snavely

APPENDIX 3

Football Entries by Place of Birth

The following lists the football entries included in the book alphabetically by their state or, in a few instances, foreign nation of birth.

ALABAMA (11)
Robert Brazile
Junious Buchanan
Vincent Dooley
Vincent Jackson
Lee Roy Jordan
Ozzie Newsome
Homer Norton
Ken Stabler
Johnny Stallworth
Bryan Bartlett Starr
Patrick Sullivan

ARKANSAS (12)

James Benton
Paul Bryant
Clifford Harris
Lamar Hunt
Donald Hutson
Roy Jefferson
Kenneth Kavanaugh
Robert Mitchell
Ralph Neely
Fletcher Joseph Perry
Billy Ray Smith, Jr.
Barry Switzer

CALIFORNIA (31)

Marcus Allen
Gary Beban
David Berry
John Brodie
Willie Buchanon
William Corbus
Glenn Davis
Thomas Fears
Thomas Flores
Daniel Fouts
Michael Garrett
Frank Gifford
Melvin Gray
Melvin Hein
John Huarte
James Lofton
Hugh McElhenny, Jr.
Ronald Mix
Haven Moses
Harold Muller

James Plunkett
Leslie Richter
Jerry Robinson
Alvin Rozelle
Bob St. Clair
Orenthal James Simpson
Richard Stanfel
James Turner
William Walsh
Kenneth Washington
Charles White

COLORADO (2)

Earl Clark
Byron White

CONNECTICUT (6)

Albert Booth, Jr.
Walter Camp
Floyd Little
Andrew Robustelli
Elmer Kenneth Strong, Jr.
Henry Williams

DISTRICT OF COLUMBIA (3)

Leonard Ford, Jr.
Lawrence Jones
William Wood

FLORIDA (9)

Ottis Anderson
Lee Harold Carmichael
Anthony Carter
Wesley Chandler
David Jones
Peter Pihos
Stephen Spurrier
George Summerall
Charles Waters

GEORGIA (14)

William Andrews
Melvin Blount
James Brown
John Franklin Broyles
James Wallace Butts, Jr.
William Fincher
Roosevelt Grier
William Ray Guy
John Hannah
Marion Motley
James Parker
Daniel Reeves
George Rogers, Jr.
Herschel Walker

HAWAII (1)

Charles Brewer

IDAHO (1)

Lawrence Wilson

ILLINOIS (35)

Frank Albert
Kenneth Anderson
Richard Barwegan
Charles Bidwill, Jr.
Richard Butkus
Anthony Canadeo
George Connor
Herbert Crisler
James Crowley
John Driscoll
Walter Eckersall
William Fischer
Otto Graham, Jr.
George Halas
Charles Harley
Jesse Harper
James Hart

William Heston
John Lattner
Edward Madigan
Mike McCormack
George Musso
Raymond Nitschke
Benjamin Owen
Frederick Pollard
Michael Pruitt
Hugh Ray
Frederick Slater
Mac Speedie
Henry Stram
George Trafton
Kellen Winslow
Albert Wistert
Anthony Ronald Yary
Claude Young

INDIANA (10)

Wilbur Ewbank
Robert Griese
Thomas Harmon
Leslie Horvath
Alexander Karras
Robert Kuechenberg
Jesse Raymond Morrison
Elmer Oliphant
Adolph Schulz
Frank Thomas

IOWA (8)

Edward Anderson
Jay Berwanger
Donald Chandler
Nile Kinnick, Jr.
Elmer Layden
Daniel McGugin
Donald Perkins
Lawrence Shaw

KANSAS (5)

John Christiansen
Ronald Kramer
John Riggins
Gale Sayers
Francis Schmidt

KENTUCKY (3)

William Alexander
Paul Hornung
George McAfee

LOUISIANA (12)

Terry Bradshaw
Christian Cagle
Thomas Casanova III
John David Crow
William Davis
John Henry Johnson
Charles Joiner, Jr.
Bertram Jones
Edward Robinson
Marchmont Schwartz
James Taylor
Gaynell Tinsley

MARYLAND (5)

Douglas Flutie
Walter Foreman
Calvin Hill
Poe Brothers
Thomas Trenchard

MASSACHUSETTS (14)

Joseph Bellino
Angelo Bertelli
Charles Brickley
Francis Cavanaugh
Edwin Coy
Charles Daly
Allen Davis

Huntington Hardwick
Edward Healey, Jr.
Louis Little
Edward Mahan
Wayne Millner
Edward Storey
Mark van Eeghen

MICHIGAN (13)

George Allen
Heartley Anderson
Richard Anderson
Earl Blaik
Peter Dawkins
Robert Devaney
George Gipp
William Hewitt
William Morley Jennings
Gene Lipscomb
Earl Morrall
Benjamin Oosterbaan
Thomas Shevlin

MINNESOTA (18)

Terry Baker
Albert Baston
Bernard Bierman
Gino Cappelletti
Gilmour Dobie
Sidney Gillman
Joseph Guyon
William Heffelfinger
Walter Kiesling
James Langer
John Madden
Clarence Munn
Ernest Nevers
Clark Shaughnessy
Bruce Smith
Edwin Widseth
Richard Wildung
Charles Wilkinson

MISSISSIPPI (8)

William Brown
William Cannon
Hugh Green
Harold Jackson
Frank Kinard
Wilbert Montgomery
Walter Payton
Jackie Smith

MISSOURI (6)

James Conzelman
Donald Faurot
Clinton Frank
Robert Cal Hubbard
Billy Sims
Lionel Taylor

MONTANA (1)

Gerald Kramer

NEBRASKA (10)

Berlin Guy Chamberlin
Francis Leahy
William Lyman
Thomas Osborne
Glenn Presnell
Dave Rimington
John Rodgers
Carl Snavely
Dean Steinkuhler
Edward Weir

NEW JERSEY (15)

Charles Berry
Louis Creekmur
Irving Fryar
Franco Harris
James McMahon

Lydell Mitchell
Marshall Newell
Drew Pearson
James Ringo
Paul Robeson
Richard David Robinson
Mike Rozier
Amos Alonzo Stagg
Joseph Theismann
Alexander Wojciechowicz

NEW MEXICO (1)

Thomas McDonald

NEW YORK (23)

Joseph Alexander
Francis Carideo
Hector Cowan
Arthur Donovan
Hamilton Fish
Daniel Fortmann
Percy Haughton
Frank Hinkey
Vincent Lombardi
Sidney Luckman
John Mackey
Timothy Mara
Mark May
Joseph Paterno
Stanley Pennock
Bemus Pierce
Daniel Reeves
Aaron Rosenberg
Lynn Waldorf
Glenn Warner
Robert Waterfield
Harold Weekes
David Belford West

NORTH CAROLINA (8)

Robert Bell
Carl Eller
Roman Gabriel, Jr.
Joe Gibbs
Christian Jurgensen III
Charles Justice
Henry Sanders
John Tatum

NORTH DAKOTA (1)

Palmer Retzlaff

OHIO (44)

Clifford Battles
Paul Brown
Robert Brown
John Cannon
Joseph Carr
Howard Cassady
Lawrence Csonka
Leonard Dawson
Daniel Dierdorf
Wesley Fesler
Joseph Fortunato
Benjamin Friedman
Robert Gain
Archie Griffin
Louis Groza
Wayne Woodrow Hayes
John Heisman
Wilbur Henry
William Clarke Hinkle
Victor Janowicz
Donald James
Calvin Jones
Howard Jones
Thomas Jones
Richard Kazmaier, Jr.
Lawrence Kelley
John Lambert
Dante Lavelli
George McAfee
August Michalske

Donald Miller
Charles Noll
Alan Page
George Parratt
Ara Parseghian
George Pfann
James Ritcher
Glenn Schembechler, Jr.
Donald Shula
Roger Staubach
Harry Stuhldreher
James Tyrer
Paul Warfield
William Willis

OKLAHOMA (12)

Paul Burris
Robert Fenimore
Steve Largent
Charles Long
Stephen Owen
Loren Owens
Robert Reynolds
Darrell Royal
Lee Roy Selmon
James Thorpe
Billy Vessels
James Weatherall

OREGON (3)

Robert Grayson
Ahmad Rashad
Victor Sears

PENNSYLVANIA (49)

Herbert Adderley
Charles Bednarik
DeBenneville Bell
Frederick Biletnikoff
George Blanda
John Brallier
John Butler
John Cappelletti
Gary Collins
Hugh Duffy Daugherty
Ernest Davis
Michael Ditka
Anthony Dorsett
Charles Engle
Lawson Fiscus
Edgar Garbisch
Charles Gelbert, Jr.
William George
Harold Grange
Jack Ham
Thomas Truxton Hare
Richard Harlow
Leon Hart
Leroy Kelly
Francis Kilroy
Charles Knox
Frank Kush
Stephen Lach
Langdon Lea
John Lujack, Jr.
Daniel Marino, Jr.
Richard Modzelewski
Joseph Montana, Jr.
Leonard Moore
Joseph Namath
James Nance
Robert Peck, Jr.
Robert Pellegrini
Michael Reid
Arthur Rooney, Sr.
Joseph Schmidt
Francis Sinkwich
Andrew Smith
Joseph Stydahar
Charles Trippi
Emlen Tunnell
John Unitas
Randy White
Adam Wyant

SOUTH CAROLINA (7)

Felix Blanchard, Jr.
Jacob Scott III
Arthur Shell
James Tatum
Young Arnold Tucker
Charles Waters
George Webster

SOUTH DAKOTA (1)

Norman Van Brocklin

TENNESSEE (9)

Douglas Atkins
Dana Bible
Joshua Cody
Claude Humphrey
Charles Moran
Jess Neely
Robert Suffridge
Lynn Swann
William Wallace Wade

TEXAS (56)

Charles Aldrich
Lance Alworth
Samuel Baugh
Madison Bell
Albert Benbrook
Raymond Berry
Clifford Branch, Jr.
Earl Campbell
Eric Dickerson
Turner Gill, Jr.
Charles Greene, Jr.
Alvis Forrest Gregg
Abner Haynes
Kenneth Houston
William Howton
Cecil Isbell
John Jefferson
John Kimbrough
Thomas Landry
Richard Lane
Robert Yale Lary
Robert Layne
Robert Lilly
Lawrence McCutcheon
Lewis McFadin
Alvin McMillin
Oliver Matson
Donald Maynard
Edward Meador
Leo Meyer
Robert Neyland
Thomas Nobis, Jr.
Robert David O'Brien
Raymond Parker
Arthur Powell
Gregory Pruitt
Joseph Routt
Frank Ryan
Delbert Shofner
Kenneth Sims
Michael Singletary
Jerald Sisemore
Charles Smith
Charles Taylor
Otis Taylor, Jr.
Yelberton Abraham Tittle, Jr.
Gerald Tubbs
Clyde Turner
Howard Twilley, Jr.
Eugene Upshaw
John Vaught
Ewell Doak Walker, Jr.
Robert Wilson, Jr.
Warren Woodson
Elmo Wright

UTAH (2)

Merlin Olsen
John Steven Young

VIRGINIA (15)

Roosevelt Brown, Jr.

Charles Caldwell, Jr.
Robert Dodd
Nathan Dougherty
William Dudley
Kenny Easley
William Beattie Feathers
Charles Follis
Robert Huff
Marvin Keyes
Willie Lanier
Clarence Parker
Gresham Poe
Francis Tarkenton
Lawrence Taylor

WASHINGTON (5)

Morris Badgro
Donald Coryell
Albert Edwards
John Elway
Raymond Flaherty

WEST VIRGINIA (11)

Frank Gatski
Marshall Goldberg
Charles Howley
Robert Huff
Gino Marchetti
George Marshall
John McKay
Alfred Earle Neale
Floyd Schwartzwalder
Curtis Warner
Fielding Yost

WISCONSIN (17)

Alan Ameche
James Bakken
Edward Cochems
Thomas Dempsey
Daniel Devine
Lavern Dilweg
Charles Dorais
Harold Grant
Merlin Harder
Arnold Herber
Elroy Hirsch
Earl Lambeau
Alphonse Leemans
John (Blood) McNally
James Otto
Erny Pinckert
Michael Webster

WYOMING (2)

Boyd Dowler
Andrew Kerr

FOREIGN NATIONS

AUSTRALIA (1)

Patrick O'Dea

BOHEMIA (CZECHOSLOVAKIA) (1)

Hugo Bezdek

CANADA (3)

Morley Drury
Bronislaw Nagurski
Arnold Weinmeister

GERMANY (2)

Ernest Stautner
Robert Zuppke

GUATEMALA (1)

Theodore Hendricks

HONDURAS (1)

Steve Van Buren

IRELAND (1)

James Hogan

ITALY (1)

Leo Nomellini

NORWAY (1)

Knute Rockne

SCOTLAND (1)

John Sutherland

APPENDIX 4

Entries Playing Professional Football

The following lists the entries who played or are still playing professional football:

Herbert Adderley
Frank Albert
Charles Aldrich
Joseph Alexander
Marcus Allen
Lance Alworth
Alan Ameche
Edward Anderson
Heartley Anderson
Kenneth Anderson
Ottis Anderson
Richard Anderson
William Anderson
Douglas Atkins
Morris Badgro
Terry Baker
James Bakken
Richard Barwegan
Albert Baston
Clifford Battles
Samuel Baugh
Gary Beban
Charles Bednarik
Robert Bell
Joseph Bellino
James Benton
Charles Berry
David Berry
Raymond Berry
Angelo Bertelli
Frederick Biletnikoff
George Blanda
Melvin Blount
Terry Bradshaw
John Brallier
Clifford Branch, Jr.
Robert Brazile, Jr.
Charles Brickley
John Brodie
James Brown
Robert Brown
Roosevelt Brown, Jr.
William Brown
Junious Buchanan
Willie Buchanon
Paul Burris
Richard Butkus
John Butler
Christian Cagle
Earl Campbell

Anthony Canadeo
William Cannon
Gino Cappelletti
John Cappelletti
Lee Harold Carmichael
Anthony Carter
Thomas Casanova III
Howard Cassady
Berlin Guy Chamberlin
Donald Chandler
Wesley Chandler
John Christiansen
Earl Clark
Gary Collins
George Connor
James Conzelman
Louis Creekmur
John David Crow
James Crowley
Lawrence Csonka
Glenn Davis
William Davis
Leonard Dawson
Thomas Dempsey
Eric Dickerson
Daniel Dierdorf
Lavern Dilweg
Michael Ditka
Arthur Donovan
Charles Dorais
Anthony Dorsett
Boyd Dowler
John Driscoll
William Dudley
Kenny Easley
Walter Eckersall
Albert Edwards
Carl Eller
John Elway
Thomas Fears
William Beattie Feathers
Robert Fenimore
William Fischer
Lawson Fiscus
Raymond Flaherty
Douglas Flutie
Charles Follis
Leonard Ford, Jr.
Walter Foreman
Daniel Fortmann
Joseph Fortunato
Daniel Fouts
Benjamin Friedman
Irving Fryar
Roman Gabriel, Jr.
Robert Gain
Michael Garrett
Frank Gatski
William George
Frank Gifford
Turner Gill, Jr.
Sidney Gillman
Marshall Goldberg
Otto Graham, Jr.
Harold Grange
Harold Grant
Melvin Gray
Hugh Green
Charles Greene, Jr.
Alvis Forrest Gregg
Roosevelt Grier
Robert Griese
Archie Griffin
Louis Groza
William Ray Guy
Joseph Guyon
George Halas
Jack Ham
John Hannah
Marlin Harder
Charles Harley
Thomas Harmon
Clifford Harris
Franco Harris
James Hart
Leon Hart
Abner Haynes
Edward Healey, Jr.

Melvin Hein
Theodore Hendricks
Wilbur Henry
Arnold Herber
William Heston
William Hewitt
Calvin Hill
William Clarke Hinkle
Elroy Hirsch
Paul Hornung
Leslie Horvath
Kenneth Houston
Charles Howley
William Howton
John Huarte
Robert Cal Hubbard
Robert Huff
Claude Humphrey
Donald Hutson
Cecil Isbell
Harold Jackson
Victor Janowicz
John Jefferson
Roy Jefferson
John Henry Johnson
Charles Joiner, Jr.
Bertram Jones
Calvin Jones
David Jones
Lee Roy Jordan
Christian Jurgensen
Charles Justice
Alexander Karras
Kenneth Kavanaugh
Leroy Kelly
Marvin Keyes
Walter Kiesling
Francis Kilroy
John Kimbrough
Frank Kinard
Gerald Kramer
Ronald Kramer
Robert Kuechenberg
Frank Kush
Stephen Lach
Earl Lambeau
John Lambert
Thomas Landry
Richard Lane
James Langer
Willie Lanier
Steve Largent
Robert Yale Lary
John Lattner
Dante Lavelli
Elmer Layden
Robert Layne
Alphonse Leemans
Robert Lilly
Gene Lipscomb
Floyd Little
Louis Little
James Lofton
Charles Long
Sidney Luckman
John Lujack, Jr.
William Lyman
George McAfee
Mike McCormack
Lawrence McCutcheon
Thomas McDonald
Hugh McElhenny, Jr.
Lewis McFadin
John Mackey
James McMahon
Alvin McMillin
John (Blood) McNally
Gino Marchetti
Daniel Marino, Jr.
Oliver Matson
Mark May
Donald Maynard
Edward Meador
August Michalske
Donald Miller
Wayne Millner
Lydell Mitchell
Robert Mitchell

Ronald Mix
Richard Modzelewski
Joseph Montana, Jr.
Wilbert Montgomery
Leonard Moore
Charles Moran
Earl Morrall
Haven Moses
Marion Motley
Harold Muller
Harry Muncie
George Musso
Bronislaw Nagurski
Joseph Namath
James Nance
Alfred Earle Neale
Ralph Neely
Ernest Nevers
Ozzie Newsome
Raymond Nitschke
Thomas Nobis, Jr.
Charles Noll
Leo Nomellini
Robert David O'Brien
Elmer Oliphant
Merlin Olsen
Thomas Osborne
James Otto
Stephen Owen
Loren Owens
Alan Page
Clarence Parker
James Parker
George Parratt
Ara Parseghian
Walter Payton
Drew Pearson
Robert Peck, Jr.
Robert Pellegrini
Donald Perkins
Fletcher Joe Perry
Peter Pihos
Erny Pinckert
James Plunkett
Arthur Powell
Glenn Presnell
Gregory Pruitt
Michael Pruitt
Ahmad Rashad
Daniel E. Reeves
Michael Reid
Palmer Retzlaff
Robert Reynolds
Leslie Richter
John Riggins
Dave Rimington
James Ringo
James Ritcher
Paul Robeson
Jerry Robinson
Richard David Robinson
Andrew Robustelli
Knute Rockne
John Rodgers
George Rogers, Jr.
Mike Rozier
Frank Ryan
Bob St. Clair
Gale Sayers
Joseph Schmidt
Jacob Scott III
Victor Sears
Lee Roy Selmon
Arthur Shell
Delbert Shofner
Donald Shula
Orenthal James Simpson
Billy Sims
Kenneth Sims
Michael Singletary
Francis Sinkwich
Jerald Sisemore
Frederick Slater
Billy Ray Smith, Jr.
Bruce Smith
Charles Smith
Jackie Smith
Mac Speedie

Stephen Spurrier
Ken Stabler
Johnny Stallworth
Richard Stanfel
Bryan Bartlett Starr
Roger Staubach
Ernest Stautner
Dean Steinkuhler
Elmer Kenneth Strong, Jr.
Harry Stuhldreher
Joseph Stydahar
Robert Suffridge
Patrick Sullivan
George Summerall
John Sutherland
Lynn Swann
Francis Tarkenton
John Tatum
Charles Taylor
James Taylor
Lawrence Taylor
Lionel Taylor
Otis Taylor, Jr.
Joseph Theismann
James Thorpe
Gaynell Tinsley
Yelberton Abraham Tittle, Jr.
George Trafton
Walter Trenchard
Charles Trippi
Gerald Tubbs
Emlen Tunnell
Clyde Turner
Howard Twilley, Jr.
James Tyrer
John Unitas
Eugene Upshaw
Norman Van Brocklin
Steve Van Buren
Mark van Eeghen
Billy Vessels
Ewell Doak Walker, Jr.
Herschel Walker
Robert Walston
Paul Warfield
Curtis Warner
Kenneth Washington
Robert Waterfield
Charles Waters
James Weatherall
George Webster
Michael Webster
Harold Weekes
Arnold Weinmeister
Edward Weir
David Belford West
Byron White
Charles White
Randy White
Edwin Widseth
Richard Wildung
William Willis
Lawrence Wilson
Robert Wilson, Jr.
Kellen Winslow
Albert Wistert
Alexander Wojciechowicz
William Wood
Elmo Wright
Adam Wyant
Anthony Ronald Yary
Claude Young
John Stephen Young

APPENDIX 5

College Football Hall of Fame Members

Many football entries have been elected to the National Football Foundation's College Football Hall of Fame in King's Mills, OH. A dagger following a name indicates that entry is in either the Indoor or Outdoor Sports volume. Through 1986, the College Football Hall of Fame members included in this or subsequent book are:

PLAYERS

Frank Albert, Stanford
Charles Aldrich, Texas Christian
John Alexander, Syracuse
Lance Alworth, Arkansas
Alan Ameche, Wisconsin
Heartley Anderson, Notre Dame
Douglas Atkins, Tennessee
Hobart Baker,† Princeton
Terry Baker, Oregon State
Albert Baston, Minnesota
Clifford Battles, West Virginia Wesleyan
Samuel Baugh, Texas Christian
James Bausch,† Kansas
Charles Bednarik, Pennsylvania
Joseph Bellino, Navy
Albert Benbrook, Michigan
Angelo Bertelli, Notre Dame
Charles Berry, Lafayette
John Berwanger, Chicago
Felix Blanchard, Jr., Army
Albert Booth, Jr., Yale
Charles Brewer, Harvard
John Brodie, Stanford
Richard Butkus, Illinois
Christian Cagle, Southwest Louisiana/Army
John Cannon, Notre Dame
William Cannon, Louisiana State
Frank Carideo, Notre Dame
Howard Cassady, Ohio State
Berlin Guy Chamberlin, Nebraska
Earl Clark, Colorado College
Joshua Cody, Vanderbilt
George Connor, Notre Dame
William Corbus, Stanford
Hector Cowan, Princeton
Edwin Coy, Yale
John David Crow, Texas A&M
James Crowley, Notre Dame
Peter Dawkins, Army
Charles Daly, Harvard/Army

Ernest Davis, Syracuse
Glenn Davis, Army
Michael Ditka, Pittsburgh
Robert Dodd, Tennessee
Nathan Dougherty, Tennessee
John Driscoll, Northwestern
Morley Drury, Southern California
William Dudley, Virginia
Walter Eckersall, Chicago
Albert Edwards, Washington State
Thomas Fears, Santa Clara/UCLA
William Beattie Feathers, Tennessee
Robert Fenimore, Oklahoma State
Wesley Fesler, Ohio State
William Fincher, Georgia Tech
William Fischer, Notre Dame
Hamilton Fish, Harvard
Daniel Fortmann, Colgate
Clinton Frank, Yale
Benjamin Friedman, Michigan
Robert Gain, Kentucky
Edgar Garbisch, Army
Michael Garrett, Southern California
Charles Gelbert, Jr., Pennsylvania
Frank Gifford, Southern California
George Gipp, Notre Dame
Marshall Goldberg, Pittsburgh
Otto Graham, Jr., Northwestern
Harold Grange, Illinois
Robert Grayson, Stanford
Charles Greene, Jr., North Texas State
Robert Griese, Purdue
Archie Griffin, Ohio State
Joseph Guyon, Georgia Tech
Victor Hanson,† Syracuse
Huntington Hardwick, Harvard
Thomas Truxton Hare, Pennsylvania
Charles Harley, Ohio State
Thomas Harmon, Michigan
Leon Hart, Notre Dame
Edward Healey, Jr., Dartmouth
Walter Heffelfinger, Yale
Melvin Hein, Washington State
Theodore Hendricks, Miami
Wilbur Henry, Washington & Jefferson
William Heston, Michigan
Frank Hinkey, Yale
William Clarke Hinkle, Bucknell
Elroy Hirsch, Wisconsin/Michigan
James Hogan, Yale
Paul Hornung, Notre Dame
Leslie Horvath, Ohio State
Robert Cal Hubbard, Centenary
Robert Huff, West Virginia
Donald Hutson, Alabama
Cecil Isbell, Purdue
Victor Janowicz, Ohio State
Calvin Jones, Iowa
Lee Roy Jordan, Alabama
Charles Justice, North Carolina
Kenneth Kavanaugh, Louisiana State
Richard Kazmaier, Jr., Princeton
Lawrence Kelley, Yale
John Kimbrough, Texas A&M
Frank Kinard, Mississippi
Nile Kinnick, Jr., Iowa
Ronald Kramer, Michigan
Stephen Lach, Duke
John Lattner, Notre Dame
Elmer Layden, Notre Dame
Robert Layne, Texas
Langdon Lea, Princeton
Robert Lilly, Texas Christian
Floyd Little, Syracuse
Sidney Luckman, Columbia
John Lujack, Jr., Notre Dame
George McAfee, Duke
Thomas McDonald, Oklahoma
Hugh McElhenny, Jr., Washington
Lewis McFadin, Texas

Alvin McMillin, Centre
Edward Mahan, Harvard
Oliver Matson, San Francisco
Donald Meredith,† Southern Methodist
Donald Miller, Notre Dame
Harold Muller, California
Bronislaw Nagurski, Minnesota
Ernest Nevers, Stanford
Marshall Newell, Harvard
Thomas Nobis, Jr., Texas
Leo Nomellini, Minnesota
Robert David O'Brien, Texas Christian
Patrick O'Dea, Wisconsin
Elmer Oliphant, Purdue/Army
Merlin Olsen, Utah State
Benjamin Oosterbaan, Michigan
Clarence Parker, Duke
James Parker, Ohio State
Robert Peck, Jr., Pittsburgh
Stanley Pennock, Harvard
George Pfann, Cornell
Peter Pihos, Indiana
Erny Pinckert, Southern California
Arthur Poe, Princeton
Frederick Pollard, Brown
Michael Reid, Penn State
Robert Reynolds, Stanford
Leslie Richter, California
Aaron Rosenberg, Southern California
Joseph Routt, Texas A&M
Gale Sayers, Kansas
Adolph Schulz, Michigan
Marchmont Schwartz, Notre Dame
Thomas Shevlin, Yale
Orenthal James Simpson, Southern California
Frank Sinkwich, Georgia
Frederick Slater, Iowa
Bruce Smith, Minnesota
Stephen Spurrier, Florida
Amos Alonzo Stagg, Yale
Roger Staubach, Navy
Elmer Kenneth Strong, Jr., New York University
Harry Stuhldreher, Notre Dame
Joseph Stydahar, West Virginia
Robert Suffridge, Tennessee
Francis Tarkenton, Georgia
James Thorpe, Carlisle
Gaynell Tinsley, Louisiana State
Charles Trippi, Georgia
Norman Van Brocklin, Oregon
Billy Vessels, Oklahoma
Ewell Doak Walker, Jr., Southern Methodist
Kenneth Washington, UCLA
George Webster, Michigan State
Harold Weekes, Columbia
Edward Weir, Nebraska
David Belford West, Colgate
Byron White, Colorado
Edwin Widseth, Minnesota
Richard Wildung, Minnesota
William Willis, Ohio State
Albert Wistert, Michigan
Alexander Wojciechowicz, Fordham
Andrew Wyant, Bucknell/Chicago
Anthony Ronald Yary, Southern California
Claude Young, Illinois

COACHES

William Alexander
Edward Anderson
Madison Bell
Hugo Bezdek
Dana Bible
Bernard Bierman
Earl Blaik
John Franklin Broyles
Paul Bryant

Charles Caldwell, Jr.
Walter Camp
Francis Cavanaugh
Herbert Crisler
Hugh Duffy Daugherty
Robert Devaney
Daniel Devine
Gilmour Dobie
Charles Dorais
Charles Engle
Donald Faurot
Richard Harlow
Jesse Harper
Percy Haughton
Wayne Woodrow Hayes
John Heisman
William Morley Jennings
Howard Jones
Lawrence Jones
Thomas Jones
Andrew Kerr
Francis Leahy
Louis Little
Daniel McGugin
Edward Madigan
Leo Meyer
Jesse Raymond Morrison
Clarence Munn
Alfred Earle Neale
Jess Neely
Robert Neyland, Jr.
Homer Norton
Benjamin Owen
Ara Parseghian
Edward Robinson
Knute Rockne
Darrell Royal
Francis Schmidt
Floyd Schwartzwalder
Clark Shaughnessy
Lawrence Shaw
Andrew Smith
Carl Snavely
Amos Alonzo Stagg
John Sutherland
John Tatum
Frank Thomas
John Vaught
William Wallace Wade
Lynn Waldorf
Glenn Warner
Charles Wilkinson
Henry Williams
Fielding Yost
Robert Zuppke

APPENDIX 6

Pro Football Hall of Fame Members

Many football entries have been elected to the Pro Football Hall of Fame in Canton, OH. As of 1986, the Pro Football Hall of Fame consists of 133 members. Through 1986, the Pro Football Hall of Fame members are:

Herbert Adderley
Lance Alworth
Douglas Atkins
Morris Badgro
Clifford Battles
Samuel Baugh
Charles Bednarik
DeBenneville Bell
Robert Bell
Raymond Berry
Charles Bidwill, Sr.
George Blanda
James Brown
Paul Brown
Roosevelt Brown, Jr.
William Brown
Richard Butkus
Anthony Canadeo
Joseph Carr
Berlin Guy Chamberlin
John Christiansen
Earl Clark
George Connor
James Conzelman
Lawrence Csonka
William Davis
Leonard Dawson
Arthur Donovan
John Driscoll
William Dudley
Albert Edwards
Wilbur Ewbank
Thomas Fears
Raymond Flaherty
Leonard Ford, Jr.
Daniel Fortmann
Frank Gatski
William George
Frank Gifford
Sidney Gillman
Otto Graham, Jr.
Harold Grange
Charles Greene, Jr.
Alvis Forrest Gregg
Louis Groza
Joseph Guyon
George Halas
Edward Healey, Jr.
Melvin Hein
Wilbur Henry
Arnold Herber
William Hewitt
William Clarke Hinkle
Elroy Hirsch

Paul Hornung
Kenneth Houston
Robert Cal Hubbard
Robert Huff
Lamar Hunt
Donald Hutson
John Henry Johnson
David Jones
Christian Jurgensen III
Walter Kiesling
Frank Kinard
Earl Lambeau
Richard Lane
James Langer
Willie Lanier
Robert Yale Lary
Danta Lavelli
Robert Layne
Alphonse Leemans
Robert Lilly
Vincent Lombardi
Sidney Luckman
William Lyman
George McAfee
Mike McCormack
Hugh McElhenny, Jr.
John (Blood) McNally
Timothy Mara
Gino Marchetti
George Marshall
Oliver Matson
Donald Maynard
August Michalske
Wayne Millner
Robert Mitchell
Ronald Mix
Leonard Moore
Marion Motley
George Musso
Bronislaw Nagurski
Joseph Namath
Alfred Earle Neale
Ernest Nevers
Raymond Nitschke
Leo Nomellini
Merlin Olsen
James Otto
Stephen Owen
Clarence Parker
James Parker
Fletcher Joseph Perry
Peter Pihos
Hugh "Shorty" Ray
Daniel F. Reeves
James Ringo
Andrew Robustelli
Arthur Rooney, Jr.
Alvin Rozelle
Gale Sayers
Joseph Schmidt
Orenthal James Simpson
Bryan Bartlett Starr
Roger Staubach
Ernest Stautner
Elmer Kenneth Strong, Jr.
Joseph Stydahar
Francis Tarkenton
Charles Taylor
James Taylor
James Thorpe
Yelberton Abraham Tittle, Jr.
George Trafton
Charles Trippi
Emlen Tunnell
Clyde Turner
John Unitas
Eugene Upshaw
Norman Van Brocklin
Steve Van Buren
Ewell Doak Walker, Jr.
Paul Warfield
Robert Waterfield
Arnold Weinmeister
William Willis
Lawrence Wilson
Alexander Wojciechowicz

APPENDIX 7

College and Professional Football Conferences, Leagues, and Associations

Since American football began in 1869, several major college and professional football conferences, leagues, and associations have developed. The first two lists cite several major college and professional football conferences and leagues that have operated since 1869. The college conferences, along with the National Football League, remain in existence. The third list cites several major football associations.

COLLEGE FOOTBALL CONFERENCES

Atlantic Coast Conference
Big Eight (formerly Missouri Valley, Big Six, Big Seven) Conference
Big Ten (formerly Western, Big Nine) Conference
Border Conference
East Coast Athletic Conference
Ivy League
Mid-American Conference
Missouri Valley Conference
Pacific Coast Conference
Pacific Ten (formerly Pacific Eight) Conference
Rocky Mountain Conference
Skyline (Mountain States Athletic) Conference
Southeastern Conference
Southern Conference (formerly Southern Intercollegiate Athletic Association)
Southwest Athletic Conference
Southwestern Athletic Conference
Western Athletic Conference

AMERICAN PROFESSIONAL FOOTBALL LEAGUES

All-America Football Conference (1946–1949)
American Football League (1926, 1936–1937, 1940–1941, 1960–1969)
National Football League (1919–)
United States Football League (1984–1986)
World Football League (1974–1975)

FOOTBALL ASSOCIATIONS

Amateur Athletic Union
American Football Coaches Association
American Professional Football Association
Football Writers Association of America
National Association of Intercollegiate Athletics
National Collegiate Athletic Association
Professional Football Writers Association of America

Index

Note: The locations of main entries in the dictionary are indicated in the index by *italic* page numbers.

Contributors

Charles C. Alexander, Professor of History, Ohio University, Athens, OH.

Frederick J. Augustyn, Jr., Subject Cataloger, Economics and Political Science, Library of Congress, resides in College Park, MD.

Marybell I. Avery, Assistant Professor, Department of Physical Education, Creighton University, Omaha, NE.

C. Robert Barnett, Professor, Department of Health, Physical Education and Recreation, Marshall University, Huntington, WV, and President, Professional Football Researchers Association.

Carl M. Becker, Professor of History, Wright State University, Dayton, OH.

William H. Beezley, Professor of History, North Carolina State University, Raleigh, NC.

Michael Bodek, Sportscaster, WDUQ FM, Pittsburgh, PA, lives in McKeesport, PA.

Dennis A. Booher, Assistant Professor of Physical Education, Pennsylvania State University, Schuylkill Campus, Schuylkill Haven, PA.

William A. Borst, Baseball Author and Television Host, resides in St. Louis, MO.

Robert T. Bowen, Jr., Retired Professor of Physical Education, University of Georgia, Athens, GA.

Frank P. Bowles, Associate Professor of English, University of Northern Colorado, Greeley, CO.

Axel Bundgaard, Professor of Physical Education, St. Olaf College, Northfield, MN.

Jim Campbell, Administrative Director, National Football League Alumni, Fort Lauderdale, FL.

Stan W. Carlson, Editor and Publisher, lives in Minneapolis, MN.

Robert N. Carroll, Teacher and Editor, *Coffin Corner*, resides in North Huntingdon, PA.

Rocco J. Carzo, Athletic Director, Tufts University, Medford, MA.

Dennis Clark, ABE Assessor, Lane Community College, Eugene, OR.

Joanna Davenport, Associate Professor of Physical Education, SUNY at Plattsburgh, Plattsburg, NY.

L. Robert Davids, Retired Federal Government Public Affairs Officer and Founder of Society for American Baseball Research, resides in Washington, DC.

Irving Dilliard resides in Collinsville, IL.

John E. DiMeglio, Professor of History, Mankato State University, Mankato, MN.

Joseph English, Professor, School of Education, St. Bonaventure University, St. Bonaventure, NY, and Eleanor B. English, Director, Olean Youth Bureau, Olean, NY.

John L. Evers, Retired High School Teacher and Administrator, resides in Carmi, IL.

Albert J Figone, Associate Professor of Physical Education and Graduate Coordinator, Humboldt State University, Arcata, CA.

Leonard Frey, Professor, Department of Linguistics, San Diego State University, San Diego, CA.

Daniel Frio, Soual Swales Teacher, Wayland High School, Wayland, MA, lives in Sharon, MA.

James R. Fuller works in the printing industry and resides in Fulton, MO.

Cappy Gagnon, Director of Special Programs, Los Angeles Sheriff's Department, and former President of Society for American Baseball Research, lives in Hollywood, CA.

Larry R. Gerlach, Professor of History, University of Utah, Salt Lake City, UT.

Daniel R. Gilbert, Professor of History, Moravian College, Bethlehem, PA.

John R. Giroski, Professor, Chabot College, Hayward, CA, resides in Oakland, CA.

Richard Gonsalves, Author, lives in Gloucester, MA.

William A. Gudelunas, Associate Professor of History, Pennsylvania State University, Schuylkill Campus, Schuylkill Haven, PA.

Brian C. Gunn resides in Waukesha, WI.

Allan Hall, Professor, Departments of Athletics, Physical Education and Health, Ashland College, Ashland, OH.

John Hanners, Associate Professor of Drama and Chairperson, Communication Arts/Theatre Department, Allegheny College, Meadville, PA.

John David Healy resides in Washington, DC.

Keith Hobson, Technical Representative, British Aerospace, resides in Tettenhall, Wolverhampton, West Midlands, England.

Adam R. Hornbuckle resides in Durham, NC.

Harry A. Jebsen, Jr., Dean, College of Arts and Sciences, Capital University, Columbus, OH.

Thomas D. Jozwik, Insurance Inspector and a Director of the Society for American Baseball Research, resides in Milwaukee, WI.

Richard S. Kirkendall, Henry A. Wallace Professor, Department of History, Iowa State University, Ames, IA.

Donald E. Kosakowski resides in Oxford, CT.

Tony Ladd, Professor, Lifetime Fitness Center, Wheaton College, Wheaton, IL.

Jay Langhammer, Account Executive, Design/Display, lives in Dallas, TX.

Mary Lou LeCompte, Assistant Professor, Physical and Health Education, University of Texas, Austin, TX.

W. Bruce Leslie, Associate Professor of History, SUNY College at Brockport, Brockport, NY.

Angela Lumpkin, Associate Professor of Physical Education, University of North Carolina, Chapel Hill, NC.

Erik S. Lunde, Professor of American Thought and Language, Michigan State University, East Lansing, MI.

Curtice Mang resides in Phoenix, AZ.

George P. Mang, Executive Vice President, Statewide Insurance Corporation, resides in Phoenix, AZ.

Douglas D. Martin, Professor of History, Towson State University, Towson, MD.

Jerry D. Mathers, Public School Teacher and Writer, lives in Lyons, NE.

Frank Mazzella, Professor, Department of Political Science, Southwest Missouri State University, Springfield, MO.

Bernie McCarty, Newspaper Writer, resides in University Park, IL.

Charles R. Middleton, Associate Dean, College of Arts and Sciences, University of Colorado, Boulder, CO.

John Muncie, Professor of History, East Stroudsburg University, East Stroudsburg, PA.

Eugene C. Murdock, Professor of History, Marietta College, Marietta, OH.

Jerome Mushkat, Professor of History, University of Akron, Akron, OH.

Douglas A. Noverr, Professor, Department of American Thought and Language, Michigan State University, East Lansing, MI.

James E. Odenkirk, Professor, Health and Physical Education Department, Arizona State University, Tempe, AZ.

Steve Ollove, Freelance Sportswriter and Author of *Sports Buff*, lives in Hamilton, MA.

Kant Patel, Associate Professor of Political Science, Southwest Missouri State University, Springfield, MO.

Edward J. Pavlick, resides in Milwaukee, WI.

David L. Porter, Louis T. Shangle Professor of History and Political Science, William Penn College, Oskaloosa, IA.

Kevin R. Porter, Student, lives in Oskaloosa, IA.

Benjamin G. Rader, Professor of History, University of Nebraska–Lincoln, Lincoln, NE.

Harold L. Ray, Professor and Coordinator, Graduate Studies, Department of Health, Physical Education and Recreation, Western Michigan University, Kalamazoo, MI.

Milt Roberts, Author, resides in Lewes, DE.

Eric C. Schneider, Program Associate, Delaware Humanities Forum, Wilmington, DE.

Edward S. Shapiro, Professor of History, Seton Hall University, South Orange, NJ.

James K. Skipper, Jr., Professor of Sociology, Virginia Polytechnic Institute and State University, Blacksburg, VA.

Joe Lee Smith, Public Information Director, Lamar University, Beaumont, TX.

Ronald A. Smith, Professor of Physical Education, Pennsylvania State University, University Park, PA, and Secretary-Treasurer of the North American Socity for Sport History.

Eric Solomon, Professor, San Francisco State University, San Francisco, CA.

Luther W. Spoehr, Teacher and Writer, lives in Providence, RI.

Jon D. Sunderland, Assistant Professor of Physical Education, Gonzaga University, Spokane, WA.

William A. Sutton, Professor, Department of Sport Management, Robert Morris College, Moon Township Campus, Coraopolis, PA.

Marcia G. Synnott, Associate Professor of History, University of South Carolina, Columbia, SC.

Frank W. Thackeray, Associate Professor of History, Indiana University Southeast, New Albany, IN.

Steven Tischler, Assistant Professor, Empire State College, New York, NY.

Robert B. Van Atta, Public Relations Management, resides in Greensburg, PA.

Bruce W. Wasem, Assistant Professor of Health, Physical Education and Recreation, Wilmington College, Wilmington, OH.

John S. Watterson, Editor, Adjunct Professor, lives in Evanston, IL.

Kendall J. Wentz, Teacher and Principal, resides in Kimberling City, MO.

James D. Whalen, Retired, Former Purchasing Agent, Credit Union Treasurer/Manager, Federated Department Stores, lives in Dayton, OH.

John D. Windhausen, Professor of History, St. Anselm College, Manchester, NH.

Jerry Jaye Wright, Assistant Professor of Physical Education, University of Wisconsin–Milwaukee, Milwaukee, WI.

Lawrence E. Ziewacz, Assistant Professor, Department of American Thought and Language, Michigan State University, East Lansing, MI.

ABOUT THE EDITOR

DAVID L. PORTER is Louis Tuttle Shangle Professor of History and Political Science at William Penn College in Oskaloosa, Iowa. He is the editor of *Biographical Dictionary of American Sports: Baseball* (Greenwood Press, 1987), the first volume of a comprehensive reference work devoted to all major American sports, and the author of *The Seventy-Sixth Congress and World War II, 1939–1940* and *Congress and the Waning of the New Deal*. His articles have appeared in such journals as *The North American Society for Sport History Proceedings*, *The Society for American Baseball Research Review of Books*, *American Heritage*, *Senate History*, *The Palimpsest*, *American Historical Association Perspectives*, and *Midwest Review*, and in such books as *The Book of Lists 3*, *Herbert Hoover and the Republican Era*, *The Hero in Transition*, *Franklin D. Roosevelt: His Life and Times*, *Sport History*, and *The Rating Game in American Politics*.